Makers of Nineteenth Century Culture

1800–1914

Also edited by Justin Wintle
Makers of Modern Culture

edited by Justin Wintle and Richard Kenin
The Dictionary of Biographical Quotation

Makers of Nineteenth Century Culture

1800-1914

EDITED BY Justin Wintle

Routledge & Kegan Paul
London, Boston, Melbourne and Henley

First published in 1982
by Routledge & Kegan Paul Ltd
39 Store Street, London WC1E 7DD,
9 Park Street, Boston, Mass. 02108, USA,
296 Beaconsfield Parade, Middle Park,
Melbourne, 3206, Australia, and
Broadway House, Newtown Road,
Henley-on-Thames, Oxon RG9 1EN
Set in Baskerville by
Input Typesetting Ltd, London
Printed in Great Britain by
Billing & Sons Ltd, Worcester

ISBN 0-7100-9295-4

In memoriam F. J. W.

Contents

Contributors

Dr Jane Aaron
257
Department of English, Polytechnic
of Central London

Dr Edward D. J. Acton
217
Department of History, University
of Liverpool

Michael J. Alexander
274, 365, 446
Department of Music, Couldon
College of Further Education, Stoke-
on-Trent

Professor Stanislav Andreski
65, 325, 377, 424
Department of Sociology, University
of Reading

Dr Rosemary Ashton
76, 95, 170, 269, 477
Department of English, University
College, London University

Joseph Bain
53, 60, 384
Department of English, Winchester
College

Zygmunt G. Barański
252, 311, 336
Department of Italian Studies,
University of Reading

Derrick Barlow
207, 211
Jesus College, University of Oxford

Dr Michael Bartholomew
4, 281
Arts Faculty, Open University

Professor John Bayley
363
St Catherine's College, University of
Oxford

Professor Harold Beaver
5, 161
Department of English, University of
Amsterdam

Professor T. O. Beidelman
420
Department of Anthropology, New
York University

Dr Christopher Bettinson
24, 163, 370, 465
Department of French, University
College, Cardiff

Professor Michael Biddiss
1, 97, 121, 162, 175, 176, 188, 302,
312, 391, 416, 422
Department of History, University of
Reading

Alan Bold
227, 245, 407
Author

Professor John Bowle
282, 366
Wadham College, Oxford, and
Collège d'Europe, Bruges

Lord Briggs
471
Provost of Worcester College,
University of Oxford

Vincent Brome
234
Author and broadcaster

Dr David Bryant
99, 287, 300, 426
Department of French, University
College, Cardiff

Dr Bryan Burns
350
Department of English Literature,
University of Sheffield

Stuart Campbell
22, 48, 187, 328, 375
Department of Music, University of
Glasgow

Dr Roger Cardinal
182, 220, 285, 331, 385
Faculty of Humanities, University of
Kent

Dr John Carroll
333
Department of Sociology, La Trobe
University

Remo Catani
345
Department of Italian, University
College, Cardiff

Dr Alan Chalmers
301
Department of General Philosophy,
University of Sydney

Dr Deborah Cherry
57
Department of the History of Art,
University of Manchester

G. H. Claridge
359
Eliot College, University of Kent

Tim Clark
219, 221
Graduate student, Department of Fine
Arts, Harvard University

Joyce Crick
159, 199, 481
Department of German, University
College, London University

Professor Philip Collins
119
Department of English, University of
Leicester

Dr Patrick Conner
362, 387
The Royal Pavilion Art Gallery and
Museums, Brighton

Dr John Cottingham
15
Department of Philosophy, University
of Reading

David Cox
41, 122, 164, 196, 197, 390, 427
Composer and writer on music

Professor Bernard Crick
18, 35, 313, 452
Department of Politics and Sociology,
Birkbeck College, London University

Professor Margaret Davies
374
Department of French Studies,
University of Reading

Dick Davis
103, 156, 258, 490
Poet and translator

R. M. Davison
253
Department of Russian, University of
Liverpool

Dr Basil Deane
85
Music Director, Arts Council of Great
Britain

Dr Robert Dingley
431, 432
Department of English, University of
New England, N.S.W.

David Dinour
218
Formerly Reader in Economics, New
University of Ulster

Dr William Drabkin
31
Department of Music, University of
Southampton

Cuthbert Hamilton Ellis
433, 447
Author and artist

Dr Colin Evans
444
Department of French, University
College, Cardiff

Duncan Fallowell
78, 262, 380, 382, 442, 487
Author

Dr Alison Finch
430
Faculty of French Studies, Cambridge
University

Professor Antony Flew
194, 195, 289
Department of Philosophy, University
of Reading

Professor J. E. Flower
193
Department of French and Italian,
University of Exeter

Dr Robert Fox
259
Department of History, University of
Lancaster

Professor Richard Freeborn
127, 454, 460
School of Slavonic and East European
Studies, London University

Ted Freeman
10, 22, 110, 308
Department of French, University of
Bristol

John Furse
73, 142, 178, 237, 355, 474
Humanities Unit, Plymouth
Polytechnic

Peter Gathercole
463
Darwin College, Cambridge
University

A. W. Gibson
104, 177, 357
Department of English, Royal
Holloway College, London University

Derek Gjertsen
13, 37, 90, 108, 243, 270, 335
Author

Dr Ranulph Glanville
25, 169, 241, 406
School of Architecture, Portsmouth
Polytechnic

Dr Anthony Glees
40
Department of Government, Brunel
University

Dr Bernhard Glienke
8
Corpus Christi College, Cambridge
University

Mike Gonzalez
296, 456
Department of Hispanic Studies,
University of Glasgow

Philip Gooden
55, 56, 118, 130, 411
Department of English, Kingswood
School

Dr David Gooding
150
School of Humanities and Social
Sciences, University of Bath

Richard Perceval Graves
228
Author

Professor Charles Gregory
6, 23, 67
Department of English, California
State University at Sacramento

C. E. J. Griffiths
75
Department of Italian Studies,
University of Manchester

Paul Griffiths
134, 417, 479
Music Critic of *The Times*

Ronald Grimsley
247, 389
Emeritus Professor, Department of
French, Bristol University

Dr Tanya Harrod
138, 152, 320
Author

Dr Cameron Hawke-Smith
148, 149, 280, 356, 401
Keeper of Archaeology, City Museum
and Art Gallery, Stoke-on-Trent

Dr Martin Hemingway
261
Department of Extra-mural Studies,
London University

Christopher Heywood
50, 96, 318, 403
Department of English Literature,
University of Sheffield

Dilip Hiro
3, 386
Author, playwright and journalist

Richard Hobbs
235, 367
Department of French, University of
Bristol

William F. M. Horsley
172
Broadcaster and Radio Producer for
the BBC

Philip Howard
326
Literary Editor, *The Times*

Professor W. D. Howarth
133, 393
Department of French, University of
Bristol

Lucy Hughes-Hallett
275, 428
Author

Richard Humphreys
19, 29, 101, 111, 115, 179, 297, 347,
409, 461
Lecturer, Tate Gallery

Dr Roger S. Huss
231, 232, 310
Department of French, Queen Mary
College, London University

G. M. Hyde
192
School of English and American
Studies, University of East Anglia

Timothy Hyman
146, 183, 209, 315
Artist and Extra-mural lecturer at
London and Sussex Universities

Professor J. C. Ireson
230, 256, 472
Department of French, University of
Hull

Dr Douglas Jarman
286
Royal Northern College of Music

Richard Jenkyns
244
Lady Margaret Hall, University of
Oxford

Dr J. Barrie Jones
151
Department of Music, Open
University

Peter Jones
316, 418
Department of Manuscripts, The
British Library

Dr Verina Jones
292
Department of Italian Studies,
University of Reading

Jonathan Keates
59, 66, 83, 125, 128, 137, 184, 201,
239, 307, 309, 340, 381, 425, 440, 449,
459, 468
Department of English, City of
London School

Barry J. Kemp
354
Faculty of Oriental Studies,
Cambridge University

Dr Peter Kornicki
388, 445
Humanities Research Institute, Kyoto
University

David Knight
113, 305
Department of Philosophy, Durham
University

A. J. Kox
278
Institute of Theoretical Physics,
University of Amsterdam

Basil Lam
61, 404
Music critic

Andrew Lamb
438
Musicologist, writer and broadcaster

Professor Lester C. Lamon
79, 129, 478
Department of History, Indiana
University at South Bend

Dr Christopher Lawrence
17, 251, 273
Wellcome Institute for the History of
Medicine

Robert Layton
38
Music Division, BBC

Professor Sir Edmund Leach
165
King's College, Cambridge University

A. Robert Lee
39, 63, 144, 208, 224, 229, 238, 277,
279, 303, 436, 451, 485
Department of English, University of
Kent

Dr David J. C. Lee
368, 493
Department of French Studies,
University of Reading

David J. Levy
20, 117, 123, 266, 453
Department of Sociology, Middlesex
Polytechnic

Calan E. C. Lewis
98, 105, 126, 410
Author

Professor U. Limentani
160
Magdalene College, Cambridge
University

Richard Littlejohns
398, 399
Department of German, University of
Birmingham

Professor Don Locke
189
Department of Philosophy, University
of Warwick

Dr W. J. Mc Cormack
49, 139, 265, 338, 343, 443
School of English, University of Leeds

Professor Hugh Macdonald
36, 405, 408
Department of Music, University of
Glasgow

Malcolm MacDonald
7, 52, 344
Author

Dr Duncan MacLeod
271, 419
St Catherine's College, University of
Oxford

Dr Roger McLure
26, 288
Department of French, University of
Keele

Helen McNeil
87, 120, 173
School of English and American
Studies, University of East Anglia

David Meakin
132, 157, 323, 430
Department of French, University of
Bristol

Dr J. G. Merquior
284
University of Brasilia

Dr John Milner
250, 464
Department of Fine Art, University of
Newcastle-upon-Tyne

R. R. Milner-Gulland
268
Reader in Russian Studies, University
of Sussex

Stuart Morgan
94, 135, 225, 378
Department of Art History, Brighton
Polytechnic

Andrew Motion
450
Poet

Professor Eric Mottram
2, 33, 77, 80, 100, 136, 140, 205, 206,
462, 480, 483, 484
Department of English, King's
College, London University

Dr Alan Munton
360
English Department, College of St
Mark and St John, Plymouth

Dr Dugald Murdoch
352, 414
Department of Philosophy, University
of Canterbury (N.Z.)

Dr W. H. Newton-Smith
74, 214
Balliol College, University of Oxford

Paul Nicholls
71, 84, 154, 185, 248, 434, 457
Author

Kaori O'Connor
32
Author and Designer

Dr Robert Olby
106, 240, 304, 346, 348
Department of Philosophy, Leeds
University

Christopher Ormell
16, 114, 174, 181, 276, 294, 324, 351,
358, 373
School of Education, University of
East Anglia

Timothy O'Sullivan
12, 47, 291
Author

Dr Dorinda Outram
107, 329
Girton College, Cambridge University

Dr Roger Parker
34, 361, 383
Department of Music, Cornell
University

Professor G. H. R. Parkinson
145, 299
Department of Philosophy, University
of Reading

Professor Richard Arthur Peace
191
Department of Russian Studies,
University of Hull

Brian Petrie
293
Author

Professor Pierluigi Petrobelli
467
School of Music, University of
Perugia, and Director of the Verdi
Institute

Professor H. R. Post
45
Department of the History and
Philosophy of Science, Chelsea
College, London University

Dr Derrick Puffett
489
Faculty of Music, University of
Oxford

Professor Patrick Rabbitt
491
Department of Psychology, University
of Durham

Philip Radcliffe
306
King's College, Cambridge University

Simon Rae
11, 91
Author

Dr Michael Redhead
46, 131
Department of the History and
Philosophy of Science, Chelsea
College, London University

T. J. Reed
190, 213
St John's College, University of
Oxford

Ann Renier
226
Author and translator

Professor James Richmond
27, 28, 68, 82, 124, 153, 200, 204, 332,
376, 400, 437, 458
Department of Religious Studies,
University of Lancaster

Professor Keith Robbins
54, 93, 186, 339, 486
Department of Modern History,
University of Glasgow

Dr Neil Roberts
143
Department of English Literature,
University of Sheffield

June Rose
171, 334
Author and broadcaster

Michael Rosen
212
Merton College, University of Oxford

Professor Christopher Salvesen
210
Department of English, University of
Reading

Dr Jim Samson
86
Department of Music, University of
Exeter

Mary Sandbach
439
Author and translator

Michael Scherk
255m, 476
Author and editor

Michael Schmidt
448
Editorial Director, Carcanet Press

Dr Clive Scott
254, 469
School of Modern Languages and
European History, University of East
Anglia

Frederick Scott
62, 349, 372, 397, 441
The Architectural Association,
London

Professor Elman Service
321
Department of Anthropology,
University of California at Santa
Barbara

Professor Donald Leslie Shaw
30, 147, 260, 353, 379, 395
Department of Hispanic Studies,
University of Edinburgh

Paul Sidey
264
Senior editor, Hutchinson Publishing
Group

C. H. Sisson
203
Poet, translator and critic

Professor Hans Sluga
166
Department of Philosophy, University
of California at Berkeley

Dr C. N. Smith
141, 215, 327, 337
School of Modern Languages and
European History, University of East
Anglia

Dr Crosbie Smith
246
History of Science Unit, University of
Kent

Ewen Smith
44
Institute of Latin American Studies,
University of Glasgow

Dr Harold L. Smith
51
Department of History, University of
Houston

Keith Smith
242, 371
Department of Economics, University
of Keele

Brian Southam
14
Publisher and author

George Spater
92
Senior Visiting Research Fellow,
University of Sussex

Paul Spencer-Longhurst
112
Barber Institute of Fine Arts,
University of Birmingham

Corbet Stewart
198, 223, 322
Department of German, Queen Mary
College, London University

Mark Storey
88, 423
Department of English, University of
Birmingham

Dr Hew Strachan
89
Corpus Christi College, Cambridge
University

Professor A. V. Subiotto
64, 249
Department of German, University of
Birmingham

Andrew Swarbrick
342
School of English, University of Leeds

Dr David Thomas
236
Department of Drama, University of
Bristol

Dr Patricia Thomson
392
Reader in English, University of
Sussex

Dr Keith Tribe
272
Department of Sociology and Social
Anthropology, University of Keele

Gerard L'E. Turner
58
Museum of the History of Science,
University of Oxford

Pat Turner
102, 158, 180, 222, 317, 319, 364, 455,
466, 473
Curator, Education Department, Tate
Gallery

Wilfried van der Will
155, 396, 402
Department of German, University of
Birmingham

Christopher Wagstaff
267
Department of Italian Studies,
University of Reading

Malcolm Warner
233, 314, 394
Author

Dr Helen Watanabe-O'Kelly
435
Department of German, University of
Reading

Giles Waterfield
263, 330, 421
Director of the Dulwich Picture
Gallery

Simon Watney
69, 81, 413, 482
School of Communications,
Polytechnic of Central London

Gray Watson
43, 168, 341
Department of Art History and
Complementary Studies, Wimbledon
School of Art

Dr Marie Wells
42, 202
Faculty of Scandinavian Studies,
Cambridge University

Michael John Wilson
116, 290, 369, 415
Deputy Keeper, The National Gallery
(London)

Christopher Wintle
475
Department of Music, Goldsmith's
College, London University

Justin Wintle
109
The Editor

Dr Hilary Wise
70
Department of French, Queen Mary
College, London University

Dr John Worrall
167, 216, 283, 492
Department of Philosophy, Logic and
Scientific Method, London School of
Economics

David Wright
72, 412
Poet and translator

Dr Gayle Graham Yates
9, 298, 429
Associate Professor, Women's Studies,
University of Minnesota

Acknowledgments

My thanks to all the contributors. Special thanks to Mike Alexander, Professor Richard Freeborn, Ted Freeman, Kaori O'Connor, Timothy O'Sullivan, Michael Redhead, Michael Schmidt and Christopher Wintle, who each gave much help and advice during the compilation. Further thanks to Professors Ernest Gellner, Richard Gregory, Norman MacKenzie and John North, and to Dr. W. H. Brock. With regard to the entry on Darwin, and the question 'who shall edit the editor?', I am indebted to Dr John Cottingham, Professor Antony Flew and Peter Gathercole for their helpful comments. I am also indebted to Mrs Jennifer Martin, who typed the entire manuscript, and to Melissa Brooks, who subbed it, as well as to staff in every department of Routledge & Kegan Paul, with a special mention for Carol Taplin for dealing both promptly and efficiently with the necessary paperwork.

Introduction

The nineteenth century was an astonishing period. America arose, Germany was unified, Africa mapped, and Japan coaxed out of her cocoon. Its revolutions in science, technology, transport, communications and commerce are the very stuff of encyclopedias. It was the Age of the Two Ms – Machines and Mobility. Railways and steamships moved colossal quantities of people, raw materials, crafted and manufactured goods from one corner of the globe to another at unprecedented speeds. Greatly improved printing techniques, especially in graphics, and the electric telegraph galvanized the quality and flow of information. Well before 1900 the ordinary well-to-do were picking up their telephones, and taking photographs. The first computers were built, and the fixed-wing aeroplane envisaged. In politics dynamic new forces were held in uneasy balance: while the huge increase in the level and distribution of material prosperity ensured not just the survival but the consummation of the bourgeois ethic in the West generally, in central Europe the ideologies of socialism were being forged. If liberalism was a characteristic response to both these currents, so too was its cousin, revolutionary nationalism. In the Old World and in South America, in country after country, the traditional forms of government were torn down and replaced with novel democratic and republican institutions. And all the while Britain and France sought to establish world-wide empires. No wonder that Karl Marx, caught up in the march of history at a climactic passage, thought that history was marching somewhere. Like an Old Testament prophet he espied the Promised Land. Yet, in another context, History, as the history of civilizations (a favourite theme among Victorians), paled into insignificance. A dramatic new conception of time itself was demonstrated, first by geology, then biology. A few thousand years of recorded history were as nothing compared to the hundreds of millions of years that it had taken the earth and its organic covering to reach their present form. Ozymandias was but yesterday's man. Evolution was a sobering, even chilling truth. Science, so lately hailed as the great means to all man's aspirations, had become an agent of his discomfort. Darwinism proclaimed the death of God. Religion, beset from within by theological disputes, struggled to retaliate. The century that had opened with Napoleon astride the wreckage of the French Revolution, ended with the search for a secular metaphysic – a search negatively proposed by Schopenhauer, strongly asserted by Nietzsche, and doubtfully accomplished by Freud.

The same century also began with Jane Austen perfecting her art in Hampshire, and closed with Paul Gauguin practising his in Tahiti. On the face of it one can scarcely imagine two more disparate figures: the one minutely engaged in her native social locale, the other removed into an other-worldly realm of sensual obsession. But there were similarities. Both strove for detachment; both embraced a limited range of subject matter; and in each case the process of image-making was a solution to a psychological isolation. Just how alike, or unalike, they are depends on your cultural point of view; and your cultural point of view will almost certainly find itself rooted in the ideas of the nineteenth century. Between Jane Austen and Gauguin new ground was broken in every field. The reigning spirit of upheaval and dislocation affected every activity. In literature and the arts the Romantic movement, with its sudden emphasis on individualism, heralded an era of irresistible genius; and individual genius continued to supply the needs of each succeeding movement – of Realism, Naturalism, Impressionism and Symbolism. Great novelists emerged everywhere – Tolstoy and Dostoevsky in Russia, Stendhal, Balzac, Zola and Flaubert in France, Scott, Dickens and George Eliot in Britain, Melville and Henry James in America. Chekhov, Ibsen and Strindberg staged a renascence in drama. Ballet became a major art form, and opera shone grandly. Music enjoyed not only an incomparable new repertoire, but new standards of virtuosity in its performance. In mathematics the boundaries fixed by Euclid were transgressed by such figures as Galois, Lobachevsky, Riemann and Cantor. Physics prepared to part company with Newton. Mendeleyev's Periodic Tables set chemistry on a solid footing. With the development of immunology, medicine too became a proper science. And science extended her territory as the humanities courted her rigour. Much philosophy was dominated by positivism; experimental methods were applied to psychology; sociology and anthropology were born.

Of course, there were currents of continuity as well – there always are. Darwin and Marx, by today's evaluation the two giants in the swell, were in a sense embodiments of the Enlightenment: each firmly believed in natural laws discernible to reason. This book is largely designed to help the reader untangle the dialectic between tradition and innovation that underlies the nineteenth-century ferment. Like its predecessor, *Makers of Modern Culture*, it does so by concentrating on the achievements of the period's leading figures; and it offers interpretations rather than an 'authoritative account' – in the view of this editor an impossible or at least unwelcome illusion. It takes 1800 as its starting point, and continues through until 1914. Both dates are as arbitrary as any others that might have been chosen, and both create moderate difficulties in deciding who belongs where (and separate from the greater difficulty of deciding who doesn't belong at all!). At the tail end many important figures who did not produce any important work before 1900, but who did produce important work before *and* after 1914, will be found in *Makers of Modern Culture*; and at the front end some important people (notably Blake, Goya and Schiller) have been omitted to await inclusion in the next volume (covering the eighteenth century) where they equally belong. In either case a double asterisk (**) in the Index signifies that the claims of a particular culture-maker are not being ignored by the project as a whole.

But the Index is there for more important reasons than to indicate editorial policies of selection and rejection. Readers are strongly urged to consult it when looking up the subject of their immediate interest if they wish to get the fullest use out of this book. There are often many references to a figure other than the entry devoted to him or her. The reader will also find that the Index contains thematic references – e.g. to 'Symbolism' or 'Evolution'. These too are given to promote both the means and an inducement to exploration.

A fuller account of my editorial concerns and procedures, including a working definition of the word 'culture' (in essence 'how we see ourselves'), will be found in the Introduction of *Makers of Modern Culture*. Inevitably, because I have stuck by the same format, *Makers of Nineteenth Century Culture* is preoccupied with the significance of its subjects for us more than with a proper historical reconstruction, although in some obvious cases (for instance, Herbert Spencer) my weighting has been influenced by a figure's prestige within the period itself. But it is as a contemporary interpretive discussion of the nineteenth century that the book is presented; and that it is just that owes much to the continuing commitment to the project of many who contributed to the first volume. To them, as to the newcomers, I am indebted.

Justin Wintle
London 1982

A

1

ACTON, John Emerich Edward Dalberg, Lord
1834–1902

British historian

At the heart of Acton's life and work was commitment
to defence of individual conscience. This permeated his
attitude not only towards the past but also towards
unduly authoritarian behaviour from secular or ecclesiastical bodies in his own age. In pursuing his convictions he exploited the advantages of inherited wealth
and influential cosmopolitan connections so that he
might take the risks which others often shunned. This
was evident, above all, in stormy dealings with his own
Catholic Church – an institution which threatened to
bear out the truth of his famed dictum, 'Power tends
to corrupt, and absolute power corrupts absolutely.'

Acton was born at Naples, to whose kingdom his
grandfather had once been premier. His mother was
widowed early, and at the age of six he acquired a
stepfather who later, as Lord Granville, became British
Foreign Secretary. He grew up socially and intellectually at ease among the great Whig families of England and among leading liberal Catholic circles both
there and abroad. He attended Oscott College and
underwent periods of private tuition in Paris and Edinburgh before embarking, in 1848, upon his most decisive educational experience. This involved spending
much of the next decade, in Munich and on wider
European travels, as the personal student of Ignaz
Döllinger*. From him was obtained a thorough
grounding in the rigorous methods of the new German
school of historical criticism.

By 1858 Acton was home in England determined to
rescue his backward countrymen, Catholic and even
Protestant too, from their intellectual insularity. Between 1859 and 1865 he sat as Liberal MP for an Irish
constituency, but he felt uneasy within the Commons
and contributed little to its proceedings. None the less
he held strong views about the way in which democracy
and nationalism might be perverted for illiberal purposes, and he won from Gladstone* a personal regard
that was reflected through the conferment of a peerage
in 1869. During the 1860s Acton's influence was exercised less through parliamentary channels than as an
essayist in this the great age of the Victorian intellectual periodical. Most significantly, he collaborated with

others like Newman* on liberal Catholic publications,
editing the *Rambler* which was soon revamped as the
Home and Foreign Review.

Acton's efforts at subjecting historical and contemporary issues to the scrutiny of the latest critical scholarship soon brought conflict with Cardinal Wiseman,
once his Oscott principal, and with the Vatican itself.
The hierarchy contested the liberal Catholic view that
such examination could only strengthen the church in
the longer term. Rome was in no mood to make concessions about the fact that the 'nephews' of certain earlier
popes were really sons, or indeed about still weightier
matters. In 1864, when Pius IX crystallized his comprehensive rejection of social and intellectual modernity into the *Syllabus of Errors*, Acton closed his journal
before the Vatican could do it for him. Even so, he
continued elsewhere his eloquent opposition to the
authoritarianism of the Curia and the pope's own obsession with preserving temporal power.

Matters came to a head in 1870, when the new
Kingdom of Italy seized most of the papal territory
only weeks after the Vatican Council had promulgated
the dogma of Infallibility. During the council Acton
was in Rome busying himself behind the scenes to
stiffen resistance from those prelates who opposed any
such proclamation either because it was 'inopportune'
or, as he himself believed, because it was still more
fundamentally erroneous in its threat to individual conscientious judgment. He made regular reports to Döllinger. Out of them his mentor moulded the *Letters of
Quirinus from the Council*, an exposure of the clerical
intrigues underpinning the Curia's Victory, which
caused instant scandal when published in Germany.
Döllinger was excommunicated, in company with his
'Old Catholics'. Although as a layman Acton was less
immediately vulnerable, he expected a similar fate. But
the blow never came, despite the fact that he remained
in some respects still more intransigent than Döllinger.
Thus the Englishman was permitted to continue from
within the church his battle to purge it of obscurantist
authoritarianism, and thus to make it a more effective
prop to freedom in spheres both spiritual and secular.

Everything which had gone before seemed but a
preparation for that great project of 'a History of Liberty' to which Acton soon turned. What he actually
accomplished of it was fragmentary. Though no book
came from him, he travelled widely, conversed brilliantly, and consolidated a formidable international

reputation. In 1886 he was among the founders of the *English Historical Review*, and by the end of the decade was an honorary graduand of Oxford and Cambridge. In 1895 he settled at the latter university, where religious intolerance had denied him any student place forty-five years before, as Rosebery's nominee to the Regius Chair of Modern History. The next six years were perhaps his happiest and most influential.

Wide acclaim greeted the famous inaugural lecture on *The Study of History*. Its peroration, proclaiming Acton's belief in the discipline as an instrument of moral arbitration, was to encourage more silliness in others than in himself. Appreciative audiences attended his subsequent courses which provided much material for the collections of his work published posthumously: *Lectures on Modern History* (1906), *The History of Freedom and Other Essays* (1907), *Historical Essays and Studies* (1907), and *Lectures on the French Revolution* (1910). His last scholarly energies were devoted to completing plans for that great collaborative undertaking *The Cambridge Modern History*, an enormous monument to one kind of positivistic learning. In 1901, exhausted and ill, he again went abroad and died in Bavaria the following year. Thus ended what Acton himself called 'the story of a man who started in life believing himself a sincere Catholic and a sincere Liberal; who therefore renounced everything in Catholicism which was not compatible with Liberty and everything in Politics not compatible with Catholicism'.

Michael Biddiss

See: Gertrude Himmelfarb, *Lord Acton: A Study in Conscience and Politics* (1952); David Matthew, *Lord Acton and His Times* (1968); and Hugh MacDougall, *The Acton-Newman Relations* (1962).

2
ADAMS, Henry Brooks 1838–1918

US historian, novelist

'Probably no child, born in the year, held better cards than he,' Adams wrote in his autobiography *The Education of Henry Adams* (1907), meaning that his great-grandfather was second President of the United States and his grandfather the sixth. The pressure of this ancestry was augmented by his father's distinction as a diplomat, one statesman brother and two others who were writers. But Adams rebelled against such family responsibility to succeed as a deadening limitation, preferring what he termed failure, on his own terms. Harvard, as he later records, taught him 'little, and that little ill', and he graduated in 1858 without honours. Studying law in Germany, he discovered that the value of Berlin's serious reception of the arts was to counter Boston, where 'every one thought Beethoven*

a bore.' Hearing his music proved to be 'among the marvels of education.' And he interviewed Garibaldi* in Italy. His real education had begun. When his father became Minister to England in 1861, Adams worked as his secretary for seven years – which included the Civil War – and experienced upper-class British culture. His letters to the American press included highly provoking remarks on the probability of war with Britain. Articles in the *North American Review* suggested a career in history, and after a spell freelancing on finance for newspapers he became, under family pressure, Assistant Professor of History at Harvard (1870–7) – hence the well-known passage in Pound's *Cantos*: 'Said Mr Adams, of the education,/Teach? at Harvard?/Teach? It cannot be done./And this from the monument' – i.e. from Henry James*.

For Adams history could be neither the conventional bore of successive royals and politicians, nor the deceptions of academic economics and war studies. *The Education*, 'The Tendency of History' (1894) and 'The Rule of Phase Applied to History' (1908), which drew on the physicist Willard Gibb's theory of change in phase and of change in equilibrium, demonstrate the operation of energies and forces: 'The historian's business is to follow the tracks of energy; to find where it comes from and where it went to; its complex course and shifting channels; its values, equivalents, conversions.' Nevertheless, he edited the *North American Review*, took a PhD at Harvard, and built a sound reputation as a historian on lives of Albert Gallatin (1879) and John Randolph (1882) and a comprehensive *History of the United States of America During the Administrations of Jefferson and Madison* (1885–91). Of his two novels, both of which appeared pseudonymously, *Democracy* (1880) tells an inside story exposing the mechanisms of Washington politics, and *Esther* (1884) concerns a woman painter's realization that freethinking, religion, art and marriage are incompatible in American society.

Adam's sense of the discontinuous and chance actions in history received a severe reinforcement with his sister's death by tetanus contracted from a carriage accident. Then the wife he had married in 1872 committed suicide in 1885 (her father's death and her own melancholy temperament were unavoidably catastrophic), an event unmentioned in the autobiography – the gap exemplifies the gaps in true history. Adams began to travel in the hope of release from anguished memory – to Japan, into continental Asia and to Europe, to Tahiti. The most celebrated work of the President of the American Historical Association had yet to come: *Mont-Saint-Michel and Chartres* (1904), *The Education* and *The Degradation of the Democratic Dogma* (posthumously published in 1919), works as coolly analytical of human social energies as his novels. His two representative unities of radiating and controlling energy were the thirteenth-century Virgin of Catholicism and the great cathedral communities, and the dynamo in the Hall of Dynamos at the Chicago Great Exposition of 1893. In order to free himself from American provinciality and an education that befitted him for the eighteenth century, he had to consider the processes of cultural synthesis rather than singularity, multiplicity and a multiverse rather than separations and a universe, to include – as historians customarily did not – science, technology and the particular force of women, in the configurations of power. Chapter six of the first volume of his *History of the United States* concludes with the peculiar problem of American potentiality:

> Could it transmute its social power into the higher forms of thought? Could it provide for the moral and intellectual needs of mankind? . . . Could it produce, or was it compatible with, the differentiation of a higher variety of the human race? Nothing less than this was necessary for its complete success.

He came to believe, as he wrote to his brother, the historian Brooks Adams, that 'science is to wreck us . . . we are like monkeys monkeying with a loaded shell.' He yearned for a cultural unity which would combine science and metaphysics – 'I am a dilution of Lord Kelvin* and St Thomas Aquinas' – and found himself a 'conservative Christian anarchist'. So he became typical of the majority of American liberal intellectuals of the twentieth century. While he remained sceptical of his own achievement, scorned American political behaviour, and rejected the inevitable destructive purposes of scientists, he retained an optimistic view of the human mind, 'itself the subtlest of all known forces', manifested in history and science.

The Pacific and Asia hardly changed him: 'I was a little bored by the calm of the tropical sea, or perhaps it was the greater calm of Buddha that bored me.' The double image of energy which appealed to his active mind was a woman, in *Esther*, gazing at Niagara. In the *History* he protested against the incompetence of 'five million Americans struggling with the untamed continent', an image of betrayal, relying on fraudulent nationalism as unified energy. His vision was more that of the twentieth century: 'Except as reflected in himself, man has no reason for assuming unity in the universe, or an ultimate substance, or a prime-motor.' Between the order of Chartres and the chaos of Washington he chooses neither, and proceeds to diagnose the major modern issues. For example, in 'Prayer to the Virgin of Chartres', found in a wallet of special papers after his death, he wrote: 'Yet we have Gods, for even our strong nerve/Falters before the Energy we own./Which shall be master? Which of us shall serve?' The poem then moves from the electricity generated by the dynamo to energy radiant from the atom – and still the problem remains: how to control power. In *The Education* Adams writes:

> From cradle to grave this problem of running order through chaos, direction through space, discipline through freedom, unity through multiplicity, has always been, and must always be, the task of education, as it is the moral of religion, philosophy, science, art, politics, and economy.

In his youth American political economy was already backward – 'No one, except Karl Marx* foresaw radical change', and 'the blackmailer alone was the normal product of politics as of business.' The future for young Americans could only be positive in accurate knowledge of the processes of change, which neither Aquinas nor Adam Smith nor Marx explained satisfactorily. There was no coherent curve of meaning encompassing everything and controlling direction, much as he would like to demonstrate: 'If a Unity exists, in which and toward which all energies centre, it must explain and include Duality, Diversity, Infinity and Sex!' But only Whitman* used sex as a force rather than a sentiment: 'American art, like the American language and American education, was as far as possible sexless. Society regarded this victory over sex as its greatest triumph.' Psychology is merely a narcissistic trap, 'the mirror of the mind', and the self itself 'a centre of supersensual chaos'. Adams concludes: 'If science were to go on doubling or quadrupling its complexities every ten years, even mathematicians would soon succumb. An average mind had succumbed in 1850; it could no longer understand the problem in 1900.' The historian therefore has no authority; he cannot teach, only learn. But Adams is certain of the utter necessity of an education to understand energy and power: 'The new American child . . . must be a sort of God compared with any former creation of nature. At the rate of progress since 1800, every American who lived into the 2000s would know how to control unlimited power.' But 'a new social mind would be needed to comprehend it.'

Eric Mottram

Other works include *Historical Essays* (1981). See also Worthington Chauncey Ford (ed.), *Letters of Henry Adams 1858–1891* (1930) and *1892–1918* (1938). See: Ernest Samuels, *The Young Henry Adams* (1948), *Henry Adams: The Middle Years* (1958) and *Henry Adams: The Major Phase* (1964); J. C. Levenson, *The Mind and Art of Henry Adams* (1957).

3

AFGHANI, Jamal Uddeen Al 1838–94

Islamic teacher and writer

An Islamic scholar, philosopher, teacher, orator, linguist, journalist and politician, Jamal Uddeen Al Afghani played a leading role in arousing anti-imperialist consciousness in the Muslim world, then dominated by European powers, and encouraging reformist and constitutional movements within Muslim countries. This brought him into conflict with not only Britain, the foremost imperialist nation of the time, but also the rulers of Egypt, Iran and Turkey.

He was a controversial figure, spartan in habits, and a life-long bachelor. His death was kept a secret for many years; and his national origin and birth-place are still a subject of debate. He claimed to have been born of Sunni parents at Asadabad near Konar, in the district of Kabul, Afghanistan, in 1838. But his critics insisted that his birth-place was Asadabad near Hamadan in western Iran, and that his parents were Shia, a minority sect, and that he lied about his Shia origin so as not to alienate the Sunni majority.

There is however no doubt that he spent his childhood and adolescence in Kabul where he studied Islam as well as philosophy and exact sciences. He left Afghanistan when he was eighteen, and was abroad for five years. He stayed in India for over a year; and after his pilgrimage to Mecca went to Karbala and Najaf in Iraq. On his return to Afghanistan, he helped the ruler, Dost Mohammed Khan, to mount a successful attack on Herat. After Khan's death in 1863, he became involved in the civil war which broke out. His patron lost; and he was expelled from Afghanistan in September 1868. He went to India and Egypt and then Istanbul, where he was well received.

Afghani lectured at such prestigious places in Istanbul as Sultan Ahmed's mosque and Aya Sofia. In one of his lectures he described imparting prophetic teachings as a human craft or skill. This offended the religious establishment, headed by the Shaikh al Islam (Wise Man of Islam), Hasan Fahmi, who was jealous of his scholarship and popularity. Under the circumstances Afghani considered it prudent to leave Istanbul.

He arrived in Cairo in March 1871, and was given an annual allowance of 12,000 Egyptian piastres by the ruler, Khedive Ismail. Besides teaching his disciples theology and philosophy, he urged them to take up journalism, since he regarded the written word as the most effective method of influencing the minds of contemporaries. Among his students were Mohammed Abdu and Said Zaghlul Pasha: the former was to become the grand mufti of Egypt, and the latter a founder of the nationalist Wafd Party. He helped establish a daily newspaper and a monthly journal. He encouraged patriotic resistance to growing British and French interference into Egypt's affairs, attacked Khedive Ismail for his spendthriftness, and proposed a parliamentary system of government.

When, in early 1879, Tawfiq succeeded his father, Khedive Ismail, the British advised him to expel Afghani. He did so. In September, Afghani was deported to Hyderabad, India, and then to Calcutta, and kept under British surveillance. This continued until the simmering nationalist movement in Egypt had burst out as an armed uprising in 1881–2, and had then been crushed by British troops.

In January 1883, Afghani turned up in Paris. Four months later he published an article in the *Journal des Débats* in which he refuted Joseph-Ernest Renan's* arguments, delivered in an earlier lecture, that Islam and science were incompatible. With the help of Indian Muslims living in Paris, he and Mohammed Abdu started a journal, *Al Urwat al Wuthqa* ('The Indissoluble Link'), in March 1884. Because of its opposition to the British policies in such countries as Egypt and India, the journal was banned by the British in their colonies. It ceased publication seven months later.

Following an invitation in 1886 by Nasir Uddeen Shah, the ruler of Iran, Afghani went to live in Tehran. But his popularity there soon disconcerted the shah. The next year he left for Uzbekistan province of tsarist Russia. There he engaged in propaganda against the British in India; and this pleased the tsar. At his urging, the tsar allowed the publication of the *Koran* and other Islamic literature in Russia for the first time.

In 1889, on the way to the Paris World Exhibition, he met the Shah of Iran in Munich. Accepting the shah's invitation, he returned to Tehran. But his stay there was short and unhappy. His plan for reforming the judiciary aroused the shah's suspicion; and he retired to a religious sanctuary near the capital. In early 1891, the shah sent a large force of cavalry to arrest him, and banish him to Khaniqin at the Iranian-Turkish border.

After Afghani had reached Basra, and recovered his health, he attacked the shah for giving tobacco concessions to a British company. His disciple, Mirza Hassan Shirazi, the first clergy of Samarra, decreed that the faithful should stop smoking until the shah had withdrawn his tobacco concession. The shah yielded.

Afghani then travelled to London, and carried out a sustained campaign against the dictatorial rule of the shah, chiefly through *Diyal al Khafikayn* ('Radiance of the Two Hemispheres'), a monthly journal published in Farsi and English. He thus helped to build a reformist movement in Iran under the leadership of the clergy, which was dedicated to the shah's overthrow.

When the Sultan of Turkey invited Afghani to Istanbul, he went. There the sultan gave him a generous monthly allowance and tried to persuade him to cease his propaganda against the shah. He refused and sought, in vain, to leave. On 11 March 1896 the Shah of Iran was murdered by Mirza Mohammed Reza, a disciple of Afghani. This led to the accusation that Afghani had guided the assassin's hand: a charge he denied in an interview with the Paris-based *Le Temps*. About a year later he died of cancer of the chin, and was buried in Nishantash. In December 1944 his body was removed from there and sent to Ali Abad, a suburb of Kabul, where it has rested since then.

Afghani made four major contributions to Islamic and secular thought and action. He argued that each believer had the right and responsibility to interpret the *Koran* and the *Sunna* ('custom') for himself. He wanted the people to help themselves, and often quoted the Koranic verse which states: 'Verily, Allah does not change the state of a people until they change themselves inwardly.' He urged Muslims to master science as a means of liberating themselves from the domination of Western nations. While he stressed the pan-Islamic concept throughout his life, in his writings and lectures on India he underlined the need for unity between Muslims and Hindus in their struggle against British rule.

As the anti-imperialist movement sharpened in Islamic and non-Islamic colonies, in the wake of the Second World War, interest in Afghani's teachings rose dramatically. The success of the Islamic revolution in Iran in 1979 reiterated the significance of Afghani and his views.

Dilip Hiro

See: E. G. Browne, *The Persian Revolution of 1905–1909* (1910); Elie Kedourie, *Afghani and Abduh: An Essay on Religious Unbelief and Political Action in Modern Islam* (1966); Nikki R. Keddie, *An Islamic Response to Imperialism: Political and Religious Writings of Sayyid Jamal ad-Din 'al-Afghani'* (1968) and *Sayyid Jamal ad-Din 'al-Afghani': A Political Biography* (1972); A. Albert Kudsi-Zadea, *Sayyid Jamal ad-Din Al Afghani: An Annotated Bibliography* (1970).

4
AGASSIZ, Jean Louis Rodolphe 1807–73

Swiss naturalist

Agassiz was born in Switzerland and had a varied European education, attending universities in Zurich, Heidelberg and Munich, and studying under the foremost European comparative anatomist, Georges Cuvier*, in Paris. He returned to Switzerland as a professor at the College of Neuchâtel in 1832, but continued to travel widely. In 1847 he moved to America to take up a professorship at Harvard University. He remained in this post until his death.

The formative influences on him were contradictory.

From his German education he picked up the *Naturphilosophie* of Schelling* and Oken. This led him to see plants and animals as temporal realizations of eternal, divine ideas: in tracing the structure of, and relations between, living things, he wrote, 'the human mind is only translating into human language the Divine thoughts expressed in nature in living realities' (*Essay on Classification*, 1859). The other influence came from Cuvier, who taught him the sober, meticulous, empirical methods of fossil comparative anatomy. These two influences combined in Agassiz's work to produce a characteristic tone: brilliant empirical studies of fossils are set in a cloudy interpretative framework. Both influences, however, together with Agassiz's own firm beliefs, acted in one clear direction: they combined to insist that naturalistic evolution, as proposed by Charles Darwin* in 1859, has not occurred. According to Agassiz, the naturalist does not see material, genetic connections between living things. Rather, the relations between species show 'the omnipresence of the Creator' (*ibid.*). Agassiz became the chief scientific opponent of Darwin's theory in America, attacking it both at the empirical level and at the level of its philosophical and religious implications. Thus, his life ended on a sour note. He had become one of the leading figures on what was, by 1873, the losing side.

But this defeat should not obscure his earlier achievements. His *Recherches sur les poissons fossiles* ('Researches into Fossil Fish', 5 vols, Neuchâtel, 1833–44) followed the methods of his master, Cuvier, and established him as a leading icthyologist (student of fish structure). His descriptive palaeontological work could be detached from its location within his metaphysics and be used independently by naturalists working in other traditions.

Agassiz also contributed to the debate about the possibility of former Ice Ages. The earth was widely believed by geologists to be slowly cooling down. The prospect, therefore, of a time in the recent geological past when conditions in Europe were spectacularly *colder* was difficult to envisage. Consequently, studies of glaciation tended to be rather idiosyncratic. Agassiz made a complex topic more complex by proposing, during the late 1830s, not just that existing glaciers had once been much more extensive, but that perhaps the whole of the northern hemisphere had, fairly recently, been blanketed in ice. Agassiz was well disposed towards the idea of vast ice-sheets, for they gave him a mechanism for the utter extinction of complete floras and faunas, leaving the hemisphere vacant for a complete new range of plants and animals to be created by God. Ice Ages were a guarantee against evolutionary continuity. Agassiz's work on glaciation was brought together in his *Études sur les glaciers* ('Studies on Glaciers', 2 vols, Neuchâtel, 1840).

When he went to America, in 1847, Agassiz's interests shifted somewhat from research towards the popularization of natural history and towards the establishment of a well-endowed university research institute. Under his guidance, and as a consequence of his fund-raising, the Harvard Museum of Comparative Zoology was founded in 1859. He also entered the debate about human origins, proposing that there were a number of distinct human varieties – or perhaps even species – and that all humans are not descended from common ancestors. The notion that blacks and whites are not genetically related was eagerly taken up by defenders of slavery. Agassiz's research on this topic reflects his own prior commitments as much as his rather scanty anthropological studies.

Overall, Agassiz's influence was mixed. His palaeontological work endured. His implacable opposition to Darwin lent scientific prestige to the case of the opponents of evolution. His campaign for the institutionalization of science in America was probably his most enduring activity. His Romantic metaphysics have not been fully explored, but they serve to show that there were competing modes of biological study during the nineteenth century: the triumph of the Darwinian mode should not obliterate the significance of *Naturphilosophie*.

Michael Bartholomew

The standard biography is E. Lurie, *Louis Agassiz: A Life in Science* (1960). A good representative work by Agassiz is L. Agassiz, *Essay on Classification* (1859, repr. edn, E. Lurie, 1962).

ALBERT, Prince Consort: see under VICTORIA and ALBERT

5
ALCOTT, Louisa May 1832–88

US novelist

Louisa May Alcott is remembered for that most seductive of all American girls' classics, *Little Women: Or Meg, Jo, Beth and Amy* (1868–9), the fictional version of her family in New England during the Civil War. But it presents a bowdlerized view of the Alcotts of Concord, Massachusetts, for her transcendentalist father, Bronson Alcott, is almost wholly eliminated though he overshadowed her life. It is impossible to understand the daughter without first confronting that unscrupulous sage and high-minded parasite.

Bronson Alcott was an educational theorist, intent on transmitting the ideas of Pestalozzi and Froebel* to America. Louisa May (the second of his four daughters) was born in Germantown, Pennsylvania, where he had founded a progressive school. On the school's collapse the family moved to Boston, where further

educational failures – and the dissolution of the experimental commune at Fruitlands near Harvard – eventually drove the Alcotts to Concord. The girls, who were educated entirely at home, received extra tuition from their new neighbours, especially from Emerson*, Sophia Hawthorne and Thoreau*.

But the family was now in dire need of finance. Louisa wrote fables and melodramas and poems. She served as a volunteer nurse in Georgetown for three months before contracting typhoid and being sent home. The resulting loss of hair and teeth made her feel old at thirty. She published her letters home from the Union Hotel Hospital as *Hospital Sketches* (1863), which won her an audience in the north. She wrote her first novel, *Moods* (1864), centred on Thoreau, on whom she had had something of a crush. All her fiction was to a large extent autobiographical. But it was with *Little Women* that she achieved runaway sales and immured herself for two decades within the code of female subservience and self-sacrifice that her novel so successfully promoted.

That was the paradox. She was a headstrong, assertive woman, an abolitionist (like her father), fighting for temperance reform and women's suffrage, editing a children's magazine (*Merry's Museum*, 1867), yet her principal theme was that of feminine self-suppression: 'moral pap for the young', she called it. Her own self-portrait is drawn in 'Jo March', the impetuous boy-girl who deliberately tames herself into a 'little woman', just as she transformed her sisters Anna, Lizzie and May into the dull Meg, the saintly Beth and shallow, complacent Amy. Yet *Little Women* is corroded by guilt and sexual inhibition. Its bottled-up aggression finds outlet in violent self-sacrifice and a desperate desire not to grow up. In Jo's own comic idiom: 'I wish wearing flat-irons on our heads would keep us from growing up. But buds will be roses, and kittens, cats.'

For women must grow up: that is the moral. They must become the cooks and nurses of family life. Little women work; it is the Tom Sawyers who shirk. It is only boys – as *Good Wives* (1871), *Little Men* (1871), and *Jo's Boys* (1886) make abundantly clear – who are free to scribble, to explore, to expound and improvidently evade the responsibilities of daily life. Women are the practical angels who protect male innocents (like father) under their sheltering wings. As a juvenile author, Louisa May Alcott retreated from guilt into permanent adolescence. As 'Aunt Jo' she compiled a *Scrap-Bag* (6 vols, 1872–82) for children. She shared the same birthday with her father and died in Boston within forty-eight hours of his death on the very day he was buried.

Yet her bibliography runs to more than 250 items, including three novels for adults. *Hospital Sketches* remains one of the most vivid mementoes of the Civil War. 'Transcendental Wild Oats', published in *Silver Pitchers* (1876), is a hilarious account of her father's

'Con-Sociate Family' experiment at Fruitlands. *Work: A Story of Experience* (1873) relates her own early life as housemaid and seamstress in Boston during the 1860s; while her anonymous gothic tales, with their scheming and sexually bewitching heroines (the very obverse of Jo March), have been collected by Madeleine B. Stern in *Behind a Mask: The Unknown Thrillers* (1976).

Harold Beaver

Ednah D. Cheney edited Louisa May Alcott's *Life, Letters and Journals* in 1889. Since then her biography has been written three times: Katherine Anthony, *Louisa May Alcott* (1938); Madeleine B. Stern, *Louisa May Alcott* (1950); and more recently, and most successfully, Martha Saxton, *Louisa May: A Modern Biography of Louisa May Alcott* (1978).

6
ALGER, Horatio, Jr 1832–99

US author

The Rev. Horatio Alger's pride in family was not fully transmitted to his son, Horatio Jr, despite the constant recountings of Algers on the *Mayflower*, marital connections with the Quincys, service in the Continental Army and the reverend's memories of days at Harvard. From his birth in Revere, Massachusetts, Alger was slated to follow in his father's footsteps. And indeed he did graduate from Harvard in 1852 while his proud father watched, having taken time off from his abolitionist activities with Theodore Parker. In August 1853, as planned, the young graduate enrolled in Harvard Divinity School despite an inclination to continue his tentative start as a writer of moral tales and poetry. He soon dropped out to pursue this writing career, returning reluctantly to the divinity school to take his degree in 1860.

In 1863 after a trip to Europe Alger made his first visit to New York City, exploring the streets and taking notes as he had done in London and Paris. All of Alger's biographers agree that he was deadly serious in his ambition to become a chronicler of the new urban life even more realistic than Dickens*; but once he forsook his potential career as a minister and settled in New York to become a writer and chaplain of a Newsboys' Lodging House, these biographers of the creator of the 'American Dream' differ widely: some insisting that he was an industrious, influential, respected humanitarian and novelist, others emphasizing his insecurity caused by a domineering father and hinting at an unusual interest in young boys, while still others talk of love affairs with various women including a married woman who eventually rejected him. It seems that when someone decides to write about Alger they do so to uphold or mock the virtues and ideals

which his tales preached. Industry, frugality, and prudence (Franklin's 'way to wealth') are the ideals offered to the poor by Alger and those that admire such preaching find much to admire in Alger's life; those who find such preachings hypocritically pious find much to criticize and speculate about.

Certain facts are clear. He accepted a pastorate at Brewster, Massachusetts, preaching, teaching and writing until 1866, when he left Brewster and the ministry to pursue his literary career. In 1868 the publication of his eighth book, *Ragged Dick: or, Street Life in New York*, established him as a best-selling author of boys' books in the rags to riches format. He became close friends with Charles O'Connor, superintendent of the Newsboys' Lodging House, which led to the close connections with those boys over the years. In 1872 his book, *Phil, the Fiddler*, courageously exposed the Italian padrones who bought boys in Italy, brought them to New York, and sent them out on the streets as musician-beggars. He also spoke publicly on that abuse and suffered threats and retaliation as a result. He won many honours and made millions for his publisher. He died a bachelor in his sister's home on 18 July 1899.

Whether he was a pederast, child molester, frustrated adulterer, lover of cabarets, or a model man of God hardly matters. What does matter is the kind of story Alger dreamed and how America responded to it. No source can agree on just how many books by Alger were sold during his life and after, but estimates range from seventeen million to three hundred million and given the wide circulation of his dime novels and magazine serials as they passed from hand to hand one can be sure that his readers did include a large number of the American population in the second half of the nineteenth century and early twentieth. And those readers told the Alger success story over and over again: anyone can become rich in the United States if they work hard enough, are moral enough and dream (want) it enough. The Alger myth stressed Individualism, Upward Mobility, and Hard Work, all taking place in the tumultuous world of the Big City. The Goal was Success: wealth, respectability, and virtue. The three were divinely interwoven and could not exist without each other. His publisher A. K. Loring wrote that Alger had portrayed 'the ambitious soul' of the country, 'the spirit of reborn America', 'the turmoil of the city streets . . . above all you can hear the cry of triumph of the oppressed over the oppressor'. While this self-serving, optimistic evaluation may be extravagant, it does strike the great chord of immigrant optimism that provided so much of the cheap labour, 'the turmoil of the city streets', and the rare genuine rags-to-riches story of that time. Alger saw his 'streets of New York' through innocent Harvard-coloured eyes and that was the preferred view. Although Alger's boys work hard and preserve their virtue, it is usually chance, in the form of a rich benefactor, that brings them reward.

Yet Alger thought he was being realistic. He wanted to show, above all, what his beloved boys of the street must suffer. He knew not only about evil padrones and the day-to-day struggles of the street urchins, but also of the particular crimes that haunted this world as they did that of Dickens. Theft, murder, brutality, child-beating, conmanship, kidnapping and shoplifting are as common in his books as are the lurid characters that make such practices their way of life, and they seem more credible and pervasive than the virtuous rich or even the criticized ideal rich. Alger knew his urban streets; he just dreamed too easily that a child could escape them.

Alger is rarely read now and yet his myth is still invoked by politicians, educators, and many religious leaders. Youth can be 'Adrift in New York', with 'The Odds Against Him', 'Shifting for Himself'; but 'Struggling Upward' if he is 'Brave and Bold', he will 'Strive and Succeed'. The Horatio Alger hero pervaded the American mind for almost a century before it finally died, if it really has. Alger never wrote the big novel for adults that he talked of and his literary style has been chuckled over for decades but he plucked from the American culture around him one of the basic heroes of his time and that is no small accomplishment for any writer.

Charles Gregory

Alger's other books include: *Mark the Match Boy* (1869, Ragged Dick Series); *Rough and Ready; or Life among the New York Newsboys* (1869, Ragged Dick Series); *Paul the Peddlar, or, The Adventures of a Young Street Merchant* (1871, Tattered Tom Series); *Risen from the Ranks; or, Harry Walton's Success* (1874, Luck and Pluck Series); *From Canal Boy to President* (1881); *Helping Himself; or Grant Thornton's Ambition* (1886). See: Herbert R. Mayes, *A Biography Without a Hero* (1928); Frank Gruber, *Horatio Alger, Jr: A Biography and Bibliography* (1961); Ralph Gardner, *Horatio Alger, or The American Hero Era* (1964); John Tebbel, *From Rags to Riches: Horatio Alger, Jr., and The American Dream* (1963); Edwin P. Hoyt, *Horatio's Boys: The Life and Works of Horatio Alger, Jr.* (1974); Malcolm Cowley, 'The Alger Story', *New Republic* (1945).

7
ALKAN, Charles-Valentin 1813–88

French composer and pianist

Among the composers rescued from obscurity by the revival of interest in nineteenth-century Romanticism, Alkan is almost certainly the most valuable discovery. Long dismissed as a writer of mere technical exercises, his music – when performed by a few dedicated artists and circulated in new editions and recordings – has amply confirmed Busoni's judgment that he stands with Liszt*, Chopin*, Schumann* and Brahms* as one of the five greatest piano composers since Beethoven*.

Born into a large and prodigiously musical Parisian Jewish family of Alsatian extraction, Alkan (he took the forename of his father, the piano teacher Alkan Morhange) became a student at the Paris Conservatoire at the age of six, made his public debut at seven (as a violinist), gained the Paris Conservatoire's first prize for piano at the age of ten, and gave his first public piano recital when he was twelve. Until the mid-1840s he was one of the most celebrated piano virtuosi in Paris, and often shared the platform with Liszt, Thalberg, and especially Chopin who, with George Sand*, became a close friend and next-door neighbour. But around the time of Chopin's death Alkan withdrew from public life and devoted himself to composition. Apart from a brief return to the concert stage in the mid-1870s, when he gave several series of recitals remarkable for their technical difficulty and imaginative programming, he remained an apparently misanthropic recluse, a vague legend in his own life-time. The traditional story of his death – crushed by a bookcase – has recently been impugned, but not disproved.

Alkan is said to have been the only pianist in whose presence even Liszt felt nervous; and Vincent d'Indy*, who heard him play near the end of his life, maintained that he surpassed Liszt in interpretative powers. He was admired for an absolute technical mastery, a striking range of colour, and most of all for a rhythmic discipline which scorned rubato and made him the supreme exponent of the French *style sévère*. All these qualities are demanded by his own music. He wrote a certain amount of orchestral music (mostly lost), some fine chamber works and a great deal for the now ob-solete pedal-piano, but his reputation rests securely on his vast output for the piano. Hummel, Cherubini* and Chopin were early influences, and Beethoven and Bach an abiding inspiration, for music which makes most imaginative use of the full range of the keyboard and often poses the performer fearsome rhythmic chal-lenges to be taken at headlong pace in absolutely un-yielding tempo (a typical example is the Allegro Barbaro from the 12 Studies in the Major Keys op.35, which inspired Bartók's similarly titled piece).

Alkan also displays striking harmonic individuality (especially in the use of diatonic dissonance) and an occasionally awesome grasp of large-scale structure. It is these features, quite as much as his uncanny skill at suggesting orchestral timbres in purely pianistic terms, which earn him the epithet bestowed by one of his pupils: 'the Berlioz* of the piano'. His originality may easily be grasped by an examination of his *Grande Sonate* (op. 33, 1847), which *begins* with a scherzo, proceeds to a vast Faustian allegro which includes, among other things, a fugue in nine real parts, and concludes with two completely contrasted slow movements. Meanwhile the key scheme takes the music further and further away from its original D major, and ends it in the remote regions of G sharp minor. Even more impressive are the Symphony for piano and, above all, the huge Concerto for solo piano (undoubtedly one of the greatest piano works of the nineteenth century) – both of which are merely part of the massive set of *12 Études dans les tons mineurs* (op. 39, 1857). Alkan also wrote many smaller pieces which show a surprisingly wide expressive and psychological range, with frequent leanings towards the bizarre, the grotesque and the sardonic. In the course of these he invented the 'cluster' chord seventy years before Henry Cowell, and anticipated some of the characteristic devices and atmospheres of both Mahler* and Sibelius.

Malcolm MacDonald

Other works include: 6 volumes of *Chants* for piano; *Sonatine* (op. 61, 1861); *Marche funèbre et marche triomphale* (op. 26, 1844); *Menuetto alla tedesca* (op. 46, 1857); *2 Capriccii* (op. 50, 1857); *Grande sonate de concert* for cello and piano (op. 47, 1857). See: Ronald Smith, *Alkan: Volume One, The Enigma* (1976); Raymond Lewenthal, editorial notes to *The Piano Music of Alkan* (1964).

8

ANDERSEN, Hans Christian 1805–75

Danish author

There are few nineteenth-century writers about whose character and development we know so much as Hans Christian Andersen's. Not only did he publish several autobiographies and accounts of his long, restless travels throughout Europe, but he also kept a number of diaries and was a prolific letter-writer. Between his private notes and the public presentation of his curriculum vitae as *The Fairy Tale of My Life* (*Mit Livs Eventyr*, 1855, trans. 1951) there exists a tension, a level of contradiction: behind the idealization we discover an earnest social climber sustained by an unshakeable faith in God's providence.

Andersen grew up in the slums of Odense, the only child of a journeyman shoemaker and a washerwoman. In such an environment (he later referred to himself as a 'swamp plant') he was fortunate to be noticed for his talents by several wealthy patrons. At the age of fourteen he moved to Copenhagen, determined to win recognition as a performing or creative artist. When he kept failing, his patrons, in particular Jonas Collins, a director of the Royal Theatre, sponsored his education at grammar school and, for a one-year introductory

course, at the university. While still a student he published several collections of poetry, prose and drama. Financially he remained unsecured until 1838, when he was awarded an annual grant from the public purse. But even then he did not change his life-style. He continued a bachelor, staying mainly as a guest in different houses between his travels.

The culture to which Andersen the outsider and underdog strove to belong was the golden age of arts and scholarship in Denmark. This period, generally reckoned to be between the years 1800 and 1864, contained, besides Andersen himself, Søren Kierkegaard* and the sculptor Bertel Thorvaldsen. The ideal of education was bourgeois classicist; German idealism supplied the criteria of ethics and aesthetics, and literary criticism derived its judgments from Schelling* and Hegel*. Danish literature itself moved gradually from Romanticism through a Biedermeier (or 'bourgeois Romantic') compromise towards realism. Andersen acknowledged Walter Scott*, E. T. A. Hoffmann* and Heinrich Heine* as his masters, although two Danish writers, Adam Oehlenschläger and Johan Ludvig Heiberg, were an equal influence on him in his formative years.

Andersen's route to the fairy tale, the form upon which his reputation so firmly rests, was indirect and multifarious. Before he chose to become a writer he tried his hand at acting, singing and dancing; and before he came to fairy tales he had already written plays, poetry, novels and travelogues. In the narrative genre he stands as a pioneer in Scandinavian literature, and it was as a novelist that he first became known, particularly after the publication of *The Improvisatore* (*Improvisatoren*, trans. 1845) in 1835. If success in the theatre was restricted to *Mulatten* ('The Mulatto', 1840), as a travel writer he was outstanding. *Skyggebilleder* ('Shadow Pictures', 1838 – cf. Heine's *Reisebilder*), about his first trip to Germany, *En Digters Bazar* ('A Poet's Bazaar', 1842), about a journey to the near orient, and *I Sverrig* ('In Sweden', 1851) are justly regarded by Scandinavians as classics.

A month after *The Improvisatore* Andersen published his first fairy tales in the form of *Eventyr, fortalte for Børn* ('Fairy Tales Told for Children', 1835), a slim volume containing four short texts: 'The Tinderbox', 'Little Claus and Big Claus', 'The Princess on the Pea' – which were reworked from folklore – and 'Little Ida's Flowers', his own creation, like nearly all his later tales. As their fame spread among the young and old, at home and abroad, he kept adding to their number, dropping in 1843 the reference 'for children' and calling them from the 1850s *Eventyr og Historier* ('Fairy Tales and Stories'). By 1872, almost forty years after the series commenced and three years before his death, and when his last collection was published (*Nye Eventyr og Historier* – 'New Fairy Tales and Stories'), their tally had swollen to 156.

It is as a writer, and not just a purveyor, of fairy tales that Andersen is revered. It was common practice in Romantic culture to set down folk tales that had survived orally (*Volksmärchen*) as well as to invent one's own (*Kunstmärchen*). The complex reasons that this was so are perhaps best summarized as a reaction to the Enlightenment, which had set greatest store on the attainment of reason. The Romantics, by contrast, tried to regain what had been lost: man's and mankind's childhood paradise. Andersen was no *poeta doctus*, living forever separated from folklore's naive and popular origins: both his background and his temperament help explain how his talent was so suited to the direction it eventually took. First, he had been born into the social class where folklore was most vigorously preserved, and many of the stories he later adapted he first heard as a child. Second, his inability to 'achieve the common' (Kierkegaard), to learn and follow a profession, to marry and settle down, meant that his childhood mind survived into adulthood to an unusual degree. Finally, his artistic strengths were for narrative, for the fantastic, and for the small-scale; epic discipline and realistic consistency were qualities he found difficult to sustain.

His aptitude for the fairy tale was first exercised in the houses he visited, where he entertained the children of his hosts with stories that were either memorized or improvised. His manner of delivery is described by a contemporary:

> He spoke continually with plenty of phrases that children used, and gestures to match. Even the driest of sentences was given life. He didn't say, 'The children got into the carriage and then drove away', but, 'So they got in the carriage, good-bye Daddy, good-bye Mummy, the whip cracked, snick, snack, and away they went, giddy up!'

In its written form Andersen's story-telling used the same grammar, spontaneity and vivacity. The mythical plots and the magical world of the fairy tale were renewed correspondingly: Andersen individualized and sentimentalized, rationalized and moralized, idyllized and humorized it. Being thus adapted to the Victorian ideology of both parents and children, it also lost its character of the original 'simple form' and gained its unique 'naivistic' sophistication.

'What author,' asked Georg Brandes in 1869, 'has a public like him?' And the same question might be asked today, over a hundred years after his death, when children throughout the world are still brought up reading 'The Little Mermaid', 'The Emperor's New Clothes', 'The Steadfast Tin Soldier', 'The Nightingale', 'The Ugly Duckling', 'The Snow Queen' and 'The Little Match Girl'. To account for his extraordinary popularity it is insufficient to point to his style alone, although in that respect the difference between Andersen and the folklorists proper (e.g. Charles Perrault and the Grimm* brothers) is as strongly marked as in the content of his tales. Indeed, the full force of his style can only be felt by the Danish reader. An immense influence on novelists and short-story writers in Denmark since the days of Naturalism and Impressionism, Andersen's prose is difficult to translate. It is rather the originality and semantic riches of his plots that guarantee his celebrity abroad.

Bernhard Glienke

Andersen's other novels include *O.T.* (1836, trans. 1845) and *Kun en spillemand* (1837, trans. *Only a Fiddler*, 1845). Among the hundreds of English translations of the *Tales*, the best are by Paul Leyssac (1937), Jean Hersholt (1947), R. P. Keigwin (1951–60), Reginald Spink (1960), L. W. Kingsland (1961) and Eric C. Haugaard (1974). See: Frederick J. Marcker, *Hans Christian Andersen and the Romantic Theatre* (1971); Reginald Spink, *Hans Christian Andersen and his World* (1972); Elias Bredsdorff, *Hans Christian Andersen: The Story of His Life and Work 1805–75* (1975); and Bø Gronbech, *Hans Christian Andersen* (1980).

9

ANTHONY, Susan Brownell 1820–1906

US feminist

It was a surprise to no one that the first face of a woman to appear on a coin of US currency was that of Susan B. Anthony (1979). In a republic where all the presidents whose faces have been the ones on the coins have been male, the best-known historical woman was the one who is justly credited more than any other with the gaining of the right to vote for women. The Nineteenth Amendment to the American Constitution giving women the elective franchise was known for years before its passage (1920) as the 'Susan B. Anthony Amendment'. Even when women's history was largely absent from education, every schoolchild was likely to know the name of Susan B. Anthony.

Introduced to the women's rights issue and the leader of its campaign, Elizabeth Cady Stanton*, two years after the historic Seneca Falls convention (1848), the first American women's rights gathering and the occasion when suffrage was first called for publicly by American women, Susan B. Anthony formed with Stanton an active partnership and a friendship that lasted more than fifty years. Stanton was the theorist, logician and stylist of the twosome; Anthony provided determination and single-mindedness. These qualities, together with deep affection for and loyalty to each other, made them ideally complementary collaborators in an important cause.

Anthony had a secure childhood in an upstate New

York family familiar with radical political action. Her mother, Lucy Read Anthony, was the daughter of a Massachusetts legislator. Daniel Anthony, her father, farmer, mill owner, insurance businessman in sequence, was an abolitionist and temperance movement activist whose friends included Frederick Douglass* and William Lloyd Garrison. She was educated in her family's Quaker faith, one of the tenets of which was that women and men are equal before God, and one of their practices was that women were allowed to speak in meetings as readily as men. Out of her years related to her father's cotton mill management, she developed an enduring interest in labour problems. Throughout her childhood, she was given emotional support and education by her parents and included in their abolitionist and temperance efforts.

When her father experienced economic setback in the late 1830s, she went out to teach. It was a matter of considerable import to her that women teachers earned much less money than men. She was involved in the state convention of schoolteachers in New York and caused a stir in 1853 when she asked to speak on the floor of its gathering, itself controversy enough, and then in that speech pointed out that the reason that teachers were paid low wages was that women were in the profession.

Susan B. Anthony tired of teaching and returned home in 1850 to be introduced by a Seneca Falls temperance editor, Amelia Bloomer, to Elizabeth Cady Stanton. Her parents and younger sister, Mary, had attended in 1848 the women's rights convention called by Stanton, Lucretia Mott and the others.

From this beginning the two women forged an alliance that saw them throughout the 1850s organizing women's rights and suffrage associations, giving Lyceum lectures and writing petitions and arguments for newspapers of the movement. They said of their rhetoric that Elizabeth 'forged the thunderbolts' and Susan 'hurled them'. For her tactical leadership Anthony was called by William Henry Channing 'the Napoleon* of the women's rights movement'. It was she who bore the brunt of greatest vilification of the women. Unmarried, plain-looking and intensely serious, she was singled out for ridicule in the press and on public platforms. The women's issues were several, including divorce, child custody and property rights for women, employment, education, household management, health and dress among them, as well as the vote. Their programme was more comprehensive in the early years than the movement's came to be between 1890 and 1920 when the vote became such a singular issue. One proposed solution to the dress question was the Bloomer costume, a tunic top with pantaloons, which Susan B. Anthony wore for a year in the face of horrendous opprobrium, finally being persuaded by Stanton that the ill-effect of the negative attention was worse for their cause than wearing long dresses.

Susan B. Anthony but dimly understood, if at all, female human reproductive questions. She jealously chided her married cohorts, Stanton, Lucy Stone and Antoinette Brown, for their 'baby-making' when there was so much work to be done. Once she wrote to Elizabeth, 'Those of you who have the talent to do honor to poor womanhood, have all given yourself over to baby-making; and left poor brainless me to do battle alone.'

Still, her affinities were deep both in particular and in the abstract, and she was open in her receptivity to new people and ideas. Her friendship with Stanton was described as life-long by both of them in the metaphors of marriage. When the Civil War came in 1861, she was willing to subordinate the women's effort into the abolition effort for 'the Negroes' hour', but after the war she was distressed to see the word 'male' put into the American Constitution in the Fourteenth Amendment giving the Negro the vote. Even so, for a time in 1870 she was willing to follow the lead of Victoria Woodhull in taking before Congress the interpretation that the Fourteenth Amendment already granted women the right to vote. However, coming to see the self-aggrandizement at the heart of Woodhull's campaign, Anthony withdrew before the failure of that effort.

After the Civil War, Anthony was a part of the American Equal Rights Association, a group led by Theodore Tilton that increasingly came to sacrifice the women's effort. Following a campaign in Kansas in which the women worked but the Republican leaders did not include woman suffrage, Anthony and Stanton started a woman suffrage newspaper, the *Revolution* (1868). In 1869, they formed the National Woman Suffrage Association. A more conservative American Woman Suffrage Association was begun the same year. For the next twenty years, the organization was the focus for hard, relentless political activity for Anthony. She organized campaigns in states across the country, travelled and made speeches, wrote and circulated petitions. In 1872, she purposefully voted illegally in a presidential election, was found guilty by a United States District Court, refused to pay the fine, but was not even taken to higher court for the violation. Near the end of that decade, she, Stanton and Matilda Joslyn Gage began a *History of Woman Suffrage*, a monumental work chronicling their effort, the first volume of which appeared in 1881, the whole work spanning six volumes, Ida Husted Harper finishing the last two after Anthony's death (1881–1922).

In 1890 the National American Woman Suffrage Association was formed as a merger of the two former associations with Stanton and Anthony continuing in leadership. Their radical positions they held with more conviction than their younger associates. As president of the association in 1896, Anthony found herself defending Stanton's *The Woman's Bible*, a project in religious interpretation and liberal biblical commentary she had not cared about as passionately as Stanton had but she defended it in the name of religious liberty.

As an active aged woman, Anthony was revered in a way she had not been when young. She received many honours, among them a gift of financial support to write a large three-volume *Life of Susan B. Anthony* with the help of Ida Husted Harper (1898, 1898, 1908). Leader of the American delegation to the International Woman Suffrage Alliance in Berlin in 1904, she was proclaimed 'Susan B. Anthony of the World'. Protégées of hers, Carrie Chapman Catt and Anna Howard Shaw, became her successors as presidents of the National American Woman Suffrage Association. Methodist minister and physician, 'Annie' Howard Shaw, was her personal favourite, and their friendship was the source for Gertrude Stein's opera tribute to Susan B., *The Mother of Us All* (1922).

Attending her last convention in 1906, she left her optimistic thematic message for women: 'Failure is impossible,' she said.

Gayle Graham Yates

See: *The Concise History of Woman Suffrage*, ed. Mari Jo and Paul Buhle (1978); Katharine Susan Anthony, *Susan B. Anthony: Her Personal History and Her Era* (1954); Alma Lutz, *Susan B. Anthony: Rebel, Crusader, Humanitarian* (1959); Eleanor Flexner, *Century of Struggle* (1959).

10
ANTOINE, André 1858–1943

French theatre director, actor and critic

By the second half of the nineteenth century the French theatre had reached its lowest ebb in modern times. As Dumas *fils** said, 'a man without any value as a thinker, moralist, philosopher or writer could be a dramatist of the first rank.' Theatre was a commercial affair, plagued by rapacious management, the star performer system and the most unambitious standards of formula playwriting. If a century later, by 1950, the French theatre had reached a peak which it had not scaled for three hundred years, credit for the first faltering steps out of the mire, and credit too for inspiring a revival of the German and English theatre at the end of the nineteenth century, must go to a young and theatrically inexperienced employee of the Paris Gas Company in the 1880s. André Antoine's career as a director and critic extends well into the present century, but his significance in theatre history, European as much as French, is attributable entirely to his success and notoriety in his earliest theatrical enterprise, the Théâtre Libre, 1887–94.

In a number of important respects Antoine sought to challenge and transform the theatre of his time. His company were essentially amateurs, highly trained and disciplined and in every way discouraged from aping the declamatory mannerisms of the flamboyant stars of the age. Just as he developed in his actors and his own personal performances a style of 'natural' speech delivery incorporating the hesitant rhythms and intonations of contemporary verbal discourse, so too movement and gesture were to be 'real', mimetic, naturalistic. Antoine was here defying the grand manner in which professionals stood up and advanced to the footlights in key speeches (to the extent that singed costumes could be a major expense, he claimed!). Antoine loathed both stagey movement and footlights. What Antoine was creating, on the contrary, was the transparent 'fourth wall' illusion of the Naturalist style, according to which the audience are simply secret observers of re-created scenes from 'real' life. Jibes about the sight of Antoine's back while he was delivering dialogue became a critical commonplace. Antoine's approach to scenic realism was consistent with his acting style. Where possible he tried to get away from painted flats and backdrops by using three-dimensional décors and props. The best example occurred in a double bill of 1888, Fernand Icres's *Les Bouchers* ('The Butchers') and a French version of Verga's* *Cavalleria Rusticana*. In the interests of Sicilian local colour a working fountain was laid on for the latter, but the French imagination retains only a notorious detail of the first play, real sides of meat.

In some seven years the Théâtre Libre performed one hundred or so plays, usually only for a few performances each on a subscription season basis. The vast majority of them were new works by little known French playwrights, often writing in the Naturalist vein associated with Zola* and his disciples in prose fiction. But although Antoine was accused by critics of presenting a drab, deterministic picture of society in the shape of a 'slice of life' (a phrase invented by one of his authors, Jean Jullien), he was not in fact doctrinaire in his aesthetics. His repertory included a fair sprinkling of poetic, religious or farcial works, and it so happens that almost the only one of his French unknowns to have survived is the eminently comic Georges Courteline. Much, perhaps too much, has been made of Antoine's failure to unearth major French talent. But his importance in bringing foreign work to Paris cannot be overstressed: Tolstoy's* *The Power of Darkness*, Ibsen's* *Ghosts* and *Wild Duck*, Strindberg's* *Miss Julie* and Hauptmann's* *The Weavers*; all these were considerably greater dramatic works than the standard fare to which French audiences had been accustomed for thirty years, Augier, Dumas and Sardou*. Cosmopolitanism, anti-commercialism, a spirit of *avant-garde* adventure, transformation of the conventions of acting and design were all developments for which French and European theatre were beginning to be indebted to Antoine in the last decade of the century.

Ted Freeman

See: A. Antoine, *Mes Souvenirs sur le Théâtre Libre* (1921); S. M. Waxman, *Antoine and the Théâtre Libre* (1926); M. Roussou, *André Antoine* (1956); J. A. Henderson, *The First Avant-garde, 1887–1894* (1971).

11
ARNOLD, Matthew 1822–88

British poet and critic

Matthew Arnold, the eldest son of Thomas Arnold*, was born at Laleham in 1822. He was educated at Winchester and, from 1837, at Rugby. In 1841 he went to Balliol College, Oxford, on an open scholarship, but neglected his work and, like his close friend Clough*, failed to take a first class degree. However, in 1845 he joined Clough as a fellow at Oriel, though he had no intention of teaching. In 1847 he became private secretary to the Marquis of Lansdowne, who later appointed him an Inspector of Schools (1851). This post enabled Arnold to marry Frances Lucy Wightman. Before his marriage Arnold had frequently visited the continent, and in 1848 and 1849 had met at Thun the mysterious 'Marguerite' about whom he wrote the love poems collectively entitled 'Switzerland'. Arnold remained a school inspector for thirty-five years. As a break from his normal duties he was occasionally sent abroad to investigate continental education. These assignments resulted in such books as *The Popular Education of France* (1861), *A French Eton* (1864) and *Schools and Universities on the Continent* (1868). He also wrote a number of official reports, selections of which were published in 1889 and 1908. Although Arnold's work was with elementary schools for the working class, his personal preoccupation was with middle-class education, improvement of which he regarded as a most pressing national priority.

In 1849 Arnold published *The Strayed Reveller, and Other Poems,* which surprised those who knew him as something of a dandy by its vein of stoical melancholy. 'The something that infects the world' ('Resignation') is a theme present in most of the poems, despite their exotic settings in myth or the classical past. *Empedocles on Etna, and Other Poems* (1852) gives further expression to a personal and general malaise, the nineteenth century being characterized as 'this iron time/Of doubts, disputes, distractions, fears' in 'Memorial Verses' (1850) commemorating Wordsworth*. Arnold's feeling that the modern intellect was inimical to man's spiritual and creative needs is most powerfully embodied in 'Empedocles' which follows the Greek philosopher and poet through a crisis of world-weariness culminating in his suicide in the crater of Etna. The volume also includes the 'Marguerite' poems which extrapolate from the lovers' predicament a pessimistic view of the individual's isolation – 'We mortal millions live *alone*' ('To Marguerite – Continued'). In 1853 Arnold brought out *Poems: A New Edition,* notable for the Preface which justified the omission of 'Empedocles' on the grounds that it was morbid. Arnold quoted Schiller – 'All art is dedicated to Joy' – and insisted that poems should be based on 'great actions, calculated powerfully and delightfully to affect what is permanent in the human soul'. In a letter to Clough of 1853 he emphasized that poetry should '*animate* and *ennoble*'. The preface also inveighed against Romantic subjectivity and what Arnold saw as the contemporary fixation with details of imagery and sensuousness of expression at the expense of over-all structure or *Architectonicè*, arising, he thought, from the deleterious influence of the Elizabethans. He wanted poets to revert to classical models and he wrote to Clough 'modern poetry can only subsist by its *contents:* by becoming a complete magister vitae as the poetry of the ancients did'. Arnold tried to live up to his own standards, producing the long poems 'Sohrab and Rustum' (1853) and 'Balder Dead' (1855) in 'the grand style' of the classical epic, and a Greek tragedy, *Merope* (1858), but the strength of his poetry remained in the personal and elegiacal mode of 'The Scholar-Gipsy' (1853), 'Thyrsis' (1866) and 'Dover Beach' (1867). Although Arnold published further collections of poetry in 1855 and 1867, his inspiration was waning and these contained little new apart from occasional poems and memorial verse such as 'Rugby Chapel' (1867) on his father, 'Heine's Grave' (1867) and 'Haworth Churchyard' (1867) on Charlotte Brontë*. 'Obermann Once More' (1867), Arnold's last major poem, shows the earlier melancholy giving way to the more hopeful meliorism of his prose.

In 1857 Arnold was elected Professor of Poetry at Oxford and he held the chair for ten years. His first published lectures were *On Translating Homer* (1861) in which he characterized Homer's distinctive qualities and laid down guidelines for translators, taking exception to Francis Newman's recent version of the *Iliad* because it failed to render Homer's 'nobility'. Another series of lectures resulted in *On the Study of Celtic Literature* (1867). In 1865 *Essays in Criticism* (First Series) appeared. In 'The Function of Criticism at the Present Time' Arnold says that the task of criticism is to 'make the best ideas prevail' in order to create a proper climate for a literature 'adequate' to the needs of a complex modern society, and to help the individual to an awareness of 'the best that is known and thought in the world'. In 'The Literary Influence of Academies' he castigates the English for their 'intellectual eccentricity' and lack of the critical spirit, while in 'Heinrich Heine' he hails 'a brilliant soldier in the Liberation War of humanity', and also acknowledges Goethe* as the outstanding critical intelligence of Europe whose 'imperturbable naturalism' was responsible for eroding the last vestiges of medieval Europe. 'Dissolvents of the old European system . . . we must all be,' Arnold declared.

Although criticism was 'disinterested' and above party, class or sectarian interests, Arnold was drawn to comment on social and political affairs. His underlying conviction was that the 'ideas' of the French Revolution were bound to prevail, that the *Zeitgeist* or 'time-spirit' was on the side of democracy as against the old aristocratic order. There was, however, a conservative element in Arnold's politics, and in *Culture and Anarchy* (1867) he warned that personal liberty must be contained by 'a principal of Authority' if anarchy were to be avoided: 'Without order there can be no society, and without society there can be no human perfection.' The state was 'sacred'. The book is most celebrated for Arnold's conception of culture as 'a study of perfection', and for his attack on the Philistinism of the English middle class, which lacked 'sweetness and light'. In contrast to their 'Hebraism', dourly concerned with work and morality, 'money and salvation', Arnold proposed 'Hellenism', the spirit of the Greek Humanism with its ideal of the wholly developed man. His onslaught on Philistinism was also carried out in a series of satirical letters to the *Pall Mall Gazette* (1866–70) which he published as *Friendship's Garland* in 1871.

In the 1870s Arnold turned his attention to religion, producing *St. Paul and Protestantism* (1870), *Literature and Dogma* (1873) and *God and the Bible* (1875). Arnold wanted to preserve Christianity, but saw that its traditional defenders were in fact imperilling its chances of survival. 'Christianity is true; but in general the whole plan for grounding and buttressing it chosen by our theological instructors is false, and, since it is false, it must fail us sooner or later.' Arnold wished to dispense with the miraculous and supernatural elements of religion which science was discrediting, clear away the accretions of dogma and *Aberglaube* ('extra-beliefs'), and return to the essentials of Christianity, the person and example of Jesus. The anthropomorphic deity of popular theology, characterized by Arnold as a 'magnified non-natural man', was to be replaced by 'the eternal not ourselves which makes for righteousness'. Religion for Arnold was *'morality touched by emotion'*, and he was writing in the tradition of Coleridge* and his father by placing the emphasis on the moral validity and 'natural truth' of Christianity. Like his father, he believed in a national church which would embrace Christians of all doctrinal persuasions.

After *Last Essays on Church and Religion* (1877) Arnold returned to social and political commentary and literary criticism in *Mixed Essays* (1879), *Irish Essays* (1882) and *Discourses in America* (1885). His concern in these last years was with 'the humanisation of man in socie-

ty', and while he saw dangers in American democracy (he visited America to lecture in 1883 and 1886), he remained convinced of the need for greater equality in England. Arnold's later literary criticism, contained in *Essays in Criticism* (Second Series, 1888), attaches great importance to poetry in a scientific world. In 'The study of Poetry' Arnold wrote, 'More and more mankind will discover that we have to turn to poetry to interpret life for us, to console us, to sustain us.' In the same essay he promulgated his system of judging poetry by 'touchstones' from the classics. Other essays give final assessments of the Romantic poets, of whom Wordsworth and Byron* were 'first and pre-eminent, a glorious pair'.

In 1883 Arnold accepted a Civil List pension of £250 and in 1886 he retired from the inspectorate. He died suddenly of heart failure at Liverpool in 1888.

Throughout his adult life Arnold read widely and his *Note-books* (ed. H. F. Lowry, K. Young and W. H. Dunn, 1952) are filled with quotations from classical, European and English writers. As a young man Arnold had delighted in the novels of George Sand*, and while at Oxford read Carlyle* and Emerson*. Goethe and Sainte-Beuve* helped form his regard for criticism while his political thought was influenced by Burke. Spinoza was an important influence on his religious writing, and he was well read in such contemporary European theologians as Renan* and Strauss*. Writing in 1872 he acknowledged Wordsworth and Cardinal Newman* as formative influences, and another was undoubtedly his father from whom he took both a strong sense of personal morality and his interests in education, religion and society. The contemporary who affected him most was Clough, to whom he wrote in 1853, 'I am for ever linked with you by intellectual bonds – the strongest of all.'

As a critic, Arnold's importance lies in his championing of the critical spirit and his insistence, against English insularity, on the concept of a European culture. Though his critical methods have not survived the various revolutions in literary criticism of this century, his essays express that critical tact and sensitivity towards literature that he sought to inculcate, and even if his evaluations have not necessarily stood the test of time, his criticism will always remain worth reading. His other prose writings shed light on major issues of the nineteenth century and are saved from the polemical excesses of some Victorian 'sages' by Arnold's urbanity and wit. Several of his phrases have passed into the language, and *Culture and Anarchy* is indisputably a prose classic.

As a poet, Arnold ranks below Tennyson* and Browning*. His output was uneven and he was handicapped by his own wilfully imposed poetic and the pressure of his work. He was right, however, when he wrote in 1869, 'my poems represent . . . the main movement of mind of the last quarter of a century', and as well as this representative quality the canon includes a number of individual poems of the highest standard.

Simon Rae

Works: *The Poems of Matthew Arnold* (2nd edn), ed. Miriam Allott (1979); *The Complete Prose Works of Matthew Arnold*, ed, R. H. Super (1960–77); *Reports on Elementary Schools 1852–1882*, ed. F. S. Marvin (1908); *Letters of Matthew Arnold, 1848–1888*, ed. G. W. E. Russell (1895); *The Letters of Matthew Arnold to Arthur Hugh Clough*, ed. H. F. Lowry (1932); *Unpublished Letters of Matthew Arnold*, ed. Arnold Whitridge (1923). See: Lionel Trilling, *Matthew Arnold* (1939); Park Honan, *Matthew Arnold: A Life* (1981); on the poetry: C. B. Tinker and H. F. Lowry, *The Poetry of Matthew Arnold: A Commentary* (1940); A. D. Culler, *Imaginative Reason: The Poetry of Matthew Arnold* (1966); W. A. Madden, *Matthew Arnold: A Study of the Aesthetic Temperament in Victorian England* (1967); see also: E. D. H. Johnson, *The Alien Vision of Victorian Poetry* (1952); on the prose: S. Coulling, *Matthew Arnold and his Critics* (1974); D. J. DeLaura, *Hebrew and Hellene in Victorian England* (1969); John Holloway, *The Victorian Sage* (1953)

12
ARNOLD, Thomas 1795–1842

British educational reformer

Arnold was born at Cowes on the Isle of Wight where his father, who died when Thomas was six, was a collector of customs. In 1807 his mother sent him to school at Winchester, whence he proceeded to Corpus Christi College, Oxford, at the unusually early age of sixteen. The fellows of Corpus, a tiny but influential college, left their pupils much to themselves and to educate one another. In an exceptional generation, which included John Keble, Arnold soon distinguished himself, though somewhat shy and stiff in manner and dogmatic in style of argument. In 1815 he became a fellow of Oriel, in the heady atmosphere of whose common room the Oxford Movement was beginning to ferment. Keble, Renn Hampden and Edward Hawkins were already fellows; over the next ten years they were joined by Hurrell Froude, E. B. Pusey and John Henry Newman*. Arnold engrossed himself in the arcana of the Oxford libraries. He was ordained deacon in 1818. The following year he moved to Laleham, where he lived with his mother, took a few pupils preparing for entry to the universities and worked among the poor of his parish. He married in 1820; the eldest of his nine children, Matthew Arnold*, was born in 1822. After eight years at Laleham he applied, reluctantly, for the headmastership of Rugby. He took up the appointment in 1828.

Arnold had been reluctant to apply for the headmastership of Rugby partly because he feared he would not be empowered to make such changes in the school as he might find necessary. 'My love for any place, or person, or institution,' he wrote a little later, 'is exactly the measure of my desire to reform them.' In supporting Arnold's application Edward Hawkins had written that he would 'change the face of education through the public schools of England'. The Rugby which Arnold took over had grown beyond recognition from the modest grammar school of its sixteenth-century origins. It was still small beside schools such as Eton, Winchester and Westminister: like them it was, in Thomas Bowdler's words, a 'very seat and nursery of vice'. These were worlds of licensed barbarism in which dozens, if not hundreds, of boys lived in common, largely subject to the unpredictable discipline of individuals and factions amongst themselves. At Eton in 1825 one boy killed another in a fight over a seat in the schoolroom. Their education was mainly aimed at achieving a parrot-like familiarity with classical literature.

Arnold arrived at Rugby with a dim view of the young: 'My object will be, if possible, to form Christian men, for Christian boys I can scarcely hope to make.' His first action was to attempt to get to know and understand his pupils. Individuals whom he found to be persistent evil influences were expelled. Thereafter, having established a stern and apparently all-knowing presence in the community, he took the older boys into his confidence and used them as his agents, with a view to awakening some sense of the responsibilities of personal authority. As a teacher Arnold tried to present knowledge as a means of understanding. His curriculum included such novelties as mathematics, European languages and modern history; and while classical languages remained predominant he used the problems of construing them to encourage his charges to think, within limits, for themselves.

These limits were described by Arnold week by week from his pulpit in Rugby chapel. His sermons were usually prepared in a hurry, yet even on paper they are extraordinarily powerful. (Three collections were published, in 1829, 1834 and 1876.) His preaching was both magisterial and perfervid. He would break down and weep openly in front of the whole school at the story of the Passion. He was obsessed with sin, and came to regard his life as a constant battle against sinning boys. ' . . . it has all the interest of a great game of chess,' he wrote of his job after two years, 'with living creatures for pawns and pieces, and your adversary, in plain English, the Devil . . . It is quite surprising to see the wickedness of young boys.' Every act in a Christian life, he warned them, was both secular in being done on this earth, and religious in being done in the presence of God. It was his mission to make religious principle the dominant feature of an education and thus of a life. 'What we must look for here,' he preached, 'is, first, religious and moral principle; secondly, gentlemanly conduct; thirdly, intellectual ability.'

In other words Arnold's theory was that of 'muscular Christianity' (though the phrase was Disraeli's*). 'What is he sent to school for?' asks the hopeful parent, Squire Brown, in Thomas Hughes's *Tom Brown's Schooldays* (1857), which describes Rugby under Arnold, 'If he'll only turn out a brave, helpful, truth-telling Englishman, and a Christian, that's all I want.' And it appears it was exactly what a great many parents wanted, especially those of the new middle classes. On the models of Arnold, his co-reformers and followers, the existing public schools grew in size throughout the nineteenth century and many new ones were established in imitation of them, including a complete network of Anglican schools on the foundation of Nathaniel Woodard. As training grounds for people, many of whom would spend most of their lives in the service of the British Empire, with Hindus at their feet and Boers across the battlefield, the public schools manifestly succeeded brilliantly. For better or worse the spirit of Dr Arnold ruled most public schools until the early 1960s.

As a religious thinker Arnold parted company with his Tractarian colleagues. Extreme ecclesiasticism did not consort at all with his own view of the essential unity of church and state. His ecclesiastical views were condensed in *Principles of Church Reform* (1833). A stream of controversial writing on church matters gave him a reputation for liberalism dangerous enough to cost him certainly a professorship of divinity and probably a bishopric.

Arnold became a national figure. Many people thought his talents were wasted on mere schoolmastering. He himself wished to be remembered mainly as a historian, especially for his *History of Rome* (1838–45). An opportunity to pursue his ambition came in 1841, when he was appointed Regius Professor of Modern History at Oxford; but he lived to give only one set of lectures before dying of a heart attack in his forty-seventh year.

Timothy O'Sullivan

See: T. W. Bamford, *Thomas Arnold* (1960); A. P. Stanley, *The Life and Correspondence of Thomas Arnold* (1844). See also: D. Newsome, *Godliness and Good Learning* (1961); D. L. Edwards, *Leaders of the Church of England, 1828–1978* (rev. edn 1978); J. Gathorne-Hardy, *The Public School Phenomenon* (1977); A. C. Percival, *Very Superior Men* (1977); Lytton Strachey, *Eminent Victorians* (1918).

13
AUDUBON, John James 1785–1851

US natural historian and artist

Audubon was born in Santo Domingo, the present Haiti, the illegitimate son of a French sea captain and planter and his Creole mistress who died shortly after his birth. He was taken by his father when aged four to France where he remained until 1803 when, to escape conscription in Napoleon's* army, he was sent to look after his father's interests in Pennsylvania.

For the next twenty years Audubon engaged in a variety of unsuccessful businesses before finally, in 1819, finding himself bankrupt in jail. 'I cannot help thinking Mr Audubon a dishonest man,' wrote the poet John Keats* after his brother had lost all their money in one of Audubon's speculations.

Whether actually dishonest or too interested in the observation and printing of nature to be successful in any business venture is far from clear at this distance. That his untutored pleasures in the drawing of birds could be anything more than a pastime became clear to Audubon when A. Wilson passed through his Louisville store in 1810 seeking subscribers for his pioneer work, *American Ornithology* (1808–14). It was not however until 1820 that he decided to produce his own portfolio of American birds and consequently spent the period 1820–4 travelling through Mississippi and Louisiana seeking further specimens for his intended work.

Finding little encouragement in America he sailed to Britain in 1826 and almost immediately found the craftsmen and entrepreneurs of Edinburgh willing to help. He began at once to produce the enormous 'Double Elephant' size engravings, 39 by 29 ins, for the portfolio. The intention was to sell at regular intervals a set of five plates for 2 guineas to any willing subscribers. In this way, first with W. Lizers of Edinburgh and after 1827 with R. Havell in London, eighty-seven sets of 435 plates were issued between 1826 and 1838. About 200 full sets were published at a price of $1,000. *The Birds of America* was complemented by a companion text *Ornithological Biography* (1831–9). A highly successful compact edition of the two works in seven volumes was issued between 1840 and 1844 in New York.

In 1839 Audubon returned finally to America where he settled down on his 35-acre estate on the Hudson. His last years were spent, in collaboration with his sons, on the three volume *Viviparous Quadrupeds of North America* (1845–8).

The distinctive feature of Audubon's work lay in the dramatic way he posed his birds supposedly against 'their natural avocations'. The accuracy claimed by Audubon for his engravings has since been challenged with some modern ornithologists claiming that virtually all his paintings were inaccurate and that, unwittingly, he has endowed his birds with human expressions, attitudes and poses.

Derek Gjertsen

The standard biography remains F. Herrick, *Audubon, The Naturalist* (1938), although there is a more readily available but slighter work, J. Chancellor, *Audubon* (1978). As the *Birds of America* (1827–38) sold for $400,000 when last auctioned in 1977 it can only be examined in the largest of libraries. Selections from it are available in many works, however, such, as D. C. Peattle, *Audubon's America* (1940), while the original paintings have been published in *The Original Water Colour Paintings of J. J. Audubon* (1966). His work is put into perspective in C. Jackson, *The Bird Illustrators* (1975).

14
AUSTEN, Jane 1775–1817

British novelist

The years of Jane Austen's lifetime coincide with a period of sharp historical change – from the 'old' world of Georgian England to the 'new' England of the Regency and the birth of modern Britain. Change, as it was marked in the daily lives of the minor landed gentry of southern England, provided the setting and the material for Jane Austen's special mode of social comedy. The scene is domestic, highly localized and class-bound. The tone is modest, the guise is entertainment. The author described herself as a laborious miniaturist, her chosen subjects '3 or 4 Families in a Country Village'. But this modesty is belied by the intellectual scope of the novels, their engagement with ideas, their largeness of mind. They challenged the prevalent assumption about society as a civilizing force and man's secular fulfilment as an enlightened social being. They provide a searching critique of the fashionable modes of thinking and feeling. They undercut the Regency boast that this period, above all, was triumphantly the Age of Improvement. The social comedy, then, is sardonic and intellectual, enforcing the belief that life is a comedy to those who think. Cobbett* and Coleridge* would have found Jane Austen good company!

In her hands, the novel itself undergoes a transformation. The primitive forms of the eighteenth century are fashioned into a unified and disciplined work of art: the crock becomes a vase – to be admired for its shapeliness, balance and completeness of form. These qualities of style and technique are evident on the small scale – in the diction, the phrasing and the structure of sentences, paragraphs and chapters – and equally in the overall narrative, thematic, ironic and dramatic structures. In this, Jane Austen is acknowledged a

supreme artist of the novel. For the ordinary reader, she is also the most accessible and constantly entertaining of great writers, to be enjoyed for the play of wit, the vitality of her characters and the easy entrance to her fictional world. The predicament of women is her overriding concern – their gifts and abilities constrained, their destinies unfree; and in this cause she stands in unpolemical proximity to the polemical Mary Wollstonecraft.

Between Jane Austen's life and art, there is a striking congruity: essentially a private person, she depicts the drama of private lives and never moves beyond the range of her own experience and observation. She came of a large and cultivated clerical family. Her father was rector of the small Hampshire village of Steventon. Amongst the eight children (of whom Jane was the second of two daughters), reading, writing and home-theatricals were household pursuits. Her earliest surviving pieces, composed when she was eleven or twelve, were written to entertain the family. They draw upon family jokes, family situations and the family reading – a tradition of family humour that runs throughout her writing.

Of Jane Austen's emotional life, we know virtually nothing. There survive a number of confused and contradictory stories of possible liaisons and engagements between 1796 and 1802. It seems possible that there was one serious relationship that ended with the man's sudden illness and death. Thus Jane Austen remained single, dedicated to the immediate family, to a growing body of young nephews and nieces and to her own writing. She travelled widely within the family, staying with the Austens and their various branches throughout southern England including London. To this limited extent, she moved in society. But she totally avoided literary circles and succeeded in preserving her anonymity as a writer and her privacy as a person. If the biography reveals a narrowness to her life, a narrowness faithfully reflected in the insularity of the novels, it is a limitation of scene which in no way detracts from the concentration and the critical detachment with which she observed society.

Jane Austen's development can be traced in her childhood works, the juvenilia contained in the notebooks *Volumes the First, Second* and *Third*, covering the period from about 1787 to 1793. In this collection come her minor masterpieces of burlesque satire, *Love and Friendship* and *The History of England*, revealing a precocious sophistication of literary judgment, a precocious maturity of style, a genius essentially critical, tempered by a childish sense of fun. The targets for her wit and literary virtuosity were the weaknesses and absurdities of contemporary writing, in particular the school of sentimental fiction and the Gothic romance. These childhood satires led on to essays in dialogue and little social sketches increasingly realistic; and, in turn, these led on to the three early novels: *Sense and*

Sensibility, begun as 'Elinor & Marianne' about 1795 and eventually published, much revised and rewritten, in 1811; *Pride and Prejudice*, begun as 'First Impressions' in 1796–7 and published, similarly reworked, in 1813; and *Northanger Abbey*, begun as 'Susan' in 1798–9, similarly reworked, in 1817.

The three major novels – *Mansfield Park* (1813), *Emma* (1815) and *Persuasion* (1817) – written between 1811 and 1816, are unmistakably works of Jane Austen's maturity. Her other minor works include verses, prayers, riddles and charades from various periods of her life: *Lady Susan*, a novel-in-letters, written about 1793; a dramatic skit on *Sir Charles Grandison*, from the 1790s; *The Watsons*, a novel abandoned about 1804–5; and a burlesque *Plan of a Novel* written in 1816. Finally, in January 1817, she began *Sanditon*, completing eleven chapters before ill-health forced its abandonment on 18 March. Five months later, to the day, she succumbed to Addison's disease. Something of her capacity for wry detachment – 'negative capability' in a minor key – is to be seen in this last creative effort. *Sanditon* is a fierce satire on health-resorts and invalidism, in a style entirely new. It continues the critique of 'improvement' that runs so strongly through *Northanger Abbey, Mansfield Park, Emma* and *Persuasion*.

Her authorship of the six novels was first made public in December 1817, in the 'Biographical Notice' contributed by her brother Henry Austen to the posthumous edition of *Northanger Abbey* and *Persuasion*. By that time, she had won a cultivated following; one admirer was the Prince Regent, who solicited the dedication of *Emma*. The reviewers had at once recognized a new writer of talent; three of the novels were reprinted in her lifetime; and in his review of *Emma* (*Quarterly Review* for March 1816), Sir Walter Scott* hailed this 'nameless author' as a master of 'the modern novel' in the new realist, anti-Romantic tradition. This line was elaborated in a review of *Northanger Abbey* and *Persuasion* (*Quarterly Review* for January 1821) by Richard Whately. Together, these two essays provided the foundations for the serious criticism of Jane Austen and they testify to the power of the novels to command serious analysis and discussion.

The six novels share a single narrative base in romantic comedy, tracing the experiences of young women on the path to marriage. But each of the novels is distinct in character and quite unromantic. The heroines encounter disillusionment and self-discovery. Their eyes are freshly opened to themselves, to the dreams they must surrender, to the truths and falsities of 'sense' and 'sensibility', of 'pride' and 'prejudice', to the betrayals of 'persuasion', to those 'duties' of family, of class and religion they must hold fast to and those which they must reject, to the compromises necessary to maintain self-respect within a harmonious existence amongst those with whom destiny has placed them. These reconciliations are not easily won. We can detect the author's anger and contempt for a society in which the pressures of social convention and expectation can threaten and destroy the integrity of the human spirit. Certainly, the muted triumphs of Jane Austen's heroines as they sail into marriage are accompanied by a tide of suffering unmitigated by the tones of comedy and by the light dismissive ironies with which, in her final chapters, Jane Austen so curtly ties up the loose ends of her characters' destinies.

One part of Jane Austen's achievement resides in the security of her authorial stance, an ironic poise, which gives the novels a special openness, a freedom and richness of meaning (particularly the three later works). Jane Austen provides space for the reader individually to experience the works, further, and anew, at each successive reading. Alongside this is Jane Austen's genius in the creation of character. Her heroines are credible. They come across as individuals in the possession of minds, with the capacity for thought, for the process of thinking, and a sharp consciousness of themselves and other people. To match them in English literature we have to go back to Shakespeare or forward to George Eliot*. A 'prose Shakespear' she has been called; and not for the heroines alone – Mrs Jennings, Mr Collins, Lady Catherine de Bourgh, Lady Bertram, Mrs Norris, Mr Woodhouse, Mrs Elton and Sir Walter Elliot. Instinct with life, it is indeed the supreme Shakespearian realm of the imagination from which these figures come. Shakespearian too is her supreme gift in mobilizing the play of ideas within the solid flesh of dramatic creation.

Brian Southam

All the works are mentioned above. The standard editions of the novels and all the juvenilia and minor works were edited by R. W. Chapman, Oxford. A later edition of the novels comes in the Oxford English Novels series. The Penguin set has some outstanding critical introductions by Tony Tanner and D. W. Harding. The new Everyman edition has equally valuable introductions by Peter Conrad. The standard biography is Elizabeth Jenkins, *Jane Austen* (1938, reprinted), while Mary Lascelles, *Jane Austen and Her Art* (1939, rev. 1954) provides *the* analytical account of the novelist's work. David Cecil, *A Portrait of Jane Austen* (1979) is *the* book, a perfectly judged life and letters. The *Letters* (1932, enlarged 1952) were edited by R. W. Chapman. The only recent discovery has been *Sir Charles Grandison*, ed. B. C. Southam (1981). See also: *Jane Austen: The Critical Heritage*, ed. B. C. Southam (1968).

15
AUSTIN, John 1790–1859

British legal philosopher

Austin was born in London and called to the Bar in 1818. He was married in 1819, and he and his wife, Sarah Taylor, became neighbours of Bentham* and the Mill* family, and were for many years associated with the Benthamite circle. Austin gave up practising law in 1826, when he was appointed to the first Chair of Jurisprudence in the newly founded University of London. *The Province of Jurisprudence Determined* (1832) was an expanded version of Austin's first series of lectures, and was the only substantial work to be published in his lifetime. Austin gave up his chair in 1832, when student interest in his lectures declined, and the rest of his life was not especially distinguished. He served for a time on the Criminal Law Commission, and later became a royal commissioner for Malta. His *Lectures on Jurisprudence, or the Philosophy of Positive Law*, reconstructed from notes by his wife, was published posthumously in 1863.

Austin's work was largely concerned with the nature of law and legal systems, and he may be regarded as the chief spokesman of the school of jurisprudence known as legal positivism. Positivism is best seen as a reaction to the older tradition of natural law theory which maintains that there is an intimate and essential connection between law and morality. On the natural law view, the law derives its normative force from certain fundamental principles of natural justice: the content of the law does and must reflect these underlying moral principles, so that, in the words of Augustine, *'lex iniusta non est lex'* ('an unjust law is no law'). The positivists, by contrast, follow Bentham in maintaining that 'the existence of law is one thing, its merit or demerit is another'. Thus, according to Austin, the 'province of jurisprudence' has to do not with the content of law but with its pedigree: positive law consists merely in the set of rules actually in force in a society, and these rules are to be defined not in terms of what moral principles they may or may not reflect but simply by reference to the mechanism by which they are generated. In the words of Austin's famous definition, law

is simply 'the command of the sovereign'. Much of *The Province of Jurisprudence Determined* consists of further analysis and clarification of this definition. A command is an order backed up by sanctions for non-compliance. The sovereign is that person or group of persons towards whom the majority in a society have the habit of obedience.

In recent times Austin's theory has been subject to the most close and searching criticism. If laws simply reflect the arbitrary will of the sovereign, backed by sanctions, then the law-maker becomes simply the 'gunman writ large'. Hence the Austinian model cannot, it seems, explain the universal obligatoriness of law: the fact that the law is binding on those who enact it just as much as on the population at large. Again, how can Austin's view explain the continuity and stability of law – the fact, for example, that the statutes of a given monarch remain in force under his successors? A further disturbing criticism is that Austin's picture seems far too simple to accommodate the diversity and complexity of modern legal systems. Laws do not simply enforce conduct; there are many laws which confer certain powers and responsibilities on people, or which (like the laws of contract or testamentary laws) enable people to do certain things (e.g. undertake obligations, or transfer their property).

Despite these criticisms, the positivist approach to law which Austin developed remains highly influential. For example, the most important modern work on jurisprudence, H. L. A. Hart's *Concept of Law*, although critical of the details of Austin's work, nevertheless takes the Austinian model as the starting point for constructing a more sophisticated and coherent positivist account of the nature of legal systems. Furthermore, Austin's insistence on separating questions of fact from questions of value has provided a powerful impetus for modern jurisprudence; whether it is possible to give a positivistic, value-free account of what law is remains a vexed and crucial issue in current legal theory.

John Cottingham

The best critical account of Austin's theory is to be found in H. L. A. Hart, *The Concept of Law* (1961), II–IV.

B

16

BABBAGE, Charles 1792–1871

British mathematician

It is possible that at some future date a film will be made of the life of Charles Babbage, polymath, tabulator and premature inventor of the computer. If such a film is made, it will dwell, no doubt, on Babbage's early, confident years – years in which our rich and handsome hero introduced continental methods of mathematics to Cambridge, helped to found the Astronomical Society, received its gold medal, became a fellow of the Royal Society (at twenty-three), was elected Lucasian Professor of Mathematics, was received by the Chancellor of the Exchequer, and was awarded an annual grant of £1,500 for work on his remarkable invention, the 'Difference Engine'. Babbage involved himself in a hundred and one practical and taxing problems, from pin manufacture to cryptanalysis, from lighthouses to statistical linguistics. He actually lived the kind of colourful, multi-sided life sometimes depicted for fictional academics on the silver screen.

The promise of Babbage's early years was not merely bright, it was astonishing. He set himself a series of large and ambitious tasks. He appeared, both to himself (no doubt) and to his contemporaries, to have the capacity to pull them off. Yet the early promise gradually turned to dust. The Difference Engine was never completed. Babbage shamelessly neglected his Lucasian chair. In his later years he became a crotchety, tiresome, disappointed and greatly impoverished man. During the 1860s Babbage must often have ruefully reflected that had he attempted less, he must have achieved more.

Babbage was born on 26 December 1792 in Teignmouth, Devon. His family was not poor, and he was educated at private schools in Alphington and Enfield. He taught himself algebra and calculus, with the aid of books, prior to entering Trinity College, Cambridge, in 1811. But after a personal mathematical preparation of this kind, Cambridge was rather a disappointment. The notation and methods of calculus used were those of Newton, and the superior flexibility and explicitness of the continental, Leibnitzian notation was totally ignored. Babbage, typically, wasted no time in trying to put this right. In 1812 he helped to form – with fellow undergraduates Herschel and Peacock – the Analytical Society, a body whose aim was to introduce Leibnitzian notation into the university. Whereas Newton represented the derivative of a function $\dot{y}$, Leibnitz denoted it dy/dx, or sometimes Dy. Babbage described the object of the new society, facetiously, as that of promoting 'the principles of pure D-ism in opposition to the *Dot*-age of the university!' The incident shows many sides of Babbage's unique personality: his impatience, his underestimation of the inertia opposing change, his courage in going for a bold solution, his capacity to reduce an issue to a slogan with the object of marshalling support, his scorn for the established wisdom.

Babbage graduated from Peterhouse in 1814, wrote three articles on the calculus of functions, and was elected Fellow of the Royal Society in 1816. In 1820 he was one of the chief architects of the foundation of the Astronomical Society. And he began to turn his attention to the problem of producing accurate tables for astronomical, navigational and mathematical purposes. The tables in use at the time had been compiled laboriously item by item and contained innumerable errors. It is true that the computation had been done on simple calculating machines, but these machines had to be set up by hand, repetitively, and it was this intervention of the human operator which was responsible for the errors. Babbage realized that it would be possible to use the method of differences to devise a machine which, once set in motion, would compute item after item, basing each new result on the preceeding one. This would effectively eliminate human error and should result in tables of superb accuracy and consistency.

Babbage's case was very powerful: such tables were evidently needed; there seemed no impediment in principle to the construction of a machine of the kind envisaged. British power was at its zenith; this, it was felt, was the kind of lead Britain *should* set – a project which would benefit her people, and also anyone who needed tables of proven accuracy, proven authority.

Babbage's methodology is hard to fault. He had a model of his Difference Engine constructed in 1820–2 and it worked admirably. He issued a volume of logarithms of natural numbers from 1 to 108,000. He drew up impressive plans of the full-size Difference Engine, and even invented a notation for recording the mode of operation of the moving parts. He travelled abroad to learn something of the clockwork and gear-wheel technology of the continent. He invented new tools for the manufacture of components. He was continually thinking of ways to streamline the design and improve its operation.

Not surprisingly, Babbage's ambitions imposed strain on those around him, and Clement, the engineer in charge of the work on the Difference Engine, rebelled openly in 1828: he even removed the special tools Babbage had designed, so that there was no way in which work could proceed. For fifteen months work on the Difference Engine was at a standstill.

It was during this period of hiatus that Babbage began to wonder whether there was not a still more dazzling goal to be achieved, only slightly beyond the Difference Engine. Instead of building a machine which would automate a *single* table-making task, why not make a machine which would work automatically on *any* arithmetic task? What was needed was a method to instruct the machine, and such a method already existed, in the cards used on the Jacquard loom. There would be two sets of cards: 'variable' cards, containing the numbers on which computation would proceed, and 'operation' cards embodying the sequence of operations required. The machine would print its own answers. Babbage called his new machine the 'Analytical Engine', and for eight years actively worked on it. Finally, in 1842, the government said no to the request for further funds.

Unfortunately the rising sun of the Analytical Engine had distracted Babbage's attention from the Difference Engine, still hopelessly incomplete. A portion of the Difference Engine was put together in 1833, was later shown at the International Exhibition of 1862, and finally moved to the Science Museum, South Kensington, where it may be seen today. The Swedish engineer, Georg Scheutz, after reading an article in the *Edinburgh Review*, built himself a less ambitious version of the Difference Engine, which worked well, and was in use in an observatory for many years.

But Babbage's heart was now in the Analytical Engine. His friend Lady Lovelace wrote programs for it. It was, in effect, a mechanical computer of ambitious power, though Babbage did not take the final step – that of arranging for the machine to modify its own program. Had Babbage done this, he would have realized that a more modest machine of this kind, being recursive, can do many things as effectively as a large machine, albeit more slowly. Altogether Babbage spent thirty-seven years on the Analytical Engine, and by his death it was still far from being a reality.

Babbage's life was a warning to any lesser mortal who might have been tempted to move towards automated calculation. If Babbage, with his incomparable gifts, failed there was only one conclusion to be drawn – the task was beyond nineteenth-century man. It may be noted that a century later, in the 1930s, it proved impossible to construct a really effective electromag-netic computer, in spite of all the advances of the preceding years and the considerable advantages of electrical operation with binary codes. The valve computers of the 1940s and 1950s were perpetually breaking down, and it was only the invention of the transistor, with its negligible current consumption, which created the near-miraculous standards of reliability needed to get a programmable computer to work in a satisfactory way.

Babbage's life was not entirely a failure. He was responsible for the logarithmic tables mentioned above; he made various minor inventions, including signalling 'by occulting solar lights' which was used by the Russians at the Battle of Sevastopol. Lord Rose commented that Babbage's engineering improvements 'more than repaid the sum expended' by the government. He wrote a number of books and numerous articles, none of which, however, became a classic. These are, of course, mere fragments of achievement resulting from a talent of impressive boldness, intelligence and verve, which broke, finally, on a task beyond its strength.

Christopher Ormell

Babbage's works include: *The Ninth Bridgewater Treatise* (1837); *The Exposition of 1851* (1851); *Passages from the Life of a Philosopher* (1864). See: *The Dictionary of National Biography*, vol. 2 (1885); Norman T. Gridgeman, 'Charles Babbage', in *Dictionary of Scientific Biography*, vol. I (1971).

17
BAER, Karl Ernst von 1792–1876

Estonian biologist

Baer, who was perhaps the most important figure in the creation of modern theoretical and experimental embryology, once said he did not know why he had decided to take a medical degree. Seen in the broadest historical context his achievement was much more than the creation of a narrow scientific discipline. Rather embryology as developed by Baer became the linch-pin that eventually secured together cell theory and Darwinian evolutionary thought and thus virtually guaranteed the successful adoption of the biological conception of man that emerged in the nineteenth century.

Baer, who came from a noble Estonian family, began his career as a medical student, and received his MD from the university of Dorpat in 1814. Soon after this he was fortunate enough to study under one of the greatest teachers of biology in the nineteenth century Ignaz Böllinger. In 1819 Baer became Professor of Anatomy at Königsberg where most of his great embryological work was done. In 1834 he moved to St Petersburg and remained there for the rest of his working life. In Russia his interests expanded to cover anthropological, geographical and medical subjects. He travelled a great deal and by the time of his death was one of the most renowned scientific figures in Europe.

Baer's most well-known embryological finding was the demonstration in 1827 of an egg in the mammalian ovary. The male reproductive elements called animacules had been seen microscopically in semen since the seventeenth century and the existence of a corresponding female product was widely presumed. Baer identified the ovum in a bitch belonging to a colleague who generously sacrificed her in the cause of science. Baer named the male products spermatozoa. His discovery demonstrated the unity of the reproductive process in the biological world. In time, improved microscopes and cell theory eventually showed ovum and sperm to be merely special cells in which it was successively established that the nucleus and then the chromosomes were the link between generations.

Baer's other major and related embryological work made clear the nature of development. Two theories of embryonic growth competed at the beginning of the nineteenth century. Preformationism posited the mature anatomical and physiological existence of the organism at the beginning of development. Growth then was essentially a process of nutrition. This theory was deeply embedded in eighteenth-century conceptions of the universe as a manifestation of divine wisdom. Organic form was assigned to the First Cause. Development was the manifestation of secondary causes, in other words mechanistic laws. Epigenesis on the other hand postulated that form as well as size develops during gestation: organs do not pre-exist. Baer's *Ueber die Entwickelungsgeschichte der Thiere* ('On the Developmental History of Animals', 1828–37) is the major nineteenth-century statement, both theoretical and factual of epigenetic doctrine.

Baer studied vertebrate development from conception to birth. He described the formation of the various germ layers in the embryo, and followed the process of organ formation by folding and tubulation of these layers. Development, he showed, proceeds from the homogeneous to the heterogeneous, from the general to the special. In other words a heart is a mammalian heart before it is a monkey, man or rabbit heart. The comparative nature of his studies showed the similarity of development in all vertebrates. Besides this general embryological account, Baer also made specific discoveries. He described the notochord, or primitive spinal column, the neural folds, the precursors of the central nervous system, and the brain vesicles.

Though Baer laid the foundations of modern epigenetic embryology the question still remained what was it that gave overall direction to embryonic development? How did organic form arise? Such a question of course did not trouble preformationists. Baer himself vigorously rejected any mechanistic explanation and postulated an intrinsic 'essence' or 'idea' controlling development. This opinion was widely shared at the time. Later in the century embryologists rejected this view and asserted that physico-chemical laws were sufficient to explain embryogenesis.

It is curious that the richness of Baer's work failed to refute a widely held nineteenth-century biological concept: the belief that ontogeny recapitulates phylogeny. In other words that the developing individual repeats its specific evolutionary history. The doctrine had a long history but was most fervently espoused by Ernst Haeckel* in his defence of Darwin*. Baer's account, however, of the general preceding the special, had already invalidated this theory.

In the end of course it was Baer's embryology itself which most closely dovetailed with the evolutionary synthesis. Cell theory explained differentiation and provided continuity between generations, and Mendelian genetics (see Mendel*) later gave an account of stability, change and biparental inheritance. Epigenetic embryology was the key that linked together these diverse elements in creating the modern view of man's place in nature.

C.J. Lawrence

To the non-reader of German, Baer, his works and accounts of them remain inaccessible. His major embryological work mentioned above is untranslated. His account of the mammalian ovum has appeared in English, 'On the Genesis of the Ovum of Mammals and of Man' trans. Charles O'Malley, *Isis*, vol. 47, 1956, pp. 117–53. About Baer: there are no specific works in English but see Jane M. Oppenheimer, *Essays in the History of Embryology and Biology* (1967). The principal German source is L. Stieda, *Karl Ernst von Baer, Eine biographische skizze* (1878, 1886).

18

BAGEHOT, Walter 1826–77

British political writer and economist

Bagehot is often thought of as an editor of the *Economist* who happened to write a couple of books reasonably well-known to the more intellectually pretentious kind of banker or MP. To bankers he is an intellectual, while to intellectuals a banker. This view lingers even after the massive *Economist* edition of the *Collected Works of Walter Bagehot* (1965, edited by Norman St John-Stevas who had earlier written a life and assessment of Bagehot. These show that his stature, depth and originality, not simply scope, had been greatly underestimated. His realism was not simply that of the knowing journalist and friend of statesmen (Gladstone* called him his 'spare Chancellor'): it had a theoretical basis in evolutionary theory which carried forward the methodological individualism of J. S. Mill* into the psychological and anthropological concerns with group behaviour of the twentieth century. His reputation for 'commonsense', writing like a 'plain, blunt honest man' with no theoretical preconceptions about political and economic institutions, is false: his realism has a theorized sense of historical development behind it. Paradoxically his essays on literature do seem to have a genuine straightforwardness, a kind of knowledgeable simplicity about them, very different from what now appears as the contrived realism of his *The English Constitution* and *Lombard Street* – quite as stylized and selective a realism as, say, Manet's* *Déjeuner sur l'herbe* of the same period.

Walter Bagehot's father was a leading West Country merchant in Somerset and his mother's family were rich, local bankers. He was educated at the local grammar school and in 1842 entered University College in the new University of London, heavily influenced by Benthamite* ideas. After reading for the Bar (but never practising), he went into the family banking business in London, but began writing for leading reviews on both literary and economic topics. In 1857 he became friendly with James Wilson, the founder and owner of the *Economist* which had established new standards of anonymous and seemingly objective reporting and commentary on economic events and institutions, writing for an intelligent but not an intellectual, not necessarily a university-educated, audience. This became Bagehot's audience and his style became that of the *Economist*, shrewd, knowing, businesslike and colloquial, realistic but impersonal. Indeed in 1858 he married Wilson's oldest daughter (just as his parents' families had gone joint stock by marriage) and by 1861 he was editor of the *Economist*, a post he held until his early death.

The English Constitution (1867) is his most famous book, but it is often misread as a simple realistic account of how the constitution actually works. He boldly put a chapter on the Cabinet before one on the Monarchy (though he did not see the growing importance of party). He mocks and exposes as a 'lawyers' fiction' the idea that the British constitution rests on a division of powers; rather it is the Cabinet that pulls it all together. He offers a realistic account of the actual *functions* of the House of Commons, not of their formal powers or rhetorical claims. 'Function' (drawn from Darwinism*) is an important concept to Bagehot, as when in the chapter on the Monarchy he begins by asking why so much attention is given to 'the actions of a retired widow and an unemployed youth', and ends by explaining that the 'dignified' aspects of the constitution (such as the Monarchy) are not merely to be distinguished from 'the efficient' (such as the Cabinet) but are of great importance: 'England could not be governed without them.' Here Bagehot's realism masks a seminal political argument; indeed the book is best read as the most subtle and brilliant of the

polemics associated with the 1867 Reform Bill controversy. A confident and knowledgeable ruling class, he implies, has no need to fear the growth of democracy so long as they can manipulate the dignified aspects of the constitution to excite 'deference'. The responsible ruling class must not retreat into their country houses and their clubs or turn reactionary, but they must come out and play popular politics, compete for the vote of the 'man at the back of the Clapham omnibus'. If they do so they will win, since they have so many built-in advantages. This view, implicit in the 1867 edition, was made fully explicit in the introduction to the 1872 edition.

Physics and Politics appeared in 1872, his most theoretical work. He argued three propositions: (1) that the strongest nations prevailed over the others and that 'in certain marked peculiarities the strongest tended to be best'; (2) that within every nation the kind of people who come to the top are those who are most admired, and 'the most attractive, though with exceptions, is what we call the best character'; and (3) he claimed that normally success in either of these competitions could not depend upon force alone, but that there were occasional adverse conditions in which both kinds of predominance, national and that of human types or characters, depended upon force. This was utilitarianism plus popular Darwinism, a Whiggish view of 'the survival of the fittest' and of 'what was fittest to survive', a view that few subsequent high theorists have taken seriously, but have ignored, almost to our peril, its great influence upon and plausibility to men of affairs. Bagehot himself was a decent liberal and had his drawing-room designed by William Morris*; he can hardly be blamed for twentieth-century uses of his theories. But his arguments as to why the specific culture of a skilled ruling elite depends upon parliamentary manipulation, a nationally controlled banking system and (on rare occasions) force, are far from trivial, at worst compelling, at best embarrassing.

His *Lombard Street* (1873) extended his political realism into the economy, unmasking, as it were, the central position of the Bank of England, and arguing that its powers should be even greater to control the other banks and to lend freely and extend credit to maintain the whole system; and also that its own rate of interest could and should be used to regulate external movements of currency. This was a remarkable (and permanently successful) injection of *étatist* views of central monetary control into an otherwise fully *laissez-faire* theory and practice of the market. He died in the middle of a major work on economics of which fragments survive. Generally he had stressed that the money-market economy of capitalism was not just an extension of the barter-economy, but depended on a specific culture and social psychology. The laws of market economics were not universal, but culture-bound – though they were, none the less, the best.

Thus he protested against economic thought proceeding by way (even then) of elaborating abstract theories and models, and he asked it to come to terms with the new anthropological and sociological knowledge in order to offer a realistic account of economic behaviour. These were precepts, however, not examples, such as he had been able to offer in describing what the House of Commons and what Lombard Street really were. Had he lived longer economic theory might have developed in a wholly different way. His political influence certainly, if malign, was immense.

Bernard Crick

See: Alastair Buchan, *The Spare Chancellor: The Life of Walter Bagehot* (1959); Norman St John-Stevas, *Walter Bagehot: A Study of His Life and Thought* (1959); C. H. Sisson, *The Case of Walter Bagehot* (1972).

19
BAKST, Léon Samölivich 1866?–1924

Russian painter and theatre designer

Bakst was born in Grodno, near St Petersburg. (There is, in fact, no certainty that this was in 1866.) He studied at the academies in Moscow and St Petersburg but always found academic standards reactionary and deadening. He was expelled from the St Petersburg Academy for painting the Virgin Mary and Joseph as contemporary Jewish peasants. The artist he admired most as a student was the religious 'Wanderer' painter Neskerov. In the early 1890s he travelled to Paris where he studied under the Finnish painter Edelfelt. Upon his return to Russia he met Benois, Filosofov, Roerich, Serov and other radical artists and became a portrait painter and theatre designer. In 1899 he joined Diaghilev's newly founded Mir Iskusstva (World of Art) group in St Petersburg and from then on until its demise in 1904 contributed to the group's magazine. The group's main aim, under the influence of the diplomat Charles Birlé, was to rejuvenate Russian art and literature by importing the most recent ideas from the rest of Europe, such as the Art Nouveau style practised by Beardsley* and Mackintosh, the Post-Impressionism of Cézanne* and Gauguin* and the Symbolism of Moreau*, Rimbaud* and others. The predominant aesthetic of Mir Iskusstva was Symbolist and Bakst's paintings, like *Terror Antiquus* (1906), reflect the impact of the poetry of Blok and Balmont as well as of painters like Puvis de Chavannes*, and the designer Victor Vasnetsov. Bakst believed, along with Benois and Diaghilev, that the arts should become reintegrated and saw an opportunity for this on the stage. He was particularly impressed by similar attempts in England by Edward Gordon Craig. In 1902 he designed his first sets and costumes for the St

Petersburg Theatre. In 1905, having travelled with Serov in Greece, the archaic art of which was a persistent influence on his mature style, he decorated the vestibule of the show of Russian art at the Tauride Palace with sculptures and a trellised water-garden. This exhibition was organized by Diaghilev who was also responsible, in 1906, for the twelve rooms dedicated to Russian art at the Salon d'Automne in Paris. Once again Bakst designed the setting. In 1908 he designed sets and costumes for Fokine. In 1909 he travelled to Paris with Diaghilev's Ballets Russes and designed the costumes for many of the series of ballets performed from then on. This year also saw his first major one-man show of watercolours at the Bernheim Gallery in Paris. Although he often quarrelled with Diaghilev he became the Russian impresario's chief and most celebrated designer. All his work was conducted in full collaboration with the musicians, choreographers and producers and this helps to explain the quite extraordinary overall visual unity which each ballet seems to have. His main designs were for *L'Aprés-midi d'un faune*, *Schéhérazade*, *Narcisse*, *L'Oiseau de feu*, *Hélène de Sparte*, and *Salomé*. Bakst's work was not confined to the stage alone and he also produced fashion and textile designs for famous houses like Worth and continued to paint portraits and to produce illustrations. His influence upon fashion design and the development of textile design during the twenties and thirties was considerable. He died near Paris.

Bakst was largely responsible during his career for the revival of costume design and theatre sets in Europe. The sources of his art are many and varied and include Indian, Persian and Hellenic period styles as well as the Sezession art of Klimt* and Schiele and Art Nouveau. The key to his work's power lies less in the technical innovation, for which he is rightly revered, than in his acute feeling for the emotional values of colour, texture and movement. He wrote, 'From each setting I discard the entire range of nuances which do not amplify or intensify the hidden sense of the fable.' His figures are never static but seem charged with a concentrated dynamism dictated by their own rhythmic logic. In talking of his use of colour he explained,

in each colour of the prism there exists a gradation which sometimes expresses frankness and chastity, sometimes sensuality and even bestiality. . . . This can be felt and given over to the public by the effect one makes of the various shadings. That is what I tried to do in *Schéhérazade*. Against a lugubrious green I put a blue full of despair, paradoxical as it may seem.

Such notions of colour show the close proximity of Bakst's ideas to those of his compatriot Kandinsky, one of the fathers of abstract painting.

Richard Humphreys

See: A. Alexandre and Jean Cocteau, *Decorative Art of Léon Bakst* (1913 trans. 1972); Raymond Lister, *The Muscovite Peacock* (1954); Charles Spencer *Bakst* (1977).

20
BAKUNIN, Mikhail Alexandrovich 1814–76

Russian anarchist

Mikhail Bakunin was born on the family estate of Pryamukhino acquired by his grandfather, a state councillor under Catherine the Great. He entered the Imperial Russian artillery academy at the age of fourteen and received his commission in 1833. Two years later he left the army and, at the age of twenty-six, Russia itself. Thus began the extraordinary Odyssey that was to end only with Bakunin's death. Drawn to the most radical of revolutionary ideas yet unable totally to escape the slavophile influences of his youth, he devoted his whole life to the cause of international revolution. Wherever he went, Berlin, Paris, Brussels, London, Italy, he wrote, organized, argued and, indeed, quarrelled for the sake of the revolutionary cause. He took part in the February 1848 Revolution in Paris. The next year found him in Saxony where he was arrested and sentenced to death for his part in the Dresden uprising. The sentence was not carried out. Instead Bakunin was extradited to Austria where he was wanted for his participation in the Czech revolt of 1848. Again he was sentenced to death but instead of carrying out the execution the Austrians commuted the sentence to life imprisonment and promptly deported Bakunin to Russia where he was imprisoned in the Peter and Paul fortress in St Petersburg in accordance with a sentence passed in 1844 when he had disobeyed the tsar's order to return to Russia. From this period there dates the extraordinary confession, written at the demand of Tsar Nicholas I. It is a document of unique interest not only because of what it tells us of the revolutionary events of 1848 and 1849 but for the insights it affords into the character and motivation of its author. Confession it was but scarcely the document of contrition which the tsar requested and required and Bakunin was sent to Tomsk in western Siberia where he lived the relatively unrestricted life of a political exile in imperial Russia. Even in Siberia he became involved with people planning for Siberian independence. In 1861 he escaped via Japan and San Francisco to London and rejoined the mainstream of the revolutionary movement. He joined the First International in 1868 but the mutual detestation between Bakunin and Karl Marx* led to his expulsion in 1872. In the meantime his frenetic activity had culminated in his abortive attempt to start the revolution in Lyons when the Commune took power in Paris in 1871. He returned to Italy in 1874 and died two years later in Berne.

With such a life it is hardly surprising that Bakunin's ideas were never expressed in a single systematic work. But the mass of occasional and semi-occasional pieces which he composed throughout his life exerted a formative influence on the development of the anarchist wing of the revolutionary movement. In Italy and Spain in particular an anarchism based largely on Bakunin's principles became a potent political force. Elsewhere Marxist and other varieties of non-anarchist socialism proved more powerful but even where this was so Bakunin's criticism of the despotic potential in the project of a socialist state provided a disturbing critique from within the revolutionary ranks. 'Government by science and men of science,' he wrote, 'even if they style themselves positivists, the disciples of Auguste Comte*, or even the disciples of the doctrinaire school of German Communism, cannot fail to be impotent, ridiculous, inhuman, cruel, oppressive, exploiting and pernicious.' Bakunin envisaged a regenerated humanity that would arise after the necessary purgation of revolutionary terror, a humanity whose life would find natural expression in the development of cooperative communities which would have no need of the repressive apparatus of state power. The possibility of this leap into post-revolutionary existence is, on the whole, taken for granted in Bakunin's writings. What he provided was a theory of political action rather than an investigation of the possibilities of universal anarchy. His negative arguments, against Marx and Mazzini* especially, are unmatched by any convincing positive defence of his own position. His anarchism is, in the last analysis, an affair of the heart, based in revulsion against every actual or potential limitation on the expresion of human life. That is the strength of his work as well as its weakness. It explains Bakunin's continuing appeal as much as the frustration of his hopes.

David J. Levy

Two anthologies provide useful selections of Bakunin's voluminous writings: *Bakunin: Selected Writings* ed. Arthur Lehning (1973); *The Political Philosophy of Bakunin* ed. G. P. Maximoff (1953). See also E. H. Carr, *Michael Bakunin* (1937).

21
BALAKIREV, Mily Alexeyevich 1837–1910

Russian composer

Balakirev's early years were spent in Nizhny-Novgorod and then Kazan, where he studied mathematics at the university. His musical education profited from his contact with the household of A. D. Ulybyshev (1794–

1858), the author of books on Mozart and Beethoven*. Having gained some practical experience of music, he made some reputation as a pianist and composer. In 1855 he moved to St Petersburg, where he met Glinka*, who formed a very favourable impression of his talent; this respect was repaid later when Balakirev was primarily responsible for editing Glinka's works for publication. Towards the end of the 1850s he played the 'Emperor' to the tsar and saw some of his songs in print. Between 1855 and 1862 he made the acquaintance of the most important members of what became known as the Balakirev circle: Cui (1835–1918), a military engineer, Mussorgsky*, a soldier and later a civil servant, Rimsky-Korsakov*, who served in the navy, and Borodin*, a medical chemist. Balakirev's enthusiasm for the greater experience of music drew these amateurs to him 'as if by magnetism', and he inspired them with his own ideals and not infrequently compelled them to comply with his prescriptions in their own compositions.

Russian composition in the 1860s is generally considered to have been polarized round, on the one hand, the conservatoires and their directors, the Rubinshteyn brothers, and, on the other, the Balakirev circle. Whereas the former aspired to give professional musicians a conventional training to internationally accepted standards, the latter were passionately committed to writing Russian music, drawing on the native folk and church music; in the former group conservative, rather old-fashioned views predominated, while the others were interested in the newer music of Berlioz* and Liszt*; whereas the first group was mainly foreign in origin and cosmopolitan in outlook, the second was aggressively nationalist; the first stressed rules and traditions, the second inventiveness and originality. This view is really too static, and does not allow for interaction between the two groups; the polarization does not take account of the position of Tchaikovsky* and Serov, who had some sympathies with each side. Nevertheless, this picture is of some help in explaining the intense rivalries of the 1860s.

V. V. Stasov, who first met Balakirev in 1856, was an important influence on his nationalist outlook, and became the most active propagandist for the circle. It was Stasov who in 1867 referred to the existence of a significant school of Russian composers, using the words 'a mighty handful' *(moguchaya kuchka)*. Though not in fact originally applied to the composers who in the West became known as 'the Five' (i.e., Balakirev, Borodin, Cui, Mussorgsky and Rimsky-Korsakov), it is now generally taken to refer to them. Stimulated by Stasov's great interest in all aspects of Russian history and art, Balakirev's group were firmly committed to the use of Russian subjects for operas and programme music, to the incorporation in art music of the rich resources of native music, and to the working-out of suitable structures for such music. While both Stasov

and Balakirev suggested subjects, devised scenarios and wrote programmes for compositions by the others, it was Balakirev's tastes in the technical field which gave the group's music a degree of homogeneity. He had strong opinions on where in a symphony folksong could be used and how it should be used; his penchants for certain harmonic devices, key schemes and even particular keys are reflected in the works of the others. As was inevitable, there came a time when the other composers were no longer prepared to tolerate Balakirev's fussy, often rude interference in their work, but he exerted a most powerful influence on their first works, and his ideas coloured their entire *oeuvre*.

Balakirev's role was accomplished more through these contacts than through institutions; he did, however, hold a number of important appointments. He was a prime mover in the establishment in 1862 of the Free (i.e., 'without charge') School of Music, whose assistant director he was until 1868. This rival to the conservatoire in St Petersburg gave more attention to vocal music and church music, encouraged students from a wider social range, and came to be known for the more adventurous programmes of its (mainly) orchestral concerts. From 1868 to 1874, and from 1881 until his death Balakirev was director of the school. From 1867–9 he was Anton Rubinstein's successor as conductor of the orchestral concerts of the Russian Musical Society. From 1883 until 1894 he was musical director of the Imperial Court Chapel. He underwent several crises, however, and was not a consistently prominent figure in the musical world. Cui opined that his career could have been more glittering had Balakirev been of less independent character and more ready to cultivate important people.

His ideas were tried out in a series of works, many of which he completed or revised up to 1905. Thus, others' works embodying Balakirev's principles appeared before his own. The First Symphonies of Rimsky-Korsakov and Borodin, and the Second Symphony of Tchaikovsky were all completed and performed before his own First Symphony (1864–6 and 1893–7, performed 1898). Some of his shorter orchestral works are based on a number of national folksongs. His greatest symphonic poem, *Tamara* (1867–82), is centred on a poem by Lermontov*. It is a magnificently evocative piece, describing how Tamara seduces passing men before tossing them into the roaring current of the river Terek. Its depiction of the wild dark forces of nature is typically Romantic, and its water-imagery and voluptuous oriental music reveal a strong affinity with *Schéhérazade* (1888).

Piano music is the other major area of Balakirev's output. *Islamey* (1869, revised 1902) and the Sonata in B flat minor stand out from a considerable number of mazurkas, nocturnes, scherzos, waltzes, etc. *Islamey*, an 'oriental fantasy', exploits folk material from the Caucasus, and is typical of the musical audacity, relentless rhythms and brilliant colours of Russian 'oriental' music; it is a virtuoso work of the first order, and Balakirev's best-known composition. The four-movement Sonata uses material from 1855 to 1857, but assumed its definitive form between 1900 and 1905; there is no real stylistic disparity despite the long span of work. It is the only major work in this genre from this generation.

Balakirev is given much more credit for his role as mentor than as a composer. He is known only for a handful of works, when there are others which deserve greater familiarity. Quite apart from their intrinsic interest, we could then see just how much the compositions of Borodin and Rimsky-Korsakov especially are indebted to his.

Stuart Campbell

Other works: incidental music to Shakespeare's tragedy *King Lear* (1858–61 and 1902–5); Overture on the themes of Three Russian Songs (first version 1858, second version 1881); Second Overture on Russian Themes (also known as *Musical Picture 1000 Years*, 1863–4, second version, as symphonic poem *Rus'*, 1884); Overture on Czech Themes (first version 1867, second version as *In Bohemia*, 1905); Piano Concerto in E flat major (1861–2, 1906–9, completed by S. M. Lyapunov); two collections of Russian folksongs, published 1866 and 1898. See: E. Garden, *Balakirev: A Critical Study of his Life and Music* (1967); G. Abraham, *Studies in Russian Music* (1933), *On Russian Music* (1939); V. Stasov, *Selected Essays on Music* (trans. 1968).

22
BALZAC, Honoré de 1799–1850

French novelist

More than is even the case with the other great French Romantics, of whom he is an exact contemporary, Balzac the writer repays some familiarity with Balzac the man. An appreciation of what his world is all about begins with the very details of his name. He was born in Tours into a family of modest origins, whose name, Balssa, had been changed to the more illustrious-sounding Balzac; Honoré in turn appropriated the noble particle *de* at the age of about thirty when he was beginning to attract attention as a writer. He soon shook off his provincial origins (although provincial milieux were to play a not inconsiderable part in his fiction), and shook off too the career for which his parents intended him, the law. Throughout the whole of the 1820s he eked out a precarious existence in Paris, writing hack, derivative fiction *à la* Scott*, Radcliffe, Fenimore Cooper* under pseudonyms. He failed to establish himself at the same time as printer and publisher, running up crippling debts in the process. These and even more hare-brained ventures (e. g. reclaiming Roman silver mines in Sardinia, cultivating pineapples commercially) were to be a prominent feature of his life and his fiction, and are not untypical of the restless, entrepreneurial spirit of the age. When after 1830 Balzac finally did establish himself in the fashionable Parisian eye as a result of his first successes, *The Physiology of Marriage (Physiologie du mariage*, 1829), *The Chouans (Les Chouans*, 1829) and *The Wild Ass's Skin (La Peau de chagrin*, 1831), he attracted too the attention of the caricaturist. The legendary Balzac was born: a man of colossal energy, eager to cut a figure as a wit and dandy in defiance of his short, fat figure; capable of prodigious bouts of creative labour but revising his works many times at the (ruinously expensive) proof stage; an intellectual butterfly, albeit a corpulent one, who read widely but hastily, familiarizing himself with all the main scientific and philosophic currents of the age, including many dubious ones: mesmerism, illuminism, the phrenology of Gall and the physiognomy of Lavater. Not the least feature of his caricatural image was the attraction he held for his women readers. When he died in 1850, an exhausted and burnt out writer, he had in fact only just married the Polish widow, Countess de Hanska, who had been an admirer of his work at first anonymously and by correspondence throughout the whole of his mature career.

In roughly twenty years of feverish activity Balzac wrote ninety-one novels and stories, painting a detailed picture of the middle and upper classes of France in the first half of the nineteenth century. Although wide, the panorama is not complete, for the peasantry and growing proletariat/artisan class are merely shadowy figures glimpsed occasionally in a corner of the canvas. But this did not diminish the enthusiasm of Engels* – 'I have learned more from Balzac than from all the works of the historians, economists and professional statisticians of the period taken together' – any more than of George Lukács in this century. A number of characteristics of the age are of some importance for an understanding of Balzac's work. First, and in this respect Balzac is himself very representative, the Napoleonic period, Restoration and July Monarchy together constituted an era in which personal dynamism, energy, indeed the most self-centred individualism, were at a premium. Not long after his death in 1821, Napoleon Bonaparte* acquired a mythic stature as the embodiment of these supposed national characteristics, and Balzac, like Stendhal* and Hugo* in varying degrees, occasionally worshipped at the shrine. Second, the July Monarchy in particular was the period when the industrial revolution fully got under way in France, and with it triumphed the spirit of *laissez-faire* capitalism. In fact long before Guizot coined what has been taken to be the slogan of the age, *'Enrichissez-vous!'*, unscrupulous entrepreneurs had made fortunes as early as the revolutionary and Napoleonic periods out of hoarding, commodity speculation and shady state contracts. Two of Balzac's most famous characters, Goriot and Grandet, enriched themselves in precisely this way. A new middle class was thus coming into being which controlled land, property, political power and, increasingly towards the end of Balzac's life, mining, manufacturing and capital. With wealth came social aggrandizement and at the top of the scale a title and ministerial status. A concomitant was a previously unknown degree of class-consciousness: the newly indebted peasantry (Balzac's *Les Paysans*, 1844) *vis-à-vis* the new bourgeois landlords *vis-à-vis* the new aristocracy *vis-à-vis* the old émigré nobility.

This then, the period 1795–1845, is the age to which Balzac aspired to be the secretary in his prose fiction (and also a handful of largely unsuccessful plays). The vast majority of his novels and stories are set in contemporary or near-contemporary France, and the enormous gallery of characters – Fernand Lotte in his *Dictionnaire biographique* has nearly 2,500 named entries – is based on a wide range of professions and occupations, human types and sub-groups of social classes. Many of his best-known novels, *Cousin Bette (La Cousine Bette,* 1846), *Old Goriot (Le Père Goriot,* 1834), *A Harlot High and Low* (the current Penguin translation of *Splendeurs et misères des courtesanes,* 1838–47) and *Cousin Pons (Le Cousin Pons,* 1847) are set mainly or entirely in Paris. Others, such as *The Black Sheep (La Rabouilleuse,* 1842) or the immense *Lost Illusions (Illusions perdues,* 1837–43), are set both in Paris and the provinces, and derive much of their power from the contrast between both settings, one of the author's major themes throughout his work. Issoudun and Angoulême respectively are the two towns in these novels, and could be joined by a long list of others which are used similarly as a powerful, brooding backdrop to the human dramas in the foreground.

The sociological value of Balzac's fiction is without parallel in literary history before Zola*. His most ambitious work, *Lost Illusions,* is at least of minor interest for its picture of the economic realities of printing and petty journalism in the provinces. But it is of even greater value for its major theme, the important new developments in intellectual life in the capital and the way in which they too are subordinated to financial considerations. With varying degrees of deliberateness Balzac points to the cynical commercialization of cultural life – journalism, publishing, bookselling, bookreviewing, and the byzantine ramifications of the theatre industry – which were one of the dimensions of that masterpiece that most impressed Marx* and have subsequently been expanded upon by Lukács. Whether or not, as in this case, it is a question of the 'recuperation' (to use a modern Gallicism) of culture by capitalism, or, as in less ambitious but not necessarily less compelling works, a matter of good men

falling among whores and lawyers, Balzac's greatest novels are a penetrating indictment of the moral standards of his times. The message seems to be that 'honesty serves no purpose . . . corruption is the general rule . . . there are no principles, just events, etc.' These, the sentiments of perhaps Balzac's most powerful character creation, the cynical Vautrin in *Old Goriot,* are echoed by other characters, and borne out time and time again in other novels. The author's imagination was at its most fertile in creating his enormous cast of opportunists who populate his world and in some of the more striking cases recur from novel to novel – one of his proudest innovations. Between the extremes of social climbers like Rastignac and Chardon – the latter eventually ennobled as de Rubempré – on the one hand, and homicidal criminals such as Vautrin and Philippe Bridau on the other, there is a huge middle ground of crooked financiers, lawyers, landowners, politicians and journalists. Baron Nucingen, du Tillet, Roguin, Fraisier, Finot, Esther van Gobseck, Valérie Marneffe ('a Machiavelli in skirts'), Gaudissart ('the Napoleon of the boulevard theatre'), these are just a few of the hundreds of characters who are committed to the hilt in the struggle to monopolize money, sex, power, ideology and culture.

In the last two examples Balzac uses one of his favourite rhetorical devices, antonomasia, to persuade us of the epic stature of his characters; elsewhere he harnesses Lady Macbeth, Dido and Don Juan in the same way. One of the most famous examples is Goriot himself, '*le christ de la paternité*', and that novel also makes use of another awesome precedent to heighten the emotional impact on the reader of seeing Goriot ruthlessly exploited by his daughters Delphine and Anastasie. 'All is true,' urges the author in English, borrowing from Shakespeare. The fate of King Lear can be witnessed any day in the seemingly banal world of bourgeois Paris; the novel has supplanted the theatre as the major cultural medium, and modern themes have supplanted ancient ones. Witnessed, that is, by any reader willing to enter into complicity with Balzac, to heed his chivvying, authorial directions, respond to his powerful, morally preempting presence, creating analogies and maxims, typologies and social categories on every page that he wrote. Prendergast has effectively demonstrated the failure of Émile Benveniste to find a page of Balzac which contains *histoire* and no *discours*. Balzac's writing is, like Benveniste's unfortunate example taken from *Gambara,* 'impregnated with the discursive mode'.

Balzac's aspiration was more grandiose than just to be the social historian of contemporary France, for the universal resonance of the title he gave to the whole corpus of his work, *The Human Comedy, (La Comédie humaine)* is inescapable. Balzac was not a man to blush at appropriating the analogy of Dante's *Divine Comedy* any more than at claiming to do with the pen what

Napoleon did with the sword. His scientific and socio-logical pretensions were similarly grand. In keeping with the growing positivist spirit of the age, the 1840's, Balzac grouped his novels as 'Studies' under major headings: 'Analytical', 'Philosophic and Manners', and subdivided the latter into 'Scenes of Private Life, Provincial, Parisian, Military Life', etc. In the manner of Linnaeus, Cuvier*, Lamarck*, Geoffroy Saint-Hilaire he sought to categorize and typify human beings, the clerk, the petty landlord, the Paris student, the southerner, etc. 'Society makes of man, according to the environment in which he functions as many different species as exist in zoology,' he tells us in the 'Avant-Propos de la Comédie Humaine' (1842), and in his manipulation of plot, character, event, milieu and theme we often detect anticipation of both Taine* and Zola. Yet sometimes he could get it wrong. The monumental seductress Lady Arabella Dudley of *Le Lys dans la vallée* is the way she is because she is, first, a woman and thus either an *ange* or a *démon* (sometimes Balzac was no subtler than Victor Hugo), secondly an *English*woman, hence either a tight-lipped puritan or a nymphomaniac, and, best of all, a native of 'Lancashire, where women die of love'.

Much of the time the conscious scientific framework of *The Human Comedy* and the determinist implications of the 'Avant-Propos' are irrelevant to an appreciation of the individual parts or even frankly at variance with the moral and aesthetic strategies to which Balzac frequently resorted when hard-pressed. He borrowed freely from a store-house of Romantic stereotypes when it suited him, and indeed the whole Romantic vogue of the occult and the fantastic *à la* Hoffmann* persisted fitfully into the 'realist' vein of his mature work. Balzac is an uneven writer, and his vices have been dwelt upon often enough: sentimentality and bad taste, artistic ineptitude, not to mention hypocrisy (deploring the opportunists in whom he lived out his most lurid social fantasies). But if an artist has the right to be judged by the peaks of his achievement rather than the troughs, Balzac must still be credited with having achieved a major advance for the novel in his time. He took it where it had never been before, and his impression on European fiction was indelible. At his best he is every bit the visionary that Baudelaire* considered him to be, more attuned to the spirit of his age than any contemporary, just as Baudelaire in turn and Flaubert* were to be in the next generation.

Ted Freeman

The best collected edition of *La Comédie humaine* in French is the Pléiade, Paris, 11 vols. Critical editions of the leading novels are also published by Classiques Garnier, Paris, and by British academic publishers (French text with notes and introduction in English), e.g. *Le Colonel Chabert* and *Gobseck*, ed. A. G. Lehmann (1955); *Eugénie Grandet*, ed. H. J. Hunt

(1967); *Le Père Goriot*, ed. Charles Gould (1967). In English translation the collected works were published by Dent, 1895–8 (almost complete, but leaving out a few minor, *risqué* titles), and Caxton, 1895–1900. The best current list (1980s) is kept by Penguin. For Balzac's correspondence see the edition by R. Pierrot, Garnier, 5 vols, 1960–9, and *Lettres à Mme Hanska*, ed. Pierrot, Paris (Delta), 4 vols, 1967–9. See also: *L'Année Balzacienne*, annually from 1960; H. J. Hunt, *Honoré de Balzac: a Biography* (1957) and *Balzac's 'Comédie Humaine'* (1964); F. Lotte, *Dictionnaire biographique des personnages fictifs de la Comédie humaine* (2 vols, 1952 and 1956); S. Rogers, *Balzac and the Novel* (1953); Peter Brooks, *The Melodramatic Imagination* (1976); G. Lukàcs, *Studies in European Realism* (trans. 1950); C. Prendergast, *Balzac, Fiction and Melodrama* (1978); D. F. McCormick, *Honoré de Balzac* (1979); M. Kanes, *Balzac's Comedy of Words* (1975).

23

BARNUM, Phineas Taylor 1810–91

US showman, publicist and author

To call P. T. Barnum the first great 'showman' is to neglect an essential part of his greatness, for Barnum was among the first to understand the nature of advertising his product not only by posters but by manipulating the existing media and word of mouth. In many ways he was the Founding Father of Madison Avenue. The small village of Bethel, Connecticut, where he was born, would hardly seem a fertile place for such talents. And yet biographers and critics have stressed the atmosphere of practical jokes and exaggerated rhetoric in which Barnum grew up. Although Barnum attended grammar school for at least six years, his first major 'lesson' for his future came from his grandfather Phineas Taylor, who gave him a property called Ivy Island when the child was four, telling him that this fabulous property would make him wealthy when he came of age. At ten he visited this 'property' and discovered it to be 'an almost inaccessible, worthless bit of barren land, and while I stood deploring my sudden downfall, a huge black snake (one of my tenants) approached me with upraised head.' Memories of this hoax combined with experiences working in a country store where he learned 'that sharp trades, tricks, dishonesty, and deception are by no means confined to the city' were the most important schooling Barnum had in his formative years.

Barnum's first adult venture was a newspaper, the *Herald of Freedom*, first published on 19 October 1831, whose critics labelled it 'Masonic and anti-priestcraft'. More formidable opponents brought three suits of libel against him, the third landing him in jail for accusing a local deacon of 'usury'. The anti-clerical stance of this tabloid would continue to be one of the major forces directing Barnum throughout his life in the rather grimly puritan days of the first half of the nineteenth century. Barnum, more than any other single man, made public entertainments popular and respectable in an age that frowned on the masses enjoying anything other than religion. In his own defence Barnum once said 'This is a trading world and men, women and children need something to satisfy their gayer, lighter moods and hours, and he who ministers to this want is in a business established by the Author of our nature.'

In 1835 Barnum began his show business career in New York city with the exhibition of an old Negro woman whom he claimed to be George Washington's 161-year-old former nurse, thus shrewdly cloaking his entertainment in the acceptable colours of science and patriotism, somewhat tarnished by later revelations that she was a fake.

Barnum continued to tour and exhibit until 1841 when he bought the American Museum in Manhattan and turned this curious old warehouse with its waxworks, freaks, animals and a lecturing 'professor' into one of the most famous entertainment places in the country. He doubled the museum space and added transient attractions such as educated dogs, 'industrious fleas, automatons, ventriloquists, living statuary . . . the first English Punch & Judy in this country, Italian Fantoccini, mechanical figures . . . dissolving views, American Indians who enacted their warlike and religious ceremonies on the stage . . .' In doing all this Barnum began to change the very nature of entertainment in America and in the process accumulated his first fortune grossing over $300,000 in the first three years.

This fortune and reputation were greatly enhanced by the tours Barnum made in the early 1840s with Charles S. Stratton, the 25 inch midget known professionally as General Tom Thumb. The general did monologues and historical and mythic roles playing everything from Cupid to Napoleon*. With Tom Thumb as his vehicle Barnum fulfilled a longtime ambition to tour England and Europe, exhibiting the advertising shrewdness that made him both rich and notorious. He let Tom perform for three nights in London and then stalled until he received the coveted invitation to Buckingham Palace for an audience with Queen Victoria* which was quickly followed by a second to see the three-year-old Prince of Wales. Barnum exploited all this quickly and broadly and soon the midget was known in the press as the 'Pet of the Palace'. Barnum snowballed this first royal audience into others on the continent and returned to the United States with an even more valuable human property, one that is estimated at selling about twenty million of the eighty-two million admission tickets sold by Barnum in his career.

Despite his success with the museum, General Tom Thumb, the famous 'Siamese twins', Chang and Eng, and other attractions, Barnum still sought to 'place himself before the world in a new light' by elevating public taste. And so without ever having heard her sing, he booked Jenny Lind, 'The Swedish Nightingale', for an American tour of 150 concerts which would earn the then astounding figure of over $700,000. No foreign artist had been so fully accepted, praised, and paid for by the American public, thus climaxing the exhibition phase of Barnum's career.

After two publicized 'retirements' in 1855 and 1868, Barnum returned to show business in 1871 to demonstrate once more his place as the premier promoter of the century. He became partners with William Cameron Coup and Dan Castello to build a travelling circus with such innovations as travel by rail, Ben Lusbie who could sell six thousand tickets in one hour, a half-ton seal, and the permanent base of P. T. Barnum's Great Roman Hippodrome in New York City. Eventually, Barnum bought out his partners and travelled as 'Barnum's own Greatest Show on Earth', slowly increasing the size until the overheads were $3,000 a day. In 1881 he merged with Allied Shows Circus owned by James E. Cooper, James L. Hutchinson and James Anthony Bailey. Thus was the *three-ring* circus born on 18 March 1881, establishing new definitions of extravagance for an age-old form. In 1882 the new partners bought 'Jumbo', a twelve-foot tall, six and a half ton elephant, from the London Zoological Gardens. Jumbo quickly became one of Barnum's biggest successes and was often presented in tandem with General Tom Thumb. Barnum is often credited with 'inventing' the circus, an institution that has existed for perhaps thousands of years. What he really did – with the help of shrewd partners like Coup and Bailey – was truly American: through money, size and advertising he simply created 'the greatest show on earth'.

During his various retirements Barnum wrote two books which reveal both his character and his interests. His frequently revised autobiography first came out in 1855 and in 1865 he published *Humbugs of the World*. The latter attacks spiritualists, quacks, swindlers, ghosts and certain religious cultists, while the former outlines 'Forty Busy Years' of providing 'Healthful entertainment to the American people'.

P. T. Barnum was that typical nineteenth-century American success, the sincere charlatan: a man who believe that all his tricks, deceptions, braggadocio, and sheer size were in the best interests of the public. He brought entertainment on a vast public scale to a nation that in his youth had shunned it. He made public spectacle and pleasure not only acceptable, but necessary and profitable.

Charles Gregory

See: *How I Made Millions: Or the Secret of Success* (1884, the last rewrite of his autobiography); *Why I Am a Universalist* (1895). About Barnum: M. R. Werner, *Barnum* (1927); Constance Rourke, *Trumpets of Jubilee* (1927); Irving Wallace, *The Fabulous Showman* (1959); Neil Harris, *Humbug: The Art of P. T. Barnum* (1973); Joel Benton, *Life of Honorable Phineas T. Barnum* (1891); Alice Curtis Desmond, *Barnum Presents: General Tom Thumb* (1954).

24

BARRÈS, Auguste-Maurice 1862–1923

French novelist, essayist and politician

Born in Charmes-sur-Moselle in Lorraine and educated at the *lycée* in Nancy, Barrès effectively combined the roles of writer and public figure until his death in 1923. In the early 1880s he embarked on a literary career in Paris, rejecting with equal vehemence the Naturalism of Émile Zola* and the Parnassianism of Leconte de Lisle. At this time his intellectual masters were Taine* and Renan*, whom he pillaged very selectively, and Schopenhauer* who taught him the limits of intellectual analysis.

By the late 1880s his literary and political vocation was on a firm footing. Inspired by the Panama scandal and by the cause of General Boulanger, he entered politics as parliamentary member for Nancy and was later to. represent a variety of constituencies, serving the Les Halles district of Paris between 1906 and 1923.

It was his literary development that had led him to political commitment. An early Symbolist, he produced *The Cult of the Self* (*Le Culte du moi*, 1888–91), a three-novel cycle in which, following Stendhal*, Byron* and Napoleon I*, he glorified energy and developed his theory of individualism. In showing the individual personality as the only tangible reality and the need for a free person to cultivate his own instincts, Barrès indicates how the alienated self, after a prolonged period of withdrawal, needs to develop conscious links with society outside.

His views concerning the spiritual and moral decline of Third Republic France were vigorously expressed in the novel cycle beginning with *The Uprooted Generation* (*Les Déracinés*, 1897), and known under the generic title *The Novel of National Energy* (*Le Roman de l'énergie nationale*). Abandoning subjective realism he moved much closer to the scientific realism of Bourget and the documentary style of Hugo* and Zola. The stress in these novels is always on the rottenness of cosmopolitan political and financial society and the imperative for the young of France to remain rooted in traditional, provincial values, symbolized in 'land and dead ancestors' ('*la terre et les morts*').

It was during the writing of these novels that Barrès played his most crucial political role as the leading advocate of French nationalism during the years of the Dreyfus Affair. As an active journalist and pamphleteer, his patriotism and his traditionalism were fused in a definition of national solidarity which defended church, army and provincial identity against the enemies of the French nation – Liberals, German influence and Jews. Eschewing the virulent anti-Semitism of Drumont and other reactionary figures he nevertheless waged unremitting war on the foreigner within who consciously or unconsciously destroyed the traditional values of France.

Never a member of the Action Française Barrès concentrated in the years before the outbreak of war on alerting French opinion to the German problem in a series of sentimental provincial novels describing the tribulations of a young Alsatian faced with the choice of serving in the German army or escaping to unoccupied France or the heroism of a young girl from Metz who responds to her national duty by refusing to marry an attractive German schoolteacher. During the war he attempted to rally Frenchmen of all creeds to the national cause and in the latter part of his life toyed with the notion of permanent Franco-German concord.

Complex in both artistic and intellectual terms Barrès was in effect a serious-minded dilettante. His literary credo was a curious mixture of Symbolism, Realism, Romanticism and Classicism. Beside the didacticism of his political writings must be set the idiosyncratic poetic meditations on religious and artistic themes and his expressive exploitation of landscape and exotic imagery.

His intellectual roots were equally heterogeneous. Weaned on Schopenhauerian idealism which he combined with aspects of the historical relativism of Taine and Renan, he looked also to contemporary associationist psychology for arguments against what he saw as the prevailing influence of Kant and his universalist ethics. Thus, acutely aware of what he saw as the political and moral decline of France since 1870, he diagnosed the 'dissociation' and 'decerebration' of his country and advanced the need to reassemble and reintegrate the scattered elements of national consciousness by renewed personal contact with ancestral and environmental factors. At the same time, his very stress on emotional and instinctual perceptions preserved him from the strait-jacket of mindless ideology, just as in his traditionalism he stopped short of the doctrinaire 'integral nationalism' of Maurras and the Action Française.

Indeed, his enthusiasm for a saviour-figure like Boulanger in the 1880s and his campaigns as a National Socialist in the 1890s stem from his belief in a plebiscitary dictatorship in the republican tradition. And among contemporary politicians he admired not only the populist poet, Déroulède, the Provençal separatist, Mistral, and the doyen of the new right, Maurras, but also the Socialist leader, Jean Jaurès, whose pre-war pacifism he nevertheless denounced as pan-Germanism.

Likewise, despite his life-long defence of the Catholic Church, he maintained his spiritual independence to the last. He possessed a deep religious sense and was convinced of the spiritual and social mission of the Catholic Church in France: for all that, however, he distinguished himself from the militancy of a Claudel or a Bourget in his admiration for one of their *bêtes noires*, Ernest Renan.

Barrès was master and guide of his generation but his influence on the twentieth century was scattered and not restricted to Mauriac and other Catholic writers. It can be detected also in the writings of Gide and Camus and, more surprisingly perhaps, in the patriotic poetry of Aragon during the Second World War. In addition, his ideas have been taken up by advocates of right-wing regionalism in France, as well as by the Welsh nationalist writer, Saunders Lewis. Finally, many aspects of his political thinking find an echo in the constitution of the French Fifth Republic framed by Debré for de Gaulle in 1958.

Christopher Bettinson

Barrès's complete works, including the fourteen volumes of personal writings (*Mes Cahiers*), were published by the Librairie Plon in Paris (14 vols, 1929–57). See: Z. Sternhell, *Maurice Barrès et le nationalisme français* (1972); P. Ouston, *The Imagination of Maurice Barrès* (1974); C. S. Doty, *From Cultural Rebellion to Counter-revolution: The Politics of Maurice Barrès* (1976).

25
BARRY, Sir Charles 1795–1860

British architect

Known as one of the leading architects of the Gothic Revival, Charles Barry was actually a pioneer of the Victorian neo-Renaissance. He introduced the 'palazzo' form into England at a time when British architecture was dominated by a Neoclassical style whose chief exponent was Sir John Soane*. Like many British architects, Barry's background afforded little advantage either by birth or by education. His mother died when he was three and his father, a London parliamentary stationer, when he was ten. In 1810 he was apprenticed to a firm of architects and surveyors in Lambeth, and it was there that he acquired the basis of his later command of the technical aspects of building. A modest legacy from his father's estate enabled Barry to embark upon a European tour in 1817. His funds were augmented in Rome where he managed to sell some sketches of the buildings he had studied, and he con-tinued his journey (as an artist-companion) to Greece, Egypt, and what is now Syria and Turkey. On his return in 1820 he married and set up in private practice. Of his four sons, two (E. M. and Charles junior) became successful architects (cf. the Scott* family architectural dynasty), one (John Woolfe) an engineer, and one (Alfred) Bishop of Sydney, principal of King's College, London and his father's eventual biographer.

Barry's early work includes several loosely Gothic churches and the Grecian design of the Royal Institution of Fine Arts in Manchester, but his first major building was the Travellers' Club in Pall Mall (1829–31). Several features distinguished this signal evocation of the palazzo spirit. Symmetrically organized around a central court (later covered), the club is, in its elevation, handled as essentially a flat surface, with columns and pilasters used only to frame the window openings. The top of the elevation is capped by a projecting cornice, and the corners emphasized by tall chimney stacks. Bolder still is the larger edifice next door, the Reform Club (1838), resembling the Cinquecento Palazzo Farnese. As well as the mirrors which are used inventively to create a play of spatial illusion around the covered central courtyard and stairs, the Reform Club is notable especially for its intricate and highly sophisticated servicing system. What Barry learnt in this regard he applied on behalf of a wholly different cause in 1841, when he was architect for Josiah Jebb's Pentonville Model Prison, an environment so thoroughly serviced (cf. Jeremy Bentham*) as to annihilate all but the most extreme changes in external conditions.

Barry continued to develop his conception of the Renaissance idiom under the Earl of Sutherland's patronage through such projects as Bridgewater House (1847–50) and the mansion at Clivedon (1851), and the Halifax Town Hall (1859–62), completed by his son E. M. Barry. But the building for which he is justly famous is the New Palace of Westminster (1835–67). The competition brief specified a Gothic design, and to a degree Barry complied. In its asymmetrical skyline and in almost every detail of its ornamentation the New Palace of Westminster is rightly cited as a neo-Gothic masterpiece. But in the symmetry of its multi-courted ground-plan (cunningly incorporating the old Westminster Hall and subtly changing its axis) and in the massing of its volumes, it simultaneously embodies strong classical elements.

To assist him Barry hired A. W. N. Pugin*. Officially Pugin's responsibility was to supervise the wood-carving, but in fact his contribution to the uniquely recognizable Houses of Parliament embraced so many aspects of their design (including the massing of Big Ben and much of the detail of the interior) that it is proper to speak of a collaboration between the two architects. Pugin's son even went so far as to claim, after Pugin's death in 1852, that the overall design was his father's and not Barry's inspiration. That this filial distortion of what was actually the case gained public credence may be interpreted as a curious homage to Barry's versatility. Pugin became the acknowledged master of Gothicism, and therefore it was assumed that a creation that looked as splendidly Gothic as the Houses of Parliament must have been essentially his. Thus from its beginning, and as befitted its future role as the symbol of democracy, the New Palace of Westminster was deceptive in its appearance, and in the best political traditions, the government of the day wrangled with Barry about his fees, refusing to pay him, beating him down, and constantly asking him for 'favour designs' in a remarkably unscrupulous way. He died, seven years before its completion, an embittered and exhausted man. Even so, the palace has managed to remain functional in spite of a vast increase in its usage, probably reinforcing the two-party form of British democracy by the layout of its two chambers.

Ranulph Glanville

See: A. Barry, *Memoir of the Life and Works of the late Sir Charles Barry, Architect* (1867); R. Dixon and S. Multhesius, *Victorian Architecture* (1978).

26
BAUDELAIRE, Charles Pierre 1821–67

French poet

Throughout his life Baudelaire maintained an intense and often anguished relation with his mother, a woman of some taste but little understanding. As a child of seven he felt deprived of her affections when in the year following his father's death she took as her second husband Colonel Aupick, a decent if unimaginative man who partly fuelled the adolescent Baudelaire's postures of revolt against conventional morality. Judging from the poet's letters, his stepfather nevertheless seems to have stood as a symbol of his deeper desire to achieve moral worth. The family background goes some way to explaining two fundamental tensions that are expressed in his poetry: his need for woman's love set against scorn for uncomprehending female superficiality; and his deep-rooted need for personal piety and worth, coupled with an uncompromising awareness of the 'worm' at the heart of virtue. His feeling of dispossession was exacerbated when to cure him of his profligate habits as a dandy in the *Bohème*, the management of his inheritance was removed from his control and entrusted to a lawyer friend of the family, Ancelle. Lumbered by debts, kept constantly short of money, unfavoured by the patronage of established men of letters, dogged by sequences of misfortunes that seem so diabolically schemed as to suggest complicity (see Sartre's study, below), Baudelaire's life is a story

of frustrations, humiliations and procrastinations. In 1841 his parents sent him on a voyage to India, in the hope of weaning him from what they judged to be his depraved Parisian life. He got only as far as Mauritius, returning to Paris in 1842. The journey proved fruitful, however, from the creative point of view, since it stocked his mind with the exotic imagery on which his poetry was to draw. Otherwise Baudelaire barely stirred from Paris during the twenty-eight years (1836–64) that he lived there continuously. He interested himself briefly in Republican politics and played a minor part in the 1848 Revolution. But he was by temperament too aristocratic and too 'metaphysical' in his conception of evil to sustain a commitment to the prevailing liberal doctrines of human perfectibility.

By mid-century Baudelaire had earned himself a reputation as an art critic and as the author of a number of essays including, as one of his most striking pieces, a non-psychological interpretation of laughter in its relation to original sin. He also produced remarkably good French translations of some of the works of Poe*, with whose ideas on the creative imagination he had felt an immediate affinity. Despite some success in placing his poems with prestigious journals, Baudelaire's reputation was by 1855 still that of an eccentric vampire of legendary lubricity (mostly his own invention) attempting to shock his way to public recognition. The same lack of understanding greeted the publication, in 1857, of the volume of poetry on which his fame rests, *Les Fleurs de mal*. He was put on trial for obscenity in the same year, fined and forced to publish an expurgated version of his collection. The ban – on six offending poems – was not lifted until 1949, though publishers contrived to incorporate them in most post-1857 editions. A second edition containing fresh poems, but not the banned ones, appeared in 1861. This being the last edition which Baudelaire was able to supervise personally, it is generally considered to be the most trustworthy guide to his intentions with regard to the thematic groupings and sequences which, he believed, would best convey the 'architecture' of the whole collection: a synopsis of human destiny in its progress through the stations of illusory salvation. The first posthumous edition, again substantially enriched, came out in 1868 (*Les Nouvelles Fleurs de mal*).

The originality of Baudelaire's achievement does not lie in any novelty of theme, versification, or even supporting theories of art. The focus on everyday life, the satanical, the macabre, the exotic and erotic, the suffering of the artist, his role as intercessor between the human and the divine, the thirst for the absolute were all part of the stock-in-trade of the contemporary Romanticism. In versification he tends to work his own variations within traditional forms of euphony, particularly the alexandrine, which gives even his lesser poems a stately dignity. His special sound effects tend to come from assonances and alliterations within the line rather than from innovations in rhyme or rhythm.

As regards his theories of art, though, if they were 'in the air' at the time they had not before been fixated by an intelligence comparable to Baudelaire's in keenness and imaginative scope. He saw clearly what the contemporary Art For Art's Sake movement failed to understand – that technique is not its own end but the servant of vision. Against the Realist aesthetics he maintained that beauty is a spiritual product of the imagination and not a property of some aspects of the world ('nothing of what is satisfies me'; 'the beautiful is always the effect of art'). Against the Parnassians, who had turned from the ugliness of modern civilization to seek consolation in the emotional and philosophical abstractions of Classicism, he maintained that beauty, although admittedly not of the world, must be wrought from it by a process of imaginative alchemy ('God gave me mud and I made gold of it'). In contrast to the Romantic poets, he believed that if nature can be made to appear beautiful it is as the result of the poet infusing it with his personal vision and not of his having made perfectly manifest God's presence in it. Baudelaire is one of the first poets consciously and philosophically to centre the poetic universe on man. In this he is an early 'modern'.

His preoccupation with evil is best understood in the light of his conviction that poetic vision is personal in its origin and bizarre in its effects: 'The beautiful is always bizarre.' Independently of both his belief in original sin as in the essential evil of the universe, and of the extent and nature of any private perversities, the *aesthetic* value which evil held for Baudelaire lay in the effects of strangeness and surprise that it would yield if it could be subjected to an imaginative transmutation. The presence of goodness, moreover, as what is found strange or surprising given its origin in evil, is indispensable to the dialectic of Baudelaire's alchemy. We find, accordingly, that the 'gold' of the poetry is suffused with a warm radiance. It has a moral or redemptive quality that is inseparable from its beauty and quite distinct from the didacticism against which he often protested.

In his concept of the poet as visionary or seer Baudelaire had been anticipated by Hugo*, and there was nothing particularly new about the idea that what the poet was gifted to 'see' and interpret for the rest of mankind was the latently visible system of universe analogy or *correspondances* placed by God in nature. On the subject of correspondences Baudelaire's thinking is at its least cogent. For one thing, his theoretical writings lump together the Fourierist* doctrine of terrestrial or 'horizontal' correspondences, such as are perceived in synaesthetic experience, with the 'vertical' or transcendental correspondences linking heaven with earth and deriving from a more ancient Platonic-Augustinian tradition. Furthermore, it is hard to reconcile

his aversion to nature with his adherence to either doctrine of analogy: for must nature not compel love and reverence if it is the repository of divinely appointed analogies? Finally, Baudelaire states that the interrelations between symbols (objects as terms of analogic relations), being providentially ordained, are 'mathematically exact'. But if this is the case, poetic vision loses the personal and creative character which he praises elsewhere, becoming a contemplative faculty for the revelation of a pre-ordained world-system. This 'objective' conception of analogy is not, however, carried over into his poetic practice, where we find the same sensory datum playing shifting and variable symbolic roles in response to changing mood, sometimes passing into its opposite. Images of flux and mobility, for example, are consubstantial now with spiritual decay, now with the fluid patternings of creation. Sensations of lulling and swaying render sometimes the hypnotic fascination of evil, sometimes the gentle swell of nascent creativity. The impression of deep tension combined with fluidity which much of the poetry gives depends in part on this deliberate play with polyvalent analogy.

Yet in the sphere of correspondence theory Baudelaire had an original and powerfully influential insight which survives the contradictions mentioned: that the poet's gift for apprehending analogies, a gift assisted in Baudelaire's case by a lifelong addiction to hashish, could and should be embodied in the literary devices of metaphor, simile, allegory, etc., which are thereby promoted from decorative effects to epistemological instruments for perfecting his analogic intuitions and transcribing them into a public medium. Baudelaire believed that the precision and intersubjective value of a metaphor had their explanation in the fact that, being 'drawn from the inexhaustible storehouse of universal analogy', it captures the mathematical exactness of a pre-existent analogic relation. But he could have justified the literary use of metaphor by pointing, less metaphysically, to the reality of synaesthetic experience. This would not, however, have been a perfect solution either, for while synaesthesia allows for subjective variations it leaves obscure the intersubjective value of successful poetic metaphors, the speculative explanation of which constitutes the attractiveness of the 'objective' theory.

From the technical viewpoint Baudelaire's originality undoubtedly rests on his suggestive use of language and of familiar, trivial objects to conjure up subtleties of feeling and thought. He excels in the art of suggesting the infinite through the finite, particularly the ugly. He regarded poetic language as an 'evocative bewitchment', magical in its effects, though as scientific as mathematics or music in the precision of the handling through which these are achieved: 'There is no chance in art . . . the imagination is the most scientific of the faculties.' Suggestion differs from description in that what it evokes leaves 'an absence to be completed by the imagination of the listener'. Here again technique is at the service of a personal vision of beauty, as possessing 'some slightly indeterminate quality . . . leaving room for conjecture.' Baudelaire is a master of the aspect of the art of suggestion which calls for a delicate striking of the balance between an over-exact use of terms that would stultify reverie and, at the other extreme, an insufficiency of definition such as would leave the reader's imagination unstimulated and inert.

The 'new shiver' which Hugo credited Baudelaire with having brought to French poetry arises from the distinctive tonality that accrues to beauty when it is extracted from ugliness. The distillations of memory, filtered through imagination, succeed in salvaging from the thwarted aspiration to perfection a value that is limited inasmuch as impregnated with the failure on which it feeds, while yet being absolute in its suggestion of mystery and invitation to renewed spiritual voyages. One lovely species of this 'flower' arises from the granting of absolute value to what is known to be in one sense illusory: it is recognized that the mysteries of a mistress's eyes are unbacked by corresponding qualities of heart and mind; they are empty – but 'emptier and deeper than even you, O Heavens'. The pit of hell is an inverted vision of the vault of heaven.

The influence of Baudelaire cannot be overstated. He is the most important forerunner of Symbolism (Mallarmé*), which adopted in an even more self-conscious and thoroughgoing style his notions of poetry as verbal sorcery with a strong emphasis on word-music, of the analogic value of objects and their indeterminacy as symbols, of the role of imprecision and of precision, as well as of that of the reader as active participant in the production of the poem.

Roger McLure

Baudelaire's complete *oeuvre* is collected in the Bibliothèque de la Pléiade edition (1961). His prose writings include: *La Fanfarlo* (a thinly disguised autobiographical novel); *Paradis artificiels*; *De L'essence du rire et généralement du comique dans les arts plastiques*; *L'Oeuvre et la vie d'Eugène Delacroix*; *Salon de 1846*; *Salon de 1859*; *Journaux intimes*. His *Sur la Belgique* is a vituperation against what he sees as Belgian pusillanimity. There is an English edition of most of the poems of *Les Fleurs du Mal* in the original French, but with good plain prose translations and an introduction: F. Scarfe, *Baudelaire* (1962). The standard English biography is by E. Starkie, *Baudelaire* (1957). The best introduction to understanding Baudelaire's poetry is A. Fairlie, *Baudelaire* (1960). Other critical studies in English include: W. F. Leaky, *Baudelaire and Nature* (1969); P. Quennell, *Baudelaire and the Symbolists* (1954). Among studies in French are: J. Prévost, *Baudelaire* (1953);

M. A. Ruff, *L'Esprit du mal et l'esthetique baudelairienne* (1955); J. Pommier, *La Mystique de Baudelaire* (1964); J. Lonke, *Baudelaire et la musique* (1975). Sartre's existential-psychoanalytical study of Baudelaire the man (*Baudelaire*, 1947) is brilliant but not conclusive.

27
BAUER, Bruno 1809–82

German biblical critic and philosopher

Born in 1809 at Eisenberg in Saxony, Bauer studied at the University of Berlin in its Hegelian* heyday, and became in his early days a conservative, 'right-wing' Hegelian. He progressively identified himself with the radical, 'left-wing' group in the Hegelian party. His academic career began in 1834 as a lecturer (*Privatdozent*) at Berlin, and he was promoted to an *ausserordentlicher* professorship at Bonn five years later. His earliest teaching and work (on the interrelationship of the four Gospels) generated intense academic and ecclesiastical controversy, on the grounds of which he was deprived in 1842 of his chair by the Prussian government, although it was unclear whether a majority of the Prussian theological faculties supported his deprivation. Bauer spent the remainder of his career in scholarly retirement, writing on the ideological and political history of the eighteenth and nineteenth centuries, and in literary vituperation directed against the Christian academic and ecclesiastical establishment of Germany. He died in Berlin in 1882.

It is enlightening to compare and contrast the life and work of Bauer with those of D. F. Strauss*, of whom he was a near contemporary. Although it is singularly difficult to summarize Bauer's complicated and technical writings, it simplifies the matter if we follow modern scholarship in distinguishing between an 'early' and a 'later' Bauer (or Bauer I and Bauer II) in interpreting his work. We deal with the former of these in the first instance. Bauer's intense interest in Gospel criticism was evoked by his earliest research on the Johannine Gospel (published in 1840 as his *Kritik der evangelischen Geschichte des Johannes*). He seizes upon the intensely allegorical, metaphorical, parabolic and analogical character of the work (which in his day had long been recognized). This he unambiguously describes as *Kunst*, which, while it may be correctly translated as 'art', carries in Bauer's usage the connotation of something 'ingenuous' or 'over-clever'. But there can be no doubt for Bauer that the description 'art' implies that the Fourth Gospel is emphatically *ahistorical*, that no part of it is to be regarded as anything but theological and esoteric fantasy. But what then of the relationship, Bauer asked, between the Fourth Gospel and the synoptics (Matthew, Mark and Luke)? Bauer adopted the position which was being vigorously and plausibly argued in his day, that the earliest 'historical' Gospel was Mark, and in his notorious second work (*Kritik der evangelischen Geschichte der Synoptiker*, 1841–2) developed and elaborated the unpopular thesis that Luke and Matthew are but expansions, elaborations and embellishments of the Second Gospel which do not contain any trace of historical material independent of or additional to that which is allegedly to be found in Mark. To be more precise, in Bauer's judgment the earlier theological expansion of Mark is Luke, which in turn functioned as the sole basis for the later literary document Matthew. Bauer was swift to realize the momentous significance of what he was saying: considered as a historical phenomenon (originating in history with the historical Jesus) the Christian religion rested, not upon the New Testament, nor upon the four Gospels, but solely and exclusively upon the very slender document, the Gospel of Mark. (This explains incidentally the extremity, not to say the savagery, of the treatment meted out to Bauer by the German establishment in 1842.)

Bauer next and predictably turned his attention to Mark, and, to the furious indignation of the establishment, proceeded radically to dehistoricize it also. It is to do Bauer no injustice whatever to summarize his conclusion on Mark by saying that the Marcan Gospel is the invention of a single author! For example, Bauer treated with extreme scepticism the received notion in theological circles that prior to the historical appearance of Jesus there existed in Jewish circles a strong, widespread expectation of the appearance of the Messiah, witnessed to in extra-Marcan circles. Undoubtedly, Bauer with incisive originality analysed the difficulties involved in making sense of those passages in which the Messiahship is a subject of discussion between Jesus and his disciples, and the entire discussion of the Messianic office of Jesus leads him to the conclusion that Messiahship was attributed to Jesus at a very late date by the Christian community, whatever that was, and whenever it may be said to have come into existence. It is important to note that at this stage Bauer is neither saying nor implying that there never was some actual flesh-and-blood Jesus of whom the religious community predicated so much. The sheer facticity of a historical Jesus is not at this stage called in question.

It is quite otherwise when we turn to consider the 'later' Bauer (Bauer II). It can no longer be seriously doubted that the later Bauer, with his bitterness and contempt and loathing for the 'theologians' and the 'apologists', was created by the treatment handed to him by the Christian establishment, which seemed to him to be a repetition of that treatment meted out to Strauss by Tübingen seven years earlier. Bauer II strives hard to understand the various episodes of Jesus's life as reflections of the experience of the early Christian community: therefore, the temptations pro-

ject upon a screen the struggles of the earliest Christians with the flesh and the devil. He strives to the point of genius to derive some of the more obscure Gospel sayings of Jesus from the experience of the later community. Whatever posterity's judgment upon Bauer was, it can no longer be denied that later biblical criticism was to benefit immeasurably from the brilliant and honest manner in which he focused attention on very real difficulties in the Marcan historical narratives as they stand – whether these concern Jesus's puzzling mission of the Twelve, certain rather obscure sayings attributed to Jesus, parables whose point is no longer clear, the order in which the Gospel materials have been arranged, the incompatibility of publicly performed material miracles with a supposedly secret Messiahship, the difficulties with which the final journey of Jesus from Galilee to Jerusalem bristles, the mysterious circumstances of the Last Supper, the irresoluble problems involved in constructing a coherent account of the resurrection appearances, which had so troubled the biblical critics of the Enlightenment. The difficulties, problems, contradictions and incompatibilities are just so numerous and excruciating that all attempts to deal with them rationally must fall to the ground, and all significant talk of a 'real' historical Jesus behind or beyond them must now be abandoned as having no meaning whatever. Bauer's meaning, as a Hegelian, seems to have been that religion has to do essentially with various episodes or movements (e.g., the reconciliation of the human with the divine) in the life of man; in the Marcan Gospel what apparently happened is that such dynamic movement has been frozen or solidified, entangled with materialistic miraculous events, and predicated of one individual (Jesus) rather than of humanity as such. Religion, according to Hegelianism, moves in the realm of 'ideas', and in the Gospels these ideas have been represented in a worldly, quasi-historical biographical form which has most seriously obscured and distorted them. The point of Gospel criticism is to disentangle the eternal ideas or enduring truths from the essentially inadequate and dangerous form in which they have become clothed.

It is no easy task to state in brief form modernity's assessment of Bauer's work. It is unquestionably true, as Albert Schweitzer complained so long ago, that the condemnation directed at Bauer II has tended to overshadow the valuable and original contribution of Bauer I to the ongoing progress of synoptic criticism in the nineteenth century. Within the history of that discipline the work of Bauer I still deserves honourable mention. Yet it is not difficult to explain the occurrence of the vehement and absolute condemnation of Bauer II within theological circles. In the case of Bauer II, as in the case of Strauss, it is reasonable to suggest that in the last analysis Bauer approached the Gospel materials with a fully-fledged, *a priori*, Hegelian philosophical scheme which predetermined for him their character and meaning. Moreover, as in the case of Strauss, the account of Gospel and Christian origins given by Bauer II simply leaves behind far too many unanswered, not to say unanswerable, questions which historians and theologians simply cannot discard. In the last analysis, Bauer II could not satisfactorily answer the question *why* the Gospels (whose central figure is a historical character) saw the light of day at that point in world history when they did in the absence of a factual historical figure which is their principal concern. Even if it were conceded that in the last analysis the author of Mark was the sole chronicler of Jesus, Bauer II's work does not satisfactorily illumine the relation between his literary achievement and the experience of that Christian community who exalted him as Lord and went to the farthest corners of the known world in order to preach his 'name'. These criticisms are uncannily similar to those directed towards the work of Strauss. Bauer II's reputation was not helped by various inconsistencies and errors in his work. For example, his defence of the existence of an earlier written record (*Ur-Markus*) which may have been used by the author of the Second Gospel is hardly consistent with his view that the latter is the sole originator of the Jesus-story who did not depend on earlier historical tradition. Moreover, his *a priori* insistence upon the lateness of the New Testament records led him eventually to date the synoptic writings in the second, third or fourth decades and the Pauline epistles in the sixth or seventh decades of the second century, which has been conclusively falsified by more modern research. And these datings involved him in giving a preposterous account of the Jesus-story as a fantasy based upon the life of the Roman moralist Seneca. On these grounds, Bauer is best remembered for his early and original contributions to biblical criticism and to the history of modern Europe.

James Richmond

Other works include: *Christus und die Cäsaren: Der Ursprung des Christentums aus dem römischen Griechentum* (1877). See: Karl Löwith, *From Hegel to Nietzsche: The Revolution in Nineteenth-Century Thought* (1965); Albert Schweitzer, *The Quest of the Historical Jesus* (1954); F. Lichtenberger, *History of German Theology in the Nineteenth Century* (1889); F. Copleston, S. J., *A History of Philosophy*, vol. VII (1963).

28
BAUR, Ferdinand Christian 1792–1860

German Protestant New Testament critic and historian of Christian origins

Born in Cannstadt in 1792 the son of a Würtemberg pastor, F. C. Baur was educated in Blaubeuren theo-logical seminary and in the university at Tübingen. He began his career as a theological tutor at Blaubeuren (1817–26), and from 1826 until his death was Professor of Historical Theology at Tübingen. He was the founder and leader of the so-called 'Tübingen School' of historical scholarship, whose other members are generally reckoned to be Schwegler, Zeller, Hilgenfeld, Köstlin, Volkmar, Holsten and, for a short period, Albrecht Ritschl*. A German academic of immense stamina and prolific capability (a colleague of his has recorded that for most of his professional life he rose daily, summer and winter, at four o'clock in order to begin his academic labours), Baur occupies an extremely important position in the development of modern critical research into the history of primitive and early Christianity and the dating of its principal documents.

Although it is almost impossible to summarize in a brief space a lifetime's scholarship like Baur's, it is beyond argument that his most significant and lasting contribution centres around his so-called 'conflict' theory of the origins of Christianity, the ancient church, and the New Testament canon. In giving his account of the evolution of the Christian religion, Baur plotted in great detail the so-called 'preparation for Christianity' in both Judaism and classical antiquity. He paid attention to the political and geographical universalism of the Roman Empire, Graeco-Roman philosophy with its interest in 'natural theology'; he carefully analysed Judaism in the immediately pre-Christian period, paying particular attention to the way in which it had been broadened and spiritualized by Greek influences from the Hellenism of Alexandria, directing it in a more universalist (as contrasted with nationalist or particularist) direction. It was into this milieu that Jesus came. Of central importance in understanding his mission is his teaching (with particular reference to the Sermon on the Mount), with its uniquely unprecedented emphasis on character and the heart, which represents almost an attack on the legalistic ethics of his Jewish contemporaries. A clash between Jesus and these becomes inevitable through Jesus's claim to universal Messiahship, which is incompatible with the narrow, materialist, almost ethnic concept of Messiahship entertained by the Jewish nation, a clash which results in Jesus's formal rejection and judicial execution. So-called 'original' Christianity begins then within an almost exclusively Jewish context – with the original twelve disciples preaching to their Jewish contemporaries Jesus's resurrection from the dead and his imminent second advent in judgment, which would bring reconciliation between him and the Jewish nation which had rejected him. This stage in the evolution of Christianity is the so-called 'Petrinist' one whose main characters are the original twelve (especially Peter, James and John), and whose principal documentary monument is the Gospel of Matthew.

The second stage in the process begins with the appearance and conversion of Paul, who understood himself as the 'Apostle to the Gentiles': that is, as the missionary of Christianity to the entire 'world' (as contrasted with 'Israel'), an understanding which at once produces conflict, disagreement and contradiction, between Paul and the 'Judaizing party'. This stage is known as the 'Paulinist' or 'Universalist' stage (marked by a breach with the Mosaic Torah, temple-worship and the necessity for cultic circumcision), whose principal literary monuments are Romans, I and II Corinthians (the genuinely Pauline authorship of Ephesians, Colossians, Philippians, I and II Thessalonians being rejected by Baur). Open and irreversible conflict was avoided by an agreement that the two parties should operate separately (Acts 15, etc.) and not overtly competitively, despite the opposition to Paul by the 'Judaizers' in Galatia.

The third and final stage of the process can only be understood in the light of Baur's contention that the principal task facing the subapostolic church was that of a mutual 'reconciliation' (*Aufheben*) of the two factions, in which their differences could be 'softened', 'superseded', 'neutralized' and 'overcome'. This is the 'mediating' or 'reconciling' stage of the process, whose literary monuments are thus described by Baur: the Gospel of Luke and Acts (the latter edited by a disciple of Paul, in order to give an idealistic appearance to primitive Christianity); the epistles to the Colossians, the Ephesians and of James, the former two of which are edited by a Paulinist, in contrast to Hebrews, an attempt at mediation by a number of the Judaizing party from an 'Alexandrine' point of view; in the much later Johannine gospel the intra-ecclesiastical struggle is left far behind, and is replaced by an account of Christianity within the framework of a cosmic conflict between God and evil, light and darkness. This third mediating stage is expressed in the old-Catholic (*altkatholisch*) Church of the second century which was to become the research-subject of A. Ritschl, which was obliged or forced (note the element of *necessity*) to develop in response to 'opposing' elements from without – namely, the two early heresies of Gnosticism (derived from Greek speculative notions), and Montanism (ecstatic and prophetic in form, incompatible with classical Christianity in its world-renouncing and rigid asceticism). The second-century church's response to those was twofold: a juridically defined historic episcopate regarded as being successive with and representative of 'the Apostles', able to apply 'original' Christianity in a rapidly changing world; and, second, ecclesiastical dogma, framed in the terminology and concepts of Greek speculative theology, which enabled the church to combat the heretics with their own intellectual weapons. But Baur's account of the emergence of the episcopate was gravely at variance with that given by the Roman Catholic Church, and this,

together with the fact that he gave a quite naturalistic account of the emergence of the papacy (that Peter was ever in Rome was dismissed as a pious but unhistorical legend, the choice of Rome as the headquarters of the ancient church being explained in terms of Rome's vast politico-geographical importance), brought him into conflict with his gifted Catholic colleague at Tübingen, Johann Adam Möhler (1796–1838), author of the notable *Symbolik* of 1832 (trans. 1843). As for ecclesiastical dogma, this reached its highest peak in the definition of Christ's person (over against a range of christological heresies) as *homousios* ('of one substance') with the Father at the Council of Nicaea in AD 325.

Even this briefest of sketches should make it clear how wide-ranging and important the researches of Baur were for the nineteenth century. The most difficult and vexatious problem is that of the relation between the thought of Baur and the threefold dialectical movement of Hegelianism. The similarity between the two is obvious, with special reference to the element of logical necessity involved in both; and that Baur had read and admired Hegel* is beyond doubt. But it is a scandal of modern 'textbook history' that Baur has been portrayed as an unyielding and mechanical 'Hegelian', insensitively and unreflectively forcing or imposing the Hegelian scheme on to his historical sources! It is greatly to the credit of much modern research that it has given us a different picture: that Baur reached his main historical conclusions (including his datings of, e.g., the New Testament books) independently of his 'Hegelianism', although it is beyond dispute that he was not unaware *a posteriori* of the similarity between the historical 'movement' reached by his researches and that which lies at the core of the Hegelian view of the historical process. Naturally, Baur's work evoked tremendous controversy both within and without Germany. But much more modern New Testament research (including, naturally, research into the so-called 'Synoptic' problem) saw the light of day in response to and sometimes in disagreement with Baur's published work. His work supplied an impetus also towards renewed research into Christian origins, the evolution of the episcopate and the papacy, the character of the creeds, the nature of early church dogma, and the history of the early heresies. It is agreeable that the recognition of the inestimably important contribution that he made to nineteenth-century historical criticism is today replacing those textbook caricatures and stereotypes which for generations obscured his name and denied to his work the place it deserves in the development of nineteenth-century theological research.

James Richmond

Works: *Gesammelte Werke*, ed. K. Scholder (1963 and following). Translation: *On the Writing of Church History*, ed. Peter C. Hodgson (1968). See: Otto Pfleiderer, *The Development of Theology in Germany Since*

Kant (1890); F. Lichtenberger, *History of German Theology in the Nineteenth Century* (1889); Edward Caldwell Moore, *An Outline of the History of Christian Thought Since Kant* (1912); Claude Welch, *Protestant Thought in the Nineteenth Century*, vol. I, 1799–1870 (1972); Peter C. Hodgson, *The Formation of Historical Theology: A Study of Ferdinand Christian Baur* (1966); Horton Harris, *The Tübingen School* (1975).

29
BEARDSLEY, Aubrey Vincent 1872–98

British illustrator and writer

Aubrey Beardsley was born in Brighton. From an early age he had tubercular tendencies and his work was often interrupted by severe attacks of haemorrhaging. As a child he was a precocious draughtsman and pianist. After attending Brighton Grammar School he took a job with a surveyor and then with the Guardian Life Assurance Company in London. He wrote verse and drama and drew in the evenings. In 1891 he introduced himself to the famous painter Burne-Jones*, who was impressed by his work and who helped and encouraged Beardsley in his career as an illustrator. Beardsley began to study in particular the drawings of Mantegna, Dürer and Botticelli. He was also greatly impressed by the 'Peacock Room' Whistler* had designed for the shipping magnate Frederick Leyland; the American artist had made especially elegant and original use of the Japanese style. Beardsley attended some evening classes at Westminster School of Art in 1892 – the only training he received. During this early period he met and was influenced by Puvis de Chavannes*, became interested in Japanese prints and Greek vase decoration, became a 'Wagnerite' and was acquainted with Oscar Wilde*.

In 1892 he received his first commission from the publisher John Dent to provide a large number of line-block illustrations to an edition of Malory's *Morte D'Arthur*. These showed the strong impact of Walter Crane, William Morris* and Burne-Jones and yet, in their extraordinary eclectic and complex effects, reveal Beardsley's own powerful and individual artistic personality. In 1893 he illustrated Wilde's *Salome*, published in 1894 by The Bodley Head, which by its form and contents shocked critics and public. *The Times* reported the edition as:

fantastic and grotesque, unintelligible for the most part, and, so far as they are intelligible, repulsive. They would seem to represent the manners of Judaea as conceived by a French décadent. The whole thing must be a joke, and it seems to us a very poor joke!

Hostility is often very accurate, at least in its empirical descriptions. In the same year Beardsley founded the *Yellow Book* with Henry Harland, and acted as art editor. In 1895 he was dismissed from the magazine by its publisher John Lane, having been implicated in the Wilde trial, and replied by founding the *Savoy* with Leonard Smithers in 1896. His other major works include illustrations to *The Lysistrata of Aristophanes* (1896), *The Rape of the Lock* (1896), and *Ben Jonson His Volpone* (1898). In 1897 Beardsley became a Catholic convert under the influence of his benefactor André Raffalovich. He died in Menton in the South of France, after chills and haemorrhaging, in 1898 at the age of twenty-five.

During his lifetime Beardsley's drawings, his friends and his habits made him a spectacular and scandalous figure. His art transforms the romanticism of artists like Morris and Burne-Jones into a bitter and erotic fantasy. He achieved this technically by using a fine steel pen and dense black ink, with which he virtually scraped his designs into the cartridge paper. He rarely sketched preliminary studies but rather drew directly with pencil and then went over this with pen and sable brush. Most of his work was executed for photo-mechanical line-block processes. His style of dramatic black and white contrasts and an extremely fine and sinuous line varied from his early complex arts-and-crafts effects, to a classical but personal art nouveau in *Salome* and finally, in *The Rape of the Lock*, to a novel reinterpretation of rococo profusion. This movement shows how far Beardsley naturally veered between extreme minimalism and a profound *horror vacui*. A disturbed but free sexuality informs almost all Beardsley's best work, even when the imagery is not explicitly erotic, and his imagery and style accurately represent the attempt by an *avant-garde* in English art and letters to wholly undermine Victorian morality and aesthetics. Not until Wyndham Lewis was England again to find such an ideologically subversive artist. Beardsley illustrated his own erotic prose story, *Under the Hill*, published posthumously, and this shows him to have had an original literary talent. The critic Roger Fry prophesied Beardsley's future fame as 'the Fra Angelico of Satanism'. His influence, however, was less in matters of immorality than in the visual arts and, significantly, in literature. Artists like Léon Bakst*, Toulouse-Lautrec*, Paul Klee and Picasso can be counted, along with Englishmen like Laurence Housman, Arthur Rackham and Eric Gill, as those directly influenced by his linear and asymmetric art. His influence has also extended to descriptive passages in the works of writers who include D. H. Lawrence, Ronald Firbank and William Faulkner. His purely formal powers as an illustrator, or perhaps interpreter, of literary texts seems to have provoked a response in many different spheres of creativity. This is the greatest testimony to his genius.

Richard Humphreys

See: Robert Ross, *Aubrey Beardsley* (1909); Brian Reade, *Aubrey Beardsley* (1967); Bridgit Brophy, *Aubrey Beardsley* (1976); Stanley Weintraub, *Aubrey Beardsley, Imp of the Perverse* (1976); Simon Wilson, *Beardsley* (1983).

30
BÉCQUER, Gustavo Adolfo 1836–70

Spanish poet

With the posthumous publication of Bécquer's *Rimas* (1871; sixth and latest trans. D. A. Altolé, *Symphony of Love*, 1974) Spanish lyric poetry turned a corner. Bécquer, born in Seville, the son of a painter, drew his inspiration from the popular poetry of Andalusia and from the example of German Lieder which had just begun to be translated. Before this, however, he had made a reputation as a writer of poetic prose. Between 1858 and 1863 he published most of his twenty-two *leyendas* (fanciful short stories). These reveal his special ability to deflect the reader's interest from the real to the fantastic by deft manipulation of details. While some of the *leyendas* are merely anecdotic and others now seem dated by their overtly religious and moral content, the best of them (trans. J. R. Carey, *The Inn of the Cats and Other Stories*, 3rd edn, 1946; C. F. and K. L. Bates, *Romantic Legends of Spain*, 1971) combine humour, pathos and irony with charming elements of fantasy. Also Bécquer created in them a unique type of Spanish lyrical prose based on the incorporation of semi-poetic rhythms and diction, emphasis on sensations rather than ideas or feelings, a colourful and pictorial approach and audacious use of figurative language.

In his literary essays and introductions Bécquer tried to analyse the creative act. Realizing that it stemmed from below the threshold of consciousness, he perceived (in contrast to his Spanish contemporaries) that poetry was born, not out of ideas, but out of a mysterious stirring in the depths of the mind. In tune with this conviction he turned away from the prevailing pattern of poetry of statement and moved towards poetry of subtle suggestion and the exploration of sensations, intuitions and non-rational experience. In this way he broke entirely new ground for Spanish poetry, and revealed to younger poets a whole range of fresh possibilities. At the same time he introduced into the Spanish lyric a new tone of quiet intimacy in contrast to the often shrill or portentous sound of much Romantic and Post-Romantic verse.

We do not know enough about Bécquer's emotional life to be able to relate the *Rimas* to it. However, we can discern a group of poems expressing the hopeful, ascendant phase of love and a second group dominated by disillusionment and bitterness. Thus a major theme

of the *Rimas* is that of the joys and sorrows of the lover. Finally there is a group of lyrics concerned with the ultimate destiny of man and related themes, such as death, immortality and religious faith. This last group is of importance as linking Bécquer with the Romantic legacy of spiritual unrest.

Bécquer's best poems are those in which, in order to convey new sensations and states of mind, he developed a new arsenal of expressive effects based chiefly on visual and auditive imagery, with a tendency away from the concrete towards the evanescent, the imprecise and the nebulous. But Bécquer's poetic technique has hitherto resisted analysis: as when an Impressionist painting is put beside earlier nineteenth-century pictures, we recognize the difference instinctively. The imprint of Bécquer's work is strong on that of Spain's finest woman poet, Rosalía Castro. Rubén Darió who is regarded as the father of modern poetry in Spanish, began by imitating Bécquer. By 1904 one of the two poets of the Generation of 1898, Machado, could call him 'the first innovator' and twenty years later the other, Unamuno, was still under his influence. Frequent re-editions of the *Rimas* attest the fact that his popularity with the general reader in Spain and Latin America is undiminished.

D. L. Shaw

See: his *Obras* (1962) and E. L. King, *Gustava Adolfo Bécquer, From Painter to Poet* (Mexico City, 1953).

31
BEETHOVEN, Ludwig van 1770–1827

German composer

The eldest of three children, Ludwig van Beethoven received his earliest musical training from his father, a music teacher and singer at the electoral court in Bonn. This instruction was supplemented by friends and relatives until about 1780, when the court organist Christian Gottlob Neefe became the boy's piano and composition teacher. At Neefe's urging, Beethoven visited Vienna in 1787, hoping to have composition lessons from Mozart; but his mother's illness hastened him back to Bonn after only a few weeks, and he was never to see Mozart again. In Bonn, Beethoven quickly established himself as a competent musician, deputizing for Neefe whenever he was away. As he reached manhood and became a court musician in his own right, he composed an important *Cantata on the Death of Joseph II* early in 1790 and a second cantata, for the election of Leopold as the new emperor, later the same year. In 1792 Haydn, returning from his first visit to London, stopped over in Bonn, where he met Beethoven and saw some of this music. As a result of this meeting Beethoven left Bonn late in 1792 for Vienna where, apart from occasional travel, he was to spend the rest of his life.

Beethoven lost no time winning a reputation as a pianist and teacher among the Viennese aristocracy. His recognition as a composer came more slowly, but by the end of the 1790s a number of works bearing his individual stamp had become popular, including the 'Pathétique' Sonata (1798–9). In 1800 he completed his first set of string quartets (op. 18) and mounted a successful concert which included the first performance of his First Symphony. But although he was triumphing as a performer and composer, he was also becoming aware of a condition that was to afflict him for the rest of his life: deafness. Though it did not surface immediately as an insuperable · professional and social handicap, Beethoven's coming to terms with his increasing deafness, expressed to close friends in touching letters in 1801 and 1802, created a turning point in his life. From then on he became less concerned with his outward appearance, more bad-tempered in the company of friends and admirers, and – eventually – more reclusive. Artistically, he was spurred on to hitherto unimaginable achievements. The 'Eroica' Symphony (1803–4), rightly described as a great watershed of musical composition, was the first result of Beethoven's new determination, and it was followed in the next five years by three more symphonies, two piano concertos and a violin concerto, the three 'Rasumovsky' string quartets (op. 59, 1806), the opera *Leonore* (1805, revised in 1806 and – as *Fidelio* – again in 1814), and numerous other masterpieces of symphonic, chamber and piano music. He continued to receive substantial (albeit at times irregular) financial support from the Viennese nobility. In the later years one of his most faithful pupil-friends and generous supporters, the young Archduke Rudolph, was made the dedicatee of several of Beethoven's greatest works, including the last two piano concertos, a piano trio, three of the last seven piano sonatas, and the monumental *Missa Solemnis* (1819–23), which was composed for the occasion of Rudolph's installation as Archbishop of Olmütz (now Olomouc).

Towards the end of his career Beethoven relied increasingly on the income received from the publication of his music. For a time he was reduced to making arrangments of folksongs of various nationalities for small chamber ensemble. The ageing composer suffered from near-total deafness, poor health, occasional periods of acute illness and more frequent ones of deep depression. His only sustained passion for another human being was for his nephew Karl, of whom he was initially made joint guardian after his brother's death in 1815 and eventually won (in an extended court case) sole custody. But the relationship, which has been interpreted as the outcome of Beethoven's failure at a love relationship with a woman, was never a completely happy one; and Karl's attempted suicide in

1826 probably helped hasten Beethoven's own end the following year.

When Beethoven was born, the current musical language – what is now called the 'Classical style' – was reaching its first maturity in the early symphonies and string quartets of Haydn. By the time Beethoven was a grown man, ready to embark on a professional career in the Austrian capital, Haydn had elevated the Classical style to serve the highest musical art, and Mozart (whose career barely spans Beethoven's childhood and adolescence) had assimilated Haydn's style and those of contemporary composers elsewhere in Europe to create some of the most sublime musical creations of all time. Thus Beethoven, though his formal training was modest, had the advantage of a fully developed musical language before him and many excellent models to emulate. In the earliest works the influence of Mozart can be clearly seen in specific compositions. Many works from the 1790s are in the same key and for the same instruments, as well as having the same overall movement structure as mature pieces by Mozart. The results of this emulation are mixed. The String Trio op. 3 and the Quintet for piano and wind op. 16 fall short of their respective models (Mozart's K.563 and K.452). Yet the 'Pathétique' Sonata, thematically and emotionally patterned after Mozart's big Fantasia and Sonata in C minor of 1785–6 (K.475 and K.457), is a high-point in Beethoven's early development. And the A major quartet from op. 18 at times approaches, at times exceeds, Mozart's K.464 in range of expression and compositional technique. But Beethoven was also conscious of Haydn's achievements, to the extent that, in the best of his early music, he is often able to combine Haydn's special ability to develop themes and motifs with Mozart's elegant formal proportions, ravishing melodic power and sensuous chromaticism. Beethoven's total absorption of his Classical inheritance culminates in the op. 18 quartets (especially no. 1, in F), in the First and Second Symphonies, and in many of the first fifteen piano sonatas.

The turn towards what is commonly referred to as the 'middle period' occurred some time between 1801 and 1803, when the composer became aware of the handicap his deafness was creating. In the second of the piano sonatas op. 31, in D minor and commonly known as the 'Tempest', Beethoven worked out an unusual solution to the problem of integrating a slow introduction into the traditional sonata structure. In the 'Kreutzer' Sonata for violin and piano, he successfully combined compositional integrity with a high degree of technical difficulty for the violinist and the pianist. (This virtuoso element becomes increasingly prominent in his later style.)

But the first fully ripened fruit of Beethoven's new artistic growth is undoubtedly the 'Eroica' Symphony. Here the scale and dimensions of classical instrumental composition are about doubled. This expansion results from an internal growth in all four movements. Even the traditionally slender minuet or scherzo movement, which preserved the eighteenth-century convention of incorporating dance music into serious instrumental composition, is expanded here: the third movement of the 'Eroica' begins in the home key of E flat, but the first actual theme we hear (i.e. a hummable tune, for the oboe) is in a different key; the resolution of this conflict, between the home key and another tonality, requires a greater expansion than 'normal' classical proportions could have predicted.

It is the first movement of the 'Eroica', however, that has most attracted the attention of musical analysts. The very opening bars seem to forecast a much bigger structure than anything that had been conceived before. The theme, which – atypically – is begun as a bass line (by the cellos) and completed as a melodic line (by the violins), contains the seeds of many of the melodic and harmonic developments which are played out in the course of the movement. And the very point at which cello and violin strands intersect highlights the crucial notes about which these developments unfold.

From the 'Eroica' on, Beethoven explored new possibilities for the wind and percussion instruments of the orchestra. In the 'Eroica' he was content to add just one new instrument to the ensemble – the third horn. But the effects of this addition are far-reaching. For not only is the sound of the horn trio exploited for its own sake (in the middle section of the scherzo), Beethoven also uses the horns to extend his musical structure. In the first movement he makes the second horn seem to enter a few bars too early with the reprise of the first theme; moments later the first horn enters, but now in the 'wrong' key.

In the Fifth Symphony (1807–8) Beethoven achieved large-scale unity not only from the pervasive employment of the famous four-note motif but also by using the brass in a special way: instead of pitching the horns and trumpets (and the timpani) in the same key as each of the individual movements, as would have been customary in the late eighteenth century, he keeps these instruments in the key of C throughout so that this tonality can be referred to at any time during the symphony. (The most striking outbursts of C occur in the slow movement, whose home key is the remote A flat.) Beethoven's later ideas on instrumentation led him eventually to use the timpani in a thematic (or motivic) role, first in the scherzo of the Seventh Symphony, then in the finale of the Eighth and the scherzo of the Ninth; in the latter two movements the timpani are tuned unprecedentedly an octave apart.

One other example of Beethoven's middle-period orchestration deserves special mention. In the Sixth Symphony, the 'Pastoral' (1808), he scores the first two movements and part of the third for small orchestra: woodwind, two horns, strings. In the middle of the third movement the trumpets are added; then during the fourth movement (subtitled 'Thunderstorm') the timpani, piccolo and trombones are brought in. Towards the end of this movement these extra instruments drop out – roughly in the order in which they were introduced – but the trumpets and trombones are brought back once more for the final movement, a 'Hymn of Thanksgiving'. This gradual building up of orchestral forces, followed by a partial dismantling, not only reinforces the external programme of the symphony but helps to show its musical architecture as being based on a single dynamic curve.

The modification of classical proportions in music, which can be seen on a large scale in the 'Pastoral' Symphony, was abandoned for a time, and Beethoven's next two symphonies, the Seventh and Eighth (1811–12), show a clear return to 'tried and true' classical formats. Yet it was a matter he returned to consistently from about 1815 onwards, albeit mainly in works for chamber or solo forces. One way he sought to bring unity to multi-movement work was to quote the opening theme of a piece just before the final movement: examples of this are found in the Piano Sonata op. 101 and the Sonata in C for cello and piano op. 102, no.1 (both completed in 1816); a further development of this idea occurs in the Ninth Symphony, whose finale contains a catalogue of themes from previous movements. Another method of unifying a large structure was to have the end of a movement resolve on to – or seem to melt into – the beginning of the next movement. The late piano sonatas opp. 109–11 (1820–2) and the song cycle *An die ferne Geliebte* (1815–16) are rich sources of this procedure. Beethoven also composed some long movements which can be subdivided into smaller parts that seem to be movements – not yet fully formed – in themselves. The Ninth Symphony finale, though held together by the tune of the *Ode to Joy*, contains such a scherzo (for tenor solo, accompanied by Turkish wind band) and slow movement (based on a particular stanza of Schiller's poem). A similar plan unfolds in the *Grosse Fuge* op. 133, which was originally the finale of another string quartet.

In all these 'new' forms Beethoven was striving after a balance of mood. This is something which could be achieved in the eighteenth century by composing a set of contrasting and complementary works and publishing them together as a single opus, each work being in a different key and one of them being in a minor key. This balance among keys, often only remotely related to one another, and between minor and major is something which Beethoven sought to achieve within the limits of a single work; success came in the late quartets.

The last five string quartets, written between 1824 and 1826, represent a culmination of Beethoven's art in the terms discussed above. Problems of large-scale structure dominate the three central works: op. 132 in A minor, op. 130 in B flat (originally ending with the *Grosse Fuge*) and op. 131 in C sharp minor. In each of these, Beethoven proposed still more radical solutions to the problems he had faced in the Ninth Symphony and the late chamber and solo instrumental works: the concept of 'movement', tonality in the large, thematic unification, even the meaning – verbal or philosophical – of musical utterances. We find some superficial resemblances to op. 132 in Mendelssohn's* early A minor string quartet (op. 13), and Richard Wagner* was more deeply affected by these works, especially op. 131. But one must look much further ahead – to the symphonies of Mahler*, and to the music of Bartók, Schoenberg and other twentieth-century masters – to observe a truly profound influence of these works.

It was perhaps to be expected that Beethoven's achievements in his last five years were not entirely understood by the next generation of musicians. For them the message of revolution, freedom and universal brotherhood was easier to grasp than the musical problems in his works, and the solutions which they offered. Such thinking about the composer prevailed in the nineteenth century, and has persisted up to our own time: commentators continue to search for, or invent, 'programmes' and other metaphors for his evidently abstract musical structures. To some extent Beethoven himself paved the way for this romanticized view, either by giving descriptive names like *sonate pathétique*, *sinfonia eroica* and *quartetto serioso* to compositions which are thoroughly classical in design, or by attaching verbal mottoes like '*Lebewohl*' or '*Muss es sein? – Es muss sein!*' to simple musical motifs. He may even be held responsible – indirectly – for the fact that discussions of the Ninth Symphony usually centre round the choral finale, with its famous Schiller text (the finale is, in effect, a multi-movement cantata for solo voices, chorus, and large orchestra including special 'Turkish' contingent), in preference to the first three movements, which are probably more innovatory in harmony, in orchestration and even in form.

It should also be emphasized that, despite Beethoven's example, there was considerable change in the techniques of composition during the first quarter of the nineteenth century. Though Beethoven himself remained faithful to the 'sonata principle', many younger composers, including Schubert*, Mendelssohn, Schumann* and Chopin*, were beginning to favour smaller forms of expression in which the creation of themes, rather than their development, was regarded as the chief process of composition. And when these composers did write in sonata form, they tended to emphasize its sectional aspect (e.g. the contrast between first and second subjects) as much as its dramatic power. Moreover, both Schubert and Schumann took some of Beethoven's less characteristic works as models for composition, especially some of the modest but gently

exploratory works of *c.* 1809–16. It was with the piano sonatas and cello sonatas from these years, and with the song cycle *An die ferne Geliebte*, that Beethoven touched these composers deeply and thereby exerted a genuinely musical influence on the Romantics.

In one major field of composition, that of opera, Beethoven did not break new musical ground. True, the score of *Fidelio*, which cost him much effort (three versions survive, the first two being called *Leonore*), is rich in profound musical utterances, and the sentiments expressed in the libretto are in perfect harmony with Romantic idealism. Yet the models for the overall design of *Fidelio* are, clearly, the mature comic operas of Mozart, which must remain the focal point for the study of classical opera.

One aspect of Beethoven's musical achievement has not ceased to fascinate scholars and laymen alike for more than a century: the record of his labours which has been preserved in the sketchbooks. In these manuscripts it is possible to trace the genesis of most of the composer's masterpieces, to observe the development of some ideas and the suppression of others. The sketches offer a kind of musical biography of the composer, one which runs parallel to the events of his life and furnishes evidence concerning the chronology of his works and insight into his development as a creative artist. Whether or not the sketches can offer analytical insight into individual works has been a matter of debate. Gustav Nottebohm, the nineteenth-century pioneer of Beethoven scholarship, used the sketches chiefly as an aid to determining chronology and resolving textual problems, yet he could not conceal his fascination with Beethoven's compositional process. Heinrich Schenker, in his critical editions of the late sonatas (1913–21), frequently transcribed and commented on the sketches as a way of amplifying his analyses. More recently the relationships between Beethoven's compositional process and contemporary analytical procedures have been defined more scientifically; and it has even been shown that, to a limited extent, the stages in the genesis of a Beethoven work are in reciprocal relation with the layers resulting from a Schenkerian analysis of that work. But criticism of this stance has been expressed with equal eloquence.

William Drabkin

The standard biography of Beethoven was written by A. W. Thayer in the nineteenth century, and was revised critically for the first time by Elliot Forbes as *Thayer's Life of Beethoven* (1964). The most up-to-date, informed and enlightening biography is Maynard Solomon, *Beethoven* (1977). There is no reliable German edition of the letters; the best edition, in English translation, is by Emily Anderson (1961). Critical: D. F. Tovey, *Beethoven* (1944), *Essays in Musical Analysis*, i–ii (1935) and *Companion to the Beethoven Pianoforte Sonatas* (1931); Walter Riezler,

Beethoven (1938); Joseph Kerman, *The Beethoven Quartets* (1967); Charles Rosen, *The Classical Style* (1971). Schenker's analyses of the Ninth (1912), Fifth (1925) and Third (1930) Symphonies offer some of the most penetrating insights into musical structure ever recorded.

32

BEETON, Samuel Orchart 1831–77

British editor and publisher

BEETON, Isabella Mary Mayson 1836–65

British journalist

Illustrated magazines and special interest publications intended for a mass market were a creation of the nineteenth century, and in England no one was more influential in their development than Samuel Beeton. Women's and juvenile magazines of today are still modelled on the Beeton prototypes which were at once the first and best of their sort, and the part-work and branded reference book industries that he pioneered are flourishing. Yet, while Samuel Beeton is not remembered, his wife Isabella Beeton is: and mainly for the cooking recipes that she did not originate.

Born in London and apprenticed there in the printing and paper trade, Samuel Beeton was well placed to respond to the needs of the larger reading public that emerged in mid-nineteenth-century Britain as a result of increased levels of literacy. What this public wanted was material that was cheap, entertaining and 'improving', consonant with the general belief in self-help, self-improvement, diligence and industry prevalent at the time. In 1852, at the age of twenty-one, Beeton launched the *Englishwoman's Domestic Magazine*. Beeton's intention, as set out in the preface to the first issue, was to provide a periodical which should 'tend to the improvement of the intellect', a radical notion in that pre-feminist era. The tone of the publication was challenging and stimulating, the object being to encourage independence and to teach the reader to think for herself. For a monthly cost of 2d women were presented with a wide range of articles which, in addition to the predictable items on cookery, gardening, and child care, included more original features such as problem pages, medical articles, coloured fashion plates and free needlework and dressmaking patterns – items that remain a mainstay of women's magazines to this day. The *Englishwoman's Domestic Magazine* also carried serializations of quality fiction, for example Hawthorne's* *Scarlet Letter*.

In 1855, Beeton launched the *Boy's Own Magazine*, the first magazine for boys. Here his aim was to 'produce pleasure and convey instruction', and through its deliberately brisk adult style it heralded a general trend in children's literature away from cloying sentimentality on the one hand and parental exhortation on the other. As well as adventure stories, *Boy's Own* featured essays on sporting subjects, on nature, on travel and on biography.

Acting as editor and publisher Beeton was to launch seven magazines in all, the other five being the *Boy's Own Journal* (1856), the *Boy's Penny Magazine* (1860), *Beeton's Christmas Annual* (1860), *The Queen* (1861) and *The Young Englishwoman*, (1864) the first magazine for girls.

In 1856 Beeton married Isabella Mary Mayson, who had grown up literally beneath the grandstand at Epsom race-course, where her stepfather was Clerk of the Course. Her education had been completed at Heidelberg, to a high standard unusual for Englishwomen at the time, and within a few months of her marriage she was writing on fashion and domestic subjects for the *Englishwoman's Domestic Magazine*.

Reference books and encyclopedias were becoming one of the mainstays of the popular publishing trade and in the early 1860s Beeton began work on a series of special interest, female and juvenile reference publications that would ultimately amount to more than a hundred titles covering such diverse subjects as cookery, religion, gardening, natural history, letter writing, the stock market and public speaking. Some of these works were volumes complete in themselves, others were introduced as related part-works which were finally reissued as one comprehensive volume. By far the most successful of these part-works was Beeton's *Book of Household Management*, conceived by Sam and compiled by Isabella, first issued in volume form in 1861.

The *Book of Household Management* was the first genuinely comprehensive digest of all matters domestic, a work which remains unrivalled for accuracy and scope. Although the cookery chapters were largely composed of recipes gathered from a variety of contemporary sources, Isabella devised a style of cookery writing notable for clarity, simplicity of preparation and emphasis on economy and nutrition that has set the standard for cookery books ever since. Among the other subjects dealt with in the *Book of Household Management* were the duties of the mistress of the household, etiquette, the arrangement of dinner parties, child and infant care, meticulous descriptions of the duties of household servants and even the buying and selling of houses. Today the *Book of Household Management* provides historians with a unique social document whose range and detail permit an accurate reconstruction of the life of the time. In a contemporary context, it was notable for its appeal to all classes of society. On the one hand it was an invaluable social guide for the *nouveaux riches*, but for the poorer classes to whom domestic service provided the only opportunity for advancement, the *Book of Household Management* purposely set out to provide, in its description of household duties, sufficient information to assist the reader to embark on a career in service. Also, in an era of industrial innovation that saw the introduction of canned foods, packet soups, roller-milled flour, gas cookers and refrigeration, the homely and economical strictures contained in the cookery section – spiced with Isabella's catchphrases 'clear as you go' and 'a place for everything' – enabled women of all classes to make the best of the new inventions.

Isabella Beeton was typical of the women for whom her husband published his magazines – a woman of feminine aspect but independent mind, who believed that education and a career could only enhance and enrich her traditional role as wife and mother. She died in 1865, at the age of twenty-nine, of puerperal fever following the birth of her fourth child, the first two having died in infancy. A year later Beeton was obliged to work as a salaried employee of a rival firm, after losing his assets in a banking collapse. He continued to produce a stream of reference books, but never recovered from his bereavement and financial reversals. In his last years he turned to publishing radical attacks on the establishment, arguing for such controversial measures as the abdication of Queen Victoria* in favour of the Prince of Wales. He died of tuberculosis at the age of forty-six.

Kaori O'Connor

See: Nancy Spain, *Mrs Beeton and her Husband* (1948); H. Montgomery Hyde, *Mr and Mrs Beeton* (1951); Sarah Freeman, *Isabella and Sam* (1977).

33
BELL, Alexander Graham 1847–1922

Scots/US inventor

Bell immortalized the words 'Watson, please come here – I want you' as the first telephonic cry for help. His grandfather had studied sound engineering and his father researched speech and the teaching of deaf children in Edinburgh, where Alexander was born. The family, decimated by tuberculosis, moved to Canada in 1870, and Bell went to America in 1871. Two years later he became Professor of Vocal Physiology at Boston University. Falling in love with a deaf student concentrated his researches.

Out of work to improve the telegraph and rethink some of Helmholtz's* ideas on hearing and sound production and Joseph Henry's electromagnetic experiments and achievements in the transmission of a steady current over long distances, Bell sought to convert sound-wave vibrations into electric current and back again. The immortal words were uttered on impulse to his assistant after an accident with some battery acid.

Watson, on another floor, heard them coming from one of Bell's instruments. Bell patented the telephone in 1876, commercialized it, married and became an American citizen. Edison* added a more efficient mouthpiece to the instrument, and at the 1876 Philadelphia Centennial Exposition the Emperor of Brazil publicized it by dropping it when it talked. Queen Victoria* helped by buying one. Bell later developed Edison's phonograph, invented a metal locator to hunt down the assassin's bullet in President Garfield (the mattress springs interfered with its success on this occasion), founded *Science*, a major journal, in 1883, supported the unfortunate Samuel Langley's airplane experiments, and looked into air-conditioning. In 1915 he said the immortal words again, opening the first transcontinental telephone. It surely could not have been from lack of imagination. And Bell kept faith in another respect: his interest in the problems of the deaf, which may be said to have inspired his revolution in communications, continued into old age. The money earned from his 'Graphophone', the first successful attempt to record sound, was used to fund the American Association to Promote the Teaching of Speech to the Deaf, renamed in 1956 The Alexander Graham Bell Association for the Deaf.

Eric Mottram

See *The Dispositions of Alexander Graham Bell* (1908); Alvin F. Harlow, *Old Wires and New Waves* (1936); R. U. Bruce, *Alexander Graham Bell and the Conquest of Solitude* (1973).

34
BELLINI, Vincenzo 1801–35

Italian composer

'Bellini is, it is true, poor in orchestration and harmony . . . but rich in feeling and in his own, individual melancholy! Even in his least known operas, . . . there are long, long, long melodies which no one had done before him.' The assessment, made by Giuseppe Verdi* in 1898, would be endorsed by many today: Bellini is a composer restricted in technical range but, particularly in melodic invention, of considerable originality and power. His masterpiece, *Norma*, remains in the repertory of the world's major opera houses, while most of his other operas enjoy occasional revivals or gramophone recordings.

Bellini came from a family with strong musical traditions. Born in the Sicilian town of Catania, his precocious musical ability was fostered by his grandfather (himself a composer), and showed itself mostly in religious compositions. A decisive move occurred in 1819 when Bellini enrolled at the Naples Conservatoire. From 1822 he took lessons there with the famous Neapolitan composer Zingarelli and in 1825 graduated with an opera entitled *Adelson e Salvini*. This was sufficiently successful to stimulate commissions for two further operas, one for Naples, *Bianca e Fernando* (1827), and one for La Scala, Milan, *Il pirata* (1827).

By the time of *Il pirata* the essentials of Bellini's mature style are all present. Early influences – inevitably Rossini*, but also Mozart and the popular idiom of southern Italy – have been assimilated, synthesized within Bellini's primary means of musico-dramatic communication: his richly individual melodic style. Typically moving in the compound metres of Sicilian folk music, with far less vocal ornamentation than Rossini, the melodic lines often seem directly inspired by the words which underpin them. In this respect it is significant that *Il pirata* also marks the beginning of Bellini's long collaboration with the librettist Felice Romani, whose poised Neoclassicism seems perfectly matched by the composer's delicately balanced vocal writing.

From 1827 until the final two years of his life, Bellini made Milan the centre of his activities. In spite of their mixed initial receptions, his next three operas, *La straniera* (1829), *Zaira* (1829) and *I Capuleti ed i Montecchi* (1830), served to consolidate his already considerable reputation within Italy. During the 1830s and early 1840s, Bellini was second only to Donizetti* in popularity, and this position was all the more remarkable in being based on so few works. The unprecedented fees he demanded became a standard for aspiring composers.

In 1831 Bellini produced two operas for Milan which many consider to be his greatest achievements. The first, *La sonnambula*, is unique in his mature output; rather than a tragic work, it is an *opera semiseria*, a rustic tale of unashamed sentimentality. *Norma*, on the other hand, shows the composer at his most dramatically varied; the heroine's opening aria, 'Casta diva', remains an unsurpassed model of classically balanced vocal lyricism, while the final act generates more dramatic power than the composer had previously attempted. Two years later came *Beatrice di Tenda*, a failure at its first performance but soon one of the most popular repertoire pieces in nineteenth-century Italy.

In 1833 Bellini moved to Paris, meeting Chopin*, Heine*, Rossini and others. His last opera, *I puritani*, was produced there in 1835. By this stage he had broken with Romani, and many consider this final opera flawed by Count Carlo Pepoli's rather clumsy libretto. Others, however, are by no means as dismissive, seeing in this last work an attempt to experiment with a completely novel musico-dramatic structure, one devoid of conflicts, with the atmosphere tending towards fable rather than melodrama. In the light of this new departure, Bellini's death from dysentery in September 1835 becomes all the more tragically premature.

Bellini's reputation and popularity, which sank to a low point in the early years of our present century, has in the past thirty years increased quite substantially. True, in an operatic career which spanned barely ten years, we are unlikely to find the stylistic developments so prominent in Donizetti or Verdi; nor would many make claims for the composer's powers of musical characterization or rhythmic invention; but his '*melodie lunghe, lunghe, lunghe*' continued to exert a powerful influence on composers as disparate as Berlioz*, Chopin, Verdi and Wagner*. As musicologists become increasingly aware of historical continuities within the nineteenth century, Bellini may well assume even greater significance.

Roger Parker

All Bellini's operas have been mentioned above (*Il fu ed il sara*, 1832, is almost certainly an unauthorized pasticcio). He also composed a number of religious works (mostly before 1825) and occasional vocal and instrumental pieces. The major collection of letters is L. Cambi, *Vincenzo Bellini: epistolario* (1943). See: L. Orrey, *Bellini* (1969), and H. Weinstock, *Vincenzo Bellini: His Life and his Operas* (1971). The most thoroughgoing critical study is F. Lippmann, 'Vincenzo Bellini und die italienische Oper seria seiner Zeit' in *Analecta Musicologica*, vol. 6, 1969.

35

BENTHAM, Jeremy 1748–1832

British philosopher and reformer

The modern edition of Bentham's works is planned in thirty-two volumes, many drawn from unpublished manuscripts; indeed some of his most influential works had not even been published in his lifetime, such a reviser, such an improver, such a perfectionist he was. His disciples were often moved nearly to despair by his failure to publish major works on which he had toiled off and on for twenty or thirty years, although they had read the manuscripts and made use of them in legal or political argument or schemes for reform. John Bowring partly remedied the situation by publishing between 1838 and 1843 eleven volumes of *The Works of Jeremy Bentham*, giving his already great influence a second wave of power. But Bentham had published enough and advised enough in his lifetime permanently to change the way we think of public law.

His father was a prosperous and ambitious London attorney. He wanted his son to be a great man, perhaps Lord Chancellor and a member of the peerage. Certainly Jeremy was an infant prodigy, reading fluently and tackling history at three and writing in Latin by five. Nor were music and literature neglected, for the social graces were needed for social advance. At seven he went to Westminster School and at thirteen to Queen's College, Oxford, as the two most fashionable and most orthodox institutions of the day. Graduating at sixteen, he returned to London to read for the Bar at Lincoln's Inn, though in the winter of 1763 he returned to Oxford to hear Blackstone's lectures on the laws of England. But the state of the law and the discipline of law both equally appalled young Bentham. Most of the Common Law appeared to him as incoherent and inconsistent nonsense, both lacking in principle and malign and uncertain in effect. He began to look to the French and Italian Enlightenment to find universal principles, initially to understand how laws in general relate to human society, and, finally to demonstrate how the whole structure of law might be rationally reformed and objective and benign criteria for legislation established according to the 'felicific calculus', the balance of pleasure and pain, 'the greatest happiness of the greatest number': in a word, 'utilitarianism'.

This enterprise, through all its intricacies and exaggerations, became Bentham's entire life work and his achievement. For when all the mocking is done about the over-precision of some of his definitions and criteria, about the impracticality of some of his schemes for reform, about his hopes to measure different kinds of pleasure and pain, and when all scepticism has been considered about whether his ideas directly influenced the course of nineteenth-century legal and administrative reform, it can hardly be denied that he was responsible for one of the great conceptual shifts in distinctively modern thinking: the move from perceiving legislation and judicial decisions as the necessary embodiments of the traditions and history of a community into thinking of them as rational instruments of change to increase public well-being.

He began work on a vast critique of Blackstone, not simply to show the incoherence of the argument from tradition and precedent, but – typical of Bentham's method – to show case by case that Blackstone's own argument did not work even on his own grounds. Small wonder that the scale of the work got out of hand and seemed endless, but he did publish in 1776 (what Leslie Stephen* was to call that 'annum mirabilis' of publishing) a digression called A Fragment on Government. This attacked Blackstone's constitutional views, especially his doctrine of 'the sovereignty of Parliament', that an unchallengeable and legally uncontrollable sovereignty was everywhere necessary and that in England it resided in parliament. Thus, if parliament made an error or committed an evil, there was simply no remedy if law and order were to be maintained (the 'sovereignty of Parliament' was indeed the keystone of the ideology of the governing class, linking both Whig and Tory). Bentham mocked: did Blackstone think that the Swiss in their Federal cantons 'know not government' because they 'knew not the blessing of sovereignty'?

Characteristic of Bentham were swift oscillations from pages of excruciatingly pedantic definitions and criticisms of other definitions into paragraphs of biting colloquiality. (Only in his Book of Fallacies, 1824, a taxonomy of the arguments reactionaries invoke against reform, did these two contrary qualities come together with an almost Swiftian vigour.) The Fragment on Government brought him to the attention of Lord Shelburne, an aristocratic reformer and salonier. Shelburne introduced Bentham to the leading parliamentary and legal reformers of the day. From that time on Bentham's influence lay as much in the advice he gave and the projects they hatched together in discussion as in his published writings. He was mentor, so long as he was active, to two great generations of reformers, those of the 1780s and of the 1820s. But his work always came first: he apologized to Talleyrand that he must ask him to dinner rather than see him in the day 'for I cannot abridge my working hours'.

His most famous and influential work was the Introduction to the Principles of Morals and Legislation (1789). It began: 'Nature has placed mankind under the governance of two sovereign masters, pain and pleasure', from which premise he famously argued that 'the Greatest Happiness of the Greatest Number' should be the object of legislation. It is easy to pick holes in this, particularly on ideal or perverse assumptions about what minorities might view as happiness; but it is still hard to think of anything better as a general principle for the mind of every legislator, the broadest possible test to be applied to the codification, amendment, retention or formulation of legislation. Most legislation in Bentham's day was nakedly and simply passed or preserved in the interests of the landowning class: almost any general principles applied to law would be emancipatory.

Certainly Bentham could over-elaborate and believed that correct definitions and the unambiguous use of words, even if it meant inventing new words, could settle argument and even allow exact and measurable comparisons of legislative pleasure and pain. His major works had to be torn from his desk, edited and often toned down or simplified by loyal disciples. The young John Stuart Mill* edited five volumes of his Rationale of Judicial Evidence (1825), probably the largest empirical study with the clearest theoretical perspective that had ever been made of what comes to count as 'evidence' in law. Through Lord Shelburne's circle he met a young Swiss reformer, Etienne Dumont, who began to translate into French and simplify many of Bentham's works, beginning with an early version of his Constitutional Code and ending thirty-seven years later in 1829 with De l'organisation judiciaire et de la codification, often working from manuscripts not published in English until after Bentham's death (and sometimes Dumont's improved versions were translated back into English). From Dumont's French versions were taken the Spanish at the very time of the break-up of the Spanish South American Empire, so Hispanic liberals and liberators took up Bentham's principles: even in his lifetime he had a world-wide fame and correspondence and knew that Spanish authors called him *El legislador del mundo*.

An early trip to Russia in 1779 did not persuade the Empress Catherine to adopt a reformed constitution (as his host had hoped). Almost from then on his influence radiated out from his study in a small house near the Palace of Westminster where he lived comfortably but simply on a small family legacy. He worked on his famous 'panopticon' scheme for a model prison for over twenty years, which began life as a plan for cooperative settlements for the unemployed. If this can be thought emblematic of the rationalistic folly of Bentham, the tale of its indirect influence over subsequent prison reform is, if complex, impressive and even at the time parliament compensated him for his efforts. He wasted much time on an attempt to promote a Thames Police Bill in the 1790s, which was really the thin end of a wedge for comprehensive local government reform: it came to next to nothing, but its principles were taken up by Sir Robert Peel in the 1829 Metropolitan Police Act. Sometimes his thought was literally far ahead of his time. In *The Principles of Morals and Legislation* he had said that the Greatest Happiness Principle implied four subordinate aims of government: subsistence, abundance, security and equality; and these in turn implied, he was quite explicit: free education, guaranteed employment, minimum wages, sickness benefits and old-age insurance, thus virtually the whole programme of the modern welfare state of industrial societies.

His influence on legal and administrative reform has been disputed. That contemporaries of intelligence and influence counted themselves his friends or disciples is obvious: Shelburne and Romilly in the older generation, the Mills, Austin*, Grote, Bowring, Dumont, Roebuck, Fonblanque, Bingham, Burdett, Graham, Eyton Tooke and Lord Brougham in the early nineteenth century. Edwin Chadwick took the details of the New Poor Law of 1834 from the unfinished *Constitutional Code* and of the Act of 1836 establishing a proper census of vital statistics for the first time. Parkes and Place drafted the Municipal Reform Bill of 1835 from the *Code*. And the reorganization of government departments, reform of the land laws, the parcel post, national secondary education, the modern police force and the establishing of a civil service based on competitive examination have all been laid at Bentham's door. But historians of the Cambridge school have doubted the claim that ideas and arguments could have such effects, suggesting instead that 'reforms' take place because of the perceived needs of government itself responding to social change. This may, indeed, explain why and when reforms take place, better than

Millite myths that reason eventually wins the day; but the *form* many of these changes took, when the need for change at all was conceded, owed much to Bentham. Such historians also return to his texts and damningly ask whether there is a single example of any of his elaborate schemes ever being put into practice as he would have wished (even the founding of London University). The answer is obvious but the point is not made. The question is, rather, would certain things have taken the form they did if Bentham had not written and had not had his active disciples? All ideas are tempered by practice, all paper projects fail in their detail but many change the whole climate of expectations. None of Bentham's disciples who entered government or administration were hundred per cent devotees, but all achieved something on his lines. Bentham's status has been diminished by using the *reductio ad absurdum*: look at the 'panopticon' scheme and where is it? But a less polemical history of ideas (on both sides) would carefully explore degrees of commitment among a great teacher's followers and degrees of influence by them in practical affairs. Nothing happened as Bentham intended, but much of our contemporary landscape in government, law and education would be unimaginable without him.

Bernard Crick

See: *Collected Works of Jeremy Bentham* (from 1968). Charles W. Everett, *Jeremy Bentham* (1969), contains useful selections as well as commentary and a brief life. See also: Mary P. Mack, *Jeremy Bentham* (1962); Elie Halévy, *The Growth of Philosophic Radicalism* (1901–4); Leslie Stephen, *The English Utilitarians* (1900).

36

BERLIOZ, Louis-Hector 1803–69

French composer

Hector Berlioz was the son of a country doctor from La Côte-St-André, between Lyon and Grenoble. He came to Paris at the age of seventeen to attend medical school and made it his home for the rest of his life. He showed early enthusiasm and aptitude for music, greatly magnified by his encounter with Parisian music, especially opera, and he soon gave up medicine for the less certain career of music; he earned his living at first by singing in a theatre chorus and by giving guitar lessons, later by writing criticism, an occupation which he sustained intensively for over thirty years despite his distaste for it, and by conducting.

His teachers in Paris were Lesueur and Reicha, both individualists from whom he learned much, although his obsessive admiration for Gluck and Spontini, later for Weber* and Beethoven*, provided the greatest stimulus to composition. He entered the Paris Conservatoire in 1826 and won its coveted Prix de Rome in 1830, the year in which his first masterpiece, the *Symphonie fantastique*, was composed and first performed. It placed him firmly in the forefront of the French Romantics, the group of writers and artists with whom Berlioz shared some social intimacy and a considerable range of tastes, especially for Shakespeare, Goethe* and the new favourites of Romantic fashion: Byron*, Scott*, Cooper* and Moore.

There followed a period of nearly two years in Italy, not productive in terms of writing music (he greatly disliked the Italian music that he heard) but useful for the maturing of his style. He returned to Paris in 1832 and in the following year he married Harriet Smithson, the Shakespearian actress who had captivated all Paris in 1827 and had already been the subject of the *Symphonie fantastique*. His compositions flowed steadily; he gave numerous concerts and wrote prolifically for the press. He received two government commissions but secured no permanent position in Paris. In 1842 he began a series of concert tours to Belgium, Germany and Austria, and for the next twenty years was frequently abroad, travelling many times to Germany, five times to London and twice to Russia. *La damnation de Faust* was composed on one such tour in 1845–6. He gradually became disillusioned and embittered about Paris, preferring to give concerts abroad, and frustrated by the general decline of taste in the later part of his life. Once the *élan* of Romanticism in the 1830s had passed he was subjected to increasing indifference and hostility. The failure of *Benvenuto Cellini* at the Opéra in 1838 discouraged him deeply, so did a similar failure of *La damnation de Faust* in 1846, and it was only with great reluctance that he embarked on *Les Troyens* in 1856, a large-scale Virgilian opera of which only a part was performed in his lifetime. His last years passed in deepening despair, especially after the death of his only son in 1867, and he died in 1869. His *Memoirs*, compiled over a long period, were published in 1870.

Berlioz was no pianist and his facility on flute and guitar was his only instrumental skill. Yet he studied orchestral technique closely and developed an orchestral style of outstanding versatility and brilliance. He published a treatise on the subject in 1844. He was also prominent as a conductor (on which he also wrote a treatise) and he strongly influenced the later course of orchestral development in the hands of Liszt* and Wagner*; Liszt was for a long period one of his closest friends. He wrote many songs with piano accompaniment, and the better ones were later orchestrated. Six settings of Gautier*, published under the title *Les nuits d'été* in 1841, illustrate to perfection his sensitive response to poetic feeling and his personal adaptation of formal procedures for expressive ends. Nearly all his music is orchestral, and he chooses combinations of instruments and voices to serve the needs of each sub-ject, since none of his music is abstract or without some indication of its poetic content. Much of it relates to his favourite literature or to personal experience. The *Symphonie fantastique* and its sequel *Lélio* (1831) sprang from two love affairs, with copious reference to other passions, particularly Shakespeare, who provided the source for a dramatic overture on *The Tempest* (1830), another overture on *King Lear* (1831), various short pieces for *Hamlet* (1844), the dramatic symphony *Roméo et Juliette* (1839) and the comic opera *Béatrice et Bénédict* (1860–2), based on *Much Ado About Nothing*. Goethe generated the *Eight Scenes from Faust* (1829) and its fuller working as *La Damnation de Faust* (1846), a large-scale concert work with chorus and soloists. From Scott came the overtures *Waverley* (1827) and *Rob Roy* (1831); Byron – and his own experience in Italy – inspired *Harold en Italie* (1834).

The *Grande symphonie funèbre et triomphale* (1840) is a ceremonial piece for large military band, relating to the stirring outdoor music of the French Revolution. That same tradition lies behind his choral works for large forces on sacred texts, notably the *Grande messe des morts* (*Requiem*) of 1837 and the *Te deum* of 1849. A choral work of a quite different kind, though still on a sacred subject, is the trilogy *L'enfance du Christ* (1850–4) which treats the story of the Holy Family's flight from Herod in a devotional yet dramatic manner, as a concert work. Although Berlioz strove most of his life to write operas, it was not in his artistic nature to devote himself wholly to a single genre, as Verdi* and Wagner more nearly did. He preferred the mixed genre, with heterogeneous elements overlapping: symphony and concerto in *Harold en Italie*, symphony and opera in *Roméo et Juliette*, song and declamation in *Lélio*. In *Benvenuto Cellini* (1836) comic and serious opera intermingle, for Cellini, the sculptor-hero, is an artist as well as a swashbuckler. The pope, in this opera, is treated in comic style, and despite revision and revival in later years, its mixed nature never disarmed criticism. In *Les Troyens* (1856–8), his greatest work and the culmination of all strands in his earlier music, there are moments of symphonic utterance amid the familiar outlines of romantic grand opera, with its heroics, its ballets and its big choral ensembles. What distinguishes it from the genre is its epic span, in both time and space, its intensity of expression and its classical serenity, qualities which Berlioz was proud to interfuse.

Although his early music was revolutionary in almost every aspect, he soon ceased to take an active interest in contemporary composers and his idolization of Gluck drew all his thoughts back to the past. He believed that music was a highly refined art fit only for cultivated minds, and he deplored the easy facility of many composers whose trivial style won them fortune and respectability. He hated the commercialization of music and the vanity of singers, and he felt that the most advanced music, such as Wagner's, was drawing the art into a world where he did not wish to follow it.

His views were lucidly expressed in his many articles for the press, sometimes with wearying persistence. But the pervasive irony is leavened by a sharp streak of humour which makes him one of the wittiest and most stylish of music critics. The human comedy of music-making and of Parisian society did not escape him. His views were ardently held and expressed. Central to his attitude to music is his belief in expression, the capacity of music to embody images, ideas and feelings. This ranges from the literalness of programme music to the less easily defined area where the music reflects its text or subject with as much veracity as possible. He regarded it as the composer's duty to convey the expressive content of his subject, a duty far more pressing than considerations of structure or abstract balance – although these were not to be neglected. Personal identification with a subject, and the composer's integrity, were paramount.

His music belongs to the French tradition stemming from Lully and Rameau and therefore sounds strange to ears expecting a style closer to that of Schumann* or Chopin*. He admired Mozart but did not imitate him; he was impatient with Bach and Handel and had no taste for quaintly medieval styles which pervade the Romantic movement, and he stood aside from the fashionable historical drama of Hugo* and Scribe. His romanticism is expressed in his assumption that the arts spill over one into another and that imagination can override reality. His attitude to women was generally to bestow on them ideal qualities which they never possessed; he saw vividly in his mind's eye things which usually call for stage presentation, hence his fondness for concert works which strike less imaginative listeners as excessively theatrical.

His ideas passed on to Liszt and thence to Wagner, and the Russians found Berlioz's music a source of inspiration, but in France his influence was negligible: neither Gounod*, Bizet*, Massenet, Franck*, Fauré*, Debussy nor Ravel reveal any debt to his music. This in part reflects the personal nature of composition, in Berlioz's view; style could not be transmitted, only a certain ideal of composition. His music only rarely sounds like either Beethoven or Gluck, even though they were the models he most aspired to emulate. His music was for a long period subject to derision, often on technical grounds, and ignorant criticism. *Les Troyens* was not staged in full until 1957, at Covent Garden, and the rediscovery of this work in particular has transformed modern attitudes to his achievement, aided by recordings – a medium well suited to his idiosyncratic blend of the seen and the unseen. He is now accepted without question as the leading French composer of the nineteenth century and as a truly representative figure of French Romanticism.

Hugh Macdonald

Berlioz's autobiographical *Memoirs* should be read in David Cairns's admirable translation (1969). His letters are currently appearing from Flammarion (3 vols since 1972, 3 to come), and English readers will find a good selection in Humphrey Searle's collection (1966). Berlioz's own compilations of his criticism have been published in scholarly editions by Gründ (Paris, 1968–71); their titles are *Les Soirées de l'orchestre*, *Les grotesques de la musique* and *À travers chants*. The first and third are found in English translations under various titles. A large recent anthology of his writings has been published under the title *Cauchemars et passions*, ed. Gérard Condé (1981). Adolphe Boschot's three-volume biography (Paris, 1906–13), with studies by Jullien (1888) and J. G. Prod'homme (1904), laid the groundwork for later writers. Jacques Barzun, *Berlioz and the Romantic Century* (2 vols, 1950), places Berlioz in his cultural milieu with great insight and breadth. Brian Primmer, *The Berlioz Style* (1973), embarks on analysis; Hugh Macdonald, *Berlioz: Orchestral Music* (1969), introduces the symphonies and overtures.

37

BERNARD, Claude 1813–78

French physiologist

Bernard was born in the heart of the Beaujolais where his parents worked in the vineyards and where, even when a distinguished Royal Academician, he returned each year for the vintage. After attending local schools Bernard was apprenticed to an apothecary of Lyons in 1832. Bernard, however, at this time had his mind set on a literary career and with the manuscript of a completed play moved on to Paris in 1833. Fortunately Bernard allowed himself to be persuaded that it would be wise to acquire another career to fall back on in case of need and consequently began the study of medicine, qualifying as an intern in 1839.

The magnetism of medicine proved stronger than that of literature and after serving for some years as assistant to F. Magendie at the Collège de France Bernard succeeded him there on his retirement in 1855 as Professor of Medicine. He also held a special Chair of Physiology at the Sorbonne. On his death in 1878 such was the eminence attained by Bernard that he became the first French scientist to receive a state funeral.

Bernard was a highly creative experimental physiologist who illuminated virtually all areas of the discipline. In particular, he revealed completely unexpected mechanisms in the areas of nutrition and control of the circulatory system. In the former field he obtained his first major success when in the period 1846–9 he succeeded in working out some of the functions of the pancreatic juices. When they were mixed *in vitro* with a substance like butter he noted that it was broken down into its constituent fatty acids. Further, if the pancreatic duct was blocked then fat would pass undigested through the animal's body. He also showed that the pancreatic juices could convert starch into the sugar maltose.

More impressive and significant, however, were Bernard's long researches on the connection between the liver and the production of sugar in the body. He began by noting that if solutions of sucrose were injected they were soon excreted; if ingested, however, it equally quickly turned up in the blood as glucose. This suggested to him that it was essential for the proper digestion of sugar that it be first exposed to the gastric juices. But what happened to it after that?

In trying to follow sugar through the body Bernard found, to his great surprise, that, even though he had removed the liver of a rabbit, carefully washed it clear of any sugar, twenty-four hours later, sugar was once more present in the liver. The conclusion was obvious: the liver could synthesize glucose from its own internal resources. In 1857 he identified a substance in the liver, glycogen, from which the glucose was synthesized.

The significance of this was that it destroyed the long standing assumption that animals cannot synthesize the chemicals they need; only plants supposedly possessed this power. Animals, by contrast, were thought to be capable of breaking complex substances into the simpler forms required by the body.

At the same time as his researches on glycogenesis Bernard was carrying out important work on the vascular system. He had noted that when the cervical sympathetic nerves were severed in rabbits there was a distinct increase in temperature of the paralysed parts. If the cut ends were stimulated artificially the temperature dropped back to normal. He went on to establish that the effect was produced by constriction of the capillaries under the control of what came to be known as vasoconstrictor nerves. Bernard also discovered that other nerves could lead to the dilation of the capillaries rather than their constriction. He had in fact discovered a completely unsuspected form of vascular control, namely, the vasomotor nerves.

In addition to these and many other lines of research Bernard also thought deeply on the nature of what he termed '*médecine expérimentale*'. He was, he declared, 'one of those who think that the laws of physics and chemistry are not violated in the organism.' He was no vitalist, stating: 'When we characterize a phenomenon as vital, it amounts to saying that we do not know its immediate cause.' For him, 'the properties of living matter are . . . either known and defined, in which case we call them physico-chemical properties, or else unknown and undefined properties, in which case we name them vital properties.'

Bernard realized that it was not so much change in but rather the control and regulation of the physiological states of an organism which might seem to call for unique, vital forces. He avoided this difficulty by introducing his idea of a distinctive *milieu intérieur*, as real as the external atmosphere, which through complex interactions between nerves, fluids and cells, as with the vasomotor reactions, maintains the equilibrium of such inner states as temperature and blood pressure.

There were however limits to his rejection of vitalism. The idea of organic development he found completely baffling, as well he might. In the development of a chicken from an egg, 'the grouping of the chemical elements . . . takes place only according to laws which govern the chemico-physical properties of matter.' But, just what makes the chemicals develop in one way rather than another belonged, Bernard ceded, 'essentially to the domain of life, rather than to chemistry or physics or anything else.'

Derek Gjertsen

Most of Bernard's work was published from 1855 to 1879 in a series of *leçons* or lectures in Paris and are not readily available. A selection can be found in J. Fulton, *Readings in the History of Physiology* (1930). Fortunately Bernard's masterpiece was *Introduction à l'étude de la médecine expérimentale* (1865), trans. *An Introduction to the Study of Experimental Medicine* (1957). See: Michael Foster, *Bernard* (1899); J. Olmsted, *Claude Bernard*, Physiologist (1939).

38

BERWALD, Franz Adolf 1796–1868

Swedish composer

Franz Berwald was the most important and original composer Sweden produced in the nineteenth century and was the finest Scandinavian symphonist of his day. The family was of German origin: the earliest recorded member being Johann Daniel (*c.* 1638–91) who is thought to have come from Bärwalde, south of Stettin. Berwald's father, Christian Friedrich Georg (1740–1825), settled in Stockholm in 1772 and became a member of the Royal Orchestra *(Hovkapellet)*. Franz showed an early aptitude for music and attracted attention as a violin prodigy. He had little formal education, which makes his subsequent wide-ranging activities and interests all the more remarkable. Like his father, he served in the *Hovkapellet* as a violinist and violist during the period 1812 to 1828. He was also active as a composer: a Septet (1818), a violin concerto (1820) and two string quartets (1818). Contemporary critics complained of the audacity and boldness of his music at this period. Although it bears evidence of strongly classical sympathies, there are many unpredictable traits that reflect an exploratory mind. In the 1820s Berwald had sought unsuccessfully a scholarship to study abroad but it was only after the performance of an act of his opera, *Gustaf Vasa* (1828), that this was forthcoming.

The 1830's was the most extraordinary decade in his life. Arriving in Berlin he busied himself with operatic plans, which largely came to nothing, and his musical career seemed to make no headway. Berwald possessed strong intellectual curiosity and later in life was a keen pamphleteer, writing on such topics as education, reafforestation, housing and so on, in terms that were in advance of his time. His early interest in orthopaedic work grew apace; by 1835 he had opened an orthopaedic institute in Berlin based on Ling's principles. This flourished for the rest of the decade. The 1840s were the most productive years musically. After closing his institute, Berwald went to Vienna and enjoyed a number of successes. These were not, however, repeated on his return to his homeland. Both the *Sinfonie sérieuse* and an opera, *Jag går i kloster*, were poorly received, but it is from this period that the bulk of the music by which he is known came into being. The *Sinfonie singulière* (1845), his masterpiece, is quite unlike anything else in the music of its time. And although its musical language is predominantly diatonic, the work has a refreshing vigour and an imaginative vitality that steps outside the comparatively pale Scandinavian musical world of the day.

There are formal innovations, too: the scherzo is integrated into the slow movement, just as the *Sérieuse* recalls the slow movement after the scherzo, and before the finale gets under way. The String Quartet in E flat (1849) takes the process a stage further: here the scherzo is embodied in the slow movement, which is in its turn enveloped in the first, so that the material of the first movement opens and closes the work. In the *Sinfonie capricieuse* (1842), he resorts to a more common structural device to secure organic cohesion, that of a largely monothematic first movement.

In the latter part of his life, success again eluded him: the Swedish musical establishment remained indifferent to his talents, and he was passed over for two key musical appointments. As a result he sought his livelihood outside music again, becoming manager of a glass works at Sandö in northern Sweden in 1850 where he was also active in running a saw mill. His main creative outlet during the 1850s was chamber music: there are two fine piano quintets, a number of piano trios and a piano concerto (1855), which can be performed by piano alone. In 1862 the Royal Opera in Stockholm mounted a performance of Berwald's *Estrella di Soria* and recognition came when the Royal Academy of Music in Stockholm made him Professor of Composition in 1867.

During his life Berwald failed to gain a secure foothold on the repertory and it was left to the present century to initiate a thorough process of discovery. The *Sinfonie singulière* was not heard until 1905 and his last opera, *The Queen of Golconda*, received its first performance a hundred years after his death. If his outlook and sympathies were fundamentally classical, he remained a forward-looking composer; when his music reminds one of other composers, one usually discovers that these passages are not echoes but prophecies. He was a voice of undoubted originality and the history of the symphony in the nineteenth century is incomplete without it.

Robert Layton

See: Robert Layton, *Franz Berwald: A Critical Study of the Swedish Symphonist* (1959); Ingvar Andersson, *Berwald* (1968); and *Franz Berwald: Die Dokumante seines Lebens*, Erling Lomnäs (ed.) (1979).

39
BIERCE, Ambrose 1842–1914?

US author and satirist

'Bitter Bierce' – in that undoubtedly too abrupt phrase Bierce's dark misanthropic attacks on human pretension were summarized for his late nineteenth-century readers both in America and abroad. From his literary base in San Francisco, in journalism, stories, verse, essays and fragments (enough in all to make a twelve volume *Collected Works* in 1912), his laconic wit – on occasion as trenchant as anything in Swift or Wilde* or his Baltimore acolyte H. L. Mencken – took aim against a gallery of targets, among them the glorification of war, the Victorian cult of family life, sentimental popular writing, entrepreneurship and Big Business, patriotism and American fads and enthusiasms of almost every variety. As an idealist soured by his grim personal knowledge of the Civil War and of the crass acquisitive ethos and mediocre politics of Gilded Age America, or as a higher species of wise-cracker whose cryptic humour derives from the frontier tall tale, or as a major American black humorist who can claim kin to Poe*, the later Melville*, the Twain* of *Pudd'nhead Wilson* and Nathanael West, as well as to popular figures like W. C. Fields and latterly Lenny Bruce and Mort Sahl, he deserves more discerning attention than has been customary in the histories of American literature.

His claims are those of a great sardonic stylist, possibly at times too mannered and fitful, who knew as if by instinct how to expose the politician's cant or the self-serving rhetoric of the petty moralist. He rarely deployed his talents other than to denounce or deflate, especially genteel moral values, a fierce opinionated satiric intelligence unwilling to let dunces hold sway either in literature or life. At times he was drawn to the eccentric rims of human existence – he had a penchant for the world of the spirit-rappers and ESP – but equally he drew upon striking powers of Gothic invention, a marvellous aptitude for *bizarrerie* and Poe-like fantasy. If at times the epigrammatic wit is simply too acerbic or Bierce's style too pared down and wooden (he had an influence on Hemingway), his morbidity, as it was popularly thought, was also, as Clifton Fadiman rightly observed in his Bierce anthology of 1946, 'exceptionally fertile', the discomforting idiom of a clear-sighted cynic.

Born in Meigs County, Ohio, but raised mainly in Indiana, of mean-spirited. Puritan farmer stock, after some early newspaper work and a spell at the Kentucky Military Institute in 1859, he enlisted as a Union soldier. A man of genuine individual bravery, he fought and was wounded in a number of frontline engagements and participated in the Battle of Shiloh and Sherman's Atlanta March to the Sea. On demobilization he went west, first as part of a military expedition into Indian country, then to a post in the US Sub-Treasury in San Francisco. There he began his first serious writing, for small-circulation papers like the *Californian*, the *Golden Era* and *News Letter*, of which he became editor in 1868. In 1871, having published his first stories in the *Overland Monthly*, he married, and in 1872, on a bequest from his father-in-law, arrived in England setting up house basically in Bristol and Bath, but in London honing with journalists like Tom Hood the literary skills which would make him internationally known within the decade. It was in London, too, that his first three books were published, *The Fiend's Delight* (1873), *Nuggets and Dust* (1873), and the delightfully named *Cobwebs from an Empty Skull* (1874), all of which served notice of his cryptic flair.

By 1875, unhappy in marriage, he was back in San Francisco, working at the US Mint, but again a frequent contributor to the West Coast journals, especially his celebrated 'Prattle' columns which appeared in the *Argonaut* and across several publications and the pieces which eventually became *The Devil's Dictionary*. Typical are his definitions of marriage: 'The state or condition of a community consisting of a master, a mistress and two slaves, making in all, two'; or of a year: 'A period of three hundred and sixty-five disappointments'; or of a lawyer: 'One skilled in circumvention of the law'. From 1881-6, he was editor of the *Wasp* before, in 1887, agreeing to write for William Randolph Hearst's *San Francisco Examiner*. Although he thought Hearst essentially a crook, a robber-baron, he was shrewdly allowed his own journalistic head and in the columns of newspapers whose editorial positions he frequently thought infamous he evolved his measure as a master of invective and the devastating satiric jibe. In 1877 he had issued his book-length hoax on the sexual dangers of dancing the waltz, *The Dance of Life*, and a literal account of one aspect of frontier gold-

prospecting, *Map of the Black Hills Region*. But it was in the 1890s, an era which also was enjoying Mark Twain, Bret Harte* and a 'Western' school of writing, that Bierce began publishing the books on which his fame has since largely come to rest: *The Monk and the Hangman's Daughter* (1891), a collaborative volume which landed him in litigation; *In the Midst of Life: Stories of Soldiers and Civilians* (1892), his view of the Civil War as *cauchemar*, bleak, hysterical human madness, and which contains exceptional stories like 'A Horseman in the Sky', 'An Occurrence at Owl Creek Bridge' and 'Parker Adderson, Philosopher'; *Black Beetles in Amber* (1892), his lively satiric verse; *Can Such Things Be?* (1893), cryptic prose narratives based on war and psychic themes; *Fantastic Fables* (1899), up-dated Aesopian fables usually with a timely modern twist; *Shapes of Clay* (1903), further satiric verse pieces written for his son; and *The Cynic's Word Book* (1906), the title given to what is now better known as *The Devil's Dictionary*, Bierce's anthology of droll philosophical definitions. To these should be added other writing from the *Collected Works*, especially tales like those under the title *The Parenticide Club*, the best known of which symptomatically begins 'Early one June morning in 1872 I murdered my father – an event which made a deep impression on me at the time.'

Bierce's later personal life was almost as bleak as his literary *persona*. His son Day was killed in a duel in 1899; he divorced his wife Molly in 1905; suffered worsening asthmatic ill-health; and engaged in a run of bad-tempered personal and literary feuds. He also went to Washington DC (1896–1909), writing for the *Cosmopolitan* and on assignment for the Hearst newspapers. By the end, though he saw his *Collected Works* through the presses, he felt increasingly unsure of his satiric touch. The old fires were growing exhausted, and in 1913, a testy, uncompanionable figure, he headed towards Mexico seeking, as he said, oblivion, which he most likely found in one of the bitter partisan skirmishes of the revolution. Behind him lay a record of work for which, amid a great deal of dross and journalistic occasional writing, he merits his due esteem as a rare American wit and ironist.

A. Robert Lee

See: *The Collected Writings of Ambrose Bierce*, ed. Clifton Fadiman (1946); Paul Fatout, *Ambrose Bierce, The Devil's Lexicographer* (1951); M. C. Grenander, *Ambrose Bierce* (1970).

40

BISMARCK, Otto von 1815–98

Prussian politician and first Chancellor of the
German Reich

Otto von Bismarck, rightly known as the Iron Chancellor, was born on 1 April 1815 on his father's estate in Prussia and died on 30 July 1898 on one of his own, Friedrichsruh. He was one of the most extraordinary politicians of modern times but the price of his many achievements was very high. Although he presided over enormous changes in Germany, his aim was to harness them so as to ensure the preservation of the ideals and the elites of the old order. Always a pragmatist, he was prepared to follow many paths and the one that he had chosen by the time he was dismissed led his successors directly to the Great War and the socialist revolution which followed it.

Bismarck is usually remembered as the father of German nationalism but in reality he was more of a reluctant midwife, whose first hope for her charge had been stillbirth. Realizing that the birth was inevitable, however, Bismarck not only named the day in January 1871, but the place, Versailles, and the conditions of birth and growth as well. And so it was that Bismarck finally brought together all the principalities of Germany. To be sure, some of them had already given up their political independence by joining in the North German Confederation of 1867. Their economic independence had been eroded too, thanks to their membership of the Zollverein, the Prussian-led customs union. But the ultimate deed which signified the completion of Bismarck's plan, the accession of the South German states to the confederation, could only take place in 1871. This, his main act, the founding of the German Reich, was far more than what it seemed, the simple culmination of the liberal ideas which had conceived it. It was, in fact, a structure which gave pride of place to Prussian militarism and feudalism: in short, to the values of Bismarck's own class.

To many contemporaries, he seemed a giant, the 'honest broker' (the epithet was his own) of European power politics, the man who had contained the excesses of democracy and socialism, an apparent champion of liberalism who gave Germany the faint outline of parliamentary institutions and practices which could, one day, produce true parliamentary democracy. The things that went wrong after the pilot had departed, so his admirers argued, were scarcely his fault. And the less savoury parts of his design, his anti-Semitism (despite early friendships with Jews), his ruthlessness towards domestic opposition, and especially his repression of the Poles, were excused as necessary evils. But what his apologists ignored were the traditions of political behaviour that Bismarck was content to establish. A recent biographer is right to call him a 'white revolutionary': for he was as much of a revolutionary as Lenin except that he fought on the side of the established Prussian order. Even his God-fearing attitude could be attributed to his alleged belief that God was a Prussian.

Without Bismarck, the values he supported could not have survived the more modern forces of nationalism and liberalism, of industrialization and socialism. During the revolution of 1848 he had gained first-hand experience of the power of new political forces and he was appalled by them for the simple reason that they threatened to abolish the world in which he believed. Out of an indifferent law student (at Goettingen and Berlin) and an aimless and uncommitted civil servant, there emerged a political genius. And the essence of that genius was Bismarck's readiness to cooperate with any group which would enable him to further his own goals and to concede as little as possible along the way.

The most dangerous period for him lasted from 1851, when he was appointed Prussian Ambassador to the German Diet, until 1877 when he began his apparent 'change of course'. This was the time when liberalism and nationalism were at their most virile and just after a revolutionary assembly had tried to forge a united Germany by parliamentary means. The thirty-nine existing political units were not, however, going to succumb to majority decisions, as counter-revolution in 1849 made quite plain. But the drive for unity was irresistible for it was not only fuelled by mass political support but also by sheer economic advantage. Although Bismarck was a known hardline opponent of any change in the existing monarchical order, he quickly realized that pure opposition would lead to the destruction of the power of monarchy. He saw that the real choice that faced Germany was a Protestant Reich led by Prussia or a Roman Catholic one led by Austria. He was determined that the former should prevail.

As Prussian Prime Minster after 1862, Bismarck set about forcing Austria out of Germany. Even though it was a sister monarchy, it was treated ruthlessly. First it was squeezed by Prussian economic strength (mainly concentrated in the Ruhr). Then Bismarck began a policy of violence which set the Prussian army against the Habsburgs. The Schleswig-Holstein issue permitted Prussia to fight in defence of German citizens and on 3 July 1866, at the Battle of Sadowa, Austria was defeated. Bismarck used one more war to complete his work; it was important for him to prove to the non-Prussian kingdoms that a Prussian-led Reich would effectively be little more than a league against external threats, from which they could not defend themselves on their own. To this end, he waged a particularly violent war against Napoleon III, whose defeat at Sedan allowed Bismarck to found the new Reich in France, an advantage of some significance.

Now that he was Reich chancellor, Bismarck began to consolidate his empire. Much of this early work was supported by the liberals since they possessed, until 1877, a majority in the Reichstag (which was elected under the – at that time – very advanced conditions of universal manhood suffrage). One important joint venture which served liberals and their chancellor well was the *Kulturkampf*, the virulent war waged against the power of the Roman Catholic Church whose interests in education and in the people of Poland made it an ideal target.

Bismarck was, however, never a liberal and he never became one even when he was unable to gain the support of his true allies on the right. At no time did he propose to turn the Reich into a liberal parliamentary democracy governed by a cabinet of elected representatives. His constitutional concept never changed: it was based on a king-emperor who ruled by divine right, who appointed a government responsible to him (and not to the people) for the execution of specific tasks about which parties and others might have a view. The state itself was above all parties and this could not be challenged. This meant that by 1877, when economic slump and electoral setbacks made the liberals incapable of providing a majority in the Reichstag, Bismarck was in a position to ignore their demands and proceed with the abolition of free trade practices and the suppression of the dynamic new force of socialism.

In foreign affairs, Bismarck wanted the fledgling Reich to mature in conditions of peace. His triumph here was twofold: first, his new Germany which did upset the *status quo* in Europe was not challenged by its neighbours; and, second, he averted a major European war over the Balkans in 1878 by holding the Congress of Berlin. His design for Germany's future, however, was more ambitious than mere peace. His treaties with Austria in 1879 and Russia in 1881 not only enhanced the international power of the Reich (it was by virtue of the former treaty that Germany went to war in 1914) but also guarded the monarchies of central Europe against the threat of revolutionary socialism.

It was perhaps ironic that it was the increasing power of German Social Democracy (flourishing despite Bismarck's repression) that produced the issue which led to Bismarck's departure from office. The new Kaiser, Wilhelm II, wanted the anti-socialist legislation toned down and to offer the working class more reforms. Bismarck's intransigence appeared so reactionary that he was now even out of step with the very monarch whose interests he was bound to uphold, and his position became untenable.

The whirlwind of Bismarckian politics were not realized fully until 1918 when Wilhelmine Germany became a defeated and ruined outcast and when socialist revolution stalked the streets of Germany. It would, of course, be wrong to blame Bismarck for policies made after he left office. But he can be held to account for producing a Germany in which those policies could be made. For it was he who enabled Prussian Junkerdom to survive in conditions which ought to have sent it into painless retirement and it was he who poured liberalism into a sinister and illiberal mould. Ultimately he placed a higher value on iron and blood than on tolerance and humanity and in so doing established traditions that Germany, and the world, learned to regret.

Anthony Glees

See: Otto von Bismarck, *Gedanken und Erinnerungen* (1898) and *Die Gesaemmelten Werke* (1924–32); Lothar Gall, *Bismarck: der weisse Revolutionär* (1980); Erich Eyck, *Bismarck and the German Empire* (1968); W. N. Medlicott, *Bismarck, Gladstone and the Concert of Europe* (1956); O. Pflanze, *Bismarck and the Development of Germany* (1963).

41
BIZET, Georges 1838–75

French composer

A great composer of diverse talents, Bizet had the misfortune to be largely misunderstood and underestimated during his short life, and was equally unlucky in the treatment of his works after his death. The beginnings were auspicious: a child prodigy who was admitted to the Paris Conservatoire at the age of ten. There his teachers included Gounod* and the composer Jacques Halévy (who later became his father-in-law). His Symphony in C, written when he was seventeen, was unrecognized until 1935, when it was at last published and performed. Its Mozartian freshness, vitality and charm have since won it ever-increasing popularity. His accomplished one-act opera *Le Docteur Miracle* (1857) won a competition sponsored by Offenbach*; and his cantata *Clovis et Clothilde*, of the same period, won him the important Prix de Rome in 1857. The three years which Bizet spent in Italy, free from financial concern, were probably the happiest of his life. At this time, also, Bizet was not only blossoming as a composer, with an *opéra bouffe Don Procopio*, and a choral symphony *Vasco de Gama*; but he was also showing great talent as a pianist. Even Liszt* was impressed.

The trouble started when, returning to Paris in 1860, he began his uneasy career as a composer for the theatre. Impulsive by nature, he withdrew and destroyed a one-act opera which the Opéra-Comique had accepted. Then his exotic full-scale operas *Les Pêcheurs de Perles* and *La Jolie Fille de Perth* (after Walter Scott*) were only moderately successful. There followed a spiritual crisis in which Bizet re-examined his whole attitude towards his art. His health, which was never good, deteriorated. Unlike Gounod, he had not been able to accept the teaching of the church; he turned for a time to a study of the history of philosophy. As a result of all this, the change in his style of composing was radical – as can be seen in what remains of his opera *La Coupe du Roi de Thulé*, a work which may well have been of outstanding importance, but was mutilated after his death and only fragments remain. These show, however, a vastly increased range of melodic and dramatic power, and an elaborate use of 'leading motifs', stemming from the powerful influence which Wagner* then had on him. The culmination was to come later. Disquieting circumstances persisted – an unhappy marriage in 1869 to Halévy's daughter, who was neurotic and emotionally unstable; and participation in the Franco-Prussian War.

During the last four years of his life, however, Bizet produced some of his finest works. The early and largely hampering influences of Meyerbeer* and Gounod were now thrown off, and a striking originality is found in the one-act opera *Djamileh* (1872). In this work, despite a poor libretto, Bizet felt he had found his true style – a form of dramatic realism through music which led directly to *Carmen*, his masterpiece. In a lighter vein he also composed at this time the witty and delightful suite for piano duet, *Jeux d'enfants*, five movements of which (with additions) were arranged as the *Petite Suite* for orchestra. A masterpiece also of this period was the incidental music which he wrote for Daudet's* *L'Arlésienne*. Certain parts of this are well known through the two concert suites drawn from the total of twenty-seven numbers. At first it was not a success: audiences predominantly interested in the drama were irritated by the (for them) unwanted intrusion of music. The *mélodrames*, however, demonstrate Bizet's remarkable capacity to underline and sum up, orchestrally, the emotional and dramatic content of the play. Unfortunately, he was not able to witness its highly successful revival at the Paris Odéon in 1885.

The four-act opera *Carmen* (1875) undoubtedly represents the summit of Bizet's achievement. Tchaikovsky's* prophecy in 1876 that it would become the most popular opera in the world has been vindicated. In this work, based on Mérimée's* novel, Bizet transformed the current concept of *opéra-comique*: drama, characterization, music were completely at one, and passion, jealousy, tragedy were all vividly represented with a 'realism' that was never crude, always artistically controlled. It was a style which had an immense influence on subsequent opera-composition. Composers as different as Puccini*, Busoni and Stravinsky have all paid tribute to the Bizet style. But to the first audiences, the originality, the unexpectedness, the 'shocking' subject matter – all proved disturbing, and the opera was initially a failure. The failure plunged the composer into a deep depression which was undoubtedly a contributing cause of his death a few months later at the age of thirty-seven. He died just when his genius had really begun to blossom: an incalculable loss to the world of music. Bizet was not a great innovator: his importance lay in his gifts as a melodist and as a musical dramatist. His work is full of original harmonic touches, and as a master of orchestration his skill was of the highest order. Another orchestral master, Richard Strauss, once advised young composers not to study Wagner's scores if they wanted to learn how to orchestrate, but to study the score of *Carmen*: 'What wonderful economy . . . and how every note and every rest is in its place.'

David Cox

Mina Curtiss's valuable study, *Bizet and his World* (1958), was based on much research into unpublished documents. Other studies include: Martin Cooper, *Georges Bizet* (1951); F. Robert, *Georges Bizet* (1965); and (particularly to be recommended) Winton Dean, *Georges Bizet: His Life and Work* (1965; rev. 1975).

42

BJØRNSON, Bjørnstjerne 1832–1910

Norwegian novelist, poet, dramatist, journalist and orator

Although in the twentieth century it is Henrik Ibsen* who stands out as the great nineteenth-century Norwegian, in the second half of the nineteenth century it was his four years younger contemporary Bjørnson who made the greater impression, not just in Norway, but in Scandinavia as a whole and in Europe. But whereas Ibsen was 'only' a dramatist, Bjørnson was a poet, dramatist, novelist, journalist, theatre director, publicist and national figure, who regarded it as his mission to educate and stimulate in growth and national feeling the emergent Norwegian nation.

Bjørnson first made his name as a writer with his stories of peasant life, *Synnøve Solbakken* (1857, trans. 1895), *Arne* (1859, trans. 1895) and *A Happy Boy* (*En glad Gut*, 1860, trans. 1896). These marked a break with the prevailing romantic epigonism, giving a less idyllic view of peasant life than was then current. Moreover they were written in a new and vigorous style which showed the influence of the narrative technique of the sagas and folk tales. At the same time and up till the 1870s Bjørnson also wrote saga dramas, which with the peasant stories were meant to express the true national spirit of the emergent nation (Norway had gained independence from Denmark in 1814) and be a kind of mirror in which the Norwegians could see themselves in the past and present.

In 1865 Bjørnson wrote *The Newly-Married Couple* (*De Nygifte*, trans. 1912), a slight one-act play which none the less was a harbinger of a new era in that it was the first domestic problem play. In 1875 this was followed by *A Bankruptcy* (*En Fallitt*, trans. 1914) and *The Editor* (*Redaktøren*, trans. 1914), realistic plays which urged greater honesty in the business world and the press, and which preceded Ibsen's first attempt in the genre by two years.

During these years Bjørnson had also been active as a theatre director and as a journalist. From 1857–9 he was director at the Norwegian Theatre in Bergen (a post he took over from Ibsen), and from 1865–7 he was director of the Christiania Theatre (Christiania being the old name for Oslo). Both in his capacity as theatre director and journalist Bjørnson fought hard to break the Danish control of the Norwegian theatre, and to foster a national dramatic tradition – Norwegian plays performed by Norwegian actors speaking Norwegian.

The other side of Bjørnson's journalistic activity was political and nationalistic, and he fought among other things for the acceptance of the party system in politics, to defend Norwegian independence *vis-à-vis* Sweden, for greater democracy as opposed to bureaucracy, and for the Folk High School Movement as opposed to the Latin-based school system. But not only did Bjørnson write in various papers and weeklies, he also enjoyed being editor, and between 1856 and 1873 was editor of five different papers and periodicals.

Someone as keen as Bjørnson to speak out on all issues and to be at the centre of all activity could hardly fail to cause controversy and raise opposition to himself, and this he did, especially in the very conservative Christiania, which he christened 'tiger city' (*tigerstaden*) because of its coldness and hostility to him. For this reason, and in order to get time to read and write, he made several extensive visits abroad, most notably between 1863 and 1865, 1873 and 1875 and 1882 and 1887.

On returning from his second visit Bjørnson had bought a farm in central Norway in order to be near his Folk High School friends. However, he eventually found their views narrow and his position isolated. It was during this time that his thinking and beliefs went through a radical transformation, which in part was due to his reading of such seminal writers of the day as John Stuart Mill*, Taine*, Renan* and Zola*. As a result he lost his childhood faith, acquiring instead a sort of evolutionary faith, which saw progress towards ever greater perfection as being part of the divine plan. Because Bjørnson was such a central figure in Norwegian life and culture and because he was so open about all he was thinking, his religious crisis did not remain a personal matter, but came to be regarded as the inauguration of a new age in Norway.

The beginning of the 1880s was another politically very active period for Bjørnson as he lent his weight to the growing liberal-left opposition which in 1884 finally toppled the conservative government which had controlled Norway ever since it acquired its own parliament in 1814.

Bjørnson's literary output from the 1880s and 1890s differs from his earlier work in that it has a more limited didactic aim. In the play *A Gauntlet* (*En hanske*, 1883, trans. 1913) he attacks the sexual mores of the day and demands the same purity of men before marriage as men demand of women. The novel *The Flags are Flying in the Town and at the Harbour* (*Det flager i Byen og paa Havnen*, 1884, trans. as *The Heritage of the Kurts*, 1892) is a plea – in the spirit of Herbert Spencer* – for a better education for girls, while *On God's Paths* (*Paa Guds Veje*, 1889, trans. 1890) is a plea for religious tolerance. However, if many of Bjørnson's works from these years are not as artistically successful as the earlier peasant stories, he did write one play which equals the best of Ibsen, namely *Beyond Our Power* (*Over Ævne, første stykke*, 1883, trans. 1913) which is an attack – made through a very lovable and ideal clergyman – on all striving and aspiration which runs counter to our limited human nature.

In the 1890s Bjørnson became more involved in social questions and in the cause of international peace and the fate of smaller oppressed nations, such as the Finns, the Czechs and the Slovaks, and his position was such that when he wrote on these issues in the international press, the world listened.

If one asks how such a central figure can today be almost forgotten outside Norway (where he is still regarded as something of a national hero) the answer is perhaps that he was eminent in many areas rather than pre-eminent in one. Moreover he was so in touch with his times, so much part of them, that, unlike Ibsen, he is almost absorbed into the history of Norway in the second half of the nineteenth century. He in no way stands apart from that history as does Ibsen. This would not have worried him, however, for to live and be able to serve in a decisive period of history was, he believed, the greatest good fortune that could befall one, and perhaps as Ibsen said of him 'his life was his greatest work'.

Marie Wells

See: B. Downs, *Modern Norwegian Literature 1860–1918* (1966).

43
BÖCKLIN, Arnold 1827–1901

Swiss painter

Böcklin was born in Basle and studied art at the Kunstakademie in Düsseldorf. His reputation within the German-speaking world, at times amounting to hero-worship, has been matched until recently by incomprehension or simply ignorance elsewhere. In his willingness to sacrifice good taste to expressive force-fulness he was indeed a typically Germanic artist. So it may seem surprising that when asked for advice on how to become an artist he should have recommended 'drinking wine rather than beer and going to Italy as quickly as possible' and that he should himself have lived for thirty years in Rome and died at a villa near Fiesole which he had bought six years previously. A large part of his subject matter was taken from classical mythology and his settings were nearly always Mediterranean. But, if the South recommended itself partly for its associations of rational calm, this was primarily useful for producing tension with the irrational violence which could always be felt below the surface and occasionally burst through in no uncertain terms, as in his late allegorical works *War* (*Der Krieg*, 1896) and *Plague* (*Die Pest*, begun 1898). This tension can be felt at its strongest in two landscapes, *Stimmungslandschaften*, each of which exists in five versions executed at different dates: *Villa on the Shore* (*Villa am Meer*) and his one internationally famous work, *Island of the Dead* (*Toteninsel*). *Villa on the Shore* shows a solitary brooding female figure standing on the seashore and behind her a partly ruined Italian villa with colonnade; the impending storm is suggested mainly by the bending cypress trees in the 1864–5 version and mainly by the waves in that of 1878. The sinister silence is even more pronounced in *Island of the Dead*, which Böcklin called 'a picture for dreaming about'. Under a lowering sky, lighter but more stormy in the later versions, an island looms up out of the sea, with tombs in its cliffs and tall dark cypresses between them, as a small boat carrying a coffin and a standing figure clad in white is rowed towards it.

It was his ability to evoke silence that was later to earn Böcklin the admiration of de Chirico. The other side of this concern with silence was the typically Symbolist synaesthetic ambition of producing paintings which would directly evoke music; typically Symbolist too were both Böcklin's interest in colour theory, especially with regard to complementary colours, and his exploration, with the help of mythology, of the fantasy world of erotic fear and desire. At times, as in the girl riding a unicorn in *Silence of the Forest* (*Das Schweigen des Waldes*, 1885), the symbolism appears an almost comic anticipation of Freud. More disturbing however is the element of deliberately used vulgarity or 'overstatement' in Böcklin's images, particularly evident in his pictures of reptilian sea-monsters and darkly lecherous nymphs or mermaids sprawling on rocks, of which *Calm Sea* (*Meeresstille*, 1887) is an outstanding example. Of all mythological figures, the one who meant most to him was Pan, the cloven-hoofed and horned God not merely of libidinous nature but also of panic and the nightmare. Genuine archetypal depths, not unconnected with male paranoia, are stirred by *Pan Frightening a Goatherd* (*Pan Erschreckt einen Hirten*, two versions,

both *c.* 1860). Even if the vulgarity of many of Böcklin's paintings represents little more than his inability to transcend the world of nineteenth-century *Bürgertum*, works such as this justify a view of him as the most important artist of the Symbolist generation within German-speaking culture, creating a link between the melancholy of Caspar Friedrich* and the more strident introversion of the Expressionists.

Gray Watson

See: Rolf Andree, *Böcklin: die Gemälde* (1977); the catalogue of the Böcklin Exhibition at the Hayward Gallery, London (1971).

44
BOLIVAR, Simon 1783–1830

Venezuelan statesman

Occasionally an individual emerges who seems to confirm Carlyle's* assertion that 'the history of the world is but the biography of great men'. Such a man was Simon Bolivar, whose military acumen secured for him just such a mythological status in Latin America's history. Against that, however, must be set a consideration of his political philosophy.

Bolivar was born in Caracas into a family of wealth and position. Orphaned by the age of nine, his upbringing came under the control of an uncle who provided him with several tutors, the most influential of whom was Simon Rodriguez, an admirer of Rousseau and other eighteenth-century liberal philosophers.

In 1800, Bolivar was sent to Spain to complete his education. Already showing the restlessness of many 'Creoles' (as the white ruling groups of Spanish descent were called) with Bourbon reforms, his discovery of the corruption of the Spanish court reduced still further his respect for the monarchy. He had become convinced that hereditary monarchy was markedly inferior to a system of life-presidents.

He married in 1802 and returned to Caracas, but his wife died within a year. By 1804, he had returned to Europe where he renewed his friendship with Rodriguez, now in exile after his implication in an earlier rebellion in 1797. His old tutor introduced him to several like-minded men, enabling Bolivar to develop his own ideas through discussion. There he met Humboldt*, whose enthusiasm for Latin America, and his conviction that conditions there were ripe for rebellion, helped the young man to see the potential of his homeland and how it might be realized.

Equally significant for Bolivar was the crowning of Napoleon*, which he saw as a betrayal of the people. Napoleon, for him, was no more than a dishonest tyrant. This, however, was a problem for the Old World; Bolivar was concerned with the New World. In 1805 he travelled around Europe with Rodriguez, and at Monte Sacro made his famous vow to liberate his country. In 1807, going by way of the United States, he returned to Caracas.

A year later, Napoleon provided the opportunity the Latin American Creoles had been waiting for; when his troops invaded the Iberian peninsula, provincial governments (the juntas) were formed in Spain, and they were soon imitated in Latin America. Initially these bodies declared themselves loyal to Ferdinand VII of Spain, but republican sympathizers soon emerged to take advantage of this break in metropolitan authority. By 1810, Bolivar was in London seeking support for Venezuelan independence. Unsuccessful at that level, his journey bore fruit in two ways: first, he persuaded Miranda to return from exile and lead the independence forces, and second, he studied British political institutions, for which he developed great admiration.

Venezuela's first republic was declared on 5 July 1811; it was short-lived. After an early setback, Miranda surrendered his troops to Spain and the republic fell. From his exile in Cartagena, New Granada (now Colombia) Bolivar published a manifesto (*El Manifiesto de Cartagena*, 1813) considering the reasons for the collapse of the republic. This he attributed to the disunity inherent in the federal system, and to the weakness of a central authority obsessed by humanitarian sentiments and unwilling 'to use force in order to liberate peoples . . . ignorant of the value of their rights'. He argued that it was now in the interests of both New Granada and Venezuela to organize an invasion force to liberate his homeland. By 1813, after a gruelling campaign, Bolivar was able to re-enter Caracas, assume political dictatorship, and declare the second republic. A bloody civil war ensued, in which the royalists were supported by the poor *llaneros* who fought *against* the rich Creoles rather than *for* Ferdinand. In 1814, Bolivar took refuge first in New Granada, and then in Jamaica.

In Jamaica he wrote his famous letter *La Carta de Jamaica*, sketching out his vision of Latin America's future. Despite the failure of two republics, he believed that independence was inevitable; it would be achieved by Creole assumption of power rather than by revolution. While seeking unity to eject Spain, he rejected the idea of full representative democracy. He envisaged a political system on the British model, with a hereditary upper house, an elected lower house, and a life-president in place of the monarch.

Denied support by both Britain and the United States, he won backing from the President of Haiti, and returned to the mainland, establishing his capital at Angostura. He now urged the Congress to prepare a constitution incorporating the ideas expressed in his *La Carta de Jamaica*, with the addition of a fourth branch of government charged with preparing the citizenry for democracy.

With his base secured, and with the support of Paez's rebel forces in the east, Bolivar altered his military strategy. Bolstered by a Foreign Legion of European soldiers, he joined with the leader of the rebels in New Granada and crossed the Andes by what was thought to be an impossible route. He then launched a successful surprise attack against the Spaniards at Boyaca and, in August 1819, triumphantly entered Bogota, capital of what was now proclaimed as the Republic of Colombia – despite the fact that two of the new republic's three provinces were still under Spanish control.

After a six-month ceasefire, Bolivar's refreshed troops defeated the Spaniards at the Battle of Carabobo and recovered Caracas for the rebels. A constitution was drawn up (1821), naming Bolivar as president; he felt it too weak, however, and returned instead to military duty, this time on Ecuadorean soil. There the assistance of Antonio José Sucre ensured the decisive victory at Pichincha in mid-1822, which secured the country's freedom.

While Bolivar had been liberating the north, the Argentine General San Martin was established as protector of the independence movement in the south. Their paths seemed fated to cross, as they did at Guayaquil on 26 July 1822. Temperamentally they were opposites – Bolivar given to dramatic gestures, San Martin quiet and introverted. Faced with Bolivar's reluctance to accede to any of his suggestions, San Martin saw this as indicative of Bolivar's desire for dominance. Assuming he now represented an obstacle to independence, San Martin withdrew into exile in Europe. Bolivar was well satisfied, and the way was clear for the Peruvian Congress to name him Supreme Military Commander.

Nevertheless, Bolivar did not feel strong enough to attack the Spaniards, entrenched in the mountains, until late 1824. Then, at the battles of Junin and Ayacucho, he again displayed his military prowess, and accepted the surrender of the Spanish army. By April 1825, Sucre had also liberated Upper Peru, which was then renamed Bolivia. Bolivar was invited to draft its new constitution, a document which provides the best example of the 'Liberator's' political philosophy. It established: (1) a life-president with the right to choose his successor; (2) suffrage limited to 10 per cent of the population; and (3) a three-body national assembly, consisting of an hereditary and an elected assembly and a body known as the Censors, charged with moral responsibility. There was no attempt at social reform.

Bolivar now turned his attention to the construction of an Andean federation, another step towards his long-term ambition of building a league of American States. However there were few who sympathized with his idea of a strong central government; unity provided the strength to conquer a common enemy, but once the enemy was removed unity was no longer necessary.

Peru resented Colombia's direction, and within Colombia itself strains were becoming apparent. In 1826, while Bolivar called for the establishment of a league of Hispanic American States, open hostilities broke out between Venezuela and New Granada. Bolivar hurried back from Peru to appease the warring factions, reluctantly conceding the need for a new constitution. He was not wholeheartedly in favour of the 1821 Constitution, but he regarded it as the best possible at that time; now he feared that the liberals would seek to weaken central authority even further.

Dissatisfied with the direction constitutional discussions were taking in the Congress, Bolivar's supporters withdrew from the convention and he once more assumed dictatorial powers. Yet he could not hold his disintegrating creation together; Peru attacked Colombia, Venezuela and Ecuador seceded. Bolivar's personal popularity was also waning, and an attempt was made on his life in 1828.

By 1830 he was badly disillusioned and, weakened by years of hardship, his health was rapidly deteriorating. Ironically, like San Martin before him, he seems to have come to see himself as an obstacle to a lasting settlement, and he too resigned all his posts and prepared to return to Europe. On learning of the assassination of Sucre, his friend and presumed successor, however, he went instead to the home of a Spanish friend in Santa Marta. There he died of tuberculosis on 17 December 1830.

Ewen Smith

See: S. de Madariaga, *Bolivar* (1951); G. Masur, *Simon Bolivar* (1969); G. E. Fitzgerald, *The Political Thought of Bolivar* (1971).

45
BOLTZMANN, Ludwig 1844–1906

Austrian physicist

Ludwig Boltzmann made a major contribution towards explaining the laws governing the human-scale world accessible to our senses in terms of the micro-world of atoms at a time when 'the existence of atoms' was a hotly debated subject. He went a long way to showing mathematically that the second law of thermodynamics follows from the theory of random processes in molecular mechanics. His work in statistical mechanics is the link in the main development of physics from Maxwell's* theory of gases to Planck's quantum theory.

Boltzmann, the son of a tax official, was born in Vienna, the capital city of the Austro-Hungarian Empire and a lively forum of philosophic schools. He studied physics at the University of Vienna, which had a great tradition in this field. One of his main teachers was Josef Stefan, the discoverer of the radiation law

named after him (which Boltzmann later derived from thermodynamic considerations). Though Boltzmann is reported by his contemporaries to have been a very good experimentalist, his central concern throughout his life was to find theoretical explanations in the form of rigorous mathematical derivations, in particular from deeper atomistic theories. This programme arose naturally from Boltzmann's personal philosophy: he was a radical atomist (*Atomist bis ins Unmögliche*) who believed even the infinitesimal calculus to be but an approximation arising from small but finite mathematical 'atoms'.

In the second half of the nineteenth century it seemed possible that the whole of chemistry and physics (except for optics and electromagnetism) might be reduced to a single atomic theory. Important successes in this direction had been achieved by Clausius* and by Maxwell (whom Boltzmann much admired), explaining the pressure of ideal gases in terms of the impact of molecules moving relatively freely apart from occasional collisions, and the heat content of gases to be the total of the mechanical energies of the molecules.

There were two laws known to govern the large-scale interconversion of mechanical energy and heat. The first law (generalized by Helmholtz*) states the conservation of energy in the sense that a certain amount of mechanical energy is always equivalent to a certain amount of heat. The second law states that not all the heat at a given temperature can be converted into mechanical work; that there is in fact an absolute limit to the efficiency of a heat engine, depending on the temperature.

Boltzmann's main work was concerned with the derivation of the second law of thermodynamics from the molecular kinetic theory of Clausius and Maxwell. He tackled this problem already in his second publication in 1866. This programme was opposed by Mach* and his followers, whose positivistic philosophy had no place for unobservable material atoms. Their phenomenalist (or rather 'sensationalist') programme reduced science to sensations as the ultimate entities. They had no patience with the construction of 'deeper' explanatory models and preferred to retain phenomenological laws, such as the firmly established second law of thermodynamics, as ultimate.

In his philosophic polemic against atomism Mach had for a decade a strong ally, the famous and influential chemist Wilhelm Ostwald. In common with most chemists, Ostwald had used the 'atomic hypothesis' in his work on ions (charged atoms), as indeed had Mach in some of his early scientific work. Ostwald's achievement included the discovery of laws of electro-chemistry on thermodynamic grounds. Such derivations have the advantage of being 'model-independent'. Ostwald was so impressed by the power of thermodynamic theory that he became the founder of a quasi-religion called 'energetics' whose commandment was essentially the first law of thermodynamics. In his text-books and public lectures Ostwald allied himself with Mach in condemning the arbitrary construction of models. He was reconverted to atomism in the light of J. J. Thomson's discovery of the electron and Einstein's explanation of the 'Brownian motion' (see Robert Brown*) of colloidal particles by the random bombardment of molecules.

Ostwald added a specific logical argument against Boltzmann's work: the second law of thermodynamics states that heat cannot flow spontaneously (i.e. without the expenditure of work from outside) from a colder to a hotter body; that on the contrary temperatures equalize under heat-exchange to a final state of thermal equilibrium. Thus heat flow is in this sense irreversible. A certain function, called entropy, of the amount of heat transferred divided by the temperature, can only increase. On the other hand, mechanics, to which Boltzmann wanted to reduce thermodynamics, is strictly reversible, in the sense that for every motion there is another motion described by reversing the sign of the variable denoting time, which is equally possible. The opponents of Boltzmann's atomism kept pointing out that you cannot expect to obtain irreversibility from a theory according to which all processes are essentially reversible.

In order to resolve this paradox, Boltzmann was increasingly forced to rely on probabilistic (or statistical) arguments. It is interesting to note that a statistical approach in science can be traced in the physics department of Vienna University from the time of Mendel*, culminating in Franz Exner's suggestion (four years after Boltzmann's death) that all laws of physics are fundamentally statistical, a notion probably inspired by the derivation of the law of radioactive decay from fundamental probabilistic assumptions by Stefan Meyer, a student of Boltzmann, and Egon von Schweidler. Boltzmann already refers to probability in his first paper on thermodynamics in 1866.

Boltzmann's essential argument was that a reverse thermodynamic process (such as heat flowing from a colder to a hotter body) was not impossible but merely exceedingly improbable, and that our direction of time was given by the fact that our immediate world happens to be in an improbable state changing in a preferred direction towards a more probable state. He developed this argument in reply to the objections raised by Ostwald, his colleague Joseph Loschmidt, and by Ernst Zermelo (a pupil of Planck).

A curious feature of Boltzmann's work is his concentration on the task of deriving already accepted results from atomistic theory without emphasizing the novel phenomena also predictable by that theory. He did refer to breaches in the second law of thermodynamics in the form of statistical fluctuations to be expected on the basis of his statistical mechanics, but the theory of such fluctuations was only developed later, notably in

the case of Brownian motion by Einstein and Boltzmann's pupil, Marian Smoluchowsky. Similarly, Boltzmann rarely referred to the key quantity required to develop an essentially atomistic quantitative theory, viz., the actual number of molecules which make up a given amount of material, such as 1 cc of a gas at standard pressure and temperature. This number had been first determined by his senior colleague Loschmidt who worked next to him in the Physics Institute in Vienna when Boltzmann was professor there. It is also interesting to note that some derivations of thermodynamics results were also achieved by Boltzmann's contemporary J. Willard Gibbs on a formally analogous statistical basis without reference to atoms.

Boltzmann firmly believed in the actual existence of material atoms. He deserves to be remembered for his painstaking use of elementary mathematics to link molecular mechanics and thermodynamics. Far from introducing arbitrary models, such a unification reduces and simplifies. One of Boltzmann's few lapses in rigour is his postulate that a certain kind of random molecular disorder is maintained during motion according to the laws of mechanics. This is not a matter for postulation, but a question of mathematical consistency to be proved or disproved.

Boltzmann's outstanding achievement was the derivation of an equilibrium distribution law which generalizes Maxwell's law of the equilibrium distribution of the kinetic energies of molecules in a gas to energies of any kind. His famous 'H-Theorem' shows, at least for a monatomic gas, that book-keeping of the increase and decrease in the number of atoms of given energy resulting from collisions leads to the monotonic increase of the average of a certain quantity defined in terms of the motion of the atoms. This quantity can be identified with entropy (the thermal quantity that according to thermodynamics theory never decreases). The increase continues until the steady state is reached. This steady state turns out to be the Maxwell distribution. Entropy turns out to be a function of the probability of the state of the system.

It is a historic paradox that around the turn of the century, near the height of the success of atomic theory, Boltzmann claimed to be overwhelmed by the popularity of his opponents. It should be stated that Ostwald claimed, in reverse, that a national scientific conference was rigged against him. At one of these conferences Boltzmann said to Ostwald: 'I see no reason why energy should not also be regarded as divided atomically.' Ostwald was 'thunderstruck' by this suggestion, and next to Ostwald stood Planck, who in 1905 first introduced quantization of energy in his law on blackbody radiation. After unsuccessful attempts to derive his law thermodynamically, Planck adopted a statistical approach differing from Boltzmann's in several points, and spuriously claimed that a statistical approach required the adoption of quantization.

Probably the happiest years of his life Boltzmann spent as Professor of Experimental Physics at Graz (Austria's 'second' university) whose rural surroundings appealed to him. He also held professorships at Leipzig and Munich for a few years, and travelled to Britain and the USA where he was honoured. He ultimately returned to Vienna where he resumed his Chair of Theoretical Physics and later took a chair in philosophy of science. The latter move was largely if not entirely to argue against Mach's philosophy. In his inaugural address attended by a record audience he showed himself a sincere, blunt and thoughtful man, but not a philosopher on a par with Mach. Both refer to Darwin* in their philosophy.

He was a very popular lecturer as well as a teacher of the next generation of physical scientists (including Walther Nernst and Svante Arrhenius). Arrhenius was awarded the Nobel Prize in 1903 for his work in ionic theory, Nernst was awarded the Nobel Prize in 1920 for his third law of thermodynamics.

Boltzmann committed suicide during a vacation in Duino (of Rilke's *Elegies*) in 1906. He had been in poor health for some years. On his tombstone is written the equation $S = k \log W$ which is Planck's formulation of Boltzmann's bridge between S, entropy, and W, probability. He is perhaps best summed up by himself: 'My whole life is devoted to the development of theory.'

Heinz R. Post

Works: *Wissenschaftliche Abhandlungen* (3 vols, 1909); *Populäre Schriften* (1905); *Vorlesungen über die Principe der Mechanik* (3 vols, 1897–1920); *Vorlesungen über Maxwells Theorie der Elektrizität und des Lichtes* (2 vols, 1891, 1893); *Vorlesungen über Gas-Theorie* (2 vols, 1923); with J. Nabl, *Kinetische Theorie der Materie* (Encyclopaedie der Mathematischen Wissenschaften, 1905). See: *Festschrift Ludwig Boltzmann*, ed. S. Meyer (1904); James Clerk Maxwell, 'On Boltzmann's Theorem on the average distribution of energy in a system of material points', in *Cambridge Philosophical Society Transactions*, vol. XII (1879); *Ludwig Boltzmann: Theoretical Physics and Philosophical Problems: Selected Writings*, ed. B. McGuiness (1974); E. Broda, *Ludwig Boltzmann* (1955); *The Boltzmann Equation*, ed. E. G. D. Cohen and W. Thirring (1973); H. R. Post, 'Atomism 1900', in *Physics Education*, vol. 3 (1968)

BONAPARTE, Napoleon: see under NAPOLEON BONAPARTE

46
BOOLE, George 1815–64

British mathematician

Boole was the son of a Lincolnshire bootmaker. He had only a rudimentary education and never attended a university. In mathematics he was almost entirely self-taught and is said to have begun reading mathematical books because they were cheaper to buy than the classics. He worked as a school teacher but he was already producing highly original mathematical papers and in 1844 was awarded a gold medal by the Royal Society for a paper published in the *Philosophical Transactions* entitled 'On a General Method in Analysis'. In 1849 he was appointed to the chair in mathematics at Queen's College, Cork, in Ireland. He was elected a fellow of the Royal Society in 1857.

The significance of Boole's work may be viewed under two related headings, his contribution to pure mathematics and his contribution to logic. In respect of mathematics Boole belonged to the flourishing school of British algebraists which had emerged in the first half of the nineteenth century. During the eighteenth century British mathematics had largely stagnated as compared with continental mathematics due to a slavish adherence to Newtonian methods, but the situation changed dramatically with innovations introduced by George Peacock, Charles Babbage*, John Herschel, Duncan Gregory, Augustus de Morgan and others who not only promoted the study of the great continental mathematicians but also developed the 'abstract' approach to algebra. Hitherto algebra had been considered as a collection of laws abstracted from the study of arithmetic, its subject matter the properties of numerical magnitudes. But in the new abstract approach the possibility was envisaged that algebra might apply to any objects which satisfy the basic laws or 'axioms'. Boole for example, following the ideas of Gregory, developed an algebra of differential operators which effectively sought to reduce the solution of certain differential equations to a purely algebraic procedure. Then in 1847 Boole published a short tract entitled *The Mathematical Analysis of Logic* in which he tried to apply the new abstract algebra to the subject matter of logic. The idea of reducing the processes of logical argument to a form of purely mathematical calculation had already been entertained by Leibniz in the seventeenth century, and also by de Morgan, but Boole was the first to arrive at a detailed practical solution of the problem. Indeed Boole's invention of what later came to be termed symbolic logic was the major advance in the subject since Aristotle's systematic treatment in his *Organon* dating back to the fourth century BC. But another very significant point emerged. The algebraic laws required for application to logic were in some respect different from those required in application to arithmetic. So Boole here contributed to the idea that abstract algebra could not only have many different applications outside the field of arithmetic, but that the laws or axioms might also be varied to suit different applications. Similar ideas of how the notion of an abstract algebra could be generalized in this way were arrived at by William Hamilton with his algebra of quaternions (1843) and by Hermann Grassmann with his algebra of extensions (1844), developments which paralleled the discovery in geometry of non-Euclidean variants by Carl Gauss*, Nikolai Lobatchevsky* and others. Boole showed how his new algebra could be interpreted both as an algebra of classes, so comprehending the classical syllogistic modes of reasoning, and as an algebra of propositions, so comprehending what is now known as sentential or propositional logic, but which also dates back to the Greeks (Stoic logic). In 1854 Boole published a revised and much enlarged account of his system entitled *An Investigation of the Laws of Thought*, which included the study of a third interpretation of his abstract algebra, namely the theory of probability. The title of this work is somewhat misleading since it is clear that Boole was not conducting an empirical study of modes of human reasoning, which might well in many instances be fallacious, but was concerned with prescribing the laws of *correct* reasoning. There were a great many gaps and ambiguities in the detailed development of Boole's ideas which were clarified by later writers such as William Stanley Jevons*, John Venn and especially Ernst Schröder in the latter part of the nineteenth century.

Boole's work in logic is often confused with a quite different development which originated with Gottlob Frege*. Instead of trying to reduce logic to mathematics as Boole had done, Frege sought to reduce mathematics to logic by defining mathematical notions like number in terms of logical notions like class. The two approaches are connected in the sense that Frege had first to present logic itself in an abstract axiomatic formulation, not unlike Boole's symbolic logic, although a much more powerful and subtle instrument (which ironically turned out to involve an inconsistency, the attempted elimination of which is a major theme in the history of twentieth-century logic).

The work of Boole and Schröder was still studied however and in the 1930s led to the modern Polish school of algebraic logic, associated with the names of Tarski, Lindenbaum, Rasiowa and Sikorski. In the meantime, 'Boolean algebra' has been extensively studied as an important branch of mathematics in its own right with applications to the design of computers and the general theory of electronic switching circuits.

In spite of the largely unrigorous and intuitive style in which Boole developed his ideas he ranks as a major figure in the history of nineteenth-century mathematics.
Michael Redhead

The Mathematical Analysis of Logic, being an Essay towards a Calculus of Deductive Reasoning (1847) is reprinted in G. Boole, *Studies in Logic and Probability* (1952). Bibliographical information is given by his grandson, Sir Geoffrey Taylor, 'George Boole F.R.S. 1815–1864', in *Notes and Records of the Royal Society of London*, vol. 12 (1956). See: N. I. Styazhkin, *History of Mathematical Logic from Leibniz to Peano* (1969); T. Hailperin, *Boole's Logic and Probability* (1976).

47
BOOTH, William 1829–1912

British founder of the Salvation Army

Booth was a native of Nottingham, although his mother was of Jewish origin. After attending numerous schools, at the age of thirteen he was apprenticed to a pawnbroker in a particularly sordid part of the city. He proved good at the trade, and developed a sharp commercial sense which he never lost. In 1843 his father, an unsuccessful speculative builder, died; his wife and daughters made a living running a small shop. Booth became bitter about the plight of the poor and his own family's struggle against penury. In later years he was to speak of his 'blighted childhood'.

Brought up as a nominal member of the Church of England, in early manhood Booth drifted into Methodist circles. A piece of sharp practice in the pawnbroker's shop preyed upon his conscience: in 1844 he made a public confession. Two years later he joined a group of young revivalists who held services in the streets of Nottingham, among whom Booth, with his great height, strikingly contrasting black hair and pale face, and passionate mode of utterance, soon became prominent. In 1849 he moved to London, still working as a pawnbroker. At times he starved himself in order to save money to send home to his mother and sisters. In the Methodist Church he became first a lay, then an itinerant, preacher.

Soon after he arrived in London Booth was introduced to a Clapham girl, Catherine Mumford, a devout Methodist with a mind unusually well stocked with theology. Their association was extremely fruitful: she in broadening the intellectual base of his thinking, although he remained almost completely ignorant of – indeed, indifferent to – theology; he in weaning her off the deference to public opinion typical of a suburban chapelite. They married in 1855.

Booth's violent style in the pulpit made the Methodist worthies uneasy. Rather than submit to their cautions Booth broke with Methodism in 1861 and, with Catherine, became an independent revivalist, establishing the Christian Mission in Whitechapel four years later. It was a chance remark of Booth's son Bramwell which led to the Mission being renamed

'Salvation Army' in 1878. From 1880, the Salvation Army spread through North America, Australia and Europe. Booth initially resisted the Army's use of uniforms, and of military titles for its officers, not least his own of 'General'; but he came to value the military technique: 'If Moses had operated through committees,' he would say, 'the Israelites would never have got across the Red Sea.' He led the Army until the day of his death, assisted by Catherine, a life-long semi-invalid, until her death in 1890. Of their seven children, Bramwell, who had been the Army's strongest organizing force from very early on, succeeded his father as General; Ballington led the Army in the United States, although he later seceded to found the rival Volunteers of America; and Evangeline was active in North America for thirty years.

Booth was a highly fastidious man (dirt and smells made him feel ill), never strong in constitution, and towards the end of his life blind. Some of his characteristics have made him vulnerable to satirists. He kept an unusually varied range of good friends, from bookies to heads of state, and many whose way of life showed no sign of the repentance and spiritual renewal which it was part of his mission to exhort (though he once persuaded Cecil Rhodes to kneel down in a railway carriage and pray with him). His profound obscurantism in almost everything made him an easy target for progressive intellectuals such as T. H. Huxley*. But his simple vigour made him a uniquely powerful figure in Victorian society. Some of the Salvation Army's early excursions into the slums had caused riots, but over the years it was handsomely financed in its crusade on behalf of what Booth called variously the 'dim millions' or the 'bottom dog'.

One of Booth's biographers wrote that he 'saw himself as a moral scavenger netting the very sewers. . . . He saw sharply what others scarcely saw at all, and felt as an outrage what others considered to be natural. . . . He unroofed the slum to Victorian respectability.' He was moved by a deep compassion and love for the poor, believing that the smallest gesture of concern from decent people could save them from despair. But even more he was moved by a 'love for souls': he did not believe that you could make a man clean simply by washing his socks. While the physical needs of the people might be cared for through the Army's hostels, shelters, hospitals, schools and farm colonies, its colourful street meetings, with their bands, banners and vehement preaching, were equally important in Booth's scheme in converting them to a way of life based on a religion which, rejecting the sacraments, relied on the basic moral precepts of Christianity.

By both action and example Booth was probably more influential than either churchmen or politicians in pioneering solutions to some of the problems of the Victorian cities. In 1896 A. F. Winnington-Ingram, soon to be Bishop of London, wrote: 'It is not that the Church of God has lost the great towns; it has never had them.' Ten years later King Edward VII asked Booth what the churches thought of him, and was told: 'Sir, they imitate me.' Indeed, E. W. Benson, Archbishop of Canterbury, 1883–96, had laboured hard to bring the Salvation Army within the fold of the Church of England.

Timothy O'Sullivan

See: H. Begbie, *Life of William Booth* (1920); W Booth (with W. T. Stead), *In Darkest England and the Way Out* (1890); C. B. Booth, *Catherine Booth* (1970); R. Collier, *The General next to God* (1965); R. Sandall and A. R. Wiggins, *The History of the Salvation Army* (1947 ff.). See also: K. S. Inglis, *Churches and the Working Classes in Victorian England* (1963).

48
BORODIN, Alexander Porfirevich 1833–87

Russian composer

No other member of the 'mighty handful' pursued his non-musical career so far as Borodin. He was a distinguished medical chemist whose first scholarly work was published in 1858 in the journal of the (Russian) Academy of Sciences, who obtained his doctorate in the same year and who held a readership (from 1862) and then a professorship (two years later) at the Medico-Surgical Academy. He was a meticulous and original scientist thoroughly wrapped up in his subject and a conscientious teacher. He had further interests besides – in the new medical courses for women inaugurated in 1872, for instance, as well as extensive family responsibilities. Borodin recorded that his musical friends were pleased to learn that he was ill, because it meant that he might have time for composition.

He had unusually extensive opportunities for foreign travel in connection with his research, and his musical horizons were extended thereby. His early songs are competently written, but without traces of the striking originality which became apparent after his exposure to Balakirev's* influence. It was in 1862 that he made the acquaintance of that composer who, almost at once, set him to work on a symphony – a preposterously ambitious project for one of his previous attainment and training. The work was completed by 1867, however, and this First Symphony in E flat proved to be an innovative demonstration of the ideals of the Balakirev circle. It employed folksong at the points in a symphony at which Balakirev considered its use appropriate (in the trio, but not in the scherzo itself, for example). It showed an awareness of the music of Glinka* and Berlioz*, and exhibited some of the melodic, rhythmic and harmonic types which were to be characteristic of Russian orchestral music. The still more remarkable Second Symphony in B minor, with its foreshadowing of Sibelius in the fragmentation and development of themes in the first movement, was written between 1869 and 1876. Borodin worked on a two-movement Third Symphony in A minor in 1882 and in 1886–7. A further orchestral work, the musical picture *In Central Asia*, dates from 1880.

Borodin's most radical harmonic experiments are to be found in some of the songs of the 1860s; indeed, it is in the songs that the progress of his music can best be observed. An early example of the epic narrative style which features strongly in *Prince Igor* occurs in the 'Song of the Dark Forest' (1868). The modal practice, free metre and non-western cadences of the oldest and most primitive layer of Russian folk music are used here, while the piano is employed in a highly original fashion. 'Abstract' musical experiment with ideas not specially characteristic of folk music (added sixth chords, unresolved seconds, etc.) is found in 'The Sleeping Princess' (1867). 'Towards the Shores of a Distant Homeland' is Borodin's tribute on the death of Mussorgsky*. 'In Other People's Houses' (1881) is a setting of verses of social relevance, akin to the satirical songs for which Mussorgsky is more famous. At no point, however, did Borodin go so far as his friend in jettisoning accepted norms in the name of graphic musical truth. All the songs, and indeed all his work, betrays a care that the formal structure should be satisfactory. His two string quartets (in A, 1874–9, and D, 1881) are exceptional examples in this genre from the 'handful'; they have deservedly outlived Rimsky-Korsakov's*.

Borodin worked much but intermittently on the opera *Prince Igor* in 1869–70 and between 1874 and his death. It was completed and partly orchestrated by Rimsky-Korsakov and Glazunov and first performed in 1890. Its subject, suggested by Stasov, is derived from the literary epic *The Lay of the Host of Igor*. The libretto, by Borodin himself, was not completed before composition began. The opera is concerned with the conflict between the Russians and the Tartars in the twelfth century. It contains much fine music in lyrical, epic, folk and primitive veins, but partly as a result of its episodic composition is richer in colourful and effective individual scenes than in cumulative dramatic impact.

Stuart Campbell

See: Gerald Abraham, *Studies in Russian Music* (1935) and *On Russian Music* (1939); Serge Dianin, *Borodin* (trans. 1963), the standard biography.

49
BOUCICAULT, Dionysius Lardner (né Boursiquot) 1820–90

Irish dramatist

Born in Dublin on 27 December 1820, Boucicault's mother was Anna Maria Darley, sister of the poet George Darley. His father may well have been her husband, Samuel Smith Boursiquot, a wine merchant of Huguenot extraction. It is at least as likely that the father was Dr Dionysius Lardner, a don at Trinity College, Dublin, and compiler of the 134-volume *Cabinet Cyclopaedia*. The boy was educated at Lardner's expense in the University College School, London. Thereafter his life sustained this early pattern of confusion and eccentricity.

Although he was an all-rounder in the best Victorian traditions of the theatre, Boucicault is now remembered primarily as a playwright. He wrote something in the region of one hundred and fifty plays, and late in his life contributed many articles on the theatre to the *North American Review* and other journals. It may be said that his work is uneven, though not perhaps uneven enough to include anything of the first rank.

Boucicault's reputation today depends on two specific areas of his work. In 1964, David Krause edited a collection of the plays with Irish settings; of these *The Colleen Bawn* (1860), based on Gerald Griffin's novel *The Collegians*, is perhaps the best known, though *The Shaughraun* (1874) has also been successfully revived in Ireland. The Irish plays are highly landscaped, the dialogue richly brogue-ish, and the action frantic.

More recently, London has seen the great commercial success of a revival of *London Assurance* (1841). Here Boucicault is seen as mediating between the erotic comedies of the Regency period and the later work of Pinero, Jones and – of course – Oscar Wilde*. In a few such plays Boucicault reveals himself capable of constructing a complex, well-made play, but his success in the 1970s is perhaps more an indicator of present needs in the commercial theatre than of any inherent quality in the work itself.

W. J. Mc Cormack

See: *The Dolmen Boucicault*, ed. David Krause (1964); D. L. Boucicault, *The Octoroon* (1970). The standard biography is Richard Fawkes, *Dion Boucicault: A Biography* (1979), which includes lists of plays and other writings.

50

BRADDON, Mary Elizabeth 1837–1915

British novelist

Possibly no writer has undergone a posthumous eclipse as complete as that which overtook Mary Elizabeth Braddon. As 'Miss Braddon' during her protracted and courageous liaison with her publisher, John Maxwell, whom she married in 1874 on the death of his first wife in a mental asylum, and subsequently as 'The Author of Lady Audley's Secret', she captivated the largest known readership of the century. Among her eighty works, many of which suffer from repetition of each other's themes and styles, none matched the bold subject matter and nervous, rapid creative energy of *Lady Audley's Secret* (1862), her best known and most inspired work. Miss Braddon's house in Richmond, Surrey, and subsequently her apartment in Pall Mall, formed the setting for a literary and social circle of considerable brilliance which included Oscar Wilde* and royalty.

The boldness of *Lady Audley's Secret* and its successor, *Aurora Floyd* (1863) gave currency to the term 'sensation novel' following an unsigned article of that title by Henry Longueville Mansel in the *Quarterly Review* (1863). Mansel's strictures were parried in the *Revue des deux mondes* in a better written article of that year by its editor, Emile Forgues. The views of Forgues and Michael Sadleir are the best, albeit the most neglected, among critical views of Miss Braddon's work. Other literary admirers included Galsworthy, Ford Madox Ford and Arnold Bennett. Though the chorus of her detractors included the young Henry James*, he subsequently made use of her themes in his novels.

In the novel, Lady Audley emerges as a victim of a hereditary nervous weakness, as a result of which she cannot endure the shocks of modern social and economic life. A poignant and skilfully dramatized exposure of her second, bigamous marriage to the ageing Sir Michael Audley is undertaken by the baronet's nephew, Robert Audley. At the third confrontation she collapses, ending her days in the Belgian mental asylum to which Robert escorts her. In subsequent works, notably *The Doctor's Wife* (1864) and *Strangers and Pilgrims* (1873), similar themes were explored with greater directness and sympathy for the heroines.

Miss Braddon pioneered the female-oriented later Victorian novel in which a limited case of characters plays out a psychological drama in a strongly depicted setting. This aspect of her art is obscured to a considerable extent by her over-indulgence in mystification and intrigue. The modernity of her achievement is reflected in her literary taste: her literary formation owed much to Balzac*, Hawthorne* and Flaubert* several decades before these writers acquired widespread Victorian currency. As the editor of *Belgravia*, a women's magazine, she contributed to female emancipation, but the crises of the 1880s were beyond her scope and her writing lost ground to a new and more demanding generation.

Christopher Heywood

See: Michael Sadleir, *Things Past* (1944); C. Heywood, 'French and American Sources of Victorian Realism', in *Comparative Criticism*, I (1979), ed. E. S. Shatter Robert Lee Wolff, *Sensational Victorian* (1979).

51

BRADLEY, Francis Herbert 1846–1924

British philosopher

Francis H. Bradley was the leading British philosopher of his generation, and he has been described as the only first-rank philosopher produced in Britain during the nineteenth century. Bradley was the son of a well-known evangelical preacher, the Reverend Charles Bradley. He was educated at two public schools, Cheltenham and then Marlborough, and at University College, Oxford. In 1870 he was elected to a life fellowship at Merton College, Oxford, a position which he retained until his death. He was the first English philosopher to be awarded the Order of Merit, a distinction which he received in 1924.

Bradley played a major role in establishing Idealism as the dominant school of British philosophy during the latter part of the nineteenth century. His first major work, *Ethical Studies* (1876), presented a biting critique of John Stuart Mill's* Utilitarian ethics, and of positivist ethical doctrines as expressed by Frederick Harrison. The title of a famous chapter in that book, 'My Station and its Duties', has been taken to imply that Bradley believed that morality consists of actions appropriate to one's social position and functions in society, but this is a misconception. Bradley held that self-realization was the true end of moral action. Man is a social being who has no existence apart from society. Self-realization is possible only in society and is the result of the development of the moral self playing its part in the moral life of the community.

Bradley's *Principles of Logic* (1883) was of major importance in undermining the Utilitarian philosophy of mind in which logic was subordinated to psychology. Utilitarians maintained that our ideas originate in our own individual sense-experience. Questions concerning the extent and certainty of knowledge thus tended to devolve into speculations about the origin of ideas. Bradley's writings contributed significantly to the rejection of this 'psychologism'. The distinction which he made between psychological theories about the working of the mind and philosophical explanations of the grounds and acquisition of knowledge marked a turning-point in the history of logic. Although his views on other points were subjected to much criticism by later students of logic, on this matter Bradley's opinions were of lasting importance and shaped the direction of subsequent work in that field.

Bradley's early writings were clearly influenced by Hegel*, and along with works by T. H. Green and Bernard Bosanquet contributed to the emergence of an Anglo-Hegelian movement in late nineteenth-century British philosophy. But Bradley denied that he was an Hegelian, and in his masterwork, *Appearance and Reality* (1893), he rejected several of the cardinal doctrines of Hegelian thought. Bradley had no use for the notion of dialectic, and insisted that the absolute could not be in the process of becoming, but existed in its final form. He also had harsh words for Hegel's identification of thought with ultimate reality and considered this notion 'as cold and ghost-like as the dreariest materialism'.

In contrast to Hegel's rationalism, Bradley claimed that the absolute could be known only through an immediate experience of feeling that transcended thought. Ultimate reality is a unity within which each category of human experience has a place. This spiritual monism drew criticism from other Idealists on the ground that it seemed to make the individual self nothing but an aspect of the absolute.

The theory of evolution created a cultural crisis in late Victorian society which some Idealists attempted to meet by substituting new metaphysical concepts for traditional theological doctrines. Although he shared the antipathy felt by many Idealists towards the philosophical assumptions underlying the new scientific theories, Bradley's metaphysics was not intended to be part of this effort to rescue theological truths by garbing them in philosophical language. He considered the absolute to be incompatible with the God of the theologians, and was pleased that *Appearance and Reality* tended to encourage religious doubt.

Few philosophers have dominated their discipline as thoroughly as Bradley did during the quarter century prior to the First World War. The impact of his arguments was enhanced by an unusually powerful and decidedly polemical style of writing which so impressed T. S. Eliot that he considered Bradley one of the outstanding stylists of all time among English authors. Although Bradley's influence was still very strong at Oxford in the 1920s, the writings of G. E. Moore and Bertrand Russell prior to the First World War had already initiated a reaction against Idealist thought which was eventually to make Bradley's theories seem largely irrelevant to the main currents of thought within twentieth-century British philosophy.

Harold Smith

Bradley's other books include: *The Presuppositions of Critical History* (1874); *Essays on Truth and Reality* (1914); *Aphorisms* (1930); and *Collected Essays* (1935). Bradley published revised editions of all the works mentioned in the text. The second edition of *Appearance and Reality* (1897) is of special importance in that it contains an appendix in which Bradley replies to many of the criticisms directed at the first edition. The best source of biographical information about Bradley is G. R. G. Mure, 'F. H. Bradley', *Encounter*, vol. 16 (January 1961). The most useful study of Bradley's thought is Richard Wollheim, *F. H. Bradley* (1959).

52
BRAHMS, Johannes 1833–97

German composer

Brahms was born in a tenement in the poorest quarter of Hamburg, son of a young town musician and a seamstress already in her mid-forties. He was always intended for a musical career, studying first with his father and a local piano teacher; at the age of eleven recognition of his unusual gifts induced the noted teacher Edouard Marxsen to accept him as a pupil for both piano and composition. The family's poverty forced Johannes to play for money in the seaport's taverns and brothels, and his health was undermined for a time, though he gave some public recitals on his own account and began teaching and arranging popular music. In 1853, his life was transformed when he undertook a concert tour with the Hungarian violinist Reményi, which led him first to a meeting at Göttingen with the composer-violinist Joachim (who became a life-long friend and champion); then to Weimar, where he met Liszt*; and finally to Düsseldorf, where he enormously impressed Robert and Clara Schumann with the playing of his own compositions. Schumann* responded with a wildly enthusiastic article in *Neue Zeitschrift für Musik* hailing Brahms as a long-awaited master, 'one who should utter the highest ideal expression of his time, who should claim the Mastership by no gradual development, but burst upon us fully equipped': which instantly made Brahms an object of controversy and scepticism. This new-found friendship was tragically clouded by Schumann's mental breakdown in 1854, which propelled Brahms into the position of chief confidant and protector of his wife and children. He fell deeply in love with Clara Schumann, fourteen years his senior – it is unclear whether this passion, which was certainly mutual, was ever consummated, but they remained close friends for the rest of their lives.

In the later 1850s Brahms was employed at the princely court of Lippe-Detmold; afterwards he lived in Hamburg before becoming conductor of the Vienna Singakademie in 1863. He resigned the post in the following year, but henceforth resided in Vienna. The première of *Ein Deutsches Requiem* ('A German Requiem', op. 45, to his own selection of texts from the Lutheran Bible), which he conducted at Bremen in 1868, marked his public acceptance as an artist who had fulfilled Schumann's early prophecies; and the appearance of a First Symphony (op. 64) in 1876 which Hans von Bülow was moved to call 'the Tenth' – suggesting that at last a worthy successor had appeared to the symphonies of Beethoven* – confirmed his position as a 'living classic' in the eyes of all but ultra-Romantics of Wagnerian persuasion.

Brahms's life after he settled in Vienna was unremarkable in its externals: despite several liaisons of varying emotional depth, he never married; and though one of the first great composers to earn a considerable fortune in his lifetime (chiefly from his immensely popular *Hungarian Dances* for piano duet) he lived a frugal bachelor's existence in a small flat, devoting much of his money to helping fellow-musicians – he was instrumental, for instance, in furthering Dvořák's* early career. Concert tours and walking holidays, often in Switzerland or Italy, varied his routine. His last years were shadowed by the deaths of several close friends, and after Clara Schumann's in 1896 he went into a decline; he himself died of cancer of the liver (as had his father) the following year.

In 1860 Brahms had been unwise enough to sponsor, with Joachim, a 'manifesto' criticizing the so-called 'New German School' of high Romantic composition, headed by Liszt. As a piece of propaganda it was a failure, but it was symptomatic of his reverential attitude towards tradition which cast him, in hostile eyes, into a 'reactionary' role; even today the image is of a solid, unadventurous composer, a classicist antipope to Wagner*. These two great figures seem in retrospect the coeval Alpha and Omega of nineteenth-century German music (though Brahms was the younger man by nearly a generation). Wagner is only too clearly the revolutionary, with his operas' strong appeal to the ungovernable emotions and his vastly enlarged harmonic language; Brahms, with his symphonies, concertos, and chamber works that sit so comfortably and immovably in the mainstream repertoire, seems by contrast the embodiment of bourgeois conservatism, even if raised to the highest power of genius. In fact he is one of the most complex, and ultimately ambiguous, figures in the history of music; and it is arguable that if he had been less lavishly endowed with sheer musicality the potent contradictions of his art would be more readily evident. He was probably the subtlest and most comprehensive musical mind since Beethoven, and it is in his music, and not before, that Beethoven's profoundest examples are fully understood and developed upon.

The nineteenth-century debate about 'Music of the Future', which ranged Brahms and Wagner on opposite sides, concerned the proposition that the traditional musical forms were exhausted, and that music must move on to 'freer' forms that would develop with the depiction of intense emotion. The classical hierarchies of tonal relationships and balanced, ordered structures were progressively loosened in Schubert's*, Chopin's* and Schumann's lyric forms; the programmatic symphonies of Mendelssohn*, Berlioz*, Raff, and Goldmark; Liszt's tone-poems and 'cyclic' forms; and ultimately Wagner's music-dramas with their leitmotivic structures and dramatic periods. The concepts of 'form' and 'content' had become distinct as they had never been in the Classical era: the idea of 'sonata-form' itself, seen as that era's most characteristic achievement, was a description *post hoc* (actually *c.* 1840) of normative practices in Haydn, Mozart and Beethoven. The early Romantics were much impressed by the vigour and intensity of Beethoven's ideas, but were either unprepared to submit to his structural disciplines (Liszt, Wagner), or attempted to apply those disciplines for the sake of their honoured associations, rather than as an organic outcome of the potential of the basic material (Schumann).

Brahms, too, was a Romantic, of the most passionate kind: his early piano works are as turbulent as Schumann's, and the massive opening movement of the First Piano Concerto (op. 15, 1854–8) is a *ne plus ultra* of *Sturm und Drang* emotionalism and tragic power. But it also deploys and organizes its explosive material, on the largest scale, with complete understanding of the fundamentally *dramatic* nature of sonata-style: and perhaps its chief model is the first movement – in the same key, D minor – of Beethoven's Ninth Symphony. Meanwhile the First Serenade for orchestra (op. 11, 1857–8) had already displayed how his melodic thinking, which possesses a very personal breadth and flexibility, could give rise to structures of Haydnesque wit and formal clarity, propelled by a Beethovenian dynamism. Brahms did not revert to the structural norms of the classical style, but built upon the foundation of its more unorthodox inspirations, which until then had exerted little influence.

This makes him a Janus figure in musical history. There is no doubt that his personal historical sense was very highly developed: he himself performed and edited music of the Baroque and Classical eras, was keenly interested in the work of contemporary musicologists, and had an intimate and admiring knowledge of Mozart, Haydn, Beethoven, and Schubert. Their example was the basis for his own language, yet he was no epigone: his historical sense included the certainty of the irrecoverability of the past. Charles Rosen has observed that 'The depth of his feeling of loss gave an intensity to Brahms's work that no other imitator of the classical tradition ever reached: he may be said to have made music out of his openly expressed regret that he was born too late.' There is a large element of truth here, but it remains a one-sided view. The intensity of Brahm's feelings was not simply for the loss of the classical style. He was a man of his own times, and his imaginative identification with aspects of earlier music was his personal approach to writing music of those times.

Brahms essayed all the traditional musical genres except opera: his major works include four symphonies, four concertos, and several choral works with orchestra; a large body of chamber music including three string quartets as well as sextets, quintets, trios, and sonatas; a great number of songs and unaccompanied choruses, including nearly a hundred settings of German folksongs; and a substantial output of solo piano music which concentrated, after his early years, on sets of variations and the smaller forms of the ballade, rhapsody and intermezzo. There is an apparent preference for 'abstract' or 'pure' designs: no avowedly programmatic works, though many private, concealed programmes may well lurk in pieces of such tightly controlled emotionality as the C minor Piano Quartet (op. 60, 1874).

But these time-honoured forms arise now from different premises, to articulate new orders of material. Brahms's harmony could be as chromatically complex as Wagner's, though arrived at from a more diatonic basis; and his treatment of tonality in large-scale forms seldom fulfils traditional expectations, but instead makes new departures which in retrospect prove justified and satisfying. His study of older music led him to create an enriched polyphonic texture in which each contrapuntal voice has an increased independence and life of its own: his success in this was due to the plasticity of his melodic gift and, especially, to his subtle and all-pervasive mastery of rhythm to point up contrasts of line and shifts of pulse.

It is precisely here that he ceases to be a classic and becomes rather the first of the moderns, the initiator of that drive for absolute polyphonic freedom which characterized the early development of Schoenberg: who revered Brahms, and summed up his importance for later generations in a classic essay with the seemingly paradoxical title 'Brahms the Progressive'. It was, perhaps above all, Brahms's infinite resource in motivic development that Schoenberg admired, and in this connection it is relevant to note Brahms's predilection for variation form, apparently as a means of fully defining the essence, and exploring the infinite latent possibilities, of any given thematic idea. The piano variation-sets on themes by Handel (op. 24, 1861) and Paganini* (op. 35, 1863), the slow movement of the First String Sextet (op. 18, 1860), the finale of the Clarinet Quintet (op. 115, 1891), and the orchestral *St. Antoni* Variations (op. 56, 1873) are all distinguished examples. Perhaps the summit is the astonishing passacaglia on a theme derived from Bach that is the finale of the Fourth Symphony (op. 98, 1885): a display of

'pure' musical invention of the utmost tragic power. But this finale is itself but a crystallization of processes adumbrated in the three previous movements: the symphony's opening idea of falling thirds is organically developed throughout its whole length with allusive ingenuity – just as, in the Third Symphony (op. 90, 1883), all movements made use of multifarious developments of a three-note figure F-Ab-F – and the *idea* of passacaglia form is already implied in the character of the counterstatement of the first movement's first subject.

At certain points in the late piano pieces (opp. 116–19, 1891–3) and the *Vier ernste Gesänge* (op. 121, 1896) motivic elaboration in melodic and harmonic spheres is almost total. It was these aspects of Brahms's practice that were the ultimate sanction for Schoenberg's rigorously motivic 12-note method. It is probable, too, that Brahms's creative mixing of old and new musical resources made a profound impression on Busoni; and the power of certain of his inspirations has continued to haunt the consciousness of twentieth-century composers (the openings of such diverse works as Carl Ruggles's *Sun-Treader* and Bernd Alois Zimmermann's *Die Soldaten*, for instance, are most likely attempts at re-creating, in their own voices, the tremendous timpani-pinned impression of the start of Brahms's First Symphony).

Brahms has generally been acknowledged one of the supreme craftsmen among composers, and he was highly self-critical, destroying all that he imagined to be sub-standard work. Even his orchestration, once unfavourably compared to the pyrotechnics of Berlioz or Tchaikovsky*, is now generally understood as brilliantly suited to the nature of his inspiration, and is one of the secrets of the quality – which he shares with Beethoven – of intimacy on a grand scale. The worst that can be charged against his music is that occasionally he relies on technique alone, and produces a dry discourse – the first two String Quartets (op. 51, 1873) are especially disappointing in this respect for a composer with Beethoven's examples before him. But the creator of such full-hearted love-music as the Double Concerto (op. 102, 1887), or merely such a sumptuous tune as the trio-melody in the scherzo of the C major Piano Trio (op. 87, 1882) can be forgiven anything. 'Such a great man! Such a great soul!' sorrowed Dvořák: ' – And he believes in nothing!' But there is nothing nihilistic about Brahms's music: rather, it is the work of a great *humanist* mystic who, aware of the tragedies, paradoxes and imponderables of existence, wrote his works to provide sustenance for the here and now.

Malcolm MacDonald

The collected edition of Brahms's works is published by Breitkopf & Härtel, Leipzig, and a large number of individual pieces are widely available in many other editions. He was a copious correspondent, and revealing collections of his letters include *Letters of Clara Schumann and Johannes Brahms 1853–1896,* ed. Berthold Litzmann (1922) and *Johannes Brahms: the Herzogenberg Correspondence*, ed. Max Kalbeck (1909). See: Karl Geiringer, *Brahms: His Life and Works* (2nd edn, 1947); Hans Gal, *Johannes Brahms; His Work and Personality* (1963); Bernard Jacobson, *The Music of Johannes Brahms* (1977); Julius Harrison, *Brahms and his Four Symphonies* (1939).

53

BRIDGES, Robert Seymour 1844–1930

British poet

Robert Bridges was born on 23 October 1844 at Walmer into a rich and well-established Kentish family. He was educated at Eton and then at Corpus Christi College, Oxord, at both of which he was happy and successful. He had at one time intended to become a clergyman – he had gone through an adolescent Puseyite phase at Eton – but in fact after two years of foreign travel he entered St Bartholomew's Hospital as a medical student, with the intention of practising medicine until he was forty. He took his MB in 1874 and worked in the Children's Hospital, Great Ormond Street, and then at the Great Northern Hospital. In 1881 he became ill and gave up his medical practice.

He settled at the Manor House at Yattendon, Berkshire, and married in 1884 Monica, daughter of Alfred Waterhouse, the well-known architect. In 1907 he moved to Chilswell, a house he had had built on Boar's Hill near Oxford. He became Poet Laureate in 1913, was awarded the Order of Merit in 1929 and died on 21 April 1930.

Apart from his own work, the most famous literary event of his life was the publication in 1918 of the *Poems of Gerard Manley Hopkins*. At one time, in the heyday of Hopkins's* posthumous fame, it used to be considered a serious blot on Bridges's reputation as friend and critic that he had not been more fulsome in his praise of these poems: though of course without his initiative they would never have been known at all.

Although dusty copies of *The Testament of Beauty* (1929) clog the shelves of second-hand bookshops, Bridges is not an entirely neglected master. Even if respectful indifference is what his poetry generally inspires among 'serious' critics, most general readers of poetry probably know a handful of his poems – 'A Passer-by', 'London Snow', 'Flycatchers', 'Nightingales' – quite well, often without being able to name the author, and to a small and not particularly influential readership he seems a fine, even a great, poet.

The patrician aloofness of his verse, its formal perfection, the traditional subject matter and diction, his fastidious avoidance for the most part of darker themes,

his concern with such matters as prosody and phonetic spelling, and perhaps above all the easy circumstances of his life have – though in themselves accurate enough – given a false impression of literary dilettante in the tradition of Edmund Gosse* and Austin Dobson.

Yet there is nothing amateurish about Bridges. His poetry was his life-long preoccupation and the perfection and beauty at which he aimed were achieved by an unsurpassed fineness of ear and technical skill. His range is not wide, but within it he achieved perfection astonishingly consistently. When in 1890 the first four books of his *Shorter Poems* were published Housman* called it the most perfect book of verse ever written – not the sort of praise that Housman distributed lightly. It is in these short lyrics that Bridges's greatest achievement lies. Essentially he is a master only of small forms, though *The Testament of Beauty* is in this, as in almost every other way, a sport. The verse dramas have deservedly sunk without trace.

Bridges was usually uninfluenced by contemporary writers: he was curiously unimpressed by the great Victorians. His major passion was Milton. Not only did Milton influence his own poetry, but his essay *Milton's Prosody* (1893) is his major contribution, and a very important one, to a true understanding of Milton's subtlety as a metrist. Shakespeare, Keats* and Shelley* were among his masters. These, with the Roman poets, Dante, the Elizabethan song-writers and the Blake of *Songs of Innocence and Experience* are the most obvious of his enthusiasms. Of contemporary poets he admired mostly his personal friends: Hopkins and one or two (largely forgotten) writers. It is perhaps this lack of contact with the general literary vogue of his day that gives his best poetry its timelessness.

He is not however a wholly traditional poet. He was keenly interested in experiments in verse and his 'neo-Miltonic syllabics' in *New Verse* of 1926 contain some very successful experiments, notably 'Cheddar Pinks'. *The Testament of Beauty*, written when he was eighty-five, is in every way an astonishing work. Uneven, and at times confusingly argued and episodic, it is still a remarkable attempt at the impossible task of justifying the ways of nature to man:

> . . . [Man] himself
> becoming a creator hath often a thought to ask
> why Nature, being so inexhaustible of beauty,
> should not be all-beauteous; why, from infinit
>   resource,
> produce more ugliness than human artistry
> with any spiritual intention can allow?

This does not sound promising, but it is a compelling poem and well worth persisting with, despite a few *longueurs*.

Bridges will probably never be read by many, but to those who can like the chamber-music quality of his poetry he is a poet who richly repays reading, whatever critical fashion dictates. He speaks to a 'fit audience, though few', which is probably what he would have wished.

Joseph Bain

Poetical Works (1953); *Collected Essays and Papers* (3 vols, 1927–33). See: R. Brett Young, *Robert Bridges* (1914); E. Thompson, *Robert Bridges 1844–1930* (1931); N. C. Smith, *Notes on The Testament of Beauty* (1931); J. Sparrow, *Robert Bridges* (1962).

54

BRIGHT, John 1811–89

British politician

John Bright was born at Rochdale, Lancashire, the son of a cotton spinner. Educated at various Quaker schools, he began work in the family business. Later he gained a national reputation, in association with Richard Cobden*, as a public speaker on behalf of the campaign for the repeal of the Corn Laws. In this connection, he became MP for Durham in 1843, subsequently representing Manchester and, after being defeated in that constituency largely arising from his opposition to the Crimean War, sat for Birmingham until his death. His ministerial career, in Gladstone's* 1868 and 1880 governments, was brief. He resigned from the former because of ill-health and from the latter in protest against the bombardment of Alexandria. He was twice married and had ample progeny. His importance lies in what he was rather than what he accomplished.

He was a life-long Quaker, vehement in his opposition to church rates and a fierce critic of the idea of an established church. To an extent, he was a spokesman on educational and allied issues for religious Dissenters. He was the first Nonconformist in modern history to enter a British Cabinet. He was not an absolute pacifist – supporting, for example, the military suppression of the Indian Mutiny – but he was a strong critic of an interfering foreign policy. His criticism of British diplomacy before the Crimean War and of the war itself gained him considerable political unpopularity and perhaps precipitated a nervous breakdown. During the American Civil War, however, he firmly identified himself with the cause of the North where his support was valued. His hostility towards colonial wars or expeditions was well-known.

It was on his capacity as an orator that his contemporary fame rested. He developed his skill in the late 1830s and early 1840s. His voice was strong and his fluency remarkable. Without a classical education, he proudly believed that he expressed himself in plain, direct English. He had a gift of humour and could coin a striking phrase. Probably not at his best in the House of Commons, his oratory was most effective in the mid-1860s when he threw himself into a public campaign for the further extension of the parliamentary franchise. His ferocious attacks on the aristocracy disturbed the occupants of royal and ducal palaces. Even so, although rightly regarded as a Radical, he was apprehensive about giving the vote to the masses. His speeches on this issue strengthened his political position and his voice was a necessary element in the Liberal administration Gladstone formed in 1868. In office, however, Bright was never happy in an executive capacity and had little taste or talent either for administration or for Cabinet manoeuvring. His speeches in the last decade or so of his life are less pungent and powerful but even so give an idea of his range of subjects and illustration. The broadening of the electorate made the ability to communicate to large but 'respectable' audiences of great importance. Arguably, he led and Gladstone, Disraeli*, Hartington and Salisbury were all forced to follow him on the platform.

After his initial onslaught on the protectionism inherent in the 1815 Corn Law, Bright remained a staunch advocate of free trade principles throughout his life. Although not an original economic thinker, he had a gift for putting the essence of an argument in a comprehensible form, although oversimplifying in the process. What was good for cotton, Rochdale and Lancashire must be good for Britain. In the debate on urban conditions, Bright claimed that the factory system in itself could not be held responsible. He resisted factory legislation and clashed bitterly with Lord Shaftesbury. He also opposed proposals for public health provision, basing his case on economy and opposition to state intervention and regulation. His target was the 'landed interest' and he certainly played a part in the lessening of its influence. Yet, when the Corn Laws were repealed in 1846 (by no means simply a success for Bright and his colleagues in the Anti-Corn Law League) Bright thereafter found it difficult to rally his commercial friends to form a 'middle-class party' distinct from Whigs and Tories. Although Bright tried hard to enlist their support, many other men did not share his distaste for the established church and were not averse to a social and political system which still substantially depended upon deference. Bright became a lonely critic rather than the leader of a new political movement. Although he could be thought to epitomize mid-nineteenth-century provincial, commercial and Nonconformist culture, Bright was not unaltered by the political prominence he gained. He latterly enjoyed the company of the aristocracy he had once denounced. In other respects too, with age, his radicalism seemed distinctly conservative. He strongly opposed votes for women and was suspicious of trade unionism. Early in his career he had taken an unusually deep interest in Ireland's problems and put forward influential plans for dealing with the land and ecclesiastical questions. However, disliking what he considered violence and sedition, he opposed Gladstone's proposals to give Ireland home rule. At the end of his life he was again a very independent Liberal. After his death, his speeches continued to be published – even as late as the eve of the First World War – and statues were erected in Manchester and elsewhere but he leaves behind no abiding legislative achievement.

Keith Robbins

See: H. Ausubel, *John Bright, Victorian Reformer* (1960); D. Read, *Cobden and Bright* (1967); K. G. Robbins, *John Bright* (1979).

55
BRONTË, Charlotte 1816–55

British novelist

Charlotte Brontë was born in 1816 at Thornton near Bradford. In 1820 the Brontë family moved the short distance to Haworth where her father had been appointed perpetual curate and where Charlotte had her home for the rest of her life. Two elder sisters died, partly as a result of the harsh and unhygienic regime at the girls' boarding school Charlotte herself briefly attended; this tragic episode is recalled in the opening pages of *Jane Eyre* (1847). Charlotte later taught at another school and spent some time as a governess, a job which the evidence of her letters and novels suggests was one of miserable dependence on indifferent and snobbish employers but which was also one of the very few openings available to a woman without means or the likelihood of marriage. The central experience of her life would seem to have been the period in Brussels (1842–3), in company with her sister Emily*, devoted to the study of languages as well as to some teaching. In Belgium Charlotte Brontë became deeply attached to the husband, Constantin Heger, of the woman who directed the school Charlotte attended. Her feelings were not returned, possibly not completely understood by their object, but their lasting effect on Charlotte is shown by the fact that the master/pupil relationship is either explicitly present in her novels (Paul Emanuel and Lucy Stowe in *Villette*, 1853) or implicitly transmuted into that between the masterful husband and the meek bride (Rochester and Jane Eyre).

Charlotte Brontë's first novel, *The Professor* (1857), was rejected by the first publishers to whom it was submitted and only appeared posthumously. Her second and most famous work, *Jane Eyre*, was an immediate success and provoked great speculation about the identity and character of its author – like her sisters Charlotte hid, at first, under a masculine pseudonym.

She completed only two further novels, *Shirley* (1849) and *Villette*. Although gratified by the attention and applause of the literary establishment and animated by her friendships with other writers (notably Mrs Gaskell*, her first biographer), her extreme reticence made success hard to enjoy. Also the deaths of her sisters and brother within a few months of each other in the late 1840s left her profoundly isolated. In 1854 Charlotte Brontë married her father's curate, A. B. Nicholls, and despite her forebodings – very different from her heroines' passionate expectations – the brief marriage brought her contentment. She died in the early stages of pregnancy in the following year. Unlike her sister Emily, whose one novel *Wuthering Heights* (1847) has no connection with the outward events of her life, Charlotte used the experiences of her circumscribed existence to the full in her novels. *Villette* and *The Professor* are set largely in Brussels and concerned with the experiences of lone English expatriates at school in the capital. *Shirley* is set in Yorkshire at the beginning of the nineteenth century and, although containing material about the Luddites and the Napoleonic Wars as well as some sketchy discussion of the state of the poor, rests on the relationship between the two heroines and the two brothers whom they marry. One, the Shirley of the title, is a portrait of Emily Brontë. *Jane Eyre* has recollections of the author's dark school-days and the frustration of the governess-heroine's marriage to the Byronic figure of Rochester – he already possesses a wife, living but mad – carries echoes of Charlotte's own situation with the Hegers in Brussels. Eventually Rochester atones for his attempted bigamy by losing both his sight and his first wife in a fire. The subsequent happy union in this novel is denied to Lucy Snowe of *Villette* by the death of her husband-to-be. These two most substantial achievements of Charlotte Brontë are alike in their Gothic paraphernalia and melodramatic incident but the more sombre conclusion of the later work is evidence of greater artistic maturity.

Another aspect of the four novels is a pervasive consciousness of the predicament of women in a male-ordered society. This is so even of *The Professor* which is unconvincingly narrated through a masculine *persona*. The feeling co-exists with a disconcerting acknowledgment of the need to defer to male 'superiority'. In reality the resources of the Brontë family were devoted to the career of the incompetent Branwell rather than to the furtherance of his sisters'; in literature Charlotte generally upholds male dominance while inconsistently lamenting the petty roles allotted to women. The response is emotional not intellectual and is most effectively conveyed not by direct statement but by the desolation which periodically overtakes the single, unprovided heroines. Charlotte Brontë's strengths lie not in her ramshackle plots nor in her characterization, but in her rhetorical force, in the sincerity with which the vicissitudes of her heroines are charted, in the power of certain episodes (the drug-induced vision of a Brussels fête in *Villette*, the attack on the mill in *Shirley*), the stamp of an individual temperament on all her work.

Philip Gooden

Biography: Winifred Gérin, *Charlotte Brontë* (1967). Criticism: David Cecil, *Early Victorian Novelists* (1934); Patricia Beer, *Reader, I Married Him* (1974).

56
BRONTË, Emily 1818–48

British novelist and poet

Emily Brontë was born in the parish of Bradford of Yorkshire; shortly after her birth her father, a clergyman, was appointed to a new living at Haworth, where the family remained (Mr Brontë outliving all his children) and where the early years in the parsonage were marred by the deaths of Emily's mother and her two eldest sisters. All the surviving sisters – Emily, Charlotte* and Anne – produced novels and poetry. The single son, Branwell, famous ironically for his personal and literary failure, died from tuberculosis in 1848, of the same disease and in the same year as Emily herself. The intense inward mental and emotional lives of the young Brontës can be traced in the elaborate epics in verse and prose which they wrote together as children and adolescents.

Emily had a fitful education, even spending a period in Brussels with Charlotte in 1842, teaching and learning languages; they planned to start a school themselves in Haworth. Some idea of the autonomous nature of Emily's only novel, *Wuthering Heights* (1847), can be gathered from the fact that none of its author's experiences as tutor or travellor are detectable in the work: the book is extraordinarily independent of the outward circumstances of her life. Emily Brontë was not in any sense a 'professional' writer. Charlotte records how she 'accidentally lighted on a MS. volume of verse in my sister Emily's handwriting'. The poems she found 'wild, melancholy and elevating' but it was very hard to persuade Emily to agree to their publication. Some of the poems are presented within the framework of the verse sagas, others are more personal. The mystical, visionary element in them is strong, as is the rhapsodic response to nature. In 'The Prisoner', for instance, the speaker describes a mystical oblivion which is also a heightened awareness; the agony is intense when consciousness returns, 'When the pulse begins to throb, the brain to think again; /The soul to feel the flesh, and the flesh to feel the chain.' Some of the seeds of Wuthering Heights can be discovered in the author's own reading – including Scott* and By-

ron* – and in local Yorkshire stories of family feuds but the book rises strangely and impressively above any sources. It describes the mingled histories of two families, the Earnshaws and the Lintons. Into the former family is introduced the foundling figure of Heathcliff, brought to the house of the title by old Mr Earnshaw. The child 'is dark almost as if it came from the devil', the first of many demonic references in relation to Heathcliff. The hero-villain forms a passionate, quasi-incestuous attachment with Cathy Earnshaw, his 'sister'. The liaison which would occur if both followed natural impulse is frustrated by the marriages of both to members of the cultivated, conventional Linton family. The child (also called Catherine) of one union, that of Cathy and Edgar Linton, is eventually linked with Hareton Earnshaw, the legitimate heir to Wuthering Heights. Heathcliff dies, an event presented largely as a feat of will, believing that he will be reunited with Cathy beyond the grave. The disciplined, symmetrical entanglements of the two families – it can best be shown diagrammatically – and the careful attention to detail, for example over calendar dates, provide for the novel an infrastructure on which Emily Brontë stages the destructive outbursts of the Earnshaws complemented by the sometimes querulous passivity and calm of the Lintons and the interpenetration of these two worlds. The complexity of the story is heightened by its presentation through two occasionally obtuse narrators and an unchronological arrangement of events. The book operates principally through contrasts: between the violence associated with Wuthering Heights and the more tepid amenities offered by Thrushcross Grange (the Lintons' home); between the characters of Heathcliff and Cathy and the unique love that animates them and the more conventional romantic attachments.

The unassimilable quality of this novel which is both lucid and mysterious is finally best suggested by the conclusion where Heathcliff's death is ambivalently presented as a consummation, not a conclusion to a relationship. At the same time, in a characteristically Victorian vignette, the younger Catherine is instructing the near-illiterate Hareton Earnshaw as prelude to a socially (and fictionally) acceptable marriage. Emily Brontë does not endorse or condemn either union – each is natural and appropriate to its participants – and in this as in so many other respects as an artist she is untypical of her age.

Philip Gooden

See: *The Complete Poems of Emily Brontë*, ed. C. W. Hatfield (1941); Winifred Gérin, *Emily Brontë* (1971); David Cecil, *Early Victorian Novelists* (1934); Frank Kermode, *The Classic* (1975).

57
BROWN, Ford Madox 1821–93

British artist

Ford Madox Brown was born of English parents in Calais. From 1835 to 1839 he studied in the Belgian academies of art attending those at Ghent, Bruges, and finally Antwerp, where he studied with Baron Henry Leys, a historical painter. These years were followed by a period of intensive personal study in Paris, and, in the winter of 1845–6, in Italy. On the way, in Basle, he inspected the works of Holbein. In Italy he looked at pre-Renaissance Italian art, and encountered the work of the Nazarenes, German painters settled in Rome who wanted to restore the principles and devotion of early art. Brown's style changed profoundly. He rejected his youthful manner with its dark and sombre tones, bravura brushwork, and flamboyant melodrama, for cool tones, bright colours, clear sunny daylight, precise and detailed brushwork, and a hieratic pictorial order.

He settled in England in 1846, and put these new principles into practice in two works, *Wycliffe Reading his Translation of the Bible* (1847–8) and *Chaucer at the Court of Edward III* (1845–51). Brown believed that art had a vital function and message for his age. In *Chaucer* he pictured a hierarchical feudal society under the government of a cultivated monarch who patronized the arts. The picture was both a protest against modern fragmentation and a utopian vision of the Middle Ages which offered a positive alternative. Neither Brown's artistic methods nor his historicism were unique. A group of painters who shared and developed these interests and with whom Brown was in contact was the Pre-Raphaelite Brotherhood, one of whose members, D. G. Rossetti*, had been a pupil of Brown in March 1848. *Chaucer* and *Wycliffe* are major artistic documents in the early Victorian movement which sought to repair social dissolution by the medieval example of community.

From the medieval world, Brown turned to paintings which tackled the nature of society in his own era. *Work* (1852–63) and *The Last of England* (1852–5) are the principal pictures of this type and the artist's greatest achievements. Both draw their subject matter from the contemporary world and their philosophic inspiration from the writings of Thomas Carlyle*, especially *Past and Present* (1843). In *Work* Brown presents a synoptic view of Victorian society centred around a group of labourers working in Hampstead High Street. (Thomas Carlyle and F. D. Maurice appear at the right.) Paradoxically he combines an unlikely combination of figures and incidents with a painstakingly literal style which is insistent on every detail in its attempt to render the scene in a convincing way, and an actual setting. The realism of the style is a vehicle for social comment. By exploring the connections and divisions between this group of people, Brown offers a pictorial equivalent and critique not only of his own society, but also of Carlyle's plea for an organic society where everyone is linked by a common sense of responsibility. *The Last of England* deals with emigration. Most of the painting was done out of doors on cold winter days in order to capture the chilly grey light, in itself a metaphor for the pain and loss of separation, experienced by the two principal figures seated on the stern of the ship. During this decade Brown also painted landscapes, such as *An English Autumn Afternoon* (1852–5) and the smaller pictures now in the Tate Gallery. He was interested in sunlight, the reflected lights in shadows, and abrupt transitions of space (concerns shared by the Pre-Raphaelites). But his landscapes are too imbued with social purpose, recording the countryside and suburbs of North London before the invasion of gas and railroad.

In the following decade, with a major retrospective in 1865, the artist's fortunes improved. His later years were mostly spent in Manchester painting the series of twelve wall paintings for the town hall. These works lack the commitment and social realism of his earlier paintings. Brown's importance lies not here but in his attempts to tackle the major issues of his age in paintings which, whilst they present life-like pictures of the Victorian world, also offer stern comment and the hope for change.

Deborah Cherry

Brown's work can best be seen at Manchester City Art Gallery, Birmingham City Art Gallery, Ashmolean Museum, Oxford, and the Tate Gallery, London. See: F. M. Hueffer (Ford Madox Ford), *Ford Madox Brown: A Record of His Life and Work* (1896); Mary Bennett, *Ford Madox Brown* (exhibition catalogue, Walker Art Gallery, Liverpool, 1964). Brown's diaries were abridged and edited by W. M. Rossetti in *Pre-Raphaelite Diaries and Letters* (1900) and *Ruskin, Rossetti, Pre-Raphaelitism* (1899).

58
BROWN, Robert 1773–1858

British botanist

Robert Brown was the son of a minister of the Episcopalian Church of Scotland, and was educated at Montrose Grammar School, and Marischal College, Aberdeen. When the family moved to Edinburgh, he entered the university there as a medical student. While there, his interest in botany was encouraged by Professor John Walker, who persuaded him to study Scottish flora; at the age of eighteen, he read a paper on the subject to the Natural History Society. This brought him to the attention of William Withering, who was preparing the second edition of his *Arrangement of British Plants*. He not only included Brown's work in the book, but also exerted an influence upon the young man which shaped his entire career. In 1795, Brown joined the Fifeshire Regiment as ensign and assistant surgeon, spending most of the next three years in Ireland. There he discovered the only European representative of an American order, *Eriocaulon septangulare*, and this find led directly to his becoming a botanist.

While travelling to London in 1798, Brown called on Withering at Birmingham, and was given an introduction to Jonas Dryander, who was librarian to Sir Joseph Banks, the President of the Royal Society, and the first botanist of the Australian region. Brown succeeded in impressing Banks to such effect that he was proposed as naturalist to Captain Flinders' expedition to New Holland (Australia). This expedition in the *Investigator* left England in 1801, returning in October 1805 with some 4,000 species of plants, notes and drawings.

At this time, the Linnean Society bought the lease of a house at 9 Gerrard Street as its headquarters, and created the threefold post of 'Clerk, Librarian and Housekeeper' at a salary of £100 a year, with compulsory residence in free quarters in the house. On 17 December 1805, Brown was elected to the post, which he held until his resignation in 1822. It has been said of him that he was the most distinguished paid servant ever to hold office in the Linnean Society. On giving up the salaried appointment, he was elected a Fellow, and he was President from 1849 until his resignation at the age of eighty in 1853.

In 1810, Dryander died and Brown succeeded him as curator and librarian to Sir Joseph Banks at 32 Soho Square, while continuing to hold his triple post with the Linnean Society. Banks died in June 1820 and Brown was one of the main beneficiaries of his will, which gave him the use of the house, with the herbarium and library, for life, after which it was to be transferred to the British Museum. In fact, it was transferred by Brown himself.

When new buildings were constructed for the British Museum, it was decided to form a separate department of botany. In 1827, Brown was appointed keeper, with the rank of under-librarian, and he then proceeded to transfer the Banksian Herbarium to the new rooms. With one assistant, J. J. Bennett, Brown had the responsibility of organizing the department and, more particularly, of defending it against the ignorance of the trustees. During the 1830s, the attempt was made to economize by placing the collections under other officers and by reducing the rank of the keepership. Brown vigorously maintained the importance of the botany collections in evidence to the Royal Commission on the British Museum of 1847. His international reputation as a scientist weighed heavily with the com-

missioners who, in effect, censured the trustees of the British Museum. The then small botany department was allowed its autonomy and the chance to grow. The point was also made that the Museum was not just for public exhibition, but was to be a research centre.

Brown's scientific achievements and influence were considerable. His work falls into three groups: geographico-botanical, structural and physiological, and systematic. His period of greatest productivity was under Banks, from 1806 to 1820. As Charles Darwin* said of him: 'His knowledge was extraordinarily great, and much died with him, owing to his excessive fear of making a mistake.'

One of his earliest publications, *Prodromus Florae Novae Hollandiae* (1810), established Brown's reputation with botanists everywhere, but particularly in Germany. At that time, the two main systems of plant classification were those of Linnaeus and Jussieu, neither satisfactory, especially with the variety and complexities of the Australian flora. Brown modified and extended the system of Jussieu, based on observations of unusual exactness.

In 1831, Brown published a pamphlet on *Observations on the Organs and Modes of Fecundation in Orchideae and Asclepiadeae*, describing microscopical studies concerning the sexuality of plants. He also identified and named the 'nucleus of the cell as perhaps it might be termed', thus proposing the concept of the nucleated cell as the building block in plants, and in a sense originating the science of cytology.

Brown's name is widely known today outside the botanical field for his microscopical observations on fine particles suspended in water that show small random movements; since 1871, this effect has been called 'Brownian motion'. During the summer of 1827, Brown was looking into the mode of action of pollen in the process of impregnation. For these observations, he used *Clarkia pulchella*, the pollen grains of which, before bursting, contain granules of unusually large size (about 5 micrometres) and oblong in shape. Observing these particles immersed in water with a simple microscope capable of magnifying 300 times, Brown saw that they were in motion. He tried many other pollens, bruised plant material, old dried plants, fossils, coal, minerals (even part of the Sphinx), and eventually glass and inorganic substances, in fact any powder fine enough to remain in suspension. He believed that he had seen a fundamental molecule, after the proposals of Buffon, but as he extended the observations, he began to realize that the effect was so widespread that it was impossible to offer a hypothesis of the cause of the minute motions. Brown published his findings in a privately printed pamphlet in 1828, with the title *A Brief Account of Microscopical Observations ... on the Particles Contained in the Pollen of Plants; and on the General Existence of Active Molecules in Organic and Inorganic Bodies*. A complete explanation came with the kinetic theory of gases and liquids. This eventually established that the particles move through bombardment by the molecules of the liquid. By studying the kinetics of the microscopic particles, the size of the actual molecules in the liquid can be deduced, as well as the number in a given volume. This was proposed in 1905 by Einstein, related to Brownian particles by Smoluchowski in 1906, and proved experimentally in 1909 by Perrin. Consequently, the evidence from Brownian motion led to an actual proof of the existence of atoms and to the development of atomic theory. Einstein's calculations involved statistical mechanics in order to handle the 'random walk' motions of the particles and, using the same mathematics and the proposition that light be considered a collection of independent particles of energy, he devised quantum mechanics to explain black-body radiation.

Brown died on 10 June 1858 in the house left to him by Banks. He never married and had no close relatives. He was a Fellow and Copley Medallist of the Royal Society, Hon. DCL of Oxford University, and the recipient of honours from many European scientific academies.

G. L'E. Turner

Prodromus Florae Novae Hollandiae was reprinted in facsimile in the series *Historiae Naturalis Classica* (no. 5, 1960). *The Miscellaneous Botanical Works of Robert Brown*, ed. J. J. Bennett, 2 vols (The Ray Society, 1866–7). See: J. B. Farmer, 'Robert Brown, 1773–1858', in *Makers of British Botany*, 108–25, ed. F. W. Oliver (1913); J. Ramsbottom, 'Robert Brown, botanicorum facile princeps', in *Proceedings of the Linnean Society*, vol. 144 (1932).

59
BROWNING, Elizabeth Barrett 1806–61

British poet

Few will nowadays quarrel with the judgment pronounced on Elizabeth Barrett Browning by an age in which high-mindedness has lost so much of its erstwhile importance. The number of those who know or care about 'The Rhyme of the Duchess May', 'The Romaunt of the Page', or 'Lady Geraldine's Courtship' dwindles yearly (it may soon reach single figures) and there is not much indication that a revival of interest is either due or overdue. To those with any notion of the outlines of English literature Mrs Browning is likely to remain enshrined as the wife of a great if currently unfashionable Victorian poet, a partner in a sensational love affair, and a woman whose likeness by Gordigiani in the National Portrait Gallery makes her uncannily resemble her spaniel Flush, of whom Virginia Woolf was later to write so affectionately.

If this seems a little unfair the fault is in part her own. A sense of humour cannot be denied her: for that we have only to look at her recently published girlhood diaries or to note the testimonies of her many friends. But neither her upbringing nor her adult life was conducive to a balanced awareness either of her role as a writer or of the inevitably limited range of her poetic gifts. Though in no sense conceited, she appears to have seen herself as a woman with a mission, and that frequently dire quality of high seriousness which clogs Victorian literature led her towards an interest in politics which not only succeeded in killing the freshness of her own poetry but also contributed to her early death.

Her father, Edward Moulton Barrett, who, thanks to the enormous success of Rudolf Besier's 1930s stage and screen hit *The Barretts of Wimpole Street*, has had a far worse press than he in fact deserves, was responsible for encouraging her early efforts as a poet. A wealthy West India merchant setting up as a country landowner, he moved, with his family, from Burn Hall, Durham, where Elizabeth ('Ba' to her adoring relatives) was born, to the exotic pseudo-Indian mansion at Hope End, near Great Malvern, where she spent a memorably happy girlhood. Something of a prodigy, she learned enough Greek to read Homer at the age of eight, and three years later produced a four-book epic on the battle of Marathon, which her father at once had published.

Happiness in a secure, loving and cultivated family atmosphere was cut short by her mother's death and Elizabeth's disastrous riding accident which, at fifteen, brought fears that she might never walk again. For at least another decade she became the archetypal sofa-bound cripple of Victorian literary imagination, tended by the other Barretts in an appropriately possessive manner. A move to London to be nearer the doctors naturally brought her into direct contact with the world of writers and publishers, and her spontaneous charm and liveliness soon created a circle of loyal friends. Among these were several women who, like herself, had successfully invaded traditionally masculine preserves of literature and education, such as Mary Russell Mitford and Anna Jameson. The unfortunate painter Benjamin Robert Haydon* showed her a posthumous respect by naming her as an executor in documents left at his suicide. A young poet Robert Browning* was induced to correspond with her through the intervention of her cousin John Kenyon.

It was some time before the pair actually met, but the intensity of their correspondence, which forms one of the most appealing series of Victorian letters, had already created an atmosphere encouraging to the affair between the 40 year-old Elizabeth and the 36 year-old Browning. The subterfuges resorted to by both, the gradual recovery undergone by Elizabeth herself, the secret marriage at Marylebone parish church, the flight to Italy with the faithful maid Wilson and the indispensable Flush, and the ludicrously out-raged reaction of the Barretts are elements of literary folklore. The success of the marriage was crowned by the birth of a son, 'Pen', in 1849.

A love of Italy was as much hers as her husband's, and she came increasingly to involve herself in the central issues of the Risorgimento, especially as it affec-ted the Grand Duchy of Tuscany, where the Brownings now lived at Florence. Though her family had broken off any substantial contact with her, she maintained strong links with England, acquiring the friendship of such figures as George Eliot*, Ruskin*, Thackeray* and Tennyson*, and being seriously proposed as Poet Laureate on Wordsworth's* death in 1850. Her com-mitment was nevertheless to the forging of Italian na-tionhood, and her emotional preoccupation with political events reached a crisis during the Franco-Aus-trian conflict of 1858, and the resultant collapse of Bourbon Naples and the duchies. Her belief in the greatness of Napoleon III, not shared by her husband, was severely shaken by his compromise treaty with Austria, and her death in 1861 is supposed to have been hastened by hearing the news of the final relapse of Camillo Cavour.

Much of her later poetry is accordingly coloured by the Risorgimento, though the crude vigour of certain pieces in *Poems Before Congress* (1860) and *Last Poems* (1862) triumphs over their need for historical footnotes. The simplicity and immediacy carried in the opening lines of *Casa Guidi Windows* (1851) create what is surely one of the most attractive beginnings to any Victorian poem of comparable length, but such promise is not followed up by the turgid political debate which ensues. Of her earlier work, 'The Cry of the Children' justifies contemporary admiration for it as an effective plea for social justice in the age of Hood and Dickens*, and 'Sonnets from the Portuguese' (in *Poems*, 1850 – Por-tuguese as spoken from a Marylebone sofa) place her with Louise Labe and Gaspara Stampa as one of the great women love poets, as well as being immeasurably the best sonnets written in the nineteenth century. Rhyme, which so often betrayed her into moments of potent bathos, serves her in this case to perfection.

Her finest work, as her admirers at once perceived, was the long verse novel *Aurora Leigh* (1856), a unique achievement in form and content, and profoundly in-fluential on later Victorian poetry and fiction both in England and in America. Echoes of it can be found in the later works of Tennyson, in the novels of George Eliot and in the poetry of Emily Dickinson*, who was warm in her praise of Mrs Browning. Partially auto-biographical, it deals, in a way which strikingly an-ticipates the more emphatically feminist impulses of the late nineteenth and early twentieth century, with the role of an independent, imaginative and cultivated woman in a society shaped by men.

Crucial as are the ideas embodied in *Aurora Leigh* to an understanding of social and intellectual currents in mid-Victorian life, its attraction as poetry lies in its author's ability to evoke a keen sense of place. We enjoy and remember moments such as the continental train journey (one of the first such to be portrayed in European poetry) or the description of a Florentine holiday, rather than the severe analysis of moral and ethical questions. The most discreet and fitting epitaph on Mrs Browning was provided by the Italian poet Niccolo Tommaseo, who said that she 'united within a woman's heart the wisdom of a sage and the spirit of a poet, and made from her verse a golden link between Italy and England'. She was not a great crafts-man, and her passions tended to cloud her aesthetic judgment, but by the consistent practice of her art she brought a much-needed dignity to the role of woman as poet in an age when women were starting to confront undreamt-of freedoms and responsibilities.

Jonathan Keates

See: Dorothy Hewlett, *Elizabeth Barrett Browning: A Life* (1952); Alethea Hayter, *Mrs Browning: A Poet's Work and Its Setting* (1962).

60

BROWNING, Robert 1812–89

British poet

It has been Browning's fate that he fell a prey in his later years to the sort of snobbish adulation which often attends obscurity of expression. After early compara-tive neglect, the poet's reputation fell into the hands of readers and critics who saw in him a seer and moral teacher with a tough but reassuringly optimistic mes-sage; a thinker who, despite – perhaps even because of – his verbal difficulty, could provide for the initiated a strenuous assurance that God was in his Heaven, that doubt could be conquered by persistent faith and that an intellectually consistent poetic argument could be adduced in defence of anti-intellectualism. Brown-ing's poetry seemed bracing, free of the morbidity of much late-Victorian art, gratifyingly taxing in its expression, but confident and life-enhancing. The tone of much Browning criticism up to the First World War tended to follow such lines, and even if George San-tayana and others reacted strongly against this fashion, the very course their criticism took tended still to attack him on his qualifications as a thinker and teacher, rather than on his artistic qualities.

Since then poets of greater obscurity have carried messages more in keeping with this present age and Browning has been largely ignored, apart from a hand-ful of well-known school anthology pieces. Even here his moral heartiness has tended to make him a poet more popular with teachers than pupils. Not having gone so deeply through the purgatorial period of critical antagonism meted out to such contemporaries of his as Tennyson*, Browning has not benefited from rediscovery and reassessment. He lacks the dark pessimism of Tennyson, the cultured melancholy of Arnold* or the metaphysical anguish of Hopkins*. He seems altogether too normal, too sane, and perhaps too verbose, while the verbal complexities that tantalized his age have become merely irritating in a century accustomed to the conundrums of Pound, Eliot, Yeats, Wallace Stevens, Empson and their followers. An enormous proportion of his verse is dismissed – unread – as unreadable. This includes all his plays, most of his poems before 1843 and virtually everything after 1869. Even *The Ring and the Book* (1868–9), considered his masterpiece, is almost certainly far more often praised than read. Not that Browning himself is guiltless in this matter: *Sordello* (1840), despite its fine passages, remains one of the most obscure poems ever written and seems to most readers a puzzle whose solution ill repays the effort, while the plays are of interest merely to students of Victorian drama, and only not inferior to most examples of that luckless genre, while *The Ring and the Book*, despite its acknowledged mastery, is terrifyingly long. The late poetry though is another matter altogether and hardly deserves the almost total neglect into which it has fallen. Not that Browning has lacked sympathetic critics and biographers: they have so far failed to carry the public with them.

Yet Browning's poetry has been extremely influential in the twentieth century: more so than has sometimes been acknowledged by his debtors. Pound's admiration for Browning is well-known and accounts for some of the worst as well as some of the best features of his poetry, but T. S. Eliot's *Journey of the Magi* and *Prufrock* and much besides are inconceivable without Browning's example; and the dramatic monologue has had a significant place in the work of many English and American poets of recent years, while in 'St Martin's Summer' and other poems in his later volumes there is more than a suggestion of Hardy*.

Browning was born on 7 May 1812 in Camberwell, then a village. His father was a clerk in the Bank of England and his mother was from Dundee, the daughter of a Scottish mother and a German father. She had a keen interest in natural history and music, which her son was to share, and was a deeply religious Nonconformist – an influence which was to prove strong but ambiguous. Between mother and son there was an exceptionally close bond. He remained all his life a man who needed the society and support of women, and to his mother he was entirely devoted. His father was an unworldly erratically scholarly man: 'My father was a scholar and knew Greek,' wrote Browning in 'Development', one of his last poems. From this poem we catch a glimpse of Browning senior's method of teaching, for it was from him rather than from his formal education that Robert learnt most, though he went to school after a fashion and, for a very brief spell, to London University. He shared his father's delight in the odd, the out-of-the-way, and from him too came his love of painting. His father's educational methods, though strangely modern and calculated to interest and stimulate a sensitive and inquiring mind, were probably not very systematic – Browning, like Yeats, had an eccentric area of knowledge – and Santayana was later to pour scorn on, and read a lot into, this unconventional education. Yet the strange by-ways of knowledge, picked up partly from his father, partly from his browsings in his father's library, partly from what he called his 'university' of Italy, give the characteristically wide range of his subject-matter. From his exceptionally sheltered childhood Browning took away a love of the unusual, a need to be mothered and an easily wounded sensibility.

Though probably too much has been made of Browning's distress over the reception of his first published poem, 'Pauline' (1833), a Shelley*-like effusion, uncharacteristic of his later work, he remained conscious of his own fear of self-revelation. He writes to Elizabeth Barrett (see E. B. Browning*), 'You speak out, *you*, – I only make men and women speak – give you truth broken into prismatic hues, and fear the pure white light, even if it is in me.' Yet the paradox of Browning is that he is at his most personal when appearing most objective. He is best known for his dramatic monologues. He did not invent the form, but he and Tennyson independently and almost simultaneously brought it to perfection in their different ways. Browning perhaps developed it more consistently, and it represents some of his finest work. Browning's art in the dramatic monologues has been compared to that of the actor assuming a role, but it is surely more than this. The characters are created from within, and poet and reader and character participate in the same ritual. The monologue is not an argument presented to the reader, but an act in which the reader is made to share. In so far as the individual poem is successful it involves a fusion of the reader's personality with that of the protagonist; we do not judge Andrea del Sarto or Count Guido, we collaborate with them. The drama of the monologue is a quarrel, not between different characters on the stage, but between the reader's desire for freedom and sense of moral order, or what Robert Langbaum (see below) refers to as 'sympathy versus judgment'. Hence Browning's fondness for disreputable characters and extreme dramatic situations. The danger of the method, and one that Browning does not always escape, is wordiness. It is this ability to make the reader identify with characters whom he cannot necessarily admire that reaches its highest point in *The Ring and the Book*. This 'theme and variations' forces one to modify one's response to a central event in such a way that the crude story is made to reveal the greatest range of interpretation – one's instinctive responses are repeatedly shaken.

Two fine and unaccountably neglected poems of his late 'unreadable' period – 'Red Cotton Night-Cap Country' and 'The Inn Album' – are again evidence of his ability to handle extreme and apparently unsuitable material with astonishing virtuosity.

It may seem odd that a writer so well-versed in drama of character, so expert at variations of speech, should have made such heavy weather of writing for the stage. Perhaps one is here misled by the term 'dramatic monologue'. The monologue is dramatic in so far as it shows conflict emerging in speech; but drama requires visual action, and interplay between characters. Browning's plays remain wordy and introspective, a series of self-explanatory speeches rather than an interplay of character, speech and action. Perhaps the monologues should be called 'psychological monologues': the drama is entirely interior and entirely self-sufficient. The poet assumes the personality of the speaker and this allows both anonymity and universality.

But it is not only the dramatic monologues that are in this sense 'dramatic': Browning's love poetry, another aspect of verse at which he is a master, is oblique too. Not usually in any conventional sense lyrical, the poems have a deep but muted sensuality and a sense of the physical, and are often concerned with a moment of union between the sexes, all too fleeting and rare: the 'good minute' is a moment of mutual illumination, endlessly sought for and as real, though the poetic means are different, as such moments in Donne's poetry. Yet again the poet avoids too direct a personal reference: the poem keeps its distance: it is 'Any Wife to any Husband' or 'One Way of Love' and 'Another Way of Love'.

One of the facts that everybody knows about Browning is his elopement in 1846 with the poet Elizabeth Barrett and their life together in Italy until her death in 1861. Italy, and particularly Renaissance Italy, gave to Browning a sense of freedom and colour and an escape from Victorian England. His poetry is a poetry of extremes, that plunges passionately into violent action. Italy provided the electric charge that his work needed:

> Open my heart and you will see
> Graved inside of it, 'Italy'.

Elizabeth and Italy were the inspiration of some of his happiest and some of his intensest poetry. Italy stimulated too his love of art. No poet writes better about the other arts, particularly music, than Browning.

Browning's mind was quick rather than profound and his philosophy is as superficial and commonplace as the 'philosophy' of most of us. His work is weakest when most concerned with abstractions, and his attempts at systematic teaching have worn badly. His insistence on the efficacy of struggle for its own sake – the 'I was ever a fighter' strain in his work – and his confessional poems such as 'Easter Day' have lost much of their appeal, but the idea of Browning as a mindless optimist is contradicted by much of his poetry: not only such poems as 'Caliban upon Setebos' and 'Childe Roland', but much of his love poetry is aware of the tragic and gloomy side of life and the frailty of relationships.

He wrote too much, too carelessly and too easily, but his own satiric comment, 'That poet's a Browning: he neglects the form', is scarcely accurate. There are few poets with a more adventurous sense of form: indeed the form of the poems is sometimes their most ingenious characteristic. Nor is he deficient in musicality: the falling cadences of 'A Toccata of Galuppi's' and the rhythmic control of such poems as 'The Last Ride Together' would give that the lie. It is a lack of pruning, an over-emphasis and long-windedness that make even such poems as 'Fifine at the Fair' tedious despite their ingenuity:

> Volubility
> With him, keeps on the increase

as he says of one of his characters.

All the same, with his colloquialisms, his Chaucerian skill as a story-teller, his liberation of poetic speech from the over-sophistication and conscious polish of much Victorian verse, his obsession with the brutal and the prosaic, his acceptance of women as partners rather than idealized mistresses, he would seem to speak very much to us today. It is true that there is a sort of brashness in his work that can repel the more fastidious: he writes too much at the top of his voice.

A young woman meeting him for the first time wrote:

> He talks everybody down with his dreadful voice, and always places his person in such disagreeable proximity to yours and puffs and blows and spits in your face. I tried to think of 'Abt Vogler' but it was no use – he couldn't ever have written it.

And there's something of that too.

Joseph Bain

See: G. K. Chesterton, *Robert Browning* (1903); B. Miller, *Robert Browning. A Portrait* (1952); W. C. DeVane, *A Browning Handbook* (1955); R. Langbaum, *The Poetry of Experience: The Dramatic Monologue in Modern Literary Tradition* (1957); B. Litzinger and D. Smalley, *Browning: The Critical Heritage* (1970); I. Jack, *Browning's Major Poetry* (1973); N. Irvine and P. Honan, *The Book, The Ring and The Poet: A Biography of Robert Browning* (1974); C. de L. Ryals, *Browning's Later Poetry – 1871–1889* (1975).

61

BRUCKNER, Anton 1824–96

Austrian composer

Bruckner's uniqueness among major composers could be defined in several ways. No one of comparable stature left so few important works; an accomplished organist in his eleventh year, he continued his technical studies until he was thirty-seven; happy to give before large audiences organ recitals consisting mostly of improvisations, in society Bruckner was totally without self-confidence. Several years after becoming principal organist at the monastery of St Florian he doubted his musical gifts to the extent of studying Latin with a view to becoming a schoolmaster. Having composed his mature symphonies he humbly permitted well-meaning conductors to make cuts during rehearsal. To the end of his days this profoundly inspired artist and consummate craftsman remained obedient to priests and respectful to the upper classes.

Anton Bruckner was born at the village of Ansfelden in Upper Austria in 1824, the descendant of a line of peasants and artisans traceable as far back as the fourteenth century. His father and grandfather were both teachers at the village school. The musically gifted father played for dancing to augment his meagre salary and became the prey of convivial drinking; in 1836 his health broke down so completely that the boy Anton had to return home from Linz where he had been sent to improve his education. After his father's death a year later Anton entered the choir at St Florian, the great Benedictine House that was to be the centre of his personal life. Here he studied organ and violin and, during a year at Linz before qualifying as school assistant, heard for the first time music by Beethoven*. With dedicated patience he copied out the whole of Bach's *Kunst der Fuge*. In 1841 Bruckner became assistant in a village school, living the life of the rural poor; besides teaching his duties included work in the fields with the labourers. He began to compose church music and, later, choruses for men's voices. In 1845 a post as regular school assistant brought the security of ten years at St Florian. Even after composing a Requiem and being confirmed in his position as first organist he continued to doubt his vocation and in 1854 applied for an administrative vacancy in the monastic chancellery. Failures in love (to the end of his life Bruckner was susceptible to the charms of too-young girls) and self-doubt drove him to the brink of collapse, though he soon recovered sufficiently to compose his first significant work, the Mass in B flat minor, performed in 1854. Almost against his will he accepted the post of organist at Linz cathedral, fearful at the thought of having to emerge from the seclusion of his beloved St Florian.

The time at Linz began with a period of comparative happiness; Bruckner conducted choral concerts, was well received in local society and, with almost fanatical diligence ('I worked seven hours daily for Sechter') perfected his technique, though in his compositions he remained cautiously derivative, modelling his style largely on Schubert* or Mendelssohn*. Knowledge of the great masters of instrumental music came from studies with Otto Kitzler, ten years Bruckner's junior. Other Linz friends made him aware of Wagner* and in 1865 he was present at the first performance of *Tristan* in Munich, having heard *Tannhäuser* three years earlier. In 1864 he completed the D minor Mass, the work which showed for the first time more than hints of future greatness. The earliest symphonies, no. 0 *(Die Nullte)* and no. 1, belong to this period; with the success of the D minor Mass, the encouragement of Wagner and a passing acquaintance with Berlioz*, Liszt* and Anton Rubinstein, anyone but Bruckner would surely have begun to feel secure in the larger world of music.

On the contrary, having completed the two symphonies and a second Mass (a commission from the Bishop of Linz) he suffered a total collapse from which he recovered completely to apply for a lectureship at Vienna University. Failure here was mitigated by an appointment at the Vienna Conservatorium, to succeed his own mentor, Simon Sechter, but the prospect of moving from the security of Linz precipitated another crisis of indecision. At Linz Bruckner was well paid and, like any worthy servant of the establishment, could look forward to the security of a pension. No disrespect for a visionary artist is intended by the observation that these intense disturbances of mind may have sprung as much from a peasant-like fear of penury as from spiritual malaise. Certainly the acceptance of the Vienna post was made less painful by an increase in the salary offered and a promise that his position at Linz would be held in suspension should he wish to return.

At first all went well in Vienna: Bruckner proved an excellent teacher and in 1872 the third of his Masses, performed in the Augustinerkirche, was praised by Hanslick, later to be a relentless opponent. Symphonies were another matter. Dessoff, conductor of the Philharmonic concerts, rejected no. 1 in 1869 and no. 2 three years later. It was Dessoff who, beginning to rehearse no. 0, had asked its unfortunate composer to tell him where the first subject began. ('And where are you going to put your brown tree?') Neither of the rejected symphonies betrayed any lack of invention or of technical skill, but the abundance of motifs and the absence, even thus early in Bruckner's maturing style, of the classical impetus preserved by Brahms*, must have seemed evidence of mere incapacity. No. 3, with its majestic trumpet theme that so impressed Wagner (in its first version the work contained quotations from the *Ring*), was still less acceptable. The doubtless inadequate performance under Bruckner himself in 1877 was a disastrous failure, promoting only the self-distrust that led to the usually regrettable revisions of many works. Isolation and incomprehension were in part the consequence of this naive artist's unforeseen involvement in the musical politics for which he could not have been worse suited. In their feud with the classicists the Wagner party needed a symphonist to set against Brahms, while Hanslick (the model for Beckmesser), though far from being a fool and more appreciative of Wagner's genius than has been pretended, found in Bruckner the unresisting victim of his brilliant and obtuse polemics. (Brahms refrained from attacking a colleague, but in private expressed his doubts as to Bruckner's sense of movement by references to 'symphonic boa-constrictors'.) If Brahm's resolution of the problem facing the composer of symphonies in the later nineteenth century still seems more convincing than Bruckner's this is because he was able to limit its scope by adhering to the harmonic rhythms of the classical masters and thus retaining the guidelines of sonata form – the distinction between exposition and development, the structural emphasis on the beginning of the recapitulation and its transition to coda. The nature of Bruckner's genius left him no choice but to embody in musical architecture the range, scope and time-scale of Wagner's mature dramas; only a profoundly thoughtful artist could have sustained the dual burden of defining and then creating a new kind of symphony containing valid equivalents for no longer available procedures.

The Fourth Symphony (composed 1874, revised 1878, performed 1881) was, in its first movement at least, the evident product of a major composer. As yet the enlargment of the classical time-scale does not preclude the observance of traditional structures, but in the symphonies that followed processes of transition became increasingly continuous until, in no. 7, the letter of sonata form had virtually disappeared, leaving its spirit all the more enhanced in the first of Bruckner's works to win acceptance. Neither the Fifth nor the Sixth was heard by the composer but the first performance of no. 7, at Leipzig, not Vienna, was immensely successful, as was the second, at Munich. Bruckner rightly feared the worldy Viennese for when they heard the work, under Richter, in March 1886, the insufferable Hanslick described the symphony, full of exalted vision and wonderful tone-colours (original, not taken from Wagner), as '*unnatürlich, aufgeblasen, krankhaft und verderblich*' ('forced, inflated, morbid and pernicious'). However, several eminent conductors were now favourable, notably Hermann Levi (Wagner's tolerated Jew) for whom Bruckner had profound regard. No. 8, even more monumental than no. 7 – it had taken three

years to write – was sent to Levi in 1887 for inclusion in his winter season, but having seen the score he rejected it as incomprehensible. Hard-won confidence was destroyed and the symphony was submitted to drastic revision, to be performed in 1892, by Richter, not Levi. No omen deterred Bruckner from planning his ninth symphony in D minor but it was never finished. Even with the fragmentary last movement it is clearly the most daringly original of the series, harsh and tormented as though all that remained of the New Testament for this devout artist was Revelation, in its most forbidding aspect. At the last concert he attended, nearly a year before his death in October 1896, Bruckner heard his own *Te Deum*.

No other great composer's fame can have rested on so few works. Of the symphonies, the first three are imperfect, the last unfinished. Three Masses, some motets, the *Te Deum*, of chamber music one Quintet.

Such is the sum of a master who, so far from being a Romantic, was perhaps the last representative in the nineteenth century of the Great Tradition, reaching back to the Middle Ages, of a music that drew life from its own nature and substance, not from the private emotions and fantasies of those who composed it.

Basil Lam

Robert Simpson, *The Essence of Bruckner* (1967); Philip Barford, *Bruckner Symphonies* (1968): Hans Redlich, *Bruckner and Mahler* (1955 rev. 1963); Erwin Doernberg, *The Life and Symphonies of Anton Bruckner* (1960).

62

BRUNEL, Isambard Kingdom 1806–59

British engineer

Of all the great engineers of the first age of the machine, Isambard Kingdom Brunel was undoubtedly the most original, and arguably the greatest. He is remembered equally for his failures as for his successes, for they both share the same qualities of grandeur, of being the produce of creative genius working always to advance the art of engineering.

His father was the celebrated French émigré, Marc Isambard Brunel. Isambard Kingdom was born in Portsea, near Portsmouth, on 9 April 1806, during the time that his father was finishing the revolutionary block-making machinery in the naval dockyard. His education was carefully overseen by his father, who encouraged him to draw as a child, and later sent him to Paris to learn mathematics and to undergo an apprenticeship with Louis Breguet, the maker of chronometers and scientific instruments. On his return to England in 1822, he began to work with his father, and also spent time working with the consummate craftsman engineer and associate of his father's, Henry Maudsley. Thus his early experience was with two of the finest exponents of the new machine technology. Consequently, Isambard Kingdom stands apart from Samuel Smiles's* ideal of self-help, of the ultimately shallow and philistine tradition of the self-taught, self-made engineer/entrepreneur.

His father began work in 1824 on the second great project of his career, the Rotherhithe Tunnel beneath the Thames in London. The undertaking was prolonged, difficult and dangerous. In 1828 there was a major flood in the tunnel, in which Isambard, by then engineer in charge, was seriously injured. His description of the accident, written shortly afterwards, contains a revealing item: 'When standing there the effect was grand – the roar of the rushing water in a confined passage, and its great velocity rushing past the opening was grand, very grand.' This appreciation of such proximity of the dark power of nature was strangely in tune with the spirit of the art of the time, with the poetry of Blake and the paintings of John Martin*. It reveals a sensibility that was to inform much of his finest work.

At the end of a long convalescence, Isambard moved to Bristol, a city whose setting, with the fantastic gorge of the Avon, must have appealed to him. He entered and finally won the competition for the design of a bridge to span the gorge. Because of problems of finance, his design was to remain unbuilt until after his death. Finally it was to be completed by a consortium of those who had been both associates and opponents of his during his lifetime. It stands today with its high suspended single span, a graceful soaring memorial, this bridge which was, in his own words, 'my first child, my darling'. After several years of frustration, he was invited, in 1833, by a group of Bristol merchants, concerned for the future of the city as a port, to survey a possible route for a railway from the city to London. He promised to discover 'not the cheapest, but the best route'. He undertook the survey on horseback. From this beginning, the Great Western Railway was formed, and Brunel was appointed engineer.

Thus began a life of continuous hectic endeavour which was to prove finally fatally exhausting, a life paralleled by many of his contemporaries in this most explosive of ages.

Isambard's essential nature as an engineer was always to innovate, always to find a fitting originality for each new problem, eschewing established solutions, always working from what he took to be basic principles. Thus the railway as it unfolded became a line of constant invention across southern England. He determined from the outset to make what he called 'the finest work in England' perfect in execution. Rejecting all precedents, he decided that the line should consist of a broad gauge of 7 feet to facilitate speed and comfort. This was to cause considerable controversy as there already existed an established gauge of 4 feet 8½ inches pioneered by George Stephenson*, and widely adopted. That this gauge had pragmatic origins in the coal mines of the north of England would have been sufficient to condemn it in Brunel's eyes. His indifference to the foreseeable problems of a mixture of gauges on a national scale is an indication of his vision of the Great Western Railway as a singular work, a demonstration of excellence. Consistent with this, he insisted on having total responsibility for all aspects of the work, and, with the exception of the building surrounding his great roof at Paddington Station, his finger was on every detail.

He moved his office to London which allowed him to exercise his love of society. Through a common interest in music he became friends with the Horsley family of Kensington, and in 1836 he married Mary, one of the daughters.

Throughout his life, until his final great work, he attracted to him devoted colleagues of almost equal brilliance to his own. Such a man was David Gooch, the designer of a series of beautifully proportioned powerful engines for the Great Western Railway. With these locomotives the railway was able to demonstrate journeys at unprecedented speeds, regularly averaging over 50 mph.

The first section from Paddington to Taplow was opened on 31 May 1838. In 1840 Queen Victoria* travelled by special train from Windsor to London, with Gooch and Brunel on the footplate. The final joining of the two lines emerging from Bristol and from London required the driving of what was then the longest tunnel in the world, through solid stone at Box Hill, near Bath. On the last day of June 1841, a garlanded train travelled the completed route in four hours.

By 1844, the extended broad-gauge line was running express trains from London to Exeter. The excellence of Brunel's conception was proven, but it was to be finally a Pyrrhic victory. Throughout England more cautious railway engineers had adopted the narrow gauge, and finally the inescapable fact emerged that in order to overcome the inconvenience of changing between the two gauges, it was easier and cheaper to narrow a line rather than broaden it. The Great Western Railway however, rather heroically, maintained the broad gauge until 1892.

West of Exeter, on the line to Plymouth, Brunel undertook what must be considered his strangest and certainly least successful work. Concerned partly by the steep inclines involved in the route between Exeter and Newton Abbott, he decided to construct an atmospheric railway. The driving mechanism he constructed was a buried tube between the lines, which was maintained as a partial vaccum by pumping stations built at intervals. Within the tube, a piston was drawn along by the unequal air pressures. This was connected through a continuous slot in the top of the tube to the carriages on the rails above. The success depended upon the linear valve remaining air tight while allowing the repeated passage of trains. This proved impossible to achieve for any length of time. While it worked it fulfilled its author's specification 'moving trains at up to 54 m.p.h. and up to 100 tons in weight at slower speeds', but its final total failure was unavoidable. It proved to be the most costly failure in the history of civil engineering. Within this defeat however, as his biographer L. T. C, Rolf has pointed out, can be detected a clear indication of his finest qualities.

He was building through a landscape of great beauty. From his efforts can be read an intention of fitting his own work into the greater work of nature. The trains would be moved by a silent force; the pumping stations were carefully considered and sited. It is as if some deeper vision urged on his vaunting inventiveness, a vision that once developed would have stood as a moral principle of harmony between nature and the machine, a principle capable perhaps of transforming the dark horror of the early industrial landscape.

It is some measure of his esteem that despite the disaster he was retained as engineer for driving the railway further westward. It is some measure, too, of his resilience that in the process he built a series of brilliant stone and wood viaducts and finally, carrying the line across the broad Tamar river at Saltash in 1849, began his last and greatest bridge. With one of the two great spans in place by 1857 he was as ever ready to move on, leaving it to be completed by his associates, who finished it in the year of his death.

As early as 1835 he had suggested to the amazed directors of the Great Western Railway that the western terminus should be New York, rather than Bristol. While intensely involved with the railways, he designed and had built by the Great Western Steamship Company in 1836 the first of his three great ships, the *Great Western*. The purpose of the ship for its designer was to prove the viability of crossings under continuous steam power. He was the first to realize the theoretical relationship between performance and form and the gain by building large ships. His ships were therefore to be big and fast, as were the locomotives that he and Gooch designed for the Great Western Railway. Each of the three ships at its launching was the largest ever built. The first two were intended for the Atlantic crossing, the third for the journey to Australia. All three, the *Great Western*, the *Great Britain* and the *Great Eastern*, were plagued by bad luck. The first two were built in Bristol and the third, the *Great Eastern*, was built at Millwall on the Thames, close to his father's tunnel, the site of his first serious work and the place where the river had nearly taken his life. The misfortunes that danced attendance around the building, launching and maiden voyage of his last gigantic ship were to exhaust him, break his spirit and kill him. Most of the

problems stemmed from Isambard's choice of contractor, who turned out to be very different from Brunel's devoted associates on previous work. Also the undertaking became a public event, prone to ridicule or praise through the newly powerful popular press. A new age had arrived, populist and disrespectful, quite out of sympathy with the intensity and integrity of his brilliance.

He collapsed aboard the great ship three days before its first sailing and died on 15 September 1859. The last report he had, hours before his death, of the *Great Eastern* out in the English Channel on her maiden voyage was that there had been an explosion on board, with several fatalities.

From the life and work of Isambard Kingdom Brunel can be discerned an image of an industrialized society free from the compulsion of mass production, producing through the concerted efforts of the people, orchestrated by genius, fine works. His finest remaining memorials, the bridge at Saltash and the route of the Great Western Railway, stand therefore also as mitigating to the first half of the nineteenth century, to the great energy of the working people of the dark enflamed first Machine Age.

Frederick Scott

See: L. T. C. Rolf, *Isambard Kingdom Brunel* (1957); L. T. C. Rolf, *Victorian Engineering* (1970).

63
BRYANT, William Cullen 1794–1878

US poet and editor

The generous, admiring view of Bryant given by Walt Whitman* in 'My Tribute To Four Poets' (1885) – 'bard of the river and wood, ever conveying a sense of the open air . . . with here and there through all, poems or passages of poems, touching the highest universal truths' – has not been the one to prevail. James Russell Lowell* probably came closer to the modern estimate of Bryant in 'A Fable For Critics' (1848) when, in also acknowledging 'a true soul for field, river and wood', he judged him cold, too formal and late eighteenth-century in manner, nowhere the equal of Wordsworth* (one of Bryant's own professed models) as a poet of nature. Yet however minor Bryant is now thought he remains, with Irving* and Cooper*, a founding early nineteenth-century voice of American literature and, as the author of 'Thanatopsis' and 'To A Waterfowl', a pastoral and contemplative poet of distinction. He was also, for the better part of a lifetime, a respected, influential force for liberalism, mainly as editor of the widely read *New York Evening Post*. The political dimensions of Bryant's editorial work are engagingly hinted at in *Burr* (1973), Gore Vidal's recent fiction of fact about the early Republic.

Born of impeccable Massachusetts Puritan stock, Bryant had the benefits of an affluent, cultured home, and the encouragement of his father, a doctor and state senator, in his first literary endeavours. Rightly enough, he has been taken to bridge his own and the previous century, in religion moving steadily away from New England's ancestral Calvinism towards a benign Unitarian faith and in politics from his region's hereditary conservatism towards a more liberal, democratic political ethos. He gave notice of precocity with his anti-Jefferson pamphlet written at fourteen, *The Embargo, Or Sketches Of The Times; A Satire* (1808); enrolled briefly at Williams College (1810–11), before practising law (1816–25), for which he felt a deep antipathy; published his first collection, *Poems*, in 1821, and in 1825 found a professional outlet for his literary inclinations as co-editor of the *New York Review and Athenaeum Magazine*. Behind him were many of his best poems, 'Thanatopsis' especially, which though written earlier was first published in 1817 in the *North American Review*. In 1826, an increasingly acclaimed man of letters, he gave his *Lectures on Poetry*, and in 1827 moved to the *Evening Post* as a staffer where, by 1829, he had become part-owner and editor-in-chief. His *Poems* (1832) confirmed his reputation and marks the best of his literary career. At the *Evening Post* he involved himself in a number of major campaigns, first as a leading Jacksonian Democrat and then as a supporter of Lincoln* and the Republican Party. He spoke out for abolition, for the Union cause, for free trade and religious liberty. Thus, as much as he was known for his poetry, Bryant was also a figure of political substance, a listened to, progressive American voice.

After *Poems* (1832), he also kept up his poetic output, mainly in the elegiac, slightly anachronistic manner of 'Thanatopsis' and his other meditative verse. His principal later volumes include the *The Fountain* (1842), *The White-Footed Deer and Other Poems* (1846), *A Forest Hymn* (1860), *Hymns* (1860), *The Little People of the Snow* (1873), *Among the Trees* (1874) and *The Flood of Years* (1877), together with his deserving blank-verse translations of the *Iliad* (1870) and the *Odyssey* (1871). A further dimension to his achievement lies in his prose writings, *Letters of a Traveller* (1850; second series, 1859), based on his European journey of 1834–6 and containing his views of contemporaries like Cooper and Irving, and his collected *Orations and Addresses*, meticulous compositions which underline Bryant's public role.

Bryant's poetic skills are undoubtedly most finely orchestrated in 'Thanatopsis', his stately, religious contemplation of death amid nature which bears comparison with Thomas Gray's 'Elegy in a Country Churchyard'. Similar in melancholic tone, and in the measured late-Augustan diction, is 'To A Waterfowl'

(1818), a vision of man's life-journey seen in the flight of the American bird. To these might be added poems like 'Inscription for the Entrance to a Wood' (1815), a spiritual vision of Godhead in nature; 'The Ages' (1821), a panoramic view of human and American destiny; 'To Cole, the Painter, Departing for Europe' (1829), an assured verse tribute to the Hudson Valley painter (see Cole*); 'The Prairies' (1832), an invocation of American landscape and space based on Bryant's visit to the Great Plains; and 'A Forest Hymn' (1861), a typically deistic nature poem. Although he lived well into the nineteenth century, and as a political animal responded acutely to the issues of his age, Bryant's poetic roots lay firmly in an earlier period. His nature poetry, and many religious verses on death and the passage of time, although frequently compared with the so-called English Graveyard School, are wholly his own. They are not, however, especially American in theme. Bryant is an important transitional voice, eloquent within limits, a worthy point of departure for the coming mid-century American Renaissance.

A. Robert Lee

See: Tremaine McDowell, *William Cullen Bryant* (1935); H. H. Peckham, *Gotham Yankee* (1950); A. F. McLean, *William Cullen Bryant* (1964).

64
BÜCHNER, Georg 1813–37

German dramatist

Georg Büchner anticipated by a century much of the dilemma of the modern intellectual consciousness, exemplifying in his short life the unresolvable tension between activist committed writing and a philosophical existential sense. Two major streams of modern drama, the political and the absurd, have a direct precursor in Büchner, whose awareness of the insistent claims of the one and the inescapable reality of the other is shared by playwrights like Beckett and Dürrenmatt, Adamov and Weiss. A cause of Büchner's ambivalent responses to life is often sought in the frustrating political situation in which he found himself. After the Congress of Vienna in 1815 Europe was plunged into the torpor of restoration; absolutism reigned supreme and made only paper concessions to the pressures of liberal constitutions. In the land of Hesse Büchner experienced at first hand this period of repression, censorship, peasant hunger, emigration, and abortive uprisings in 1830 and 1833 that foreshadowed the Revolutions of 1848. The Marxist historian Heinz Kamnitzer attributed Büchner's 'peculiar combination of revolutionary power and wild despair' to his position between political disillusionment and hope, but this only partially explains the utter despondency about human existence that erupts in both his imaginative work and his letters.

At school Büchner already gave indications of his dissatisfaction with existing society and during his medical studies at the Universities of Strasbourg and Giessen he engaged in the student agitation against the political conditions in Germany. In 1834 Büchner founded a Society for the Rights of Man and met Ludwig Weidig, with whom he wrote a short, inflammatory pamphlet, *The Hessian Courier* (*Der Hessische Landbote*), designed to incite the local peasantry to rise against the exploiting aristocracy. With its catchy slogan 'Peace to the hovels! War on the palaces!', factual tax statistics and rousing invective, it is direct political propaganda that could hardly be bettered now. It also illustrates Büchner's conviction of the ineffectiveness of high literature to influence society and his scorn of theoreticians and intellectuals, who only play a peripheral role in changing the world. Büchner had already expressed his fury at the impotence of the masses, condemned to toil for the princes and liberals, and he 'prayed every night to the rope and the lamp-posts'. He adopted an unequivocal materialist stance, seeking the impetus to revolution in the need of the poor masses, once they could free themselves from the 'two levers of material misery and religious fanaticism' with which their rulers oppressed them. Long before Marx* this impetuous young man, who thought with his heart not his head, attempted with *The Hessian Courier* an isolated uprising of the impoverished agricultural proletariat that was doomed to failure. Indeed, the instigators of the pamphlet were betrayed and several arrested; Büchner managed to stay free though constantly under police suspicion and investigation. He wrote the drama *Danton's Death* (*Dantons Tod*) in 1835 as the police net closed in on him in Darmstadt, and soon after he fled precipitately over the frontier to Strasburg, followed by a warrant for his arrest. Here Büchner worked on his novella *Lenz* and the comedy *Leonce and Lena*. Late in 1836 he gained political asylum in Switzerland and was awarded a doctorate at the University of Zürich, where he became a lecturer for the remaining months of his life. Just as he had earlier recognized with absolute clarity that 'the only revolutionary factor in the world is the relationship of the poor and the rich' he went straight to the heart of the matter in his scientific considerations. The lecture he gave in Zürich prior to his appointment opened without prevarication with a succinct opposition of the teleological and ontological views of life, the essential question in natural philosophy. In that winter Büchner wrote the fragmentary tragedy *Woyzeck* and died of a fever early in 1837.

Büchner's idiosyncratic literary imagination and expression were out of tune with his time, and performances of his plays did not come until the turn of the century: *Leonce and Lena* in 1895, *Danton's Death* in 1902,

Woyzeck in 1913 (with Alban Berg's powerful opera a few years later). Büchner's political acumen, his philosophy of history and existential view of man, and his repudiation of idealism all stamp him as a forerunner of the sensibility of the later nineteenth and twentieth centuries. *Danton's Death* is a historical play about the French Revolution, but although Büchner thought of the dramatist as a chronicler neutrally documenting the facts of history, his studies of these turbulent events engendered in him a deep and passionate sense of man's powerlessness to impose his will on the world:

I felt as though crushed beneath the fatalism of history. I find in human nature a terrifying sameness, and in the human condition an inexorable force, granted to all and to none. The individual is no more than foam on the wave, greatness mere chance. . . . The word *must* is one of the curses with which mankind is baptized. . . . What is it in us that lies, murders, steals?

These sentiments are voiced almost word for word by Danton as he plays out his historical role. The futility of action – even of the purposeful 'idealists' like Robespierre – brings men face to face with their naked existence, stripped of ethics, morality and free will. Intellectual deprivation is intensified by each man's isolation: as Danton says to his mistress, 'We know little enough about each other. We're thick-skinned creatures who reach out our hands toward one another, but it means nothing – hide rubbing against hide – we're very lonely.' The baring of human experience and the absurdity of action exemplified by the unheroic hero Danton is redeemed at the close by Lucille's defiant 'Long live the King!', an *acte gratuit* forestalling Camus and Sartre by a century.

Woyzeck, the almost clinical account of a lowly soldier who stabs his common law wife to death through jealousy, is loosely modelled on a real case which intrigued Büchner because of a legal tussle over the issue of an individual's responsibility for his actions. It allowed Büchner to develop the theme adumbrated in *Danton's Death* of human beings as automata, 'puppets manipulated on wires by unknown powers'. This theme merges with Büchner's fierce sympathy for the weak and down-trodden. Woyzeck is a passive hero, indigent and inarticulate, subjected to the degradation of the underdog. But he is not alone in his sorry state; all the characters are caught in the trap of humanity, the overbearing doctor and melancholic captain no less than Woyzeck and Marie. Woyzeck starts a long line of dramatic heroes who are the victims of circumstance, unable to express themselves adequately and incapable of asserting their will on the world. In structure, too, the play is uncompromisingly committed to realism and presages Expressionist techniques and the 'epic' theatre developed by Brecht with its sequence of loosely linked scenes enacting an objective process.

Even *Leonce and Lena* is permeated by irony and realism. It purports to be the fairy-tale story of a prince and princess coming together in fulfilment of what has actually been planned and destined by others. They return to their own country pretending to be automata, and this occasions a light-handed satire on robots, puppets, masks and roles in human life. A witty play on words relieves the intense ennui that composes the fabric of existence. The prose piece *Lenz*, based on diaries kept by a pastor in Alsace, is a documentary evocation of crucial months in the life of the eponymous eighteenth-century playwright. Büchner presents this near-clinical case of a passionate talent whose potential is stultified by the society around him, analysing it coolly, precisely, minutely in all its phases. Its tension is due to Büchner's 'imaginative exactness' and the implicit reference to the smothering of his own driving realism in the stifling artificiality of the restoration period. Through Lenz Büchner proclaimed his own aesthetic credo: literature as the presentation of life, stark, unadorned, stripped of preconceptions and philosophical musings and pretensions. What is, is.

Büchner's 'doctrine of realism' rejected an easy, abstract idealism and spoke for humanity in real terms, seeking the amelioration of life through the overthrow of existing structures. His indignation and political activism, no less than the emancipatory passion of his creative writing, run counter to his sombre insight into the senselessness of existence; the dynamic balance of this polarity is the source of the energy in Büchner's work that has been so potent in the twentieth century.

Arrigo V. Subiotto

All Büchner's main works are mentioned above; the most definitive edition is W. R. Lehmann, *Georg Büchner: Sämtliche Werke und Briefe* (from 1967). Translations: C. R. Mueller, *Complete Plays and Prose* (1963); M. Hamburger, *Lenz* (1966); V. Price, *The Plays of Georg Büchner*. See: Maurice B. Benn, *The Drama of Revolt: A critical study of Georg Büchner* (1976); A. H. J. Knight, *Georg Büchner* (1951).

65
BUCKLE, Thomas Henry 1821–62

British historian

In the middle of the nineteenth century Buckle was the only known continuator in Britain of the great Scottish thinkers of the eighteenth century (such as Adam Ferguson to whom Buckle attributed the idea of inductive study of history) who sought to discover the conditions of progress by comparing civilizations and nations and who (together with their French contemporaries such

as Montesquieu, Turgot and Condorcet) can be regarded as the founders of comparative sociology. Like his senior contemporary August Comte*, Buckle saw in the applications of reason and the growth of knowledge the chief source of progress, but he did not think that there was much progress in the sphere of morality or religion, and condemned Comte's authoritarian utopia. He produced neither a philosophical system nor a programme of reform and confined his task to explaining the past and discovering the conditions of progress, on the basis of a much wider and more exact knowledge of history. He collected masses of factual information to back his theories and died on an expedition to obtain first hand knowledge of oriental civilizations.

Although he did not use these expressions, Buckle believed that the chief motors of progress were freedom of thought and freedom of enterprise. This was a widespread view and his originality lies in his explanations and theories about the fluctuations on these scores. He attributed to the monarchs with their officials, the priests and the nobility, a perennial tendency to constrain these freedoms, which he labels 'the protective spirit'. When these forces are in alliance, or any of them preponderant, the protective spirit stifles progress. The latter is possible only when, through many-sided conflicts, they somehow neutralize one another and one side has to ally itself with the townsmen and the lower classes, and in consequence leaves them more freedom.

The first two volumes of his unfinished work were published shortly before his death under the title *History of Civilization in England* (1857–). Only one chapter, however, deals specifically with England, while one third of the work is devoted to a discussion of methodological and theoretical problems such as the possibility of historical induction, statistical regularities as the basis thereof, the influence of geographical environment on culture, the nature of progress, the relations between government, religion and the progress of knowledge. The rest of the work, as well as most of the short pieces and unfinished fragments contained in the posthumously published two volumes, are comparative analyses of history. He starts by comparing Europe with Asia and then deals with England, France, Germany, Spain and Scotland, drawing comparisons between them and offering explanations of their different paths. Death at forty-one prevented him from widening the field of comparisons.

Despite various conceptual and factual errors, Buckle ranks as one of the great masters of comparative method, surpassing on this score all his contemporaries with the exceptions of de Tocqueville* and Marx*. De Tocqueville made fewer errors and had more general ideas but dealt with a narrower range of cases. Buckle gives almost as much room to class conflict and the play of economic interests as does Marx, but pays less attention to the mode of production. He is weaker than Marx in the ability to formulate theories but freer from dogmatism. Unlike Comte, Marx and Spencer*, Buckle has no scheme of evolutionary stages. Connected with this is his focus on a more detailed study of changes recorded by history, rather than classification or static description of primitive societies, which was the dominant preoccupation of nineteenth-century evolutionists. From this viewpoint, Buckle appears as the forerunner of the great exponents of comparative study of history without evolutionist presuppositions who appeared at the end of the nineteenth century: Gaetano Mosca* and Max Weber. In an incidental remark, Buckle anticipated the latter's thesis about the influence of Protestantism on accumulation of capital. In his analyses of causation, Buckle attaches much weight to contacts between cultures and steers clear of circular explanations in such terms as national soul, destiny or race which were fashionable then and until recent times.

His belief in the laws of historical change and the relative unimportance of individuals, as well as his irreligious rationalism, made him a target of bitter attacks by conventional historians in many, now little known, books and articles. His influence was greater on the continent than in Britain where he found a follower and defender only towards the end of the century in the person of John Mackinnon Robertson*, the author of *Buckle and his Critics* (1895) which still remains the best study of Buckle. Robertson also edited a reprint of Buckle's masterpiece with a very valuable introduction and notes which constructively rectify the latter's errors, dispel various misunderstandings and are essential for understanding Buckle.

Son of a prosperous merchant and, therefore, free from the need to earn a living, Buckle led the rather secluded life of a sober and frail bachelor, very attached to his highly intellectual mother, dedicating all his energies to extraordinarily voracious reading and the preparation of his work on which he embarked when still almost a child.

Stanislav Andreski

See: *The Miscellaneous and Posthumous Works of Henry Thomas Buckle*, ed. Grant Allen, 2 vols (1885); *Introduction of the History of Civilization in England*, ed. J. M. Robertson (1904).

66
BULWER-LYTTON, Edward, 1st Baron Lytton
1803–73

British author and politician

It was Arnold Bennett who once observed that 'we read Anatole France* to find out what Anatole France

has been reading', and this is nowadays as good a reason as any for examining the works of Jorge Luis Borges. The well-known catholicity of Borges's reading has made him almost legendarily *au fait* with the literature of England and he is one of a mere handful of those who can still confidently allude to the novels and stories of Edward Bulwer-Lytton. It was not, of course, always thus. Before the hardening of literary taste by university dogma made fiction respectable and replaced its associations with guilty pleasure by those of moral duty, it was possible to turn to Lytton's voluminous *oeuvre* without a nagging sense that in doing so one was somehow wasting one's time on an author whose work was not strictly 'relevant to central concerns'. Now that a broader view is beginning to obtain of the novel's role as a reflector of social issues and of the influence of popular fiction on critically hallowed writers, it would be foolish to disregard the immense vogue and significance enjoyed by Lytton among the nineteenth-century reading public.

The son of General Bulwer of Wood Dalling, Norfolk, he assumed his mother's maiden name of Lytton when in 1838 he inherited her estate at Knebworth in Hertfordshire, where, like others of his generation, he gave vent to his late Romantic fantasies in the grandiose adornments of the house. In various respects Knebworth is the essence of its creator, who, though several of his major works were produced during the early Victorian decades, belongs in spirit and tone inalienably to the world of those who survived Lord Byron*, the world inhabited and written about by Benjamin Disraeli*, who knew and worked with Lytton and felt his effect as a writer.

Perhaps the most important event of Lytton's early life was one which itself was suffused with the quality of those silk-bound bijou annuals, *The Keepsake* and *The Book of Beauty*, for which several of his first works were produced. In 1827 he married Rosina Doyle Wheeler, an Irish girl whose already considerable eccentricities were further encouraged by her friendship with Lady Caroline Lamb and the fervid poetess Letitia Landon ('L.E.L.'). Rosina had already broken off the engagement three times before consenting, and the marriage, opposed by Lytton's mother, took on a sinister resemblance to that of the Byrons some ten years previously, ending, similarly, in divorce. Of Lady Lytton's thirteen published novels, practically all were coloured by a desire to proclaim her husband's disgrace, but the world tended to side with him rather than with a wife determined to claim that he had wished to have her commited as insane.

Politics offered a welcome relief from the marriage and its aftermath. Initially a Whig, Lytton sat as MP for St Ives and Lincoln, but joined the Tories in 1852 and became colonial secretary in Lord Derby's second ministry, 1858–9, a post to which he brought a typical administrative skill. He was made a baron in 1866 and was buried in Westminster Abbey. His son Robert was a distinguished diplomat and a controversial Indian viceroy, and, true to family traditions, his granddaughter Constance became a heroine of the suffragette movement.

As an author Lytton was one of the most prolific and assiduous of his day and his popularity was commensurate, as the number of reprinted editions implies. He was gifted with an extraordinarily wide general knowledge, an excellent sense of history and an expert's hand at turning a good plot. He was, conversely, as vulgar, verbose and sensation-seeking as the most catch-penny of Victorian fiction writers, but unlike Dickens*, whose enjoyment of a comparably wide readership led him to appreciate Lytton, after whom he named one of his children, he never mastered the art of crude colouring.

Besides his contribution to popularizing German scholarship in England and his encouragement of the young Browning*, he is noteworthy for having revitalized the theatre with plays such as *Richelieu* (1838) and *The Lady of Lyons* (1838), both for the great actor Macready, and his superbly racy comedy *Money* (1840), and for having demonstrated the true versatility of the novel as a genre. The dandy novel *Pelham* (1828) with its truculent maxims on dress (the source, as much as his verse satire *The New Timon*, 1846, of Tennyson's* famous condemnation of 'the padded man that wears the stays') is still richly enjoyable, as is *The Last Days of Pompeii* (1834), perhaps the most successful attempt by any novelist at using newly discovered archaeological evidence as material for a story. *Paul Clifford* (1830) and *Eugene Aram* (1832) explore the criminal Newgate world, and *The Caxtons* (1849) and *Night and Morning* (1852) investigate the field of social realism. Of his three later historical novels *Rienzi* (1835) became the source of Wagner's* first major opera and *Harold, the Last of the Saxons* (1848) suggested a play to Tennyson. A continuing interest in the occult led to *The Haunters and the Haunted* (1857), a classic among ghost stories, and in the prophetic *The Coming Race* of 1871 he anticipated certain effects of Wells and later science fantasists.

It is hard not to admire Lytton's combination of energy and enthusiasm, as characteristic of its period as the interests reflected in the novels themselves. He is by no means a refined or discerning artist – some might even say that he was not an artist at all – but his achievement was to broaden the areas in which the novelist could work and to dilute, in an accessible form, a wide spectrum of the principal concerns of his age.

Jonathan Keates

Other novels include: *The Last of the Barons* (1843); *Ernest Maltravers* (1837); *My Novel* (1853). See: V. A. G. R. Bulwer-Lytton, *The Life of Edward Bulwer, First Lord Lytton* (2 vols, 1913); Michael Sadleir, *Bulwer: A Panorama, 1803–1836* (1931); ed. C. H. Shattuck, *Bulwer and Macready* (correspondence, 1958).

67
BUNTLINE, Ned (Edward Zane Carroll JUDSON)
1823–86

US writer and politician

Judson's biographers cannot even agree on the place and date of his birth and so one arbitrarily selects from all the listed dates the one on his tombstone – 1823. The place is equally vague: either Harpersfield or Stanford. How appropriate for a myth-maker who used pseudonyms, had at least two wives at the same time, and founded the Know-Nothing Party. E.Z.C. Judson wrote dime novels under many names, acted in pseudo-Wild West shows, and created fictions about his own life as easily as he wrote stories of the sea and the American West.

Judson's early years were spent in rural New York in a contentious atmosphere encouraged by his family's pro-Mason, anti-Catholic beliefs. He joined the US Navy and fought (with distinction according to him) in the Seminole Wars. He resigned in 1842 and drifted into the insecure world of journalism where he was a jack-of-all-trades hack writer, editor and printer. In May of 1844 he published in Pittsburg a monthly literary journal called *Ned Buntline's Magazine*, the first appearance of his best-known pseudonym.

In the 1850s Buntline's income was augmented by temperance lectures and the organization of the 'nativist' political party known first as the 'Know-Nothing' Party for its instructions to reply 'I know nothing' when asked about their party's principles. The party's organizers were in favour of prohibition, anti-abolition, anti-Catholic, anti-foreign and in general represented the not-so-secret fears that have haunted American until today. No one could be sure just how powerful they were since they were not officially organized until the convention of 1854, but the defeat of many local Democrats and Whigs were claimed as victories for Know-Nothingism in states from New Hampshire to Texas. In 1854 their convention declared themselves the 'American Party' and in 1856 they ran the renegade Whig Millard Fillmore for president. Buntline organized fervently for the party, to the point that in some areas party members were called 'Buntlinites', and is credited with giving the party its original 'Know-Nothing' name. In 1855 Buntline read himself out of the party claiming that the once firm principles of the 'native American' party had been corrupted as political office and power became more feasible.

In 1860 Erastus Beadle issued the first 'dime novel', a series of cheap paperbacks designed to exploit the growing literacy and desire for romance among the masses. Beadle's rules included the following caveats: 'We prohibit all things offensive to good taste in expression and incident; we prohibit subjects or characters that carry an immoral taint; we require grace and precision of narrative and correctness in composition.' Buntline had been doing such adventure writing in his journals and for newspapers, and so in 1865 he signed with Hilton's Ten Cents Books, a Beadle rival, and in 1869 decided to investigate the Western material popularized in early Beadle novels. Buntline was looking for a real Indian fighter as subject matter. Major Frank North, the hero of a fight at Summit Springs, Nebraska, had nothing but contempt for writers and suggested to Buntline that a young man sleeping under a wagon nearby would be more suitable material. And thus William F. Cody (soon to be Buffalo Bill) was awakened by his creator, who was immediately struck by the physical beauty of the long-haired 23-year-old scout. Months later Street & Smith published a new serial in the *New York Weekly* entitled 'Buffalo Bill: The King of Border Men; the Wildest and Truest Story I Ever Wrote'. This story and its immediate successors created the image of Buffalo Bill which would quickly fall into line with Natty Bumpo, Daniel Boone, and Davey Crockett as one of the basic Western heroes. Indeed, the first Buntline Buffalo Bill story was still selling through Sears, Roebuck & Co. as late as 1928 for only 22c. Other authors took up the character in such forms as the weekly 'Buffalo Bill Stories' and a play (by Fred G. Maeder) based on Buntline's first Buffalo Bill story. Buntline quickly plagiarized this play based on his own novel to create *The Scouts of the Plains* and summoned Cody and his friend Texas Jack Omohundro to star in it. The play opened in Chicago on 16 December 1872 to sneering critics and cheering audiences. Buntline himself co-starred with the real scouts as part of a trio of Westerners defending themselves against the dastardly savages. Financially the play was a roaring success and proved to Cody that show business was the place for him. He would become internationally famous as the centrepiece for his own Wild West Show which never really escaped the framework of his Buntline-created legend.

After an unsuccessful effort at legend-making with two scouts named Arizona Frank and Texas Charlie, Buntline decided to move from the Scouts versus Indians legends to the cattletowns of Kansas and Nebraska, seeking out the famous marshalls and gunfighters of that era. Thus the new confrontations would be between lawmen and cowboys, gunfighters and outlaws. Rather than the hand-to-hand struggle with knives, the combatants would face off for the fast draw with six-shooters. To ingratiate himself with these gunfighters, Ned Buntline had the Colt factory make him some guns he modestly called Buntline Specials, .45 six-shooters with 12-inch barrels. Once again Buntline had more new material to pour out to his various

markets under his seemingly endless stream of pseudonyms. And the cowboy and the gunfighter became the new focus for the Western myth, pushing the scout, the cavalry and the Indian into the background.

Buntline settled down somewhat after that in Stanford with the last of his wives while continuing to fulfil contracts for both Beadle and Street & Smith, to send long letters to the press, dabble in politics, and grant interviews to young reporters about the literary life and the Wild West. He died on 16 July 1886 with the self-serving legends, myths, half-truths and gossip still circulating. Given his numerous contracts, pen-names, and fecundity, one can only wonder if the 'official' estimate of four hundred dime novels does justice to this output. What can be measured more easily is his contribution to the myth of the American West. Exploiting the newspaper stories of Indian clashes and the need for heroes, Buntline dramatized the essential conflict of the lone scout against the savage hordes as the thrusting point of the nation's manifest destiny. Buntline's particular genius was to combine real people and place names with the typical hyperbole of the frontier and journalism. For him to fantasize in print about Buffalo Bill and then to produce him live for a touring production of Cody's supposed life was to satisfy the starving easterners with more legend than they could possibly digest.

Charles Gregory

Buntline's titles include: *The Black Avenger of the Spanish Main* (1847); *Agnes; or the Beautiful Milliner* (1866); *Buffalo Bill: King of the Border Men* (1881); *Little Buckshot, The White Whirlwind of the Prairie* (1981); *Red Dick, The Tiger of California* (1890); *Red Ralph, The Ranger* (1870); *The Red Warrior; or Stella Delorme Comanche Lover* (1869); *Texas Jack, The White King of the Pawnees* (1891); *Wild Bill's Last Trail* (1900). See: Thomas V. Paterson, *The Private Life, Public Career, and Real Character of that Odius Rascal Ned Buntline!* (1849); Fred E. Pond, *The Life and Adventures of Ned Buntline* (1919); Albert Johannsen, *The House of Beadle and Adams and Its Dime and Nickel Novels* (1950); Jay Monaghan, *The Great Rascal* (1951).

68
BURCKHARDT, Jacob Christoph 1818–97

Swiss historian of art and culture

Burckhardt was born, the son of a Swiss Reformed pastor, in Basel on 25 May 1818. Educated in the *Gymnasium* in Basel, he began the study of theology at the university there: he soon abandoned any thought of a theological career, and transferred to the University of Berlin, where he studied history under the distinguished historians Franz Theodor Kugler (1808–58) and Leopold von Ranke* from 1839 until 1843. He completed his studies of the history of art and architecture at the University of Bonn. He visited Italy in 1846, and then again in 1847–8 and 1853–4; it is no exaggeration to say that he fell completely in love with the remnants of classical and Renaissance civilization he found there, and that his Italian experiences completely dominated his life's work. He commenced his teaching career as a *Dozent* in the University of Basel (1844–55) and it was during this period that he published *The Age of Constantine the Great* (*Die Zeit des Konstantins des Grossen*, 1853, trans. 1949). He spent a short spell as Professor of Art History in Zürich Polytechnic (1855–8), and in 1855 published his work on Italian art history, *Der Cicerone*. He was appointed Professor of History and the History of Art in the University of Basel in 1858, a post which he held until his retirement thirty-five years later in 1893. In 1860 he published his best-known work, *The Civilization of the Renaissance in Italy (Die Kultur der Renaissance in Italien*, trans. 1929 and 1951). During the period 1868–73 he worked on the manuscript of his reflections on the philosophy of history, *Reflections on History* (*Weltgeschichtliche Betrachtungen*, trans. 1943), which was not published posthumously until 1905. He died at the age of seventy-nine in Basel.

Burckhardt's sensitive and scholarly works on classical and Renaissance art, architecture and culture remain important and well-known in art history circles; but in more academic and scholarly circles he has commanded more attention and interest for his not terribly systematic nor consistent observations on the historical process published in his *Reflections on History*. It is for this reason that he has sometimes been classified among the 'philosophers of history', although the title 'philosopher' was always one which he disclaimed. It is not impossible to select out of his rather untidy thoughts on the historical process (which first saw the light of day as university lectures at Basel) certain key terms and themes.

In the first place, it is important to note that Burckhardt expressed scepticism about finding 'the ultimate meaning' of history: unlike, say, St Augustine or Hegel*, he did not believe that man could possibly transcend the historical panorama to that point where he could perceive some pattern or motif being portrayed in and through it. He did not share St Augustine's conviction that through faith and revelation man could identify history's beginning (the Creation), middle (the Incarnation) and end (the Last Things). Nor was he impressed by the claim of the Hegelians to be able to survey the historical process *as a whole* and discern in dialectical movements within it the achievement of self-consciousness by the Absolute. But scepticism about an 'ultimate' goal or meaning emphatically did not imply, for Burckhardt, that history, or historical epochs or episodes, do not have 'meaning' or 'significance' for us. To the contrary, he insisted, the opposite

is the truth: there are, in history, eras and episodes pregnant with significance and meaning for us and our lives today, and it is the task of the historian to engage in sifting, in value-judging, in interpretation, in order to lay bare precisely what these eras are and what their relevance is for us, although Burckhardt made it transparently clear that in doing so the critical historian is anything but infallible.

History then is there to be appropriated by generation after generation. But if so, there arises a logical necessity for continuity in history, and in Burckhardt's view such continuity is incompatible with vast and violent revolutions which, however valuable and necessary they may seem to their perpetrators, are always in danger of abandoning the enrichment accumulated by past generations and epochs. A few examples of how such a view worked out in practice may be given. A little reflection informs us that our own Western European civilization derives from the marriage of Hellenistic thought, the law and political genius of Rome, and Christianity. The combination of these three provides the common cultural heritage of the Middle Ages, with a universal religion (Catholicism), a universal language (Latin) and a universal absence of mindless nationalism. (To be fair to Burckhardt, he did not altogether approve of the bloodshed caused in the achievement of Roman unity any more than he approved of everything which appeared to be necessary to maintain the supremacy of Catholicsm in the Middle Ages.) The historical process then involves discontinuity as well as continuity. But when we come down to modern times, we are struck by the increasing frequency of discontinuity, which pleased Burckhardt hardly at all. If, for instance, we contemplate the sixteenth-century Reformation (celebrated by so many Germans of Burckhardt's generation as glorious and God-given progress), we should not fail to observe its bleakly negative aspect: the mindless rejection and destruction of a world-denying, ascetic culture which had taken hundreds of years to build, carried out, not indeed mainly or solely by Luther or by an informed élite, but by a mass, a mob, whose motives were far removed from Lutheran 'justification by faith alone'. Burckhardt therefore fastened upon the Reformation confiscation of ecclesiastical properties, its destruction of ecclesiastical art, its iconoclasm, its invocation of rebellion against tradition and authority, its obsession with 'turning everything upside down'. As for Luther himself, whatever his original motives may have been, the empirical results of his obsessional emphasis upon justification *sola fide* were antinomianism and the abhorrence of good works. Similar strictures were directed by Burckhardt against that doctrine which united a wide range of Reformers – namely, divine predestination. And in support of his thesis, Burckhardt pointed to the anarchy which he believed was the inevitable consequence of one of the radical branches of the Reformation, namely Anabaptism.

Another classic target of Burckhardt's gloomy diagnosis of modernity was the 1789 Revolution in France. In spite of the lofty and humanitarian motives of many who longed for and initiated it, there was still the ghastly phenomenon of mob rule and the Reign of Terror, the mindless rejection of tradition and order, the ridiculous coronation of Napoleon*, who was in the last analysis no more and no less than a vulgar military dictator. He was equally gloomy about the 'revolutions' which punctuated the nineteenth century, each one of which was in his view yet another episode of discontinuity with a past pregnant with human enrichment, partly at least a victory for philistinism. Possibly he reserved his most scathing words for the Second Reich and for Bismarck's* Germany: he rejected uncompromisingly German enthusiasm for disrespect for the past, the bureaucracy, the bourgeois philistinism, the militarism and the lust for power which he discerned in the German Empire which emerged after the defeat of France in the Franco-Prussian War. On the theological side, he was little short of contemptuous of so-called liberal protestant theology – of that theological century which began with Schleiermacher* and ended with Ritschl*. For Burckhardt, such liberal protestants, whose ultimate aims were to respectabilize Christianity, to compromise with shallow nineteenth-century optimism, to undergird contemporary bourgeois ideals, compare miserably with the Christians of the earliest centuries, whose world-renouncing asceticism compelled the admiration and commitment of their contemporaries, whose willingness to die for their supernatural faith in an unseen world helped to 'Christianize' and inspire the secular order, who far from flirting with pagan society attempted to cleanse and discipline it and mould it into the image of the Kingdom of God.

Of course, such a defectively brief résumé of Burckhardt's views is in grave danger of giving a disastrously one-sided and distorted picture of his mentality and opinions. For Burckhardt was too great a historian not to see the other side of the coin: naturally, he was aware of gain as well as loss within the historical process; of course, he had reflected upon human motivation and considered the mechanics of historical necessity. Nevertheless, his mature over-all judgment led him into profound disagreement with the majority of his European contemporaries, and it is not in the least surprising that many of these regarded him as an impossibly conservative eccentric and excessively pessimistic Jeremiah, a judgment which seemed to be corroborated by his solitary, reclusive and ascetic lifestyle. Yet, in hindsight, from the closing decades of the twentieth century, it is perfectly intelligible that today there should be a certain resurgence of interest in Burckhardt's reflections on history. It is not going too far to say that, in the light of the events of the past one hundred years, Burckhardt speaks to our generation more clearly and disconcertingly than he did to his own: he spoke much of *Machtsinn* (the lust for power) and *Erwerbsinn* (the lust for gain) and their evil consequences; he predicted the cultural dangers of mindless egalitarianism; he identified in nineteenth-century life the seeds of future despotisms, military dictatorships and intolerable bureaucracies; he warned that the time was at hand when peoples would believe 'not in principles but in *Führers* . . . and in saviours'; he prophesied that unrestricted materialism and unrestrained devotion to money-making business would be lethal for spiritual contemplation and the cultivation of inwardness. From this point of view it is arguable that today Burckhardt deserves to be read and pondered alongside Schopenhauer*, Kierkegaard*, Dostoevsky* and Nietzche*.

James Richmond

Other translated works include *On History and Historians* (1965). See: Karl Löwith, *Meaning in History* (1949); *From Hegel to Nietzsche: The Revolution in Nineteenth-Century Thought*, trans. David E. Green (1964); Eda Sagarra, *Tradition and Revolution: German Literature and Society 1830–1890* (1971).

69

BURNE-JONES, Sir Edward 1833–98

British painter

Edward Jones was born in Birmingham on 28 August 1833. He incorporated 'Burne' to his surname in the 1860s, although he did not hyphenate the two until he was knighted in 1894. He was educated at King Edward's School in Birmingham. His childhood was not happy, largely due to his mother's death soon after, and as a result of, his birth. He drew prolifically and attended drawing classes at the Government School of Design in Birmingham in 1848. In 1853 he entered Exeter College, Oxford, intending to take Holy Orders. But in the same year he came under the influence of Ruskin* through his friend William Morris*, who had also intended to become a priest. Both men were profoundly influenced by the work of the Pre-Raphaelite painters, and decided to leave university in 1855 in order to pursue careers respectively as a painter and an architect. The following year Jones met both Ruskin and Rossetti*, and attended art school evening classes whilst living with Morris at 17 Red Lion Square. In 1857 the two men helped decorate the Oxford Union, and this experience soldered their desire to work together as decorators. In 1859 he made his first visit to Italy, and in the late 1850s became a part of the Little Holland House set, an influential *avant-garde* grouping which included Watts, Tennyson* and many of the Pre-Raphaelites. In 1860 he married a childhood friend, Georgiana Macdonald. They had one son, Philip, and a daughter, Margaret.

In 1861 he became a founder of Morris, Marshall, Faulkner & Co., better known simply as the 'Firm'. He worked steadily as a painter and designer of stained glass, furniture, tapestries, and ceramics for the next four decades, producing many book illustrations. He became famous overnight as the result of his contributions to the first Grosvenor Galley exhibition in 1877, and his name was henceforth invariably associated with the 'greenery-yallery' current of the Aesthetic movement. In 1878 he gave evidence for Ruskin in the notorious Whistler* v. Ruskin libel trial, which subsequently placed him in an invidious position in the eyes of younger artists, who none the less, like Duncan Grant, continued to be profoundly influenced by both his style and his subject matter. He accepted a baronetcy in 1894, and died in 1898, two years after Morris, and his remains are buried to the right of the porch of the church at Rottingdean in Sussex, where he had bought a house in 1880.

Burne-Jones's protestation that 'the more materialistic science becomes, the more angels I shall paint' typifies one characteristic tendency in high Victorian culture towards that industrialism on which it was so dependent. As for many of his contemporaries, the results of the capitalist division of labour were seen as offences against good taste, offences which would only be remedied on the transcendent plane of art. Hence it was entirely in keeping with his painting that Burne-Jones should have thought of himself as a young man as Celtic Jolyn, and even Eduardo della Francesca. His eventual surname admitted him vicariously to an aristocratic society with medieval values, largely imaginary, of which all his art is an extended wish-fulfilment fantasy. He was fully conscious of this when describing his work as 'a reflection of a reflection of something purely imaginary'. Yet his imagination was clearly structured within the iconographic and ideological framework of late Pre-Raphaelitism, with all its introspective anxieties and ideal resolutions to real nineteenth-century social problems such as housing, marriage and sexuality. That his own sexuality was complex and obscure cannot however be satisfactorily explained by a crude 'repression' hypothesis, since he was evidently as exhibitionistic about his obsessions as he was secretive. In this respect his work constitutes a kind of inventory of the Victorian bourgeois sexual imagination, a gazetteer of what were, after all, highly popular fantasies. His work remains captivating by the sheer force of its power to condense social and sexual, public and private issues.

There is a marked tendency in Burne-Jones's images for things to happen 'elsewhere'. He provides a peripheral or oblique view of dramatic events. Thus in *The Wine of Circe* (1863–9) Circe is seen drugging the wine whilst Odysseus's ships are glimpsed through a window approaching the island, thus forming a picture within a picture, a device which enabled Burne-Jones to contain dramatic narrative action by implication. Other examples of this dramatic displacement include the *Laus Veneris* of 1873–8, in which Venus lounges broodingly whilst Tannhauser and his companions are seen, approaching on horseback, through a window which again repeats the proportions of the whole picture. Even the family portrait of his wife and children from 1883 cuts off Lady Burne-Jones completely from her children who are glimpsed far away behind her through a doorway. This effect of distancing is at its most pronounced in *The Baleful Head* of 1886–7 which depicts Perseus showing Andromeda the Medusa's head in safe reflection, as they in turn gaze at themselves and one another in the same well-water. It is not sexuality which he repressed, but social relations as a whole. In this context it is worth considering the relation between his elaborate and frequently highly detailed preparatory drawings, and the more abstract and generalized paintings which derive from them in a process of systematic denial. His favourite themes were of exclusion and quest. He employed emblematic signs with fixed cultural associations and seems never to have been interested in landscape painting, though he drew the human figure from the life. His brilliant ability to fill space decoratively is most apparent in his numerous roundel designs, which frequently anticipate the Art Nouveau work of Obrist and the Vienna school, as well as paralleling in some respects the very French modernists with whom his art has been so often contrasted. Burne-Jones finally makes best sense within the overall European climate of Aestheticism, and it is in relation to Gauguin* and even Van Gogh* that his work is viewed to its best advantage.

Simon Watney

The best source on Burne-Jones's life remains his wife, Lady Burne-Jones's, commentary *Memorials of Edward Burne-Jones* (2 vols, 1904). A recent biography is Penelope Fitzgerald, *Edward Burne-Jones: A Biography* (1975). See: Martin Harrison and Bill Waters, *Burne-Jones* (1973). The November 1975 issue of *Apollo* magazine contains many useful articles, and the Arts Council of Great Britain catalogue of the same year is also available.

70
BURTON, Sir Richard Francis 1821–96

British explorer and translator

Burton's achievements range over a quite astonishing variety of fields. With his immense physical energy, acute powers of observation and boundless curiosity, he carried out pioneering work in areas as diverse as archaeology, falconry, mining and zoology. His expeditions were anthropological field studies rather than geographical surveys; he observed meticulously the customs, beliefs, language and dress of his hosts and fellow travellers, noting with particular relish details likely to shock his Victorian audience. His translations, too, from European and oriental languages, are usually annotated with lengthy footnotes which demonstrate the breadth of his interests and draw frequently on his personal experiences.

Of an Anglo-Irish family with aristocratic connections but limited means, Burton had an erratic education in France and southern Europe, picking up a number of languages and becoming a formidable boxer and swordsman. He survived less than two years as an undergraduate at Oxford, where he did however become proficient in Latin, Greek and Arabic. A commission was arranged in the Bombay Native Infantry and he spent the next six years in India, acquiring another half-dozen languages and immersing himself in Indian society as far as was possible for an English officer. To this end he perfected the art of disguise, which he was to use so effectively on his travels in Africa and Arabia. But an over-explicit report on the activities of eunuchs and pederasts in the brothels of Karachi, although officially commissioned, put an end to his army career. It took him nearly two years to recover from a severe bout of cholera and a painful eye disease; typically, he put the time to good use, publishing three books of his observations in India.

In 1852 he offered his services to the Geographical Society, to explore Arabia; his real objective was to visit the holy city of Medina and penetrate the Great Mosque of Mecca. He was not the first European to bring off this highly dangerous exploit, but he was the first to describe with objective sensitivity the complex religious rites observed, and the emotional reactions of his fellow pilgrims.

Instead of returning at once to London to savour his triumph he set about planning a new expedition to a holy city – this time Harar, in the heart of Somalia. It proved an even more arduous and dangerous journey, but Burton emerged from encounters with murderous tribesmen and waterless deserts as the first white man to enter the city, gain an audience with the Amir, and escape unscathed. A further expedition, across Somalia to the Nile, was abandoned when the party was attacked and one of their number killed and others wounded. It was on this trip that he first encountered John Hanning Speke, with whom he mounted the famous 1857 expedition in search of the source of the Nile. Despite appalling hardships they discovered Lake Tanganyika and Lake Victoria, but the strain of illness and the incompatibility of their personalities resulted in an atmosphere of hostile rivalry. On their return to the coast Burton dallied in Aden while Speke took the first boat to London to claim sole credit for the expedition. The vituperative exchanges between the two men only ended five years later with Speke's mysterious death just before the pair were to confront one another in a public debate before the British Association.

After the Nile expedition, in disgust and disappointment, Burton took himself off to North America where he travelled widely from Canada to the southern states. Much of the inevitable weighty volume which later appeared chronicles his impressions of the community of Latter Day Saints in Salt Lake City; he expressed particular approval of the practice of polygamy, and took the opportunity of getting in some ironic digs at more orthodox religions. On his return he married Isabel Arundell, of an aristocratic Catholic family, whom he had courted in a sporadic fashion for ten years. Romantic, snobbish and bigoted, but blessed with immense reserves of energy, Isabel proved a fiercely devoted wife whose motto was to 'pay, pack and follow' in her husband's wake. Due in part to Isabel's connections, the couple were taken up by London society, and Burton formed a lasting friendship with Swinburne* who shared his taste for erotic literature.

Lacking private means, Burton was obliged for the rest of his life to accept minor diplomatic posts, first in West Africa and later in Brazil. These he invariably used as bases for long expeditions, which resulted in a constant stream of books and articles. At last Isabel managed to procure the consulship in Damascus – a city much closer to Burton's heart. There the local Turkish viceroy interpreted Burton's restless curiosity as dangerous interference in the country's affairs, and he succeeded in engineering his ignominious dismissal after less than two years in the coveted post.

For the remaining twenty-four years of his life he was based in Trieste, though his official duties occupied him less than his constant travels, including two ill-fated expeditions – one to the Red Sea coast and one to West Africa – in search of gold deposits. As failing health forced him to curtail his physical activities he devoted his energies to writing up past expeditions, and especially to a project he had toyed with for many years – the unexpurgated translation of a vast number of oriental folk tales, *The Book of a Thousand Nights and a Night*, better known as *The Arabian Nights*. He had already translated anonymously the *Kama Sutra* and *The Perfumed Garden*, with the cooperation of the orientalist Arbuthnot. But it is his ten-volume translation of *The Arabian Nights* that is generally considered his *magnum opus*; laced with archaisms and passages of florid hyperbole, it nevertheless has a freshness and vivid directness which make it the most readable of the English versions. It is an anthropological as much as a literary work: footnotes often outrun the text; they range from notes on points of grammar and style to scholarly essays on the beliefs and traditions of the Arab world to autobiographical reminiscences. The popular and critical success of the work made up to some extent for the official neglect which had embittered his later years. The knighthood he was awarded ten years before his death he considered a belated and inadequate consolation prize, but it was balm to Isabel's pride.

On his death his wife insisted on a Catholic burial, and ever protective of her husband's reputation, she systematically burned virtually all his journals and manuscripts, including his recently completed revision of *The Perfumed Garden*. His marble mausoleum – a bedouin tent hung with camel bells and bleeding hearts – is to be seen in the graveyard of the Church of St Mary Magdalene in Mortlake, Surrey.

Hilary Wise

Burton's works include: *Personal Narrative of a Pilgrimage to El Medinah and Meccah* (memorial edition, 1893); *First Footsteps in East Africa; or an Exploration of Harar* (1856); *The Lake Regions of Central Africa* (2 vols, 1860); *The City of the Saints and Across the Rocky Mountains to California* (1861). Translations: *The Kama Sutra of Vatsyayana* (1883); *The Perfumed Garden of the Cheikh Nefzaoui, A Manual of Arabian Erotology* (1886); *A Plain and Literal Translation of the Arabian Nights' Entertainments, Now Entitled The Thousand Nights and a Night* (1885–8). See: B. Farwell, *Burton* (1963); F. M. Brodie, *The Devil Drives: A Life of Sir Richard Burton* (1967).

71

BUTLER, Samuel 1835–1902

British novelist and essayist

'Every man's work . . . is always a portrait of himself.' The author of these words was born in Langarin, Nottinghamshire, the son of the Reverend Thomas Butler, and grandson and namesake of a former bishop of Lichfield (concerning whom he wrote *The Life and Letters of Samuel Butler* in 1889). A lonely childhood at home was interrupted by Butler's attendance at Shrewsbury School, and finally ended when he entered St John's College, Cambridge, in 1854. Butler's father intended his son to continue the family tradition by joining the clergy; he refused, however, on the ground of religious doubts. In 1859 Butler emigrated to New Zealand where, with financial aid from his father, he established a successful sheep-run, doubling his capital in five years. While at Cambridge Butler had contributed to undergraduate newspapers, and he now began writing for the New Zealand press. He became acquainted with the recently published theories of Charles Darwin*, and in 1862 wrote an article entitled 'Darwin and the Origin of Species'. He also produced a number of shorter pieces, among them 'Darwin among the Machines' (1863), which were later to form the basis of his popular novel, *Erewhon* (1872). In 1863 the Reverend Butler edited and published a volume of his son's letters from New Zealand under the title *A First Year in Canterbury Settlement*, but Butler always refused to acknowledge this as his first book. In 1864 he returned to England, taking rooms in Clifford's Inn in London, where he lived for the rest of his life. In the early 1870s Butler speculated badly, and was in financial difficulties for some years, until his father's death, and a subsequent inheritance, absolved him in 1886.

As an undergraduate, Butler had considered becoming a professional painter. Following his return to England he began to study the subject seriously, attending Heatherley's School of Painting, and later exhibiting at the Royal Academy. It was at Heatherley's that Butler met Eliza Mary Anne Savage. She became his closest friend, and they corresponded regularly until her death in 1885. Attached as he was to Eliza Savage, Butler never showed any inclination to marry, and once wrote, 'Brigands demand your money or your life; women require both.' In later life, Butler's closest acquaintance was his eventual biographer, H. F. Jones, with whom he collaborated on a number of musical compositions. Butler spent most of his last years writing and travelling. He had a particular affection for Italy, about which he wrote several volumes. He also became fascinated by the work of Homer, which he translated into colloquial English.

Butler's interest in the work of Charles Darwin served to accentuate the religious doubts which had prevented him from entering the church. These doubts centred upon the question of the literal truth of the gospels. Since David Strauss* had published *Das Leben Jesu* in 1835 (translated by George Eliot* in 1846), controversy had surrounded the problem of reconciling rationalism and Christianity. Butler's major contribution to this debate was *The Fair Haven* (1873), a tract on theology prefaced by a fictional memoir of one John Pickard Owen. Written with an irony which many Christians failed to detect, *The Fair Haven* indicates the way in which belief in a beneficent Providence was being threatened by rapid scientific growth. Butler personally rejected orthodox Christianity because he could not accept its superstitions; but he continued to believe in God: 'As long as there is an unknown there will be a God for all practical purposes.' Butler's doctrine was pantheistic, in that he saw each individual human being as a part of a universal which goes under the name of 'God'. He believed that conscious will, or 'cunning', in every cell of that universal made it capable of shaping its environment to suit its own best interests. The theology of *The Fair Haven* has probably lost its immediate relevance for most modern readers, but its fictional framework contains some of Butler's most amusing satire.

Samuel Butler's only commercial success as a writer was *Erewhon*. Although more a novel in the nineteenth-century sense than *The Fair Haven*, *Erewhon* is nevertheless primarily a series of satirical set-pieces, with a story woven around them. It was Butler's philosophy never to take anything on trust; he regarded unthinking acceptance as the great enemy of any society, and in *Erewhon* used an imaginary country as a background against which to examine, and undermine, dominant Victorian concepts of moral, religious and social behaviour. Higgs, the novel's central character, is a bourgeois Christian, motivated, at least at the outset, by a desire for profit. Like Swift's Gulliver, Higgs brings ingrained preconceptions to an alien society, one which is an almost negative image of that from which he has come: poverty and sickness are punishable as crimes, for example, while thieves are given hospital treatment. Competition, ruthless ambition and greed, the 'virtues' of Victorian England, have no place in Erewhon. Yet this imaginary land is no Utopia: inhumanity and hypocrisy make it as illogical as any other society. Butler's doctrine of 'permanent scepticism' would not allow him to indulge in idealism. A central chapter in *Erewhon* is 'The Book of Machines', deriving from one of the Darwinian articles Butler had written in New Zealand. It here becomes a mock treatise by an Erewhonian scholar, justifying his country's abolition of machines on the grounds that they pose a threat to man's supremacy. In effect Butler extends Darwin's theory concerning the survival of the fittest to encompass the development of machines, and in so doing was tapping a widespread, if unconscious, Victorian fear of technological progress: he wrote, 'I fear none of the existing machines; what I fear is the extraordinary rapidity with which they are becoming something very different to what they are at present.' 'The Book of Machines' rivals Swift's 'Modest Proposal' as a sustained piece of logical argument vitiated by a single, elusive flaw. In 1901 Butler published *Erewhon Revisited*, in which Higgs returns to Erewhon twenty years after his first visit, and discovers, to his horror, that he has been deified as the 'Sunchild', and that 'Sunchildism' is now the national religion. Butler was himself returning, after a similar interval, to the problematic of the relationship between rationalism and Christianity. He considered *Erewhon Revisited* to be more of an organic whole than its predecessor, and indeed its character and plot development are far superior; but he concluded that, while *Erewhon Revisited* showed a marked improvement in style, '*Erewhon*, with all its faults, is the better reading of the two.'

Butler's masterpiece is undoubtedly his semi-autobiographical novel *The Way of All Flesh*, published posthumously in 1903. He here turned his attention to the tyrannies of Victorian family life, and, perhaps because many of his targets were taken from personal experience, his satire is seen at its most savage; one critic has described Butler as 'an expert in demolition'. The novel is built upon Butler's theory, deriving from his study of Darwin and other evolutionists, that heredity transmits habits and modes of behaviour which are stored up by the unconscious. The eccentricities of the Pontifex family are traced from one generation to the next: Thomas Pontifex is persecuted by his father, and in turn becomes a despot to his own son Ernest (Butler's fictional alter-ego). Butler's evolutionary ideas do not, as is often claimed, mar the novel; without them it would be a qualitatively different, and probably less wickedly funny, book. If *The Way of All Flesh* does have a major weakness, it is that it displays to the full Butler's obsession with money, and his faith in financial independence as a panacea for all social ills. Like most of his work, Butler's final book found little favour with the reading public. But then he had always despised authors like Dickens*, who were conventionally popular. Butler was closest in nature and style to Jonathan Swift: both were relentless in pursuit of their chosen targets, and historically both were, in Thackeray's* words, 'alone and gnashing in the darkness'.

Paul Nicholls

Butler's other works include: *Life and Habit* (1877); *Evolution Old and New* (1879); *Unconscious Memory* (1880); *Luck or Cunning?* (1886); *The Humour of Homer* (1892); *On the Trapanese Origin of the Odyssey* (1893); *The Authoress of the Odyssey* (1897); *Shakespeare's Sonnets Reconsidered* (1899). See: H. F. Jones, *Samuel Butler: A Memoir* (2 vols, 1919); P. N. Furbank, *Samuel Butler* (1948); and B. Willey, *Darwin and Butler: Two Versions of Evolution* (1960).

72

BYRON, Lord (George Gordon Noel) 1788–1824

British poet

When Byron died in 1824 the newspapers in France remarked that two of the greatest men of the century – Napoleon* and Byron – had gone at almost the same time. In Germany, Goethe* said that Byron 'must unquestionably be regarded as the greatest talent of the century'. Neither of these extreme claims is justifiable, but they both point to the fact that almost from the beginning the myth of Byron has been more potent than his poetry, despite the immense contemporaneous popularity of the latter. The poems that continentals like Goethe and Alfred de Musset* most admired were Byron's worst – his Gothic melodramas like *Lara* (1814) or *The Corsair* (1813), and his unplayable plays, *Cain* (1821), *The Deformed Transformed* (1824) – all of them practically unreadable today. Those that constitute his real achievement as a poet – for the modern reader at least – brought him more obloquy than reputation at the time: in particular the irreverent, rambling, unfinished, and probably unfinishable, *Don Juan* (1819–24).

George Gordon Byron was born with a deformed foot in London in 1788, the son of Captain John Byron, a rake and fortune-hunter, whose uncle, 'The Wicked Lord', was the fifth Lord Byron of Newstead Abbey near Nottingham. Byron's mother was Captain Byron's second wife, the first having died after giving birth to a daughter, Augusta. The second Mrs Byron, like the first, was an heiress. Catherine Gordon of Gight was a raw, provincial girl whose father, a Highland laird, belonged to the notorious reiving clan of the Gordons. The marriage was unhappy. The captain's debts and extravagance swallowed up most of his wife's money, and he died, possibly by his own hand, when Byron was three. By then Mrs Byron had withdrawn to Aberdeen where she was just able to make ends meet on a meagre income. She was a vulgar and violent woman. Their poverty in Scotland, where Byron imbibed 'too much Calvinism for faith or unfaith in Christianity', and the attentions of his nurse, who initiated him to sexual practices very early, marked Byron for life. He was highly sexed, bisexual, and at the same time affectionate ('I must have something to love'): Unlike Shelley* he did not make his women miserable; it was the other way round, for most of Byron's ladies, except the Countess Guiccoli, were termagants: for instance Lady Caroline Lamb, Annabella Milbanke, and Shelley's sister-in-law Claire Clairmont.

Owing to the unexpected death of the heir, Byron inherited the title and estates in 1798, when he was ten. In 1801 he was sent to Harrow, where he read widely – Rousseau's *Confessions*, Locke, Bacon, Hume, Berkeley, and 'all the British Classics . . . with most of the living poets, Scott*, Southey*, &c. – Some French, in the original, of which the Cid is my favourite', as well as Pope, Cervantes, Fielding, Smollett, Richardson, Sterne and Rabelais. He formed some passionate friendships, and despite his lameness became a noted swimmer and played cricket for Harrow at Lord's. All portraits and descriptions of Byron agree that he was remarkably handsome. But he had a tendency to fatness, and there was his deformed foot; points on which he was sensitive. On account of the one he would diet rigorously, living for weeks on nothing but biscuits and soda-water; on account of the other he sought to excel in bodily exercises, especially swimming. The conquest of his lameness may be one reason why he was in love with the idea of himself as a man of action rather than a poet.

He went to Cambridge in 1805, where he published a collection of juvenilia, *Hours of Idleness* (1807), which was well received except for a scathing notice in the *Edinburgh Review*, one result of which was his satire on contemporary poets and critics, dressed in rather wooden heroic couplets: *English Bards and Scotch Reviewers* (1809). There are some good hits, including the lines on Wordsworth* (an easy and popular target), but Byron came to regret the poem, especially when he became friends with some of its victims – Coleridge*, Moore, and Scott. At Cambridge he formed some solid friendships, notably with the reliable John Cam Hobhouse, later Lord Broughton (1786–1869), who was to be his fidus Achates during his life and after his death. Like any other Regency buck, he also had a taste for low life, and frequented the company of pugilists like Gentleman Jackson and other *demimonde* characters. Newstead Abbey he made the scene of some rather scandalous parties, on the lines of Sir Francis Dashwood's 'Hellfire Club'.

When Byron attained his majority in 1809 he took his seat in the House of Lords and almost immediately set off with Hobhouse on a long and adventurous Grand Tour of the continent, a journey that was to be as crucial to his development as Wordsworth's equally unconventional, though less well-heeled, travels in France and Switzerland nearly twenty years earlier. Byron was away for two years, travelling as far as Constantinople by way of Portugal, Spain, Greece and Albania. While in Albania – then even more than now a wild, remote, little-visited region – Byron began his long semi-autobiographical travel poem, *Childe Harold's Pilgrimage* (1812), written in spenserian stanzas, filled with lush romanticism and projecting an image of himself as the melancholy outcast, satiated and vaguely Satanic – in short the prototype of the Byronic hero that became the central figure of his popular verse tales like *The Corsair* which were to thrill so many bosoms for the next two or three decades. It is a formless poem threaded upon his own wanderings, but laced with vivid topographical description and stirringly denunciatory political comment. But the language is full of poetical clichés, and Byron never managed to handle the spenserian stanza with conviction.

When he returned to England in 1811 he was met by a series of personal losses – the deaths of his mother and several Cambridge friends – which intensified his feeling of isolation. A beginning at politics (he opposed a bill to make the destruction of factory machinery a capital offence) was abandoned after the publication of *Childe Harold* early in 1812. The success of the poem was immense. The limping, never-quite-accepted young aristocrat found himself being invited everywhere and exposed to an adulation almost equivalent to that offered to pop stars in our day. He began to frequent the fashionable salons of the Whig aristocracy, and became involved in an affair with the gamine, spoiled, unpredictable Lady Caroline Lamb, the wife of Queen Victoria's* future prime minister, Lord Melbourne. Their affair was both notorious and spectacular, but her violent caprice soon wore him out. It was at Melbourne House that Byron met his future wife,

Annabella Milbanke. Like Caroline Lamb, she was a spoiled child, but unlike her an intellectual prig. Byron entered into a correspondence that developed into a courtship in spite of his entanglement with other affairs: Lady Oxford, his half-sister Augusta, and his difficulty in disengaging from Lady Caroline. It was Annabella's complacent belief that she could reform the wicked poet that led her to accept his hand after more than once refusing it; and on New Year's Day 1815 he married 'The Princess of Parallelograms'.

The marriage lasted a year and a fortnight. He was moody, irascible, capable of humiliating his wife in front of others, and given to Grand Guignol posings (Sir Walter Raleigh once remarked, 'The man Byron tried to be was the invention of Mrs Radcliffe'). She was humourless, gullible, puritanic and completely self-absorbed. Matters were not helped by Byron's temporary but acute financial embarrassment – they had a bailiff camping in their London house a few weeks before Annabella gave birth to a daughter. Byron was drinking heavily and Annabella convinced herself that he was mentally deranged. A month after their daughter was born Annabella left London with the baby to visit her parents. The parting was amicable; she wrote him affectionate letters; but on her arrival home her account of Byron's behaviour so outraged her parents that they refused to allow her to return.

No specific charges were ever brought against Byron by Annabella; it was enough for her to hint and for others to speculate, then and thereafter. Sodomy, incest with his half-sister Augusta, have been among the more popular conjectures to account for her moral horror of Byron. At any rate Byron found himself a social outcast as suddenly as he had become a celebrity. A few days after signing a deed of separation from his wife he left England for good in April 1816.

A week before he left England, Shelley's future sister-in-law Claire Clairmont threw herself at Byron's head and succeeded in having an affair with him. Having learnt where he was going, Claire persuaded Shelley and her sister, who were leaving England, to take her with them and go to Geneva in Switzerland. There they found Byron. This was the beginning of a mutually valuable friendship between the two poets. Like Wordsworth and Coleridge, if not on so exalted a level, they complemented and educated one another, Shelley taking Coleridge's role of ideas-man and junior partner. He opened Byron's eyes to Wordsworth's poetry; the later and better half of *Childe Harold's Pilgrimage* owes much to Shelley, and *Don Juan*, even more.

From Geneva Byron moved to Venice, where he spent three years in wild dissipation, but finished *Childe Harold* and produced *Beppo* (1818) – a light satirical narrative poem in *ottava rima* which was the dummy-run for *Don Juan* and furnished him with the ideal vehicle for the wit and colloquial eloquence which was

his true gift. He became the *cavaliere servente* or gentleman-friend of the young Countess Teresa Guiccoli, whom he followed to her elderly husband's palazzo in Ravenna in 1819. Here he lived for two years, when Teresa's estrangement from her husband and her family's involvement with the Carbonari – a revolutionary group seeking to free Italy from the Austrians, with which Byron was also actively engaged – forced them to remove in 1821 to Pisa, where Shelley had invited them.

At Pisa Shelley persuaded Byron to help finance the impecunious radical editor, Leigh Hunt, by bringing him out to Italy to edit a magazine to be called the *Liberal*. No sooner had Hunt and his family arrived than Shelley was drowned in the Bay of Lerici, leaving Byron more or less responsible for the maintenance of the Hunts and of the *Liberal*, which ran to four numbers, and to which Byron contributed *The Vision of Judgment* (1822), a hilarious take-off of Southey and one of the best acerbic satires in the language. It is not so much a satire as a 'flyting' in the tradition of Scotch poets like Dunbar (T. S. Eliot has noted that Byron is best regarded as a Scotch poet).

After Shelley's death Byron removed to Genoa, where he was approached by an emissary from the Philhellene London Greek Society to go to the aid of the Greeks who had risen against their Turkish oppressors in 1821. Byron, one of the few Philhellenes who knew Greece, its language and problems at firsthand, was soon persuaded. He sailed for Greece in 1823, taking with him medical supplies and considerable funds from his own purse for the partisans. The Greek insurgents were divided into rival, almost warring, factions and brigand armies. Byron delayed cautiously before deciding to back the party led by Prince Mavrocordato, whose headquarters were at Missolonghi, a miasmal seaport of Western Greece. Here, having accomplished nothing, he caught a fever and died – bled and purged to death by his doctors – on 19 April 1824. Nevertheless his death proved to be the crucial event of the Greek War of Independence, for it provoked an international wave of enthusiasm for the Greek cause. Three years later a combined British, French and Russian fleet defeated the Turks at the Battle of Navarino, and Greece was free.

The only poet to get a chapter to himself in Bertrand Russell's *History of Western Philosophy* (1946) is Byron. There he is seen as the type of aristocratic rebel, an apostle of Romanticism, a forerunner of Nietzsche*. Russell even asserts that 'nationalism, Satanism, hero-worship, the legacy of Byron, became part of the complex soul of Germany'. All this has more to do with Byron's life than with his poetry. As with Oscar Wilde*, his legend and personality are more powerful than his literary remains: more has been written about the lives of these two than about their works.

Byron's death in Greece for the cause of freedom, his

exile, after the wreck of his marriage for unnameable or at any rate unnamed wickednesses, made him the type of figure of the Romantic movement, the beautiful and damned youth whose griefs and remorse are the subject of his art, the heroic martyr laying down his life to fight despotism. His great vogue derived from his ability to reflect the contemporary mood, and from his dilution and popularization of Romantic sensibility – a coarsening of sentiment into sentimentalism. Wordsworth justly complained that Byron borrowed his pantheism in the last two cantos of *Childe Harold*. But Byron's real and valuable contribution to the Romantic movement was, paradoxically, his anti-Romanticism: the gaiety and realism of poems he wrote in the last six years of his life – *Beppo*, *The Vision of Judgment* and above all *Don Juan* which Montale has called 'the only readable poem left by Byron' and of which W. H. Auden remarked 'it is as much the dramatized story of the education of Byron's mind as *The Prelude* is a direct account of the education of Wordsworth's'. The hero of *Don Juan* is not Don Juan but the discursive narrator, Byron himself; not the Romantic mask, but the real man, from whom the histrionic sentimentalism of Childe Harold had been cauterized, who is presented – in a way that scandalized Wordsworth – in 'language really used by men'. One does not read *Don Juan* for its story or descriptions, but for its asides – in a word, for Byron's conversation, which elsewhere is only to be found in his letters – endlessly entertaining, witty, unpretentious, colloquial, earthy, drily and profoundly comic. Indeed, as a master of the informal style, Byron has a claim to be regarded, even with Keats, Gray, Cowper, Horace Walpole, Coleridge and Dorothy Wordsworth in the field, as the best letter-writer in the language; a claim currently being underlined by Leslie

A. Marchand's monumental edition of his correspondence. As an admirer of Napoleon* (the ideal-type of the Romantic man of action), Byron was not the foe of tyranny that he thought he was and is thought to be. But for all his attitudinizing he was, and in his letters and in *Don Juan* remains, the foe of cant.

Byron's influence on the development of English poetry has been negligible. Of his successors, only A. H. Clough* matched his throwaway, colloquial tone. But on the continent his influence was widespread and profound, even if (as in the case of Poe*) the most admired poems were not very good. His poems were translated into French, German, Russian, Italian, Dutch, Spanish, Polish and Hungarian during his lifetime and afterwards; continental poets influenced by him include Victor Hugo*, Lamartine*, Alfred de Musset*, Heine*, Leopardi*, Pushkin*, Lermontov*, and Mickiewicz*.

David Wright

The Works of Lord Byron, Poetry, (ed.). E. H. Coleridge (1898–1904); *Byron's Letters and Journals*, (ed.), Leslie A. Marchand (11 vols, 1973–81). About Byron's life: Thomas Moore, *The Life of Lord Byron* (1830) is well worth reading though it is superseded by Leslie A. Marchand, *Byron: A Biography* (1957); see also Doris Langley Moore, *The Late Lord Byron* (1961) and *Byron and Shelley: The History of a Friendship* (1970). Critical assessments of Byron's work include: G. Wilson Knight, 'The Two Eternities', in *The Burning Oracle* (1939), and *Byron, Christian Virtues* (1953); T. S. Eliot's essay on Byron is *From Anne to Victoria*, (ed.), Bonamy Dobrée (1957); A. Rutherford, *Byron: A Critical Study* (1962); Leslie A. Marchand, *Byron's Poetry: A Critical Introduction* (1965).

C

73

CANOVA, Antonio 1757–1822

Italian sculptor

The smoothly elegant Neoclassical carvings of Canova are very much an acquired taste though there is no doubting their technical virtuosity and sophistication. Trained in Rococo Venice the early decorative tendencies were abandoned by 1781 when he settled in Rome, where he completed the first major works – the two Papal monuments to *Clement XIV* (1782–7, SS Apostoli, Rome), and to *Clement XIII* (1787–92 St Peter's, Rome) – both much prized commissions and the most important that could be given to a sculptor in Rome at the time. The style is simple and deliberately formal and there is none of the passionate flow of Roman Baroque epitomized by the full-blooded clamour for attention of Bernini. It is as though Canova needed to purify the art of carving from all excesses of temperament and instead of the ornate richness expected in such important monuments there is a subdued air of profound grief and a detached funereal silence. The working method is far from simple and during the long and often tedious process much of the carver's spontaneity is inevitably lost. Overworked, Canova needed to employ a team of capable assistants and he left much of the day-to-day work to them. He made small wax models – *bozzetti* – and later life-size clay maquettes, but left much of the interpretation into marble to others, returning only to apply the finishing touches and to complete the piece in the true Neoclassical manner. This he did with great care and attention, even to the extent of hiring readers to read from the literature of the Ancients as he polished away at the near completed work. A further detachment and lack of awareness of the innate quality of the stone results from an obsession for staining the marble with soot in order to give the dull mellowed effect he thought necessary to soften its natural luminosity. In the more serious works this is less noticeable but it does little to enhance the attempts at life-like naturalism of the more light-weight pieces which can have a certain undeniably erotic attraction. *Cupid and Psyche* (1787–93 Louvre, Paris), is an attempt to idealize the interwoven forms of two lovers and the *terracotta sketch* (1787 Gipsoteca, Possagno), reveals a knowing sense of immediate intimacy. The finished work for all its delightful touches is far from successful and the stylized harmonious composition lacks any real understanding of what is taking place. Psyche reaches elegantly upwards to hold her winged lover as though to stop him being wafted away on the wind. Cupid reaches elegantly round to caress a breast that seems awkwardly out of reach. Both are clearly bored and we sympathize with accusations of erotic frigidity. Canova's fear of excess is partly to blame but more important is the detachment of the working method which for all its delicacy and refinement only succeeds in withdrawing all life from the two participants. At times the eroticism verges on necrophilia. At times the lifeless method and stilted compositions make for bizarre exaggeration as in the cumbersome *Hercules and Lichas* (1795–1802 Galleria d'Arte Moderna, Rome), with its overblown heroics and pointless symbolism but we are easily impressed by the virtuoso carving in the *Monument to the Archduchess Maria Christina* (1799–1805 Augustiner-Kirche, Vienna), with its simple pyramid form and illusionistic effects. There is even a hint of drama as the slowly moving figures with their transparent draperies ease towards and through the open door and whatever lies beyond. This dramatic sense is evident in the works made for Napoleon* in Paris after he accepted the emperor's invitation to visit in 1802, but once again the most successful piece is more modest. The carving of *Pauline Bonaparte Borghese as Venus* (1808 Borghese Gallery, Rome), is full of tenderness and obvious delight which reflects the sculptor's intense admiration for Napoleon and his family. The slender body of the reclining woman is barely contrasted with the flowing lines of the drapery and the effect is of truly classical semi-nudity and as such utterly convincing. The austerity of the large set-pieces is forgotten and here we have the cool technician in complete control dedicated to re-creating the image of a beautiful woman for our delight. He needed no assistance. There is still no obvious excess – there is none of the French Rococo wit of Boucher – but equally there is none of the dead soot-stained dullness of which he was only too often capable. In many ways it is the least obviously *neo-classical* of his works, and this is why it succeeds.

After the fall of Napoleon in 1815 Canova visited London and was very much impressed by the newly acquired Elgin Marbles in the British Museum, which he saw as being of the utmost importance to European art. These Greek fragments clearly revealed the scope of the ancient classical sculptors with their perfect ad-mixture of cool objectivity and a sensitive awareness of observed natural order. Canova was overworked and at his least convincing merely encouraged others to interpret what he had in mind but at his best he was a keen observer and no strict dogmatist. Neoclassicism when tempered with personal involvement came close to the ideal form so beloved by those who saw it as the only answer to Romantic self-indulgence, but the influ-ence of Canova at his most unenlightened was insidious and can be seen in much banal Victoriana.

John Furse

See: Hugh Honour, *Neo-Classicism* (1968); Rudolf Wittkower, *Sculpture* (1977).

74

CANTOR, Georg Ferdinand Ludwig Philipp
1845–1918

German mathematician and logician

Georg Cantor, the creator of set theory, was born in St Petersburg in 1845 and moved with his parents to the south of Germany in 1856. Against his father's wishes he studied mathematics at Berlin University from 1863 to 1869. There he was greatly influenced by Theodor Weierstrasse's seminal lectures on the real numbers. After obtaining a doctorate for work on number theory he settled in Halle where he spent the remainder of his life, becoming Professor Extraordinary of the Univer-sity of Halle in 1872 and Professor Ordinary in 1879. His most productive decade ended in 1884 when he suffered a breakdown of health. He was subsequently plagued by mental illness and largely ceased math-ematical work in 1897.

During his lifetime his highly original work in logic and mathematics received a mixed reception. The sev-ere criticism of Leopold Kronecker and Poincaré*, among others, greatly distressed him and may have contributed to his breakdown. Poincaré regarded Can-tor's set theory as 'pathological' and confidently pre-dicted that it would come to be regarded as a disease from which mathematics had recovered. However, in time his work gained general acceptance, particularly through the support of David Hilbert, and Cantor is now regarded as one of the greatest logicians and math-ematicians of the nineteenth century. Cantor's diffi-culties in gaining a sympathetic hearing from the mathematical establishment prompted him to become a founder and first president of the Deutsche Mathe-matiker Vereinigung (German Mathematical Assembly).

Prior to Cantor and Dedekind* there was no adequate theory of the real numbers. In particular a satisfactory definition of the notion of an irrational number was lacking. Following a suggestion of Weier-strasse, Cantor defined irrational numbers as certain infinite ordered sets of rational numbers (fractions). On this approach $\sqrt{2}$ can be taken to be the sequence of rational numbers 1.4, 1.41, 1.414, ..., the squares of which progressively approximate the value 2. This led Cantor to develop a theory of sets within which to study infinite sets which, he maintained, existed actually and not merely potentially. His theory was based on the simple but powerful notion that two sets have the same number of members just in case the members of the two sets can be placed into a one-one correspondence. Cantor defined an infinite set as one which can be put into a one-one correspondence with a proper sub-set of the set (i.e. to a selection of some members of the set). For instance, the set of natural numbers 1, 2, 3, ... is infinite for it can be put into a one-one correspondence with the set of even natural numbers 2, 4, 6, ..., a result which also shows that these two sets have the same number of members. Cantor defined denumerable sets to be those that can be put into a one-one correspondence with the natural numbers and used the symbol α_0 for the number of members in any such set. He established the counter-intuitive result that the set of all rational numbers is denumerable and using his famous diagonal method showed that the infinite set of all real numbers is not denumerable. Using the symbol 'c' for this larger in-finite number which gives the size of the set of all real numbers Cantor laboured in vain to answer the ques-tion as to whether there are any infinite numbers be-tween α_0 and c. The continuum hypothesis which states that there are no such infinite numbers is now known to be consistent with the postulates of set theory but not a consequence of them.

Cantor discovered the existence of an infinite hier-archy of ever larger infinite sets which Hilbert referred to as 'Cantor's Paradise'. The crucial element in this is Cantor's theorem which states that the number of members of the power set of a given set A is greater than the number of members of A. The power set of A is the set of all sub-sets of A. It turns out, as Cantor showed, that the power set of the set of all natural numbers is the same size as the set of all real numbers. By Cantor's theorem the power set of the set of real numbers is an infinite set of even greater size. Taking the power set of that set in turn gives a still larger set. And repeating this operation gives an endless sequence of ever larger infinite sets. Cantor went on to develop the laws of arithmetic for the resulting hierarchy of infinite numbers.

In the course of his work on infinite sets Cantor attempted to prove that the infinite set of points on a line of unit length was smaller than the infinite set of points in a unit square. However, in 1877 he estab-lished that in fact these sets are of the same size, a result which he said he saw but did not believe. Indeed this result holds if one moves to three or more dimensions. This meant that one could no longer understand an increase in dimension in terms of an increase in the number of points. While Cantor was himself unable to produce a satisfactory alternative account of dimension his work prompted others to do so.

In his development of set theory Cantor had defined a set to be 'a collection into a whole of definite distinct objects of our intuition or our thought'. Cantor became aware that on this understanding of a set the resulting theory had problematic aspects, discovering in 1895 what is now known as the Burali-Forti paradox and in 1899 the paradox that bears his name. This latter paradox arises if one posits (as the definition would seem to allow) the existence of a set S consisting of all sets. By Cantor's theorem, the power set of S must be larger in size than S itself. But by the definition of S the power set of S must be a sub-set of S and hence it cannot be larger in size. Mathematicians have had to add restrictions to Cantor's theory of sets to prevent these and other paradoxes. However, these restrictions do not affect Cantor's results concerning infinite sets which remain the basis of our understanding of infinities in mathematics.

W. H. Newton-Smith

Gesammelte Abhandlungen, ed. Ernst Zermelo (1932), contains Cantor's collected works. His most influential papers appear in translation in *Contributions to the Founding of the Theory of Transfinite Numbers* (1955), which contains an introduction to his work by P. E. B. Jourdain.

75
CARDUCCI, Giosuè 1835–1907

Italian poet, orator and literary critic

Giosuè Carducci spent his childhood years at Bolgheri (Tuscany), a time and place remembered with nostalgic affection in many of his poems and recalled frequently in autobiographical reminiscences. In 1856 he graduated from the Scuola Normale di Pisa and the following year published his first collection of poems, *Rime*. In 1860 he was appointed to the Chair of Italian in the University of Bologna, a post he held, with distinction, until 1904. For much of his life Carducci was, on account of his irascibility in general and his uncompromising political and literary views in particular, a focus of controversy. As a result, acceptance and respectability came relatively late (he was made a senator only in 1890) and wider recognition outside Italy was only conferred a few months before his death with the award of the Nobel Prize for Literature in 1906.

Any survey of Carducci's work is inevitably condi-

tioned by the poet's own concern with spiritual unity, reflected in the painstaking care with which he arranged his poems into collections, having little regard to their individual chronology. Indeed poems were often moved from one collection to another, as new groupings were perceived by the poet, until the definitive arrangement was arrived at in the single volume collection of his poetry edited by Carducci himself (*Poesie*, 1901).

The earliest collection, *Juvenilia 1850–60* (1871), is notable on the one hand for the poet's obvious knowledge of and admiration for both the classical and Italian poetic traditions, and on the other, for his early support of the Piedmontese monarchy in the final traumatic years of Italian Unification. Discontent and disillusionment with the leadership and policies of the new Italy, together with his recent adherence to the Masonic movement, led swiftly, however, to a conversion to democratic republicanism, which combined with a vibrant anti-clericalism, characterize the poems of *Levia Gravia 1861–71* (1868, revised 1871) and *Giambi e epodi 1867–79* (1882). Not even the successful completion of Italian Unity with the occupation of Rome in 1870 changed Carducci's attitudes. In fact, his scorn at the manner of its acquisition was outspoken (see 'Canto dell'Italia che va in Campidoglio' in *Giambi e epodi*) but he gave voice, certainly, to the feelings of many of his compatriots.

None the less, the 1870s eventually saw a softening of his political rhetoric as a result both of his acceptance of the monarchy's role in the Italian State and of the emergence of new poetic concerns in the *Rime nuove 1861–87* (1887) and the *Odi barbare* (1877, revised 1893). These two collections represent the pinnacle of Carducci's poetic achievement. The former reflects the poet's love of the Italian countryside ('Il bove', 'San Martino') which sometimes develops into a mood of self-analysis, especially in relation to the places remembered from his childhood ('Attraversando la Maremma toscana', 'Davanti San Guido'). In the *Odi barbare*, so-called because of the attempt in these poems to imitate, in modern Italian, the rhythms of Latin poetry, some of the major themes of his work: patriotism, disdain for the mediocrity of his contemporaries in comparison with the greatness of their Roman forebears and love of the natural scene, are uniquely combined in single poems ('Dinnanzi alle terme di Caracalla', 'Alle fonti di Clitunno'). Other poems draw out a sense of individual human suffering from historical events ('Per la morte di Napoleone Eugenio', 'Miramare') or mundane occurrences, such as the departure of a train ('Alla stazione in una mattina d'autunno').

The poems of his last collection, *Rime e ritmi* (1899), are those of an accomplished artist rather than of the mature poet of the two previous collections, and here literary reminiscences and sentimentality predominate.

Although Carducci's reputation has traditionally

rested on his poetry, during his lifetime he was famous, and sometimes notorious, as a teacher, literary critic and orator. As a teacher and critic, while lacking a basic philosophy of art, he was, none the less, perceptive and stimulating: he never shrank from condemning in other writers what he felt to be the feeble conventionalities of latter-day Romanticism, nor, as a native Tuscan, from exposing the ridiculousness of those who sought artificially to Tuscanize the language of poetry. Mention ought also to be made of his edition of Petrarch's poems *Le Rime* (joint editor with S. Ferrari, 1899), which still provides a valuable insight into the poetic language of Petrarch, and of his work on Leopardi*, particularly his role in the publication of the poet's Commonplace Book (*Pensieri di varia filosofia e di bella letteratura*, 'Philosophical and Literary Thoughts', 1898), a landmark in Leopardi studies.

Carducci's abilities as an orator are amply attested by the great number of occasions on which he was invited to speak, and even in printed form the magic of his words in many instances can still be felt. His commemoration of Garibaldi* pronounced *ex tempore* in Bologna, two days after the general's death in 1882, not only captures the spirit of what Garibaldi meant for Italians, but also manages to turn sadness at such an irreparable loss into a triumphant exhortation to lay aside all that was detrimental to the life of the nation.

In the last three-quarters of a century Carducci's fame as a poet has suffered, both inside and outside Italy, from the difficulties presented by his poetic language, the sheer volume of his writing and a seemingly obsessional concern with political issues long felt to be irrelevant. Yet even granted that there is much in his work which, for various reasons, may be dismissed, there remains a central core of his poetry which is both accessible and abidingly relevant, with its themes of nostalgia, the search for peace and a contempt for mediocrity in any form. And finally, as an articulate expression of the ideological and moral crises of the first half century of the history of the Italian State, Carducci's work will always be of fundamental importance.

C. E. J. Griffiths

The first complete edition of his works was *Opere* (20 vols, 1889–1909). The definitive edition is *Opere di Giosuè Carducci* (30 vols, 1935–41), uniform with which is the definitive edition of the poet's letters, *Lettere di Giosuè Carducci* (1938–60). A useful single-volume, annotated anthology of his works, prose and poetry, is still *Antologia carducciana*, ed. G. Mazzoni and G. Picciola (1907), and a selection of translated poems is to be found in G. Bickersteth, *The Poetry of Giosuè Carducci* (1911), which also contains a useful introduction. The key critical work on Carducci is B. Croce, *Giosuè Carducci* (4th edn. 1946), a collection of

studies first published in reply to the criticisms of E. Thovez, *Il pastore, il gregge e la zampogna* (1910). A recent biography is M. Biagini, *Vita di Giosuè Carducci* (1971).

76
CARLYLE, Thomas 1795–1881

British man of letters

Carlyle was born in the Dumfriesshire village of Ecclefechan, the son of a stonemason. His parents were members of the Secession Church, a dissenting offshoot of the Presbyterian Church which stresses the importance of the Bible as a text and as a guide to individual action, and, though unlettered, they were pious and articulate people. Both exercised a strong influence on Carlyle; as he recalled in his 'Reminiscence' written on his father's death in 1832, James Carlyle was 'a natural man, . . . healthy in body and mind, fearing God, and diligently working on God's earth with contentment, hope, and unwearied resolution'. Carlyle attended Annan Academy, going on to Edinburgh University in 1809. It was his intention, and his parents' wish, that he should become a minister after completing his general arts degree. But his experience at the 'Rational University', where Hume's sceptical empiricism was influential on the teaching, made him give up the divinity course after a year's attendance. From 1818, Carlyle lived by freelance tutoring and reviewing. He started learning German in 1819, and taught it to Jane Welsh, whom he met in 1821 and who was later to become his wife.

This period in Edinburgh, at the university and after, he later fictionalized in the semi-autobiographical *Sartor Resartus* (1833–4). Tempted to intellectual doubt by his reading of Hume and Gibbon, undecided about his future career, hesitant in his up-and-down courtship with Jane Welsh (whom he married in 1826), Carlyle experienced a phase which he dramatized in *Sartor* as 'the Everlasting No'. In the words of the hero Teufelsdröckh, 'Doubt had darkened into Unbelief', the world had become 'all void of Life, of Purpose, of Volition, even of Hostility: it was one huge, dead, immeasurable Steam-engine, rolling on, in its dead indifference, to grind me limb from limb'. Carlyle's conversion to 'the Everlasting Yea', like Teufelsdröckh's, was effected largely by his reading of Goethe*. In 1823 he began translating *Wilhelm Meister's Apprenticeship*, a work which puzzled and, because of its lack of overt moral teaching, repelled him, yet which he could admire for its mature wisdom. Moreover, the task itself was therapeutic for him. His notebook for 1823 carries some meditation of suicide. By concentrating on the translation, he struggled through to a more balanced frame of mind. Though he had lost his spiritual bearings, he found in reading Goethe (and Schiller, Novalis and Fichte*) 'a new Heaven and a new Earth' (*Sartor Resartus*).

The translation of *Meister*, in spite of some errors and occasional bowdlerizing, remains the best and most spirited rendering of the work. It was largely through Carlyle's translation and reviewing that Goethe became properly known in England, as G. H. Lewes* acknowledged by dedicating his *Life of Goethe* (1855) to Carlyle, 'who first taught England to appreciate Goethe'.

Throughout the 1820s Carlyle made his career from reviewing, becoming known as the foremost mediator of German literature in England when Francis Jeffrey, editor of the influential *Edinburgh Review*, invited him to 'Germanize the public'. This Carlyle did in a pioneering article, 'The State of German Literature' (1827), in which he persuaded readers to look, as he had done, to German literature for relief from materialism. The best examples of German literature offered a secularized spirituality, what he called in a famous chapter in *Sartor* 'natural supernaturalism'. He pursued this theme in other articles in the *Edinburgh Review*, 'Signs of the Times' (1829), 'Characteristics' (1831), and in *Sartor*. The age was for Carlyle a 'Mechanical Age', in its philosophy as well as its industry. He warned again and again against the mechanical, empirical philosophy of Hume and Hartley (the mind a 'passive engine', 'a sort of thought-mill to grind sensations into ideas'), against atheism, against the Utilitarians' measuring of pleasures and pains. Carlyle often used the grinding-mill metaphor, with its pun on James Mill's* name. His works of the late 1820s and early 1830s – some of the best writing he did – preached the urgency of attending to the question of the 'condition of England'.

Though Carlyle was making his name by reviewing, he became increasingly dissatisfied with that 'despicable business', and wanted to 'give *work* for reviewing' (1828). His first original work, *Sartor Resartus*, was composed during the years at Craigenputtoch, an isolated farmhouse in Dumfriesshire to which he and Jane moved in 1828. In *Sartor*, Carlyle dramatized both his own spiritual upheaval and what he saw as the ills of his age. The work is at once idealistic and satirical, 'mystical' and rational. Contemporaries found it puzzling, and some objected to the stylistic idiosyncrasies, the mixture of Scottish, biblical, Miltonic and Germanic rhetoric, with many coinages and naturalizations of foreign words (e.g. 'backwoodsman', 'philistine', 'maelstrom'). He offered the manuscript to several London publishers without success, but the work was finally serialized in *Fraser's Magazine* (1833–4), and first published in book form in America in 1836, through the good offices of Ralph Waldo Emerson*, who had made a pilgrimage to the 'Sage of Craigenputtoch' in 1833. Readers in England and America

responded to the 'philosophy' of *Sartor*, its call to duty and rejection of faithlessness. As George Eliot* wrote in the *Leader* (1855),

there is hardly a superior or active mind of this generation that has not been modified by Carlyle's writings. . . . The character of his influence is best seen in the fact that many of the men who have the least agreement with his opinions are those to whom the reading of *Sartor Resartus* was an epoch in the history of their minds.

Having moved to London in 1834, the 'Sage of Chelsea', as he was soon called, set to work on his imaginative reconstruction of the French Revolution. This history, the first volume of which was accidentally used to light a fire when Carlyle had lent the manuscript to J. S. Mill*, having to be rewritten from scratch, appeared in 1837 and secured his reputation. For Carlyle history was the biography of great men, and though he could not give the revolutionary leaders or Napoleon* full approval, he saw them as necessary 'heroes' thrown up by circumstances. This was again the theme of *On Heroes, Hero-Worship, and the Heroic in History* (1841). In 'Chartism' (1839) and *Past and Present* (1843), Carlyle continued his preaching and prophecy; urging the need for reform but fearing a revolution, he advocated the rise of a new, enlightened aristocracy which would practise a modern version of feudalism.

During the 1840s and 1850s Carlyle continued his self-appointed task of warning his contemporaries of the dangers of political and economic *laissez-faire* on the one hand and social revolution on the other. Predictably, he admired Cromwell, whose *Letters and Speeches* he edited in 1845, and Frederick the Great of Prussia, of whom he wrote a massive biography (1858–65). Many of those who had admired the early essays, *Sartor* and *The French Revolution* – like Mill, George Eliot and Matthew Arnold* – regretted the increasingly violent rhetoric ('Carlylese') and the increasingly illiberal message of his work. Trollope* caricatured him in *The Warden* (1855) as Dr Pessimist Anticant, who 'instituted himself censor of all things in general. . . . His theories were all beautiful . . . but when he became practical, the charm was gone.' In *Latter-Day Pamphlets* (1850) he saw dangers in democracy, regretting, for example, the humane treatment of offenders in 'model prisons', because their conditions were better than those of the uncriminal poor living outside the prison walls. Sharing his father's view of the sanctity of work, he wrote that the rebelling West Indian sugar workers had 'inherited' their duty as slaves and should be compelled to work ('Occasional Discourse on the Negro Question', 1849). When Eyre, Governor of Jamaica, brutally put down a native riot in 1865, leading English liberals pressed for his prosecution. Carlyle (with Tennyson* and Ruskin*) supported the governor's action.

On Jane's death in 1866, Carlyle recorded his misery and guilt. Theirs had been in some ways a stormy marriage; both were insomniac and hypochondriac, and Carlyle was particularly sensitive to disturbance. Jane had nobly arranged for the soundproofing of his study while he escaped to Scotland (1853), and she had once saved his nerves by appearing on his behalf before an income tax tribunal. Carlyle prepared her papers for publication, but could never decide to print them. In 1871 he handed them over to his young admirer, J. A. Froude*, with the ambiguous injunction to publish them or not after his death, as Froude saw fit. His later years saw few publications but many honours; in 1865 he was elected Lord Rector of the University of Edinburgh, he was awarded the Prussian Order of Merit in 1874 and an Honorary LLD from Harvard in 1875. On his death in 1881, burial in Westminster Abbey was offered but declined in accordance with his wishes. He was buried without a service in Ecclefechan.

Controversial in his lifetime, Carlyle was the subject of fierce argument after his death, for Froude's free publishing of Jane's letters, of Carlyle's *Reminiscences* (1881) and of a four-volume biography of Carlyle almost immediately after his death scandalized relatives and readers alike. Froude was frank about the Carlyles' squabbles, even hinting at sexual impotency on Carlyle's part. Others sprang to Carlyle's defence, and a stream of biographies, reminiscences and letters appeared in the 1880s and 1890s. Carlyle's influence on his contemporaries had been enormous. Emerson owed much of his 'transcendentalism' to Carlyle; for Froude, Clough*, George Eliot, and others, *Sartor* had dramatized their own religious doubts and had given them secularized hope. Though interest in Carlyle declined during the first half of the twentieth century (for his political opinions seemed to foreshadow fascism), he is now the subject of much scholarship. A complete edition of his and Jane's letters is in progress. No one can doubt that, for all his intolerance and his faults of style and logic, Carlyle was one of the most influential writers of the nineteenth century.

Rosemary Ashton

The standard edition of Carlyle's works is the Centenary Edition edited by H. D. Traill (30 vols, 1896–9). Froude's biography (4 vols, 1882–4) remains the best, though Ian Campbell, *Thomas Carlyle* (1974) is a short, clear guide to the main events of Carlyle's life. *The Collected Letters of Thomas and Jane Welsh Carlyle*, ed. C. R. Sanders and K. J. Fielding (7 vols, 1970), is in progress. See: Basil Willey, *Nineteenth Century Studies* (1949); John Holloway, *The Victorian Sage* (1953); C. F. Harrold, *Carlyle and German Thought 1819–1834* (1934); Albert J. LaValley, *Carlyle and the Idea of the Modern* (1968). *Victorian Prose: A Guide to Research*, ed. David J. DeLaura (1973), contains a bibliography of Carlyle studies.

77

CARNEGIE, Andrew 1835–1919

US industrialist and philanthropist

Born in Dunfermline, County Fife, Scotland, Andrew Carnegie spent his first twelve years in a family whose economic security had deteriorated rapidly. Both of Andrew's parents came from families of craftsmen, but his father, a skilled handloom weaver, saw the demand for his craft in the linen industry disappear almost completely with the rise of steam mills and the factory system. Will Carnegie never adjusted to this blow, and his wife, Margaret, took charge. In 1848 she borrowed money from friends, sold the household effects, and embarked upon a six week voyage with her husband and two sons to the United States. Margaret had two sisters and several Scottish friends in Pittsburgh, Pennsylvania, and this dirty young city became the base of operations for Andrew's meteoric career.

Andrew took a job almost immediately after arriving in Pittsburgh, and he quickly demonstrated the qualities that would bring him such great success. He began working for $1.20 a week in a textile mill, but his alertness, diligence, intuition, courage and opportunism became evident even in the lowly unskilled jobs of a twelve-year-old youth. He learned double-entry book-keeping in night school after putting in a fourteen hour day at the factory job. And when he found a new position as a messenger boy for a telegraph company, he used his idle time sweeping out the office and learning to read the 'sound' of the telegraph key. By age sixteen he had been promoted to full-time telegraph operator, a position secure and financially rewarding enough for a life's work. Good fortune, however, had positioned Andrew Carnegie in the 'mainstream' of America's rapid economic development. The telegraph, together with the railroad, was 'revolutionizing' the pace and potential for commerce and industry. Carnegie recognized what he saw and entered into the dynamic situation without looking back.

From his position in the Pittsburgh telegraph office, Andrew became a keen observer of business practices and personalities. 'He knew who sold what to whom, at what price, and on what terms.' He observed failures and successes, and his alert mind evaluated and retained what his eyes and ears received. Carnegie was also being observed. One of the important business figures in Pittsburgh was Tom Scott, superintendent and later president of the Pennsylvania Railroad. In 1852 Scott hired Carnegie as his personal telegrapher and secretary. For twelve years Andrew assimilated and applied the vast knowledge to be learned from his central location in the management of what was not only 'the standard railroad of the world', but also the largest business firm in the world. As such it represented the organizational model for financing and managing modern large-scale enterprise. Carnegie's skills, dedication, capacity for work and good connections caused him to follow Scott rapidly up the corporate ladder. In 1859, at age twenty-four, he became superintendent of the Pennsylvania Railroad. Carnegie recognized very quickly that the keys to a profitable large corporation were costs – knowing them, controlling them, reducing them. Cost accounting became a near obsession with him and would be an essential ingredient in his later success as the world's pre-eminent industrialist. Carnegie, however, was also introduced to the art of capitalism – investment allowed one to make money (or lose it) without actually working for it. Money itself could be a commodity that was bought, sold or used, and he saw how the officials of the Pennsylvania Railroad manipulated money to their firm's and their own advantages.

By 1865 Carnegie had become very wealthy, but he chose to leave the railroad for a career as a full-time investor. He moved in the ranks of the Morgans and other financiers, marketing tens of millions of dollars in stocks and bonds in the United States and Europe. He made a substantial fortune through speculation and commissions and established important business relationships, but in 1872 he changed career courses again. He had tired of the unsettled nature of the financial world, and the speculative side of his work clashed with a steadily maturing view of wealth and purpose in life. He expressed his desire, instead, 'to make something tangible.'

Nothing could have been more tangible than steel. The American iron industry had received a great boost from the Civil War, and the rapid expansion of railroad building after the war increased this demand. Furthermore, Carnegie's European business activities had acquainted him with the Bessemer innovations in the British steel industry. In 1872 he consolidated some earlier investments in iron and formed a company to produce Bessemer steel. For the rest of his long career, he adhered reasonably well to his own advice to 'put all your eggs in one basket, and then watch that basket.' Carnegie transferred his exceptional qualities of diligence, courage and intuition to the steel industry, but more importantly, he carried the knowledge and experience gained from his intimate association with the Pennsylvania Railroad. Andrew Carnegie brought rational management, precise organization and the benefits of strict cost accounting to his new firm. He had learned from Tom Scott that success came to those managers who hired the best men, paid them well, and let them go to work. Carnegie prided himself in evaluating his staff and in choosing partners. He always retained a majority of the company's stock, but he

rewarded efficient, thrifty and innovative employees with promotions and limited partnerships. He urged his staff to keep a sharp eye out for cost-cutting inovations, even replacing almost new equipment if more efficient processes could be achieved. For many years, Carnegie was the super-salesman for his firm, ruthlessly negotiating against his competitors to deliver the most steel for the lowest price. He succeeded. By 1900 Carnegie Steel produced more than the entire British steel industry. Andrew Carnegie had not reached such success, however, without forcing many people unwillingly to pay his price. His own partners, especially the brilliant and hard-nosed Henry Clay Frick, complained of his conservative and autocratic control of company stock, and his unskilled workers suffered generally from low wages and lack of job security.

'By mastering the new art of large-scale management and by fathoming the mysteries of capitalism,' however, Andrew Carnegie had set a high standard for industrialists in the future. And he had become fabulously wealthy. In 1901 he sold Carnegie Steel to the new holding company of United States Steel; his share amounted to $250,000,000 in interest-bearing gold bonds.

Carnegie worked hard and had few peers in the industrial world, but he was not a one-dimensional man. He inherited a radical political tradition (Chartism) from his father and uncles, and he demonstrated in his own life a genuine inquiry into the nature of social progress. Carnegie formed close friendships among literary and political figures on both sides of the Atlantic, and he regularly published his views on national political systems, the function of wealth, and world peace. His most revealing works were *Triumphant Democracy* (1886), in which he extolled the virtues of American republican institutions, and 'Wealth' (*North American Review*, 1889), in which he argued that personal riches were held only as a 'trust' for the community good. Carnegie did not deny himself nor his family the amenities of his material success, but after his retirement in 1901 he pursued seriously his own philosophy of wealth. His gifts to libraries, colleges, organizations seeking inter-racial and international peace, and the Carnegie Corporation amounted to $350,000,000. Most of his gifts went to the United States, but he built the Peace Palace at The Hague and was also generous to his native Scotland.

The First World War was a shattering blow to Carnegie's optimism; he died on 11 August 1919 less than a year after the armistice. Andrew Carnegie left his wife (Louise Whitfield Carnegie), one daughter and an indelible mark upon the business and social institutions of modern society.

Lester C. Lamon

See: Joseph Frazier Wall, *Andrew Carnegie* (1970); Burton J. Hendrick, *The Life of Andrew Carnegie*

(1932); Harold C. Livesay, *Andrew Carnegie and the Rise of Big Business* (1975); Andrew Carnegie, *Autobiography of Andrew Carnegie* (1920); and *The Gospel of Wealth and Other Timely Essays*, ed. Edward C. Kirkland (1962).

78
CARROLL, Lewis (Charles Lutwidge Dodgson)
1832–98

British children's author

The life of the Rev. Charles Lutwidge Dodgson, alias Lewis Carroll, is uneventful: birth in Cheshire, the son of a clergyman; Richmond Grammar School; Rugby; Christ Church, Oxford, where he became a tutor in mathematics and logic until his death at his sisters' house in Guildford. He travelled abroad only once, to Russia, preferring Eastbourne or the Isle of Wight. Much photography and writing, including many academic books – *Euclid and his Modern Rivals* (1879) is the best known of these. No love affairs – a sigh in the direction of the young Ellen Terry is usually jumped on by biographers eager for material. As a result his diaries, letters, and the biographies of him are dull. More stimulating are those books which seek to partake of the imaginative world he created as Lewis Carroll, a world of such mythic force that it became self-propagating and beyond conventional critique: *Aspects of Alice* by Robert Phillips (1971), *The Magic of Lewis Carroll* by John Fisher (1973), *The Philosopher's Alice* by Peter Heath (1974), *The Raven and the Writing Desk* by Francis Huxley (1976), *Fragments of a Looking-Glass* by Jean Gattégno (1978). The most successful of these, the least beset by psychological triteness, is *The White Knight: A Study of C. L. Dodgson* by Alexander Taylor (1952).

Dodgson was a shy and fastidious bachelor with a marked stammer, sometimes priggish or melancholy, not especially likeable. Like Ruskin*, he loved young girls. In their company he was unusually animated. His letters to them are full of brilliant nonsense, unlike his other correspondence. Later in life he liked to photograph them unclad. But as they entered puberty he lost interest, and young boys he actively disliked. Dodgson's most famous companion was Alice Liddell, daughter of the Dean of Christ Church. The stories he extemporized for her on boating trips from Oxford were the basis for *Alice's Adventures in Wonderland* (1865) and *Through the Looking-Glass, and What Alice Found There* (Christmas 1871, dated 1872). With the long nonsense poem *The Hunting of the Snark* (1876), they form the essence of his literary output.

This work is the characteristic Victorian attempt to enter the dream world – and it succeeds utterly. Part poet, part logician, Lewis Carroll was better adapted to this tale than any comparable writer and the outcome is an autonomous creation free from the folksiness of the Brothers Grimm*, the sentimental realism of Hans Andersen*, or the tendency towards inconsequential whimsy which one finds in Edward Lear*. Carroll is a precursor of Surrealism (Aragon translated him) and Absurdism (their humour is his invention), hence the enormous increase in his status among intellectuals since the Great War. The ages of Freud and Jung transformed the *Alice* books from a children's story into something profoundly mysterious and there is no doubt that the title 'children's author' has always been incorrect, despite Dodgson's own modest intentions ('I meant nothing but nonsense,' he said). None the less, it is true that to notice, for example, that the trial of the Knave of Hearts is father to Kafka's *Trial*, or that Humpty Dumpty's 'portmanteau' language is the prototype of the punning technique of *Finnegans Wake* (dubbed 'superjabberwocky' by Anthony Burgess enlarging Edmund Wilson's connection), does not really get one very far. It throws some light on Kafka and Joyce but none at all on Carroll whose creations always remain gleefully superior to this kind of exercise.

More than most works of genius, the *Alice* books defy explication, because they travel with us from childhood, changing as we change, comforting, disturbing, each aspect acting as the foil for the other, and in that tension we are spellbound. They are short, very pure works, outside time, concrete, written without discursiveness at a level of inspiration that is effortlessly high. They are always fresh – with every reading a new visita springs up in the landscape. Yet there is virtually no background. They are all character and drama, full of dialogue and action, which the illustrations of Sir John Tenniel (1820–1914) exactly reinforce. Like minor deities these characters move mischievously in a clatter of laughter between our world and their own, and the chief of them is Alice herself, sensitive and robust, one of literature's archetypal figures. She returns us to the uncynical state of wondrous curiosity associated with childhood and, like a genuine goddess, leads us into strange, eternal places without leading us astray.

Duncan Fallowell

The Lewis Carroll Handbook (1970) is the standard bibliographical reference work. See also: Stuart Dodgson, *The Life and Letters of Lewis Carroll* (1898); Derek Hudson, *Lewis Carroll* (revised 1977).

79
CARVER, George Washington 1860–1943

US agricultural scientist and educator

Born a slave, of slave parents, George Washington Carver was orphaned as an infant and raised by his white owners on a farm near Diamond Grove, Missouri. As a young boy, he took Carver, their family name, as his own. Frail and frequently sick, Carver could not do heavy farm work, but he displayed considerable interest in the more tedious tasks of cooking, laundry and knitting. He enjoyed painting and music, but above all else, he had an affinity for plants. Even as a child, he became known in his rural Missouri community as the 'Plant Doctor'.

As a black youth, Carver found few opportunities for formal education in Missouri. He left home and pursued a difficult path through several elementary and secondary schools and an unsuccessful two-year effort at homesteading in Kansas, before winning admission to Simpson College in Indianola, Iowa, in 1890. After a year at Simpson, George Carver transferred to the Iowa State College of Argriculture. He received BS and MS degrees from Iowa State, and his work in cross-fertilization of plants and the collection and identification of fungi won considerable praise from his instructors and colleagues. Carver's work attracted the interest of Booker T. Washington*, and in 1897 Washington hired him as director of agricultural work at Tuskegee Institute in Alabama.

George Washington Carver's contributions to education and agricultural science sprang from and yet, at the same time, were limited by his unorthodox methods and great personal modesty. Carver shared Washington's view that black Americans could 'lift themselves' by becoming more efficient farmers and artisans. To this end, he wrote countless bulletins, leaflets and circulars, explaining in non-technical terms how southern farm practices could be improved. Since illiteracy ran high among black farmers, he encouraged the use of demonstration techniques in changing poor habits. Carver designed a 'movable school of agriculture' which conducted demonstrations and carried exhibits throughout the rural counties of the South. Carver became a frequent speaker at agricultural institutes and conferences. His real love, however, was experimentation, and he preferred to avoid public attention.

In 1910, George Carver became director of a new department of research at Tuskegee. For the next thirty-three years Carver worked with dyes, soils, fertilizers, and plant hybrids. His knowledge of plants and their distribution was impressive, his capacity for work was enormous, and the number of products coming from his laboratory was overwhelming. His work attracted interest from several sources, and his reputation soon brought considerable attention to the man and to Tuskegee Institute. In 1916, the Royal Society of Arts (London) elected him a fellow, on the recommendation of Sir Harry H. Johnston, the celebrated naturalist. In 1921, Carver drew national attention when he presented expert testimony before the House Ways and Means Committee of Congress.

Carver's reputation came to centre upon his work with peanuts and sweet potatoes. He astounded journalists, visiting observers and countless audiences with the many uses he described for peanuts, sweet potatoes and other southern crops. He eventually listed 282 peanut products, 159 uses of the sweet potato, and seventy-five products from the pecan. Carver was not always original, but he was imaginative, and he argued convincingly that the cotton-based agriculture of the South had to be diversified extensively, if it was to become profitable for small farmers. He saw his research as missionary work under the banner of agricultural diversification. As a student of new uses for plants, George Washington Carver was one of the earliest and most outstanding figures in the newly recognized field of chemurgy. His contributions to this field unfortunately were restricted, however, by his unorthodox research procedures, his unwillingness to publish in scientific journals, and his failure to build a group of students or colleagues around his laboratory. Carver never recorded the formulas for his discoveries, and when pressed by interviewers, the devoutly religious scientist often gave the impression that his successes were based upon divine inspiration and revelation.

Nevertheless, Carver's reputation gained momentum, and he became a folk hero. To black Americans, he was a symbol of success and acceptance in a predominantly hostile white world. His genuine and presumed accomplishments in this regard caused him to be awarded the Spingarn Medal by the National Association for the Advancement of Colored People in 1923. For white Americans, Carver represented a patient, humble and conservative approach to race relations which made it safe to recognize his accomplishments and encourage his build-up as an heroic example for other blacks to emulate. He received honorary doctorates from Simpson College and the University of Rochester and drew the praise of presidents and other political figures. And, not unimportantly, for organized peanut growers, Carver's findings and reputation provided a bonanza of publicity to be encouraged and even embellished. Their trade journals released numerous accounts of his work, and these articles were, in turn, picked up by the popular press.

When Carver died in 1943, he was eulogized by President Franklin D. Roosevelt and other leading figures from around the world. Congress provided funds to build a national monument at his birthplace, something previously done for only two other Americans: George Washington and Abraham Lincoln*. As a scientist, Carver's contributions do not often measure up to his legend, but as an educator and as an internationally recognized public figure he played an important role in American society.

Lester C. Lamon

See: Rockham Holt, *George Washington Carver: An*

American Biography (1943); Lawrence Elliott, *George Washington Carver: The Man Who Overcame* (1966); and Barry Mackintosh, 'George Washington Carver: The Making of a Myth', *The Journal of Southern History*, Vol. XLII (November 1976).

80

CAYLEY, Sir George 1773–1857

British inventor and flight pioneer

Cayley prepared the foundations of modern aerodynamics. Between 1799 and 1805 he built and tested full-scale fixed-wing gliders, having grasped the principles that a practical craft should have rigid wings rather than ornithopter's flappers, and that a cambered aerofoil provides more lift than a flat one. In 1781 a German ornithopteric glider probably made brief flights but, in Cayley's words, the necessity remained 'to make a surface support a given weight by application of power to the resistance of air'. His sense of space equalled his sense of flight: 'an uninterrupted navigable ocean, that comes to the threshold of every man's door, ought not to be neglected as a source of human gratification and advantage' (1816). He was the first to understand the implications of bird propulsion through the propeller action of outer primary wing feathers; first to apply the dihedral angle of bird wings – two planes meeting at an angle – to airplane possibility, for lateral stability in both kite and glider; first to suggest cycle-type tension wheels for undercarriage; first to investigate the movement of the centre of pressure on an aerofoil; first to investigate aeronautical streamlining for least resistance; first to suggest an internal combustion engine for aircraft. In 1850 Cayley published illustrated instructions on how to fly a full-sized glider (in *Mechanic Magazine*). He pioneered in agriculture, architecture, artificial limbs, artillery, a hot-air engine, a caterpillar tractor, and so forth. But his major field remained the application of scientific methodology to flight techniques, working out the basic configuration of the powered, pilot-controlled craft by separating lift, propulsion and control systems. Out of his discoveries he constructed the first successful model glider and two full-scale machines capable of piloted flight. Curiously, his notebooks contain retrogressive designs for flight by paddle and flapper power, and he promoted no long-term research programme towards efficient aircraft – although he did found the Polytechnic Institution in Regent Street, London, 1839.

Cayley was one of the last aristocratic landowning virtuosi whose enthusiasm and knowledge engendered essential lines of invention out of a multiple interest rather than a singular specialization. In 1802 he worked on wings to sustain a man and a 2 hp engine with a view, as he wrote, to end the failure of flight by

muscular strength 'from the time of Daedalus to that of Bishop Wilkins'. Against characteristic ridicule he maintained belief in 'aerial navigation' as an undoubted future accomplishment: 'mechanical *power* within certain limits as to weight, is that which is wanting to realize mechanical as well as aerostatic flight on a scale for human use.' He pioneered the *modern* helicopter in 1796 but did not transfer his vertical airscrew research to lateral propulsion. His first (1799) design is a sketch on a small silver disc of a pilot sitting between the cambered wings of a biplane with tailplanes and a fin, the most important pioneering design in aviation history, even if the fixed planes are thrust forward from manually operated paddles. His hot-air engine was less bulky than the current steam-engine and less dangerous than the gunpowder engine. His tension wheel (the later bicycle wheel) avoided splintering and distortion from shock to the rim, and his tubular beam construction reduced frame weight. He derived his notion of 'a solid of least resistance' from the action of a trout, a dolphin and a woodcock. His essay 'On Aerial Navigation' is the foundation of aerodynamic theory for heavier-than-air flight (dihedral wings, vertical and horizontal rudders for control and stability). His man-carrying glider was launched, however, by a running pilot 'taking advantage of a gentle breeze in front', as he reported, which 'would frequently lift him up, and convey him several yards together' – that is, hang-gliding ninety years before Lilienthal, Chanute and the Wrights. In 1843 Cayley criticized William Henson's aircraft design (tailplane as rudder-elevator, 25–30 mph light engine operating two six-blade propellers, tricycle tension wheel undercarriage, etc.) as impractical for its size (150 foot wingspan), lack of lateral stability, need for downhill take-off, and low-rated engine, but suggested a three-decker wing structure (he himself built triplane gliders, a major influence on Chanute and the Wrights). In 1849 he sent a ten-year-old boy up in a full-sized plane – the first human being to leave the ground in a heavier-than-air machine perhaps – descending a hill for several yards, and in 1853 his 'New Flyer' took his coachman across a valley on the Cayley estate in Yorkshire for about 500 yards. The car overturned on landing and the coachman shouted, oblivious to the historic occasion, 'Please, Sir George, I wish to give notice. I was hired to drive and not to fly.' Cayley appears to have behaved wrongly in his major profession on one wretched occasion. In 1842, the young American, Robert B. Taylor, described to him a proposal to patent a helicopter which ascended by two contra-rotating rotors on a single axis, a double hollow perpendicular shaft. The vanes would close into a disc and a propeller would then operate the craft as a monoplane. Taylor had reached beyond Cayley's principles and beyond his own pioneering machine, never reconsidered. Sir George replied that he had anticipated the machine thirty years earlier but had put the project aside. Then he checked that Taylor had no British patent, and announced that he had invented the craft himself – producing an admittedly superior design. Nothing further was heard of Taylor.

Eric Mottram

J. L. Pritchard, *Sir George Cayley: The Inventor of Aeronautics* (1962).

81
CÉZANNE, Paul 1839–1906

French painter

Paul Cézanne was born in Aix-en-Provence on 19 January 1839, the third of five children. His parents did not marry until 1844. He received a traditional classical French education at a local lycée, where a close friend and contemporary was Émile Zola*. His artistic training was also highly traditional. He studied at the Aix Drawing School, but having failed to achieve a credit at his matriculation he succumbed to his father's wishes and registered at the local faculty of law. A Wagner* enthusiast, he played second cornet in an orchestra for which Zola was flautist. Two years later he finally persuaded his father to let him go to Paris to study painting. His early academic style was quickly called into question as the result of his getting to know the Impressionist painters Armand Guillaumin and Camille Pissarro*, and he was duly rejected by the École des Beaux Arts.

After a brief flight back to Provence, where he worked for a time as a clerk for his father's bank, he returned to Paris in 1862, extending his circle of colleagues to include Sisley*, Monet*, Renoir*, and Bazille. The next ten years were divided between Paris and Provence, with a strong gravitational pull southwards. In 1874 he exhibited at the 'First Exhibition of the Société Anonyme des Artistes, Peintres, Sculpteurs et Graveurs', the first Impressionist exhibition. He thus acknowledged his own position outside the official French art world. With a monthly allowance of 300 francs from his father he was able to work exclusively as a painter, and was largely untroubled by the poverty which affected so many of his acquaintances. Spending most of his time now in and around Provence, he became increasingly reclusive and estranged from the Parisian *avant-garde* of which he had been a member. A difficult and querulous man, he quarrelled with most of his former friends, including Zola and Monet, retreating increasingly into the life of a semi-recluse, though he assiduously cultivated his growing reputation with younger painters as a solitary genius. In 1906 he died of pneumonia, contracted whilst out painting *sur le motif*, and was buried in the cemetery of Aix. He was given one-man shows in 1904 and 1905 at the Salon d'Automne and the Indépendants, and in 1907 the first major retrospective of his works was also shown at the Salon d'Automne. He left a wife, Hortence, whom he had married after the birth of their only child, Paul, who also survived him. In 1894 the French government refused a legacy of three Cézanne paintings. In 1936 *The Card Players* was bought by an American collector for five million francs.

The facts of Cézanne's working life are important in relation to the various received images of his achievements and influence as a painter. Writing in 1917 Roger Fry described him as 'the type of the artist in its purest, most unmitigated form . . . in a world where everyone else is being perpetually educated the artist remains ineducable – where others are shaped, he grows' ('Paul Cézanne', in *Vision and Design*, 1920). Fry valued Cézanne's work in so far as it represented to him a way of painting in which 'all is reduced to the purest terms of structural design'. For this reason he described him, together with such other artists as Gauguin* and Van Gogh* and Seurat*, as a 'Post-Impressionist', an appellation which has stuck owing to its immense convenience. Convenience is not, however, necessarily an unmixed blessing. For in combining the work of such very different artists of the same generation Fry was able to create a stick with which to beat the dog of academic naturalism, which he detested in the collective name of Impressionism. It has also ensured that the work of this generation has in general been regarded until recently in primarily formal terms, to the exclusion of any very penetrating consideration of the differences between these artists, or the social context in which and for which they worked. It also, interestingly enough, recycles the traditional Romantic picture of the artist as a particular kind of person, a heroic individual outside society, for twentieth-century consumption. It is around such myths that the legend of Cézanne has been sustained, and it is a myth to which Cézanne himself undoubtedly subscribed. He explained in a letter to Émile Bernard on 12 May 1904 that 'Art addresses itself to an excessively small number of individuals.' And to Joachim Gasquet on 30 April 1896: 'To be sure an artist wishes to raise his standard intellectually . . . but the man must remain in obscurity.' Many critics and artists have employed these beliefs to 'explain' the complex sociology of modern art and its tiny public in terms of a theory of the supposed nature of the artist, and of art itself. This was Cézanne's lasting significance – he preserved intact the person and the ideology of the aesthete drained of all connotations of languor and lilies.

Throughout the paintings of the 1860s Cézanne can be seen to be working his way through the gamut of alternatives available to him to the dominant styles of French official Salon painting. In particular he looked at Courbet*, violently exaggerating that artist's break with traditional means for constructing the illusion of space. The violence with which the means of painting are themselves stressed is paralleled by a subject matter of complex social and especially sexual significance, for example *The Rape* of 1867, in which a naked man carries off a woman into a landscape which makes no pretensions whatsoever to actuality. In the 1870s Cézanne worked in a more recognizably Impressionist manner, particularly in relation to his friend Pissarro, laboriously building up his picture space in related tints, already hatching his brush-strokes in groups which possess an identity of direction which is unrelated to their representational function. He was working very much against current conventions of landscape painting and the sense of the picturesque of his day, rejecting chiaroscuro modelling in favour of a sense of space constructed through the tonality of colour. As he wrote in evident excitement to Pissarro from the south on 2 July 1876: 'The sun is so terrific here that it seems to me as if the objects were silhouetted not only in black and white, but in blue, red, brown and violet. I may be mistaken but this seems to me the opposite of modelling.'

In this way he developed away from a mainstream Impressionist emphasis on the single moment of sensory perception as the cardinal criterion for aesthetic authenticity. For an ideal truth to the moment he exchanged a concern with the flow of observation over an indefinite period of time, a value he came to describe as the sense of 'duration', borrowing a term from the philosopher Henri Bergson. Hence his retention of profiles and contours which are frequently out of alignment with one another, but 'true' in so far as each registered a different, and equally valid moment, in the production of the picture which, by definition, could never be finished. In this respect again he embodies the Romantic view of art as an unachievable ideal. Cézanne's stress on the primacy of his 'little sensation' bears witness to his own belief in the uniqueness of the artist as a person, best summarized in his friend Zola's definition of a work as 'a man: I wish to find in this work a temperament, a particular and unique accent.' Such a philosophy fitted very well with the increasing formal daring of his compositions, such as the various late *Baigneuses* pictures of the 1880s and 1890s. And in the criticism of Fry and many of his French contemporaries Cézanne emerges as a model for a new kind of Bohemianism, in which the artist's essential greatness is seen to reside not in living life to the full, but in his (or her) abstemious devotion to aesthetic sensation to the exclusion of life altogether. Hence Cézanne can emerge as heroic in his way as Rimbaud* – and how much more palatable to a bourgeois audience!

Cézanne's late paintings offer a wealth of suggestions of how we are to think the problem of pictorial space. Gone are all the last vestiges of comfortable reassuring Renaissance perspective, with its endless homogeneous vistas and solid tangible forms. He insisted that pictures are not true to the objects they depict, but to the sensation the painter has of them. In this manner Cézanne wrote off the nineteenth-century Realist tradition and opened up the prospect of a grand Romantic revival, albeit a revival which continues to call upon the tones and values of classicism. Indigestible in his own time for Naturalists and Symbolists alike, he was able to draw on both as theoretical resources with which to bolster his own increased fascination with the conventions of European art themselves. His late pictures, such as *The Bathers* of 1900–4, push the sense of duration to its most extreme and vulnerable point – the exchange of a mark of paint for an object in space in an almost totally arbitrary relation. This was Cézanne's importance to the next generation: he legitimated the practice of painting as an end in itself. He made 'art for art's sake' respectable and, more to the point, modern. At the same time his remark in April 1906 to the German collector Osthaus that he had tried 'to render perspective uniquely through colour' pointed the way to the subsequent achievements of Matisse and all his followers. It should however be pointed out that this same goal of creating a universal pictorial language, in opposition to speech and writing, of rejecting hierarchies of genre and letting nature 'speak' was nothing new. Rather, Cézanne realized one strand of the Romantic tradition, and carried it across to this century triumphantly draped with legends of innovation and timeless value which remain as misleading as they are ubiquitous.

Simon Watney

Cézanne's *Letters*, ed. J. Rewald (trans. 1941), were republished in 1976. The standard biography remains that by Ambroise Vollard, *Paul Cézanne* (1914, trans. 1924). The best recent collection of Cézanne criticism is Theodore Reff, Laurence Gowing and others, *Cézanne, The Late Work* (1977). The most influential British study of the artist was Roger Fry, *Cézanne, A Study of His Development* (1927).

82

CHAMBERLAIN, Houston Stewart 1855–1927

British pan-Germanic theorist and propagandist

Chamberlain was born in 1855 in Southsea, near Portsmouth, into a family with a distinguished Service record, his father being an admiral and his uncle the British military attaché in Buenos Aires. His rather infirm disposition disqualified him for both a traditional English school education and a Service career, so he was at an early age sent abroad to be educated at the hands of tutors, one of whom was a fanatical

Prussian nationalist. After periods in Versailles and Geneva, he spent the years 1885 to 1889 in Dresden, and in the latter year settled in Vienna, where he was deeply influenced by certain racist and anti-Semitic biologists (especially Professor Julius Wiesner) then teaching at the university there. During these years he became completely captivated by the music and political writings of Richard Wagner*, whom he had already celebrated in his book *Richard Wagner* (1895). In 1905 he published his book on Kant, *Immanuel Kant*, (trans. 1914) and in 1912 his *Goethe*, both of whom he eulogized as gigantic manifestations of the German spirit. In 1908 he had married Eva Wagner, the youngest daughter of the composer, and in the following year the couple moved to Bayreuth, which was to be Chamberlain's home until his death, and in which he had much to do with the annual production of Wagner's musical works in the Festspielhaus. He remained a British subject unil the eve of the First World War, when he became a German citizen, receiving shortly afterwards, through the influence of his close personal friend Kaiser Wilhelm II, an honorary colonel's rank in the German army, which enabled him to practise officially as a pamphleteer on behalf of the German war cause, which he defended vigorously as the attempt to dominate the Western world by that nation which was demonstrably superior to all others in art, music, literature, philosophy and science. The anglophobic Chamberlain was profoundly depressed by Germany's defeat in the world war and the terms imposed upon her by the 1919 Treaty of Versailles. In October 1923 Chamberlain was visited at Wagner's Haus Wahnfried by the comparatively unknown Hitler in the company of Alfred Rosenberg. Chamberlain was completely overwhelmed by Hitler's exposition of his racist mystique and political plans, which moved him to write: 'My faith in the Germans had never wavered for a moment, but my hope, I must own, had sunk to a low ebb. At one stroke you have transformed the state of my soul' (see Alan Bullock, *Hitler: A Study in Tyranny*, 1952). Hitler and Rosenberg immediately recognized in Chamberlain the prophet and seer of the Third Reich, and there is no reason to doubt that Rosenberg regarded his own *magnum opus*, *The Myth of the Twentieth Century*, (*Des Mythus des 20ten Jahrhunderts*) as having been laid upon the foundations of Chamberlain's *The Foundations of the Nineteenth Century (Die Grundlagen des 19ten Jahrhunderts)* and believed that the mantle of Chamberlain, as chief pan-Germanic and anti-Semitic mystagogue, was about to fall upon his own shoulders. Chamberlain died in Bayreuth on 9 January 1927, and after his death his body lay in state there for a considerable period to be viewed by far-travelled pan-Germanic disciples and devotees.

Chamberlain's reputation rests principally on the forementioned two-volume work *The Foundations of the Nineteenth Century*, first published in German in 1899 (trans. 1910). Although this purports to be a 'philosophy' of history, it is in actual fact a ridiculous mixture of distorted historical fact and fanatical pan-Germanic mysticism inextricably intertwined with an unqualified anti-Semitism. Almost Manichaean in its dualism, it sees world history as the arena for a bitter struggle between two opposed and incompatible principles or ethnic groups, the 'Aryans' and the 'Jews'. The intellectual contortions in which Chamberlain had to indulge in order to define and delimit these two groups were quite ludicrous. He attempts to trace the history of the West in the light of his fundamental conviction that everything of worth, dignity and beauty has been produced by those of 'Aryan' stock, and that all that is worthless, lacking in beauty, not to say downright evil, has been the product of the 'Jews'. Every national or world disaster is shown to have been caused by 'Jewish' influence. But in proclaiming this message to the German peoples Chamberlain rightly recognized a serious obstacle – the Christian religion, rooted in the Old Testament, founded by a Jew who had become the centre of the Christian cult. He tried to remove the obstacle by portraying Jesus as an 'Aryan' northerner (i.e., from Galilee) who in his peripatetic ministry collided violently with 'Jewish' southerners in the Jewish capital of Jerusalem, whose hideous crucifixion on religious grounds symbolizes the irreducible incompatibility between his pure, spiritual teaching and the dogmas of orthodox Jewry. Accordingly, Chamberlain heavily underscores those New Testament narratives and passages which highlight the violent collision between the Galilean Jesus and the Jewish 'race'. It was predictable therefore that in his treatment of the German Reformation in the *Foundations* he should interpret it overwhelmingly as the glorious revolt of the *northern* Saxon Luther and his fellows against the ecclesiastical and dogmatic dictatorship wielded by 'non-Aryan' southerners. In such ways Chamberlain attempted to demonstrate the compatibility of his racist *Weltanschauung* with orthodox Protestantism, and to win support for the implementation of his views by the German churches. But Chamberlain's work was no theoretical academic treatise or analysis, but an optimistic testament prophesying world-progress based upon adoption of the 'German way'.

It is difficult to quantify Chamberlain's influence upon subsequent European events and thinking. In Germany, because of the ardent patronage of Wilhelm II and the enthusiastic helpfulness of the Munich publisher F. Bruckmann, cheap popular editions of most of Chamberlain's works reached an astounding number of German households. Although he was neither an 'historian' nor a 'philosopher', Chamberlain wrote in a pseudo-academic and persuasive style, which did much to respectabilize Aryan and anti-Semitic nonsense in the literate, if uncritical, bourgeois classes of Germany. It has often been protested that he was not,

like Rosenberg or Julius Streicher, a crude or barba-
rous anti-Semitic. This is true, but nevertheless he
stands, with Gobineau*, Adolf Stoecker and Wagner,
as one of the theoretical architects and (in Georg
Schott's word) 'prophets' of the Third Reich and the
Nazi State. The translation of certain of his works into
English was encouraged and financially supported by
Lord Redesdale, who recommended them vigorously
to those of his compatriots who were sympathetic to
European 'Aryanism' and anti-Semitism, and indeed
Chamberlain's works were assiduously studied by
many within the British Fascist movement. And in the
German *Kirchenkampf* of the 1930s and 1940s the so-
called *deutsche Christen* (German Christians) could
appeal, over against their opponents in the Confessing
Church, to the religious writings of Chamberlain for
justification in propagating the myth of an 'Aryan'
Jesus basically at odds with the 'Jews', and in creating
a version of 'Nordic' Christianity which dispensed with
the Old Testament and certain Jewish concepts as
necessary prolegomena for the Christian faith.

James Richmond

Other works include: *Mensch und Gott: Betrachlungen
über Religion und Christentum* (1921); *Rasse und
Persönlichkeit* (1917). See: Georg Schott, *H.S.
Chamberlain der Seher des dritten Reiches* (including his
address to Hitler on the latter's birthday on 20 April
1924, 1933); *Die Nordische Welt*, ed. Adolf Blunck
(1937); Richard Gutteridge, *Open Thy Mouth for the
Dumb: The German Evangelical Church and the Jews,
1879–1950* (1976).

83
CHATEAUBRIAND, Françoise René, Vicomte de
1768–1848

French author

It was General de Gaulle, in one of the more pronounced phases of his anglophobia, who chose, during
an interview with a British journalist, to designate
Dante, Goethe* and Chateaubriand as the three great
European writers. National honour required Shakespeare to be omitted and a Frenchman to be chosen to
complete the trio, but his compatriots may be forgiven
for having thought their leader's choice a little eccentric. What of Voltaire, Stendhal*, Racine or Balzac*?
Why select a romantic aristocrat with a limited talent
for fiction and a fatal tendency towards distinguished
political failure as the finest international exemplar of
his country's literature?

The answer, as so often with the artistic figures of
the Romantic era, has less to do with what Chateaubriand left behind in purely literary terms than with his
own vividly dramatized realization of a powerful per-

sonality. For all the subtlety and polish of his narrative
prose, almost without equal among French writers during the last two hundred years, it is the animating ego
of its creator which ultimately arrests the reader. Like
Byron* and Napoleon* he typifies an age, but his fascination for us, unlike theirs, is to be found in the
enduring tension between what his imagination
prompted him to achieve and what the restraints imposed by his background, upbringing and inherited
prejudices prevented him from achieving. A strange
quality of distance, of remoteness from the immediacy
of experience, runs both through his life and through
his interpretation of it in the vast and monumentally
absorbing *Mémoires de'outre-tombe* (lit. 'Memoirs from
beyond the Tomb') which form his chief legacy as a
writer.

'I have found myself between two centuries,' he once
wrote, 'as though at the confluence of two rivers; I
have plunged into their troubled waters, pulling away
with regret from the bank on which I was born, and
swimming hopefully towards an unknown shore.' This
vivid historical sense, remaining with him to the end,
was conditioned by the vicissitudes of early life. Born
at Saint-Malo as the youngest in a family of proud
Breton aristocrats, he was brought up at his father's
dismal château and entered the army at the age of
eighteen. The following year he was presented at court
and watched (he was the archetypal spectator) the last
days of the Ancien Régime and the beginnings of the
revolution before leaving, in 1791, on a tour of North
America.

His American visit was limited to five months spent
principally at Philadelphia, Boston and New York,
with a trip up the Hudson and a sight of the Niagara
Falls, where he broke an arm. It is typical that he
should have converted the experience into the altogether more romantic, but wholly fictitious background
to his stories *Atala* (trans. 1952), *René* (trans. 1952)
and *Les Natchez*, set in the savage backwoods of the
vast French Louisiana territory of the Mississippi, none
of which he ever actually saw but which, like several
other contemporary novelists (notably Mrs Radcliffe,
who created the French and Italian settings of *The
Mysteries of Udolpho* from a London parlour), he was
able fully and convincingly to imagine.

He returned to Europe as a result of the worsening
political situation in France, joining the royalist army
and taking part in the Thionville campaign in 1792.
In the same year he married Céleste Amable Buisson
de la Vigne, a wife chiefly memorable for tolerating a
long series of infidelities and for earning thereby a
species of penitent respect from her husband. Several
of these liaisons took place in England, where Chateaubriand joined the mass of impoverished émigré
nobility in 1793 and remained for seven years, working,
for part of that period, as a teacher at Beccles, Suffolk,
and writing his *Essai sur les Révolutions* ('Essay on Re-

volutions'), characteristically mixed in its religious and political outlook.

It was the appearance of his *Génie du Christianisme* ('The Genius of Christianity') in April 1802 which drew him to the attention of Napoleon Bonaparte, to whom he dedicated the second edition a year later. His return to France had been followed by the success of the short novel *Atala* (originally part of the *Génie*) and it is tempting to see in Chateaubriand's reconciliation of Christianity with the exigencies and ideas of Bonapartist romanticism a species of political sail-trimming which marks his career to the very last. Naive as some of his calculations may have appeared, he never lost sight of reality and was, as he himself readily acknowledged, a survivor. Like other active young Frenchmen of his day, he was ready to admire Napoleon, but was rewarded with the unpromising post of secretary to the First Consul's uncle, Cardinal Fesch, in Rome. He renounced his diplomatic career soon after the execution of the Duc d'Enghien, which alienated so many of Bonaparte's royalist admirers, and spent the remaining years of the empire as one of Napoleon's most outspoken critics, though the two respected one another deeply enough for him to remain unmuzzled.

His political life under the restored Bourbon monarchy was a series of misjudgments and disasters. Though his commitment of French arms to the war in Spain in 1823, leading as it did to his dismissal as Foreign Affairs Minister, was at least well-intentioned, his spell as ambassador in London the previous year had been marked by a serious misreading of the situation in South America. He seems to have been as incapable of repressing a tendency to let the visionary Romantic get the better of him in politics as he was unable to commit himself wholeheartedly to the interests and sympathies of the class to which he belonged. After his involvement in the Duchesse de Berry's preposterous attempt to raise La Vendée on behalf of the exiled Bourbons in 1832, he took no further part in the national life of his country and retired to complete his memoirs.

Chateaubriand was aided in the task by the good sense of his wife and the inspiration of the celebrated salon hostess Madame Récamier, to whom he was sentimentally attached until death (she herself survived him by barely a year). Among the earliest sections to be completed were his accounts of the Congress of Verona in 1822 and of the Spanish crisis. The whole nature of the work, in a more or less continuous state of revision and amendment from 1834 onwards, was significantly affected by the fact that much of it was designed for reading aloud to admiring friends in the Récamier circle at L'Abbaye-aux-Bois. Such beneficial effects upon Chateaubriand's prose style are further enhanced by an element of coolness and detachment, a legacy from that Enlightenment of which he was an heir and perhaps also from his appreciative reading of eighteenth-century English prose, which serves to soften and balance his portrayal of characters and events.

Like many other Romantic artists he was an autobiographer in everything he created. The degree of objectivity in his writings on politics and religion is invariably subordinate to the measure of personal crisis which prompted their composition. His most ambitious, and in its own day his most successful, work was undoubtedly the historical romance *Les martyrs*, published in 1809, which combines, via the tale of Eudore and Cymodocée, Greek Christians under Diocletian, a highly experimental and rhapsodic style, featuring passages of bravura description, and an episodic narrative method culminating in the appearance of the Gaulish prophetess Velléda in books IX and X. This work contributed a great deal to the promotion of a strain of Christian Romanticism which has never since wholly faded from French culture, but a far more original treatment of a religious subject appears in the *Vie de Rancé*, the biographical study of a seventeenth-century monk which Chateaubriand published four years before his death, and which is inevitably less of a biography (the method, as Sainte-Beuve* noted, is distinctly wayward and inconsistent) than an exploration of the author's personal concerns.

Of his shorter essays in fiction, the best is probably *Atala*, less by virtue of its narrative element than for the power of its descriptive writing. This too is what ultimately attracts the modern reader to the *Mémoires d'outre-tombe*, one of whose more extraordinary achievements is (just as in *Atala*) to re-create events of which the writer had no first-hand knowledge. Thus we recall the account of the retreat from Moscow or Bonaparte's flight from Elba with often far greater relish than the more minutely exact relations offered by the professional historian. The potency of Chateaubriand's work as a memorialist is to suggest that if he was not present on all the occasions he describes, then he surely ought to have been. By the sheer overwhelming inclusiveness of his fantasy he succeeds in embodying the collective European imagination of the period in a way rivalled only by Byron and Goethe. With Alexander Herzen's* *My Past and Thoughts*, which they must surely have helped to inspire, the *Mémoires d'outre-tombe* rank as one of the greatest autobiographical documents ever produced.

Jonathan Keates

Robert Baldick's *The Memoirs of Chateaubriand* (1962) is a recommended translation of *Mémoires d'outre-tombe*. See also: André Maurois, *Chateaubriand, Statesman, Lover* (trans. 1938); Friedrich Sieburg, *Chateaubriand* (trans. 1961); Victor L. Tapié, *Chateaubriand par lui-même* (1965); G. D. Painter, *Chateaubriand: A Biography, Volume I 1768–92* (1977).

84

CHEKHOV, Anton Pavlovich 1860–1904

Russian dramatist and short-story writer

Anton Chekhov was the third of six children born to Pavel and Yevghenia Chekhov in Taganrog in the North Caucasus. His father, a shopkeeper, had a great interest in the arts, which he pursued to the neglect of his business. This resulted in financial difficulties, and physical hardships for his children. Chekhov attended secondary school, but his home was not conducive to study and he had to stay on for two extra years to work up to standard. In 1876 his father went bankrupt, and the family moved to Moscow, leaving Chekhov behind to finish school. Already a prolific writer, he became editor of the school magazine called the *Stutterer*. In 1879 he re-joined his family, entering the Medical Faculty of Moscow University. In his spare time Chekhov continued to write for publication, but he worked hard at his medical studies, and not until 1883 was there any marked increase in his literary output. During this period he was mostly writing humorous short stories, poor in quality, and viewed by Chekhov simply as a means of earning extra money. It was around 1886 that he began to take writing seriously, and from then on it increasingly absorbed his time, at the expense of his medical practice.

Chekhov had written his first play, 'The Fatherless', (*Bezzotsovshchina*) in 1877, while still at school. His brother Alexander, whose opinion Chekhov always valued, disliked it, and the play was neither performed nor published during the author's lifetime. The same fate befell *On the High Road* (*Na Golshoydorage*, 1886), adapted by Chekhov from his own short story, 'Autumn'. From 1887 onwards he began to devote more attention to drama, and produced a series of one-act comic sketches known collectively as the 'vaudevilles'. These were well received by the public, and one in particular, *The Bear* (*Medved*), was quite profitable. Chekhov's first full-length play, *Ivanov*, was performed in 1887, but he was by now becoming dissatisfied with the over-theatricality of the contemporary stage, believing that actors should 'show life and men as they are, and not as they would look if you put them on stilts.' However, he found it difficult to convey these ideas to actors, and the first production of *Ivanov* was not to his liking, although a reasonable success with the public. Chekhov drastically rewrote it, and the new version was staged in 1889, to critical acclaim. In his next play, *The Wood Demon* (*Leshy*, 1889), Chekhov eschewed most of the stage conventions of the day in a search for a new 'structure of feeling'; the work failed to repeat the success of *Ivanov*, and he withdrew it. Eight years later a rewritten version was to appear as *Uncle Vanya* (*Dyadya Vanya*). After a tour of Western Europe, Chekhov bought a small estate near Moscow,

and wrote his next play, *The Seagull* (*Chayka*), in 1895, a production of which was very badly received in St Petersburg the following year. Chekhov wrote afterwards: 'I left Petersburg full of doubts of all kinds.' His self-confidence, never great, had been severely shaken. Shortly afterwards he fell ill; tuberculosis was diagnosed, and after a period in a Moscow clinic, Chekhov left for the South of France, returning to Russia in 1898. That same year the face of Russian theatre was radically altered by the birth of the Moscow Art Theatre, established by Konstantin Stanislavsky and Vladimir Nemirovich-Danchenko as a protest against the current artificiality of Russian drama. Like Chekhov, they looked for sincerity in acting rather than flamboyance and trickery. Nemirovich-Danchenko persuaded Chekhov, against both his and Stanislavsky's better judgments, to allow them to include *The Seagull* in their opening season. Stanislavsky co-directed and also took the part of the writer Trigorin. It proved to be the most successful play in their repertoire. The Moscow Art Theatre went on to establish a reputation as the greatest exponent of Chekhov's art, though the writer himself was not always satisfied with Stanislavsky's interpretations. Chekhov did not actually see them perform his work until 1900 when they toured the Crimea, where he had moved for the sake of his health shortly before the first night of *The Seagull*. In 1899 Stanislavsky had staged *Uncle Vanya*. It did not repeat the triumph of *The Seagull*, and indeed, Moscow audiences tended to be slow to appreciate any of the works of Chekhov's maturity.

In 1900 Chekhov began work on *Three Sisters* (*Tri sestry*), but ill-health made writing an exhausting task, and he described the play as 'dreary, long, and awkward'. Nevertheless, he took the manuscript to Moscow himself, and played an active part in rehearsals, although he was again out of the country, this time in Nice, when it was premièred in January 1901. Later that year Chekhov married Olga Knipper, an actress with Stanislavsky's company. It was a happy marriage, though they were apart for much of the time, he in Yalta, she in Moscow. They had no children.

Chekhov found working on his final play, *The Cherry Orchard* (*Vishnyory sad*), extremely difficult: 'I write about four lines a day, and even that costs me an intolerably painful effort.' The play was finally performed on 17 January 1904, Chekhov's birthday. He had again attended rehearsals, where there had been serious disagreements between himself and Stanislavsky. Chekhov insisted that the play was 'a light comedy', while the director saw it as a 'serious drama of Russian life'. However, Chekhov attended the opening night and was fêted by the audience, at considerable cost to his health. He died six months later, and his remains were buried in Moscow.

Chekhov's major plays focus upon the lives of the privileged landowning class of tsarist Russia, and all are set on or around provincial estates. Yet they were written during a period of political ferment. They are therefore frequently held to be 'elegies' for the passing of an age. It is argued that Chekhov presents the cultural values of the Russian upper class in their struggle for survival against the social transformation urged by middle-class intellectuals and business men. Hopeless though the struggle may be, it is at least, so the theory goes, the occasion for a heartening idealism, the expression of belief in traditional virtues. But this interpretation wrongly labels Chekhov's drama as reactionary and sentimental. The later plays are certainly concerned with resistance to social change: the three sisters create a myth around their Muscovite past, to insulate themselves against the ugly realities of provincial life; an axe fells the trees of the cherry orchard, and a social order approaches its end. But far from mourning its decline, Chekhov's work exhibits a profound understanding of the necessity of its passing. He portrays a class becoming painfully aware of its own impotency and inability to change. Self-delusion is no escape because, as Gayev remarks in *The Cherry Orchard*, 'the greater the number of cures you suggest for a sickness, the more certain you can be it's incurable.' Unlike Ibsen*, Chekhov placed no faith in personal rebellion, and the last plays have no clearly defined central character. He rejected the possibility of heroic action: 'Our life is provincial, the cities are unpaved, the villages poor, the masses abused. In our youth we chirp rapturously, like sparrows on a dung heap, but when we are forty, we are already old and begin to think about death. Fine heroes we are!' The ruling class in Chekhov's plays is presented as morally stagnant, capable only of looking to its own past; that is its tragedy. But the plays themselves are clear-sighted and far removed from sentimentality.

A leading dramatist, it should also be remembered that Chekhov ranks alongside Joyce as one of the greatest of short-story writers. His best fiction, notably 'Lady with a Lapdog' ('Dama s sobachkoy', 1899) and 'The Darling' ('Dushechka', 1898), display his ability to combine tragedy and comedy in a fine balance. 'Ward 6' ('Palata No. 6' 1892) presents a ward in a mental hospital as a symbol for Russian society. Ragin, a doctor, condones the neglect and cruelty rampant in the hospital, but is tricked into himself becoming a patient, a victim of the logic that, while there are mental wards, patients must be found to fill them. An austere work, 'Ward 6' was much admired by the young Lenin.

In all his writing Chekhov was able to convey depths of feeling – the enormity of personal tragedy, the joy of hope, the absurdity of human behaviour – through a word or a gesture. He fought, often against his own inclinations, to remove the melodramatic from his work, relying on atmosphere rather than action; it was his boast, of *The Cherry Orchard*, that there is 'not a single pistol shot in it'. Few dramatists have equalled his understanding of people's fears and weaknesses, while rejecting any indulgence in pessimism or despair.

Paul Nicholls

Chekhov has not always been well served by his English translators. The best edition of his work remains Ronald Hingley, *Oxford Chekhov* (1961–75), but there is an adaptation of *The Cherry Orchard* by the playwright Trevor Griffiths which deserves to be read widely. The authoritative biography is E. J. Simmons, *Chekhov: A Biography* (1962), but see also R. Hingley, *A New Life of Anton Chekhov* (1976), and R. Williams, *Drama from Ibsen to Brecht* (1952).

85
CHERUBINI, Luigi 1760–1842

Italian composer

Son of a Florentine musician, Cherubini showed early musical talent, and studied theatre and church music with the composer Sarti. He made a successful début as an operatic composer in 1779, and other performances in Italy established his reputation. After a visit to London he settled in Paris in 1786, at the invitation of his compatriot Viotti. He became a leading figure in operatic activity, and in 1791 his French opera *Lodoiska* was widely acclaimed. During the years of the revolution and the republic he produced a series of works, culminating in *Médée* (1797) and *Les deux Journées* (1800). In 1795 he was appointed to the staff of the newly formed Paris Conservatoire, an association which was to continue for nearly fifty years.

In 1802 a season of his operas in Vienna made a notable impact, not least upon Beethoven*, who remained his life-long admirer. But at home his fortunes declined, largely through a mutual antipathy between Cherubini and Napoleon*. He turned from the stage to the liturgy, and began to produce various compositions for church use, including settings of the Mass. The restoration of the monarch saw a revival of his fortunes. In 1816 he was appointed joint superintendent of the royal chapel, and in 1822 became director of the reconstituted Paris Conservatoire. He took his administrative duties seriously, and as these consumed more of his time and energy, so his compositional output decreased. His last opera, *Ali-Baba* (1833), was an anachronistic survival of an earlier style. But his second Requiem, in D minor, written in his seventy-ninth year, is a work of sustained fire and imagination. He died, laden with honours, in 1842.

Cherubini's importance rests upon his work as an opera composer, and an administrator. His theoretical treatise on counterpoint and fugue, though much used in the nineteenth century, was conservative in its outlook. His church music, too, was imbued with the spirit of an earlier age, with the exception of the two splendid Requiem settings, and had no influence upon later composers. It was otherwise with his operatic achievement. Almost alone he transformed the French *opéra comique*, an essentially limited and lightweight genre, into a vehicle for the expression of contemporary ideas through music of great emotional and dramatic intensity. His *Médée* remains in these respects one of the supreme challenges in the operatic repertoire. That his other works have not been taken into the operatic repertory is due more to the dominance of the Italian and German traditions in the world of opera than to any objective assessment of their intrinsic worth (although it must be said that Cherubini was in general wretchedly served by his librettists). But his influence was far-reaching. Beethoven's *Fidelio* owes much to Cherubini's dramatic style, in its subject and its orchestration, and other admirers who were not untouched by his achievement included Weber* and Wagner*.

As an administrator he must be credited with the elevation of the Paris Conservatoire to the leading position among nineteenth-century musical teaching establishments in Europe. The institution reflected his personality and interests, and (as Berlioz* pointed out) was not without its bureaucratic side. But its continued pre-eminence is a memorial to the expatriate Italian who served French music so faithfully for more than half a century.

Basil Deane

Cherubini's works include: about thirty stage works, alone or in collaboration; church music, including seven surviving Mass settings; two Requiems, and numerous smaller works; secular cantatas, choral pieces and songs; instrumental music, including one symphony and six string quartets; various pedagogical works, including a course in composition and fugue (jointly with his pupil Halévy). See: E. Bellasis, *Cherubini: Memorials illustrative of his Life* (1874); R. H. Hohenemser, *Luigi Cherubini: sein Leben und seine Werke* (1913); L. Schemann, *Cherubini* (1925); G. Confalonieri, *Prigionia di un artista: il romanza di Luigi Cherubini* (1948); B. Deane, *Cherubini* (1965).

86
CHOPIN, Frédéric 1810–49

Polish composer

Born of mixed French and Polish parentage, Chopin spent his early life in Warsaw, studying privately with Adalbert Żywny and at the Warsaw Conservatoire with Józef Elsner. His home was staunchly middle class, but his exceptional gifts gained him access to the most aristocratic households in Poland from an early age, and he continued to move freely in such circles when he moved to Paris in 1831. At the time Paris was a stronghold for Polish artists and aristocrats, many of them exiled from their politically turbulent homeland, and it remained Chopin's home until his death in 1849. His close relationship with the writer George Sand*, romanticized to absurdity by many later commentators, had ended two years earlier.

For most of his life Chopin enjoyed a comfortable income and a life-style to match. He was one of the few composers at that time to earn a substantial sum from sales of his published music, and he was the most sought-after piano teacher in Paris; only Liszt* could command comparable fees. His reputation as a performer was legendary, though curiously enough it was based on relatively few public appearances. Unlike most composer-pianists in the early nineteenth century, he shunned the public concert, preferring the more intimate surroundings of fashionable society drawing-rooms, where he could perform, and above all improvise, to small groups of initiates. Contemporary accounts of his playing stress its lyrical, flowing quality, the remarkable delicacy of his touch and the subtlety of his dynamic shading and pedalling.

The enduring popularity of Chopin's music, surviving many changes in receptive attitudes, is the more remarkable when we consider that he rarely ventured beyond the security of his own instrument. His exploration of the largely unexploited sonorities of the piano, itself undergoing important technical refinements at the time, was right at the heart of his creativity. At the same time he was not slow to absorb into the world of the piano gestures culled from symphonic and operatic composition, as well as from popular and folkloristic materials. His use of such materials and his strong nationalist commitment reflected, of course, a wider tendency of the age. Yet in other respects Chopin's tastes and attitudes differed markedly from other early Romantic composers, suggesting rather an affinity with the century of enlightenment. He had little interest in the big, abstract ideas which fired Beethoven's* imagination, or in the early Romantic literature which formed a direct source of inspiration for Berlioz*, Schumann* and Liszt. If his music reflected, in its sheer intensity of feeling, the ardour and idealism of the age, and its restless, yearning spirit, it did so without resort to cheap emotional effects or extravagant rhetoric, and certainly without the aid of a programme.

Chopin's earliest works – mainly polonaises and mazurkas – owe a good deal to Polish composers such as Ogiński and Maria Szymanowska, but he very soon came under the influence of a more international *style brillante*, cultivated by composer-pianists such as Hummel, Field and Kalkbrenner, and composer-violinists such as Paganini*. Both Hummel and Paganini gave concerts in Warsaw during Chopin's student days.

This influence is particularly marked in the three early rondos (opp. 1, 5, 73) and the four sets of variations, including the *La ci darem* variations for piano and orchestra, op. 2. It also informs the two piano concertos (opp. 11, 21) which brought his years in Poland to a close and which were intended to launch his career on the concert platforms of Europe.

The concertos marked the end of Chopin's apprenticeship. With the works written during his early years in Paris he achieved full maturity as a composer, discarding in the process many of the surface mannerisms associated with the *style brillante*. The different genres in which he worked for the rest of his life reflected in their different ways some of the deeper, more lasting influences which helped to shape his musical thought. The *Twenty-four Preludes*, op. 28, and the two sets of studies (opp. 10, 25), for instance, demonstrate his debt to Bach and the French clavecinists, both in matters of texture and configuration and in their unitary conception of form. The nocturnes, borrowing a title and manner from John Field, reveal the importance of early nineteenth-century Italian opera in helping to shape his wide melodic arches, his *fioritura*-like ornamentation and his instrumental recitative. Operatic styles may also have influenced Chopin's whole approach to thematic working. In general he was less interested in thematic dissection and reintegration on the German model than in the decoration and elaboration of melodic 'arias', often repeated against changing harmonic and textural backcloths. In his mazurkas Chopin turned to yet another musical background, the folk music of the Mazovian plains of central Poland. The rhythmic and modal patterns of the *mazur*, *oberek* and *kujawiak*, together with the characteristic melodic intonations and *dudy* drones, are all stylized in these mazurkas. Here Chopin evoked, often with ineffable poignancy, the spirit of rustic Poland, just as the polonaises suggested the idealized splendour of an earlier Grand Poland. Finally, in his waltzes and other popular dance-types (bolero, tarantella, écossaise), he turned to the 'light music' of the day, raising it to a level of sophistication which had not been attempted in similar essays by the classical masters and Schubert*.

It is perhaps predictable that in his more extended compositions Chopin should have depended more heavily on forms and procedures developed within the German tradition. It is arguable that the three mature sonatas (opp. 35, 58, 65), the last of them for cello and piano, are less successful in this respect than single-movement extended works such as the four ballades (opp. 23, 38, 47, 52), the *Fantasy* in F minor, op. 49, the *Fantasy-impromptu*, op. 66, and the *Polonaise-fantasy*, op. 61. In these works Chopin achieved a subtle and discreet dialogue between his own 'narrative' manner and classical formal archetypes, often blending elements of rondo, variation-form and sonata-form with remarkable resource and ingenuity.

Chopin had a succession of imitators among later Polish composers, most of them adopting the external characteristics of his style without penetrating its essence. But his influence reached far beyond Poland. As one of the most advanced harmonists of his time, he explored within the restricted framework of the piano miniature chromatic and modal devices which were later to be embraced by Wagner*, Brahms* and a whole generation of late-Romantic composers. His piano textures, so different from those of Beethoven, Schumann, Mendelssohn* and Brahms, were no less influential, instigating a tradition of piano writing on which many later composers were to build. These textures were characterized by a tendency towards lightness and clarity of sound, by a limitation of the low register, by the prominence of widespread arpeggiation and of filigree configuration, often achieved in piano or pianissimo levels. In these respects the piano music of composers such as Fauré*, Debussy, Scriabin* and Szymanowski took its stylistic starting-point from Chopin.

The connection with Debussy is of special interest, for it reveals the deeper significance of Chopin's work in relation to evolving nineteenth-century methods. The connection extends beyond undoubted parallels in the *character* of keyboard textures and configurations to include a parallel in their *function*. In Chopin texture often assumes an unprecedented responsibility for structure, helping to model the form of a piece in a way which foreshadows directly the 'emancipation' of texture and colour in Debussy more than half a century later. In this sense we can view his work, along with that of Berlioz and Liszt, as one of the earliest contributions to a growing body of creative 'criticism' of the Austro-German mainstream in the nineteenth century. That body of criticism was to gather support from the Russian nationalists later in the century and was eventually to culminate in major changes in the language of music in the work of early twentieth-century composers such as Debussy and Ravel in France, Bartók and Stravinsky in Eastern Europe.

Jim Samson

See: K. Michalowski, *Bibliografia Chopinowska, 1849–1969* (Cracow, 1970); M. J. E. Brown, *Chopin: An Index of his Works in Chronological Order* (1960). Source writings: *Selected Correspondence of Fryderyk Chopin*, collected B. Sydow, ed. and trans. A. Hedley (1962); J. J. Eigeldinger, *Chopin vu par ses élèves* (1979). Biographical studies in English include: F. Niecks, *Chopin as a Man and Musician* (1888); A. Hedley, *Chopin* (1947); G. Marek and M. Gordon-Smith, *Chopin* (1979). Analytic studies in English include: G. Abraham, *Chopin's Musical Style* (1939); *Frederic Chopin: Profiles of the Man and the Musician*, ed. A.

Walker (1966). Studies in Polish include: *The Book of the First International Congress devoted to the works of Frederick Chopin* (Warsaw, 1963); Z. Lissa, *Studia nad twórczościa Fryderyka Chopina* (Cracow, 1969); and J. Chomiński, *Chopin* (Cracow, 1978).

87
CHOPIN, Kate 1850–1904

US writer

In her day, Kate Chopin was widely praised as a Southern regional writer, but her work was then forgotten so completely that her name did not even appear in the nine hundred pages of Jay F. Hubbell's magisterial *The South in American Literature 1607–1900* (1954). Since the 1960s, however, Kate Chopin's novel *The Awakening* (1899) has come to be considered one of the most important American novels of the later nineteenth century, both for its daringly subversive treatment of female sexuality and for its economic structure and limpid prose style. This dramatic rise in Kate Chopin's reputation has come about partly through feminist reassessment of American literary history. Yet since Chopin consistently used specific cultural detail to convey complex issues of human relationships, her accomplishment also implicitly revalues underestimated American regional or 'local colour' writers like Chopin's more nostalgic fellow Creole George Washington Cable (1844–1925), the black American novelist C. W. Chesnutt (1858–1936) or Sarah Orne Jewett (1849–1909) whose work Chopin admired.

Born Kate O'Flaherty, Kate Chopin grew up in St Louis, Missouri, in a Catholic household where French was the spoken language. Through her mother Chopin was half Creole, a term which describes the French speaking descendants, whether black or white, of the original Spanish and French settlers in the Gulf of Mexico. Kate Chopin's direct but highly cadenced English prose invites comparison with the Flaubert* of 'Un Coeur Simple' while her characteristically confident alternation of colloquialism, dialect and elegant description is lacking in the American naturalists William Dean Howells* and Theodore Dreiser.

After marrying the successful Creole cotton factor Oscar Chopin, Kate Chopin lived in New Orleans and then at a shop and plantation in north-western Louisiana. Following her husband's death in 1883, Kate Chopin managed the plantation for a year and then returned with her six children to St Louis, where she began to write in earnest, initially modelling her stories upon those of Maupassant* which she read in 1888–9. 'Here was life not fiction; for where were the plots, the old-fashioned mechanism and stage trapping.' Chopin's themes of self-fulfilment derive, however, equally from a libertarian tradition which she located in both Madame de Staël* and in Walt Whitman*. She criticized the naturalist 'reformist' dependence upon 'social problems, social environments, local color and the rest'.

Kate Chopin's first novel, *At Fault* (1890), portrays a young widow almost destroying the man who loves her by too thorough an insistence on his obligation to his alcoholic wife. *At Fault* shows considerable psychological insight, and the setting, based upon the Chopin plantation, is vividly realized, but plot and background do not always work together. The stories collected in *Bayou Folk* (1894) and *A Night in Acadie* (1897) depict the Creoles, Cajuns, Acadiens and blacks among whom Kate Chopin lived. Often very short, these stories are distinguished by clear-sighted perception of male and female desires (as in 'The Story of an Hour', 'A Vocation and a Voice', 'At the 'Cadian Ball' and its late, uncollected sequel 'The Storm'). Although she avoided the issue of black-white conflict, Chopin's treatment of racial themes is unusually honest for the period, since she accorded blacks the same emotional range as whites (as in 'Desirée's Baby', 'La Belle Zoraïde' and 'Nég Creole').

Kate Chopin's literary career lasted only ten years; accepted by St Louis literary society, Chopin was ostracized after some critics called *The Awakening* 'poison', 'essentially vulgar', and 'sex fiction' (others praised its honesty). She stopped writing, and died in 1904. In general plot and theme, *The Awakening* resembles both Maupassant's 'Réveil' and Flaubert's *Madame Bovary*: a *femme de trente ans* commits adultery and is destroyed by her folly. But the resemblance stops there. While Emma Bovary is the victim of her romantic fantasies, Chopin's Edna Pontellier is seen as representative. One early hostile reviewer remarked acutely that 'there is throughout the story an undercurrent of sympathy for Edna, and nowhere a single note of censure for her totally unjustifiable conduct.'

The Awakening is a story of both cultural and sexual conflict. Edna, an 'American woman' from Kentucky, is married to a stolid Creole businessman who regards her sunburn 'as one looks at a valuable piece of personal property which has suffered some damage'. At a summer resort Edna is surrounded by Madonna-like 'mother-women' like the constantly pregnant Madame Ratignolle, and the chatelaine Madame Lebrun, who is 'busily engaged' in sewing by having a 'little black girl' sitting on the floor 'who with her hands worked the treadle of the machine'. Failing to understand the Creole mixture of sensuousness, propriety and 'utter absence of prudery', Edna begins to fantasize about young flirtatious Robert Lebrun. She also learns to swim; and in a number of the novel's metaphoric passages, her new physical freedom is likened to a Whitmanesque oceanic emotion: 'The voice of the sea is seductive. . . . The touch of the sea is sensuous, enfolding the body in its soft, close embrace.' Later, ominously, 'As she swam she seemed to be looking for the unlimited in which to lose herself.'

Edna's romantic illusion is irrevocably linked with both sensuous awakening and with her discovery of will and identity. Although Edna gradually distinguishes between these three impulses, and understands their interplay, she lacks the will to make a new life for herself; *The Awakening* continues where Ibsen's* *A Doll's House* leaves off, finding Edna unable to become an artist like the resolutely unmarried Mademoiselle Reisz. When she sleeps with another man, it is not Robert, whom she loves, but the *roué* Arobin. Edna recognizes that 'it was not love which had held this cup of life to her lips.' Later, when Robert proposes to ask Pontellier to let his Edna go, Edna replies that she 'would laugh at you both' since she now disposes of herself. But her 'freedom' overshoots naturalist goals into a curiously impersonal desire. Recognizing that Robert would only be one of many interchangeable lovers, Edna chooses a more immediately annihilating embrace, by swimming out naked 'like some new-born creature' into the 'seductive' Gulf waters and letting herself drown. It is characteristic of Chopin's modernity that her heroine's death is neither a triumph nor a punishment, but sheer experience, mingling fantasy, sensuousness and a failing will.

Helen McNeil

Kate Chopin, *The Complete Works*, vols I and II, ed. and introduced by Per Seyersted (1969). See: Per Seyersted, *Kate Chopin* (1977). See also: Ernest Earnest, *The American Eve in Fact and Fiction 1775–1914* (1974).

88
CLARE, John 1793–1864

British poet

John Clare has suffered from simplification, misrepresentation and sentimentality. It has been all too easy to stick to the labels of his own day, and shuffle him off as the Northamptonshire 'peasant poet', or as the mad poet of the lunatic asylum. Lack of complete editions of his work has encouraged, as it has been a symptom of, such casual neglect.

The critical difficulties we have with Clare are a reflection of his own uncertainties as to his place in society and the literary world: he is an instructive, if depressing, instance of the way in which society and literature interlock, even whilst such a thing is being denied. His pedigree, after all, was not promising for a poet: a thresher's son in the Northamptonshire village of Helpstone should expect no more than to amble through the available jobs – ploughboy, gardener, thresher, limeburner. But that other thresher of the

eighteenth century, Stephen Duck, had set a fashion with his poem 'The Thresher's Labour' (1730), which might have become a tradition, with writers like Burns and Bloomfield showing that it was possible to be a labourer, to be poor, and to write about it. When a Stamford bookseller, Edward Drury, 'discovered' Clare in 1818, and passed him on to his cousin, the influential London publisher John Taylor, Clare could be seen as fashionable, as 'hot property'. So it proved. His *Poems Descriptive of Rural Life and Scenery* (1820) went into four editions of 1,000 copies each within a year: Keats's* 1820 volume from the same publisher sold barely 500. The fashion and the popularity waned. The better (increasingly so) later volumes (*The Village Minstrel*, 1821, *The Shepherd's Calendar*, 1827, *The Rural Muse*, 1835) sold less and less well. Clare first entered an asylum in 1837 (High Beech, Epping Forest), and then, after a dramatic escape in 1841 and six months at home in Northborough (where he had moved in 1832 in the hope of establishing himself on a smallholding), he was committed to the asylum at Northampton, where he remained until his death: very few people were aware of his existence.

It is against this background of brief success and long neglect that Clare has to be seen. Clare depended on too many people who thought they knew what was best for him, and he was frequently helpless against the pressures of patrons and publishers, let alone his inner conflicts. As he was to say in a late poem, 'Child Harold' (1841) – Clare claimed he was Byron*, Shakespeare, Lord Nelson, Tom Spring, the prize fighter – 'My life hath been one chain of contradictions': that about sums it up. He was forever trying to establish himself, to assert himself: with a wife who did not understand him, a growing family, and an idealized Muse figure from his childhood (the Mary of so many of his poems), such assertion was hard, especially when a decision to live by writing increased dependence on the wealthy patrons who could afford to treat him as a curiosity. His assertion was also a literary matter. He wanted to write about the countryside as he knew it to be; along with his unbridled scorn for sentimental city-dwellers and city-poets went a reverence for a wide range of poets, particularly Thomson, Goldsmith, Collins, Gray and Cowper. He had to find his own voice (which always meant a recognition of the direct simplicities of the ballads he collected and the twang of colloquial speech), but he knew that individual talent only made sense in the context of a tradition.

It was in *The Shepherd's Calendar* (1827) that he first achieved this fusion: a month by month account of the year, with some narrative tales attached, the poem is a remarkable portrayal of the year in the country. It is a social document, a celebration of the labourer's life and place, an acknowledgment, too, that especially since enclosure, life as a labourer involves deprivation and suffering. The satirical poem 'The Parish' (unpublished in his own lifetime, but written at the same time) underlines Clare's awareness of his role as spokesman for the underprivileged: interestingly, his attempt at satire (like his later 'Don Juan', 1841) is only a partial success. His evocation of loss and despair is always most powerful when focused on the individual experience, whether of himself or the isolated figures in his landscape.

Isolation is a recurrent theme: like other early nineteenth-century poets, Clare explores the implications of the self at the centre of the poetry. His most anthologized poem, 'I am', written in the asylum in the 1840s, is a triumphant assertion, but it is against all odds and Clare knows its tenuousness. He had experienced commotion too often to rest easily on apparent solutions: the Enclosure Act of 1809 as applied to his native village he saw as the loss of Eden; the move to Northborough in 1832 he regarded as symptomatic of the loss of poetry (some of his most spare and moving poems date from this period: 'Remembrances', 'Decay', 'The Flitting'). And yet, in spite of that 'chain of contradictions', culminating in the madhouse and the belief he was married to Mary Joyce (the long-dead girl of his childhood dreams), Clare produced an extraordinary body of work that has its own inner coherence, from the early, sharply delineated sonnets ('descriptive' is the inadequate word used to describe them) to the visionary poems of the asylum. As his poem 'A Vision' declares, he 'kept his spirit with the free'. Dream, aspiration, hope; loss, despair, dependence. Out of these conflicts he forged a poetry that should make none of us feel complacent about justice being done.

Mark Storey

Poems, ed. J. W. Tibble (1935); Letters and Prose, both ed. J. W. and Anne Tibble (1951). New texts of poems, letters and prose are in preparation; but see especially The Shepherd's Calendar (1964), Later Poems (1964) and Selected Poems and Prose (1967), all ed. Eric Robinson and Geoffrey Summerfield; The Midsummer Cushion, ed. Anne Tibble (1979). About Clare: J. W. and Anne Tibble, John Clare: A Life (1932, rev. 1972); John Barrell, The Idea of Landscape and the Sense of Place (1972); Mark Storey, Clare: The Critical Heritage (1973) and The Poetry of John Clare: A Critical Introduction (1974).

89
CLAUSEWITZ, Carl von 1780–1831

Prussian writer on war

Carl von Clausewitz was born in 1780, the son of a retired lieutenant. Shortly before his twelfth birthday, he entered the Prussian army and in 1793 came under

fire for the first time. In 1801 he entered the War College at Berlin. Here he fell under the paternal influence of the greatest of German military reformers, Scharnhorst. Scharnhorst stressed the need to see war as it really is, and that for this history, not theory, should be the guide. Clausewitz also encountered the products of the Sturm und Drang movement. Although his subsequent combative prose style was more suggestive of Hegel*, his direct contacts were with Kiesewetter, a popularizer of Kant. In 1806 he witnessed the eclipse of the old, unreformed order of Prussian absolutism by the revolutionary forces of France. Disgusted by his monarch's complaisant attitude to the French, in 1812/3 he threw in his lot with the Russians. 1815 found him restored to the Prussian army and serving at Ligny. All these were experiences crucial in the formation of his ideas on war. In 1818, Gneisenau secured for him the appointment of director of the Kriegsakademie. Here was a base which allowed him to devote the remainder of his life to his studies of military history and the nature of war, and above all to his principal work, On War (Vom Kriege, 1832). In 1831 Gneisenau asked Clausewitz to serve as his chief of staff in the Polish campaign of 1831. Both contracted cholera and died.

Suffering and sadness were major themes in Clausewitz's life. Blessed with a wife, Marie von Bruhl, whose devotion ensured the posthumous publication – albeit unrevised and unfinished – of On War, he none the less had to undergo an eight-year courtship and the prolonged separations military service imposed. He coveted noble status and yet did not achieve it until 1827. He never commanded an army in the field; he never won the plaudits due to a conquering hero. And yet his thirst for military glory, coupled perhaps with its destructive aspects (especially his hatred for the French), revealed the inner tension in a man whose forte was as a student and thinker. Much of Clausewitz's brilliance lies in this personal torment, in his embodiment of seemingly irreconcilable poles.

It is not therefore surprising that in On War the individual general is depicted as a hero. Clausewitz dismissed his contemporaries, the strategic theorists searching for general principles of war. For him war was above all uncertain, an area in which the individual is always striving to rationalize the inchoate forces he encounters. This he does by understanding the essence of war itself. Therefore the role of theory in the education and preparation of the soldier should not be prescriptive or utilitarian. Rather it should facilitate understanding. It should be closely related to history. History enables the student to see how things occur, while theory provides a tool to clarify its most important points.

This Socratic approach allowed Clausewitz to consider the study of war as a tabula rasa. The nature of war is violent: killing and maiming are absolutes. War could not therefore be limited of itself. For Clausewitz's own generation Napoleon* had given fresh and horrific meaning to what in previous generations might have been only concept. Even if fought for limited aims, the belligerents could not justify the employment of limited effort. The other side might use all the means at its disposal, and therefore the most direct and immediate way to victory was best.

In practice, however, the ideal of absolute war was unattainable. The first and most pervasive limitation on war's conduct was its subordination to politics. Political circumstances gave rise to war, political consequences accrued from it, and therefore politics should determine the direction and course of its strategy. The insight was not new. The absolutism of eighteenth-century monarchs gave them control of both the military and political spheres, and their conduct of strategy represented the interplay of the two. Clausewitz's contribution was to give it priority, and to show its relationship to 'absolute' war. It is the contribution to strategic thought for which Clausewitz is justly most celebrated, and, if he had lived, it would have become the main theme throughout On War. However, the fact that he had started but not completed this revision has left inconsistencies which confuse the argument.

Clausewitz argued that the ideal of 'absolute' war was limited in a second, much more immediate way, which he dubbed 'friction'. 'Four elements make up the climate of war,' he wrote, 'danger, exertion, uncertainty and chance.' These inbuilt characteristics thwart the achievement of great conceptions in war. The problems of the individual, sickness, exhaustion, human error, and poor morale, are multiplied many times over in an army of thousands. The general himself is prey to 'friction' in innumerable forms; his skill as a commander lies in his acceptance and understanding of its constraints.

The ideal of absolute war caused Clausewitz to see the destruction of the enemy's forces as war's implicit objective. The true commander should put aside all prevarication, and seek battle at the earliest possible opportunity. Napoleonic battles fought by mass armies had tended towards attrition. Therefore numerical superiority was central, and the victors must pursue – as they did after Jena – so as to make defeat really crippling.

Eventually, however, the drive of the attack exhausts itself. Victory no longer seems imminent. Clausewitz dubbed this phase 'the culminating point of victory'. If success has not yet been secured, a period of defence must now follow. Clausewitz, almost alone among military theorists, saw defence as the stronger means. The moral importance of the attack, which Clausewitz himself embraced, has led soldiers to regard it as necessarily the first stage in a war. Clausewitz, however – mindful of the 1812 campaign – saw that the first stage might be to wait. Allow the enemy to exhaust himself

and his men: he advances, his communications lengthen, his fear of counter-attack increases. Eventually the attack passes the 'culminating point of victory', and the defender, his strength concentrated and husbanded, counter-attacks.

Clausewitz's assertion that defence is the stronger means sets up an apparent tension with his earlier emphasis on the will to battle. Similarly his unrevised treatment of the relationship between war and politics left his work open to misinterpretation. Soldiers looking for specific guidelines tended to disregard On War (its first edition of 1,500 was still not sold out twenty years after its publication in 1832) or to use it selectively. This was the case in the years leading up to the First World War, when its association with the rise of the Prussian general staff elevated it to the pre-eminent status it still enjoys. But it was a status that saw Clausewitz as the advocate of the decisive attack carried through by superior morale and ultimately as the exponent of war as a political end in itself. In recent years the true nature of Clausewitz's discussion of the relationship between war and politics has ensured that his reputation has been freed from the worst associations of militarism, and has inspired a fresh generation of strategic thinkers.

Hew Strachan

Clausewitz's collected works appeared as *Hinterlassene Werke des Generals Carl von Clausewitz über Krieg and Kriegführung* (10 vols, 1832–7). Werner Hahlweg is preparing an edition of Clausewitz's papers, *Schriften – Aufsätze – Studien – Briefe* (vol. 1, 1966). The best translation in English of *On War* is by Michael Howard and Peter Paret (1976); it includes valuable essays on Clausewitz and his influence. Peter Paret, *Clausewitz and the State* (1976), is brilliant. See also: Hans Rothfels, *Carl von Clausewitz: Politik und Krieg* (1920); Werner Hahlweg, *Carl von Clausewitz* (1957); Raymond Aron, *Penser la Guerre, Clausewitz* (1976).

90

CLAUSIUS, Rudolf Julius Emmanuel 1822–88

German physicist

Clausius, the son of a pastor, was born in the then Prussian town of Köslin which is now, as Koszalin, part of Poland. He was educated at the Universities of Berlin and Halle where he obtained his doctorate in 1847. The rest of his life, apart from active service in the Franco-Prussian War of 1870, was spent in a number of academic posts beginning with his appointment in 1850 to the Chair of Physics at the Royal Artillery and Engineering School, Berlin. In 1855 Clausius moved to the Zurich Polytechnic but returned to Germany in 1867 and held Chairs of Physics at Wurzburg and from 1869 until his death at the University of Bonn.

In 1850 Clausius published one of the classic papers of modern physics *Über die bewegende Kraft der Wärme* ('On the motive force of heat'). It was the first of nine substantial memoirs on heat and began with the position adopted by Sadi Carnot in his *Réflexions sur la puissance motrice du feu* (1824), a work Clausius only knew at second hand. Carnot had shown that whenever 'work is done by heat . . . a certain quantity of heat passes from a hotter to a colder body.' This Clausius could accept but the further point made by Carnot that 'no heat is lost in the process . . . the quantity of heat is conserved' he rejected on the obvious ground that the heat produced by friction was almost 'impossible to explain . . . except as an increase in the quantity of heat'. Further, the work of Joule* had shown the 'possibility of increasing the quantity of heat'.

The important conclusion drawn by Clausius from this apparent conflict between Carnot and Joule was that 'the accomplishment of work requires not merely a change in the distribution of heat, but also an actual consumption of heat.' In 1850 it was clear to Clausius as it could not have been to Carnot a quarter of a century earlier that it was energy that was conserved, not heat. This allowed him to take the further step and make the first formulation of the second law of thermodynamics: 'It is impossible for a self-acting machine unaided by any external agency to convey heat from one body to another at a higher temperature, or heat cannot of itself pass from a colder to a warmer body.' Heat processes were irreversible.

The implications of such a law were profound and not lost on Clausius. After struggling with a variety of terms in which to express the law Clausius finally introduced in 1865 the term entropy, 'as similar as possible to energy', to describe that fraction of a system's energy converted into wasteful heat in contrast to the 'free energy' converted into useful mechanical work. He could at last express the basic laws of thermodynamics in a form unrivalled for their brevity, poetry and bleakness: 1. *'Die Energie der Welt ist constant'* (the energy of the universe is constant); and 2. *'Die Entropie der Welt strebt einem Maximum zu'* (entropy tends to a maximum).

Clausius had in fact created a new universe. The universe of classical physics established by Laplace* out of the basic Newtonian cosmology emphasized its stability. God no longer had to intervene like a watchmaker to maintain the accuracy of his mechanical timepiece; in his wisdom he had created an harmonious and stable cosmos. The work of Clausius revealed a different picture, a universe in which ultimately all useful heat would have been dissipated and entropy totally maximized, a world which would end without sufficient energy to produce bang or whimper.

Other work of Clausius made substantial contributions to the kinetic theory of gases. It was Clausius, for example, who in 1858 first worked out the mean free path, the distance travelled by a particle between collisions. He further, in 1857, anticipated the later work of Svante Arrhenius when he argued that molecules in an electrolytic solution move just as molecules of a gas, colliding, separating and re-forming. Thus, at any given time there will always be a number of ions which in the presence of an applied potential would naturally flow to the appropriate pole and thereby produce an electric current.

Derk Gjertsen

Clausius' writings on thermodynamics are collected in *Die mechanische Wärmetheorie* (2 vols, 1865–7), trans. T. Hirst as *The Mechanical Theory of Heat* (1887). A translation of his classic 1850 paper is available in *Reflections on the Motive Power of Heat*, ed. E. Mendoze (1960). The rise of thermodynamics and the place of Clausius in its history is treated most fully in D. Cardwell, *From Watt to Clausius* (1971).

91

CLOUGH, Arthur Hugh 1819–61

British poet

Arthur Hugh Clough was born in Liverpool, but he spent his early childhood in Charleston, South Carolina, where his father had business interests. He was sent back to England when he was nine and in 1829 he went to Rugby where he became Dr Arnold's* outstanding schoolboy. After a brilliant scholarship performance he went up to Balliol in 1837, but he failed to take the expected first class degree or to win a Balliol fellowship. His undergraduate career was complicated by the influence of his tutor, W. G. Ward, a powerful intellect and an outspoken Tractarian. Although Clough did not become a proselyte the turmoil of controversy undoubtedly unsettled the religious certainties implanted by his mother and consolidated by Dr Arnold.

In 1842 he gained a fellowship at Oriel and began a period of outward contentment, enjoying his teaching and forming a circle of intimate friends which included Matthew Arnold*. He became interested in social and economic affairs, publishing a pamphlet on the Irish crisis in 1847 (*A Consideration of Objections against the Retrenchment Association*), and gaining a reputation as a radical. Nicknamed 'Citizen Clough' by Arnold, he went to Paris with Emerson* in 1848 to see the revolution for himself, but his republican ardour waned as can be seen from his letters of this and the following year when he was in Mazzini's* Rome.

His theological views became increasingly liberal during the forties and the influence of D. F. Strauss's*

Life of Jesus (Jesu Leben, 1835) is apparent in such poems as 'Easter Day' with its refrain, 'Christ is not risen, no,/He lies and moulders low.' In 1848 he resigned his Fellowship over the requirement to subscribe to the Thirty-nine Articles. This scrupulousness informs the poems he published in *Ambarvalia* (1849) and resulted in his being labelled a 'poet of doubt'. The brighter side of his temperament is shown in *The Bothie of Tober-na-Vuolich* (1848), a 'Long-vacation Pastoral' whose lively hexameters were praised by Arnold as having Homer's 'buoyant rapidity'. While in Rome Clough started *Amours de Voyage* (though it was not published until 1858). This '5 act epistolary tragi-comedy or comi-tragedy' follows the prevarications of Claude who is trapped (as Clough was) in the besieged Republic. He evinces all his creator's indecisiveness in his half-hearted pursuit of Mary Trevellyn.

Clough's character is also reflected in the next long poem he wrote. *Dipsychus,* started in Venice in 1850 but not published in its entirety until this century, adopts the structure of the Faust story, with the eponymous hero, 'the tender conscience', being tempted by the Mephistophelian 'Spirit'. In the end Dipsychus 'submits' to the world and the flesh, but a light-hearted epilogue sheds ambiguous light on his 'fall' and suggests that perhaps the Spirit 'wasn't a devil after all'. Certainly many of the Spirit's attitudes correspond to those Clough expressed in his lectures and essays, while his songs are in the satiric vein of one of Clough's best-known short poems, 'The Latest Decalogue'.

After leaving Oxford Clough became Principal of University Hall and Professor of English at University College, London, but resigned in 1852. After a short period in Cambridge, Massachusetts, with Emerson, he returned to England, married Blanche Smith in 1854, and settled down to a job in the Education Office. He was much taken up with work for his wife's cousin, Florence Nightingale*, and he also produced a new edition of Plutarch's *Lives.* He wrote little poetry until his final continental expedition when he composed the verse tales in *Mari Magno.* He died in Florence in 1861.

His early death and his failure to consolidate his boyhood brilliance led easily to the myth of the promising failure. Matthew Arnold compounded this with his reference to the 'too quick despairer' in 'Thyrsis' (1866). However, it was Clough's openness to the intellectual currents of the time that produced his artistic success, and though his poetry was found lacking in beauty, or even offensive, by contemporaries, its stark honesty, its relativism, its satire and its sense of the mind in flux have led to a revaluation and the claim that Clough was a precursor of the 'modernists'. Though he published little, Clough's poetic range was wide and his output considerable (he wrote as much poetry as Arnold). *The Poems and Prose Remains* were brought out by his wife in 1869, but it has not been

until the last thirty years that Clough has attracted the editorial and critical attention his work merits.

Simon Rae

Modern editions: *The Poems of Arthur Hugh Clough,* ed. F. L. Mulhauser (2nd edn, 1974); *The Correspondence of Arthur Hugh Clough,* ed. F. L. Mulhauser (1957); *Selected Prose Works of Arthur Hugh Clough,* ed. B. B. Trawick (1964). *The Letters of Matthew Arnold to Arthur Hugh Clough,* ed. H. F. Lowry (1932), is also an important source. See: Katherine Chorley, *Arthur Hugh Clough: The Uncommitted Mind* (1962); R. K. Biswas, *Arthur Hugh Clough: Towards a Reconsideration* (1972); W. E. Houghton, *The Poetry of Clough: An Essay in Revaluation* (1963); M. Timko, *Innocent Victorian: The Satiric Poetry of Arthur Hugh Clough* (1963); E. B. Greenberger, *Arthur Hugh Clough: The Growth of a Poet's Mind* (1970); *Clough: The Critical Heritage,* ed. Michael Thorpe (1972); R. M. Gollin, W. E. Houghton and M. Timko, *Arthur Hugh Clough: A Descriptive Catalogue* (1966).

92
COBBETT, William 1763–1835

British journalist, essayist, political reformer, agriculturalist

Cobbett was born in Farnham, Surrey, the son of a yeoman farmer and the grandson of a farm labourer. He joined the army as an uneducated youth and quickly rose from private to sergeant-major, finding time between military duties to teach himself grammar, mathematics and French. On obtaining an honorary discharge in 1791 he brought charges of embezzlement against several of his superior officers in the naive belief that his disclosure would be welcomed by the army hierarchy. When he learned that this was not the case, and that he had placed himself in jeopardy, he left England for France with his newly married wife. Within six months the bloody progress of revolution in France drove them on to America where they spent the next eight years. There Cobbett discovered his journalistic talents, becoming the country's most powerful writer. Under the name 'Peter Porcupine', and later under his own name, he courageously defended the unpopular British position in the new republic.

When Cobbett returned to England in 1800 he was greeted as a celebrity, dined with Pitt, was offered the editorship of a government-owned newspaper, and was extolled in parliament as one who deserved a statue of gold for the services he had rendered his country in America. Shortly, however, Cobbett learned that the whole government was as corrupt as its military services, and he became the champion of political reform, fearlessly exposing corruption and waste, and fighting until the end of his life for personal liberties and justice. In 1810 he was imprisoned for two years and heavily fined for protesting against the flogging of English militia men under the bayonets of German mercenary troops. With the end of the Napoleonic Wars in 1815, great economic distress descended on the country, and the government acted to stifle all protest. Suspension of the Habeas Corpus Act forced Cobbett to flee to America where he spent two and half years in exile. His life there is described in an amusing book, *A Year's Residence in the United States* (1818–19). After returning to England in 1819 he became a principal adviser to the flighty Queen Caroline in her battle royal with her husband, the dissolute George IV. Cobbett took a leading part in the fight for Catholic emancipation which was won in 1829, and in the first step toward reformation of parliament accomplished by the Reform Act of 1832. From 1833 until his death in 1835, Cobbett served as a member of parliament – probably the first from the working class to do so on his own merits, having neither money nor the backing of one of the great political parties.

Cobbett's influence as a journalist was exerted principally through his *Political Register,* which was issued weekly with only minor disruptions from 1802 to 1835. The *Edinburgh Review*, no great admirer of Cobbett, declared in 1807 that he had more influence than all the other journalists put together. His influence extended in two directions, affecting both the press and their readers: he fought the rampant corruption of the press, its practice of accepting payments and subsidies from government, from political parties and from private sources; he fought the anonymity of authorship, signing his articles with his own name; he was an important influence in the development of the modern leading article by which the views of the newspaper are expressed on current affairs. Looking at his impact on the public – he produced the first newspaper cheap enough to be easily available to the working classes; through that paper and his books, he educated those classes in their rights and gave them a sense of their worth. Even such a rival as the *Westminster Review* begrudgingly admitted the validity of Cobbett's boastful assertion that he had been the 'great enlightener of the people of England'.

As essayist, he produced some of the finest unaffected and entertaining prose that has graced the English language. 'He could make a cow's tail interesting,' Brougham once said. And his writing skills were productively engaged: he promoted a new cottage industry – the manufacture of straw hats which brought financial relief to many families living on the edge of starvation – for which he received the medal of the Royal Society of Arts; his *Cottage Economy* (1822) provided useful advice on how to manage efficiently a small house on a small income; in his *Emigrant's Guide* (1829) he told potential emigrants what they needed to know

before undertaking their great adventure; in his *Advice to Young Men and (incidentally) to Young Women* (1830) he set forth some provocative precepts for living a happy life. He produced a highly successful book on English grammar (1818) for the use of 'soldiers, sailors, apprentices, and ploughboys'; a book by which English speakers could learn French (1824), and another for French-speaking people who wished to learn English (1795); all of which went through dozens of editions and were found useful by many thousand readers. He was also the founder of the reports of parliamentary debates now known as *Hansard*, and of the standard legal work known as *Howell's State Trials*.

Cobbett's principal reform activities (his support of Catholic Emancipation and parliamentary reform) have already been mentioned. His constant harassment of wrong-doing also led to other reforms such as increased financial responsibility in government, the discontinuance of sinecures and unmerited pensions, and the selection of civil servants on the basis of merit rather than influence.

Cobbett was at heart a farmer, and kept returning to farming and gardening, and to writing about both. He was influential in the adoption of the Swedish turnip and mangel-wurzel for use as animal fodder in both America and England. He tried, unsuccessfully, to convince the English farmer of the value of maize for the same purpose, but it took another hundred years before maize found any wide acceptance in England. Cobbett's *American Gardener* (1821) was the standard authority in the United States for many years; his *English Gardener* (1828) is still in print and still useful. He also wrote of the cultivation of maize in *Cobbett's Corn* (1828) and produced a fine book on the cultivation of trees: *The Woodlands* (1828).

Cobbett's *Rural Rides* (first edition 1830), his most celebrated work, delightfully mixes a description of the English countryside of the 1820s with an idiosyncratic comment on the politics of the day, demonstrating his transcendent skill as a writer, his salty humour and his unpredictable prejudices.

George Spater

The standard biography is G. D. H. Cole, *William Cobbett* (1924). See also: James Sambrook, *William Cobbett* (1973); and George Spater, *William Cobbett, The Poor Man's Friend* (1982).

93
COBDEN, Richard 1804–65

British politician

Richard Cobden was born near Midhurst in Sussex, the son of a farmer. After schooling at Bowes Hall in Yorkshire, he went into commerce as a clerk and then as a traveller. His journeys throughout Britain convinced him that the most exciting developments lay in the north of England. He set up in business as a calico printer in Manchester – the symbol and centre of industrial transformation. Not averse to making money, his enterprise in the late 1830s was profitable. At the same time, bent on self-improvement, he was an avid reader of economic and political subjects with a keen interest (which never left him) in travelling. He journeyed widely in Western Europe, the Near East, Russia and the United States. He published his impressions in a series of pamphlets which attracted more than local interest.

Failing to gain election to parliament for Stockport in 1837, he threw himself into Manchester politics, playing a leading part in its incorporation under the terms of the 1835 Municipal Corporations Act. At the same time, he was drawn into the campaign for the repeal of the 1815 Corn Laws. This struggle, from 1838 until 1846 (when Peel introduced their repeal), became the major concern in Cobden's life, involving him in much travelling and public speaking. He was elected MP for Stockport in 1841. This campaign, while it brought public reputation, meant that his business suffered severely. Only public subscription, in recognition of his services to free trade, saved him from insolvency, though he was not thereafter successful in business or as an investor. It was a rather odd position for someone widely seen as the apostle of commerce during a period of expansion. He subsequently represented the West Riding and Rochdale in parliament but, although offers of ministerial posts were made during the 1850s, they were declined. However, in 1859–60, he was British plenipotentiary in the negotiations for a Franco-British commercial treaty whose purpose was not only to extend free trade but to improve relations between the two countries. His travels and correspondence brought him into contact with economists, politicians and princes, making his name very well-known in North America and Europe. Even though he remained in religion a member of the Church of England and returned to live in the south of England he seemed to be the most lucid spokesman of the 'Manchester School'.

Cobden's reputation rests upon his ability as an orator, organizer, pamphleteer and economic thinker. In the campaign against the Corn Laws, his speeches were invariably carefully argued and delivered. He sought to persuade by relentless reason rather than by sheer power of speech or vivid illustration. If he lacked the touch of robust genius possessed by his colleague Bright*, he nevertheless supplied him with much of his argument. As an organizer and strategist he showed a sure touch in limiting the campaign against the Corn Laws to that one objective. Press and post were skilfully used to develop an extra-parlimentary agitation of great sophistication. His commercial colleagues were persuaded to part with a good deal of money in order

to defeat the Corn Laws – the symbol of aristocratic and landed supremacy. His political writings from *England, Ireland, and America* (1835) and *Russia* (1836) to his exposure of the 'panics' of 1847–8, 1851–3 and 1859–61 contain both perceptive comments on the likely development of those countries and on 'how wars are got up'. The 'balance of power' as spoken by a statesman was little more than superstition. Britain had been too ready to interfere all over the world. Nothing but trade could make or save a country. Peace meant trade and trade made for peace. Restraints on trade were obnoxious. Goods had to be produced at the cheapest rate to supply the markets of the world at the lowest price. Of course, Cobden saw Britain as being ideally placed to take advantage of the world as it then stood but he clearly realized that such a condition might not last for ever. It was probable that a country would be found whose cottons and woollens would be produced cheaper than those in England, in which case, no human power, neither fleets nor armies, would prevent Manchester, Liverpool and Leeds from sharing the fate of their once proud predecessors in Holland, Italy and Phoenicia.

After the repeal of the Corn Laws, Cobden's political direction was uncertain. More adept at articulating opinions than interested in the processes of politics he wrote privately that he preferred pioneering for his convictions to promotion at the expense of them. He knew that his convictions whether on the Crimean War or the Indian Mutiny placed him in a minority. While opposed to the aristocratic predominance in politics he did not expect to see its replacement in his own lifetime. Ill-health meant that he did not play a prominent role in the years just before his death and his views on the nature and extent of further parliamentary reform can be variously interpreted. Less pugnacious and more subtle than Bright, there was a time in the 1840s when he appeared to be the most attractive embodiment of a provincial middle-class commercial culture whose values would become politically dominant as industrialism proceeded. Yet, in the age of Palmerston, he was acutely aware that 'middle-class' opinion could not be welded into a coherent political grouping. It was useless to throw on the aristocracy the entire blame for the wars in which Britain had been engaged, for the aristocracy never governed a people by opposing their ruling instincts. It would take the British people a long time to understand that they had been the most combative and aggressive community 'since the days of the Roman dominion' but their empire would not last indefinitely.

Keith Robbins

See: H. Ashworth, *Recollections of Richard Cobden* (1877); J. Morley, *Life of Richard Cobden* (1903); D. Read, *Cobden and Bright (1967).*

94

COLE, Thomas 1801–48

US painter

Born in Lancashire, Cole was taken to America at the age of eighteen. After a spell at the Pennsylvania Academy of Fine Art in Philadelphia he arrived in New York in the spring of 1825. Another three years' study in Europe followed before he returned to the United States in 1832 and set up home at Catskill on the Hudson where be became the accepted head of the 'Hudson River School'.

In 1825 three paintings he had placed in a New York shop-window were bought by painter Asher Durand, John Trumbull, President of the American Academy of Fine Arts, and William Dunlap, author of the first book on American art, *The History of the Rise and Progress of the Arts of Design in the United States*. After this sudden success, Cole was recognized as a leading nature painter. Despite his defence of landscape in his 'Essay on American Scenery' and the autobiographical statement he prepared for Dunlap's *History*, however, he persisted in his allegiance to the historical mode, considered superior at the time. His triumph was to transfer the prestige and techniques of one form to the other. The key element in both was for Cole their moral content. He had begun his career in 1818 by illustrating Bunyan's *Holy Way*, maintained his religious tendencies and even increased them in his work after his baptism as an Anglican in 1842. In his funeral oration his friend the poet William Cullen Bryant* said, 'The paintings of Cole are of that nature that it hardly transcends language to call them acts of religion.' While his rich, brushy panoramas demonstrated the insignificance of man as he confronted God's handiwork, their programmatic organization stressed the vanity and brevity of his existence. His proudest achievements – *The Course of Empire, The Departure and the Return, The Past and the Present, The Voyage of Life, The Cross and the World* – were all in series, and the relationship between Cole's 'narratives' and contemporary dioramas is obvious. Both were popular; Cole's career coincided with an upsurge of enthusiasm for American landscape. Asher Durand painted Cole and Bryant as *Kindred Spirits*, high on a cliff, admiring the view. 'America is a poem in our eyes,' wrote Emerson*, 'It's ample geography dazzles the imagination.'

Cole too was dazzled. Yet while his predilection was for idealized compositions – Arcadia and the Garden of Eden – his audience demanded realism. The unsaleable series were usually painted alongside the landscapes, worked up from notebook sketches after a lapse of time. Oddly, these were affected by clichés from Claude and Salvator Rosa until the year of his death. For all the talk of unsullied nature in his poems and letters, Cole, more than any other painter of his era,

recognized the complexity of his own relation to nature; perhaps, after all, he was more dangerous than either railways or settlers. Such self-awareness makes it clear why Barbara Novak called him America's first 'fully-equipped' landscapist.

Stuart Morgan

See: Esther Seaver, *Thomas Cole 1801-1848: One Hundred Years Later* (1949); Louis L. Noble, *The Course of Empire, Voyage of Life and Other Pictures of Thomas Cole, N.A.*, ed. Elliott S. Vessell (1964); Barbara Novak, *Nature and Culture: American Landscape and Painting 1825–1875* (1980).

95

COLERIDGE, Samuel Taylor 1772–1834

British poet and critic

Coleridge was the youngest of the ten children of the vicar of Ottery St Mary in Devon. After his father's death, he was sent in 1782 as a charity boy to Christ's Hospital School in London. There he was a daydreamer and precocious reader, who, according to his schoolfellow, Charles Lamb*, 'conjured' over neo-Platonism and Boehme's mysticism. In 1791, already with a reputation for fabulous learning, he went up to Jesus College, Cambridge, where he came under the influence of the Unitarian William Frend, a campaigner for the opening of the universities to Dissenters. For a combination of reasons, including his sorrow at Frend's dismissal in 1793, the deaths of his only sister and his brother Frank, his unhappy love for Mary Evans, and debts accumulated from a life of idleness and 'debauchery', he ran away from Cambridge in 1793. He took the drastic step of enlisting in the Fifteenth Light Dragoons under the pseudonym Silas Tomkyn Comberbache. His parade of classical learning led his superiors to suspect his identity and his sanity, and he was bailed out in 1794 by his older brothers.

Although he returned to Cambridge, Coleridge did not stay to complete his degree. In the summer of 1794 he met Robert Southey*, an Oxford student and poet who shared Coleridge's enthusiasm for the egalitarian ideals of the French Revolution and the belief in human perfectibility as expressed by William Godwin* in *Political Justice* (1793). Together they planned to set up a commune in America to practise these theories. The Pantisocracy scheme included three Fricker sisters of Bristol: Mary, Edith, whom Southey was courting, and Sara, whom Coleridge set about wooing, the more intensely because of the loss of Mary Evans. Pantisocracy was soon given up; Southey became less enthusiastic about the sharing of property and suggested a preliminary experiment of joint farming in Wales. Meanwhile Coleridge was wavering in his attachment to

Sara, though when admonished by Southey he promised grimly, 'I will do my Duty.' In October 1795 he married his unsuitable Sara.

Meanwhile Coleridge was lecturing on politics and religion in Bristol, and in 1796 he worked singlehanded at his periodical, the *Watchman*, commenting on political events and attacking Pitt's war on France and his repressive policies at home. By 1798 Coleridge himself was disillusioned by events in France and shared the general fear of the invasion of Britain. In 'France: an Ode' he expressed his new condemnation of France, while still upholding 'the spirit of divine Liberty'. Thereafter Coleridge engaged no more in political polemics, but settled into political, and religious, orthodoxy. Though he briefly considered becoming a Unitarian preacher in 1798, even delivering some sermons in Shrewsbury (where Hazlitt* heard and admired him), he was happy instead to accept an annuity of £150 offered by the wealthy Wedgwood brothers. Later Coleridge attacked Unitarianism as a 'cold' religion in its denial of the divinity of Christ and of the doctrines of Original Sin and Atonement.

The 1790s were the years of Coleridge's best poetry. From early attempts at 'bardic' poems celebrating Liberty, Piety, and Philosophy and denouncing Oppression, Slavery, and Corruption (e.g. 'Religious Musings', 1794, 'The Destiny of Nations', 1796), Coleridge turned to the more original and flexible form of the conversation poem. In 'Religious Musings' he praised the necessitarian philosopher David Hartley (after whom he named his first child in 1796) as the man who first 'marked the ideal tribes/Up the fine fibres through the sentient brain'. Coleridge had read Hartley's *Observations on Man* (1749) in 1794 and announced to Southey, 'I am a compleat Necessitarian.' That is, he accepted Hartley's explanation of the mind's function as a passive register of sensations, arranging those sensations into ideas according to their association in time and space. His importance for Coleridge, and for Wordsworth*, whom Coleridge met in 1795, lay in his stress on the primacy of sensation and the associational nature of memory and imagination. Thus it was clear to the two poets that childhood held the key to adulthood, that a youth spent wandering 'like a breeze/By lakes and sandy shores' was morally and imaginatively more beneficial and educative than one spent, like Coleridge's own schooldays, 'in the great city, pent 'mid cloisters dim' ('Frost at Midnight', 1798).

In the conversation poems Coleridge imaginatively imitates Hartleian associationism, letting his poet's mind ramble from the present to the past and a hypothetical future, concluding in optimism about the healing powers of nature, which, in words close to those of Wordsworth in 'Tintern Abbey' (1798), 'ne'er deserts the wise and pure' ('This Lime-Tree Bower My Prison', 1797). At the same time Coleridge flirted not only with Unitarianism but also with pantheism. As he speculated in 'The Eolian Harp' (1795):

> And what if all of animated nature
> Be but organic Harps diversely fram'd,
> That tremble into thought, as o'er them sweeps
> Plastic and vast, one intellectual breeze,
> At once the Soul of each, and God of all.

But in the poem itself he repudiates such unorthodoxy; the 'mild reproof' of Sara reminds him to put aside 'these shapings of the unregenerate mind' and 'walk humbly with my God'. As with politics, so with religion and philosophy. Coleridge soon came to distrust pantheism as a spiritless faith, a 'living Atheism' which allows no room for a personal God atoning for man's sins. And by 1801 he was struggling against the mechanical nature of Hartley's philosophy. Much later, in *Biographia Literaria* (1817), he recalled how he had embraced, then rejected, the Hartleian scheme, by which 'the soul is present only to be pinched or stroked'. The metaphor of the aeolian harp, earlier dear to him and Wordsworth as applied to the creative imagination touched off by external impulses, he also soon found uncongenial. His insistence in 'Dejection' (1802) that 'I may not hope from outward forms to win/The passion and the life, whose fountains are within' expresses the chief difference between his own and Wordsworth's views of the relationship between mind and nature.

The friendship with Wordsworth was the most important of Coleridge's life. William and his sister Dorothy settled near Coleridge in Somerset in 1796, and the poets planned epics and prose tales together. During their *annus mirabilis*, 1797–8, they collaborated on *Lyrical Ballads*. As Coleridge recalled in *Biographia Literaria*, his task was to write supernatural poems in which he would 'transfer from our inward nature a human interest and a semblance of truth' which would achieve in the reader 'that willing suspension of disbelief for the moment, which constitutes poetic faith'. Wordsworth's complementary aim was 'to give the charm of novelty to things of every day'. Of Coleridge's contributions the most original was 'The Ancient Mariner', a ballad operating on psychological, moral, and aesthetic levels by means of clusters of symbols: moon, sun, stars, the animal world, good and evil spirits. Coleridge himself, as well as his contemporaries, came to see the figure of the lonely Mariner, with his 'glittering eye', his strange hold over his audience, and his tale of guilt and atonement, as an emblem of his author, the 'damaged archangel' whose table-talk was 'as an angel's' (Charles Lamb).

Lyrical Ballads was at first ill-received. For the second, enlarged edition of 1800 Wordsworth displaced Coleridge's poem, appending an editorial apology for its 'strangeness'. Coleridge's new supernatural poem,

'Christabel', remained unfinished and did not appear. By 1800 Coleridge had lost confidence in his poetic powers, and was by now addicted to opium.

To 1797–8 belongs also the mysterious fragment 'Kubla Khan', called by its author a 'psychological curiosity' and supposedly written on his awakening from an opium-induced dream. This poem, allusive and elliptical, illustrates Coleridge's famous definition of poetry, formulated in *Biographia Literaria*, as that which excites in the reader a 'pleasurable activity of mind' by means of the 'reconciliation of opposite or discordant qualities', so that the reader himself carries on the creative activity. Its influence has been immense. Tennyson's* 'Palace of Art' and Yeats's Byzantium poems would be unthinkable without 'Kubla Khan', the first great non-discursive poem with its celebration of the poet who 'on honeydew hath fed,/ And drunk the milk of Paradise'.

In September 1798 Coleridge and the Wordsworths travelled to Germany. Coleridge studied physiology, anatomy, and natural history at the University of Göttingen, returning in July 1799 to several troubles. He met and fell in love with Sara Hutchinson, and found life with his own Sara increasingly impossible – 'two unequal Minds' and 'two discordant Wills' (first draft of 'Dejection', 1802). The association with the prolific Wordsworth nourished Coleridge's doubts about his own poetic genius; he wrote dramatically to Godwin in 1801, 'the Poet is dead in me'. Jealousy of Wordsworth, illness, debts, and the opium addiction completed his misery. His period of happy creativity was over. Ironically, the most successful poems he was still to write were painful celebrations of his failure as a poet. 'Dejection' genially combines sorrow at the suspension of 'my shaping spirit of Imagination' with pious hopes for the continuing 'Joy' of the addressee, who in the manuscript version was Sara Hutchinson, in the second version Wordsworth, and in the final poem an unnamed 'Lady'. It was published on 4 October 1802, the day of Wordsworth's wedding to Sara Hutchinson's sister Mary, and the anniversary of his own wedding. His other fine poem of these years was 'To William Wordsworth' (1807), a generous response to Wordsworth's reading of 'The Prelude', the great epic dedicated to Coleridge. He paid Wordsworth the compliment of writing in Wordsworth's own mode. Having listened 'like a devout child,/My soul lay passive, by thy various strain/Driven as in surges now beneath the stars,/With momentary stars of my own birth'.

In 1800–1 Coleridge, having moved to the Lakes to be near Wordsworth (his 'god', as Lamb commented), intensified his study of philosophy. He soon claimed to have 'overthrown the doctrine of Association, as taught by Hartley'. Kant was the chief source of his freedom from what he now saw as his 'imprisonment' in necessitarianism. Coleridge used Kant's transcendentalism, combined with Platonism and traditional Christianity, to argue for the freedom of the will and reason, while accepting that associationism accounted for memory. Later, in *Biographia Literaria*, he added 'Imagination' to the list of free, active faculties, and 'Fancy' to those determined by association. As John Stuart Mill* wrote in his important essay on Coleridge (*Westminster Review*, 1840), 'the Germano-Coleridgian doctrine' was the most influential answer to eighteenth-century empiricism. Coleridge was thus, according to Mill, one of the 'great seminal minds' of his age.

Coleridge went to Malta in 1804 in search of health. On his return in 1806 he separated finally from his wife, and lived mainly in London until his death. He soon broke with the Wordsworths too; they were distressed by his opium-taking and consequent dilatoriness. Yet Coleridge's career was not over. He became celebrated as a public lecturer; on Shakespeare and literature generally in 1808 and 1811–12, on philosophy in 1818. Undoubtedly his second Shakespeare lectures owed much to those recently given by A.W. Schlegel* in Vienna, but his Shakespeare criticism has become duly celebrated as a truly 'Romantic' view of Shakespeare in opposition to the eighteenth-century emphasis on genre and the dramatic unities. Coleridge again tried his hand at a one-man periodical, the *Friend* (1809 and 1818), and again the venture was shortlived because of bad management, lack of support, and the obscurity of which many contemporaries complained. Coleridge's vast learning, particularly his embracing of German transcendentalism, caused his critics to smile; Byron* wrote wittily of Coleridge 'explaining metaphysics to the nation -/I wish he would explain his Explanation' (*Don Juan*).

Biographia Literaria (1817) contains Coleridge's famous theory of literature as organic, with the imagination as the faculty which reconciles opposites. In spite of its obscurity (caused by Coleridge's attempt to retell in detail his philosophical and aesthetic education), the work is, as I. A. Richards has said, a 'lumber-room' of wisdom containing 'more hints towards a theory of poetry than all the rest ever written upon the subject' (*Principles of Literary Criticism*, 1924). After 1817 Coleridge concentrated on philosophy and religion, publishing *Lay Sermons* (1817) and *Aids to Reflection* (1825). These, with his last work, *On the Constitution of Church and State* (1830), exercised an immense influence on Victorian thinking. The Broad Church Movement, Christian Socialism, the ideas on education of Thomas and Matthew Arnold (both*), all owed and avowed debts to Coleridge's emphasis on the organic nature of society, his progressive conservatism, and his insistence on the compatibility of reason and faith. Coleridge achieved posthumously the fame and influence that were due to what Wordsworth aptly called his 'marvellous' intellect. With his mysterious symbolic poetry and his philosophical theory of literature, he stands as the great representative of Romantic poetry and criticism.

Rosemary Ashton

The definitive edition is still in progress: *The Collected Works of Samuel Taylor Coleridge*, ed. Kathleen Coburn, 16 vols in progress, 1969–). See also: *The Notebooks of Samuel Taylor Coleridge*, ed. Kathleen Coburn, (3 double vols, 1957–); *The Collected Letters*, ed. E. L. Griggs, (6 vols, 1956–71). A good biography of the early years is John Cornwell, *Coleridge: Poet and Revolutionary 1772–1804* (1973). Two classics in criticism are: I. A. Richards, *Coleridge on Imagination* (1934); John Livingston Lowes, *The Road to Xanadu* (1927, repr. 1930). See also: John Beer, *Coleridge's Poetic Intelligence* (1977); Thomas McFarland, *Coleridge and the Pantheist Tradition* (1969).

96
COLLINS, William Wilkie 1824–89

British novelist

The most brilliant of the circle of young writers working with Charles Dickens* was Wilkie Collins, elder son of William Collins, RA, a successful painter who died young. Wilkie Collins's work combined narrative exuberance with tenacious observation and a rich pictorial imagination. His fiction moves freely among the classes of society and reflects his preoccupation with physical handicaps and disorders of mind and body. The later writings of Dickens bear many traces of the gifted younger writer's impact on his patron, especially in the move of the later 1850s towards an interlocking narrative form and a sombre sensationalism. The success of *All the Year Round* in its early years from 1859 was due mainly to the serialization of *The Woman in White* (1860), Collins's most successful novel and his favourite among his own works.

Collins's achievement as a novelist was buttressed by his work as essayist, critic and writer of melodramatic plays. His essays on literary and other topics were reprinted in *My Miscellanies* (1863). His essay on Balzac* in *All the Year Round* (1859), together with Routledge's issue of a good translation of *Eugénie Grandet* in that year, was the culmination of the shift of taste in the 1850s which paved the way for the fiction of Henry James*, George Moore* and Joseph Conrad. The play *The Frozen Deep* (1857), Collins's most successful work of collaboration with Dickens, was a melodramatic tale of male rivalry ending in reconciliation and death. Other writings for the stage were failures which attracted ridicule. In the novels and short fiction which form his main work, Collins pioneered the closely woven tale of detection and multiple viewpoint. Though sympathetic to the problem of women's disa-

bilities in society, he was only rarely able to portray female characters with warmth and sympathy.

Collins's major novels span the 1860s and are among the most important writings of the decade. In *The Woman in White*, *No Name* (1862), *Armadale* (1866) and *The Moonstone* (1868) he established himself as a master of narrative but retained the social commitment of his masters, Dickens, Victor Hugo* and Balzac. In the critical essay which dominated the critical discussion of fiction for two decades until the advent of Zola*, Henry Longueville Mansel ('Sensation Novels', *Quarterly Review* 1863) took the negative view of Collins which reappeared in Ruskin's* essay 'Fiction, Fair and Foul' (*Contemporary Review*, 1880). 'Sensation' writing was, however, an integral part of the move towards realism and was inseparable from the main development of the novel in the century, as Trollope* argued in an essay which later formed part of his *Autobiography*. The most judicious among early views of Collins was that of Émile Forgues, editor of the *Revue des deux mondes*, whose essay 'Le roman anglais contemporain' (*Revue des deux mondes, 1863*) recognizes the *balzacien* elements of the genre and tacitly acknowledges its affinity with New England romantic fiction, in which Forgues was adept.

The Woman in White explores the exposure of two women to the machinations of two scheming villains, Sir Percival Glyde and Count Fosco. Like the plays of Webster, with which it has many affinities, it owed its germ to an account of a judicial trial; Collins owned and treasured a copy of Maurice Méjan's *Recueil des causes célèbres*, from which he took his principal motif. In showing the abuses associated with private asylums, Collins gave direction to an important strand in the social literature of his age. In *No Name* he showed how a vengeful quest for the retrieval of property by a disadvantaged woman (another important 'sensation' theme) can be tempered by the effects of romantic love. In *The Moonstone* he inaugurated the modern cult of the detective novel. His novels of the 1870s increasingly shed the paraphernalia of suspense and detection. In *Man and Wife* (1870), *The New Magdalen* (1873), *The Law and the Lady* (1873) and *Fallen Leaves* (1879), Collins developed further the interest which he first explored in *No Name*, in the penalties imposed by society on illegitimate or compromised women.

The close relationship between Collins's fiction and the facts of his life was carefully screened from view until the appearance of recent biographical studies. The dominance in his life of an over-protective mother, herself the victim of early widowhood, undoubtedly contributed to his incapacity to form stable domestic relationships. His meeting with the first of two mistresses is vividly told in the opening of *The Woman in White*. His second mistress bore his three children. Myopic, of slight stature and tenacious manner, Collins never lost the combination of eloquence and tortuousness which undoubtedly owed much to his training as a barrister, a profession he never practised. Though principally associated with the 'sensation' writer's creed as expressed in a phrase attributed to him, 'make 'em cry, make 'em laugh, make 'em wait', his novels made a distinctive contribution to the pictorialism and psychological intensity which dominated the fiction of the second half-century.

Christopher Heywood

See: Michael Sadleir, 'Wilkie Collins', in *Excursions in Victorian Bibliography* (1922); T. S. Eliot, 'Wilkie Collins and Dickens', in *Selected Essays* (1945); Kenneth Robinson, *Wilkie Collins: A Biography* (1951); N. P. Davis, *The Life of Wilkie Collins* (1956).

97

COMTE, Auguste 1798–1857

French social thinker

The nineteenth century was the great age of 'positivism'. Comte not only coined the term and took the lead in popularizing the broad movement which it was designed to cover, but he also revealed through his own achievements and failures many of the most significant problems associated with this whole attitude of mind. At the core of positivist philosophy was a vision of progress which indicated the imminent triumph of scientific attitudes over the previously dominant forces of delusive theology and metaphysics. The manner in which contemporaries expressed this vision oscillated between scrupulous modesty and sublime assertiveness. Thus the philosophy embodied a tension which had previously strained the foundations of the Enlightenment, a movement to which it was clearly much indebted. In its more subtle empiricist forms positivism aimed merely to establish rules about the conditions and methods proper to the pursuit of knowledge. But this emphasis on consistency in the sources and procedures of cognition as the major sign of scientific maturity was challenged by a countervailing tendency to seek that ripeness above all in the unitary pattern which would inevitably emerge from the actual findings of science. The latter, uncritical, version of positivism was to underpin the nineteenth century's most dogmatic and presumptuous exercises in monolithic synthesis. Among major manifestations were the cruder varieties of Social Darwinism, the efforts of Engels* to tidy up the Marxist* canon, and the most grandiose aspects of the Comtean quest to restore certainty to a civilization afflicted with political, social, and moral disorientation.

Comte himself was the son of a tax-receiver for the district of Montpellier and was educated at a boarding school in the same locality. Relations with his family were complicated by his early rejection of both their royalist and their Catholic sympathies. At sixteen he distinguished himself in the entrance examination for the École Polytechnique at Paris, which had been founded in 1794 as a centre of excellence for the training of engineers but which had rapidly won high repute for its work across a still wider range of modern sciences. Despite showing considerable talent as a mathematician, Comte survived at the École Polytechnique for only two years, being expelled in 1816 for indiscipline during the royalist reorganization of the institution. Over the next year or so, while scraping together a living from occasional teaching and journalism, he built up his reading of history and philosophy, especially work by Condorcet, Turgot, De Maistre*, Cabanis and the school of *idéologues*, and the chief luminaries of the Scottish Enlightenment. In 1817 there occurred his momentous meeting with Henri de Saint-Simon*, to whom he became secretary. It is perhaps surprising that this relationship between two such brilliant, moody, and unstable characters should have lasted for as long as seven years. Up to the bitter quarrel that parted them in 1824, Comte did much by way of lending tidier form to the ideas springing so luxuriantly from his employer's often over-fertile imagination. Later on, the former secretary would protest rather too stridently that the elder man, now posthumously dismissed as 'a deranged charlatan', had exercised no significant influence on his own thinking. This was, at best, a half-truth, as can be seen from Saint-Simon's pioneering references to 'positive philosophy' and from Comte's early *Plan of the Scientific Works Necessary to Reorganize Society* (*Plan des travaux nécessaires pour réorganiser la société*, 1822). The whole exercise in repudiation seems highly symptomatic of the general arrogance, even megalomania, into which the latter figure regularly fell. During 1826–7 there was even a bout of indisputable madness. Its most bizarre episode was the one in which Comte's mother, egged on by Lamennais at his most religiously intoxicated, forced her deranged son to undergo a Catholic solemnization of the civil marriage that he had previously contracted with a former prostitute, Caroline Massin. Though convalescence was disrupted when he attempted suicide by drowning, Comte eventually made a recovery. By the end of the 1820s he was again earning something as a tutor, to add to financial aid from his parents and, it is alleged, from the occasional guest appearances which Caroline made for rich clients needing the services of her old profession.

Comte's breakdown had interrupted work on what turned out to be the earlier and greater of his two main undertakings as a writer. The lecture course on 'positive philosophy' which he had begun to give in April 1826 before a distinguished private audience was not resumed until two years later. The first volume arising from this *Cours de philosophie positive* appeared in Paris in 1830, and there were five further instalments before the publication of the whole project reached completion in 1842. Comte acknowledged Montesquieu and Condorcet as major influences on his project, in which he declared that 'the fundamental character of positive philosophy is to regard all phenomena as subject to invariable natural laws, whose precise discovery and reduction to the smallest number possible is the aim of all our effort'. There was, in fact, a further goal – that of using such discoveries as a guide towards a social and political reorganization appropriate to the new conditions of scientific-industrial civilization. Thus it was to an essentially intellectual transformation, rather than to violent revolution in anything like the Marxist sense, that Comte looked as the engine for his version of progress.

In the *Cours* Comte proposed a hierarchy of the sciences, structured according to the increasing generality, complexity, and variability of the material treated. This structure, in which successive new disciplines enrich themselves by utilizing appropriate insights from the ones founded earlier, runs upwards from mathematics through disciplines with an increasingly direct bearing on the human condition. Astronomy and physics are followed by chemistry and biology, with the whole series culminating in 'social physics', or 'sociology' (another term invented by the author). Unlike Saint-Simon who purveyed a single model of scientific method heavily dependent on Newtonian mathematics, Comte insisted that each discipline should be considered as having its own somewhat distinct version, whose evolution must be studied in an emphatically historical way as part of the overall progress of the human mind. However, when generalizing about the nature of this same advance, he did borrow a vital concept from his former employer, even while giving it crisper expression and more substantial content. This was 'the law of three stages', deemed applicable to progress in every branch of knowledge. Here Comte suggests that in the first or 'theological' phase men treat phenomena as products of immediate action by supernatural beings. During the transitional 'metaphysical' period the latter are replaced by abstract forces. Finally, in the 'positive' stage, the vanity of all absolute notions and underlying causes is recognized and the mind applies itself through rational observation to studying more modestly the invariable relations of resemblance and succession among phenomena. All this amounts to an argument not merely that the study of society is the most complex branch of knowledge, but also that it is now about to enter upon its most sophisticated phase. Thus, under Comte's guidance, sociology will fulfil its destiny of bringing every science into proper overall perspective and of providing clear orientation as to the best principles for social reconstruction. Speculation about society as conducted in the two earlier modes seemed to point naturally towards a need to deposit power in the hands of clerics, soldiers, or lawyers; the positivist version should indicate just as readily the necessary predominance of men drawn from science, commerce, and industry.

When on his best intellectual behaviour, Comte was careful to emphasize the modesty of the 'laws' generated by positivism's mode of understanding. Sociological knowledge, for example, would have nothing about it that was absolutely final even at this mature stage. It should not seek to deal in the rhetoric of inevitable trends, and its insights must remain subject to constant reassessment in the light of the changing nature of men's circumstances. What will make our comprehension of society in the third phase distinctly better than before are our more refined notions about how truths should be tested according to a framework embracing both the 'static' resemblances between phenomena existing at any given moment and the patterns of their 'dynamic' succession through time. Unfortunately from the outset Comte himself did not consistently heed these valuable prescriptions concerning self-critical limitation of judgment. His neglect of them tended to get progressively greater, and this was due in no small measure to events having a bearing upon his private life. During the 1830s he had enjoyed a modest prosperity, based on the success of the *Cours* and on the tutorial and examining work which this had helped to bring his way at the École Polytechnique. But parts of the 1842 volume offended his patrons there and diminished the prospects of further occasional employment from the institute. In the same year, Caroline brought their increasingly unsatisfactory marriage to an end. The subsequent efforts by his friends to provide him with a regular stipend were weakened by his own often arrogant attitudes towards them. It was while living in this troubled condition that he became passionately but platonically besotted with Madame Clotild de Vaux. On her side, the liaison lasted less than two years, until her death early in 1846; yet, for Comte, it extended obsessively even beyond her grave. He paid weekly visits to her tomb, and daily penned to her a series of meditations that amounted virtually to prayers. He fell ever more deeply victim to a mysticism that could not fail to have some deleterious effect on the substance of his later writing.

Such was the atmosphere in which Comte composed most of his second ambitious work, *The System of Positive Polity* (*Système de politique positive*, 4 vols, 1851–4). Here he sought to develop and round off the argument of the *Cours*, by elaborating his ideas about sociology and about the novel political and moral structure to which the discipline now pointed. He felt that this effort was all the more urgent because of contemporary society's failure to transcend its condition of conflict between the forces of 'order', which he interpreted as pressing for a reversion towards feudal-Catholic hierocracy, and those of a 'progress' that had become indistinguishable from mere radical anarchism. Comte claimed that his approach indicated a new basis for consensus – an objective that helped to make him an important influence on such later sociological functionalists as Durkheim. He described this foundation as 'the religion of humanity'. Its authoritative scientific stature would be such as to convince men that they had within their grasp a compass reliable enough to let them rescue themselves from disorientation both intellectual and institutional. The resulting insistence on altruism (yet another of his coinages) and on a compassionate concern for fellow-humans contained much that was noble, and much indeed which foreshadowed twentieth-century secular humanism in its finest senses. As Gilbert Murray later remarked, 'I cannot but feel, first, that his system forms a wonderful achievement of sincere and constructive thinking and, secondly, that the thing he is trying to say, *if only he could succeed in saying it*, is not only sublime, but true' (my italics). That qualifying clause is, however, crucial. For Comte's aspirations were indeed badly vitiated by his inability to free himself from two leading features of religion in its more conventional guise: ritualistic panoply, and a hankering after dogmatic certainty.

Much of what resulted ('Catholicism without Christianity', in T. H. Huxley's* famed dismissal) was dangerously silly. Comte envisaged, for instance, that temporal power should reside ideally with a triumvirate of bankers. Their authority would then be checked by a 'spiritual' elite of philosophers and scientists, whose further duty would be to nurture an ethos of universal affection throughout the social order. There should be no need for legal prohibition against dissent on the part of those who stood beyond these charmed circles of temporal and spiritual power: such would be the self-evident rectitude of the expert guidance offered that conflict was unlikely to be other than minimal. All this was made worse by Comte's determination to devise a calendar of positivist saints (1849), and even a catechism (1852). When the latter came out couched in the form of a dialogue between a female believer and 'the High Priest of Humanity', critics were quick to identify the first character with Clotild and the second with the author and his pretentiousness. Among contemporary commentators J. S. Mill* was not untypical of those who had been drawn sympathetically towards the earlier writings (especially as vindicating man's capacity to exercise some substantial measure of rational control over his social destiny), but who regarded the later work as testimony largely to the melancholy decline of a once formidable intellect. It was not to a new religion, as such, but to the anti-individualistic implications of the Comtean version, as eventually elaborated, that the Englishman objected when he wrote that here one had 'the most complete system of spiritual and temporal despotism that ever issued from the brain of any human being – except, perhaps, Ignatius Loyola'. Comte's welcome to the anti-parliamentary policies of the Bonapartist Second Empire in its least liberal phase further strengthened the force of such strictures. Many of the criticisms levelled against him, by Christians and non-Christians alike, were tantamount to suggesting that the law of three stages had gone into circular motion, that the Comtean religion of humanity (including Clotild as a barely secularized version of Our Lady) had become itself boundless in pretensions, and that within it the scientist had taken over the arrogance as well as the explanatory functions of an earlier priesthood.

Comte himself spent his very last years in something close to ascetic seclusion, disappointed at not having pushed further the conversion of his contemporaries. Certainly positivist 'churches', as such, were to have a very limited future. But in a less institutional and more diffuse sense the positivist mood did manage to become perhaps the most outstanding feature of European intellectual life down to the final decade or so of the nineteenth century. Among those who did much to promote it in Comte's homeland were Émile Littré, Claude Bernard*, and Hippolyte Taine*. More widely still, as Owen Chadwick has remarked, 'The fame of Comte became a symbol, like the names of Darwin* or Voltaire; a symbol which by 1870 carried a power far beyond the intellectual influence of the lectures which he gave or the books which he published.' No other Frenchman rivalled his impact on later nineteenth-century thought abroad, especially in Britain and Germany. Even well into our own times he has continued to exercise an influence on the form of knowledge closest to his heart – the discipline of sociology, whose current practice still betrays much of that same Jekyll-and-Hyde alternation between caution and credulousness which ultimately proved to be the principal hallmark of Comte's own endeavour.

Michael Biddiss

The English edition of the *Cours*, prepared by Harriet Martineau, appeared as *The Positive Philosophy of Auguste Comte* (2 vols, 1853). Note also Comte's *Catechism of Positive Religion* (*Catéchisme positive*, 1852) and his *Religion of Humanity: Subjective Synthesis* (*Synthèse subjective*, 1856). The outstanding assessment by a contemporary is J. S. Mill, *Auguste Comte and Positivism* (1865). Among later works, see: Henri Gouhier, *La Vie d'Auguste Comte* (1931); Frank E. Manuel, *The Prophets of Paris* (1962); W. M. Simon, *European Positivism in the Nineteenth Century* (1963); D. G. Charlton, *Positivist Thought in France during the Second Empire, 1852–70* (1959); Raymond Aron, *Main Currents in Sociological Thought*, vol. 1 (trans. 1965); and Ronald Fletcher, *The Making of Sociology*, vol. 1, part 2 (1971).

98
CONSTABLE, John 1776–1837

British painter

'A nasty green thing' is what a member of the Royal Academy selection committee called Constable's *Water-meadows near Salisbury*, an opinion baffling to us today who regard Constable as much a part of our English rural heritage as cheddar cheese. It is exactly the quality of unglamorized naturalism, which we so admire, that alienated the sympathies of the Royal Academician who found the work too much of a landscape and too little of a landscape painting.

Constable was born in East Bergholt, Suffolk, the son of a mill owner whose properties in East Bergholt, Flatford, Dedham and Langham later provided so many of his motifs. 'I associate "my careless boyhood",' he wrote in October 1821, 'with all that lies on the banks of the Stour; those scenes made me a painter and I am grateful.'

His school career at Lavenham and the grammar school at Dedham was unexceptional, draughtsmanship counting for little, and in 1793 he entered the family business. His decision to take up painting seriously occurred in 1796 after meeting two artistic personalities, J. T. Smith and John Cranch, at Edmonton, while on a visit connected with the business. Both, for a time, guided his taste and introduced him to writings on art, including Leonardo's treatise on painting. Constable sketched a number of Suffolk cottages which he sent to Smith in the hope that they would be included in the latter's work then in preparation, entitled: 'Remarks on rural scenery with twenty etchings of cottages from nature'. The theme fitted perfectly within Constable's interest in modest and rustic scenes rather than the then more popular classical landscapes. Smith, however, for unknown reasons did not include them. Constable entered the Royal Academy as a student in 1799, already knowing full well what type of painter he wanted to become. 'There is room enough,' he confidently announced, 'for a natural painter.'

Though sure of his direction, Constable's stylistic means shift during these years under the influence of varying artists, experimenting with traditional landscape 'notations', sometimes looking to Gainsborough whom he sees 'in every hedge and hollow tree', at other times to Ruisdael or Rubens.

An introduction to Sir George Beaumont in this year was decisive, allowing him to study at leisure the latter's superb collection of works by Girtin, Richard Wilson and Claude (whose *Hagar and the Angel* in the National Gallery influenced the composition of *Dedham Vale*, 1802). He was bidden particularly to admire the 'breadth and truth' in Girtin's watercolours, the assimilation of which can be seen in the watercolours Constable painted while on a sketching tour of the Lake district in 1806.

The facts of Constable's subsequent biography are unsensational – he was happily married to Maria Bicknell (1816), and spent most of his life in and near London, frequently visiting his brother in his native Bergholt. The only other important places which feature in Constable's art are Brighton and Salisbury.

One of the surprising features of Constable's life is his 'stay-at-home' mentality. The Lakes tour was the last time he painted away from the few places mentioned above – places connected with his boyhood, his family and friends. *The View of Hadleigh* is one of the few later motifs not drawn from this repertoire.

This was not an accident of circumstances. Constable was deeply suspicious of the 'tourist' painter who felt the need of a scenic thrill in the setting before him. Thrill-hunts, known at the time as 'picturesque travels', took artists to particular types of scenery – the wild, the mountainous and dramatic. By contrast Constable, according to Leslie, his friend and first biographer, was oppressed by the solitude of mountain scenery. He required to feel associative qualities in landscape. When, for instance, he writes, 'painting is another word for feeling', he means by 'feeling' the associations aroused by known, habitable and farmed land. With Constable the kitchen garden becomes a fit subject for painting. On the other hand Constable found the artifice of the landscape garden equally unsympathetic. Views of houses and parks such as *Malvern Hall* were commissioned and not the choice of the artist: 'a gentleman's park is my aversion, because it is not nature.'

On other subjects Constable was equally opinionated and didactic, feeling a personal commitment to the future of English landscape painting. On the subject of the old masters of landscape he is enthusiastic but cautious, making it clear which old masters are to be studied and how.

This is the subject of his ten lectures delivered between 1833 and 1836 in Hampstead, Worcestershire and London, which he gave because he felt 'a duty to tell the world that there is such a thing as landscape in art.' The 'naturals' – Rubens, Claude, Poussin and Ruisdael – are to be studied, the 'prettifiers' Bercham and Both are to be burned. It was fear of mechanical repetition that made Constable suspicious of the formation of the National Gallery which he felt to be a poor substitute for the 'Natural Gallery'.

It is the uncomplicated study of nature which Constable felt to be the base of all landscape painting – this is the message of his introduction to a series of twenty-two mezzotints of his work executed by David Lucas and published in five parts between 1830 and 1832. Here Constable refers to 'the primitive source, nature'. This introduction contains another famous Constable phrase – the 'chiaroscuro of nature'. This does not refer simply to illusionistic effects of light and dark but to the expressive qualities in nature, the 'changing, transient qualities' – 'the day, the hours, the sunshine and the shade'.

Constable's works exhibit an unswerving application of these principles. The works from the Lakes tour previously mentioned, though exhibiting a bold use of the watercolour, betray a certain looseness of suggestion. Constable soon, however, evolved a more literal approach with an almost sculptural use of oil paint, preferring for instance to give a strong boundary line to an area of foliage rather than suggesting the transparency of the outer leaves. No artist before or since has had such an intuitive feel for the material presence of natural objects, for the heavy flatness of a field and the vigorous reach of a branch. Out of these units of rural architecture he constructs the monumental six-foot landscapes for which he is famous, five of the six depicting scenes he knew as a child – *The White Horse* (1819), *Stratford Mill* (1820), *The Hay Wain* (1821), *View on the Stour, near Dedham* (1822), *The Leaping Horse* (1825), and *Chain Pier, Brighton* (1827).

The importance he attached to these paintings, and the struggle he experienced with working on such a scale, is revealed by his making full size sketches on canvas for some of the compositions, a practice unknown previously. In these works he employs a compositional rigidity with verticals given by houses and tree groups, recession by broadly painted areas of sunlit field.

His experiments in watercolour lead naturally into the famous series of oil sketches of 1810–12. On the vigorous surface, the skies here acquire a plasticity equal to that of the objects on the land. This interest in 'skying' as he called it is taken up more methodically in studies of clouds, the majority done between 1821 and 1822, while living at Hampstead, his home from 1819. In a letter of 1821 he writes, 'the sky . . . must and always shall with me make an effectual part of the composition . . .[it is] the keynote, the standard of scale, and the chief organ of sentiment. . . . The sky is the source of light in nature, and governs everything; even our common observations on the weather of every day are altogether suggested by it.'

It is typical of Constable's almost scientific interest in nature that he should have referred to Luke Howard's analysis of cloud formations contained in Thomas Forster's book *Researches about Atmospheric Phaenomena* (2nd ed. 1815) – according to Constable 'the best book' on the subject although 'far from right'.

This research began to have a decisive effect in Constable's finished paintings during the late twenties and thirties, where Constable shows a heightened awareness of the sky's varying conditions.

Instead of midday calm with detail blurred by brightness, one finds times before and after storms depicted, with a sharper focus and plunges from light to dark both in the ground and in the sky. *Salisbury Cathedral from the Meadows* (1831) is an example of this more swirling and dramatic mode, well illustrating the 'chiaroscuro of nature'. Depth of shadow peppered with specks of white highlight is one of the mannerisms of late Constable referred to by critics as the 'snowstorm effect'.

Constable remained largely unacknowledged in England during his lifetime. His buyers were usually his friends and he was only elected to full membership of the Royal Academy in 1829, aged fifty-three. Even then the president, Sir Thomas Lawrence*, thought him 'particularly fortunate' as 'there were historical painters of great merit on the list'.

Strangely enough it was in France that his work was given its due acclaim. *The Hay Wain* and *View on the Stour* won a gold award at the Paris Salon of 1824. Gericault*, who had seen his work in England, encouraged Delacroix* to study him, and the latter was so impressed that he made alterations to the sky in *The Massacre at Chios*.

It was also only in France that Constable's work found followers – as he was one of the sources of inspiration for the Barbizon school.

Calan Lewis

Other works by Constable include: *The Mill Stream* (1814); *Boat-building near Flatford* (1815); *Wivenhoe Park* (1817); *Dedham Lock and Mill* (1820); *Hampstead Heath* (1820); *Salisbury Cathedral from the Bishop's Grounds* (1823); *A Boat Passing a Lock* (1826); *The Cornfield* (1826). See: C. R. Leslie, *Memoirs of the Life of John Constable* (2nd edn 1845, ed. and annotated by J. Mayne 1951); *The Published Mezzotints of David Lucas after John Constable*, ed. and introduced by the Hon. Andrew Shirley (1930); *John Constable's Correspondence*, ed. and annotated by R. B. Beckett (6 vols, 1962–8). About Constable: Kurt Badt, *John Constable's Clouds* (1950); Sir Charles Holmes, *Constable and his Influence on Landscape Painting* (1902); Graham Reynolds, *Catalogue of the Constable Collection in the Victoria and Albert Museum* (1960).

99

CONSTANT DE REBECQUE, Henri Benjamin
1767–1830

French writer and politician

Benjamin Constant was born in Lausanne, into a protestant émigré family. The untimely death of his mother led to an unsettled childhood, which was divided between his father, a Swiss officer in the service of Holland, his maternal grandmother and a procession of bizarre private tutors. None of this inhibited him from developing his precocious talents and becoming one of the most widely cultivated Europeans of his age. Brief stays at the Universities of Oxford and Erlangen preceded a settled period of study at Edinburgh University (1783–5) where, as an active member of the Speculative Society, he encountered many of the ideas that he was later to defend. In 1794, after an ill-suited post as chamberlain to the Duke of Brunswick and a broken marriage, his political career was given positive shape and direction by his meeting with Germaine de Staël*. In his first political pamphlet, *De la force du gouvernement actuel et de la nécessité de s'y rallier* ('On the Strength of the Present Government and on the Need to rally to it', 1796), he defended the republican programme of the Directory and shortly after helped to found the *Cercle constitutionnel*. A year after obtaining French nationality in 1798, he was appointed to the Tribunate where, until his expulsion in 1802, he assumed the dangerous role of representative of the liberal conscience.

Until the Restoration, Constant, exiled from France, remained very much in the political wilderness, travelling widely in Germany, where he met Goethe* and Schiller at Weimar, or with Madame de Staël at Coppet. Helped by the Schlegel* brothers, both he and Germaine became key figures in the dissemination of German Romantic ideas in France.

After 1813, Constant was actively preparing his political comeback. His support for Bernadotte, the publication of *De l'esprit de conquête et de l'usurpation* ('On the Spirit of Conquest and Usurpation', 1814), and the diatribe against Napoleon* in the *Journal des Débats* (1815) identified him as a committed opponent of Napoleon's arbitrary political methods. However, on Napoleon's return in 1815, he accepted an appointment to the Council of State and was involved in drawing up constitutional amendments. In his *Mémoires sur les cent jours* ('Memoirs on the Hundred Days', 1820) he gives a reasoned defence of this but there remains a lingering suspicion that political opportunism lay behind this volte-face.

In *Principes de politique* ('Principles of Politics', 1815) and subsequent writings, he showed himself to be a liberal pragmatist who firmly believed in certain essential individual freedoms. Through his pamphlets and articles, and, after 1819, as a riveting debater in the Chamber of Deputies, he became an outspoken defender of liberal ideas. Faced with the royalist reaction after the assassination of the Duke of Berry (1820) and particularly after the succession of Charles X (1824), his fierce opposition to any whittling away of personal liberties made him a popular and respected figure and helped to bring about the July Revolution (1830) and the establishment of a more liberal monarchy. He became President of the Council of State until his death at the end of that year.

Although recognized as one of the founders of the European liberal ideal, perhaps Constant's most enduring achievement lies in the pages of his psychological novel *Adolphe* (1816) written in 1806. Central to this analysis of his experience of love and of the tragic inevitability of human suffering is his break with Madame de Staël in 1806 and his relationship with Anna Lindsay. Both lucid and self-delusory, *Adolphe* encapsulates modern man's ambiguous moral relationship with himself and others. Its dense psychological structure ensures it a place not only in the European analytical tradition but as one of the finest achievements of French literature. *Cécile* (1951), discovered in 1948, although more overtly autobiographical, also displays Constant's ability to create a meaningful literary experience from an analysis of his tempestuous relationship with Madame de Staël and the rival claims of Charlotte von Hardenberg, whom he married in 1808.

Ironically, Constant's life work *De la religion considérée dans sa source, ses formes et ses développements* ('On Religion considered in its Source, Forms and Developments', 1824–31), which was to have ensured his posthumous fame, has never generated great enthusiasm. Erudite and perceptive, it is a vast comparative inquiry into the shifting forms of religion, which, nevertheless, identifies a permanent religious feeling common to all men (*le sentiment religieux*). Perhaps of more appeal to the modern reader are his autobiographical writings, *The Red Note-Book* (*Le Cahier rouge*, 1907) and his *Private Diaries* (*Les Journaux intimes*, 1952), in which he portrays himself in all his contradictory moods and leaves the impression of a complex, indecisive but never petty or shallow human being.

David Bryant

There is no complete edition of Constant's works. For the major works see: *Oeuvres* (1957); *Écrits et discours politiques* (1964); *Recueil d'articles* (1972); and *Cours de politique constitutionnelle* (1979). For English translations see: *Prophecy from the Past: Benjamin Constant on Conquest and Usurpation* (1941); *Adolphe* (1964); *Cécile* (1952); and *The Red Note-Book* (1948). On Constant: P. Bastid, *Benjamin Constant et sa doctrine* (1966); H. Gouhier, *Benjamin Constant* (1967); G. Poulet, *Benjamin Constant par lui-même* (1968); and J. Cruickshank, *Benjamin Constant* (1974).

100
COOPER, James Fenimore 1789–1851

US novelist

James Fenimore Cooper is the earliest major American novelist to dramatize 'the march of civilization' on 'those distant and ever-receding borders which mark the skirts and announce the approach of the nation', the process from 'new barbarity' on the Frontier to a primary urban society. He dramatizes the nature of law in the peculiar conditions of a new society, encroaching on wilderness and the Indians but inheriting Europe, while resisting it.

This deeply romantic conservative grew up in the wilderness of Otsego Lake, New York, where his father was judge and landowner in a region which later became Cooperstown. Indians could still be observed and to some extent known, although white anthropology had as yet made no inroads on their cultures and the understanding of them. After private tuition, Cooper went to Yale in 1807, was expelled for a prank, and, after two years at home, was sent into the new navy. A spell as seaman on a sailing ship from Maine to England preceded his naval commission. He served on the Great Lakes (later to be used in *The Pilot*, 1823, and other novels) until Judge Cooper's death left him and his brothers a large estate – which they squandered. When Cooper married in 1811, his wife insisted that they settle on her farm at Scarsdale, New York, and raise a family. To produce a better novel than the one he found himself reading to his wife he wrote *Precaution* (1819), a slight and faintly parodistic version of the average current lady's novel. But he had found a vocation and the following year wrote *The Spy*, and in 1823 the first of the Leatherstocking series, *The Pioneers*. In New York, he became the focus of the Bread and Cheese Club of writers. But he still needed an income to support his wife and educate his daughters. He accepted an appointment as consul in Lyons, but apparently never went there and spent the first two of his seven years abroad in Britain (Walter Scott* became an acquaintance). In Paris his main friend was Lafayette. He gained a reputation for being litigious and disputatious; his romantic and historical novels were followed with hefty satires with unpopular criticisms of his fellow countrymen. America he loved, but it had already deteriorated. He brought libel suits against his critics, wrote a *History of the Navy of the United States of America* (1839), and managed to keep a fairly stable Cooperstown circle of family and friends from which to compose the rest of his large *oeuvre*, including the rest of the Leatherstocking saga among his thirty-two novels.

His sea fiction, especially *The Red Rover* (1827), *Afloat and Ashore* (1844) and *The Sea Lions* (1849), are solid and innovative enough to prepare the way for Dana, Melville* and Conrad, treating the ship itself with more detail and concern than before, exploiting naval nationalism, and using marine materials for moral idealism and both social and religious allegory. The Cooper seaman is as imagined as the Cooper Indian. In *Homeward Bound* and *Home as Found* (1838) he analyses social distinction on an ocean liner within the structure of a sea adventure (Arab raiders, an English sloop of war, and so on), and then satirizes American manners, dress, business and law. One critic called the latter novel 'a skinning alive'. Cooper sued him suc-

cessfully for libel. *The Crater* (1847) moves from sea voyage to that perpetual nineteenth-century theme of Utopia within America, interpreted as an English society ameliorated by the pioneer spirit. Democracy intervenes as a kind of fallen human nature, but all is saved by an underwater eruption: let those 'who vainly imagine that the masses are sufficient, remember their insignificance and tremble'. Cooper pioneered in fiction that radical conservatism which has remained central to a nation which, while priding itself on its bourgeois revolution as origin, has sought to halt further developments ever since. Reflecting on the British mutinies at the Nore (which Melville used in his last novel), Cooper believed that the American seamen were better protected and 'of a much better origin'; moreover, 'the American nation is a mild and reasoning nation, and is everywhere governed with bayonets. God knows what they may become, but that is their character at present.'

Melville, a fellow wary conservative, praised Cooper's 'great robust soul' and that energy was placed at the disposal of cultural power through the novel – as the preface to Cooper's first novel stated: 'Books are, in great measure, the instruments of controlling the opinions of a nation like ours. They are an engine alike powerful to save or to destroy.' His America would be an agrarian class society run by property-owning liberals who refuse 'the besetting, the degrading vice of America . . . the moral cowardice by which men are led to truckle to what is called public opinion'. Natty Bumpo or Leatherstocking or Hawkeye or Deerslayer is a mythopoeic figure of pioneer wariness and conservative self-reliance, based on the eighteenth-century belief in the sacredness of unspoilt nature and in the presence of a vestigial Noble Savage. Leatherstocking is a romantic aristocrat, related to Jefferson's nature's aristocrats, a huntin' gentleman with an old seadog's scorn for both the masses and the officers. And his loneliness is his author's. 'Manners, education and refinement are positive things,' Cooper writes, and Natty Bumpo is created to prove the fact in the American wilderness and to recognize it in those Indians who retain nature's reason. He is a good shot and a sentimentalist with women, ancestor of John Wayne. *The Deerslayer* (1841) shows the young Mohican warrior risking his life for his beloved *and* for his white hunter friend, opposed by the 'fiendish' Mingoes, Indians who have rejected Mohican moral standards. Nevertheless, Cooper is fascinated by both scalping rituals and self-discipline as part of the structure of Indian honour. *The Last of the Mohicans* (1826) deals with the ends of an ancient race as Hawkeye witnesses them. Scalping is given as 'the gift and natur' of an Indian', 'not to be denied' to nature's chivalric warrior. Cooper also supplies massacre, killing children and drinking blood – with some account of Indian culture. In *The Pathfinder* (1840), forest and sea supply a double location, with rather secondary Indian material: a sailor is taking a friend's daughter Mabel through the forests to her father, an army sergeant, in camp on Lake Ontario. Pathfinder and Chingachgook guide them. The second journey takes the principals to an island (from which French ships are raided) and allows them to survive a brutal attack by Indians in French pay. The sergeant wants Mabel to marry the white hunter, but Pathfinder remains solitary. Within this structure, Cooper affords an extraordinary compendium of contemporary social and cultural attitudes. *The Pioneers* (1823) concerns degenerate Frontier settlement Indians, Natty Bumpo in decline, and the Mohican warrior, Chingachgook, now seventy, baptized by the Moravians and succumbing to drink. In *The Prairie* (1827), in many ways the most interesting of the saga, the location is west of the Mississippi, and the focus is on Ishmael Bush, a migrating patriarchal settler at the head of his 'tribe'. Cooper shows Leatherstocking in sharp conflict with these tree-felling, nature-conquering settlers, but it is they who are the community, forerunners of civilization, as he cannot be. He may be a law to himself but the Bush group can create communal law, without irrational belief in natural virtue or some innate sense of justice. America needs both the pioneering community and the calm teaching of the eighteenth-century moralist-hunter if the land is not to yield to rapacious exploitation and the bad Indian.

The society of the ship and the solitary hunter, English gentry and the pioneering settler community, the noble savage and the skilled seaman: out of such an enterprising set of rich criteria Cooper made his impressive body of romances, to a large extent overcoming a style pitted with early nineteenth-century sentimentality and convention, and a lack of psychological penetration beyond stereotypes. He was the first American author to gain international fame, and the configuration of American life in his fictions gave Europe its first influential image of the state of the early republic.

Eric Mottram

Works: *The Works of James Fenimore Cooper* (1895–1900); *Letters and Journals of James Fenimore Cooper*, ed. James F. Beard (6 vols, 1960–8). See: James Grossman, *James Fenimore Cooper* (1949); Donald A. Ringe, *James Fenimore Cooper* (1962); George Dekker, *James Fenimore Cooper, the Novelist* (1967).

101
COROT, Jean-Baptiste-Camille 1796–1875

French painter

Corot was born in Paris. His parents were prosperous milliners and cloth dealers. They encouraged Corot to follow them into the family trade by apprenticing him to a cloth merchant in 1817. For the next five years Corot pursued his interest in art by taking evening classes at the Académie Suisse. In 1822, however, he was reluctantly given an annual allowance by his parents and was thus enabled to become a professional painter. He bought a studio and studied under the Classical landscape painters Michallon and Bertin. In 1825 Corot travelled in Italy and painted landscapes in Rome, Tivoli, Naples and Venice. He studied in Rome under Caruelle d'Aligny, whom he always considered his real master. Two more trips to Italy, in 1834 and 1843, took him to the Alpine lakes, Genoa and Florence. After his return to France in 1828 Corot began his many *plein air* works on tours of France, particularly in Brittany, Normandy, and the Fontainebleau Forest. He fled Paris during the July Revolution of 1830 and while resting at Chartres painted his first recognized masterpiece, a view of the cathedral. It was not until the 1840s that Corot began to receive any wide acclaim. *Little Shepherd* (1840) was the first picture of his to be bought for a state museum and in 1846 he was awarded the Legion of Honour after the great success of *Homer and the Shepherds* (1845), based on a poem by André Chenier and inspired by the precepts of Classical landscape. Corot also began to receive commissions for mural work, notably at Louis Robert's house in Mantel (a decoration for the bathroom now in the Louvre), a *Baptism of Christ* (1844–5) for a Parisian church and a mural at Ville-D'Avray, where his parents lived. In the fifties his popularity increased still further as his painting became more lyrical and literary in tone. Napoleon III paid 18,000 francs for *Solitude* in 1867. Younger radical artists like Degas* and Monet* began to recognize the importance of both his figure and landscape work. His acquaintances included Daubigny, Daumier*, Delacroix* and Courbet*, and throughout his life he was renowned for his immense generosity to struggling fellow artists and even to those many plagiarizers who made a living by forging his work. He bought Daumier's rented cottage at Valmondois for him when the artist was destitute and even gave 10,000 francs to Millet's* widow, though he held her husband's work in little esteem. Corot had a few pupils such as Lépine and Chintreuil, but more famous artists, such as Pissarro*, also sought his advice and he gave a number of lessons to one of the female Impressionists, Berthe Morisot, until she left him to study under Manet*. He spent his last years in Coubron and died after a struggle with stomach cancer in 1875. He never married for, as he wrote to a friend in 1826, it would have interfered with his one love – landscape painting.

Like Cézanne* Corot presents in his work a re-working of interest in empirical visual research. He spent hours working out of doors and his painting bears close affinities to that of the Barbizon artists from whom, nevertheless, he remained aloof. He rejected Romanticism and realism (though he knew both Courbet and Delacroix, who called him the 'father of modern landscape') and the greater part of his work finds its tradition in the Classicism of Poussin and in a pantheistic revision of Watteau's lyricism which he seems to have nurtured through a reading of Rousseau. Fritz Novotny has described Corot as searching for a 'mysticism of the real' and his depiction of transparent atmospheres by almost infinite tonal gradation does give his work a timeless quality entirely missing from either Romantic or Naturalist and Impressionist art. A key to his art is his persistent mixing of white lead with all the other hues to create a consistent density and sense of atmospheric weight. Corot completed his images within the frame, as it were, and thereby imposed absolute temporal and spatial limits upon them which many other nineteenth-century painters sought to undermine. Degas, however, a leading exponent of these aesthetic subversions, admired Corot's art a great deal and considered his *Reclining Nymph* (1855) matchless. This is a significant interest as Degas was the most conservative of the Impressionist generation in a number of ways and the painter who held most regard for seventeenth- and eighteenth-century formulae. Although he is best known today, perhaps, for his calm French and Italian landscapes, the range of Corot's oeuvre is very wide, from the almost proto-Cubist *Outer Harbour of La Rochelle* of 1851 to the contemporaneous *Morning: Dance of the Nymphs*, a haunting combination of *plein air*, Watteau and Poussin. These 'souvenirs' which reflect the revival of interest in rococo during the Second Empire relate to Corot's passion for the opera and ballet and often seem theatrical in their overall effect. His art was also influenced by photography and one of his favourite graphic techniques was that of *cliché-verre* (to which he was introduced by his friend, the lithographer Constant Dutilleux, in 1853) in which the design is engraved on collodion-coated glass plate which is then placed on sensitized photographic paper and exposed to light. This process certainly contributed to the misty chiaroscuro effects typical of Corot's later work.

In summary there are four main areas in Corot's output – the history landscapes, the 'natural' landscapes, the 'souvenirs' and the figure and portrait paintings. Throughout, as Baudelaire* pointed out, there runs, despite Corot's undoubted sophistication, a curious and unique naivety in both the artist's character and art. His drawing and composition are never slick and he even seems to share with other French painters, like Poussin and Cézanne, a certain manual clumsiness. Berenson based a theory of 'the ineloquent in art' upon this type of charm. Corot's influence on later artists is so varied and pervasive that it is difficult to trace. Aside from the painters already mentioned, Boudin, Utrillo* and Seurat* all benefited from a study of the different aspects of his art. At an exhibition of Corot's work in 1897 Monet told an acquaintance, 'There is only one person here, that's Corot: we, we are nothing when compared to him. This is the saddest day of my life.'

Richard Humphreys

Alfred Robant, *L'Oeuvre de Corot: Catalogue raisonné* (4 vols, 1905); François Fosca, *Corot, sa vie et son oeuvre* (1958); *Corot*, Arts Council Catalogue (London 1965); Jean Leymaire, *Corot* (trans. 1974).

102
COURBET, Gustave 1819–77

French artist

Courbet's art for much of his life provoked scandalized comment and reactionary responses. In some measure this was due to the particularly unstable period in French politics when the young Courbet's work was coming to fruition. His brand of 'realism' was considered highly revolutionary and treated with suspicion.

Born at Ornans, a small village in the Jura mountains, Courbet began to paint whilst at the Royal College in Besançon. He then moved to Paris to study law but instead continued his life as an artist, drawing from the works of old masters in the Louvre and the live models at the Académie Suisse. After exhibiting a self-portrait at his first Paris Salon in 1844 Courbet continued to study and whilst so doing journeyed to Holland in 1847 to survey the art in the Dutch museums.

Returning to Paris he became part of a lively group of intellectuals who included Baudelaire*, Champfleury and Proudhon*. The revolutionary uprising in February of 1848 which removed the existing government was in turn swept away by a more reactionary group of politicians, so that friends of Courbet, including Proudhon, were imprisoned. However, Courbet had not yet produced works to warrant his own arrest. It was not until the joint Salon of 1850 and 1851 that he was to exhibit his first two large-scale controversial pieces.

At this period the conventional subject matter for a great painter was either historical or romantic and to be treated in a grand style. Courbet, having learnt much from the past, worked on a large scale in a manner deriving from 'great' work. His subject matter though was neither heroic nor idealized. It was that of peasant people who lived and worked around Ornans and because he did not sentimentalize or make them picturesque the paintings could not fall into the category, which held some degree of appeal, known as *genre*. The Parisian public when faced with the realities of provincial working-class life, shortly after a revolution, were greatly disturbed. The two paintings which provoked such furious comment were the *Stonebreakers* and the *Funeral at Ornans*, and these were hung along with seven other works by Courbet at the 1851 Salon.

The *Stonebreakers* are two peasants, dispassionately and accurately recorded at their roadside work. The nature of their occupation is clearly evident and, manifestly poor in their torn clothing and sabots, they fill almost the entire canvas. The other even larger work depicting a village funeral procession at a graveside is immensely impressive. The viewer of the painting is not shown who has died. The gaping hole in the earth sinks out of sight below the lower edge of the picture's frame. To the left of the grave are the attendant richly robed clergy, in sharp contrast to the sombre phalanx of villagers. Behind the figures in the middle distance runs a parallel line of heavy white crag, as hard as the life of the people who farm the area. This subject matter pre-empts by thirty years similar humanistic but visionary concerns painted by Van Gogh* and Gauguin*. To elevate the poor to the scale and grandeur of the wealthy was, in 1851, decidedly shocking.

However, Courbet avoided imprisonment because he had secured the patronage of the Duc de Morny, half-brother of Napoleon III. In addition, a further wealthy patron, Alfred Bruyas, gave him financial support so that he could continue painting and attempt a further huge canvas that was to be Courbet's claim to the origination of the final form of modern art. This work, completed by 1855, is called *The Studio*. It was rejected by the jury adjudicating works for the Exposition Universelle to be held in Paris. Characteristically Courbet held his own one-man show in a separate pavilion.

Despite certain uncompromisingly new aspects in the work, much of it remains traditional, owing something to Rembrandt, Velasquez, David* and Ingres*, amongst others. It could be said to make its revolutionary nature clear by containing both the norm and that which broke with it. Out of the thinly painted darkness, strong contrasts of dark and light stamp their presence upon the viewer. The space, like that of the funeral at Ornans work, is enclosing, yet empty except for the humanity that inhabits it. Most uncompromisingly new is Courbet's positioning of himself as the central focus of the picture. He is shown painting a landscape, considered to be another low form of art. As the central motif of the painting, the artist had become, in that moment, prince of all his world. No longer artisan, called upon to record the whims of the wealthy or to produce propaganda for church or state, he was his own master. He had gained, as he himself stated, 'his intellectual freedom'.

Behind Courbet, a buxom model stands in his studio, watching admiringly, whilst a small boy looks up in fascination from his position at the seated artist's knee. Surrounding these three are a number of friends such as Bruyas and Champfleury but in addition representatives of the world at large are also depicted, a Jew, a pauper, a burgher and his wife, and many others who add the social spectrum to the work.

This wholly new admixture, all treated in the same manner, giving pride of place to no one but the artist, was admired by few and championed only by the astute Delacroix* who as both great painter and critic had considerable insight into Courbet's thought. Even Champfleury, himself a realist writer, could not fathom the seemingly unreal juxtapositioning of such disparate characters.

Courbet's reputation declined a little but he continued to paint and to find some purchasers for his work. Having acquired the freedom to paint as he pleased he concentrated upon so doing. In 1858 he visited Germany to paint hunting scenes and in 1860 he was back in Paris exhibiting. His works submitted to the 1863 and 1864 Salons were rejected, one for being anti-clerical, the other for its alleged indecency. However, *The Covert of the Roe Deer* and the *Woman with Parrot* were enthusiastically received in 1866, a year after he had met Monet* and Whistler* in Normandy. This latter district of France attracted Courbet considerably from that year onwards. In 1870 the King of Bavaria decorated the painter for his services to Art and the following year Courbet was elected to the Commune whilst he was holding office as elected president of the Federal Commission of Artists whose task it was to safeguard works of art.

From such a position of eminence it seems extraordinary that Courbet should be involved in the revolutionary razing of the Vendôme column in May of that year. Arrested and tried, he spent six months in prison where he became ill. His paintings were by then totally rejected by officialdom and he was ordered to pay the expenses of the rebuilding of the column. To carry out this order the authorities confiscated Courbet's property and the artist left Paris to retire in Switzerland to the small town of La-Tour-de-Peilz where he was buried in 1877.

Pat Turner

Other works include: *The Young Ladies from the Village* (1851–2); *The Meeting* (1854). See: *Courbet and the Naturalistic Movement*, ed. G. Boaz (1967); *Courbet in Perspective*, ed. Petra ten-Doesschate Chu (1977); T. J. Clark, *The Absolute Bourgeois* (1973); T. J. Clark, *Image of the People: Gustave Courbet and the 1848 Revolution* (1973); J. Lindsay, *Gustave Courbet: His Life and Art* (1973).

103

CRABBE, George 1754–1832

British poet

George Crabbe was born on 24 December 1754, the eldest child of a collector of salt-duties in the then tiny fishing village of Aldeburgh, on the Suffolk coast. Though he was to spend most of his adult life in other parts of England the bleak East Anglian coastal life he witnessed as a child remained the source of much of his finest poetry. After a brief education at local schools he was apprenticed to a surgeon at the age of thirteen; he found the work uncongenial and abandoned it after seven years. His true adolescent interests were botany and poetry; in his late teens he published his first lengthy poem, *Inebriety*. In 1780, determined to find a patron, he arrived in London with £3 in his pocket. He was almost destitute when he was finally taken up by Edmund Burke who helped him to publish *The Library*; on Burke's advice he was ordained and returned to Aldeburgh as its curate at the end of 1781. He later became chaplain to the Duke of Rutland at Belvoir Castle, and of villages in Leicestershire. In 1783 he married Sarah Elmy, to whom he had been engaged for eleven years; the publication of *The Village* in the same year marked the first appearance of his distinctive poetic voice. *The Newspaper* (1785) was a return to the style of his earlier more derivative work and thereafter he published virtually nothing for twenty-two years.

In 1792 an inheritance (from his wife's family) made Crabbe more financially comfortable, but the numerous fatalities among his children and his wife's gradually increasing nervous illness were a severe emotional strain for him. During his long poetic silence he wrote and destroyed three novels and a botanical work.

In 1807 *The Parish Register* appeared; despite the gap in time between this poem and *The Village* it is remarkably similar to its predecessor in both subject-matter (reflections on the lives of the inhabitants of a particular parish) and tone (sympathetic but never sentimental). The poem was an immediate success and established Crabbe's reputation. It was followed in 1810 by *The Borough* (the borough in question being Aldeburgh) and by *Tales* in 1812. In 1813 his wife died and shortly afterwards he moved to a living in Trowbridge, where he remained for the rest of his life. In 1819 his last substantial work, *Tales of the Hall*, appeared.

Crabbe's early poems were praised and corrected by Dr Johnson; as an old man he met Scott* and Wordsworth*, both of whom admired his poetry; his career links the age of Johnsonian reason with that of Romanticism – he outlived Keats*, Byron* and Shelley* and did not die until 1832.

His use of the heroic couplet indicates his eighteenth-century allegiances; but unlike the Augustans he does not use it to point general truths so much as to convince us of the reality of highly localized lives and circumstances. His most compelling subject matter – the lives of the rural poor – seems to mark him as a Romantic, but he lived through the American and French revolutions and showed sympathy for neither. He hated Jacobinism and his attitude towards religious enthusiasm and dissent was one of contempt. He had no time for the Romantic cultivation of feelings for their own sake – disaster in his poems is usually the result of the protagonist's lack of self-control: the even flow of his couplets – what one may call his metrical chastity and sense of propriety – is the stylistic counterpart of the behaviour he implicitly recommends: sober, patient, self-aware.

Crabbe entirely lacked the Romantics' visionary view of reality: for him truth did not lie behind the daily life before our eyes (as it did for Wordsworth and Coleridge*) – it *was* that daily life. Reality was for Crabbe the quotidian, immediate world; it was neither exotic nor arcane. This confidence in the substantial truth of the world about him separates him from the Romantics in a further crucial way; his subject is not, as it is for almost all of the major early nineteenth-century poets, himself and the nature of his own feelings. His world is peopled by characters in the same way that Chaucer's is and we believe in their individuality: the subject 'matter of his poems is not at the mercy of a Romantic ego unsure of where its own reality ends and that of the external world begins.

In so far as his poetry changed it was in a gradual deepening of characterization which approaches the novelistic (his poetry has been admired by many novelists including Jane Austen* and E. M. Forster): at the same time a quietly understated humour becomes more prominent. In keeping with his own gradually improved circumstances the characters in his last two books are on the whole more prosperous than those in the earlier works. His great strength is his use of the telling particular; in presenting the details of the world he describes he convinces us of their reality and at the same time makes them function as indicators of the psychological truth of the poems' characters: this is the source of the power of a story like, for example, *Peter Grimes* (from *The Borough*) in which the landscape exactly reflects Grimes' sluggish despair while never for a moment ceasing to exist as a real landscape in the real world.

The best introduction to Crabbe, apart from the poems themselves, is undoubtedly the biography of him written by his son, who also published the *Posthumous Tales* left by his father, in 1834.

Dick Davis

See: P. New, *George Crabbe's Poetry* (1976); George Crabbe the Younger, *The Life of George Crabbe* (1834).

104

CRANE, Stephen 1871–1900

US novelist, poet and short-story writer

Stephen Crane was born in Newark, New Jersey. His education was of less significance in his life than his move, in 1891, to New York City. In New York, he frequented the slums and sampled the poverty and squalor of life in the Bowery. It furnished the material for his first novel, *Maggie: A Girl of the Streets*. Printed at Crane's own expense in 1893, *Maggie* displayed some of the distinctive features of a Naturalist novel. Crane concentrated, for instance, on the sordid details of low life, and emphasized the determining power of heredity and environment. But he adopted a technique very different from that of the Naturalists, a selective and oblique method of presentation which was to prove characteristic of his best prose. *Maggie* aroused no interest, however. In 1895, Crane published *The Black Riders*, a volume of unrhymed poems, written in free verse and occasionally blasphemous. It caused a stir and provoked some abuse. But Crane won fame only late in that year, with the publication of the full version of *The Red Badge of Courage*. A finely crafted tale of a young soldier's baptism by fire, it is remarkable for its Tolstoyan* attention to the details of experience in battle. But, at the same time, it is also a subtle portrayal of psychological tumult. It brought Crane instant renown, and he swiftly became an international literary celebrity.

In 1896, Crane published *George's Mother*, a novel in the mould of *Maggie*, but a slighter one. It was followed, in the same year, by a collection of stories entitled *The Little Regiment*, by *The Third Violet*, and by various tales and poems. Success, however, was accompanied by a decline in creative power. As Crane became a public figure, so he began to cater to public demand. The result was a succession of inferior war stories, and pot-boilers like *Active Service* (1899) and *The O'Ruddy* (completed by Robert Barr, 1903). But some of Crane's finest tales were written during this period. It was in these that his talent chiefly emerged, in his last years, though a second volume of poetry proved to be of a quality comparable to that of his first.

Critics have fretted over the question of how to classify Crane: whether he is most fitly deemed a Realist, a Naturalist or an Impressionist. All of these terms are in some respects appropriate. There are clear affinities between *Maggie* and *George's Mother* and Zola's* novels. But Crane himself claimed that his aesthetic creed was indentical with William Dean Howells'* 'realism' and Hamlin Garland's 'veritism'. The influence of Howells and Garland is clearly discernible in his early work. Crane referred to his method, however, as that of an Impressionist. His habit of rendering stories as se-

quences of fleeting sensations and perceptions would seem to justify the word.

But to place Crane within a school or movement is to say little about the original nature of his achievement. Crane's world is a haphazard one, a world of the chance event and the unforeseen occurrence. Experience is patternless and random. Crane evolved a narrative technique perfectly adapted to this vision. He dispensed with the conventions of plot, its chain of cause and effect, the sense it fosters of orderly sequence. He gave his fiction an episodic structure. He passes quickly over apparently crucial matters, and highlights the incidental. The unexpected and outlandish becomes mere matter of fact. The commonplace becomes marvellous. The inevitable result of such a technique is a view of the individual as less actor than victim, exposed to the vicissitudes of a capricious world. The corollary of this is irony – an irony aimed at the postures men strike in their attempt to salvage a pride, a dignity or self-assurance from the muddle of their lives.

The anti-heroic bent of so much of Crane's work identifies it as part of a trend in late nineteenth-century American fiction, a reaction against romanticism and idealism also found in the work of Howells and Garland. But the romanticism Crane revolted against was present in his own temperament. His work is never entirely free of it. It emerged more clearly in his later writing, as he espoused and proclaimed a doctrine of self-reliance. The Crane inclined to subject courage to ironic scrutiny came increasingly to applaud it. Crane's poetry reflects this complexity in attitude. The attacks on self-importance and affirmations of the value of a stoical humility are interspersed with celebrations of a Promethean self-assertiveness. In theme and form, Crane's poems are unorthodox and iconoclastic in a manner that is reminiscent of Emily Dickinson*, whose influence on Crane has been remarked on by critics. Stark, spare and direct, often relying for its effects on an art of juxtaposition, the poetry in some ways anticipates the work of the Imagists. Crane's influence has been detected in the work of Conrad, Willa Cather, Dreiser, Sandburg and Sherwood Anderson. But the writer most obviously indebted to Crane is Hemingway. Hemingway's bare, terse, concentrated prose style, his ability to convey simple impressions clearly, owe much to the example of Crane.

Andrew Gibson

Other works: 'Sullivan County Sketches' (published serially, 1892); *The Open Boat and Other Tales of Adventure* (1898); *War is Kind* (poems, 1899); *The Monster and Other Stories* (1899); *Whilomville Stories* (1900); *Wounds in the Rain* (1900); *Great Battles of the World* (1900); *Last Words* (1902). See: J. Berryman, *Stephen Crane* (1950); E. Solomon, *Stephen Crane: From Parody to Realism* (1966); J. Cazemajou, *Stephen Crane*

(1969); M. Lafrance, *A Reading of Stephen Crane* (1971); F. Bergon, *Stephen Crane's Artistry* (1975).

105
CRUIKSHANK, George 1792–1878

British caricaturist, illustrator and etcher

'Cradled in caricature' (his own phrase) by his father Isaac, George Cruikshank became the most important political caricaturist of the Regency, taking the place of Gillray (d. 1815). He had to hand two distinct styles: one a quick, jagged style that complemented an 'off-the-cuff' joke, and one a more finished tonal style compared by Ruskin* to the etchings of Rembrandt.

Having graduated from children's lottery tickets and other cheap ephemera, he entered the political scene at an opportune moment – Napoleon's* (or 'Boney's') retreat from Moscow. From this he turned to home affairs attacking the English Court and the government, getting good mileage from the extravagances of the Prince Regent.

From 1815 he collaborated with William Hone*, a radical publisher and social reformer. Together they produced such works as the *Bank Note, not to be Imitated* (1819) – an imaginary note featuring a line of men and women hanging from the gallows – a protest against the executions for passing forged one-pound notes. Their publications also included the successful *The Political House that Jack Built* (1819).

His work was found to be so potentially harmful to the Crown that Cruikshank in 1820 received £100 'in consideration of a pledge not to caricature his majesty in any immoral situation'. Cruikshank took the money more seriously than the pledge.

From the 1820s he turned increasingly towards social comment – a major work being *Life in London* (1820), the text by Pierce Egan and illustrated by himself and his brother Robert. The engraved scenes show Tom and Jerry, accompanied by Logic, an Oxonian, experienceing the high and low life of the metropolis. No doubt because of its success (it was even adapted to the stage) he began to direct his humour towards the politely amusing, rather than the scurrilous, creating such works as *The Humourist* (1819–20), *Points of Humour* (1823), and fairy tales including *German Popular Stories* (1824–6), *Peter Schlemihl* (1824). Through such works his caricatures gained such popularity that he could for a time become his own publisher and dispense with a text altogether; examples are *Phrenological Illustrations* (1826), *Illustrations of Time* (1827), *Scraps and Sketches* (1828–32).

With the vogue for popular editions of classic works Cruikshank was commissioned to illustrate authors such as Scott*, Smollett, Fielding, Defoe – principally for Roscoe's Novelists' Library (1823–3). His most fa-mous collaboration with an author, however, was with that 'Cruikshank of writers' (the *Spectator*) Charles Dickens*, then a mere journlist known as Boz. Cruikshank first illustrated *Sketches by Boz* (1836) and in so doing guaranteed its success. He then illustrated his one Dickens novel, *Oliver Twist* (1838), later claiming he played a part in its creation. The book contains the famous engraving of Fagin, 'the dreadful Jew that Cruikshank drew' (Thackeray*).

His association with the writer of historical fiction, W. Harrison Ainsworth, was longer lasting and with Bentley as publisher they produced popular sellers, including *The Tower of London* (1840) and *Jack Sheppard* (1839).

From 1835–53 he worked on *Cruikshanks Comic Almanack*, one of a series of magazines depending for sale on the popularity of his name. However, during its running his popularity was already on the wane. *Punch* appeared in 1841 and began to take his audience.

The last part of his life was taken up advocating teetotalism: *The Bottle* (1847), a Hogarthian episodic narrative, illustrates the consequences of a first sip of 'strong drink'; they are, we are not surprised to discover, eventual murder and insanity.

His major work advocating sobriety, a large canvas *The Worship of Bacchus*, was exhibited along with other selected works of his carreer in 1863. The poor attendance showed that he had outlived his popularity. Fame had already passed to John Tenniel, Charles Keene, Millais* and Rossetti*.

Calan Lewis

Other works illustrated by Cruikshank include: Dr Syntax, *Life of Napoleon* (1814–15); J. Wight, *Mornings at Bow Street* (1824); William Hone, *The Table Book* (1827–8); William Clarke, *Three Courses and a Dessert* (1830); *George Cruikshank's Omnibus*, ed. Laman Blanchard (1841–2); *Ainsworth's Magazine*, ed. William Harrison Ainsworth (1842–4); *George Cruikshank's Table Book*, ed. Gilbert Abbott á Beckett. See: Blanchard Jerrold, *The Life of George Cruikshank* (1882); W. Bates, *George Cruikshank: The Artist, the Humourist, and the Man* (1878); A. M. Cohn, *George Cruikshank, A Catalogue Raisonné of the Work Executed during the Years 1806–77* (1924); G. W. Reid, *Descriptive Catalogue of the Works of George Cruikshank* (3 vols, 1871).

106
CURIE, Marie Sklodowska 1867–1934

Polish-French physicist

Marie (Polish Maria) was the fifth child of the schoolteacher and inspector Wladyslaw Sklodowska. Until the birth of Marie, her mother Bronislawa Bognska was the director of a private school for girls in Warsaw. Continuing the family tradition of academic excellence Marie won a gold medal at school, and worked as a governess to help finance her elder sister Bronya's medical studies in Paris. In 1891, not long after Bronya's marriage, Marie joined them in Paris in order to study physics and mathematics for the *Licence és Sciences*. There she met the young physicist, Pierre Curie, and in 1895 they married. They had two daughters, Irène the physicist and Nobel Laureate, and Eve the writer and author of the well-known biography of her mother.

In 1897 Marie decided to embark on research for the Paris doctorate and chose as her topic the spontaneous radiation from uranium slats which Henri Becquerel had discovered in 1896. Soon it became clear that Marie had chosen a very good topic; by the spring of 1898 Pierre had abandoned other researches and was devoting his energies to uranium radiation. That year they announced the discovery of two new elements, polonium and radium, and Marie coined the term 'radioactivity'. The discovery of induced radioactivity followed in 1899, and at the International Congress of Physics in 1900 they presented a review of their work which became widely known within the physics community.

After four years of unremitting effort Marie obtained a tenth of a gramme of pure radium chloride from which the atomic weight of this new element could be measured. The next year – 1903 – she defended her thesis: 'Recherches sur les Substances Radioactives'. Running to some 40,000 words the French text was reprinted and revised four times over the next twelve months; translated into English it appeared in Britain (1903) and America (1904); German and Polish editions followed.

The remarkable results of the couple's five years of toil (autumn 1897 to spring 1903) led to the award of the Davy Medal of the Royal Society of London and the Nobel Prize for Physics (with Henri Becquerel) in 1903. Eight years later Marie was awarded the Nobel Prize for Chemistry for the discovery of radium and polonium.

Pierre taught at an annexe of the Sorbonne – the School of Physics and Chemistry – but his salary was inadequate for the couple's needs, so Marie taught physics to girls at the École Normale Supérieure in Sèvres from 1900 to 1904. That year a chair of physics was created for Pierre with Marie as his assistant. When in 1906 he was killed in a road accident Marie succeeded him to become the first woman to teach at the Sorbonne.

Although fame had come to the couple in 1903 they were so utterly selfless and uncommercial that they deliberately filed no patents, reaped no fees for technical advice, but readily aided the industralist, Armet de L'Isle, when he set up a radium factory on the outskirts of Paris, and the American mining engineers

when they started radium extraction in Buffalo, New York State. When war broke out in 1914 Marie, who had left her second Nobel Prize money in Sweden, used it to buy national bonds. The little savings she had kept in the form of gold she took to the bank to be melted down for the war effort. Meanwhile the new Radium Institute built for Marie had been completed, but remained empty until war was over. Marie's energies were devoted to equipping ambulances with X-ray equipment and with training medical staff in its use.

In 1921 Marie visited the United States to receive from President Harding the 1 gramme of radium which had been purchased for her by a national subscription of £30,000.

As Marie aged her health declined and symptoms of the effects of radiation damage began to show – cataracts, skin lesions and finally leukaemia, from which she died shortly after being taken to a sanatorium in the French Alps.

Marie's researches can be divided into three phases: 1894–7, 1897–1903, 1903 onwards. In the first she studied the magnetic properties of steel, in the second radioactivity and the isolation of radium salts, in the third she continued within the field of radioactivity, but her most creative period was over. She played a part in the standardization of radium, the unit of radioactivity being termed the curie in her honour. Her lecture course at the Sorbonne was published posthumously under the title *Radioactivité* in 1935.

When Marie took up the study of the spontaneous radiation of uranium – the 'Becquerel Rays' – it was known that such radiation was characteristic of uranium, and was distinguished from other examples of fluorescent substances by the fact that it did not require previous exposure to light. Its special significance in Becquerel's view was that it was a property of uranium metal as well as of uranium salts. Marie decided to test the activity of a wide range of uranium compounds including uranium minerals. She measured their activity by the degree to which they ionized the atmosphere around them; the greater the ionization the greater the conductivity. Using Pierre and Jacques Curie's piezo-electric quartz balance and a gold-leaf electroscope they showed that some samples of the traditional uranium ore – pitch-blende – were nearly eight times more active than uranium metal. This suggested to the Curies the presence of other elements in the ore which like uranium gave off Becquerel rays but more vigorously. Since the radiation was unaffected by physical and chemical changes it must be an atomic phenomenon, therefore unlikely to be unique to one element. Accordingly they began a search for other active stubstances in pitch-blende. From Bohemia they received a ton of the residues from the extraction of uranium from pitch-blende, the chemical treatment of which yielded the Curies two fractions, one of the bismuth fraction 400 times more active than uranium, the other barium fraction 7,500 times more active. The first, they suggested, contained a new 'radioactive' element which they christened 'polonium', the second a new element 'radium' which was highly radioactive. It was decided to concentrate work on radium in order to prepare a sufficient quantity for the determination of its atomic weight. This daunting task, carried out under primitive laboratory conditions and with virtually no assistance, yielded 0.12 gms of the chloride of radium from which the atomic weight of 225 (actually 226) was calculated. Radium could then be placed in the Periodic Table of the elements among the alkaline earths and following barium. Marie had shown that an element although present only in minute quantities could be purified by successive concentrations in the barium fraction using its radioactivity as the mark of its presence.

The majority of the work on the radiation from radioactive substances was carried out by Pierre. The Curies made more progress on this aspect of their subject than over the cause of the phenomena. Rutherford and Soddy championed the disintegration theory according to which radioactivity was a product of atomic disintegration of one element into another. Initially the Curies doubted this because the parent element showed no signs of losing its activity and becoming exhausted with lapse of time. They were not receptive to Rutherford's explanation of this apparent inexhaustibility in terms of a very slow rate of disintegration. Instead Marie imagined radium gaining energy to replace its losses from the energy of gravitation or from some unknown cosmic radiation which only radioactive substances could absorb. However, in her *Traité de radioactivité* of 1910 she fully accepted the disintegration theory and consequently she joined with Rutherford, Soddy and others in rejecting the assumed constancy of the chemical elements.

Robert Olby

See: Eve Curie, *Madame Curie* (trans. 1937). Biographical information will also be found in Marie Curie's biography of her husband, *Pierre Curie* (trans. 1923, reprinted 1963). Marie Curie's thesis has been reprinted by van Nostrand, *Radio-active Substances* (1966).

107

CUVIER, Léopold Chrétien Frédéric Dagobert, called Georges 1769–1832

French naturalist and administrator

Like his exact of contemporary Napoleon*, Cuvier was born into an environment on the fringes of metropolitan France. The town of Montébeliard, now within the département of the Doubs on the Swiss border,

formed part of the German state of Württemburg, and was only annexed to France in 1793. Cuvier grew up in an almost exclusively Protestant milieu, and his expectations in early life were of a career in the service of the government of Württemburg. His education at the university in Stuttgart emphasized subjects such as technology, law, economics and foreign languages needed for the making of a career in bureaucracy, and included natural history only as an adjunct to the courses on forestry management. In natural history, apart from some teaching by the great German physiologist Kielmeyer, Cuvier was self-taught. However, he certainly regarded his Stuttgart training as the basis of his successful administrative career in France.

In spite of a successful career at the university, Cuvier could obtain no immediate position in Germany. To support his family, otherwise dependent on his father's meagre military pension, he was forced to take a position in France as tutor to a Protestant family living in Normandy. Here, his vocation as a man of science preoccupied with the problem of classification gradually began to emerge. In 1795, he went to Paris and after a long series of minor positions became Professor of Comparative Anatomy at the Muséum national d'Histoire naturelle in Paris in 1802. In the same year he also became professor at the Collège de France. Elected to the Institut in 1795, he became one of its permanent secretaries in 1803. Cuvier also occupied many posts in the administration of education. He organized the establishment of many of the earliest *lycées* in 1802–3, and under the French Empire introduced many reforms into the educational systems of Holland, Italy and Germany. He was also closely involved with the establishment of the Faculty of Sciences in Paris in 1809, and campaigned for most of the Restoration for the state support of education for the poor. After 1814, Cuvier's administrative power reached its peak. He kept his responsibilities for education, and in addition became the head of the most important section of the Conseil d'État. In 1817, he refused the offer of the Ministry of the Interior. After 1822, Cuvier at various times combined the direction of the University of France with the directorship of the non-Catholic religions of France, the vice-presidency of the Medical Faculty of Paris, and the grand-mastership of the Protestant Faculties of Theology. Such a concentration of office was unusual even in Restoration France, and frequently gave rise to public attacks. However, these positions, combined with those in science and with his membership of most Parisian, provincial and foreign learned societies of any note, meant that Cuvier was able to exercise patronage over an astonishingly wide range of affairs.

Cuvier's enormous achievement in science is peculiarly hard to evaluate. His command of a clear yet emotional expository style, his commanding institutional position in science which enabled him to suggest research programmes and insist strongly on positivistic norms in natural science, have often tempted historians to mistake rhetoric for achievement, or to fall into the opposite error of assuming that Cuvier's public roles could not have allowed him the time and concentration for substantive scientific work.

When Cuvier arrived in Paris, the most important problem facing natural historians was that of classification. Thanks to the voyages of exploration of the eighteenth century, numbers of known species had increased rapidly. Two major systems of classification had been put forward to explain the relations between these species, by the Swede Linnaeus and the Frenchman Buffon, but neither was regarded as wholly satisfactory. Particularly in the case of animals, the reliance of both men on external characteristics as a means of establishing groups produced many obvious absurdities of animals being classified together who had little in common except colour of fur or arrangement of teeth. It was Cuvier's achievement to suggest ways of classifying animals which were based on far more profound similarities. His classifications were concerned with internal rather than with external characteristics, and were overwhelmingly concerned with the identification and correlation of physiological systems. He applied these ideas over the full range of the animal kingdom in a flood of papers and in two lengthy books, the *Leçons d'anatomie comparée* (On Comparative Anatomy; 1800–1805) and the *Règne animal* ('The Animal Kingdom,' 1817). In much of his work, Cuvier drew on the new physiology which was being taught in the Faculty of Medicine in Paris by Xavier Bichat. He shared with Bichat an idea of the nature of life itself which deeply influenced his work in classification. Life for them consisted of self-consciousness and of sensation. This meant that the nervous system was felt automatically to head the hierarchy of physiological systems and to provide the most obvious way of forming the major groups of animals. In 1812, Cuvier put forward the idea that there were four major groups in the animal world, which he called *embranchements*. The vertebrates, insects, molluscs and *rayonnés*, or animals like starfish which radiated from a central point, were distinguished one from another by the arrangement of their nervous systems and by the way that system interrelated with the major physiological functions.

Cuvier also tried to raise the status of comparative anatomy as a science by equipping it with predictive laws for the first time, thus ending its position as a science of pure observation and description. He pointed out that the components of the living economy were so tightly interrelated that it should be possible, given any part of the animal's body, to predict the rest of its organization. These laws of the 'conditions of existence' and of the 'correlation of parts' remain linked to Cuvier's name.

However, in spite of his deep insights into the structure of nature, and his unrivalled skill as an anatomist, Cuvier's ideas never commanded the unchallenged position that many biographers have sought to ascribe to them. There were many real difficulties in his classificatory ideas. A physiological classification could only produce the major divisions of the animal kingdom; it was of little use in establishing the relations between animals already within the same major classification. In the main body of his work on classification Cuvier in fact tended to rely almost exclusively on detailed observation of minute differences of bone and teeth structure. This kind of approach was, however, of basic importance in his work in palaeontology. Although not the first person to take an interest in extinct species, Cuvier certainly offered more convincing reconstructions of such species in greater numbers than any of his forerunners, and more sharply realized their importance for the reconstruction of the history of the earth. It was also in this role that he made his greatest impact upon the contemporary imagination. Balzac* amongst others hailed him as the resurrector of a whole lost world of animal life. Cuvier also increased the unity of the life-sciences by being the first person fully to realize the importance of comparative anatomy for the reconstruction of extinct species, and the first person to use it to prove the fact of extinction.

Cuvier's life was also marked by controversy. Lamarck* argued against him that extinction did not occur, but that animals gradually changed their form over time due to the pressures of the environment. Cuvier, for whom the gaps between the major groups of animals were unbridgeable, refused to believe in such transformations. In no way an evolutionist, Cuvier believed that the succession of different forms of life was caused by geological upheavals which destroyed entire populations and allowed others to migrate in order to take their place. The second great conflict of Cuvier's life was that with his colleague Étienne Geoffroy St Hilaire, which came to a head in 1830. This was really concerned with the nature and objectives of classification. Geoffroy attacked Cuvier's *embranchements* formed in relation to physiological criteria, with the idea that, considered morphologically, all animals could be reduced to the same basic scheme. This debate posed the question of whether the business of natural history was to consider animals as closed physiological systems, or in terms of analogies which leaped over the boundaries between the *embranchements* and which often gave suggestive pointers towards the history of species. Modern biologists tend to adopt a mixture of the two approaches; but in the nineteenth century the conflict between Cuvier and Geoffroy was viewed as symptomatic of an irreconcilable division of approach.

After his death, Cuvier's reputation was variable. The French, annoyed at their failure to pre-empt the theories of Darwin* which dominated the last half of the century in natural science, often portrayed Cuvier as an inferior scientist who had used his political power to undermine the work of Lamarck, who was seen as Darwin's forerunner. In recent years, however, writers such as Michel Foucault have tended to ascribe to Cuvier a dominant role in the change from the natural history of the eighteenth century to that of the nineteenth, with its concern with the inner nature of the animal economy and its willingness to see the animal world as existing in and for itself without reference to ideas of divine creation or human needs. Cuvier's reputation rests solidly in any case on his work in classification, almost all of which is still accepted today.

Dorinda Outram

Other works include: *Recherches sur les ossements fossiles des quadrupèdes* (1812); *Discours dur les révolutions du globe* (1812, and six subsequent editions during Cuvier's lifetime). Secondary work on Cuvier is abundant and highly repetitive and is surveyed by Dorinda Outram in *History of Science* (1976); the best study of his classification is Henri Daudin, *L'idée de série animal* (1926); see also: William Coleman, *Georges Cuvier: Zoologist* (1964); Dorinda Outram, *Politics and Vocation: Georges Cuvier and the Life of Science in Post-Revolutionary France* (1982); Michel Foucault, *The Order of Things (Les mots et les choses,* 1966, trans. 1970).

D

DALTON, John 1766–1844

British chemist

It would be hardly possible to overestimate the influence of Dalton on modern science. What bestows a unity on the various scientific disciplines is a commitment to three specific assumptions. The first two, that the language of nature is mathematical and that it can be deciphered by experiment and observation, were clearly formulated in the seventeenth century. The third, that matter everywhere is reducible to its basic atomic constituents was first proposed by Democritus in fifth-century BC Athens. Despite much opposition from many quarters the atomic tradition never completely disappeared from Western thought and when revived by Gassendi in the 1620s found widespread support. It was however only with the work of Dalton that the atomic hypothesis began to take on a recognizably modern form.

He was an unlikely figure to play such a radical role in the history of science. Born in the small Cumberland village of Eaglesfield, Dalton was the son of a cottage weaver. The Cumberland of his day was undoubtedly backward, rural and impoverished; it was not, however, unlearned. In Dalton's own Quaker community considerable value was placed on education and he was fortunate to be encouraged by such local scholars as Elihu Robinson, who lent him scientific texts, and the famous blind Jack Gough who stimulated his interests in meteorology.

Dalton began work at the early age of eleven in the career he pursued for the rest of his life, as a teacher, first at the local village school and from 1781 to 1793 in Kendal. He moved to Manchester in that year when he accepted a post at New College, a dissenting academy founded in 1786. He resigned in 1800 and spent the rest of his life, until incapacitated by a stroke in 1837, working as a private tutor, teaching the young of Manchester Latin, French, Euclid or anything else they required.

That one of the greatest scientists in Europe was forced to earn his living by teaching schoolboys simple arithmetic was an indication of the total absence of academic scientific posts outside Oxford, Cambridge and London rather than a failure on the part of society to recognize his true worth. In fact Dalton's work was suitably recognized by his countrymen and he not only received the appropriate medals and honorary degrees but also, from 1833, was in receipt of a royal pension.

Under the influence of blind Jack Gough, Dalton had begun keeping regular meteorological records in 1787. These he published with much other material in his first book, *Meteorological Observations* (1793). There was no indication at this time that Dalton had in any way formulated his atomic theory.

In fact, the precise route taken to the theory is far from clear, for Dalton left more than one account of its genesis. It is likely however that consideration of a problem concerning the atmosphere first set him seriously thinking about atoms. The chemists of the eighteenth century had established that the atmosphere was not an homogeneous 'elastic fluid' as supposed by Newton but rather a mixture of oxygen, nitrogen and water vapour. Why, Dalton asked, did they not settle into distinct layers with the densest at the bottom? As a good Newtonian it was natural for Dalton to seek an answer in the *Principia*. There Newton had taught that a gas consists of small particles which repel each other with a force which increases as the distance between them diminishes. If, Dalton claimed, it is also assumed that this applies only to atoms of the same gas and that atoms of different gases neither attract nor repel each other then a situation like the mixture of atmospheric gases would arise.

This was published in 1801 and, at this point, although Dalton had begun to think atomically he had not yet made the crucial step of thinking in terms of atomic weights. When, however, he wrote in 1803 on the absorption of gases by water the step had been taken. He posed the question, 'Why does water not admit its bulk to every gas alike? and answered that it probably depended on the '. . . weight and number of the several gases: those whose particles are lightest . . . being least absorbable and the others more as they increase in weight.' Dalton was well aware of his originality, adding in a footnote, 'An enquiry into the relative weights of the ultimate particles of bodies is a subject, as far as I know, entirely new: I have lately been prosecuting this enquiry with remarkable success.' He even added his first determination of atomic weights.

Dalton's actual procedure consisted in analysing a compound like water into its constituents. He found that whatever quantity he took it always contained 8 parts of oxygen, by weight, to 1 of hydrogen. The same also held for all other compounds: they too were always reducible to the same constituents in some specific, unvariable proportion. Further, Dalton found that these were always simple numerical proportions like 2 to 1, 3 to 2 and never such ratios as ¾ to 1.

To get from such measurements to atoms required Dalton to make an additional assumption. If two elements A and B combine in only one way, as with hydrogen and oxygen to form water, he insisted they must be binary compounds, AB, made from precisely one atom of each. If they combined in just two ways, as with carbon and oxygen forming to make carbon monoxide or carbon dioxide, then one compound must be binary, CO, and the other ternary, that is either C_2O or CO_2. Three compounds would yield one binary and two ternary and the process can obviously be extended to cover more complicated cases.

With this assumption Dalton could advance from the fact that water is made from 8 parts of oxygen, by weight, to 1 part of hydrogen to the conclusion that, as water was a binary compound, the individual atoms themselves must share this property. Thus if we assign an arbitrary value of 1 to the weight of hydrogen, then oxygen must inevitably have a weight of 8. The first atomic weights in history had been assigned. It mattered little that Dalton, unaware that oxygen is diatomic and the correct formula of water is not HO but H_2O, had assigned incorrect values; these could be corrected; the importance lay in the fact that he was able to make an assignation of weights at all.

On this basis Dalton, in his account of his theory, *A New System of Chemical Philosophy* (Part I, 1808) could give a beautifully simple account of matter: '. . . the ultimate particles of all homogeneous bodies are perfectly alike in weight, figure etc . . . every particle of water is like every other particle of water.' Equally he could distinguish between different elements such as hydrogen and mercury by pointing out that the atoms of mercury were some 167 times heavier than hydrogen.

Dalton's theory found widespread and rapid acceptance. There were of course many errors in his work, some of which took decades to correct; there were also leading scientists who for the whole of the nineteenth century refused to accept atoms as anything other than a useful heuristic device. There were however technically better chemists than Dalton such as A. Avogadro, J. Gay-Lussac and J. Berzelius who were able to take his insight and use it to work out some of the basic laws of chemical combination. Once this had been achieved science had finally adopted its modern form.

Derek Gjertsen

There is an excellent biography: F. Greenway, *John Dalton and the Atom* (1966). A number of useful papers are to be found in: *John Dalton and the Progress of Science*, ed. D. Cardwell (1968). There is also an important monograph: A. Thackray, *John Dalton* (1972). As for his own writings, *A New System of Chemical Philosophy* (1808, 1810, 1827) is available in facsimile (1953), while substantial extracts are to be found in *Harvard Case Histories in Experimental Science*, ed. J. Conant (1950).

109
DARWIN, Charles Robert 1809–82

British naturalist

Darwin made the doctrine of the evolution of species, which until the publication of *The Origin of Species* in 1859 had existed only as a sporadic and uncertain hypothesis, overwhelmingly probable by showing that natural selection, as an evolutionary mechanism, is and must be operating. Because his theory convincingly replaced religious doctrines about the special creation of each species, its dissemination and acceptance marked a significant as well as substantial expansion of the role of empirical science within our culture. Just as the terms evolution and Darwinism have tended to become synonymous, so too has an antithesis between science and religion aptly been laid at Darwin's door.

Charles Darwin was born in Shrewsbury, the son of a doctor, Robert Waring Darwin, and grandson of both Erasmus Darwin and of the industrialist Josiah Wedgwood. In 1818 he entered Shrewsbury School, where, according to his mildly disingenuous *Autobiography*, he was a very average pupil who preferred dogs, angling and shooting to the prescribed classical studies. In 1825 he was sent by his father to study medicine at Edinburgh University; but, nauseated by the one surgical operation he attended, young Charles was obviously unsuited to the profession, and in 1827 he was transferred to Cambridge to prepare for holy orders. However, although at this period Darwin entertained a belief in 'the strict and literal truth of every word of the Bible', he was no more minded to take up the cloth than he had been the stethoscope (an invention of 1816), and he continued to cause his family concern by his 'idle, sporting' behaviour. But in reality his time at the two universities was by no means wasted. At Edinburgh he had mixed with several naturalists, among them Robert Edmund Grant, a supporter of the evolutionary views of Lamarck*, views which Darwin had already encountered in Erasmus Darwin's *Zoönomia* (1794–6); and at Cambridge he came to be known by some of the dons as 'the man who walks with Henslow'. The Rev. John Stevens Henslow was Professor of Botany, and, although entirely conservative in his adherence to the doctrine (most widely disseminated at the time through William Paley's *Natural Theology* of 1802) that all species were separately created and immutable, a field observer of considerable acumen. Darwin's friendship with him, which he described as the 'circumstance which influenced my career more than any other', was fruitful in three respects: it sharpened Darwin's own powers of observation; it directed his attention toward geology; and it secured him a berth on the *Beagle*.

This last was all-important, for the five years (from December 1831 until October 1836) Darwin spent aboard HMS *Beagle* furnished the material and experience without which *The Origin of Species* could not have been written. He was taken on as ship's naturalist by the ship's master, Captain Robert Fitzroy, after an introduction by Henslow. Fitzroy, later sacked as Governor of New Zealand for defending Maori land claims, was commissioned by the Admiralty to conduct a detailed survey of the coasts of South America and to set up chronometrical stations around the globe. This journey gave Darwin a prolonged exposure to an area of the world radically different in its fauna and flora from his native England, as well as a more general sweep of the entire southern hemisphere. Darwin seems to have endured the hazards of the voyage remarkably well; but within a few months of his return home he became a semi-invalid. His illness, which has sometimes been identified as Chagas' Disease (his symptoms were lassitude, digestive disorders and vomiting), affected the rest of his life. From 1842, three years after his marriage to his cousin Emma Wedgwood (by whom he had ten children, eight surviving infancy), he lived in near-reclusion at Down House in Kent. The success of his father's practice combined with a judicious investment policy more than enabled him to live independently, and to the end of his days he maintained a firm belief in the social benefits of an intelligensia freed from the burden of employment.

From the notes, observations and collections made during the *Beagle's* long circumnavigation Darwin worked on a number of publications that gave him a solid position in the British scientific community. These included *The Structure and Distribution of Coral Reefs* (1842). But the first work to reach a wider audience and which is remembered by non-specialists is the *Journal of Researches into the Geology and Natural History of the Various Countries Visited by H.M.S. Beagle* (1839, rev. 1846), better known as *The Voyage of the Beagle*. Quite apart from its virtues as the most informed travel book of its time and the most readable of all Darwin's output, it can be seen as setting the stage for the theory that was to come. Beneath its light and often anecdotal surface, *The Voyage* displays a remarkable familiarity with existing botanical, zoological and geological literature; and behind its scholarship lurk those acute questions which led its author toward an evolutionist explanation of speciation.

Paley had used an analogy to summarize the orthodox position. Finding a watch in a field, it would be reasonable to infer that the object owed both its gross design and intricate mechanism to the inspiration and labour of a watchmaker. And so it was with the world and its organic contents. All had been made and designed by a God, each species having its place in a grand hierarchy of living beings, in which man, by his rationality, enjoyed special pre-eminence. Each species was suited to its climate and habitation by its special characteristics; or, put another way, geographic and climatic diversity existed in order to support the broadest possible spectrum of living things, knowledge of which best equipped man to learn of the existence of his creator.

There was nothing original in Paley's teleological formulation. In the main it harked back to such works as John Ray's *Wisdom of God Manifested in the Works of Creation* (1691); and, in its adherence to Usher's biblical chronology that dated the Creation in 4004 BC, it proved vulnerable to two immediate threats: the discovery of extinct species in the fossil record, and the emergence of a geology that described the inorganic world as having changed through periods of time far greater than anything suggested in Genesis. Here the decisive publication was Sir Charles Lyell's* *Principles of Geology* (3 vols, 1830–2), the first volume of which Henslow had urged Darwin to take with him on the *Beagle*. In it Lyell argued that, far from being designed, the features of the contemporary earth have emerged from, and are explicable wholly by, the gradual accumulative operation of such forces as earthquakes, volcanic eruptions and the weather.

Lyell's non-catastrophic model of evolution Darwin made his own. In his work on coral reefs he embraced it directly, showing how polyps-built atolls are signposts for submerged islands; and in the *Voyage* he adopted it as his perceptual framework. It was precisely the apprehension of current appearances through a corridor of projected past time that generated his famous observations on the Galapagos Islands. There he found that not only were many species unique to the archipelago, but they were often unique to the individual islands. But what mattered was the degree of relationship between species: for whereas the closest ties existed between species on separate islands, the fauna and flora of the Galapagos resembled that of South America much more than that of any comparable basaltic larval terrain, for instance the Cape de Verd islands. Darwin's comments on the Galapagos finches show clearly the direction of his thoughts: 'Seeing the gradation and diversity of structure in one small, intimately related group of birds, one might really fancy that from the original paucity of birds in this archipelago one species had been taken and modified for different ends.' Why is it, he asks elsewhere, that living marsupials are found only in South America and Australia (which had once been joined)? And why is the closest relation of the South American rhea the South African ostrich?

In fact, when the *Voyage* was first published, Darwin had already come to the main conclusions of his theory of descent with modification. He opened his first note-book on evolution in July 1837, and in 1838 a reading of Malthus's* *Essay on the Principle of Population* suggested to him the mechanism of natural selection. In 1842 he wrote a thirty-five-page sketch on the subject, which in 1844 he elaborated into a 230-page essay that he showed to the botanist Joseph Dalton Hooker (both are published in Gavin de Beer, *Evolution by Natural Selection*, 1958). But it was not until 1856, on the advice of Lyell himself, that he began preparing his views for publication. And even this bore only an indirect relation to what finally appeared, for Darwin originally intended writing a work three or four times the length of the *Origin*, which he referred to as an 'abstract' only. The delay, between 1844 and 1856, can be explained by Darwin's keen awareness of the momentousness of the issues at stake, and his recognition that acceptance of his theory would depend on the maturity of its presentation; although during the interim much of his time was devoted to four monographs that set out to classify the different orders of living and fossilized bar-nacle. What forced his hand was the arrival from the Malay Archipelago of Alfred Wallace's* paper, ex-pressing ideas identical to his own. With Wallace's consent, papers by both men were read at a meeting of the Linnaean Society on 1 July 1858. *The Origin of Species* was then written and published on 24 November of the following year. The first edition of 1250 copies sold out on the same day.

If caution was Darwin's strategy, his instinct was faultless, for *The Origin of Species* is still, in its close argument, an impressive piece of advocacy, the more so as its author took particular pains to forestall his enemies by previewing their likely criticisms. Evolution by natural selection, or descent with modification as Darwin often calls it, is extrapolated from three broad areas of fact: the 'struggle for life', variation and in-heritance. Malthus, in his *Essay*, had argued that so long as human populations are permitted to increase geometrically while the food supply increases only ar-ithmetically, famine and death are inevitable. And this, says Darwin, is exactly what happens in the animal and vegetable kingdoms, on the largest possible scale: 'as more individuals are produced than can possibly survive, there must in every case be a struggle for existence, either one individual with another of the same species, or with the individuals of distinct species, or with the physical conditions of life.' Nature 'red in tooth and claw' (the phrase is Tennyson's*) affords no 'artificial increase of food, and no prudential restraint from marriage'. From this it follows that 'any being, if it vary however slightly in any manner profitable to itself, under the complex and sometimes varying con-ditions of life, will have a better chance of surviving, and thus be *naturally selected*.' Finally: 'From the strong principle of inheritance, any selected variety will tend to propagate its new and modified form.' Let this pro-cess of random adaptation to a dynamic environment continue long enough and new species, new genera, new families and new orders will be co-evolved.

The most difficult term in Darwin's tripartite equa-tion was variation, and to this topic he devoted the opening chapters of his book. Variation is first demon-strated not among feral creatures, but among the do-mesticated, such as dogs and pigeons; for every trainer knew that by careful selecting new breeds could be developed within fairly short periods of time. Thus, all varieties of tame pigeon are known to derive from a single species of rock-pigeon. In the wild, human con-trol is merely substituted by the struggle for life. A powerful support for this view can be found in the vagaries of classification itself. Ever since Linnaeus had provided naturalists with a system for ordering the different species, arguments had raged about what did and what did not constitute a distinct species. Darwin concluded that if hard and fast lines between species and sub-species are difficult to draw, then that is be-cause hard and fast lines do not naturally occur. Rather, species are separated by degree, not kind. As Linnaeus himself had said, it is the characteristics that make the genus, not the genus that makes the characteristics.

Having thus presented his theory, Darwin moved on to corroborate it with circumstantial evidence from four important areas: the fossil record, the distribution of species, morphology and embryology. For the theory itself, as Darwin himself admitted, could never be proved: the great span of evolutionary time was simply irrecoverable. Indeed, one of the hardest tasks facing him was the reconciliation of his thesis with contem-porary palaeontology: for whereas fossils provided am-ple evidence of the extinction of species, which one would predict from the theory, few if any of them could be identified unequivocally as 'intermediate' varieties – although one fossil discovery, that of the archeopte-ryx, unexpectedly linking birds back to reptiles, was hailed as irresistible confirmation of the evolutionary position. Yet, quite apart from the fact that the fossil record was as yet relatively unexplored, Darwin was able to point out that the record never would be 'com-plete' because geologically it was impossible: sedimen-tary beds are not laid down continuously, and however long it might take for a species to become modified, the period during which it remains unchanged is incom-parably longer. On the other hand, affinities between extinct and living species greatly enhanced the theory, particularly with regard to distribution: for the fossils of one area are generally more closely allied to living species of the same area than those of any other. And fossil resemblances formed only a part of the larger morphological picture: for, throughout nature, diversity of function is consistently located in similarity of structure. The wings and legs of a bat, like the legs of a horse and the arms of a chimpanzee, are not only built up from the same basic bone units, but the bone units always appear in the same sequence. In embryology we can virtually see such implicit adaptation taking place, for the embryos of different species are frequently alike in their early stages. 'Thus, community in embryonic structure, reveals community of descent.' Or, as Darwin's German champion, Haeckel*, put it (much too crudely): ontogeny recapitulates phylogeny.

The morphological and embryological arguments applied as much to man as to any other species. Although The Origin of Species carefully refrained from making a point of this, it became, in the public's mind, the key issue in the controversy that followed publication. Darwin himself took very little part in the great debate, and willingly allowed T. H. Huxley* to lead the evolutionist charge. It was Huxley too who first gave an extended account of man the primate in his Evidence As To Man's Place In Nature (1863). But Darwin did take up the subject himself in his widely influential The Descent of Man, and Selection in Relation to Sex (1871).

In The Descent of Man Darwin offered the first comprehensive account of sexual selection, an accomplice of natural selection, operating among many of the more developed species. In such species striking differences between males and females are said to have come about adaptively. Thus, the peacock's tail has evolved by virtue of the advantage it bestows on the peacock's chances of attracting a peahen. Among some species of beetle the two sexes appear so unlike that previously naturalists had been misled into assigning them to different species altogether. Among humans, too, sexual selection is used to explain why women are generally smaller, less hairy, less muscular and, according to Darwin, less well-equipped mentally. Darwin also ascribes racial differences to the same cause, while proposing that the various races (many of which he refers to as 'savages') be regarded as subspecies. He does not, like so many of his contemporaries, argue that the different races represent originally different species; yet the characteristic that separates man from all other species is his moral sense – in a famous passage he describes how man alone possesses the capability to judge his own actions; and this quality, he says, has only been brought to a pitch among Caucasians.

Clearly The Descent of Man exhibits some of the white supremacism and the sexism regarded by many commentators as an unfortunate consequence of the application of Darwin's ideas during the last decades of the nineteenth century. But while some of what he says must be put down to the prejudices of his age, and while 'Social Darwinism' derived at least so much from the laissez-faire philosophy of Herbert Spencer*, his plea for human sub-speciation needs to be regarded as an attempt to reinforce his main scientific argument – man's commonality with nature. In the same spirit, and prefiguring the main concerns of ethology, his chapter on 'Mental Powers' describes the incidence of such behaviour as curiosity, fear, imitation, attention, memory, imagination, reason, language, even the sense of beauty, and above all the 'social instinct', among many animals other than man. What sets the latter apart is merely the concentration of all these qualities (which act together to produce moral sense) in one species.

Darwin's vivid account of man as one species among many underpins the social sciences; his picture of man's mind as the product of different and variously developed biological skills serves as an antidote to idealist philosophies; his rejection of orthogenesis constitutes a repudiation of the Judaeo-Christian concept of God; and his theory of evolution provides the framework of the modern understanding of the life process. While together these ideas make up the core of 'Darwinism', separately they each had clear antecedents in an increasingly materialist European culture. Atheism was a widespread, age-old phenomenon. By the mid-nineteenth century discoveries in prehistoric archaeology had already abetted geology's rejection of biblical chronology (the Frenchman Boucher de Perthes in the late 1830s established the dates of the Stone Age); early ethnologists, like some social theorists (notably Condorcet, and later Marx*), had embarked on stadial models to explain the route from 'savagery' to 'civilization'; at least two physical anthropologists, W. C. Wells (in a paper given to the Royal Society in 1813), and James Cowles Prichard (in the second edition of Researches into the Physical History of Mankind, 1826), had proposed theories of natural selection; and Spencer, who coined the tautological phrase 'Survival of the Fittest', had espoused Lamarck's theory of the inheritance of acquired characteristics throughout the 1850s. Although Darwin drew relatively little upon sources outside the natural sciences (the major exception being his reading of Malthus), the implications of his work were quickly apprehended, and often assimilated, by a very broad cross-section of the intellectual community at home, in Europe and in America.

The reason why this was so lies as much in the quality of Darwin's thought as in any contemporary disposition toward loosely evolutionist attitudes. In both the Origin and the Descent, as in the early notebooks, his great strength lies in his ability to discern broad patterns amidst a mass of observation; and it is the compatibility of his theory of adaptive modification with findings from a very wide range of scientific inquiry that has stood surety for its proof, and which explains why it has so often carried the day against creationism. It is for example quite remarkable that the major discoveries in experimental biology and chemistry, from Mendel* to Watson and Crick's work on DNA, have squared comfortably with the Darwinian hypothesis. Indeed modern biology is founded upon the synthesis of Darwinian natural selection and Mendelian genetics effected by the statistical analyses of Sir Ronald Fisher and J.B.S. Haldane in the late 1920s and early 1930s. That is not to say that in some respects Darwin's theory has not itself been modified. It is now thought by some that he placed too much emphasis on the graduality of evolution and on species rather than individuals; and a leniency toward Lamarck exhibited in later editions of the *Origin* was exorcized in the 1890s after advances in cytology offered a convincing refutation of the French biologist. But the principle of evolution by natural selection is still accepted by a vast majority of biologists, and fundamentalist criticisms of Darwin tend also to be a fundamental rejection of scientific logic.

In the years immediately after 1859 attempts were made to reconcile Darwinism with traditional religious dogma, by asserting that natural selection was God's chosen method of creation – what John Dewey dubbed 'design on the instalment plan'; and even today there are those who interpret spontaneous mutation as a form of sublime intervention. In general however it remains one of the great ironies that natural history, which flourished in the early nineteenth century as the handmaiden of religion, turned traitor on its cause. Indeed, what distinguished Darwin's theory of evolution from others of the period, and what provoked so much hostility, was precisely its insistence that the growth of complex out of simple forms is a matter of chance rather than design. Even Lamarck had upheld the ordinary teleological view of progress as necessary progress.

Darwin himself worked indefatigably on during the 1870s, publishing works of high scientific value, among them *The Expression of the Emotions in Man and Animals* (1872), *The Effects of Cross and Self Fertilization in the Vegetable Kingdom* (1876), containing an explanation of the adaptive advantages of sexual selection, and *The Formation of Vegetable Mould through the Action of Worms* (1881). He died in 1882, of a heart attack, and upon the intercession of twenty MPs was buried in Westminster Abbey.

Justin Wintle

The full text of Darwin's *Autobiography* first appeared in *The Autobiography of Charles Darwin, ed. Nora Barlow (1958),* although a theologically 'expurgated' version was included in *Life and Letters of Charles Darwin,* ed. Francis Darwin (3 vols, 1887). Darwin's other works include: *Geological Observations on the Volcanic Islands Visited During the Voyage of H.M.S. Beagle* (1844); *Geological Observations on South America* (1864); *A Monograph on the Subclass Cirripedia* (2 vols, 1851 and 1854) and *A Monograph of the Fossil Lepudidae, or*

Pedunculated Cirripedes of Great Britain (1851); *A Monograph of the Fossil Balanidae and Verrucidae* (1854); *On the Various Contrivances by which British and Foreign Orchids are Fertilized by Insects* (1862). For Darwin's 'Notebooks' see *Bulletin of the British Museum (Natural History),* vol.2 (1960) and vol.3 (1967). See: Julian Huxley, *Evolution: The Modern Synthesis* (1942; 3rd edn, 1974); Gavin de Beer, *Charles Darwin: A Scientific Biography* (1963); John Maynard Smith, *The Theory of Evolution* (2nd ed. 1966); Lynn Barber, *The Heyday of Natural History* (1980); Ronald Good, *The Philosophy of Evolution* (1981); Peter Brent, *Charles Darwin* (1981); Jonathan Howard, *Darwin* (1982); and Wilma George, *Darwin* (1982). Two collections of essays by Stephen Jay Gould are also recommended: *Ever Since Darwin* (1977) and *The Panda's Thumb* (1980).

110
DAUDET, Alphonse 1840–97

French writer

At the peak of his career in the 1880s, Daudet was possibly the most successful writer of his time in France. He was firmly established alongside Zola* and Edmond de Goncourt* as one of the leading figures of his profession, and enjoyed a reputation that had spread beyond France to be endorsed by Meredith*, Stevenson* and Henry James* among others. He owed his success to a steady output of novels about contemporary life, mostly set in Paris, but with occasional (and significant) excursions to his native region, Provence: *Young Fromont and Risler Senior (Fromont Jeune et Risler Aîne,* 1874), *Jack* (1876), *The Nabob (Le Nabab,* 1877), *Les Rois en Exil* (1879), *Numa Roumestan* (1881), *L' Évangéliste* (1883), *Sapho* (1884), *L'Immortel* (1888), etc. In these works the dramas and hypocrisies of contemporary politics, business, religion and fashionable society were dwelt upon with no great depth of analysis either morally or psychologically but with enough skill and insistence to appeal to the expanding middle-class readership of the Third Republic. Like his friend Zola, with whose Naturalist movement he was often associated, Daudet made use of detailed documentation, often stored in notebooks until needed. The different *quartiers* of Paris with its mushrooming suburbs, the increasingly subtle stratification of middle-class society, and the new urban professions, all of these are evoked by Daudet with a fair degree of accuracy tinged with humour and sentimentality. Sometimes *causes célèbres* were given a fictional treatment, and well-known personalities were thinly disguised. Thus in *The Nabob,* amongst other transformations, the famous Second Empire politician the Duc de Morny (to whom the young Daudet was for a while private secretary) became the 'Duc de Mora', and the financier François

Bravay was the big-hearted, ambitious, 'méridional' Bernard Jansoulet, the nabob of the title. But, although a brief mention of this novel may suggest a comparison with Zola's *His Excellency Eugène Rougon*, nowhere in Daudet's work can one find the Naturalist's detailed, epic treatment of the proletariat and the peasantry – nothing at least to compare with *Germinal* and *The Earth*.

If Zola had written nothing better than *Eugène Rougon* he might well have experienced the same fate as Daudet – almost total eclipse within twenty years of his death. Outside France Daudet is now known almost solely as the author of the sentimental *Letters from My Windmill* (*Lettres de mon Moulin*, 1866) and the four Tartarin novels (*Tartarin de Tarascon*, 1872; *Tartarin sur les Alpes*; 1885; *La Défense de Tarascon*, 1886; and *Port Tarascon*, 1890). In these works, as notably in *Numa Roumestan*, Daudet propagated the myth of southern panache, bravado, verbal intoxication. The southern character, sometimes called 'méridional', sometimes 'provençal' by Daudet is portrayed with mixed feelings: affection because of the warmth, generosity and spontaneity that animate Tartarin, Numa, Jansoulet and the various characters of the *Letters*; disquiet because of the suffering and destruction that often follow in the wake of their mendacity. In fact not all of Daudet's southerners are boastful windbags. Some of them may be brooding, inarticulate peasants who explode in passion and violence, as in *L'Arlésienne* (1872), for which Bizet* composed the famous incidental music. The contrast between the hot-blooded southerner and the principled, level-headed northerner is expressed most strikingly in the misalliance between Numa and his wife Hortense Le Quesnoy. Numa is a southern politician of the Third Republic, an opportunist who rises to dubious eminence in Paris, and symbolizes in Daudet's words 'the re-conquest of Gaul by the Latins'. As Clogenson has observed, the time was ripe for such a theme. Taine* had given an intellectual impetus to the notion of racial character, and in particular Mistral and the Félibrige group were championing the cause of Provençal culture. Furthermore it was a curious fact – in a century when France was being increasingly dominated by Paris and northern industry and commerce in general – that a number of men of southern origins were prominent in the political life of the nation, Guizot, Thiers, Émile Ollivier, Gambetta, etc.

If this southern theme in Daudet's work is now the only one to which we may feel inclined to attach importance a century later, its authenticity is due to the fact that Daudet was exploiting his earliest autobiographical material. Like Guizot, he was born in Nîmes. His tribulations *en route* to Paris via Lyon and Alais, and unhappy experiences in schools as both pupil and teacher (he was small and picked upon) are recounted in the first part of *Le Petit Chose* (*sic*, i.e. 'Little What's 'is Name', as he was always called by

a particularly insensitive teacher). Occasional echoes of Dickens* in this and other works of Daudet will strike readers in the English speaking world. Certain other derivations too – Balzac*, Mérimée*, Zola, not to mention the quixotic fantasies of Tartarin – have provoked a hostile response in recent times, nowhere more so than in one of his fellow-countrymen, Jacques Vier, who considered him in 1956 to be 'one of the most ingenious parasites in our literature'. This is a harsh judgment: likewise, the opposite view, that of Daudet's latest English translator – 'though not quite the equal of his friends Zola and Flaubert, he remains today a major figure in French literature' (Frederick Davies, 1978) – is an overstatement. But in its combination of intellectual aberration and generosity of spirit it is not an inappropriate reward for the auther of *Tartarin de Tarascon*.

Ted Freeman

See: *The Novels, Romances and Writings of Alphonse Daudet* (20 vols, 1898 – 1903); *Letters from My Windmill*, ed. F. Davies (1978). See also: J.H. Bornecque, *Les Années d'apprentissage d'Alphonse Daudet* (1951); Y.E. Clogenson, *Alphonse Daudet, peintre de la vie de son temps* (1946); Murray Sachs, *The Career of Alphonse Daudet* (1965); A. Roche, *Alphonse Daudet* (1976, containing an excellent bibliography).

111
DAUMIER, Honoré-Victorin 1808–79

French artist

Honoré Daumier, painter, sculptor and political cartoonist, was born in Marseilles. His father was a glazier who also wrote poetry. In 1816 the family moved to Paris where Honoré worked as an office boy for a notary. In 1822 Daumier was taught drawing by a family friend, the collector Alexandre Lenoir, and in the next few years he studied with Suisse and learnt the new art of lithography with the printer Belliard. In 1830, after the revolution, King Louis-Philippe, in the words of Marx*, 'formed a stock company for the exploitation of France's wealth, whose dividends were divided among ministers, Chambers, 240,000 electors (from a population of 28 million), and their followers, and Louis-Philippe was their director'. Daumier at this point became a political cartoonist for Charles Philipon's Republican *La Caricature* and began his career as a fierce satirist of *juste milieu* France. Despite the apparent freedom of the press Daumier was imprisoned for six months in 1832–3 for his satirical print *Gargantua* which presented the king eating the entire wealth of France and was a comment on the new civil list of 1832. During his internment by the government Daumier was also kept briefly at a sanatorium after which he produced *Chimeras of the Imagination*, a Goyaesque fantasy of the madhouse. After his release Daumier set about modelling an extraordinary series of clay 'masks' based on the members of the Assembly for use by himself and the other cartoonists at *La Caricature*. After the appalling massacre of the inhabitants of a Parisian tenement in 1834 Daumier produced his famous *12 rue Transnonian* print. In the following year press censorship was enforced and Daumier began work of a less political and more generally satirical variety for the magazine *Le Charivari*. He invented 'Robert Macaire', based on a stage character, who represents the 'promoter', the dishonest bourgeois and whose catch-phrase is 'I adore industry'. In 1841 Daumier moved to the 'artist's isle' of Saint-Louis where he lived until the mid-sixties. In 1846 he married 'Didine', a glazier's daughter. Daumier lived simply among the people and was quiet and reserved by temperament. After the 1848 revolution the censorship laws were abolished and Daumier's graphics became more specific again. At this time he also began to paint more seriously, partly as a result of new liberal policies initiated at the Salon. Daumier invented 'Ratapoil' ('ratskin'), a satirical figure symbolizing the new president, Louis-Napoleon. Daumier's criticisms were fully justified when Louis-Napoleon pulled off his *coup d'état* in 1851 and made himself emperor. Twenty-six thousand of his opponents were exiled and press censorship restored. The 1850s were a depressing decade for Daumier and his work seems temporarily to lose some of its earlier power. In 1858 he nearly died of a mystery illness. He stopped working for *Le Charivari*, 1860–3, but with revived spirits produced an enormous amount of work in all his usual media. During the 1860s he met the younger radical artists like Manet* and Monet* and also began to spend his summers in Valmondois where he became acquainted with Corot*, Rousseau* and Daubigny. By this time Daumier's lithographic work had become far more general in both form and content and also more tragically intentioned as the domestic and international situation seemed to deteriorate. He refused the Legion of Honour in 1870, as did Courbet*, and then witnessed the siege of Paris after the fall of the emperor at Sedan in the Franco-Prussian War. Shortly after the suppression of the Commune in 1871 and the establishment of the Third Republic under Thiers, Daumier became almost totally blind and stopped work. By this time he was living permanently in the country. A large retrospective of his work in 1878, a year before his death, confirmed his immense reputation among fellow artists. During his life he had produced 4,000 lithographs, a few hundred paintings, innumerable drawings and a great number of sculptures and reliefs.

Since his death Daumier's reputation has fluctuated and his place in French art as one of the first 'moderns' has never been easily explained or convincingly proposed, perhaps because his art is inextricably linked with a complex and confusing period in French history. Although he was of a retiring nature his work touches upon all the major issues of his times. He is probably best known for his grotesque and disturbing characterizations of Parisian lawyers. Baudelaire* wrote:

> Every little meanness, every absurdity, every quirk of the intellect, every vice of the heart can be clearly seen and read in these animalized faces; and at the same time everything is broadly and emphatically drawn. Daumier combines the freedom of an artist with the accuracy of a Lavater.

As usual with Baudelaire's criticism this pinpoints an essential feature of Daumier's art and the one which has divided his critics ever since. Formalist critics like Roger Fry have been disappointed by the emphasis on 'psychological' and 'literary' matters in his work and have seen his necessary output as a cartoonist as diverting him from important issues of form. This would seem to be historically and aesthetically a narrow and even naive viewpoint. Daumier's art is surely humanistic and based upon a deep reading of psychological motivation and social conditioning. His massively modelled forms, his superb exercises in black and white oppositions and his capturing of facial and bodily movement in a complex spatial composition are part of a unified vision. This is always present even in his most topical cartoons. It was this dedicated style of work and intense tragi-comic sense which made Daumier a genius in the eyes of his most important contemporaries and friends – from Michelet* and Balzac* to the Goncourts* and Baudelaire, and from Delacroix* to Degas*. Henry James* wrote of his drawing style, based on remembered observation rather than direct copying, that it attained a 'certain simplification of the attitude or gesture which has an almost symbolic intensity. His persons represent only one thing, but they insist tremendously on that, and their expression of it abides with us.' It was this classic ability to grasp inwardly his targets and reinvent them alive and ghastly that distinguishes Daumier's achievement from that of other cartoonists and illustrators of the period like Doré*, Gavarni and Cham. Daumier had studied Rubens, Rembrandt, the Venetian painters of the sixteenth century, Hals, Goya and Delacroix. All these artists were masters of chiaroscuro, vivid drawing and an imaginative transformation of the mundane and psychologically hidden aspects of human character. Like them also, Daumier, in his painting, drew with the brush on an even ground, and used a complicated series of glazes to create subtle moods out of monochrome or ghostly mixtures of grey, brown, lavender and white. His *Laundress* is a secular madonna figure rising from the Quai d'Anjou like a spectre against the hazy background of the far bank of the Seine. The picture anticipates the mature work of Degas where the subtlety of the drawing and massiveness of the figure, echoing masters like Massacio and Michelangelo, are wedded to a realist vision of mid-nineteenth-century urban life. One of Daumier's few recorded sayings had been 'Il faut être de son temps.' The furthest Daumier seriously wandered from his times was in the series of paintings based on *Don Quixote* in which he contrasted the 'lean' and the 'fat', the ideal and the pragmatic, in man and, as in his pictures of the theatre and of clowns, projected his own convictions about the general neglect of his work and the general notions he held concerning the human condition which he shared in his own way with writers like Balzac, Baudelaire and Flaubert*.

Daumier pointed a new way for French artists in his classical sense of form and his concern with contemporary social reality. His influence was felt not only by artists like Manet, Degas, Pissarro*, Van Gogh* and Rouault but also by writers like Flaubert, Champfleury and Daudet*.

Richard Humphrys

See: J. Adhémar, *Honoré Daumier* (Paris, 1954); O. Larkins, *Daumier: Man of his Time* (1966); *Daumier, Catalogue Raisonné*, ed. K.E. Maison (2 vols, 1968); H.P. Vincent, *Daumier and his World* (1968).

112
DAVID, Jacques-Louis 1748–1825

French painter

The greatest French painter of the eighteenth century, David is also a crucial figure in the development of art in France during the nineteenth. He is conventionally regarded as the prime exponent of French Neoclassicism, although attention has increasingly been drawn to the Romantic element in much of his work and to the phenomenon of his consistently superb portraits. By the painters and writers of the nineteenth century itself he was seen as a leader who had, by his stylistic innovations and high seriousness, rescued French art from triviality and a merely decorative function and established the status it was to enjoy during their own period. Géricault*, for instance, referred to David as '*le régénérateur de l'école française*' and Delacroix* dubbed him '*le père de toute l'école moderne en peinture et en sculpture*'.

As an artistic personality, David emerged slowly from the milieu of Boucher, Fragonard, Greuze and Chardin. To the vision and methods of these artists his own work owes a considerable debt, most marked in his early pictures, such as *The Combat of Mars and Minerva* (*Le Combat de Minerve contre Mars*, 1771), but still detectable in many later paintings. He was born in Paris of bourgeois parents and was originally intended for the architectural profession, to which end he re-

ceived a good education, but by 1766 he had enrolled as a pupil of J. M. Vien, a professor at the Royal Academy of Painting and Sculpture. Vien, who claimed an interest in the revival of Classical art, accompanied David when, having at his fourth attempt secured the Prix de Rome offered by the Academy, the young artist left for Italy in 1775. There it was that David's vision underwent a complete transformation – an operation for cataract, as he himself called it. The style most frequently associated with him began to develop, stimulated by the architecture and sculpture of ancient Rome, the discoveries at Herculaneum and Pompeii, the work of the artists of the Renaissance and seventeenth century, notably Raphael and Poussin, and the aesthetic of Neoclassicism, propounded by the followers of J. J. Winckelmann. His habit of painstaking study after nature was also formed during these years.

Returning from Rome in 1780, David secured full membership of the Academy three years later on the presentation of his *Andromache mourning Hector* (*La Douleur d'Andromache*), a painting which paved the way for his future success as a purveyor of highly dramatic death-scenes. His position as the leading artist of his day was confirmed when, in 1785, he exhibited at the Paris Salon his most important Neoclassical work, *The Oath of the Horatii* (*Le Serment des Horaces*). Here, as in the paintings which immediately followed it, David's economy of statement and strict subordination of colour to drawing epitomized the new severity of taste engendered by the reaction to rococo excess. The subject gave pictorial expression to the cult of civic virtue, preached by Rousseau and the *philosophes*, which stressed self-sacrifice, devotion to duty, honesty and austerity. Simultaneously the painting was intensely natural and supremely elevated, passionate in content yet meticulous in form. It was the perfect response to the demands of Diderot and other critics for a more serious and didactic art.

On the outbreak of the French Revolution, David rapidly came to sympathize with many of its aims. He became a member of the Jacobin party, a deputy, voted for the death of Louis XVI and played a large part in the organization of public festivals. He began to look to the contemporary world for his subject matter, which he then proceeded to elevate to the stage of epic history and to imbue with a powerful moral charge, the most celebrated example being his commemorative portrait of the *Dead Marat* (*Marat assassiné*, 1793). Echoes of this modern *pietà* recur in the work of the Romantics, such as Gros, Géricault and Delacroix – indeed, David's ability to illustrate the heroic quality of contemporary events was perhaps his greatest gift to succeeding generations. Throughout the nineteenth century, French writers from Stendhal* to Zola* were preoccupied with the concept of modernity, though only Baudelaire*, who went so far as to ally Romanticism with the heroism of modern life, had the imaginative equipment to interpret David effectively.

David's ability to convey a moral or political message was exploited by Napoleon*, who gave him official status as *Premier Peintre* and for whom he painted works of distinctly propagandist intent, such as *Bonaparte crossing the St Bernard Pass* (*Bonaparte franchissant le Grand-Saint-Bernard*, 1801) and the *Coronation* (*Le Sacre de l'Empereur*, 1805–7). Once more his work responded to his environment, changing in technique and mood from the earlier Republican style, becoming larger and more highly coloured than hitherto and expressing a new interest in pageantry. His heroic and emotional interpretation of current events was to be highly influential on younger painters such as Delacroix and shows David himself in a Romantic light.

David himself, however, came to regret his departure from classical subjects. Even before the fall of the Empire he returned to his half-finished *Leonidas at Thermopylae* (*Léonidas aux Thermopyles*), which he had laid to one side at the height of his enthusiasm for Imperial commissions in 1804. He brought the painting to completion in 1814 and thereafter remained firm in his devotion to Antiquity. Throughout the remaining years of his life he concentrated on scenes taken from classical literature, though now consisting of episodes from love stories and consequently lacking the moral tension and high seriousness of his former work. He recommended classical subject matter to his pupils and adherents and his advice was widely respected, particularly after his exile to Brussels in 1816, which was viewed by many of his followers as itself a symptom of the current deterioration in artistic taste and abandonment of the *beau idéal*. Gros, who was left in charge of David's studio in Paris, was particularly guilt-stricken at his own success as chief illustrator of the Napoleonic epic, forsook contemporary life and reverted to weak classical set-pieces. Ingres*, too, a former pupil of David, became increasingly adamant in defence of the classical tradition, which he linked with the supremacy of drawing in composition. The stage was thus set for the academic or Salon art of the Second Empire and classical works, more or less feeble, continued to be produced in France throughout the entire nineteenth century.

The reputation of David, however, need not depend on such misconceived derivations. His true contribution to the development of French paintings lies rather in his call to moral grandeur and artistic commitment, in his instinct towards the contemporary and in his advocacy of study from nature combined with meticulous compositional method. In the latter connection, his portraits are of enormous moment. Throughout his career he produced works in this field of unparalleled brilliance, coupling superb technique with acute sensitivity to personality and environment, for example, *Lavoisier and his Wife* (1788).

David is a difficult artist to interpret, for he is really several artists in one, yet his adaptability is masked by a deceptive simplicity of imagery. Although he appears in every general survey of French art, few satisfactory books have been devoted to him alone. Some parts of his *oeuvre* have been thoroughly examined, for example his career as a designer of festivals during the French Revolution, by D. L. Dowd in his *Pageant-Master of the Republic* (1948), but much research remains to be done on certain other aspects of him.

Paul Spencer-Longhurst

The classic French monograph, L. Hautecoeur, *Louis David* (Paris, 1954), containing only one plate, has recently been joined by the profusely illustrated *David, Témoin de son Temps* (1980) by Antoine Schnapper. The best account to date in English is Anita Brookner, *Jacques-Louis David* (1980), which contains excellent background material in addition to its other merits.

113
DAVY, Sir Humphry 1778–1829

British chemist

Davy was born in Penzance in Cornwall, then a remote part of England; his father was a wood-carver, frequently unemployed, and after his death Davy was apprenticed in 1794 to a local apothecary and surgeon. He met James Watt's son Gregory, who had come to Cornwall for his health; and through Watt and others' patronage was appointed to the Pneumatic Institution in Bristol, financed largely by the Wedgwoods, where experiments were being done on the administration of various newly discovered gases to the sick. Here Davy carried further the work of Joseph Priestley, publishing in 1800 *Researches . . . concerning nitrous oxide* in which he analysed and synthesized the various oxides of nitrogen, and described the pleasurable and anaesthetic effects of laughing gas. Largely on the strength of this work he was invited to the Royal Institution in London, newly founded for lecturing and research chiefly in applied science, where he began as assistant lecturer in 1801 and by 1802 was professor. He proved a brilliant lecturer, attracting enormous crowds; when he later lectured in Dublin there was a black market in tickets.

For work mostly on tanning and agriculture, he was elected to the Royal Society and awarded its Copley Medal; and in 1806 he turned his attention again to the relation of electricity to chemistry. In 1799 Alessandro Volta had invented the first electrical battery, and Davy had been among those who believed that a chemical reaction led to the production of electricity. In 1806 he was invited to give the Bakerian lecture to the Royal Society, and in research for this he proved that an electric current decomposes pure water into oxygen and hydrogen only. To avoid by-products, he used apparatus of silver, gold and agate. His conclusion was that chemical affinity was electrical; and indeed he found that positively charged silver was reactive, and negatively charged zinc inert – a reversal of their roles when neutral. In 1807, preparing for another Bakerian Lecture, he found that fused potash could be decomposed yielding globules of the new and highly reactive metal potassium. Davy danced about the laboratory in ecstatic delight, and made good use of this spectacular substance before his lecture audiences. He was awarded a medal for his work by Napoleon's* government, although Britain and France were at war; and in 1812 went to France to collect it.

Meanwhile, he had in 1810 succeeded in proving that chlorine, believed by A. L. Lavoisier and his successors to be an oxide, was also an element; and thereby overturned the existing theory of acidity, according to which oxygen was a necessary component of acids. Davy believed that electrical forces underlay chemical properties, and that composition was relatively unimportant; as his early work on the oxides of nitrogen, including laughing gas and the nasty brown fumes of nitrogen peroxide, also indicated. In 1812 he married Jane Apreece, a cousin of Sir Walter Scott*, and was knighted – one of very few men of science to be so honoured at this period. He also took on a bookbinder's apprentice, Michael Faraday*, as his assistant; and the three of them set off for France.

On his return, Davy was asked to do something about mine explosions, and in a typical burst of activity he invented the safety-lamp, in which the flame is surrounded by wire gauze which conducts away the heat so fast the gas mixture does not explode. In 1820 he was the obvious candidate to be President of the Royal Society; but his term of office (like his marriage) was not altogether happy, and in 1827 he became seriously ill and resigned. He died in Geneva on another continental tour, in search of fishing and health. His career shows how a highly talented man could rise to the top in Regency England; and yet his social relations were uneasy, and he was relaxed chiefly on fishing trips with a few close friends, mostly doctors or country gentlemen with an interest in science. He was the friend of Coleridge*, Southey*, Scott and Byron*, and was with Stamford Raffles the founder of the London Zoo. His work can be seen as a series of brilliant fragments; he was far from being a methodical or plodding person, and he illuminated everything he touched. To historians as to contemporaries, he remains controversial, dazzling, and enigmatic.

D. M. Knight

There is no recent full-length biography of Davy, nor an edition of his letters. Probably the best short biography is H. Hartley, *Humphry Davy* (1966). For bibliography, see J. Z. Fullmer, *Sir Humphry Davy's Published Works* (1969); and for current scholarship, see *Science and the Sons of Genius: Studies on Humphry Davy*, ed. S. Forgan (1980).

114
DEDEKIND, (Julius Wilhelm) Richard 1831–1916

German mathematician

Richard Dedekind was born in Brunswick in 1831, son of a professor of law. At first his interests lay mainly in physical science, but soon he began to gravitate towards mathematics. From the local *Gymnasium* he progressed in 1848 to the Collegium Carolinum, where Gauss* had been a student, and from thence to Göttingen University, where Gauss was now the famous professor. Gauss, in fact, examined Dedekind for his doctorate in 1852 and commended the young man's 'independence' of view.

In later years Dedekind was often referred to as 'Gauss's last student'. Richard – he had by now abandoned his first two christian names – taught at Göttingen for four years, from 1854, and later at Zürich Polytechnic. However in 1862, for reasons which are not entirely clear, he moved back to his home town of Brunswick to accept the modest post of Professor of Mathematics in Brunswick Technical High School. There he stayed for fifty years; a bachelor, he was looked after by his novelist sister Julia. He was probably the first professional mathematician to give a series of lectures (1857–8) on Galois's* theory of equations.

Although he eventually became, by reputation, one of the leading mathematicians of Europe, he never accepted a post commensurate with this fame. He led what appeared to be a contented, and was certainly a mathematically productive, life. His field of research was algebraic numbers, and he did important work in that area, particularly in developing his idea of the algebraic system known as an 'ideal'. But the contribution for which he is really famous is his theory of irrational numbers: the concept which is fundamental to modern mathematics, the 'Dedekind Cut', a way of defining numbers. Dedekind published his work on this in 1872 under the title *Stetigkeit und Irrationale Zahlen* ('Continuity and Irrational Numbers').

Dedekind's work on numbers might appear at first glance to be highly technical and of strictly limited interest even within mathematics. But to interpret Dedekind's work in this way is to take it out of context. Dedekind should be seen, rather, as the second giant in that remarkable trio whose other members were Frege* and Cantor*. These three logician-mathematicians exerted a joint influence on modes of thought which stretches far beyond the narrow confines of technical mathematics. They created, in effect, the Neoplatonic interpretation of mathematics. Frege laid the foundations of this approach with his concept of numbers as classes of classes. But that was fairly easy going. The hard problem, which had stumped the Greeks, was how to handle irrational numbers; that is, numbers like $\sqrt{2}$ which, it had been known since Pythagoras, could not be expressed as fractions, as ratios of natural numbers.

Such numbers could, of course, be expressed as decimals, but these decimals were never fully 'given', because they went on and on, to ever more decimal places, without recurring. Thus: $\sqrt{2} = 1.414213662373095 \ldots$. But how could one begin properly to *define* numbers like this which, as it were, no one could ever completely *see*, let alone write down?

Given an intellectually rigorous treatment of such irrational numbers, the Neoplatonic account of mathematics would really make sense: its ideas would begin to be taken seriously. It was Richard Dedekind who hit upon the solution, who managed to provide just such a treatment. Then Cantor added the extraordinary discovery of a kind of sense and pattern in transfinite classes: in numbers, that is, 'beyond infinity'. This was a piece of mathematical conjuring combining logic, power and mystery – or rather of a profound mystery suddenly and remarkably opened up.

That such knowledge of the *transfinite* was possible – this was at first hard to believe. It was almost transcendental. David Hilbert later declared that nothing would induce him to abandon the 'paradise which Cantor has opened to us'.

But this was only the crowning achievement of mathematical Neoplatonism: beneath this exotic theory lay the less spectacular – but more practical – edifice constructed by Frege and Dedekind. It provided an unexpected, firmly reasoned backing for all those late-nineteenth-century thinkers who were in any case temperamentally eager for a return to a broadly classical view of things. A kind of Platonic epistemology appeared to rise suddenly, like a phoenix, from the wreckage of paradoxes and contradictions which, since the time of Zeno, had laid it waste.

To see the size of the problem Dedekind solved we need to return to consider the original problem of irrational numbers. It was typical of the subtlety of early Greek mathematics that the essential relativity of numbers had been grasped by Pythagoras and his school. The Pythagoreans realized that whenever we use numbers we implicitly refer to a unit. One cannot simply say 'There are three in the room'; one has to say *what* there are three of, e.g., chairs, people, rugs, cushions. So, the Greeks reasoned, in measuring things, we are always measuring *relative* to a unit, which is in itself essentially arbitrary. This, then, was a sophisticated, logically advanced view of number. For the Pythago-

reans it provided a kind of *Weltanschaung* – ratio could be found in everything, in measurements, weights, values, volumes, liquids, speeds, even music.

This philosophical honeymoon was, however, rudely shattered when one of the brotherhood discovered that the diagonal of a unit square, which was of length $\sqrt{2}$ units, could never be expressed as a ratio of natural numbers. If $\sqrt{2}$ could be written as p/q, where p and q were natural (whole) numbers without any common factor, it would follow that $p^2 = 2q^2$, that p was even, that q was also even. This was a fundamental contradiction, because p and q by definition had no common factor. (Two even numbers would have the common factor 2.)

It is hard to realize today the effect of this discovery. The brothers were sworn to secrecy. It was expressed thus: 'That God had made a mistake in creating the universe.' Later Greek mathematicians were unable to solve the riddle, and it remained an unsolved, grumbling problem for more than two and a half millennia. It defeated Archimedes, Newton, Leibnitz, Gauss, all the mathematical giants.

Dedekind began by accepting that irrational numbers were of a different species from rational numbers, yet somehow mixed among them. (And mixed very densely, because between any two rational numbers (fractions) it was possible to find an infinite number of irrational numbers.) How could such numbers be defined?

Dedekind hit on the idea of these numbers as being merely 'cuts' or partitions of the rationals. For example, rational numbers could be divided into two sets, a set L whose squares were less that 2, and a set R whose squares were more than 2. Both L and R were well-defined; every rational number belonged to either L or R; and all the Ls were less than the Rs. Thus a cut of the set of rational numbers dividing them into L and R was thinkable, though there was no rational number which made this cut.

Like all the best ideas this was very simple: yet it did the trick. The set of all 'cuts' of the rational numbers in this sense clearly formed a well-defined set of numbers of two types: the rationals themselves and the irrationals. The new set was henceforth called the set of 'real' numbers, perhaps because this set formed the category of numbers we use to represent magnitudes in the real world.

Dedekind was also responsible for another important step in the construction of Neoplatonic mathematics. It was he who first defined an infinite set as a set which could be put into one-to-one correspondence with a part of itself. Dedekind communicated this idea to Cantor, and this was the trigger which set Cantor off on his investigation of infinity.

The two pioneers met at Interlaken in 1874, and thereafter became great friends. At the time they were both considered to be minor, way-out, unconventional, slightly eccentric nobodies. Then, gradually, the mathematical world began to wake up to the fact that Dedekind had settled a millennia-old question. Dedekind's idea graduated to the position where it was not merely part of the conventional wisdom, but became the bedrock from which any rigorous approach to higher mathematics must begin.

Meanwhile Dedekind lived on. His work became so fully accepted and so obviously essential reading for students of the subject that he became a legend decades before his death. Twelve years before his demise Teubner's *Calendar for Mathematicians* listed Dedekind as having died on 4 September 1899. Dedekind, who was actually in excellent health, was much amused at this. He wrote to the editor saying that while the day might possibly prove to be correct, the year was certainly wrong. 'According to my own memorandum,' he wrote, 'I passed this day in perfect health and enjoyed a very stimulating conversation ... with my luncheon guest and honoured friend Georg Cantor of Halle.' Dedekind died eventually on 12 February 1916, aged eighty-five.

Christopher Ormell

Works: *Gesammelte Mathematische Werke* (3 vols, 1930–2). Translations include *Essays on the Theory of Numbers* (1901) and 'Irrational Numbers', in *The World of Mathematics*, vol. I, pt III, ch. 8 (1956). A classic statement of Dedekind's theory of real numbers may be found in G. H. Hardy, *Pure Mathematics* (1908). See also: E. T. Bell, *Men of Mathematics*, vol. 2 (1937); Carl B. Boyer, *A History of Mathematics* (1968); Kurt R. Biermann, 'Richard Dedekind', in *Dictionary of Scientific Biography*, vol. IV (1971).

115
DEGAS, Edgar 1834–1917

French painter and sculptor

Edgar Degas was born in Paris, the eldest child of a banker. His grandfather, whose family bank it was, had fled to Naples during the Revolution. Degas's mother was a Creole from the United States and died when the artist was thirteen. After a sound classical education Degas enrolled as a law student in 1853 but soon abandoned his studies in favour of painting. He copied the drawings of masters like Mantegna and Leonardo in the print-room of the Bibliothèque Nationale and began to frequent the studio of an Ingres* disciple, Louis Lamothe. As a boy Degas had met Ingres who greatly impressed him and who advised him to 'Faites des lignes et des lignes.' For Ingres, as for Degas, drawing was the 'probity of art'. From 1857 until 1860 Degas spent much time in Italy where he continued to study drawing and painting. He became intimate with the group of French artists, writers and

musicians who stayed at the Villa Medicis and met great luminaries such as Gustave Moreau*, Bizet* and Edmond About. Moreau particularly influenced Degas's early preference for history painting. Examples of these early works include *The Young Spartans* (1860) and *The Daughter of Jephthah* (1861–4). In *The Young Spartans* Degas's concern with contemporary reality can be discerned in the deliberately Montmartre-style snub-noses of the children. Degas's return to Paris in 1859 decisively altered the course of his career. He became familiar with the newly fashionable Japanese prints which were available at the print-shop of Mme Desoye in the rue de Rivoli and began to form contacts with the more radical realists and future Impressionists. Men like Manet* and Renoir*, the painters, and Zola* and Duranty, the writers, became his closest intellectual companions. The masterpiece of his early career is probably the group portrait *The Belleli Family* (1860–2), in which one can see his various interests perfectly balanced. The drawing is classically cool and precise; the grouping of the figures against the rectangles of the background and the slight tensions between the poses of the figures show an interest in Japanese composition, as does the use of the patterned wallpaper; and the youngest girl's left leg 'replaced' as it were by the legs of the chair she is sitting on reveals Degas's slightly bleak humour and his sense of the artificiality of his work. During 1860s Degas began to draw and paint race-horses, theatre scenes and ballet dancers. In 1870, during the Franco-Prussian War, Degas served in the Garde Nationale and may have injured his eyesight while sleeping out in the cold. In 1872–3 he visited his mother's home town of New Orleans in America and was greatly exhilarated by the change of culture. His *Cotton Market* (1873) shows his increasing concern for the canons of naturalism and his great skill with a limited palette. In 1874 his father died and he was forced to sell some of his now large drawings collection to help the family. It was during this year that he played a decisive part in organizing the first Impressionist exhibition, held at the old studio of the photographer Nadar. Degas was not an Impressionist *pur sang* for, although he was friendly with Monet*, Renoir and others, he believed deeply in the virtues of fine draughtsmanship and in the necessity for deliberated composition. He preferred artificial to natural light and was more interested in the movement of the human figure than in landscape or *plein air* effects. Very late in his life he said, 'If I were the government I would have a company of police watching out for men who paint landscapes from nature', adding good-humouredly that his friend Renoir could do as he wished. Degas, however, contributed many works to all the remaining Impressionist shows, including decorated fans and sculpture. His later life was spent producing an enormous amount of work. He became interested in photography which he used as an aid in composition and was particularly fascinated by the work of Muybridge whose chronophotography allowed one to catch the progressive changes of movement in a human body performing an action. This was of great use to Degas in his studies of dancers and horses. Degas was also a remarkable technical innovator and may be said to have radically expanded the possibilities of the graphic arts. Like a number of artists often dubbed 'conservative' he believed that a very great part of the artist's power lay in his craft knowledge and dedication to study. He told Vuillard*, 'A painting is an artificial work existing outside nature and it requires as much cunning as the perpetration of a crime.' In 1887 he travelled in Spain and Morocco. In the 1890s, although he drew and painted (often using curious techniques like pastel brushed with hot water on to the paper), his eyesight was deteriorating seriously and he executed more sculptures, in wax and plaster, which were easier for him to work. He continued to extend his superb collection of art. He virtually stopped work in 1908 and died in Paris in 1917. He had told a friend to avoid making a long oration at his funeral and that 'You might just say he loved drawing'.

Degas's influence on the visual arts has been very great. He brought to perfection the possibilities of the naturalist aesthetic while retaining those traditional elements of painting he so greatly valued. He sought an art which combined rigorous drawing with realist subject matter. His style is as greatly informed by a study of Titian and Delacroix* as it is by a temperamental preference for Ingres and Mantegna; as much by Leonardo's observation of surface as by the snapshot of photography and Duranty's realist credo. Although he was a political conservative, being an anti-Dreyfusard and holding a dandyish contempt for the masses, he was concerned with men and women in their social aspect. His influence on painters like Sickert*, Gauguin*, Toulouse-Lautrec*, Bonnard, Vuillard and Picasso is perhaps incalculable. His celibacy and utter dedication to his art, his prizing of the intellect and inherited sensibility and taste, were the qualities that drew the poet Valéry to him. In his story *An Evening with Monsieur Teste* Valéry tells of an aloof and lonely figure who observes the audience at the opera with a visionary precision and control and whose personal habits are few and astringent. He has Leonardo's intellect and Mallarmé's* remote imagination. Monsieur Teste was in part Valéry's idealized perception of Degas's mind itself.

Richard Humphrys

See: *Lettres de Degas*, ed. M. Guérin (1945, trans. 1947); John Rewald, *Degas' Sculpture: The Complete Works* (1956); J. Adhémar and F. Cachin, *Edgar Degas: Gravures et Monotypes* (Paris, 1973); *Notebooks of Degas*, ed. T. Reff (2 vols, 1976); T. Reff, *Degas: The Artist's Mind* (1976).

116
DELACROIX, Eugène 1798–1863

French painter

Delacroix is regarded as the leading painter of the Romantic movement in France, and in his own lifetime he was typed as a rebel. His violent subjects and vigorous technique shocked the critics and he was excluded from the Institut until 1857, when at the seventh attempt he was finally admitted. Throughout his life he was seen as the opponent of Ingres*, the acknowledged leader of the Classical school. But Delacroix repudiated his own reputation and claimed to follow in the tradition of the great masters of the Renaissance and the seventeenth century. He venerated Raphael, Michelangelo, Titian and Correggio, and the influence of Rubens runs throughout his work. In later life, in particular, he presented himself as a man of conservative tastes, and the *Journal* which he kept from 1822 until his death confirms his preference for classical art over the painting and literature of his own day.

Delacroix was born into a well-to-do family of good standing in French Empire society. He had a thorough education and, at the suggestion of his uncle, the painter Henri-François Riesener, entered the studio of Pierre-Narcisse Guérin in 1815. There he befriended the slightly older Géricault*, whose work was to have a profound effect on him. In 1822 Delacroix exhibited at the Salon for the first time. The picture, *Dante and Virgil crossing the Styx*, brought critical acclaim and was purchased by the state. Delacroix's reputation was made and he thereafter appeared regularly at the Salon. The movement and colour of his work was seen as a riposte to the Neoclassical school. In 1824 his rivalry with Ingres began, when they both exhibited important works: Ingres his *Vow of Louis XIII*, a devout picture owing much to Raphael and Philippe de Champaigne, and Delacroix his *Massacres at Chios*, a recent incident drawn from the Greek War of Independence, and treated in a manner strongly influenced by Géricault and the older Baron Gros. Delacroix's painting caused a stir because of its modern subject and its energetic treatment. It is said that at the last minute he retouched much of the sky after seeing Constable's* *The Haywain*, also on exhibition at the Salon.

English art and literature provided an inspiration for Delacroix which other painters still sought in Italy. He was a friend of Bonington and in 1825 visited England and met Sir Thomas Lawrence*. Such works as *The Execution of Marino Faliero* (1826) and the *Portrait of Baron Schwiter* (1826–30), painted on his return, show Lawrence's influence in their colouring and the liquid handling of the paint. Many of his subjects, too, Delacroix derived from British writers, notably Byron*, Walter Scott*, and Shakespeare, and over the next twenty years he was to produce paintings and lithographs after *Hamlet*. He also produced a series of lithographs based on Goethe's* *Faust*, a favourite theme with French artists. The subject of his Salon exhibit of 1827, a massive painting of *The Death of Sardanapalus*, derives from a play by Byron, and the sadism and eroticism of the theme – the slaughter of the oriental king's horses and concubines at his own command – shocked the French public. Delacroix was reprimanded by the Superintendent of Fine Arts and warned that if he failed to change his ways he would receive no official support. The picture is turbulent, chaotic and colourful, and contravenes all the canons of classical art. While he did subsequently choose less *risqué* themes, Delacroix could not moderate his style and it continued until his death to earn him official disapprobation.

The Revolution of 1830 brought with it a change of administration, and Delacroix's painting of *Liberty leading the People* was bought by the state, but, as a potentially subversive image, was never afterwards exhibited. In 1832 Delacroix travelled to Morocco and Algeria as attaché to a diplomatic mission. He brought back seven albums of watercolours and drawings which are brilliantly concise and evocative. In Morocco Delacroix felt he had discovered the true life-style of the ancients, natural, noble and violent, and he drew upon his memories for the subjects of pictures for the rest of his life. The paintings he produced soon after his return, *Women of Algiers* (1834) and *The Jewish Wedding* (1837), are amongst his greatest in their brilliant use of colour and in the re-creation of the exoticism of the Arab world. As time went on his African paintings were to grow less concrete and more purely imaginative, a retreat into a world of unbridled passion that he valued above the bourgeois society of Paris.

On his return to Paris, Delacroix continued to paint large canvases for the Salon, such as *The Return of Columbus from the New World* (1839), *The Entry of the Crusaders into Constantinople* (1840) and *The Justice of Trajan* (1840). As if designed to show an orthodox talent, the subjects are dignified episodes from classical and medieval history. Delacroix also found favour with the government of Louis-Philippe. Adolphe Thiers, who had favourably greeted *Dante and Virgil* in 1822, now directed important commissions his way. There are good reasons for thinking that Delacroix's real father was in fact the statesman, Talleyrand, and, if true, this may account for his success in the face of academic disapproval. His first large-scale commission was for the decoration of the Salon du Roi and library of the Chamber of Deputies in the Palais Bourbon (1833–47). It was followed by the library of the Palais de Luxembourg (1840–7) and the ceilings of the Galerie d'Apollon in the Louvre (1850–1) and the Salon de la Paix in the Hôtel de Ville (1852–3; destroyed in 1871).

Delacroix gave great thought to the philosophical programmes of his mural decorations. They are alle-gorical in concept, and heroes of history and mythology are used to stand for noble virtues. The Palais Bourbon library, for example, has two half-domes representing peace and war, the one showing *Orpheus civilizing the Greeks*, the other *Attila and his Barbarians trampling Italy and the Arts*, with, in between, five ceiling bays devoted to science, philosophy, legislation, theology and poetry. His treatment is inspired by the great decorative painters of the past, Raphael, Michelangelo and Rubens, but the mood is modern. Like all Delacroix's work, his decorations have a nervous, almost frenetic energy, and reflect a belief in the decadence of modern civilization.

As he grew older, so Delacroix became more pessimistic. He never married and led an increasingly isolated existence, supported by his housekeeper Jenny Le Guillou and maintaining contacts with just a few close friends, amongst them George Sand* and Dumas *père*. But as he retired from society, so began Baudelaire's* championship of his art in Salon reviews and articles, which consecrated Delacroix's reputation as the supreme poet of Romanticism. His late work is a private, imaginative outpouring. It includes lion hunts, battles, African scenes, subjects from Byron, Shakespeare and the lives of artists, and religious themes – *Daniel in the Lion's Den*, *The Martyrdom of St Stephen*, *Christ on the Sea of Galilee*, *The Crucifixion* and *The Entombment* – into which he projects his own loneliness and suffering. At his last Salon, in 1859, he exhibited *Ovid among the Scythians* which shows the exiled Roman poet in a distant wilderness, surrounded by uncomprehending barbarians – and it is moving chiefly because it speaks of the plight of Delacroix, the painter.

Delacroix's last major work was the decoration of the Chapel of the Holy Angels in the Church of St Sulpice, Paris. The project took six years to execute, and, by the time it was finished in 1862, his health was ruined. He died a year later. In certain respects the chapel is his most radical work. It shows on one wall *Jacob wrestling with the Angel*, and on the opposite wall *The Expulsion of Heliodorus from the Temple*, with *Michael the Archangel Vanquishing the Devil* on the ceiling. Here Delacroix's technique is carried to its extreme, with bright strokes and dabs of colour enlivening the shadows and creating a rich, scintillating harmony.

Delacroix had few pupils and, by the time of his death, his mode of painting with themes taken from history, mythology and literature was all but overtaken by the vogue for naturalism. The Symbolists, and above all Gustave Moreau*, certainly benefited from his example but the Impressionists, too, confessed a great debt to him. Renoir's* odalisques owe as much to Delacroix as to Ingres, but it was chiefly in his free execution and bold use of colour that Delacroix demonstrated to Manet* and the Impressionist circle where an answer to the outworn conventions of the academic masters might be found.

Michael Wilson

See: *Journal de Eugène Delacroix* ed. André Joulin (3 vols. 1932); *Correspondance générale* (5 vols 1936–8). See also: Charles Baudelaire, *Delacroix: His Life and Work* (trans 1947); Raymond Escholier, *Delacroix: Peintre, graveur, écrivain* (3 vols 1926–9); Lee Johnson, *Delacroix* (1963); George P. Mras, *Eugène Delacroix's Theory of Art* (1966); Frank Anderson Trapp, *The Attounment of Delacroix* (1971).

117

DE MAISTRE, Joseph 1753–1821

French writer

In his life and work Joseph de Maistre embodies, more than any other, the spirit of reaction against the French Revolution which dominated Catholic and conservative political thought in continental Europe throughout the nineteenth century. A master of striking imagery his powers of argument commanded the respect of many who were far from sharing his political outlook. He was born in Savoy, the son of a judge, and followed his father into the magistracy. Savoy was ruled by the King of Sardinia and when the armies of revolutionary France invaded in 1792 de Maistre chose the path of exile. He lived four years in Lausanne where he wrote and published his *Considerations on France* (*Considérations sur la France*, 1796), a fierce attack on the French Revolution and its works which won him a reputation as a powerful writer. These years also saw the composition of his *Study on Sovereignty* (*Étude sur la Souveraineté*, 1870), a more systematic work which, like so many of de Maistre's writings, was only published long after his death. In 1802 he was appointed Sardinian representative in St Petersburg where he remained for fourteen years. This Russian period was the most intellectually productive of his life. A succession of published and unpublished works poured from his pen including the highly original *St Petersburg Dialogues* (*Les Soirées de Saint-Petersbourg*, 1821).

So radical was de Maistre's opposition to the revolution that when monarchical restoration came in 1814–15 he found himself rejected by the very sovereigns he had worked so hard to restore. The difference in attitude between de Maistre and the regime of Louis XVIII is brought out well in a letter written in 1815:

The problem being raised on every side is this: to find the means of re-establishing order while interfering the least possible with the revolutionaries and their acts, while the real problem is on the contrary: to find the means of destroying the revolutionaries and their acts, as thoroughly as possible, without exposing the legitimate sovereignties.

Too royalist for the king, de Maistre found that he was too ultramontane for the pope who refused the dedication of his study *Du Pape*.

From the beginning there are two shaping elements in de Maistre's thought: a deep-rooted suspicion of the rationalism and individualism of the Enlightenment and an unshakable belief in the existence of God. He combines an empirically grounded pessimism concerning the likely short term course of events with a cosmic optimism founded in belief in divine providence. Providence, though only explicable in terms of divine will, is not incomprehensible to man. Its logic is the logic of God and not that of man but events are patterned in ways men can grasp. The justification of their course is theological yet men are capable of discerning the regularities which the world reveals. As in the work of his contemporary Louis de Bonald, belief in the reality of the Creator reinforces the suspicion that the created world, social and political as well as natural, is subject to certain immutable laws from which men stray at their peril. This emphasis on the regularity of social phenomena exerted a considerable influence on the development of sociology through the work of Auguste Comte* who was an admirer of de Maistre's writings.

De Maistre's opposition to the form taken by the Restoration settlement was based in a positive belief in the value of certain forms of government and an acute understanding of the support such systems need in the realm of ideas and the structure of social relations. His theory of sovereignty remains a challenge to all liberal and democratic conceptions of political power as something which can be limited and even exercised by the majority of a population. His work on the historical roots of effective political institutions ranks with that of Edmund Burke as a reproach to every idea that sound institutions can be designed by legislators at will. De Maistre's works retain their interest because he was not content to answer revolutionary ideas on the level of polemic but sought to ground his own in a profound and disturbing analysis of man's nature and place in the universe. The regimes for which he fought have passed into history but the problem of political order with which he grappled throughout his life remains recognizably the same.

David J. Levy

Jack Lively's anthology, *The Works of Joseph de Maistre* (1965), provides an excellent selection from his writings for the English-speaking reader.

118

DE QUINCEY, Thomas 1785–1859

British essayist

Thomas De Quincey was born in Manchester into a prosperous middle-class family. The early period of his life is fitfully described in his *Autobiographic Sketches* (almost everything that De Quincey wrote was for magazine publication; he himself superintended the first collected edition of his work in book form, 1853–60, but there were later and fuller editions published in England and America). He ran away from Manchester Grammar School at the age of seventeen, as he recounts in his most famous book *Confessions of an English Opium Eater* (1822, revised 1856), led a nomadic existence in Wales and then in London. It was there in 1804 on a visit from Oxford University, to which he had gone as an undergraduate in the previous year, that he first took opium – that 'dread agent of unimaginable pleasure and pain' – as a remedy for neuralgia. For many years afterwards he was intermittently dependent on the drug. Although De Quincey rhapsodizes over the 'infinite repose' and intense imaginative experiences provided by opium, then easily and legally available as a medical panacea, the defensive tone of some of his writing on the subject (see, for example, his attack on fellow addict Coleridge* at the beginning of the *Confessions*) and his attempts to free himself from the addiction show his awareness of its perilous glamour. In 1809 De Quincey moved to the Lake District, drawn there partly by the presence of Wordsworth* whom he had always idolized at a distance. The relationship between hero and worshipper, described after it had cooled in a series of articles for Tait's *Edinburgh Magazine*, forms one of the most coherent and continous elements in De Quincey's fragmented output. It was also in the Lake District that De Quincey married, fathering a large family. Later they moved to Edinburgh where the essayist, haunted by debt, wrote with his furious facility for various journals and where he died in 1859.

In the *Confessions* De Quincey describes his considerable conversational powers as deriving from 'a prodigious memory', 'an inexhaustible fertility of topics' and a capacity for detecting remote analogies, as well as 'a prematurely awakened sense of *art*' applied to conversation'. All these attributes are evident in his writing which has the zigzag undisciplined and intimate quality of good talk. In the story of his friendship with Wordsworth he did not restrict himself to an admiring account of the poet's work but included a miscellany of information on, say, the poet's legs – 'certainly not ornamental' – or Dorothy Wordsworth's stutter. This sort of gossipy aside coexists with philosophical discussion, critical commentary, formal biography and the manic exactitude De Quincey could display, especially in his rambling footnotes. Because he used the essay form and because he wrote rapidly his work is necessarily episodic, connected not 'by ropes and cables but by threads of aerial gossamer'. De Quincey could not resist the trail of a digression wrapped within a digression and this sometimes makes for a clumsy structure in his writing but it does not preclude a narrative and didactic talent which enables him to explore entertainingly the ramifications of a story or a theory. To the commonplace De Quincey brought an expansive elaborate style: see the mock-heroic description of childhood fights in the chapter 'Introduction to the World of Strife' in his *Autobiographic Sketches*. Any material brought under his inquisitive eye – for instance, the Irish uprisings of 1798 or the encounter of one of his brothers with a ghost in the Galapagos Islands – he treated lucidly and analytically. This capacity for introspection and analysis, coupled with his nervy sensibility and drug-taking produced the visionary rhetoric which captures the waking dreams where the author moves passively in a landscape of grand tranquillity or horror (the last section of the *Confessions*, the section 'Levana and Our Ladies of Sorrow' in *Suspiria de Profundis*, 1849, the essay *The English Mail Coach*). It is a paradox of De Quincey's work that, although little of himself is revealed directly in his writings, his gaze being turned outward to the world or inward to the dark and impersonal interior of dreams, all his work is expressive of an inquiring and brilliantly intelligent stylist.

Philip Gooden

De Quincey's *Collected Writings* were published in 14 vols (1896–7). These are supplemented by *The Uncollected Writings*, ed. James Hogg (2 vols, 1890), and *The Posthumous Works*, ed. Alexander H. Japp (2 vols, 1891–3). See: Alethea Hayter, *Opium and the Romantic Imagination* (1968); Grevel Lindop, *The Opium Eater, A Life of Thomas De Quincey* (1981).

119

DICKENS, Charles John Huffam 1812–70

British novelist

Dickens's lengthy career as an author, during all of which he manifestly was at the top of the tree, occupied the middle third of the nineteenth century – from 1836–7 when *Pickwick Papers* (his first novel and, as many contemporaries thought, his best) became a bestseller of unprecedented popularity and established him immediately as a literary eminence, to 1870 when he died suddenly while writing *Edwin Drood*. Thus, as Humphry House remarked, 'his writing life coincided almost exactly with the rule of the Ten-Pound Householders', that is, between the Reform Acts of 1832 and 1867 (*The*

Dickens World, 1941), and many contemporaries saw him as the product, and the voice, of this period of reform. Immediately before becoming a full-time novelist, he had been on the staff of the Benthamite* *Morning Chronicle*, and though he was never an avowed Utilitarian, or Philosophical Radical – 'Isms!' he once exclaimed: 'oh Heaven for a world without an *ism*' – his critique of Victorian society and its institutions owed something to that intellectual tradition. Not, of course, that his significance was only, or even primarily, political. He was a prolific creator of characters, a compelling narrator, the greatest of English humorists, a master of pathos, a highly original stylist, and a wide-ranging depictor of the urban life of his age: and in all these respects he had a large influence. Outside his fiction, he was brilliantly and energetically active in many areas, as a magazine editor and journalist, an amateur actor, a remarkable solo recitalist, an eloquent public speaker, and a philanthropist.

Lower-middle-class in origins (his father was a Royal Navy pay-clerk), he experienced in his childhood a sudden and painful though impermanent descent into the working class when, in 1824, his father's financial ineptitude landed the family in bankruptcy and himself in jail. Charles, who had ceased attending school, was sent to work in a bottling warehouse. As his intimate friend and official biographer John Forster commented, the 'very poor and unprosperous' in his novels 'were not his clients whose cause he pleaded with such pathos and humour . . . . but in some sort his very self.' The boy hero of his second novel *Oliver Twist* (1837–9) was the first of a series of lost, bewildered and oppressed children in his fiction, inspired by this experience. He indeed virtually introduced the child, the child's-eye view upon life, and the school into English fiction, and in this, as in much else, was soon followed and imitated. Oliver had been born in a workhouse, Dickens thus creating an opportunity to attack the controversial Poor Law Amendment Act (1834). Such topicality, and this concern with social institutions, were to be characteristic of his fiction, where characters are often seen in relation to institutions: schools, prisons, the churches, the money market, the law courts, the civil service, and officialdom in general.

Oliver is born in the provinces and comes to and stays in London: so do many Dickens heroes, who thus repeat the pattern of his own life. (Born in Portsmouth and raised mostly in Chatham, he moved finally to London when aged ten.) This immigration from the country to the large town or the metropolis was moreover a conspicuous feature of Britain at this time; as the 1851 Census showed, the majority of people now lived in large towns, for the first time in history. 'Dickens describes London like a special correspondent for posterity,' observed Walter Bagehot* in 1858. London was much the most frequent, and successful, setting for his fiction; his presentation of the countryside is perfunctory, but he writes with verve about some overseas environments, the America of *Martin Chuzzlewit* (1843–4) for instance, or the Italy of *Little Dorrit* (1855–7). Eminently he was the novelist of urban experience, to a degree and with a density achieved by no predecessor. London specially suited his genius, being the country's political, commercial, administrative and artistic centre, and presenting conspicuously such extreme contrasts between affluence and destitution, power and powerlessness, and containing both cosy and quaint neighbourhoods and the possibility of urban *anomie*. He was at his most powerful as an explorer of urbanism in certain novels of his maturity: *Bleak House* (1852–3), *Little Dorrit* and *Our Mutual Friend* (1864–5). He is interesting though less knowledgeable and effective on the purely industrial town, in *Hard Times* (1854) and incidentally elsewhere.

From the start, he offered in every novel a variety of contents. Comedy, including the farcical, was prominent in *Pickwick*, and is never absent thereafter, though later is is less pervasive: and its narrative tone, which is rarely self-effacing, is most characteristically comic or ironic. Pathos, often centring on a child or some other disadvantaged or easily oppressible character, provided an important element in his original popularity, though it was less admired and less conspicuous later. Violence, crime, murder, hidden secrets and skulduggery added excitement and suspense to his narratives, and gave opportunities for him to present human nature in its most extreme forms. (Dickens was much concerned with, and perceptive about, criminal psychology, mental disturbance, and madness, as well as with the more common reaches of individual and social behaviour.) Most of his novels refer to, or have as a prominent subject, contemporary political or social issues, generally treated from a reformist standpoint, though on some issues, such as 'the Woman Question' then emerging, he was conservative or retrograde. Very young when he achieved fame, he developed greatly in technique and in intellectual command of the large swathe of society and emotionally varied materials which, ambitiously, he took as his province. Love and marriage are generally less central and less impressive in his novels than in most fiction, but are more prominent in his two first-person (and partly autobiographical) novels *David Copperfield* (1849–50) and *Great Expectations* (1860–1).

The wide diffusion of his novels to a heterogeneous audience was much assisted by their all being serialized. They were thus bought by many who could never have afforded the lump-sum purchase of a hardback book, and they became a regular topic for conversation over a lengthy period. (The impact of radio and television series and serials presents obvious analogies.) 'His current serial was really a topic of the day; it seemed something almost akin to politics and news – as if it belonged not so much to literature as to events'

(*Daily Telegraph*, 18 June 1872). The publishers of *Pickwick* created what remained Dickens's favourite serial form: twenty monthly numbers, each with two illustrations – and these illustrations, mostly by 'Phiz' (Hablot Browne), were, and remain, important in providing unforgettable visual images of his people and places. This serial pattern was much imitated, as was Dickens's invention of the Christmas book with *A Christmas Carol* (1843); he was an influential pioneer in the forms, as well as the content, of popular literature, as Robert L. Patten (cited below) most amply demonstrates. Similarly his giving public readings from his works, from 1853, led to a vogue for such author-recitals.

His attachment to Christmas, evident throughout his career, was notable and significant. In Christmas are concentrated many of his fondest tastes and beliefs: the stress upon family and the hearth, and the special care for children's happiness; simple unsophisticated good living and jollity; benevolence and generosity; hope, in a dark world; a stress on what unites rather than distinguishes people (for all classes celebrate Christmas in similar ways). His special feeling for Christmas, as novelist, magazine editor, public reader, and paterfamilias, is a prime instance of his being the spokesman for a widespread popular sentiment or conviction. (Anthony Trollope* nicknamed him, with unkindly intent, 'Mr Popular Sentiment', in *The Warden*, 1855). As indeed his vast – and soon international – popularity suggests, his artistic temperament was far from that of an outsider or a crier in the wilderness. In denouncing social evils, he was articulating the conscience of his times, but rather as a member of a loyal opposition than as a rebel or revolutionary: and the shortcomings of his sympathies corresponded to common English prejudices – against blacks, for instance, or Jews, or the Irish, or Roman Catholicism.

Shortly before his death, he had an audience with Queen Victoria*. A courtier briefed her for this meeting with 'the author whose name will hereafter be closely associated with the Victorian era' – a sound forecast, for his novels take in so many of the central preoccupations of the times that 'Dickens's England' remains a meaningful concept. Queen Victoria would like him, this courtier advised: 'he, too, has the most anxious desire to raise what we call "the lower classes"; and would sympathize with Your Majesty in many of the Queen's views and aspirations.' She found it so, and on his death wrote in her diary: 'He is a very great loss. He had a large, loving mind and the strongest sympathy with the poorer classes. He felt sure that a better feeling, and much greater union of classes would take place in time. And I pray earnestly it may.' Dickens was not so 'safe' or conformist as this community of outlook with his queen might suggest, but this anecdote better suggests his standpoint than some more exciting recent views represented by the influential Edmund Wilson's assertion that 'Of all the great Victorian writers, he was probably the most antagonistic to the Victorian Age itself' (*The Wound and the Bow*, 1941) – unless Wilson was implying that no great Victorian authors were much at odds with their age. Without insincerity, Dickens gave his large public much what it wanted, both in entertainment and literary satisfactions, and in eloquent and impatient reformism. His enormous literary skills and his standing as a much-loved as well as admired personality gave wide currency, and weight, to his ideas, which in general were not far in advance of public opinion. Certainly he was credited with great influence: 'pen in hand, he wielded a power superior to that of a whole House of Commons,' wrote one obituarist, somewhat extravagantly; 'In his own inimitable way,' wrote the radical publicist Charles Knight, 'he has perhaps done more to expose wrong and injustice and to improve society socially and morally than any other worker or writer of the present century.'

To adapt a line of Wordsworth's*: 'He gave them eyes, he gave them ears', making the reading public more vividly aware of the world – including its submerged tenth – around them; imposing upon them, indeed, a new way of seeing, hearing and interpreting. But, very sensitive visually and aurally, and widely exploratory in his range of perception, his was a highly imaginative, not merely a recording, mind. Characteristically he spoke of his mind's taking 'a *fanciful* photograph' of a scene; his natural tendency was thus to yoke the imaginative with the literal, for example, demanding 'a little standing-room for Queen Mab's Chariot among the Steam Engines', or 'blessing the South-Eastern Railway Company for realising the Arabian Nights in these prose days' (when railway speed had a magic-carpet effect). His art straddled, and at its best uniquely combined, the journalistic and the poetic; his narrative prose was much more intense and more highly metaphoric than any of his predecessors' in the novel. Not only in content and in reformist rhetoric but, more fundamentally, in vision and in imaginative construction, he enlarged the forms of fiction and the sensuous capacities of English prose. His influence was apparent in Russian and French as well as in Anglo-Saxon fiction: see George Ford, *Dickens and his Readers* (1955) and *Dickens and Fame* (centenary issue of *The Dickensian*, 1970). As House concluded his seminal study *The Dickens World*: 'he made out of Victorian England a complete world, with a life and vigour and idiom of its own, quite unlike any other world there has ever been'.

Philip Collins

Dickens's novels, much reprinted and widely translated, are most conveniently available in trustworthy annotated form in the Penguin English Library (1966–78). Five novels have so far appeared in the textually authoritative Clarendon Press

Dickens (1966–). The Clarendon Press also publishes the scholarly editions of his *Speeches*, ed. K. J. Fielding (1960), *Letters*, ed. Madeline House *et al.* (from 1965), and *Public Readings*, ed. Philip Collins (1975). His plays and poems, few in number, are of negligible interest, but his essays are often excellent and very relevant to his fiction: *Reprinted Pieces* (1858), *The Uncommercial Traveller* (1861, 1868, 1875), *Miscellaneous Papers*, ed. B. W. Matz (1908), all reprinted later. See: John Forster, *Life of Dickens* (1872–4), the official biography, often reprinted; G. K. Chesterton, *Charles Dickens* (1906); Edgar Johnson, *Charles Dickens: his Tragedy and Triumph* (1952), the standard biography; John Butt and Kathleen Tillotson, *Dickens at Work* (1957); J. Hillis Miller, *Charles Dickens: the World of his Novels* (1958); Angus Wilson, *The World of Charles Dickens* (1970); F. R. and Q. D. Leavis, *Dickens the Novelist* (1971); *Dickens: the Critical Heritage*, ed. Philip Collins (1971): Robert L. Patten, *Charles Dickens and his Publishers* (1978).

120

DICKINSON, Emily 1830–86

US poet

Emily Dickinson and Walt Whitman*, the two greatest nineteenth-century American poets, were contemporaries who appear not to have read each other's work. Both rebelled successfully against the limited subject matter and traditional form of poetry in their society, but they used almost diametrically opposed methods. Whitman dilated his ego into a national and universal self, embracing a potentially hostile audience with his long, free-verse poems. Dickinson's highly condensed, often ironic first person lyrics set forth alternately exuberant, tormented and fragmented selves. She deliberately turned her back on a public that encouraged even more insipid 'Dimity Convictions' (poem 401) of its 'refined' 'Brittle' 'Gentlewomen'. 'Civilization—spurns—the Leopard!/Was the Leopard—bold?' she asked sarcastically (492). Knowing that 'Much Madness is Divinest Sense' (435), Dickinson damned the 'majority':

> Assent—and you are Sane—
> Demur—you're straightway dangerous—
> And handled with a Chain—

Of the more than 1700 lyrics that Dickinson wrote (some 500 or so during 1862–3) she published only seven, anonymously, during her lifetime; many of her poems were hardly 'written' at all – inscribed on scraps of paper or bound into eight-poem packets. In 1890 a much-acclaimed selection of Dickinson's poems appeared, edited and regularized by Mabel Todd and

Col. T. W. Higginson, a minister, Civil War hero, and the 'Preceptor' who had advised Dickinson in 1862 to 'delay' publishing what he felt to be her 'spasmodic' verse.

Only with T. H. Johnson's *Complete Poems* (1955) were Dickinson's poems printed as they were written, with irregular rhythms, slant rhymes, capitalization and, most valuably, with the dashes which give even her shortest lines a floating, resonant quality. Dickinson's rich, elliptical letters first appeared in 1958. Thus Dickinson's reputation, like Herman Melville's*, has relied upon twentieth-century assessments; neglect during her lifetime has made her in effect a modern poet. Since Dickinson is the most important American woman poet, her deliberate testing of the range and intensity available to a female poetic have made her work a challenge to the critic and an inspiration and warning to the poet; her influence, unmistakable in the work of Theodore Roethke and Sylvia Plath, increases annually as critical studies based on her complete works appear.

Since Dickinson almost never titled or dated her poems, Johnson's chronological numbering, based upon internal evidences and handwriting, is necessarily conjectural. Nevertheless it is possible to distinguish three overlapping phases in Dickinson's work. First was a celebratory phase, influenced by Ralph Waldo Emerson*, in which Dickinson's voice is often an Emersonian imperial self, or a joyous child in a nature where 'Apprehensions—are God's introductions—/To be hallowed—accordingly—' (797). A second, more psychological phase in the early to mid-1860s depicted torment, estrangement, and occasional passionate affirmation. In a third phase from the late 1860s to Dickinson's death in 1886, earlier themes were expressed more epigrammatically, with a stable and often scathing irony: 'Far from Love the Heavenly Father/Leads the Chosen Child' (1021).

Emily Dickinson grew up in western Massachusetts as part of the New England professional, political and intellectual elite. Her lawyer father, treasurer of Amherst College and member of the US House of Representatives, dominated an oppressively closely knit family, with an invalid wife and two daughters, Emily and Lavinia, who never married. Emily Dickinson's beloved brother Austin, also a lawyer, lived next door with his vivacious wife Sue; when Emerson lectured at Amherst in 1858, he stayed with Austin and Sue (but Emily did not attend the lecture). For a woman of her day, Emily Dickinson had an excellent education, first at Amherst Academy, then at the Mount Holyoke Seminary (later College), where she cut short her studies after a year to return to the parental home where she lived for the rest of her life. As Dickinson's confident poetic allusions to astronomy, botany and geology show, she was a serious student of the natural sciences, influenced by the Amherst scientist Edward Hitchcock's view of 'natural language' as well as by Emerson's more ecstatic celebration of the legible 'hieroglyphic' of experience and nature. Dickinson once remarked that she did not understand why it should be necessary to read anyone but Shakespeare, but aside from Shakespeare, the pervasive Emerson, and the inevitable – and deeply absorbed – Bible, she read and used contemporary writers such as George Eliot* (her poetry as well as her novels), Robert* and Elizabeth Barrett Browning*, the Brontë sisters*, and Henry Wadsworth Longfellow* (for his novel *Kavanagh* as much as for his poetry).

Even when Dickinson's poems doubt her personal worthiness, they never question her intellectual powers or fear her ability to express herself. Dickinson's notorious reclusiveness freed her from conformist demands imposed by her class, sex and religion; it was a strategy as well as a fate. 'The Soul selects her own society/Then—shuts the Door—' (303). In 1862-3 Dickinson appears to have suffered a severe crisis of identity which her poetry both expressed and to some extent probably healed; she often uses writing and speech as metaphors for life, while erasure and silence signify death, loss, or destruction of self. 'They shut me up in Prose,' poem 613 recounts, 'As when a little girl/They put me in the closet—/Because they liked me "still"—'. But, the poem continues, she has 'abolished' her captivity. Many poems and the famous 'Master' letters, addressed to an unknown recipient (possibly Rev. Samuel Bowles) set love next to a self-annihilating despair. 'She dealt her pretty words like Blakes,' Dickinson wrote (479), probably referring to her insensitive sister-in-law.

Yet Dickinson's love poems, like her many poems on the 'flood subject' death, make joy or sorrow secondary to sheer intensity of experience. 'I like a look of Agony,/Because I know it's true—' (241). But she asserts even more strongly in 'Wild Nights—Wild Nights!' (249) that 'Were I thee/Wild Nights should be/Our luxury!' Dickinson was aware that she used emotion, even victimization, to generate her power. 'Power is only Pain—/Stranded, thro' Discipline' (252). In one remarkable poem she wrote, 'My life had stood a loaded gun' until 'The Owner passed—identified—/And carried, me away—!. Although now 'I speak for him', her lover will die some day. The 'Vesuvian' poet, however, is immortal: 'For I have but the power to kill/Without—the power to die—' (754). Dickinson's greatest terror is of 'Bandaged Moments' when the Soul is 'too appalled to stir' and submits to the caress of 'Goblin' 'Horrors' (512). Repression, substitution or 'balm' only exacerbate anguish:

To fill a Gap
Insert the Thing that caused it—
Block it up
With Other—and 'twill yawn the more—

You cannot solder an Abyss
With Air (546).

Dickinson is sometimes carelessly called a Puritan poet; aside from her loathing of the self-proclaimed Elect or 'meek members of the Resurrection' (216) and her distaste for the 'Eclipse . . . whom they call their "Father" ', (letter to Higginson, 1862), Dickinson never accepted original sin and was repelled by the concept of Heaven as a 'great schoolroom in the sky' – though of course she did find it necessary to attack these concepts in quatrains parodic of the Bay Psalm Book and sermon citation. Dickinson's Puritan inheritance shows up positively in her concentration on joy in experience of the created world, in her bouts of self-denial, and in her love of dialectic – whose terms she characteristically inverts in mid-poem.

The Dickinsonian speaker witnesses the present moment: noon, sunset, ecstasy, death, recognition. Even Dickinson's shortest poems employ several image systems; she is anti-Platonic; her metaphors function as facets of an action defined by the poem's 'circuit'. Her condensed, often ambiguous syntax, riddling word plays, omissions and shifting emblems all embody the flux of complex processes which were her great subjects. More deeply even perhaps than Whitman (because she dealt with less tractable material), Dickinson was a poet of experience.

Helen McNeil

See: Richard B. Sewall, *Emily Dickinson* (2 vols, 1974), which is the definitive biography. See also: Ruth Miller, *The Poetry of Emily Dickinson* (1968); Robert Weisbuch, *Emily Dickinson* (1975); Sharon Cameron, *Lyric Time: Dickinson and the Limits of Genre* (1979). And also: *The Manuscript Books of Emily Dickinson* ed. R. W. Franklin (2 vols. 1982).

121
DILTHEY, Wilhelm 1833–1911

German philosopher and historian

Dilthey might properly have applied to himself the observation he once made upon Goethe*: 'For him everything was a problem; every solution contained a new problem – nothing left him in rest.' He was one of the intellectual giants of the late nineteenth century, producing a diverse range of writings on epistemology, ethics, aesthetics, psychology, literature and the history of ideas. His chief claim on our continuing attention derives from his concern, towards the end of European positivism's golden age, to clarify the relationship between natural science and the domains of the humanistic disciplines – those that focus on the behaviour and creativity of men. No one wrangled more scrupulously than he with the teeming problems raised by the quest for symbiosis between 'lived experience' and conceptual thinking. The intellectual turmoil to which he thus exposed his own mind stands in marked contrast to the smoothness of his professional advancement in the external academic world. He was born in the Rhineland, the son of a Protestant pastor, and attended school at Wiesbaden. His university education began with a year of theology at Heidelberg, and was then enlarged by sustained philosophical and historical studies at Berlin where he encountered directly the spell of Ranke*. By 1866 Dilthey had obtained a professorial appointment in philosophy at Basel, and he subsequently took up posts at Kiel (1868) and Breslau (1871). Finally, in 1882, he was chosen for the Berlin chair that had once been Hegel's*, and from it he pursued his outwardly uneventful career of teaching and research for another quarter-century.

The pre-eminent monument bequeathed to us by Dilthey is his *Einleitung in die Geisteswissenschaften* (1883). This 'Introduction to the Sciences of the Mind' (or 'Human Sciences') was conceived as the first part of a still more substantial 'critique of historical reason'. He toiled over numerous further portions until his death, constantly agonized by his inability to round off the project. In Stuart Hughes's words, 'Like Weber – and less successfully than Weber – he attempted a synthesis too mighty for the human mind.' Still, the *Einleitung* was a work whose own stature grew with time, exerting an influence on philosophers like William James*, Benedetto Croce, and Martin Heidegger, intellectual historians such as Friedrich Meinecke, and on sociologists particularly of Weberian persuasion. Dilthey's undertaking followed the neo-Kantian principles which then characterized much of German philosophy, and marked especially the comparable attempts of Wilhelm Windelband and Heinrich Rickert at devising some convincing historical epistemology. The differentiation between the phenomenal and noumenal spheres, in Kant's terms, was deemed to be reflected in that between the modes of study appropriate to the natural sciences on the one hand and to the human sciences on the other. The latter required the investigator to probe beyond the surface of observable actions in order to tackle questions of thought, desire, and emotion – to make linkages between lived experience, and the manner in which it is both expressed and comprehended. As Dilthey declared, 'Thucydides, Machiavelli, and Ranke opened the world of history to me, a world telling its own story . . . . The philosophical concepts based on natural science could not do justice to this world which stirred within me.'

Thus Dilthey postulated two roads towards knowledge, separate but equal in status. In order to explain how social and cultural activity might be grasped independently of borrowings from natural scientific method, he resorted to the often fruitful but also vulnerable concept of *Verstehen*, a form of inner understanding or even sympathetic intuition. This was employed most centrally in regard to the study of history as the basis of humane reality. There it conveyed how the historian, though circumscribed by his own time and manners, could evoke the past through in some sense 'experiencing' it. Problems certainly remained, particularly in so far as such experience was inseparable from the interpreter's own system of values. Unlike Rickert, Dilthey freely accepted the relativity of these; indeed, it was precisely by heightening men's self-awareness about such presuppositions that he hoped to banish metaphysics from the human as well as the natural sciences. He sought to establish through the processes of *Verstehen* a case for the autonomy of history and for the dignity of humanistic scholarship at large, without resort to that framework of seemingly rigid and universal law derived from pre-Einsteinian physics which he considered inappropriate within the sciences of the mind. As José Ortega y Gasset summed up Dilthey's insistence on the glorious variability of his object of study, 'Man does not have a nature; man has a history.'

In the last resort, Dilthey failed to effect an acceptable compromise with positivism. His assertion of human science's equality with and independence from natural science went so deep as to imply conflict rather than the condominium that he actually hoped to inspire. To what extent did *Verstehen*, for instance, risk succumbing to a relativism of a fundamentally irrationalistic kind? Or, again, did not Dilthey sometimes attribute to positivism as a whole, including its more truly critical versions, certain failings that were intrinsic only to its crudely uncritical manifestations? Concerning the general relationship between humane and natural scientific scholarship from this time onwards, Gerhard Masur has commented: 'The two halves of man's cognitive effort were divorced from each other, neither half paying great heed to the labours of the other. It was the first time in the history of Western civilization that such a separation had occurred.' If the twentieth century has suffered greatly from this intellectual schism, then it is only proper to reiterate that this was not the outcome which Dilthey himself intended. As Michael Ermarth has crisply stated, 'His adversary was not science but scientism, not reason but the kind of rationalism which restricts reason solely to the methods of physical science and then extends these methods to all forms and features of reality'.

Michael Biddiss

Notable among other works appearing in Dilthey's lifetime are *Das Leben Schleiermachers* (*Life of Schleiermacher*, 1870); *Ideen über beschreibende und zergliedernde Psychologie* (1894; excellently presented, with another shorter monograph, in an edition by R. Makreel under the title *Descriptive Psychology and*

Historical Understanding, 1977); and the essay collection *Das Erlebnis und die Dichtung* (*Experience and Poetry*, 1905). Most, but by no means all, of his work has been slowly gathered together in the *Gesammelte Schriften* (18 vols, 1914–77). English samplings are available in H. A. Hodges, *Dilthey: An Introduction* (1949), and H. P. Rickman, *Dilthey: Selected Writings* (1976). The most recent and best secondary accounts are Michael Ermarth, *Wilhelm Dilthey: The Critique of Historical Reason* (1978), and H. P. Rickman, *Wilhelm Dilthey: Pioneer of the Human Studies* (1979).

122

D'INDY, (Paul Marie Théodore) Vincent
1851–1931

French composer and educationist

In his artistic aims and ideals, Vincent d'Indy was a direct follower of César Franck*. He became a devoted pupil of Franck when he was twenty-one, remaining with him for nearly ten years. Before this, d'Indy – who was a patriotic descendant of an aristocratic family of the Ardèche region of the Cévennes – had had instruction in piano and harmony since the age of eleven, and at sixteen had become acquainted with Berlioz's* *Traité de l'Instrumentation*. Some early compositions of d'Indy's were published when he was nineteen. His family, however, wanted him to study law, and not to become a professional musician. But after a period of serving as a soldier in the Franco-Prussian War, the call of music was too strong – and although Franck's opinion of his abilities was originally somewhat discouraging ('You have ideas, but can't do anything with them!'), d'Indy joined the master's organ classes at the Paris Conservatoire, which were in fact more like composition seminars. At the same time he earned his living (and enlarged his experience) by various freelance musical activities – as a timpanist, then as a chorus-master for the famous Colonne Concerts. And Franck was not the only powerful influence: d'Indy attended *The Ring* at Bayreuth in 1876, and from then on the music of Wagner* was to be of tremendous importance in shaping his own composition style. Besides this, he spent some time with Liszt* in Weimar, and met Brahms* in Vienna.

Such, briefly, was the background of Vincent d'Indy, who for half a century was a major figure in the musical life of France, as composer, teacher, conductor, theorist, and writer on music. His output was extensive: operas, symphonies and other large-scale orchestral works, much secular and sacred vocal music, chamber music, songs, keyboard music. As a pioneering editor, he made performing versions of operas by Monteverdi, Gluck and Rameau, and transcribed and edited much other early music; he also completed and orchestrated

certain works of his contemporaries – for example, works by Chausson and Lekeu left unfinished at their death.

While still a student, d'Indy had joined the Societé Nationale de Musique, founded for the advancement of French music. Franck was president, but d'Indy became the leading spirit behind the Societé. As a writer on music he did much to vindicate the music and the teaching of Franck, and in 1897 he helped to found the Schola Cantorum. As director of the Schola, d'Indy could put into practice his Franck-based theories of musical education founded on the classics, the Beethovenian* principles of cyclic form, and the Austro-German symphonic approach – as applied also to opera. It was an eclectic approach in relation to French music and naturally met with some opposition. But composition pupils as different as Roussel, Satie, Auric, Turina and Varèse all profited from this broad-based teaching, which was more imaginative and more creative than that of the Paris Conservatoire. D'Indy's theories and methods are fully explained in his writings – in books and articles describing the work of the Schola Cantorum (which eventually became the École César Franck), in his book *César Franck* (1906), and in the monumental and influential *Cours de composition musicale* (in four volumes).

In his compositions d'Indy was faithful to his own academic principles: structure, craftsmanship, orchestration are consistently admirable. Musically – despite the sincerity and commitment – even his finest works, such as the operas *Fervaal* (1888–93) and *L'étranger* (1898–1901), do not easily stand up to the test of time. In art, as in religion and politics, d'Indy's basic conservatism could be over-dogmatic, and even at times chauvinistic. The musical content of his work is often felt to be intellectual and 'contrived' rather than inspired. Besides Franck and Wagner, another very positive influence is found in much of d'Indy's best music – namely, the folksongs which he collected from the Cévennes region where his family originated. He makes use of this material in, for example, the symphonic triptych *Jour d'été à la montagne* and the *Symphonie sur un chant montagnard français* (also known as the *Symphonie cévenole*), and in these a strong and attractive individuality is found.

David Cox

See: Léon Vallas, *Vincent d'Indy* (2 vols, 1946 and 1950); Norman Demuth, *Vincent d'Indy* (1951); J. Canteloube, *Vincent d'Indy* (1951).

123

DISRAELI, Benjamin, Earl of Beaconsfield 1804–81

British statesman and writer

Benjamin Disraeli, the least likely and one of the greatest of British Prime Ministers, was the son of a well-liked *littérateur* Isaac D'Israeli, whose own father had come to England from Italy in 1748 and prospered in the straw hat trade. Disraeli liked to surround his origins, and much else beside, with a cloak of glamorous fantasy but he was in truth descended on both sides from families of well-established Italian Jews. He was circumcised as an infant in the synagogue but following the death of his grandfather Isaac D'Israeli (as he spelt the name) had the young Benjamin baptized when the whole family converted to Anglicanism in 1817. As a youth Disraeli became involved with a number of unsuccessful business ventures including an attempt to found a rival to *The Times*. His first success came with the publication of his novel *Vivian Grey* in 1826. The writing of novels was an activity which was to continue to occupy him at intervals throughout his life. Many of their titles are scarcely known today (*Alroy, Contarini Fleming, The Young Duke*, etc.) but they sold well in their time as lively sketches of social and political life. Some were rather weightier, though none is without its absurdities. Notable among the better known was the famous trilogy of the 1840s *Coningsby* (1844), *Sybil* (1845) and *Tancred* (1847), in which Disraeli skillfully interwove his complex story lines with an exposition of his ideas on politics, industrialism, race and history. The mixture of realism and fantasy is wholly characteristic as is the lively pace of the narrative and dialogue. Even as an elderly, retired statesman he wrote and published *Endymion* (1880) – and received the handsome sum of £10,000 for doing so.

Using the money from his second novel the young Disraeli travelled in the Levant, but after his companion (and sister's fiancé) died of smallpox in Cairo he returned to England in 1831. He stood as a Radical under the unreformed franchise in June 1832, receiving twelve votes to his opponent's twenty. It was now his overwhelming ambition to enter the House of Commons and after trying twice more in the same constituency and once, as a Tory, in Taunton, he was elected for Maidstone in 1837. Passed over for office by Peel when he formed his ministry in 1841, Disraeli became one of the leaders of a group of young Tory MPs known as Young England. Combining a devotion to the landed interest with a deep concern for the condition of the newly urbanized working class – concerns that bulk large in *Coningsby* and *Sybil* – Disraeli and his colleagues felt themselves betrayed when, in 1845, Peel announced his intention of repealing the protective duties on corn. This was the opportunity Disraeli had

needed. In a succession of brilliant and bitter speeches he helped to topple the prime minister. The Tory Party was split, but Disraeli was now a major force in what remained and when Lord Derby became prime minister in 1852 he was made chancellor of the exchequer and leader of the House of Commons, offices which he also held in Derby's second (1858–9) and third (1866–8) ministries. Only after Derby's retirement in the latter year did Disraeli become prime minister for the first time though he had already been the moving force behind the 1867 Reform Act which enfranchised the urban working class. The paradox of a Conservative Parliamentary Reform Act can be explained by the predominantly Liberal character of the middle-class electorate enfranchised in 1832. Disraeli looked to the factory workers to redress the balance against their employers and, in the medium term, he was not to be disappointed. His major term of office ran from 1874 until 1880. These were years of great achievement. In foreign policy he purchased the Suez Canal, acquired Cyprus and had Queen Victoria*, with whom he always maintained the friendliest of relations, crowned Empress of India. Disraeli's efforts at the Congress of Berlin in 1877 did much to avoid the outbreak of a general European war. In home affairs the record was even more impressive with a major series of acts designed to improve living conditions, standards of work safety, and regulation of food and drugs. The work of Disraeli's great six-year ministry did much to assure the future of the Conservative Party as a mass force in the emerging world of democratic politics. He was made Earl of Beaconsfield in 1876 – his wife, twelve years older than he, had earlier been granted the title Countess of Beaconsfield. She died in 1872, and Disraeli himself died on 19 April 1881. He was buried beside the church on the estate he owned at Hughenden in Buckinghamshire.

Disraeli was one of the founders of the modern British Conservative Party and as such a major influence on the future of the nation. He was more a man of principles than of principle, unlike his great Liberal rival William Gladstone*. That is to say that he regarded short term consistency in policy as less important than the furthering of a number of broad political ends. These included the expansion of British power abroad and the preservation of a hierarchical social fabric at home. The lengths to which he would go to achieve these goals – the introduction of parliamentary reform for instance – could lead some even among his political supporters to forget the essentially conservative purpose of his work, while opponents, like Mrs Gladstone, thought him a cynic of the worst type. This is certainly untrue: for while Disraeli was always concerned with what he said and where and was capable of the grossest flattery when he felt it would suit his interests he was governed throughout maturity by a

DÖLLINGER, JOHANN JOSEPH IGNAZ VON / 171

steady devotion to his country and its monarch who became his friend.

David J. Levy

Works include: *The Vindication of the English Constitution* (1835); *Novels and Tales by the Earl of Beaconsfield* (11 vols, 1881), including *Lothair* (1870); *Lord Beaconsfield's Letters 1830–1852*, ed. R. Disraeli (1887); *Selected Speeches of the Earl of Beaconsfield*, ed. T.E. Kebbel (2 vols, 1882). W.F. Monypenny and G.E. Buckle, *The Life of Benjamin Disraeli, Earl of Beaconsfield* (6 vols, 1910–20), is the official biography, but there is a splendid newer life by Robert Blake, *Disraeli* (1966).

124
DÖLLINGER, Johann Joseph Ignaz von
1799–1890

German Catholic theologian and church historian

Born in Bamberg, Bavaria, in 1799, the son of a physiologist who later became Professor of Anatomy at Würzburg, Döllinger was ordained to the Catholic priesthood in 1822, and for a short period (1823–6) taught church history at the seminary at Aschaffenburg. In 1826 he was called to the church history chair at Munich, in which he was to achieve immense fame as one of Germany's greatest church historians. During the early part of his career Döllinger adopted extreme Ultramontane positions, and in 1831 won considerable respect from the Roman authorities for his defence of the ultra-conservative Catholic position with regard to the contentious issue of mixed marriages. But during the next twenty or so years there occurred a marked change in his mental and intellectual attitudes, brought about by his gigantic researches into the history of the Catholic Church, which rendered Döllinger increasingly sceptical about the temporal and spiritual claims being made for the Bishop of Rome. In 1854 he was alarmed, like many other Catholic Liberals in Germany, by the promulgation in Rome of the Dogma of the Immaculate Conception, and in 1861 he published his important *Über Kirche und Kirchen: Papsthum und Kirchenstaat* ('Church and Churches: Papacy and Church State'), an examination of the papacy's claim to temporal power, which concluded with a plea to the papacy to give up its Hildebrandine claims to such power and other monarchical trappings. In the book Döllinger, who as late as 1851 had published a narrow, bigoted and unjust 'Life of Luther' (*Luther: Eine Skizze*), speaks almost eulogistically, not to say lyrically, of the German Reformation.

Döllinger and his Catholic sympathizers were alarmed by the promulgation by Pius IX in 1864 of the Bull *Quanta Cura* to which was appended the famous *Syllabus Errorum*, regarded by many German Catholic Liberals not merely as an attack on theological errors typical of the nineteenth century, but as an Ultramontane assault upon modern Western culture, philosophy, science and research. Döllinger was particularly and severely alarmed by the fact that thesis thirteen in the *Syllabus* seemed to be directed against certain of his own opinions, and that the covering letter attached to it seemed to make the encyclical dogmatically binding upon the whole Catholic Church. During the next five or six years Döllinger and his theological sympathizers in the German Catholic faculties observed Roman developments carefully, correctly predicting that events were rushing along towards the official ecumenical predicating of infallibility of Pius IX. During these years Döllinger intensified his researches on the basis of which he fearlessly expounded his opinion: any doctrine of personal papal infallibility is not at all, as maintained by its defenders and advocates, an ancient Catholic truth, implicit in the common doctrine of the ancient church, which might now appropriately (that is, in view of the agnosticism, atheism, materialism and relativism typical of much nineteenth-century thought) be made explicit by a formal definition in an ecumenical council, and binding upon all the faithful. To the contrary, insisted Döllinger, the doctrine is a relatively late one, which he described as 'new', advanced during the medieval period, and buttressed by 'fables' (*Fabeln*) and 'forgeries', and now receiving fantastic emphasis *vis-à-vis* the person of Pius IX himself. Throughout his academic career, Döllinger continued, he had taught the contrary of the doctrine, and had even tried to refute the 'coarse' Protestant accusation that the Catholic Church was secretly, or in some underhand way, committed to the doctrine. Of great importance is Döllinger's vehement claim that a Catholic Church committed to any publicly promulgated doctrine of papal infallibility *de fide* would have ceased to be in a significant sense that Catholic Church into which he personally had been baptized, confirmed and ordained. Such views were published first anonymously in a series of articles in an Augsburg newspaper, and then in July 1869 in the expanded form of a book, *The Pope and the Council*; (*Der Papst und das Konzil*, trans. 1869) under the pseudonym of 'Janus', although no one seriously doubted that the author was Döllinger (aided possibly by several collaborators).

When the doctrine was finally promulgated by Vatican I in 1871, Döllinger was predictably one of the first and most vigorous dissenters. It is of great importance to notice that Döllinger was not a straightforward member of the formidable opposition group known in 1870 as the 'Inopportunists', those who pleaded that the formal definition might split the Catholic Church, arouse political opposition, cause church-state crises in Protestant countries, and evoke theological acrimony in the church. Naturally, he was in absolute agreement with these opinions: but he went much further than the Inopportunists in his insistence that the dogma was inequivocally false, and he did not hesitate to describe it solemnly as a 'lie'. Such views he maintained up to his formal and full excommunication by Archbishop G. von Scherr of Munich on 17 April 1871. There has been considerable controversy among theologians and historians whether the excommunication edict against Döllinger may have been over-hasty. After his exclusion from the Catholic Church he was generously accoladed with both academic and civic honours. From 1871 until his death various unsuccessful efforts were made to reconcile him with the church, and Pope Leo XIII* was concerned to facilitate his return to the fold. During the early part of his career as an excommunicate he evinced some interest in the Old Catholic Church, but became progressively disillusioned with what he regarded as the abandonment by it of essential elements in the ancient Catholic tradition. He died in his ninety-first year, almost twenty years after his excommunication, never having said Mass nor approached the sacraments during that period.

James Richmond

Other works include: *The First Age of Christianity* (2 vols, London, 1866; 3rd edn, 1877); *Fables Respecting the Popes in the Middle Ages*, trans. A Plummer (1871); *Church History*, trans. E. Cox (2 vols, 1839); *Hippolytus and Callistus; Or the Church of Rome in the First Half of the Third Century*, trans. A Plummer (1876); *The Gentile and the Jew in the Temple of Christ* (2 vols, London, 1862). See: *The Catholic Encyclopedia*, vol. V (1909); Geddes MacGregor, *The Vatican Revolution* (1958); Josef L. Altholz, *The Liberal Catholic Movement in England* (1960); Dom Cuthbert Butler, *The Vatican Council 1869–1870* (1930 and 1962).

125

DONIZETTI, Gaetano 1797–1848

Italian composer

Of all musical forms Romantic Italian opera is perhaps the least readily accepted or understood by the average twentieth century music lover. Paradoxically so, since its gestures and rhetoric are of the simplest and its conventions there to be grasped with the greatest of ease. Yet it is these very conventions and this same simplicity which repel those for whom music must achieve a scientific profundity before it is to be countenanced. Histrionics, melodrama, melody itself take on, in *bel canto* opera especially, the rawness of a direct assault upon the senses which many find embarrassing or positively frightening. Yet the genre has a vast and ardent following, and no composer more nakedly embodies both its seductive charm and its primitive vulgarity than Gaetano Donizetti.

The story of his life is the more tragic since, alone among the great nineteenth-century Italian masters, his fundamental good nature, allied to an extraordinary tenacity and industriousness, made him especially deserving of good fortune. He was wholly without the cold, fretful paranoia of a Bellini*, the fierceness and uncommunicativeness of a Verdi*, or the heartless epicureanism of a Rossini*. But for a single, disastrous sexual adventure his life might have been a bourgeois idyll of honest theatrical craftsmanship, tinged with a vein of melancholy following the death of his wife.

His early musical education was of the soundest. In the city of his birth, Bergamo, lived Giovanni Simone Mayr (or Johannes Simon Mayr), a noted Italian operatic master in the grandiloquent Neoclassical vein of the Napoleonic era. At his newly-opened music school Donizetti, a pupil for some eight years, received a thorough grounding in elementary disciplines and was also exposed to the music of Haydn, Mozart and Beethoven*. His earliest compositions included string quartets, which are mostly technical exercises, and a number of short operas, though few of these student works bear the marks of a personal style.

He was already, however, beginning to impress other musicians by his fecundity and assuredness, and to win the patronage of local aristocrats, and it was one of these, Marianna Pezzoli-Grattaroli, dedicatee of several of his salon pieces, who helped buy him out of military service in 1818. Four years later, at the Teatro Argentina in Rome, he achieved his first substantial operatic triumph with *Zoraide di Granata*, and was immediately signed up in Naples by the Milanese impresario Barbaja. Even if none of his Neapolitan operas during the 1820s was a particular success, Donizetti had now entered upon the career of an early nineteenth century Italian stage composer for which his *oeuvre* and his experiences offer something of a paradigm.

True recognition came in 1830 with *Anna Bolena*, to a text by the doyen of *bel canto* theatre poets, Felice Romani. The work is a thoroughly polished essay in Italian Romantic taste, with its story based with characteristic freedom on English history, its formal alternations of aria and ensemble, its dramatic conflicts and its flexibility as a vehicle for vocal display. These and other elements were thereafter to form the basis for the Donizettian operatic formula, providing, with little serious variation, the recipe for most of his remaining stage works.

With operas such as *Parisina*, *Torquato Tasso* and *Belisario* he established his reputation not merely in Italy but in Germany and Austria (despite some predictable criticism of the thinness of his musical resources), France and England, where, though he never visited London, his works provided the mainstay of the operatic repertoire during the early nineteenth century.

His two most enduring lyric dramas of the period are *Lucrezia Borgia* (1833) and *Lucia di Lammermoor* (1835) in which the librettists, Romani and Salvatore Cammarano respectively, capitalized upon the literary successes of the Hugo* and Scott* originals to produce vivid, resilient plots and characters, perfectly matched by the limpid grace and agility of Donizetti's scores.

It was during these years as well that the composer developed his matchless gifts for comedy in music. An apt turn for neat situations and a sense of the bizarre showed itself from the very beginning of his career, and it is no surprise to discover, in *Le convenienze ed inconvenienze teatrali* (1827, more familiar in Italy nowadays as *Viva la Mamma*), *Il campanello di notte* (1836) and *Betly* (1836) that Donizetti stitched together his own libretto for each. Surely the finest of the comedies produced during the 1820s and 1830s is *L'elisir d'amore*, a classic alloy of *opera buffa* with the wistful sweetness of *opera seria* in the tale of the village lovers Adina and Nemorino united by the machinations of the quack doctor Dulcamara and his magic elixir.

In 1837 Donizetti received the offer of the directorship of the Naples Conservatoire, but this was not confirmed, owing to partisan interests in favour of Mercadante. The overstated piety of the Queen of Naples resulted in the banning of *Poliuto*, based on Corneille's religious drama, for its representation of martyrdom – a fact made more ironical through Donizetti's noted lack of interest in the type of political issues in which the censor of Italian opera librettos was normally called upon to interfere. In the following year the composer left for Paris, where his work gained instant popularity and he himself adapted easily enough to the specific formal demands of French lyric drama.

Donizetti's idea seems to have been that of earning enough from his Parisian commissions to retire from professional life altogether, but by now the serious decline of his mental powers was making it necessary for him to concentrate on bursts of intensive work on a series of ambitious operatic projects. In 1842 he was given the coveted post of court *kapellmeister* in Vienna, while still maintaining links with Paris, Naples and Milan. To this final period belong such lofty and compelling scores as *La favorita* (1840), *Maria Padilla* (1841) and *Linda di Chamounix* (1842), as well as two delightful comic masterpieces, the French *opéra comique La fille du regiment*, and *Don Pasquale*, which brought the Italian *opera buffa* genre to a perfection from which it could only decline subsequently.

In 1828 Donizetti had married Virginia Vasselli, to whom he was a devoted husband and whose death was a severe loss. Experts seem undecided as to whether it was before or after her death that he contracted syphilis, whose final stages started to take hold of him during the early 1840s. During the rehearsals for his grand opera *Dom Sebastien* (1843) his behaviour began

to attract concern by its eccentricity and his friends noted the beginnings of a serious mental and physical decline. By 1846 medical examination had confirmed the worst, and the composer, tended by his nephew Andrea, was removed to a sanatorium at Ivry, and thereafter to Bergamo, where he died in 1848. A last photograph, one of the most poignant representations of an artist as the victim of mental relapse, shows him as a paralytic vegetable wrapped in tartan rugs. He inscribed his own epitaph when he signed one of his last, mad letters '*le pauvre Donizetti*'.

Among those most deeply moved by his final condition was Verdi, who acknowledged his failure of nerve in not going to visit Donizetti while he was in Paris. Though Bellini has often been invoked as an influence on the development of the Verdian style, it is the mature Donizetti who most obviously marks the pages of works such as *Nabucco*, with its note-for-note borrowings of phrases from *Lucia di Lammermoor*, *I Lombardi* and *Ernani*. Using Bellinian and Rossinian models Donizetti crystallized the forms of early nineteenth century Italian opera, and though seldom a pioneer or an innovator in any significant sense, he developed for himself an unmistakable idiom through modifying existing structures.

Certain formal devices quickly became Donizettian trademarks. He seems to have been particularly excited by the possibilities of the ensemble finale, and many of his middle and later operas, notably *Lucia di Lammermoor*, *Maria Stuarda* and *Maria di Rudenz*, contain the typical slow sextet followed by a closing section with chorus in a faster tempo. He is the master of the smoothly-flowing, well placed vocal line, grateful to the singer and supported by the simplest of rhythmic accompaniments but is never afraid to allow an aria to dissolve into a less orthodox mould should the dramatic situation require it. As an orchestrator he is invariably imaginative, throwing his instrumentalists into concertante and obbligato relief, and showing a greater willingness than most of his Italian contemporaries to experiment with effects of timbre and contrast.

This sensitivity to orchestral resources is as readily displayed in the comic operas as in the grander works after *Anna Bolena*. Though Donizetti's own nature must inevitably have distanced him from the satirical bite of Rossinian *opera buffa*, his ability to blend a gentle sentimentality with a riotous sense of the absurd shapes for us a world in which indulgence towards human foibles and an affectionate mockery of them, seen at best in *La fille du regiment*, are forever paramount.

A mixture of comic and serious tinges his most fascinatingly individual work, *Linda di Chamounix*, a love story involving such typical French Romantic stage elements as an Alpine village, scenes of Parisian life, and a mad scene in which the heroine is recalled to sanity by the hero's reminiscence of their earlier love duet. Like all his later operas this shows the powerful influence of French and Austro-German styles upon Donizetti, typified by the appearance of ballet, greater participation by the chorus, a freer treatment of recitative, and ampler orchestral sonorities, shown at their best in the excellent overtures to *Maria di Rohan* and *La Favorita* (the latter featuring conscious allusions to Beethoven's *Leonora* overtures, no doubt prompted by the fact that Donizetti's heroine bears the same name). There is every reason to suppose, on the basis of his work during the late 1830s and early 1840s, that Donizetti would have moved towards a far more supple and elastic treatment of lyric drama, if his tragic illness had not intervened.

Donizetti was a man of the theatre, intelligent, well-read, but neither a visionary nor an intellectual. He never saw any of his dramatic works as an inviolable creation, and certainly did not scruple to transfer passages from one opera to another wherever he saw the need for it. His compositions were written with singers in mind and with the possibility of being adapted to suit the needs of other singers. His prolific talent led him occasionally into troughs of mediocrity (he seems to have been more or less incapable of surmounting the problems posed by inadequate librettos) and into a formulaic repetitiveness. His more tiresome mannerisms, such as the tendency to end every minor piece on a major resolution (this effectively ruins the tragic close of an opera such as *Maria Stuarda*) his use of what Wagner* called the 'big guitar' technique of accompanying arias with *arpeggiando* figures, and his excessive tolerance of the much-abused conventions of the nineteenth-century Italian theatre, have all made him a continuing butt for criticism in the post-Bayreuth era, and he remains the favourite target for those who imagine that purity of artistic intention necessarily guarantees good opera.

Jonathan Keates

See: H. Weinstock, *Donizetti and the World of Opera in Italy, Paris and Vienna in the First Half of the Nineteenth Century*; W. Ashbrook, *Donizetti* (1965).

126
DORÉ, Gustave 1832–83

French illustrator

Doré could invent a sketch with as much ease as he was reputed to be able to pick up tunes on his violin. As an infant prodigy of draughtsmanship he went to Paris, soon to become the most sought after illustrator in France.

He was born in Strasbourg, the second son of middle-class Alsatian parents. When, in 1841, his father was appointed chief engineer for the department of L'Ain the family moved to Bourg-en-Bresse. It was

here that Gustave received his only instruction in drawing, at Mlle Jeannot's Academy of Art. On a visit to Paris in 1848, he so impressed the celebrated publisher Charles Philippon with his drawings that he was given a three year contract. He was to contribute a weekly page to the *Journal pour Rire*, a harmless follow-up to *Le Charivari* which had closed down after libel action (see Daumier*). From 1853 he contributed to the *London Illustrated News* and so became known to the British public, a connection which was strengthened in 1869, with the opening of the Doré gallery at 35 New Bond Street, now Sotheby's. In 1854, he published engravings of Rabelais which marked the transition from caricature to serious illustration. In 1861 he was awarded the Legion of Honour for his work on Dante's *Inferno*, and this, together with his illustrations of the Bible, secured his European fame.

He was a great social light in Paris. His soirées were renowned, as were his impromptu gymnastic displays. His violin playing was admired by no less a judge than Rossini*. Yet his personal life was jealously guarded by his mother and for this reason some have felt that emotionally he never grew up. Her death was a tragedy to him, and he died only two years later in 1883.

His illustrated works can be divided into four main categories: caricature, illustrations to fairy tales, the classic texts, and finally those of contemporary life.

His early caricature sketches for *Journal pour Rire* show a debt to Grandville and Cruikshank*. The cartoons illustrate the foibles of human nature, substituting a light-hearted wit and cheek in place of Daumier's biting satire. Although he soon specialized in book illustration a number of his caricatures were published later in 1867 as *Two hundred Sketches – Humorous and Grotesque*.

His illustrations to fairy tales include engravings for Perrault's *Fairy Tales* (1862); Thomas Hood's *Fairy Realm* (1865); and La Fontaine's *Fables* (1867). In these he shows his easy capacity for entry into the child's world. By using a 'Tom Thumb' perspective the minutest details are given a false scale. These are among the most delightful illustrations of his work.

Within this category can be included Balzac's* *Contes Drôlatiques* (1861). Here he conjures up the romantic scenery of the Middle Ages, in part dependent on his childhood memories of Alsace. He shows a disturbing tendency to linger over gruesome and cruel scenes, which introduce a Teutonic element to this type of illustration.

His illustrations of the classic texts include: Rabelais' *Oeuvres* (1854); Shakespeare's *Tempest* (1860); Dante's *Inferno* (1861); Cervantes' *Don Quixote* (1863); Milton's *Paradise Lost* (1866); the Bible (1866); Tennyson's* *Idylls of the King* (1868); and Coleridge's* *Ancient Mariner* (1875).

Of these Dante's *Inferno* is his most famous. Yet his melodramatic staging of the circles of hell cannot, on an artistic level, bear comparison with Blake's visionary illustrations of the same theme, and they fall short of the imaginative scale of the original.

Gustave Doré's greatest achievement is his illustration to Blanchard Jerrold's chatty guide, *London: A Pilgrimage* (1872). Although Doré illustrates every walk of life the work is justly famous for the relatively few dealing with the abject poverty Doré encountered in the East End. In these scenes Doré combines social reportage with the gift of cosmic fantasy he had developed in his Dante illustrations; so that the half lit and mouldering façades of an East End street such as Bluegate Fields appear as a circle of hell inhabited by gibbering shades.

Despite his success as an illustrator, Doré from the beginning coveted recognition as a painter. His large academic religious works failed to grant him such acclaim. They only allowed him a personal right to the title 'misunderstood genius'.

Calan Lewis

Other works illustrated by Doré include: Le Baron Charles Davillier, *L'Espagne* (1874); Dante, *The Vision of Purgatory and Paradise* (1866); E.A. Poe, *The Raven* (1883); and H. Taine, *Voyage aux Eaux des Pyrénées* (1855). See: B.W. Jerrold, *Life of Gustave Doré* (1891); N. Gosling, *Gustave Doré* (1973); E. de Maré, *The London Doré Saw* (1973).

127
DOSTOEVSKY, Fyodor Mikhailovich 1821–81

Russian writer

Born in Moscow, the second son of a doctor at the hospital for the poor, his early life appears to have been enclosed and solitary. Deliberately segregated from local children, he was educated at home and at local schools, always in the company of his elder brother Mikhail. His father was short-tempered, domineering and fond of drink, but well educated by the standards of the time; his mother was more cultivated and of finer breeding. Apart from the Bible, the Dostoevsky family had reading tastes which embraced Russian literature and some of the most important journals of the day. Probably the most significant of Dostoevsky's childhood recollections concerns a visit to the theatre at the age of ten to see a production of Schiller's *The Robbers*. The dramatic qualities of the work and its romantic plea for freedom were to have enduring and profound meaning for Dostoevsky's development as a writer. Of equal importance was the fact that his father acquired in 1831 an impoverished estate of two peasant villages in the province of Tula on which the Dostoevsky family used to spend their annual holidays. This was Dostoevsky's only real introduction to the Russian people, or *narod*, about whom he was to write so eloquently. From Schiller and the wretched Tula estate grew themes and incidents stretching the length of Dostoevsky's life and receiving their fullest treatment in the last of his novels, *The Brothers Karamazov* (*Brat'ya Karamazovy*, 1878–80).

The death of his mother in 1837 was followed by the death of his father two years later, supposedly murdered by his peasants. The Dostoevsky family broke up. Dostoevsky himself had already entered the military engineering institute in St Petersburg where, though he received a technical education, he seems to have devoted a great deal of his time to reading the Russian classics and an assortment of European writers from Walter Scott* to Hoffmann*, De Quincey* and Balzac*. A predilection for the horrific and supernatural is evident in his tastes at this time. When he had completed his engineering training, he obtained permission to retire from army service and devoted himself to a literary career. A translation of Balzac's *Eugénie Grandet* was quickly followed, in 1846, by Dostoevsky's first original work, *Poor folk* (*Bedniye lyudi*), which received the accolade of high praise from the leading critic V.G. Belinsky, and established the author's place in Russian literature almost overnight. The first success was not repeated with his second work, *The Double* (*Dvoynik*, 1846), and on the whole his career showed signs of dribbling away into various unsatisfactory experiments with such themes as the power of legend (*The Landlady*, *Khozyaika*, 1847) or the power of dreams (*White Nights*, *Beliye nochi*, 1848). Towards the end of the 1840s he was drawn into discussions about utopian socialism and revolution at meetings of the Petrashevsky group. He was certainly influenced by such ideas at the time, though there are no grounds for assuming that he was ever sincerely committed to revolutionary views. In the spring of 1849 he was arrested along with other members of the Petrashevsky group, imprisoned, summoned before a military tribunal and sentenced to death. The evidence against him was based principally on his having read aloud at a meeting Belinsky's famous 'Letter to Gogol' in which the critic had attacked Gogol* for his religious mania and declared that the Russian people were profoundly atheistic. It was not so much the content of the 'Letter' as its illegality which condemned Dostoevsky. The enactment of the death sentence, a horrific charade devised on Tsar Nicholas I's orders to strike terror into the convicted men, ended with the announcement that the sentences had been commuted to terms of penal servitude and exile.

At the beginning of 1850 Dostoevsky was put in chains and carried away to Siberia to spend four years in the penal settlement at Omsk. The experience was shattering. Whether or not it was a major cause of his epilepsy, which may have manifested itself earlier, remains unclear, but there is no doubt that for the rest of his life Dostoevsky was to suffer terribly from epileptic attacks. His account of his four-year incarceration in the penal settlement is a classic of prison literature (*Notes from the House of the Dead, Zapiski iz myortvogo doma*, 1861–2), telling both of the literal privations, chiefly the sheer absence of privacy, and of the stoic nobility of the convicts. When he was released in 1854, he was still confined in Siberia but able to live a relatively free life, especially after being commissioned as an officer. He married the widow of a colleague and was finally permitted to return to European Russia in 1859.

His marriage was on the whole unhappy. Moreover, he was now faced by the task of rehabilitating his reputation as a writer in a Russia dominated by talk of reform and possible revolutionary changes. His experiences had strongly confirmed in him the religious feelings latent in him during the 1840s and when with his brother's help, he launched a journal, *Vremya*, (*Time*) in 1861 his politics were conservative, jingoistic and vaguely 'populist' in the sense that they advocated a belief in the Russian peasantry and urged the intelligentsia to learn from them. It was in *Time* that he published his first novel, *The Insulted and Injured* (*Unizhenniye i oskorblyonniye*, 1861), as well as his account of his first trip to Western Europe, *Winter Notes on Summer Impressions* (*Zimniye zametki o letnykh vpechatleniyakh*, 1863). The metropolitan capitalism of the West, particularly as he encountered it in London, shocked him and aroused in him strong anti-Western, anti-radical attitudes. Infatuated with a young woman, Polina Suslova, he gambled on his European trips and became addicted to it. Indebtedness increased and misfortunes followed. His journal was closed down by the authorities for printing an article on the Polish rebellion of 1863 and the following year, despite receiving permission to launch a second journal, *Epoch* (*Epokha*), disasters befell him in the shape of his wife's death, his brother's death and the death of one of his closest collaborators, Apollon Grigor'yev. Though he published his most oustanding work to date, *Notes from the Underground* (*Zapiski iz podpol'ya*, 1864), in *Epoch*, his journal soon faltered and then failed completely, leaving him with heavy debts which he attempted to recoup by gambling sprees abroad. In desperate straits, in Wiesbaden, in the early autumn of 1865, he conceived a project for a long novel, *Crime and Punishment* (*Prestupleniye i nakazaniye*, 1866), which he wrote the following year. In order to fulfil a contractual obligation for a novel to be completed by a deadline in 1866, he temporarily abandoned his major work to write *The Gambler* (*Igrok*, 1867), a novel which he dictated to a young stenographer. This young lady, Anna Snitkina, became his second wife early the following year and despite the quarter of a century which divided their respective ages it proved to be an exceedingly happy and successful marriage.

It began inauspiciously with the newly married couple forced into European exile in order to escape Dostoevsky's debtors. Four years were spent abroad, chiefly in Dresden, during which he completed two major novels, *The Idiot* (*Idiot*) (1868) and *The Possessed* or *The Devils* (*Besy*, 1871–2). On returning to Russia in 1871 his wife assumed the role of his publisher and created a stable, tranquil home life. Her careful, devoted management of Dostoevsky's finances gradually brought an end to his indebtedness. Although the early deaths of some of his children and serious epileptic attacks clouded the last decade of his life, his literary reputation prospered both through his publicistic activity (his *Diary of a Writer, Dnevnik pisatelya*, begun in 1873; continued, with intervals, until his death) and through his public readings, his editorial work (of the journal the *Citizen, Grazhdanin*, 1873–4) and his work as a novelist (*The Raw Youth, Podrostok*, 1875), crowned by the appearance of his greatest novel, *The Brothers Karamazov*, in 1879–80. His greatest triumph occurred during the celebrations associated with the unveiling of the Pushkin* memorial in Moscow in June 1880 when his speech was greeted by an enormous popular ovation. His funeral on 1 February 1881, after his death on 28 January, was an occasion for large-scale mourning.

Dostoevsky's first work, *Poor Folk*, may have the old-fashioned appearance of letters between an impoverished middle-aged clerk, Devushkin, and a much younger girl, but this simple formula is given psychological depth and its particular Dostoevskian character through the way in which Devushkin's letters become intricate confessions not only of his passion for the girl but also of a dawning awareness of his own identity, his social place and the meaning of his poverty. Devushkin's sense of alienation in an urban world is the first instance of a major concern of Dostoevsky: the problem of human identity in urban society. Dostoevsky's second work, *The Double*, demonstrated on a pathological level a confusion over identity already discernible in Devushkin, though in this case the dilemma of Golyadkin senior persecuted by his malicious double, Golyadkin junior, has as many comic as schizophrenic features and is on the whole more noteworthy for its dramatic concentration of events in time and its use of the *skandal* scene than for its psychology. The greatest of Dostoevsky's works all have such a 'dramatic' time-scheme and are built on successive 'scandalous' scenes involving the public humiliation of one or another character. Dostoevsky experimented with many forms and themes in his work of the 1840s, but strictly speaking he became master of none. Nor is there any real evidence of prominence being given to socio-political or religious ideas, and it is hard to discern more than the faint lineaments of the writer's future greatness in these beginnings.

On his release from penal servitude in 1854 he confessed to a correspondent his doubts and his faith in one of the most remarkable testaments of the nineteenth century:

> I will tell you about myself that I am a child of the age, a child of disbelief and doubt up to this time and even (I know) to the end of my life . . . . And yet God sometimes sends me moments when I am completely at peace; at those times I love, and I find that I am loved by others, and in such moments I have composed for myself a symbol of faith, in which everything for me is lucid and holy. This symbol is very simple, it is: to believe that there is nothing more beautiful, profound, loving, wise, courageous and perfect than Christ, and not only is there not, but I tell myself with jealous love there cannot be. What is more, if someone proved to me that Christ was outside the truth, and it was *really true* that the truth was outside Christ, then I would still prefer to remain with Christ than with the truth. (Letter to N.D. Fon-Vizina, February 1854.)

This testament only began to achieve a specific literary relevance in his work some ten years later when, in his *Notes from the Underground*, he proclaimed his doubts about the scientism, materialism and radicalism of the 1860s by opposing the notion of man as an essentially rational creature with his own concept of man as essentially capricious, sceptical and wilful. But his first successful realization of this concept in a literary characterization came with Raskolnikov, the student drop-out of the novel *Crime and Punishment* who commits murder in order to prove his right to be a self-willed Napoleon but eventually discovers his fallibility and the nihilistic futility of his motives. Raskolnikov is confronted by a dilemma of choice which is reflected also in his own divided character. These choices are between the arrogance of man who has usurped the place of God (Svidrigaylov) and the humility of the prostitute Sonya who acknowledges the need for faith and forgiveness. Whether or not Raskolnikov achieves moral regeneration under Sonya's influence must remain in doubt, but the dramatic power of this majestic novel-tragedy, the profundity of its ideas and its nightmarish blending of a squalid urban reality with the characters' fevered subconscious has made it the basis of Dostoevsky's reputation as Russia's leading nineteenth-century novelist.

In his second major novel, *The Idiot*, Dostoevsky attempted to embody his concept of a contemporary Christ in the child-like 'idiot' Prince Myshkin whose gospel is a mixture of salvation through the power of beauty and Russian messianism. Brilliant though the first and final parts of the novel are, as a whole the work is overburdened with talkative, polemicizing characters and sub-plots. If there is hope for Russia through the promise of a Russian Christ in *The Idiot*, in Dostoevsky's third great novel, *The Possessed* (or *The* *Devils*), the future of Russia is projected as one of turmoil in which an intelligentsia, poisoned by Western ideas and nihilistic influences, cannot discover a faith in itself or in the God-carrying Russian people. Stavrogin, the supposed saviour of the intelligentsia, is apparently torn between a nihilistic vision of freedom (represented by his disciple Kirillov) and the possibility of religious faith (embodied in the faith-seeking Shatov), but is eventually manipulated by the terrorist Pyotr Verkhovensky to serve his own destructive ends. As a diagnosis of the political tyranny awaiting Russia as a result of revolution this novel has proved to be the most difficult of Dostoevsky's novels for Soviet critics to interpret.

After this powerful, if black, comedy Dostoevsky aspired to reappraise the situation of Russia in more positive terms, but his study of an 'accidental family' (*A Raw Youth*) contributed little to this process and it was not until he attended the trial of the terrorist Vera Zasulich in 1878 that he found the formula for his last and greatest novel, *The Brothers Karamazov*. This novel is built around the trial of Dmitry Karamazov for the murder of his father. The result was a miscarriage of justice and the novel is so structured as to reveal, through an analysis of motive, why such a miscarriage should have occurred.

The Karamazov family is treated as a microcosm of the Russian situation. The three legitimate brothers represent, in Dmitry's case, mundane contemporary Russia, in Ivan's, the influence of the West and, in Alyosha's, holy Russia with its spirit of true Christian faith. Though Ivan's critique of the church and denial of God (especially in the famous 'Grand Inquisitor' chapter) appear to make an unanswerable attack on the injustice of the world, it is counterbalanced by the vision of a just world based on mutual responsibility for the world's sinfulness which Alyosha's mentor, Father Zosima, offers in his teaching. The ultimate guilt rests with those, like Ivan, who incite humanity to a total nihilistic freedom in the moral sphere.

The Brothers Karamazov, as the culmination of his achievement, sets in relief Dostoevsky's lifelong concern with the paradoxes of choice which confront mankind. Posed always in highly dramatic confrontations for and against, in fictional worlds that are as resonantly polyphonic as they are teeming with characters, Dostoevsky's heroes live their convictions and commitments at fever pitch; and in this intensity of commitment to life, as if to an act of faith that has passed through all the crucibles of doubt, lies Dostoevsky's greatness.

Richard Freeborn

Other works: (in Constance Garnett translation) *The Eternal Husband, and Other Stories, An Honest Thief, and Other Stories, The Friend of the Family, and Other Stories*; (in Jessie Coulson's translation) *The Gambler/Bobok, A*

Nasty Story; translations of Dostoevsky's notebooks for his major fiction are available in editions by the Chicago University Press and Ardis, Ann Arbor, Michigan. About Dostoevsky: the best biographies available in English are by L. Grossman (trans. Mary Mackler, 1974), R. Hingley (1978) and K.V. Mochulsky (trans. M.A. Miniham, 1967). Of critical works available in English among the most important recently published are: M.M. Bakhtin, *Problems of Dostoevsky's Poetics* (trans. R.W. Rotsel, 1973); D. Fanger, *Dostoevsky and Romantic Realism* (1967); J. Frank, *Dostoevsky, The Seeds of Revolt, 1821–49* (1976); a chapter on *Crime and Punishment* in R. Freeborn, *The Rise of the Russian Novel* (1973); M. Holquist, *Dostoevsky and the Novel* (1977); M. Jones, *Dostoevsky, The Novel of Discord* (1976); R. Peace, *Dostoyevsky: An Examination of the Major Novels* (1971); *Dostoievsky: A Collection of Critical Essays*, ed. R. Wellek (1962).

128
DOUGHTY, Charles Montagu 1843–1926

British traveller

The crowning irony of Doughty's achievement is that he should now be remembered for his contribution to our understanding of the Arab world rather than for the celebration of the English race by which he set such store. It is no very wild overstatement to say that nobody nowadays reads the long and diffuse poems he published during the last decades of an equally long and varied life, and that the niche he expected to find in the annals of literature, one embodying the classic traditions of Chaucer, Spenser and Shakespeare, was denied to him. His ambitions in this direction, however, make him no less typically English by their slightly pathetic solemnity, reminiscent on a much reduced scale of Milton's during his more emphatically political phase.

Charles Montagu Doughty was born in 1843, the son of a Suffolk clergyman, and educated at Cambridge. His gift of lucidly expressed observation showed itself early in his study of Norwegian glacier action, given in a paper to the British Association while he was still an undergraduate. Fervent patriotism determined his subsequent aim, which was to write a series of poems worthy to be placed beside *Paradise Lost*, *The Faerie Queene* and *The Canterbury Tales*. Intensive preparations for this sent him as a traveller throughout Europe, and, in 1874, on his first journey to the East.

Wandering on foot through Syria and Palestine he became increasingly absorbed by the rhythms and textures of desert life, and in 1875 he crossed the Sinai peninsula as a member of a camel caravan. A request to the Turkish authorities to let him make the journey to Mecca was turned down, and funds were denied him by the Royal Geographical Society and the British Association. With typically heroic tenacity, and on limited resources, Doughty stayed a year at Damascus perfecting his Arabic and then set off in disguise as Khalil, an Arab Christian physician, on his momentous twenty-one-month journey from Medain Salih to Jiddah.

His extraordinary courage and endurance, constantly tested not only by the need to sustain his incognito and by the incidental hardships of a desert crossing, but also by the constant raiding and brigandage which formed an essential component of nomadic life, were matched by an uncanny preciseness of observation which allowed his narrative of the whole adventure to assimilate an astonishing variety of detail. We learn, as Doughty learned, an immense range of physical facts about Arabia, its rocks, sand and water, its landscapes and contours. So far from being monotonous, the desert, under his penetrating gaze, assumes a clearly marked identity which shapes the men who cross it. Digging in the sand for deposits of dried camel dung, drinking foul water, getting stoned by children – 'Ya, Nasrany! thou shalt be dead!' – and having his medical equipment pilfered, he was a traveller rather than a tourist and as such directly, though surely unwittingly, contributed to a snobbery on this distinguishing point which survives among English travel writers to this day.

The results of his experience were chronicled in *Travels in Arabia Deserta*, a work of 1,150 pages, at first rejected by various publishers but hailed as a masterpiece by William Morris* and Robert Bridges* when it came out in 1888. By then Doughty had married and retired to the life of poetic seclusion in England which he was to lead until his death in 1926. Popularity only really arrived for *Arabia Deserta* with Edward Garnett's 1908 abridgement, and among those who were significantly influenced by this was T.E. Lawrence. It was he who prevailed upon Jonathan Cape to reprint the work in its entirety.

Despite its singular quirks of style, the inevitable results of saturation in the Elizabethan and Jacobean writers Doughty so admired, *Arabia Deserta* soon became established as one of the monuments of English travel literature. Its pervasive influence can be felt not only in such classics of Orientalism as Gertrude Bell's *Persian Pictures*, Robert Byron's *The Road to Oxiana* and Wilfred Thesiger's *Arabian Sands*, but as conditioning the whole nature of a romantic relationship with the Levant which had begun with Lady Hester Stanhope, Robert Curzon and William Kinglake and which was to inspire Englishmen haunted by the need for a simpler and tougher life, whose values perpetuated those with which their education had imbued them. Doughty's signal achievement was to have created within a nineteenth-century context a pattern for the twentieth.

Jonathan Keates

See David G. Hogarth, *The Life of Charles M. Doughty* (1928).

129
DOUGLASS, Frederick 1818–95

US racial leader

Frederick Douglass began life as Frederick Augustus Washington Bailey, a slave in Talbot County, Maryland. His mother was a black slave and his father was an unknown white man. At age seven Frederick's owner sent him to work and live with a family in Baltimore, and in this urban setting he first glimpsed the implications of freedom. He learned to read with the help of his mistress, and he recognized, even as a child, that slavery was not a natural state, but a restriction imposed by one person upon another. This knowledge made his bondage even more unbearable when, at age fifteen, he was forced to return to farm life as a field hand. His independent manner quickly earned him the pain and humiliation of the lash, and he vowed to escape. His first attempt failed, and after being returned to Baltimore and trained in the shipyards as a caulker, he made good on his second try in 1838.

Frederick went to New York where he was soon joined by Anna Murray, a free black woman from Baltimore. They were married and moved to Massachusetts. Frederick changed his last name to Douglass and sought to support a growing family as a free labourer. He discovered, however, that as in Baltimore, white workers resented having to compete as equals with a black man. But Massachusetts was also the centre of abolitionist activity in the United States, and although he could find no steady work, Douglass took time to attend such meetings and read William Lloyd Garrison's influential newspaper, the *Liberator*. His articulate witness to the inhuman abuses of slavery soon attracted Garrison's attention, and Douglass's own career as an abolitionist and civil rights leader quickly took shape. He was a powerful and effective speaker, yet many whites doubted his story of bondage; he seemed too intelligent and self-confident to have spent his life as a slave. In answer to these critics he published his first autobiography in 1845. The *Narrative of the Life of Frederick Douglass* argued persuasively that slavery was unnatural and depended upon ignorance (the slave's and the non-slaveholding public's) to sustain itself. The *Narrative* brought great publicity to Douglass in America and abroad. And since he was an escaped slave, it put his own freedom in considerable jeopardy.

At the urging of his abolitionist friends, Douglass left his family behind and spent the next two years travelling in England, Scotland and Ireland. For the first time in his life, he felt himself accepted as a man and an equal. The reform spirit burned brightly in Britain during the 1840s, and Douglass was profoundly influenced. An end to slavery now implied more than emancipation; it meant full social, political, economic, and spiritual opportunity. Furthermore, he became sensitive to all forms of human bondage, speaking out in favour of women's rights, temperance and Irish home rule. While in Britain, Douglass not only broadened and deepened his commitment to liberal reform, he also made very important intellectual and financial friends. When his independent judgment and expanded goals caused conflict with Garrison and other abolitionists upon his return to America, his English friendships helped sustain him during some very difficult times. These same friends also provided funds to purchase his freedom and to launch his dream of an abolitionist newspaper of his own. He established the *North Star* in Rochester, New York, in 1847 and published it through several name changes for seventeen years. Frederick Douglass was now the best-known black abolitionist in America. He insisted upon an end to slavery and the recognition of blacks as equal participants in the nation's future. He lectured widely, attacked schemes to colonize blacks outside the United States, participated in woman suffrage forums, and became a confidant of John Brown. When Brown's raid upon Harper's Ferry, Virginia, stirred up great controversy in 1859, Douglass again had to flee to England in order to avoid arrest. The issue of slavery, however, was coming to a crisis.

The rise during the 1850s of the Republican Party as a force hostile to the slave South had given Douglass an opportunity to influence national policy. He distrusted the depth and commitment within the national political organization, but he made his decision to join its ranks. When the Civil War broke out, Douglass used every ounce of his personal prestige and political influence to turn the war into an attack upon slavery and a campaign for freedom. To this end he lobbied President Lincoln* concerning emancipation and the use of black troops. When Lincoln finally yielded on both issues, Douglass energetically recruited black army volunteers. He was not content, however, for blacks simply to serve; he complained bitterly, for example, when black soldiers did not receive promotion or equal pay. Freedom was essential, but Douglass wanted equal opportunity as well. The period of Reconstruction following the war, therefore, would be a time of frustration for Frederick Douglass. Lincoln and his successors in Washington had been hesitant to strike down slavery, and they were even more uneasy with ideas of racial equality. Douglass recognized that racism was not just a 'southern problem', and he agitated among his fellow Republicans urging their support of meaningful suffrage and civil rights legislation for all blacks as well as former slaves. He was pleased with the passage of constitutional amendments guaranteeing these rights, but he was soon disappointed in the failure of the federal government to enforce the new laws.

Personally, Frederick Douglass's last twenty years were spent in honour and comfort. He was recognized as the elder statesman among black Americans and was widely sought as a lecturer and guest. His loyalty to the Republican Party earned him appointments to a commission studying the annexation of Santo Domingo, as marshal and then recorder of deeds for the district of Columbia, and as minister and consul-general to Haiti. When his first wife died, he married Helen Pitts, a white woman, and in spite of criticism for this breach of racial custom, their marriage was quiet and strong. Personal comfort, however, did not relieve Douglass's genuine concern for the insecurities of the vast majority of black Americans. On the eve of his death in 1895, he was again speaking with outrage against the lack of enforcement of those Reconstruction laws he had pursued so vigorously twenty-five years earlier. As his career ended, Frederick Douglass saw black Americans facing an increasingly rigid caste system instead of enjoying the equal opportunities he had expected.

Lester C. Lamon

See: Philip S. Foner, *The Life and Writings of Frederick Douglass* (4 vols, 1950–5); Nathan I. Huggins, *Slave and Citizen: The Life of Frederick Douglass* (1980); Benjamin Quarles, *Frederick Douglass* (1948); and Dickson J. Preston, *Young Frederick Douglass: The Maryland Years* (1981).

130
DOYLE, Sir Arthur Conan 1859–1930

British novelist

Arthur Conan Doyle was born in Edinburgh in 1859. A member of an Irish Catholic family, he was educated at Stonyhurst in Lancashire and studied medicine at Edinburgh University. For a few years, before the success of his writing gave him a substantial income, he had a medical practice near Portsmouth. An adventurous temperament and an innate curiosity had already prompted him to spend several months as ship's doctor on an Arctic whaler. These qualities, together with his humanitarianism, later took him to South Africa during the Boer War. His work there as a doctor and, more importantly, his polemical writings on behalf of the British cause earned him his knighthood in 1902.

It was the Sherlock Holmes stories that gave Doyle his first public success and it is with Holmes and his narrator, Dr Watson, that their creator is lastingly associated. Doyle was, however, a prolific and tireless worker who wrote historical romances, supernatural tales, a series of short stories featuring the bombastic Brigadier Gerard, and a group of novels and tales about Professor Challenger, the irascible scientific genius whose theories (like Holmes's) are always proved right. Ironically Doyle expended more creative effort on historical works while the Holmes stories were produced quickly and to order. Doyle put much research into such novels; from his mother and his childhood reading he inherited a love of an age of romantic and chivalrous simplicity which in a novel such as *The White Company* (1891) is qualified by a mild irony. Also evident in this early production is his narrative dexterity. Another side of Doyle's nature is suggested by the words of the story-teller in the short tale of the supernatural, *The Leather Funnel* (1900): 'I have myself, in my complex nature, a hunger after all which is bizarre and fantastic.' This is exemplified by some of the memorably odd concepts to be found in Doyle's work: the survival in South America of a dinosaur-filled plateau in *The Lost World* (1912); the notion that the earth is the shell of a monstrous animal like a sea-urchin (*When the World Screamed*, 1929). Bizarre mysteries and riddles abound in the Holmes canon and elsewhere, for example the complete disappearance of a train in *The Lost Special* (1919) or the reasons behind the existence of a society which promotes the welfare of red-headed men (*The Red-Headed League*, 1891). The riddles are soluble but a trace of the grotesque and of the Victorian macabre still clings to facts which can be rationally explained. Doyle also attempted scientific investigations himself in the miasma of spiritualism, of which he was a fervent proponent in the last years of his life. This is reflected in the Professor Challenger story, *The Land of Mist* (1926).

The model for Sherlock Holmes, and in part for his deductive methods, was Dr Joseph Bell, a surgeon and lecturer at Edinburgh University. Holmes's principal literary antecedent is Auguste Dupin, the amateur detective created by Edgar Allan Poe*. Holmes and Watson first appeared in *A Study in Scarlet* (1888), subsequently in three novels and over fifty short stories. What distinguished Doyle from his predecessors in the genre and from most of those who have come after is narrative pace, directness and simplicity of characterization, the ability to create economically a sense of place. Almost invariably the stories begin with Holmes's being offered a problem by an anguished or baffled client; the detective's importance is suggested by the frequency with which the famous find their way to Baker Street, his chivalry and benevolence by a willingness to help the underdog. Holmes's eccentricities, his powers of observation, his application of logic to situations where whimsy seemed the dominant factor became as familiar to British and American readers as his appearance, 'that pale, clear-cut face and loose-limbed figure'. The detective's popularity was so great that when Doyle, anxious that his literary energies should not be directed too much into one channel, killed Holmes off in *The Final Problem* (1893), public entreaties and financial inducements caused the author to bring him back to life (the resurrection is made plausible in *The Empty House*, 1903). The problems in the stories, although central to their interest, never overshadow every other element. The best illustration of Doyle's vigorous, often sombre imagination is the Holmes novel, *The Hound of the Baskervilles* (1902), in which the author transforms Gothic nightmare into Victorian crime. The Holmes stories perhaps provided for their public a heightening of the details of an everyday life threatened by the bizarre and criminal but ultimately controlled by an heroic intelligence.

Philip Gooden

Conan Doyle's other works include: *Uncle Bernac* (1897); *The Adventures of Gerard* (1903); *The Poison Belt* (1913); *The Maracot Deep* (1929). See: Erik Routley, *The Puritan Pleasures of the Detective Story* (1972); Julian Symons, *Bloody Murder* (1972); Charles Higham, *The Adventures of Conan Doyle* (1976).

DUCASSE, Isidore-Lucien: see under
LAUTRÉAMONT, Comte de

131
DUHEM, Pierre-Marie-Maurice 1861–1916

French physicist, historian and philosopher of science

Pierre Duhem was born in Paris, the son of a commercial traveller. After a brilliant student career at the prestigious École Normale Supérieure, he wrote a doctoral thesis attacking the work of the influential French chemist Pierre Berthelot. His thesis was rejected and this led to a life-long animosity between Duhem and the French educational authorities. He was appointed lecturer at Lille University in 1887, taught briefly at Rennes (1893–4), and finally became full professor at Bordeaux in 1894, where he remained until his death. It was only in 1913 that he was elected one of the first non-resident members of the French Académie des Sciences, belated recognition in his own country of his outstanding contributions to French science. There is no doubt that Duhem's own ungenerous attitude to scientific opponents, and generally acrimonious disposition, contributed to his isolation from the academic establishment in Paris. Moreover Duhem was a devout Catholic with strongly held right-wing political views and hence quite out of sympathy with the free-thinking, liberal attitude of most of his colleagues.

Duhem is now best known as a philosopher of science, but he thought of himself primarily as a physicist, and made numerous important contributions in thermodynamics, hydrodynamics, the theory of elasticity and physical chemistry. On the basis of this purely scientific work Duhem must be regarded as a major figure in French nineteenth-century culture. But Duhem's interests went far beyond the narrow confines of strict research in theoretical physics. His ideas on the philosophy of science were presented in his most famous work, *La Théorie physique, son objet et sa structure* (1906, trans. *The Aim and Structure of Physical Theory*, 1954). A number of themes can be distinguished. In the first place Duhem sought to separate physics sharply from metaphysics. The purpose of a physical theory was not to go behind the veil of appearance, to capture the reality behind the appearances, to say what the physical world was *really* like, but simply to comprehend in as economical and convenient a way as possible the collection of experimental laws, correlations of directly observable aspects of phenomena, which was the starting point of science. The claim here looks like an appeal to positivism in the form held by Ernst Mach*, for example, that science does not explain anything but merely describes correlations between 'sensations'. But Duhem differed from Mach in a number of important respects. In the first place he believed that highly developed sciences like physics were essentially 'theoretical' in the sense that the entities involved were mathematical representations of, or abstractions from, anything directly observable, and in other cases were constructed by mathematical calculations from such abstractions. The aim of science then was to arrive at these 'abstractive' or 'phenomenological' *theories* which would entail by strict logical deduction a wide variety of lower-level 'experimental laws'. The prime example for Duhem of such a process was thermodynamics in which a few theoretical connections between abstract quantities like energy, entropy and temperature, could comprehend an enormous variety of experimental laws in physics and physical chemistry. Duhem thus championed the so-called 'energeticist' school of Wilhelm Ostwald, Georg Helm and others as opposed to the atomists who tried to explain the macroscopic behaviour of matter in terms of unobservable entities like atoms and molecules of which it was said to be 'in reality' constituted. One reason why Duhem's own scientific work has been underestimated until recently was his scornful attack on atomic theories of matter, which, with the benefit of hindsight, turned out to be more fruitful than the purely phenomenological energeticist approach. Duhem also affirmed his belief that science could arrive, via phenomenological theories, at classifications of phenomena, which he called 'natural', and which he regarded as reflecting an ontological order. In this he went beyond the tenets of positivism, but believed that 'natural' classifications were indicated by and indeed could explain the otherwise inexplicable fact that science could often make successful novel predictions of hitherto unsuspected experimental laws. Furthermore Duhem recognized the very important point that the interpretation of any experimental observation in science already involved a number of theoretical assumptions concerning the measuring apparatus, and that the naive view of a bedrock foundation of certainty in science at the level of observation is quite unrealistic.

The second major theme in Duhem's work was conventionalism. This was the view that any *particular* hypothesis in a theory could never be shown to be false by experiment, but could always be held on to as a matter of 'convention'. This situation arises because the deduction of an observational prediction by the theory will always involve utilizing a number of hypotheses additional to the one under test, either because of the theoretical assumptions involved in the experimental procedures just referred to, or because the deduction of any experimental law from a theory will in general involve several component hypotheses in the total theory. At all events if observation does not agree with the predictions of the theory this can always be ascribed to the falsity of one of the *additional* hypotheses rather than to the falsity of the hypothesis under test. The decision as to which element in the total theoretical structure we regard as suspect is not forced on us by logic, but is ultimately made by fiat, a matter of convention rather than fact. In particular Duhem claimed there was no such thing in science as a crucial experiment for deciding between two competing hypotheses. As an additional argument for this Duhem remarked that just as no hypothesis could be refuted, also no hypothesis could be unambiguously verified, since there would always be many other possible theories that could explain all the relevant experimental data. On this view we arrive at certainty in science, but a certainty of stipulation or convention rather than the factual certainty which the alternative inductivist approach to the philosophy of science would regard as approachable, if not actually attainable. However Duhem recognized that continued defence of a particular hypothesis in the face of recalcitrant observation might lead to an excessively complicated and 'unnatural' scheme of hypotheses for the total theory, and remarked that the question of when to abandon an hypothesis was a matter not of logic but of 'good sense' on the part of scientists. Duhem's support of conventionalism was closely argued, and indeed the arguments were somewhat different from those employed by the other main proponent of this approach to the philosophy of science, Henri Poincaré*. Duhem's arguments suggested that the empiricist conception of a sharp distinction between synthetic and analytic propositions might be called in question. This step was specifically taken by Willard Quine in the present century and the resulting 'Duhem-Quine thesis' has been a major debating point in current discussions of empiricism.

A third important theme in the book is Duhem's attitude to models in science. In the latter part of the nineteenth century a remarkable difference had emerged between the practice of mathematical physics in Britain and on the continent. In Britain the fashion was to produce elaborately detailed mechanical models of the way electrical and magnetic forces might be transmitted through the aether, for example. Until a mechanical model had been produced of some abstract theory, physicists like Lord Kelvin* and James Clerk Maxwell* felt that the theory could not be properly grasped or understood. Duhem contrasted here what he calls the 'broad weak' minds of the English physicists, comprehending a wide variety of facts with the aid of many different and possibly contradictory but nevertheless visualizable models, with the 'narrow strong' continental mind, admired by Duhem, in which the ideal of science was a small but powerful and quite abstract set of mathematical hypotheses. Duhem conceded that models might play a part in discovering theories, but should then be discarded as a quite inessential part of the final product. Duhem's somewhat dogmatic views on this question were the background for important discussions by philosophers of science in this century on the true role of models and analogies in the development of science.

Duhem's discussions of philosophy of science were particularly characterized by detailed historical examples of the way science was actually practised. This reflected the third main area of Duhem's wide-ranging interests, the history of science. He undertook very extensive researches in this field with particular reference to documenting ideas about scientific theories which corresponded with his own conception of devices, not for arriving at literal truth, but for 'saving the phenomena'. He was one of the first people to make a serious study of medieval mechanics, and to trace links between the Paris school of fourteenth-century mechanics, associated particularly with the names of Jean Buridan, Albert of Saxony and Nicole Oresme, and the Renaissance work of Leonardo da Vinci and Galileo. Although some of Duhem's detailed conclusions in this field are not now generally accepted, he was undoubtedly a major pioneer in the detailed study of primary source material in the history of medieval science.

Michael Redhead

Other works: history and philosophy are charmingly combined in *Essai sur la notion de théorie physique de Platon à Galilée* (1908), trans. as *To Save the Phenomena*; the major historical works are: *Études sur Léonard de Vinci* (3 vols, 1906–13) and *Le Système du monde* (10 vols, 1913–59). Biographical information is given by P. Humbert, *Pierre Duhem* (1932), and by his daughter, Hélène-Pierre Duhem, *Un Savant Français: Pierre Duhem* (1936). The Duhem-Quine thesis is presented in W.V.O. Quine, 'Two Dogmas of Empiricism', reprinted in *From a Logical Point of View* (1953).

132

DUMAS, Alexandre (*père*) 1802–70

French playwright and novelist

One of the most colourful of the French Romantics, Dumas impresses by his immense energy and output rather than by the depth of any individual achievement. Entertainment was his prime aim, and he succeeded in it: one of literature's great opportunists, he was superficial and facile, but vigorously so, and not without originality. Inheriting the dynamism of his father, the half-caste General Dumas whose eventful career had taken him from San Domingo to brief glory in Napoleon's* army, Alexandre was to write tirelessly: his complete works (some produced in collaboration, though debate rages as to how extensively) total some 300 volumes, mostly plays, fiction, memoirs, travel accounts. In addition, he founded newspapers and a theatre, indulged in political adventure with Garibaldi* and numerous love-affairs, one of which produced Alexandre Dumas (*fils*)*, the future dramatist.

Under the cover of a bureaucratic career, Dumas began writing hack vaudeville plays until inspired by the visit of a British Shakespearian company in 1827–8 to tackle a clumsy verse tragedy, *Christine*, and the historical drama, *Henry III and his Court* (*Henri III et sa cour*, 1828) which proved an instant success; despite its crude 'historical' colour, shallow psychology and plagiarized incident (there are strong echoes of Schiller and Shakespeare), the sheer pace of action, the manipulation of melodramatic curtainlines made it as much a landmark in the brief but tempestuous triumph of Romanticism on the French stage as Hugo's* later, more poetic *Hernani*. Other quasi-historical plays were to follow, including the much-performed *The Tower of Nesle* (*La Tour de Nesle*, 1832) – a lurid melodrama exploiting legends of royal orgies in the reign of Louis X, involving incest, murder, even filicide, all dominated by the sinister, suggestive presence of the tower itself. It has more to do with the conventions of Gothic horror than with real history, but did encourage the vogue for the Middle Ages in this period. Of more lasting importance was *Antony* (1831), an innovatory contemporary prose tragedy, launching a genre that would later produce Ibsen* and Chekhov*. Pace, passion and simplicity of structure ensured the impact of this adulterous 'episode of love, jealousy and anger in five acts'. The play boasts an archetypal Romantic hero – the bastard, the outsider, superior to the society that has spurned him; Dumas evokes problems of illegitimacy and the position of women in a spirit of anti-social rebellion that finally veers into apparent, if tragic, recognition of prevailing values. With less tragedy and more humour, *Kean* (1836) presents the familiar Romantic theme of the alienation of the artist/genius, though again with a final reconciliation to society. Perhaps Dumas was too much of a natural opportunist to sustain a position of consistent revolt.

The sense of pace, movement – and opportunism – to which his theatre testifies was also to guarantee the perennial success of Dumas's historical romances, to which he turned from 1840 onwards. Just as his plays had adroitly catered for the new middle-class theatregoing public, so his romances caught the vogue for serialization in popular newspapers such as *La Presse*, *Le Siècle*, etc. Dumas's gift for cliff-hanging suspense made him one of the most sought-after writers in the peak years of serial-mania, 1840–8.

His stories take their subjects from: the Middle Ages – *The Bastard of Mauléon* (*Le Bâtard de Mauléon*, 1846); the sixteenth century – *Marguerite de Valois* (*La Reine Margot*, 1845), *Chicot the Jester* (*La Dame de Monsoreau*, 1846), *The Forty-Five* (*Les Quarante-Cinq*, 1848); the seventeenth century – *The Three Musketeers* (*Les Trois Mousquetaires*, 1844), *Twenty Years After* (*Vingt Ans après*, 1845); the eighteenth century – *Joseph Balsamo* (1846), *The Queen's Necklace* (*Le Collier de la Reine*, 1849); and the early nineteenth century – *The Mohicans of Paris* (*Les Mohicans de Paris*, 1855). The historical sweep is undeniable, but the treatment of history is – as in the plays – superficial. First, he admitted, came the idea for a dramatic story, and only then did he seek a historical frame to fit it. History is romanticized: passion becomes the mainspring of conflict, duels and heroic deeds appear to be the stuff of the past. F.W.J. Hemmings is right to remark that 'history is for Dumas, paradoxically, a means of projecting his novel out of real time completely', and it is for this that he is not a novelist so much as an author of romance. He concentrates on incident and movement rather than description (in contrast with Balzac* and the main development of serious fiction), indulges in extensive but rapid exchanges of dialogue, sketches simple but vigorous characters and relies heavily on melodrama. These elements are skilfully combined in his contemporary romance *The Count of Monte-Cristo* (*Le Comte de Monte-Cristo*, 1844–5), offering us the ultimate in wish-fulfilment heroes, the wronged outsider who comes for a time to dominate society, an embodiment of Romantic myth.

When Dumas eventually read Flaubert's* *Madame Bovary*, he rejected it resentfully. Even in his incomprehension, there was insight: that novel pronounced him finally out of date.

David Meakin

See: H. Clouard, *Alexandre Dumas* (1954); R.S. Stowe, *Alexandre Dumas père* (1976); F.W.J. Hemmings, *The King of Romance*: *A Portrait of Alexandre Dumas* (1979).

133

DUMAS, Alexandre *fils* 1824–95

French playwright

The illegitimate son of the prolific and successful dramatist and novelist of the Romantic generation, Dumas *fils* benefited as a young man from his father's wealth and social connection; but his early years were unhappy, and his sufferings on account of his irregular birth were to provide an autobiographical basis for his novel *L'Affaire Clémenceau* (1866). A brief liaison when he was aged twenty with the celebrated courtesan Marie Duplessis led (after her death) to the novel *La Dame aux camélias* (1848 trans. as *Camille* 1934) and to the play of the same name which, written in the following year, launched Dumas on a distinguished theatrical career. However, this play had had to overcome the imperial censor's ban, and was not staged until 1852. Not only did Dumas revert to a favourite theme of the Romantic dramatists of the 1830s, that of a great love which is a law to itself, transcending the normal conventions of society; but by choosing to illustrate this theme by dramatizing the life of such a well-known contemporary personality (rather than a historical courtesan like Hugo's* Marion Delorme) he was deliberately challenging the attitudes of a puritanical, if hypocritical, age. The success of *Camille* was, however, no mere *succès de scandale*: Dumas's is an honest portrayal of an empty and frivolous way of life: the debate between Marguerite Gautier and M. Duval, the father of her lover Armand, gives full weight to the moral imperative, even if emotional sympathy remains with Marguerite; and the play has a human warmth that still gives it an appeal to audiences (in the theatre and on television) well over a hundred years later. Dumas's play provided the basis for one of the most moving of nineteenth-century operas in Piave's libretto for Verdi's* *La Traviata* (1853), and has also been the subject of several film adaptations (notably Greta Garbo's *Camille*, 1936).

Dumas was never to recapture the warmth and spontaneity of his first play; and the rest of his theatrical output, up to 1887, together with prefaces written for his published works from 1867 onwards, shows an increasing preoccupation with the notion of a didactic drama, and a growing conviction of the playwright's role as a moral teacher. His name is often linked with that of Emile Augier (1820–89) as an adherent of *le théâtre utile*, a reaction against the amoral individualism of Romantic drama. Their objectives were certainly similar; but whereas Augier studied a wide range of social issues, Dumas showed an obsessive concern with sexual problems – adultery, prostitution, illegitimacy and divorce – which he treated in an increasingly didactic manner. He was fond of proclaiming the 'mathematical' quality of his plots, and declared that the dénouement of a play should be the *quod erat demonstrandum* of a logically worked out equation. Distinctive stages in the evolution of Dumas's dramatic manner can be seen in *Le Demi-monde* (1855), which paints a telling, if sententious, portrait of that social no-man's-land; *Le Fils naturel* ('The Natural Child', 1858), a play whose subject obviously meant much to Dumas in view of his own birth, but in which the thesis (that the illegitimate suffer a grave social handicap) is hardly borne out by the plot; *Les Idées de Madame Aubray* (1867), in which there is perfect integration of the plot with the theme: the contrast between worldly morality and that of the New Testament; and *La Femme de Claude* ('Claude's Wife',1873), whose melodramatic plot treats in a heavily symbolic manner the humiliating national defeat in the Franco-Prussian War (which Dumas ascribes, in an apocalyptic preface to this play, to the sapping of moral fibre by the sexual degeneracy of the Second Empire). Dumas's thesis-plays were the most vigorous examples of the socially conscious theatre of his day; but now the issues they deal with are things of the past, as a result of changes in legislation and in public attitudes, the plays themselves are no more than museum-pieces. There remain two or three plays – *Les Idées de Madame Aubray*, and the late *Denise* (1885) and *Francillon* (1887) – in which the overt moralizing is tempered by human understanding; and above all *La Dame aux camélias*, which deserves to stand among the half-dozen masterpieces of nineteenth-century French drama.

W.D.Howarth

See: *Théâtre complet*, 7 vols (1868–98); R. Doumic, *De Scribe à Ibsen* (1912); P. Lamy, *Le Théâtre d'Alexandre Dumas fils* (1928); F.A. Taylor, *The Theatre of Alexandre Dumas fils* (1937).

134

DVOŘÁK, Antonin 1841–1904

Bohemian (Czech) composer

A butcher's son, Dvořák was slow to make his way as a composer, producing nothing significant until he was in his thirties. Once started, however, he wrote copiously in all the standard genres: ten operas, nine symphonies, a host of other orchestral works, several quartets, a variety of large-scale choral works, numerous songs and many sets of piano pieces. Indeed, like Schubert* he gives the impression of having composed spontaneously and with ease. He had a great gift for melody, and he had no problems with orchestration, having in his youth worked as a professional viola player in the Prague opera orchestra under Smetana* (1866–73). And it was Smetana's example that was to be so useful to him in giving a distinctively Czech flavour to his music.

However, at first he was most influenced by Wagner*, as is evident in the early symphonies that were never published during his lifetime: no. 1 in C minor (1865), no. 2 in B flat major (1865), no. 3 in E flat major (1873) and no. 4 in D minor (1874). The third won him an Austrian national prize and brought him to the attention of Brahms* who was on the jury. Brahms became a personal friend and champion of his music, but it was only when he had taken note of Smetana, in the *Three Slavonic Rhapsodies* and *Eight Slavonic Dances* for orchestra (all 1878), that his mature style began to form, and indeed the great majority of his most familiar works were composed after the mid-1880s. Of his later symphonies, for example, nos 5 in F major (1875) and 6 in D major (1880) have never been as popular as nos 7 in D minor (1885), 8 in G major (1889) and 9 in E minor (1893). No. 7, unusually dramatic and firmly unified, was consciously composed in emulation of Brahms, whereas the other two later symphonies concentrate on what came most naturally to Dvořák: flowing melody and fresh woodwind scoring redolent of the countryside.

His Ninth Symphony bears the subtitle *From the New World* (*Z noveho světa*) and was one of the works he composed in America as director of the National Conservatory of Music in New York (1892–5). In it he was stimulated by Black American and Indian music, though the feeling is just as much Czech: the case of the 'American' Quartet in F major (also 1893) is precisely similar. For Dvořák's procedure was to use general features of folk music rather than quote specific melodies, and his American material offered the same kind of modal patterns that he found in the music of his own country. In matters of rhythm, though, he was more inclined to borrow directly from folk music; for example, the scherzos of both his Sixth and his Seventh Symphonies use the crossed metres, triple and duple, of the *furiant*, a Czech dance.

Dvořák's period in America was productive, seeing the composition not only of the 'New World' Symphony and 'American' Quartet but also of his Cello Concerto (1895), his last great essay in standard symphonic form. Moreover, as the first distinguished European composer to spend time in the New World, he had a notable influence on the emergence of American music, encouraging composers to seek stimulus in the music they found around them, as he had done. But he felt a strong need to return to his own territory, and he spent the last decade of his life teaching at the Prague Conservatoire. The major works of this period were a set of symphonic poems based on fairy tales

and three operas, *The Devil and Kate* (*Čert a Káča*, 1898–9), *Rusalka* (1900, another fairy-tale piece) and *Armida* (1902–3), all of which show some return of his Wagnerism.

These interests of his late years draw attention to the strain of Liszt*-Wagner descriptiveness in Dvořák's musical character, for although his orchestral output is dominated by works in the abstract forms – symphonies, concertos (one for piano, 1876, and one for violin, 1879, as well as that for cello) and the Symphonic Variations (1877) – he also wrote a triptych of overtures under the title *Nature, Life and Love*, comprising *Amid Nature* (*Vpřírod*, 1891), *Carnival* (*Karneval*, 1891) and *Othello* (1891–2), apart from the final symphonic poems: *The Water Sprite*, (*Vodník*, 1896), *The Noonday Witch* (*Polednice* 1896), *The Golden Spinning Wheel* (*Zlatý kolovrat* 1896), *The Wood Dove* (*Holoubek* 1896) and *Heroic Song* (1897). In all but the last of these he derived melodies from lines of Czech verse, a conscious intensification of his normal practice of letting Czech speech patterns influence his melodic thinking.

Inevitably this happened most conspicuously in his operas. The first of them, *Alfred* (1870), was a Wagnerian piece with a German libretto, but in all the others he used his native language, contributing with Smetana and Fibich to the great flowering of Czech opera in the last three decades of the century. These operas include two comedies, *The Pig-Headed Peasants* (*Tvrdé palice*, 1874) and *The Peasant a Rogue* (*Selma sedlák*, 1877), and two grand operas, the tragedy *Vanda* (1876) and the historical epic *Dimitrij* (1881–2), which continues the story of Mussorgsky's* *Boris Godunov*. But his operatic masterpiece was *The Jacobin* (*Jakobin*, 1887–8), concerned with life in a Bohemian village and filled with romantic melody, especially associated with the figure of a schoolmaster-musician with whom the composer obviously identified.

Among his other vocal works were two popular sets of songs, the four *Gypsy Songs* (1880, including 'Songs my Mother Taught me') and the ten *Biblical Songs* (1894, texts from the psalms), as well as three bigger pieces composed for English audiences: the cantata *The Spectre's Bride* (Birmingham 1885), the oratorio *St Ludmila* (Leeds, 1886) and the *Requiem* (Birmingham, 1891). Like Mendelssohn* before him, Dvořák enjoyed great favour in England, not only on account of the melodiousness of his contributions to the oratorio tradition – including also a *Stabat Mater* (1876–7), a Mass in D (1887) and a *Te Deum* (1892) – but also for his symphonies, among which the Seventh and Eighth were given their first performances by the Philharmonic Society of London.

Unlike his colleague Smetana, therefore, Dvořák was established internationally long before his death and was able to prove the possibility of a Czech voice in all the customary musical forms. And though his own brand of romantic nationalism barely outlasted him, his work as a teacher (of his son-in-law Josef Suk among others) encouraged others to take up the challenge presented by his achievements.

Paul Griffiths

Other works: Seranade for string orchestra, 1875; Seranade in D minor for wind and low strings, 1878; *Legends* for piano duet or orchestra, 1881; Scherzo capriccioso for orchestra, 1883; Piano Quintet in A major, 1887; Piano Trio in E minor 'Dumky', 1890–1; String quartets in A flat major and G major, both 1895. See: John Clapham, *Dvorak: Musician and Craftsman* (1966); Robert Layton, *Dvorak Symphonies and Concertos* (1978).

E

135

EAKINS, Thomas 1844–1916

US painter

Born in Philadelphia, Eakins spent his entire life there except for a period of study under Gérome at the École des Beaux Arts 1866–9) which included visits to Italy, Germany and Spain. On his return he attempted to reconcile a *plein air*, Luminist-indebted approach with his personal 'scientific' bias. For Eakins mathematics and experiment were indispensable aids to observation. His lifetime of dissection was referred to explicitly in *The Gross Clinic* (1875) and *The Agnew Clinic* (1889), both, despite the precedent of Rembrandt, attacked for alleged brutality. More hard-won data resulted from his association with Eadward Muybridge in 1884; his apparatus for studying motion has led some experts to credit Eakins with the invention of the first film camera. Complicated perspectives, an obsession with precise measurement, lectures on refraction or definitions of muscular movements in horses, suggest that Eakins was an academic. In the twentieth century Barbara Novak called him 'perhaps the most philosophical and conscientious of American artists'. Yet in his own time his friend Walt Whitman* said, 'Eakins is not a painter, he is a force.'

Critics have neglected the strong autobiographical strain in Eakins. *The Agnew Clinic* contains a portrait of him by his wife, *The Swimming Hole* included a self-portrait with his dog Harry, and he made another appearance in *The Artist and His Father Hunting Reed Birds*. Relationships with sitters, family, friends and pupils were strong. When they broke down, equally powerful feelings of justice were aroused. Use of nude male models resulted in his resignation in 1886 as head of the Pennsylvania Academy School. The disgrace haunted him. At the end of his life, still determined to prove his good intentions, he returned to an earlier, historical theme, *William Rush Carving His Allegorical Figure of the Schuylkill River*. The old artist politely offering his hand to the naked female model is easily interpreted as an idealized Eakins, respectful as ever of the indeterminate line of demarcation between himself and others.

He seldom ventured into history. When he did, as in *The Crucifixion*, a portrait of his pupil J.Laurie Wallace, the feeling of daily life triumphed over expected pomp. In *Spinning*, one of his few sculptures, the young girl seems to belong to both past and present. Lost in her task, she hovers somewhere between Eakins's sportsmen – boxers, baseball players, swimmers, oarsmen, chessplayers, hunters – and the subjects of his portraits, which came to preoccupy him from the late 1870s. *Professor Leslie W.Miller*, *Samuel Murray* or *Mrs Edith Mahon* are alone with themselves, oblivious of the painter's presence. Like sportsmen, they are absorbed in a non-intellectual kind of thinking which cuts them off from other people.

In Eakins the relation between motion and stillness, the ideal and the 'brutally' real, between thought and action, his own life and his art, all seem quite different from that of any other American painter. The act of examining these relations is complicated by the variety of the work, the vicissitudes of fortune which led him, for example, from the nude to the portrait, and a natural reticence which he also respected in others. It is hardly surprising that his ideal critic has yet to appear.

Stuart Morgan

See: Sylvan Schendler, *Thomas Eakins* (1967); Lloyd Goodrich, *Thomas Eakins: Retrospective Exhibition*, Whitney Museum of American Art catalogue (1970); Gordon Hendricks, *The Life and Work of Thomas Eakins* (1974); *Arts Magazine*, special Eakins issue (May 1979).

136

EASTMAN, George 1845–1936

US inventor and manufacturer

When a friend suggested Eastman should take a camera on holiday in Santo Domingo, he envisaged a popular device for what later infested the world as holiday snapshots. Born into a poor New York family, supporting himself at fourteen, he concentrated his general enterprise and ability in a single area: film. Previous emulsions had to be smeared on glass and did not last. Photography remained largely in the laboratory or studio. In 1878 Eastman mixed in gelatine and the unmessy emulsion became long-lasting. Two years later he commercialized it. In 1884 emulsified paper replaced heavy glass; four years later he produced the first popular camera or *kodak* (a trademark he also invented). But to develop the film and reload, you had to send the whole instrument to Rochester, New York – hence the slogan: 'You press the button – we do the rest.' In 1899 celluloid – invented by John Wesley Hyatt for billiard balls in 1869 – replaced paper. Edison then used this film for stills on a reel, or early movies. Celluloid proved a grim fire hazard but only in 1924 did Eastman produce cellulose acetate to replace it. By this time he controlled a huge company and interested himself in progressive labour organization – sickness benefits, retirement annuities and life insurance. He donated large sums to education, – including the Massachusetts Institute of Technology – so that some youngsters would not suffer from lack of schooling, and to dental clinics in Europe. He committed suicide apparently out of loneliness and a drying inspiration.

Eric Mottram

See: H. and A. Gersheim, *The History of Photography* (1955).

137
EÇA DE QUEIROZ, Jośe Maria 1845–1900

Portuguese novelist

The course of nineteenth-century Portuguese literature both imitates the principal European trends reflected in the cultures of France, England and Germany, and manages to convey something of the uniquely turbulent and complex character of the national experience during the decades of civil war, constitutionalism and colonial conflict, culminating in the fall of the monarchy in 1910. Thus we find a Romantic poet such as Almeida Garret, a Symbolist like the tragically shortlived Cesario Verde, and a genre novelist in Julio Diniz, all three of whom present significant viewpoints on the moods and trends of society in Lisbon, Oporto and the provinces. Yet, good as these may be and strong as are the traditions of Portuguese writing as a whole, it is to a writer of far greater detachment than they, a voluntary exile from his country, to whom we turn for the most consistent illumination of the decadent and confused atmosphere of nineteenth-century Portugal.

Jośe Maria Eça de Queiroz was the illegitimate son of a magistrate living in the small town of Povoa de Varzim in northern Portugal. The rugged northern regions in which the nation had originally been established were traditionally a centre for rebellion and dissent, and Eça's schooling in Oporto, with its classic revolutionary tradition, and at Coimbra University encouraged the dissident outlook which found its expression in his early articles written for the controversial journal *As Farpas* edited by his friend Ramalho Ortigão. A vein of gentle nostalgia, allied to a continuing

pleasure in literary experiment, also inspired the composition of a set of lyric prose poems, *Prosas Barbaras* (1905).

The inspiration for these derived additionally from Baudelaire*, and the heavy impress of French culture, always so dominant in Portugal, drove Eça naturally towards the type of Flaubertian fiction being produced in the Paris of the Second Empire. His essay *Realism As A New Expression of Art* (1871) heralded the novels on which his subsequent reputation has been largely based. In 1875 he produced *The Sin of Father Amaro* (*O Crime do Padre Amaro*, trans. 1962), a highly effective and brilliantly cynical account of the sexual lapses of a country priest, and three years later *Cousin Bazilio* (*O Primo Basilio*, trans. 1953) transferred the basic idea of Emma Bovary to lower-middle-class Lisbon. His most ambitious work of this type, however, was undoubtedly *The Maias* (*Os Maias*, 1888, trans. 1965), a story based on the incestuous passion of a brother and sister, and using a broad canvas to satirize the follies of Portuguese society both Francophile and Anglophile. Eça's experience of England was acquired largely through periods spent as consul in Newcastle and Bristol, with extensive travels throughout the country and prolonged visits to London. He was a shrewd and amused commentator on English life, and his *Cartas da Inglaterra* ('Letters from England'), only published in 1945, present an agreeably dispassionate view of matters literary, social and political. A comfortable income and a natural penchant for a life of fashionable ease, however, led Eça to take his family to Paris, where he spent the last years of his life.

There is evidence that the move to France was at least in part prompted by an increasing disillusionment with life in Portugal, riven as the country was with political strife created substantially by the problems of international alliance and colonial involvement in Africa. The plot of *The City and the Mountains* (*A Cidade e As Serras*, 1901, trans. 1955) plays upon the ambivalent feelings of the sophisticated, pseudo-Parisian Portuguese hero towards the life of his native mountains in the Minho district of the north, to which he eventually returns. Significantly, though Eça did not follow in his protagonist's footsteps, this was the favourite among Portuguese readers during the intensely chauvinistic and parochial decades of Salazar's dictatorship.

The monument to Eça in Lisbon, a model of grandiose bad taste which would greatly have tickled the novelist's wry sense of humour, shows the half-naked figure of Truth prostrating herself before him, and not for nothing was his meticulous and unsparing realism admired by Zola*, who described him as 'far greater than my own dear master Flaubert*'. As a prose stylist, even in casual correspondence, he is unrivalled by any other nineteenth-century Portuguese writer, and his eye for telling minutiae contributes to a descriptive atmosphere which never descends to fussiness or over-writing.

His most immediately striking characters and plots are those provided by *Cousin Bazilio* and *The Sin of Father Amaro*. The former shows the heaviest influence on Eça of the French 'clinical' manner of detached dissection from which he was ultimately to draw away. The latter, perhaps his best work in terms of construction, is more deliberately intended to act as an inclusive vision of Portugal's failure to sustain the social and economic recovery during the short reign of Pedro V (1854–9), and the passionate bitterness which animates the book reaches its climax in the extraordinary final chapter, one of the most hauntingly conceived of any European novel of the period.

The Maias marks a distinct departure from the tautly organized universe of the earlier books. It is altogether more rambling and episodic in structure and more indulgent in tone, and the humorist always latent in Eça breaks frequently to the surface, nowhere better perhaps than in the closing vision of two men running for a tram which we are never entirely sure they will catch. This has frequently been invoked as an image of Portugal's own experience, given symbolic life in the writer's most individual utterance, the novel *A Illustre Casa da Ramires* ('The Illustrious House of Ramirez'), published posthumously in 1901. It is here that Eça not only breaks new ground, in a book whose lack of incident relates more to this century than to the last, but crystallizes his tender, regretful view of the bizarre historical experience of the country and people he had observed with a dispassionate precison and a warm affection.

Jonathan Keates

See: E. Guerva da Cal, *Lengua y Estilo de Eça de Queiroz* (1954); J.G. Simões, *Eça de Queiroz* (1964).

138
EDDY, Mary Baker 1821–1910

US Founder of the First Church of Christ Scientist

Mary Baker Eddy was born at Bow, near Concord, New Hampshire, the sixth and youngest child of Mark and Abigail Baker, both Congregationalist descendants of old New England families. She married three times; firstly in 1843 to George Washington Glover who died the following year before the birth of her only son George Glover; secondly to Daniel Patterson, a dentist, whom she divorced on grounds of desertion in 1873; thirdly in 1877 to Asa Gilbert Eddy, a sewing machine agent who predeceased her in 1882.

She was a sickly imaginative child who suffered from violent seizures which were probably hysterical in origin. She was tormented by her father's belief in pre-

destination. The fact that she was received into the Congregationalist Church despite her denial of this doctrine is a sign of her powerful personality whilst still a young girl. Her schooling was frequently interrupted by illness but she received a smattering of education from an elder brother and in later life remembered studying 'natural philosophy, logic and moral science'. From an early age she wrote poetry and prose and as a young woman was to build up a modest reputation as a local authoress.

Following the death of her first husband she and her family were so convinced of her ill-health that she was judged incapable of caring for her child and after his sixth birthday she played no part in his upbringing. Her second marriage brought her little happiness and she lived the life of an invalid, tortured by a 'spinal weakness' and still prone to mysterious seizures. In 1862 she was temporarily cured by a gifted healer, Phineas Parkhurst Quimby. Her meeting with him transformed her life. She was befriended by him, sat in on his healing sessions, lectured on his work and when he died she possessed some of his writings in manuscript. Quimby held that the origin of all disease was mental. He wrote: 'I deny disease as a truth, but admit it as a deception, started like all other stories without any foundation and handed down from generation to generation till people believe it.' If he could convince the patient of this he believed that he invariably effected a cure.

Clearly his theories influenced Eddy although she was to deny this emphatically in her short autobiography, *Retrospection and Introspection* (1891). She imposed a Christian framework upon his ideas and by forbidding the laying on of hands she disassociated Christian Science from popular faith healing. She dated the discovery of Christian Science to 1866 (the year of Quimby's death) when after a bad fall which temporarily paralysed her she turned to the Bible and cured herself. Her revelation was set down in *Science and Health* which she continually revised in her lifetime and which together with the Bible still forms the basis of Christian Science teaching. Written in conditions of uncertainty and poverty and finally published in 1875 it undoubtedly reflects many of the preoccupations of her girlhood. The unyielding religion of her childhood contrasts with the optimistic and, at times, ecstatic tone of *Science and Health*. Her obsession with illness is worked out in the central doctrine of Christian Science: that matter does not exist, that man is incapable of sickness, sin and death, that they are illusions caused by erroneous thinking. The logical consequence of this – the rejection of medical assistance – is perhaps the most controversial aspect of Christian Science teaching.

In 1870 Eddy established a partnership with Richard Kennedy and began to teach and lecture on a regular basis charging considerable sums for a course of tuition. She was a dictatorial leader, banishing students she believed guilty of malpractice (she broke with Richard Kennedy in 1872). She became obsessed with a perversion of her own belief in the power of the mind which she was to call malicious animal magnetism, that is the mental projection of harmful forces. Thus she was convinced that her husband Gilbert Eddy died of arsenic poisoning administered mentally.

The disputes, lawsuits and scandals surrounding the Christian Science movement in her lifetime make melancholy, and occasionally risible reading. Yet her achievements were astounding considering she began to promulgate Christian Science when she was an obscure invalid of forty-five. She founded and dissolved a teaching institute, the Massachusetts Metaphysical College, established the First Church of Christ (Scientist) in Boston, founded a monthly, weekly and daily newspaper (the last being the much respected *Christian Science Monitor*). She died an immensely wealthy woman.

She became keenly aware of the dangers of a cult of personality and spent her last years in seclusion not far from her birthplace. The directives she issued in those years form the *Manual of the Mother Church* which like *Science and Health* is regarded by Christian Scientists as being divinely inspired. The church today is ruled by a board of directors set up by Mrs Eddy before her death.

Her last years were evidently not free from physical and mental torment. Her authoritarian approach and her concern to root out error from among her disciples may be compared to Freud's suspicion and distrust of his followers. Both, it has been argued, suffered from a psychoneurosis, the self-cure of which produced the ideas which brought them fame. None the less the relief and happiness which Christian Science brings to its followers must not be underestimated. Growing readiness to accept the psychosomatic nature of many illnesses has interested doctors in Christian Science.

Tanya Harrod

See also: *Miscellaneous Writings 1883–1896* (1904). See: Robert Peel, *Mary Baker Eddy: The Years of Discovery* (1966), *Mary Baker Eddy: The Years of Trial* (1971), *Mary Baker Eddy: The Years of Authority* (1977); Sir George Pickering, *Creative Malady* (1974).

139
EDGEWORTH, Maria 1767–1849

Anglo-Irish novelist and miscellaneous writer

Born in Oxfordshire to a happy-go-lucky Anglo-Irish father, Maria Edgeworth was reared in the nearest imitation of an Enlightenment atmosphere that her father's caste could provide. Returning with the family to Ireland in 1782, she was for the rest of her life engaged with the responsibilities of a landed intelligentsia in a disaffected landscape. Her early work lay in the field of education and literature for children, and her career as novelist only began in 1800 with the publication of *Castle Rackrent, A Hibernian Tale taken from the Facts, and from the Manners of the Irish Squires before the year 1782.* This wonderfully ironic, savage and oblique narrative remains the starting point for any reconsideration of Anglo-Irish literature and its historical configurations. Other Irish novels followed, *Ennui* (1809), *The Absentee* (1812) and *Ormond* (1817), though the description 'novel' is really the focus of an unresolved critical dispute about the nature of Irish fiction. *Patronage* (1814) is the most remarkable of her 'English' novels.

A contemporary of Jane Austen*, and daughter of an Irish radical, Maria Edgeworth brings together vitally significant strands of literary and social development in the years after the French Revolution. Her fiction charts a gathering antipathy to reform or change, though at all times it incorporates a subversive criticism of fashionable convention and the *status quo*. Her most important contribution to current discussion of Anglo-Irish culture should be a vivid fictional enactment of the necessarily *dual* bonds which tied England to Ireland in the early nineteenth century; in this respect a subdivision of her work into 'Irish' and 'English' areas is to be deplored. Nevertheless, the work set in Ireland retains a brilliant sense of phrasing and social observation which to some degree relates to her disenchantment.

W.J.Mc Cormack

The standard life is Marilyn Butler, *Maria Edgeworth; A Literary Biography* (1972). Michael Hurst, *Maria Edgeworth and the Public Scene* (1969), covers in detail her social and political position from the 1820s onwards. Marilyn Butler, *Jane Austen and the War of Ideas* (1978), discusses her effectively in a literary context.

140
EDISON, Thomas Alva 1847–1931

US inventor, engineer and manufacturer

As a boy in Ohio Edison gained a reputation for being odd, asking so many questions which infuriated his teachers that his mother, a teacher herself, decided to educate him at home. He read quickly and memorized easily; at twelve, only Newton's *Principia* seems to have floored him. To afford chemicals for his home laboratory he worked as a newsboy on the railroad between Port Huron and Detroit, and then, graduating to a printing press, issued his own newspaper, the first to be printed and published on a train. After his baggage coach laboratory caught fire, he and his gear were thrown off. In 1862, a station agent, father of a boy he had rescued from train rails, offered to teach Edison to be a telegrapher. He became the fastest in America; with the earnings he reinforced his technological knowledge, buying (amongst others) Faraday's* writings. During the Civil War years he wandered the central states, one of those tramp operators – skilled, in demand and intellectually alert – who were transforming American communications and thereby the structure of society. He liked *Othello* and copied plays for a Cincinatti theatre. In 1868 in Boston he patented his first invention – a mechanical vote-recorder, which failed because Congress did not particularly want voting procedures speeded up: lesson number one for the young inventor – only invent what is needed. Waiting to be interviewed in New York City in 1869, he repaired a telegraph machine (basic for speculation) and immediately got a job. During the speculation burst that year, the president of a Wall Street firm paid him 40,000 dollars for a stock ticker. So, at the age of twenty-three, he could found the first firm of consulting technologists, and for six years in Newark, New Jersey, invented continuously – practical quadruplex telegraphy in 1874, the mimeograph, telegraphic improvements, waxed paper, etc., always basing invention on social justification and commerciality. In 1876 he founded Menlo Park, New Jersey, the first industrial research factory – to produce, he planned, an invention every ten days, from a technological and scientific team. This method was a major advance on the tradition of chance individual cleverness. Before his death 'the wizard of Menlo Park' had issued nearly 1,300 inventions including radio aerials (purchased by Marconi*), the dictaphone and gummed paper. In one four-year period the rate became one every five days. He had converted the lonely study, partly resulting from his deafness, into a group industry.

In 1877, he worked on and improved Bell's* telephone to make it practical. Then he put tin foil on a cylinder, connected the waves from a needle skimming it to a receiver. The sound wave track on the foil was reproduced – the basic phonograph, for which Edison wrote out ten uses, including phonographic books for the blind. (His London company staff at this time included Bernard Shaw). In 1878, he improved on Sir Joseph Wilson Swan's incandescent bulb, with carbon filament, by a wire filament which would heat to white light in a vacuum without melting. Patent No.222,898 thus ruined the gas market: two months after its invention, the electric light bulb illuminated the main street of Menlo Park. Then Edison worked to invent a generating system for the variable power needed – achieved in 1881, the year he encouraged one of his employees, a car enthusiast named Henry Ford. Edison's peculiar need for controlled enterprise now

moulded his character in battle with his one-time associate Nikola Tesla. The latter backed alternating current against Edison's direct current in electricity transportation. He lost the electric-chair contract to Tesla and George Westinghouse (who obtained the alternating current victory to develop Niagara Falls power). The struggle was bitter and neurotic. In 1899, Edison recorded a series of images on an Eastman* film-strip, flashed their projection on a screen in rapid succession, controlled by perforations fitting sprocket wheels turning at regular speed. In 1903 the Edison Company issued the first story film, *The Great Train Robbery* (director, Edwin S.Porter; length, 800 feet; with Marie Murray in the first screen cabaret; Harry Davis opened his Pittsburg nickelodeon with it in 1905).

The electronic industry in fact begins with Edison's flair for concentrated, resistant absorption of each invention in the field in order to change it – 'genius is one per cent inspiration and ninety-nine per cent perspiration': his most famous maxim summarizes his method. He made technological inventions practical for the mass public as never before and confirmed the American legend of the poor boy becoming the self-made wealthy industrialist. It took him 8,000 experiments to produce a better storage battery than Gaston Planté's 1859 and Charles Francis Brush's 1881 inventions: the steel alkaline battery of 1905. To the public he became, according to *Harper's Weekly* in 1897:

a midnight workman with supernal forces whose mysterious phenomena have taught men their largest elemental power; a modern alchemist, who finds the philosopher's stone to be made of carbon, and with his magnetic wand changes everyday knowledge into the pure gold of new applications and original uses.

The sinister isolated genius, prominent in earlier American fiction, is characteristically offset by the boy Edison, tinkering with gadgets and delivering newspapers, and by the adult engineer technocrat and tycoon. Edison became, like Franklin, a certain kind of American mythic ideal in his own lifetime. In old age he could remember seeing the prairie schooners, or covered wagons, in Milan, Ohio, setting out for the Californian gold fields. At the end of his life he worked for nine years on the magnetic separation of iron ore from rock. But the method did not work for the rich ores in the Missah Range. His vision of controlling the world steel industry failed, his savings of two million dollars were lost. He turned to cement manufacture, hoping to produce prefabricated concrete houses in large numbers at low cost.

Eric Mottram

See: Thomas Alva Edison, *Diary and Sunday Observations* ed. D.D.Runes (1948). Also: Matthew

Josephson, *Edison: A Biography* (1959); Ronald W.Clark, *Edison: The Man who made the Future* (1974).

141

EICHENDORFF, Joseph von 1788–1857

German Romantic poet and novelist

Born into the landed gentry of Upper Silesia, Eichendorff spent his boyhood at the family home, Schloss Lubowitz. The atmosphere there was still that of the Ancien Régime, and the idyll was sustained by untroubled Catholicism. Images reminiscent of the castle and its surroundings are recurrent in Eichendorff's writings as he conjures up the beauty of its landscape and the easy relationships between all who lived on the estate. After secondary education at the Catholic *Gymnasium* in Breslau, Eichendorff began university studies at Halle. The most significant incident of his two years there was a walking tour in the Hartz Mountains. In 1807, moving to Heidelberg to complete his university course, he fell under the sway of Joseph Görres (1776–1848) who was then deeply involved in the German Romantic revaluation of the folksong tradition. To Görres must go much of the credit for helping Eichendorff towards the realization that in Romantic literature he might find apt expression for his sensibility and his dissatisfaction with the realities of life in the nineteenth century. In 1810 Eichendorff went to Vienna in order to prepare for the Austrian civil service examinations; these he passed, only to discover there was no vacancy available. He had, however, met Friedrich and Dorothea Schlegel* who encouraged him to write, and he began work on the novel *Ahnung und Gegenwart* ('Intimations and the Present Age'), first published in 1815. Meantime he had seen military service in the final campaigns against Napoleon*. At last, in 1816, Eichendorff obtained a minor civil service appointment. He held a number of posts, in Breslau, Danzig, Königsberg and Berlin, but he found scant satisfaction in scrupulously fulfilling his duties. Retiring from public service in 1844, he died in 1857.

Eichendorff went on writing all his life, and if his works are not strictly autobiographical, they reflect nostalgia for the lost contentment of his youth and, indirectly, frustration in his subsequent career. His best lyrics are evocations of nature, of rapt moments when man and nature are in perfect accord and time stands still, or else they sing the delights of the open road. The style, derived from folksong, is deceptively simple in vocabulary and rhythm, and Eichendorff achieves his finest effects by the sheer musicality of his language. His most famous prose work is *Memoirs of a Good-for -Nothing* (*Aus dem Leben eines Taugenichts*, 1826, trans. 1955). This tale of the aimless wanderings of a lad who leaves his father's mill one sunny spring morn-

ing and his inconsequential meetings with travelling artists and mysterious ladies owes something to the picaresque tradition, even more to the *Bildungsroman*, the novel of personal development which Goethe* had made a central literary genre in Germany with *Wilhelm Meister*. But nothing so positive as personal development emerges from *Taugenichts*; Eichendorff is content to develop the Romantic concept of the quest as a joyous, wondering journey, with hardly a hint of anxiety or neurosis. He presents a more serious side of Romanticism in the long conversations with which the improbable incidents of his novels are interspersed (*Ahnung und Gegenwart* and *Dichter und ihre Gesellen*, 'Poets and their companions',1834). Eichendorff is, however, remembered chiefly for less pretentious works, and his lyrics and *Taugenichts* are among the most successful manifestations of the German Romantic creative fascination with folk literature.

C.N.Smith

Works, *Neue Gesamtausgabe der Werke und Schriften*, 5 vols (1957–60). See: O.Seidlin, *Versuche über Eichendorff* (1965); *Eichendorff heute*, ed. P.Stöcklein (1960); and, in English, E.Schwarz, *Joseph von Eichendorff* (1972); L.Radner, *Eichendorff: Spiritual Geometer* (1970); G.T.Hughes, *Eichendorff: 'Aus dem Leben eines Taugenichts'* (1961).

142

EIFFEL, Gustave 1832–1923

French engineer

A construction engineer of great ingenuity and versatility Gustave Eiffel is justly renowned as the builder of the dramatic 300.51 metre Eiffel Tower which still dominates the city of Paris. Designed for the Universal Exhibition of 1889 it symbolizes French recovery from humiliating defeat in the Franco-Prussian War and is both a supreme technical achievement and a bizarre structure that aptly reflects the frivolity of the Belle Époque. It was however as a builder of railway bridges and train-sheds of a strict functional simplicity that he made his prime contribution to the French Industrial Revolution. The railways were the vehicles of that revolution and a new approach to architectural engineering was essential and vital to it. In 1867 he opened his own metal-working shops in Levallois-Perret, an industrial suburb outside Paris, and Eiffel and Company soon established an international reputation. The high bridge across the Sioule river north of Clermont-Ferrand, completed in 1869, is the direct ancestor of the Tower with its wrought-iron trusswork, its careful attention to wind bracing and the utilization of a system of rollers and rockers to launch the structure pier by pier across the wide chasm. In 1876 the magnificent

span across the Douro river at Oporto was completed
for the Portuguese National Railway, the challenge of
the 525 foot width surmounted by building the two
halves of the arch out towards each other supported
from above by steel cables attached to piers set on
either bank. Its success led to further important undertakings, not all linked to the ever expanding railway
system, including a gasworks at Clichy, a covered market in Bordeaux and the enlargement of the Bon
Marché department store in Paris in 1879.

1884 saw the completion of the bridge at Garabit
400 feet above the Truyere river and until the construction of the tallest tower Eiffel considered it 'one of the
victories of modern engineering' and thought of it as
his masterpiece. The subtle design for the highest
arched bridge in the world left nothing to chance and
the same method used at Oporto again proved effective
and the daunting project was completed in less than
five years. In 1881 Eiffel had played an important part
in the making of another dramatic national symbol,
'Liberty Enlightening the People', and his iron skeleton
for the hollow Statue of Liberty designed by Frédéric
Auguste Bartholdi with the supporting beams for the
extended right arm running through the body to counterbalance the upward thrust is one of his most inventive solutions. A complete understanding of the
capabilities of a given material enabled him to overcome the most complex structural problems and when
he came to build his finest work it was to wrought-
iron, the material that had revolutionized nineteenth-
century industrial construction, that he turned. Above
all it is the Tower that we see as the high point of
Eiffel's career and it remains a triumphant reminder
of the ties between the engineer who made it possible
and the painters who came to see it as a symbol of
hope for the new opportunities offered by twentieth-
century technology.

John Furse

See: Joseph Harriss, *The Tallest Tower* (1975); Jean
Roman, *Paris 1890s* (1961).

143
ELIOT, George (Mary Anne or Marian Evans)
1819–80

British novelist

The hero of George Eliot's greatest novel, *Middlemarch*,
is a scientist: a medical practitioner and researcher
whose attempts to introduce modern medicine are
thwarted by his entrapment in the complex social network of an ignorant, conservative provincial town. In
the same novel she gives tragic portrayals of the corrupted conscience of an Evangelical zealot and the
emotional sterility of a theological scholar, self-induced

by wilful blindness to the futility of his labours. These
are some of the fruits of a life that encompassed most
of the stresses and intellectual dramas of the mid-nineteenth century. The daughter of the steward of a landed
estate in Warwickshire, she fervently espoused Evangelical Christianity – the Christianity of Wilberforce*
and Hannah More – in her teens, and in her early
twenties rejected Christianity in favour of an equally
committed quest to reconcile a causal, scientific interpretation of the world with the ethical imperatives
of her former religion. In the next fifteen years she
translated two of the major German critiques of Christianity: David Strauss's* *Life of Jesus* (trans. 1846) and
Ludwig Feuerbach's* *Essence of Christianity* (trans.
1854). A statement of George Eliot's own, 'The idea of
God, so far as it has been a high spiritual influence, is
the ideal of a goodness entirely human', is a précis of
Feuerbach's thesis.

Despite the serious strain caused by her loss of religious faith, she remained close to her family until her
father's death in 1849, after which she moved to
London to pursue full-time literary work. This was
still, and was to remain for a few years, of a 'secondary'
kind: translating and literary journalism. These were
however of the most serious and demanding kind and
her lengthy reviews (the best of which are collected in
her *Essays*) helped to prepare her for novel-writing by
requiring her to articulate her thoughts on literature,
religion and the study of society. Most of this work was
done for the *Westminster Review*, the leading organ of
secular, moderately radical intellectuals. She was effectively its editor for a few years in the early 1850s.

A major influence that helped her to crystallize her
views was the work of Auguste Comte*. His combination of scientific materialism, humanized religion,
altruism (his coinage) and reverence for the past, and
his elevation of feeling over intellect, were ideally suited
to a secular intellectual of George Eliot's temperament.
His espousal of 'sociology' (another coinage), the scientific study of humanity, was to be particularly influential on the novels. But she was not a slavish follower
of Comte. She was never a regular attender at the
Positivist Church established by friends of hers in
London, refused the request of a friend to write a
positivist Utopia and, most importantly, she radically
modified one of Comte's major dogmas. He claimed
that the individual does not exist, only humanity is
real. Eliot, as a novelist whose attachment to theory
was subordinate to her imaginative absorption in experience, embodied in her fiction a more subtle, dialectical understanding of the mutual dependence of the
individual and the group.

The second great crisis in George Eliot's life came
in 1854 when she fell in love with George Henry
Lewes*. Lewes was legally married but George Eliot
acted out her own belief in marriage as a voluntary
commitment by eloping with him and living as his wife

until his death in 1878. She was ostracized, particularly by women, and her family broke with her. This isolation was undoubtedly painful and possibly damaging, but Lewes crucially helped her to work up the confidence to start writing fiction.

One essay written in this period is a manifesto for the kind of fiction George Eliot was about to start writing. It is a review of a German work of social documentation, and in it she argues that a novelist who adopted the methods of the social scientist, and studied the actual behaviour, motives and circumstances of the various classes, particularly the common people, would succeed in fostering in his readers a fruitful sympathy for men and women as they are, rather than a false and vitiating sympathy for ideal types. 'Realism' is upheld above all for its *moral* value. The essay is significantly titled 'The Natural History of German Life': her model for the practice of fiction is the science of organisms in relation to their environment.

The hallmark of the early creative work that followed is the recovery of the world of her childhood in the analytic light of her subsequent development. At the same time the ideas she had absorbed from Comte, Feuerbach and other sources are dissolved in the dense medium of that recovered world – so that it was possible for enthusiastic early readers of *Adam Bede* to suppose that 'George Eliot' was a country clergyman, rather than the atheistic and adulterous translator of Feuerbach and Strauss.

Most of her fiction is historical, not simply because it is set in the past, but because an apparently stable and entrenched social world is presented with a consciousness of the historical forces that are about to change it. In most of them the action takes place at an historically pregnant moment for the community it studies – the arrival of Evangelicalism in a provincial town in *Janet's Repentance*, the First Reform Bill in *Felix Holt* and *Middlemarch*, the impact of Savonarola on Florence in her most recognizably historical novel, *Romola*. Even *Daniel Deronda*, set in the present, works a similar process projectively, prophesying the State of Israel. Her narratives frequently represent the dilemma of individuals who have risen spiritually and intellectually above the level of their communities, who embody 'development' (like many of her contemporaries George Eliot interpreted evolution as a mechanism of moral progress) but are incapable of changing their world and are moreover tied to it 'by the strongest fibres of their hearts'. Maggie Tulliver in *The Mill on the Floss* is an obvious example.

George Eliot began with a series of three *Scenes of Clerical Life* (echoing Balzac*). The first of these, *Amos Barton* (1857), shows her most literal practice of the doctrine stated in 'The Natural History of German Life'. She attempts to win the reader's sympathy for a provincial clergyman who is as plain, unintelligent and ineffective as she can make him. She achieves a limited success but seems quickly to have realized that such a medium was inadequate to her larger themes. In subsequent work she focuses on more exceptional protagonists and in the third of the *Scenes*, *Janet's Repentance* (1857), she anticipates most of the characteristics of her mature work.

Adam Bede (1859), the first major novel, which secured George Eliot's reputation while she was still anonymous, is the most nostalgic and overtly moralistic of her novels. Although there is evidence of her powers of social analysis, particularly in the relations between the squire and his tenants, the presentation of the rural world of Hayslope is strongly influenced by pastoral models. It is not, like most of her communities, seen historically; it is rather a secular and plausibly imperfect paradise from which the sinners Arthur and Hetty are expelled in punishment. The process of self-deception by which the well-meaning young squire destroys both his own life and Hetty's without ever intending to exemplifies George Eliot's understanding of moral action. The portrayal of Hetty's vanity, fantasies and egocentricity, though harsh, is equally convincing. The relentless causal sequence of pregnancy, infanticide and death-sentence is, however, too evidently selected to favour a moral *parti-pris*.

The world of *The Mill on the Floss* (1860), her second novel, is much more analytically presented and firmly rooted in historical processes. Maggie's mother and maternal aunts are not only great comic creations but subjects of an anthropological study of class customs. In contrast to the morality-fable design of *Adam Bede*, where the virtuous hero Adam is perfectly adapted to his environment and the sinners Arthur and Hetty are expelled from it, Maggie, the most morally developed character, can neither fit into her world nor leave it. The limbo into which the logic of her dilemma drives her anticipates the open endings of many twentieth-century novels (such as D.H. Lawrence's *The Rainbow*, which was clearly influenced by *The Mill*) but George Eliot, who had planned a tragedy, resolves all with the *deus ex machina* of the flood. George Eliot's attachment to the Comtean principle of 'continuity' shows here not in overt nostalgia but in the overwhelming power of the past over the moral and emotional lives of the characters. Maggie herself asserts the principle that makes escape impossible for her: 'If the past is not to bind us, where can duty lie? We should have no law but the impulse of the moment.'

Silas Marner (1861) is the last of the novels to draw freely and spontaneously on the impressions of George Eliot's childhood. Its composition interrupted work on her first consciously researched novel, *Romola*. It is her most successful attempt at overtly poetic narrative, strongly indebted to Wordsworth*, grounded less on analysis of motive than on apprehensions of spiritual growth that defy analytic presentation. The scene in which the embittered and alienated miser gropes for his lost gold and feels the blond curls of the little girl who is to redeem him is one of the most moving and pregnant images in English fiction.

With *Romola* (1862–3) George Eliot begins a major development. As *Villette* is to *Jane Eyre* and *Little Dorrit* to *David Copperfield*, so are her last four novels to her first three. She leaves behind the peculiarly English and Victorian type of novel that overlaps with 'children's classics' and begins to develop into a major European writer. *Romola* itself does not put George Eliot in that class, but it signals her refusal to repeat her successes or pander to her audience. It is a detailed and deeply informed study of Renaissance Florence, and is interesting for that reason alone. But despite the mass of circumstantial detail with which George Eliot strives to emulate the density of her earlier fictional worlds, the didactic and emotional drives behind the book stand out too nakedly. On the one hand in Romola herself she indulges a craving for ideal action that she had analysed in Maggie Tulliver and would once again in Dorothea Brooke. On the other she hunts down Tito Melema (a more sinister and accomplished Arthur Donnithorne) with a cold and abstract ruthlessness.

The didactic and schematic treatment of Tito contrasts markedly with the portrayals of the varied, variously reprehensible egotists in her last three novels. Mrs Transome in *Felix Holt*, Casaubon, Lydgate and Bulstrode in *Middlemarch*, and Gwendolen Harleth in *Daniel Deronda* are portrayed with a new kind of depth and intimacy. This is achieved mainly by what F.R. Leavis called 'psychological notation', an essentially poetic method of giving the most private and tenuous experience the status of a perceived reality: '[Mr Casaubon's] soul was sensitive without being enthusiastic: it was too languid to thrill out of self-consciousness into passionate delight; it went on fluttering in the swampy ground where it was hatched, thinking of its wings and never flying.' Judgment is not withheld, but the exposure of the inescapable self, the knowledge that in real life is matched only by self-knowledge, constitutes an authentic tragic vision.

In *Felix Holt* and *Daniel Deronda* these achievements belong to the less obviously ambitious parts of the novels. The treatment of industrial unrest in *Felix Holt* (1866) is a failure. Industrialism is the one major aspect of Victorian life that defeated George Eliot's imagination, and on this subject she compares unfavourably with less gifted novelists such as Mrs Gaskell* and even Charles Kingsley*. The stiffness in the characterization of Felix himself reflects the failure to grasp the larger reality. The sympathetic portrayal of Zionist idealism in *Daniel Deronda* (1876) is more interesting because it is unparalleled, because it springs from a nobler impulse than the industrial part of *Felix Holt*, and because it entails a bolder imaginative experiment.

Nevertheless George Eliot fails with this theme for the same reason that she failed with the heroine of *Romola*: when stripped of her entirely creditable sympathy for the Jews, the story amounts to an indulgence of the desire for ideal action unhampered by the psychological, circumstantial and material complexities that are the very substance of her creative genius.

The other half of *Daniel Deronda* concerns Gwendolen Harleth, a more profoundly analysed Emma whose vitality and intelligence are channelled by narrowness of circumstance into ignorant egocentricity. Her nemesis in the form of the numbingly but tenaciously lifeless Grandcourt is a strikingly original study of evil. Her story, with its account of moral growth, is perhaps Eliot's greatest single achievement, but *Middlemarch* (1871–2) is undoubtedly her greatest novel. Its doomed scientist hero Lydgate is quoted as saying, 'a man's mind must be continually expanding and shrinking between the whole human horizon and the horizon of an object-glass.' This describes the method of the novel. It is conceived between the poles of intimate psychological detail and historical events of national importance (the First Reform Bill, the spread of the railways). The latter are there not so much to influence the action as to remind the reader that the resistant world of *Middlemarch* will suffer change regardless of the fate of people such as Lydgate and Dorothea who have a vision of a better future. George Eliot did not unequivocally think that the world was better in 1870 than in 1830. The question is not whether change will come but whether it will come through morally responsible vision such as that of her protagonists rather than through the random forces of political and economic expediency. In the novel we see the former happening only to a very small degree. Between the poles are the subtly distinguished circles of the social world, themselves constantly shifting, which shape, confine and resist the inner selves of the characters. If realism can be defined as the creation of a fictional world which seems to be continuous with the real world of history, *Middlemarch* is a model of realistic technique. There not only seems to be but is in the mind of the author an enormous range and depth of knowledge beyond the pages of the book, to which we are directed by the subtlest hints. Behind the stories of Lydgate, Casaubon and Bulstrode, for example, there is far more knowledge of medical history, theological controversy and Evangelical religion than George Eliot directly exploits in the novel.

By the end of her life George Eliot was respected and by some almost worshipped not only as a novelist but as a moral teacher. This helped her to overcome the isolation caused by her union with Lewes but it contributed to a decline in her reputation after her death when her work was misrepresented as heavy moralizing in laboured prose. Despite this she was a formative influence on Hardy*, James* and Lawrence, and the authority of *Middlemarch* is an important reason for the lure that realism still has for English novelists today.

Neil Roberts

Other works: 'The Lifted Veil' (1859); 'Brother Jacob' (1864); *The Spanish Gypsy* (1868); *The Legend of Jubal and Other Poems* (1874); *Impressions of Theophrastus Such* (1879); *The George Eliot Letters*, ed. Gordon S. Haight (7 vols, 1954–5); *Essays of George Eliot*, ed. Thomas Pinney (1963). See: Gordon S. Haight, *George Eliot: A Biography* (1968); Jerome Beaty, *Middlemarch from Notebook to Novel* (1960); Barbara Hardy, *The Novels of George Eliot* (1959); *Middlemarch, Critical Approaches to the Novel*, ed. Barbara Hardy (1967); R.T. Jones, *George Eliot* (1970); F.R. Leavis, *The Great Tradition* (1948); Neil Roberts, *George Eliot: Her Beliefs and Her Art* (1975); Rosemary Ashton, *The German Idea* (1980).

144
EMERSON, Ralph Waldo 1803–82

US author and Transcendentalist

If Transcendentalism, that especially American nineteenth-century credo of New World optimism with its emphasis upon human perfectability and upon nature as the expression of a benign 'transcendent' universal order, claims any single custodial voice, it belongs inescapably to Ralph Waldo Emerson. Throughout his prolific essays, addresses, poems and journals (first published in 1909–14 and currently being reissued in a modern edition by Harvard University Press), Emerson sought to articulate a new perception of man's spiritual meaning, a trust in the propitiousness of his appointed destiny. And it was in his own country, the America as he saw it favoured by history and abundant material wealth, that he believed this destiny would best come to fulfilment. He spoke of America's 'optative mood', its 'exceptional' hope to mankind. Whether or not for his contemporaries much of his essential programme – 'Self-Reliance', 'The Over-Soul', Transcendentalism as an unchurchly belief in the divine shaping spirit behind all matter – was entirely free of vagueness, even ethereality, it was Emerson who undoubtedly caught the confidence and forward expectations of his time. In urging the birth of a new individual selfhood, a new and 'American' spirit to redeem the world, he represents one of the great classic, luminous voices of American idealism.

To admirers, both at home and abroad, he seemed indeed an American Victorian sage, the prophet of a new dawn. To the less enchanted, however, Poe*, Melville* and Hawthorne* pre-eminently, he might have meant perfectly well, but was the dupe of an uncritical,

almost extravagant, optimism. Charles Dickens*, writing in his *American Notes* (1842), saw both defects and strengths. Emerson could be 'dreamy and fanciful', yet equally offer 'much more that is true, manly, honest and bold'. However Emerson is best understood: as a neo-Platonist and Kantian (he credited Kant with the term 'transcendental') America's most eminent philosophical intelligence, or as a late heir to European Romanticism in the line deriving from Wordsworth*, Coleridge* and his particular favourite Goethe*, or as a homegrown Yankee enthusiast urging spiritual good cheer in despite of the evident human capacity for evil and pain, his influence upon American thought has been undeniable. He foreshadows a whole body of debate about individual and national identity, about American 'mission', art, history and belief. And in arguing for a Transcendentalist 'theology' which dispensed with all formal church institutions and liturgy in favour of direct human and religious experience, he spoke not only to a deeply Protestant but deeply American inclination.

At the same time, Emerson connects nineteenth-century America with its New England and Puritan past. His own Massachusetts family ancestry stretched back nearly three centuries to the founding drama of America. In rejecting first the sin and punishment doctrines of Calvinism and theocratic 'Covenant' theology, then the more liberal Unitarianism in which he trained at Harvard as an intending minister, Emerson also made borrowings, notably the Puritan missionary style of high moral seriousness and emblematic manner of deciphering the world. His exhortations he pitched uncompromisingly at an elevated level, the oratory of a New England Brahmin practised in the arts of the sermon and Lyceum address and well read in Eastern works like the Vedas and *Bhagavadgita* as well as classic European literary tradition, which won him an almost legendary reputation in his own lifetime. He came to personify, too, the importance of Boston, and satellite towns like Cambridge and Concord, to the nation's cultural life, albeit an importance which waned as the century progressed. In Emerson Americans believed they detected a beacon for the age – a quintessential WASP and New England beacon, to be sure, lofty, distant, often given to barely accessible, high-soaring rhetoric – who had responded exhilaratingly to the great surges of the nation's historical energy, especially the settling of the frontier and America's vast Western spaces. For his countrymen, as for Emerson, these were happenings perfectly literal in themselves, but also metaphors of America's millennial promise. Fearing that materialism might damage America's spiritual chances, he made a typical idealist appeal in his address 'The Young American', delivered in 1844: 'I call upon you, young men to obey your heart, and be the nobility of this land.'

In developing his theories of Transcendentalist belief

and personality, Emerson was seeking, as he said in 'The Transcendentalist' (1842), for 'the whole connection of spiritual doctrine', the essence behind any single cause, whether abolition, temperance, or the many other American and New England expressions of reform. This search led him, almost inevitably, into the workings of the creative imagination, and the nature of literary form and language. He evolved appropriately 'organic' theories of inspiration and composition, and found himself calling for a specifically American literary tradition. In this, he added another claim to his achievements. He heralded the mid-century flowering of the American Renaissance which was to include not only himself and a gallery of minor Transcendentalist figures, but the names of Melville, Hawthorne, Whitman* (who addressed him as 'dear Friend and Master'), and his fellow New England poets, Thoreau* and the Amherst-born Emily Dickinson*. Emerson's star has unquestionably now faded, despite occasional efforts to re-argue his importance. Yet from within his New England time and place, he spoke as one of his culture's 'representative men', a landmark presence in the American intellectual tradition.

Despite his reputation to the contrary, Emerson knew adversity intimately and from an early age. He lost his father at eight; took on the lasting care of a mentally retarded brother; had to work his way through Harvard (1817–21), then teach school for a living while enduring bad health; and, having become junior pastor at Boston's Second Unitarian Church and married Ellen Tucker in 1829, lost his wife to tuberculosis in 1831. Shortly after he learned of the deaths of two of his brothers. In 1832, no longer able to believe in the sacraments of the Lord's Supper, he resigned his pastorate; travelled in Europe and visited the Lake poets and Carlyle*, with whom he maintained a lifelong correspondence; took up lecturing as a livelihood, and in 1835, remarried, to Lydia Jackson, a marriage helped by a considerable bequest from his first wife's will, but later saddened by the tragic early death of his son Waldo in 1842. The Transcendentalism he had been evolving in his talks and in the journals he had begun in 1820, and which had caused his abandonment of the ministry, found a first written and public expression in his anonymous piece, *Nature* (1836), whose rhapsodic opening paragraphs called for 'an original relationship to the universe', and 'our own works and laws and worship'. By 1837, he was a mainstay of the 'Transcendental Club', which attracted the likes of Bronson Alcott, reformer and key influence on American pedagogy and child education, Margaret Fuller*, the feminist who wrote *Women In the Nineteenth Century* (1845), poets like Jones Very and William Ellery Channing, and Elizabeth Peabody, whose Boston bookshop became a Transcendentalist gathering-place, who provided America with its first kindergarten and

whose sister Sophia married Hawthorne. To these, somewhat later, must be added Emerson's friend and boarder, Thoreau. With the advent of their journal, the *Dial* (1840–4), and the widening circle of discussion and lectures, Transcendentalism, in so far as it even became a 'movement', could be said to have been launched.

Emerson himself had certainly found his stride. In 1837 he delivered the Phi Beta Kappa Address at Harvard, 'The American Scholar', a call for the emergence of 'Man Thinking', and for 'a nation of men [which] will for the first time exist, because each believes himself inspired by the Divine Soul which also inspires all men'. He advocated especially that Americans 'write their own books' and repudiate 'the courtly muses of Europe'. In 1838, again at Harvard, he argued for an inspirational, near-mystic religion which repudiated most church institutions and saw Jesus as but one exemplary religious teacher among many, unmiraculous and historical – opinion of a heady subversive order to offer a graduating class of ministers and immediately a source of outrage to orthodox Unitarian and protestant theologians. By 1841, he was the father of two daughters, and had published his *Essays: First Series*, in which the major dialectics of his thought were set forth in detail. Of these 'Self-Reliance' ('Whoso would be a man, must be a non-conformist'), 'The Over-Soul' ('The simplest person who in his integrity worships God becomes God') and 'Compensation' ('Whatever is evil, malignant, brutal has its positive, salutary counterpart') are perhaps the most bracing and characteristic. In 1844, well on his way to becoming a national institution as a Transcendentalist and pro-abolition speaker, he published his *Essays: Second Series*, nine meditations of which the deservedly best-known is 'The Poet', a vital manifesto as to the status and possibilities of poetry in its broadest sense. 'It is not metres,' he suggested, 'but a metre-making argument that makes a poem.' He also invoked the challenge offered by the New World to the creative sensibility:

Our log-rollings, our stumps and their politics, our fisheries, our Negroes and Indians, our boats and our repudiations, the wrath of rogues and the pusillanimity of honest men, the northern trade, the southern planting, the western clearing, Oregon and Texas, are yet unsung. Yet America is a poem in our eyes; its ample geography dazzles the imagination, and it will not wait long for metres.

Of all the American writers who responded to Emerson, no one perhaps better heeded appeals of this sort than Walt Whitman. Emerson by now was truly in pursuit of his own 'first-person singular', as he expressed it, to the point of turning down an offer to join the Transcendentalist and utopian communitarians of

Brook Farm, the Fourierist* enterprise which Hawthorne later made the setting of *The Blithedale Romance* (1862). He continued to speak out for emancipation and reform; travelled busily in Europe and then the western states of America; took up the defence of John Brown in public and attacked the Fugitive Slave Act often to noisy abuse; and spoke movingly at the funeral of his so-called 'practical disciple', Henry David Thoreau, in 1862.

Emerson went on lecturing and publishing well into his later years, still a harbinger of hope and uplift, despite what he had seen of slavery, Civil War carnage, the rise of an America increasingly won over to industrialization and capital profit. His *Poems* (1846) contains essential Transcendentalist miniatures like 'Each And All', 'The Snow-Storm', and 'Bacchus'. In 1850, he published *Nature: Addresses and Lectures*, a compendium of past work, then *Representative Men*, six portraits of world-figures, Plato, Swedenborg (for whose doctrine of 'correspondences' he professed an important affinity), Montaigne, Shakespeare, Napoleon* and Goethe. Oddly he did not include a scientist, despite his own keen interests in natural science. In selecting these typological men, he was doubtless also reflecting the influence of his admired Carlyle's 'On Heroes, Hero-Worship, and the Heroic in History' (1841). In *English Traits* (1856), he issued a volume to compare with Hawthorne's *Our Old Home* (1863). Three later works, *The Conduct of Life* (1860), *Society and Solitude* (1870) and *Letters and Social Aims* (1875), betray a distinct drop in intellectual acuity yet remain consistent in their advocacy of a trustful, confident metaphysics.

To fellow Transcendentalist believers, Emerson offered a crucial message of hope and spiritual renewal. Whitman spoke for many in thinking him no less than the architect of a new human and social personality, and of an America truly the 'new-found land'. Others, like Hawthorne, who knew him as a neighbour, thought Emerson the prisoner of his own rhetoric, a victim of unguarded optimistic fervour, as he indicated in his story 'The Celestial Omnibus'. Melville was yet more brutal, pillorying Emersonianism in the figure of Mark Winsome in *The Confidence Man* (1857), the Transcendentalist as hollow man, bland and fundamentally evasive. Yet if he did not persuade everywhere, or entirely bestride his age, Emerson was a wholly essential factor in America's cultural coming-of-age (Oliver Wendell Holmes*, no undue lover of Transcendentalism, called 'The American Scholar' 'our Intellectual Declaration of Independence'). He was a genuinely singular intelligence, and a considerable literary stylist in his own right, as not only his essays and poems but the rich aphoristic notations of his journals bear witness. No account of American culture and ideas can offer itself as complete without reference to his ample contribution.

A. Robert Lee

See: F.O. Mathiessen, *American Renaissance; Art and Expression in the Age of Emerson and Whitman* (1941); Ralph Leslie Rusk, *The Life of Ralph Waldo Emmerson* (1949); Perry Miller, *The Transcendentalists* (1950); Vivian Hopkins, *Spires of Form: A Study of Emerson's Aesthetic Theory* (1951); Paul Sherman, *Emerson's Angle of Vision* (1952); Stephen Whicher, *Freedom and Fate: An Inner Life of Ralph Waldo Emerson* (1953); Milton R. Konvitz and Stephen E. Whicher (eds), *Emerson, A Collection of Critical Essays* (1962); Tony Tanner, *The Reign of Wonder: Naivity and Reality in American Literature* (1965); Quentin Anderson, *The Imperial Self: An Essay in American Literary and Cultural History* (1971); Lawrence Buell, *Literary Transcendentalism: Style and Vision In The American Renaissance* (1973); David Porter, *Emerson and Literary Change* (1979).

145
ENGELS, Friedrich 1820–95

German historian, philosopher and revolutionary

Friedrich Engels, the lifelong friend and colleague of Karl Marx*, was born in Barmen on 28 November 1820. The eldest son of a wealthy cotton manufacturer, he went to Manchester at the end of 1842 to work in a branch of his father's firm. This, his first stay in England, lasted until August 1844. It brought Engels face to face with the conditions under which the English working class lived, and laid the foundations of his book, *The Condition of the Working Class in England* (*Die Lage der arbeitenden Klasse in England*, 1845). Engels was already a Communist before his first meeting with Marx in Paris in August 1844, but there is no doubt that his views were substantially modified by Marx, whose intellectual superiority Engels readily admitted. 'Marx,' he wrote, 'stood higher, saw farther, and took a wider and quicker view than all the rest of us.' But Engels did much to help Marx. He collaborated with him in a number of important works – *The Holy Family* (1845), *The German Ideology* (written 1845–6, published 1932) and *The Communist Manifesto* (1848). More than this, he was for many years Marx's chief source of financial support. After a short spell of revolutionary activity on the continent, Engels resumed work in the Manchester branch of his father's firm in 1850, and helped to support Marx out of his income. He continued to work with the firm until 1869; late in 1870 he moved to London, to be near Marx. He died in London on 5 August 1895.

'Marx,' said Engels, 'was a genius; we others were at best talented.' This is a fair self-assessment. Engels was not a great original thinker, but he was a man of many talents, and he was able to make good use of other men's ideas. He did important work as a Marxist historian, writing *The Peasant War in Germany* (*Der* *deutsche Bauernkrieg*, 1850, trans. 1926), in which he gave a Marxist interpretation to data drawn mainly from the work of the German historian Wilhelm Zimmermann, and *The Origin of the Family, Private Property and the State* (*Der Ursprung der Familie, des Privateigentums und des Staats*, 1884, trans, 1902), which relied heavily on *Ancient Society* (1877), a book by the American anthropologist Lewis H. Morgan*. More important than these, however, were Engels's philosophical works. If one seeks the philosophical views of the founders of Marxism, one must look above all to Engels's works, and in particular to his book *Herr Eugen Dühring's Revolution in Science*, usually called *Anti-Dühring* (*Herrn Eugen Dührings Umwälzung der Wissenschaft*, 1878, trans. 1934). This, an attack on the views of a German socialist, was intended to be a short encyclopedia of Marxist views about philosophy, science and history. Engels tried to give a more detailed account of the philosophy of science in his 'Dialectics of Nature' (begun in 1873), but he abandoned the work after Marx's death in 1883, to allow himself more time in which to edit the last two volumes of Marx's *Capital*. However, he did publish in 1886 an important essay on the relations between Marxism and the philosophies of Hegel* and Feuerbach*, *Ludwig Feuerbach and the End of Classical German Philosophy* (*Ludwig Feuerbach und der Ausgang der klassischen deutschen Philosophie*, trans. 1934).

The philosophy expounded by Engels is now called 'dialectical materialism' (he himself did not use the term, but he did speak of a 'materialist dialectic'). This philosophy owes much to Hegel's dialectic, but rejects Hegel's view that mind is the ultimate reality. In speaking of a *materialist* dialectic, Engels means that matter has primacy over mind. Matter is not a product of mind; rather, mind is the highest product of matter. But though Hegel was wrong on that point, the laws that govern the movement of matter are close to some of those stated by Hegel. In a way which parallels Hegel's distinction between understanding and reason, Engels distinguishes 'metaphysical' from 'dialectical' thinking. The metaphysician thinks of things in isolation from each other, and as rigid and fixed. For him, a thing either exists or it does not; a thing cannot both be itself and something else. But this way of thinking, Engels argues, is unduly abstract and leads to insoluble contradictions. This is precisely because it does not see beyond individual things to their connections, and beyond their existence to their generation and destruction. The dialectician, on the other hand, views things as part of the whole vast interconnection of things, and as moving rather than fixed.

Engels recognizes three laws of dialectics – laws, he notes, that had already been stated by Hegel, 'but in his idealistic fashion'. As in Hegel, these laws are universal in their application; they are said to be true, not only of conscious beings, but of inanimate nature also. The first law is that of the transformation of quantity into quality. This asserts that an increase in quantity suddenly produces, at a certain 'nodal point', a difference in quality; as when, for example, water, which has been growing steadily hotter (quantitative increase) suddenly changes into steam (qualitative change). The second law, that of the interpenetration of opposites, displays the difference between the metaphysician and the dialectician. Identity and difference, says Engels, are not irreconcilable opposites. One has to recognize (whatever the metaphysician may say) that things are *both* the same *and* different. The last law is that of the negation of the negation. Here, the underlying idea is Hegel's concept of *Aufhebung* ('sublation'). Development, according to Engels, proceeds by way of repeated negations. One state of affairs is negated by another, and this by another; but the second negation does not re-establish the first state of affairs, but leads to one that is new and higher. One of the examples cited by Engels is Marx's account, in volume I of *Capital*, of the origin and supersession of capitalist private property. This sort of private property is said by Marx to be the negation of individual private property that is based on individual labour. But capitalist production, 'with the inexorability of a law of nature', begets its own negation. This negation of a negation does not re-establish private property for the producer; rather, it gives him individual property that is based on cooperation and the common ownership of land and of the means of production. That is, it leads to a new, and higher, form of society.

Engels also had important things to say about the nature of human freedom. Marx's view that social change obeys necessary laws might seem to take away human freedom, but Engels replies that this is not so. Borrowing again from Hegel, he says that there is no real opposition between freedom and necessity. Freedom does not consist in being independent of necessary laws; rather, freedom is the insight into necessity. It consists in the knowledge of the laws that determine the actions of human beings, and in the possibility that this knowledge gives of making these laws work towards human ends. For Engels, then, freedom is a form of the ability to achieve one's ends; it is an ability that is based on knowledge.

The dialectical materialism that is still the official philosophy of the countries of the Soviet bloc is, in essence, the philosophy of Engels. Many Western Marxists, however, regard Engels's philosophy as seriously defective. They do not, on the whole, object to Engels's three laws viewed as descriptive of society, but they criticize Engels for extending these laws to cover inanimate matter. Some Western Marxists, indeed, say that not only was Engels wrong in this, but that in so doing he failed to grasp the true nature of Marx's thought. This, however, is hard to accept, unless one supposes that Marx himself did not grasp the true nature of his own thought. It is undeniable that

Marx's writings pay almost no attention to the philosophy of the natural sciences. Yet Engels wrote in 1885 that, since the kind of outlook expounded in *Anti-Dühring* belonged in large measure to Marx, he read the whole manuscript to Marx before it was published. One may surely assume that what was printed had Marx's approval; that is, that there was no fundamental division between the two men in respect of their views.

G.H.R. Parkinson

For editions and translations of the works of Engels, see the article on Karl Marx. See also: W.O. Henderson, *The Life of Friedrich Engels* (1976); D. McLellan, *Engels* (1977); L. Kolakowski, *Main Currents of Marxism*, vol. 1, *The Founders* (1978); Terrell Carver, *Engels* (1981).

146
ENSOR, James 1860–1949

Belgian painter and graphic artist

Born into a bourgeois family in Ostend and of partly English descent, Ensor had a stormy training at the Académie Royale in Brussels. Though rejected by the Antwerp Salon in 1882, he was almost simultaneously accepted in Paris; he became a member of 'Les XX' and from 1893 exhibited at the Libre Aesthétique. Apart from visits to London and Paris, he scarcely left his home town. Having begun as an anarchic and farouche rebel, he shrank after 1900 into a provincial grand old man, was created a baron, and by 1920 was embarked on almost thirty years of creative impotence.

Even in his earliest genre paintings Ensor emerges as an artist of great distinction. *Russian Music* (1881) is ambitious in scale and suggests the sophisticated cultural milieu in which he was formed; the sober colour and broken handling reveal his interest in the Barbizon School. Throughout his early development, especially in his etchings, Ensor pursued two parallel but interdependent tracks; he was both the very convincing and sensitive heir to the landscapes of Rembrandt and the townscapes of Charles Meryon, as well as, more strikingly, the inventor of a contemporary demonology. *Rooftops of Ostend* or *Sunset* (both from 1885) show a completely individual calligraphy, and already his characteristic palette is revealed, with its dominant pinks, and light tonality (which owes much to his study of Turner*). A later still-life such as *The Ray* (1892), with its mesmerizing fish-face is as intense and disturbing as any of his imaginative works.

But his central achievement remains the creation of a satiric vision, a modern equivalent to the moralities of Bosch and Brueghel, which also feeds on the gross humour of Low Country carnival. From the beginning this vein sometimes crossed the borderline of sanity, and images like *Roman Soldiers Discovering a Dead Body* (1880) or *Demons Tormenting Me* (1895) represent a deliberate regression; he invited the charge of madness, and in his 1887 etching of himself urinating, *Le Pisseur*, the graffiti include '*Ensor est un Fou*'. The remarkable *Tribulations of St Anthony* (1887), now in New York, shows the pink-cowled figure huddled in the lower left, looking anxiously over his shoulder at the phantasms clustering towards the frame; as he turns his back, across the empty marsh-like space another cloud of fragmentary images – women at café tables, insects, devils – comes to overwhelm him.

In 1888 he completed his masterpiece, *Christ's Entry into Brussels*, where a canvas 12 feet by 9 is stuffed from top to bottom with leering faces; the masks of carnival come to signify the grotesque folly and hypocrisy of society, unredeemed by the socialist banners which adorn the streets. In his etchings the same socialist Christ appears among beggars in limbo, while demons sniff at one another's anuses or perform enemas. Masks also confront death, and skeletons are a constant motif, performing farces, quarrelling over a bone, or in one mysterious little picture, examining Chinoiserie in a crowded library.

Ensor's vision proved influential from the 1890s onwards, especially in Germany; Emil Nolde visited him in Ostend in 1902, although he would later use masks to quite different ends; and immediately after the war, the 'Dadantesque', George Grosz, along with contemporaries like Dix and Beckmann, would again employ carnival to lash their contemporaries into shame. By that time Ensor's creative years were over; a few late paintings such as *Dolls* (1916) retain some of the old fire, but his misanthropy had been diverted into resentment at a rising generation, while alcoholism and premature senility contributed to the pathos of his decline.

Timothy Hyman

Paul Haesaerts, *James Ensor* (1957); *James Ensor, Etchings* (Arts Council, 1978).

147
ESPRONCEDA, José de 1808–42

Spanish Romantic poet

The son of an officer in the Spanish army, Espronceda was educated by the timidly liberal poet and critic Lista, later a fierce adversary of many of the ideas of the Spanish Romantics. Growing impatient with his teacher's prudent political outlook, at thirteen he joined a youthful conspiracy to avenge the Liberal martyr Riego and was banished to a monastery. There he began writing *El Pelayo*, a Neoclassical epic on the

Moorish invasion of Spain, fortunately left unfinished. Between 1827 and 1833 he lived in exile in London and Paris. During this time he began a tempestuous and eventually adulterous love affair with the daughter of a fellow-exile which later produced the *Canto a Teresa*, the most famous emotional outpouring in Spanish Romantic poetry. After his return to Spain he continued to belong to the conspiratorial Left of the Liberals and then became a founder member of the then extremist Republican Party. Shortly before his death he showed signs of moderation and was elected to parliament.

A historical novel, *Sancho Saldaña* (1834), imitating Walter Scott*, contains indications of the growing spiritual and intellectual malaise which was to distinguish Espronceda and Larra* from the more traditionalist Romantics, such as Zorrilla. Its development into strongly pessimistic insight can be followed in Espronceda's lyric poems. Three groups stand out. The first of these is patriotic and libertarian, including laments for the deaths of fellow-revolutionaries and the intemperate 'Dos de mayo', celebrating the rising of the Spanish people against Napoleon* in 1808. But the aggressive tone of these poems suggests in retrospect an attempt to find in political commitment a means of relief from the poet's deeper view of life. A second group of lyrics on figures such as the corsair, the beggar, the headsman and the condemned criminal illustrate the Romantics' hostility to social restraints and conventions. The criminal, condemned to execution, however, may also suggest Everyman, in the prison-house of existence, condemned by fate to inevitable death. The headsman may also symbolize a force of evil called into being by a cruel God. The lyrics of the third group are more specifically philosophical and include a hymn to the sun which culminates in the poet's rejection of the idea that anything can be thought of as absolute and enduring. Our ideas, beliefs and certainties have no time-defying existence.

The first of Espronceda's two masterpieces is *El estudiante de Salamanca* (1836–7, trans. E.O. Lombardi, *The Student of Salamanca*, 1953). It is a dramatic narrative poem in a great and novel variety of metres on a theme similar to that of Byron's* *Don Juan*. The hero, Don Félix de Montemar, after killing the brother of his abandoned mistress, is drawn by a spectre to a macabre and fatal punishment, meeting his own funeral on the way. But in spite of his role as a rake and a gay seducer, Don Félix emerges also as a figure of cosmic rebellion, and the poem contains a memorable outcry against the bitter reality of life. Technically the poem is a virtuoso piece, with superb use of light-effects and cold colours to evoke a phantasmagoric and nightmarish world. It also contains highly inventive imagery, startling contrasts and strikingly innovatory rhythmical patterns.

El diablo mundo ('The Devil World'), which began to be published in 1840 and remained unfinished at the poet's death, is a Byronic mock-epic in the form of an allegory of the life of man. Set in nineteenth-century Madrid, its hero Adán (Adam), who stands for man, is granted the choice between death (and understanding) and eternal life on earth. He chooses the latter and the poem records the unhappy consequences. Coming afresh naked and guileless into the world, Adán finds himself not only mocked and ill-treated by his fellows, but also – inevitably – immured, literally and figuratively, in a prison. Youth and love's illusion liberate him, but disillusionment, first with society and then with existence, follows. Awareness of death brings him to the quest for a satisfying answer to life's enigma. Here the poem breaks off. The most original and modern feature of *El diablo mundo* is the coexistence in it of two outlooks. In the first, Espronceda assumes the characteristic Romantic stance of the artist-philosopher-magus, the mouthpiece of the human spirit, satanically rebellious but at the same time deeply anguished, striving to express a profoundly tragic insight into the human condition. In the second we perceive a conscious reaction against this self-projection, as the poet satirizes himself and questions both the validity of his own aims in the work and the sincerity of his Romantic attitudes. The contrast between the two outlooks marks Espronceda's maturity, his capacity to view even his own spiritual malaise with detachment and irony.

D.L. Shaw

See: *Poesía completa* (1975); also M.A. Rees, *El estudiante de Salamanca* (*A Critical Guide*) (1979). The best general introduction in English is R.A. Cardwell's *Espronceda's El estudiante de Salamanca and Other Poems* (1980).

148
EVANS, Sir Arthur 1851–1941

British archaeologist

Like many members of Victorian industrial families Arthur Evans never had to contend with the problem of making a living. His father, Sir John Evans*, provided him with a comfortable income, and at the age of fifty-seven he inherited the entire Dickinson paper-mill fortune.

As a young man, newly down from Oxford, Evans travelled widely in the troubled parts of Eastern Europe, reporting for the *Manchester Guardian* on the successful rebellion of the peoples of the Balkans against their Turkish overlords. He was a flamboyant Liberal who identified himself closely with the nationalist cause and thrust himself forward in all the trouble-spots. Throughout this time Evans's interest in archaeology was growing (he had inherited the collector's curiosity and acquisitiveness from his father) and he undertook several small-scale excavations in the Dubrovnik district. In 1883 he visited Greece and met Schliemann*. He began to be fascinated by Mycenaean civilization and determined to prove that such an advanced society must have had some form of writing.

In the late 1880s Evans concentrated his energies on transforming the Ashmolean Museum, of which he had been elected curator, into the 'home of archaeology in Oxford'. He fought stubbornly for the study of prehistory against the opposition of Jowett* and the Oxford classicists, who refused entry of every kind of archaeology but that of Classical Greece. Evans rightly observed that 'the great characteristic of modern archaeological progress has been the revelations as to periods and men as to which history is silent'.

It was not until 1894 that Evans revisited Greece and reported on the evidence for a Bronze Age writing system. In the same year he began negotiations for the purchase of the site at Knossos, recorded in Homer as the labyrinth of the legendary King Minos. In 1899, after the successful Cretan rebellion, the transactions were complete and the excavations began. What he found at Knossos was to occupy Evans for the remaining forty years of his life.

What his excavations revealed (they were substantially complete by 1905) was a hitherto unknown Bronze Age civilization far more ancient than anything yet found on the Greek mainland. The palace at Knossos was undoubtedly the centre of this culture, which Evans named 'Minoan'. Many thousands of clay tablets with linear scripts were discovered, including the 'Linear B' scripts deciphered in the 1950s by Michael Ventris. But one of the most splendid achievements of Minoan civilization was its art, revealed in pottery designs, metalwork, wall-paintings and gemstones. This art expressed a lyrical appreciation of nature that was alien to both the Mycenaean and Classical Greek worlds and which was readily enjoyed at a time when European taste was assimilating the art of the Impressionists and the Japanese.

Schliemann had proved that the Homeric poems reflected a real world whose memory had been all but obliterated for the Classical Greeks. Evans showed that beyond this world lay another of which there was hardly a mention in Homer. The origin of this civilization could be traced back almost as far as that of Egypt. This was dramatic proof, not merely of the ability of the spade to demonstrate the historical reality of legendary events (as with Schliemann), but to document totally unrecorded events of the distant past.

Unlike his father, Evans did not believe that the archaeologist should do his best to eliminate the subjective element in reconstructing the past: the Romanticism of his Balkan period can still be felt in many passages in his major work, *The Palace of Minos* (1921–

35). He was an exponent of a literary and imaginative tradition in archaeology, which persisted until the mid-twentieth century, where scientific rigour was sometimes neglected for the shallow satisfactions of make-believe history.

C.F. Hawke-Smith

Other important works include: *Scripta Minoa* (1909 and 1952). For a recent exhaustive review of Minoan-Mycenaean civilization see Colin Renfrew, *The Emergence of Civilisation* (1972). A more popular account can be found in Sinclair Hood, *The Minoans* (1971). See: Joan Evans, *Time and Chance* (1943).

149

EVANS, Sir John 1823–1908

British archaeologist

As the younger son of an impoverished schoolmaster and antiquarian John Evans avoided the shallow learning of early nineteenth-century Oxbridge. Instead he was apprenticed to his maternal uncle, John Dickinson, who had pioneered and patented a new technique of mass-produced paper. Having married Dickinson's daughter he spent his entire working life as managing director of the paper mill, and his geological, numismatic and archaeological researches were undertaken in off-moments of his business life. His early interest in geology was stimulated by a long legal wrangle with a canal company about the supply of water to the mill from the neighbouring chalk. It was while he was travelling as a geological consultant that he met Joseph Prestwich, another amateur geologist serving a rival firm. Prestwich became his associate in extensive archaeological fieldwork. Evans was a leading member of the Royal Society, becoming vice-president in 1876. He was knighted in 1892.

In 1859 Evans made a trip with Prestwich to the Somme valley in France to examine the claims of Boucher de Perthes that humanly shaped flint tools (now known as Palaeolithic handaxes) had been found stratified in gravels in association with the bones of extinct animals. Within a week they were back to report to the Royal Society, where many of the leading scientists, including Lyell* and Huxley*, were convinced by their presentation of the evidence. From this time the high antiquity of man – the evidence for which had been steadily accumulating over more than fifty years – could no longer be doubted. The authority of the biblical account of human beginnings was increasingly questioned, even outside scientific circles. The following decade saw immense progress in the study of Palaeolithic man, particularly in France through the work of Lartet* and De Mortillet.

Evans's earliest work was on the subject of pre-

Roman coinage in Britian. His attempt to apply Darwinian* principles to archaeological material was the exemplar of many subsequent typological studies concerned with the chronological ordering of artifacts on the basis not of associations but internal variability (cf. Petrie* and Pitt-Rivers*). His major works were *The Ancient Stone Implements* (1872) and *The Ancient Bronze Implements* (1881), both compendious volumes presenting in great detail the bare artifactual data on which the prehistory of Western Europe is largely based.

Evans's achievement was finally to rescue human prehistory from the antiquarian and dilettante and to show that it could become a proper subject of scientific investigation. The objects in the collector's cabinet were shown to be documents as valid in their own way for the prehistory of man as written documents were for history. In opening up a vast perspective on human development archaeology gave credibility to the Darwinian doctrine of the gradual evolution of man from the lower animals and the Spencerian* idea of the progressive development of human societies.

C.F. Hawke-Smith

See: Joan Evans, *Time and Chance* (1943); Glyn Daniel, *One Hundred and Fifty Years of Archaeology* (1975).

F

FARADAY, Michael 1791–1867

British experimentalist and natural philosopher

Born the third child of a blacksmith in Newington, Surrey, Faraday became an eminent experimentalist, consultant, and lecturer on science. His rise from humble origins to greatness epitomized the Victorian ideal of self-help through self-improvement, contributing more to his popularity than scientific achievement alone could have done. The crucial turning point in his fortunes came at the end of his apprenticeship as a bookbinder when, in 1813, he persuaded Sir Humphry Davy* to make him an assistant in the laboratory of the Royal Institution. In 1826 Faraday became director of the laboratory. A year later he published his only book, the *Chemical Manipulation* (1827). He emulated Davy's response to the growing public appetite for scientific knowledge, seen to be improving, useful, and profitable. Yet in many of his lectures Faraday emphasized the moral and religious significance of science as a search for truth, rather than its utility. He established the Friday Evening discourses, delivering over a hundred of these between 1825 and 1861, on topics ranging from Brunel's* Thames tunnel to flatworms, colliery disasters, and the wave nature of light. Like the Christmas lectures for children (the last of which he gave in 1861), these discourses continue at the Royal Institution today. He became the institution's first Fullerian Professor of Chemistry in 1833. He also taught chemistry at the Royal Military Academy at Woolwich (1829–53), reported on lighthouse illumination for Trinity House (1836–65) and was a senator of the new London University (1836–63).

Faraday was an artisan of ideas who taught his contemporaries not only new facts but how to see old facts in new ways. He used experiment to evoke phenomena which he then expressed in a language tied closely to laboratory procedures. These seem to have been as great a source of innovation as his eclecticism in ideas. The radical physical implications of his visual language of lines of force were tempered by the reassuring fact that 'Faraday's lines' rested on the firm basis of experimental practice. His overtly experimental style led contemporaries such as Helmholtz* to confer on Faraday an undeserved honour for banishing metaphysics from science. He usually justified his new ideas

through practical demonstrations rather than abstract arguments. Thought and practice are interwoven in the work described in the three volumes of his collected *Experimental Researches in Electricity* (1839, 1844, 1855) and the seven volumes of *Faraday's Diary* (1932–6). These reveal his experimental ingenuity and an extraordinary receptiveness to visual experience, but show neither the methodological purity nor the intellectual commitments postulated by some interpreters. As much a nonconformist in his science as he was in his religion, Faraday distrusted the powers of human intellect, especially when used to anticipate nature. Experiment was needed to challenge orthodoxy and to contain the excesses of abstraction.

In 1816 Faraday published his first scientific paper, on an 'Analysis of the native caustic lime of Tuscany'. He soon gained a reputation as a chemical analyst with studies on the liquefaction of gases, hydrocarbons (including the discovery of benzene in 1825), alloys of steel, and the production of high quality optical glass. Many of these are collected in his *Experimental Researches on Chemistry and Physics* (1859). This early work was eclipsed by the stream of basic discoveries that began in 1831 with Faraday's demonstration that an electric current is induced when a circuit moves relative to the lines of magnetic force that fill the space around a magnet. He showed that these lines are independent of the matter in which they originate and terminate (unipolar induction) and used them to state his law of electro-magnetic induction in 1832. In that year he proved the identity of the five known forms of electricity (static, voltaic, galvanic, thermal, and magnetically-induced). In 1833 he established two laws of electrolysis which relate the amount of chemical action of a current to the quantity of electricity passed through a solution, and the masses of the chemical products to their chemical equivalents. James Joule* later developed the implications of these discoveries for a theory of energy conservation. In 1834 Faraday showed that the shock produced by breaking a long conducting circuit (also noticed by Joseph Henry) is a case of magnetic induction in which the magnetic lines of the current act on its own conductor instead of a neighbouring one. In 1835 he began to experiment on electrostatic phenomena, formulating the view that induction is an active state of the region between charged bodies rather than an interaction of discrete electric fluids. This led him to prove that insulators are not impervious to electricity but have specific inductive capacities (1836–7). He failed to get similar results with magnetic forces but was persuaded to resume this search by William Thomson (Lord Kelvin*) in 1845.

Overwork brought on an illness that lasted from 1839 to 1843. Faraday challenged traditional atomic and materialistic doctrines in two lectures of 1844. He argued that material properties are not localized in discrete particles of finite extension but are distributed throughout space, so that two atoms may pass through each other just as 'two sea waves of different velocities' combine and separate. In 1846 he further dematerialized atoms by extending his argument to inertia and gravitation and by hypothesizing that light and heat travel as vibrations in the lines that carry these powers through space. The optical aether is really just attenuated 'matter'. On his view entities such as atoms or magnetic poles do not exist in their own right. They merely define the boundaries of physical relationships, which are exchanges of force. The influence of these arguments, although delayed, was to set laboratory experience of current-magnet interactions above everyday experience of inert objects, making forces more real than brute matter.

The 1846 lecture followed an experimental breakthrough. In 1845 Faraday showed that a ray of plane-polarized light is rotated in a strong magnetic field (the Faraday effect) and that all matter is susceptible to magnetic influence (diamagnetism). Extending this work to crystals in 1848, he developed a general theory of magnetism. Published in 1850, this gave the first explicit definition of the magnetic field (a term Faraday had been using since 1845) and placed his magnetic researches on the same theoretical footing as the electrical work of 1836–7. He built instruments to demonstrate the quantitative, geometrical relationships between electric and magnetic lines, and sharpened his arguments of 1844–6, against the rival, action at-a-distance theories of electromagnetism. In 1852 he developed the earlier insight (based on discoveries of Oersted and Ampère) that electricity and magnetism are mutually perpendicular components of a field of force, perpendicular to a third axis which defines the direction in which they act. This geometrical synthesis showed the 'oneness' of apparently distinct forces. Faraday's life's work had been to include all forces in this synthesis, from atomic 'relations' to gravitational attractions. His last paper, a 'Note on a possible relation of gravity with electricity or heat', was rejected by the Royal Society in 1860, but Faraday continued his search until he retired to Hampton Court in 1862, on a pension from Queen Victoria*. Faraday's interlocking systems of electric and magnetic lines gained wider acceptance as the subject of James Clerk Maxwell's* mathematical theory of the electromagnetic field. An asymmetry in Maxwell's formal treatment of magnetic induction prompted Einstein's 1905 reformulation of electrodynamics.

David Gooding

Other works: examples of Faraday's lectures include *A Course of Six Lectures on the various Forces of Matter* (1860) and *A Course of Six Lectures on the Chemical History of a Candle* (1860 and many later editions), both ed. William Crookes. For others see: A.E. Jeffreys, *Michael Faraday, A List of his Lectures and published Writings* (1960). Extracts of letters and diaries can be found in the first biography, H. Bence-Jones, *The Life and Letters of Faraday* (2 vols, 1870). A contemporary appreciation emphasizing scientific style is J. Tyndall, *Faraday as a Discoverer* (1868). *The Selected Correspondence of Michael Faraday*, ed. L.P. Williams (2 vols, 1971), is indispensable. A comprehensive recent biography is L.P. Williams, *Michael Faraday, A Biography* (1965).

151
FAURÉ, Gabriel Urbain 1845–1924

French composer

Gabriel Fauré was the youngest of six children. His father was first a schoolmaster and then the director of a teachers' training college in the southern *département* of Ariège. At the age of nine Fauré was sent to the Niedermeyer School in Paris, where the teaching was more thorough and comprehensive than that at the Conservatoire, with its traditional bias towards opera. Among Fauré's teachers Saint-Saëns* did much to encourage his early efforts in composition. Fauré was to spend much of his life as an organist, but in 1896 he was appointed to a professorship of composition at the Paris Conservatoire when his influence on a whole generation of French composers started to bear fruit. He became director of the Conservatoire in 1905, the administrative duties of which left him less time for composition. Unfortunately, increasing deafness led to his resignation in 1920, and his final years were spent in semi-retirement. His last work, the String Quartet, was completed only two months before his death in November 1924.

As with many composers, Fauré's work can be divided into three periods, with the inevitable consequent overlapping. The most characteristic music of Fauré's earlier years (to *c.* 1884) is undoubtedly the chamber music, particularly the First Violin Sonata (1875–6) and First Piano Quartet (1876–83). Their originality is due to the fact that Fauré had very few French models to serve as a guide, save for the earlier chamber works of Saint-Saëns. The continuity of the accompanimental figurations show Fauré's indebtedness to Baroque movements of the single *Affekt* type, rather than to the Romantic sonata where a single movement will often unfold several 'new chapters' during its course. The clarity of the textures and the quiet inevitability of the music are astonishingly assured. Of Fauré's hundred or so songs, thirty-five date from this period; while a few add little to their Gounodesque models, the best of them (particularly *Après un Rêve*, c. 1875, and those set to the sensitive poetry of Sully-Prudhomme) display a subtle correlation between poetry and music which has remained a model in French song-writing. Apart from the ambitious *Ballade*, Op. 19 (1879), Fauré's earlier piano works, while beautifully written, are more derivative: particularly the first four Nocturnes and the first three Impromptus, where Fauré's model was Chopin*. The first two Barcarolles, however, are more Fauréan in their sensuousness, the composer preferring to utilize his own vivid imagination of this most romantic of musical genres rather than depend on the more elaborate *Barcarolle* of Chopin.

The second period (c. 1885–1900) saw the consolidation of Fauré's techniques as a composer. Gone are the occasional reminiscences of Gounod* in the songs, and Chopin in the piano works. In particular, the songs demonstrate that the exquisite poetry of Paul Verlaine* all but belongs to Fauré's music: the *Five Venetian Songs* (1891) and the nine songs of *La Bonne Chanson* (1892–4) scale the peak of Fauré's art in this form. In both, the subtle employment of thematic transference from one song to another, along with the sensitive treatment of voice and piano and the sheer fertility of Fauré's musical invention make these cycles a landmark in the history of French song. The *Requiem* (1886–90), intimate, restrained and already showing that austerity and tenuity of texture which was to be a hallmark of the music of Fauré's third period, is still the best known of his large-scale works. The Sixth and Seventh Nocturnes for piano (1894 and 1898) are an enormous advance on the earlier Nocturnes: the latter is particularly interesting in its interrelation of material from one theme to another, and in the bold employment of passing notes in contrapuntal textures. The *Dolly Suite* (1893–6) for piano duet shows in its cheerfulness and lightness of touch a different side to Fauré. The almost unknown Second Piano Quartet (1886) is even finer than its predecessor with its large-scale opening Allegro, an almost barbaric scherzo, a long nocturne-like slow movement, and a finale which again looks ahead harmonically and texturally to Fauré's final period. The First Piano Quintet (1890–4 and 1903–5), mostly composed in the 1890s as a projected third piano quartet, was first performed in Brussels in 1906, and belongs spiritually to the last period. As in all but one of the late chamber works, there are only three movements: the gravely beautiful first movement is remarkable for a recapitulation 'so varied as to take away all feeling of repetition' (Aaron Copland); while the ternary slow

movement, beginning in 12/8 time, gradually mixes it with 4/4, in which time signature the movement ends. The free variation form of the finale is perhaps the least successful part of the quintet.

The production of the lyric drama *Prométhée* in 1900 marks the start of Fauré's final period. He had gradually been moving towards the ultimate refinement of his art, the paring down of all inessentials, resulting in limpid textures whose frequently contrapuntal lines had brought a new and unique quality of sound to music. The last four song cycles have never been popular either with singers or audiences, for this is essentially intimate music. The same is true of much of the piano music from this period. The almost unknown *Nine Preludes* (1909–10), the elegiac Eleventh Nocturne (1913), the tortuous harmonies of the middle of the Fourth Impromptu (1905), the surprisingly dissonant accented passing notes of the stormy Twelfth Nocturne (1915), all these epitomize the enormous variety even of Fauré's later piano music, which as a whole in both quality and quantity is in every way comparable with that of Chopin, Debussy or Ravel. But it is in the last six chamber works that one can see the most complete picture of the composer. The Second Violin Sonata (1916–17) contains one of Fauré's most powerful and compelling first movements; the glory of the Second Cello Sonata (1921) is the noble lyricism of its central movement; while the large-scale Second Piano Quintet (1919–21) provides the most comprehensive view of every facet of Fauré's genius.

Comparing the idiom of the earliest song with that of the String Quartet of over sixty years later, one can see immediately the enormous strides made by Fauré over this period: the two pieces seem almost to suggest two different composers. And yet by proceeding chronologically from one piece to the next, it is evident that his development was perfectly logical, indeed inevitable. The influence of the Niedermeyer School on his employment of modal techniques has been somewhat overstressed: the First Piano Quartet and the *Requiem* use modal themes, but they are works which have become popular to the exclusion of many others which do not. Harmonically Fauré was in fact a late Romantic, but in other respects he was very different from his contemporaries. He was one of the first to pare down the non-essentials of music at a time (c. 1890) when in general music was at its most opulent; and thus, like Debussy, he forestalled the Neoclassicism of the 1920s. He took considerable trouble over accompanimental figures, where often tunes will emerge against the main melody almost in a contrapuntal manner. Like Beethoven*, his fondness for contrapuntal and canonic devices increased as he grew older. Fauré was particularly skilful in his employment of thematic metamorphosis, usually accomplished in a quiet way, displaying that reticence and refinement which is so characteristic of much French music in general and of Fauré in particular. He suppressed several of his early orchestral pieces, but his interest in orchestration was greater than is often imagined. When writing his only opera, *Pénélope* (1907–12), he wrote to his wife: 'The orchestration . . . will be a pleasure, a relief and a relaxation.' Unlike his pupil Ravel, Fauré never 'searched for new harmonies'. His technique of moving rapidly from one chromatic chord to another was a favourite one, but his aim was never to subvert the tonal system. He often 'looks at' rather than 'states' a new key; and thus it is not so much the language which is new, it is rather the syntax, the order of words. In this respect he was a potent force for the twentieth century. It is unlikely that Fauré will ever be as popular as Debussy, in France or elsewhere. Fauré's music never imposes itself by brute force, and therefore it will probably be always to a minority that his work will appeal. Nevertheless, like Rameau, he remains one of the great underrated figures in French music.

J. Barrie Jones

See: Charles Koechlin, *Gabriel Fauré* (1945); Norman Suckling, *Fauré* (1946); Jean-Michel Nextoux, *Fauré* (1972); Vladimir Jankélévitch, *Fauré et l'inexprimable* (1974); Robert Orledge, *Gabriel Fauré* (1979).

152
FAWCETT, Millicent Garrett, Dame 1847–1929

British suffragist

Millicent Garrett Fawcett was a leading member of the constitutional branch of the women's suffrage movement: from 1897 she was President of the National Union of Women's Suffrage Societies (NUWSS).

She was born in Aldeburgh, the fifth daughter of Newsom Garrett, merchant and shipowner. Her schooling was cut short when she was fifteen but her marriage in 1867 to the blind MP and Cambridge economist Henry Fawcett brought her into radical political circles and in itself provided her with a specialized education. In 1868 her first article, 'The Lectures for Women at Cambridge', appeared in *Macmillan's Magazine* and in 1870 she published a short primer, *Political Economy for Beginners*. In 1867 she joined the London National Society for Women's Suffrage with the full support of her husband who with John Stuart Mill* had presented the first of many women's suffrage petitions to the House of Commons in the previous year. Her sister Elizabeth Garrett Anderson's struggle to obtain medical qualifications and Elizabeth's friend Emily Davies's fight for women's secondary and higher education profoundly influenced her thought. She believed that women's rights were best upheld by education, by an equal moral standard for men and women, by professional and industrial liberty and by political status.

Millicent Fawcett played a major part in the establishment of the Cambridge lecture scheme which was to develop into Newnham College. (In 1890 her daughter Philippa was placed above the Senior Wrangler in the Mathematics Tripos.) With her husband she campaigned for the right of married women to own property and for the amendment of the Factory Acts to allow women equal working hours. After his death in 1884 she joined the National Vigilance Association formed to combat criminal vice. But she was continually reminded that all efforts to protect women's rights were hampered by their lack of political power. She joined the Liberal-Unionists in 1887 and her active role in the party kept her in contact with politicians during the decades when women's suffrage seemed to make little progress. Between 1887 and 1895 she visited Ireland regularly and made many speeches attacking Home Rule. In 1901 she was invited to lead a committee of women sent to investigate conditions in the concentration camps in South Africa; the commission's report did much to improve the appalling conditions in the camps.

The achievement of at least limited suffrage for women seemed possible in the 1870s (Jacob Bright's Women's Disabilities Bill passed a second reading in 1870) but in the 1880s and 1890s votes for women were continually baulked by party politics, in particular by the hostility of the Liberal leadership towards women's suffrage. In 1905 Mrs Pankhurst founded the Women's Social and Political Union. From the start the WSPU was seen to be militant and by 1908 was adopting a campaign of deliberate violence. As head of the NUWSS Millicent Fawcett condemned, while fully understanding, the suffragettes' tactics. She wrote: 'What is called militancy is "political unrest" caused by the mishandling and misunderstanding by politicians of one of the greatest movements in the history of the world.' The suffragists benefited from the publicity given to women's suffrage by the militants. Membership of the constitutional societies increased and Mrs Fawcett led a series of impressive marches culminating in the 1913 'Pilgrimage'. After the failure of the Conciliation Bills of 1910–12 the NUWSS decided to abandon its policy of non-alignment and to back the Labour Party which actively supported women's suffrage.

Mrs Fawcett suspended suffrage activities during the Great War in order to release women for war work. She was faced with a pacifist majority on the NUWSS council but succeeded in remaining president whilst all her fellow officers resigned. She maintained contact with friends of women's suffrage in parliament and gained the support of Lord Northcliffe thus ensuring the backing of *The Times*. In 1918 limited suffrage for women was included in the Representation of the People Act. In 1928 Dame Millicent witnessed the culmination of a life's work – the enfranchisement of women on equal terms with men.

Millicent Fawcett's strength as a leader lay in her moderation. She gained the respect of politicians and was politically more sophisticated and consistent (although less imaginative) than the Pankhursts. Yet her old-fashioned *laissez-faire* liberalism was to seem out of place in the twentieth century and characteristically she left the NUWSS in 1924 because she opposed their advocacy of mothers' pensions and family allowances.

Tanya Harrod

Millicent Fawcett's important works are (with Henry Fawcett) *Essays and Lectures on Social and Political Subjects* (1875); *Women's Suffrage* (1911); *The Women's Victory* and *After: Personal Reminiscences, 1911–1918* (1920); *What I Remember* (1924); (with E.M. Turner) *Josephine Butler* (1927). See: Ray Strachey, *The Cause* (1928) and *Millicent Garrett Fawcett* (1931); Constance Rover, *Women's Suffrage and Party Politics in Britain 1866–1914* (1967).

153
FEUERBACH, Ludwig Andreas 1804–72

German philosopher and religious thinker

Born in Landshut in 1804, the son of a Bavarian lawyer who became a judge, Feuerbach studied theology at the University of Heidelberg before transferring to the University of Berlin in 1824, where he sat at the feet of G.W.F. Hegel* and F.D.E. Schleiermacher*. His thought was deeply influenced by them both, and it is recorded that he was an enthusiastic listener to the sermons of the latter delivered in the Holy Trinity Church (Dreifältigkeitskirche, now the ruined Kaiser-Wilhelms-Gedächtniskirche) in Berlin, which he described to the day of his death as 'holy ground'. His short-lived academic career (1828–32) as *Privatdozent* in theology at the University of Erlangen ended when he was pressurized to resign owing to his extremely heterodox Hegelian views on death and immortality. He spent the remainder of his life in private scholarship, mainly in Rural Bavaria, and died in 1872 in the village of Rechenburg near Nuremberg. Feuerbach is commonly and not incorrectly classified as belonging to the 'left-wing', radical, branch of the Hegelian School, which included in its membership D.F. Strauss*, Bruno Bauer*, A. Ruge, M. Stirner and, later, Marx*. His central and best-known work is *The Essence of Christianity*, (*Das Wesen des Christentums*, 1841, trans. 1854).

The starting-point for understanding Feuerbach's thought is undoubtedly the philosophico-religious thought of Hegel and Schleiermacher. For Hegel, 'God' is the Absolute Mind or Spirit (*Geist*) achieving self-consciousness through the ongoing, sublime, progressive thinking of the totality of finite minds of humanity, a view which has attracted the title 'panlogical immanentism'. For Schleiermacher, 'God', identified as 'the All', 'the Spirit of the All', or 'the World-Spirit' (*Weltgeist*), is immanent within all that is and moves around man, makes contact with man in and through the pressure of his environment, creating in and evoking from man 'holy (or pious) feeling', which forms for Schleiermacher the essential substance of all genuine religion. It is essential to notice that both Hegel and Schleiermacher, while they did not explicitly repudiate the notion, had precious little to say of God's *transcendence* over the world, his 'otherness' over against the world of everyday common experience. Feuerbach's thought may be said to begin from this apparent lack or omission in the thought of his two masters. He argued therefore that the thought of them both, Hegel's in particular, tends unmistakably towards the affirmation of the non-objective quality of God's existence and being. The main substance of their teaching, with minor, not to say negligible, qualification, is Man; human thinking, human reflection, human feeling and human striving. They hardly utter, that is, the word 'God', except in the closest possible conjunction with human activity, to the virtual exclusion of 'God' conceived of as a transcendent, 'other' being.

From this Feuerbach drew the radical conclusion that both Hegel and Schleiermacher (although they both just failed to realize it) were substantially and really talking about man *sub specie aeternitatis et divinitatis* rather than about the God of traditional supernaturalistic theism. Feuerbach therefore in *The Essence of Christianity* announced his programme of doing what his philosophical mentors had shrunk from doing – to transform completely theology into anthropology, the love of God into the love of man, the service of God into the service of man. Man must be persuaded to turn his attention away from the other-worldly to the worldly, from some life which is allegedly to come to this present life, from heaven towards earth. It is not that what Hegel and Schleiermacher had said about God was false – rather that the sublimity and divinity and perfection which they had predicated of a transcendent deity (whose factual existence, in Feuerbach's view, had been falsified by the critical philosophy of the *Aufklärung*) should now and in the future be predicated of their only and proper subject, Man himself. The basic, but incalculably huge, error of most traditional Western theistic religion has been to project the inestimable worth and sublimity which belongs to the human species on to an imaginary, non-existent deity 'beyond' or 'over' or 'behind' the world of nature. Feuerbach by no means wishes to abandon or discard theological terminology or discourse; he simply wishes to have it all transferred to man from 'God'. Feuerbach was sharply critical of Hegel's philosophical idealism: not only did it imply contempt for the epistemological value of sense-experience (the basis of modern science), but it also understood man in a ludicrously spiritual (*geistlich*) sense, as some kind of disembodied spirit lacking, or despising, bodily needs, comforts and drives. Hence we have Feuerbach's celebrated anti-Hegelian aphorism, '*Mann ist was er isst*' ('Man is what he eats'). The contribution here of Feuerbach towards a certain kind of materialism is undeniable. If we combine these two fundamental notions of Feuerbach together, the quite erroneous and pernicious concentration of thought, effort, devotion, materials and money (e.g., in the building of churches, cathedrals, shrines and sanctuaries) upon a non-existent transcendent deity, and the fantastically spiritual and non-material understanding of man in idealism, we have the celebrated Feuerbachian doctrines that God is worshipped at the expense of man, that heaven can be contemplated only by ignoring the earth, that there is not merely mutual incompatibility but hostility between traditional religious supernaturalism and the welfare of the human species understood in its widest possible sense. And clearly, the aspiration for life after death can easily become a worthless compensation for the endurance of allegedly irremediable sufferings and unjustices in this present worldly life. Such reflections lead naturally to Feuerbach's extremely important notion – that of human 'self-alienation'. Empirically, man is all too vividly aware that he is not what he ought to be: but what he ought to be or to have become he has disastrously projected on to an other-worldly but non-existent God. But the distance between such a deity and man means that man is permanently alienated from self-realization, and the abiding importance of religion for Feuerbach is that it is the area not only where self-alienation takes place, but where it is recognized for what it is.

Paradoxically perhaps, Feuerbach returns to the Christian religion in order to glean from it concealed but highly significant anthropological insights. Christianity must now be subjectivized, or 'anthropologized'. If we approach it in the light of its indispensable anthropological or existential contribution we see it in its true light for the first time. 'God', we must realize, is the epitome or quintessence of all human realities or perfections or potentialities which belong to the human species as such; 'God' is the symbol of human perfectibility. The doctrine of the incarnation must be turned upon its head: it signifies not God becoming man, but the deification of man, the possibility of man becoming God. The contemplation of miracles signifies the drive within the human spirit towards the fulfilment of human desires, aspirations and ambitions. The Holy Spirit doctrine is the projection, the objectification, of the crying out of the human spirit for the fulfilment of profoundly cherished aspirations. Prayer, properly

understood, is man's self-analysis in the light of his unique needs and capabilities. Sacraments utilizing water and bread and wine point to human belief in the curative, therapeutic powers immanent in nature. In other words, Feuerbach's re-examination and reinterpretation of Christian doctrines represents his programme of translating theology into anthropology, in his view the only programme to prevent Christianity from disappearing into oblivion.

The contemporary estimate of Feuerbach's worth and significance is a singularly contentious, not to say emotive, matter, and depends in the last analysis upon the philosophical, theological and ideological standpoint of the critic. For twentieth-century Protestant neo-orthodox theologians like Karl Barth, for example, Feuerbach's work stands as a grim, but important, warning to all theological thinkers who attempt to move from a theory of human nature (theological anthropology) to a doctrine of God; Barth held uncompromisingly that this slippery slope, which has been trodden by many 'existentialist' theologians from Schleiermacher to Bultmann, leads inevitably to a sublime humanism, and was charted with startling clarity for the first time by Feuerbach. Then again, many traditional philosophical theists have bluntly labelled Feuerbach 'atheistic', on the grounds of his denial of the transcendence of God. But in his lifetime Feuerbach vehemently rejected the title as misleadingly unfair: his predication of divinity of the human species was in his view profoundly religious. On the other hand, many modern reformist Christians of liberal, even left-wing, persuasion have used Feuerbach positively to warn modern Christendom of the perils of so emphasizing divine transcendence, or the 'spiritual' or 'other-worldly' aspects of Christianity, that unconcern is directed towards man as a psychosomatic creation who lives in a political and economic order that may be in need of radical, even revolutionary, reform. The link between Feuerbach's work and the critique of religion formulated by Marx and Engels* is so obvious as hardly to need comment. In the religious dimension, Feuerbach is *the* link between Hegel and Marx, and to this day Feuerbach occupies an important position in the Soviet and Eastern bloc philosophical pantheon. And his use of the term 'projection' inspired Freud in his construction of a psychogenetic account of religion.

James Richmond

Translations: *The Essence of Christianity* (1957), with introductory essay by Karl Barth; *Lectures on the Essence of Religion*, trans. Ralph Manheim (1967). See: James Collins, *God in Modern Philosophy* (1960); Jacob Tauber, 'The Copernican Turn of Theology', in *Religious Experience and Truth*, ed. Sidney Hook (1962); James Richmond, *Faith and Philosophy* (1966); James C. Livingston, *Modern Christian Thought* (1971); Karl

Barth, *Protestant Theology in the Nineteenth Century* (1972).

154
FEYDEAU, Georges (Léon Jules Marie)
1862–1921

French dramatist

During the late nineteenth century, French theatre was at its strongest in the field of light comedy, and no one wrote more successfully or skilfully in this vein than Georges Feydeau. Born in Paris, the son of Ernest Feydeau (himself a well-known author), he was educated by private tutors, later entering the Lycée Saint-Louis. Feydeau first visited the theatre at about the age of seven, and is said to have begun writing a play upon his return home. He later claimed to have done so in order to avoid schoolwork. By the time he entered the Lycée, Feydeau was already in possession of considerable technical skills, notably in the writing of dialogue.

Through the Window (*Par la fenêtre*, 1881) was the first of Feydeau's plays to be staged, followed by a production of *Love and a Piano* (*Amour et Piano*) in Paris in 1883. The following year Feydeau began National Service, but continued to write, and out of this period came *A Gown for his Mistress* (*Tailleur pour dames*, 1887), which won some critical acclaim. This was followed, however, by five lean years of rejection, until 1892, when *Monsieur Goes Hunting!* (*Monsieur chasse!*) and *Champignol in Spite of Himself* (*Champignol malgré lui*) began runs of over a thousand performances. The latter was written with Maurice Desvallières, Feydeau's most frequent collaborator.

A string of lucrative successes made Feydeau the most popular playwright in France. But a fascination for the stock market, inherited from his father, meant he had to keep on working to cover his financial losses. His last play, *Hortense Said: 'I don't give a damn!'* (*Hortense a dit: 'Je m'en fous!'*) was performed in 1916. He died in Rueil, following a cerebral haemorrhage, five years later.

Feydeau ranks with Eugène Labiche and Georges Courteline as one of the great French farceurs. Written during a period when the 'well-made play' dominated French drama (see Sardou*), a Feydeau farce is like a clock made with all its works on display: it is the creation of a highly skilled craftsman taking every opportunity to show off. As in all farces, Feydeau's humour is drawn primarily from physical situations, rather than from the study of character. An audience is always distanced from the proceedings, observing the smoothly mechanical manipulation of figures on the stage, rarely becoming involved with them as individuals. Feydeau's finest work – *A Flea in her Ear* (*La*

puce à l'oreille, 1907), for example, or *Keep an Eye on Amélie* (*Occupe-toi d'Amélie*, 1908) – have been likened to jigsaw puzzles, each separate piece designed for a specific effect, but also forming part of a minutely detailed whole.

Feydeau understood well the workings of the theatre of his time, and knew how to make best use of the stage and its properties. His plot devices – mistaken identity, overheard conversation, and so on – are unoriginal, but in his hands become unique, as they are frenziedly piled one on top of another. Few companies outside France have ever mastered the necessary style for Feydeau: a measured effect appearing through apparent chaos. As a result, much of the work of one of the masters of the one-act comedy remains unknown in the English-speaking world.

Paul Nicholls

Feydeau's other plays include: *Jailbird* (*Gibier de potence*, 1884); *Budding Lovers* (*Fiancés en herbe*, 1886); *The Schoolgirl* (*La lycéenne*, 1887); *A Household Bath* (*Un bain de ménage*, 1888); *A Pig in a Poke* (*Le chat en poche*, 1888); *How to Get rid of your Mistress* (*Un fil à la patte*, 1894); *Our Future* (*Notre futur*, 1894); *The Dupe* (*Le dindon*, 1896); *Good Intentions, Bad Effects* (*Les pavés de l'ours*, 1896); *Night Session* (*Séance de nuit*, 1897); *Sleep, I Tell You!* (*Dormez, je le veux!*, 1897); *The Girl from Maxim's* (*La dame de chez Maxim*, 1899); *The Duchess of the Folies-Bergère* (*La duchesse des Folies-Bergère*, 1902); *Pass the Deal!* (*La main passe!*, 1904); *The Bud* (*Le bourgeon*, 1906); *Madame's Late Mother* (*Feu la mère de madame*, 1908); *Going to Pot* (*On purge Bébé*, 1910); *A Hundred Million from Heaven* (*Cent millions qui tombent*, 1911); *'Don't Go Walking Around Naked!'* (*'Mais n'te promène donc pas tout nue!'*, 1911); *Léonie is Fast, or, The Pretty Affliction* (*Léonie est en avance, ou, Le mal joli*, 1911); *We're Going to Play Cocotte* (*On va faire la cocotte*, 1913); with Maurice Desvallières he wrote: *The Lovers of Loches* (*Les Fiancés de Loches*, 1888); *The Édouard Affair* (*L'affaire Édouard*, 1889); *It's a Woman of the World* (*C'est une femme du monde*, 1890); *Barillon's Wedding* (*Le Mariage de Barillon*, 1890); *The Ribbon* (*Le ruban*, 1894); *Hotel Paradiso* (*L'hôtel du libre échange*, 1894); and *The Golden Age* (*L'âge d'or*, 1905); with Maurice Hennequin: *The Ribadier System* (*Le système Ribadier*, 1892); with Francis de Croisset: *The Circuit* (*Le Circuit*, 1909); and with René Peter: *I Don't Cheat on my Husband* (*Je ne trompe pas mon mari*, 1914).
During the late 1960s a number of one-act farces by Feydeau were adapted for British television by Ned Sherrin and Caryl Brahms, who are perhaps his most sympathetic translators.

155
FICHTE, Johann Gottlieb 1762–1814

German philosopher

Fichte was one of the most popular philosophers of nineteenth-century Germany. His popularity stemmed not from the speculative boldness of his philosophical writings, but from his inspiring achievements as a revolutionary and patriotic orator, i.e. as the author of such speeches, pamphlets and essays as *Beitrag zur Berichtigung der Urteile des Publikums über die Französische Revolution* ('Contribution to the Correction of the Public's Judgments Regarding the French Revolution'), published anonymously in 1793; *Zurückforderung der Denkfreiheit von den Fürsten Europens, die sie bisher unterdrückten* ('Reclamation of the Freedom of Thought from the Princes of Europe, Who Have Hitherto Suppressed It'), likewise published anonymously in 1793; *The Vocation of the Scholar*, (*Einige Vorlesungen über die Bestimmung des Gelehrten*, 1847 trans. 1974; and *Reden an die Deutsche Nation* ('Addresses to the German Nation', 1807–8). The latter and his social utopia of 1800, *Der geschlossene Handelsstaat* ('The Exclusive Commercial State'), made it possible for Fichte to be subsequently requisitioned as an early exponent of their political programmes by such extreme ideological adversaries as Socialists and National Socialists. In the face of such twentieth-century claims it is as well to bear in mind that Fichte's political position, which certainly did not shy away from partisanship, belongs to a historically different constellation. The socialism he advocated was a kind of guild socialism, with elaborate contractual arrangements between the different estates and guilds in society, arrangements decreed by reason and guaranteed by the state (the 'Reichsstaat', i.e. the constitutional state, a notion central to the Weimar Republic and even more so to the Federal Republic of Germany). The patriotism he advocated had nothing to do with the wild imperialism and enslavement of other nations envisaged by Adolf Hitler. What we can say for certain is that Fichte was a Jacobin *manqué*. The bold, subversively agitatory title of his essay on the freedom of thought bears the subtitle *Heliopolis, im letzten Jahre der alten Finsternis* ('City of the Sun, in the Last Year of its Old Obscurantism'), indicating that Fichte regarded the days of the absolutist petty princes as numbered. He was a cosmopolitan humanist and, for most of his life, an ardent republican, although there were moments when he seemed prepared to make his peace with constitutional monarchy. At the time of the Napoleonic occupation of Prussia he did much to help build a patriotism which would unite all Germans, a necessary precondition for defeating Napoleon*.

It is astonishing that a man like Fichte, who came from very humble origins – his father was a poor ribbon weaver – should have risen to such eminence in a country whose rulers did everything to keep in check the spread of the revolutionary ideas from France. Two moments of lucky chance altered Fichte's life: as a young boy he was recognized for his extraordinary intelligence by a wealthy aristocrat who undertook to pay for a first-class education of this young talent. Later, when Fichte had completed his studies at the University of Jena and Leipzig, having failed to get a position as preacher, he went to Königsberg (in 1791) where he submitted a treatise to Immanuel Kant, *Versuch einer Kritik aller Offenbarung* ('Attempt at a Critique of all Revelation'), which, quite in accordance with Kantian philosophy, based religion on the moral law and argued that revealed religion was a practical postulate because without the authority of religious revelation some men were incapable of acting morally. With Kant's recommendation this treatise was published in the following year. It was widely held to be by Kant himself as the author's name had been omitted by accident. Kant felt obliged to have a correction printed in the *Allgemeine Literaturzeitung*, naming the real author, expressing his respect for him and asking the public to give him his due. Fichte's reputation was made and when, in 1793, the University of Jena was looking for a philosopher, preferably with Kantian leanings, Fichte appeared to be the obvious unavoidable choice. The state authorities elected to turn a blind eye to the fact that Fichte was also the author of some very subversive pamphlets. Fichte held this position only until 1799. As co-editor of the *Philosophisches Journal* he had allowed publication of an article which was indicted as atheist by the state authorities in Weimar. Fichte, fearing a limitation of academic freedom, threatened to resign. His resignation was promptly accepted and he had to leave the university. He turned to Berlin which, not least because of the guarantees of religious tolerance by the King of Prussia, was becoming a major centre of intellectual and literary culture. Fichte was now unquestionably the most important and famous philosopher in Germany next to Kant. The direction of his thinking had taken a sharp turn away from Kant's *Critiques* towards a philosophy of absolute idealism. This he expounded in his *Grundlage der gesammten Wissenschaftslehre* ('Foundations of the Entire Science of Knowledge'), the first version of which was published in 1794. He was the leader of a young German intelligentsia which considered Schiller and Goethe* too cautiously conservative and was prepared to challenge the repressive domination of the old aristocracy through the leadership given by an aristocracy of intelligence and scholarship, as Fichte had taught in his lectures on the vocation of the scholar. In Berlin he associated with writers of the early Romantic movement such as Dorothea Veith, Schleiermacher*, Tieck, August Wilhelm Schlegel* and Friedrich Schlegel*. At the turn of the eighteenth to the nineteenth century the latter declared that the major tendencies of the age were indicated by the French Revolution, Fichte's *Wissenschaftslehre* and Goethe's *Wilhelm Meister*. In his social utopia of 1800, the 'exclusive commercial state', Fichte attempted to keep alive the Jacobin ideal of equality, including that of happiness, while the 'realm of reason' in France had turned into a realm of the bourgeoisie after the fall of Robespierre and Saint-Just. In 1805 he was given a professorship at the University of Erlangen.

The collapse of Prussia in the face of the Napoleonic armies occasioned a major reorientation in Fichte's attitude. Even in his lectures *The Characteristics of the Present Age* (*Die Grundzüge des gegenwärtigen Zeitalters*, 1844), which had first been delivered shortly before in 1804–5, Fichte had proclaimed that for the man of intellect – as distinct from the 'man of the soil' – the true fatherland in Europe had to be the state which at a given time was culturally the most advanced. When these lectures were published in 1806, Fichte fled first to Königsberg and then to Copenhagen to escape from 'the most awful despotism'. Napoleon was a betrayal of the humane ideals which the revolutionary French Republic had stood for. Hence France was no longer the pinnacle of culture in Europe. Fichte hoped that that distinction might pass to Germany, although he considered as late as 1813, not without a little pessimism, that without the abdication of the petty princes there could be no united German people. But Fichte's view of history was optimistic. Mankind was basically locked on a positive trajectory of an even higher realization of ethical humanity. The philosopher, by the sheer power of his thought, might push mankind towards this goal. If Marx* could call Kant's philosophy of right 'The German theory of the French Revolution', then Fichte's philosophy of right must be considered the highest articulation of radical Jacobinism. Fichte's philosophy might be merely a reflection of the separation of intellectual labour from manual at the inception of bourgeois society, but Fichte was certainly not content merely to interpret the world. His project was to change it.

Fichte's main philosophical achievement was to shift German philosophy decisively towards absolute idealism. He was dissatisfied with Kant's critique of reason because it contained a deep-seated contradiction: all intellectual apprehension was dependent on sense perception, which in turn depended on things outside the perceiving subject. Fichte proceeded to argue that all perception is the realization of the pure self, of which the individual ego is but a part. Without the pure, absolute self, i.e. without pure knowledge, there is nothing. Being and the absolute self are identical. The latter is in constant activity, an activity of positing the non-self, of opposing it and of forming a synthesis with it in absolute knowledge. The individual is but a part of this dialectical process of the absolute self. In other words, Fichte established the triple step of dialectical

thought which, via Hegel, became the basis of both idealist and materialist nineteenth-century German philosophy. Philosophy itself, before it was dismantled by the critique of political economy in the writings of Marx and Engels*, was intended by Fichte to be the science of knowledge, i.e. the foundation of all particular sciences. To the extent that these theories, under Fichte's direct influence, were written into the constitution of the newly founded University of Berlin (1810) – which in turn helped to transform the university system both in Germany and in Britain – Fichte contributed greatly to the spirit of theoretical inquiry that pervades the production of knowledge. He was one of the first elected vice-chancellors of Berlin University. He died from an infection passed on to him by his wife whilst she was nursing German soldiers engaged in the battle against Napoleon.

Wilfried van der Will

J.G. Fichte, *Gesamtausgabe*, ed. Reinhard Lauth and Hans Jacob (1962 *et seq.*). English translations include: William Smith, *The Popular Works of Johann Gottlieb Fichte* (2 vols, 1848–9); Peter Heath and John Lachs, *Fichte: Science of Knowledge* (1970); Garrett Green, *Attempt at a Critique of All Revelation by J.G. Fichte* (1978). See: Robert Adamson, *Fichte* (1981); F. Coppleston, *Fichte to Nietzsche* (vol. VII of *A History of Philosophy*, 1963).

156
FITZGERALD, Edward 1809–83

British poet

Edward FitzGerald was born on 31 March 1809 near Woodbridge in Suffolk, where he was to spend most of his life. His mother's side of the family was sufficiently wealthy for him never to have to work for a living. He was educated at King Edward VI Grammar School, Bury St Edmunds, and Trinity College, Cambridge; he did not distinguish himself scholastically but at both institutions he met people who became lifelong friends. Such affectionate relationships – often with famous literary figures, including Alfred* and Frederic Tennyson, Carlyle* and Thackeray* – became the centre of his life; but he tended, and the tendency increased as he grew older, to keep his friends at arm's length – preferring the exchange of letters to meetings. His letters overflow with kindliness and quiet wit, revealing a man of great sensitivity, scepticism and innate good-nature; they are among the finest in English.

In 1856 he married Lucy Barton – she had misinterpreted a remark he made at her father's death-bed as a promise of marriage and typically he felt compelled to honour the 'promise'; the couple separated after a year, FitzGerald providing handsomely for his wife.

Two friends, neither remotely connected with the literary world of his more famous acquaintances, were particularly important to him. The first, William Kenworthy Browne, was an amiable squire who was killed in a hunting accident in 1859; FitzGerald was severely depressed by this and only began to recover his spirits when, in the early 1860s, he met Joseph Fletcher, a Lowestoft fisherman who, FitzGerald said, strongly resembled Browne physically. FitzGerald had a seagoing yacht built – named, significantly enough, 'The Scandal' – in which he went sailing with 'Posh', as he called Fletcher.

His reputation rests on his translations from Persian, in particular of a selection of the quatrains of Omar Khayyam (*Rubáiyat of the Omar Khayyam*, 1859). He was introduced to the language by E.B. Cowell, later Professor of Sanskrit at Cambridge. The Khayyam translation was made in the late 1850s, immediately after the failure of his marriage; the disillusioned agnosticism of Khayyam obviously appealed to him (he rejected all 'mystical' interpretations of the quatrains), and the sexual ambiguity of the 'Saki' perhaps contributed to his deep affection for the poems which, as he wrote, he 'ingeniously tessellated into a sort of Epicurean Eclogue in a Persian garden'. As in all his translations FitzGerald enters into a dialogue with his author – he does not merely reproduce what is already there. He also made versions of Attar's 'Parliament of the Birds', Jami's 'Salaman and Absal', six plays by Calderón and works by the Greek dramatists. His other productions include a Platonic dialogue on education (*Euphranor*), an anthology of aphorisms (*Polonius*) and an edition of Crabbe's* poetry, which he greatly admired. He was a man who lived by cherishing others – at a distance; letters and translations were his chosen forms, and both live on the stimulus of another mind. The extraordinary popularity of the *Rubáiyat* had hardly begun when he died, peacefully in his sleep, in 1883.

Dick Davis

See: *Letters of Edward FitzGerald* (1901); Thomas Wright, *The Life of Edward FitzGerald* (1904); A.M. Terhune, *The Life of Edward FitzGerald, Translator of the Rubaiyat of Omar Khayyam* (1947); Alethea Hayter, *FitzGerald to his Friends* (1979).

157
FLAUBERT, Gustave 1821–80

French novelist

'Flaubert, creator of the "modern" novel, stands at the crossroads of all our literary problems of today,' wrote Sartre. Few nineteenth-century writers command the attention and status accorded Flaubert today; yet it is anything but the complacent status of a fixed, classified reputation. It has more to do with anxiety and questioning, and Sartre rightly stressed the problematic aspect of Flaubert's example: not only as a creator of modern fiction but as a pioneer in the modern problematics of writing in general. Even his influence is contradictory and diverse. Each generation finds it own Flaubert: a sign of greatness, but a disturbing greatness.

No doubt this vocation to disturb has its origin in the estrangement at the heart of Flaubert's own experience. The second son of a prestigious Normandy doctor, he was painfully aware of his position in the family: his elder brother was destined by the family structure to succeed the father, while Gustave, the unneeded child, experienced his existence as superfluous. 'We are superfluous, we workers in the field of art,' he would write in 1870. This sense of superfluity Sartre saw as the *leitmotif* of Flaubert's whole life, and the cause of his early problems with language, experiencing words as alien, non-natural. Later this would take the form of his anguished difficulty in writing, the protracted agonies of style so amply documented in his letters.

His adolescent writings were wholly in the Romantic mode; in them recurred the theme of the absent God, the resentment of creature against Creator, of 'monstrous' child against the sadistic parent who has created it for nothing. The pessimism was not merely conventional: it expressed what was to be a lifelong sense of passivity, an estrangement from praxis and a deep resentment against the world of social success, the world of the bourgeois. At the age of twenty-three, Flaubert underwent a nervous seizure, and experienced it as a significant rite of passage, cutting him off from ordinary life and leaving him with the world of art, the ivory tower of passive, ironic observation of reality, the struggle to transform that observation and that irony into language: 'my poor life, in which sentences are the only adventures.'

Not that his retreat was total – in 1849–50 he undertook a journey through Egypt, Palestine, Syria and the Lebanon. On his return began the long ordeal of *Madame Bovary*, as charted in his letters to Louise Colet, so rich in reflections on the problems of fiction. The novel's publication in 1856 created a scandal not unlike that of Baudelaire's* *Fleurs du mal*, a notorious trial for obscenity, ending in acquittal. Thereafter, apart from the brief episode of a second trip to Africa, Flaubert's life was one of anguished, never-satisfied dedication to his art. Each successive work was a long labour, involving heroic – sometimes disproportionate – feats of documentation to be transmuted into fiction: *Salammbô* (1857–62); *Sentimental Education* (*L'Éducation sentimentale*, 1864–9); the final version of *The Temptation of Saint Anthony* (*La Tentation de Saint Antoine*) was published in 1874, the *Three Tales* (*Trois contes*) in 1877. On his death

Flaubert left unfinished the major work of his last years, *Bouvard et Pécuchet*.

Few works fascinate yet resist criticism as much as these novels: above all they show the hopeless inadequacy of the label 'realist' that contemporaries pinned on Flaubert. Though in his later years he came to be regarded as a master by Maupassant* and Zola*, the implications of his work defy labelling altogether, and evoke only doubt. The theme of his novels is the difficulty of interpreting experience: aptly, the reader is brought up against the problem of interpreting the novels themselves. They are singularly lacking in authorial guide-lines – 'Stupidity consists in drawing conclusions,' Flaubert was fond of repeating. The ideal he strove for was the impersonality of a Shakespeare, works giving such an illusion of autonomy that he hoped the reader would be astounded by them, wondering how they had come into being. Yet the profound irony of Flaubert's creative intelligence is everywhere, a destructive, vengeful force, undermining and devaluing the lives of his characters; constantly he seeks out the grotesque, 'that ridiculousness intrinsic in human life itself'.

Madame Bovary is an epic of frustration, a deeply unconventional novel about someone who tries to live her life as a conventional novel: the country doctor's wife who, like Don Quixote, sees the world through the prism of literature. Her mind is full of the bric-à-brac of Romantic illusions and stereotypes, so much so that her aspiration away from the desperately humdrum world of provincial respectability – the world of the bourgeois – can express itself in no other, more authentic way. The cycles of disillusionment are charted with pitiless irony, through marriage, adultery, up to her horrible, clinically observed death by poisoning. Cycles indeed: the overwhelming impression is one of lack of progression, as Emma inevitably fails to find an authentic language for her aspiration. She does not speak, but *is spoken* by the clichés of her culture; she is a victim of those 'received ideas' which Flaubert delighted in collecting as a vengeful gesture against the world. The writing itself embodies a sense of non-progressive nihilism: he reduces the importance of dramatic events, exploits the imperfect tense with striking originality to freeze action into *tableaux*, to emphasize the static at at the expense of the dynamic. Flaubert saw his study as critical, even anatomical, but ironic detachment is only half the picture. The effectiveness of the novel depends on his ability to feel himself into his character (what Henry James* would call 'the creative effort to get into the skin of the creature'), to become Emma Bovary in the very movement, the almost physical vibration of her sensibility and her illusions, by an amazing power of empathy that allows him to capture the near-inexpressible texture of experience. The technique he enlists is that of the mobile point-of-view, dramatizing consciousness through description of what is perceived in a way that strikingly prefigures the modern 'phenomenological' novel. Narrative perspective is decentralized to such a degree that a sense of relativity reigns, perfectly embodying the phenomenon of non-communication with which the novel deals. Flaubert's style is, then, a constant tension between irony and empathy, detachment and intimate narrative involvement. The irony is all the more devastating for being held in tension with the uncanny ability to become the sensibility that is the object of that irony. If Flaubert saw the artist as God, it is God simultaneously as ironic observer and pantheistic penetration into the whole of creation.

Flaubert saw his own personality as a tension between two contrasting tendencies – the lyricist and the critical realist-observer. Critics once made much of the oscillation in successive works between apparent predominance of one tendency or the other: this was misleading, as the basic method is always the tension itself. While writing *Bovary* he railed against the banal subject matter, expressive of the modern world he despised, and dreamed of a mode more 'natural' to him; to this he turned in the sumptuous exoticism of *Salammbô*, only to find just as much labyrinthine difficulty in the writing as he had experienced over the earlier work. This story of the struggle between ancient Carthage and the mercenary armies, centring on the passion of the barbarian Mathô for the priestess Salammbô, was in a sense sheer self-indulgence, allowing Flaubert to indulge his love of documentation and his quasi-sadistic taste for descriptions of cruelty, violence and lingering death – to the extent that the reader who enjoys the novel must question his own motives for doing so. Ambivalence is everywhere: the violence shades into eroticism, Salammbô's mysticism is also sexual, and Flaubert typically wrote that the book would be both 'dirty and chaste, mystical and realistic'. Yet for all the over-richness of detail, he had the experience, faced with his longed-for subject, of confronting a void; and the effect left by the novel is that of an unnervingly petrified world in incongruous contrast with the violence of passions and action. The narrative surface remains oddly impenetrable and places obstacles in the way of interpretation: when, we ask, is Flaubert being ironic? The characters are constantly 'bewildered', 'dumb-founded' in the face of experience, and this mirrors the position of the reader faced with the text. In this respect it is strikingly unlike the normal run of historical novels in the nineteenth century.

If *Salammbô* left many contemporary readers nonplussed, Flaubert's return to the modern world in *Sentimental Education* met with almost universal incomprehension. He conceived the novel as a revenge against his age, and this story of a young man's illusions and the mediocrity of his existence in a world fated to mediocrity makes disquieting reading indeed. Such pusillanimity and anti-heroism were shocking enough in themselves (and Henry James criticized Flaubert's concentration on 'abject human specimens'), but in addition the work reads as an 'anti-novel' in that the very concept of 'plot' seems inappropriate to it. Events arise and disappear without sense of causality or purpose, so that in spite of constant agitation, nothing appears to happen. The twenty-seven years of the narration are twenty-seven years of anti-climax. In the devastatingly ironic epilogue, after a stunning 'blank' in time, the whole of the novel is, as it were, short-circuited out of existence as the 'hero' evokes his youth, 'the best times we ever had', situated before the opening of the novel itself! The historical dimension receives the same pessimistic treatment: Flaubert portrays the 1848 Revolution from the periphery, and sees it, too, as a non-event, a vicious circle of envy, greed and misplaced idealism. The overall effect of the novel for the modern sensibility is absurdist; it subverts the structures of significance of conventional fiction, constantly frustrating expectation in a way that will inspire much twentieth-century writing.

For all the difference in subject, *The Temptation of Saint Anthony* is an equally bewildering work, though less effective in that it does not even appear to fall into the category 'novel' and so never raises expectations to be frustrated. Part narrative, part drama, it owes much to Goethe's* *Faust*, and again shows Flaubert at his most self-indulgent, one 'hermit' creating another, revelling in temptations, exotic varieties of religious experience, the ambivalence of mystical and sexual, grotesque and sublime. Ambiguity is its keynote – especially when the Saint utters his final wish to 'be matter': are we to interpret it as ironic nihilism, or ecstatic pantheism, a religious equivalent of Flaubert's own aesthetic method? Similar questions face the reader of the exquisitely wrought *Three Tales*, stories of destinies biblical, medieval and modern with a narrative surface of such blank impersonal perfection that the reader can never be sure when – and how much – irony is being directed at the subject. For all the variety in setting, in each story we find the same tendency to freeze action into *tableaux*, the unique process of petrification.

In *Bouvard et Pécuchet* Flaubert faced an almost impossible task, problematic in its very conception. It was to extend and eventually include the 'Dictionary of received ideas', and to represent his most extreme onslaught on bourgeois culture. The two retired clerks who undertake an absurd quest for knowledge, working haphazardly and platitudinously through subjects as vast and various as medicine, archaeology, literature, philosophy, are no doubt grotesque, but not simply grotesque; for they, too, come to experience the doubts that were Flaubert's own, and he himself was obliged to read the books (1,500 of them!) that they absorb in their quest, duplicating their folly in one of the strangest and most paradoxical enterprises in the history of

literature. Here Flaubert came as near as he could to his ideal of 'a book about nothing', whose unity and essential subject matter would be language itself.

Writing in the post-1848 world, when social upheavals had cast doubt on the values and permanence of the bourgeois order, Flaubert more than any contemporary expressed that doubt, but not by adopting – like Zola – the optimistic role of social reformer or revolutionary (indeed, he was a victim of the received ideas of his class when it came to alternatives to the bourgeois order); instead, he allowed that doubt to infect the very structure of the main organ of bourgeois culture – the novel; producing texts that defy causal patterning, resist summary or reductive labelling. They are books that force us to question the nature of reading, the operation of language, the business of interpretation. Not for nothing is Flaubert seen as one of the fathers of modernist awareness, a subversive force within his own culture.

David Meakin

For Flaubert's letters, see *Correspondance* in *Oeuvres complètes* (1974). See also: V. Brombert, *The Novels of Flaubert* (1966), *Flaubert par lui-même* (1971); J. Culler, *Flaubert: The Uses of Uncertainty* (1974); J.-P. Sartre, *L'Idiot de la famille* (1972); R.J. Sherrington, *Three Novels of Flaubert* (1970); E. Starkie, *Flaubert: The Making of the Master* (1967), *Flaubert the Master* (1971); A. Thibaudet, *Flaubert* (1964).

158
FONTAINE, Pierre 1762–1853

French architect

Fontaine worked largely in Paris with his partner, the architect Charles Percier. However, as favourites of Napoleon*, they were asked to remodel the interiors of a number of his private residences. More importantly they were also called upon to produce façades for the rue de Castiglione, the rue and place des Pyramides and the rue de Rivoli. Work was begun on the rue de Castiglione in 1801 and the whole scheme, similar in style, continued until mid-century. It was part of Napoleon's grand scheme for Paris. The design of the colonnades was a central feature of this work of Fontaine and Percier who derived their form in large part from Rome. In 1798 the two architects had published a book, well illustrated, called *Maison et Palais de Rome Moderne*, ('Houses and Palazzi of Modern Rome'). The style known as Romantic Classical in architecture straddled the beginning of the nineteenth century. It combines Roman strength and simplicity, even severity, of detailing with classical repeating arches and feeling for long vistas. The later Renaissance revival of the mid-nineteenth century is more Hellenistic and softer in style.

Fontaine was one of a number of architects who supervised the designs for the Arc de Triomphe de l'Étoile, memorial to his mentor, Napoleon himself. The enormous scale and solid weightiness of this monument belie some of the later work to be carried out by Fontaine.

In 1816–24 Fontaine was working under the Restoration for a new patron, Louis XVIII. His commission was for the Chapelle Expiatoire in memory of Louis XVI and Marie Antoinette. Lying close to the Boulevard Haussmann in Paris, it also has a Roman quality, although the funereal starkness is relieved by complex relief sculptures in the domed ceiling and mosaic flooring.

Before his death Fontaine, who was a remarkably adaptable architect, a necessary quality in one who needed to survive a succession of differing political regimes, was able to experiment with the new methods of building deriving from the use of iron and glass. He was responsible for the wide roof of the Galerie d'Orléans which he built in the garden of the Palais Royal. This was as early as 1829–31 and, although the building is no longer in existence, it would seem that Fontaine, with his knowledge of dome construction, of curved roofs in the rue de Rivoli, was able to become a fore-runner of much later iron, then steel, and glass architecture. His Romanesque classical style beginnings provided important understandings for construction of a lighter, more airy kind.

Pat Turner

See: N. Pevsner, *An Outline of European Architecture* (1942 and 1960); M.L. Birer, *Pierre Fontaine, premier Architecte de l'Empereur* (1964).

159
FONTANE, Theodor 1819–98

German novelist

Born in Neuruppin, Prussia, of French Huguenot stock, Henri Théodor Fontane was the only son of the apothecary Louis Henri Fontane. He received his earliest education from his father, a lively intelligent man, though not a very reliable provider. He followed his father's profession, moving to Berlin for his apprenticeship. His earliest verses from the early 1840s were in the revolutionary style of the *Vormärz* – he even joined a Herwegh-Club – but he soon established a reputation as a writer of patriotic historical ballads after the manner of Sir Walter Scott*. 1848 saw him part-observer, part-participant in the revolutionary events in Berlin; he was even chosen to be a preliminary elector for the new Prussian parliament. Political

restoration and family responsibilities struck him at much the same time: in 1849 he decided to risk earning a living by his pen, but married in 1850 and soon with a small son to support he swallowed his republican principles and in 1851 accepted an appointment in the newly formed Prussian Press Office. He continued as a member of the literary club *Der Tunnel über den Spree*, wrote patriotic historical ballads, and began to develop into a literary critic of some stature.

In 1852 he was sent for a season to London as an official correspondent. This produced his first travel book: *Ein Sommer in London* ('A Summer in London', 1854). His next stay lasted four stimulating and fruitful years, freelancing as well as official, and he returned in 1859 only when his patron, the conservative Prussian Prime Minister Manteuffel, was dismissed from office by the new Regent. On returning, Fontane transferred his skills as a travel writer to his own country. He found his own distinctive voice in his *Wanderungen durch die Mark Brandenburg* ('Travels in the Brandenburg March', 1861-1881), part history, part topography, part character-sketches, part urbane conversation with the reader. Drawn towards novel-writing, the need to earn a living still held him to journalism. He was employed by the conservative newspaper *Die Kreuz-Zeitung*, and later from 1870 by the more congenial liberal paper *Die Vossische Zeitung*. He became a war correspondent in Bismarck's* three wars – against the Danes in 1864, against Austria in 1866, and against France in 1870, where, wandering in search of Joan of Arc's birthplace, he was arrested by the French as a spy, and only released after Bismarck had used the good offices of the US ambassador to get him out. Each campaign produced its book, the last, *Kriegsgefangen* ('Taken Prisoner of War', 1871), causing some displeasure in Prussia on account of its humane presentation of his captors as human beings, not enemy monsters. Whoever might be employing him, Fontane looked through his own tolerant, sceptical eyes.

Back in Berlin, he became the *Vossische*'s drama critic, and was one of the first to welcome the new Naturalism of Ibsen* and Hauptmann*. But the pull to novel-writing grew stronger, and, after a disastrous short stint as secretary to the Academy of Arts, in 1876 he made the great decision to turn to fiction full-time. In 1878, aged fifty-nine, he published his sprawling four-decker: *Vor dem Sturm* ('Before the Storm'), an historical novel set in Prussia on the eve of Napoleon's* defeat, nourished by his ballads, the *Wanderungen* and Sir Walter Scott.

And he never looked back, writing novels into ripest old age. With hindsight one can see the teleology of this late development – late for him, and for his country: to make him a novelist he needed the variety of experience that journalism, travel, social encounter brought; he needed the congenial years in the outside world, experiencing a world power and a great literary tradition in England. Moreover, the social novelist required a society to chronicle. Not until the end of the century did Germany – Bismarck's Prussian Germany, unified in 1871 – offer it; only then did Fontane's Berlin become the urban and urbane centre that could match Thackeray's* London. Sociable, tolerant, ironical, disliking the absoluteness of principle, enough of a compromiser himself to understand all and forgive all (to work for the *Kreuz-Zeitung* and the *Vossische* is the sign either of no character or of very great character indeed), he became the loving and sceptical chronicler of lives bent or broken by the social code, epitomized in the tensions of ill-matched marriages (*Irrungen Wirrungen*, 1888; *Effi Briest*, 1895, trans. 1968, his masterpiece); the humorous critic of social pretension (*Frau Jenny Treibel*, 1892); the profound analyst of the hollowness of Prussian formality (*Schach von Wuthenow*, 1882). Fully aware, as a good realist, that other minds cannot ultimately be known, he nevertheless shows great psychological insight, particularly in respect of his woman characters. But they are mainly presented not from within but in interaction with the world: husband, lover, social gathering. He is as much a master of the intimate exchange as of the set-piece dinner party. His is a subtle art of allusion and suggestion, of figures not characterized directly but reflected in act, comment and conversation. In the perspectivism of his last, most characteristic, work, *Der Stechlin* (1898), the figures dissolve into a multiplicity of mutually refracting mirrors. Like an Impressionist painter, he presents not the object, but the light upon it. Written on the brink of the new century, it is focused on a dying Junker of the old, humane school, and raises question after question about the social and moral nature of the new Germany. It is his most radical novel in theme, of old and new, as well as in form. He lived just long enough to see it published.

Fontane is regarded as virtually the creator of the modern German social novel. The way his example has been absorbed by two of Germany's greatest twentieth-century novelists is index enough of his achievement. Heinrich Mann polemically claims his ancestry in compelling a society to know itself. Thomas Mann, to whom his irony was deeply congenial, continues his exploration of the precariousness of the late bourgeois, from *Effi Briest* to *Buddenbrooks*, and of the hollowness and ambiguity of the Prussian ethic from *Schach von Wuthenow* to *Tod in Venedig*. Though the writers with whom he has greatest affinity wrote in English: Jane Austen*, Thackeray, Henry James*, he has not been sufficiently translated.

Joyce Crick

Other works include: travel: *Jenseit des Tweed* ('Across the Tweed', 1860); war reporting: *Der Schleswig-Holsteinische Krieg im Jahre 1864* ('The War in Schleswig-Holstein 1864', 1865); *Der deutsche Krieg von 1866* ('The German War in 1866', 1871); *Der Krieg gegen Frankreich 1870–71* ('The War against France 1870–71', 1872–5); further novels: *L'Adultera* (1882); *Unwiederbringlich* (*Beyond recall*, 1891, trans. 1964); *Die Poggenpuhls* (1896); memoirs: *Meine Kinderjahre* ('Years of Childhood', 1893); *Von Zwanzig bis Dreissig* ('From twenty to thirty', 1898); collected works: *Sämtliche Werke* (28 vols, from 1959). Biography: H.H. Reuter, *Theodor Fontane* (2 vols, 1968). Criticism: W. Müller-Seidel, *Fontane* (1975); Peter Demetz, *Formen des Realismus: Theodor Fontane* (1864).

160
FOSCOLO, Ugo 1778–1827

Italian poet, novelist and critic

Foscolo was born in Xanthe, Ionian Isles; after an early education in Greece, he was taken to Venice by his Greek mother in 1792, following the death of his Venetian father. His upbringing had been classical in his native land and continued on the same lines in Venice; there was, however, a romantic strain in his temperament and this was enhanced when he became a disciple or friend of such leading exponents of pre-Romantic taste as Melchior Cesarotti, the author of the renowned translation of the Ossianic poems, Ippolito Pindemonte and Aurelio Bertòla. Of these, the famed and authoritative Cesarotti, then professor in the University of Padua, was perhaps the most influential, while Pindemonte provided at least the first stimulus for the composition of Foscolo's most acclaimed poem, *Dei sepolcri*. Foscolo, however, remained faithful to his classical ideals till the end of his life and never subscribed to Romantic tenets.

Classical elegance above all is, indeed, apparent in his early odes 'A Luigia Pallavicini' and 'All'amica risanata', while autobiography and self-portrayal are an integral part of his twelve matchless sonnets (1798–1803); they supply further evidence of the duality within him (classical training and romantic temperament). Disillusionment replaced enthusiasm for the ideals of the French Revolution after Napoleon* surrendered Venice to Austria (1797). This feeling of betrayal and the theme of unrequited love were coupled in his youthful work *Le ultime lettere di Jacopo Ortis* (1798–1802), in which he followed the European fashion of the epistolary novel; here, too, there is a largely autobiographical element, in so far as the author's moods and some of his vicissitudes are reflected in those of the protagonist of the novel. Although very many influences can be detected, Goethe's* *Werther* was the real model, with the notable difference that the protagonist of *Ortis* is deeply affected by two passions instead of only one (love for his country as well as for his adored Teresa, already destined to be married to another). While this detracts from its unity, the novel vibrates with eloquently expressed feelings and with all the hatreds and enthusiasms of young Foscolo; it had a profound influence on generations of Italians and deeply affected Giacomo Leopardi*.

Foscolo lived in Milan, Bologna and Florence in 1797–1806, engaged in intense literary and political activity; he also fought against the Austrians, and spent two years in France as a soldier; at this time he began his translation of Sterne's *Sentimental Journey*. Tenure of a university chair in Pavia (1808–9) was cut short by Napoleon.

Many of the ideas outlined in his novel find new poetic expression in his celebrated ode *Dei sepolcri* (1806; published in 1807). Its immediate motive (French-imposed burial laws), main sources (English sepulchral poetry, Lucretian thought, Vico's philosophy) and even its recurring themes (negation of an after-life; and anti-Napoleonic spirit) are subservient to its main purpose – Foscolo's belief in the importance for posterity of the memory of great men and, ultimately, the affirmation of his faith in man and spiritual values, in the sense that the noblest deeds and highest achievements of the past are seen as a perennial source of inspiration. His epigrammatic and magnificently rhetorical style rises from an elegiac and meditative beginning, in a truly pre-romantic vein, to a lyrical and epic climax, celebrating the glories of Renaissance Italy and Ancient Greece.

His other extended poetic work, *Le Grazie*, remained unfinished; it was meant to have a vaguely didactic purpose and to convey the poet's outlook on life and art in an essentially classical style oscillating between epic and lyrical overtones. Long fragments containing passages drafted with consummate artistry and real inspiration are extant; but, as it is, the poem lacks unity and the very fact that, in spite of Foscolo's efforts over many years, it was never completed is an indication that the author gradually lost confidence in his ability to produce what he had originally conceived; the allegorical structure which he tried to superimpose on poetic expression was too replete with symbols and metaphysical notions to generate sustained poetry. His three tragedies (*Tieste*, 1797; *L'Aiace*, 1814; *Ricciarda*, 1815) had varying degrees of success.

Foscolo left Italy for Switzerland in 1815, a self-imposed exile from Austrian domination, and settled in England in 1816. His early social and literary success owed something to the welcome he received in Whig circles as a champion of liberty who had dared to stand up to Napoleon. His major critical works were published in Britain, some of them in the leading periodicals of the time (*Quarterly Review*, *Edinburgh Review*, etc.) or as introductions to editions of Dante and Boccaccio; but his *Essays on Petrarch* (privately printed, 1821; first edition, 1823) were issued as a separate volume. They mark a turning point in the history of

criticism of Petrarch's poetry on account of their insight and erudition. The 'Historical Discourse on the text of the "Decameron"' and the 'Discourse on the text of the "Divine Comedy"', both of 1825, are remarkable in their turn for the novel historical outlook Foscolo brought to the consideration of their respective subjects and can be said to inaugurate modern criticism of Dante's *Comedy* and Boccaccio's *Decameron*. After the brilliant social life of his first few years in Britain, hardship and poverty supervened through his own improvidence. He died in 1827 and was buried in Old Chiswick Church, whence his remains were removed in 1871 to Santa Croce in Florence, the church he had celebrated in *Dei sepolcri* as the repository of Italian national glories.

U. Limentani

A major critical edition of all Foscolo's works and letters is nearing completion, *Edizione Nazionale delle Opere* (1933–); an earlier edition of Foscolo's collected works in eleven volumes is: *Opere edite e postume* (1850–62). Biography: G. Chiarini, *La vita di Ugo Foscolo* (1910); E.R. Vincent, *Ugo Foscolo – an Italian in Regency England* (1953). Critical: A. Donadoni, *Ugo Foscolo pensatore, critico, poeta* (1910); M. Fubini, *Ugo Foscolo* (1928); E.R. Vincent, *The Commemoration of the Dead* (1936); O. Macrí, *Semantica e metrica dei 'Sepolcri' del Foscolo* (1978); T. O'Neill, *Ugo Foscolo's 'Dei sepolcri': On Virgin Muses and Love* (1981).

161
FOSTER, Stephen Collins 1826–64

US song writer and composer

Blackface minstrel shows became an essential ingredient, by the mid-nineteenth century, in forming the white conception of Negro character and humour. An essential element of their prodigious success were the songs of Stephen Collins Foster. He was born near Pittsburgh, Pennsylvania, and received no formal musical training. His first surviving song, 'Sadly to Mine Heart Appealing' (composed at the age of thirteen), struck the key-note of sentimental balladry which he maintained all his life. But it was not until he joined his brother in Cincinnati, in 1846, that he began his successful exploitation of Negro ballads.

What turned this young book-keeper to black folk material? Cincinnati, in the decades before the Civil War, was something of a crossroads between north and south, east and west. While Foster was attending Negro camp meetings, Harriet Beecher Stowe* (another resident) was stirred by anti-slavery propaganda and the memoirs of slave fugitives. Certainly two of the decisive forces in the white take-over of black causes and black performances were for a time contemporary in Ohio.

In 1848 Foster presented his first collection of ballads (including 'Louisiana Belle', 'Oh, Susanna!', 'Uncle Ned' and 'Away Down South') gratis to a local publisher, who issued them anonymously as *Songs of the Sable Harmonists*. The following year 'Nelly was a Lady', published in *Foster's Ethiopian Melodies*, was popularized by Christy's Minstrels. That was the turning-point.

Edwin P. Christy (1815–62) of Philadelphia had formed a blackface troupe, originally known as 'Virginia Minstrels', which had toured west and south with their repertoire of Negro songs, dances and jokes. Christy claimed to be 'the first to harmonize and originate the present type of minstrelsy': that is, he took the part of 'interlocutor', seated at the centre of a semi-circle of performers whose 'end men' were called Brudder Tambo (with the tambourine) and Brudder Bones (with the castanets). These three maintained a crossfire of repartee while the entire company presented songs and farces to the accompaniment of banjo or fiddle. Some such vaudeville Christy presented, to rapturous applause, at New York's Palmo's Opera House on 27 April 1846. His reception in London was to be equally enthusiastic. It was to Christy that Foster, in 1851, sold the privilege of singing his songs from manuscript; they were even published with Christy's name as author.

Some 175 songs were presented in this manner throughout that pre-war decade, including 'Old Folks at Home' (*Swanee Ribber*) in 1851, 'Massa's in de Cold, Cold Ground' in 1852, 'My Old Kentucky Home' and 'Old Dog Tray' (which sold 125,000 copies within eighteen months) in 1853, as well as 'Camptown Races', 'Hard Times Come Again No More', 'Jeanie with the Light Brown Hair' and many more. Foster's trip to New Orleans in 1852 seems to have been his only visit south. With 'Old Black Joe' in 1860 he deserted the composition of dialect songs, as if the outbreak of Civil War had finally undermined his nostalgia for plantation idylls. He continued to turn out melancholy songs by the dozen, but they were mainly repetitive and commonplace. He started drinking heavily, became separated from his wife, sold his songs to music stores for cash, and died at the age of thirty-eight in a Bowery ward.

Harold Beaver

His brother, M. Foster, published *Biography, Songs and Musical Compositions of Stephen Foster* in 1896. J.T. Howard corrected much of the detail in *Stephen Foster, America's Troubadour* (1934, revised 1953). See also Raymond Walters, *Stephen Foster: Youth's Golden Gleam, A Sketch of his Life and Background in Cincinnatti* (1937) and Evelyn Foster Morneweck, *Chronicles of Stephen Foster's Family* (2 vols, 1944), as well as Robert C. Toll, *Blacking Up: The Minstrel Show in Nineteenth-Century America* (1974).

162
FOURIER, Charles 1772–1837

French social thinker

None of those earlier socialist thinkers whom Marx* and Engels* viewed as 'utopian' better deserved the title than Fourier. His character might well have been invented by Charles Dickens*, or even Lewis Carroll*, and the fact that he did really exist has never ceased to be a cause for astonishment. Despite his many denunciations of the *philosophes*, Fourier never hesitated to take eighteenth-century ideas on harmony to their ultimate logic, and his thinking can well be treated as one of the most curious eddies in the area of confluence between the currents of Enlightenment and Romanticism. Here was a dogmatist who insisted upon a firm linkage between his social analysis and a fanciful cosmology which even encompassed copulating planets; a visionary who could conceive of our globe being organized in such a way that it would habitually possess 'thirty seven million poets equal to Homer, thirty-seven million geometricians equal to Newton, thirty-seven million dramatists equal to Molière', and who (perhaps even more remarkably) could regard such a prospect as beatific; an incorrigible optimist who believed that the adoption of his proposals about communal living would trigger off zoological and climatic changes such as would transform lions into benevolent anti-lions and the seas into something resembling lemonade. Nobody has been able to write about this prophet of universal contentment, whose vocabulary and conceptions were pervaded by the fantastic and bizarre, without questioning the man's sanity.

Fourier's own external career was necessarily less frenzied than these imaginings. He was born at Besançon, into the family of a cloth merchant, and educated at the local Jesuit college. During the opening phase of the French Revolution he lived in the great southern manufacturing centre of Lyon, and then in 1794 began two years of military service as a conscript. Between 1796 and 1826 he held various commercial jobs in the Besançon and Lyon regions, living as a bachelor and dedicating all his spare time to study and writing. Supported by a modest family legacy, he was able to spend his final decade in Paris working solely at the publicization of his utopian projects. The broad outlines of his vision had been formed as early as 1800, and then sketched for others through journalistic articles over the next few years. In 1808 there appeared Fourier's first book, *The Social Destiny of Man* (*Théorie des quatre mouvements et des destinées générales*, 2 vols, published at Lyon despite the title-page reference to Leipzig which was inserted, characteristically, to baffle suspected plagiarists). The subsequent *Treatise on Agrarian-Domestic Fellowship* (*Traité de l'association domestique-agricole*, 2 vols. 1822) provided the fullest exposition of his views. But, in terms of relative clarity, these were most effectively presented in *Le nouveau monde industriel et sociétaire* (perhaps best translated as 'the new world of communal activity', 1829). Prominent among Fourier's final writings are *Pièges et charlatanisme* ('snares and quackery') *de deux sectes Saint-Simon et Owen* (1831), an attack on the prescriptions of two of his foremost socialist rivals, and *The False Division of Labour* (*La fausse industrie morcelée*, 2 vols. 1835–6) which reveals him at his most quirky.

At the root of Fourier's hostility towards contemporary society was his certainty about both the wastefulness and the immorality of the business world that he knew so well. 'Truth and commerce,' he observed, 'are as incompatible as Jesus and Satan.' Against 'Civilization', conceived as such a scene of internecine cheating and competition, he asserted his own principle of collaborative 'Harmony'. Revealing no small debt to Rousseau, he argued that misery and vice stemmed merely from the artificial restraints imposed by 'civilized' versions of social organization. Transformation could come only through an unfettering of the passions, which he then labelled under thirteen headings with his usual taxonomic obsessiveness. The benefits of such liberation could be enjoyed, however, only within a meticulously structured context of communal life and labour. Fourier thus pleaded for the establishment of 'phalanxes', each containing a carefully balanced population of about 1,600 persons. An individual's existence within the 'phalanstery' building and its surrounding cultivable grounds would be geared to diverse forms of cooperative activity within an overall pattern which would turn out to be concordant with each person's natural talents, passions, and inclinations. The ingenuity of Fourier's approach is exemplified most famously in his 'Little Hordes', teams of children whose passion for muckiness would be rendered socially beneficial by unleashing them upon that residue of unavoidably dirty tasks with which even a perfect community must contend. It was not envisaged that the phalanx should abandon altogether the habit of private ownership, but certainly there would need to be a far less unequal distribution of wealth than hitherto. Such inequalities as remained would cease to be divisive inside a community where people could enjoy prompt and diverse gratification of every passion, and especially those relating to board and bed: liberation from rigours of climate and of bourgeois marriage conventions meant that the phalanstery promised to be the scene for a constant feast of good food and free love.

A few contemporaries found this prescription for social organization so alluring that they overlooked the cosmological corollaries (something which annoyed Fourier greatly) and concentrated on trying to establish somewhat pale imitations of the phalanstery. During the early 1830's, when the Saint-Simonian* movement was splitting, Fourierist notions won over a number of disciples led by Victor Considérant and a newspaper was founded to promote the cause. The one major French effort at running a phalanstery, opened near Rambouillet in 1834, was under-capitalized and went bankrupt after two years. More interesting were the American imitations, especially that launched by George Ripley at Brook Farm in Massachusetts (1841–6) which attracted attention from such literary figures as Hawthorne* and Emerson*. On balance, however, Fourier's main influence was not institutional in this sense at all. His considerable impact on later decades is apparent not in any substantial subscription to the phalanstery idea but rather in the way that particular Fourierist insights stimulated sympathetic comment from a diverse range of socialists, anarchists, feminists, pacifists, internationalists, and proponents of educational and psychological reform. Even if his stress on small agrarian communities made much of his work increasingly marginal to many concerns of an industrializing world, there was still power in his eloquent moral outrage and in his negative critique of bourgeois civilization. It is not difficult to see how Fourier, as student of repressed passion rather than as father of the phalanx, helped Marx to think more forcefully about 'alienation'. We can no less readily appreciate why, treated from the same angle, he has often been considered as an important forerunner to Freud, and indeed why André Breton should have adopted him as an ancestor of twentieth-century Surrealist protest.

All of this would have been little consolation to Fourier himself, who was concerned not just with diagnosis but with implementing quite precisely his own particular version of the cure for society's ills. He reiterated unsuccessful appeals to rulers in France and beyond, and sought constantly for some other benefactor who would fund a really rigorous and sustained trial of the phalanstery concept. In his last years he made known that at noon each day he would be available *chez soi* for the purpose of greeting this patron. Not surprisingly, the saviour never came.

Michael Biddiss

Most of Fourier's writings are available in the *Oeuvres complètes* (12 vols, 1966–8). Jonathan Beecher and Richard Bienvenu have edited a good English selection, *The Utopian Vision of Charles Fourier* (1972). See: Hubert Bourgin, *Fourier: Contribution à l'étude du socialisme français* (1905); Frank E. Manuel, *The Prophets of Paris* (1962); David Zeldin, *The Educational Ideas of Charles Fourier* (1969); and Nicholas V. Riasanovsky, *The Teaching of Charles Fourier* (1969).

163

FRANCE, Anatole (pseudonym of Anatole-François Thibault) 1844–1924

French writer

The son of a self-educated peasant with Catholic/monarchist affiliations, France studied for eight years at the Collège Stanislas in Paris, showing great enthusiasm for classical literature. Inspired equally, however, by Voltaire, Diderot and the sensationalists, France distanced himself from parental orthodoxy. A great admirer of the Parnassian poets, he served his literary apprenticeship on a number of specialized journals and, under the influence of Leconte de Lisle, wrote literary criticism and poetry. From 1876, when he held the sinecure of assistant librarian at the Senate, he developed wide interests in journalism and literary composition, notably short stories, novels and semi-autobiographical works. His *The Crime of Sylvestre Bonnard* (*Le Crime de Sylvestre Bonnard*, 1881) is a diaristic account portraying in gently humorous vein the preoccupations of an old pedant. A combination of parody, burlesque and occasional preciosity, this quasi-autobiographical work was much admired for its classical assurance and stylistic distinction, for which it received the accolade of the French Academy in 1884.

A free-wheeling, sceptical aesthete, France's firm belief in rationalism and individualism placed him, alongside Renan* and the Scientists, in opposition to the developing Catholic revival (Bourget, Huysmans*, Claudel *et al.*). Thus *Thaïs* (1890), a philosophical tale, was attacked on religious grounds by the Jesuits, but also on literary grounds by Zola* and his Naturalist associates. France continued in the 1890s to publish novels, wide-ranging essays, and short stories, in which the style ranged from neo-Romantic aestheticism to Rabelaisian exuberance and Voltairean satire. Admired in France by the conservative Maurras and the socialist Jaurès, he was seen as a major European figure by Edmund Gosse*, who presented him to English readers as intelligent but entertaining, ironic yet civilized.

The urbane tone of his *causeries* in *On Life and Letter*, (*La vie littéraire* 4 vols. 1888–92, trans. 1911–24) reveals an intellectual dilettantism of the highest order and a marked catholicity of literary taste. Here France a whole range of topics in a personal, anecdotal style reminiscent of the humane scepticism of Montaigne. His attacks on both Zola and the Symbolists were in the name of 'honest realism' and intelligibility: at the same time, maverick-like, he defended his own subjective, impressionistic view of art against the dogmatism of Brunetière with its emphasis on 'objective', historically based literary criticism.

France's ironic detachment and intellectual flexibility characterize also his political and social attitudes.

Liberal under the Second Empire, hostile to the Commune, he supported Thiers's republicanism in 1871, moving in a more radical direction only during the Dreyfus Affair. A great admirer of Zola's Dreyfusard convictions, he gradually veered towards militant socialism. Courted by the Communist wing of the Socialist Party in 1921, he was soon to be attacked for deviationism. His centrality in French culture, however, is confirmed by his election to the Academy (1896), the Nobel prize award (1921), the eightieth birthday celebration at the Trocadero (1924) and, finally, the scale of his state funeral six months later.

His Dreyfusard involvement in the 1890s clearly marked his literary development. His four-volume *Contemporary history* (*Histoire contemporaine*, 1897–1901) is a satire of French life through the observations and ironic comments of a philosopher. In it France combines historical chronicle, dramatic dialogue and an episodic, short-story technique. He criticizes dominant ideologies in the light of his firm attachment to principles of non-violence, justice and tolerance, the main butts of his attack being the nationalism and implicit militarism of the anti-Dreyfusards. This attack, combined with a rationalistic critique of religious superstition, is found again in his *Life of Joan of Arc*, (*Vie de Jeanne d'Arc*, 1908) and France extended his burlesque and ironical treatment to the whole history of France in *Penguin Island*, (*L'Ile des Pingouins*, 1908). This novel, directed against the 'official' history of Bainville and Lavisse, contains a mixture of Enlightenment rationalism and olympian detachment which has clear Marxist overtones. It was followed by *The Gods are Athirst* (*Les dieux ont soif*, 1912), which condemns the violence and fanaticism of the French Revolution, and *The Revolt of the Angels* (*La révolte des anges*, 1914), in which, somewhat cynically, Satan renounces the violent battle with the tyrant God for love of the earth. These last three novels disconcerted socialist friends and *bien-pensant* critics alike.

Anatole France is distinctive by the variety and range of his writings, as well as by the controversial quality of his ideas and attitudes. His novels, whether historical or contemporary in subject, reveal both the intellectual guru and the innovator in novelistic practice. Equally, his several volumes of short stories display a sureness of touch and technical expertise which make him a major figure in the development of the genre. France was influential in forming public opinion in literary, religious and political matters. In one sense very much of his age, France was in addition a very distinctive voice – sceptical, ironical, analytical and cerebral, but with a subtly modulated comic vision of his fellow men.

Christopher Bettinson

The English translation of France's complete works was published by John Lane at Bodley Head, (1908–28). See: E.P. Dargan, *Anatole France, 1844–1896*

(1937); C. Jefferson, *Anatole France: The Politics of Skepticism* (1965); D. Tylden-Wright, *Anatole France* (1967); R. Virtanen, *Anatole France* (1968); and M. Sachs, *Anatole France: The Short Stories* (1974).

164

FRANCK César (Auguste Jean Guillaume Hubert) 1822–90

Belgian (naturalized French) composer

In three different ways, Franck was an important figure and exercised a far-reaching influence: as composer, as organist, and as teacher. It was as pianist, however, that he first showed immense promise at the Conservatoire of Liège, the city of his birth, and then at the Paris Conservatoire. In his early years his father wished him to become a professional pianist, rather than a composer; and in 1842 and 1843, somewhat against the grain, Franck was mainly concerned with concert-giving in his home country. But at the same time a set of three Trios for violin, cello and piano (published as opus 1) became known in France and Germany, and this was followed soon after by a 'biblical eclogue', *Ruth*. At the age of twenty-six, in Paris, at the midst of the 1848 French Revolution, he freed himself from his father's influence, married, and settled down to a life given up mostly to teaching and to his work as a church organist. Composition had to be done in the early morning and during holidays.

Franck's organ compositions date from 1858, when he became organist of Sainte-Clotilde, Paris. There he had a fine instrument of the famous French organ-builders, Cavaillé-Coll; and the particular characteristics of it, including the solo stops and 'reed' choruses, stongly influenced the music he wrote. French organ music at the time was not of much significance. Franck laid the foundation of a French school of organ music which, passing to other composers, has continued vigorously to develop in scope and variety up to the present day. Franck's own organ works are not numerous, the principal ones being *Six Pièces* (1862), *Trois Pièces* (1878), and his last work, *Trois Chorals* (1890) – and the finest compositions from these sets are firmly established and treasured in the repertoire of organists everywhere. All the ingredients of Franck's highly personal style are found there: an imaginative variation technique, intense chromatic expressiveness (owing much to Wagner*), pastoral beauty contrasting with heroic utterance, fugal and other contrapuntal skills, and at times vigour and brilliance. Over all is a deep seriousness of purpose and what has been described as a sort of mystical exaltation.

It was in his organ classes that Franck exerted most of his influence as a teacher: classes in improvisation became in fact composition seminars for a cluster of pupil-disciples known as the 'Bande à Franck'. This activity was further extended from 1871, when Franck was made Professor of Organ at the Paris Conservatoire. An idea of the extent of his influence on the course of French music can be gathered from the list of his pupils, which included such names as Duparc, Dukas, d'Indy*, Pierné, Chausson, Bréville, Lekeu, Ropartz, Guilmant, and many others. In 1896, d'Indy, with Charles Bordes and Guilmant, founded the Schola Cantorum (later the École César Franck) as a perpetuating memorial to Franck and his teaching. As a personality, Franck was generally unassuming, calm and benevolent – a disposition which brought him the nickname 'Pater Seraphicus' or 'le Père séraphique'.

Franck wrote four operas, some large-scale choral-and-orchestral works, and a good deal of other sacred and secular vocal music – but it is not by these that he is remembered. His dramatic sense and his feeling for musical characterization were not strong. But it was natural that his early association with the piano should bear fruit – as we find particularly in two substantial works for that instrument: the *Prélude, choral et fugue* (1884) and the *Prélude, aria et final* (1886–7). The former was the result of a wish to write a prelude and fugue in the style of Bach: it became a personal structure which is still a satisfying concert item today. The latter is virtually a sonata in 'cyclic' form – material from the first section reappearing in different guises throughout the work, giving purpose and unity to the whole. The same cyclic principles are found in the Symphony in D minor, which was badly received on its first appearance in 1889. Now, however, Franck's Symphony and Berlioz's* *Symphonie Fantastique* are the only two symphonies of France established in the international orchestral repertoire. The other large-scale orchestral work which is heard regularly is the skilful and delightful *Variations Symphoniques* (1885) for piano and orchestra. These works belong to the last ten years of his life: this was indeed a rich creative period for him, and included also the String Quartet (1889), one of the few works which found real success in the composer's lifetime; the Sonata for violin and piano, an essential part of every professional violinist's repertoire; and the imaginative symphonic poems, *Le Chasseur maudit*, *Les Djinns*, and *Psyché*. When he died (following a street accident) he was at the height of his creative powers.

David Cox

See: Vincent d'Indy, *César Franck* (1906); Norman Demuth, *César Franck* (1949); Léon Vallas, *La véritable histoire de César Franck* (1950, trans. 1951); Laurence Davies, *Franck* (1973).

165
FRAZER, Sir James George 1854–1941.

British folklorist, anthropologist and classical scholar

Throughout the last forty years of his life Sir James Frazer was widely believed by English men of letters and the general educated public to be a man of vast erudition, towering genius and outstanding originality who had, almost single-handed, created a whole new academic discipline – that of social anthropology. The reality was rather different. Frazer was indeed appointed to a titular, non-stipendiary Chair of Social Anthropology at Liverpool University in 1907 which was the first of its kind, but he abandoned the post almost immediately and he was never otherwise engaged in ordinary academic duties. The prize fellowship at Trinity College, Cambridge, to which he was appointed in 1879 (for a thesis on Plato) was later extended into a life fellowship and, except for a period during the First World War, when he lived in London in the Middle Temple (where he had chambers by virtue of being an Honorary Bencher), he lived in Cambridge for most of the next sixty-two years.

His literary output was continuous and prodigious but it was based almost entirely on secondary sources. Frazer had no first-hand experience of the primitive customs which provide the subject matter for most of his writings and he was so carefully shielded from the ordinary problems of living by his highly eccentric wife that he was quite naive about many matters of common knowledge. In retrospect we can see that his great reputation derived very largely from the skill which he exercised as popularizer of his predecessors' ideas. He illustrated these ideas with countless entertaining examples which he was able to assemble through his indefatigable capacity for searching out obscure ethnographic sources. In Frazer's view the originals were usually uncouth so he remodelled his quotations into a florid literary style which appealed to the literati of his day and which carefully avoided every reference to human sexuality. Frazer explicitly prided himself on the fact that his books were a genteel form of literature rather than dry scholarship. The emphasis which Frazer placed upon the childishness of primitive customs had, in its period, an added appeal, since it served to justify the paternalistic rule of European colonial powers over the 'savages' of Africa, Oceania and elsewhere.

In his maturity Frazer, who had been brought up in a pious Presbyterian household, became a cautious agnostic. In the pages of The Golden Bough Christianity is, by implication, just one of a whole family of religious systems which had flourished at different times in the Middle Eastern region over a period of several millennia. Heresy of this modest sort was not at all new but, whereas many of Frazer's contemporaries used this line of argument as part of a general aggressive attack on the whole of Christian theology, Frazer expressed his agnosticism with great tact. Thus sceptics who were of conservative rather than radical persuasion found nothing in his writings which could possibly cause offence to elderly church-going parents. On the rare occasions when Frazer overstepped the mark in this respect he was always careful to delete or modify the offending passage in the next edition! The Golden Bough, which was finally expanded to thirteen fat volumes and which was by far the most influential of Frazer's works, has two central constantly recurring themes: (1) magico-religious performances designed to enhance 'fertility'; (2) religious practices relating to the sacrificial killing of kings who, during their lifetime, are considered to be incarnations of deity. Since the first of these topics is directly connected with human sexuality while the second could be directly exemplified by Christianity, Frazer was on dangerous ground, but he managed to treat the first theme as if it referred exclusively to the fertility of vegetation, while the second, at least in the form in which it appears in the abridged, one-volume edition of 1922, is pursued without any reference to Christianity at all. To modern readers much of the resulting circumlocution seems both smug and prurient but in the early years of the century it had a strong appeal.

Some of the features of Frazer's theories about totemism, magic and divine kingship have by now become assimilated into the general background of professional anthropological thinking, but, for the most part, these are details which he took over from his mentor William Robertson Smith*. His personal contributions to the general store of serious anthropological thinking have proved to be almost nil. But the secondary and puritanical quality of Frazer's anthropological writings had its compensations even for the professionals. Frazer's achievement was to make anthropology respectable. In the long run this served to unlock the financial resources which made possible the first-hand field research on which modern post-Frazerian social anthropology is based.

But in fields other than that of professional anthropology Frazer's influence was very considerable. Just as Picasso and his friends in Paris, in the period from 1907 onwards, managed to adapt the formal qualities of African sculpture to their own art without understanding anything at all about the social context from which their models had come, so also many major literary figures in the England of the same period found that when Frazer transformed incomprehensible 'savage customs' into imitation fairy-tales they became treasure trove for the poetic imagination. A.E. Housman* was making this point when he described Frazer's work as 'a museum of dark and uncouth superstitions invested with the charm of a truly sympathetic magic'. Kipling, T.S. Eliot, Ezra Pound and D.H. Lawrence, to name only a few, all made plundering expeditions of this kind into the pages of *The Golden Bough.*

The biographical details which follow are supplementary to those which have been indicated already. Frazer was born and received his early education in Glasgow where his father was principal owner of a prosperous chemist's shop in the centre of the city. He entered Glasgow University to read for a Master of Arts degree at the age of fifteen. There was nothing exceptional about this as the stereotyped curriculum involved was similar to that of a modern high school. He already showed a bent for classical studies and in 1874 he entered Trinity College, Cambridge, with an entrance scholarship. As an undergraduate he read classics but afterwards, at his father's behest, he qualified for the Bar and was admitted to the Middle Temple in 1881. But he never practised, for by that time he had already gained his fellowship at Trinity.

Frazer would doubtless have continued his career as an orthodox classical scholar had it not been for the arrival at Cambridge in 1883 of a fellow Scot, the extraordinary polymath William Robertson Smith, whose principal occupation at that time was as editor of the ninth edition of the *Encyclopaedia Britannica.* Smith and Frazer became close friends and Frazer's earliest writings in the field of anthropology were articles prepared for the 'T' volume of the encyclopaedia. These articles were themselves sub-edited by Smith who was an admirer of the recently deceased Scottish anthropologist J.F. McLennan. Almost the whole of Frazer's anthropological thinking originated during the period 1887–94 when he was closely associated with Smith.

In 1896 Frazer married a French widow, Mrs Lilly Grove, who thereafter became his extremely domineering business manager. Frazer's public success, as expressed in honours and decorations and honorary degrees, owed much to his wife's persistent campaigning but she was greatly disliked by most of Frazer's closest admirers. He maintained a vast international correspondence but was allowed to have few close friends. He was knighted in 1914.

Frazer's most substantial contribution to classical studies was his six-volume translation and commentary, *Pausanias's Description of Greece* (1898, second edition 1913). He was also responsible for an edition of *Sallust* (1884), the two-volume Loeb edition of *Appolodorus* (1921) and a five-volume edition, including translation and commentary, of *Ovid's Fasti* (1929, Loeb edition 1931).

The full bibliography of Frazer's anthropological writings is very long and very repetitive. Apart from various works which were assimilated into the final structure of the full scale version of *The Golden Bough* (original 1890 edition, 2 vols), the most important items are *Totemism and Exogamy* (4 vols, 1910); *The Belief in Immortality and the Worship of the Dead* (3 vols, 1913–24); *Folklore in the Old Testament* (3 vols, 1918).

Edmund Leach

See: R.A. Downie, *James George Frazer: The Portrait of a Scholar* (1940); T. Besterman, *A Bibliography of Sir James George Frazer, O.M.,* (1934).

166
FREGE, Friedrich Ludwig Gottlob 1848–1925.

German mathematician and philosopher

Frege was born in Wismar, East Germany, and died in Bad Kleinen, near his home town. After studying chemistry, philosophy and mathematics at the University of Jena from 1869 to 1871, he went to the University of Göttingen where he pursued further studies in physics, mathematics and philosophy and obtained a PhD in mathematics in 1873. His most important teachers were the mathematicians Ernst Abbe and Ernst Schering, and the philosophers Kuno Fischer and Hermann Lotze. With the help of Abbe, who remained his lifelong supporter, Frege obtained a teaching position in mathematics at the University of Jena where he remained from 1874 to his retirement in 1918.

From his doctoral dissertation onwards Frege displayed a keen interest in the conceptual clarification of the foundations of mathematics. In pursuit of this aim he developed a new symbolic logic, subjected the concept of number to philosophical and formal analysis, investigated the fundamental concepts of logic, and constructed a theory of meaning. Personally shy and without charisma as a teacher Frege had considerable difficulty in communicating his ideas. His only known student was the philosopher Rudolf Carnap through whom Frege's logical techniques and mathematical logicism became known to the members of the Vienna Circle and the movement of logical positivism. Though Frege wrote with great precision and an unusual philosophical clarity, his writings were generally ignored by his contemporaries. Nevertheless he influenced a number of seminal figures in early twentieth-century philosophy, such as Edmund Husserl, Bertrand Russell and Ludwig Wittgenstein. Because of his influence on Russell, Wittgenstein and Carnap he can be considered one of the sources of twentieth-century analytic philosophy. When analytic philosophers after the Second World War focused their attention on the theory of meaning, Frege's work in that area drew increasing attention. His essay 'On Sense and Reference' of 1891, a masterly exposition of his views on meaning, is still today his most widely read work. Frege's influence in this area can be seen clearly in the writings of such diverse philosophers as Carnap, Alonzo Church, John Austin, and Michael Dummett. His influence is indeed so pervasive that Dummett could write just a few years ago that Frege's work 'provides the terms in which the basic problems can still most fruitfully be posed'.

Philosophically Frege was most strongly motivated by the ideas of Leibniz and Kant. Like Kant he tried to show that empirical knowledge presupposes principles of a non-empirical, a priori kind. For that purpose both sought to establish that the propositions of geometry and arithmetic are true a priori. But while Kant held both to be synthetic a priori, Frege argued that only geometrical truths were such while arithmetical truths were analytic, logical truths. This so-called logicist thesis he had, probably, taken from Lotze who, in turn, was influenced by Leibniz. Almost all of Frege's work can be seen as an attempt to establish the truth of the logicist thesis. Nevertheless, many of Frege's ideas remain interesting apart from the now discredited logicism.

In order to establish the logicist thesis Frege considered it necessary to radically improve logic itself. Departing from both traditional syllogistic logic and from George Boole's* somewhat earlier algebra of logic, he designed a new symbolic logic that contains the essential elements of contemporary logic. His *Begriffsschrift* ('Conceptual Notation') of 1879, in which he first expounded his ideas, is comparable in its significance for logic only to Aristotle's *Prior Analytic*. Employing the Leibnizian idea of a logical calculus, the book provides the first precise axiomatization of a logical theory, constructs a truth-functional logic of propositions, and advances an analysis of general propositions that removes the philosophical puzzles that had surrounded such propositions since the time of Aristotle. In order to show the potential fruitfulness of his new logic Frege concluded the *Begriffsschrift* with an analysis of the notion of mathematical series.

In 1884 Frege published his second book *The Foundations of Arithmetic* (*Die Grundlagen der Arithmetik*). The work possesses a critical acumen and analytical vigour that makes it attractive even to those not concerned with the philosophy of mathematics. In the first half of the book Frege gave a critique of various traditional views on the nature of arithmetical propositions and the concepts of number and of unity. His particular target of attack were naturalistic conceptions, such as John Stuart Mill's* account of mathematical truths as high level abstractions from observations. He argued that false conceptions of numbers originated frequently from considering number terms in isolation. In contrast he formulated a context principle asserting that 'words have meaning only in the context of a sentence.' This principle was later employed and generalized by Wittgenstein, Willard van Orman Quine, and the ordinary language philosophers.

Frege also criticized psychological conceptions of arithmetic. Drawing on ideas contained in Lotze's writings on logic, he insisted on a sharp distinction between logic and the psychological and argued that concepts and numbers, while not real, were nevertheless objective. His attack on psychologism anticipates Husserl's better known critique in his *Logische Untersuchungen* of 1901 which it may have influenced.

In the second half of the *Foundations* Frege developed his own, positive account of the natural numbers. He argued that the natural numbers are primarily used for counting and that this fact should be reflected in their definition. Counting, he insisted further, is the establishing of an equinumerosity relation between sets of objects. Since sets are specifiable by concepts, natural numbers must be defined via such set-specifying concepts. Finally, he held that numbers are themselves objects in the sense that identity claims can be made about them. They are, however, not empirical, real objects, but abstract objective entities. With these considerations in mind, Frege proceeded to define the natural numbers as extensions of concepts under which equinumerous concepts fall. With this result, he believed, he had come close to the proof of the logicist thesis.

In order to show that the notions used in the definition of the natural numbers were indeed logical notions Frege published a series of highly original essays in the early 1890s. In 'Function and Concept' he tried to clarify the notion of concept in terms of the more general notion of function. Characterizing functions as incomplete or unsaturated, he contrasted them sharply to objects (in his abstract sense of the term) which he called complete or saturated. In the same essay he also set out to clarify the notion of the extension of a concept. In the most celebrated of the essays, the essay 'On Sense and Reference', he argued persuasively for the need to distinguish between the meaning of an expression and what the expression stands for and showed how such a distinction could remove certain logical puzzles about identity statements and oratio obliqua.

With these preparatory undertakings completed, Frege felt ready for the precise proof of the logicist thesis. In his main work, the *Grundgesetze der Arithmetik* ('The Fundamental Laws of Arithmetic', vol. 1, 1892; vol. 2, 1902), he set out to show in a completely formal manner how the propositions of arithmetic could be derived from five logical axioms. In the second volume he indicated how the analysis could be carried beyond the natural numbers to the reals, treating them as measuring numbers. When the second volume was almost ready for publication, Frege received a letter from Bertrand Russell containing Russell's celebrated set-theoretical antinomy and pointing out that the contradiction could be derived also from one of Frege's axioms. In an appendix to the work Frege tried to sketch a way out of the difficulty which has, however, since been shown unsuccessful.

Frege himself eventually concluded that the contradiction undermined the logicist thesis. In the writings after 1902 he set out to explain in new ways the philosophical ideas of his logic that were unaffected by the contradiction. And in the last years of his life he outlined a revised view of mathematics. Arguing now that the foundations of arithmetic had to be sought in geometry and that the latter was, in Kant's sense, synthetic *a priori*, he hoped to have found a more successful way to defend the original claim that empirical knowledge presupposes *a priori* foundations. These final reflections have not so far been influential.

Hans Sluga

See: *Translations from the Philosophical Writings of Gottlob Frege*, ed. P. Geach and M. Black (1952); G. Frege *The Foundations of Arithmetic* (trans. J. Austin, 1950); M. Dummett, *Frege; The Philosophy of Language* (1973); H. Sluga, *Gottlob Frege* (1980).

167
FRESNEL, Augustin Jean 1788–1827

French physicist

Fresnel was born, the son of a successful Norman architect and builder, in Broglie in 1788. Intending a career in engineering, he went to the École Polytechnique in 1804 and subsequently joined the government service as a member of the Corps des Ponts et Chaussées. He began to think about optics seriously only in 1814 and had to set his studies aside entirely the following year when, seeing Napoleon's* return from Elba as 'an attack on civilization', he left his engineering post and offered his services to the Royalist forces. The re-establishment of the Empire saw him, naturally enough, rather unpopular with the authorities; he was suspended from duties and put under police surveillance. He spent his enforced leisure studying optics again. With the second restoration he was reappointed to the Corps des Ponts et Chaussées and therefore he could spend time on optics only during periods of leave (of which he got rather more than his share, thanks to the intervention of Arago, who had become his friend). He was assigned to Paris in 1818 and was there enabled to work quite hard on his research. This lasted until 1824, when he became involved again with government work (on lighthouses) and the demands of this job, plus failing health, meant that he did little or nothing on physical optics from 1824 until his death (from tuberculosis) at the age of thirty-nine, in 1827.

Despite the brevity of his research life, Fresnel produced in the years from 1818 to 1824 paper after paper which together contribute surely the longest step forward in optics ever made by a single individual. He discounted the Newtonian, corpuscular theory of light and became firmly convinced that light consists not of particles but of oscillations set up by luminous bodies and transmitted through an all-pervading medium – the 'luminiferous aether'. Fresnel determined to take seriously the idea that this medium is an ordinary elastic medium and hence that the disturbances in it, which constitute light, obey ordinary mechanical principles.

Fresnel first developed a detailed theory of diffraction – of the fringes that are produced when a light beam is partially obstructed by an opaque object. After a few false starts, Fresnel hit on the idea that, contrary to earlier theories, light is not 'bent' by the opaque object, the latter's only function is to suppress that part of the light which falls on it; the fringes are produced by the wave nature of light itself – rectilinear propagation (hitherto thought to be light's most basic property) is only an approximate effect.

Fresnel submitted his theory of diffraction to the French Academy for its prize competition in 1818. One of the most famous stories in the history of science is of how one of the Academy's judges – Poisson (the others were Laplace* and Arago) – showed that Fresnel's theory has the 'absurd' consequence that the shadow of a small opaque disc should have a bright spot of light at its centre. On performing the experiment to refute Fresnel's ideas, the judges were astonished to find that the prediction is in fact correct. Fresnel was awarded the prize.

By the time Fresnel had heard of the similar work of Thomas Young* he had already gone far beyond what Young had achieved. He produced new, wave-theoretically correct theories of reflection and refraction and produced new and striking experimental confirmations of the interference of light.

Certain properties of so-called polarized light (which had been 'discovered' by Malus in 1808) had long worried Fresnel and, in 1821, he finally decided that his original theory – that the oscillations constituting light occur in the *same* direction as the overall propagation of light – was wrong. He developed instead the transverse theory, according to which the oscillations occur at right angles to the direction of propagation. This led to a massively impressive general theory of the transmission of light in transparent media and, in particular, to a theory of the phenomenon of double refraction (some crystals produce two refracted beams from one incident beam) as well as to major advances in crystal optics. The transverse theory has the consequence, however, that the light-carrying ether must be a solid – but then how do the planets move so freely through it? Fresnel had also raised the problem of whether opaque and transparent bodies in motion 'drag' the ether along with them. These problems were to keep Fresnel's successors busy for the rest of the century. Fresnel had, almost single-handedly, brought about one of the major scientific revolutions: he had convinced his contemporaries and successors that the corpuscular theory of light had to be abandoned and that the way forward lay with the wave theory – no matter what difficulties this might bring in its trail.

John Worrall

Literature on Fresnel is surprisingly scarce given his importance. There is no full length biography. There is, however, an edition of his Complete Works, *Oeuvres complètes*, ed. H. de Senarmont, E. Verdet and L. Fresnel (3 vols. 1886), the first volume of which contains a very useful introduction by Émile Verdet.

168
FRIEDRICH, Caspar David 1774–1840

German painter

If landscape became the principal genre for expressing the spiritual aspirations of the Romantic movement in painting, this was due as much, if not more, to Friedrich as to his contemporaries Turner* and Constable*. Now generally regarded as the foremost German Romantic artist, he put detailed observation of nature at the service of a poetic and transcendental vision. Some of his symbolism was a little conventional: for example, leafless oaks representing the transitoriness of the body and evergreens the life everlasting of the spirit; asymmetrical monastic ruins recalling the contingent and time-bound character of the historical church in contrast to the perfect and symmetrical image of the ideal church. But the power of his paintings derived from his ability, using these and other motifs, to evoke particular moods and feelings with concentrated intensity.

His bold compositions, often with a upward-pointing triangle in the centre foreground, bear witness to his strong graphic sense. Another striking instance of this is his schematic treatment of the sun's rays in *The Cross in the Mountains* (*Das Kreuz im Gebirge*, 1807–8). It is noteworthy that this, one of his most famous paintings, depicts not the crucifixion – Friedrich never painted biblical scenes – but a crucifix such as might be found in the mountainous forests of Central Europe. There is an intended universal meaning but this is conveyed through means proper to landscape painting: for example, Christ's blood and hence the archetypal connection between sacrifice, the death of the sun-hero and fertility, is hinted at by the red light in which everything, including the forest floor, is bathed.

One of Friedrich's most remarkable technical gifts was the depiction of mist in such a way that only as one stares at the picture does one gradually register the depth of ground and notice figures or objects looming up in it, thus re-creating with an almost uncanny accuracy the experience of confronting actual mist.

Aesthetically, the mist supplies a counterpoint to the precise, linear Neoclassical style of draughtsmanship, which can be compared to the rectilinear precision of Schinkel's* architecture and which Friedrich had inherited from his student years (1794–8) in Copenhagen. He had been born into a pious Protestant environment in the Pomeranian coast town of Greifswald which, together with the nearby island of Rügen, was to feature in many of his later paintings. The nature mysticism whose seeds had been sown there was greatly encouraged by the literary and philosophical environment of Dresden, where he moved in 1798, which reflected the influence of Tieck, Novalis and the Schlegel* brothers.

Friedrich was not interested in the naturalistic depiction of actual landscapes, although his intense concern with the rendering of realistic detail can be seen in his studies of plants, trees and rocks as well as certain buildings, notably the Abbey of Eldena. Typically, one picture shows this building transferred unaltered from Pomerania to the Riesengebirge. Typically too, in *Morning in the Riesengebirge*, (*Morgen im Riesengebirge*, 1810–11), the landscape is made up of mountains, rocks and other elements derived from sketches done at different times and in different places. What interested him rather was the reflection in nature of the human soul and in particular the passage of the human soul through stages in time. Thus there is a close correspondence of meaning between his *Times of Day* (*Tageszeiten*) cycle (1821–2) and his pictures of the four seasons on the one hand and paintings such as *The Stages of Life* (*Die Lebensstaufen*, c. 1835) on the other. The latter shows five figures on a characteristically triangular promontory and beyond them the sea on which there are five ships, the largest of which is drifting towards the shore representing, it has been suggested, the artist's own coming death. Even in his earlier paintings, death had been a predominant theme, explicitly in the frequent depiction of graveyards and dolmens, implicitly in the melancholy which pervades the majority of his work. It is problematical how much to interpret this as evidence of a morbid and pessimistic sensibility and how much as evidence of a profound resignation linked to a belief in redemption. Certainly, symbolic references to redemption abound but they seldom dispel the sombre mood and it is even possible to detect a streak of desperation in works such as the early woodcut *The Woman at the Precipice* (*Die Frau am Abgrund*, 1803–4) and the powerful black chalk self-portrait of c. 1810. Consistent with both interpretations is the sense of longing evident in pictures as divergent as the quiet *Woman at the Window* (*Frau am Fenster*, 1822) and the dramatic *Two Men Contemplating the Moon* (*Zwei Männer in Betrachtung des Mondes*, 1809) with its sinister gnarled tree roots beneath the waxing moon.

Friedrich is both marked as typically Romantic and

at the same time separated from his lesser contemporaries in Germany by his extreme sensitivity. His direct influence was far less than his stature would suggest, being confined essentially to a small circle in Dresden, where most of his paintings are still to be seen. His spirit, however, shorn of its lingering traditionalist and Christian trappings, was resurrected in the Surrealist landscapes of Max Ernst.

Gray Watson

See: L.D. Ettlinger, *Friedrich* (1967); the catalogue of the Friedrich Exhibition at the Tate Gallery, London (1972); Helmut Börsch-Supan, *Caspar David Friedrich* (1974); Roger Cardinal, *German Romantics* (1975).

169
FROEBEL, Friedrich 1782–1852

German educationalist

Froebel, best remembered as the originator of kindergartens (literally 'child gardens'), was born in Oberweisbach, Thuringia, the son of a Lutheran minister who, after Froebel's mother's death, remarried. Froebel did not get on with his stepmother, and at the age of ten was sent away to live with an uncle and aunt. Like many lonely, isolated children he developed a strong and lasting fascination with nature, undertaking an apprenticeship in forestry when he was fifteen. In 1800, however, he spent two terms at the University of Jena, and then went on to Frankfurt to study architecture, knowledge of which he later put to good use in designing his own houses and school buildings.

Froebel's working life may be divided into three parts: a somewhat directionless beginning; an extended period during which he acquired a broad base of experience from which to develop and publish his theories; and his final years, when he put his ideas into practice.

Having tried his hand at surveying and land management he was taken on as a teacher at a Frankfurt school which had adopted the progressive principles of the Swiss educationalist Johann Pestalozzi. A more important appointment, perhaps, came in 1806, when he became private tutor to the children of the Baron von Holtzhausen: it was in this post that he realised his vocation and began elaborating ideas which emphasized the uniqueness and individuality of each child as a learner. To improve his overall qualifications, and to study science and mathematics, he returned to university, this time to Göttingen and Berlin. After military service in the War of Liberation, he worked in Berlin's Museum of Mineralogy before opening his first school at Griesheim in 1816. In 1819, a year after marriage to a fellow teacher, Wilhelmina Hoffmeister, the school was moved to Keilhau. It was not until 1837

however that the first kindergarten was established, at Blankenburg.

Having posted a general account of his ideas in *The Education of Man* (*Die Menschenerziehung*, 1826, trans. 1886), a book formidable to read even in its original German, and having been obliged by the authorities to relinquish control of the Keilhau school in 1832, Froebel spent several years in Switzerland training others in his methods. It was not until the opening of the first kindergarten however that he was able to demonstrate the range of his theories for the education of young children.

In contrast to the generally held views of the time, Froebel thought of play and children's games as a basic means of learning. So thoroughly has this liberal idea, with its antecedents in the writings of J.-J. Rousseau, become enshrined in our attitude toward children that in order to grasp how revolutionary it was in the mid-nineteenth century we need consciously to evoke memories of pit children and prints of the well-regulated Victorian nursery. But that it was certainly felt to be radical at the time is reflected by the disciplinarian Prussian government's ban imposed on Froebel-style kindergartens from 1851 until 1860; an ineffective ban, as even in this decade the kindergarten movement spread rapidly throughout other areas of Western Europe, largely as a result of the efforts of the Baroness von Marenholtz-Bülow, an early disciple.

For his kindergartens Froebel assembled and invented a number of techniques and pieces of apparatus. These include the 'Occupations' and 'Singing Games' (outlined in *Mother-play and Nursery Songs, Mutter und Koselieder*, trans. 1895), but perhaps the most famous are the eight 'Gifts', devices such as soft balls and wooden blocks which are manipulated so as to develop manual-spatial dexterity and knowledge of assembly, relationship and use. The child is given the gifts in sequence, so that the various skills involved are acquired progressively. (The constructional emphasis within Froebel's programme for structured play grew out of his early studies in architecture and mathematics. In this context it is perhaps worth noting that the twentieth-century architect, Frank Lloyd Wright, was specifically trained by his ambitious mother in the 'Gifts'; and one of Wright's own children designed and manufactured a set of building blocks that are clear descendants of the forms used by his father.)

Froebel's ideas on primary education were part and parcel of a much larger concern he had with social reform in general and a German resurgence in particular. Like many great teachers he was a humble yet inspiring person, well classified as a liberal optimist for his view that:

under each human fault lies a good tendency which has been crushed, misunderstood or misled. Hence the infallible remedy for all human wickedness is first to bring to light this original good tendency and then to nourish, foster and train it.

His profound respect for every child as a 'necessary member of humanity', prefiguring certain aspects of mainstream twentieth-century psychology, was an aspect of his love of nature and belief in a divine order. 'Look after my flowers – and my weeds,' he exhorted at his death, 'for I have learnt from them both.'

Ranulph Glanville

See: *Friedrich Froebel: A Selection from his Writings*, ed. Irene M. Lilley (1967); William H. Kilpatrick, *Froebel's Kindergarten Principles Critically Examined*, (1916).

170
FROUDE, James Anthony 1818–94

British historian and man of letters

The story of Froude's life is one of recurrent scandal and controversy. He was the son of the Archbishop of Totnes and younger brother of Richard Hurrell Froude, Newman's* friend and fellow Tractarian at Oxford. In 1830 Froude went to Westminster School, where he was lonely and bullied. His strict father was unsympathetic, and Froude dramatized this period of his life in his first (pseudonymous) work, a short story called 'The Spirit's Trials' (in *Shadows of the Clouds* by 'Zeta', 1847). In it, Canon Fowler whips his schoolboy son, Edward, and then thwarts his marriage plans. Edward dies of consumption, having rejected the Thirty-nine Articles, largely because he cannot believe in a God who decrees eternal punishment for a large part of mankind.

As in fiction, so in life. Froude had gone up to Oriel College in 1836, soon after the early death of his brother Richard. He came under Newman's influence, and contributed a life of St Neot to Newman's *Lives of the English Saints* (1844). When Newman converted to Rome in 1845, Froude was not tempted to follow him, but he was beset by religious doubts. He could not accept the sacredness of the Bible, partly as a result of reading the German higher criticism, and partly because he was disinclined to worship a God who appeared in Old Testament scripture as an arbitrary despot. Froude later recalled this difficult time in Oxford in the 1840s in 'The Oxford Counter-Reformation' (*Short Studies on Great Subjects*) and in his biography of Carlyle*:

All round us, the intellectual lightships had broken from their moorings, and it was then a new and trying experience. The present generation . . . will never know what it was to find the lights all drifting,

the compasses all awry, and nothing left to steer by except the stars (*Thomas Carlyle: A History of his Life in London*, 1884).

For Froude, as for so many of his generation, the man who rescued them from the brink of unbelief was not the Anglo-Catholic Newman, but the advocate of secularized spirituality, of 'natural supernaturalism', Carlyle: 'Amidst the controversies, the arguments, the doubts, the crowding uncertainties of forty years ago, Carlyle's voice was to the young generation of Englishmen like the sound of "ten thousand trumpets" in their ears.' Thus Carlyle appears as a modern prophet in Froude's novel, *The Nemesis of Faith* (1849), offering a faith without a church. Under his influence the protaganist, Markham Sutherland, resigns his clerical position, preferring 'the religion of Christ' to 'the Christian religion'. Sutherland goes to Italy where he falls in love with a young married Englishwoman. Her husband obligingly goes away on business; the young couple declare their love; in an episode in a boat on Lake Como they neglect her child, who dies from a wetting in the lake. The would-be lovers part in despair.

The Nemesis of Faith shows signs of formal influences from Goethe's* *Wilhelm Meister* and Carlyle's *Sartor Resartus*, with its device of an editor-cum-friend of the hero collecting and editing his fragmentary memoirs. It also borrows its climax from Goethe's *Die Wahlverwandtschaften* (*Elective Affinities*), which Froude later translated anonymously for Bohn's Library (1854). It is hard to know whether *Nemesis* caused a scandal more because of the religious doubts of Sutherland or because of the Goethean theme of adultery. William Sewell, vice-rector of Exeter College, burnt it ceremonially, and Froude resigned his Exeter Fellowship. In fact, Froude never fully lost his faith. As he said of *Nemesis*, 'It did not maintain any heretical doctrines . . . . It was a mood, not a treatise.' Charles Kingsley*, whose wife's sister Froude married in 1849, thought he had been foolish to make public his 'spiritual diarrhoea', and Carlyle, displeased at figuring as Froude's hero, was scornful of his 'spiritual agonising bellyaches'.

In his revulsion from Oxford and Newman, Froude turned to writing a twelve-volume *History of England from the Fall of Wolsey to the Death of Elizabeth* (1856–70). His extreme pro-Protestant bias and his admiration of the strong hero (in the manner of Carlylean history) led him to blacken Mary Stuart and whitewash Henry VIII. Though his *History* rivalled Macaulay's* in popularity, it was attacked by professional historians for its cavalier treatment of materials and its extreme interpretation of events. Indeed, Froude thought, like Carlyle, that writing history was an imaginative act: 'the most perfect English history which exists is to be found, in my opinion, in the historical plays of Shakespeare' (*Short Studies*). Like Carlyle, Froude supported strong action by those in power, expressing this view in *The English in Ireland* (1872–4) and *Oceana, or England and her Colonies* (1886). It was natural that Froude should want to write biography, and his most important attempt in the genre was, fittingly, the life of Carlyle.

Froude had met his 'hero' in 1849, and Carlyle later made him his literary executor. The first two volumes of the biography were published with what appeared to contemporaries to be indecent haste in 1882 (Carlyle died in 1881). Froude followed with *Letters and Memorials of Jane Welsh Carlyle* (1883) and volumes three and four of Carlyle's life (1884). His portrait was that of an irascible, brooding man, and Carlyle's family and admirers responded with a number of anti-Froude biographies and memoirs of Carlyle. But Froude's work, though careless with documents, was the best written, most interesting, and on the whole least partial of the many accounts of Carlyle. Froude's talents as a fine stylist and lively narrator may disqualify him as a serious historian but they claim our admiration in what is still the best biography of Carlyle.

Rosemary Ashton

Froude's works were published by the New Universal Library in 1905. The standard biography is Waldo H. Dunn, *James Anthony Froude: A Biography* (2 vols. 1961–3). See also: Walter E. Houghton, *The Victorian Frame of Mind* (1957); and Robert Lee Wolff, *Gains and Losses; Novels of Faith and Doubt in Victorian England* (1977).

171
FRY, Elizabeth 1780–1845

British prison reformer

Known as 'the Angel of the Prisons', Elizabeth Fry became a symbol of saintliness soon after she began to visit Newgate Prison in December 1816. Her influence on the degraded women prisoners and the improvements she made in their living conditions astounded the nation. Lord Lansdowne described her in parliament as 'the Genius of Good'; George Crabbe* wrote a poem about her; and fashionable London flocked to the prison to see her reading the Gospels to the female convicts.

In the aftermath of the Napoleonic Wars, the government was alarmed by a London crime wave of unprecedented proportions and anxious to quell the mood of unrest in the country. Mrs Fry's 'miracles' were seized upon as a model of the way in which to deal with the restive lower classes.

She was a matron of thirty-six with nine children by a Quaker minister when she first began to visit Newgate. Her compassion was aroused at first by the plight of the babies born in the gaol, most of them naked and wretched. She appealed to their mothers to help them to have a better start in life and to the prison authorities to allow her to work with the prisoners. Her concern as a religious was to retrieve souls from eternal damnation; however she was equally concerned with the prisoners' welfare in this life. In exchange for a promise from the women to forsake their wicked ways, swearing, drinking and gaming, she pledged herself to set up a school to teach reading, writing and sewing and also to provide employment for the prisoners. She actually appealed to the prisoners for their approval of her scheme and, despite male scepticism, the experiment flourished.

Her school for prisoners and their children was adopted as a part of the prison system of the City of London. Her care for all prisoners, particularly those condemned to death, had a profound effect on penal reformers who came to see her work at Newgate. She always reserved the front bench at her Bible readings for women awaiting the death sentence.

In 1818 she travelled to Glasgow, visiting local prisons and magistrates *en route* and founding local Ladies' Associations for Prison Visiting, modelled on Newgate, everywhere she went. With her brother, Joseph John Gurney, who had accompanied her, she published *Notes on a Visit made to some of the Prisons in Scotland and the North of England* (1819), which drew public attention to the filth, overcrowding and corruption of the prison system. She portrayed the prisoners as wretches to be pitied rather than feared.

For twenty years she and her band of helpers inspected every female convict ship before it sailed. She worked to improve conditions an board ship by practical measures and also by influencing parliamentary opinion. Several times she was invited to give evidence to parliamentary committees on prisoners and punishments.

In 1827 she published *Observations on the Visiting, Superintendence and Government of Female Prisoners*. In it she pleaded in thinly veiled terms for a more useful life for women. 'During the last ten years much attention has been successfully bestowed by women on the female inmates of our prisons. But a similar care is evidently needed for our hospitals, asylums and our workhouses.' Although she always insisted that her authority to work in the prisons sprang from a divine source, Elizabeth Fry had opened up opportunities for women to work in a man's world and pioneers like Florence Nightingale* were directly inspired by her example.

From 1820 until her death she was seen as the figurehead of most of the philanthropic endeavour in England. She founded Benevolent Societies for the Poor, instituted a nursing order and provided libraries for coast guard stations.

Her most creative years in the prisons in England were between 1817 and 1819. Later, much of her work was taken over by government and the prisons came under the surveillance of the Home Office. Prison officials were sceptical of her religious influence and out of sympathy with her desire to rehabilitate the prisoners. The government was more interested in making prison sentences a deterrent.

Abroad her reputation was still high and in her late fifties she began to tour prisons on the continent. Everywhere she went she drew attention to excesses of neglect and cruelty and suggested reforms. She was given a rapturous reception by prison officials and the aristocracy alike in France, Germany, Prussia, Denmark, Holland and Belgium. Some concrete results were achieved. Female prisoners were placed under the care of women warders in France and in Denmark, the prisoners were given employment and the king issued orders that the prisons should be heated in winter.

Before Elizabeth Fry's intervention in the prisons, prison authorities had regarded their charges as wild beasts to be caged. Her personal recognition of the prisoners as individuals, capable of self-respect and rehabilitation, changed society's attitudes profoundly.

She was born in Norwich, the daughter of a wealthy Quaker banking family. Since Quakers believe that men and women are equal in the sight of God, her education was more intellectually stimulating than was usual for girls at that time. In her married life her large family (she bore eleven children) frequently felt neglected, but domestic duties were not allowed to stand in the way of her religious mission. She was of nervous temperament and dependent on stimulants and sedatives all her life. Her own writings reveal her to be a far more complex and contradictory human being than the saintly image of the nineteenth century would suggest.

June Rose

See: John Kent, *Elizabeth Fry* (1962), and June Rose, *Elizabeth Fry* (1980).

172
FUKUZAWA Yukichi 1835–1901

Japanese educator

Yukichi Fukuzawa was a philosopher, writer and educator whose ideas strongly influenced the Japanese after the opening of Japan to the West. He did much to guide the popular attitudes and emerging institutions of Meiji Japan. But he never held high office or took part directly in politics. And though he developed almost single-handed an intellectual framework for a liberal modern state based on individual freedom and representative government, this was not the path that Japan was to choose in his lifetime.

Fukuzawa was a gifted and clear-sighted teacher. In a static and feudal society he urged *dokuritsu jison*, 'independence and self-respect'. And in a country still dominated by the teaching of the Chinese classics he compaigned for *jitsugaku*, 'practical learning', in every sphere from physics to foreign languages. Fukuzawa's very readable autobiography is the story of his battle with the reactionary forces of his age. Born the youngest child of a low-ranking samurai from a provincial clan in Kyushu, he felt at first hand the injustice and frustration bred of the rigid social hierarchy of the time. Those of lower rank had to abase themselves before their superiors on all occasions.

Fukuzawa went to Nagasaki and then Osaka to study Dutch. He was dismayed at the material and social backwardness of the Japanese, and at the ignorance of their leaders, who were resisting Western pressures to open up the country. But he believed, in common with the utilitarian thinkers of the West, that progress was inevitable. And later, in *Gakumon no Susume* ('The Encouragement of Learning', 1872–6), he proclaimed the then revolutionary tenet that all men are born equal.

The anti-foreign fever in Japan reached a peak in the years around the overthrow of the shogunate and the restoration of the Emperor in 1868. But Fukuzawa, while studying and teaching English in Edo (Tokyo), thrust himself into the centre of Japan's dealings with the outside world. He took part in the first overseas voyage of a Japanese mission, which crossed the Pacific to America in 1860, and went as an official translator on subsequent journeys to Europe and the United States. He used the experiences to write *Seiyo Jijo* ('Things Western', 2 vols, 1866 and 1870), the first authoritative book about Western society, which became a best seller. In this and other early works Fukuzawa reported and explained Western customs and many of the principles of science and ecomomics which were still new to the Japanese.

But Fukuzawa realized that Japan would be able to re-create Western institutions only after a revolution in social values, and here he was only partly successful. Still, in the thirty years after the Restoration he made detailed studies of many Western ideas and institutions, from police and currency systems to education and politics. Even as the civil war raged in Edo, Fukuzawa pointedly did not take sides, but went on teaching at the private school he had set up there. That school still survives as Keio University. Fukuzawa also founded his own newspaper, published his own books and started up many public debating societies. He was offered the job, effectively, of Minister of Education, but turned it down out of his deep-rooted aversion to the exercise of power.

Fukuzawa's enthusiasm for the benefits of Western culture led him to be over-optimistic about his own country's future in two respects. The first was the question of the Japanese peoples's political emancipation. Fukuzawa helped to persuade the government to agree to the establishment of a 'diet' or parliament. He wanted this to be the heart of a parliamentary system along the British model, with governments being formed from members of the majority party. In fact the Meiji oligarchy clung stubbornly to power in the emperor's name and party politics failed to take root, yielding instead to totalitarianism some thirty years after Fukuzawa's death.

Secondly, Fukuzawa supposed that since Westerners were guided by reason in so many areas of life, this would also apply to their conduct of international affairs. He even justified Britain's Opium War against China, laying the blame on Chinese decadence in resisting open trade. But in later life Fukuzawa became convinced that white racism was working against Japan too. He concluded that Japan, the most advanced country in the Far East, was destined to lead Asia. He was a leading advocate of Japan's expansion in Korea and the Sino-Japanese War of 1894–5. And he turned against the movement for 'people's rights' because it interfered with the growth of Japan's military strength.

Fukuzawa was himself an outstanding example of what he sought to teach his fellow-countrymen – critical reason and independence of mind. But when he saw the ideals of freedom and equality in conflict with Japan's struggle for a place among the leading nations of the world, he sided with nationalism.

William Horsley

Fukuzawa Zenshu (the collected works) were published in Tokyo in two parts, 1926 and 1933. *Fukuo Jiden* (1899) has been translated as *The Autobiography of Fukuzawa Yukichi* (1966). See: G.B. Sansom, *The Western World and Japan* (1950); Donald Keene, *The Japanese Discovery of Europe* (1952); Carmen Blacker, *The Japanese Enlightenment* (1964); Wayne H. Oxford, *The Speeches of Fukuzawa* (1973).

173
FULLER, Margaret 1810–49

US writer and feminist

As the so-called 'high priestess of Transcendentalism' Margaret Fuller excited wild admiration and derision in her lifetime and since. For many, her complex and peculiarly symbolic life has seemed of far greater interest than her writing; a brilliant conversationalist and orator, she admitted that she often felt constrained in print. Today Fuller may look like a recognizable type of charismatic personality, a natural leader and proselytizer. During her lifetime, however, public life was not open to women: it took Fuller's highly public efforts to find roles adequate to her talents to convince mid-

century Americans that women could partake in intellectual and public life.

Recently Fuller's *Woman in the Nineteenth Century* (1845) has been recognized as both an eloquently argued and highly influential feminist tract; also Fuller (with Poe*, who resented her competition) was the only American literary critic of her age to write consistently from principles; and her translations and articles on German literature, particularly Goethe*, made her the most important nineteenth-century American interpreter of German culture.

When Margaret Fuller met the British feminist Harriet Martineau* in Concord, Massachusetts, in 1835, Fuller had already been forcibly introduced to the harsh realities of life; her father, a once-powerful, then embittered Jeffersonian lawyer, had educated her like a boy; by age seven she was reading Virgil and Caesar in Latin. After withdrawing to the country, Timothy Fuller had died suddenly, leaving Margaret to run a failing farm and then support her invalid mother and younger brother by her pen. When Ralph Emerson* met Fuller at Martineau's recommendation, he found her (as he wrote later) laden with disadvantages: 'a woman, an orphan, without beauty, without money'; but they became friends, and Fuller developed into one of the leaders of the Transcendentalist movement.

Fuller was always clear that her goal in both her writing and her life was to grow; her life was a search for a role, just as her writing was a search for a method. Fuller both believed and exemplified the Unitarian and Transcendentalist doctrine of 'Self-culture', as set forth by William Ellery Channing, Bronson Alcott, and, most influentially, by Emerson in 'Self-Reliance' (1840). 'Very early I knew that the only object in life was to grow,' she wrote. 'I was often false to this knowledge, in idolatries of particular objects, or impatient longings for happiness, but I have never lost sight of it, have always been controlled by it, and this first gift of thought has never been superseded by a later love' (*Memoirs*, 1852).

In 1836 Fuller began to teach at Bronson Alcott's Temple School, an experimental school which operated according to Socratic method; in 1839 her translation of Goethe's *Conversations with Eckermann* appeared; in 1840, Emerson and Fuller decided that the Transcendental movement needed its own magazine, so they founded *The Dial* (1840–4), which Margaret edited for two years as an eclectically inclusive journal, publishing Emerson, Alcott, Orestes Brownson, Thoreau*, and oriental sacred writings, amongst others. At the same time (1839–44) Fuller instituted her unique 'Conversations' or seminars for educated women in Boston, seeking 'to systematize thought and give a precision and clearness in which our sex is so deficient' because of women's lack of opportunity to use or 'reproduce' intellect. In a society dominated by the pulpit, by political oratory, and by the lyceum lecture, Fuller invented a female discourse.

By their example Fuller and her pupils demonstrated that women could develop arguments and speak in public; in 1845, Fuller's pioneering feminist work, *Woman in the Nineteenth Century*, argued an analogy between black slavery and female subjection which was already becoming historical reality in the link between abolitionism and the emergent American feminist movement (as in the Declaration of Principle at Seneca Falls, 1848). Fuller never joined the Brook Farm utopian experiment, but she visited frequently and held Conversations; Nathaniel Hawthorne*, her friend at the time (after her death he wrote a bilious attack in his journal), mythologized her critically but probably accurately as the tragically magnetic feminist Zenobia in *The Blithedale Romance* (1852).

In 1844, Fuller moved to New York to become (in another 'first') lead literary reviewer for Horace Greeley's crusading *New York Tribune*. *Woman in the Nineteenth Century*, her farewell to the New England ethos, was conceived as a legal debate between real and ideal (Man and men, Woman and women); it developed into a critique of marriage for creating a 'Model-woman of bird-like beauty and softness, fitted to please or at least not disturb her husband'.

Fuller had recognized that the meditative and questing transcendental self was in practice male and she claimed for women an equal right to find the spark of divinity in their own selves and to seek fulfilment in work; her book created a sensation. Like Mary Wollstonecraft's *Vindication of the Rights of Women*, whose tradition it continued, *Women in the Nineteenth Century* is an analytic work, but it lacks in broad social vision; like

Simone de Beauvoir in *The Second Sex* a hundred years later, Fuller argued the case for all women by citing exceptional women.

Two years of writing criticism and investigative reporting for a large public politicized Fuller. When she went to Europe in 1847, an apocryphal conversation had her telling Thomas Carlyle* 'I accept the universe' and Carlyle replying 'By Gad Madam, you'd better' – but by this stage Fuller's 'acceptance' was no mere Transcendentalist's condescension. In Italy in 1847–8 Fuller became deeply involved with the Republican cause, sending back passionate reports to the *Tribune*. She had become a friend of Mazzini*, and then married the Republican Marchese Ossoli, and had a son (though there was gossip about the order of these events). With the French invasion of Italy, Fuller and Ossoli left for the United States, but their ship sank, and they and their child were drowned within sight of the American shore. Her shocked friends Emerson, William Ellery Channing and James Freeman Clarke quickly published the *Memoirs*(1852), which turned Fuller into a Romantic heroine.

Helen McNeil

Fuller's selected works are most readily available in Perry Miller's anthology, *Margaret Fuller: American Romantic* (1963), and in *Margaret Fuller: Essays on American Life and Letters*, ed. Joel Myerson (1978). See: Wade Mason, *Margaret Fuller: Whetstone of Genius* (1940); Bell Gale Chevigny, *The Woman and the Myth: Margaret Fuller's Life and Writings* (1976); David M. Robinson, 'Margaret Fuller and the Transcendental Ethos: *Woman in the Nineteenth Century*', *PMLA* 97, no. 1 (January 1982).

G

GALDÓS, Benito Pérez: see under PÉREZ
GALDÓS, Benito

174
GALOIS, Evariste 1811–32

French mathematician

The life of Evariste Galois is a tragedy of the bitterest and most poignant kind, and of this tragic life the last four years from 1828 to 1832 were the essence. In 1828 Galois was seventeen, haughty, high-spirited, aware of his own exceptional mathematical talent, and with some important mathematical studies already below his belt. In 1832 he was left dying in an obscure field, unattended, after an unsought and squalid duel. No one at the time was aware that one of the greatest mathematical talents had been savagely cut down before he had had a chance to put his gifts to work. Galois's death was not, however, a freak event: the whole of his short life was dogged by an inexorably evil luck.

He was born at Bourg-la-Reine, outside Paris. His father was a staunch Republican, his mother a woman of spirit too. At the age of twelve he was sent to the grim *lycée* of Louis-le-Grand in Paris. At first Galois, who had already been admirably taught by his mother, shone in this environment, winning prizes in literature and the classics. But then there was a rebellion in the school, and a group of older children were expelled. This gave Galois an indelible impression of injustice, an impression which soon hardened into automatic expectation. He lost interest in the curriculum, and at thirteen suffered the indignity of demotion. Yet it was at this time that he read Legendre's *Éléments de géométrie* (1794), generally reckoned to represent two year's work for the brightest mathematical scholar, but which Galois absorbed in a matter of weeks.

He soon progressed to Lagrange's *Algebra*. Being already in the world of advanced mathematics, he took little interest in the ordinary mathematical curriculum, and was frequently admonished for poor or mediocre work. He did however win the school maths prize. He then took the examination for the Polytechnique, where he was sure that his genius would be recognised. But the examiners could not understand Galois's methods, and failed him. At last, at the age of seventeen, he had the good fortune to fall under the influence of a perceptive man, L.P.E.Richard, a teacher of advanced mathematics at Louis-le-Grand. Richard gave Galois every possible encouragement, and the result was a great flowering of the youth's skill. He published a paper on continued fractions, but his most startling discoveries were put in a longer paper, which he submitted to Augustin-Louis Cauchy, the leading mathematician of the age. Cauchy promised to present Galois's paper to the Academy; but then Cauchy 'forgot', and somehow mislaid the manuscript. Another crushing blow followed when he was again failed by the Polytechnique. At the same time Galois's father, by now mayor of Bourg-la-Reine, fell victim to a poison-pen campaign, developed a persecution mania, and committed suicide.

Galois submitted a brilliant memoir for the Grand Prize in mathematics offered by the Academy. The secretary received it safely, but died before he had time to read it, and when his papers were searched it had disappeared. Then the final blow fell. A third memoir was sent to another leading mathematician, Siméon-Denis Poisson, who had shown interest in young Galois. But Poisson failed to grasp the point of the new paper, and returned it with a note saying it was 'incomprehensible'. At this Galois decided to abandon mathematics. He threw himself instead into revolutionary politics, and was soon arrested and imprisoned. On being released he was seduced by a 'coquette', and it was probably this liaison that led to the fatal duel, although even the identity of his duellist has never been satisfactorily established. At any rate he died eighteen days after receiving his wounds, having been found by a passing peasant. When his younger brother arrived at the hospital, Evariste admonished him: 'Don't cry! I need all my courage to die at twenty.'

Those papers and manuscripts that survived were collected and published in the *Journal de Mathématiques Pures et Appliquées* in 1846. Since then Galois has been acknowledged as an outstanding pioneer of modern mathematics. The years between 1828 and 1832, when his work was done, may in retrospect be seen as years of mathematical metamorphosis, for it was during this short spell that mathematics emerged from the chrysalis of post-Newtonian physical representation and began to take on the character of a free and independent science. The exploration of formal possibilities, without any ties to descriptive reality, became an end-in-itself, even providing a new intellectual aesthetic. Although more than a decade passed before his findings became generally known, Galois can now be seen as the chief proponent of this transformation. It was actually the young Frenchman who took the first breathtaking steps towards the use of abstract algebra in a bold, rigorous, convincing non-representational way.

At about the same time Gauss* had developed 'complex' (imaginary) numbers and Lobachevsky* was developing non-Euclidean geometry. Thus mathematics acquired three new potential branches all at once: non-representational algebra, non-numerical arithmetic and non-Euclidean gemetry. What was achieved may be seen in perspective when one considers that in each of the three cases the knowledge established had allegedly been proved logically impossible by Kant. Of the three, it was the idea that algebra could be pursued as a formal system in its own right which was the most uncompromising. Gauss's complex numbers could be thought of as a kind of calibration of near-misses in trying to solve insoluble equations. Lobachevsky's non-Euclidean plane was capable of visual representation – up to a point. But Galois's new, synthetic algebras were pure invention; there was no lingering possibility that they might partially 'represent' anything. They showed that algebraic systems, rigorously developed, acquire a life of their own, and are not ultimately dependent on patterns observable in physical reality.

Yet these non-representational algebras could be used to dazzling effect in solving problems in classical algebra. They acted like mysterious catalysts, freeing blocked processes in numerical algebra, and leading to results which the most conventionally minded mathematician could hardly deny. Galois's systems are nowadays known as 'Galois Fields' and 'Galois Groups'. The idea of a Galois Field is that one produces a purely abstract system of 'polynomials' (expressions like $X^3 + 2X^2 + X + 1$) in which the symbol X does not stand for a number of any kind, but is simply an uninterpreted mark. If one then adds a fundamental identity, like $X^3 + X + 1 = 0$, one gets an abstract system which begins to generate interesting results, e.g., the polynomial mentioned above becomes equivalent to $2X^2$. Galois showed that systems of this kind obey the rules for a 'field', which means roughly that the ordinary operations, $-, \div, \times$ are always possible, except in the single instance of division by zero. The idea arose from an extension of the notion of a complex number, part 'real', part 'imaginary'. This was equivalent to a system of polynomials $2X + 1$, $5X - 11$, $-3X + 12$, etc., together with the fundamental equation $X^2 + 1 = 0$.

The power of Galois Fields is shown by the fact that they enable one to establish two celebrated impossibilities, the impossibility of solving quintic equations algebraically (in the general case), and the impossibility of trisecting the angle. The great intellects of the ancient world, Euclid and Archimedes, probably spent hundreds of fruitless hours trying to trisect the angle with ruler and compasses. Galois's method shows at a stroke that the quest was unattainable: it is logically *impossible* that there could be such a construction.

Christopher Ormell

For a modern edition of the works see *Écrits et Mémoires mathématiques d'Evariste Galois*, ed. R. Bourgne and J.-P. Azra (1962). See: E.T. Bell, 'Genius and Stupidity: Galois', in *Men of Mathematics*, vol.2 (1937); and W.W. Sawyer, *A Concrete Approach to Abstract Algebra* (1959).

175
GALTON, Sir Francis 1822–1911

British scientist

When we think of Galton the word 'genius' readily springs to mind. It not only captures something of his extraordinary versatility and inventiveness but also indicates one of the chief objects of his investigative concerns. We need scarcely be surprised that the grandson of Erasmus Darwin and the half-cousin of the even more famous Charles Darwin* should have devoted so much of his own career to examining the origins, nature, and transmission of exceptional talent.

Galton was the precocious son of a prominent Midlands banker and amateur of science. He attended private academies in Boulogne and Kenilworth before completing his pre-university education at the Free School (later King Edward's) in his native Birmingham. Between 1838 and 1840 he prepared for a medical career by making a tour of hospitals on the continent, spending some time at Giessen in the laboratory of the great organic chemist Justus von Liebig*, and attending courses at King's College, London. Over the subsequent four years he studied mathematics at Trinity College, Cambridge, where his progress was hindered by a breakdown due to obsessive overworking. Any remaining idea of becoming a doctor was abandoned when, in 1844, his father died and left him with ample independent means.

During 1845–6 Galton explored the Nile from Cairo to Khartoum, and travelled in Syria and the Holy Land. He then passed some years endeavouring, through an excess of hunting and shooting, to turn himself into an ordinary English country gentleman. Fortunately wanderlust managed to prevail, and in 1850 he embarked upon that exploration of South West Africa which won him his first significant scientific repute. *Tropical South Africa* (1853) was followed two years later by the splendid and soon classic handbook *The Art of Travel: or, Shifts and Contrivances Available in Wild Countries*. Already a luminary of the Royal Geographical Society, he was in 1856 elected FRS. Further distinction as an explorer was denied to him by recurrent ill-health. Instead, he moved deeper into the work of the British Association for the Advancement of Science (being general secretary, 1863–7), while also diversifying his personal scholarly activities in a quite remarkable way.

Among the many topics to which Galton made useful contributions over the following decades were meteorology (where he coined the word 'anticyclone' and pioneered systematic weather mapping), the establishment of identity through study and classification of finger prints, the development of correlation theory in statistics, and investigations into taste, smell, colour blindness, composite photographic portraiture of types, word association, and the functioning of visual memory. There were even 'Statistical Inquiries into the Efficacy of Prayer', whose rather negative import caused squalls when they were published in the *Fortnightly Review* (1872). An increasingly dominant theme in his work from the later 1860s onward was, however, the elaboration of techniques for the measurement of physical and mental attributes – procedures which eventually became a leading source of inspiration for early twentieth-century British and American psychologists concerned with intelligence testing and other forms of aptitude scaling. For Galton it was obvious that the scientist should also be asking how to ensure that the best of these attributes could be transmitted to posterity. It was he himself who gave to such study of improved human breeding that label of 'eugenics' which stuck thereafter.

Leading items from his many publications in the field are *Hereditary Genius* (1869); *English Men of Science: Their Nature and Nurture* (1874); *Inquiries into Human Faculty and Its Development* (1883); *Record of Family Faculties*, (1884); *Natural Inheritance* (1889); *Noteworthy Families* (with E. Schuster, 1906); and *Essays in Eugenics* (1909). Galton's most fundamental contention, evident already in the first of these books, was that important mental characteristics (intelligence especially) were inherited in exactly the same way as physical attributes, and that there existed a clear hierarchy of such talents both within and between races. He believed that those who were best endowed among the higher stocks must resist competition from inferiors of their own population as well as from outsiders. Success here was, in Galton's view, inseparable from the question of differential breeding rates. Thus he sought to promote more intensive reproductive activity amongst those whom he deemed superior, on a scale of values that broadly reflected his own upper middle-class background. To this end he advocated special allowances and other incentives for those of higher quality, and conversely he aimed to discourage the inferior from having offspring. The object was to develop a stock physically, mentally, and morally better than anything known hitherto. Galton had no doubt that conscious direction from the state was essential to make any such eugenic campaign effective. This sort of control was required precisely because 'civilization' as conventionally understood tended constantly to diminish the rigour with which the processes of Darwinian natural selection would otherwise operate. On one hand, it artificially protected an effete and idle landed aristocracy; on the other, it also allowed the lowest orders the opportunity of excessive reproduction. Civilization in this sense thereby served only to confuse proper patterns of hierarchy. Taken to their logical conclusion, his eugenic proposals point in the longer run not towards an elitist dominance of superiors over inferiors but rather towards a world in which the latter have disappeared altogether and in which the improved breed enjoys a genetic monopoly.

In his final years Galton sought to ensure the continuance of eugenic research by founding a relevant laboratory at University College, London. He also provided in his will for the endowment of a professorship to be held there by his collaborator and former pupil Karl Pearson*. The chief weaknesses of the approach which Galton himself had laid down are easily detectable. He cannot be blamed, of course, for completing most of his work before the belated recognition of Mendel's* significance at the turn of the century – but, equally, the fact must be faced that Galtonian eugenics had been devised on the basis of a defective theory of inheritance. Altogether less defensible was the naivety of Galton's approach towards the moral and political issues entailed by his proposals: for example, even if one suspects that he would have had no truck with the Nazi version of a eugenic New Order, he did certainly leave some important hostages to later totalitarian fortune. No less notable was his consistent underestimation of the complexity of the interaction between nature and nurture, and especially of the extent to which data on 'noteworthy families' and suchlike were skewed under conditions of gross inequality in educational opportunity. There was sublime smugness in the observation that 'the men who achieve eminence, and those who are naturally capable, are, to a large extent, identical.' All too often Galton's work reads like a complacent paean to the Victorian 'establishment', or at least to that non-aristocratic portion of which he himself was such a distinguished ornament.

Michael Biddiss

See: Galton's autobiographical work, *Memories of My Life* (1908), and Karl Pearson's predictably reverential account, *The Life, Letters, and Labours of Francis Galton* (3 vols, 1914–1930). D.W. Forrest,

Francis Galton: The Life and Work of a Victorian Genius (1974), provides a more balanced assessment.

176

GARIBALDI, Giuseppe 1807–82

Italian patriot and soldier

Among the 'freedom fighters' and 'national liberators' of the last 150 years Garibaldi stands in the very first rank. He achieved vast fame in his own lifetime both because of his dramatic deeds and on account of his personal qualities. He inspired loyalty from Italians, and respect from much farther afield, through his courage, his dignified simplicity, and his capacity for disinterested self-sacrifice.

Garibaldi was born in Nice, shortly before its transfer from French to Piedmontese rule. As a young merchant seaman he soon came into contact with radical patriotic activists in Genoa, Piedmont's leading port, and in the refugee community along the coast at Marseilles. Here in the early 1830s he first encountered the recently exiled Mazzini*, who was then launching his new republican nationalist organization known as Young Italy. Inspired by its ideals, Garibaldi participated during 1833–4 in unsuccessful risings against the monarchy of Sardinia-Piedmont. The next decade or so was spent fighting dictatorship in Uruguay and elsewhere in Latin America, at the head of a band of fellow-exiles soon renowned as his 'Redshirts'. In these years he trained himself for the career of professional rebel, perfected his techniques of guerilla combat, and adopted that gaucho costume which would thereafter become an integral part of his image as romantic liberator.

The European revolutions of 1848 brought Garibaldi and some sixty of his veterans hurrying home. The Piedmontese government spurned his offer of aid against the Austrians, so he concentrated on supporting the radical rising in Milan where Mazzini was already engaged. Having fought well but unavailingly, the Garibaldians then re-emerged to undertake during May and June 1849 an heroic role in the defence of Mazzini's short-lived Roman Republic. Further exile followed, and it was not until 1854 that Garibaldi returned to Italy. By then he was reluctantly coming to accept, as Mazzini could not, that the Piedmontese monarchy offered the most realistic point of focus for Italian nationalism. In the war of 1859 against Austria he fought with distinction at the head of a semi-independent volunteer force while holding the rank of major-general in the king's army.

By the spring of 1860 Piedmont had gained Lombardy, together with much of Central Italy. Yet Garibaldi himself felt deeply insulted by the fact that the premier, Cavour, had rewarded France for its support by ceding Savoy and his very own birthplace of Nice. Relations were already strained when in May Garibaldi, with the 'Thousand Redshirts', sailed from Genoa for Sicily aiming to seize the opportunity given by an anti-Bourbon rebellion in that island. Cavour feared lest the expedition endanger the gains already made, but equally he felt unable openly to oppose the scheme of a soldier who was already attaining the status of the Risorgimento's only truly popular hero. King Victor Emmanuel and his chief minister chose to sit on the fence until events made Garibaldi's own fate clearer. The sheer speed and scale of the guerillas' success both in Sicily and on the Neapolitan mainland during the next four months staggered observers everywhere. Many suspected that Garibaldi might even now try to establish a Mazzinian republic in the liberated territories or unintentionally provoke hostile foreign intervention by launching his own assault against Rome. Thus Cavour was relieved when a pre-emptive southwards advance by Piedmontese troops led to a peaceful link-up and a confirmation of the king's overall authority.

Garibaldi's only major request was that he might act as viceroy in Naples until conditions were fully stabilized. His response to the resulting refusal – and to what he regarded as some ungenerous treatment of his volunteers – was a dignified withdrawal to his island home at Caprera, from whence he observed subsequent events with increasing disillusionment. He felt slighted by Cavour and his successors, but he was now undeniably a patriot-liberator of international stature. He was hugely fêted on his English visit of 1864, and soon after turned down President Lincoln's* offer of a command in the US Army. In the war of 1866 between Piedmont and Austria he commanded well a virtually independent group in the Tyrol. He made two raids on the Papal States, in 1862 when he was blocked by Piedmontese forces, and then again five years later when Napoleon III's troops opposed him. In 1870–1 he was active once more, this time in France on behalf of the republican resistance to Prussian occupation.

The final years were spent, in simple manner, at Caprera. Garibaldi became more sympathetic towards socialism, the quest for women's rights, and even the cause of pacifism – as if to suggest that his own victories by the sword had proved hollow. Certainly, like Mazzini, he died disappointed about the way in which the newly united Italy was turning out. Whatever the map might suggest, the actual quality of the unification left much to be desired. Above all, the South was being treated as an area for quasi-colonial exploitation by the North. Put otherwise, there was precious little fellow-feeling between the portion of Italy which Cavour had unified and that other half which, in the almost miraculously triumphant expedition of 1860, had been liberated through the deeds of Garibaldi.

Michael Biddiss

See: *Autobiography of G. Garibaldi*, ed. A. Werner (3 vols., trans. 1889); also the selection of memoirs in *Garibaldi*, ed. Denis Mack Smith (1969). Among secondary works, there is still much of value in G.M. Trevelyan's trilogy, *Garibaldi's Defence of the Roman Republic*, *Garibaldi and the Thousand* and *Garibaldi and the Making of Italy* (1907–11). Note also Denis Mack Smith, *Cavour and Garibaldi, 1860* (1954); and John Parris, *The Lion of Caprera* (1962).

177

GASKELL, Elizabeth Cleghorn 1810–65

British novelist

Elizabeth Gaskell was born Elizabeth Cleghorn Stevenson, in Chelsea. She was brought up by an aunt, in Knutsford, and attended Avonbank School in Stratford. In 1832, she married William Gaskell, then an assistant minister in the Unitarian church. They settled in Manchester, which was to provide the setting for some of her most important work. In 1837, with the help of her husband, she composed *Sketches Among the Poor*. Ten years elapsed, however, before she returned to literature, contributing three short stories to the recently launched *Howitt's Journal*. It was only in *Mary Barton*, though, that, in 1848, her talent decisively emerged. A story of love and murder in Manchester, *Mary Barton* broke new ground, dwelling on the squalor, the deprivations and discontents of working-class life in the 1830s. Though she denied any wish to promote discord, Mrs Gaskell seemed to espouse the cause of the oppressed, and scandalized some of her public.

Mary Barton made her a celebrity, and won her some hostility and the acquaintance of the famous. At Dickens's* invitation, she submitted stories for his periodical *Household Words*, including a collection with a recognizably Knutsford setting. Out of these grew *Cranford* (1851), an ingenious comic fantasia. After her death, it became her most popular work, and has commonly remained so. It was followed, in 1853, by *Ruth*, a novel about the seduction and betrayal of an innocent girl, and her attempt to live on with her illegitimate son in peace and with dignity. Deeply religious in tone, it was none the less widely and vigorously attacked for its subject matter and its supposedly lax morality. She was defended, however, by eminent literary and religious figures, and her aims, her courage and talent all gradually won respect.

North and South was serialized in *Household Words* in 1854. It dealt with contrasts and conflicts: between rural south and industrial north, between masters and men. But it gave the masters' point of view as well as that of the workers, and advocated conciliation. After the death of her friend Charlotte Brontë* in 1855, Mrs Gaskell was asked to write her biography, and com-

plied, publishing it in 1857. Once again, she found she had courted trouble. Reviewers chorused their praise, and the book met with a sensational reception. But it angered some of those it referred to, and they threatened court cases. Mrs Gaskell was forced to revise it. But her public had been disconcerted by the uproar, and proved reluctant to buy the revised edition. Later works caused less fuss. *Sylvia's Lovers* (1863) was set in Northumberland, and dealt with passion and mismarriage. It won little applause from reviewers, and was seen as a sign of incipient decline. Serialized in the *Cornhill Magazine* in 1863–4, *Cousin Phillis* uncontroversially returned to the Knutsford of Mrs Gaskell's childhood. So, too, did the meticulously crafted *Wives and Daughters*, of which one chapter remained to be written at the time of her sudden death.

Elizabeth Gaskell has sometimes been chiefly appraised as a novelist concerned with social problems. Acutely sensitive to the changes taking place in contemporary society, she explored some of their more distressing consequences with frankness and urgent concern. In *Ruth* and *Mary Barton*, she took the Victorian novel into territory that had previously remained largely unexplored. She examined the plight of the poor and the powerless with precision and compassion. But her workers and common folk are more than hapless victims. They are richly endowed with shrewdness and vitality, a culture and lore of their own. Profoundly sympathetic to working-class anger, she distrusted the unions and shrank from mob violence. She was more inclined to emphasize the responsibilities of the masters than the need for labour to act and organize in defence of its own rights.

She was often critical of sheltered southerners, intransigent bosses, the cosseted middle classes. Yet she was by nature inclined to think well of others, irrespective of their class or background. She rarely challenged the social order with radical forcefulness, arguing, instead, for moderation and mutual tolerance, and appealing to reason. Her keen sensuous awareness made her peculiarly well-equipped to document the details of lives spent in stinting and misery. But it also meant that she was readily captivated by luxury, and inclined to make the meagre comforts of the poor seem opulence. She was endlessly fascinated, too, by subtleties of thought and feeling. But she found them in rich and poor alike.

The 'Knutsford' fiction has often been seen as an imaginative retreat into the world of her childhood. Yet, if it is a pastoral milieu, it is by no means an idyllic one. Evoked with lavish care, it is also a commonplace, workaday world. Impressions of arcadian seclusion are adulterated by a sense of hard economic realities, of the effects of changes in social circumstances. But to emphasize any of these factors is to diminish the originality of the 'Knutsford' novels. The allure of *Wives and Daughters* lies in the delicacy with which it charts the intricacies and slight shifts in relationships within a small community. *Cranford*'s is a world of whims and quirks, where trifles take on a delightfully exaggerated importance and the ageing are childlike in their occupations and pleasures. Sadness stalks on the edges of *Cranford*, but is deftly kept at bay. In *Cousin Phillis*, however, tragedy unfolds, strangely and starkly, amidst the daily business of farming and domestic life. Central to the 'Knutsford' fiction – as to most of Mrs Gaskell's work – is an imagination constantly intrigued by the curious complexities of unremarkable lives.

There were different Mrs Gaskells, as she herself admitted. She appreciated resolution, determination and enterprise, but often deplored their effects. She warmed to strength and rude vigour, but valued a civilized sensibility and was covertly attracted to refinement. A foe to puritan austerity, she could occasionally be prim and censorious herself. Inheriting some of Jane Austen's* satirical wit, she is none the less commonly charitable to her characters, disposed to seek out contexts in which they can display their virtues. Her cheerful good faith has its drawbacks: the *Life of Charlotte Brontë*, for instance, sometimes seems mere hagiography. Yet Mrs Gaskell was not consistently sanguine. There is a vein of melancholy and morbidity in her writing, and she was sometimes sickened by evil, by a 'hard, cold, populous world'. The works, however, are also shot through with a sense of the charm of the remote and the exotic. But she was imaginatively most engrossed by small and circumscribed worlds, limning them with a finesse that is perhaps her most notable achievement.

Lines of development in the English novel have been traced from Mrs Gaskell on through Trollope* and George Eliot* to Hardy* and Lawrence. She has sometimes been placed in the tradition of English socialist writing, as a predecessor of Ruskin* and William Morris*. Yet she was not an influential figure. Her affinities with contemporaries are obvious. Her 'social problem' novels, for instance, beg comparison with *Coningsby* and *Alton Locke, Felix Holt, the Radical* and *Hard Times*. But she is also something of an anomaly in Victorian letters. Her temperament and her Unitarian faith made her trustful, and her natural optimism saved her from the predicaments shared by many Victorian artists and intellectuals. It tended to keep her both from their despondencies and doubts, and the sometimes rather strained affirmations by which they sought to counter them. In certain respects, it blunted her analysis of social ills and curtailed her powers of insight. But it also made for much of what is most valuable in her: her sanity, her humanity, her sparkling sense of enjoyment.

Andrew Gibson

The Works of Mrs. Gaskell, ed. A.W. Ward (8 vols,

1906), includes most of the shorter stories. See also: *The Letters of Mrs. Gaskell*, ed. J.A.V. Chapple and A. Pollard (1966). See: E. Wright, *Mrs. Gaskell, The Basis for Reassessment* (1965); W. Gerin, *Elizabeth Gaskell: A Biography* (1976); and A. Easson, *Elizabeth Gaskell* (1979).

178

GAUDI, Antoni 1852–1926

Spanish architect

Gaudi was a Catalan architect capable of flights of fancy and dramatic effects of great structural complexity and it is unwise to categorize him too precisely. It is equally irresponsible to see him as a fantasist outside the European tradition as the links with the Art Nouveau movement and with the Gothic Revival epitomized by Viollet-le-Duc* are strong. Links too with the writings of John Ruskin* and William Morris* are well documented and his lifelong friend and patron Count Eusebo Guell was a man of advanced taste and the possessor of an extensive library which reflected current progressive thinking. Catalonia is in spirit neither French nor Spanish, and Gaudi's Separatist sympathies are known through his association with the Catalan Cooperative Movement. At the 1878 Paris World Fair he exhibited a project for workers' housing linked to a factory and social services based on the cooperative idea.

Catalan Gothic is essentially Mediterranean, full of deep shadows and sculptured details dependent for their dramatic effects on strong sunlight. Gaudi was a great admirer of its bold vaulting and decorative feats of engineering, and though comparison might be made with the excesses of Roman Baroque there is no evidence that Gaudi looked to Bernini for inspiration. The use of natural forms to extend the flow of the building up and out into seemingly infinite space is the basis of both methods and it seems sensible to leave it at that.

Catalan Art Nouveau, known as 'Modernismo', like its mainstream European counterpart was a reaction against the materialism of the age and concerned with more imaginative ideas related to poetry and fanciful decoration. It is a mistake to see Gaudi as being alone in his thinking and much of the building in and around Barcelona at the time was in similar vein.

When Gaudi built he built in brick and stone and only resorted to iron and steel when the natural materials were incapable of stretching to the limits asked of them. There is a strong tradition of bricklaying in Catalonia and the insistence that the buildings should grow from the specific natural environment encouraged Gaudi to use local stone quarried by local labour. In his most extensive scheme, the Parc Guell, conceived in 1900 as an organic 'garden city' development for a suburb of Barcelona, the natural landscape was exploited to the full in the manner of the Romantic gardeners of late eighteenth-and early nineteenth-century England. Recent interest in Gaudi is centred on this scheme with its total involvement in the progressive stages of cooperative design and the ingenious manner in which the hill into which it is set dictates the plan. The method is simple and the elements are welded together piece by piece as necessity demands. Individual sections are linked together by the use of a variety of natural forms which not only look like trees but can be seen to behave like trees. The tilted columns which hold the paths against the undulating contours of the hill seem literally to grow in answer to structural requirements. The use of materials is based on strict economy and the splendid decoration is made from a mosaic of broken fragments of china cups and plates, glass and other bizarre bits and pieces. Much of the decoration is the work of a fellow architect, Josep Jujol, and Gaudi's role in much of his work was that of a master mason concerned to draw from the ideas and expertise of others rather than to dominate a scheme with his own personality. It is unwise to see him as a wilful expressionist.

His continuing awareness of human scale is well seen in the terrace over the proposed market place where the serpentine bench running around the rim is shaped to the human body and offers scope for private conversation in what has become an open playground.

Work stopped on the scheme in 1914, and, though it must be seen as a failure in that few houses were built and the 'garden city' concept was unrealized, there is much to be admired in the excesses of imaginative structural play and the way the architect has allowed both the architecture and the human need to have equal say.

Gaudi was a model maker and the complicated wire and canvas lead-weighted constructions made in preparation for the Guell Colony Chapel show how the suspended linear designs, when inverted, accurately describe the intricate vaulting and delicate columns of the final project. The deliberate sculptural quality of the architecture is important and in this respect the monumental *Sagrada Familia* – Gaudi's 'Cathedral of the Poor' to which he dedicated his life from 1883 until his death in 1926 – must be seen as his masterpiece. With no support from the clergy, 'El Temple della Sagrada Familia', built and supported by subscription, is an animated mixture of traditional revivalist Gothic and the florid naturalism which so typifies the architect at his most fanciful. It embodies all the answers set by other projects and the enormous structural difficulties surmounted in its building reflect not only the intense feeling of the architect but the remarkable craftsmanship of the anonymous Catalan workers who were encouraged to stretch their capabilities to the limits in carrying out such a vast undertaking. It is part sculp-

ture on the grandest scale and part modern industrial Gothic and reflects clearly the basic nineteenth-century fear of the new materials and the optimism for the future which those same materials offered. Slowly and steadily Gaudi realized his dream, working from the models made of wire and canvas through the many plaster casts of sculptural details out on to the building itself with the dramatic cluster of towers over the eastern gate. The unfinished building is indeed fantastic and there is nothing quite like it in modern times. Only the models hint at what it might have been, but it is well loved by the poor of Barcelona and this is its true testament.

Gaudi's appeal is understandable and in an age of functional austerity there is an undeniable attraction in the concept of a style deliberately derived from a specific human need to suit a specific known environment. When it is allied to the use of simple materials worked by local skilled labour then an overall rightness is almost inevitable. A true balance between the traditional building style of the past and an awareness of the possibilities offered by new technology is the legacy handed on to the twentieth-century architect by the nineteenth-century engineer. Le Corbusier, very much a kindred spirit, saw Gaudi as 'the constructor of 1900, the professional builder in stone, iron, or bricks', a man who well realized the necessity for cooperative effort in order to draw from the site its full potential and in so doing build intelligently on an apt human scale.

Gaudi was no freak but an astute workman who well understood the lessons of the past and had the imagination to relate them clearly to the needs of his own time.

John Furse

See: J.J. Sweeney and J.L. Sert, *Antoni Gaudi* (1960); J.M. Richards and N. Pevsner, *The Anti-Rationalists* (1973)

179

GAUDIER-BRZESKA, Henri 1891–1915

French painter and sculptor

Henri Gaudier was born in St Jean de Braye, near Orleans. His father was a master carpenter. Henri was educated in Orleans and in 1907 won a scholarship to study English at a school in Bristol. His earliest works are studies made at Bristol Zoo of birds and animals. Throughout his career he found his greatest inspiration in natural forms and particularly those of animals. In 1909 he studied in Munich and in Paris, where he worked in a library. The following year he met Sophie Brzeska, a Polish girl, and first took her home to France and then to London with him in 1911. They lived as 'brother' and 'sister'. It was now that he changed his name to Gaudier-Brzeska. Henri worked in the city for a shipping broker and practised as a sculptor and painter in the evening. He met the artist Horace Brodzky and the writers Middleton Murry, Katherine Mansfield and Frank Harris. In 1913, when he lived under a railway arch in Putney, he met Ezra Pound and Wyndham Lewis, and through these contacts exhibited his sculptures and drawings at the Allied Artists' exhibition in July 1913. The same year he joined Lewis's Rebel Art Centre and in 1914 was a member of the Vorticist group and contributed illustrations and an article to the magazine Blast. In September he joined the French army and went to the front. He was given two promotions for gallantry, exhibited at the London Group and Vorticist exhibitions and contributed more work to the second and final issue of Blast. On 5 June 1915 he was killed in a dawn infantry charge at Neuville-Saint-Vaast.

Gaudier's life was short but of immense activity and, finally, had a powerful symbolic value. He came to represent, for men like Lewis and Pound, the quintessential modern artist and personality of the 'New Age' which abruptly ended in August 1914. Lewis, who called Gaudier 'preternaturally alive', and Pound, who said in discussing the sculptor's death, 'the real trouble with war is that it gives no one a chance to kill the right people', saw him as a faun-like spirit of energy and intuitive intelligence crushed by an enormous economic and political conspiracy on behalf of mediocrity. The Imagist poet Richard Aldington summed up his intellectual qualities when he wrote, 'He thinks in form – abstract form – instead of in things and ideas'.

Gaudier's knowledge of the history of art was purportedly forbidding and his many changes of style, from Hellenic to African, from Chinese to Cubist, show his wide range of reference and his natural ability to find strong self-expression in any form. Of his contemporaries he particularly admired Epstein, Archipenko, Brancusi and Modigliani. Like all modern sculptors he was indebted to Rodin's* pioneering researches in form. It was, however, as a carver that he saw himself and his art fully represents the reaction against modelling that took place at the same time the Cubist painters were reinventing the basis of their art and rediscovering the values inherent in primitive art styles. 'The sculpture I admire,' Gaudier wrote in a review of 1914, 'is the work of master craftsmen. Every inch of the surface is won at the point of a chisel – every stroke of the hammer is a physical and mental effort.' Carving in stone or marble was the appropiate medium for the new ideas he had to express. In his late work he aimed at geometrical simplification and compression of form. His drawings for these works, with their harsh thick lines, adequately convey the sense of primitive monumentality and precision he was aiming at. Unlike the Futurist artists he was not seeking to represent real movement. Unlike the Cubists he wanted 'significant

activity', as the Vorticists called their notion of the energy the best art captures. His studies of birds and animals show him searching for a plastic equivalent for movement as a dynamic but potential and arrested power. His enormous Hieratic Head of Ezra Pound (1914), although partly executed as a jest (in profile it represents a phallus), is a dramatic example of the primitive and totemic qualities Gaudier wished to introduce into the natural image. Similarly, his Birds Erect (1914), in limestone, actually based on some cacti in the artist's studio, and Bird Swallowing a Fish(1913), in bronze, are compact, almost emblematic pieces in which Gaudier, in his own words, sought to present his emotions, 'by the arrangement of my surfaces, the planes and lines by which they are defined'. In his essay in the first number of Blast he called for an elemental but fecund simplicity of form, asserting, 'Sculptural feeling is the appreciation of masses in relation. Sculptural ability is the defining of these masses by planes.' His ideas echo those of the Imagist poets.

Gaudier produced superb line drawings in pen and ink, a number of semi-abstract paintings, and chalk studies, which all bear witness to his great talent and curiosity. His essays in Blast are important historical and critical pieces, written almost in a style prophetic of the prose of Charles Olson. His influence on his own generation was perhaps slight, despite his strong and disturbing personality. His influence on the later generation of sculptors like Barbara Hepworth and Henry Moore, however, was very significant. Although Gaudier-Brzeska was a Frenchman he was probably the father of the abstractionist carving school in England.

Richard Humphrys

See: H. Gaudier-Brzeska, Drawings and Sculpture, Introduction by M. Levy (1965). See also: Ezra Pound, Gaudier-Brzeska: A Memoir (1916); H.S. Ede, Savage Messiah (1931); H. Brodzky, Henri Gaudier-Brzeska (1933).

180
GAUGUIN, Paul 1848–1903

French artist, ceramist and writer

Although born in Paris, Gauguin spent his early childhood in Peru. Later, as a youth, he travelled extensively as a merchant seaman and in the navy, before starting to paint in 1873 at the age of twenty-five. Working at first purely as an amateur Gauguin, like his guardian Gustave Arosa, was able to collect paintings, amongst which were works by the Barbizon school and by Pissarro* with whom Gauguin painted during three summers. During this time he met the other Impressionist painters and adopted their style which was just reaching the high point of its development.

Gauguin also gave up his career in banking and concentrated upon his painting. He began to feel, as he worked more intensely, that a realistic or naturalistic style such as that of either the Barbizon school of Courbet and Corot or of the Impressionists was sufficient in some measure. Aware of the preoccupation with volumetric structure with which Cézanne* was struggling, Gauguin also experimented with these ideas as a way of avoiding pure description of the visual world as practised by Monet* and Renoir*.

In 1885, having visited England and probably aware of Whistler's* interest in Japanese art, Gauguin produced an important work for the development of his style. This was *Still Life with Horse's Head*. The subject matter of this painting combines a Japanese doll with the plaster cast of a horse's head from the Elgin Marbles seen at the British Museum. A letter to his friend Schuffenecker that year expresses Gaugin's realization that for him art must have some inexplicable content and convey more than a rationalist approach to ideas of sensation. These conclusions signify a rejection of the positivist tendencies of Impressionism for a more subjective, emotional and imaginative art.

The following year this trend continued. As a result of seeing Kate Greenaway's book illustrations the forms in Gauguin's painting became less volumetric and considerably flattened. The effect was decorative and more abstract. Areas of canvas were covered with a single rich colour whereas his Impressionist style had been composed of a myriad multi-coloured marks.

There still remained to be solved the problem of the relationship of volume and light to decorative abstract elements. To attempt a synthesis Gauguin made some ceramics and applied the simple peasant patterns he had seen whilst visiting Brittany to the swelling forms of his ceramics. However, dissatisfied with the situation in Paris, Gauguin's increasing restlessness led him briefly to Martinique. As a result his painting gained a still brighter colour intensity and spatial qualities were produced by the superimposition of layers of flat shapes one upon another.

Returning to Brittany to live amongst a group of artist friends, Gauguin's work became prolific as he moved towards a fuller synthesis of the many ideas and influences that engaged him. Aware of the new Symbolist poetry, exemplified by the writings of Mallarmé*, in which the 'feeling of the thought' or 'the Idea' was more important than the subject matter, Gauguin responded by making his work evocatively allusive.

At this time the ideas of Émil Bernard became particularly necessary to Gauguin. Bernard had worked out a style of painting which he termed 'cloisonnisme'. This blending of flat richly coloured shapes with a simplified linear definition in something of the manner

of stained glass windows fulfilled Gaugin's need for an art form which was both ideal and exotically primitive.

The important painting which first fully incorporated the symbolist aesthetic and produced the complete synthesis he required was *The Vision After the Sermon* produced during the summer of 1888. The subject of Jacob wrestling with an angel is a recurrent theme in European art, Gauguin presented it in a unique manner. The two wrestling figures which form the vision are seen small in the right half of the painting against a brilliant flat red field. The work is divided into two diagonally by a serpentine tree trunk. On the left in the foreground is a group of Breton peasant women in traditional white bonnets. Only the heads and shoulders of these peasants are included and turned away from the person viewing the painting who is therefore in the position of joining the crowd watching the visitation.

To Gauguin, who identified strongly with the simple, impoverished and religious peasants amongst whom he was living, the wrestling man and spirit symbolized not only the struggle of the peasants but also his own on two levels. In the first instance Gauguin was also poor and trying to succeed in a life away from the increasing materialism of urban civilization. In the second he was struggling in his art with a number of difficulties, in particular that of empirical naturalism which seemed to him opposed to spiritual abstraction. The painting of the Vision therefore demonstrates two main preoccupations that dominate the remainder of Gauguin's life, the relationship of innocence to knowledge and of primitivism to sophistication.

It was through Bernard's introduction that the painter Sérusier met Gauguin and was instructed how to paint the work now known as the *Talisman* of 1888. Whilst Sérusier was sitting in front of the landscape, painting, Gauguin demanded of him, 'How do you see that tree? It's green? then choose the most beautiful green on your palette, – And this shadow? It's more like blue? Do not be afraid to paint it with the purest blue possible.' Upon his return to Paris, Sérusier's little painting met with much interest from the younger painters at the Académie Julian, who later formed a group known as the Nabis. Sérusier commented upon the *Talisman* that it was 'Thus we learned that every work of art was a transposition, a caricature, the passionate equivalent of a sensation received.'

Shortly after this instruction to Sérusier, Gauguin who had corresponded and exchanged portraits with Van Gogh* throughout the summer journeyed south to Arles. However, although fruitful in terms of painting for both men, the few months they were together proved unhappy and ended in the tragedy at Christmas of Van Gogh's first phase of insanity. Gauguin returned north and exhibited his work in the Café Volpini at the Paris Expo Universelle.

Although financially unproductive these new paintings again caused excitement amongst younger artists. Gauguin, however, felt himself to be a failure and subsequent paintings in Brittany of the *Yellow Christ* and *Christ at Gethsemane* are the equivalents for his sense of loneliness and persecution.

At last, because of continuing disregard by the art establishment in Paris, Gauguin auctioned his paintings and left for Tahiti in 1891. The works produced there were at first questioning and pessimistic in mood. None the less the form and aesthetic were still developing so that volume became more obviously synthesized with the decorative elements. The native people, painted with a simple monumentality, are directly expressive. It was not until after a return to Paris to collect more money, and an unsuccessful suicide attempt when back in the South Seas that Gauguin's art achieved its final serenity, which appears to have been maintained until his death in 1903.

Faa Ihe Ihe of 1898, in the Tate Gallery collection is the first of these more optimistic paintings of a primitive life. It is a work that is long horizontally and shallow vertically giving the effect of a frieze. The trees and Javanese figures stand singly and unevenly spaced along the length with an almost musical sense of rhythm to the spacing, echoed by the lyrical undulations of branches and outlines of figures. These are set against a unifying golden yellow background. The title means 'to adorn', the kind of beautifying that precedes a feast or celebration. The central goddess figure appears as a motif and derives from a photograph in Gauguin's possession depicting a frieze in the Buddhist temple of Barabadour. This central motif reappears in a similar fashion to the dog derived from a Courbet painting in his guardian's possession and the horse and rider in other works. Memory, imagination and reality mingle to produce a Garden of Eden on earth in which man is joyously united with both art and nature.

Gauguin's influence throughout Europe was extensive. Indeed it may well be that of all the artists in the latter half of the nineteenth century, Gauguin, as the foremost artist of the key Symbolist movement that was the turning point for the development of art in the twentieth century, was the most important.

In France alone his ideas were propagated by a number of disciples who lived with him in Brittany. Many of these continued to work there and people from all over Europe visited the North of France to meet them and to absorb the atmosphere of those rural surroundings that Gauguin had projected in his paintings. Rather later the Fauves and Cubists, in particular Matisse, Braque and Picasso, drew upon Gauguin in their speculations concerning primitivism. This interest was manifest in England and artists of the *avant-garde*, many of them connected with the Slade, prior to the 1914–18 war, paid great attention to Gauguin's work.

Whilst Cubism was developing in France, Expressionism was gaining ground in Germany and the Brücke in particular in their drives toward a primitive outdoor life-style and a preoccupation with the raw technique of woodcuts also saw themselves as following in Gauguin's footsteps. Primitivism, simplicity and subjective concerns with imaginative vision and memory abound in the first years of the twentieth century and in the visual arts they draw their strength in large measure from Gauguin.

Pat Turner

Gauguin's works include: *Self Portrait With Cherries* (1888); *Where do we come from? What are we? Where are we going?* (1897). See: John Rewald, *Gauguin* (1938); Ronald Alley, *Paul Gauguin* (1961); Marete Bodelson, *Gauguin's Ceramics* (1964); Alan Bowness, *Gauguin* (1971); H.R. Rookmaaker, *Gauguin and 19th Century Art Theory* (1972).

181
GAUSS, Carl Friederich 1777–1855

German mathematician

Gauss was much more than just a 'mathematician' in the modern sense. His work ranged freely over pure mathematics, mathematical physics, experimental physics, astronomy, statistics, even technology. In the course of a long life he made a vast number of mathematical and scientific discoveries, though he kept many of these to himself. If he had announced all his discoveries it is probable that nineteeth-century mathematics would have moved forward fifty years: but there could have been *fewer* mathematicians, because the sheer efficiency of Gauss's mathematical perception and creativity was of a kind which might well have discouraged lesser mortals if it had been widely known.

Gauss is generally conceded to be one of the three greatest mathematicians, alongside Archimedes and Newton. But his main achievements in mathematics and mathematical physics were much more technical than those of Archimedes and Newton, and he wrote no book of such inescapable centrality to theoretical science as Newton's *Principia*. The result is that we honour Gauss today in the names of things associated with two of his least important triumphs: a unit in electricity and the Gaussian ('Normal') distribution in statistics.

Gauss was born in Brunswick in 1777 to a poor family. His immediate ancestors on his father's side were peasants and gardeners: there was no trace of intellect or culture. His mother Dorothea and his uncle Friederich, however, were more unusual. His mother was quite single-minded in shielding and guiding her clever son. His uncle was a man of artistic talent and a lively mind, who found that he could draw out the young Carl's talent. He died early, and Gauss later remarked sadly of the uncle who had done so much to encourage his early development that 'a born genius was lost in him'.

The first signs of precocious talent in arithmetic showed when Carl was only two: he corrected his father's reckoning in some accounts. Carl's knowledge was almost all self-acquired and during his childhood he continued to make rapid strides in calculating facility and understanding arithmetical patterns. But his unusual talent showed only intermittently and it was not till he was nine (two years after starting school) that the schoolmaster sat up and took notice that he had a potential genius on his hands. Gauss soon progressed in mathematics far beyond the level of his teachers in the school, and his case was brought to the attention of some leading citizens of Brunswick, who in turn managed to interest the Duke of Brunswick in the boy. As a result of meeting Carl in 1791 (when Gauss was fourteen) the Duke generously promised to pay for his education.

Gauss was sent to the Collegium Carolinum (a *Gymnasium*) in 1792, and to Göttingen University in 1795. Four years later he was a doctor of the University of Helmstedt, after submitting a thesis offering the first rigorous proof of the 'fundamental theorem of algebra', which says roughly that an equation of degree *n* must have *n* real or complex roots. The rigour of Gauss's proof stemmed from the fact that he had discovered how to handle complex numbers in a logically consistent way. (Complex numbers are numbers composed of real and imaginary parts mixed together). During the same period Gauss virtually finished his first masterpiece on number theory, *Disquisitiones Arithmeticae* (1801).

For several years Gauss continued his research in mathematics, supported by a pension from the Duke of Brunswick, and in 1809 became Director of the Göttingen Observatory. From the beginning of the nineteenth century and for a period of about twenty years Gauss's main work lay in calculating difficult astronomical orbits. He was capable of prodigious feats of calculation and his extraordinary talent in this direction probably gave his work a greater degree of comprehensibility to the Duke, and his own family, than the abstruse research in number theory. Nevertheless Gauss from time to time resumed his 'pure' research, and increasingly after 1820. His discoveries, however, are of an extremely technical nature. Gauss was largely responsible for creating the modern idea of mathematics as an autonomous abstract subject.

But, like Newton and Archimedes, Gauss himself was equally at home in the so-called 'pure' and so-called 'applied' parts of mathematical science. He set the subject of electricity on a proper basis, devised the method of least squares in statistics, invented the heliotrope, the bifilar magnetometer and the electric telegraph. In a word he set a formidable example of

sustained intellectual genius which a few later figures have approached but never equalled.

Christopher Ormell

Carl Friedrich Gauss Werke (12 vols, 1863–1933). See: Heinrich Mack, *C.F. Gauss und die Seinen* (1927); E.T. Bell, ch. 14, 'The Prince of Mathematicians', in *Men of Mathematics* (1937); Tord Hall, *Carl Friedrich Gauss: A Biography* (1970)

182
GAUTIER, Pierre-Jules-Théophile 1811–72

French writer

Théophile Gautier entered French literary history in 1830 in the legendary red waistcoat he wore at the opening night of *Hernani*, that highpoint of militant Romanticism. Admirer of Hugo* and intimate of Nerval*, Gautier was a Romantic Bohemian *par excellence*, a rhapsodic lover and devotee of things beautiful and bizarre. He made his initial reputation as one of the rare French Romantics to make their reader laugh, with the comic verse narrative of *Albertus* (1832) and the ironic novel *Mademoiselle de Maupin* (1835), and as the champion of eccentrics like Villon in his survey of forgotten pre-Classical writers, *Les Grotesques* (1834–5).

Not long after these boisterous beginnings, Gautier became a regular newspaper columnist, and though he lamented the irksome regularity of his duties, continued to earn a living as a journalist-critic for the rest of his life. In some curious way, editorial commissions and constraints excited his verbal facility; there are stories of Gautier penning his copy in the printshop itself, quipping that 'you should never have yourself guillotined before time'. His literary output is coloured throughout by this paradox of writing on demand coupled with a febrile imaginativeness.

The youthful novel *Mademoiselle de Maupin* is Gautier's masterpiece. Based on the true story of a girl who dresses as a man in order to experience life (and especially love) from a contrary viewpoint, the novel is a witty parade of sexually ambiguous incidents interspersed with poignant speculations on Gautier's *idées fixes*: female beauty, the fatefulness of passion, the condition of poetic reverie. Constructed on the principle of capricious improvisation (it was completed in a rush to meet a publisher's deadline, as ever), the novel conflates letters from different characters with comic digressions and authorial interventions – often *in medias res* during a seduction scene, in classic comic-erotic style. Though full of hilarious improbabilities and jokes, the novel does cohere around a serious principle, Gautier's unequivocal adoration of ideal beauty. Thus the suffused sensuality of the book is actually grounded in a strict aesthetics of preference for certain archetypes of beauty, exemplified in Renaissance painting and classical sculpture. The narrative climax comes when the heroine at last gives herself – for one night only – to the entranced hero D'Albert. He thereby experiences the marvellous fusion of aesthetic ideal and tangible reality as Madeleine de Maupin undresses for him, revealing the living perfection of her beauty – portrait, sculpture and body in one. The theme was to obsess Gautier throughout his life: how could an ideal nurtured by art be convincingly reconciled with the imperfections of material existence?

The tension between yearning and frustration – endemic to Gautier's generation, as witness the work of Nerval or Musset* – is the pivot of many of Gautier's stories. In the poetic narrative 'Arria Marcella' (1852), a dreamy young hero discovers the imprint of a woman's flawless breasts and thigh in the museum of lava-casts at Pompeii; when that night he sleepwalks in the streets of the dead city, he passes into a state of euphoric hallucination so intense that the city comes alive and the 'retrospective ideal' of the long-dead Arria Marcella appears before him as a flesh-and-blood reality. This fulfilment of a passion at once aesthetic and erotic bridges a vast stretch of time, as if Gautier were playing out in narrative form the manifesto later articulated in the poem 'L'Art':

> All things pass. -Robust
> Art alone embraces eternity,
> The sculpted bust
> Survives the city.

The transcendence of time is the theme of the late novella *Spirite* (1865), where the hero finds that the only way to enjoy union with his beloved is to meet her on a supernatural plane. This eerie consummation on a level outside earthly existence may be read as Gautier's haunted answer to the real-life frustration he felt in his love for the elusive Carlotta Grisi, a dancer whom he had earlier cast in the role of an ethereal sprite in his ballet *Giselle* (1841).

This compulsive toying with chimeras makes of Gautier one of the foremost exponents of the 'fantastic' in France (and in this respect a rival as well as a disciple of Hoffmann*). His focal theme is that of the point of transition between the real and the unreal. In 'La Toison d'or' ('The Golden Fleece', 1839), a man hesitates between two dissonant loves, an absorbing spiritual passion for the figure of Mary Magdalen seen in a Rubens painting in Antwerp Cathedral, and a flirtation with a pretty lace-maker called Gretchen. Only when the latter dresses up for him in the same old-fashioned clothes as Ruben's model can a magic transference take place and a dangerous aesthetic fixation be safely rerouted into a terrestrial embrace. In 'La Morte amoureuse' (1836, trans. 'The Priest'), Gautier sounds a more panic note when he tells of a priest who,

at the moment of taking his vows of chastity, is smitten with lust for the glamorous seductress Clarimonde. When the latter dies, the priest is called out at night to administer the last rites; kneeling beside the beautiful corpse, he cannot resist kissing its cold lips, whereupon Clarimonde's eyes flicker open and she releases a voluptous sigh . . .

The frivolity of many of Gautier's ghost stories should not belie the seriousness with which throughout a long career he defended certain values against what he felt to be the encroaching gracelessness and philistinism of French culture. The hard-hitting preface to *Mademoiselle de Maupin* gave early notice of his contempt for those who disdained true beauty and wished to reduce art to servile social ends: 'Nothing is truly beautiful unless it is useless; everything useful is ugly, for it expresses a need, and the needs of man are ignoble and disgusting . . . the most useful place in a house is the lavatory'. The primacy of ideal beauty gave rise to the doctrine of 'art for art's sake' which the austere Parnassian school was to take as its watchword in the 1860s, in opposition to the increasing dominance of Realism. To this school Gautier may be assigned honorary membership, on the strength of the finely polished verse of his *Émaux et Camées* (*Enamels and Cameos*, definitive edition 1872), which comprises such exemplary verbal artefacts as the poem 'Symphonie en blanc majeur' ('Symphony in White Major').

Gautier had once contemplated a painter's career, and although his journalism covered all the arts, including theatre, ballet, music and literature, he most relished reviewing the visual arts and, in particular, contemporary painting. As an art critic, Gautier helped determine the definition of the modern sensibility as it arose out of the crucible of Romanticism, anticipating Baudelaire* in his celebration of Delacroix* as the master of radiant colour, while finding time to discuss with equal enthusiasm the sharp outlines and tranquil poise of more classically inclined or 'sculptural' painters such as Ingres* and Chassériau. Like Diderot before him and Baudelaire after, Gautier was an art critic of impulse and temperament, not an analyst of painterly techniques so much as an enthusiast of types of beauty to which he was instinctively drawn. His lyrical descriptions of paintings – often landscape paintings, a Romantic genre which he was one of the first to recognize – are a fascinating example of the pen vying with the brush.

This practice of *transposition d'art* may indeed be seen as the fertilizing principle of much of Gautier's best work, since, whether in fictions like *Mademoiselle de Maupin* or in travel sketches like *Voyage en Espagne* and *Voyage en Italie*, he never writes so brilliantly as when he is depicting real experience in terms of the idealizations of painting. The man 'for whom the visible world exists' was also a lifelong exponent of Romanticization, the rendering of actual experience in terms of a dream-like perfectibility, exemplified in art.

The remarkable thing about Gautier's work is the way it thrives on apparent conflicts. Behind Gautier the Romantic explorer of the wayward and the fantastic, and Gautier the traveller in a hurry to jot down his copy, stands Gautier the unperturbed stylist, the magician who can always find the *mot juste* for the sentence in hand, boasting that 'I throw my phrases into the air like cats, I know they will always come down on their paws'. It was precisely as the impeccable master of French prose for whom 'there is no such thing as an inexpressible idea' that Gautier was admired by the fastidious stylist Flaubert* and saluted in a raptuous dedication in Baudelaire's *Les Fleurs du mal*. Few writers can have earned such widespread praise for their style as Gautier, there being further testimonials from such varied sources as the Goncourt brothers*, Mallarmé*, Pierre Loüys, Zola*, Swinburne* and Rossetti*, with, later still, Ezra Pound and T.S. Eliot, whose homage took the form of pastiche. Sadly, such praises reflect the existence of an elitist cult since, in terms of actual publications, Gautier has remained practically ignored since his death. For while it is true that his major texts can be found in print, the bulk of Gautier's voluminous *oeuvre* remains more or less buried in the archives of the newspapers for which he slaved for most of his career.

Roger Cardinal

Major works in print: *Contes fantastiques* (1962); *Mademoiselle de Maupin* (1966); *Poésies complètes* (3 vols, 1970); *Spirite* (1970). Translations: *Mademoiselle de Maupin*, trans. J. Richardson (1981); *My Fantoms*, trans. R. Holmes (1976). See: Serge Fauchereau, *Théophile Gautier* (1972); Albert B. Smith, *Théophile Gautier and the Fantastic* (1977); Joanna Richardson, *Théophile Gautier: His Life and Times* (1958); Michael C. Spencer, *The Art Criticism of Théophile Gautier* (1969); Rita Benesch, *Le Regard de Théophile Gautier* (1969).

183
GÉRICAULT, Théodore 1791–1824

French painter

The child of a rich Rouen lawyer, and a mother who died when he was ten, Géricault was trained under Carle Vernet and a follower of David*, Guérin. In 1816 after a liaison with a married woman, he spent a year in Italy; in 1818 he commenced two years' work on *The Raft of the Medusa*, while at the same time becoming involved with his uncle's wife, who bore him a child. In 1820 he came to England, where the *Raft* was exhibited, netting him 25,000 francs. He returned

after eighteen months, but fell from a horse, and never fully recovered. Dying at thirty-three, he left unfinished projects for major paintings on the *Slave Trade* and the *Liberation of Victims of the Inquisition*; but in his final months he completed as testament his astonishing *Portraits of the Insane*.

Géricault both in life and work belongs to the same European current as Byron*, Lermontov*, Stendhal*. As a painter his real exemplar was not the Neoclassicist David, but the proto-Romantic Gros, whose epic canvases (*Napoleon at Eylau* or *The Pest Hospital at Jaffna*) provided a standard to which he might aspire; and Gros's warm, essentially tonal naturalism is the only French precedent for Géricault's own vehement style. The tension of his art derives from the strictest classical disciplines being imposed upon a ferocious temperament; embarking from the brilliant early studies of cavalry officers, Géricault in Italy took Raphael on board, to create the powerful crowd scenes of *The Race of the Riderless Horses*.

But at the same time he must have looked hard at Caravaggio, and when he began work on his own great *machine*, it was cast essentially in the dramatic chiaroscuro of the Baroque style. *The Raft of the Medusa* presents an exemplary *proces*. His subject was a contemporary political scandal; unlike Gros, Géricault had no living hero to apotheosize and his liberal and Bonapartist sympathies found expression in attacking a reactionary government's incompetence. Documentary accounts of survivors were examined, a moment selected, the composition sketched out; then Géricault immersed himself in the world of death, making terrifying oil studies of severed heads and limbs. The *Raft* is a highly schematic composition, a single diagonal rhythm leading us from the dead at bottom left, to the living at the apex; yet for his individual figures Géricault (like Caravaggio) painted directly from the model, ensuring an almost shocking physicality. In its enormous scale, simplicity, and monumentality, the storm-tossed *Raft* becomes an archetype, a universal metaphor for the fate and predicament of mankind.

In England Géricault's art changed. With his own lifelong mania for the horse, he admired Stubbs and James Ward; the near monochrome of the *Raft* is exchanged for a silvery richness that owes much to English painting. The truly mature Géricault emerges after 1820, in the portraits of inmates at the Paris asylum of the Salpêtrie, commissioned by his friend the alienist Georget (whose physiognomical theories would later influence Lombroso). Only five out of the original ten survive, but they are among the most psychologically penetrating ever painted. A work like the *Child Murderess* now in Lyon presents us with the naked individual stripped of all class and social identity, becoming in John Berger's phrase an 'anti-social' portrait.

The promise held out by Géricault was only partly

fulfilled by his much longer lived friend Delacroix*
who lacked his breadth and stark clarity. It was only
in the 1920s that Géricault's full stature began to be
appreciated, with a centenary exhibition and important
publications by Elie Faure, Foçillon and others. Bal-
thus is Géricault's true heir among contemporary
painters; but his life has been the subject of a novel by
Aragon, and Henze has composed an oratorio on *The
Raft of the Medusa.*

Timothy Hyman

The best compilation on Géricault is in the Fabbri
Opera Completa series (Milan, 1978). See: Klaus
Berger, *Géricault and his Work* (trans. 1955) and
Lorenz Eitner, *The Raft of the Medusa* (1972).

184
GILBERT, William Schwenck, Sir 1836–1911

British humorist and playwright

It has been Gilbert's singular fate to have become
associated with the operettas produced in collaboration
with Sir Arthur Sullivan* during the 1880s and to have
been judged accordingly. His considerable significance
in the history of the Victorian theatre as a whole has
been ignored, as much by ardent 'G & S' enthusiasts
as by those for whom the Savoy operas represent one
of the most embarrassingly trivial aspects of English
culture. It is fair to say, however, that even if the
chosen format of his plays remained heavily traditional
their content reveals Gilbert's weirdly original imagination as a highly important contribution to the
nineteenth-century English world of the bizarre, satirical and grotesque.

His babyhood was marked by an incident later dramatized to happy effect in *H.M.S. Pinafore* and *The
Gondoliers*, when he was captured by some Neapolitans
who attempted to obtain ransom money from his parents. Childhood and youth were less eventful than dis-
piriting, dominated by a mother whose imperious
manner provided her son with the original of the 'elderly ugly lady' figure to whom his invention constantly
returned and to which Sullivan was finally forced to
make a reasonable objection. After serving as a militia
officer and junior civil service clerk, Gilbert turned to
journalism, writing for the comic magazine, *Fun*, one
of several rivals to *Punch* set up during the mid-century.

It was in *Fun* that he published a series of absurd
tales in verse, with his own illustrations, later collected
(1869–73) as the *Bab Ballads* ('Bab' was a personal
nickname) which at once marked him out as a perceptive and ascerbic humorist. At the same time he turned
to the writing of small burlesque dramas designed as
theatrical afterpieces, such as *Dulcamara or The Little

Duck and the Great Quack and *Robert the Devil or The Nun,
the Dun and the Son of A Gun.*

A short step from the popularity of these pieces took
Gilbert into full-length play-writing, and he became
adept at practically every kind of drama then in vogue,
though his own estimate of his work often differed
seriously from the theatre-going public's. For example,
he viewed with dismay the failure of his turgid adaptation of the Faust story, *Gretchen*, but was relatively
unmoved by the success of *The Happy Land*, a comedy
written in collaboration with Gilbert à Beckett in 1873.
A profound interest in plots involving magic, fantasy
and transformations, almost amounting to an obsession, showed itself in works such as the verse dramas
Broken Hearts and *The Palace of Truth*, and in *Pygmalion
and Galatea*, designed as a vehicle for the talents of
Helen Faucit.

Gilbert's penchant for the type of play best adapted
to showing off a statuesquely attractive young actress
to advantage made him the perfect craftsman for such
noted performers as Madge Kendal, Mary Anderson
and Julia Neilson. Though he never lost a residual
fondness for the vein of sentimentality exploited in
these works (mostly produced at the Court Theatre in
Sloane Square) he was beginning to develop the species
of richly extravagant comedy of the absurd which was
to link him, however indirectly, with the values and
outlook of the century to come. His highest achievement in this field before his collaboration with Sullivan
is *Engaged*, unquestionably the finest and funniest English comedy between Bulwer-Lytton's* *Money* and
Wilde's* *The Importance of Being Earnest*, which is directly inspired.

Gilbert first met Sullivan in 1871; despite temperamental differences, the pair shared a highly sophisticated sense of the value and effectiveness of parody
which was put to magnificent use in the series of 'new
and original comic operas' (as Gilbert always described
them) beginning seven years later with *H.M.S. Pinafore*.
The partnership continued successfully for more than
a decade, each showing some measure of respect for
the other's artistic demands and limitations. Gilbert
learned to accommodate his librettos to Sullivan's
affectionate guying of Italian and German operatic
conventions, and practically all the Savoy operas
(named after the theatre specially built to house them
by Gilbert and Sullivan's manager Richard D'Oyley
Carte in 1881) contain the extended buffo finale of
linked numbers which reflects the collaboration at its
happiest. From a purely textual point of view, the most
polished in the aptness and wit of lyrics and dialogue
are *Patience* (1881), a hilarious spoof of the 'high art'
craze of the period, and *Iolanthe* (1882), fusing the
House of Lords, the Grenadier Guards, Wagnerian
fairies and Arcadian shepherds in a tissue of triumphant absurdity.

The last twenty years of Gilbert's life were soured

by his quarrels with Sullivan and Carte over the administration of the Savoy and by his realization (corresponding to Sullivan's own) that neither could work successfully without the other. His death as the result of heart failure brought on after a life-saving attempt on behalf of two lady bathers at his Norman Shaw* designed house at Grims Dyke, Harrow Weald, ended a career whose distinctions were tinged with a sense of almost Swiftian bitterness.

Gilbert's contribution to the theatrical life of his day was varied and immense. He gained experience as an actor, a manager and a director, as well as building his own theatre, the Garrick, in 1889. As a producer he set new standards of precision in diction and movement, and his obsession with the minutiae of stage presentation became legendary. Nevertheless it is as a comic imagination that he has best endured, whether as satirist, parodist or creator of that uniquely personal world defined by his contemporaries as 'topsy-turvey-dom'. His comedy mingles the world of Dickens* and Thackeray* with the darker and more haunting strains of Lewis Carroll* (who thought *Pinafore* grossly profane) and looks forward to comic viewpoints as diverse as those of Shaw (a life-long admirer), Saki and European Surrealism (the Savoy operas were given in Germany, Austria and France during Gilbert's lifetime). An acquaintance with his work is essential to an understanding of late Victorian shibboleths and apprehensions.

Jonathan Keates

See: Sidney Dark and L. M. Rowland-Brown, *W. S. Gilbert: His Life and Letters* (1923); A. H. Godwin, *Gilbert and Sullivan: A Critical Appreciation of the Savoy Operas* (1926); Hesketh Pearson, *Gilbert: His Life and Strife* (1957).

185
GISSING, George Robert 1857–1903

British novelist and short-story writer

The tone of George Gissing's fiction is one of anger and despair. More than any other Victorian novelist he was at odds with his society, unable personally to conform to its standards, and indignant at the constraints it placed upon the majority of its people. Born in Wakefield, Gissing was educated at the Quaker boarding school at Alderley Edge, and at Owens College, Manchester, from where he was expelled for misconduct. In 1876 he went to the United States, where he worked as a private teacher for two years. After his return to England Gissing lived with Helen Harrison, whom he had met while at college; they married in 1879. But he was not prepared to devote himself to domestic life, his writing always being of primary im-

portance, and when his wife fell ill in 1882 Gissing placed her in a home, refusing to live with her again. She died in 1888.

In 1880, while living in London, Gissing published his first novel, *Workers in the Dawn*. At the time he was involved with various socialist movements, and most of his early novels are radical studies of the industrial proletariat. *The Unclassed* (1884) is a typical example of Gissing's concern over the destructive effect on the human personality of material deprivation. It is a bleak work, and he was soon to lose faith in socialism, viewing it as hopelessly optimistic. *Demos* (1886) charts the rise and, to Gissing, inevitable moral decline of a working-class socialist.

In 1891 Gissing married Edith Underwood, with whom he lived until 1897, when he left her and their two children and sailed to Italy. It was shortly after meeting Edith that he wrote his best-known work, *New Grub Street* (1891), in which he turned his attention to the poverty of the professional author. More humorous than his working-class fiction, *New Grub Street* is none the less a cynical and, ultimately, depressing novel. Gissing spent the years from 1897 until his death in Italy, Greece and France. He lived for most of that time with Gabrielle Fleury, who had originally written to him with a view to translating *New Grub Street* into French. Gissing died at St Jean de Luz in the Pyrenees on 28 December 1903. He had published twenty-one novels during his lifetime, and two more were to appear posthumously, along with several volumes of short stories.

Gissing was amongst the most prolific of nineteenth-century novelists. A number of his works are undeniably 'pot-boilers', notably *Sleeping Fires* (1895), but whatever their variations in quality, Gissing's novels exhibit a persistent concern for personal freedom and the destructive forces of industrial society. *The Emancipated* (1890) contains a bitter irony in its title, presenting the newly enfranchised idle classes as victims of the materialistic system they struggle to preserve. Friedrich Engels* had written that, so great is the avarice of the British bourgeoisie, 'it is not possible for a single human sentiment or opinion to remain unstained'; *The Emancipated* exemplifies this statement. Gissing's earlier novels had dealt with the urban working class, Jack London's 'people of the abyss'. The finest of these is *The Nether World* (1889), unrelenting in its presentation of the direst poverty. But while Gissing pitied the working classes, he also despised what he saw as their viciousness and barbarity. In concentrating more on the poor middle class, Gissing dramatized his own plight, that of the principled writer adrift in a sea of commercialism. He tackled this theme directly in *New Grub Street*, the work in which he best achieved a balance between his habitual indignation and a convincing realism. But it is there even in Gissing's last novel, *Will Warburton* (1905), the bourgeois

hero of which moves down the social ladder, and discovers that it is the ruthless and unscrupulous who best survive.

George Gissing was the literary heir of Elizabeth Gaskell*, and of Dickens*, of whom he wrote a critical appreciation in 1898. In many ways their inferior as a writer, his insights into the nature of poverty are more complex, as is his presentation of lower- and middle-class characters. Throughout his life Gissing refused to compromise with a social system he abhorred, and, while an undoubted egotist, nevertheless saw his own lifelong indigence as just part of a general and inexorable process of de-humanization.

Paul Nicholls

Gissing's other published novels are: *Isabel Clarendon* (1886); *Thyrza* (1887); *A Life's Morning* (1888); *Denzil Quarrier* (1892); *Born in Exile* (1892); *The Odd Women* (1893); *In the Year of the Jubilee* (1894); *Eve's Ransom* (1895); *The Paying Guest* (1895); *The Whirlpool* (1897); *The Town Traveller* (1898); *The Crown of Life* (1899); *Our Friend the Charlatan* (1901); *The Private Papers of Henry Ryecroft* (1903, and quasi-autobiographical); and *Veranilda* (1904). Amongst his volumes of short stories are *Human Odds and Ends* (1898) and *The House of Cobwebs* (1906). See: J. Korg, *George Gissing: A Critical Biography* (1963); M. Collie, *George Gissing: A Bibliography* (1975); and R. Williams, *Culture and Society 1780–1950* (1958).

186
GLADSTONE, William Ewart 1809–98

British statesman

William Ewart Gladstone was born in Liverpool, the youngest son of a Scotsman who had made a substantial fortune in the city – wealth which came substantially from West Indian plantations. His father opposed the abolition of the slave trade. In religion, William was brought up as an evangelical Anglican and in politics as an admirer of Canning – who represented Liverpool at Westminster. The young Gladstone was sent to school at Eton and then on to Christ Church, Oxford. There was always a sense in which he was 'Oxford on the surface, Liverpool underneath' and much of his subsequent success in public life can be traced to his ability to combine the virtues of provincial and commercial life with those of Oxford and the metropolis. As an undergraduate he impressed his contemporaries at the newly founded Union by his oratory and fine physical presence. He developed a zeal for work which never left him, showing an early mastery of facts and detail. That ability was reflected in his examination success – a double first – and was in turn repaid by a deep and abiding love for Oxford. He then

went on an Italian tour in 1832 much exercised as to whether his future lay in politics or in the ministry of the Church of England. The choice was not easy, involving as it did the aspirations and outlook of different members of his family. Although his university days strictly anteceded the 'Oxford Movement' in religion, Gladstone had already moved away from the evangelicalism of his youth. Theological and ecclesiastical issues remained of paramount importance but he accepted the offer of a parliamentary seat at Newark which was in the patronage of the Duke of Newcastle, the father of a school and university friend. He entered the Commons in 1832 – in the first election under the new franchise – and represented that constituency until 1845. He was thought of as an Ultra-Tory, the rising hope of all those who feared for the stability of church and state. However, his industry and ability soon came to the notice of Peel (whose own background was not dissimilar) and he held junior office in the brief ministry of 1835. Peel never professed to understand Gladstone's ecclesiastical preoccupations and the expression of them in *The State in its Relations with the Church* (1838) did not advance his political career. His stress upon the extent to which full citizenship entailed membership of the Church of England was coming to seem somewhat anachronistic. Nevertheless, after 1841, Peel made him vice-president and subsequently president of the Board of Trade – a task which Gladstone relished and where his capacity for work was displayed to the full. In 1845, however, he resigned because of the government's intention to make a grant to the Roman Catholic seminary at Maynooth in Ireland. Such a proposal conflicted with the argument of his book. He no longer adhered to that view but would not be thought to be clinging to office for its own sake. Many contemporaries, not least the prime minister, were mystified by the workings of Gladstone's conscience. After a short interval, he returned to office as colonial secretary, only to go into the political wilderness a few months later when Peel's government was defeated in the Commons in 1846.

Over the next thirteen years, Gladstone was only in office for two. There were many who thought that a promising career had fizzled out. He had married in 1839 the daughter of a landed family from North Wales (politically of Whig outlook) and he devoted himself to wrestling with some intractable problems of estate management mixed with a fascination with classical history which produced *Studies in Homer and the Homeric Age* (1858). His political sympathies and ambitions in this mid-century period seemed extremely confused – in part a reflection of the puzzling state of party combinations. The Conservatives had split on the issue of the repeal of the Corn Laws. Gladstone supported the repeal and in this matter and other aspects of government and administration found himself close to Peel. But Peel died in 1850, leaving those who regarded themselves as 'Peelites' drifting uneasily without clear allegiance either to the Tories or to the Whigs. Gladstone represented Oxford University from 1847 to 1865 and this was not particularly conducive to 'liberalism', but the direction his mind was taking on ecclesiastical, commercial and foreign policy matters seemed to be 'liberal'. Personal calculations cannot have been absent either. Disraeli* seemed to block the way in the Tory party and it seemed likely that Palmerston and Lord John Russell might leave the Whig/Liberal leadership vacant earlier. As chancellor of the exchequer from 1859 to 1865 he consolidated his reputation as a master of detail and an expositor of unrivalled power. His sympathies also seemed to extend to those upright working-men who could not be thought of any longer as beyond the pale of the constitution. What that meant precisely in terms of the franchise was another matter. Defeated at Oxford in 1865 he was then returned for South Lancashire – a change which symbolized a further broadening of his outlook. After the first election held under the Second Reform Act he was the only man capable of uniting the disparate Radical and Whig elements into the first Liberal government, properly speaking, of 1868.

Gladstone was prime minister from 1868 to 1874, from 1880 to 1885, in 1886 and from 1892 to 1894. His capacity in government was enormous, taking a detailed if excessive interest in the workings of all departments of state. He showed equal facility on the public platform in an age when oratorical power was of great importance; the speeches he delivered during his campaign in Midlothian in 1880 being most conspicuous. It may be said that late nineteenth-century Liberalism was welded together by Gladstone. Although he remained a High Anglican (and a vigorous and public opponent of the claims of the Church of Rome) his moral convictions and his belief in their relevance to policy appealed to Protestant Nonconformists. Opponents and colleagues nevertheless detected a good deal of cunning in his political behaviour – not least in his abortive attempt (which split his party) to introduce Home Rule for Ireland, both in the mid-1880s and in his final ministry. Although Gladstone's career can in a sense be seen as a rejection of Conservatism, at the end of his career he was no friend of contemporary Radicalism. In his first ministry, the essential purpose of his policies can be seen to be the eradication of 'privilege' but it subsequently became more difficult to define the positive mission of Liberalism. The passion which he brought to certain issues of foreign policy, as for example in *The Bulgarian Horrors and the Question of the East* (1876), did also have certain personal political advantages. To suggest that is simply to make the point that despite his deep (if a little eccentric) learning Gladstone was first and foremost a politician. As such, whether in or out of office, he dominated the late-Victorian age. Its political culture

was largely shaped by his outlook – and even those who attempted to take a new direction were not very successful in doing so. If his powers waned somewhat in his final phase, his eloquence, executive capacity, financial acumen, religious devotion, and political cunning made him indeed the 'Grand Old Man'.

Keith Robbins

See: John Morley, *Life of Gladstone* (3 vols, 1903); P. Magnus, *Gladstone: A Biography* (1954); S. G. Checkland, *The Gladstones: A Family Biography 1764–1851* (1971); *The Gladstone Diaries*, ed. M. R. D. Foot and H. C. G. Matthew (1968 and continuing).

187
GLINKA, Mikhail Ivanovich 1804–57

Russian composer

Glinka's education in music was extremely unsystematic. In common with other well-to-do Russians at the time, he developed various musical talents as social assets, and in due course took them beyond the level of dilettantism. Singing and piano-playing were his highest performing accomplishments, though he gained valuable early experience through directing a serf orchestra. He became acquainted with the folk music practised in the vicinity of the family estate, with the concert and theatre life of St Petersburg, and with the repertory of classical music current in domestic performance. A stay in Italy from 1830 to 1833 deepened his knowledge of contemporary Italian operatic practice, though it eventually led to his disillusionment with it. Other foreign travels brought him into contact with Berlioz*: each composer professed a high regard for the work of the other. In 1833–4 and 1856–7 Glinka studied with the celebrated contrapuntist Dehn in Berlin, from whom he received the most thorough training of his career in compositional skills. A spell in Spain (1845–7) introduced him to the rhythmic, melodic and colouristic qualities of Spanish folk music. His only major musical appointment, indeed his only major appointment of any sort, was as musical director of the Choir of the Imperial Chapel from 1837 to 1839.

This background gives no hint of Glinka's vital importance in Russian musical history. To some degree in parallel with Moniuszko in Poland and Smetana* in Bohemia, Glinka demonstrated the possibility of forging a distinctive national musical idiom. He arrived at this idiom by using features of indigenous folk music against a background of the norms of European art music; in the case of *Kamarinskaya* (1848), he allowed the character of a folk theme, rather than received ideas of structure, to play the major part in determining the form of a composition. Lacking the conventional musical education which he might have obtained in

Western Europe, Glinka was better able to see the possibilities of enrichment offered by folk music. Although the climate of his time and his own inclination favoured the creation of a body of Russian national music, the two Spanish Overtures (*Capriccio brillante on the Jota aragonesa*, 1845, and *Recollection of a Summer Night in Madrid*, 1851) reveal that he was alive to other openings. Certain of his own works exhibit weaknesses, not all of a musical character, which have kept them out of the international repertory. Yet many of the ideas with which the next generation of Russian composers stunned the musical world may be traced directly to the compositions of Glinka. The debt was generously acknowledged, and the task of making known and publishing his works willingly undertaken by the later composers.

Glinka's career coincided with a period in which the attention of the Russian intelligentsia was focused on the question of Russia's identity. Pushkin*, his contemporary and friend, had carried out for the Russian language and literature a task analogous to Glinka's in the development of Russian music and inaugurated a distinguished line of writers. Investigation of the Russian past flourished. History was examined for clues to the interpretation of Russia's present and future. Geographical, archaeological and ethnographical research was encouraged by new institutions. The specimen-gathering of enthusiastic amateurs was quickly superseded by more thorough assessment to professional standards. The random jotting of folksongs (words and music separately and together) was followed by a more systematic and critical approach to collecting and recording. Historical, social and cultural study and speculation proceeded apace.

In his rebellion against the lingua franca of Italian opera, still promoted on a lavish scale in Russia during his lifetime, Glinka's intention was to begin to create a corpus of music which would be rooted in Russia. This music would be flesh of Russia's flesh, as Italian opera was of Italy's. Opera afforded the broadest canvas for this nationalist ideal. *A Life for the Tsar* (1836) recounts the self-sacrifice of a Russian peasant for his country. Ivan Susanin, a genuine historical character, led the Poles who invaded Russia in 1613 into the depths of a forest, and thus enabled the tsar to escape and his country's independence to survive. The scope for authentic characterizations of such a story by means of costume, designs, setting and music is obvious. Both Russians and Poles are so characterized. The original title, *Ivan Susanin*, is restored in the version with new text (1936) now in use in the Soviet Union. The title was changed in the first place in an attempt to harness the opera on behalf of the policies of Nicholas. The nationalist implications, effectively realized in song, dance and pageantry, are clear, whether the subject is understood generally, or as offering propaganda support for the autocracy.

Pushkin's imitation of a folk fairy tale, *Ruslan and Lyudmila* (opera – 1842), opens up a different avenue. This has a fantastic subject in which the supernatural is carried to comical lengths. But it represents an important genre of folk art, and as such enabled Glinka to extend his tribute to the national culture. It is most unfortunate that both operas were put together in an extremely amateurish fashion. In both cases, much of the music was composed not just before the words were written but before the precise course of the plot had been worked out. It seems characteristic of the essential triviality of the composer's personality – obvious from his *Memoirs* and many letters – that he did not raise his sights from the business of setting down notes on paper to the much larger issues involved in creating an opera. The eventual librettos were the work of several writers, most of them drawn from Glinka's circle of convivial friends, and none of them first-rate literary talents. The dramatic integrity of the resulting operas (especially *Ruslan*) is such that they rely on their musical quality alone for survival. It is only in the composer's homeland that they are a regular part of the repertory.

Vestiges of Italian vocal writing, the French taste for ballets in opera, the reminiscence motives and supernatural elements of German Romantic opera may all be discerned in Glinka's works. Folk-song-influenced melodies and harmonies, dance rhythms and imitations of folk instruments play an important role, however, together with other musical devices not yet found in Western art music (the whole-tone scale, certain harmonic fingerprints). Glinka's instrumentation, perhaps influenced by that of Berlioz, favours thin, clear textures and bright unblended colours. The 'orientalism' of later composers is already exploited by Glinka in *Ruslan*, where he draws ideas for the Eastern Dances from the folk dances of peoples adjoining the Russian part of the Russian Empire. A major line in Russian opera stems from each of Glinka's operas: such grand national spectacles as *Boris Godunov*, *Khovanshchina*, *Prince Igor* and *The Maid of Pskov* are descended from *A Life for the Tsar*, whereas the example of *Ruslan* led on to *The Golden Cockerel*, *The Tale of Tsar Saltan*, *The Love for Three Oranges* and others.

Stuart Campbell

Other works: *Valse-fantaisie* (for orchestra, 1839–56); incidental music for *Prince Kholmsky*, a tragedy by N. Kukol'nik (1841); *Farewell to St Petersburg*, a song cycle (1840); many songs, including *Midnight Review* (1836), 'Where is our rose?' (1837), 'I remember a wonderful moment' (1840), *Adel'R/* (1849) and *The Gulf of Finland* (1850). Glinka's *Memoirs* may be read in a translation by Richard B. Mudge (1963). See David Brown, *Glinka: A Biographical and Critical Study* (1974).

188

GOBINEAU, Arthur de 1816–82

French author and political thinker

To the twentieth century Gobineau has become known as the 'Father of Racism'. Such a description clearly oversimplifies the question of intellectual origins, but it does crystallize his claim to be a seminal figure in the history of ideas about the vital role of race as a social determinant. He is remembered, in addition, as a talented author of travel books and of novels and short stories charged with an irony very reminiscent of Stendhal*.

Gobineau was born near Paris into an impoverished gentry family sympathetic to Bourbon legitimism and the vanishing values of the Ancien Régime. After being privately educated he sought to earn his living as journalist and historical novelist. In 1849 he became *chef de cabinet* to Tocqueville* during the latter's spell as foreign minister, and he then spent the next thirty years combining authorship with the demands of diplomatic service in locations as varied as Switzerland, Germany, Persia, Greece, Brazil, and Sweden. His two missions to Tehran stimulated the informative works *Trois Ans en Asie* ('Three Years in Asia', 1859) and *Religions et Philosophies dans l'Asie Centrale* ('The Religions and Philosophies of Central Asia', 1865), and the romanticist orientalism of his youth remained apparent in such imaginative writings as the *Tales of Asia* (*Nouvelles asiatiques*, 1876). Prominent among many other creations are the novel *Sons of Kings* (*Les Pléiades*, 1874) and the drama *The Renaissance* (*La Renaissance*, 1877), in both of which the case is put for an elite-morality along lines not dissimilar to those followed later by Nietzsche*.

The central statement of Gobineau's belief in the need to speak up for hierarchical principles against the levelling tendencies of nineteenth-century mass society is the four-volume *Inequality of Human Races* (*Essai sur l'inégalité des races humaines*, 1853–5). Here he treated racial competition in much the same way that Marx* and Engels* were already regarding class struggle – as the fundamental key to an understanding of society's past development and present problems, indeed to a grasp of every aspect of politics, culture, and morality. The resulting monistic synthesis pivoted around the historical achievements of that supposedly superior 'Aryan' stock which alone possessed true civilizing potential and a proper conception of honour. Now, however, this breed stood irrevocably debilitated by miscegenation, under threat from lesser white elements within Europe and still more destructive coloured hordes beyond. The process of decline into universal mediocrity might be slowed but no longer halted; thus the chief task of the elite with which Gobineau iden-tified himself was the assertion of a dignified if ultimately unavailing defiance.

The work's most perceptive critic was Tocqueville, who condemned its determinism and predicted that its ideas might prove most dangerously alluring in Germany. There indeed it was that Gobineau was most enthusiastically taken up, not least because of the friendship which he enjoyed with Richard Wagner* during their last years and on account of subsequent propagandist activities by the Bayreuth Circle. By the turn of the century a loose rhetoric of racial causation, owing much to the Frenchman, was quite widely current in Europe. A Gobineau Society had been formed in Germany by 1894, and a chain of personal and intellectual links then stretched on from the Wagnerites via Houston Stewart Chamberlain* and Alfred Rosenberg to Hitler himself. Gobineau's belief in the modern age as the twilight of the Aryans tended to be played down, even while his conviction that race held the key to history was being more than ever exploited. Whereas the author of the *Human Races* had despaired of the world and virtually withdrawn from it, Hitler pledged himself to policies of more positive racial redemption. Never was hope more harmful. From much the same 'facts' about race the two men drew very different practical conclusions. But, then, the facts were comparatively unimportant – it was the symbol that was the same.

Michael Biddiss

Gobineau's letters to Tocqueville, published as vol. 9 of the latter's *Oeuvres complètes* (gen. ed. J.P. Mayer, 1959), are especially valuable. The most accessible starting point in English is *Gobineau: Selected Political Writings*, ed. Michael Biddiss (1970). The chief secondary studies are: Jean Gaulmier, *Spectre de Gobineau* (1965); Janine Buenzod, *La Formation de la pensée de Gobineau* (1967); Michael Biddiss, *Father of Racist Ideology* (1970); and Jean Boissel, *Gobineau* (1981). The *Études Gobiniennes*, ed. Jean Gaulmier (1966 onwards), provide a more or less annual review of relevant work.

189

GODWIN, William 1756–1836

British philosoper and novelist

Godwin was a minor political journalist until the publication of *Political Justice* (1793) at the peak of the debate over the revolution in France. His powerful arguments and extravagant conclusions made him for a time the most famous, or most notorious, radical thinker in Britain, his devotees including Wordsworth*, Coleridge* and Southey*. A novel, *Caleb Williams* (1794), designed to illustrate the themes of the political treatise, was an equal success, followed by a collection of essays on education, morality and literature called *The Enquirer* (1797). That same year Godwin married Mary Wollstonecraft, and their happiness together is lovingly evoked in both his *Memoirs* of Mary (1798) and the novel *St Leon* (1799). But Mary died in childbirth six months later, and in the changed political atmosphere Godwin now found himself an object of ridicule and satire, as well as being the subject of a number of theoretical critiques, most notably Malthus's* *Essay on Population*. Even former friends like Mackintosh and Parr turned against him, though there were Coleridge and Lamb* to take their place. The *Reply to Parr* of 1801 is a measured, judicious, and largely successful response to all these critics.

In 1801 Godwin married a formidable widow, Mrs. Clairmont, and with a family of five to support they set up as publishers of children's books, several of which Godwin wrote himself under pseudonyms, though, among others, the Lambs contributed their *Tales from Shakespeare*. By 1812 Godwin was such a forgotten figure that Shelley* was astonished, and delighted, to learn that he was still living. Shelley seemed willing to use his unearned wealth to support so great a figure, Godwin was all too eager to accept, and continued to do so even when Shelley, to Godwin's great distress, eloped with his daughter Mary in 1814. There was a reconciliation of sorts when Shelley and Mary married two years later, and Godwin continued to request, and sometimes get, Shelley's help until the latter's death in 1822. Through his sixties and seventies Godwin continued to write roughly a book a year, including a further volume of essays called *Thoughts on Man* (1831). In 1833 the Whig Reform government provided him with an official post and lodgings, as Yeoman Usher of the Receipt of the Exchequer.

Godwin is best remembered now as the friend of Sheridan, Wordsworth, Coleridge, Lamb and Hazlitt*, and as the 'venerable horseleech' who sponged off Shelley. But his intellectual reputation must depend ultimately on *Political Justice*, a fascinating *tour de force* which combines pioneering statements of philosophical anarchism and utilitarian ethics with extreme and unorthodox opinions about honesty, gratitude, promises, marriage, private property, personal cooperation, and the future development of man and society. The first edition of 1793, printed while it was written, shows us a thinker being led ever further and further, from premises which were at first implicit to conclusions which were originally unanticipated. The second edition of 1796 is more polished, containing a number of important new arguments which represent his most substantial, albeit largely forgotten, contribution to philosophy.

The fundamental principle in Godwin's thinking is the omnipotence of truth, leading to the perfectibility of man. Men cannot help but recognize the truth,

Godwin believes, if it is presented clearly to them, and their judgment is not distorted by social and political pressures. And once they recognize the truth, they cannot but act on it. In this way man is perfectible: vice and error – which are, for Godwin, much the same thing – will disappear, as the truth becomes more widely known and available. But the main obstacle is the coercion and imposture of political institutions, which seek to prevent men from forming their own opinions and acting independently on them. Indeed once political institutions wither away men will find they have no need of them. Instead we will be governed by individual judgment and conscience, by reason, truth and justice, in an ideal state of society which Godwin calls 'political justice'. But while Godwin is, ultimately, an anarchist, he was no revolutionary, believing in gradual reform rather than the sudden overthrow of authority. This was certainly the line that he followed in practical politics, to the incomprehension or distress of some of his more radical acquaintances like Thelwall or Shelley.

This philosophical anarchism provides the backbone of *Political Justice*, but there are, in addition, any number of other discussions of equal, if not greater, philosophical interest, especially his moral theory which combines Helvetian utilitarianism with a Calvinist rejection of what he later came to call 'the private and domestic affections'. If morality is concerned with providing the greatest benefit for the greatest number, and individual affections lead me to prefer my family and friends when I could actually have done more good for others, then individual affections are positively immoral, ultimately to be dispensed with in a state of political justice. Similar conclusions are drawn concerning gratitude and the keeping of promises, though the extreme position of *Political Justice* is considerably (and consistently) modified in the *Reply to Parr*. Other topics discussed by Godwin include free-will and necessity, benevolence and self-love, and the nature of virtue. There are also important and original discussions of education, both in *The Enquirer* and in an early pamphlet, the *Account of the Seminary* (1783).

Godwin's major fictional work is *Caleb Williams*, which influenced the development of both the modern detective novel and the modern psychological novel, and remains excitingly readable even today. *St Leon* is of interest for its fictional portrayal of the Godwin-Wollstonecraft marriage, and its change of mind, and heart, about the private and domestic affections.

Don Locke

F.E.L. Priestley's edition of *Political Justice* (1946) contains the variant texts from all three editions published in Godwin's lifetime. See: C. Kegan Paul, *William Godwin: His Friends and Contemporaries* (1876); Ford K. Brown, *William Godwin* (1926); C.H. Driver, 'William Godwin', in *Social and Political Ideas of the*

Revolutionary Era, ed. F.J.C. Hearnshaw (1931); H.N. Brailsford, *Shelley, Godwin and Their Circle* (1931); David Fleischer, *William Godwin: A Study in Liberalism* (1951); J.B. Boulton, *The Language of Politics* (1965), ch. 11; B.R. Pollin, *Godwin Criticism: A Synoptic Bibliography* (1967); and Don Locke, *A Fantasy of Reason: The Life and Thought of William Godwin* (1980).

190

GOETHE, Johann Wolfgang von 1749–1832

German writer

Goethe dominates German literature by the quality, range and originality of his work, and by its historical timeliness and effect. In large measure he created the national literature. At his birth in 1749 it had no European standing, its post-medieval achievements were mere erratic blocks on a local landscape. By the rough mid-point of his life he had produced major works, set new poetic standards, and with Schiller as his partner in the decisive years of 'High Classicism' (1794–1805) established Weimar as the authoritative centre of a politically and culturally fragmented German-speaking world. At his death in 1832 German literature was translated and emulated in England and France and widely accepted as a major component in world literature, with himself its most internationally respected figure.

Goethe was born in a Free Imperial City, Frankfurt am Main. He studied in Leipzig and Strassburg and practised law briefly on his return home. At twenty-five he was attracted to the court of Weimar by Duke Karl August of Sachsen-Weimar. What was planned as a visit became lifelong residence, its only interruption a long stay in Italy from autumn 1786 to mid-1788. It was an outwardly uneventful life, devoted to literature, science and administration. The administrative work, while never amounting to 'statesmanship' (the Duchy of Weimar was simply not that significant) was of value to the writer as a varied contact with life. His scientific studies were extensive and, at least in biology, influential. He pressed beyond Linnaeus's fixed classification of species to a more dynamic view of plant-forms as stages in a continuous organic metamorphosis, an advance which has been compared in importance with that from alchemy to chemistry. But in literature his work is of a different order again. In sixty years of creativity, he so amply made good Germany's deficit in every literary genre that his successors were faced with a quite different problem – how to find some area for originality not overshadowed by his genius.

In drama, though often at odds with the traditional formal requirements, he produced an impressive corpus. The prose chronicle-play *Götz von Berlichingen*

(1771) puts German history on the stage in a manner claiming descent from Shakespeare, inspiring in turn Scott's* historical novels and initiating an alternative, 'non-Aristotelian' line in German drama that leads down to Brecht's epic theatre. *Egmont* (1787), though torn between character-study and political history, has some fine dialectic and splendid crowd scenes. *Iphigenie auf Tauris* (1787) gives classical (verse) shape and a humane ethical resolution to conflicts which might have had a drastically tragic 'Greek' ending; *Torquato Tasso* (1790) treats with similar outward control the inner and social disharmonies suffered by a poet, the prototype for countless successors in works about artists down to modern times. Goethe's *magnum opus*, *Faust*, both in its genesis (1770–1832) and in its final mass (12,111 lines) goes beyond all known measure, making up its own laws of dramatic form and thematic scope, which it fulfils with supreme poetic virtuosity. Other, minor, dramas and fragments abound. Goethe almost always starts from a conception of character rather than a pattern of action, generating drama from the antitheses of temperament between protagonists (Faust-Mephistopheles, Faust-Gretchen; Egmont-Oranien, Egmont-Alba; Tasso-Antonio). The lack of a completely preconceived action can make for formal untidiness, which is often increased by a complex and intermittent process of composition; but in return he offers us some of the most fully realized and convincing human studies in the whole of drama.

The novel was still only half accepted as a serious genre when the young Goethe created one of its masterpieces, *Young Werther* (*Die Leiden des jungen Werthers*, 1774; revised version 1787). He takes the epistolary form common in the eighteenth century (Richardson, Rousseau) but transforms its brittle conventions into something wholly plausible: Werther's persuasively 'authentic' letters express and analyse an over-sensitive, anchorless mind driven by unhappy love and other discordant experiences to suicide – a climax enhanced by the late switch to barely disguised omniscient narration by an 'Editor'. *Werther* was a European sensation, largely through its emotive subject and its subtle enlisting of sympathy; it remains inexhaustible for its perfect prose and its almost total harmony of theme and technique. *Wilhelm Meisters Lehrjahre* (1796) and its sequel *Wilhelm Meisters Wanderjahre* (1829) make up the first fully self-aware *Bildungsroman*, or novel of individual development. The hero is gradually weaned away from his love of the theatre, an involvement more whole-heartedly and colourfully conveyed in the fragmentary original version, *Wilhelm Meisters Theatralische Sendung* (c. 1777, published 1911). His education, and with it the novel-sequence itself – especially the *Wanderjahre* – escape progressively from the realities of society into the abstractions of Utopian thought. Goethe's example set a trend for the novel, reinforcing the non-social tradition of German art even in this most potentially social of the literary forms. Analysis was turned inward to states of soul and mind in isolation from the state of the world, and where society was thought of as a school, some kind of acceptance was bound to be the lesson. Goethe came closer to the European norm of what a novel is and does in *Kindred By Choice* (*Die Wahlverwandtschaften*, 1809), a profound and still enigmatic study of marital and extra-marital relationships through which the unstable ethos and conflicts of an era can be sensed.

Over the years, Goethe's narrative prose becomes less sensitively flexible, more measured, sage and monumental. The same is true of his autobiographical writings, except where he quotes direct from the letters and journals of an earlier phase he is describing, as in the *Italian Journey* (*Italienische Reise*, 1816/27). That work documents the crucial Italian months which brought him to his 'Classical' maturity. The *Kampagne in Frankreich* (1822) describes the German princes' abortive incursion into revolutionary France in 1792 and brings out the confusions and futilities of war with an often Tolstoyan* touch. *Poetry and Truth* (*Dichtung und Wahrheit*, 1814, 1831) treats Goethe's childhood and early manhood up to the turning-point of his departure for Weimar in 1775; it is an intriguing exercise in perspective, late wisdom observing and reflecting on early experience. The gaps between these scattered though massive autobiographical fragments can be filled with the aid of some 14,000 extant letters. Many of these are without equal in German prose – for their vigour and spontaneity in his youth, their zest and balance in his middle years, their subtlety and serenity in his old age.

Goethe is thus a dramatist and prose writer of grand and varied achievements. But his real genius and unsurpassed greatness is as a poet; and it is in the development of his poetry that his deepest nature and value as a writer appear.

Here practically all was still to be done. The glories of German medieval lyric were forgotten, the grandeur of Baroque religious rhetoric was fading. 'Poetry' in mid-eighteenth century meant either the emotionally and poetically trivial flirtations of Rococo verse, or the earnest reflections of popular philosophy all too deliberately put into lengthy stanza-sequences. Klopstock, it is true, had brought a new intensity of emotion, especially religious, into this drab scene, limbering up a potentially agile poetic language with new expressive demands. Yet much of his poetry too feels constructed, the emotion induced; he has few softer tones and rarely descends from a high rhetorical horse. A natural voice speaking in an unforced yet poetically concentrated way about universal human concerns, the voice of 'a man speaking to men' as Wordsworth* later puts it, is hardly to be heard in these years. Herder, who was to be the age's most influential critic, sought it in the folk poetry of the past, simple, haunting, and – with the

lightest of touch – profound. It is Goethe's quite uncalculating originality that he begins to speak with just such a voice, to the point of writing his own ballads and seeming folksongs. In this the acquaintance with Herder's theories, great though their impact was, had not made him damagingly self-conscious: his poetry was not so much the creation as the almost providential illustration of the theories. His youthful letters had already achieved direct expression even while he was briefly toying with the Rococo verse-modes to which he was brought up. Dropping these, he takes immediate experience as his material and explores it as if it were a new continent. Love, aspiration, human encounters, nature – to be more precise, the sense of being vigorously alive in the real world and the first intuitions of an order in which man is securely rooted – these are his subjects. So is reflection, but a reflection which now has the full human reality it had not been given by his predecessors: embodied in myth and symbol, and often in a monologue which fuses the poet's individual perceptions with the imagined ones of an archetypal figure – Prometheus, Ganymede, Mahomet – Goethe's reflection is itself enacted as an experience. All this provides one obvious sense in which his early lyric is *Erlebnisdichtung*, the poetry of experience. It is already, through the freshness and intensity with which he expresses his perception, revolutionary. But in a striking way experience also shapes the poetic form: 'free' verse, stanzas slight or massive, *ad hoc* patterns born of a single moment, all show the minute responsiveness of the verbal medium to the inherent structure of the subject. This is 'inner form', no longer something imposed but an organic part of the recorded experience, in part organizing it but even more strongly organized by it. Feeling and perception are not just stated but mapped. This is an even more important sense of *Erlebnisdichtung*, and one not so open to dismissal by over-cautious critics as leading us into 'biographism', the substitution of the poet's life for his art.

Goethe's expressive aesthetic and his individualism of theme and form make him appear a Romantic, as in a broad European context he is often said to be. Certainly no writer more fully and repeatedly fulfils the Romantic ideal of poety as the 'spontaneous overflow of powerful feeling' (Wordsworth again), and not just in his early poems. But no other poet's work – and this is less clearly a Romantic feature – can better sustain minute scrutiny as the formally perfect result of such (one might think) undiscriminating impulse. In other words, he resolves the potential conflict between flux and form, process and product, the Romantic appeal to an internal criterion of value and the Classical appeal to an external one. This means that his 'Romantic' beginnings contain the seed of his 'Classical' maturity. Then in the period of his Italian journey, he observes the coalescing – identity, even – of growth and form in everything: in the natural phenomena he studies as a scientist, in ancient art and architecture as offshoots of nature, in the social patterns of Mediterranean culture. Art, nature and society appear informed by the same laws. He becomes consciously committed to norms, as Classicists usually are. Yet even his Classicism remains strongly individualistic. The constants he discovers at every turn are appreciated in the light of the perceiver's own present experience. Antiquity itself, usually the unquestioned keystone of Classicism, is revered not as a sacrosanct part of culture but as an archetypal humanity which modern man may restore in himself, as the *Roman Elegies* (*Römische Elegien*, 1788) illustrate. The Classical phase, with its high degrees of reflective awareness, is thus a restatement of the early work on a spirally higher plane – an example of what Goethe called *Steigerung*. Crucially, his creative powers are unimpaired by the reflection that situates his experience in broader contexts. He remains (to use Schiller's famous critical term) a 'naïve' poet. His verse of the Classical decade, whether didactic ('Metamorphose der Pflanzen', 'Metamorphose der Tiere', 'Dauer im Wechsel'), epic in the ancient tradition (*Hermann und Dorothea*, 1797) or lyric, combines serenity with power, the excitement of perceiving single phenomena with the calm satisfaction of knowing their place in a harmonious order. Goethe's sense of harmony can be linked with intellectual influences (Leibniz, Spinoza) and it is a central part, whether as cause or effect is hard to determine, of his scientific work; but in the end it is always an immediate poetic insight that renders it real. The profoundest thoughts are conveyed through simple objects and perceptions; poetry becomes consistently and unforcedly symbolic.

These essentials do not change in the post-Classical phase, when the externals of graeco-latin metre and subjects are sloughed off and the ageing Goethe's virtuosity turns to other modes, to the Persian of the *West-eastern Divan* (*Westöstlicher Divan*, 1819, trans. 1914) collection, or the Chinese of *Chinesisch-deutsche Jahres-und Tageszeiten* (1830), or the almost exhaustive range of poetic forms which the dramatist displays in *Faust II*. The Classical appropriation of the world through contemplation, enjoyment, scientific analysis and poetic sensibility remained as a once-for-all achievement, serious and secure beneath the play of forms. Yet security does not mean stasis, for in the late philosophico-scientific poems the great theme is change and movement, albeit within an overarching order; we glimpse the evolution of organic forms and forces through which the universe persists. Nor does security mean a withdrawal from dangerous areas of experience: at seventy-four Goethe falls in love yet again, and the shattering effect of losing a seventeen-year-old girl he was too bewitched to renounce gives rise to his one great tragic lyric, the 'Trilogie der Leidenschaft' (1821). Here it is as much as the poet can do to assemble fragments of consolation by invoking the sufferers he himself created – Werther, Tasso – and even they prove insufficient. He thus draws on a mythology of his own making, achieving instinctively what German Romantic theorists had aspired to in vain in their recipes for cultural rejuvenation and poetic vigour.

That is a sign how rich and canonical his *oeuvre* now was. And since his day, the figures and phases of his work and career have practically constituted a mythology for German (and to some extent, with *Faust*, European) writing, which returns to them compulsively for material, example, stimulus and challenge. This is hardly surprising. Whether we think of the quality and variety of his literary work, or the multifariousness of his intellectual interests, or the range of eminent contemporaries in all fields of endeavour which his correspondence brings into a unifying focus, or the transformations of German poetry which he witnessed over his creative lifetime and was in large measure responsible for himself – in any and all of these senses, Goethe was and is (as Nietzsche* said) not so much a great individual as a culture.

Germans in recent years, driven by the catastrophes of their history into reproachful retrospects on their cultural past, have found Goethe wanting as a classic – wanting precisely because he *is* such a classic, so stable, rounded, harmonious, untragic in outlook and (especially) unpolitical in his commitments. This is already to see him as more serene, less problematic than he actually was and felt himself to be, though it is true he lacks the axiomatic and sometimes facile pessimism of so much European culture since his day. It is also true that, as a virtually lifelong courtier, he was politically conservative as far as his personal influence and his conscious views about contemporary society are concerned. Yet his *work* is essentially dynamic and liberating; and if we are truly to avoid biographism, it is in the poet's work that we must see his contribution to human thought, feeling and ultimately action.

Very much this distinction was made by Matthew Arnold* when in 1863 he tried to assess Goethe's effect in comparison with Heine's*, who aspired to influence the world by more direct means. Of course, Goethe's influence was bound to be slower and more gradual. Yet his individualism and 'profound imperturbable naturalism' were for Arnold 'absolutely fatal to routine thinking'; and he concluded:

Nothing could be more really subversive of the foundations on which the old European order rested; and it may be remarked that no persons are so radically detached from this order, no persons so thoroughly modern, as those who have felt Goethe's influence most deeply.

Much has changed since 1863, ways of being even

more 'radically detached' have emerged. But Arnold's judgment still essentially does justice to the nature and potential effect of Goethe's work.

T.J. Reed

See: G.H. Lewes, *The Life and Works of Goethe* (1855); Richard Friedenthal, *Goethe, His Life and Times* (Trans. 1965); Barker Fairley, *A Study of Goethe* (1969); E.M. Wilkinson and L.A. Willoughby, *Goethe, Poet and Thinker* (1962); T.J. Reed, *The Classical Centre: Goethe and Weimar 1775–1832* (1980).

191

GOGOL, Nikolai 1809–52

Russian (Ukrainian) prose fiction writer and playwright

By common consent one of the most enigmatic, yet seminal, writers in Russian literature, Gogol is Russia's classic comic author whose 'laughter through tears' suggests deeper, darker emotions, and whose life, as strange as his writing, is full of tragic absurdities. Personal themes lie submerged in his art. Thus the family name was Yanovsky, but his grandfather, who was of clerical origin, had tacked the Cossack name Gogol to the Polish-sounding Yanovsky to claim the right to own serfs. The grandson later renounced his true surname in favour of this 'noble' appendage which was not only bogus but comic (*gogol* is a species of duck). Comic names and overweening social pretensions figure prominently in his writing, and the plot of *Ivan Ivanovich and Ivan Nikiforovich* (*Povest' o tom kak Ivan Ivanovich possorilsya s Ivanom Nikiforovichem*, 1835) hinges on the adding of 'gander' to another 'noble Cossack' name. When his father, an amateur Ukrainian playwright, died in 1825, Gogol was worshipped by a young and adoring mother. Her son treated her with a mixture of affection and aloofness, but explored the theme of incest explicitly in *The Terrible Vengeance* (*Strashnaya mest'R/, 1832*) and implicitly in *Viy* (1835).

After an undistinguished school career in the Ukraine Gogol left in 1828 for St Petersburg to find fame. A poem 'Hanz Kyukhelgarten' which he printed privately under a pseudonym in 1829 was badly reviewed. Gogol took back all the copies and burned them. Inspiration ending in conflagration is a recurrent motif in Gogol's life, as is escape through travel: that summer he went on a mysterious spree to Germany on money entrusted to him for mortgage repayments by his mother. Success came in 1831 with *Evenings in a Village near Dikanka* (*Vechera na khutore bliz Dikan'ki*), a collection of rumbustious tales of Ukrainian life, for which he had solicited ethnographical material from his mother. His art often needed the stimulus of others, and it was at this time that he made the acquaintance

of Pushkin*. Later, he would claim that Pushkin had given him the themes both of his play *The Government Inspector* (*Revizor*, 1836) and of his novel *Dead Souls* (*Mertvye dushi*, 1842). Gogol shamelessly cultivated the powerful and the rich and in 1834, with no obvious qualifications, he managed to gain appointment as a lecturer in history at St Petersburg University. After a brilliant inaugural lecture he resorted either to absences or mumbling from ill-prepared notes, and at the final oral examinations appeared with a bandaged head claiming to be incapacitated by toothache. He resigned in 1835, but this brief period was the most productive of his literary career: nearly all his mature work was either written or planned between 1834 and 1835.

Mirgorod (1835) develops the earlier Ukrainian theme through four contrasting stories: 'The Old World Landowners', 'Taras Bulba', 'Viy' and 'Ivan Ivanovich and Ivan Nikiforovich'. A microcosm of the Ukraine projected in four contrasting modes (idyll, epic, folklore, comedy), it is, nevertheless, permeated by the author's own neurotic preoccupations: sexuality as a demonic force and anxiety about origins and status.

Arabesques (*Arabeski*, 1835), a collection of stories and essays, contains three of the so-called 'St Petersburg Tales'. 'The Portrait' (*Portret*) is a Hoffmannesque* allegory about the demonic in art (rewritten 1842). 'Nevsky Prospekt', a diptych of two contrasting stories sets the amorous adventures of the painter Piskarev against those of the lieutenant Pirogov, and exposes the vulnerability of romantic and artistic idealism in a world of vulgar banality. Gogol's depiction of people as mere moustaches, sleeves, etc. admirably illustrates a central device of his comic manner – synedoche, and the theme of St Petersburg as an unreal city was taken up by later writers, notably Dostoevsky* and Andrey Belyy. *The Diary of a Madman* (*Zapiski sumasshedshego*) is at once a comic and pathetic account of a civil servant's descent into madness: it is Gogol's only sustained attempt to portray psychology from inside.

The Nose (*Nos*, 1836), a story of Kafka-like absurdity, is often interpreted as expressing a castration complex, but the theme of a personified nose being of higher rank than its owner may be related to Gogol's double life as writer/lecturer and a sense of his 'having run away with himself'. In his most famous story *The Overcoat* (*Shinel'*, 1841) a poor government clerk makes improbable sacrifices to buy a warm winter coat, of which he is robbed almost immediately. His efforts to recover it end in his death, completely overcome by the words of an important (i.e. 'significant') person. The story is traditionally seen as championing the victim of an oppressive society, but the hero's poverty is presented with grotesque hyperbole and his true indigence is psychological. He is a man without content, inarticulate; yet as a copy clerk he is obsessed with words in their outward calligraphic form, and is crushed by the verbal effects of a 'significant' person. This subtext reveals the author's growing neurosis about the lack of significance in his own writing. The earlier story *The Carriage* (*Kolyaska*, 1836) is not set in St Petersburg, but like *The Overcoat* it reveals the hero's vacuity through his attitude to a possession – a carriage.

In the play *The Government Inspector* Khlestakov, a foolish young nonentity, is mistaken for a government inspector by the corrupt officials of a provincial town, who think they have bought him off only to be confronted with the arrival of the real inspector. Gogol parodies the stock device of mistaken identity: Khlestakov, although a beneficiary, is also a dupe of the situation, and the more incredible his stories, the more he is believed. Conventional love intrigue is also parodied in Khlestakov's indiscriminate pursuit of the mayor's daughter and his wife.

Gogol, displeased with the play's reception, fled abroad, where he remained (based in Rome but constantly travelling) until 1848. In 1842 the first part of *Dead Souls* was published. The title, deliberately ambiguous, ostensibly refers to the dead peasants (souls) which still officially exist for tax purposes, and whose documents the rogue hero Chichikov is buying to use as a pledge for a mortgage. Travel allows the 'Hero' to see Russia, and chapters 2–6 constitute a portrait gallery of Russian landowners, who, though grotesque to a degree greater than the characters of Dickens*, have a vivid reality which has won them broad acceptance as national types. There is much play with the reader, which is reminiscent of Sterne, and there are long digressions and extended similes. Gogol called the work a 'poem' (*Poema*) and planned two further parts which would show positive aspects of Russia and the path to regeneration. Although he laboured on this task until his death, he was not satisfied, and twice burned the fully written second part. He claimed that the second burning was an error and went into a prolonged fast for Lent, from which he died, further tormented by the grotesque medical practices of the day. His death, however, is often attributed to the influence of religion, which together with a growing sense of his own mission dominated his latter years. The publication of *Selected Passages from Correspondence with Friends* (*Vybrannye mesta iz perepistki s druzyami*, 1847) revealed Gogol as bigot, obscurantist and reactionary. It shocked many of his erstwhile champions.

Gogol's reputation as a scourge of corruption rests on *The Government Inspector*, *Dead Souls* and *The Overcoat*. Because sordid details appeared in his work he was dubbed by his enemies a writer of the 'natural school', but the designation was taken up in a positive sense by such champions as Belinsky. It is obvious that Gogol's grotesque presentation of reality is far removed from naturalism as it is usually understood, but to equate Gogol's fiction with the actualities of Russian life was a polemical standpoint of those seeking social change.

If few critics take Gogol's own pronouncements on his art at face value, his works have nevertheless received acclaim from an incredibly wide spectrum of critical positions. For the Russian Symbolists Gogol was a precursor and an initiator of poetic prose. The Formalists saw his works as substantiating their theories on the self-sufficiency of literary form. Psychologists have viewed them almost as Freudian constructs whilst others have seen his works as essays in the absurd and the grotesque, and yet others have looked for spiritual or social messages. Most Soviet scholars resolutely see him as a critical realist. 'We have all come out of Gogol's overcoat' is an apocryphal remark attributed to Dostoevsky, but it has its own truth. Dostoevsky recognized the submerged psychology in Gogol's writing and brought it to the surface by his own methods. Both he and Tolstoy* succumbed to the Gogolian concept of the author as preacher, and both completed what Gogol could not himself achieve, the novel of spiritual regeneration. Turgenev*, Goncharov*, Saltykov-Shchedrin, Leskov and many others owe a great debt to Gogol, and his influence can still be strongly felt in the Soviet literature of the twentieth century.

Richard Peace

Recommended translations: *Collected Works*, trans. Constance Garnett (6 vols, 1922–8); '*Taras Bulba*' and *Other Tales*, '*The Inspector General*', introduction by Nikolay Andreyev (1962); *Dead Souls*, trans. with an introduction by David Magarshak (1961); *The Divine Liturgy of the Eastern Orthodox Church*, trans. Rosemary Edmonds (1960); *Selected Passages from Correspondence with Friends*, trans. Jesse Zeldin (1969); and *Diary of a Madman and Other Stories*, trans. Ronald Wilks (1972). About Gogol: Henri Troyat, *Gogol, The Biography of a Divided Soul*, trans. from the French by Nancy Amphoux (1974); Richard Peace, *The Enigma of Gogol* (1981).

192
GONCHAROV, Ivan Alexandrovich 1812–91

Russian novelist

The output of Ivan Goncharov was not large, three novels, some short stories and a volume of travel notes, yet his place in the history of Russian literature is secure. His reputation rests upon his second novel, *Oblomov* (1859, trans. 1974), and it is a mark of the classic status of this work that it has been subjected to widely divergent interpretations, from the politically committed to the absurdist, without exhausting its possibilities. The Russian 'sociological' critic Dobrolyu-bov, in an essay entitled *What is Oblomovitis?* (1860), took a strictly diagnostic view of the novel, seeing it as the product of and commentary upon an identifiable tendency in Russian society and literature born of class divisions and the institution of serfdom. He praises the disinterested objectivity of its author, whose realism, the 'ability to convey the complete image of an object', makes it possible for him to write about his indolent and apathetic hero in such a way as to hold the reader's attention, despite the fact that the novel contains 'hardly any action'. Goncharov, in Dobrolyubov's view, attributes his hero's indolence to the privileged position of the hereditary landowner, accustomed all his life to be waited on hand and foot and to have all his needs supplied. Russian society is full of such 'overgrown children' as Oblomov, with 'chaos reigning in their heads'. Dobrolyubov demonstrates how the natural impulses of the hero were thwarted by his mother, that he was not by nature a 'dull, apathetic type' but was spoilt by over-indulgence; and this in turn is held responsible for Oblomov's failure to see 'the meaning in life in general' (the logic and psychology of this argument are questionable).

Dobrolyubov thus connects Oblomov with other representatives of a type known to Russian critics as 'superfluous men': characters from Pushkin's* Onegin to Turgenev's* Bazarov and beyond, who symbolize the failure of Russian society to provide a place for men of original intellect and imagination. It is the great achievement of Goncharov, on this view of his work, to have shown in his true colours the figure whom previous writers had tended to romanticize, since Oblomov's apathy is a 'realistic' variant of the 'romantic' cynicism and destructiveness of earlier 'superfluous men'. An interesting component of the thesis is Dobrolyubov's comment on Oblomov's attitude to women: he expects them to be 'dolls' and recoils from women who demand that he should 'respect their rights': the weak/strong woman syndrome is compared to the work of Turgenev (whom Goncharov was to accuse, quite irrationally, of stealing his ideas). But the 'positive' figure of Stolz, the active and efficient counterpart of Oblomov's inertia, is rightly censured by Dobrolyubov as shadowy, an inadequate representative of the 'simplicity and clarity of thought' that will characterize the 'new life'.

Influential as this analysis of *Oblomov* may have been, it fails to account for Goncharov's humour, his irrationalism, and his obsession with certain recurrent metaphors and symbols. These three elements are present already in his first novel, *The Same Old Story* (*Obyknovennaya Istoria*, 1847, trans. 1975), which opens with the hero Aduyev fast asleep. Its plot concerns his departure from the country for St Petersburg to pursue a bureaucratic career of the type Oblomov swiftly abandoned as overtaxing. Aduyev's mother tries to

prevent him leaving, pointing out to him the beauty and bounty of the surrounding fields, thus foreshadowing the less sentimental and psychologically more complex evocation of regressive drives in *Oblomov*. Beyond the realistic treatment of the social milieu we recognize (as the title indicates) an archetypal drama of son and mother. This drama is intrinsic to the 'sociological' concerns of Goncharov's work, especially in so far as he contrasts the abstract activity ('male') of St Petersburg with the organic intimacy ('female') of rural life within which intricate networks of cause and effect link even the most disparate and arbitrary incidents. It is true that Goncharov evokes rural life without nostalgia; but at the same time there is an immense, indeed pathological, sense of loss at the severance of the hero from this 'matrix' of life. The experience of the womb-like estate as both freedom and constraint is at the root of the incongruities of Goncharov's world, especially the comic contrast of stasis and mechanical gesture in *Oblomov*. Aduyev's uncle converts the hero from youthful romanticism to hard-headed realism: but it is significant that this same uncle should experience a spiritual crisis late in life. Goncharov's social theme is thus related always to the inner life of feeling and imagination.

Aduyev's love for Nadya is undermined by jealousy of his rival, the Count: and this is a conventional plot. But his fear of losing Nadya is outweighed by his fear of winning her: and this confirms the point made by Dobrolyubov. The hero of each of Goncharov's novels experiences a kind of emotional devastation in the presence of the woman to whom he is attracted, and the author, who suffered himself from a similar kind of depression, explores this state of mind with exceptional insight, throwing new light on the misogyny of the 'superfluous man'. When, in *Oblomov*, the hero surrenders Olga to Stolz, he turns for consolation to Pshenitsyna, the earth-mother figure in whose name can be discerned the Russian word for 'wheat'. This catastrophic return to the mother, ending in death, is marked by the recurrence of the ambivalent symbol of the ravine which was only a hundred yards from the parental home, which allured the young Oblomov but was associated with guilt and punishment. Stolz, the Germanic super-ego who embodies a deep-seated Russian anxiety, has the will to steer Olga through the 'ravines' of life's depressions: but his clear-sightedness is seen as a poor thing by comparison with the enchanted narcissism of Oblomov's poetic inertia. Dobrolyubov was right to call Oblomov an 'overgrown child', but was seemingly unaware of the meaning of the games that he and Zakhar play.

The Precipice (*Obryv*, 1869, trans. 1915) again introduces a 'superfluous' hero, Rayski, and a forceful anti-hero, the nihilist Volokhov, who gets the girl (Vera) who then leaves him for the Stolz-like Tushin. The 'Precipice' of the title, though not the same word in Russian as Oblomov's 'ravine', has a similar symbolic function as a correlative of the hero's impotence and the imputed immorality and destructiveness of women.

Goncharov died in 1891 after an uneventful life spent in the Civil Service and Censor's Office. His visit to Japan and voyage around the world in 1852–5, though the subject of a book *The Frigate Pallas*, (*Fregat Pallada*, 1856), seem to have had little permanent effect on a personality shaped once and for all by the early milieu of prosperous merchant and landowner from the Volga city of Simbirsk.

G.M. Hyde

Critical studies of Goncharov include: Janko Lavrin, *Goncharov* (1954); Helen Rapp, 'The Art of Ivan Goncharov', in *The Slavonic and East European Review*, vol. XXXVI (June 1958); and A. and S. Lyngstad, *Ivan Goncharov* (1971).

193
GONCOURT, de, Edmond 1822–96
and Jules 1830–70

French essayists, novelists and diarists

Although Edmond was older by eight years and outlived Jules by twenty-six, the Goncourt brothers are, like the Rosny and Tharaud brothers, always thought and spoken of in terms of an inseparable pair. Financially independent they were able to devote their lives to a study of social history (especially that of the eighteenth century), art and literature, and they built up an interesting and impressive collection of *objets d'art*. From the early 1860s they organized the *dîners* Magny at a Parisian restaurant over which Sainte-Beuve* presided and which were attended by many of the leading writers and artists of the period. After his brother's death Edmond continued this tradition with the regular Sunday meetings in the Grenier des Goncourts at Auteuil, a kind of literary salon frequented by, amongst others, Flaubert*, Taine*, Gautier* and the Russian writer Turgenev*. In his will Edmond left money for the foundation of the Goncourt Academy (in some ways rival to the French Academy) and from 1903 an annual prize (the Prix Goncourt) was (and continues to be) awarded in the autumn for the best imaginative prose work – preferably a novel – to have been published during the previous year. (Although the prize itself is today worth only the equivalent of a few pounds, the award guarantees huge sales.)

In spite of such apparently sociable activities as these the brothers were, according to many of their contemporaries, strange, sensitive men. They believed themselves to be misunderstood, despised and persecuted. Afraid of women, neither of them married. They were,

however, far from sexless and Jules contracted syphilis at the age of nineteen from which he eventually went insane and died.

The Goncourt's work can usefully be divided into three categories: social-historical studies, novels, and above all diaries. They shared a passion for the eighteenth century and did much to rescue from near oblivion painters such as Boucher, Fragonard, Chardin and especially Watteau in their monumental study *French XVIII Century Painters*, (*L'Art du dix-huitième siècle*, 1859–75, trans. 1948). They also wrote with sensitivity about Japanese art of the same period in works like *Outamuro* (1891) and *Hokusai* (1896). Of a more conventional social-historical nature were their studies of women, love and social customs: for example *The Woman of the Eighteenth Century*, (*La femme au dix-huitième siècle à la société, l'amour et le ménage*, 1882, trans. 1928) and *Portraits intimes du XVIIIᵉ siècle* ('Intimate Portraits of the eighteenth century', 1862). In those works they relied heavily on detail and trivial information to convey a degree of authenticity. This same approach is apparent in the novels as well. These, they believed, should be constructed from real events in the same way as historical studies are elaborated from documents (diary entry, 24 October 1864). They spent much of their time, therefore, in the collecting of factual evidence and in the observation of people close to them. Thus, for example, their best known novel, *Germinie* (*Germinie Lacerteux*, 1864, trans. 1955), is based on their servant Rose Malingre whose secret life of debauchery and squalor they accidentally discovered; *Sister Philomene*, (*Sœur Philomène*, 1861, trans. 1921) on hospital conditions and life of a Rouen nurse; *Madame Gervaisais* (1865) on one of their aunts; *Renée Mauperin* (1864, trans. 1888) partly on their father. In their novel writing they belonged to those generally grouped together and known as Naturalists. The style of their novels, however, is often distinctly their own and is similar to that found in their works on painting – often excessively descriptive, episodic and sometimes impressionistic. A concern for language resulted in what became known as their *écriture artiste* (artistic writing), in which neologisms, rare words and contorted syntax all too often obscure the general development of the intrigue. (This style was later parodied by Proust in the final volume of *À la recherche du temps perdu*.) After Jules's death Edmond produced several novels in much the same mould of which the most notable are *La fille Elisa* (1877), based on the life of a prostitute imprisoned for murder, and *The Zemganno Brothers* (*Les Frères Zemganno*, 1879, trans.1886), an interesting study of the close relationship between two circus performers.

Of particular interest, however, is their diary, serialized in the *Echo de Paris* and published in volume form from 1887 until Edmond's death. Subtitled 'Mémoires de la vie littéraire' and described by them as a 'documentary novel', it is a social record of considerable value. Their mania for thoroughness and accuracy caused difficulties, however, and a good deal of material had to be withheld. As Edmond remarked, it would not be possible to have the absolute truth about certain things and people revealed until twenty years after his death. Even so in its truncated form the diary still produced some bitterness and anger on the part of some (the Daudet* family, for example) who felt that they and their friendship with the brothers were being betrayed. The diaries were not to be published in their entirety until 1956.

In spite of their prolific output and general role as animators the Goncourt brothers never really enjoyed the influence of many of their contemporaries. As novelists they are today largely forgotten though they were highly regarded by Sainte-Beuve and by Zola* and their claim made in the preface of *Germinie* to have been the first to write seriously and realistically about the working class does have some justification. It is, however, as observers of society that they are of particular value and no student of late nineteenth-century France can afford to ignore their diaries.

J.E. Flower

Other works: novels: *En 18--* (1851); *Charles Demailly* (1860); *Manette Salomon* (1867); *La Faustin* (1882); *Chérie* (1884); essays: *Histoire de la société française pendant la Révolution* (1854); *Les Maîtresses de Louis XV* (1860); *L'Italie d'hier: Notes de voyage 1855–1856* (1894); plays: *Henriette Maréchal* (1865); *Germinie* (1888); *La Patrie en danger* (1873). The best edition of the diaries is by R. Ricatte (4 vols, 1956). In English: *Pages from the Goncourt Journal*, trans. Robert Baldick (1962). See: P. Sabatier, *L'esthétique des Goncourt* (1920); G. Rovon, *Les Frères Goncourt* (1953); R. Ricatte, *La Création romanesque chez les Goncourt* (1953); A. Billy, *Les Frères Goncourt* (1954); J.-P. Richard, *Littérature et Sensation* (1954); R. Baldick, *The Goncourts* (1960); E. Caramaschi, *Réalisme et impressionisme dans l'œuvre des frères Goncourt* (1971).

194
GOSSE, Edmund William 1849–1928

British writer

The future Sir Edmund was the only child of Philip Henry Gosse*, and the conflicts and confinements of his childhood are unforgettably described in the autobiographical masterpiece *Father and Son* (1907). Until he left home at seventeen to take up his first job, in the cataloguing section of the British Museum, the son's reading of secular poetry and literature had been only spasmodic and surreptitious. From then on it became wide and thorough, both in English and in the several western European languages of which he became mas-

ter. In 1871 in the course of a trip to the Lofoten Islands Gosse happened to pick up a volume of Ibsen* in a Trondheim bookstore. Teaching himself Norwegian as he went he proceeded to publish the first English translations (1891 and 1892) of both *Hedda Gabler* and *The Master Builder*. In 1875 he left the British Museum to work as a translator in the Board of Trade. Further publications followed: among others an edition of Gray and lives of Swinburne*, Thomas Browne, Ibsen, Congreve and his own zoologist father P.H. Gosse. In 1884–5 there was a lecture tour in the USA. This resulted in his being offered, and refusing, the Chair of English Literature at Harvard. In 1904 he was made Librarian to the House of Lords. Continuing to produce a mass of short occasional literary criticism and literary biography he died in 1928, heavy with years and with honours. These honours included the French Legion of Honour, the Order of the Polar Star from Sweden, and the Order of St Olaf of Norway. Gosse's portrait by J.S. Sargent* hangs in the National Portrait Gallery.

The real claims of Sir Edmund Gosse to space in the present volume are: that he introduced Ibsen to the wider English-speaking world; and that in *Father and Son* he produced the most haunting representation of a type of generational conflict most typical of its century.

Antony Flew

See: *Gide and Edmund Gosse: Correspondence 1904–1928* ed. L.F. Brugmans (1959); *Transatlantic Dialogue: Selected American Correspondence of Edmund Gosse* ed. P.F. Mathiesen and M. Millgate (1965). See also: E. Charteris, *The Life and Letters of Sir Edmund Gosse* (1931).

195
GOSSE, Philip Henry 1810–88

British naturalist

Just as his only child Edmund Gosse* is chiefly read and remembered as the author of *Father and Son* (1907), so the father is now seen only through the eyes of the son. The single achievement ever recalled by any non-specialist is the book *Omphalos* (1857); perennially mentioned in footnotes to the history of ideas although never, it seems, actually read. Yet both father and son were, each in his own right, makers of nineteenth-century culture.

Philip Gosse was humbly born – his father was a talented miniaturist whose writings were not bought. At seventeen the young man took off for Newfoundland, where an undemanding office job allowed him to begin his true life's work as a natural historian. After an unsuccessful interlude farming in (mainland) Canada (1835–8) he was in 1840 able to sell his first book, *A Canadian Naturalist*, for a good sum, and returned to England. He established a small private school near London, managing to produce his *Introduction to Zoology* in 1843. The British Museum then sent him on a mission to Jamaica (1844–6). In 1848 he married Emily Bowes, a writer of widely used devotional manuals. In the following year she produced Edmund. In 1852 the father undertook a study of the *Antiquities of Assyria* for the Society for the Propagation of Christ's Kingdom, and in the same year retired to south Devon.

However, nervous dyspepsia notwithstanding, he continued to work with almost obsessional energy. 1854 saw the publication of the most popular of all his books, *The Aquarium*. He was here the first to show people how they could preserve marine creatures alive in their own homes. So, in large numbers, they did. In 1855–6 a two-volume *Manual of Marine Zoology* appeared, and in the second of these years he was elected a Fellow of the Royal Society. His first wife died in 1857, but he married again in 1860. In 1858–60 he published *Actinologia Britannica*, the standard work on sea anemones.

The story of his life is typical of Victorian England at its best: someone self-taught rises from modest beginnings to considerable scientific achievement and distinction; with these labours supported almost entirely from the sales of writings bought mainly by individuals, striving to improve themselves through an instructive hobby. But the father was also a Plymouth Brother: a member, that is, of an extreme fundamentalist sect, accepting 'the precious book from cover to cover', and always in the most literal reading.

Omphalos is the Greek for navel, and refers to ancient discussions of whether Adam could have been created bearing all the physiological signs of a past which, by the hypothesis, he had not had. The author of *Omphalos* drew on a far wider biological and geological knowledge to show how the doctrine of Special Creation, upon which he still insisted as revealed truth, must generate innumerable further paradoxes of the same kind. A stratum of sedimentary rock, for instance, would presumably have to be specially created to include fossils of organisms which had never lived. *Omphalos* has been almost universally ridiculed both in its own time and since. Of course its position is incredible and preposterous. Nevertheless the great mass of contemporaries, who themselves accepted Special Creation – Darwin's* *The Origin of Species* came out only in 1859 – had no right to smirk and jeer. Philip Gosse was honourably honest and forthright in seeing, stating, and accepting implications which his inferiors preferred to evade or ignore.

Antony Flew

196
GOUNOD, Charles (François) 1818–93

French composer

Gounod believed France to be 'essentially the country of precision, neatness and taste; that is to say, the opposite of excess, pretentiousness, disproportion, longwindedness'. Whether 'precision, neatness and taste' can be accepted as a general description of Gounod's output as a composer is debatable. He certainly had remarkable gifts as a melodist, and a sure instinct for producing what was effective. His instrumental writing was resourceful, and he knew how to explore the capabilities of the human voice. The particular kind of religious feeling expressed in much of his work led to a harmonic style which has often been described as cloying, but which (together with excellent craftsmanship) had a powerful influence in many other countries besides France. And at times the influence amounted to a reaction *against* the characteristic Gounod style.

Gounod's family background was artistic: his father was a distinguished painter and his mother a fine pianist. From his mother he had his first lessons in music. He entered the Paris Conservatoire when he was eighteen, displayed immense promise, and after three years was awarded the important Prix de Rome. Unlike Berlioz*, a previous recipient of this prize, Gounod responded in a positive way to the atmosphere of Rome, and during his period of study there he became immersed in sixteenth-century polyphonic church music – that of Palestrina in particular. As a result of this, his first composition of note was a three-part Mass, with orchestra, performed in Rome in 1841. There were other important formative influences during this Rome period: he met Mendelssohn's* sister, Fanny, who introduced him to the poetry of Goethe* (in translation), and to music of Bach, Beethoven*, and of her brother; he met the versatile singer Pauline Garcia, and was impressed by the scope of her work. And on the religious side he came into contact with the Dominican Père Lacordaire, to whose teaching he at once felt a warm response. After Rome, Gounod went to Vienna, Berlin, and Leipzig, where he met Mendelssohn and heard him play the organ. He returned to Paris with a good knowledge of the important international musical styles of the time. But at first, religion was clearly paramount, and besides becoming organist and choirmaster of the Église des Missions Étrangères Gounod devoted himself to the study of theology with the object of becoming a priest. This course, however, was finally abandoned, after several years during which he had neglected composition. From 1850 he was drawn to the worldly ambition of becoming a successful opera-composer rather than a composer of Masses. At the start, under the influence of Meyerbeer*, his operas were not successful. Then, by turning from the Paris Opéra to the Théâtre-Lyrique, and finding a lyrical, unpretentious style which was nearer to his true nature, he achieved his ambition – especially in *Faust* (1859). His librettists, Jules Barbier and Michel Carré, had devised a superficial and popularized version of Goethe's great drama, which with a sprinkling of religiosity, was well suited to the tastes of his audiences. The work has endured as one of the most universally successful of all operas. Some of the operas that followed – notably *Mireille* (1864) and *Roméo et Juliette* (1876), after Shakespeare – enjoyed a good deal of acclaim in their day, but he was never able to repeat the kind of success achieved by *Faust*.

For five years, from 1870, Gounod lived in England, and made himself very much at home there. *Faust* was Queen Victoria's* favourite opera; but it was the sacred music of Gounod which really achieved popularity in Britain – especially the oratorios *La Rédemption* (1882) and *Mors et Vita* (1885), both of which had their first performance at the Birmingham Festival. Gounod became so much a part of the English choral tradition that he even founded his own choir, which became later the Royal Choral Society. He wrote several more Masses (including the famous *Messe à Sainte-Cécile*), a Te Deum, various motets, and some songs of a rather maudlin religiosity. One of the most famous of these was the *Ave Maria*, a melody superimposed upon Bach's first Prelude, in C, of the *Forty-Eight*.

Today, besides the composer of the ever-popular *Faust*, Gounod is remembered for some of his finest songs, such as the 'Sérénade', 'Le Premier Jour de Mai', 'L'Absent' – which combine melodic freshness, gracious simplicity, and many felicitous personal harmonic touches. Some of his earlier instrumental writing still lives – for example, the *Petite Symphonie* for wind instruments (1855). In such music we do indeed come near to that 'precision, neatness and taste' which Gounod considered to be characteristic of French art.

David Cox

See: the composer's autobiographical *Mémoirs d'un Artiste* (1895); various collections of letters; Norman Demuth, *Introduction to the Music of Charles Gounod* (1950); biographies by J.-J. Debillemont (1864), H. Busser (1961), J. Harding (1973).

197

GRIEG, Edvard (Hagerup) 1843–1907

Norwegian composer and pianist

From the middle of the nineteenth century, many composers from different parts of Europe, who had come under strong Austrian and German musical influences, sought to express individuality by incorporating in their compositions melodic and rhythmic elements from their native folksongs and dances: Smetana* and Dvořák* in Bohemia; Rimsky-Korsakov* and others in Russia, Vaughan Williams in England; Bartók and Kodály in Hungary; and none more clearly and strikingly than Grieg in Norway.

Grieg was not a major talent; the emotional and expressive range in his music is limited. He did not have the ability of a Smetana or a Dvořák to build up powerful dramatic musical structures. The feeling of development, of organic growth, in his music is restricted. He wrote no symphonies. The movements of a large-scale work such as the Piano Concerto are episodic rather than symphonic in style. At the same time his essentially small-scale constructions often display great originality, and elements of his technique were used and developed in many ways by composers who followed him. For example, his use of harmony, his highly characteristic chord sequences, without which (for example) the work of Delius and even Debussy undoubtedly would have been different. 'The realm of harmonies was always my dream-world,' Grieg once said; 'and the relationship between my harmonic sensibility and Norwegian folk-music was a mystery even to myself.' Sometimes the titles of pieces – *Norwegian Bridal Procession* or *Norwegian Peasant March* – convey explicitly the music's character. At other times – as in the chamber music – the influence of his national heritage is more subtle, permeating the more classically constructed musical textures. The romanticism of Schumann* and Chopin* was an important influence for Grieg. His treatment of folk-material owed much to the clear-cut musical textures of, for example, Chopin's mazurkas. In his early years he came, also, under the inevitable influence of Wagner*. He attended the *Ring* cycle at Bayreuth in 1876 – an experience which made him long for a similar national theme and the establishment of a Norwegian national opera. But this remained an unrealized dream.

Grieg's mother, whose maiden name was Hagerup (the composer's middle name), was an accomplished pianist. It was she who gave him his first piano lessons when he was six years old. Encouraged by the Norwegian violinist and composer Ole Bull, he later went to Leipzig, where his teachers included Ignaz Moscheles. Grieg became famous as a pianist – as soloist in his Piano Concerto and numerous piano works; but particularly as an accompanist, which temperamentally he found more congenial. His wife, Nina, was a gifted singer, and their musical partnership was a very special one. Grieg's 149 songs are a vitally important part of his output. He had a remarkable gift for being able to catch precisely the atmosphere of the poems he set – amorous, pastoral, or dramatic – enhancing them by simple lyrical and harmonic means, guided by a sure musical instinct.

In 1869 Grieg received a letter from Liszt*, con-

gratulating him on his Violin Sonata, op. 8, and inviting him to Weimar. But it was not until the following
year that the meeting took place – in Rome. This was
an important occasion for Grieg. Liszt's enthusiasm
gave the young composer (by nature somewhat reticent) a feeling of confidence and purpose. By 1874
Grieg was able to give up the irksome tasks of teaching,
and devote his time to writing music, because he had
been awarded a special state pension.

Grieg's association with Ibsen* led to a collaboration
which for the composer was particularly rewarding,
both artistically and financially. The playwright asked
Grieg to write incidental music for *Peer Gynt*. The result
is Grieg's most widely enjoyed music – though the two
orchestral suites heard in the concert hall represent
only eight of the twenty-three musical pieces in the
play. Likewise, his association with another writer,
Bjornson*, led to music for *Sigurd Jorsalfar* and a work
for reciter and orchestra, *Bergliot*.

Grieg's instrumental music also included Norwegian
Dances for orchestra, and the *Holberg* Suite for strings
– an essay in Neoclassicism several decades before
Stravinsky started to explore this style of composition.
The chamber-music works of Grieg were not numerous, but they form one of the most satisfactory sides of
his output: three violin sonatas, a cello sonata, and two
string quartets (one of them unfinished). What gives
them strength and permanence in the chamber-music
repertoire is primarily their melodic and rhythmic variety; but there is also in these works a formal cohesion
and purposeful musical development which is less evident in his other music.

David Cox

An immense amount has been written about the
composer in many different languages (see the *New
Grove's Dictionary*, 1980). Biographies: Henry T. Fink,
Grieg and His Music (1929); David Monrad-Johansen,
Edward Grieg (1938); John Horton, *Grieg* (1974);
Gerald Abraham, *Grieg – a Symposium* (1948).

198
GRILLPARZER, Franz 1791–1872

Austrian dramatist

Born in the year of Mozart's death, Grillparzer, apart
from occasional journeys abroad, spent his entire life
in Vienna, his work being nourished on the rich theatrical traditions of that city. He studied law and his
early professional appointments were tutorships in jurisprudence; for over twenty years (1832–56) he was in
the Austrian Civil Service, working as a court archivist.
But such employment was essentially ancillary to his
literary and dramatic work. The enormous success of
his early plays, *Die Ahnfrau* ('The Ancestress', 1816)

and *Sappho* (1817), led to his appointment as *Theater-
dichter* at the famous Burgtheater, where a number of
his other plays were first performed. But the failure of
his only comedy, *Weh' dem, der lügt* (literally 'Woe to
him who tells lies') in 1837, caused him to withhold
his subsequent dramatic work from the public. His last
three plays were published posthumously.

There is no necessary correlation between a melancholic temperament and a predilection for tragedy: but
in Grillparzer's case a lifelong tendency to depression
and self-doubt (which were partly hereditary – both
his mother and one of his three brothers committed
suicide) are clearly linked to a profound pessimism
concerning the human condition as a whole. Not surprisingly, then, his plays dwell frequently on those
traditional preoccupations of the tragedian, *hubris* and
vanitas; are sceptical about the value of ambition in the
individual and notions of progress in mankind as a
whole; and are not, when such topics are in question,
without a certain moralizing element. Also evident,
particularly in his earlier plays, is a tendency to see
and present life in terms of antitheses: contemplation
and action, Spirit and Life, etc. In *Sappho*, for instance,
the great poetess, laurel-crowned and dedicated to the
gods, finds that human love, at first a source of solace,
shatters her creative existence; *King Ottokar, his Rise and
Fall* (*König Ottokars Glück und Ende*, 1822–3, trans.
1962) presents two opposing ideals of kingship: for the
protagonist, Ottokar, the ruling power is an extension
and projection of his own egoism; for his rival and
eventual conqueror, Rudolf I of Habsburg, it involves
the subjugation of selfhood to an ideal of service.

But the oppositions in Grillparzer's work are seldom
quite so clear-cut: for Grillparzer was as much a psychologist as a moralist, acutely aware of the power of
human emotions, in mutability or inconsistency, to
blur distinctions. Hence, in the trilogy *The Golden Fleece*
(*Das Goldene Vliess*, 1818–20), which is concerned with
Jason's capture of the fleece from the island of Colchis
and his relationship with the Colchian princess and
sorceress, Medea, the opposition between civilization
(Greece) and barbarism (Colchis) is combined with a
more psychologically differentiating element: the study
of the developing love-hate relationship between the
mutually incompatible protagonists. Medea, first seen
as a headstrong young girl, is emotionally drawn into
happy union with the ruthless Jason; returning with
him after several years to Greece, and now mother of
two sons, she is driven, by a combination of marital
unhappiness and gradual social ostracism, to revert to
barbarism in acts of manic savagery. The psychological
development is impressively charted; the structure of
the trilogy, however, is somewhat cumbersome, suggesting a slightly uneasy relationship between psychological treatment and mythological material. But in
Hero and Leander (*Des Meeres und der Liebe Wellen*, literally
'The waves of the sea and of love', 1827–31, trans.

1962) psychology is more happily united to myth. The young Hero, having withdrawn from the world to consecrate herself to the service of Aphrodite, comes to realize, when the impetuous Leander enters her life, that she has withdrawn too soon, not because of any real dedication, but because of her ignorance of life's full potentialities. Her uncle and mentor, the priest, attempting to guard her purity, takes measures which result in the death of both lovers. But the priest, lacking though he be in ordinary compassion, yet acts in defence of values which seem to him unassailable: and thus the tragedy as a whole, so far from being reducible to a simple conflict between love and duty, is an example of that tendency towards moral relativization which becomes increasingly evident in Grillparzer's later work.

It is seen, for example, in his most famous nondramatic work, the novella *The Poor Musician* (*Der arme Spielmann*, 1848), a subtle and poignant study of the ambiguous nature of worldly failure (and, by implication, success). And the last three plays might roughly be described as studies in the complexity of human motive. *Libussa*, (1872) a play which moves in the atmosphere of legend, is concerned with the events leading up to the founding of Prague at the point where the contemplative queen, Libussa, cedes the ruling power to her beloved Primislaus, the man of action and believer in progress: or, to put it in a more abstract form, the point where myth gives place to history. *The Jewess of Toledo* (*Die Jüdin von Toledo*, 1872 trans. 1953) is a delicate study of the consequences of sexual attraction. King Alfonso VIII of Spain is diverted from monarchic responsibility by the kittenish charms of the Jewish girl, Rahel; Rahel, on the orders of the puritanical and censorious queen, is murdered. The king mourns a while, then forgets; is cursed by Rahel's sister, Esther, who, when she observes that her father's greed exceeds his grief, revokes her curse to end the play on a note of ironic and weary forgiveness.

The protagonist of Grillparzer's last and perhaps greatest play, *Family Strife in Habsburg* (*Ein Bruderzwist in Habsburg*, 1872 trans. 1940), is the Emperor Rudolf II, uneasily placed at the confluence of tendencies and events which will result, in the play's closing scenes, in the outbreak of the Thirty Year's War. A contemplative, more aware of the broad movements of history than of its immediate occasions, a devout Catholic with a respectful sympathy for the integrity of Protestant belief, by turns crusty, compassionate, unyielding and incautious, Rudolf is by far Grillparzer's most complex figure. The 'family strife' of the title arises from a plot by some of Rudolf's relatives to end a foreign war which, in the emperor's view, will stem internal dissension. In the end, and after his death, Rudolf is proved to have been right; and his brother, the ambitious but irresolute Mathias, one of the leading figures in the conspiracy, finds that his aims are indeed realized: yet, as he ascends the throne, the country collapses into the horrors of civil war.

Recurrently in Grillparzer's work, the protagonists are ejected from a state of primal goodness or innocence into a world of moral and emotional confusion (*Verwirrung*, together with cognate forms, is a key term, especially in the later work). Almost all of his plays are therefore implicitly variations on the theme of the Fall. Insight is gradually and painfully attained, and it is usually a pessimistic insight. The most positive value in Grillparzer's world tends to be a quality which he calls *Sammlung* (literally 'collectedness' or 'composure'), a quality which is difficult to define briefly, but which amounts to a kind of spiritual integrity, a gathering of the human faculties around a firm moral centre. A tendency towards quietism is often involved, but it must be emphasized that quietism in Grillparzer is not simply a state of negative withdrawal; like its opposite, ruthless ambition, withdrawal too is at times presented as morally problematic.

Grillparzer's scepticism and the political conservatism which accompanied it (in his younger years he had frequently been in conflict with the Metternich regime, but viewed the 1848 uprisings with disfavour; in his later plays both Libussa and Rudolf II are given speeches in which they grimly foresee the degeneration of mankind into a shallow egalitarianism) may not appeal to all readers: but the perpetration of overt 'messages' is a relatively minor part of this writer's endeavour. What matters far more is his sense – his realized *dramatic* sense – of the complexity, the confusion, at times the sheer muddle of life as it is actually lived and the sympathetic understanding with which his finest depictions of this are imbued.

Corbet Stewart

Other plays: *The Faithful Servant of his Master* (*Ein treuer Diener seines Herrn*, 1826 trans. 1941); *Life's a Dream* (*Der Traum ein Leben*, 1831, roughly based on Lope de Vega's *La vida es sueño*). Translations are by Arthur Burkhard. *Medea*, the final part of the *Golden Fleece* trilogy, has been translated by F.J. Lamport in *Five German Tragedies* (1969). See: Walter Naumann, *Franz Grillparzer: das dichteriche Werk* (1964); W.E. Yates, *Grillparzer: A Critical Introduction* (1972).

199
GRIMM, Jacob Ludwig Carl 1785–1863
GRIMM, Wilhelm Carl 1786–1859

German philologists and folklorists

Born in Hanau, the brothers were the first and second surviving sons of the lawyer Philipp Wilhelm Grimm. Inseparable from earliest childhood, they were sent away to school together at Cassel, and on their father's death studied law together at the University of Marburg, Jacob under the great conservative jurist Savigny. Already as students they were caught up in the high tide of the second generation of Romantics. Part of the Romantic response to the Napoleonic invasions had been to discover and affirm a German national literature and a German national identity. Savigny's view of law as the product of national custom and as the expression of a national culture was readily transferable to folk poetry and folk tales, as Herder had first perceived. The brothers became the friends of Achim von Arnim and Clemens Brentano, poets and compilers of the great German folksong collection *Des Knaben Wunderhorn* (1805–8), and contributed to their journal *Zeitung für Einsiedler*. One early essay of Jacob's, 'Gedanken, wie sich die Sagen zur Poesie verhalten' ('Thoughts on the relationship of legends to poetry'), appeared there, making the seminal distinction between 'art-poetry' and 'folk-poetry'. The romantic quest for the natural 'folk' origins of language and literature was to be one driving force of their long life's work of scholarship; the other was their sense of the unity of German national culture.

As young men they entered the service of the Elector of Hesse as librarians at Cassel, and continued in the office when Napoleon* invaded and made his brother Jérome King of Westphalia. They made their earliest editions and collections at this time: Jacob's *Über den altdeutschen Meistergesang* ('On the ancient German Master-song') and Wilhelm's translation of Danish heroic lays and ballads in 1811; in 1812 and 1815 their famous shared collection of fairy tales *Kinder- und Hausmärchen*, which has gone round the world. The first English edition, illustrated by George Cruikshank*, came out as early as 1823–6. They listened to the tales from the old peasants of Hesse – one Dorothea Viehmann in particular – and got their friends to do the same. They took them down with minimal editorial rewriting, but the later expanded editions, Wilhelm's work, show signs of marked literary working-over. Those years of romantic antiquarianism also produced their collection of German legends (*Deutsche Sagen*, 1816–18), a pioneering edition of the eighth-century Old High German poems *Das Hildebrandslied* and the *Wessobrunner Gebet* (1812), an edition of the twelfth century epic by Hartman von Aue, *Der arme Heinrich*, and their own journal *Altdeutsche Wälder* (1813–16).

The story of their lives is largely the story of their scholarship, its most remarkable external events themselves epitomizing the crises and recoveries of liberal intellectuals in Restoration Germany. The cultural nationalism of the young conservative Romantics modulated without disharmony into the anti-aristocratic liberal nationalism of the men of 1848. After Napoleon's defeat, they returned to the service of the restored Elector of Hesse, Wilhelm still as librarian, but in 1815 Jacob was sent on diplomatic missions to Paris and to the Congress of Vienna. He did not omit to visit the libraries either. But 1815 was as important for their work as it was to the restored princelings, for it was then that A.W. Schlegel* published his attack on their *Altdeutsche Wälder* for cloudy conceptualization and amateurish historical speculation when what was most urgently needed for lucid and accurate literature and language studies was an exact historical grammar.

This marked the turning-point from dilettante collecting to scholarly discipline. Jacob took up the challenge. While Wilhelm, always the more 'literary' of the brothers continued with his editions of ancient poetry (*Grâve Ruodolf*, 1828; *Vrîdankes Bescheidenheit*, 1834; *Der Rosengarten*, 1836; *Ruolands liet*, 1838; *Konrad von Würzburg*, 1840 and 1841), Jacob turned almost wholly to philology. Building on earlier work by Rasmus Rask and Franz Bopp he produced his major achievement, his historical *Deutsche Grammatik* ('German Grammar,' 1819–37). He did not give up his collecting – of German legal monuments (*Deutsche Rechtsaltertümer*, 1828) and German mythology (*Deutsche Mythologie*, 1835) and his collector's habit of mind served him well in the Grammar. It was the patient accumulation of detailed instances rather than new theorizing that led him to formulate the law which bears his name of the regularity of consonantal shifts in the historical stages of the German language, and of consonantal correspondence in all the Germanic languages.

Passed over for promotion in Cassel by an unappreciative and contemptuous prince, they accomplished much of this work at the University of Göttingen, in Hanover, where in 1830 Wilhelm had been appointed librarian and Jacob professor. But the whims of petty rulers were to follow them there. Under pressure after the revolutions of 1830, William IV, King of Great Britain and Elector of Hanover, had granted a limited constitution. His death in 1837 brought the young Victoria* to the English throne, and her wicked uncle Ernst August to Hanover. Arbitrary and brutal, with little sense of the liberal nationalism emerging in Germany, he was not long in abrogating the constitution. The Grimms, mindful of their oath to it, and of their responsibility to their students, signed a protest, in company with the other five of the 'Göttingen Seven': the historian Dahlmann, the jurist Albrecht, the literary historian Gervinus, the physicist Weber and the orientalist Ewald. But despite strong support from liberal circles elsewhere in Germany, the Elector of Hanover promptly dismissed them from their posts and banished them. 'Professors, actors and whores are always to be had' was his comment. Jacob's account of the episode, 'Über meine Entlassung' ('On my dismissal', 1838) is a noble exposition of the values of a scholar on the one hand devoted to making known the past, but on the other fully aware of the political demands of his own day.

In the wilderness, Jacob conceived the huge collaborative project that was to occupy them both for the rest of their lives: the great historical dictionary that bears their name. Rescued in 1840 by appointments to the Academy of Sciences and the University of Berlin by the new Prussian King Wilhelm IV, who was, as it turned out, more fond of the liberal gesture than of liberal politics, the brothers settled down to research and teaching, becoming virtually the founders of the new study of German language, literature, history and institutions known as *Germanistik*. Jacob presided at the first big professional meetings at Frankfurt in 1846 and at Lübeck in 1847. In 1848, with many of his academic colleagues, including Gervinus and Dahlmann, he was back in Frankfurt at another gathering: with the outbreak of the March Revolution, he had been elected a member of the new liberal parliament. After the failure of the revolution's attempt at extending political liberties and unifying the fragmented German states, Jacob returned in disappointment to the privacy of his study and the comfort of Wilhelm's family, and to the public activity of teaching. The dictionary consumed their days and nights. Part of the impetus behind it now was to build a philological monument to a German unity that was a linguistic, but not a political, reality. 'What else do we have in common but our language and literature?' he queries sadly in the preface to the first volume (1854). Jacob saw the first three volumes published (1860, 1862), but the mighty work outlived them both. Wilhelm, who had suffered intermittently from ill-health all his life, was the first to die, in 1859. They had lived together under the same roof all their lives, even after Wilhelm's marriage. Jacob outlived him by four years, driven by the dictionary. He was working on the article on the word *Frucht* when he died. The work was continued by teams of philologists for another century, and the collaboration of scholars from East and West Germany brought it to an end in 1961.

Between them, with Jacob as the main driving force, they founded the study of *Germanistik*, established Germanic philology as an academic discipline, pioneered editorial techniques, and on the brink of the industrial century rescued the material of rural folklore. Convinced of the unity of language and literature, and of the primacy of both in a national culture, they were characterized by a dedication, a scrupulousness, a liberality and a sweetness which have left fitting monuments in Grimm's law, Grimm's *Dictionary*, and Grimm's *Fairy Tales*, and in the memory of the Göttingen protest, which has itself become a German legend.

Joyce Crick

See: Hermann Gerstner, *Die Brüder Grimm* (1952): Ludwig Denecke, *Jacob Grimm und sein Bruder Wilhelm* (1971); Murray Peppard, *Paths through the Forest. A Biography of the Brothers Grimm* (1971); Josef Dinninger, 'Geschichte der deutschen Philologie', in *Deutsche Philologie im Aufriss*, ed. Wolfgang Stammler (vol. I, 1952).

H

200

HAECKEL, Ernst Heinrich 1834–1919

German biologist

Born in Potsdam in 1834, Haeckel moved from the study of medicine to zoology and physiology at the Universities of Würzburg, Berlin and Vienna. At the early age of twenty-eight he was appointed director of the Zoological Institute at Jena and three years later Professor of Biology at the University of Jena, a post which he was to hold until 1909. During his forty-four years' tenure of this chair various attempts were made, inspired by the ecclesiastical and scientific establishments, to have him dismissed. From 1859 onwards Haeckel espoused Darwin's* theory of natural selection and the philosophical implications which he perceived in it. He published his views on this in a treatise of general morphology in 1866, and in a more substantial form in his *The Natural History of Creation* (*Natürliche Schöpfungsgeschichte*, 1867, trans. 1892). During the closing decades of the nineteenth century he was involved in various intellectual disputes, on the philosophical front with the neo-Kantians, and on the theological front with the Ritschlians. His views on the nature of the physical universe and of man achieved an outstandingly widespread hearing in his semi-popular book *The Riddle of the Universe*, (*Die Welträtsel*, 1899, trans. 1901), which was re-issued many times in cheap, popular versions and was translated into many languages. Towards the end of his life Haeckel was involved with the Nobel prize-winning chemist Wilhelm Ostwald (1853–1932) in the foundation of the so-called *Deutsches Monistenbund* ('German Society of Monists'), which held its first and only world congress in 1912. Haeckel embarked upon several long zoological journeys during his lifetime during which he exercised his considerable artistic skill with pen and brush, although it has been well remarked that his artistic imagination and philosophical assumptions took priority over pure scientific observation in the production of his highly impressive pictures of biological organisms. These pictures were published in two popularly influential and beautiful volumes, *Kunstformen der Natur* ('Art forms in Nature', 1904) and *Wanderbilder* ('Pictures', 1905). He died in Jena in 1919.

Haeckel's thought-system, to be described as metaphysical rather than scientific, is generally and rightly classified as 'evolutionary naturalism', and deserves to be considered together with not dissimilar systems of his period, notably those of Ludwig Büchner (1824–99), Karl Vogt (1817–95) and Jakob Moleschott (1822–93). German historians of science are agreed that this powerful vogue of materialistic and naturalistic metaphysics was rooted partly in the amazing advances of nineteenth-century experimental science and in the philosophical vacuum which followed the collapse of Hegelian speculative idealism shortly after 1850. Haeckel's system then is 'naturalistic' in that he completely and exhaustively identified reality, or ultimate reality, with physical 'nature', or 'nature' as this is studied in the physical sciences. More narrowly, ultimate reality is to be identified with 'substance' (*Substanz*). But modern scientific inquiry reveals that substance is not static, but dynamic, forever manifesting itself in a bewildering myriad of shapes, forms, processes and interactions. Biological organisms appear and disappear; they undergo extremely complicated mutations producing singularly complicated manifestations, the highest, qualitatively speaking, being *Homo sapiens* himself, as explained by Darwin in his *Origin of Species* and *The Descent of Man*. But Haeckel wished to push beyond Darwin's purely *scientific* categories (as did, for example, T.H. Huxley* and Herbert Spencer*) towards a more *philosophical* understanding of the ultimate constitution of nature. Haeckel attempted to do so by saying that we never find 'matter' (*Materie*) on its own, but always combined with 'spirit' (*Geist*); or that every atomic particle is a combination of 'stuff' (*Stoff*) and 'force' (*Kraft*). In the evolutionary story as told by Darwin we actually observe matter being activated by spirit, stuff being shaped, altered and empowered by force. Haeckel did not shrink from applying such categories to the origin and nature of man himself, asserting that human consciousness, mind and spirit were but highly sophisticated manifestations of *Geist* or *Kraft*, completely immanent within man's physical constitution, and in no sense transcending it, as asserted by the various forms of philosophical idealism from Plato to the Hegelians. Since Haeckel believed that ultimate reality was 'one' (Greek, *monos*), 'forceful nature', his completed system became known as 'monism', and as such incompatible with all forms of 'dualism', whether that between God and man, or God and the world, or mind and body. Hence the deity of traditional theism was dubbed by

268

Haeckel a 'gaseous vertebrate', and he explicitly denied the three classical postulates of Kant's moral interpretation of man, the freedom of the will, the immortality of the soul, and the existence of God.

Haeckel objected vehemently to the epithet 'atheist' which was flung at him by philosopher and theologian alike, and insisted that his metaphysical system was not only compatible with religion but was in fact a type of religion, namely 'pantheism'. For, he argued, if reality as a whole were regarded in the light of his scientific categories, we perceive that the world (physical nature) is pervaded by a living *Kraft* or *Geist*. So that a certain reverence for the world, regarded as 'God', becomes a live option. But despite this claim, it is beyond dispute that Haeckel's thought is so crudely materialistic in essence that it does not deserve to be classified with, for example, that of Hegel*, Feuerbach* or Spinoza. Nor does his claim that monism is compatible with a form of 'social ethics' derived from the social instinct of man command respect, in the light of his forementioned rather unreflective dismissal of the freedom of the will. In the light of the thinness and superficiality of Haeckel's monistic pantheism, and the rather pathetic incompetence he displayed in his approach to complex philosophical issues, it is not difficult to understand the hostility which he evoked from the intellectual and academic establishment of his day.

It is probably indisputable that, in the words of one historian of science, Charles Singer, many of Haeckel's theories 'now raise only a smile' and that 'most of his works rest undisturbed on the less accessible shelves of libraries' (*A Short History of Scientific Ideas to 1900*, 1959). Be that as it may, in the second half of the nineteenth century Haeckel's work was a significant ingredient within a powerful evolutionary-naturalistic-materialistic tide of thought which helped to evoke, by opposition and criticism, important developments in both philosophy and theology. On the philosophical side, such work helped to call into being neo-Kantianism, associated with the names of Hermann Cohen (1842–1918) and Wilhelm Windelband (1848–1915): such thinkers, over against contemporary naturalists and materialists, attempted to revive and reinterpret Kantian idealism, and explored that unavoidable dualism between, on the one hand, the world of natural facts, entities and laws, and, on the other, the realm of the human will and mind, and of moral, aesthetic and religious values. And on the theological side, the absorption of human existence into the impersonal world of matter and natural process implied by much evolutionary and naturalistic thought evoked from many liberal protestants the notion that the role of religion is to elevate man 'over nature' or to assist man to achieve moral and spiritual perfection in 'lordship over the natural world' (see Ritschl*).

James Richmond

See: F. Copleston, SJ, *A History of Philosophy*, vol. VII (1963); W. Tudor Jones, *Contemporary Thought of Germany*, vol. I (1930); J. Macquarrie, *Twentieth-Century Religious Thought* (1963); Joseph A. Beet, 'Scientific Agnosticism', in *The Credentials of the Gospel* (1889); Franklin Baumer, *Modern European Thought* (1977); F. Loofs, *Anti-Haeckel* (1900, trans. 1903).

201

HAGGARD, Sir Henry Rider 1856–1925

British novelist

On 2 August 1886, Henry James* wrote to Robert Louis Stevenson* of Rider Haggard's recently published *She*: 'More even than with the contemptible inexpressiveness of the whole thing I am struck with the beastly *bloodiness* of it – or it comes back to the same thing – the cheapness of the hecatombs with which the genial narrative is bestrewn. Such perpetual killing and such perpetual ugliness! ... *Quel genre!* They seem to me works in which our race and our age make a very vile figure.' James's disgust was not generally shared, perhaps because, more than any other popular novelist of the late nineteenth century, Haggard effectively caught the mood of jingoistic ruthlessness with which the English colonialists set about their business. Just as the roots of the Jameson Raid and the exploits of Rhodes, Milner and others lay in the fateful aftermath of English Romanticism, so Haggard too can be seen as a writer in a tradition initiated by Byron's* *Childe Harold* and Trelawny's* *Memoirs of a Younger Son*.

Born at West Bradenham, Norfolk, the son of a barrister with strong local connections, Haggard was groomed for the Foreign Office at a London crammer and it was during this period (he was only eighteen) that he fell in love with Mary Elizabeth Jackson, a Yorkshire heiress. His departure for Africa the following year (1875) as secretary to the Governor of Natal was marked by an unofficial engagement to 'Lilly' Jackson, but he returned three years later to find her married to the singularly undeserving Francis Archer, who finally levanted with the family trust money leaving his wife to bring up their children. Though she eventually settled near Haggard in Norfolk, he himself had made a marriage of convenience, but their mutual attachment respectably and discreetly endured. Such a situation inevitably provides the basis for similar moments throughout his published fiction, and the central narrative idea of a man held by the love of two contrasted women will be familiar enough to readers of *She*, *Allan Quartermain* and *Montezuma's Daughter*.

Haggard's life in Africa during the late 1870s and early 1880s was marked by participation in several major episodes calculated to strengthen British colonial commitment. For example, as a member of Sir Theophilus Shepstone's staff, he was to witness the annexation of the Transvaal in 1877. His sympathies were generally conservative, and in 1895, having practised for eleven years as a lawyer, he offered himself as a Unionist candidate for Norfolk. Concern for the management of his estate and a sincere interest in agriculture served to relate his politics to the species of rural conservatism, neo-feudalist and often unabashedly sentimental, which finds echoes in the 'back-to-the-land' notions of writers and artists whose viewpoints are otherwise diametrically opposed to Haggard's. The synthesis of such ideas is *The Farmer's Year* of 1899, one of the most readable and informative books of its kind, and partially instrumental in making his reputation as a seriously considered authority on rural questions. He was knighted in 1912 and died in London thirteen years later at the age of sixty-nine.

It is as a writer of romantic adventure stories, however, that his fame has principally endured, though even these formed only a part of his total fictional output, covering as this did practically every species of novel then known. In the annals of English fiction his name is inextricably linked with the tradition of stirring exploits in exotic locations begun by Captain Marryat* in the 1830s, taken up and intensified at a level of unrivalled sophistication by Joseph Conrad, and adapted for the needs of British schoolboys by R.M. Ballantyne and G.A. Henty.

In the unequivocal simplicity of his moral and ethical outlook, indeed, Haggard can scarcely be said to surpass either of these two writers. His heroes, Allan Quartermain, Leo Vincey or the protagonists of *King Solomon's Mines*, his most popular book, have since become archetypes of the mustachioed colonial Englishman, undaunted in courage and impeccable in manners. There is, as James rightly observed, a substantial quantity of gratuitous blood-letting, as well as, here and there, a certain amount of lofty 'tushery' whenever natives or members of lost tribes are required to speak. Africans are either villainous, grotesque or paragons of primitive nobility and throughout Haggard's work, especially in such novels as *Benita*, runs an unsavoury current of anti-Semitism very much in tune with the spirit of the period, particularly among those who, like Haggard himself, believed that the pressure of Jewish finance had helped to cause the South African war.

All this, however, is not to deny the author's overwhelming power as an imaginative story-teller, as much at home in the historical past of works such as *Montezuma's Daughter*, set in sixteenth-century Mexico, as in the colonial milieu of *King Solomon's Mines*. To the 'deeds-of-derring-do' world of public school heroics, Haggard adds the strong colours of his own singular fantasy, peopled by lost civilizations and coloured by a heady sexuality, the whole mixture seen at its best in *She*, one of the classics of *fin de siècle* romance, *Nada*

the Lily, with its Bantu tribal background, and *Heart of the World*, with its strongly Conradian overtones. To understand and appreciate Rider Haggard is to understand the hankering for sheer, uncomplicated sensation and adventure which is a crucial and often disastrous element in the character of the Englishman.

Jonathan Keates

Haggard's *Private Diaries 1914–1925* were edited by D.S. Higgins (1980). See: M.W. Cohen, *Rider Haggard: His Life and Works* (1960); Peter Beresford Ellis, *H. Rider Haggard: A Voice from the Infinite* (1978); D.S. Higgins, *Rider Haggard: The Great Story Teller* (1981).

202
HAMSUN, Knut 1859–1952

Norwegian writer

Born Knut Pedersen, Hamsun grew up in northern Norway, and the seasons and scenery there, the short intense summers, the woods and the hills, were to provide the setting and mood of many of his works. He had plied many trades both in Norway and in the USA before his first novel, *Hunger* (*Sult*, 1890, trans. 1899 and 1967), announced the arrival of a major new literary figure. It is a semi-autobiographical account of a starving writer, who makes no complaint against society, but who notes how hunger heightens and distorts his reaction to people and events around him, and who, with the aid of a rich imagination, tries to retain a modicum of self-respect. Men of heightened nervous sensibility are also the main characters in Hamsun's next two novels, *Mysteries* (*Mysterier*, 1892, trans. 1927 and 1971) and *Pan* (1894, trans. 1920 and 1955), though the latter is also a rich poetic evocation of the seasons and nature of northern Norway. Although love plays a part in both these novels, in *Victoria* (1898, trans. 1923 and 1969), a delicate love story is the main element, and this is interwoven with often highly poetic variations on the nature of love. In addition to these novels which many consider Hamsun's greatest, he also wrote two satirical novels in the 1890s, *Redaktør Lynge* ('Editor Lynge', 1893) and *Shallow Soil* (*Ny Jord*, 1893, trans. 1914).

A mellower tone pervades the 'Wanderer' trilogy, *Under the Autumn Star* (*Under Høststjærnen*, 1906, trans. 1922), *On Muted Strings* (*En Vandrer spiller med Sordin*, 1909, trans. 1922) and *Look Back on Happiness* (*Den siste Glæde*, 1912, trans. 1940), for the first person narrator, who bears Hamsun's own name of Knut Pedersen, has now become middle-aged, more resigned and capable of self-irony. At this time Hamsun was also developing his second voice, that of the epic story-teller, detached, humorous and ironic, especially at the expense of the foibles, vanities and social ambitions of people in small communities. This is the voice of *Mothwise* (*Svermere*, 1904, trans. 1921), *Benoni* (1908, trans. 1926), *Children of the Age* (*Børn av Tiden*, 1913, trans. 1924) and *Segelfoss Town* (*Segelfoss By*, 1915, trans. 1925).

The Growth of the Soil (*Markens Grøde*, 1917, trans. 1920), the novel which won Hamsun the Nobel Prize for Literature in 1920, is a great hymn to the land, and somewhat more ironically to man the farmer, who starts by breaking new ground, and gradually develops more complex patterns of culture and technology. After the First World War there followed a period of crisis for Hamsun, and this is reflected in such bitter works as *The Women at the Pump* (*Konerne ved Vandposten*, 1920, trans. 1928 and 1978) and *Chapter the Last* (*Siste Kapitel*, 1923, trans. 1930), both of which express a very cynical view of mankind. However, good humour and exuberance return in the 'August' trilogy, *Vagabonds* (*Landstrykere*, 1927, trans. 1931 and as *Wayfarers* 1980), *August* (1930, trans. 1932) and *The Road Leads On* (*Men Livet lever*, 1933, trans. 1934), which tell of the projects started by the fantast August, who wants to bring the spirit of commercialism and the modern age to a small community in northern Norway. Hamsun disapproves of the rootless August and his attempts to change the stable rural economy, but he cannot withhold his affection from a character so full of vitality and imagination.

No one who has read Hamsun would deny that he is a master of style. In the early works the style is intense and lyrical, often approaching prose poetry, and there is a rhythm and vocabulary unique to Hamsun. In the later works the style has strong oral elements, with Hamsun using many of the techniques of story-telling, the confidential relationship with the reader, rhetorical questions, and the feigned ignorance of the motives of his characters in order to create suspense. The novels rarely lead to great climaxes, but Hamsun is a master at sustaining one's interest in a series of minor events. Usually his mockery of human frailty is good-natured, as in the 'August' trilogy, but in some works such as *The Women at the Pump* the all-knowing author distances himself from his characters to such an extent that he seems like a cynical puppeteer.

The setting of many of Hamsun's novels is a non-particularized town or community in northern Norway, the period the final years of the last century, and a recurring theme the transition from the old patriarchal self-sufficient agrarian economy to the new commercial and consumer society, with Hamsun's sympathies – on the surface at least – being very much with the former. Another recurring motif is that of the outsider or wanderer. In the four major novels of the 1890s the main characters are all outsiders, who are ill at ease in society and whose relations with women are intense and complex yet distant. In the later novels the wanderer is seen in contrast to the farmer, the settled man.

Ultimately, however, what makes Hamsun more than just a good story-teller and superb stylist are his insights into the 'almost imperceptible movements of the soul', and his sense of the mystery of life. In the novels of the 1890s this awareness is expressed positively, but in many of the works from this century there is an underlying sense of the meaninglessness of life in a post-religious age.

A problem, particularly for the Norwegians, has been Hamsun's sympathy for the Nazis during the Second World War. However, it now seems clear that the views he expressed then were latent from very early on. In the 1890s he was interested in the unique individual of heightened sensibility and so had little time for democracy, and later a nostalgic love for the primitive and vital elements of life became a marked feature of his work, though there is little trace of anti-Semitism. After the war Hamsun was tried and sentenced for treason, the whole of which prolonged ordeal he transformed into literature in *Paa gjengrodde Stier* ('On Overgrown Paths'), a work which he completed in 1949, his ninetieth year.

Marie Wells

The Wanderer (1975) contains a translation of the first two novels of the 'Wanderer' trilogy. See J.W. McFarlane, *Ibsen and the Temper of Norwegian Literature* (1960).

203
HARDY, Thomas 1840–1928

British poet and novelist

Thomas Hardy was born near Dorchester on 2 June 1840. His birth-place in Higher Bockhampton was a substantial cottage, at the end of a lane and on the edge of a piece of heath-land. His father was a builder and mason working on his own but, by the time Hardy was twenty, employing half a dozen men; his mother, a cook and serving-maid. The marriage took place less than six months before the child was born. Thomas Hardy the elder was said to have got more than one village girl into trouble, but Jemima's mother was more than a match for him. She was the disowned daughter of a yeoman farmer, left to a widowhood of great poverty with seven children. These social ramifications are of some importance, because Hardy's work, like the man himself, was strongly marked by his origins. He was a delicate child, after a difficult birth. He went to the village school and then, for seven years, to a school in Dorchester which he left at the age of sixteen with a knowledge of Latin. He was articled to an architect and church-restorer, a man for whom his father had done building work. During this time he continued his education with the help of Horace Moule, the son of a local clergyman, and did some reading in the Greek dramatists. There was a spell with an architect in London, from 1862–7; Hardy then went back to his original employer in Dorchester. He married Emma Gifford, whom he met while on an architectural assignment in Cornwall, and shortly afterwards gave up architecture to write novels. Emma was of a clerical family and the marriage seems to have confirmed Hardy's sensitivity about his social position; his wife died in 1912. In 1914 Hardy married Florence Dugdale, with whom he conspired to write *The Early Life of Thomas Hardy* (1928 and 1930), published under her name after his death – a book designed to conceal from posterity all he did not want people to know about himself and in particular whatever he regarded as inadmissible about his family. In his later years Hardy seems to have been obsessed with the notion that the family had gone down in the world, from gentle origins.

If Hardy's social life has its elements of rather depressing comedy, there are few writers who have so long and consistent a record of un-selfconscious devotion to their work. His first surviving poem, 'Domicilium' – which describes the cottage where he grew up – was written before 1860. When Hardy died in 1928 he was preparing the volume which appeared posthumously as *Winter Words*, and although the volume concludes with a poem called 'He resolves to say no more', his introductory note says merely that this is 'probably' his 'last appearance on the literary stage'. So we have nearly seventy years of writing by a man who, even at eighty-eight, had not definitively given up. The whole corpus of his work is made up of 947 poems, besides a huge dramatic epic, *The Dynasts* (1904–8), and a score of novels and volumes of short stories. Hardy's work stretched well into the twentieth century, and has been accepted by the new century as by the old. His reputation has grown and his readership continued to spread so that his works are still a valuable property in the paperback market. His poems, the high value of which was recognized early in the present century by such figures as Ford Madox Ford and Ezra Pound, have been a living influence on poets after the Second World War and indeed up to very recent times.

For the nineteenth century, Hardy was a novelist almost exclusively. Yet he is on record as saying that he would never have written a line of prose if he could have made a living by poetry. It was not until 1898 that the first and only volume of verse he published during the nineteenth century, *Wessex Poems*, appeared, but all his volumes contain, in revised if not in the original form, poems he wrote in the 1860s. The reception of both the volume of 1898 and of its successor of 1902 – *Poems of Past and Present* – was grudging. By then Hardy had long established himself, in two continents, as a major novelist. After what might be regarded as false but – to the author – no doubt

instructive starts with an unpublished story called *The Poor Man and the Lady* and with *Desperate Remedies*, the publication of which he paid for himself, Hardy found his true *métier* with *Under the Greenwood Tree* (1872). The essential elements of this novel were provided by the scenes of Hardy's childhood and the persons and traditions of his immediate family and acquaintance. It was in this novel that Hardy began the creation of a 'Wessex' which corresponded in remarkable detail with the geography and manners of Dorset and the bordering lands; for many readers the fictional names are more familiar than the real ones. Hardy's own parish came to enjoy, as Mellstock, a fame it had never known as Stinsford. There is a touch – but no more – of Shakespearian comic dialogue about some of the talk in *Under the Greenwood Tree*; for the most part Hardy was making an adaptation of the dialect familiar to him as a child. Indeed, although Hardy shows a more practised hand in several of the later novels, the language of *Under the Greenwood Tree* is exemplary, showing nothing of the occasional stiltedness which marks Hardy's forays into cosmological reflections or into the social milieux which, for all his later dinners in London and membership of a London club, were never close to his imagination.

Under the Greenwood Tree was published anonymously, but its considerable success gave Hardy confidence to launch his further works under their author's name. *A Pair of Blue Eyes* followed in 1873, then in 1874, what may be regarded as the second of the essential books in the Hardy canon – *Far from the Madding Crowd*, with its memorable picture of sheep-farming in old Dorset. The third is *The Return of the Native* (1878), more sombre in tone, with its evocation of Egdon Heath which is, so to speak, a presiding spirit in the book. *The Trumpet Major* (1880) introduces a new historical element; it is set in the days of the Napoleonic wars, which interested Hardy deeply and which later provided the subject matter of *The Dynasts*. In *The Trumpet Major* the local scene is still central and, once again, crucial characters such as Sergeant Troy seem to have been drawn from life – Troy himself apparently from the husband of Hardy's aunt – one of those whom, with the social pressures of marriage and his own aspirations, he came to regard as socially ineligible. *The Mayor of Casterbridge* (1886), probably the greatest of Hardy's novels and a tale of great tragic force, with its roots in the immediate past of Dorset and in what Hardy had learned of its inhabitants, is on a scale which lifts plot and characters far out of any merely local interest. The scene is set in the town in which fate had set Hardy himself only because it is through the local minutiae that Hardy is best able to present the universalities of human nature – as Dante, it might be said, sees so much of the destiny of man in the streets of Florence. *The Woodlanders* (1887) is an altogether less powerful book, but presents aspects of the picture, or myth, of Wessex not to be found elsewhere. *Tess of the D'Urbervilles* (1892) not only does that but gives us the second of the great tragic characters of Hardy's novels – Tess herself, whose mythic force is not lessened by the portentous epitaph with which Hardy saw fit to end her history. Hardy's final novel – *The Well-Beloved*, though published the year after, was written earlier – was *Jude the Obscure* (1896). It is a book in which the Wessex landscape, though still significantly present, becomes a muted background to a plot which evolves almost entirely out of the interaction and final explosion of the interlocked characters.

From the first, Hardy felt the drive to include in his novels elements of social and in particular sexual relationships which the ethos of the times was inclined to suppress. He remained preoccupied by then 'modern' ideas and absorbed a good deal of the rationalism of Darwin*, Mill*, Spencer* and Huxley*. He was 'churchy', as he said, and soaked in the language of the Bible and the Prayer Book, but from an early age without religious belief, as Jude himself became. With *Jude* he ran into dramatic – though, it must be said, comic – trouble. Poor Emma was scandalized; in the United States Mrs Oliphant deplored the outrage to morality. It has often been said that Hardy gave up writing novels because of these troubles; it is more likely that he now found that his novels were doing so well that he could devote himself to poetry, his great work in prose being anyhow in a sense completed.

The enduring importance of Hardy is certainly not in any set of abstract ideas – 'enlightened' or otherwise – which may have attracted him more or less as they attracted many of his contemporaries. It is in the imaginative body of his work where life is presented with a closeness of observation possible only to a man working within a milieu he knew intimately and from the cradle. There are romantic excesses which sometimes amount to absurdities, but the great novels remain solid in spite of them and these faults hardly touch the poems. Many reasons combine to give Hardy's work not only significance but popularity in our own day. One is that he was a genuine provincial, and the importance of that is being realized at last by a world in which local differences are threatened with extinction. The reality he saw is a very solid one. He speaks on behalf of a class – what might be called the lowest middle class of the countryside, below any pretension to gentility – which had scarcely made its voice heard in literature before. It is the very class from which he had tried to distance himself, socially. He lived through immense changes, in the economy as in the social life of the countryside, and the impact of urbanization, now world-wide, was perceived by him in a manageable local setting. Finally, whether in prose or verse, he could tell a good story.

C.H. Sisson

The Complete Poems of Thomas Hardy were published in 1978. There were numerous printings of the earlier *Collected Poems*, and there is an excellent *Selected Poems*, ed. David Wright with introduction and notes (1978). See: Robert Gittings, *Young Thomas Hardy* (1975) and *The Older Hardy* (1976); F.B. Pinion, *Hardy Companion* (1968). Mervyn Williams, *Thomas Hardy and Rural England* (1972), is also recommended.

204
HARNACK, Adolf von 1851–1930

German Lutheran theologian and ecclesiastical historian

Born in 1851, Harnack held many academic appointments during his long life, in the universities of Leipzig, Giessen, Marburg and Berlin, this last appointment being opposed by the church, because of certain radically 'liberal' tendencies in his work, but upheld by the state. In 1911 Harnack was appointed president of the prestigious research centre, the Kaiser Wilhelm Stiftung. He retired from his Berlin chair in 1921, and when he died aged seventy-nine was one of the most celebrated figures in academic and literary Germany, with a quite remarkable international reputation.

The most obvious way in which to classify Harnack's theological position is to describe him as a historian of ecclesiastical dogma deeply influenced by the work and standpoint of Albrecht Ritschl*, whose school acknowledged Harnack as one of its most distinguished leaders. Harnack seized upon Ritschl's conviction that Christian teaching, almost from its inception, had been 'hellenized' (*hellenisiert*) and that the entire history of church dogma needed to be 'dehellenized' (*enthellenisiert*), although Harnack preferred to speak of Christian doctrine having been 'secularized'. Indeed, Harnack saw the beginnings of such secularization reflected in the New Testament itself, in statements about the status of Christ's *person* as the eternally pre-existent *Logos* who entered the historical dimension in the person of Jesus, a doctrine which he treated rather similarly to his master Ritschl. Accordingly, Harnack had much to write about the hellenization of Christianity in the ecclesiastical discussion and definition of the person of Christ as the union of the divine nature (Greek *phusis*) with the human nature in the incarnate Son of God, as the *locus classicus* of the application of Greek philosophical categories to the primitive Galilean phenomenon of ethico-spiritual Christianity. In similar vein, Harnack dealt with the emergence and use of credal formulae (e.g. the Apostles' creed), the affirmation that bishops through tactual succession were a prolongation of the apostolic office and authority into modernity, the rigidly hierarchical and strictly delimited character of the Christian Church, and the eucharist as a sacrifice perpetrated in the ministrations of an exclusive sacerdotal caste. All of these, insisted Harnack, can be seen as resulting from the encounter, even the conflict, between the Christian community and the hellenistic-gentile world which constituted the community's environment and sphere of evangelization – in Harnack's own luminous words, ecclesiastical dogma represents 'the formulation of Christian faith as Greek culture understood it and justified it to itself': it is 'the work of the Greek Spirit on the soil of the gospel'. Not that Harnack as a great historical critic failed to recognize the necessity, in their contemporary setting, of propositional dogmas as defences against hazardous misunderstandings of or even pernicious attacks upon the Christian faith; what he deplored was that the Christian faith became permanently crystallized into such propositions and in this form was transmitted to succeeding generations as the timeless faith itself. Such a process quite obscures and distorts that primitive gospel once delivered to the apostles by Christ himself. It is one thing to say that a set of dogmatic formulae was *in situ* a necessary restatement of Christian truth to guard against heresies such as Gnosticism, Nestorianism, Monophysitism, Eutychianism and the rest. It is quite another to impose these formulae as the timelessly valid expressions of that truth which demanded the intellectual assent of succeeding generations of Christians down to modernity. Such misunderstandings and perversions Harnack expounded and documented with great erudition in the three volumes of his *Lehrbuch der Dogmengeschichte* between 1886 and 1889 (trans. *History of Dogma*, 7 vols, 1894–9), which treats of the history of dogma down to the period of Luther's Reformation. As a Lutheran, he entertained a very high estimate of Luther's work in so far as it defended the *Sola Scriptura* as the basis for Christian theology, from which resulted 'when measured by the multifarious things which the Church proffered as "religion", primarily a stupendous *reduction*'. There is no more typical sentence of Harnack's than the following: 'Out of a multiform system of grace, performances, penances and reliances he [Luther] extracted religion and restored it to simple greatness' (*History of Dogma*). Not that he was uncritical of Luther: for all his greatness, Luther transmitted to the modern world 'not a new building . . . but a modification of the traditional structure' (*ibid.*), a curious mixture of the rediscovered original gospel and old dogma. Accordingly, Luther can be credited only with 'a partial beginning of a reformation' at best. As for post-Reformation times, Harnack is clear that the *Aufklärung*, with special reference to the critical and moral philosophy of Immanuel Kant, made a quite tremendous contribution towards liberating essential Christian faith, as primarily ethical monotheism, from its timeworn dogmatic dress and disguises, a contribution which he saw being prolonged into his own lifetime by the theology of Ritschl and the work of neo-Kantians such as Cohen and Natorp.

It is clear from all of this that Harnack saw the Christian faith as consisting of some irreducible essence which in successive generations and epochs became clothed in some historical form or other, and then the theologian's perennial task is to break away the husk in order, so to speak, to get at this kernel. It is in this sense that Harnack approved of the dictum that 'we must overcome history by history'. It is reasonable to ask about the nature of this essence. Harnack answered this question in his best-known book *What is Christianity?*, (*Das Wesen des Christentums*, 1900, trans. 1901), which originated in a series of public lectures delivered to the University of Berlin in the year 1899–1900. (The vast popularity of the book is attested to by the well-documented fact that at one point in 1900 the railway terminal of Leipzig was brought to a standstill by goods trains loaded with printed copies of it!) The message of Harnack's book is well known: the essence of Christianity consists of the Fatherhood of God, the infinite worth of the individual human soul, and the Kingdom of God. The significance of Jesus for Harnack, since it cannot be christological in any metaphysical sense, seems to have been that of an incomparable religious genius or religious leader (not unlike one of the 'religious heroes' of Schleiermacher*) who stood in an incomparably close relation to God, and able to impart in a unique way the fatherly providential care of God (a notion much stressed by Ritschl), who values infinitely each single individual, a belief which helps the believer to transcend all worldly cares and trials (yet another notion central to Ritschl's system). And Jesus proclaims and brings into being the Kingdom of God, regarded by Harnack as a community organized according to the principles of moral growth, brotherly love, and compassion for the poor. Harnack's book is correctly described as *the* classic turn-of-the-century expression of so-called 'liberal protestantism'. And although twentieth-century theological critics have affirmed that the presuppositions of his history of dogma are nowadays quite untenable, and that his account of the Christian gospel is both simplistic and reductionist, his work retains considerable importance for the historian of modern Protestantism. Amongst other subjects written upon by Harnack during his long career were the Apostles' Creed, New Testament Introduction, the teaching of Jesus, the Lucan writings, Marcion and Paul.

James Richmond

Other translations: *Luke the Physician* (1907); *The Sayings of Jesus* (1980); *The Acts of the Apostles* (1909). See: Wayne Glick, *The Reality of Christianity: A Study of Adolf von Harnack as Historian and Theologian* (1967); John Macquarrie, *Twentieth-Century Religious Thought*

(1963); James C. Livingston, *Modern Christian Thought: From the Enlightenment to Vatican II* (1971).

205

HARRIS, Joel Chandler 1848–1908

US writer

As a child Joel Chandler Harris preferred rabbit hunting to school learning, but he did apprentice himself to a typesetter, Joseph Addison Turner, editor of the *Countryman*, the only newspaper printed on a plantation. Harris immersed himself in the agrarian culture of the Old South, including Negro memories of African lore, transformed into folk tales, and local dialect, for which he had a good ear: in fact he published a letter in dialect denouncing Lincoln*. In 1865, his Confederacy savings having turned to mere paper, he turned to work on the New Orleans *Macon Telegraph* and the *Crescent Monthly* (he knew Lafcadio Hearn slightly at this time). In 1867 he returned to his hometown, Eatonton, Georgia, worked on the *Monroe Advertiser*, became associate editor of the Savannah *Morning News*, married (1873), and escaped yellow fever in 1876 by shifting to Atlanta where he registered at a hotel as 'J.C. Harris, one wife, two bow-legged children and a bilious nurse'. The *Atlanta Constitution* asked him to continue a column featuring 'Uncle Si', a Negro character who developed into Harris's world-famous 'Uncle Remus' (the tar-baby tale appeared in African dialects and Bengali). After *Uncle Remus: His Songs and Sayings* (1880) he would have accompanied Twain* and George Washington Cable on a lecture tour but for a speech impediment. His popularity consolidated in the series which included *Nights with Uncle Remus* (1883), *Uncle Remus and his Friends* (1892), *The Ray-Baby and Other Rhymes of Uncle Remus* (1904) and *Uncle Remus and Br'er Rabbit*. But he also wrote an account of a Sea Island hurricane, drawn from Negro witnesses, in 1883, and *Mingo, and Other Sketches in Black and White* (1884), the first of a number of books on Georgia's upper class, poor whites and ex-slaves (1896–1902). In 1902 he joined the McClure Phillips Company, and then, with his son Julian, founded *Uncle Remus's Magazine*, whose writers included Don Marquis and Ludwig Lewissohn. Harris's public shyness prevented him from personally accepting a degree from the University of Pennsylvania. His strength lay in the penetration of public taste, and as he said, 'humour is a great thing to live by, and other things being equal, it is a profitable thing to die by.'

The Remus stories were among the first to exploit Negro folk narratives, based on local story-telling in local language, told with shrewd humour in authentic locations. But *Nights with Uncle Remus* registers a problematic change in Harris's career. Written in the Gullah dialect of the story-teller, Daddy Jack, the tales are less easy to understand. Moreover, they take place in slavery days rather than the post-Civil War times of Harris's other fictions. Uncle Remus remained a complex voice – not the stereotypical devoted black but an alert, superstitious and humorous adult. *Free Joe and Other Sketches* (1887) further extends the image by dealing with the freed and therefore desocialized slave, an ironic version of Harris's well-known axiom, 'You er what you is en you can't be no is-er.' His total work constitutes an early major definition of a possible Southern literature, including what Ralph Ellison calls 'the wily rabbit of Negro American lore'.

Eric Mottram

See: Julia C. Harris, *The Life and Letters of Joel Chandler Harris* (1918); P.M. Cousins, *Joel Chandler Harris: A Biography* (1968).

206

HARTE, Francis Bret 1836–1902

US writer

In 1854 Bret Harte left Albany, New York, for San Francisco, worked a bad claim in the Mother Load, taught, appears to have been a guard on a pony express for Wells Fargo goods, took up journalism in 1857 and rapidly achieved popular fame with verse and fiction. He wrote for the *Californian*, edited the *Overland Monthly* and *Outcroppings*, a celebrated anthology of Californian verse, and published his *The Lost Galleon and Other Tales* in 1867, and *The Luck of Roaring Camp* in 1870. To take up the *Atlantic Monthly*'s offer of an annual 10,000 dollars for whatever he wrote, he moved to Boston and lost his flair and his contract. The novel *Gabriel Conroy* (1876) and the play *Ah Sin* (in collaboration with Mark Twain*) did not rescue him – and the latter was based on the highly popular poem 'Plain Language from Truthful James', better known as 'The Heathen Chinese', only begetter of scores of such dialect poems. Harte served as consul in Krefeld and Glasgow (1878–85) and then lived in the London area, lecturing and writing. *Condensed Novels* – parodies of popular novelists – appeared in 1902, and he died from throat cancer in Camberley, where he had been living with Mme Van de Velde, a French noblewoman.

'The Luck of Roaring Camp' (in the second issue of *Overland Monthly*) made his name – the tale of Luck, a mining camp prostitute's child, which challenged sexual and class hypocrisies (the religious press condemned it), but compensated with a self-sacrificial morality which could be popularly accepted. In fact Harte's success frequently depended on the renouncing sinner in the Gold Rush West. Violence, drunkenness and hysteria are somewhat redeemed in an atmosphere of picturesque local colour with picturesque types. His version of the Far West is a melodrama of the sordid and sentimental, nicely blending pathos and humour with accurate language, derived from bars, camps and stores. But once the manner had been achieved, he repeated it. Henry Adams* admired Harte, with Whitman*, for using sex as a force rather than simply a sentiment, and his sympathy with ethnic minorities, especially the Chinese, remains creditable. His influence on the Western movie is unlimited, and his freedom in treating prostitutes, drunks and foul-mouthed kids, roughs of all kinds, is decently unmoral and looks forward to a good deal of twentieth-century American realist fiction.

Eric Mottram

See: George R. Stewart, *Bret Harte: Argonaut and Exile* (1931); Richard O'Connor, *Bret Harte* (1966).

207
HAUPTMANN, Gerhart 1862–1946

German dramatist and novelist

Born in Silesia, the son of a hotel proprietor, Hauptmann was already determined to become a writer at quite an early age. His first works were all written under the influence of the then fashionable Naturalist school. Later he began to develop a more imaginative style and the realist element in his work receded. When Hitler came to power in 1933 Hauptmann chose to stay in Germany, and although he was basically out of sympathy with the regime, he remained unmolested by the authorities. His last years, which he spent as a recluse, were characterized by bitterness and despair.

Like many of his contemporaries, the youthful Hauptmann fell under the spell of Zola* and Ibsen*. Zola's view of art as being a corner of nature seen through a temperament, as well as his concern for the poor and the oppressed, both find expression in Hauptmann's first play *Vor Sonnenaufgang* ('Before Sunrise', 1889), where human degradation, brought on by greed and materialism, is pitilessly exposed. The two works which followed, *Das Friedensfest* ('Peace Celebrations', 1890) and *Einsame Menschen* ('Lonely People', 1891), on the other hand, bear unmistakable traces of Ibsen's individualistic ethic. In these dramas progressively minded characters strive to assert their own identity within the stifling conformist milieu of contemporary bourgeois society. But it was with *Die Weber* ('The Weavers', 1893) that Hauptmann achieved what is generally regarded as his greatest triumph. What gives this drama its special strength is the relentless concentration on human suffering inflicted on the weavers by social, economic and political forces which they are powerless to resist and do not even understand.

For a number of years Hauptmann continued to produce Naturalist works, and plays like *Fuhrmann Henschel* ('Henschel the Drayman', 1898) and *Rose Bernd* (1903) are typical examples of the genre. Yet already before 1900 he had begun to show signs of impatience with the more doctrinaire theorizing of Naturalism. Moreover, he was becoming increasingly alienated by the Naturalist tendency to see man as the helpless victim of his environment. At any rate, *Hanneles Himmelfahrt* ('Hannele's Assumption', 1893) heralded a change of direction. In the second half of this play realism is completely abandoned as the dying heroine, in a series of ecstatic visions, leaves all her earthly sufferings behind her to enter into paradise.

Eroticism plays a central role in *Hanneles Himmelfahrt* and from now on Hauptmann becomes increasingly obsessed with the power of love and suffering to enable man to transcend the depressing world of physical reality. Unfortunately he never succeeds in convincing us that the metaphysical certainties, which he struggles to incorporate into his writings at this time, have anything other than a purely relative validity based on the individual, and even hallucinatory, experiences of particular characters. It is perhaps for this reason that dramas like *Die versunkene Glocke* ('The Sunken Bell', 1896), *Michael Kramer* (1900) and *Und Pippa tanzt* ('Pippa dances on', 1906) make little impact today. The same may be said of most of the narrative works which fall within this period: *Der Narr in Christo Emanuel Quint* ('The Fool in Christ', 1910), *Atlantis* (1912) and *Der Ketzer von Soana* ('The Heretic of Soana', 1918).

As he grew older Hauptmann became fascinated by the world of magic and myth, a tendency which had already been fostered by a journey to Greece in 1907. He also began to lose faith in the redemptive power of love and suffering. *Indipohdi* (1920), based on Shakespeare's *Tempest*, is an unequivocal statement of despair. Whereas Shakespeare's hero wins through to a triumphant faith in human goodness, Hauptmann's Prospero, despairing of mankind, symbolically plunges to his doom in a volcanic crater. Hauptmann's last major work was the *Atriden-Tetralogie*, a cycle of plays dealing with the Atreus myth, and it marks the logical culmination of this trend. Completed in 1944, it depicts a world in which man's surrender to evil has replaced any call to redemption.

Although Hauptmann remained a prolific writer until the end of his life, his reputation rests mainly on the dramatic works composed before 1910, and it was during this period that his influence on German literature was most pronounced. With a ruthless refusal to compromise, he showed that the theatre could deal effectively with the most unpromising and often sordid material of everyday life and, what is perhaps more important, that it could treat issues which had hitherto been regarded as unacceptable by the respectable middle-class audiences of the day. In retrospect some of his work may appear crass and melodramatic, but his impact on the theatre was enormous and its effect is still felt today.

Derrick Barlow

The definitive edition of Hauptmann's works is the *Sämtliche Werke*, ed. H.-E. Hass (from 1962). Translations: *The Dramatic Works of Gerhart Hauptmann*, ed. Ludwig Lewisohn (9 vols, 1912–29). See: H.F. Garten, *Gerhart Hauptmann* (1954); M. Sinden, *Gerhart Hauptmann: The Prose Plays* (1957); J. Osborne, *The Naturalist Drama in Germany* (1971).

208
HAWTHORNE, Nathaniel 1804–64

US writer

'A man of a deep and noble nature', 'this Portuguese diamond in our American Literature' – in these, and similar warm, acclaiming phrases Herman Melville* announced his celebrated 'shock of recognition' on first reading Hawthorne (in his pseudonymous review of *Mosses from an Old Manse* for the influential New York weekly, the *Literary World*, 17 and 24 August 1850). He wrote as an enthusiast, and doubtless in extravagant homage to a fellow author and countryman whose powers he thought exceptional, at times even Shakespearian. But it was a rare act of tribute, as eloquent as it was generous. It was also prophetic, for in Hawthorne's own time, on both sides of the Atlantic, he tended to be judged a voice pitched essentially in minor key, too bound by ancestral New England Puritanism, that determining American legacy of Calvinist theology and conscience, profound sexual suspicion, heresy and witchcraft, which began in seventeenth-century Massachusetts and the founding colonies of the eastern seaboard and which cast its shadow deep into Hawthorne's own time. And if not depicted as merely the custodian of America's supposed gloomy Puritan past, he was thought a narrow homespun 'allegorist', an adept in the art of the 'picturesque' and the 'quaint'. In each of these characterizations, almost unwittingly, Hawthorne's critics drew on the *persona* he took great pains first to bring into being, then foster, that of the reticent, unavailing, 'occasional' writer. The 'inmost Me', however, as he refers to himself in *The Scarlet Letter* (1850), too rarely won recognition.

If Melville allowed his generosity to get slightly the better of him in designating Hawthorne 'a commanding mind', he was right to think him anything but 'harmless', an easily accounted for New England local colourist. For Hawthorne brooded long, even obsessively, over his craft, a challenging literary as well as moral intelligence who is now properly regarded, with Melville himself, as belonging to the 'American Re-

naissance', the mid-nineteenth-century efflorescence of thought and letters inaugurated by Ralph Waldo Emerson's* *Nature* (1836) and which embraces landmark American works like *Moby-Dick* (1851), Henry David Thoreau's* *Walden* (1854), Walt Whitman's* *Leaves of Grass* (first edition, 1855), Emily Dickinson's* nearly two thousand 'hidden' poems, and Hawthorne's own crucial *The Scarlet Letter*, his three subsequent romances, and his short-story collections. To Henry James*, writing in his 'English (*sic*) Men of Letters' monograph, *Hawthorne* (1879), it was Hawthorne's mastery of his pictographic stories and of the romance form which – albeit with major reservations – led him to pronounce the New Englander no less than 'a beautiful, natural, original genius', a subtle and admired forbear. From a yet later perspective, in *Studies in Classic American Literature* (1923), D.H. Lawrence also paid tribute to Hawthorne, insisting like Melville upon his 'daemonic' and far from picturesque qualities, his watchful insights into human psychology and dark, ensnaring equivocations and chiaroscuro. Of this 'duplicitous' Hawthorne, wonderfully disingenuous and full of covert meanings, he writes engagingly 'blue-eyed Nathaniel knew disagreeable things in his inner soul. He was careful to send them out in disguise.'

Hawthorne was born into old Massachusetts family stock (one ancestor was a judge in the Salem witch trials). He lost his sea-captain father at four; developed his characteristic penchant for solitude and inward self-doubt and contemplation in childhood sojourns at Lake Sebago, Maine; numbered the poet Longfellow*, and a future president, Franklin Pierce, among his classmates at Bowdoin College (1821–5); after which, in his 'haunted chamber' at his mother's gabled house in Salem, he pursued a life of intense private study, mainly in literature and American Puritan and revolutionary history (1825–37). In 1828, he published *Fanshawe*, a derivative Gothic adventure-narrative, which he later sought to withdraw from circulation, but which gave notice of his coming skills as a romancer. The mainly anonymous stories he had been publishing since 1832, and others hitherto unprinted, were issued as *Twice-Told Tales* in 1837. In this event, and his engagement to Sophia Peabody, invalid sister of the influential Transcendentalist luminary and educator, Elizabeth Peabody, he believed the world 'had called me forth'. In 1839–40, he worked as measurer of salt and coal in the Boston Custom House. He returned to print in 1841 with his child's history of New England, *Grandfather's Chair*, the same year he bought $1,000 worth of shares in (and briefly lived and worked at) Brook Farm, the utopian, Fourier*-inspired, Transcendentalist community experiment led by George Ripley, which attracted the likes of Margaret Fuller* and Orestes Brownson, and to which he hoped to take Sophia. *The Blithedale Romance* (1862) casts an ironic backward glance at that experience. Having married Sophia, a marriage to which both gave themselves devotedly over a lifetime, in 1842 he moved into the Old Manse at Concord, formerly the Emerson family home, in which he composed most of the stories for *Mosses from an Old Manse* (1846).

In 1846 the Hawthornes returned to Salem, where, until 1849, when the incoming Whig administration of General Zachary Taylor, as Hawthorne said, 'politically decapitated' him, he served as surveyor of the Custom House – a post he held for party efforts on behalf of the Democrats. His unceremonious expulsion from office evidently spurred his creative energies (his imagination he describes as having become 'a tarnished mirror'), for in 1850 he published his masterpiece, *The Scarlet Letter*, whose prefatory 'The Custom House', among other things, casts a rueful eye upon the precariousness of political appointment. In high dudgeon, with Sophia and their two children, Julian and Una (the model for Pearl in *The Scarlet Letter* – a third child, Rose, was born in 1851), he left Salem for Lenox, in western Massachusetts, and from there was able to witness – no doubt with wry added satisfaction given the circumstances which led to its composition – the widespread praise elicited by *The Scarlet Letter*. Within a couple of years he had written his second romance, *The House of the Seven Gables* (1851), a 'history' ostensibly of two New England dynasties, the Pyncheons and the Maules, which like *The Scarlet Letter* mediates brilliantly between the nineteenth and seventeenth centuries, a story of memory and heritage exploring the 'wizardry' of art as against 'authority', the uses and dangers of vested individual power. There followed in turn another story collection, *The Snow Image And Other Twice-Told Tales* (1852), and two volumes for children intriguingly adapted from classical mythology, *A Wonder Book* (1852) and *Tanglewood Tales* (1853).

During the stay in the Berkshires, Melville's 'Hawthorne and His Mosses' appeared (by a fortuitous stroke Melville and his family were living on a farm in nearby Pittsfield), which led to an immediate, congenial exchange of visits and letters. For all that the relationship was more sought, and acted upon, by Melville ('The divine magnet is on you, and my magnet responds,' he wrote to Hawthorne in November 1851), and despite Hawthorne's native reticence and his diplomatic efforts to check the younger author's effusiveness, it remains a relationship as momentous as any in the literary history of America. In 1852, Hawthorne published *The Blithedale Romance*, a querying, radically ironic narrative about motive and idealistic community schemes for human progress, which embodies in its narrator, Miles Coverdale, an authorial 'presence' as masked as Hawthorne himself was often thought to be. He also, in 1852, wrote a campaign biography, symptomatically conservative in emphasis, for his college friend, Franklin Pierce, whose Democratic presidency led to a consular appointment for him in Liverpool

(1853–7), which he interpreted not as a sinecure but a set of duties to be performed with scrupulous care and energy. After a three-year term, and in worsening health, he moved his family to Italy (1857–9), the setting for his last full-length work, *The Marble Faun* (1860), a story of murder and New World initiation into the 'fallen' world of Rome and almost Jamesian in its working of 'the international situation'. These European years also yielded his shrewd portrait of English life and manners, *Our Old Home* (1863), his *French and Italian Notebooks* (1871) and *English Notebooks* (1870) which – when taken with the *American Notebooks* (1868) and despite the careful pruning by Sophia and her advisers – are indispensable to an understanding of Hawthorne's view of his role as author, and his compositional habits and major themes. Against failing spirits, he continued to write, leaving behind four fragments, all posthumously published, *Septimius Felton* (1872), *The Dolliver Romance* (1876), *Dr Grimshawe's Secret* (1883) and *The Ancestral Footstep* (1883). At his funeral, in May 1864, the mourners included Emerson and almost every writer of consequence in New England.

The sources of Hawthorne's fictional art, whether his romances or short stories, lie in his reading of the great Reformation allegorists, Bunyan, Spenser and Milton especially, and of the King James Bible and the vast 'typological' and emblematic literature of the American Puritans – sermons, annals, meditations – in which he steeped himself. Of nearer writers, he looked to Goldsmith, Washington Irving*, and pre-eminently Sir Walter Scott*. But he sought always his own cast of narrative, neither allegory entirely, nor the novel or story as evolved in nineteenth-century England and Europe in which life could be portrayed three-dimensionally and from the perspective of society dense in manners and historic tradition. Most often, thus, his fiction is pageant-like, narration as dialectical sequences of 'pictures', 'tableaux', emblematic moments and exchanges. His *Notebooks* and different prefaces set out this fictional domain with considerable precision. In *The House of the Seven Gables* he speaks of claiming 'a certain latitude, both as to . . . fashion and material, which he would not have felt entitled to assume, had he professed to be writing a Novel'. *The Blithedale Romance* he situates 'a little removed from the highway of ordinary travel, where the creatures of his brain may play their phantasmagorical antics, without exposing them to too close a comparison with the actual events of their lives.' Perhaps more explicitly still, in 'The Custom House', he proposes his fictional world as 'neutral territory, somewhere between the real world and fairyland, where the Actual and Imaginary may meet, and each imbue itself with the nature of the other.' Nowhere better does Hawthorne exploit his 'neutral territory' than in his major romance, *The Scarlet Letter*. The triangulation of Hester Prynne, Arthur Dimmesdale and Roger Chillingworth, their shifting relationship with the elfin child Pearl, the play of Puritan values as against those of the 'forest', individual freedom as against community regulation – all are set within an 'intermediate' narrative world whose ambiguous centre is the dazzling scarlet 'A' worn by Hester, an emblem at once a source of conflicting definition and a means of defining its very definers.

Hawthorne's principal stories rely equally upon an equivocating play of viewpoint, language and tone, throwing the burden of 'interpretation' with unusual sharpness upon the reader. He once aptly likened his stories to mosses, implantings meant to take root, and grow, almost unnoticed, in the reader's consciousness. They offer, time and again, meticulous, contemplative picturings of hidden guilt, isolation, the will-to-power, sexual and creative self-expression brought into conflict with the prevailing community standard. In his tales of the 'Unpardonable Sin' (defined as a 'want of love and reverence for the Human Soul'), he depicts the lonely, 'scientific' man of power, usually a Chillingworth-like figure, estranged from the necessary values of the heart – tales like 'Ethan Brand', 'The Birthmark', 'Egotism; or the Bosom Serpent', or 'Rappaccini's Daughter'. His more overtly historical stories, which rework Puritan and revolutionary material – 'The Maypole of Merry Mount', for instance, or 'Endicott And The Red Cross', or 'My Kinsman, Major Molineux' – seek from the American past more enduring meanings, about the place of art in society, about crime and punishment, or about the losses and gains in the birth of any nation. Others look to Puritanism as a continuing and representative body of behaviour which can close down mutual sexual trust as in 'Young Goodman Brown'; or to the folly of an uncritical belief in progress as in his Bunyanesque satire of Transcendentalism, 'The Celestial Railroad'; or to the artist's role itself, one of ambiguous, self-knowing power, as in 'The Artist of the Beautiful'. If Hawthorne's equivocations occasionally border on mystification, or suggest unsureness or simple sleight-of-hand, they work far more often to striking imaginative effect. He belongs in the central line of Poe*, Melville, Twain* and James, the shaping – and resonantly American – intelligence behind the romance and his own 'disguised' New World visions of perennial human frailty.

A. Robert Lee

See: Randall Stewart, *Nathaniel Hawthorne: A Biography* (1948); Roy R. Male, *Hawthorne's Tragic Vision* (1957); *Hawthorne Centenary Essays*, ed. Roy Harvey Pearce (1964); *Hawthorne: A Collection of Critical Essays*, ed. A.N. Kaul (1964); *Studies in the Novel*, Nathaniel Hawthorne Special Number, vol. 2, no. 4 (Winter 1970); Frederick C. Crews, *The Sins of the Fathers: Hawthorne's Psychological Themes* (1966); *Nathaniel Hawthorne: New Readings*, ed. A. Robert Lee (1982).

209
HAYDON, Benjamin Robert 1786–1846

British painter

The only child of a Plymouth bookseller, Haydon read Reynolds's *Discourses* and aspired despite partial blindness to become a great history-painter. At the Royal Academy Schools he found a dangerous mentor in Fuseli, while his closest friend was the moralizing Scottish *genre*-painter David Wilkie; and his work would remain throughout his life an unconvincing combination of sublime and banal, of baroque rhetoric with visual journalese. His polemics against the polite taste of the Connoisseurs were instrumental in the government purchase of the Elgin Marbles in 1816. But by 1821 he was in debt, and by 1823 in prison, the first of several spells. Paintings such as *Punch* or *May Day* (1829) were famous in their time, and Haydon held a much-discussed retrospective at the Egyptian Hall in 1832. But he never found the public employment he hoped for. Passed over in 1841 for the Houses of Parliament Mural Commission, he was reduced to recopying his own indifferent *Napoleon on the Way to St. Helena*: 'Began and finished a Napoleon* in two hours and a half; the quickest I ever did, and the twenty-fifth.'

Five years later, begging a state pension for his family, he slit his throat. As a painter Haydon's was a cautionary tale. He had an obsession with scale – 'Without a new large canvas to lean on, I feel as if deserted by the world' – and he had hoped to be heir to the visionary Fuseli – later characterized by him as 'a grotesque mixture of literature, art, scepticism, indelicacy, profanity and kindness'. But in practice Haydon had a rather literal mind, and a composition like *The Black Prince Thanking Lord James Audley after the Battle of Poitiers* is as lugubrious as its title, blandly complex and anecdotal, a congested mass of portrait heads pinned to a murky ground. Its timidity becomes glaring beside the sweep of a Romantic contemporary such as Géricault*. Technically inept, his works have darkened and are today seldom shown; his own favourite, *The Judgment of Solomon*, has been destroyed.

But Haydon's posthumous legacy was his marvellously candid *Autobiography* (published in 1853) where all his weaknesses – indiscretion, naivety, factuality – are turned to strengths. Written in a fresh colloquial style, it is the best account we have of his intellectual milieu, a London made up not only of artists but also of literary contemporaries such as Wordsworth*, Lamb* and Keats*. Haydon may have been, as Macaulay* wrote, 'exactly the vulgar idea of a man of genius', yet his book stands as a human document – an energetic open-hearted ardent man, consumed (in his own words) by 'the agony of ungratified ambition', who wins through to a kind of tragicomic grandeur.

Timothy Hyman

Popular editions include the World's Classics *Autobiography* (introduced by Edmund Blunden). Haydon's complete diary is available in 5 vols (1960–3). See also: *Autobiography and Journals* ed. M. Elwin (1950). See: C. Olney, *Benjamin Robert Haydon, Historical Painter* (1952); Eric B. George, *The Life and Death of Benjamin Robert Haydon* (1948, 2nd edn 1967).

210

HAZLITT, William 1778–1830

British essayist, critic and lecturer

The French Revolution and the English tradition of Dissent are the major shaping forces in Hazlitt's career. His father was a Unitarian preacher whose sympathy with American independence led him to New England in 1783. After four years Hazlitt senior returned with his family to Wem in Shropshire. In 1793 the young Hazlitt was sent to the Unitarian New College at Hackney where he asserted his own independence by declining to prepare for the ministry. His basic training in political and abstract thought was largely self-developed. He read Locke, Rousseau and Burke; he read the English poets and novelists. Towards the end of his life he remarked, 'I am by education and conviction inclined to republicanism and puritanism. In America they have both'; but, he went on to ask, 'can they . . . produce a single head like one of Titian's Venetian nobles?' The tension between intellect and imagination is the vital characteristic of Hazlitt's voluminous work.

He thought of himself to begin with as a metaphysician. He had met Coleridge* who had come to preach a Unitarian sermon at Shrewsbury (see 'My First Acquaintance with Poets'). Hazlitt always felt that he owed to Coleridge, embittered though their relationship became, the awakening of his understanding and the discovery of a language in which to express himself. His first book was *An Essay on the Principles of Human Action* (1805). He had also started out as a painter; a London exhibition of Italian masters had been a revelation. Only gradually did he become the foremost prose-writer of his time; much of his best work is represented by the periodical essays of his last decade, as collected in *Table Talk* (1821–2) and *The Plain Speaker* (1826), and by the masterful studies of his contemporaries in *The Spirit of the Age* (1825).

'A man who thinks to gain and keep the public ear by the force of style, will find it very up-hill work': Hazlitt's statement in 'On the Qualifications necessary to Success in Life' (1820) indicates his main aesthetic aim. But he first came to prominence as a reviewer, lecturer and political journalist. He was a radical, a Jacobin, a man of the French Revolution with which, he claimed, he had 'set out in life'. He had seen 'the dawn of a new era' and he would have no part in the political reaction which followed it. He was a hero-worshipper of Napoleon*; he was a Rousseauesque lover of the Millennium which he had glimpsed on the very verge of adolescence and to which he returned again and again with all the pathos of deeply remembered emotion – 'my earliest hopes will be my last regrets'. A backward-looking temperament is combined with continuously energetic argument and incisive prose.

Hazlitt's power as a critic was recognized when in 1815 he was invited to write for the *Edinburgh Review* and to contribute an article on the Fine Arts to the *Encyclopaedia Britannica*. He was particularly influential as an art critic, in his lifetime and after. George Eliot* refers to him in *Middlemarch* as 'the most brilliant English critic of the day'; Ruskin*, though reluctant to acknowledge it, was strongly influenced by his ability to unite subjective evocation and analysis. Hazlitt, writing about his favourite painters – Poussin, Rembrandt, Titian – and about particular paintings, decisively extended the vocabulary of critical description: words like 'tone' and 'texture' are used with a new expressive flexibility. He introduced the enormous development of the art of art criticism in the nineteenth century, yet his sympathies with painting were traditional rather than advanced ('I am irreclaimably of the old school in painting') and he had little to say about Turner* or Constable*. As a literary critic Hazlitt covered a great deal of ground. His *Characters of Shakespear's Plays* (1817) is not his best work though it had some reputation both at home and on the continent (Heine* refers to Hazlitt as the only significant Shakespearian critic in England) and the essay on *Coriolanus*, which originally appeared in the radical journal the *Examiner*, is a masterpiece of political reflection. Hazlitt's most comprehensive criticism is contained in *Lectures on the English Poets* (1818), *Lectures on the English Comic Writers* (1819) and *Lectures chiefly on the Dramatic Literature of the Age of Elizabeth* (1820). As a lecturer Hazlitt is a striking figure in a developing and characteristically nineteenth-century mode of public education. He is particularly good on Milton (a clear example of Romantic sympathy with that poet) and on Crabbe*, Wordsworth* and contemporary poetry in general. He is excellent on the English novelists, both on the theoretical issue of what they contribute to the idea of reality and the historical accuracy and value of their vision. Hazlitt's own sense of history, always alert, is one of the things which give such a keen edge to his broader criticism of life and society – that and his intense personal consciousness of time.

This latter feeling Hazlitt consciously shares with Rousseau; it is the main reason for his lifelong devotion to that writer, especially to the Rousseau of *La Nouvelle Héloïse* and the *Confessions* – though of course he also honours him as the genius of the French Revolution. What is most political in Hazlitt is often closest to his most personal emotions; yet he can keep politics and his own personality tellingly distinct in the practice of his art. He admires and learns from Burke's style while deploring the opponent of the French Revolution; he differentiates pointedly between Sir Walter Scott* and the author of *Waverley*. One other homage paid to Rousseau was Hazlitt's *Liber Amoris* (1823), an exhibitionistic, documentary account of his infatuation with Sarah Walker, his landlord's daughter and an impassive flirt. Formally the work is interesting but unsatisfying; written too close to the events it is describing, it reveals Hazlitt as both so obviously deluded and so overwrought that he fails to gain much of the reader's sympathy. Its publication added a certain uneasy colouring to the view of Hazlitt which persisted throughout the century. He remained in the consciousness of Victorian writers in various ways: an uncomfortable vivid personality, a supreme critic, a master of prose at once speaking and impassioned. Carlyle* was troubled by him, seeing the working man of letters, metropolitan, totally immersed, and sensing the earnestness, the conviction, of his writing which yet lacked 'the God-like': 'how many a poor Hazlitt must wander on God's verdant earth, like the Unblest on burning deserts; passionately dig wells, and draw up only the dry quicksand; believe that he is seeking Truth, yet only wrestle among endless Sophisms.' Something of Hazlitt's eighteenth-century heritage provokes this picture; something also of the strenuous intellectual side of his personality, that personality which it was the purpose and informing principle of the Hazlitt essay to embody as a whole. The essays are his great achievement. In style and form they have no equal. Many later nineteenth-century writers came to feel that prose had more future as a medium than verse – less had been done with it, there was more room for experiment. R.L. Stevenson's* admiration for Hazlitt's writing is well known and Hazlitt's individual voice, always plain-speaking, occasionally rhapsodic, set new standards in prose style.

Christopher Salvesen

Other works by Hazlitt: *A Reply to the Essay on Population, by the Rev. T.R. Malthus* (1807); *The Round Table* (1817); *A View of the English Stage* (1818); *Political Essays, with Sketches of Public Characters* (1819); *Sketches of the Principal Picture-Galleries in England* (1824); *Notes of a Journey through France and Italy* (1826); *The Life of Napoleon Buonaparte* (4 vols, 1828–30); *Conversations of James Northcote, Esq., R.A.* (1830). There is a *Complete Works*, ed. P.P. Howe (21 vols, 1930–4), as well as *Selected Essays*, ed. G. Keynes (1930), *Selected Writings*, ed. R. Blythe (1970), and *Selected Writings*, ed. C. Salvesen (1972). See: P.P. Howe, *Life of William Hazlitt* (1922, rev. 1928); E. Schneider, *The Aesthetics of William Hazlitt* (1933); H. Baker, *William Hazlitt* (1962); R. Park, *Hazlitt and the*

Spirit of the Age (1971); J. Houck, *William Hazlitt: A Reference Guide* (1977).

211
HEBBEL, Friedrich 1813–63

German dramatist

Hebbel was born in 1813 in Schleswig-Holstein. The son of a stonemason, he had to endure privation in his early years. After studying law at university, first in Hamburg and later in Heidelberg, he decided to devote himself entirely to literature. Initially his work met with little success, and his first play *Judith* (1841) was considered too sexually provocative to be performed in its original version. Gradually, however, his popularity increased and during his last years, spent in Vienna, he was generally recognized as the leading German dramatist of his day.

Although he always obstinately refused to admit it, Hebbel's views on the nature and function of drama were strongly influenced by Hegel* and Schelling*. They are expounded principally in two essays, *Mein Wort über das Drama* ('My Views on the Drama', 1843) and the preface to *Maria Magdalena* (1844). Hebbel conceives the world in a state of constant flux occasioned by the conflict of two opposing forces which he terms the Idea and the Individual. At the same time the Individual is not totally separate from the Idea but forms a constituent part of it. Conflict arises only when the Individual, through an act of individuation, seeks to detach itself from the Idea which, in its turn, strives to reassert its original harmony and unity. Hebbel emphasizes that this struggle can have but one outcome: the destruction of the Individual and the restoration of equilibrium within the Idea. Whilst the terminology of the theoretical essays is strictly metaphysical, reference to Hebbel's diaries and letters suggests that he viewed the dualism within the Idea in religious terms. The postulation of the Idea at war with itself is really another formula for a divided godhead, a concept also found in Schelling. In any case the conclusion for Hebbel is inescapable: man's guilt is existential and suffering is inevitably bound up with the human condition.

The notion of existential guilt places Hebbel at the end of a long line of development in German literature and links his work closely with that of his contemporary Georg Büchner*. Like Büchner, Hebbel is deeply disturbed at the prospect of innocent suffering. But whereas Büchner's characters tend to see creation as the product of a gigantic cosmic error, Hebbel, whilst never losing sight of man's tragic position within the world, is able to accept suffering as a necessary constituent in a wider universal process. Indeed, one of the main purposes of the theoretical essays is to demonstrate that drama, and more particularly tragedy, has a vital role to play in the moral education of man; for by presenting what is necessary and unalterable in the cosmic process it can reconcile us with our existential guilt and its concomitant suffering. In this way, Hebbel argues, it eliminates all forms of dualism in life and unites us with the Universal.

The extent to which Hebbel incorporated these theories into his creative writings is still a matter for dispute. *Judith*, written before they were fully matured, certainly seems to contain little evidence of them. On the other hand, later works like *Maria Magdalena*, *Herodes und Mariamne* (1850), *Agnes Bernauer* (1852) and *Gyges und sein Ring* (1856) are often interpreted as unequivocal illustrations of the theory. In each of these dramas the central figures come to grief, not primarily as a result of any innate moral failings, but because they happen to be in conflict with the prevailing ethos of their age. They can be said, in fact, to embody moral values for which their time is not yet ripe. But perhaps the clearest expression of the Hebbelian dialectic is to be found in *Die Nibelungen* (1862). In this, his most ambitious work, Hebbel shows how two irreconcilable ethical codes not only clash with each other with catastrophic consequences, but also bear within themselves the seeds of their own dissolution.

Although nearly all Hebbel's plays are based upon biblical, historical or mythological themes, the psychology is utterly modern. Tortured characters wrestle with each other in a never ending agony. For this reason Hebbel has sometimes been regarded as a forerunner of Strindberg*. Yet it is probably more reasonable to look upon him as a typical child of his time. On the one hand he was instinctively drawn towards the values of an earlier age which still firmly believed in the moral and educative function of art. On the other he was caught up in the growing pessimism which began to dominate German thought and literature after the decline of Kantian idealism. The impasse into which he was inexorably driven is reflected in the anguish of his characters.

Derrick Barlow

Apart from plays and essays Hebbel also wrote a number of stories and poems. The definitive edition of his works is the *Sämtliche Werke*, ed. R.M. Werner (1920). See: G.B. Rees, *Hebbel as a Dramatic Artist* (1930); E. Purdie, *Friedrich Hebbel* (1932); M. Garland, *Hebbel's Prose Tragedies* (1973).

212
HEGEL, Georg Wilhelm Friedrich 1770–1831

German philosopher

Hegel was the son of an official in the service of the Duke of Baden-Württemberg. He studied from 1788–93 at the Tübinger Stift, a higher education seminary specializing in the training of young men for public service. There he formed close friendships with Friedrich Hölderlin* and Friedrich Schelling*. The three shared a common intellectual outlook. Politically, they hoped for a regeneration in Germany to correspond to the revolution in France. Culturally, they contrasted the fragmentation of contemporary art and religion with the harmony of Greek life. Only in philosophy did they consider Germany a leading force, thanks to the work of Immanuel Kant. 'Kant is the Moses of our nation,' wrote Hölderlin. He had led his people out of bondage; others must take them into the Promised Land.

In the years to 1806, when he completed the *Phenomenology of Spirit* (*Phänomenologie des Geistes*, 1807, trans. 1977), Hegel worked as a tutor and as a lecturer at the University of Jena. He wrote several minor works (see *Early Theological Writings*, trans. 1948; *The Difference between Fichte's and Schelling's System of Philosophy*, trans. 1977; and *Political Writings*, ed. Z. Pelczynski, 1964) in which he pursued the need for a reintegrated cultural and religious life and for a systematic, post-Kantian philosophy.

The *Phenomenology* has always been the most admired of Hegel's works. Though difficult, it has a breadth and grandeur of presentation which carries the reader through its complexities. On one level the *Phenomenology* represents a rejection of Kantian philosophy and the conception of experience on which it is based. According to Kant, our experience is composed of two elements: a *content*, received from outside, through the senses, and a *form*, imposed on the content by the activity of the mind. The mind, therefore, sets limits on possible experience. Philosophy, by examining the mind's structure, gains knowledge of the structure of reality, in so far as it can be given to us.

For Hegel, this conception of philosophy makes use of a model - of the mind imposing its form on an essentially non-mental reality - which is psychological, rather than philosophical, in origin. Kant misconceives the mind as if it were an instrument or medium. Yet, though it rejects the Kantian conception of experience, the *Phenomenology* is, at another level, Kantian in inspiration; Hegel, too, aims to disclose the governing structures underlying experience. But, for the reasons given, he cannot proceed by trying to isolate the form of experience and treating it as something to be analysed independent of its content. Instead he adopts a historical approach. The *Phenomenology* traces the different forms which mind's relation to the world takes at each stage of historical development. The mind Hegel is dealing with he calls *Geist* (standardly translated as 'spirit'), for it is not the individual mind but that common intellect in which, he claims, all men, as individual intelligences, participate.

Thus, men's political and cultural relations (which,

from *Geist's* point of view, are forms of its own self-relation) are as much part of the *Phenomenology's* subject matter as the traditional philosophical questions of body and mind, etc. The final stage, presented at the end of the *Phenomenology*, is Absolute Knowledge: the individual becomes aware that *Geist's* structure permeates all of reality, nature as well as history. So a recognizably Kantian project – the discovery of structures of experience – has been carried, by non-Kantian means – the description of the development of consciousness – to a quite anti-Kantian conclusion: the claim that it is possible to give a philosophical account of the absolute structure of reality.

The *Phenomenology's* description of *Geist's* development leads to an important difficulty, however. The standpoint which sees the stages of consciousness as forming, together, a single, unified development is not that of the individuals who actually undergo the process. But what entitles Hegel to adopt it? It appears that Hegel is assuming his conclusion; making use of a philosophical perspective which the *Phenomenology* itself should derive.

Hegel does not deny this apparent circularity: 'the road to science [*Wissenschaft*] is science itself,' he writes. But it is only apparent. What is assumed and what is derived are, in fact, different. What is assumed at the beginning is a form of consciousness with the ability to retrace its own development when presented to it philosophically. What is derived – Absolute Knowledge – is a consciousness with a full awareness of its own nature and capacities.

Two important points follow: that the *Phenomenology* depends on the *historical* assumption that consciousness has reached the stage at which it can participate in 'science'; and that the *Phenomenology* is not the ultimate philosophical statement. It leads beyond itself, as Hegel intended it should, to the fully conscious unfolding of knowledge in the *Science of Logic*.

Hegel hoped that the *Phenomenology* would secure him a permanent academic appointment. But it was not to be. As he finished his masterpiece, the philosopher of history's career was disrupted by history itself, in the shape of the Battle of Jena. The Napoleonic campaign spoiled Hegel's chance of a university post (he was first appointed to a professorship at Heidelberg in 1816) and he worked as a journalist and then as a schoolteacher.

It was during the latter period that Hegel published his *Science of Logic* (*Wissenschaft der Logik*, 1812, trans. 1969), the work which was intended to present the structures of the Absolute in pure form – 'the exposition of God as he is in his eternal essence before the creation of nature and a finite mind', as he puts it. Even philosophers sympathetic to Hegel have generally found such claims on behalf of the *Logic* excessive. It seems that Hegel is pre-empting the function of the scientist and attempting to settle *a priori* what are really matters for practical investigation.

However that may be, there can be no doubt of the central importance the *Logic* has for Hegel. By its means the philosopher is enabled to see clearly those essential features of reality which others grasp obscurely and intuitively. This conception resembles Plato's vision of the philosopher as one who turns away from the world of shadows to the world of pure forms. But, unlike Plato, Hegel does not see these forms as a separate realm, lying behind, as it were, our own world. The philosopher sees them as part of the single 'Idea' which, developed and articulated, unifies the apparent diversity of reality. The 'immanent self-constructing path' of this pure Idea is what the *Logic* aims to chart.

In 1818 Hegel was called to the chair in Berlin where he remained till his death. The works of his later years are systematizations and recapitulations, compared to the *Logic*: attempts to show the rationality of various disciplines by discerning in them the lineaments of the *Logic's* structure. Many were given as lectures and only published posthumously. (See *Lectures on the Philosophy of History*, trans. 1956; *Philosophy of Right*, 1821, trans. 1942; *Aesthetics*, trans. 1975; *Encyclopaedia of the Philosophical Sciences*, 1817, trans. 1970–5; *Lectures on the History of Philosophy*, trans. 1892–6).

The most significant of the later works are the *Philosophy of Right* (*Grundlinien der Philosophie des Rechts*) and the *Lectures on the Philosophy of History*, which have had a disproportionate influence on Hegel's received image. On their evidence Hegel has been seen as an apologist for Prussian militarism and, even, as an incipient Fascist. These claims are based on various statements, for example, 'What is rational is actual and what is actual is rational', which appear to place established power beyond criticism. Such remarks should be set in context, however. Certainly, Hegel believes that whatever exists – and thus any existing political structure – has its place in a divinely rational scheme of things. But this does not make him an unreserved apologist for authority; if Caesar is the embodiment of historical destiny, so too is Brutus.

Yet it must be admitted that the 'rational' state described in the *Philosophy of Right* strongly resembles Prussia. Moreover, Hegel is open to two serious theoretical criticisms.

The first concerns the theological dimension of his view of history – his claim to have provided a demonstration of its beneficent, providential character. Even if Hegel succeeds in showing, as he claims to, that events which seem to be purely evil (the sufferings of innocent children, for example) are necessary for some desirable end, this does not, it can be objected, justify them theologically. To accept the sort of reasoning which justifies evil as part of the price which must be paid for good would be to accept that the realization of God's purposes is subjected to the constraints of necessity; implicitly, the divine is reduced to the human level.

The second criticism is sociological; to the idea of authority in the rational state. Hegel is committed to the view that social authority will be acknowledged directly and spontaneously by the state's citizens. (The alternative, a fully explicit justification, can only be provided at the level of philosophy; but not all the state's citizens can be expected to be philosophers!) Yet it can be objected that hierarchical societies of the sort Hegel envisages do not show such natural and spontaneous cohesion.

These objections, in the hands of Kierkegaard* and Marx* respectively, have been the starting point for the two strongest surviving post-Hegelian intellectual movements. Soon after Hegel's death philosophers influenced by him divided into right and left camps. The right interpreted Hegel, as far as possible, in terms compatible with orthodox Christianity; the left argued that the truth of Hegelianism lay in a critique of theology. Something like the ideas of the Hegelian right were embodied in the movement of British Idealism at the end of the century. Marx, Kierkegaard and Nietzsche* were all, in different ways, successors of the Hegelian left.

Philosophers outside the Marxist and existentialist traditions have tended to regard Hegel's system as, at best, a mausoleum of misplaced ambition. Although Marxists and existentialists have been more sympathetic to Hegel, they have seen little value in the commitment which Hegel himself regarded as paramount: to a universal, philosophical conception of rationality. Hegel was aware that the scientific progress of the Enlightenment had at the same time led to a loss of meaning from other areas of life. But he was no romantic; he did not seek to return to a world of myth and poetry. Only knowledge would heal the wound it had opened.

Michael E. Rosen

Most of Hegel's works have been translated (see references in text). The modern translations are very good, although unfortunately not mutually consistent in their rendering of key terms. The best comprehensive study is Charles Taylor, *Hegel* (1975). Its lucid presentation makes it also the best introduction. H. Marcuse, *Reason and Revolution* (1955), and A. Kojève, *Introduction to the Reading of Hegel* (1969), are outstanding interpretations from a Marxist and an existentialist perspective respectively.

213
HEINE, Heinrich 1797–1856

German poet

Heine is a Romantic and a Realist, a master of lyrical music and of ironic dissonance, a committed satirist and a doubter of all commitment – a deeply divided mind reflecting the complexity and conflicts of his age.

To be born in 1797 meant being brought up simultaneously in two worlds, that of the Romantic literary imagination, devoted to folksong simplicity, fairy-tale fantasy and a mistily perceived Germanic medieval past; and that of modern society, commercial and ideological, seeking stability after the upheavals of the French Revolution and the Napoleonic Wars in a phase of reactionary politics. The one world was as uncompromisingly hard as the other was seductively soft; they offered a choice of real and unreal, between which no compromise was possible. Heine first learned the Romantic poetic game, to the point of mastery; in the *Buch der Lieder* ('Book of Songs', 1827) he revelled in manipulating its rhymes and rhythms and images, and in treating its stock themes, wistfully erotic or macabre. But even in the earliest poems, dream and visions are followed by rude awakening. Soon he begins to undo the Romantic illusion, changing tone and register or stepping cynically outside convention to show the falseness of his own artefact. Yet debunking of a superseded mode is not the whole story, this is not gleeful, literary satire: the disillusion is painful, because the poetic world he undoes is the only one available to the poet. That is the reason why some poems are kept untouched by irony and can still be read as wholly Romantic, pastiches so perfect that they transcend that term (e.g. 'Der Tod, das ist die kühle Nacht'). Many of them inspired superb settings by Lieder composers, especially Robert Schumann*. It is also the reason why occasionally the poet turns irony on irony and triumphantly unmasks the real feeling concealed behind the unmasked pretence ('Nun ist es Zeit . . . '). In serving as a tool of reluctant exposure, irony becomes a means of sincere expression.

While still caught up in this love-hate affair with Romantic convention, Heine found a different liberty in prose. His *Reisebilder* ('Travel Sketches', 1826–31) are travelogues in the manner of Sterne's *Sentimental Journey* but venturing more boldly into matters of society and politics – though always with the light, brief touch that relies on a quick reader and a slow censor. Heine acquired a reputation with both. The potential dangers of being a marked man in the darkened Germany overseen by 'Prince Mitternacht' (Metternich), plus the failure of some half-hearted commercial and professional beginnings, plus the permanent problem of being a Jew in German society, drove Heine into exile. From 1831 to his death in 1856 he lived in Paris, divided again between nostalgia for the harmlessly beautiful aspects of Old Germany and pleasure in what the capital of European culture and social progress could offer. It offered Heine acquaintance and high standing with the leading figures in art, affairs and intellectual life – Balzac*, George Sand*, Dumas *père*, Gautier*, Chopin*, Liszt*, Guizot, Rothschild, Michelet* and many more; and also contact with the new socialist sects – the Saint-Simonians and later Karl Marx*, to whom his essentially Enlightenment liberalism was attracted. Paris also offered special opportunities for a brilliant exile seeking to live by his pen. Heine wrote surveys of German philosophy, religion and poetry for a French readership, and of French art and current affairs for German journals. Though conceived as journalism or *haute vulgarisation*, these works – *Zur Geschichte der Religion und Philosophie in Deutschland* ('On the History of Religion and Philosophy in Germany', 1835), *Die Romantische Schule* ('The Romantic School', 1836), *Französische Zustände* ('Conditions in France', 1852), and later *Lutezia* (1854) – are classics of sharp perception and glittering style. Their sharpness penetrates deep, it is not all surface wit; Heine's choice of detail to focus on and his shrewd snap judgments have roots in a profound grasp of society, politics and culture and of the historical and continuing relations between them.

Paris also inspired poetry of a frank sensualism and an equally frank hangover mood which suggests that physical fulfilment was no answer, personal or poetic, to the unrequited love which the *Buch der Lieder* so persistently lamented. With this cynical vein soon exhausted and his Romantic vein deeply compromised, Heine the poet was virtually at a loose end. Gradually his poetry followed his prose into political action. It is remarkable, and a sign of yet another inner division in Heine, that it took so long to do this, that the Romantic tradition of poetry as a realm separate from social reality kept so strong a hold on his 'progressive' mind. So much so that the prelude to his major political satire was a satire on political satire. *Atta Troll* (1841) is a mock-epic about an escaped dancing bear of radical opinions. Between grand digressions, it pilloried Heine's own presumed ideological allies of young Germany for their artistic deficiencies (ultimately, that is, for the inflexibility, vagueness and hollowness that they had allegedly brought into art). Understandably, they declared Heine to be characterless and unreliable. Certainly he was not of the stuff which parties are made of – a man who found it so hard to agree with himself was unlikely to agree for long with anyone else.

But the defiant play of imagination in its digressions which made *Atta Troll* a 'midsummer night's dream' was a last fling of his Romantic sentiment. Heine's continuing drift towards politics, reinforced by a flying visit to Germany in 1843, resulted in a complementary 'winter's tale', *Deutschland* (1844), a terse, pungent verse-travelogue which fused the best things from his poetic and prose past. The old simple rhymed folksong stanza proves wickedly effective for satire. Social and political targets are precisely observed and neatly transfixed, but all within an imaginative framework of dreams and visions, ghosts and *Doppelgänger*, also taken from the Romantic stock-in-trade, but all now ideologically charged. *Deutschland* is a classic of satire, one of the few in world literature that live by their sheer verve and wit and need no laborious resuscitation by historical footnotes. Equally sharp and often more scurrilous are the *Zeitgedichte*, the last part of Heine's second verse-collection, *Neue Gedichte* ('New Poems', 1844). Heine uses alternately rapier and club to attack the respect for personalities and institutions on which political passivity rests. Among the voluminous committed poetry of these years before 1848, his is much the richest and funniest (although the common opinion that Heine's is the *only* good political poetry of that phase comes from too many critics taking his word for it).

Disillusionment with the failure of the 1848 Revolutions, and the steady encroachment of a wasting disease that finally brought him to a dragging 'mattress-grave', drove Heine in upon himself. In these last years he found a new unified style, strengthened as well as overshadowed by the sense of finality. Irony became nearly superfluous. This is bitter poetry, some of it personal lyric, but more of it objective narrative – the hard truths of human nature and human history are shaped in stories from fact and legend that compose the last dark picture of a realist who is now at the end of his strength and the height of his powers.

No other major German writer is as readable as Heine, and none certainly is so urbanely amusing. Few writers anywhere combine such brilliance of surface with so uncannily penetrating an eye for the deeper truths and larger implications of what is seen. Heine's sketches, poetic, critical or social, in appearance so lightly dashed off, can contain a long history or deliver an ominous prophecy. With his mixed experience and divided allegiance, Heine bridges the gap between Romanticism and Realism; between absorption in the imagination and involvement in society; between the age of artistic patronage and the age of the literary market; between the fading Enlightenment and rising socialism. He faces the issues these changes produce with ironic integrity; and there is no better illumination for them than the fireworks of his wit.

T.J. Reed

Translations include: *The Complete Poems of Heinrich Heine*, trans. Hal Draper (1982); *Heinrich Heine: The Poems* trans. Louis Untermeyer (1937) and *The Prose Writings of Heinrich Heine* ed. Havelock Ellis (1887). See: E.M. Butler, *Heinrich Heine: A biography* (1956); Jeffrey L. Sammons, *Heinrich Heine: A Modern*

Biography (1979); Barker Fairley, *Heinrich Heine: An Interpretation* (1954); S.S. Prawer, *Heine the Tragic Satirist* (1961).

214
HELMHOLTZ, Hermann Ludwig von 1821–94

German scientist and philosopher

Helmholtz, one of the most versatile scientific genii of the nineteenth century, was born in Potsdam and educated at Potsdam Gymnasium where his father taught philology and classical literature. His family lacked the financial resources to provide him with a university education and he was obliged to accept a government scholarship to study medicine at the Royal Friedrich-Wilhelm Institute of Medicine and Surgery from which he obtained a doctorate in medicine at the age of twenty-one. The holders of such scholarships were normally required to spend ten years as physicians in the Prussian army. However, in recognition of his abilities, Helmholtz was allowed to conduct research in lieu of his regular duties. In a laboratory constructed at his barracks in Potsdam he worked on fermentation and the conversion of food into energy in animals. In 1847 he was released from the army to become an instructor in anatomy at the Academy of Arts in Berlin. He was appointed professor of pathology and physiology at Königsberg in 1848; of physiology and anatomy at Bonn in 1855; of physiology at Heidelberg in 1858; of physics at Berlin in 1871. In 1888 he became president and first director of the Physico-Technical Institute in Berlin, a post which he held until his death.

Helmholtz's greatest achievement was his formulation of the principle of the conservation of energy which states that ultimately energy is never lost nor gained but only transformed. This, which represents one of the most important scientific developments of the nineteenth century, was presented in a paper, *The Conservation of Force* (*Über die Erhaltung der kraft*, 1847, trans. 1853), to the Physical Society of Berlin when Helmholtz was twenty-six. Initially the importance of this work was not recognized and the paper was refused publication as a most fantastic speculation. While the idea of the conservation of energy for inanimate matter was not new, Helmholtz was the first to give a sufficiently broad formulation of the principle, writing that 'all that occurs is described by the ebb and flow of the eternally undiminished and unaugmentable energy supply of the world.' More specific forms of the principle were used by him to obtain substantial results in physics, chemistry and physiology. Helmholtz saw that it applied to both inanimate and animate matter and deployed it in arguing against the vitalists who thought of the soul as capable of creating energy. For Helmholtz the principle was a source of the unity of

science for he argued that it meant that all sciences ultimately reduce to mechanics. This influenced Sigmund Freud who spent a term in Berlin to hear Helmholtz's lectures to adopt the view that all mental processes are explicable in terms of underlying physical and chemical processes in the brain.

Helmholtz was the first to make a serious experimental study of the eye. In the course of this he invented the opthalmoscope which made possible the observation of the retina of the eye. Among other successes he explained the mechanism of the focusing of the eye and the co-ordinated movement of the eyes which produces a single vision. He developed Thomas Young's* theory of colour vision showing that there are three primary colours, red, green and violet, detected by three different systems of optical nerves. His three-volume *Handbook of Physiological Optics* (*Handbuch der physiologischen Optik*, 3 vols, 1856–67, trans. 1924–5) is the classical text on the eye. Helmholtz then turned his attention to the ear, explaining the role of the bones of the ear in the perception of sound. His greatest success in physiological acoustics was his pioneering work on the perception of tone presented in his *On the Sensations of Tone as a Physiological Basis for the Theory of Music* (*Die Lehre von den Tonempfindungen als physiologische Grundlage für die Theorie der Musik*, 1863, trans. 1875). Helmholtz's work covers an astonishing range including meteorological physics. Kelvin* used Helmholtz's results in hydrodynamics to develop his model of the atom. The science of thermodynamics was created by Rudolf Julius Emmanuel Clausius*, Ludwig Boltzmann* and Lord Kelvin from Helmholtz's studies of entropy. He was an influential contributor to the study of electromagnetism where his work was extended by his student Heinrich Rudolf Hertz*. Helmholtz saw that the investigation of the geometry of space was an empirical matter and, working independently of Georg Riemann*, he produced a non-Euclidean geometry of the Riemannian type. In all he produced over two hundred books and papers, in addition to giving numerous popular lectures explicating the implications of contemporary scientific developments.

Helmholtz's work on the eye and the ear provided the basis for later scientific endeavours which have superseded his own. In physics he represents an impressive refinement of the classical Newtonian approach, an approach which has been abandoned. However, in philosophy his writings are not merely of historical interest but contain insights of contemporary importance. Influenced by Kant and by the British empiricists, Helmholtz sought to turn the prevailing Hegelian* tide by developing an empiricist philosophy infused with the discoveries of science. His belief in the importance of a partnership between philosophy and science led him to urge the appointment of philosophically minded scientists to chairs of philosophy in Germany. It was imperative, he held, that each age pursue the primary aim of philosophy by examining the sources of our knowledge and the degree of its justification. His work in physiology led him to the view that there are two distinct processes in perception: the transmission of physical messages to the brain and the interpretation of these messages by the mind. He had discovered that a white page illuminated with green light produced the same visual sensation as a white page illuminated with a mixture of blue and yellow light. This showed that a sensation could not be construed as providing a copy or image of what caused its production. The sensation is a sign which need not have any kind of similarity to what it is a sign of. Consequently perception is a matter of learning to decode on the basis of experience the sensations given in experience. We are not normally aware of carrying out such decoding and Helmholtz introduced the notion of unconscious inferences to account for this fact. This seminal alternative to the popular representative theory of perception is the basis of many contemporary philosophical accounts of perception. Among those influenced by it was Ivan Petrovich Pavlov* who took the process of unconscious inference to correspond to the mechanism of conditioned reflex. Helmholtz's writings on perception and other aspects of epistemology together with his desire to integrate work in science and philosophy provided part of the inspiration for the development of the Vienna Circle and logical positivism.

W.H. Newton-Smith

See his *Epistemological Writings*, ed. R.S. Cohen and Y. Elkana (1977), which includes an introduction to his work and a bibliography. For other scientific writings see *Popular Lectures on Scientific Subjects* (1865 and 1871, trans. 1881) and *Selected Writings of Hermann von Helmholtz* (1971). On Helmholtz see Leo Koenigsberger, *Hermann von Helmholtz* (3 vols, 1902–3, abridged trans. 1906).

215
HEREDIA, José-Maria de 1842–1905

French poet

Heredia was born in Cuba. His father was of Spanish extraction, and the family proudly traced its descent from a conquistador who had served under Cortés; his mother was a Frenchwoman of respectable, but not illustrious, stock. Though Heredia spent some time in Cuba as a child and as a young man, it was in France that he received his education, attending a Catholic college in Senlis, then the École des Chartes, and in his maturity and old age he lived in Paris. He took no interest in the running of the coffee plantations owned by the family and, though he embarked on legal stud-

ies, he did not complete the course and never practised. He preferred to devote his leisure to literature. Yet, though a leading literary figure of the day, becoming a member of the Académie Française in 1894, he wrote comparatively little. Between 1877 and 1887 he published the four volumes of his version of the sixteenth-century *True History of the Conquest of New Spain* by Bernal Diaz de Castillo, and he translated a few other works from the Spanish. His reputation is, however, founded on little more than one hundred sonnets. Most of them were first published separately; then, in 1893, they were brought together, along with a handful of longer poems, to form the collection to which Heredia gave the title *Les Trophées* (*The Trophies*).

In *Les Trophées*, and the aesthetic inspiring it, may be seen a reflection and even a harmonization of the contrasts and contradictions evident in Heredia himself. While young, he came under the influence of Leconte de Lisle and, finding perhaps a father figure, he was never to waver in personal attachment or in adherence to his mentor's literary doctrines. Recoiling from the emotional exhibitionism of much Romantic poetry and the shoddiness of its versification, Leconte de Lisle saw merit in an impersonal manner and in a return to traditions of conscientious craftsmanship. These views, which are stated explicitly in the preface to his *Poèmes antiques* (1852) and exemplified in that collection and in his *Poèmes barbares* (1862), attracted a following in the 1860s. The group that emerged became known as the Parnassian poets, because much of their early work appeared in the various issues of *Le Parnasse contemporain*. Heredia was a thoroughgoing exponent of Parnassian principles.

Les Trophées is, as its title hints, a celebration of triumphs, and Heredia sets out to encapsulate in language of unfading brilliancy the most precious spots of time. The vision is wide, and the work invites comparison with Hugo's* *La Légende des siècles*. Heredia first evokes the myths of Ancient Greece; then he recalls stirring episodes from Roman history; next he turns his gaze on the Middle Ages, the Renaissance and the romance of the conquistadors; the Far East too offers grandiose visions of mankind, while nature and works of art afford privileged moments of rapt tranquillity. The colouring is vivid; details are closely observed and minutely described. The force of these impersonal poems is all the greater because vast subjects and titanic emotions are encompassed within the strict confines of a sonnet. Heredia was profoundly responsive to heroic example and great art. He loved words too, glorying in their precision as well as in their sound. In the Parnassian programme he found the discipline he needed, so that the seeming impassivity and the objectivity of stern technique could bring out, by contrast, the deep emotions of what he described. Because of his habit of fastidious revision, publication of *Les Trophées* was delayed until well after the initial wave of enthusiasm for Parnassian poetry had passed. *Les Trophées* was lauded for a time, but it marked the end of an evolutionary process: Heredia had no French successors.

C.N. Smith

The best edition of Heredia's poetry is: *Poésies complètes* (1924); see too *Les Trophées*, ed. W.N. Ince (1979). Translations of *Les Trophées*: E.R. Taylor (1902), Merle St Croix Wright (1927) and – fifty sonnets only – Brian Hill (1962). See: M. Ibrovac, *José-Maria de Heredia: sa vie, son oeuvre* (1923) and *Les Sources des 'Trophées'* (1923); Alvin Harms, *José-Maria de Heredia* (1975); W.N. Ince, *Heredia* (1979).

216
HERTZ, Heinrich Rudolf 1857–94

German physicist

No technological advance of the last two hundred years has had a greater cultural effect than the discovery of our ability to transmit electrical disturbances over enormous distances via 'radio waves'. It was in the 1890s that Guglielmo Marconi* read of the epoch-making experiments of Heinrich Hertz which demonstrated the possibility of such 'electric (or Hertzian) waves'. Marconi's work was an attempt to exploit practically the effect which Hertz had demonstrated.

The experiment for which Hertz is chiefly remembered was performed in Karlsruhe in 1887. He set up two polished metallic spheres so that there was a small air gap between them and connected the spheres by wires to an induction or 'spark' coil. This meant that large electric charges of opposite signs were built up on the two spheres. Very rapidly, the potential difference between the two spheres became so large that the air in the gap between them became ionized and hence produced a conducting path along which a spark occurred. This spark oscillated between the two spheres until equilibrium was restored; the potential difference between the two would then be built up again and the process repeated.

According to the theory of electromagnetism developed by James Clerk Maxwell* an electromagnetic pulse should be produced by each spark and the series of sparks should produce electromagnetic waves of a frequency determined by the oscillation of the charges. Hertz set up a simple unclosed loop of wire some distance from the sparking gap and observed a faint spark in the 'receiver' circuit, indicating an induced current in the detector just as Maxwell's theory predicted.

Maxwell himself had made no explicit reference to unclosed electrical circuits although the existence of these electric waves is definitely predicted by his theory. Indeed, according to that theory, light itself is such a wave – though one of enormously high frequency. The most thrilling aspect of his experiments for Hertz himself was his ability to show (by measuring the wavelength of his electric waves and computing their frequency from the oscillations of his spark) that the velocity of these waves was equal to that of light – hence confirming the Maxwellian prediction of the essential identity of the two forms of radiation. Hertz went on to show that his electric waves could be reflected, refracted, polarized and diffracted just like light.

The most fascinating incidental discovery which Hertz made during this series of experiments was that the spark in the detector circuit was stronger when that circuit was exposed to the light of the spark in the primary circuit. He performed a series of experiments in 1887 which convinced him that this effect was caused purely by the ultraviolet light emitted by the primary spark. Although its significance was obscure to him, Hertz had in fact discovered the 'photoelectric effect' – the ability of light to release electrons from the surfaces of metals.

Aside from the enormous practical consequences which Hertz's experimental results turned out to have, they were also of crucial theoretical importance. At the time Hertz began his experiments, the electromagnetic theories of Weber and F.E. Neumann were more widely accepted in Germany than the theory of Maxwell. According to the former theories, electrodynamic action was an instantaneous action-at-a-distance effect like Newtonian gravitational attraction, whilst according to Maxwell the origin of electrodynamic actions was the condition of the medium (the electromagnetic ether) between ponderable bodies. Hertz's demonstration of the existence of 'electric waves' with a finite velocity was a direct confirmation of the Maxwell contiguous-action-through-a-medium view: and although, strictly speaking, the action-at-a-distance view could (as Riemann* demonstrated) be reconciled with electric waves of finite velocity, there is no doubt that Hertz's experiments effectively brought about the downfall of this view.

Hertz himself did very important theoretical work in electrodynamics, which, if less heralded outside the scientific community than his experimental work, was almost equally influential within that community. The precise import of Maxwell's theory was still a matter of great dispute in the 1880s. Hertz set out to clarify the foundations of that theory notably by excising from it what he saw as traces of the action-at-a-distance view. He eliminated Maxwell's distinction between the polarization of, and the electric force in, the free ether, insisting that the polarizations of the medium are the only entities which really exist. His crystal clear formulation of electromagnetic theory helped others to spot clear difficulties in it – H.A. Lorentz's* electron theory, for example, emerged in this way.

In a famous lecture given in Heidelberg in 1889 Hertz suggested that his ether-theoretic elimination of the electric force should be taken as a paradigm for further developments; gravity, too, for example, should be eliminable in proper ether-based physics. Indeed, much of his later work – inspired by Mach* and particularly by Helmholtz* – was concerned with the complete elimination of forces from mechanics. His work was contained in a posthumously published book, *The Principles of Mechanics* (*Die Principien der Mechanik, in neuem Zusammenhange*, 1894, trans. 1899). Hertz's elimination programme never really bore fruit but the axiomatization of mechanics and the methodological discussions it contains make it a notable achievement of nineteenth-century philosophy of science.

Hertz had been born into a prosperous and cultured Hanseatic family in Hamburg in 1857. He was educated at the universities of Munich and Berlin (where he came under the influence of von Helmholtz who was his main inspiration and who introduced him to the problems of electromagnetism). He held posts at Kiel, Karlsruhe (where most of his important experiments were performed) and Bonn. He died in Bonn at the age of thirty-six on New Year's Day 1894, having for several years suffered from some obscure malignant bone condition.

John Worrall

Hertz's collected works were published in three volumes: *Schriften vermischten Inhalts* ('Miscellaneous Papers', 1895); *Untersuchungen über die Ausbreitung der elektrischen Kraft* ('Electric Waves', 1892); and *The Principles of Mechanics, Presented in a New Form* (*Die Principien der Mechanik, in neuem Zusammenhange* 1894, trans. 1899).

217
HERZEN, Alexandr Ivanovich 1812–70

Russian revolutionary thinker, journalist and memoirist

Alexandr Herzen was born in Moscow, the son of Ivan Alexandrovich Iakovlev, a wealthy Russian nobleman. His surname was Iakovlev's invention, since the boy was illegitimate. But he was given every attention and became heir to a considerable fortune. He was educated at home and then studied natural science at Moscow University. He became involved in radical student politics and later spent two periods of exile in provincial Russia. At the age of twenty-six he married his first cousin, Natalie Zakharina, and in 1847 he left Russia and took his family to the West where he witnessed the Revolutions of 1848. He settled briefly in Nice but the discovery that his wife was having an affair with his closest western friend, the German poet Georg Herwegh, under his own roof, engulfed his private life. The case became a *cause célèbre* and Natalie died amidst a public struggle between Herzen and Herwegh for support amongst Western revolutionaries. Deeply shaken, Herzen moved with his children to London in 1852, only returning to the continent in 1865. He died in Paris.

An immensely gifted, vivacious and self-confident young man, Herzen reacted strongly against the denial of individual rights in autocratic Russia. His own frustrations opened his eyes to the plight of the enserfed peasantry. Western ideas intensified his protest and provided him with a vocabulary for articulating his aspirations. He was highly receptive to Romantic and idealist currents of thought, to Goethe*, Schiller and Schelling*. He wrote the most important critique from the Russian left of Hegelianism, which he christened 'the algebra of revolution'. One of the first members of the Russian intelligentsia to adopt socialism, he acknowledged a major debt to Fourier*, the Saint-Simonians, Blanc and Proudhon*. Initially he looked to the West to inaugurate an era of socialist justice and individual liberty. The failure of the Revolutions of 1848 affected him profoundly. His commentary on them, *From the Other Shore* (*C togo berega*, 1850), ranks with those of Marx* and Tocqueville*. Its finest lines explored the tension between an unqualified affirmation of the individual and the sacrifices demanded by the revolutionary cause.

In view of the West's setback, Herzen began to concentrate upon the revolutionary potential in Russia. It is for his distinctive vision of Russia's socialist future that he is best known. Nineteenth-century Russia was overwhelmingly a peasant society, and it was to the peasantry that Herzen looked for revolutionary upheaval and socialist construction. Central to his vision was the existence of the Russian peasant commune. In most parts of the empire the peasantry lived in small village communes where the land was owned by the commune and was periodically redistributed among individual households along egalitarian lines. In this he saw the embryo of a socialist society. If the economic burdens of serfdom and state taxation were to be removed, and the land of the nobility made over to the communes, they could develop into flourishing socialist cells. Unlike the West, Russia had preserved an elementary solution to the evils of proletarianization and class exploitation. Moreover, since the commune was internally self-governing and showed democratic tendencies, the decisions of the elders being subject to a popular veto, he saw in it the basis for a political panacea as well. The oppression of the central state could be done away with altogether and replaced by a socialist society of independent, egalitarian communes. There was no need for Russia to follow in the footsteps of the West, to pass through the purgatory of capitalist, industrial and urban development or of bourgeois constitutional government. She could benefit from her late arrival on the historical scene and avoid the mistakes of others.

At first Herzen urged his case upon the Western circles among whom he was now moving, notably Mazzini*, Proudhon and Michelet*. But following the catastrophe which emigration to the West brought to his private life, he turned his full attention towards Russia. In 1853 he established in London the first Free Russian Press. He produced a stream of publications which were smuggled into Russia to spread his vision of Russia's future and to stimulate immediate pressure for reform and for emancipation of the serfs. His periodical *Poliarnaia zvezda* ('The Polar Star') with its famous fortnightly supplement *Kolokol* ('The Bell') became the major forum for free discussion of public affairs and the guiding source of inspiration to radical opinion in Russia. Herzen's peasant socialism was the goal of the revolutionary intelligentsia from the 1860s to the 1890s. The heirs of these 'populists', the Social Revolutionary Party, attracted the largest mass following before being crushed by their Marxist rivals.

The historical significance of Herzen's 'Russian socialism', and his pessimism during the 1850s about socialist prospects in the West, have encouraged historians to attribute to him a dominant messianic nationalism. To do so is to divert attention from the well-spring of his life's work: a passionate sense of the value of individual liberty. He refused to subordinate the individual to the demands of capitalist progress or to the utopian formulas of 'revolutionary schematics'. He rejected the use of oppression to achieve even the most desirable ends. The time has come, he said, to cease 'taking the people for clay and ourselves for sculptors'. It was his ability to maintain this commitment whilst devoting his life to revolutionary change which set him apart not only from liberals but also from all the major revolutionary sects. It makes him impossible to categorize. But it provided him with a remarkable and distinctive platform from which to observe the men, the ideas, the events of his time. Moreover, standing midway between Russia and the West, between literature and politics, between the euphoric spirit of the Romantic movement and the pragmatic mood which followed the revolutionary débâcle of 1848, he commanded a panoramic view of mid-century Europe. Gifted with a scintillating literary style, outstanding even amongst the galaxy of Russian writers of the nineteenth century, he published widely in French, German, Italian and English as well as in Russian. His works, running to thirty volumes in the Soviet edition published between 1954 and 1965, include a vast range of historical, philosophical and political essays, biographical sketches, short stories and two novels.

His greatest achievement was *My Past and Thoughts* (*Byloe i dumy*, 1861, trans. 1968). A loosely constructed autobiography, which he began in 1852 and continued to expand and revise for the rest of his life, it proved the perfect vehicle for his rare blend of *joie de vivre* and political involvement. In its pages the pattern of his own life was skilfully woven into the fabric of political, social and ideological developments around him. His account of the series of disillusionments through which he passed – in the Revolutions of 1848, in the exemplary personal life shipwrecked by Herwegh, in the Russian revolutionaries of the 1860s tainted by elitism – embraced the history of a generation. It played a major role in acquainting radical Russia with the West and in introducing the Russian intelligentsia to Western Europeans. In fusing his personal experience with the history of an era, Herzen created a literary and political masterpiece which shows no signs of losing its force.

E.D.J. Acton

The four-volume edition of *My Past and Thoughts: The Memoirs of Alexander Herzen* (1968), trans. Constance Garnett and Rev. Humphrey Higgins, contains several works apart from the memoirs, as well as a splendid introduction by Isaiah Berlin. Berlin also introduced *From the Other Shore and The Russian People and Socialism* (1956), trans. M. Budberg and R. Wollheim. In addition, see *Selected Philosophical Works* (1956), trans. L. Navrozov. On Herzen: M. Malia, *Alexander Herzen and the Birth of Russian Socialism 1812–1855* (1961); E.H. Carr, *The Romantic Exiles: A Nineteenth Century Portrait Gallery* (1968); E. Lampert, *Studies in Rebellion* (1957); E.D.J. Acton, *Alexander Herzen and the Role of the Intellectual Revolutionary* (1979).

218
HERZL, Theodor 1860–1904

Zionist leader

The founder of political Zionism and of the World Zionist Organization, Theodor Herzl was born in Budapest. He grew up in a culturally assimilated, middle-class family, and studied law at Vienna University, where he took a doctorate in 1884. Pursuing a literary and journalistic career, he spent some years writing plays which, though performed, enjoyed little success, before becoming Paris correspondent of the Vienna *Neue Freie Presse* in 1891.

Up until the Dreyfus affair Herzl believed that the only answer to the Jewish question was the complete assimilation of Jews within the countries of their residence. During 1894, however, he witnessed at first hand the vicious, anti-Semitic behaviour of the Paris mob, and his views changed dramatically. The emotional shock of what it was his responsibility to observe resulted in the famous pamphlet *Der Judenstaat* ('The Jewish State'), published in 1896. In this he identified two major factors – one external, one internal – that would always militate against the possibility of successful assimilation. The first, anti-Semitism, would never be eradicated as long as Jews lived in abnormal social and economic conditions: 'If they let us alone for just two generations .... But they will not let us be. After a brief period of toleration, their hostility erupts again and again.' And the second factor, Herzl now perceived, was a will amongst Jewish people to survive as a separate nation. The true solution, therefore, would be to establish a Jewish state. This could only be accomplished with the help of existing states, and so Herzl argued for international support, to be won through political action. In particular, since Palestine was chosen as the new homeland, it would be necessary to obtain a charter from the Sultan of the Ottoman Empire, and to this end every other activity should be subordinated. To achieve this end Herzl envisaged two necessary institutions: a 'Society of Jews', providing political leadership and legal representation (and forming, eventually, the sovereign body of the proposed state); and a joint-stock 'Jewish Company', providing finance for the immediate diplomatic moves, and eventually coping with the practicalities of migration and resettlement.

Although a liberal, Herzl saw that decision-making, at least initially, must be entrusted to the upper strata, 'to our intelligentsia'. While stressing the necessity of equal and non-discriminatory treatment of all citizens, irrespective of race and creed, and opposing religious interference in any matter of state, he nevertheless foresaw that, at the local level, it would be the rabbis who would provide direction. Beyond these prescriptions, *Der Judenstaat* offered little or no coherent social programme, but was rather a rag-bag of analysis and liberal principles. Thus, while advocating work as the right and duty of everyone, he envisaged a national flag composed of seven stars in a white field, symbolizing the seven hours of the working day – at a time when the eight-hour day was still an unachieved ideal throughout most of Western Europe.

Before Herzl's 'conversion' to Zionism, Jewish settlements were being founded in Palestine, and a movement (*Hoveve Zion* – 'The Lovers of Zion') advocating a return to Zion was already active in Eastern Europe. But its policy was simply to continue the practical work without waiting for official recognition. This Herzl opposed. Pursuing the programme he had set out in the *Judenstaat*, he laboured instead on three fronts: diplomacy, to achieve the charter; the creation of the 'Society of Jews'; and publicity. He proposed that in exchange for the payment of Turkey's foreign debts, the Sultan should allow Palestine to become a Jewish

dependency. Negotiations in Constantinople in 1896 were inconclusive, but left Herzl with sufficient confidence to embark on stage two. Despite opposition from *Hoveve Zion*, and from a majority of rabbis who denounced his views as a distortion of Judaism, the first Zionist Congress assembled in Basle in August 1897, and the World Zionist Organization was founded soon after. Most importantly, the Congress adopted Herzl's recipe for its own programme: 'Zionism seeks to secure the Jewish people a publicly recognized, legally secured home in Palestine for the Jewish people.'

'In Basle I created the Jewish state,' Herzl wrote in his diary: 'In Basle I created the abstraction which, as such, is invisible to the great majority.' Since the state itself did not yet exist, the abstraction had to be kept alive – through publicity. *Die Welt*, first published a few months before the Congress, now became the organ of the World Zionist movement, and Herzl himself was mainly responsible for the decision to hold a World Zionist Congress annually. At the same time he worked indefatigably, though with rather fewer results, to sustain diplomatic and financial activities. Following an unsuccessful attempt to enlist the support of the Kaiser (Palestine would become a German protectorate), he turned once more to the Sultan, who granted him several audiences in 1901 and 1902, but still no charter. These were followed by meetings with Joseph Chamberlain, but after an abortive plan to allow a Jewish settlement in Wadi el Arish, a Sinai valley near Palestine, and a rejected alternative suggestion, made by Chamberlain, to create a Jewish state in Uganda, the territorial objective remained unaccomplished at Herzl's death. And the Jewish Company, though registered in the form of 'The Jewish Colonial Trust' in London in 1899, fared little better. In three years it succeeded in selling only £250,000 worth of shares, and in 1902 its main functions were transferred to the Anglo Palestine Company.

Notwithstanding these setbacks, Herzl's ideal remained intact, as can be seen in the utopian *Altneuland* (trans. *The Old New Land*, 1960), his one serious novel, published in 1902. Here he described life in a future Jewish state in Palestine in 1923. Steering a middle road between capitalism and collectivism, almost all economic activities are conducted within a cooperative framework ('mutualism'). All land is publicly owned, but leased for periods of fifty years. There is complete sexual equality, and every inhabitant is covered by a general social insurance which includes sickness, old age and life. Punishment has been replaced by re-education, and, since both parties profit from the flourishing state, antagonism between Jews and Arabs is non-existent.

In this, as in most of Herzl's political thinking, there was little that was new: indeed it was almost the standard production of a late nineteenth-century West European liberal, and in some quarters the book met with fierce criticism precisely because of its seeming divorce from Jewish culture and traditions. Even the *Judenstaat* had very little new to offer when compared with Leo Pinsker's *Autoemanzipation*, published in Berlin in 1882. And yet the fact remains that Herzl's contribution to the Jewish national revival was greater than anyone else's. It was his perseverance, dynamism and above all his personal charm and charisma that led to the transformation of small groups of East European Jews into a mass movement that finally succeeded in bringing about the establishment of the Jewish state. 'If you will it, it is no legend': these words he had attached to *Altneuland* as the book's motto; and they became one of the most popular slogans of the Zionist movement.

David Dinour

A translation of *The Complete Diaries* was published in 1960. See: A. Bein, *Theodor Herzl* (1957); D. Stewart, *Theodor Herzl* (1974); and W. Laqueur, *A History of Zionism* (1972).

219

HIROSHIGE UTAGAWA (ANDŌ) 1797–1858

Japanese print artist

Hiroshige was the art name adopted in 1812 by Andō Tokutarō, son of an official in the Edo (modern Tokyo) fire service, soon after he was accepted as a pupil of Utagawa Toyohiro, a designer of modest and refined woodblock prints in the *Ukiyo-e* or genre style. Although his earliest extant signed work – a book illustration – dates from 1818, it was not until 1831 with the issue of his first series of landscape prints that Hiroshige was to discover his true forte. The productions of intervening years were generally uninspired imitations of the work of contemporaries: warrior prints after Kuniyoshi; prints of women after Eizan; and portraits of actors in the style of Kunisada.

All this changed with the publication of the great series *Thirty-six Views of Mount Fuji* (*Fūgaku sanjū-rokkei*, c. 1829–33) by Hokusai* which quickly established the landscape print as a separate and immensely popular genre. Despite his huge debt to Hokusai, Hiroshige's landscapes were in a very different style from those of the elder artist, as is evinced by the already highly accomplished set of ten views of *Famous Places in Edo* (*Tōto meisho*, 1831). Hiroshige, like Hokusai, had been trained in the *de rigueur* classical *Kanō* of ink-painting, but compositions from this early set such as *Moonlight at Takanawa*, with its flock of geese crossing the moon, owe much more in mood and subject matter to the purely Japanese *Shijō* style of painting that reached its peak in Kyoto during the early nineteenth century. *Shijō* influence is even more clearly discernible in the

narrow vertical *tanzaku* and *kakemono* prints – often of birds and flowers – that he was to produce periodically throughout his career.

In 1832 Hiroshige undertook a journey as a minor retainer in an official mission along the main artery that linked Tokyo and Kyoto, the *Tōkaidō*. Lively sketches he made of the stopping-places along the way were worked up into a series of prints entitled *Fifty-three Stations of the Tōkaidō* (*Tōkaidō gojūsan-tsugi*, 1833–4) which proved his most enduring masterpiece. The landscapes of both Hokusai and Hiroshige are realistic to a higher degree than had been normal in Far Eastern art, in the sense that they were representations of actual named locations that would be well known to an itinerant Japanese. The key word here, however, is *representations* since both artists considerably distorted what they saw in order to achieve a convincing design. Commentators have stressed the overriding importance of composition to Hokusai, contrasted with what has been described as 'poetic mood' in the work of Hiroshige. In the best prints of the younger artist this 'poetic mood' is a blend of several components: it is often created by a particular meteorological phenomenon; described using tricks of composition just as startling as those of Hokusai; and finally executed and anchored by the exceptionally subtle ministrations of a colour printer. The two most famous designs from the first *Tōkaidō* set (he was to design dozens more) – *Shōno* and *Kambara* – manifest all three of these elements.

Hiroshige seems to have been a far more placid individual than the eccentric Hokusai, and having hit upon a successful formula there followed a steady stream of landscape prints to satisfy an eager public: *Famous Views of Japan* (*Honchō meisho*, c. 1832, 1837–9); *Famous Views of Kyoto* (*Kyōto meisho*, 1834); *Eight Views of Lake Biwa* (*Ōmi hakkei*, 1834); and *Sixty-nine Stations of the Kiso Highway* (*Kiso-kaidō rokujūkyū-tsugi*, late 1830s), all of which contain designs on a par with those of the *Tōkaidō* series. Three later sets – distinguishable by their upright rather than horizontal format – have been less appreciated, and criticized as being the attenuated result of over-popularity and over-production. These are: *Famous Places: The Sixty-odd Provinces* (*Rokujū-yoshu meisho-zue*, 1853–6); *Thirty-six Views of Mount Fuji* (*Fuji sanjū-rokkei*, 1858–9); and *One Hundred Famous Views of Edo* (*Meisho Edo hyakkei*, 1856–9). But Hiroshige's powers as a draughtsman were certainly not on the wane, as is attested by the three triptychs on the subjects of Snow, Moon and Flowers that he designed in the year before his death. They are among the greatest landscape designs of nineteenth-century Japan.

It was the perverse tricks of composition of the *One Hundred Famous Views of Edo* set which prompted Van Gogh* in 1888 to make 'copies' in oils of two of the designs, and the almost arbitrary combinations of bright, flat colours to produce 'realistic' effects of atmosphere and light drew many other Impressionist painters to Hiroshige's prints; Whistler's* *Nocturnes* were directly inspired by them. Indeed, the triumvirate of Hokusai, Hiroshige and Utamaro (1753–1806) have had far more impact on Western graphic design than in their country of origin.

Tim Clark

See: E.F. Strange, *The Colour Prints of Hiroshige* (1925); M. Uchida, *Hiroshige* (in Japanese, 1930); M. Narazaki, *Hiroshige* (1969); J. Suzuki, *Utagawa Hiroshige* (1970); R. Lane, *Hokusai and Hiroshige* (1976).

220
HOFFMANN, Ernst Theodor Amadeus 1776–1822

German writer and composer

The life of E.T.A. Hoffmann was coloured by the demands of two separate careers: that of an artist dedicated to an ideal world of beauty, and that of an able though scarcely enthusiastic official in the Prussian Civil Service. For a few years in his mid-thirties, Hoffmann did manage to devote himself full-time to art, after landing the post of musical director of the municipal theatre at Bamberg; but before he was forty, he had settled for a position as deputy judge in Berlin, apportioning his energies between his legal duties and his more and more engrossing literary work.

Known today above all as a writer, Hoffmann nourished a lifelong ambition to be a successful composer. His musical works are now practically forgotten, but they were not unimpressive and included nine operas, several choral works, a symphony, and various chamber and piano pieces. His opera *Undine* (*The Water-Sprite*, 1816), based on a fairy tale by his friend Fouqué, is the first German Romantic opera, predating Weber's* *Der Freischütz* by five years. It was highly acclaimed, but ran for only twenty-three performances before the accidental burning-down of the theatre put an end to Hoffmann's one real hope of musical fame.

Hoffmann wrote music criticism of great verve and originality, reviewing contemporary work by such composers as Haydn and Mozart (whose middle name he admiringly adopted as his own). His pioneering essay 'Beethovens Instrumentalmusik' ('Beethoven's Instrumental Music', 1813) celebrates Beethoven* as a 'pure Romantic composer' and openly proclaims a peculiarly Romantic conception of the function of music: 'Music opens up to us an unknown realm, a world which has nothing in common with the outer world of the senses which surrounds us; through music, we leave behind all specific feelings, and surrender to inexpressible yearning.'

As the medium of access to the ineffable world of the 'ideal', music did indeed offer Hoffmann a marvellous trans-temporal alternative to the difficulties of empirical existence. And once it dawned on him that his musical ambitions were not to be realized, and he began to turn to writing as a compensatory activity, the higher medium remained for him a constant touchstone of all that he valued.

In his first published tale, 'Ritter Gluck' ('The Chevalier Gluck', 1809), Hoffmann depicts a musician who, fancying himself to be a reincarnation of the composer Gluck, performs the latter's works at the piano from a totally blank score, claiming to have been inspired by a visit to the Realm of Dreams. This eccentric foreshadows Hoffmann's most celebrated creation, the musician Johannes Kreisler, hero of the *Kreisleriana* cycle (1815) and embodiment of a quintessential myth of German Romanticism – the artist as a visionary madman, one whose insight into invisible higher truths is at the price of pathological imbalance. Kreisler is both genius and neurotic, a man of discordant extremes, and through him Hoffmann paints an ironic self-portrait, mocking and yet exalting his own creative ambitions. The inherent duplicity of Kreisler's temperament is brought out in the queerly structured novel *Lebensansichten des Katers Murr* ('My Views on Life by the Tom-Cat Murr', 1819–21), where Kreisler's wild loves and frustrations are whimsically juxtaposed with the dull ruminations of Hoffmann's pet cat, whose memoirs had, according to a mock-apologetic editorial note, been accidentally bound in with the Kreisler material. The Murr section of this experimental novel is a satire on reason, orderliness and Biedermeier philistinism, in contrast to Kreisler's adventures, which reflect Hoffmann's poetic equation of the passionate, the mystical and the irrational.

The Romantic vision of a rift between actual experience and a yearned-for ideal runs throughout Hoffmann's work. In 'Der Goldene Topf' ('The Golden Pot', 1814), the student Anselmus is torn between his commitment to the tangible reality of Dresden and the allurements of Atlantis, the enchanted realm of poetry and art; it is only after many trials that he gains access to the latter, sustained by his love for Serpentina, the serpent-daughter of Archivist Lindhorst, a splendid salamander-sorcerer who also poses unconvincingly as a respectable citizen. It is true that the tale is full of Hoffmann's typical drolleries – Anselmus is repeatedly shown to be a bungler who sprawls headlong in the street or spills ink over the page he is copying. Yet such slapstick cannot conceal Hoffmann's fundamentally earnest attachment to the theme of metaphysical initiation facilitated by the transcendent vision of art.

Hoffmann was fascinated by paranormal states of consciousness and in his tales often exploited contemporary studies in the fields of hypnotism and psychopathology, some aspects of which he had observed at first hand in an asylum near Bamberg. With states of ultra-sensory vision attributable to mesmerism or psychotic hallucination may be listed dreams, poetic euphoria, alcoholic delirium and amorous trances: all are envisaged as potential modes of understanding which lucid common sense cannot expect to rival.

The phenomena of mental derangement thus appear in Hoffmann with an aura of the glamorous as well as the fearful. *The Devil's Elixirs*, (*Die Elixier des Teufels*, 1816, trans. 1963) is a lurid novel in the Gothic idiom of M.G. Lewis, full of fateful lusts and vile murders. It tells of the monk Medardus and his efforts to redeem himself after falling under the thrall of his malefic *Doppelgänger*. To the discerning reader, the novel is a psychological analysis in the form of a sensational thriller, Hoffmann's way of dramatizing the discrepancies of intellect and instinct, good and evil, within his own psyche. The novel's harmonious ending may be taken as an earnest of Hoffmann's resolve to reconcile the most discordant impulses or themes.

Hoffmann's reputation was well established in his own time as that of a purveyor of the macabre and the horrid, with a technique based on a repertoire of shock effects: doubles, spectral apparitions, vampires, robots, black magic, spells, nightmares, sleep-walking and so forth. However his best stories are those where horror is less flagrant and more insidious, stories where the marvellous and the daemonic are filtered little by little into a basic context of normality. The instrusion of the unreal into the real is Hoffmann's forte. When in 'Der Goldene Topf' Anselmus wakes up to find himself sealed in a glass bottle sitting on the archivist's library shelf, or when, in 'Das Majorat' ('Rolandsitten, or The Deed of Entail', 1817), the credulous Theodor distinctly hears groanings and shuffling steps coming from behind a walled-up door in a castle hall, the reader too is being coaxed into recognizing the impossible and learns gradually to take pleasure in the inherent ambiguity and giddiness of Hoffmann's fictional world.

The persuasiveness of Hoffmann's manner may in part be explained by the buoyancy and pace of his style, with its hyperbolic vocabulary of the weird and the uncanny, and its brusque detours into the grotesque or the droll. Hoffmann knows well how to sustain a generalized perplexity without letting his tale collapse into sheer chaos. He is often at pains to disarm his reader by a series of cavalier interventions which ostensibly seek to reassure him: as author, he manages to disclaim responsibility for the improbabilities of the narrative at the same time as he is, quite manifestly, manufacturing them! The resultant self-conscious foregrounding of the writing process is itself not the least significant factor in his reputation as one of the most astute practitioners of the 'fantastic'.

Hoffmann's literary work exerted considerable influence within the German speaking world, both on contemporaries like Chamisso and Contessa and later writers like Meyrink, Kafka and Bergengruen; abroad,

it had a remarkable impact, affecting such major writers as Nerval* and Gautier*, Poe* and Hawthorne*, Gogol* and Dostoevsky*. Schumann* recorded his admiration in a piano suite entitled *Kreisleriana* (1838), the musical counterpart to the story-teller's glittering switches of tempo and tone. Hoffmann's tales found their way into ballets by Delibes (*Coppélia*, 1870) and Tchaikovsky* (*Nutcracker*, 1891–2), and an opera by Hindemith (*Cardillac*, 1926). It is however in keeping with Hoffmann's self-deprecating sensibility that he is best known to the general public as the hero of Offenbach's* comic opera *Les Contes d'Hoffmann* (*The Tales of Hoffmann*, 1881), where he is portrayed as an amusing but superficial fantasist.

Roger Cardinal

Works: *Poetische Werke*, 12 vols (1957–62); *Sämtliche Werke*, 5 vols (1960–5); *Schriften zur Musik* (1963). Translations: *The Best Tales of E.T.A. Hoffmann*, ed. E.F. Bleiler (1967); *The Devil's Elixirs* (1963); *Selected Letters of E.T.A. Hoffmann*, trans. Johanna C. Sahlin (1977). See: Thomas Cramer, *Das Groteske bei E.T.A. Hoffmann* (1966); Lothar Köhn, *Vieldeutige Welt: Studien zur Struktur der Erzählungen E.T.A. Hoffmanns* (1966); Hermann Korff, 'E.T.A. Hoffmann', in *Geist der Goethezeit*, vol. IV (1956); Ronald Taylor, *Hoffmann* (1963); Gabrielle Wittkop-Ménardeau, *E.T.A. Hoffmann* (1966).

221

HOKUSAI KATSUSHIKA, 1760–1849

Japanese artist

Hokusai was born in the Honjo district of Edo (modern Tokyo) and adopted at an early age into the artisan family Nakajima. As a youth he worked in a lending bookshop, and between the ages of fifteen and eighteen he was apprenticed to a woodblock engraver. The only artistic training open to one of his class was in the *Ukiyo-e* or genre style of painting and, in 1778 Hokusai became a pupil of Katsukawa Shunshō, then the leading designer of prints of *kabuki* actors.

Hokusai's principal and most successful medium was to remain that of the woodblock print, for which an artist would supply little more than the initial sketch from which colour blocks were cut and several hundred, or even thousand, impressions of varying quality taken. With characteristic eclecticism, however, he took lessons under Yūsen in the hybrid Sino-Japanese *Kanō* style, whose exponents formed a sort of academy to the ruling Tokugawa family. Other influences included traditional Japanese styles of *Tosa* and the new re-vamped form it had assumed under Sōtatsu and Kōrin (now called *Rimpa*), immaculately executed bird and flower paintings from Ming and Ching China, and even Western copper-plate engravings that had introduced an alien system of perspective to an earlier generation of woodblock print artists. Hokusai's attempts to synthesize these various elements reached maturity in his landscape series of the late 1820s and early 1830s, the most famous of which is *Thirty-six Views of Mount Fuji (Fūgaku sanjū-rokkei, c. 1829–33)*.

Aside from his stature as a graphic artist in such series of prints, Hokusai contributed much to Japanese art as an innovator. In the 1790s he popularized the genre of *surimono* prints, specially commissioned vignettes whose purpose was to act as an adjunct to humorous *kyōka* poems, record a change of name, or simply serve as a greetings card. He was also a prolific illustrator of novels, picture books and poetry albums, as well as an original designer of prints of women and erotica. Particularly worthy of note among the illustrated books are: *Views of Both Banks of the Sumida River (Sumidagawa ryōgan ichiran, c. 1805); Album of Drawings from Life by Hokusai (Hokusai shashin gafu, 1814); and One Hundred Views of Mount Fuji (Fugaku hyakkei, 1834–5)*. Throughout his life Hokusai produced sketches, which have an immediacy and spontaneity perforce lacking in the woodblock prints, as well as autographed brush paintings in a much more polished style.

His greatest achievement was undoubtedly the *Thirty-six Views of Mount Fuji*, which was followed by other series of landscape broadsheets of generally lesser stature: *Wondrous Views of Famous Bridges in all the Provinces (Shokoku meikyō kiran, 1831–2); A Journey to the Waterfalls of all the Provinces (Shokoku taki meguri, 1831–2); A True Mirror of Chinese and Japanese Poems (Shika shashin-kyō, 1832–3); and The Hundred Poems (by the Hundred Poets) explained by the Nurse (Hyakunin isshu uba-ga-etoki, 1839)*. Also well loved in the West are the two series known as the 'large' and 'small' series of bird and flower prints whose exquisite colouring owes much to Chinese models.

The landscape prints are significant both as a much needed shot in the arm for the woodblock print and as a new departure in the depiction of landscape, a traditional forte of Far-Eastern artists. The lack of sophistication of early perspective prints (*uki-e*) has been refined into a unified, convincing amalgam of styles from East and West at the service of the master draughtsman. The three most famous designs of the *Fuji* set: *Under the Wave off Kanagawa (Kanagawa-oki nami ura); Fine Wind, Clear Morning (Gaifū kaisei); and Rainstorm beneath the Summit (Sanka haku-u)* are of a drama and loftiness of conception quite alien to *ukiyo-e*, but are very untypical of Hokusai in that they ignore the human element in landscape. Some of the credit for this or any other series of woodblock prints must go to the printer for his finesse at wiping the blocks, and particularly here for his exploitation of a new strong blue pigment. The set was an immediate popular success.

Acting as he did as standard-bearer of the *ukiyo-e* artists, the influence of Hokusai on Western art from the mid-nineteenth century to the present day has been phenomenal, and out of all proportion to his acclaim in Japan. He remains, perhaps undeservedly, the best known Far-Eastern artist in the West. Felix Bracquemond was putting designs from *Manga (Random sketches, 1814–78)* on to ceramics from the Rousseau service during the late 1860s, and with their flat areas of colour and startling tricks of composition Japanese prints did much to encourage the experiments of the Impressionists. F.W. Dickins published a reprint of *One Hundred Views of Mount Fuji* in London in 1880.

The basis of critical acclaim of Hokusai's works has shifted ground over the past century away from admiration of the prodigious fecundity that characterizes the *Manga* cartoons, to an appreciation of the sheer graphic power and sense of composition of the 'Great Wave', which itself has become one of an international repertoire of design motifs. In his *L'art japonais* (1883) Louis Gonse wrote: 'The complete works of Hokusai would be the glory of any print collection and could be placed beside those of Rembrandt . . . . ' Few would disagree today.

Tim Clark

See: H. Iijima, *Katsushika Hokusai Den* (1893); M. Narazaki, *Hokusai Ron* (1944); J. Hillier, *Hokusai: Paintings, Drawings and Woodcuts* (1955); M. Narazaki, *Hokusai* (1968); M. Forrer, *Hokusai: A Guide to the Serial Graphics* (1974); R. Lane, *Hokusai and Hiroshige* (1976); J. Hillier, *The Art of Hokusai in Book Illustration* (1980).

222
HOLABIRD, William 1854–1923
ROCHE, Martin 1855–1927

US architects

It was in Chicago that the first skyscraper appeared in 1885, built by William Jenney whose office was to produce two of the most influential of the Chicago skyscraper architects, Holabird and Roche. Possibly it might have been thought that New York would be the first city to build a ten-storey building; however in the 1830s Chicago became the more important commercial centre due to railways and increases in the Great Lakes traffic. When in 1871 a fire decimated the city there was an opportunity for experimental building. The increase in the cost of land meant that clients pressured architects for maximum usage of the site and therefore building heights started to rise. However skyscrapers only became possible with the new technology which provided for steel frame buildings that were strong enough to carry the weight of curtain walls that were not self-supporting. This was an improvement on the original frame buildings which were of weaker construction, being made of cast and wrought iron. It was an Englishman, Henry Bessemer, who invented the process which produced mild steel beams which first appeared in the United States in the 1880s.

Holabird and Roche in 1888–9 were able therefore to build the Tacoma building, thirteen storeys high with projecting bay windows from the first floor to the roof. For lightness most of the curtain walling is window glass. By 1894 the two architects had produced the far simpler flat faced fifteen-storey Marquette building with slight recessions for the windows which are horizontally stressed, leaving the vertical emphasis to the piers which shoot dramatically from the bottom to the top. However, compared with their next design, the Marquette building appears heavy and rather rustic in style.

This next, only nine-storey skyscraper, known as the McClurg building of 1899–1900, displays a fully modern twentieth-century style. The glass expanse is far larger and piers and mullions are narrow and linear leaving the horizontal load-bearing frame to be expressed by the greater width. It is a particularly fine example of an early skyscraper and the pattern for many more that follow.

Perhaps the most well-known skyscraper architect was Louis Sullivan*. He worked for a time in Chicago with various architects including Holabird and Roche. He produced the frontage for a frame designed by the latter at No. 18 South Michigan Avenue in 1898–9. This is the third frontage section of three adjoining frame buildings produced by the partnership and Sullivan's third is similar to theirs in style in terms of weight and proportion and his windows are as long horizontally but not so high. In addition the cross beam frontage has a typical although restrained repeat decoration set at wide intervals on the horizontals and a veritable flourish of plant forms at the top of the two dividing piers. The whole of Sullivan's frontage is clad with terracotta moulding, and the effect is rather richer and more subtle than the adjoining two buildings.

In general the 'Chicago style' was to become more severe and express a more open appearance than skyscraper building in New York.

Pat Turner

See: W.A. Starrett, *Skyscrapers and the Men who Built Them* (1928); C.W. Condit, *The Chicago School of Architecture* (1964); H.R. Hitchcock, *Architecture: Nineteenth and Twentieth Centuries* (1971).

223
HÖLDERLIN, Johann Christian Friedrich
1770–1843

German poet

Although he survived well into the nineteenth century, Hölderlin was essentially the child of the so-called Classical era of German literature. That engagement with the culture of classical antiquity which had exercised some of the finest minds in eighteenth-century Germany finds in Hölderlin its latest, perhaps most intense and certainly most problematic expression: problematic partly because his profoundly personal preoccupation with Greek religion and civilization clashed with the imperatives of his pietistic upbringing and partly because his vision of Greece made him more acutely aware of the disharmonies of his own time. The result is a poetry in which a deep sense of reverence is combined, in varying degrees, with a kind of pain: the poet's dream of unity and wholeness being constantly countered by his experience of separation and division.

Hölderlin was born in the small town of Lauffen in Swabia; educated at the *Lateinschule* (or grammar school) in nearby Nürtingen, at theological seminaries in Denkendorf and Maulbronn and finally at the Tübingen *Stift* where he formed friendships with his fellow-students, Hegel* and Schelling* and obtained a Master's degree with a thesis on the history of the fine arts in ancient Greece. Despite the wishes of his pious mother, he refused to become a cleric and his professional life consisted, in the decade following the year 1793, of a series of private tutorships. In 1794, on taking his pupil, the rather difficult young son of Schiller's friend, Charlotte von Kalb, to Jena, he came under the kindly, but not altogether sympathetic, influence of Schiller and briefly, but without notable consequences, met Goethe*. A far more significant influence for his personal life was to arise in the following year, when he was appointed tutor to the children of the wealthy Frankfurt banker, Jakob Friedrich Gontard. Hölderlin's passionate, and reciprocated love for Gontard's wife, Susette, became for a time the all-dominating focus of his life. He called her Diotima – the ideal woman who, in Plato's *Symposium*, holds discourse with Socrates on the nature of love – and made her the central figure, not only of much of his poetry, but also of his novel, *Hyperion* (2 vols, 1797 and 1799, trans. 1965).

This novel relates in epistolary form the two major concerns of a young modern Greek: his love for Diotima and his desire to liberate his country from the Turkish invaders. Betrayed by his companions in arms, Hyperion returns from battle to be confronted by the fact of Diotima's death. He then travels to Germany, whose cultural shortcomings he describes in a scathing chapter and, in the book's closing pages, seeks solace in nature. Despite many poignant and beautiful passages, the novel has appealed to modern taste considerably less than Hölderlin's poetry – the tone of exalted lamentation becomes somewhat wearisome – but, like the poetry, it conveys a sense of the interconnectedness of the elements of life. 'Du wolltest keine Menschen . . . du wolltest eine Welt' ('You did not want human beings . . . you wanted a world') Diotima tells Hyperion at one point: the statement is not meant as a rebuke.

The happiness which Hölderlin enjoyed with Susette for over two years was finally shattered when her husband discovered their liaison. Hölderlin left the Gontard household in 1798, but lodged with a friend in nearby Homburg, where he continued to see Susette in secret and to work on his never completed tragedy, *Der Tod des Empedokles* ('The Death of Empedocles'), of which three versions exist. In May 1800 the lovers agreed on a final separation. Two further tutorships followed, one in Switzerland (St Gallen), the other in Bordeaux; but in June 1802 Hölderlin returned to Swabia in a state of mental derangement. In the same month, Susette Gontard died. During the years 1803–6 Hölderlin was looked after partly by his mother and partly by his friend, Isaac Sinclair, and recovered sufficiently to write a number of poems and to produce translations of Sophocles's *Antigone* and *Oedipus Rex*. But a second and more serious breakdown caused Sinclair to entrust him to a clinic in Tübingen from which he was dismissed as incurable. Under the care of a carpenter, Zimmer, he spent the last thirty-six years of his life in a tower-like wing of a house on the banks of the Neckar.

The most intensely creative years of Hölderlin's life were from 1797 to 1803. The poems of his maturity are classical not only in a formal sense (there is a frequent predilection for the alcaic ode and the elegiac distich) but also in a curious eschewal of the personal note. This is not to say that personal experience, such as the poet's love for Diotima or his feeling for the natural world, plays no part in these poems: it is rather that the personal element becomes a constituent factor in a larger fusion, so that, for instance, a poem like 'Da ich ein Knabe war' ('When I was a boy', 1798), whose opening line suggests purely individual reminiscence, soon develops into the presentation of a representative 'I' growing to maturity under the aegis of the (Greek) gods. Or again, in 'Menons Klagen um Diotima' ('Menons Lamentations for Diotima', 1800) the loss of love, though formalized by the classical framework, becomes no less immediately poignant for that. In Hölderlin there is no disjunction between private experience and the experience of history; he does not have one voice for personal emotion and another for historical or cultural reflection: the one is part of the other. Hence in the other two great odes of 1800, 'Der Archipelagus' ('The Archipelago') and 'Brot und

Wein' ('Bread and Wine'), both of which might glibly be described as reflections on classical and modern culture, the tone is far from abstract. 'Der Archipelagus' is a long, magnificently sustained meditation on ancient Greece, which is presented both historically – the central passage of the poem is a vivid depiction of the Greeks' defeat of Xerxes at the Battle of Salamis and the subsequent reconstruction of Athens – and as a permanent and pervasive force. In 'Brot und Wein' Hölderlin effects a remarkable poetic synthesis between Greek religion and Christianity. Day and night symbolize respectively the presence on earth and the withdrawal from it of the divine element; Christ is shown as the last manifestation of that day of divinity which irradiated Greek culture; the night of the modern world can still find solace in bread and wine, symbols both of Christian communion and Bacchic munificence.

The three great odes of 1800, then, are notable for wholeness, fusion, balance; but the balance was precarious. For one thing, Hölderlin seems not to have been permanently satisfied by the synthesis of Christian and pagan elements achieved in 'Brot und Wein': there are reasons for supposing that it instilled in him a sense of guilt. The later ode 'Der Einzige' ('The Only One', 1802–3), a meditation on Christ, contains the complaint: 'Und jetzt ist voll/Von Trauern meine Seele/Als eifertet, ihr Himmlischen, selbst/Daß dien' ich einem, mir/Das andere fehlt' ('And now my soul is full of mourning, as if, you divine ones, you yourselves urged that if I serve the one, I shall lack the other'). The last great completed ode, 'Patmos' (1802–3) (Patmos being the island in the Aegean sea to which the Apostle John was banished), opens with the strange syntactical contortion: 'Nah ist/Und schwer zu fassen, der Gott' ('Near is, and hard to grasp, the God'), where the unexpected conjunction 'and' in itself makes divine inscrutability a condition of divine immanence. The poem is thereafter concerned with the illumination of mystery by the dissemination of the Word, and ends, 'Dem folgt deutscher Gesang' ('Upon this follows German song') – a suggestion confirmed, for instance, by the opening of the earlier 'Germanien' (1801) that German song should concern itself, not so much with past (pagan) gods as with the poet's native land and the possibilities it offers for reverence. But the later odes of 1803 become ever more fragmentary, a series of fascinating shards. In Hölderlin's best-known short poem, 'Hälfte des Lebens' ('The Middle of Life'), the sense of disconnectedness is made the subject of the poem: the two stanzas present, respectively, a scene of summer fruition and one of hibernal desolation; the speaker's question at the halfway point in life – what fulfilment may he expect now? – remains unanswered: 'Die Mauern stehn/Sprachlos und kalt, im Winde/Klirren die Fahnen' ('The walls stand speechless and cold, in the wind the weather-vanes clatter'). Communication ceases, the sense of direction is lost.

And this may suggest one important reason why Hölderlin's poetry, largely ignored during the nineteenth century, has had to wait until the twentieth for its full rehabilitation. (In German literature he has had a marked influence on such major figures as Stefan George, Rilke, Trakl, Benn and Celan.) Hölderlin's Classicism is not a matter of resting comfortably within an approved tradition: like all visions of wholeness it is aware at once of its precariousness and its indispensability. That awareness is conveyed in a poetic language of great range, from the idyllically serene to the daringly innovative (startling compounds, jagged rhythms, expressive contortions of syntax, etc.). Hölderlin, as our century may claim credit for having realized, is not an easy poet, but he is a great and necessary one.

Corbet Stewart

English-speaking readers of Hölderlin are particularly indebted to the work of Michael Hamburger: for his translations see *Poems of Hölderlin* (2nd edn, 1952) and *Hölderlin* (the Penguin Poets series with plain prose translations, 1961). See also: E.L. Stahl, *Hölderlin's Symbolism* (1945); L.S. Salzberger, *Hölderlin* (1952); Michael Hamburger, *Reason and Energy* (1957); Ronald Peacock, *Hölderlin* (2nd edn, 1973); R.B. Harrison, *Hölderlin and the Greeks* (1979).

224
HOLMES, Oliver Wendell 1809–94

US author and physician

Although, to modern taste, Holmes deserves no better literary reputation than that of a minor belle-lettrist and unexacting 'Fireside Poet' in the vein of Bryant*, Whittier*, Lowell* and Longfellow*, for nineteenth-century America, and often beyond, he enjoyed the widest esteem as the stylish 'occasional' man of letters, the incarnation of Boston urbanity. A high New England Brahmin by birth who numbered the seventeenth-century poet Anne Bradstreet among his ancestors, and a Harvard MD and justly eminent Professor of Anatomy and Physiology, he found favour not only as wit, versifier and essayist (his fiction was less read), but also for the entertainment of his frequent lyceum and club lectures. James Russell Lowell spoke for the general opinion when, in 'A Fable for Critics' (1848), he praised the 'fancy' and 'fun' of Holmes's lyrics, the general 'vigour' of his writing.

Born in Cambridge, the son of Abiel Holmes, a Congregational minister and scholar ousted from his parish by doctrinal hard-liners (an event which in-

stilled in his son a lifelong detestation of Calvinism), Holmes studied at Harvard (1825–9), for whose class reunions from 1851 onwards he wrote a celebrated annual poem; tried his hand as a law student (1829–30); and graduated an MD from Harvard Medical School in 1836, having studied also in Paris (1833–5). His medical career was distinguished, and often controversial. He contributed to the *Bolyston Prize Dissertations for the Years 1836 and 1837* (1838); was the first to suggest the term 'anaesthesia' for use of drugs like chloroform; became Professor of Anatomy at Dartmouth Medical College (1839–40); and, from 1847 until retirement in 1882, was Dean (1847–52) and Professor at Harvard Medical School. Throughout his career he was to the fore of medical research as he gave evidence in publications like *Homeopathy and Its Kindred Delusions* (1842), *The Contagiousness of Puerperal Fever* (1843), in which he was bold enough to argue that unhygienic doctors could themselves transmit disease, and his *Medical Essays* (1883). The scientific rationalism which marked out his medical work he applied equally to religion. Repelled by Calvinism, but not won over by Emerson's* Transcendentalism, for all that he thought highly of his fellow Brahmin's intellect, he adopted the broad middle ground of orthodox Unitarianism, a firm enough believer but always the humanitarian and tolerant of theological difference.

His literary aspirations, which he never considered other than perfectly congruent with his medical duties, gained major impetus when he won national praise for his poem 'Old Ironsides' in 1830, a protest against the destruction of a battleship prominent in the war of 1812. In 1831–2, in the *New England Magazine*, he began the series 'The Autocrat of the Breakfast Table', familiar, discursive pieces which he took up again with the birth of the *Atlantic Monthly* in 1857, and which, over time, became acclaimed full-length volumes, *The Autocrat of the Breakfast Table* (1858), *The Professor at the Breakfast Table* (1860), *The Poet at the Breakfast Table* (1872) and *Over the Teacups* (1891). In each of these, and in the magazine originals, Holmes affects a tone of almost Augustan ironic ease, amiable observations on New England life and general domestic manners and foibles.

In all three of Holmes's 'medicated novels', as he was pleased to have them called, his essential subject was personality disorder – to be explained not, as so often in Calvinist New England tradition, by reference to 'Original Sin' and the like, but by medical inquiry and diagnosis. In this, the physician in Holmes blended to good purpose with the novelist. In *Elsie Venner* (1860), the best, he explores the 'case' of a village girl cruelly ostracized as a snake-like witch, in fact a schizophrenic and victim not of supposed Godly wrath but poison. Similarly, in *A Guardian Angel* (1867) and *A Mortal Antipathy* (1885), he looks into the workings of multiple personality and different kinds of phobia, fiction of no great imaginative import but markedly intelligent in its anticipation of later psychiatric knowledge. Holmes's other prose includes his essay-collections from *Atlantic Monthly*, *Soundings from the Atlantic* (1864) and *Pages from an Old Volume of Life* (1883); his two biographies, *John Lothrop Motley* (1878) and, for the American Men of Letters Series, *Ralph Waldo Emerson* (1885); and a vast further miscellany reprinted in *The Writings of Oliver Wendell Holmes* (1891).

Holmes's poetry, which with undue optimism he hoped to be best remembered for, amounts essentially to low-key *exercices de style* – verse for the occasion like his class poems and the poems he wrote for national celebrations, or 'historical' offerings like 'The Last Leaf' on the Boston Tea Party, or mild satires in the manner of his anti-Calvinist 'The Deacon's Masterpiece', or 'medical poems' like 'The Stethoscope Song' or 'Rip Van Winkle M.D.', or his ballads and ditties written in couplet-form, notably 'The Ballad of the Oysterman'. These, and the poems he worked into his 'Autocrat' series, in the title of one of his efforts, are 'after dinner' pieces, period light verse. His collected *Poems* went through several editions and includes such volumes as *Songs in Many Keys* (1862), *Songs of Many Seasons* (1875), *Bunker-hill Battle and other Poems* (1877), *The Iron Gate and other Poems* (1881), and *Before the Curfew* (1888). Holmes again tried to apply his medical insights to literature in *The Physiology of Versification* (1883), a theory as to the connection between metrical rhythm and the human pulse-rate and respiration. In his poetry, as in his other writing, Holmes has not particularly endured, eclipsed in part by the greater fame of his son and namesake, Oliver Wendell Holmes Jr (1841–1935), Supreme Court Justice and major legal theoretician.

A. Robert Lee

See: Clarence P. Oberndorf, *The Psychiatric Novels of Oliver Wendell Holmes* (1943); Miriam Rossiter Small, *Oliver Wendell Holmes* (1962)

225

HOMER, Winslow 1836–1910

US painter

Homer's biography and motivations are frequently obscure. After an apprenticeship to John Bufford, a Boston lithographer, he became a freelance illustrator. Contributions to *Harper's Weekly* continued for eighteen years. In 1859 he moved to New York, attended a drawing school in Brooklyn, then the National Academy of Design, and in 1861 decided to paint, helped by Frédéric Rondel. For twenty years he spent summers in the country, collecting material, and winters in New York, painting. Two journeys were crucial –

ten months in France (1866–7) where he exhibited at the Exposition Universelle, and two visits to Teignmouth in Devon (1881, 1882) when he exhibited at the Royal Academy in London. No proof exists that Homer ever saw a Japanese print or an Impressionist painting, even in France. Despite strong similarities with Monet*, he was less intent on questioning the solidity of the three-dimensional world than his French counterparts. At this time, in pictures such as *Croquet Scene* (1866), rituals of polite behaviour served as excuses to study the emotional resonance of gestures, glances or simply empty space. Unusual compositions and irresolute perspectives foreshadowed the style of Edward Hopper, an admirer of Homer's 'weight'. A temporarily high-keyed palette (1868–9), evident in paintings such as *Long Beach, New Jersey*, has been explained as a reaction to French painting. A period of more severe classicizing followed (1871–5); *Waiting for Dad* of 1873, in which a Gloucester wife and two children await a fisherman's return, has been compared to Piero della Francesca. Commonplace themes abounded. The flippant yet amazed manner of Henry James's* criticism in 1875 barely concealed a sense that Homer's task resembled his own as seen in the early study of Hawthorne* – to colonize America as a subject for art. At the height of his fame as an illustrator Homer unaccountably stopped. Henceforth his new medium, watercolour, would occupy as much of his attention as oil on canvas. While staying in Teignmouth he abandoned his genteel, sunlit themes for grey seas and heroic figures. In 1883 he moved to Prout's Neck, Maine, where he lived alone, concentrated on the elements and embarked on another new medium, etching. The late work was strongly post-Darwinian. Human beings disappeared almost completely; only a dynamic play of natural forces mattered. *The Fox Hunt* (1893) shows a flock of starving crows attacking a fox during a bleak Maine winter. From the 1890s onwards Homer spent part of each winter in a hotter climate. Together with one or two of his etchings, the late Bermudan watercolours seemed to him to represent his finest work. Sensuous, harmonic, joyous, translucent, *Rum Cay* (1898?) or *The Turtle Pound* (1898) are oddly reminiscent of Greek art. Homer died alone at Prout's Neck aged seventy-four.

In his lifetime Homer transformed genre painting into a means of conveying subtle emotion and produced masterpieces of woodblock engraving as well as watercolours, etchings and oil paintings. Subjects included Negro life, the Civil War, hunting, fishing, children, sport and nature. Yet these were utilized for their possibilities for formal invention. It is difficult to describe Homer's technical brilliance as an artist. Barbara Novak has argued that his career in general demonstrates a duality which combines 'indigenous conceptualism with a perceptual realism that was developing with teleological authority in the Western world at that moment.' Perhaps the struggle between eye and idea, 'making' and 'matching', the conflicting demands of innate classicism and *plein air* observation account for much in his art. It is as good a definition as we are likely to get of the historical significance of the talent of the greatest painter of nineteenth-century America.

Stuart Morgan

See: Lloyd Goodrich, *Winslow Homer* (1973); Lloyd Goodrich, *The Graphic Work of Winslow Homer* (1968); Barbara Novak, *American Art of the Nineteenth Century* (1969).

226
HONE, William 1780–1842

British writer and publicist

William Hone, writer, bookseller and publisher, was born in Bath. His father, a solicitor's clerk, moved to London in 1783, and, after little formal schooling, Hone was apprenticed in 1790 to an attorney. The French Revolution of 1789 had attracted many people to the cause of reform in England, among them Hone. He joined the radical London Corresponding Society in 1796 and became interested in the 'new philosophy' propounded by William Godwin*.

Taking rooms in Lambeth Walk, in 1800 he married his landlady's daughter and opened a bookshop and circulating library. Hone was no businessman and the project failed. He then tried to set going a scheme for popular savings banks, which came to nothing. He turned to publishing, issuing *The Lash* in 1809, but again failed. He became auctioneer for the book trade; he interested himself in the deplorable conditions in lunatic asylums; in 1815 he took up the case of Eliza Fenning, a maidservant accused of poisoning her employers and hanged, despite Hone's plea for her innocence in *The Maid and the Magpie*. In 1816 he began publishing pamphlets on topical events such as the marriage and death of Princess Charlotte; piracies of Lord Byron's* poems; and reports of trials.

On 18 January 1817, he issued *Hone's Weekly Commentary*, airing political and social abuses and criticizing the ministers regarded as responsible for them. After two numbers, he changed it to *Hone's Reformists' Register*, which ran from 1 February to 25 October 1817. He was also publishing squibs and parodies, and in April 1817 three ex-officio indictments for blasphemy were issued against him for the publication of *The Late John Wilkes's Catechism of a Ministerial Member*, *The Political Litany* and *The Sinecurist's Creed*, parodying the Athanasian Creed. The prosecution claimed that they were likely to undermine public morals and to bring the prayer book and religion into contempt. In the following December, Hone was tried three separate times; in

each trial he defended himself, and each time was acquitted by the jury.

In preparing his defence, Hone came upon much curious information and began working on *A History of Parody*, which he never finished, *The Apocryphal New Testament* (1820) and *Ancient Mysteries Described* (1823). Meanwhile, he published several political satires, ably illustrated by George Cruikshank*, including *The Political House that Jack Built* (1819), *The Man in the Moon* (1820); *The Queen's Matrimonial Ladder* and *Non Mi Ricordo*, both in favour of Queen Caroline against George IV who was attempting to divorce her on the grounds of her adultery.

In 1825, Hone began issuing *The Every-Day Book* in weekly parts, followed by a second volume in 1826, *The Table Book* (1827) and *The Year Book* (1831–2). In compiling these volumes of folklore, legends and miscellaneous information, Hone called upon his readers to send him accounts of their personal experiences or memories of popular customs, an innovation to which they eagerly responded. But Hone himself made little money out of it, as he had gone bankrupt in 1826. The four works were reprinted in volume form and remained in print until 1878.

Hone continued his literary work with *Full Annals of the Revolution in France* (1830) and an edition of Joseph Strutt's *The Sports and Pastimes of the People of England* (1830). In 1834, an illness turned his mind to religion, and he became a devout Congregationalist. Financially unsuccessful he may have been, yet Hone bequeathed to posterity a compendium of folklore and legend which holds its place in the reference libraries of today, and a number of apt satires on the political events of his day.

Anne Renier

Radical Squibs and Loyal Ripostes: Satirical Pamphlets of the Regency Period, 1819–1821, ed. Edgell Rickword (1971), contains five reprints of Hone's publications: *The Political House that Jack Built*; *The Man in the Moon, with a Political Christmas Carol*; *The Queen's Matrimonial Ladder*; *Non Mi Ricordo*; *The Political Showman – at Home*. See: Frederick William Hackwood, *William Hone: His Life and Times* (1912); Harold Herd, *Seven Editors* (1955).

227
HOPKINS, Gerard Manley 1844–89

British poet

Gerard Manley Hopkins was born in Stratford, Essex, on 28 July 1844, the first of eight children of an affluent Victorian couple: his father, Manley, worked in shipping, wrote poetry, published a book on Hawaii (whose Consul-General in London he became in 1856), and practised a tolerant Episcopalianism; Gerard's mother, Kate, was a doctor's daughter, a conscientious Christian, and a lover of music and literature. The family moved to Oak Hill, Hampstead, in 1852 and, two years later, Gerard went as a boarder to Highgate School. There he won the poetry prize for his Keatsian* set-piece 'The Escorial', courageously resisted the sadistic authority of the headmaster, earned the nickname 'Skin' (Hop*kins* anagrammatized to suggest his skin-and-bones physical frailty), attracted attention by his nightly devotion to the New Testament, and won an exhibition to study classics at Oxford.

In 1863 Hopkins arrived at Balliol College and delighted in the theologically charged intellectual atmosphere of Oxford. He became friendly with fellow undergraduate Robert Bridges* and fell under the influence of Edward Bouverie Pusey who, after the defection of John Henry Newman* to the Church of Rome in 1845, was the leader of the High Church Party (or Puseyites). Hopkins was not content to adhere to the Anglican *via media* for long, however, and on 28 August 1866 wrote to Newman telling him, 'I am anxious to become a Catholic'; two months later Newman received him into the Roman Catholic Church. The following year Hopkins, the 'star of Balliol', took a First in Greats and seriously contemplated his religious future. On 30 May 1868 he was accepted as a novice by the Society of Jesus and began his nine years' training for the priesthood.

Although he had chosen a life of dedication and strict discipline Hopkins continued to take an interest in aesthetics and the outside world. From 1868 he began to develop his own theory of natural beauty; he used the word *inscape* to describe the quintessential, intrinsic character of natural things; and *instress* to denote the dynamic energy that informs the *inscape*. He was so distressed by the social conditons prevailing in Victorian England that he wrote to Bridges on 2 August 1871:

Horrible to say, in a manner I am a Communist . . . it is a dreadful thing for the greatest and most necessary part of a very rich nation to live a hard life without dignity, knowledge, comforts, delight, or hopes in the midst of plenty – which plenty they make.

In fact Hopkins was a man who took art and life very seriously indeed, and he discussed his philosophical development in his journal and his fascinating correspondence.

Whereas the philosopher officially approved by the Jesuits was St Thomas Aquinas, Hopkins preferred to read the medieval Franciscan philosopher Duns Scotus. In 1872 Hopkins read the *Scriptum Oxoniense super Sententiis* and excitedly endorsed the Subtle Doctor's principle of individuation and his conviction that

Christ was motivated more by love than filial duty. Hopkins adored Christ as a supreme creator, a great artist: in a sermon of 1879 he described Christ as 'the greatest genius that ever lived . . . nowhere in literature is there anything to match the Sermon on the Mount.'

In 1874 Hopkins was sent to St Beuno's College, north Wales, to study theology: he also studied the Welsh language and the complexities of classical Welsh prosody. As a Jesuit he had renounced the writing of poetry 'as not belonging to my profession' and this self-denial was typical of Hopkins (who, on reading Stevenson's* *Dr Jekyll and Mr Hyde*, said 'my Hyde is worse'). He was obsessed by the idea of sacrifice: Christ's sacrifice, his own sacrifice of the flesh in cultivating the Jesuit spirit, the sacrifice of his artistic gifts. On 7 December 1875 another sacrifice occurred when five Franciscan nuns were drowned after the iron-vessel *Deutschland* was wrecked in the sands of the Kentish Knock. The rector of St Beuno's remarked that the subject was worthy of a poem and Hopkins accordingly produced *The Wreck of the Deutschland*, his first great poem and his most sustained imaginative effort.

For some time Hopkins had been formulating a new theory of poetry. Instead of the ding-dong predictability of traditional English iambic verse he substituted what he called 'sprung rhythm' which, as he explained in a letter of 5 October 1878 to R.W. Dixon, 'consists in scanning by accents or stresses alone, without any account of the number of syllables'. Hopkins was, temperamentally, an ecstatic poet dogmatically attached to the notion of self-discipline. He felt an obligation to justify his poetry by an elaborate theory, so he coined the term Sprung Rhythm, invoked labels like 'reversed feet' and 'counterpoint rhythm', insisted on the use of 'outriding half-feet or hangers', and generally attempted to hide his spontaneity behind a front of pedantry.

What Hopkins's sprung rhythm amounted to, in action, was a combination of oral rhythm and literary style; he wanted his poems to sound right and told Bridges on 21 May 1878, 'you must not slovenly read . . . with the eyes but with your ears.' He used alliteration, internal rhymes and enjambment to create a rich verbal texture and his poetry reads as if the torrential flow of inspiration could hardly be contained by technical means. This section from the eighth stanza of *The Wreck of the Deutschland* indicates his method, with each burst of sound provoking its own echo:

How a lush-kept plush-capped sloe
   Will, mouthed to flesh-burst,
Gush! – flush the man, the being with it, sour or
                     sweet
Brim, in a flash, full! – Hither then, last or first,
   To hero of Calvary, Christ's feet -
Never ask if meaning it, wanting it, warned of it –
                     men go.

Hopkins offered *The Wreck of the Deutschland* to the Jesuit journal the *Month* but, in his own words, 'though at first they accepted it, after a time they withdrew and dared not print it.' Thereafter Hopkins felt free to write though without any hope of publication. Although resigned to lack of recognition he took an ambivalent attitude to poetic celebrity: on 13 June 1878 he told R.W. Dixon, 'The only just judge, the only just literary critic, is Christ'; yet he ended one of the sombre sonnets of 1885 by saying, 'to hoard unheard,/Heard unheeded, leaves me a lonely began.' These late sonnets (especially when contrasted with the early sonnets in celebration of a world 'charged with the grandeur of God') show how Hopkins experienced, in an agonizing way, acute spiritual crises:

O the mind, mind has mountains; cliffs of fall
Frightful, sheer, no-man-fathomed. Hold them cheap
May who ne'er hung there. Nor does long our small
Durance deal with that steep or deep. Here! creep,
Wretch, under a comfort serves in a whirlwind: all
Life death does end and each day dies with sleep.

In 1889 Hopkins contracted typhoid fever and, after the onset of peritonitis, died on 8 June. His last words were: 'I am so happy, so happy.' His *Poems*, edited by his lifelong friend and correspondent Robert Bridges, were posthumously published in 1918 and his astonishingly fresh work helped change the shape and nature of modern verse. Though chronologically a Victorian he was one of the most influential figures in twentieth-century poetry.

Alan Bold

The poetry is collected in *Poems* (1970), ed. W.H. Gardner and N.H. Mackenzie; the prose in *The Correspondence* (2 vols, 1935), ed. C.C. Abbott; *Further Letters* (1956), ed. C.C. Abbott; *The Journals and Papers* (1959), ed. Humphry House and Graham Storey; and *The Sermons and Devotional Writings* (1959), ed. C. Devlin; the life of the poet is discussed in W.H. Gardner, *Gerard Manley Hopkins* (2 vols, 1944–9).

228
HOUSMAN, Alfred Edward 1859–1936

British poet and classical scholar

A happy early childhood in a typical middle-class Victorian family was followed by the death of his mother on his twelfth birthday. Housman's private misery was partially alleviated by academic success at Bromsgrove School, where Herbert Millington inspired him with a love for the classics, and where he also won prizes for English verse. In 1877 he went up to St John's College, Oxford, with an open scholarship to read classics. In

1879 he took a First in Mods, but two years later, after arrogantly ignoring those parts of the syllabus which failed to interest him, and working instead upon the pure scholarship of textual emendation, he failed in Greats.

In 1882 he took a Pass degree, and was reduced to accepting an ill-paid clerkship in the Patent Office in London. For three years he lived in Bayswater with Moses Jackson, his greatest friend from Oxford; but moved out when his affectionate feelings for Jackson deepened into a love which he realized would never be fully reciprocated. Jackson went to India in 1887 and Housman, now living in Highgate, wrote poems sadly about lost love and his own 'flawed' nature, and nostalgically about the countryside of his Worcestershire childhood. And now, in a major effort to redeem his failure in Greats, he applied himself to his classical studies, reading at the British Museum in the evenings.

An article on Propertius in 1888 was the first of numerous papers which he published every year until his death. In 1889 he was asked to join the Cambridge Philological Society; and in 1892, after ten years of obscurity, he was appointed Professor of Latin at University College, London, where his Introductory Lecture was well received. From this time he concentrated his classical efforts upon the Latin poets from Lucretius to Juvenal; and in 1894 he edited Ovid's *Ibis*.

In that year his father died; and the first five months of 1895 brought a flood of poetry for *A Shropshire Lad*, published by Kegan Paul in 1896. In 1898, after disappointing sales, the book was taken over and promoted with increasing success by Grant Richards. Richards became a close friend, sometimes accompanying Housman on the pleasure-seeking continental holidays which he began in 1897, and during which he discreetly indulged his gastronomic and homosexual tastes. Between 1900 and 1902 Housman wrote many poems about the Boer War in which his youngest brother, Herbert, died fighting.

Housman was also friendly with Arthur Platt, the Professor of Greek, and W.P. Ker, the Professor of English; and in 1900 he took a leading part in resolving a crisis in the affairs of University College. Teaching took up much of his time, but in 1903 he published the first volume of his *magnum opus* on Manilius, a Latin poet whom Housman did not rate highly, but whose work afforded the greatest possible challenge to his genius as an emendator. His scathing attacks upon the incompetence of other classical scholars damaged his reputation on the continent until the 1920s; but in 1905 his edition of *Juvenal* was warmly received in England, and in 1911 he was elected a Fellow of Trinity on his appointment as Kennedy Professor of Latin at Cambridge, and gave his Inaugural Lecture.

Wishing above all to be respected, he discouraged intimacy and became known in Cambridge as an aloof and formidable figure; though in 1919 membership of a dining club known as 'The Family' enabled him to relax in the company of friends. His wider circle of acquaintances included Thomas Hardy* and M.R. James; and he devoted much time to helping and encouraging his family, and in particular his brother Laurence Housman, the poet and dramatist. Housman still corresponded with Jackson, and news of his impending death in 1922 brought further inspiration, and the appearance later that year of *Last Poems*, which confirmed Housman's popularity as a fine poet of nostalgia, of the bitterness of life, of the sustaining power of nature, of the strength of the human spirit, and of the courage to endure.

In 1926 he published his *Lucan*, and in 1930 the final volume of his *Manilius*. In 1933 his Leslie Stephen* lecture, 'The Name and Nature of Poetry', which exactly described the nature of his inspiration, and declared that poetry could best be detected by the physical reaction it provoked in the listener, brought down the critical wrath of F.R. Leavis. From then on Housman suffered from heart trouble, and after his death in 1936 his reputation as a poet was further injured by the inclusion of inferior material in *More Poems*. The high standards of his scholarship are a legacy of permanent value to the world of classical scholarship.

Richard Perceval Graves

See: Katharine Symons and others, *A.E. Housman: Recollections* (1936); A.S.F. Gow, *A.E. Housman, A Sketch* (1936); Laurence Housman, *My Brother: A.E.H.* (1937); Percy Withers, *A Buried Life* (1940); Grant Richards, *Housman 1897–1936* (1941); *The Letters of A.E. Housman*, ed. Henry Maas (1970); Richard Perceval Graves, *A.E. Housman: The Scholar-Poet* (1979).

229
HOWELLS, William Dean 1837–1920

US author

Although far from being the mediocrity H.L. Mencken judged him – 'the author of a long row of uninspired and hollow books' (*Prejudices: First Series*, 1919) – Howells no longer enjoys a serious reputation. Yet throughout his own best years in the late nineteenth century, he was a figure of considerable eminence, both in America and abroad, a pioneer realist in his fiction, a seasoned editor, a widely read theorist and critic. The hundred or so volumes he had behind him at his death include thirty-eight novels, collections of his journalism and reminiscence, his travel writing, and his minor versifying and drama. He pursued a lifelong friendship and correspondence with both Henry James* and Mark Twain*, and was mentor to a distinguished gallery of later American realists and naturalists, most notably Hamlin Garland, Bret Harte*, Frank Norris and Stephen Crane*. By his last two decades, essentially for him valedictory years, he was widely referred to as 'the Dean of American Letters', a genuinely respected literary presence. In the kindly open letter he wrote in 1912 for Howells's seventy-fifth birthday, Henry James paid honour to his ' rare lucidity' and to his 'studies of American life, so acute, so direct, so disinterested, so preoccupied with the fine truth of the case'.

Howells's early years in frontier Ohio, as printer with his father, fledgling journalist and autodidact (he became an accomplished linguist by his own efforts and lectured at Harvard 1869–71) are engagingly remembered in works like *A Boy's Town* (1890), *My Year in a Log Cabin* (1893), *My Literary Passions* (1895) and *Years of My Youth* (1916). In 1860, after contributing to a range of Ohio and literary newspapers, he published *Poems of Two Friends*, the same year he made his first important trip to the east of America to meet James Russell Lowell*, editor of *Atlantic Monthly*, and the New England circle of Emerson* and Hawthorne*. His biography of Lincoln* (1860), on Lincoln's election to the presidency, secured for him the consulship at Venice which in time yielded travel volumes like *Venetian Life* (1866), *Italian Journeys* (1867), his critical study *Modern Italian Poets* (1887), and his Italian 'international' novels, *A Foregone Conclusion* (1875), *The Lady of the Aroostook* (1879), *A Fearful Responsibility* (1881), and his own favourite, *Indian Summer* (1886). In 1865, and never free of guilt for having avoided war service in the Union cause, Howells returned to the United States where his work as an influential editor began in earnest. Although he wrote voluminously and published in many journals, his principal efforts went to the *Nation*, then *Atlantic Monthly*, where he became editor-in-chief in 1871 – a position first held by Lowell – and finally, *Harper's*, for whom he appeared under two well-known by-lines, 'Editor's Study' and 'Editor's Easy Chair'. His own move, with his family, from Boston to New York in 1888, was widely taken to signal the coming demise of New England as America's natural cultural centre and the rise of a different, more metropolitan, American literary life.

The fiction which establishes Howells's main claim to attention began with *Their Wedding Journey* (1871), a congenial if unremarkable domestic tale of travel and manners based on the marriage between Basil and Isabel March, a family to whom he returned in *A Hazard of New Fortunes* (1890), *An Open-Eyed Conspiracy* (1897) and *Their Silver Wedding Journey* (1899). Each of these works suggests Howells's ease in depicting a sense of American place, and his shrewd, encompassing eye for middle-class custom. Three novels in particular, however, show him at strength. In *A Modern Instance* (1881), he portrays a relationship gone sour, the marriage, divorce and killing of the journalist, Bartley Hubbard, and the subsequent mixed fortunes of his widow, Marcia. If occasionally unsure in design, it aroused great controversy on publication, the anatomy of a 'modern' unsatisfactory marriage. *The Rise of Silas Lapham* (1885), Howells's most considerable effort and a 'business' novel to compare with Henry James's *The American* (1877), or Theodore Dreiser's Cowperwood trilogy, *The Financier* (1912), *The Titan* (1914) and *The Stoic* (1947), or Sinclair Lewis's *Babbitt* (1922), tells the financial 'fall', but moral 'rise' of a Yankee entrepreneur, the self-made man of business not as villain, but, for once, as a figure of genuine conscience. In *A Hazard of New Fortunes*, set in a newspaper office, Howells explores the clash of capitalism with the cause of labour, a sure, often vivid, account of strikes, violence, American urban and industrial life. Howells's other 'social' fiction – novels like *A Chance Acquaintance* (1873), *The Undiscovered Country* (1880), *Dr Breen's Practice* (1881), *Annie Kilburn* (1889), or his later reminiscent work like *The Landlord at Lion's Head* (1897) and *The Kentons* (1902) – though rarely free of defect, deserve better than their present total eclipse. Howells's benign socialist-utopian vein, shaped as much by Tolstoy* and William Morris* as by Marx*, or American socialists like Henry George and Edward Bellamy, yielded two other kinds of fiction – his so-called 'Shaker' novels, *The Undiscovered Country* (1880), *The Day of Their Wedding* (1896) and *A Parting and a Meeting* (1896), and his utopian allegories each sharply critical of capitalism, *A Traveler from Altruria* (1894) and *Through the Eye of the Needle* (1907). Although Howells took as his rallying cry 'truth and sanity in fiction', and undoubtedly paved the way for a subsequent generation of American realists, his own writing displayed distinct areas of sexual and political reticence, unlike that of Dreiser about whom he remained disapprovingly silent.

Honoured in later life with degrees from Yale, Oxford and Columbia, the first President of the American Academy of Arts and Letters, and a continuing visitor (and writer of popular guidebooks) to Europe and an esteemed international man of letters, Howells persisted not only in taking principled stands against the suppression of striking workers but in developing the case for literary realism. Books like *Criticism and Fiction* (1891) and *Literature and Life* (1902) led to his being perceived as much for the critic as the novelist. His prodigious output marks a writer of unflagging application for all that by the turn of the century, as he himself recognized, he was a figure of the past. He addressed himself, as he observed with justice, to 'the smiling aspects' of American life, the 'democratic' everyday social average. If his fiction lacks the passion of Zola* or the psychological nuance of James, or Twain's* vigour of idiom, Howells none the less deserves better than a mere passing footnote in American literary history. He remains, in his stolid, workman-like way, a founding voice of realism and the depiction of American manners.

A. Robert Lee

See: Lionel Trilling, 'W.D. Howells and The Roots of Modern Taste', *Partisan Review*, 18, September-October 1951, pp. 516–37; Everett Carter, *Howells and the Age of Realism* (1954); Clara Marburg Kirk, *W.D. Howells and the Art of His Times* (1965); Kenneth S. Lynn, *William Dean Howells: An American Life* (1971); George N. Bennett, *The Realism of William Dean Howells* (1973).

230
HUGO, Victor-Marie 1802–85

French poet, dramatist and novelist

Hugo's father rose to be a general in the Napoleonic army; his mother came from a bourgeois family centred on Nantes. The youngest of a family of three, all sons, Victor-Marie was born at Besançon where his father was stationed briefly in 1802. His early years were strongly marked by the instability of his family life in which he and his brothers were pulled between the opposing influences of his parents whose increasing estrangement culminated in a separation in 1812. Some time was spent in Italy (1808), some in Spain (1811–12), some in Paris. Hugo's education, necessarily patchy, was concluded by a period (1816–18) at the *lycée* Louis-le-Grand. A gift for verse, which had manifested itself when he was about fourteen, determined him to make his way as a writer, which he proceeded to do with determination and enterprise. A successful periodical which he ran with his brothers, *Le Conservateur littéraire* (1819–21), foundered for lack of money on the death of Madame Hugo. But a growing reputation and some shrewdly composed works – poetry on public themes, and a novel, *Han d'Islande* (1823) – earned him official prizes, the favour of Louis XVIII and two pensions. These material benefits were sufficient to launch him into his ardently desired marriage to Adèle Foucher and towards an increasingly impressive career as a poet.

By the end of the 1820s, Hugo had established himself in the front rank of the poets of the time and had imposed his authority on the French theatre which, from the beginning of the century, had been the centre of attempts to find a form to replace the tragedy on the classical model. Hugo revitalized the ode, turning it towards contemporary subjects and attitudes, developed a freer form of the *ballade*, and experimented with the historical tragedy (*Cromwell*, 1827, *Amy Robsart*, 1827, the first unsuited to the stage, the second failing at the first performance). More important than the plays themselves was the extended preface which he published with *Cromwell* in December 1827, and which has long been read separate from the play itself as a work of major importance in the development of the theory of the modern drama. The *Préface de Cromwell* presents three sets of ideas, all of them challenges to tradition: the background and importance of modern art; the concept of a drama freed from artificial constraints; the case for a new criticism freed from the eighteenth-century canons of taste. The background to the modern drama is derived from a hasty conspectus of human history seen as developing over three epochs, each having a characteristic form of expression: the primitive ages (lyric), the time of antiquity (epic), the Christian era (dramatic). Each period is thus marked by a form of poetry, and is further characterized by the presence of a work of universal importance; the Bible, Homer, Shakespeare. The modern sensibility, based on the Christian view of the duality of man, seeks to accommodate opposed tendencies: sentiment and analysis, beauty and ugliness, the sublime and the grotesque. The new drama requires a new complexity. The literary genres, particularly comedy and tragedy, should be amalgamated. The unities of time and place, which had dominated the classical stage, should be abolished. The new freedom should be reflected in the unrestricted choice of subject, the one requirement being the need to present events and characters with as much authenticity as possible (hence the theory of 'local colour'), and in the use of a more natural and varied verse style.

By 1832, Hugo was at the first high point of his career as a writer, the dominant figure of the French Romantic school, which had swept into prominence towards the end of the 1820s, particularly in the theatre, where the theories he had promulgated were triumphantly vindicated by the success of his play *Hernani* (1830), theatrically Spanish in its subject, colour and action. But his most brilliant work at this time had been done in poetry, with *Les Orientales* (1829) and *Les Feuilles d'Automne* (1831), and in the novel, with *The Hunchback of Notre-Dame* (*Notre-Dame de Paris*, 1831). The two works of poetry represent opposed facets of his imagination, *Les Orientales* taking its general shape from contemporary events (the Greco-Turkish conflict) and projecting a powerful visual fancy on to the landscapes and events of the Near and Middle East; *Les Feuilles d'Automne* ('Autumn Leaves'), introspective and meditative, with suggestions of visionary depths behind the surface of life. *The Hunchback of Notre-Dame* is arguably the finest historical novel produced in France, with its surface realism presenting the architecture, atmosphere and topography of late fifteenth-century Paris, its deep structures evoking the conflicts of a period of transition, and its characters working out a scheme of fatality inseparable from medieval superstitions.

It is as a poet that Hugo develops most clearly in the years between 1832 and 1840. *Les Chants du Crépuscule* ('Twilight Songs', 1835), *Les Voix intérieures* ('Interior Voices' 1837), *Les Rayons et les Ombres* ('Lights and Shadows', 1840), mark the development of his view of the range and responsibility of the writer and above all the poet. The *chef d'école* of 1830 aspires, by 1840, to the role of spokesman of the nation, reflecting in his verse private life, the importance of art, awareness of a spiritual dimension and of the deep sense of political events.

From about 1832 also there appears a growing ambition to play a direct role in public life, and apart from the continued literary successes, in the theatre as well as in poetry (four new plays were staged between 1832 and 1835), Hugo became more and more clearly an establishment figure. From 1836, he stood for election to the French Academy three times before being received in 1841. He was given a title (*pair de France*) in 1845, was favourably viewed by Louis-Philippe and intervened progressively in political debates. When the Second Republic was set up on the fall of Louis-Philippe in 1848, Hugo gave his support to Prince Louis-Napoleon's campaign for election as president, but switched to uncompromising opposition when the prince began to move clearly towards the assumption of permanent power. In the aftermath of the military *coup d'état* in 1851, Hugo escaped from France, first to Belgium then to Jersey (1852). Expelled from Jersey with other political exiles in 1855, he went to Guernsey where he stayed, inflexibly hostile to Louis-Napoleon and to the Second Empire, returning after the French defeat of 1870 when the Third Republic came into being.

1853 to 1859 are the years which mark the second high point in Hugo's literary life. His creative writing had been much reduced in the 1840s under the influence of public responsibilities and also of private reverses, chief among which were scandals caused by his sexual behaviour and the enduring grief at the death of his daughter Léopoldine with her husband in a boating accident in 1843. The shock of political events and the blazing enmity towards Louis-Napoleon revived his literary verve which immediately expressed itself in *Châtiments* ('Punishment', 1853), a work of poetic satire of sustained inventive power, aimed at discrediting the emperor and his entourage and weakening his regime, but also counselling against violent reprisals and presenting an idealistic prospect of progress. *Les Contemplations* (1856) projects into lyrical form the 'spectrum' of Hugo's life over a span of twenty-five years, centred on 1843, the year of Léopoldine's death. The preoccupations of the poetry of the 1830s are concentrated into two volumes (*Autrefois, Aujourd'hui*) and brought towards universal or archetypal pattern of experience, particularly in the last part of the work, where the poetic imagination is used to suggest a visionary understanding of the ontological and eschatological problems. The historical and visionary imagination of the poet dominates in the works which follow. *La Légende des Siècles* ('Legends of the Ages', 1859) is a work of epic quality and proportions, but composed of a number of separate pieces which Hugo called 'small epics' (*petites épopées*). This is the first of three series, the other two being published much later (1877 and 1883) and filling out the original design, which was to present the progress of the human consciousness, from the Creation and the dawn of history, through the early periods recounted in the Old Testament, through the medieval period to the French Revolution and the age of modern inventions. Two great poems, 'La Fin de Satin' and 'Dieu', were intended to extend the *Légende des Siècles* through the symbolic treatment of the themes of human liberty and the search for God, but remained incomplete and were not published until after Hugo's death, appearing respectively in 1886 and 1891.

Two novels appeared during the 1860s: *Les Misérables* (1862), published thirty years after its conception, and *Les Travailleurs de la mer* (1866), begun in 1864. In a prefatory note (1866), Hugo links these two novels with *The Hunchback of Notre-Dame* through the theme of fatality, working through superstition (*The Hunchback of Notre-Dame*), society and its laws (*Les Misérables*) and the forces of nature (*Les Travailleurs de la mer*). These are Hugo's greatest works of prose fiction, each obtaining popular success through the characters and surface events – Quasimodo as the familiar spirit of the cathedral, Jean Valjean's long contest with the police agent Javert, Gilliatt's struggle to raise the wreck of the *Durande* and his fight with the giant octopus, for example – but each developing a message about the underlying sense of these events, with the visionary and poetic power that progressively dominated all his writings.

Madame Hugo, who died in 1868, had followed her husband into exile, with their sons Charles and François-Victor and the surviving daughter Adèle. Hugo's mistress, Juliette Drouet, a former actress whom he had first met during the period of his theatrical triumphs, was installed discreetly near the house on Guernsey, which he bought from the money made by *Les Contemplations*. 'When liberty returns, I shall return,' said Hugo, and this vow was kept, despite the amnesty proclaimed by Napoleon III in 1859. On 5 September 1870, four days after the emperor's surrender at Sedan and one day after the proclamation of the Third Republic, Hugo was in Paris, welcomed by large crowds.

In his public life, Hugo's reputation was immense. His greatest literary works were now behind him, but important books continued to appear, some, like *L'Année terrible* (1872, poems on the war of 1870 and the Commune), of recent composition, others, like the poems of *Les Quatre vents de l'esprit* (1882), drawn from previously written material. His creative powers failed after 1878, though the years up to his death in 1885 continued to be marked by publications. He was given the funeral of a national hero.

Although he always considered poetry as the dominant literary genre, the strongest impact of his work in his own time was in the theatre which, as already shown, he revolutionized, and in the novel. In poetry, his greatest achievements came during the twenty years of exile, when he was cut off from literary developments in Paris. Despite the commercial success of *Les Contemplations*, this work, mainly because of the religious philosophy advanced in the sombre, visionary poems of the last part, did not find the response that Hugo had hoped for, so that he was led to postpone the publication of other works of this kind. Two successive schools of poetry reacted against him, the Parnassian school, led by Leconte de Lisle, occupying the period of the Second Empire and the early years of the Third Republic, and the Symbolists, inspired by Baudelaire* and Mallarmé*, and dominating the 1880s and 1890s. Denigrated by the Naturalist critics, Hugo became, in the early twentieth century, firmly identified as the leader of the Romantic movement and confined to a few plays, his more popular novels and the more accessible parts of his work in verse. Since about 1945, the efforts of a number of scholars, writing mostly in French, have succeeded in focusing attention upon the social and political commitment of his work, and upon the later poetry developing his philosophical and religious ideas, which amalgamate elements from several systems in order to present a vision of a fallen universe drawn by its creator towards ultimate integration, its guiding principle, the divine spirit or essence, manifesting itself in reincarnation. Relatively little known poems, such as 'Dieu and 'La Fin de Satin', are now beginning to be valued among the great philosophical and epic poems of Europe. Meanwhile, Hugo's early plays, despite periodic critical reaction, have retained their appeal, as have his best-known novels. *Ruy Blas* (1838) and *Hernani* are in the repertoire of the French national theatres. There are also signs of a return of critical attention to his early poetry.

Clifford Ireson

Other works: *Bug-Jargal* (1820 and 1826), novel; *Odes et poésies diverses* (1822); *Nouvelles Odes* (1824); *Odes et ballades* (1826); *le Dernier jour d'un condamné* (1829), novel; *Marion de Lorme* (1831), *Le Roi s'amuse* (1832), *Lucrèce Borgia* (1833), dramas; *L'Événement* (1848–51), newspaper run in collaboration with his sons; *Les Chansons des rues et des bois* (1865), poems; *Quatre-vingt-treize* (1874), novel; *Mes Fils* (1874), autobiography; *Actes et paroles* (2 vols, 1875; vol. 3, 1876), autobiography; *L'Art d'être grand-père* (1877), poems; *Le Pape* (1878), poem; *La Pitié suprême* (1879), *Religion et religions* (1880), *L'Âne* (1880), all poetry; *Torquemada* (1882), drama; *L'Archipel de la manche*

(1883), essays on Guernsey. Works published posthumously include: *Théâtre en liberté* (1886), drama; *Choses vues* (first series, 1887; second series, 1900), journal; *Toute la lyre* (first series, 1888; second series 1893), poetry; *Correspondance* (vol. I, 1896; vol. II, 1898); *Les Années funestes* (1898), poetry; *Postscriptum de ma vie* (1901), autobiography. For the complete works of Hugo see *Oeuvres complètes* (4 vols, 1961–4) and *Oeuvres complètes* (18 vols, 1967–70). Recommended translations: *William Shakespeare*, trans. M. B. Anderson (1906 and 1973); *Les Misérables*, trans. N. Denny (1976); *The Hunchback of Notre-Dame*, trans. Jo Sturrock (1978). See: E. Grant, *The Career of Victor Hugo* (1945); A. Maurois, *Victor Hugo* (trans. G. Hopkins, 1954); J. P. Houston, *Victor Hugo* (1974); J. Richardson, *Victor Hugo* (1976); P. Berret, *Victor Hugo* (1939); J.-B. Barrére, *Hugo: L'Homme et l'oeuvre* (1952); H. Guillemin, *Victor Hugo par lui-même* (1964).

231

HUMBOLDT, (Friedrich Heinrich) Alexander von, Baron 1769–1859

German scientist, explorer and geographer

Younger brother of Wilhelm von Humboldt*, Alexander von Humboldt was born in Berlin, the son of a Prussian army officer, and came from a line of provincial administrators. He was educated privately by tutors and later attended the University of Göttingen where he studied physics and chemistry and also became interested in geology and mineralogy. He developed these interests further at Freiberg (Saxony) Mining School, where he also found time to investigate magnetic phenomena and carry out botanical experiments in a subterranean environment. Not regarded by his widowed mother as the intellectual equal of Wilhelm, whom she intended for high public office, Alexander nevertheless soon distinguished himself. When he obtained an appointment in the Prussian Mining Department he devoted his great energy to the improvement of mining methods, designing a safety lamp and setting up a technical school for miners funded from his own pocket. His real urge was, however, to travel (his friend George Forster had been a member of Cook's second expedition) and after his mother's death his share of a considerable inheritance enabled him to resign from the mining service and realize this ambition.

From 1799 to 1804 he explored Central and South America in the company of the botanist Bonpland, and on his return settled in Paris – with its remarkable concentration of intellectual and scientific life, his spiritual home – where he spent much of the next quarter century organizing the publication (in French for the most part) of the results of his great expedition (an

undertaking twice as costly as the publication of Napoleon's* lavish *Description de l'Egypte*).

Unlike his brother, Humboldt never married, but he enjoyed lasting attachments to the French scientists Gay-Lussac and François Arago, the latter being the chief affection of his life. By 1827 Humboldt's fortune had become so depleted that he was compelled to return to Berlin and the duties of court chamberlain. There he was mistrusted by many for his cosmopolitanism and his liberal views. He made a great impact however, on the non-scientific public of Berlin with a course of popular lectures on natural history (1827–8) which formed the basis of his great panorama of nature *Cosmos* (*Kosmos*, 4 vols, 1845–62, trans. from 1848) composed during his declining years. In 1828 he also organized one of the first international scientific conferences (the highly successful Berlin meeting was the model for the first conference of the British Association in 1831), and in 1829 he led an expedition to Central Asia and Siberia.

During the later part of his long life Humboldt's dwindling financial resources made him more and more dependent on his appointment at court. His sympathies for the shortlived revolutions of 1848 were well known and while he continued to enjoy a great international reputation he had to endure the hostile philistinism of the *ultras* at court. He died in his Berlin apartment which was mortgaged to his own valet, who at the end acted as a screen between him and the steady flow of admirers from abroad.

Today Humboldt appears to us as one of the last great figures of the Enlightenment, admirable for his encyclopedic scientific culture and commitment to the empirical study of nature rather than for the discovery of any single organizing principle or theory. Yet, like his less celebrated contemporary Karl Ritter (1779–1859), he helped lay the foundations of modern physical geography in his synthesis of the numerous factors which determine the character of a country, and was the originator of systematic meteorology (the first to use isothermal lines in mapping temperature) and of plant geography. He has also been described as the first ecologist and his writings stimulated Darwin* in his own studies of plant and animal interrelationships.

Humboldt represents more than a stage in the history of science and ideas, for his conception of the panorama of nature and of man's place in it still induces respect as well as nostalgia in the modern reader. His accounts, for example, of the Inca and Aztec civilizations are true to the best traditions of the Enlightenment and show none of the ethnocentricity which characterizes many nineteenth-century encounters with foreign cultures. In his descriptions of the physical world Humboldt, although a tireless measurer, recorder and experimenter, also conveys a sense of the wonder of nature, particularly in the tropics, and echoes the poetic evocations of Bernardin de Saint-

Pierre and Chateaubriand* without succumbing to their self-indulgent rhetoric. His exemplary essay, 'De l'étude et de la contemplation de la nature' (1845), a version of his introduction to *Cosmos* specially written by Humboldt for the French audience he valued so highly, communicates a complex intellectual and sensuous enjoyment of nature in a style whose poise and lucidity has few equals in nineteenth-century French prose.

Roger S. Huss

Works: *Views of Nature* (*Ansichten der Natur*, 1808, trans. 1880); *Personal narrative of Travels to Equinoctial regions of America*, (*Relation historique du Voyage aux régions équinoxiales du nouveau continent*, 3 vols, 1814–25, trans. 1852). See: Lotte Kellner, *Alexander von Humboldt* (1963); Douglas Botting, *Humboldt and the Cosmos* (1973).

232

HUMBOLDT, (Karl) Wilhelm von, Baron
1767–1835

German scholar and statesman

Elder brother of Alexander von Humboldt*, Wilhelm von Humboldt was born in Potsdam, the son of a Prussian army officer, and came of a family of provincial administrators. Privately educated by tutors, he subsequently read law at Göttingen University and studied Kant and the *philosophes* in Paris before entering public service in Berlin in 1790. Ambassador to Rome (where he began a collection of classical sculpture which was later to adorn the family home Schloss Tegel) from 1801 to 1808 and later Prussian Minister to Austria and delegate to the Congress of Vienna, he had considerable political influence but found his liberal positions increasingly difficult to defend in the climate of reaction after 1815; following a brief period as Prussian Ambassador in London he fell from grace in 1819. Although he was an important figure in the diplomatic history of the Napoleonic period his most important contribution was in the field of domestic policy: between 1808 and 1810 he undertook a fundamental reform of the Prussian education system. Humboldt felt that all should benefit from the same basic primary education and supported many of the ideas of Pestalozzi. He established the *Gymnasium* (an institution admired abroad by educationists such as Matthew Arnold*) in which a humanistic curriculum would promote *Bildung*, the development and cultivation of the individual, a key concept of the *Aufklärung* and a preoccupation of such members of Humboldt's circle as Goethe* and Schiller. In Humboldt's reforms vocational training was provided for but remained clearly separate from and subordinate to a humanistic edu-

cation, the main route to university; this was consistent with Humboldt's view that the state existed essentially for the sake of the individual — see his *The Limits of State Action* (*Ideen zu einem Versuch die Gränzen der Wirksamkeit des Staates zu bestimmen*, 1851, trans. ed. Burrow, 1969). He also helped establish a new University of Berlin which now bears his name.

In the last twenty years of his life Humboldt devoted his time to his linguistic, historical and aesthetic interests, in his favourite setting, Schloss Tegel, which has been compared with Jefferson's Monticello for its central place in the scholar's life. In his writings on the philosophy of history he expressed a view of history which was empirical and eschewed the search for final causes; the historian's task was rather to reveal the forces of nature and man as they shaped events, to seek the idea but not at the expense of fact. More significant, however, were his linguistic activities which embraced the study of Chinese, Sanskrit, Basque, Amerindian languages and the languages of South-East Asia, Indonesia and Polynesia. His most substantial linguistic work, a study of Kawi, the hieratic literary language of Java, is prefaced by a lengthy introduction on the differences in the structure of languages and the influence of such differences on the intellectual development of mankind *Linguistic Variability and Intellectual Development* (*Über die Verschiedenheit des menschlichen Sprachbaues*, 1836, trans. 1971). Humboldt's contribution to linguistics is the subject of a considerable modern literature. He had a dynamic conception of language which he saw as an *energeia* rather than an *ergon*; for him languages are the creative expressions of particular world views, each language having its own 'inner form'. In this he looks forward to the relativism of certain modern theorists. He also produced a study of Schiller as well as poetry of his own and an extensive correspondence.

Roger S. Huss

Works: *Werke* (5 vols, 1960–4). See: W. H. Bruford, 'The idea of *Bildung* in Wilhelm von Humboldt's letters', in *The Era of Goethe, Essays presented to J. Boyd* (1959). Paul R. Sweet, *Wilhelm von Humboldt* (2 vols, 1978–80), is an outstanding biography.

233

HUNT, William Holman 1827–1910

British painter

Lacking both natural facility and parental encouragement, Hunt found becoming an artist a struggle; when he managed to gain admission to the Royal Academy Schools in 1844, it was at the third attempt. Even at this early stage in his career, he was remarkable not so much for his aesthetic sense (no one has ever accused his work of being decorative or pretty) as for his sense of intellectual and moral purpose. Self-educated, widely read and highly receptive to new ideas, he was particularly excited by the writings of Ruskin*, which articulated the view of art he himself had already been developing, as a moral, even religious activity in which truth to nature and the bearing of some spiritual message were of equal importance; he held to this view for the rest of his life. His first step towards its realization was the subsequently much repainted *Christ and the Two Maries*, which was begun in 1847, left unfinished and, unfortunately like many of Hunt's pictures, taken up again when he was an old man.

In 1848 Hunt joined his lifelong friend John Everett Millais* Dante Gabriel Rossetti* and four others of lesser importance in forming the Pre-Raphaelite Brotherhood. Hunt was at pains to point out that the term 'Pre-Raphaelite' was not meant to imply the adoption of some archaic style but an attempt to recapture the spirit of early painting, revering nature and abjuring the artificiality – the subdued, usually brownish colour-schemes, studio lighting, stereotyped figure in theatrical poses and landscape painted to a formula – that seemed to him to plague painting from Raphael onwards. Hunt's first Pre-Raphaelite painting, *Rienzi*, a scene from the life of the Italian patriot, was exhibited at the Royal Academy in 1849. The figures in *Rienzi* are almost exaggeratedly individualized portraits of actual people, including Millais and Rossetti; the colour is brilliant, giving a real impression of clear, even sunlight; and natural detail is observed with near-microscopic care. Though perhaps artistically less successful than contemporary works by Millais and Rossetti, *Rienzi* is the earliest Pre-Raphaelite picture to be painted largely outdoors and as such holds a special place in the history of Pre-Raphaelitism. Hunt maintained the principle of painting directly and meticulously from nature throughout his career, long after Millais and Rossetti had moved on to quite un-Pre-Raphaelite styles.

Hunt's next major picture was *A Converted British Family sheltering a Christian Priest from the Persecution of the Druids* (1849–50). Characteristically, many of the objects in the scene are at once parts of the setting justifiable on naturalistic grounds and elements of an elaborate symbolic programme; the fishing nets hanging on the wall, for example, are quite normal features of a riverside fisherman's shed, but they also point metaphorically to the priest's role as a missionary or 'fisher of men'. *The Hireling Shepherd* (1851–2), which shows a temporary shepherd neglecting his flock in order to flirt with a shepherdess, also has more than one layer of meaning. The shepherd represents those members of the church who concern themselves with sectarian disputes and vain theological speculations at the expense of their pastoral duties. Both the *Christian Priest* and *The Hireling Shepherd* carried deliberately top-

ical implications at a time when the High Church Tractarian movement, with which Hunt sympathized, was provoking bitter, often hair-splitting disputes within the Church of England, and even occasional acts of apparent persecution. They probably also reflect Hunt's view of his own role as a missionary of good art up against the Druids and hirelings of the 'Raphaelite' establishment.

The Light of the World (1851–3) is the work for which Hunt is best known, and indeed the most popular religious image created in the nineteenth century. Christ, carrying the lamp of truth, is shown knocking at the weed-choked door of the human soul; a huge full moon both illuminates the background, all of which was of course painted at night from an actual place, and, ostensibly by chance, makes a halo around Christ's head. The symbolism of light connects *The Light of the World* to its counterpart *The Awakening Conscience* (1853), in which a kept woman gazes out into a sunlit garden, thinks of the innocence of her childhood and realizes the depths of immorality into which she has sunk. Unaware of its effect, her lover is singing her a song, 'Oft in the Stilly Night', about memory and 'the light of other days'. *The Awakening Conscience* was immensely influential upon British art in opening up modern life as a source of subject-matter every bit as serious and morally significant as the time-hallowed themes from history, literature, mythology and the Bible. But, curiously, Hunt chose not to follow his own lead. Henceforth his subjects were for the most part to be drawn directly from the Scriptures.

The key to understanding much of Hunt's work from the mid-1850s onwards is typology, a then quite familiar means of interpreting biblical events symbolically in relation to the redemption of Man in Christ. *The Scapegoat* (1854–6), painted by the salt-encrusted shallows of the Dead Sea, was the first fruit of Hunt's experience of the Holy Land, which he visited four times; the point of the picture lies in the fact that the sacrificial goat chased out into the desert by the Israelites to carry away their sins is a 'type' of Christ crucified. The full meaning of the rest of Hunt's most important later paintings, *The Finding of the Saviour in the Temple* (1854–60), *The Shadow of Death* (1869–73) and *The Triumph of the Innocents* (1876–87), is similarly accessible only through typological interpretation. The problem Hunt faced as a painter of biblical subjects was that of reconciling Pre-Raphaelite authenticity with the effective communication of spiritual truth. He believed that the conventions and symbolism of traditional religious painting were wholly inappropriate to the modern age – everyone knew that the Holy Family were Jewish, working-class people and they should be painted as such, not as stereotypes of beauty wearing haloes – and yet that there should be more to a religious painting than mere archaeological reconstruction. Typological symbolism was the ideal solution because by associating the event depicted with the greatest of all Christian events, the Passion, it elevated its meaning without interfering with its actuality.

Malcolm Warner

Hunt is his own characteristically painstaking biographer in *Pre-Raphaelitism and the Pre-Raphaelite Brotherhood* (1905). See also: Mary Bennett, *William Holman Hunt* (catalogue to the exhibition at the Walker Art Gallery, Liverpool, and the Victoria and Albert Museum, 1969); George P. Landow, *William Holman Hunt and Typological Symbolism (1979)*.

234
HUXLEY, Thomas Henry 1826–95

British biologist

T. H. Huxley was an English biologist whose work and thinking led him into public battles over Darwinism and many other leading questions of the day. Inspired as a boy to become a mechanical engineer, his career led him to study the mechanism of living bodies and his enemies claimed that he came to treat human beings as machines. His medical studies began at Charing Cross Hospital when he was seventeen and on graduating in 1845 he at once published a paper about the hitherto unrecognized layer on the inner sheath of hair subsequently known as 'Huxley's layer'. He was granted a commission in the Royal Navy and set out on board the *Rattlesnake* to make a prolonged survey voyage to Australia, arriving in Sydney in 1848.

There he fell in love with Anne Heathorn and at the age of twenty-two proposed to her. She accepted in the full knowledge that years must pass before a struggling and almost penniless scientist could marry her. Success came early but did not make marriage any easier. His first important paper, 'On the Anatomy and the Affinities of the Family of Medusa', was printed by the Royal Society in its *Philosophical Transactions* (1849) and to his surprise at the very early age of twenty-six he was elected a Fellow of the Royal Society. Within a few years he began exchanging papers with many leading scientists and correspondended regularly with men of the calibre of Darwin*.

During his first interview with Charles Darwin, who was to publish his great book *The Origin of Species* in 1859, Huxley expressed his belief in the sharpness of the line of demarcation between natural groups and was disconcerted when Darwin received the statement with a smile. When he married Anne Heathorn in 1855 Darwin said to him: 'I hope your marriage will not make you idle: happiness I fear is not good for work.' The warning was unnecessary. Mrs Huxley sometimes levelled against her husband that age-old cry from the wives of dedicated men that he was not only as much

married to his work as to her but that his work often came first.

Huxley's most important published work at this time was the Croonian lectures, *The Theory of the Vertebrate Skull* (1858), in which he developed the principle he was to follow all his life of not hazarding any statement beyond those revealed by the facts. Employing this inductive method in the Croonian lectures, he successfully demolished the idealistic views of the origin of the skull held by the leading comparative anatomist, Richard Owen. Incapable of the flexibility required to qualify orthodox thinking, Owen asserted that man was clearly marked off from other animals by the anatomical structure of his brain. Huxley undermined if not destroyed this approach and summed up his view in *Man's Place in Nature* (1863).

By 1860 Huxley was defending Darwin's theory of evolution against the attacks of Bishop Wilberforce. His brilliant polemic not only resulted in a victory for science over obscuranticism; it made scientific theorizing respectable in a way it had never been before. Wilberforce had challenged Huxley: 'If anyone were willing to trace his descent through an ape as his grandfather would he be willing to trace his descent through an ape on the side of *his grandmother*?' Huxley replied:

If the question put to me is 'would I like to have a miserable ape for a grandfather or a man highly endowed by nature and possessed of great means and influence and yet who employs these faculties and that influence for the mere purpose of introducing ridicule into a grave scientific discussion,' I unhesitatingly affirm my preference for the ape.

Huxley's attitude to religion changed over the years. At one period he was quoting an eighth-century Hebrew prophet: 'And what doth the Lord require of thee but to do justly, to love mercy and to walk humbly with God.' Two years later he stated: 'There is no evidence of the existence of such a being as the God of the theologians.' On purely philosophical grounds he considered atheism untenable and adopted a brand of agnosticism which subordinated belief to evidence and reason. His personal creed gradually developed into a kind of scientific Calvinism.

In 1876 he visited America where his favourite sister already lived. America seemed more prepared than England to receive his agnosticism, scientism and full-blooded belief in empirical investigation as the only means of establishing real truth.

Over the years his scientific work continued unabated, concentrating on paleontology and his many studies of fossil fishes established far-reaching morphological facts. Among other publications, *Elementary Physiology* (1866) and *Anatomy of Vertebrate Animals* (1871) were masterpieces of lucidly ordered exposition.

From 1870 onwards public duties drew him away from scientific studies and between 1862 and 1884 he sat on no less than ten royal commissions. From 1871 to 1880 he was secretary of the Royal Society, from 1883 to 1885 president of the Royal Society and in 1870 to 1872 a member of the newly constituted London School Board where he wielded wide influence and propounded relatively revolutionary ideas. A man dedicated to work, his values were otherwise highly unconventional. He was against the theological conception of God, conventional religion, privilege, elite education, normal university teaching and had serious doubts even about royalty.

His appearance was described by Professor Osborn of Columbia College: 'His eyes were heavily overhung by a projecting forehead and eyebrows, and seemed at times to look inward. His lips were firm and closely set. . . .' Late photographs show a formidable person – brooding, disillusioned, given to stern discipline.

His working habits could be erratic: 'He was not one of those portentously early risers who do a fair day's work before other people are up,' his son wrote. There were royal commissions, committee meetings, lectures and research but 'the greater part of the work by which the world knows him best was done after dinner.'

His early resilience and energy eventually gave place to tiredness and bouts of depression. Aspects of his life remain a mystery. What did he mean for instance when he said: 'Few men have drunk more deeply of all kinds of sin than I'? Despite this, person after person was struck by what they referred to as his domestic happiness.

Illness troubled him from 1885 when indeed he nearly died, and his last years were plagued with the usual troubles of old age. Challenged whether – in the face of death – he still did not believe in God, he said that if there was a God waiting for him he hoped he would turn out to be Darwinian and believe in hard work.

Since his day the mind-body problem has undergone revolutionary re-examination in depth but two schools are still divided, the mechanistic believing that mind is little more than a function of brain, and the dynamic that psychological concepts like intentionality remove the whole question from such reductionist simplicity.

Huxley will be remembered as a great scientific teacher, a brilliant expositor and a man who made the scientific approach to human nature and social affairs not only respectable but desirable.

Vincent Brome

The Scientific Memoirs of T. H. Huxley ed. Michael Foster and E. Ray Lankester (5 vols, 1898–1903). Leonard Huxley, The Life and Letters of Thomas Henry Huxley (1900); Cyril Bibby, T. H. Huxley: Scientist, Humanist and Educator (1959); Cyril Bibby, The Essence of T. H. Huxley (1967); Cyril Bibby, T. H. Huxley on Education (1971); Cyril Bibby, Scientist Extraordinary: The Life and Scientific Work of T. H. Huxley (1972).

235
HUYSMANS, Joris-Karl 1848–1907

French novelist

Huysmans was the son of a Frenchwoman and of a lithographer and miniaturist of Dutch origin. He described himself as 'an inexplicable amalgam of a refined Parisian and a Dutch painter', and, although baptized Charles-Marie-Georges, chose to be known as Joris-Karl. Both the North and the visual arts permeate his writings. He worked as an obscure official in French government ministries, following early law studies and brief involvement in the Franco-Prussian War, until he retired prematurely in 1898. From then until his death he sought unsuccessfully a way of life that would reconcile his needs as a writer with his increasingly monastic religious beliefs. This search was the last stage of a longer quest, undertaken outside his conventional duties as a ministry official, that led him through often bizarre encounters and reflections and that is the central subject of his books.

Huysmans's fame rests largely on one novel: Against the Grain (À Rebours 1884, trans. 1922, Against Nature, 1959), which established him as the supreme exponent of a controversial theme: decadence. The vain attempt of des Esseintes, the novel's hero, to create for himself a totally artificial existence produces an interaction between nihilistic pessimism and perverse delectation that is the essence of the decadent sensibility, surpassing earlier models by Gautier*, Poe* and Baudelaire*, and never matched by later variants such as Wilde's* The Picture of Dorian Gray (1891). In addition, Against the Grain points to major developments in French fiction, as is clear from the sequence of Huysmans's own novels.

Huysmans's first novel, Marthe, the Story of a Woman (Marthe, histoire d'une fille, 1876, trans. 1948), owes much to the example of the Goncourt* brothers and his second, The Vatard Sisters (Les Soeurs Vatard, 1879), to that of Zola*. He was then a fervent advocate of Realism and Naturalism. His subjects were taken from contemporary Paris. Marthe describes an actress's descent into prostitution with a directness that casts derision on the Romantic image of the love-lorn courtesan. In The Vatard Sisters, two working-class sisters lead lives of humdrum labour and experience unglamorous love affairs. In both novels Huysmans aims to depict the reality of modern life; he tends to minimize peripeteia and vicissitudes of plot, and to concentrate on description. At this time, he became a champion of the Impressionists, who were then painting subjects from modern urban life. He published art criticism in the press, vigorously defending the Impressionists and virulently attacking their opponents. These articles were published in book form as *L'Art Moderne* (1883), a major work of art criticism, notable particularly for its defence of Degas*. Passages of description in *The Vatard Sisters* echo Degas and the other painters of modern life, and could be termed Impressionist writing. Huysmans was well aware that this provided a further parallel between himself and Zola, who had earlier defended Manet* and had allied literary description to painting. In the late 1870s he considered himself a disciple of Zola. He became the leading figure in a group of five young writers, including Maupassant*, who formed a loose-knit school around the Master and visited Zola at his Médan home. All six writers contributed a short story to a collection entitled *Les Soirées de Médan* (1880), Huysmans's story being 'Sac au Dos' ('Knapsack').

Huysmans later described his commitment to the Naturalist novel as a stifling experience from which he had to escape. Premonitions of this change exist in *Marthe* and *The Vatard Sisters*; in each novel a minor male character expresses profound disappointment with what modern life has to offer. They are prototypes of des Esseintes and reflections of Huysmans himself. One of them is Cyprien Tibaille, a disappointed artist in *The Vatard Sisters*, who reappears in Huysmans's next novel *Living Together* (*En Ménage*, 1881, trans. 1969) where his gloomy outlook and the hero André Jayant's disgust with marriage are presented with a black humour later admired by the Surrealist André Breton. The brief *Downstream* (*À Vau-L'Eau*, 1882, trans. 1956) concentrates specifically on the despair of one individual, here called Folantin, in the face of an unbearable and nauseating world. Modern life is no longer simply depicted by Huysmans; it stands accused of being the cause of the wretched unhappiness of the individual. *Against the Grain* investigates the only apparent alternative to this unacceptable reality: artifice. This too fails to produce anything but decay, despair, and pessimism. Religious belief, at this point in Huysmans's development, is impossible.

In all the rest of his novels Huysmans traces this crisis of the individual through a particular situation, both psychological and geographical, each work being a fictional projection of a stage of his own quest for a solution to the problem of suffering. *En Rade* (*At Harbour*, 1887) dismisses the solace of nature by deflating the notion of a rustic retreat. *Down There* (*Là-Bas* 1819, trans. 1924) stresses the increasingly spiritual nature of this crisis by disclosing the presence of Satanism in modern Paris. It also introduces the final version of Huysmans's hero, Durtal, a fusion of aspects of his earlier heroes and features of himself. Durtal, the central character in all Huysmans's remaining novels, is, like Huysmans, a writer experiencing a lengthy personal crisis, but is not simply autobiographical since he typifies a more general sensibility and predicament. In *En Route* (*En Route*, 1895, 1896) Durtal, having discovered Satan, discovers God in a retreat in a monastery and undergoes conversion to Roman Catholicism, as Huysmans had done in 1892. In *The Cathedral* (*La Cathédrale* 1898, trans. 1898) Durtal lives in Chartres and investigates a major factor in his and Huysmans's conversion: medieval art and architecture. In *The Oblate* (*L'Oblat*, 1903, trans. 1924) the quest for personal fulfilment is carried into the interior of a monastery but only to be abandoned in favour of Huysmans's final position: the acceptance of suffering for the expiation of sin.

Despite the changes of subject matter from Naturalism to Catholicism, the aesthetic of the Huysmans novel is coherent. He rejected early on the conventional plot and the traditional love theme, regarding the novel as a framework that should contain a variety of documented material, all of which illuminates a central character. In this he is using some of the methods of Naturalism to an end that is foreign to Zola's advocacy of science, and that includes both dream experience and religious thought. He referred to his religious works as 'Mystic Naturalism'. *Against the Grain* is the first full expression of this aesthetic, being both a rejection and an extension of Naturalism. The documented material in Huysmans's novels includes the visual arts throughout, and also literature, hagiography and other domains where relevant. The non-fictional works written by Huysmans, including reflections on modern Symbolist painting and medieval religious art, studies of Paris, and Catholic essays, are all germane to this documentation. The structural problems of such a novel are considerable, and Huysmans's later novels do become unwieldy and excessively static. But his novels of the 1880s demonstrate clearly an innovatory move away from the achievements of Flaubert*, the Goncourt brothers and Zola towards a focusing on the self through a reflexive world that points towards Proust. Like other members of his generation, particularly the Symbolists, he lost faith in Naturalism and positivism, and embarked upon an investigation of the individual as an irrational and mysterious entity.

Huysmans's influence in the twentieth century has been confused by an exaggerated desire to see his conversion in 1892 as a watershed separating irreconcilable elements of his work. His self-consciously esoteric and elaborate style, carried to the lengths of prose poetry in *A Dish of Spices* (*Le Drageoir à Épice*, 1874, trans. 1927) and *Parisian Sketches* (*Croquis Parisiens*, 1880 and 1886, trans. 1960), has also divided opinion sharply. But the modernity of his experiments with the novel form is widely acknowledged and in des Esseintes he created an archetype of modern fiction: a neurotic hero for whom the world is nauseous and absurd.

Richard Hobbs

Other works include: *Certains* (1889) and *Trois Primitifs* (1905), both about the visual arts; *Un Dilemme* (1887), an uncharacteristic *conte; La Bièvre* (1890), a study of Paris's second river; *Sainte Lydwine de Schiedam* (1901, trans. *St Lydwine of Schiedam*, 1923) and *Les Foules de Lourdes* (1906, trans. *Crowds of Lourdes*, 1925), both Catholic works. The standard critical biography is Robert Baldick, *The Life of J.-K. Huysmans* (1955). Other important studies are: Helen Trudgian, *L'Esthétique de J.-K. Huysmans* (1934); Pierre Cogny, *J.-K. Huysmans à la Recherche de l'Unité* (1953); Fernande Zayed, *Huysmans Peintre de son Époque* (1973). A *Bulletin de la Société J.-K. Huysmans* has appeared regularly since 1928.

I

236

IBSEN, Henrik 1828–1906

Norwegian dramatist

Ibsen was born into the family of a rich merchant in the southern Norwegian town of Skien in 1828. He spent his early childhood in large houses filled with the sound of laughter and entertainment. By 1833, however, his father's business empire had collapsed, and the family was obliged to move out of town and eke out a miserable existence in an isolated country property. The years of bitterness and recrimination that followed left an indelible scar on Ibsen's consciousness. Repeatedly in his mature work, he returned to the formative experiences of these years, tracing out the politics of family life within the context of an aggressively competitive capitalist world.

After an apprenticeship lasting six years as an apothecary's assistant in the small coastal town of Grimstad, followed by an unsuccessful attempt to pass the matriculation exam for university study in the capital city Christiania in 1850, Ibsen worked as a resident playwright and director in the newly founded Norwegian National Theatre in Bergen between 1851 and 1857. In 1857 he returned to Christiania to take over the post of artistic director of the Christiania Norwegian Theatre. This decade of theatrical work gave him invaluable experience as a playwright, but also left him with mixed feelings towards the contemporary theatre. It was the start of a love-hate relationship he never managed to resolve. Ibsen's ambitious plans to offer an exciting and challenging repertoire in Christiania were thwarted by cash-flow problems and the indifference of the theatre-going public. By 1862 he was completely demoralized. He began drinking heavily and neglected his work, which provoked hostile comment from the press and his own staff. In May 1862 the theatre was forced to close, leaving Ibsen almost destitute. For the next two years, he somehow managed to provide for his young wife and son, acting as a poorly paid literary adviser to the rival Christiania Theatre. But it was with a sense of relief that he left Norway in 1864, armed with a small travel grant and the donations of a few well-wishers, to begin a period of exile that was to last for twenty-seven years.

Ibsen's first play *Catiline* (*Catilina*) had attracted very little attention when it was published under a pseudonym in April 1850. A few months later, his second play, *The Warrior's Barrow* (*Kæmpehøjen*), was accepted for performance by the Christiania Theatre and was given its successful première in September 1850. For the remainder of the 1850s and until his departure from Norway in 1864, he wrote a steady flow of plays: *St John's Night* (*Sankthansnatten*, 1852); a revised version of *The Warrior's Barrow* (1854); *Lady Inger of Østråt* (*Fru Inger til Østråt*, 1855); *The Feast at Solhaug* (*Gildet på Solhaug*, 1856); *Olaf Liljekrans* (1857); *The Vikings at Helgeland* (*Hærmændene på Helgeland*, 1858); *Love's Comedy* (*Kærlighedens Komedie*, 1862); and *The Pretenders* (*Kongs-Emnerne*, 1863). In almost all of these plays, there were characters and themes that were to recur in his later work. But there was also a gulf, an incommensurateness, between form and content. Romantic melodrama and the Scribean intrigue play proved to be an inadequate base from which to undertake a probing exploration of human aspirations and human interaction. Even in *The Pretenders*, by far the most ambitious work of this early period, there is no real balance in the play between the dynamics of the spiritual exploration (centred on the theme of vocation) and the remorseless pace of the complex Romantic intrigue.

Ibsen's poems from the 1850s and 1860s take up similar themes to those explored in the plays, examining the nature of the poet's vocation and the clash Ibsen felt between the demands of art and life. Generally the poems suffer from Ibsen's all too quick facility for rhyming verse: the shape, the highly patterned structure of his verse forms, inhibiting the relaxed development of complex themes. But in a few poems, notably in *The Miner* (*Bergmanden*, 1851) and *On the Heights* (*På vidderne*, 1859–60), there is a muscular precision in the verse and imagery that impresses.

When Ibsen left Norway in 1864, he travelled to Rome where he was to make his home for the next four years. The landscape, the architecture, the impact of new friendships had a liberating effect on him. He worked now at a furious pace, publishing within a very brief space of time two magnificent verse plays that were to establish his international reputation as a writer: *Brand* (1866) and *Peer Gynt* (1867). *Brand* was a play that challenged the religious and political orthodoxies of the contemporary world. It explored the demands and the limits of human will-power, posing a number of crucial questions for Ibsen and his readers. How can one fulfil oneself with a heritage of guilt? How does one reconcile will-power and a sense of vocation with love? How can one oppose the crass limitations of accepted social and political doctrines without being driven to extremes? *Peer Gynt* brought an exuberant treatment of a similar complex of themes. Structured like a morality play, it explored images of selfhood in a fanciful kaleidoscope of scenes: selfishness and selflessness are juxtaposed dialectically until the dialectical triad is resolved in the notion that 'to be oneself is to slay oneself'. Where *Brand* was lean and rugged in texture, *Peer Gynt* was effervescent and sparkling.

Ibsen marked this turning point in his career as a writer by changing both his style of handwriting and of dress. Casting aside his earlier Bohemian image, he adopted a neat, dapper façade behind which he took refuge from the memory of the bitter failures and humiliations that had marked his earlier career. There were still difficult years ahead of him, but from now on his social and financial position became increasingly stable. In 1868 he moved with his family to Dresden; he was to remain in Germany for ten years, in order to ensure that his son had suitable schooling.

After settling in Germany, he wrestled with the problem of finding a dramatic form more in tune with the increasingly naturalistic temper of the age. His first steps towards modern prose drama were hesitant and tentative. A popular political comedy, *The League of Youth* (*De Unges Forbund*, 1869), was followed by a somewhat turgid philosophical work in two parts, *Emperor and Galilean* (*Kejser og Galilæer*, 1873). It was not until 1877, when he completed *Pillars of the Community* (*Samfundets Støtter*), that he began to achieve that mastery of modern prose dialogue for which he was to become famous. *Pillars of the Community* was a witty and devastatingly accurate reckoning with the ruthless entrepreneurs who were spearheading the advance of industrial capitalism in Norway. In the figure of Consul Bernick, Ibsen exposed the personal and social lies that lay behind the forging of an industrial and mercantile empire. Two years later, after leaving Germany for Rome, he completed *A Doll's House* (*Et Dukkehjem*, 1879), an equally devastating reckoning with contemporary bourgeois marriage. Nora, the main character in the play, rejects her role as a bank manager's wife, in which she is reduced to the status of a mere commodity, and leaves her husband and children to discover her own identity.

In his next play, *Ghosts* (*Gengangere*), written in Sorrento in 1881, Ibsen painted a sombre picture of what happens when a woman who has left her husband is forced, by social pressure, to return. In a classically taut form, Ibsen reveals the horrifying details of Mrs Alving's marriage and fleshes out in the action a chain of events that leads inexorably to the madness of her son Osvald. The play provoked a storm of abuse when it was published. In openly attacking the sanctity of marriage, Ibsen was threatening the very basis of patriarchal society and was duly savaged for his temerity. His response was to write an ironic riposte in *An Enemy of the People* (*En Folkefiende*, 1882), where Dr Stockman declares that the strongest man is the one who stands alone.

Two years later, when he completed *The Wild Duck* (*Vildanden* 1884), his passionate involvement with social and political issues had mellowed. He now concentrated his attention on the politics of family life, showing how easily a fragile nexus of family relationships in the Ekdal home is disturbed by the clumsy intervention of a neurotic outsider, Gregers Werle. There are numerous echoes in the play, in terms of character and setting, of Ibsen's own childhood experiences. In its use of overt symbolism and its blending of tragicomic effects, the play also marked a new, and for many a puzzling, departure.

In 1885 Ibsen moved from Rome to Munich. Before doing so, he visited Norway. It was a visit that prepared the way for his eventual return home to his native land in 1891. The immediate effect of the visit was to influence the mood and setting of his next two plays, *Rosmersholm* (1886) and *The Lady from the Sea* (*Fruen fra Havet*, 1888). Both plays are set in a small town in western Norway, clearly reminiscent of Molde where Ibsen spent two months in the summer of 1885. Both also explore complex states of mind, particularly in respect of the two main women characters, Rebecca West and Ellida Wangel. Rebecca West and her platonic lover, John Rosmer, act out in *Rosmersholm* a lethal drama of thwarted and diseased love and passion that ends with their suicide in the mill race. Ellida Wangel, by way of contrast, rejects her longing for freedom and emotional fulfilment, encapsulated in the mysterious figure of a seaman to whom she was once betrothed, and commits herself to her loyal but unexciting husband. There is a distinctly elegiac, late summer feel to the happy ending of the play.

The mood of *Hedda Gabler* (1890) is decidedly autumnal. Here the major character, a general's daughter, finds herself trapped in a conventional bourgeois marriage and decides, quite literally, to shoot her way out. A strong sense of black comedy runs through the action right up to the very last line when Judge Brack reacts to Hedda's suicide with the comment, 'But, good God! People don't do such things.'

Ibsen's last four plays reflect an increasingly icy soulscape. In *The Master Builder* (*Bygmester Solness*, 1892), Solness the main character fears the threat of youth and, in failing at the end of the play to climb successfully the high tower he himself has designed, expresses something of Ibsen's own fears of artistic and personal impotence. *Little Eyolf* (*Lille Eyolf*, 1894) is dominated by themes of vibrant but thwarted eroticism. Much of the play explores a sustained incestuous fantasy involving Asta and her supposed half-brother Alfred Allmers. By the end of the play, it is only in renouncing overt sexuality that the main characters can achieve any form of mental equilibrium. In *John Gabriel Borkman* (1896) the winter landscape mirrors expressionistically the spiritual state of the protagonists. Borkman is a former industrial magnate who overreached himself and had to serve a lengthy prison sentence for speculating with money and shares belonging to others. He also ruthlessly sacrificed the woman he loved for the sake of personal ambition, for the power and the glory. There are many echoes in the play of *Pillars of the Community*. Borkman is like an ageing Bernick who has fallen victim to his dreams. *John Gabriel Borkman* was Ibsen's final reckoning with the destructive values of contemporary capitalist society and, at the same time, an oblique criticism of his own commitment to art in preference to a life of emotional fulfilment.

Finally, in *When we dead awaken* (*Når vi døde vågner*, 1899) Ibsen returned yet again to the clash of art and life, vocation and personal happiness. It was the major theme that had preoccupied him throughout his creative life. An ageing sculptor Rubek is confronted by the woman he rejected when he was a young and aspiring artist. Irene was his youthful inspiration. But he rejected her for the sake of artistic and material advancement. He now discovers that what he lost in rejecting her was the only thing that matters: complete authenticity of response. It is too late to live his life again, but in the final scene of the play he commits himself to Irene irrevocably, passionately in a *Liebestod*, that achieves mythical stature. In this final play, there is an expressionist blend of myth and reality.

Ibsen often shocked and bewildered his contemporaries. The daunting complexity of his work baffled critics who were unwilling or unable to probe below the surface detail of his plays to seek out the hidden patterns of meaning beneath the dialogue, the hidden poetry. Many failed to see that his vision of life was ultimately life-affirming, despite the sombre tonality of his work. But there were some, notably George Bernard Shaw and Georg Brandes, who understood and appreciated the scope of his genius.

The impact of Ibsen's work on twentieth-century theatre has been enormous. Directors have explored approaches to his plays ranging from the naturalist to the expressionist, while playwrights as diverse as Harold Pinter and Arthur Miller have been influenced by his ideas. Critics have made good their initial rejection of his work and have explored his plays from almost every conceivable angle: historical-biographical, Freudian, new critical, Marxist, sociological, existentialist. If one accepts Longinus's definition of literary merit, namely that which pleases 'all men at all times', then it is clear that Ibsen fully deserves his status as a modern classic.

David Thomas

Works: *Samlede verker, hundreårsutgave* (22 vols, Oslo, 1928–58); *The Oxford Ibsen* (8 vols, 1960–77).
Biographies: Halvdan Koht, *The Life of Ibsen* (2 vols, 1931): Michael Meyer, *Henrik Ibsen* (3 vols, 1967–71).
Critical: John Northam, *Ibsen's Dramatic Method: A Study of the Prose Dramas* (1953); James McFarlane, *Ibsen and the Temper of Norwegian Literature* (1960). For a Freudian interpretation see Hermann J. Weigand, *The Modern Ibsen* (1925), and for a Marxist interpretation Horst Bien, *Henrik Ibsens Realismus* (Berlin, 1970). See also: *Contemporary Approaches to Ibsen*, vol. 4 ed. Daniel Haakonsen (Oslo, 1979), essays; and Maurice Valency, *The Flower and the Castle: An Introduction to Modern Drama* (1963).

237
INGRES, Jean Auguste Dominique 1780–1867

French painter

A pupil of David* and obsessively Neoclassical in spirit – he knew no Greek and little Latin – Ingres came to worship Raphael with a puritanical single-mindedness. He believed in the absolute superiority of line over colour and was the main opponent of the ideas expressed by his French contemporary, the Romantic Eugène Delacroix*. Winner of the Prix de Rome in 1801, much of his long life was spent in Italy and it is the splendours of the High Renaissance rather than the ideals derived from Roman antiquity that influenced his distinctive style. History painting he considered to be the peak of artistic achievement, though his reputation as a precise and skilful portrait painter was well established by the time he first left his native France. The early portraits are not only extremely perceptive likenesses but hint at another side of his complex personality. Stylistically they show an increasing emphasis on the taut outline learnt from his preoccupations with the austere line-engravings of the English sculptor John Flaxman, together with the mannered serpentine sweep of his beloved Raphael. This sinuous 'S' line he saw as the essence of feminity and above all Ingres was the painter of beautiful women.

Madame Rivière (Louvre), painted in Rome in 1805, is far more than a fine arrangement of well observed decoration held in place by a crisp incisive line. Inside the dress underneath the finery is the smooth flesh that the painter understood so well and the cool manner in which it is depicted only serves to accentuate its living warmth. It is this contrast between the method and the subject that clearly makes Ingres less than the arch classicist he so proudly professed himself to be. In many of the earlier works there is an overt eroticism and in the portrait of *Mademoiselle Rivière* (Louvre), despite the cool detachment, we can sense that the young girl is only too well aware of her latent sexuality.

As a draughtsman Ingres was particularly meticulous and many of the drawings made in Rome are complete in themselves. He drew them for money and they are the holiday snap-shots of their day. We have little doubt that they are acceptable likenesses of the sitters and treasured mementos of the Grand Tour. The eye for detail is apt when considering the rich costumes of those able to afford the luxuries of European travel and sophisticated composition of the various group portraits emphasized their correct social status.

The drawings made for the paintings are more complicated and again reflect the unhappy admixture of the rigid self-imposed linear austerity and the sensual delight in the human body. Studies made from the model are openly descriptive and among the finest drawings of modern times. They are nineteenth century in mood and clearly the inspiration for similar observations made later by Degas*. Those for the *Grande Odalisque* (Louvre) and *Angelica saved by Ruggiero* (Louvre) are extremely beautiful but often refined to the point of disbelief. When further abstracted to enhance their elegance they lose their credibility. Angelica's head is thrown far back to stress the forward thrust of her nakedness and we are far from convinced. In the *Odalisque* the curve of the back from neck to thigh is unbelievable, however tenderly handled the half-hidden breast. The paintings fail because they raise too many doubts. We are titillated by the eroticism and stunned by the sheer virtuosity of the brushwork as we are in the *Grande Baigneuse* (Louvre) with its so smooth back and subtle delicacy of tone, but this is 'art for art's sake' and this is what the painter railed against.

The Apotheosis of Homer (Louvre), painted in 1827 – three years after Constable* had exhibited his *Hay Wain* at the Paris Salon – was clearly meant to be the masterpiece to dispel all doubts. Intended as part of a comprehensive plan to decorate nine new rooms in the Louvre it shows Homer surrounded by artists, musicians and patrons of the arts. Fame holds aloft the laurel wreath and at the foot of the writer's throne sit two female personifications of the *Iliad* and the *Odyssey*. Comparison with Raphael's *School of Athens* is inevitable but unlike that truly great painting this has no life of its own. The colour is insipid and the composition unimaginative, and the two female figures in the foreground are dull and stolid. Drawings for the painting show the expected delight in the animated interplay of so complicated a grouping and there is a fine nude study for the *Odyssey* (Jules Mommeja collection, Paris) which hints at what might have been.

In *The Romantic Rebellion* (1976) Kenneth Clark argues that Ingres's obsession with style left him with 'absolutely nothing to say about life' and this seems perfectly true. Faced with a model or a client he was supremely capable but in terms of nineteenth-century picture making he had lost his way. 'A Chinese painter lost amidst the ruins of Athens' was how a contemporary, Théophile Sylvestre, put it.

Raphael was not the answer and *The Vow of Louis XIII* (Musée Ingres, Montauban), painted in 1820, proved it; but in an age of industrial revolution there was a need for easy escapism and at this Ingres excelled. The *Bain Turc* (Louvre) embodies all the fruitful elements of the early years but by now the painter was in his seventies and the result is sad parody. A seething mass of naked women lie alongside the bath. Openly fondling each other they listen to music played on the lute by a seated lady reminiscent of the Grande Baigneuse. Indolently they leer out at the spectator who is made to feel very much the voyeur. There is little or no evidence of observation or study from life.

In his obdurate determination to reject what Romanticism had to offer he killed his own considerable talent and when he died in 1867 he was a man of the past.

John Furse

See: W. Friedlander, *David to Delacroix* (1952).

238
IRVING, Washington 1783–1859

US author

In *The Sketch-Book of Geoffrey Crayon, Gent.* (1819–20), the collection of essays and vignettes on English and American life with which he consolidated his reputation and which contains his legendary 'Rip Van Winkle', Irving carefully fashioned the persona by which he wished to be understood. In 'The Author's Account of Himself', affecting the voice of the Augustan familiar essayist, he writes:

> I have wandered through different countries, and witnessed many of the shifting scenes of life. I cannot say that I have studied them with the eye of the philosopher, but rather with the sauntering gaze with which humble lovers of the picturesque stroll from the window of one print shop to another, caught sometimes by the delineations of beauty, sometimes by the distortions of caricature, and sometimes by the loveliness of landscape.

This typical genial ease of tone, and Irving's engaging trope of the writer as stroller, endeared him to readers both in America and abroad, even though, in his many lesser productions, he gave in to indulgence, the risk of sounding banal and no more than a slightly precious antiquarian. But if by inclination a belle-lettrist, Irving is properly thought, with Bryant* and Cooper* (all three were born in the 1780s), a founding voice of early

American literature, both on the basis of his several short-story masterpieces and as the first wholly professional author to emerge from the new world.

Precocious, and early to make his mark as a wit, he was born into a large and wealthy merchant family in New York city where he shied away from his father's Calvinist work-ethic in favour of bookish pursuits. After a private education, a journey to Canada (1803), and a desultory spell studying law, he began writing for his brother's newspaper, the *Corrector*, and for the *Morning Chronicle*, to which he contributed a number of small-scale satires on New York society and manners under the pseudonym of Jonathan Oldstyle, Gent. (1802–3). In indifferent health, and funded by his family, he then travelled for two years in Europe (1804–6), a journey soon to be followed by many others and which installed him as the first of a long line of major American literary expatriates. On his return to America he was admitted to the Bar, but did not practise; took again to satire in the pieces he wrote for *Salmagundi* (1807–8), a collaborative venture with his brother William and the novelist J.K. Paulding; and in 1809, a figure of coming reputation, published his *History of New York, by Diedrich Knickerbocker*, a lively, burlesque 'history' of the Dutch-American settlement of his home state and into one of whose dynasties he himself had been born.

It was, however, as Geoffrey Crayon that he came fully into his imaginative own, after a brief period in government service during the war of 1812 and further European travel. *The Sketch-Book* established him as the best known of all American men of letters, a book symptomatically first published in London under the patronage of Sir Walter Scott* and in which he brought to fine effect the style he had learnt from Addison and Steele and from poets like George Crabbe*. Not only does *The Sketch-Book* offer a view of early nineteenth-century trans-Atlantic literary relations ('English Writers on America') and of the American writer's ambiguous sense of connection with the legacy of the past, it reprinted two quintessential Irving stories, 'Rip Van Winkle' and 'The Legend of Sleepy Hollow'. In the former Irving transformed his German folk source into an American fable, the deeply mythic account of the hen-pecked New York Knickerbocker villager who falls asleep for twenty years, misses the revolution, and re-enters the community as the eternal American boy-man. Irving's familiar quizzical humour equally marks out 'The Legend of Sleepy Hollow', another Dutch-American fable based on the fate of Ichabod Crane who believes he sees an apparition, that of a ghostly headless horseman, and in the shenanigans that follow, loses his bride-to be.

Despite his continuing posture as the languid, picturesque, merely occasional author, Irving in fact wrote voluminously, though little which matches the grace and economy of his principal stories. In 1822, he pub-

lished *Bracebridge Hall*, an unconvincing, idealized portrait of the English squirearchy, which he followed in 1824 with *Tales of a Traveller*, thirty or so pieces of adventure each with a European or American setting, which contains the striking 'The Devil and Tom Walker', the Faustian legend adapted to a New England setting. Under some financial pressure, after considerable travel in Europe, he accepted in 1826 the offer of an embassy post in Spain, living first in Madrid then the Alhambra for three years. This was a productive move which yielded his *History of the Life and Voyages of Christopher Columbus* (based on the translation work he did of the Spanish historian Navarrete); *A Chronicle of the Conquest of Granada* (1829); *The Companions of Columbus* (1831); and *The Legends of the Alhambra* (1832), further testimony to his ability in turning European – and here Moorish – material to his own fictional purpose. In 1829–32, he moved to England to become secretary of the American Legation in London, before returning to America after an interval of seventeen years. The America he returned to, almost a Rip Van Winkle figure himself, took some adjustment, especially as he had to adapt to the transformations brought on by Jacksonian democracy, many of which ran counter to his own conservative, genteel origins. He did another Spanish diplomatic tour of duty as minister in Madrid (1842–5) before settling for his last thirteen years in his native land.

In 1835, he published *The Crayon Miscellany*, selections from prior work, and *A Tour of the Prairies*, his Western travel book. None of his later productions has particularly lasted, largely because Irving, if a fastidious writer, rarely displayed any serious largeness of vision. In 1836, under commission from the Astor family, with his nephew and official biographer Pierre Irving (*The Life and Letters of Washington Irving*, 4 vols, 1862–4, 1869), he wrote *Astoria, or, Anecdotes of an Enterprise beyond the Rockies*, the saga of the rise and fortune from the fur trade of a powerful American dynasty, for which he was handsomely paid but suffered harsh critical rebuke. In turn followed *The Adventures of Captain Bonneville, U.S.A.* (1837), based on the life of a former West Point officer and frontiersman; *Oliver Goldsmith: A Biography* (1849), his admiring account of an important literary mentor; *Mahomet and his Successors*, lacklustre biographies based on his researches in Granada and the Alhambra; *A Book on the Hudson* (1849) and *Wolfert's Roost* (1855), two volumes of previously published essays; and a number of posthumous pieces, especially *Spanish Papers and other Miscellanies* (1866). Shortly before his death, he completed the fifth volume of his *Life of George Washington* (1855–9), a work which reads patchily and without any clear point of interpretative arrival. Throughout his last years, at Sunnyside, his home in Tarrytown, New York, to the chagrin of James Fenimore Cooper and others who thought him too much the dilettante and adulator of things European, he was treated as a national literary institution, the first American writer to have gained high trans-Atlantic honour. In this the world flattered him. He was of real but limited talent, a nice hand with the quaint and lightly humorous and satiric, but never a writer to equal the succeeding literary generation of Melville*, Poe* and Hawthorne.

A. Robert Lee

See: *Washington Irving: Representative Selections*, ed.

Henry A.Pochman (1943); Stanley T. Williams, *The Life of Washington Irving* (1935); Van Wyck Brooks, *The World of Washington Irving* (1944); Edward Wagenknecht, *Washington Irving: Moderation Displayed* (1962); Lewis Leary, *Washington Irving* (1963); William L. Hedges, *Washington Irving: An American Study, 1802–1832* (1965); *Washington Irving Reconsidered: A Symposium*, ed. Ralph Aderman (1969); *Washington Irving: A Tribute*, ed. Andrew B. Myers (1972).

J

239
JAMES, Henry 1843–1916

US novelist

It is entirely typical of Henry James that he should belong to nowhere in particular. An abundant solitude haunts both his life history and his fiction, and in this respect he appears like a kind of belated avatar of the Romantic exile or the doomed wanderer so familiar as a cultural cliché in the early decades of the nineteenth century. The fact that the wanderings and the exile were both self-imposed and eminently comfortable is beside the point: it is his role as the lonely, half-alien observer which gives shape and vividness to his creations, and the direction of much of his early life seems to have tended towards the successful achievement of such a stance. His works continue to exhale an air of half-intimated confidence which is central to our appreciation of his unique viewpoint. 'A work of art that one has to *explain*,' he told a friend in reference to *The Awkward Age* (1899), 'fails in so far, I suppose, of its mission.' Both the italicizing and the subjective qualifier in this sentence are characteristic of its author's retreat into the kind of verbal labyrinth which anticipates the monumental inarticulateness of twentieth-century English, with its host of qualifiers and its mass of unfinished sentences. That there was something both intensely understood and supremely inexpressible in fiction was an idea to which James gave prominence in several stories, including the archetypal 'The Figure in the Carpet', in which the hidden meaning conveyed in the work of Hugh Vereker perishes in obscurity. Interest in James's writing has so far recovered from a preoccupation with his stylistic obliquity (all too easily parodied – see, for example, H.G. Wells's *Boon* and the squibs of Max Beerbohm) as to accept this aspect of his later novels as one of the most consistently rewarding.

It matters little, in the last analysis, whether he is or is not an American novelist (he became a naturalized Englishman a few months before his death). That markedly eccentric and almost too careful use of English which has characterized the American novel from its beginnings down to our own day, and which is seen at its most mannered in the writings of Melville*, Hawthorne*, James Fenimore Cooper* and others of their period, undoubtedly bit deep into the Jamesian style,

for better or worse. American too is his mingled reverence and censure of England and the English, revealed at its strongest in the correspondence of the early 1890s and in the curious sense of challenging menace conveyed in *English Hours* (1905) and stories such as 'The Turn of the Screw' (1898). In the end his preoccupations do not label him as either particularly American or especially Anglicized. More obviously and intractably than any novelist of either tradition, he belongs (if indeed he has to be made to belong anywhere) to currents altogether more emphatically European.

Europe, or at any rate the notion of it, played a significant part in his spiritual development from the beginning. His father, Henry James senior, the wealthy son of a millionaire, gave his children a broadly based education within the lively milieux of mid-century New York and New England. He himself was an amateur theologian of an eccentrically Swedenborgian cast and was keen to encourage his family to think for themselves and to shun pattern and system. In 1856, when Henry junior was thirteen, his father removed them to Europe 'to absorb French and German and get a better sensuous education than they are likely to get here' as he told Emerson*, but the boy had already based his earliest memory on sight of the column in the Place Vendôme when he was two years old.

A more fruitful experience of the Old World, indeed it may be said, the crucial encounter with it, took place in 1869 when James set sail for England. He was already a published American author, his first story, 'A Tragedy of Error', having appeared in 1864 and his first review being issued in the *North American Review*. He had begun to contribute stories to the *Nation* and the *Atlantic Monthly*, whose editor, William Dean Howells*, was a friendly and beneficial influence upon his style and his career. In addition, as has been convincingly suggested, the fact that he had *not* fought in the American Civil War was something which both affected his future detached and critical attitude towards America and determined his posture of passivity. The mention of an 'obscure hurt' sustained in manipulating a rusty fire-engine has prompted some absurd speculations designed to connect James's apparent remoteness from sexual contact with some sort of castration. There is no evidence for this, any more than there is evidence for a pronouncedly homosexual bias, and his life in this respect retains its secrets to the last.

He, was, however, deeply attached to the idea, as

much as to the substance, of his cousin Minnie Temple, the news of whose death he received while undergoing treatment at Great Malvern for his recurring constipation. His letters suggest that the emotional upheaval created by Minnie's death, experienced amid landscapes whose threatening loveliness is memorably portrayed, created for him that sense of brilliance and liveliness being crushed by acquisitiveness and greed which is at the heart of some of his greatest work. Certainly it may be said that Isabel Archer in *The Portrait of A Lady* (1881) and Milly Theale in *The Wings of the Dove* (1902) derived significant inspiration from Minnie Temple herself.

The richness of James's experience of England, France and Italy during the 1870s is almost without a parallel in the history of the growth of creative personality, and to read it through the medium of his incomparable letters, probably the best in English after Byron's*, is to feel a profound envy, mingled with inevitable admiration. In London he dined with Ruskin* and met George Eliot*, in Paris he enjoyed the company of Flaubert*, Maupassant*, Daudet* and the Goncourts*, as well as making the acquaintance of Turgenev*, and in Italy he made good friends among the American expatriate circles of Rome, Florence and Venice. It is as well to mention here that important, though frequently overlooked sense of place which manifests itself in works such as *A Little Tour in France* (1884) and *Italian Hours* (1909) and surprises those who think of James purely as a 'psychological' novelist, devoid of any interest in the visual. After settling in England in 1876 James had few serious thoughts of returning to live in America, and though his view of Europe and Europeans was significantly modified in later years he already perceived the extent of the inspiration both offered to the exercise of his talent.

The novels and stories of the late 1870s and early 1880s play to the full upon what their author called 'the international situation', the idea of the moral confrontation of cultivated Americans with the Old World. In *The Europeans* (1878) this takes place in America itself, but his fullest and most magisterial exploration of the theme appears in *The Portrait of A Lady*, often taken to be his finest work. Of the mass of short stories based on this idea the best is probably 'Daisy Miller' (1878), in which the essential vitality of an American girl is overwhelmed by the stuffiness of censorious Roman society and symbolically extinguished by a fever caught during a louche moonlight escapade in the Coliseum. It was a subject which, in varying forms, he was to return to in his last great period during the early 1900s.

An increasing absorption with the severe contrasts presented by London society both rich and poor, and by the English in general, found reflection in *The Princess Casamassima* (1886), James's most ambitious book and the nearest he ever came to the type of French realism practised so thoroughly by his friends Alphonse Daudet and Paul Bourget. *The Tragic Muse* (1890), begun two years later, mirrors his continuing amazement at the depths of English philistinism, in an analysis of the confrontation between the artist and the world.

It was to be this very philistinism which brought to an abrupt close the most confused and agonizing period of James's literary career, when, during the early 1890s, he dabbled extensively in writing for the stage. He was not, *pace* even his most fervent admirers, a good playwright, and his naive belief that he could dazzle the hidebound London theatrical public with the sophistications of French boulevard drama à la Sardou* was rudely shattered by the spectacular failure of *Guy Domville* in 1895, one of the most memorably disastrous first nights in English stage history. He returned with relief to fiction and produced in rapid succession *The Spoils of Poynton* (1897), *What Maisie Knew* (1897), *The Awkward Age* and 'The Turn of the Screw', a series of works firmly concentrated on English backgrounds and situations.

In 1896 he moved from London to Lamb House at Rye in Sussex, where he was to remain for the rest of his life. Even if his readership had never been of a 'popular' extensiveness and despite complaints as to his increasing stylistic obfuscations, he was a highly regarded figure in England, and a naturally sociable manner had won him the friendship of Robert Louis Stevenson*, Rudyard Kipling, Edmund Gosse* and other distinguished men of letters. His growing inability to express himself in any but the most parenthetical of utterances became legendary, enshrined within the reminiscence of friends such as the novelist Edith Wharton and the various small children who were taken to tea with him. During his residence in England he had remained on comparatively good terms with his family: thus the death of his sister Alice was another in the series of catastrophic blows to serenity at that time. A return to America in 1904 was an experience both vivid and horrifying, which produced *The American Scene* (1907), a travel document of fascinated revulsion.

James's last great burst of creative energy brought forth *The Wings of The Dove*, *The Ambassadors* (1903) and *The Golden Bowl* (1904), novels which powerfully revive several of his earlier thematic concerns in new ways. He wrote little of importance thereafter, beyond a handful of short stories and an unfinished novel, *The Ivory Tower*, abandoned owing to his sense that the First World War had effectively destroyed the world celebrated by the book. He returned to London and immersed himself in charitable work connected with the British war effort, becoming a naturalized subject in 1915 and receiving the Order of Merit on his deathbed a few months afterwards. He was buried in Chelsea Old Church, where a plaque commemorates him as a 'lover and interpreter of the fine amenities, of brave decisions and generous loyalties'.

He was finely prophetic in supposing that the Great War had annihilated his world, and it is difficult to imagine what he could have made of that which succeeded it. Interest in the whole nature of his work becomes enhanced by the tension sprung within it between the deliberate rhythms of a nineteenth-century life and the sense of barely suppressed hysteria authentic to the twentieth. A story like 'The Turn of The Screw', nowadays groaning under the weight of post-Freudian analysis of its unnamed governess's sexual traumas, is archetypally the creation of the man who had gone 'reeling and moaning' among the monstrous horse-drawn equipages of Papal Rome in its last days and who was to whirl through Italy as a delighted passenger in Edith Wharton's motor car. His stories and characters need and are given their due of expansiveness.

James's fiction falls very loosely into a series of moments related to his various journeyings and preoccupations. During the late 1860s and early 1870s it is still heavily marked by the influence of Nathaniel Hawthorne, and a distinctively Jamesian stance only properly emerges in his first major novel, *Roderick Hudson* (1875), which expresses his 'international' theme in fairly simple terms through the story of an American sculptor's love for a cosmopolitan beauty, Christina Light (subsequently to return as the Princess Casamassima). The nature and role of artists, indeed, dominates many of James's novels and tales during this and the following decade, but its supreme articulations in his work are not to be found until the later 1880s, when stories such as 'The Author of Beltraffio', 'The Real Thing', 'The Lesson of The Master' and the wryly comic 'The Death of The Lion' act as finely wrought pendants to our understanding of the flawed brilliance of *The Princess Casamassima* and *The Tragic Muse*.

Related to his interest in the threats and challenges of art is James's concern with the notion of innocence, not only among his wandering Americans who, like Isabel Archer in *The Portrait of A Lady*, gather wisdom through experience, but as embodied by children. His treatment of childhood is unique among nineteenth-century writers for its singularly penetrating comprehension of the child's vision of the adult world. Startling as a work like *What Maisie Knew* may at first appear through imposing the machinery of mature analysis upon a little girl's view of her mother's sexual adventures, it persuades by the overwhelming consistency of its method. The theme was to be resumed in *The Awkward Age*, a novel of marmoreal perfection in its technical finish, but perhaps the most successful of James's briefer explorations of the subject is the short story 'The Pupil', in which the sophisticated perceptions of a small boy are contrasted with the surprised naivety of his tutor.

The corruption which menaces such innocence is better suggested by James than by almost any other contemporary writer, and underpins the triumph of a work such as *The Wings of The Dove*, in which greed and sexual intrigue drive Merton Densher and Kate Croy to prey upon the goodwill of the dying Milly Theale. James's art, distancing him from the fictional traditions to which he was heir, is to suggest the extent and inclusiveness of such corruption through his minute disclosure of viewpoints rather than through a series of gestures and vicissitudes. None of his novels better demonstrates his complete understanding of evil than *The Bostonians*, whose failure in 1886, though it shocked him, was in part due to the severity with which he had caused his readers to scrutinize the characters surrounding his heroine Verena Tarrant.

'She wasn't born to know evil. She must never know it', cries Fanny Assingham of Maggie Verver in *The Golden Bowl*. In at least one respect, all James's major works can be seen as concentrating upon the conflict between living and knowing, between energy and consciousness, a dangerous duality encapsulated at its best in the famous boating scene in *The Ambassadors*. The completeness and refinement of his moral apprehensions, and his singular and obsessive determination that we should grasp the nature of their truth in its entirety, give his work, both in statement and expression, a pre-eminence whose dignified solitariness is wholly typical of James himself.

Jonathan Keates

Other works include three autobiographical studies: *A Small Boy and Others* (1913); *Notes of Son and Brother* (1914); and *The Middle Years* (1917). James's *Notebooks* (1947) were edited by F.O. Matthiessen and K.B. Murdock. Four volumes of a new edition of James's *Selected Letters*, ed. Leon Edel (from 1978) have so far appeared. Leon Edel, *The Life of Henry James* (5 vols, 1953–72) is the standard biography. See: F.O. Matthiessen, *Henry James: The Major Phase* (1944); F.R. Leavis, *The Great Tradition* (1948); Dorothea Krook, *The Ordeal of Consciousness in Henry James* (1962); and *Henry James: A Collection of Critical Essays*, ed. Leon Edel (1963).

240
JAMES, William 1842–1910

US psychologist and philosopher

The first son of Henry James Sr, William absorbed the religious, philosophical, and humanistic concerns of his father and his father's friends. In Paris, where the family lived from 1843 to 1860 James developed the ambition to become an artist. To enable him to study under William Morris Hunt in Newport, Rhode Island, the whole family returned to the United States. Within a year James transferred to the Lawrence Scientific School in Harvard to take up chemistry. A further move, this time to medicine, came in 1864, and led to his medical degree in 1869.

Under the spell of Harvard's great zoologist, Louis Agassiz*, James had looked forward to a career in biological research. The opportunity to test his enthusiasm came in 1865 when he joined Agassiz's Brazilian expedition, the experience of which seriously undermined his resolve. Instead he turned to physiology; once again interrupting his medical studies in Harvard, he spent eighteen months in Germany (1866–8); in Berlin he attended the lectures of the great Du Bois-Reymond; he visited but did not tarry in Heidelberg where Wundt* and Helmholtz* worked. More important, he read Hermann Lotze's *Medizinische Psychologie* and Griesinger's *Pathologie und Therapie der psychischen Krankheiten*, was introduced to the philosophy of Charles Renouvier, and, freed from the influence of Agassiz, he became a decided Darwinian*. In Germany James's health had been poor despite frequent visits to Teplitz for medical treatment. Returned to America he suffered three further years of depression before he accepted the position of instructor in anatomy and physiology at Harvard in 1873. Two years later he added a graduate course on 'The Relations between Physiology and Psychology'. In the undergraduate course on physiological psychology which he introduced in 1876 he used Herbert Spencer's* *Principles of Psychology* as the text. Like Spencer his approach to psychology was biological but in contrast to that great synthetic philosopher James worried about the steps in an argument, the use of analogies, the precision of terms. On every count he found Spencer wanting. Spencer's one virtue, he remarked, was his belief in the universality of evolution. His one thousand crimes were 'his 5000 pages of absolute incompetence to work it out in detail'. James's published critique of Spencer began with 'Remarks on Spencer's Definition of Mind as Correspondence' in the *Journal of Speculative Philosophy* in 1878. Here he stressed what was to become a central feature of his psychology – the active role of the mind in contrast to the passive mirror-image model of Spencer. Mind did not simply *correspond* to external relations; by its own activity it transformed those relations. To mind belonged spontaneity and creativity.

In 1879 James started a course on 'The Philosophy of Evolution', in which he tackled Spencer's *First Principles* (1862); he criticized Spencer's famous law: 'Evolution is an integration of matter and concomitant dissipation of motion; during which matter passes from an indefinite, incoherent homogeneity to a definite, coherent heterogeneity.' James reformulated the statement as: 'Evolution is a change from a no-howish untalkaboutable all-alikeness to a somehowish and in general talkaboutable not-all-alikeness by continuous

stick-togetherations and something-elseifications.' Nor did Spencer's conception of the 'unknowable' find favour with James. Spencer had relegated all attainable knowledge to that which is relative. The absolute, not being relative, was therefore unknowable. James saw that such a negative view offered no satisfaction to our emotional needs and theistic beliefs. It was, he said, as if a watchmaker were to say: 'Your watch is relative. Here is an absolute one that will not go at all.'

From 1877 onwards James's teaching on psychology was transferred to the philosophy department and in 1880 the subject title of his post was altered from physiology to philosophy. Having introduced the new physiological psychology to the American academic world and given laboratory instruction in experimental techniques, James was able to hand over such instruction to the young Freiburg psychologist, Hugo Münsterberg, whom he attracted to Harvard in 1892. Together with his pupil Stanley Hall, James was thus a central figure in the introduction to the United States of the new psychology so successfully developing in Germany. To teach the subject successfully, he told the college president, called for the union of the two disciplines of physiology and psychology in one man, a tradition set by Lotze in Göttingen and Wundt in Heidelberg.

James's work is difficult to summarize because it covered so many fields, psychological, philosophical and theological. In addition to the early articles in *Mind* and the *Critique philosophique* James edited his father's posthumous essays in 1885. He respected the deep theological aspects of his father's Swedenborgian system but he wanted to see it fashioned into a more articulately scientific form. He had long been familiar with Swedenborg through his father's studies and his own reading of this mystic author. James's subsequent preoccupation with the central role of the will, the function of belief, the existence of the supernatural, the rejection of determinism, and the espousal of moral freedom show the conformity of his fundamental concerns with those of his father. All James's subsequent writings can be viewed as contributions towards the elaboration of a philosophical position incorporating these features.

This position lay midway 'twixt the two extremes which James labelled the tender– and the tough-minded. The former were rationalists devoted to abstract and eternal principles, to monism, free will and religion. The tough-minded were empiricists devoted to facts, to pluralism, fatalism and irreligion. As examples of the tender-minded rationalists he had in mind philosophers of the school of Hegel* such as McTaggert and T.H. Green in England and Josiah Royce in Harvard. James found the rationalists' search for the real world, one infinite folio – that *édition de luxe* of all the finite distorted editions of the world – suffocating in its 'infallible impeccable all-pervasiveness'. It was discouraging that in this absolute world 'where all that is *not* is from eternity impossible, and that *is* is necessary, the category of possibility has no application.' He called this the 'through-and-through universe' and it stifled him emotionally.

Hegelian philosophy had taken root in the English-speaking world late in the nineteenth century owing to the entrenched position of British empiricism. James was therefore reacting to a contemporary movement. Equally his opposition to the tough-minded empiricists was a reaction to positivism in the materialist and evolutionary form in which T.H. Huxley*, W.K. Clifford and Herbert Spencer presented it. These positivists, James opined, had an impoverished view of the extent and variety of truth because they ruled out of court all knowledge that was not reducible to the factual data of experience, and they cautioned against belief in unproved statements. To Clifford's 'duty' not to believe, Spencer's doctrine of the unknowable, and Huxley's agnosticism James replied with his famous address granting the 'will to believe' that for which we lack adequate empirical evidence. The positivists' dependence on the empirical data of science led to a materialistic and depressing vision. What was higher was explained by what was lower. In Herbert Spencer's hand the world's history became a redistribution of matter and motion; in the writings of Ernst Haeckel* God became a 'gaseous vertebrate'. The course of evolution was in Spencer's synthetic philosophy as inevitable as the Hegelians' conception of history. Social changes were for Spencer impersonal; they were due to environment, i.e. physical geography and the like. Man's mind developed in a fatalistic, passive manner, moulded by its experience of the 'outer relations'. This philosophy of evolution, James declared, was a metaphysical creed. Against this Spencerian predestination of all human actions James put the Darwinian conception of spontaneous variations, due to 'internal molecular accidents'. The cycle of influences which acted upon the germ to cause such variations was not directly deducible from the visible external conditions of the environment. We could not therefore predict the emergence of given variations, including those geniuses which became the great men of history. Their existence was a given datum for the social philosopher just as spontaneous variations were for the biologist. James concluded that history was not an inevitable process determined in advance but the result of many unpredictable events.

James's *Principles of Psychology* (1890) was deliberately positivistic and non-metaphysical. His acceptance of the empirical parallel between states of consciousness and brain processes was, he declared , no more than a 'mere admission', but we may note in its conformity with his pluralistic ontology. Central to his conception of mind was its place in the basic structure of behaviour. Although he criticized Spencer's formu-

lation of the essence of mental life as 'the adjustment of inner to outer relations' he approved the way it pictured minds inhabiting environments 'which act on them and on which they in turn react'. The *Principles* was also crucially dependent upon the facts of immediate experience as revealed by introspection. This is particularly evident in James's theory of emotion and the ideomotor theory of will. In the former he identified emotion with the sensation of the bodily changes which follow perception of the exciting fact. We are not afraid and tremble, he declared, but tremble and are afraid. Emotion is then the mental correlate of bodily responses, not the cause of such responses. According to the ideomotor theory introspection reveals to us that in addition to the element of consent or fiat the only psychic state which precedes our voluntary acts is an anticipatory image of the sensorial consequences of the movements which that act will involve.

In both these theories physiological processes played an important part, but the most important physiological element in *Principles* was the reflex arc. As early as 1881 in an address to Unitarian ministers entitled 'Reflex Action and Theism', James claimed that the most fundamental conclusion to be drawn from physiological research was that our will dominates both our thought and our feeling. The reflex was a triad made up of incoming impressions, contemplation or thinking, and outward discharges. Thinking was thus a place of transit, 'the bottom of a loop', the ends of which were applied to the external world. The purpose of thinking was to bring about action. The theorizing faculty, he declared, 'functions *exclusively for the sake of ends* that do not exist at all in the world of impressions we receive by way of ourselves, but are set by our emotional and practical subjectivity altogether'. It effected a transformation of sense data 'in the interests of our volitional nature'. Hence the subjugation of thinking to willing, and the fallacy of considering thought in isolation from action. Anticipating the doctrine of pragmatism which he was later (1898) to define, James claimed that 'if two apparently different definitions of the reality before us should have identical consequences, those two definitions would really be identical definitions, made delusively to appear different.'

James considered two further aspects of the physiological reflex – the automaton theory and the concept of instinct. The former was included in his lectures at Johns Hopkins University in 1878 and appeared in print in *Mind* a year later entitled 'Are we Automata?'. Here he rejected T.H. Huxley's claim that consciousness was a mere epiphenomenon like the whistle of a steam engine and that no state of consciousness caused any change in the motion of the organism. In the state of psychology at the time James considered this theory an 'unwarrantable impertinence'. If, as Spencer asserted, our actions are determined by our consciousness of pleasure and pain, then it was easy to see how by the principle of selection those individuals whose pleasures were derived from actions conducive to their survival would predominate. Consequently consciousness, by playing a causal role in steering a nervous system grown too complex to regulate itself, played a vital part in the evolution of man. This was only possible, however, if our will could act on our body. Without such causal influence consciousness could have played no such role. James's treatment of instincts was also evolutionary. They all conformed to the general reflex type; they were present in all animals including man. He listed thirty human instincts and declared that 'no other mammal, not even the monkey, shows so large an array'. He sided with Darwin against Spencer in believing that instincts originated by spontaneous, heritable variations and were not acquired from acts originally executed intelligently. This was in line with James's general distrust of the alleged inheritance of acquired characters. His long list of instincts was later severely pruned by the behaviourists who gave a prominent role to the Pavlovian* conception of conditioned reflexes. James merely allowed for the modification and inhibition of reflexes due to experience, leading to the development of a variety of habits which might displace the original instinct entirely.

Two aspects of James's treatment of consciousness deserve comment. The first concerns its evolution, the second its continuity. He criticized the vagueness of Spencer's representation of the emergence of consciousness by the term 'nascent' and the analogy of the ultimate unit of consciousness with the nervous (mental) shock. James rejected any such atomistic hylozoism, and he found the assumed self-compounding of mental units 'logically unintelligible'. It just was not true that the roar of the sea was compounded in our minds from the perceptions of many little waves. Nor was it admissible to distinguish unconscious from conscious mental states. To allow this would be to turn psychology from becoming a science into 'a tumbling-ground for whimsies'. The least objectionable view was to admit the soul 'as a medium upon which the manifold brain-processes combine their effects'. Since consciousness was unitary and integral from the outset there was no need for the self-compounding of separate feelings.

James emphasized the continuity of consciousness in the metaphor 'the stream of thought'. He denied that anyone ever had a simple sensation by itself. Each sensation was accompanied by relations both spatial and temporal to other sensations. We do not hear thunder *pure* but 'thunder-breaking-upon-silence-and-contrasting-with-it'. Thought was like a bird's life made up of flights and perchings. The perchings were the substantive parts; and the flights were the transitive parts of the stream of thought. Our words and images might appear discrete and our thoughts divisible into substantive elements, but in reality they were 'fringed' with the 'overtones' of their relations with each other. James went on to underline the quality of wholeness which characterized thinking. Like the Gestalt psychologists twenty-three years later James urged that 'whatever things are thought in relation are thought from the outset in a unity.'

We have noted that the basic strands of James's philosophical thinking were present in the *Principles*. His functional view of thought and its subservience to will also marked his more mature exposition of pragmatism in 1898. Equally his discussion of perception of time and space in the *Principles* contained the essence of his later development of radical empiricism. Against the rationalists he argued that we have no intuition of space and time. Empty time and empty space meant nothing to us. Against Hermann Lotze he raised objections to the doctrine of 'local signs' as cues to the spatial location of sense data. There was no independent entity known in our minds as space into which spaceless sensations could be dropped. The sensations themselves brought space and duration with them; they were the psychic fringes. Thus the rhythmic repetition of our heart beat, our pulse and our breathing give us a sensation of duration when all else is still. Likewise our bodily sensations carry an element of varying degrees of 'vastness' or 'voluminousness' which 'is the original sensation of space, out of which all the exact knowledge about space that we afterwards come to have is woven by processes of discrimination, association and selection'.

Although the most consistent target of James's criticism was the school of Hegelian rationalists, we have seen that he attacked the crudities of the old associationist psychology. As for the elaborate, technical development of psychophysics he reckoned its proper psychological outcome was nothing. Yet he welcomed the signs of a return to a revised empiricism in philosophical circles, for he sought to promote what in 1897 he had called 'radical empiricism', of which he gave a systematic account in *The Meaning of Truth* (1909).

In his latter years James gave a fuller, more explicit development of his philosophical position, stressing pluralism, pragmatism and anti-intellectualism. Pluralism denied that there was any one entity – the absolute – embracing all reality, but admitted that 'the constitution of reality is what we ourselves find empirically realized in every minimum of finite life'. It was reality 'in distributive form', the 'strung-along unfinished world in time'.

James defined pragmatism as a method for attaining clarity of thought: 'To attain perfect clearness in our thoughts of an object . . . we need only consider what conceivable effects of a practical kind the object may involve . . . . Our conception of these effects . . . is then for us the whole conception of the object.' Theories then become instruments not answers to the enigmas of nature. But pragmatism also constituted a theory of truth. Just as scientists were coming to recognize the provisional character of all scientific laws and theories – 'a conceptual shorthand . . . in which we write our reports of nature' – so pragmatists held that all our ideas and beliefs 'become true just in so far as they help us to get into satisfactory relation with other parts of our experience.' Purely objective truth lacking any such function did not exist. In so far as theological beliefs did prove of value in concrete life they were to be considered true.

James admitted willingly that his views were anti-intellectual in the sense that the role he allowed for logic was severely limited. Against the Hegelians he urged that logic cannot help us to become acquainted 'with the essential nature of reality'. There was no objective fixed reality waiting to be discovered; it was in the making. Truth might happen to an idea. Faith in a fact could help create the fact. Thus did James fuse together in pragmatism his evolutionary, religious and positivist concerns, creating thereby a strong current in the anti-intellectualist thought in America at the turn of the century.

Robert Olby

Most of James's essays and books are still in print. Among the best accounts of James's philosophical writings is A.J. Ayer, *The Origins of Pragmatism* (1968). On Darwin's influence on James see Philip P. Wiener, *Evolution and the Founders of Pragmatism* (1949). The definitive biography is Ralph B. Perry, *The Thought and Character of William James* (2 vols, 1935, reprinted 1974). James's influence upon American thought is discussed by Morton White, *Pragmatism and the American Mind* (1975).

241
JARRY, Alfred 1873–1907

French writer

Alfred Jarry is one of those people whose fame is legendary, whose influence vast, and yet whom it is hard to locate precisely. Furthermore, his work is very badly misconstrued, in that most of it is almost unknown. He is known largely for his cycle of Ubu plays (*Ubu enchaîné*, 1900; *Ubu sur la butte*, 1901; and particularly *Ubu Roi*, 1896), for his black dress, for shooting cigarettes out of people's mouths while riding his bicycle, for intentionally living a life of 'drink as life style/work of art', i.e., for being, although physically tiny, an outsized character in turn-of-the-century Paris. Yet, his collected works add up to eight substantial volumes and cover an extraordinary range.

Jarry was born in Laval in 1873, the son of a cloth merchant. His family eventually moved to Rennes

where he went to school before going to the Lycée Henri IV in Paris in 1891. At the school in Rennes there was a very fat and, by all accounts, bullying master called Monsieur Hérbert – known to the pupils as '*le père Ebé*'. The fortuitous collision of this unloved man and the tiny, iconoclastic and outrageous schoolboy Alfred Jarry led directly to the creation of one of the theatre's legends, *Ubu Roi*. The character of Ubu, a conscienceless (in *Ubu Cocu*, Ubu flushes his tiresome conscience down the wc), vast and truly gross cad who will stop at nothing and who gets away with whatever he can, is the creation for which Jarry is best known. And while this bombastic play, and its presentation at the Théâtre de l'Oeuvre in 1896, with its absurd and cartoon-like personages, abrupt switches of scene, delight in masks (surely a reflection of the times but equally surely a precursor to Picasso and the advent of pictorial Cubism) and de-personalization of the actors (prefiguring the automaton technique used by Beckett in directing his own plays), was undoubtedly revolutionary, it seems as though the scandal still associated with it has come, in general view, to overshadow completely the rest of Jarry's work. For all its influence on what we now still call the 'Theatre of the Absurd' *Ubu* should also be seen as something of a schoolboy piece, almost on the level of a prank, marking the beginning of a versatile career, and not as is usually the case as the single creative high-point of an intentionally eccentric prodigy.

In order to discuss the main body of Jarry's work, it is probably best to use, as vehicles, two novels that are available in (excellent) English translations, *The Supermale* (*Le Sûrmale*, 1902, trans. 1968) and *Exploits and Opinions of Dr Faustroll, Pataphysician* (*Gestes et Opinions du Docteur Faustroll, Pataphysicien*, 1911, trans. 1965 in *Selected Works of Alfred Jarry*). But there is little point in attempting to explain the plot of either novel. *The Supermale*, which has been called the only real Surrealist novel, concerns the life and exploits of one André Marcueil (the supermale) and others such as the inventor, William Elson, his daughter, Ellen, and his adversary, Dr Bathybius; contains a 10,000 mile race between an intercontinental express train and a five seater bicycle, the riders of which machine (including one who dies during the race but keeps on pedalling anyhow) are fed on Elson's 'Perpetual Motion Food'; and ends in an orgy as amazing as it is strangely touching. *Faustroll* ('Faust' plus 'troll') is an episodic series of visits paid to many extraordinary 'lands' (but not in Gulliver's satirical sense) by Dr Faustroll, the bailiff, Panmuphle, who commences the story trying to serve a writ on the doctor and ends up as both storyteller and slavish oarsman in Dr Faustroll's skiff (a sieve), and the (literally) arse-faced baboon, Bosse-de-Nage, who punctuates the book with his all-purpose language (analysed in one of the chapters) consisting of the single morphemic repeat 'ha ha' whenever Dr

Faustroll is talking for too long without a break. Where *Supermale* is Surrealist, the later *Faustroll* may be taken, in a reversal of chronology, to be Cubist.

Apart from their beauty, both these novels have an external importance in the way in which they preshadow or even anticipate so much that comes later. The reviewer and critic always runs the risk of drawing analogies that infer influences that were, perhaps, never there, but there are some most remarkable similarities that can be found. Of course, many are at once obvious and acknowledged. While Jarry himself is Rabelaisian and clearly takes a lead from the Symbolists, the French Surrealist school of the 1920s and later, and particularly Apollinaire, Eluard, Jacot, Breton, Gide, Queneau and, in a somewhat different manner, Artaud all owe a debt to him, as do the Dadaists, with whom he so clearly shares feelings of outrage and enjoyment of *spectacle-per-se*.

Nevertheless, the most interesting similarities lie outside French twentieth-century literature. This is not as surprising as it may, perhaps, seem: Jarry's inspirations came from, amongst other things, the amazing imaginations of a remarkable collection of contemporary British physicists (as opposed to the French physicists of the time, e.g. Poincaré*). In *Faustroll*, he has the doctor, now dead, communicate telepathically with Kelvin* on the subject of some of Kelvin's recent scientific papers. And the sieve-skiff is a direct interpretation – albeit at an absurdly inflated scale – of a demonstration concerning surface tension by C.V. Boys, in which a sieve was actually floated in a tumbler of water.

The nearest parallel to *The Supermale* must be Flan O'Brien's (Brian O'Nolan alias Myles na Gopaleen) *The Third Policeman*. Not only are both macabrely and disjointedly funny, not only do both depend on remarkable experiences both with and of bicycles (a strangely recurrent obsession in Irish literature), not only do they also share a love of ostensive learnedness, but also both exist in fabulous worlds, built with devastating logic from (minor adjustments to) existing physical principles, which create alternative realities of great credibility. And, if *Supermale* presents such a set of alternative realities with an external scientific reference, how much further does the 'Pataphysical' logic of the internally consistent fantasy worlds of *Faustroll* go? For, in *Faustroll*, Jarry takes his vision to the extreme absurd (this is the contrast to Swift's *Gulliver*), and presents short chapters (mostly dedicated to a friend *or* enemy), each of which shimmers like some jewel, bringing to mind the exact quality of Italo Calvino's *Invisible Cities*. Could it be that, just as each city Calvino describes becomes apparent as some facet of Marco Polo's Venice, the different worlds that Dr Faustroll and his companions (surely not the model for *Three Men in a Boat*) visit – without apparently leaving Paris – are, in fact, facets of that city?

Jarry was also a considerable critic and theorist. His views, particularly on theatre, as expressed in, for instance, his various introductory talks written to precede performances of *Ubu Roi*, are still of contemporary value. He was, too, a scurrilous satirist, and his *The Passion considered as an Uphill Bicycle Race* is a triumph. He was a master of verse, both pornographic and Surrealist, and he produced charming woodcuts to illustrate his own works. But, above all, there stands his invention of that science above science which permitted his mind to roam in the fields of his imaginary worlds: 'Pataphysics' – which has survived him and is enshrined in the College of Pataphysics in Paris. In *Faustroll*, he defines it thus:

> An epiphenomenon is that which is superinduced upon a phenomenon. Pataphysics . . . is the science of that which is superinduced upon metaphysics, extending as far beyond metaphysics as the latter extends beyond physics . . . pataphysics will be, above all, the science of the particular, despite the common opinion that the only science is that of the general.

And, again, 'DEFINITION. Pataphysics is the science of imaginary solutions, which symbolically attributes the properties of objects, described by their virtuality, to their lineaments.' In a pataphysical universe, the distinction between the real and the hallucinatory is blurred.

And so it is also with the man, Alfred Jarry, himself. It is true he was iconoclastic, and while he developed himself into the gross persona of Ubu, in Paris, he drank as a discipline, bicycled, shot, lived fast, was genuinely anarchistic and Dadaistic. But there is another side, demonstrated in his later writings. Photographs reveal that the surprise one gets, knowing only *Ubu*, on reading the delicate prose of these later works is the surprise of discovering the person behind the *persona*, for the soft eyes you see are those of a small, sensitive, intensely aware man. Nevertheless, he never ceased to hide behind his bombastic sense of irony. When he died in 1907, poor and suffering from tubercular meningitis, his last act was, appropriately enough, to ask for a toothpick. His motto could well have been his definition of art. 'Art,' he said, 'is a stuffed crocodile'.

Ranulph Glanville

See: *Oeuvres complètes* (8 vols, 1948). Translations other than those mentioned above include: *Ubu Roi* (trans. Barbara Wright, 1951) and *The Ubu Plays* (trans. Cyril Connolly and Simon Watson Taylor, 1968), including *Ubu Roi*, *Ubu Cocu* and *Ubu Enchaîné*.

242
JEVONS, William Stanley 1835–82

British economic theorist

By the mid-nineteeth century a certain complacency had entered economics and political economy. There were, it is true, some sharp disagreements concerning in particular the theoretical legacy of David Ricardo*, but in terms of scope and method writers on economics were largely in accord. The development of the discipline was seen to a great extent to concern the extension of a given doctrine and method to new areas of investigation, rather than the investigation of the theoretical bases of the doctrine itself. William Stanley Jevons was one of a small group of economists who changed all that. He is usually associated with the Austrian Carl Menger and the Swiss-French Léon Walras as one of the (independent) founders of modern economics. Among a wide range of other achievements, Jevons developed and systematized the 'marginal principle', and its forms of mathematical representation, which later became the hallmark of mainstream economics.

W.S. Jevons was born in 1835, into an educated, non-conformist family with a history of interest in economic and social affairs; he was educated, however, in the natural sciences and mathematics. From an early age he seemed happy with bold conjecture: his journal at the age of seventeen, for example, contains an outline of a theory of evolution (this being seven years before the publication of Darwin's* The Origin of Species). Unfortunately his education was cut short as a result of family financial difficulties and he had to go to work: in 1853 he left for New South Wales to become assayer at the Sydney Mint. He remained in Australia for five years. This was a solitary, lonely period for him, and probably an unhappy one. Yet it was also a period of intense and original thought: such episodes are not uncommon in the early lives of truly creative thinkers. His main intellectual achievements in economic theory were developed, at least in outline, over this period, and Keynes was probably right to say that 'the last third of Jevons's life after he was thirty was mainly devoted to the elucidation and amplification of what in essence he had already discovered'.

Jevons's achievements were various, but two in particular stand out. The first was his use of statistical material for economic analysis focusing on the explanation of cyclical phenomena. This work began with a paper read to the British Association in 1862, and developed into a wide investigation of monetary and production trends, with the object of understanding the phenomenon of the trade cycle. In this work Jevons originated many of the investigative methods which have been subsequently refined in the discipline of applied economics. Unfortunately his remarkable achievements in this area have tended to be overshadowed by a bizarre theory developed towards the end of his career: Jevons noticed (who else would have even bothered to look at the data?) a strange correlation between the periodicity of commercial crises and the sunspot cycle. This led to a 'sunspot' theory of economic crisis, based on a connection between sunspot 'bursts', bad harvests (as a result of subsequent climatic variation) and economic recession. The easy ridicule which can be directed at this has mitigated against a balanced assessment of Jevons's pioneering contributions to applied economics.

He had, however, another string to his bow. This consisted of nothing less than the elaboration of a new system of theoretical political economy, first outlined in a paper in 1862 and subsequently published in book form – as The Theory of Political Economy – in 1871. This work has been correctly described as the first modern book on economics.

The innovations of The Theory of Political Economy reside in two features. The first consists in a theory of value – a general theory of the formation of prices – couched in terms of a now familiar supply and demand analysis. Unlike classical political economy, which saw prices primarily in terms of costs, Jevons introduced a new theory of demand, based on a concept of utility, as a primary determinant of the prices of commodities. The second innovation derives from the manner in which costs and demand are introduced: they are discussed not in terms of average (average costs, average degrees of utility, etc.) but in terms of marginal increments (the utility derived from the consumption of one extra unit of a good, at the margin). This approach makes it possible to use mathematical methods of analysis based on the differential calculus: the 'marginal revolution' thus established has dominated English economics ever since.

These achievements, though spectacular, were quantitatively only a small part of Jevons's work. He published numerous books on economics and logic, and also had a major influence on popular understanding of the issues in these fields through a series of works – for a general audience – on logic, economics and scientific method. These popular books had a sale of several hundred thousand copies. Jevons died in 1882, at the early age of forty-six, after a swimming accident in Sussex.

Keith Smith

Other works include: The Coal Question (1865) and Principles of Science (1874). See: J.M.Keynes, 'William Stanley Jevons', in The Collected Writings of John Maynard Keynes, vol. X, Essays in Biography (1972); R.D.C. Black, A.W. Coats and C.D.W. Goodwin, The Marginal Revolution in Economics (1973).

243
JOULE, James Prescott 1818–89

British physicist

Many scientists, like Joule, discover laws of nature; far
fewer succeed, as Joule did, in seeing behind those laws
to the much deeper and more general mechanism by
which nature operates. He was born in Salford into a
wealthy brewing family. Somewhat sickly and suffering
from a minor spinal ailment, Joule was educated by a
number of private tutors including, from 1834 to 1837,
the seventy-year-old John Dalton* from whom he
apparently learnt more mathematics than chemistry.

Scientific research was for Joule an 'essentially holy
undertaking'. So devout was he that even on his honeymoon at Chamonix in 1847 he was observed with his
especially sensitive thermometer trying 'for elevation
of temperature in waterfalls'. Initially he worked in the
family brewery and could only spend his spare-time in
scientific research but when, in 1854, the family business was sold Joule could devote himself to full time
research in his private laboratory. The only public
institution he was ever connected with was the Manchester Literary and Philosophical Society.

Joule's earliest significant researches, reported in
1841, were concerned with his supposition that 'electromagnetism will ultimately be substituted for steam
to propel machinery'. But to his surprise he found that,
whereas the consumption of 1 lb of coal would raise
1.5 million lbs 1 ft, it needed 5 lbs of zinc to generate
an equivalent amount of power with a battery. From
this point onwards Joule began to consider the electric
motor as a physical system rather than a source of
useful power.

He next moved on to consider the heating effect
produced by passing an electric current through a wire
and after careful measurement was able to formulate
in 1841 the law that the heat produced is proportional
to the resistance of the wire and the square of the
current ($H \propto I^2R$). But Joule saw something more
than the simple law, namely, that as the heat generated
was proportional to the current and as the current was
itself proportional to the amount of zinc consumed in
the battery, it followed that the heat was proportional
to 'the number of atoms (whether of water or zinc)
concerned in generating the current'. It was in fact
becoming clear to Joule that 'the mechanical and heating powers of a current are proportional to each other',
a hypothesis Joule began to explore in the 1840s in a
wide variety of experimental situations. This soon led
him to the important conclusion that mechanical power
was not just proportional to the heat generated but
was actually converted into it.

This was Joule's great insight, that the heat produced in a system derived from the work done, whether
that work was chemical, mechanical, electrical or

whatever. The point was quite general and meant that,
in any system, the same amount of work should produce the same amount of heat, that is, they were equivalent and interconvertible. As one of the most skilled
experimenters of his day Joule's next task was to confirm this insight and to determine precisely the value
of his proposed mechanical equivalence of heat.

In numerous experiments in the early 1840s Joule
forced water through pipes, compressed and expanded
gases, passed currents through wires of various sizes
and heated fluids by rotating in them a paddle wheel
driven by a falling weight. In each case he measured
the amount of work performed, in foot-lbs, and the
quantity of heat produced and did in fact find that the
same amount of work always yielded the same amount
of heat. His first determination in 1843 was that 838
ft-lbs was needed to increase the temperature of 1 lb
of water 1°F. but in 1849 he announced his definitive
measurement of the equivalence as 772 ft-lbs, a figure
in broad agreement with the currently accepted value
of 778.

Joule's ideas met initially with a largely indifferent
reception. They were well received by Lord Kelvin*
but it was only with the formulation of the basic principles of the new science of thermodynamics by such
physicists as R. Clausius* that Joule's work received
in the 1850s the international recognition it deserved.

Joule's work had been enormously influential. With
it and the related principles of thermodynamics it was
possible to see that such apparently diverse phenomena
as the growing of corn, the operation of a steam engine,
the passage of a current through a wire, the emission
of solar radiation and the contraction of muscle are in
fact all examples of the same basic physical process.

Derek Gjertsen

There is surprisingly no biography of Joule. His
collected *Scientific Papers* (2 vols, 1884, reissued 1963)
are available and there are accounts of his life and
work in J. Crowther, *British Scientists of the 19th Century*
(1935), and by R. Fox in *Mid-19th Century Scientists*,
ed. J. North (1969). See also H.J. Steffens, *Joule and
the Concept of Energy* (1979).

244
JOWETT, Benjamin 1817–93

British theologian, Greek scholar and educator

Jowett was born into a merchant family at Peckham
and educated at St Paul's School, from which he proceeded in 1835 to Balliol College, Oxford, where he
was to spend the rest of his life. He was elected a fellow
of the college while still an undergraduate in 1838 and
made a tutor in 1842. In 1854 he was appointed Regius
Professor of Greek by Palmerston, but suffered bitter

disappointment earlier in the same year when he failed to achieve the mastership of Balliol, a post to which he was ultimately to be elected, unopposed, in 1870. For some years he had to endure a wrangle over the emoluments of his chair, an increase to which was opposed by the Tractarian party on the grounds of his religious opinions; and in 1863 Pusey unsuccessfully attempted to have him tried before the vice-chancellor for heresy. Otherwise, his life was uneventful. He never married.

His importance is threefold. As a theologian, he was a prominent representative of liberal thought in the Church of England, rejecting for example the doctrine of eternal punishment for the damned. His commentary on three epistles of St Paul (1855) provoked a storm of controversy because it contained an essay attacking both the morality and the scriptural basis of the orthodox doctrine of the Atonement. His contribution to the celebrated *Essays and Reviews* (1860), entitled 'On the Interpretation of Scripture', excited further hostility; this was a powerfully argued call for the use of critical reason in the study of the Bible, and seems unexceptionable today. His opponents – wrongly, it is now clear – suspected him of a covert agnosticism; this view is unforgettably represented by the brutal but very funny caricature of him as 'Dr Jenkinson' in W.H. Mallock's *The New Republic*. After 1860 Jowett wrote nothing more on theological matters.

To Greek studies he made no original contribution; indeed, he was contemptuous of what he called 'useless learning', and opposed to the desire of other Oxford dons, such as Mark Pattison, to encourage academic research in the modern sense. Instead, he devoted himself to translations, of which the most important was his complete Plato (1871), a work which helped to encourage the shift of philosophical fashion in England from empiricism to idealism. It is significant that Jowett was also one of the first Englishmen to champion the work of Hegel*. The introductory essays that he wrote to the Platonic dialogues show him, again, not as a scholar in the strict sense but as an educator and proselytizer; for instance, the notorious awkwardness of his attempt to adapt the Platonic theory of love to contemporary circumstances should be seen as the product of a desire, admirable in itself, to insist upon the continued, living value of ancient thought for the modern world.

However, his permanent place among the ranks of the eminent Victorians is earned not by anything that he wrote but by his influence as a teacher and personality. He could be cutting, and he made enemies, but as a tutor he was adored by many of his pupils (the most enthusiastic of whom were nicknamed the 'Jowett-worshippers'), and as master of Balliol he presided augustly over what was increasingly recognized to be the most outstanding college in Oxford. Jowett cannot be personally credited with the rise of Balliol from obscurity to the front rank, since the crucial reforms were made mostly before he became a fellow, but his magnetism and distinction stamped upon the educated consciousness the idea, still not quite eradicated, of the Balliol man as the possessor of a highly trained and polished mind, conscious of its own superiority, a man whose dedication to public service was matched by a sense that eminence and authority were his natural due. It should be added, however, that Jowett enjoyed an equal success with Balliol's more raffish elements: Swinburne* and John Addington Symonds were among his devoted admirers. He was also active both inside and outside Oxford in promoting the education of boys of poor family, both publicly and by a private generosity so well concealed that to this day very little is known about it. He was the greatest 'Oxford figure' of the nineteenth century, and his position has no exact parallel before or since.

Richard Jenkyns

There are two important biographies of Jowett: Evelyn Abbott and Lewis Campbell, *The Life and Letters of Benjamin Jowett* (2 vols, 1897); and Geoffrey Faber, *Jowett: A Portrait with Background* (1957). See: Basil Willey, *More Nineteenth Century Studies* (1963), on Jowett's theology; and Richard Jenkyns, *The Victorians and Ancient Greece* (1980), pp. 246–52, on his Greek studies and religious attitude.

K

245

KEATS, John 1795–1821

British poet

The popular image of the poet as a fragile creature constitutionally incapable of surviving for long in a brutally hostile world was virtually supplied intact by the life and legend of Keats. He produced, in only three years, the verse that was to ensure his exalted place 'among the English poets after my death' (as he hopefully put it in a letter of 14 October 1818) and he died at the age of twenty-five in circumstances that allowed his friends to make him the supreme martyr to hypersensitivity. Keats succumbed, finally, to consumption in Rome on 23 February 1821 but Shelley's* elegy *Adonais*, published soon afterwards, suggested that in death he had found the peace cruelly denied to him in life:

> And that unrest which men miscall delight
> Can touch him not and torture not again.

All that was needed to complete the tragic picture was a poignant epitaph and Keats himself had requested the inscription 'Here lies one whose name was writ in water', which duly appeared on his tombstone in the protestant cemetery in Rome. 'It might make one in love with death,' said Shelley whose ashes were placed in the same cemetery after he had been found drowned with a copy of Keats's 1820 collection in his pocket, 'to think that one should be buried in so sweet a place.'

More than any other poet, with the possible exception of Dylan Thomas who had qualities in common with him, Keats has been presented to posterity as a symbol. The earliest biographical sketch, in Leigh Hunt's *Lord Byron and Some of His Contemporaries* (1828), erroneously established inauspicious beginnings for the future sacrificial victim claiming 'Mr Keats's origin was of the humblest description'. Modern biographical research has refuted this excessively romantic notion. The poet's father, Thomas Keats, was socially acceptable enough to make a financially advantageous marriage to Frances Jennings and thereby acquire a position running the business and stables attached to the Swan and Hoop Inn in Finsbury, London. Thomas Keats died, in an accident, in 1804 and Frances remarried shortly after her first husband's funeral, possibly in order to cope with four children: John (the eldest, born 31 October 1795), George, Tom and Fanny. John went to school and developed, perhaps as a traumatic reaction to his father's death and rapid replacement by a stepfather, a melancholic manner. In 1811 he became apprenticed to Thomas Hammond, a surgeon; in 1815 he entered Guy's Hospital as a student.

At the age of eighteen Keats began to write poetry or, rather, effortlessly imitative verse recalling Spenser's deliberately gorgeous diction. When, on 5 May 1816, he had a poem published in Leigh Hunt's radical journal the *Examiner* he considered his future quite self-consciously. Though licensed to practise as surgeon and apothecary he decided he had too much sympathy to invade, medically, another individual's privacy and opted instead for the precarious life of a full-time poet. This decision was applauded by his new friends Leigh Hunt and the painter Benjamin Haydon*. Keats always tended to depend on personal relationships though two of those closest to him brought him most anguish: his brother Tom suffered from, and died of, the same disease that killed Keats; and the poet's love for Fanny Brawne caused him to question continually the reasons that had led him to such a financially insecure choice of career. Yet as an archetypal Romantic Keats felt he had little choice but to obey his poetic impulse.

At his best Keats was an original though he had an extraordinary mimetic gift: he was a writer who combined an inquiring modern mind with an almost Elizabethan response to the sheer luxury of language. He gathered together in his poetry all those stylistic ingredients that contributed to an impressive literary texture. The result disturbed the taste of his time. Keats's artful attempts to produce seemingly spontaneous poetry, verse that apparently emerged fresh from the inspirational moment, seemed emotionally indecent to literary minds conditioned by the metrically precise prosody of Pope. The Neoclassical ideal eliminated self-indulgent obscurity and encouraged clarity so the reader was forcefully directed to the subject matter of the predictably measured verse. Keats was unwilling, and temperamentally unable, to conform to this artificial tradition. His models were Spenser and Shakespeare and he attempted to duplicate their verbal density by producing poetry that ostentatiously drew attention to itself. He threw euphony and alliteration, sensuousness and sensitivity together with such enthusiasm that the finished product possessed an abundant verbal charge. In addition to his sense of the musical power of words, Keats had a strong pictorial imagination so that the poetry he composed was constantly alive to the possibilities of synaesthesia, as witness this description of a posy from the first item in his first collection of *Poems* (1817):

A bush of May flowers with the bees about them;
Ah, sure no tasteful nook would be without them;
And let a lush laburnum oversweep them,
And let long grass grow round the roots to keep
                                          them
Moist, cool and green; and shade the violets,
That they may bind the moss in leafy nets.

This egregiously rejected the criterion of 'a complete couplet inclosing a complete idea' as demanded by John Wilson Croker, co-founder of the influential Tory journal *Quarterly Review*.

At any time such idiosyncratically expressive talents would have provoked comment but Keats managed to turn his position into a predicament by setting his texts in controversial contexts. From the beginning Keats's reputation was discussed in terms of his relationship with Leigh Hunt; and for the Tory literary establishment the Hunt connection contaminated Keats's poetry. Hunt's *The Story of Rimini* (1816) caused offence for two reasons: first it was written in prison as he served a sentence for an attack on the Prince Regent; second it rationalized the poetic liberties clumsily taken by Hunt in the name of a pseudo-Wordsworthian theory insisting on 'a free and idiomatic cast of language'. Hunt championed Keats in the *Examiner* as a new poet who seemed to embrace all his radical ideals. In 1816 Hunt drew his public's attention to Keats's 'ardent grappling with Nature' as shown in the sonnet 'On First Looking into Chapman's Homer'. Then Keats's volume of *Poems* (1817) was ecstatically received by Hunt as the production of 'a young writer of genius' with 'an intense feeling of external beauty'. The fact that the book was dedicated to Hunt, began with a line from *The Story of Rimini*, and included a sonnet 'Written on the Day that Mr Leigh Hunt Left Prison' categorized Keats as a willing disciple and made it easier for colleagues to dispose of him. Wordsworth* told Haydon that Keats was 'a youth of promise too great for the sorry company he keeps', while the more irascible Byron* was initially more extreme for he wrote to John Murray that Keats was a 'miserable Self-polluter of the human mind' (4 September 1820) and that 'such writing is a sort of mental masturbation' (9 September 1820). Actually Keats was too deeply imaginative to take Hunt seriously as an artistic mentor though he was obviously grateful for the older man's encouragement; his attraction to Hunt's political style and poetic

pace amounted to a passing fancy rather than a permanent infatuation.

During 1817, the year in which his first collection materialized in print, Keats was formulating a theory that would describe how his own method of work involved an enormous and overwhelming aesthetic response to whatever happened to stimulate him. In a celebrated letter to his brothers George and Tom, written on 22 December, Keats said, 'at once it struck me what quality went to form a man of achievement, especially in literature, and which Shakespeare possessed so enormously – I mean *negative capability*, that is, when a man is capable of being in uncertainties, mysteries, doubts, without any irritable reaching after fact and reason . . . with a great Poet the sense of Beauty overcomes every other consideration, or rather obliterates all consideration.' Keats believed in an immediately expressive poetry because he was personally prepared for every creative emergency and his poetic faculty was trained to pursue his aesthetic ideal. Hardly surprisingly, then, he began his new long poem with a credo:

A thing of beauty is a joy for ever:
Its loveliness increases; it will never
Pass into nothingness.

Endymion (1818), a poem brooding on a mythological theme, became less of an achievement than a polemical exhibit. Between them Shelley and Byron perpetuated the myth about Keats's death being directly caused by its adverse criticism. In his preface to *Adonais*, Shelley stated, 'The savage criticism on his Endymion, which appeared in the *Quarterly Review*, produced the most violent effect on his susceptible mind; the agitation thus originated ended in the rupture of a blood vessel in the lungs; a rapid consumption ensued.' In 1823 Byron published Canto XI of *Don Juan* and endorsed Shelley's opinion in a memorable couplet:

Tis strange the mind, that very fiery particle,
Should let itself be snuffed out by an article.

Inevitably subsequent critical discussion of Keats cast the commentators into one of two opposing camps: those (eventually forming the majority) who sought to make posthumous amends by placing Keats's poetry way above criticism; and those few who felt he had been justly put in his place. However much Keats resented the attacks on his work he was sufficiently tough-minded to cope with literary antagonism. What he mainly resented was the slight on his supposedly inferior social status. Thus it was not the attack in the *Quarterly* that mainly depressed him but the prior notice in an intellectually ambitious Scottish periodical.

Endymion was prefaced by an apologia in which Keats crassly anticipated criticism by describing his poetic romance as 'a feverish attempt, rather than a deed accomplished' and identifying himself as an inexperienced adolescent (though he was all of twenty-two). This concession was quickly taken up by *Blackwood's Edinburgh Magazine* of August 1818 which published, over the cryptic signature 'Z', John Gibson Lockhart's attack on the 'Cockney School of Poetry'. Lockhart diagnosed the disease of *Metromanie* (or compulsive poetry-writing) and found Keats to be a chronic victim on the evidence of 'the calm, settled, imperturbable drivelling idiocy of *Endymion*'. Lockhart, aware of Keats's social origins, also observed that Keats's 'Endymion is not a Greek shepherd, loved by a Grecian goddess; he is merely a young Cockney rhymester, dreaming a phantastic dream at the full of the moon.'

As usual Keats was attacked as an associate of the 'worthless and affected' (and, of course, politically motivated) Leigh Hunt, author of the 'odious and incestuous *Story of Rimini*'. Lockhart dismissed the whole Keatsian package by stamping it with his personal seal of political disapproval: 'Keats belongs to the Cockney School of Politics, as well as the Cockney School of Poetry.' Keats took grim exception to this insult to his integrity and heartily despised Lockhart for it. A month after Lockhart's review came John Wilson Croker's unsigned piece in the *Quarterly Review* (dated April 1818 but delayed until late September). Again Keats's work was used as a weapon with which to beat the dangerous Leigh Hunt: 'This author is a copyist of Mr Hunt, but he is more unintelligible, almost as rugged, twice as diffuse, and ten times more tiresome and absurd than his prototype.' Whereas Lockhart's scorn had been withering, Croker's criticisms concentrated on Keats's supposed technical limitations and the poet was enough of a craftsman to concede that he was not yet an absolute master.

However, in an incredibly short time Keats had come an astonishingly long way as a creative artist. In July 1820 he saw the publication of his third and finest collection, *Lamia, Isabella, The Eve of St Agnes, and Other Poems*. This volume added to the title pieces the great Odes (to a Nightingale, on a Grecian Urn, to Psyche, on Melancholy) and 'the unfinished poem of Hyperion' and established Keats as a poet who had finally evolved various formal solutions to his own artistic challenges. His early death aroused feelings of confusion and even guilt and Keats's literary remains were scrutinized for their material contribution to a myth that had become a cult for the Victorians who drooled over Keats's beautiful textural effects. His influence on the image of the poet as heroic martyr was enormous and his verbal approach coloured all subsequent lyrical poetry. In the twentieth century there was a reaction against the uncritical acceptance of all things Keatsian and, with the appearance of a definitive edition of the letters, the poet was at last credited with intelligence as well as an insatiable appetite for beauty. Keats is now regarded as the most balanced of the Romantic poets; a Romantic, indeed, who achieved classical status.

Alan Bold

The poems appear in *Poetical Works*, ed. H.W. Garrod (1956); the prose in *The Letters of John Keats*, ed. H.E. Rollins (2 vols, 1958); the life of the poet is entertainingly and exhaustively examined in Robert Gittings, *John Keats* (1968); and the changes in his reputation are documented in *Keats: The Critical Heritage*, ed. G.M. Matthews (1971).

246
KELVIN, Lord (William Thomson) 1824–1907

British physicist

Lord Kelvin's intellectual life – during which he published some 660 scientific papers – extended over a period longer than the reign of Queen Victoria*. His capacity to combine pure science and technology placed him among the most eminent of Victorians, as well as among the foremost of nineteenth-century men of science and engineering. His position at the centre of a major correspondence network of elite Victorian physicists – G.G. Stokes, James Clerk Maxwell*, Hermann von Helmholtz*, and P.G. Tait, for example – gave him a leading role in the emergence of physics as a new nineteenth-century discipline. His employment of models and analogies within physical theory constituted a crucial phase in the development of scientific methods – both in his own time and for more recent philosophers of science. And his active part in geological and cosmological debates following the publication of Darwin's* *Origin of Species* placed him in the mainstream of nineteenth-century concerns about man's place in nature.

As an undergraduate at both Glasgow and Cambridge Universities, the Irish-born William Thomson received the best education available in Britain for a future mathematical physicist. Encouraged throughout his early years by his father – Professor of Mathematics at Glasgow – Thomson moved easily from the wide-ranging philosophical education of a Scottish university to the much narrower, more intensive mathematical training characteristic of Cambridge in the first half of the century. Having come second in the Cambridge mathematics tripos of 1845, and having spent some months in Paris learning the techniques of experimental science, Thomson – at the age of twenty-two – was elected to the Glasgow Chair of Natural Philosophy (physics) in 1846, a post which he retained until his retirement in 1899.

Thomson's achievements in theoretical and applied physics were as impressive in their range as in their quantity. His greatest intellectual debt was to the works of the influential French theoretical physicists of the early nineteenth century, most notably to Joseph Fourier's *Théorie analytique de la chaleur* (1822). Begun before the age of twenty, Thomson's earliest original work employed flow analogies from the theory of heat conduction – developed in Fourier's famous 1822 treatise – in the elucidation of electrostatic phenomena. Although never presented as a fully-fledged theory of electricity and magnetism, Thomson's imaginative use of analogical reasoning provided a historical stepping stone from Michael Faraday's* qualitative interpretation of such physical phenomena to James Clerk Maxwell's celebrated mathematical work on electromagnetism during the 1860s and 1870s.

Of more immediate significance for William Thomson's career was his application, during the 1850s, of Fourier's mathematical methods to the analysis of electrical pulses in very long telegraph wires. Overland telegraphy had spread rapidly since its birth in 1837. Greater practical and theoretical problems, however, attended the development of underwater telegraphy. When the first attempts were made to lay an Atlantic cable in 1857–8, it was apparent to Thomson that the theory of such long submarine telegraphs was not understood by the practical engineers of the day, and the project was doomed to failure. With his unrivalled knowledge of the subject, however, Thomson could advise on the optimum dimensions and operating conditions of the next attempt in 1865–6. This time the success of the venture was guaranteed, and, in recognition of his services to the nation, Thomson was knighted by Queen Victoria in 1866.

A second major strand in Thomson's theoretical work was his contribution to the new science of thermodynamics. During the late 1840s, Thomson established an absolute scale of temperature – a scale which depended not on any particular substance such as mercury or alcohol, but on theoretical laws of physics. Today, of course, every student of science refers to the Kelvin scale of temperature with its units of degrees Kelvin. At the same time, Thomson also introduced the term 'energy' in its modern sense. By 1851, two new fundamental laws of physics had been enunciated. The first law of thermodynamics stated that heat and work were mutually convertible according to an exact equivalent, a more general version being the law of energy conservation: that energy can neither be created nor destroyed by any material agency. The second law of thermodynamics, or law of energy dissipation, stated that energy, when left to itself, always tended to move from a state of concentration to one of diffusion. Although Thomson was by no means responsible for the single-handed formulation of these laws, he did bring together the work of several important predecessors and colleagues – most notably that of Sadi Carnot, James Joule*, Rudolf Clausius*, and W.J.M.

Rankine – whose separate achievements had hitherto received scant recognition from contemporaries.

Thomson was, in short, an entrepreneur in scientific ideas as much as in technology. He had a remarkable ability to discern the significance of scientific work which his contemporaries had neglected. Without Thomson's recognition, the value of much of the physical and mathematical work of Sadi Carnot, Michael Faraday, George Green and others could easily have passed unnoticed. Having thus discerned the importance of such work, Thomson would then proceed to exploit and develop its potential for as wide a range of science as possible. Thermodynamics was a striking illustration of his scientific ability. Once he had integrated the achievements of others into an established framework of mathematical and physical laws, he then developed and applied the new science to subjects as diverse as thermoelectrical phenomena and the age of the earth. At the same time, a joint project with his Edinburgh colleague, P.G. Tait, *A Treatise on Natural Philosophy*, was an attempt, never completed, to redefine the subject matter of physics as the study of energy and its transformations.

Although Thomson was not opposed to evolutionary biology as such, he was convinced that the uniformitarian geologists – whose views were well exemplified by James Hutton's remark concerning earth history: 'no vestige of a beginning, no prospect of an end' – had ignored the laws of physics. In other words in setting indefinite limits to the age of the earth, the geologists had taken no account of the new laws of thermodynamics. Thomson therefore employed these physical laws, together with available data, to calculate an approximate figure for the age of the earth and solar system, a figure which varied between twenty and a hundred million years. Whatever the actual figure, the implication was that the terrestrial time scale was too short for evolution by *natural selection* to have occurred, and that some other mechanism, such as the inheritance of acquired characteristics, must be at least as fundamental to the evolutionary process. The discovery of radioactivity in the early twentieth century, of course, demanded a new approach to the age of the earth question and thereby released biology and geology from the restraints imposed by nineteenth-century physics.

In his later years, Thomson had become very much an establishment figure in British science. He sat on numerous committees of the British Association for the Advancement of Science and played a leading role in the establishment of absolute standards of electrical measurement. Closely allied to this work were his business interests in the patenting and manufacture of scientific, navigational and electrical instruments. As though in recognition of his mature status, he became Baron Kelvin of Largs in 1892. In fact, his peerage owed much to the prominent part which he played, as an Irish-born scientist, in opposing Gladstone's* proposals for an independent Irish parliament during the 1880s. Yet his political commitments were never sufficiently dominating to divert him from his primary interests in theoretical and practical physics, interests which he maintained right up to his death. Thus it was that this Imperial scientist ended an immensely varied career with a place not far from Sir Isaac Newton in Westminster Abbey.

Crosbie Smith

Most of Kelvin's scientific papers are reprinted in William Thomson, *Mathematical and Physical Papers* (6 vols, 1882–1911), in *Popular Lectures and Addresses* (3 vols, 1891–4), and in *Reprint of Papers on Electrostatics and Magnetism* (1872). The standard 'life-and-letters' biography is S.P. Thompson, *The Life of William Thomson, Baron Kelvin of Largs* (2 vols, 1910), which contains a very full chronological list of Kelvin's publications and patents. See: J.D. Burchfield, *Lord Kelvin and the Age of the Earth* (1975), an important study of Kelvin's influence upon geological science.

247
KIERKEGAARD, Søren Aabye 1813–55

Danish writer and thinker

Kierkegaard was born in Copenhagen on 5 May 1813, the seventh and last child of Mikel Pedersen Kierkegaard, who, after being a poverty-stricken shepherd boy on the Jutland heath, became such a prosperous hosier that he was able to retire at the early age of forty and devote himself to intellectual and religious pursuits; his sombre view of Christianity, with its strong emphasis on the figure of the suffering Christ, made an indelible impression on his youngest son. Entering the University of Copenhagen in 1830 with the intention of studying theology, Søren rapidly widened his cultural interests and soon abandoned all thought of entering the church; there followed a period of uncertainty and dissipation. Shocked by the unexpected discovery of his father's moral fallibility and still more by his death in 1838 at the age of eighty-two, he turned to serious study and rapidly passed his examinations, eventually qualifying for the Master of Arts degree with a thesis, 'On the Concept of Irony with constant reference to Socrates'. It was about this time (1840) that he fell in love with a young girl called Regina Olsen, to whom he became engaged, only to break off the engagement almost immediately afterwards because of the mysterious 'secret' which he believed to debar him from marriage. His first major work was *Either/Or* (*Enten-Eller*, 1843, trans. 1944), the significant title of which already anticipated one of the main themes of his later philosophy of life. This was

followed by *Repetition* (*Gjentagelsen*, 1843, trans. 1941) which is, at the same time, the history of a young man whose poetic character makes him abandon the girl he loves, and the discussion of a new religious category indicated by the title; in 1845 appeared *Stages on Life's Way* (*Stadier paa Livets Vej*, trans. 1939) which forms a kind of sequel to *Either/Or*. Other works, published either pseudonymously or with Kierkegaard as the alleged 'editor', included *Fear and Trembling* (*Frygt og Bæven*, 1843, trans. 1941), a series of meditations inspired by Abraham's intended sacrifice of Isaac; *Philosophical Fragments* (*Philosophishe Smuler*, 1844, trans. 1936), which dealt with the relations between reason and existence and, more broadly, philosophical idealism and Christianity; and the very substantial *Concluding Unscientific Postscript to the Philosophical Fragments* (*Af sluttende uvidensk abelig Efterskrift*, 1846, trans. 1941), a sustained and sometimes humorous attack upon the metaphysics of Hegel*. *The Concept of Dread* (*Begrebet Angst*, 1844, trans. 1944) was a concise, difficult but penetrating study of a notion which has played a vital role in modern existentialism, while *The Sickness unto Death* (*Sygdommen til Doden*, 1849, trans. 1941) provided a remarkable analysis of the psychology of religious despair. Written with a more specifically Christian purpose was *Training in Christianity* (*Indovelse i Christendom*, 1850, trans. 1941), which emphasized the role of offence as a decisive religious category. Kierkegaard also published under his own name a series of orthodox Christian *Discourses* which were meant, as he said, for 'edification'. From 1834 until some months before his death he kept an extensive private journal which constitutes an important part of his complete works.

The events of his life were few. In 1846, however, a scurrilous attack by a journal called the *Corsair* which sought to hold him up to public ridicule – a task made easier by his somewhat unprepossessing physical appearance – caused him considerable distress. During his last years he launched a bitter campaign against the state church which he mercilessly berated for having acquiesced in worldly values instead of upholding true Christianity. More specifically, he directed his wrath against a distinguished member of the church, Bishop Mynster, who upon his death in 1854 had been described by one of his contemporaries as a 'witness to the truth'. Kierkegaard's polemical articles appeared first of all in the *Fatherland* and then in a series of broadsheets entitled *The Instant*. On 22 October 1855, while he was still involved in this anti-clerical campaign, he collapsed in the street, dying in hospital a few weeks later.

Kierkegaard encountered two major cultural influences in his formative years. The first was Romanticism, especially in its German form. He saw it as a movement which had opened up the resources of the inner life by releasing emotion and imagination. More especially, Kierkegaard shared the Romantics' antipathy to the philistinism of the bourgeoisie and its indifference to spiritual values. The Romantic emphasis on the notion of the infinite seemed to express a new idealism by revealing the meaning of 'passion' to a culture which had become completely enslaved by worldly preoccupations. Kierkegaard was constantly attacking the debasing effect of a materialism that ignored the force of human individuality and reduced all people to a common denominator. Nevertheless, he soon became aware of the dangers of the Romantic attitude and sharply criticized its undisciplined indulgence in feeling and fantasy as well as its partiality for an emotionalism which, as he put it, 'overflowed all boundaries'. Already in his Master's thesis he had called attention to the shortcomings of Romantic emotions which failed to acknowledge the need for morality. He pointed out that dreaming and imagination could have damaging effects upon the individual when they made him the victim of fleeting moods which deprived him of all spiritual roots. Although Romantic irony had served a useful function by liberating men from the power of false gods, it had remained too negative and destructive in its ultimate effects.

The second – and even more decisive – cultural encounter was with the philosophy of Hegel. The title of the *Concluding Unscientific Postscript* is itself a criticism of the pretensions of the Hegelian 'system'. While admitting its fascination as an imposing intellectual edifice, Kierkegaard condemned Hegelianism for its abstract and remote character; its rationalism discussed the meaning of reality in such a wide metaphysical context that it took no account of the individual human being. Kierkegaard mocked at Hegel for grandiose intellectual claims which ignored the very factor which is every man's first concern – his own reality. Although Hegel recognized the presence of contradictory and dialectical elements in human life, Kierkegaard thought that he had mistakenly sought to reconcile them by an appeal to an all-embracing absolute.

To the Hegelian preoccupation with being, Kierkegaard opposes the power of 'existence' – one of the principal notions of his whole philosophy. This explains his great sympathy for Socrates as a thinker who did not use irony as a mere intellectual device but as a means of bringing people back to the reality of the human condition. Socrates, in Kierkegaard's eyes, had the great merit of acknowledging 'the essential significance of existence, of the fact that the knower is an existing "individual"'. To exist, for Kierkegaard, is not simply to think, but to be actively engaged in deciding the meaning of one's life: every man has to choose the meaning of his existence, whether he consciously recognizes this need or not. Yet choosing one's existence means actively moving from one 'state' or 'sphere' to the next. According to Kierkegaard, there are three main 'stages of existence': the 'aesthetic', at which a man obeys only his emotions and senses while ignoring the need for any higher values; then comes the 'ethical' phase, that of the 'universal human' through which the individual is made aware of his moral obligations to other people and the need to subject his selfish impulses to some higher purpose; the third and last stage of human existence is the religious, through which the individual comes into a direct personal relationship with God. A man cannot move from one stage of existence to the next by reflection or a gradual transition but only through a kind of 'leap'.

Because the act of choice always involves uncertainty, the expression of human freedom will always be accompanied by a sense of anguish or 'dread' – a notion that has played an important role in modern existentialism. Unlike fear which is a psychological phenomenon, dread is of 'nothing' or more precisely of 'a nothing vaguely hinted at'. 'Nothing', however, is not mere negation, but an undefined awareness of the infinite possibilities of the human self – possibilities which can be realized only when the individual has moved on to the next stage of his existence. Yet such possibilities, being inseparable from freedom, arouse ambiguous feelings which Kierkegaard compares to dizziness: 'Freedom gazes down into its own possibility and grasps at finiteness to sustain itself'. The desire to choose a higher stage of existence is accompanied by apprehension in the face of the risk involved.

A category akin to dread, and yet different, is 'despair', which Kierkegaard defines as a sickness of the spirit since it involves a disruption of the proper balance between the finite and infinite elements in the human personality. The man who despairs clings defiantly to the finite elements in his being, obstinately refusing to face the demands of spiritual reality; or, if he accepts such demands, seeks a merely imaginative and abstract relationship with them. To avoid despair the individual has to allow the temporal element within him to take its meaning from the eternal, recognizing that his existence is grounded in a transcendent power greater than itself.

In view of this, it is not surprising that Kierkegaard should attach so much importance to the category of the 'individual'. By this term he does not mean some kind of excessive 'individualism', but the man who has fulfilled the authentic possibilities of his inner being, ultimately concentrating all his energies on achieving an effective relationship with God. The essential characteristic of such an individual is his 'inwardness' or 'subjectivity' (not to be confused with the more superficial concept of 'subjectivism' which is a wilful refusal to face objective reality); subjectivity involves an intense effort to grasp the absolute meaning of existence through an act of personal appropriation. That is why, for Kierkegaard, it can be identified with 'truth'. While Kierkegaard does not deny the importance of scientific knowledge, he insists that it cannot be made a criterion for the establishment of the truth which determines the meaning of human existence.

Partly for personal reasons (he felt himself to be different from other men and was prevented by his 'secret' from sharing their full humanity), partly because of the difficulty of achieving genuine individuality in a corrupt world, Kierkegaard devoted considerable attention to the idea of the 'exception' and tended to see himself increasingly in that role. Nevertheless, his writings dealt primarily with problems of the human condition and not with those of a few gifted or abnormal individuals. The religious requirements of human existence, and especially of Christianity, meant that Kierkegaard's work constantly offered a radical challenge to any form of complacency. This is especially apparent in his specifically Christian works. In the *Training in Christianity* he points out that to be a Christian means to be 'contemporaneous' with Christ. No compromise is possible with a religion whose message must be 'uttered, plainly set forth and heard'. The absolute demands upon both the individual and the church entail a steadfast refusal to compromise with worldly values. Christ himself as the God-Man cannot be idealized or distorted since he will always constitute an 'offence' to reason and common sense. Kierkegaard's growing dissatisfaction with established Christianity was bound up with what he believed to be its rejection of the absolute demands involved in the honest acceptance of Christ himself through a living act of faith. Faith, the possibility of offence and the presence of the God-Man are the three essential constituents of a Christianity that may require the individual to accept suffering as a condition of salvation.

Kierkegaard's work thus involves a decisive break with the philosophical rationalism which had culminated in the work of Hegel, and it has often been compared with that of Nietzsche* who also opposed a philosophical outlook concerned with the exclusive search for objective, rational certainty. As an 'existential thinker', Kierkegaard recognized the dialectical aspects of human consciousness and the challenging nature of the human will. It is particularly through 'philosophers of existence' such as Martin Heidegger and Karl Jaspers and an 'existentialist' like Sartre that Kierkegaard has exerted an important influence on modern thought, even though he himself never used the term 'existentialism' and would certainly have been shocked by the secular and atheistic application of his ideas. The 'dialectical theology' of Emil Brunner and Karl Barth remains much closer to his original intentions. In general, however, Kierkegaard's conception of human nature as tension and paradox and his insistence on the uniqueness of human freedom and personal commitment, anguishing though they may be, have endeared him to many writers and thinkers who are not necessarily sympathetic to his Christian aims.

His radical challenge to the complacent acceptance of rational principles has led to an experience capable of giving new meaning to the 'tragic' aspects of the human condition.

Ronald Grimsley

The main Danish sources are *Søren Kierkegaards Samlede Vaerker*, 3rd edn by A.B. Drachman, P.H. Rohde *et al.* (20 vols, Copenhagen, 1962–4); *Soren Kierkegaards Papirer*, ed. P.A. Heiberg, N. Thulstrup *et al.* (25 vols, Copenhagen, 1968–78). The most comprehensive bibliography of Kierkegaard studies is J. Himmilstrup, *S. Kierkegaard, International Bibliografi* (Copenhagen, 1962). Translations of Kierkegaard's major writings have been published by the Princeton University Press which is currently preparing a new edition of the collected writings. Important selections from the journals are *The Journals of S. Kierkegaard*, ed. A. Dru (1938) and *S. Kierkegaard's Journals and Papers*, trans. H.V. and E.H. Hong (7 vols, 1950–78). See: W. Lowrie, *Kierkegaard* (1938); James Collins, *The Mind of Kierkegaard* (1953); J. Hohlenberg, *S. Kierkegaard* (trans. T.H. Croxall, 1954); G.E. and G.B. Arbaugh, *Kierkegaard's Authorship: A Guide to the Writings of Kierkegaard* (1968); R. Grimsley, *Kierkegaard: A Biographical Introduction* (1973).

248
KINGSLEY, Charles 1819–75

British novelist and poet

Charles Kingsley was born at Holne Vicarage in Dartmoor, the eldest son of a Devonshire clergyman whose two younger children, Henry and George, also became well-known writers. Kingsley spent most of his childhood in Devon, but attended King's College School in London after his father moved to the rectory of St Luke's at Chelsea in 1836. In 1838 he entered Magdalene College, Cambridge, and was ordained four years later, obtaining a curacy at Eversley in Hampshire. In 1846 Kingsley married Fanny Grenfell, and was made rector. Eversley remained his home for the rest of his life, although he made many excursions abroad, most memorably to the West Indies in 1869, a journey commemorated in *At Last* (1870). Kingsley was a writer of verse, drama, and essays, but is best remembered for his novels, the first of which, *Yeast*, was serialized in *Fraser's Magazine* in 1848, appearing in book form three years later. In 1859 Kingsley was made chaplain to Queen Victoria*, and from 1860–9 was Professor of Modern History at Cambridge, where he was a popular, if unscholarly, lecturer. Vehemently anti-Catholic, from 1864 onwards Kingsley engaged in a heated debate with John Henry Newman*, an equally zealous convert to Catholicism, the chief result of which was the latter's famous autobiography, *Apologia pro Vita Sua* (1864). Kingsley was made Canon of Westminster in 1873, two years before his death.

During the 1840s Kingsley had some sympathy with radical politics, especially Chartism, and once asked, 'What is the use of preaching about Heaven to hungry paupers?' This concern for the poor is apparent in his first two novels, *Yeast* and *Alton Locke* (1850). Both are highly polemical, and in *Alton Locke* the aspirations of the Chartists are presented with an understanding which led to Kingsley's views being labelled 'dangerous'. This was far from the truth. While aware of the material conditions out of which Chartism arose, Kingsley himself placed no faith in charters or working-class agitation, believing change would come only from God. *Alton Locke*, tailor and poet, moves from revolutionary politics to a position essentially that of Christian Socialism, a movement of which Kingsley was one of the co-founders in 1848. Christian Socialism was a form of humanitarianism which held that social change, while desirable, was only possible through spiritual enlightenment of the ruling class; it was therefore supportive of the *status quo*. Kingsley wrote many articles in support of Christian Socialism under the pseudonym 'Parson Lot'. But as he grew older he became a pillar of the establishment, espousing many unprogressive causes, including that of the Confederate South in the American Civil War.

Kingsley was the author of several historical novels which were once popular amongst young people, though not primarily intended for them. *Westward Ho!* (1855) is an Elizabethan adventure story, culminating in the arrival of the Spanish Armada, and providing Kingsley with ample opportunity to display his anti-Catholicism. *The Water Babies* (1853) was written by Kingsley for his fourth, and youngest, child, and is a classic of children's fiction, although the delights of the unabridged version may have palled somewhat for the modern reader. The hero of *The Water Babies*, Tom, is a chimney-sweep, and the early chapters dealing with his life under the evil Grimes are excellent. But following Tom's escape and subsequent drowning, the novel moves into a world of fantasy beneath the waters of the Thames, becomes overladen with symbolism, and Kingsley gradually loses his grip on his material. The evocative detail of the river scenes testifies to Kingsley's knowledge of the natural sciences, but as a work of fiction, *The Water Babies* must be seen as a heavily flawed masterpiece.

Kingsley never wrote a wholly satisfying work of literature, and some of his novels, notably *Yeast*, are extremely clumsy. He is at his best in *The Water Babies* and *Alton Locke*, the latter being an interesting, if minor, contribution to that group of 'industrial' novels which includes Elizabeth Gaskell's* *Mary Barton* and Disraeli's* *Sybil*.

Paul Nicholls

Kingsley's other works include: *The Saint's Tragedy* (1848); *Phaeton, or, Loose Thoughts for Loose Thinkers* (1852); *Hypatia* (1853); *Glaucus* (1855); *The Heroes* (1856); *Two Years Ago* (1857); *Andromeda and Other Poems* (1858); *Hereward the Wake* (1866); *The Hermits* (1869); *Prose Idylls* (1873); and *Health and Education* (1874). See: G. Kendall, *Kingsley and His Ideas* (1947); and U. Pope-Hennessy, *Canon Charles Kingsley* (1948).

249
KLEIST, Heinrich von 1777–1811

German dramatist

Like Franz Kafka a century later Kleist experienced life as an open wound, exposed to the constant abrasions of everyday existence. There are indeed characteristics common to both that suggest parallels between them: a strict upbringing in the conventions of a rigid family; inefficiency and lack of interest in handling practical matters like money; an intensity of personal relationships and an unremitting need for love, reflected in long engagements that yet came to nothing; single-minded pursuit of artistic creation that refused to compromise with ruling tastes and expectations, leading to incomprehension and lack of immediate recognition. Kleist committed suicide at the age of thirty-four after a lifetime's unsuccessful struggle to achieve an equilibrium between his driving ambition to literary fame, intense emotional involvement in the minutest of preoccupations, and a total dedication to resolving fundamental moral and philosophical questions.

Kleist was born into an ancient military family and was initially destined for a career in that tradition, joining the Prussian army as an ensign and taking part in the Rhine campaign in 1793. His distaste for the military led him to resign his commission in 1799, after which he engaged in desultory but intensive studies in science and philosophy, partly at his home university at Frankfurt-Oder. Contact with the work of Kant and Fichte* rapidly undermined the optimism of the Enlightenment – already wavering in Europe – and induced in Kleist a despairing feeling that man is exposed to unpredictable forces, unable to control his own destiny. He discovered in the *Critique of Pure Reason* that 'we cannot decide whether what we call truth is truly true or whether it only appears so to us', and the impact of this revelation of the futility of intellect and knowledge led to the famous 'Kant crisis' of 1801, the bitter recognition that instability and uncertainty are the overriding dominants in human life. Kleist tried to dictate his own 'plan of life' in dread of becoming a 'puppet of fate', but the remaining decade of his life only reflects the haphazard nature of his activities and the turmoil of his attitudes. He engaged in restless travel and study, with fitful intermissions actually earning a living; he was even imprisoned in France as a spy in 1807. Earlier, in 1801, Kleist had wanted to join the French forces mustering in Boulogne for an attack on England, and by 1808 the Napoleonic Wars overrode his theoretical intellectual preoccupations, and he turned from speculation on the metaphysical condition of man to write about concrete situations in the context of national causes. He turned on Napoleon*, now the oppressor, 'the parricidal spirit risen from hell', with a fanatical hatred which permeated his later plays with patriotic fervour. In his last year he started a journal, *Berliner Abendblätter*, with his friend Adam Müller, but this too foundered after confrontations with the censors.

While the optimistic certainties of the Enlightenment were being crowned by the classical humanism of Goethe* and Schiller, Kleist was introducing an uncomfortable and insistent note of doubt into values that appeared rock-fast. His literary creations erupted with little warning, seemingly impelled by pathological and psychological forces that welled up from his unconscious. His work showed the disastrous effects that could follow from the lability of empirical evidence, the fragility of personal relationships, unfathomed psychological motivations and the disconcerting incursions of chance in human affairs. Not surprisingly, Goethe balked at Kleist's 'morbid mind' which aroused 'horror and revulsion in him, like a body intended by nature to be beautiful but gripped instead by an incurable disease'. Goethe and Kleist were the antipodes of the early nineteenth century: where the former sought reconciliation, resolution, synthesis, harmony and tolerance, the latter probed the vulnerability of human life, the impotence of men to master the impenetrability of existence.

In one way or another all of Kleist's works reflect his intellectual and existential convictions that it is a perilous illusion to think men are in control of their destinies. In his first play, *Die Familie Schroffenstein* ('The Schroffenstein Family', 1802), where a chain of chance and errors leads to a gruesome event, the echoes of warring families from *Romeo and Juliet* are obsessively intensified. Kleist aimed high: he worked feverishly on *Robert Guiskard*, a grandiose dramatic project that was to reconcile the ancients and moderns, Sophocles and Shakespeare. But it fell short of his vision and he destroyed the manuscript. The uneasy interaction of delicacy of feeling and harsh happening that characterized *Die Familie Schroffenstein* reappeared later; in *Amphitryon* (1807) the faithful Alkmene is subjected to a 'confusion of feelings' in her bewildering experiences with her actual husband and the god who usurps his bed. This wry 'comedy' skirts tragedy, juxtaposing a deceptive reality with the genuineness of inner feelings. Another perverse comedy, *The Broken Jug* (*Der zerbrochene Krug*, 1811, trans. 1977), displays the unreliability of experi-

ence even more acutely. A village judge finds himself in the paradoxical situation of having to elicit the truth in a case where he is the culprit. With ironic inevitability and reluctance he meticulously establishes incontrovertible facts that only deepen the confusion, for he is both pursuer and pursued.

It was in sensitivity of feeling, particularly in female characters, that Kleist found both authenticity of human nature and helpless exposure to the perplexing brutalities of existence. *Käthchen von Heilbronn* (1810), with its romantic medieval setting, is a masterly study of the total surrender and instinctive acts of a being in love, defenceless against the hard malice of life, but self-sufficient in her own inner conviction of feeling. In *Penthesilea* (1808) Kleist pursued his articulation of feminine psychology into the extreme area of pathological obsession with sado-masochistic overtones. The Amazons' leader dismembers Achilles in an overwhelming surge of love-hate, sparked off by deception, and then symbiotically succumbs herself to self-destruction. Affinities with the Romantics as well as anticipations of much later psychology are evident here, as they are in the handling of unconscious states in Kleist's masterpiece, *Prince Friedrich of Homburg* (*Prinz Friedrich von Homburg*, 1821, trans. 1978). Again the action hinges on paradox: the young Prussian soldier prince, impelled by ambitious visions and waves of love, acts as instinct and feeling dictate, but clashes with the authority and discipline of commands. He is a victor, but condemned to death. After knife-edge suspense the prince comes through to voluntary recognition of his blame, and the serene harmony of the close appears to be symbolic of Kleist's own reconciliation with the Prussian state and the reality of the *status quo*.

The strength of passions and abysses of motivation, the arbitrary consequences of error, chance and deception in human life, the random violence and fickleness that the incomprehensibility of events and behaviour produce, all mark the handful of prose stories that Kleist wrote. Taut, spare, economical, they demonstrate the dangers of rational beliefs and the precarious logic of existence. Kleist was always aware of the conflicting dichotomy in man of naive feeling and intellectual reasoning, nowhere better expressed than in the influential essay 'On the Marionette Theatre' (*Über das Marionettentheater*, 1811). He dreaded losing control of his identity, beliefs and actions, and his turbulent life and work is an enduring articulation of his struggle to come to terms with the bewilderingly enigmatic quality of existence.

Arrigo V. Subiotto

Most of Kleist's plays are mentioned above. His stories were published in two volumes (1810 and 1811). See: *The Marquise of O. and Other Stories*, trans. D. Luke and N. Reeves (1978). On Kleist: E.L. Stahl, *Heinrich von Kleist's Dramas* (1961); W. Silz,

Heinrich von Kleist: Studies in his Works and Literary Character (1961).

250
KLIMT, Gustav 1862–1918

Austrian artist

Born at Baumgartner in 1862, Klimt became the leading figure in the dynamic and forceful decorative art that characterized late nineteenth-century Vienna. He was not however simply a painter of murals for his easel paintings were equally decorative; they in turn were informed by the grave and erotic personal preoccupations that provided a driving force for the portraits, landscapes and subject paintings evolved in his studio. Indeed Klimt was to be active in many fields scarcely distinguishing between art and design, uniting the visionary themes of Symbolist art inspired by Moreau*, Toorop and Khnopff with the rhythmically lavish decorations of international Art Nouveau and Jugendstil. He designed clothes, posters and publications as well as paintings.

Klimt's initial artistic impetus came from his father, the Bohemian engraver Ernst Klimt. He studied at the School of Arts and Crafts of the Austrian Museum in Vienna, and his early commissions included decorative panels, amongst which were spandrels for the Kunsthistorisches Museum in Vienna executed in deliberately archaic styles. Klimt's tastes were subsequently to embrace many cultures from Byzantine mosaics to the asymmetrical clarity of Japanese prints. He shared with the Post-Impressionists a love of paint as pigment and employed dense firm colour, yet immense professional and academic facility ensured the continuing importance of line and drawing in his painting. All of these diverse elements were combined with great vigour in stylized compositions that were as evidently talented and competent as they were daring, for Klimt was, above all, a virtuoso of consummate skill.

His subjects owed much to the Symbolist movement that spread throughout Europe in the 1880s and into the 1890s, an introspective and fantastic art that evoked the images of imagination more often than it reflected the world of visual observation. This background permitted Klimt to revitalize allegorical painting in Austria re-enforcing its themes with personal expressive force and ravishing effects of decoration. Klimt synthesized the myriad tendencies and tastes of his day, but his art, not least as a result of sheer talent, was wholly his own.

Music (1895) exemplifies these qualities. A decisively contemporary Viennese girl plays a stylized version of an ancient lyre. Greek sculptures are depicted at either side, whilst behind the figure a riot of curling organic patterns spread out across the flat surface of the board on which Klimt has painted, appearing not simply to decorate the background wall but to spill across the painting as embodiments of sound, a symbol or equivalent of music itself. The work is at once expressive and decorative: the two were never separate in Klimt's art where design and emotion combine.

Allegory was used by Symbolist painters and writers as a vehicle for emotional expression. Klimt seized upon this to embody his own meditations upon life, love and death. Frequently morbid and erotic themes combined and made his most public works intelligible and disturbing to a wide public, projecting his fears and longings beyond the confines of personal preoccupations on to a level of public awareness that made Klimt a key figure in the cultural life of late nineteenth-century Vienna.

He was an unapologetic artist whose every mark, including abstract decorations, was informed by suggestions of the wealth and the frailty of life. *Hope* (1903) depicts with an unprecedented and immodest directness the profile of a naked contemporary and heavily pregnant young Viennese girl, who stares frankly at the viewer, with flower-studded hair, against a background of anguished figures, a large fish and a skull. The theme of fecundity and hope confronting death is extended to flat and decorative motifs. This is allegory but is also shocking in its emotionally expressive directness, at once beautiful and intensely sinister.

In 1897 Klimt became president of the newly formed Vienna Secession (Vereinigung Bildender Künstler Österreichs), the designer of its first poster and a regular contributor to its square-format periodical *Ver Sacrum*. The Vienna Secession under Klimt embraced design and architecture as much as painting, establishing a brilliant and distinctly Viennese contribution to Jugendstil.

Major undertakings by Klimt during the Vienna Secession period included murals for the Great Hall of Vienna University (*Philosophy*, 1899–1907; *Medicine*, 1900–7; *Jurisprudence*, 1903–7) which caused a scandal, and the *Beethoven Frieze* designed around Max Klinger's polychrome sculpture of the seated Beethoven* displayed at the Vienna Secession in 1902, Klimt's frieze attempting a visual equivalent of Beethoven's music and a homage to the composer whose imagination inspired so many Symbolists.

His last major decorations were no exception. In 1908 he collaborated with the architect Josef Hoffmann at the Palais Stoclet in Brussels, enclosing its dining room in a frieze that extended the tendrils of a tree of life in curling branches round the entire room, catching in their flow two embracing lovers in precious robes so densely linked and intertwined as to be visually inseparable, a single unit, allegorical, expressive and decorative.

Klimt travelled widely and received many honours. He was an honorary professor at the Academies of

Munich and Vienna in 1917. He died the following year.

John Milner

See: Fritz Novotny and Johannes Dobai, *Gustav Klimt* (1956); Werner Hofmann, *Gustav Klimt* (1972).

251
KOCH, Heinrich Hermann Robert 1843–1910

German bacteriologist

Koch, to whom modern bacteriologists turn in search of paternity, did a great deal of his most brilliant work whilst still a practitioner in Wollstein, a town in present day Poland. Koch came from a family of pious industrious Lutherans. From an early age his mother fostered in him an interest in natural history. He studied medicine at the University of Göttingen in the early 1860s and here was deeply influenced by Jacob Henle who, twenty years earlier, had written a classic defence of the theory of contagion. After a distinguished career as a medical student Koch took up a series of economically unrewarding provincial medical posts interrupted with a brief episode as a field hospital physician during the Franco-Prussian War. In 1872, by now married, he settled in Wollstein.

During the 1870s the theory that febrile diseases were caused by parasitic agents began, after a period of relative dormancy, to be heatedly debated. In France, Louis Pasteur* had asserted the fermentative activity of the fungi and in England Joseph Lister* had described his antiseptic treatment. By the 1870s many bacteria had already been observed though their relation to disease remained questionable. Koch, a partisan of the parasitic theory, had part of his home equipped as a laboratory and in 1873 began a study of anthrax.

Koch developed techniques for culturing the bacteria known to be found in the blood of diseased sheep. He described their life cycle, the formation of spores, and the capacity of these latter to resist marked environmental changes. He then showed anthrax only developed in mice when inoculated with viable organisms or spores. Koch's report on the aetiology of anthrax was published in 1876 with the help of the botanist Ferdinand Cohn. At this time Koch was also investigating the question of wound infection and in 1878 published a monograph on the subject. This essay first stated the criteria, later known as 'Koch's postulates', which are necessary for a disease to be identified as bacterial in origin.

Bacteriological success brought social rewards and in 1880 Koch moved to an important government post in Berlin in the Imperial Department of Health. Here with a small army of disciples, Koch worked out and perfected most of the basic laboratory techniques of modern bacteriology. In 1882 he announced his greatest triumph, the demonstration of the infectious nature of tuberculosis and the identification of the bacillus, an organism particularly uncooperative in attempts to culture it. In 1884 during scientific trips to Egypt and India Koch described the bacillus associated with cholera, isolating it both from victims of the disease and their drinking water. In 1885 he became Professor of Hygiene at the University of Berlin. Further social and scientific success flowed his way until his death. Most notable was his identification of the causal organisms in a variety of tropical diseases, his inspiration and training of a whole generation of famous bacteriologists and immunologists, and his receipt of the Nobel Prize.

Koch's life, however, was far from serene. Pugnacious and arrogant, his relationships with Louis Pasteur and Rudolph Virchow were marked by their acrimony. In the domestic arena his unhappy marriage ended in 1893 after his infatuation with a young actress. Scientifically his claims for the therapeutic value of 'Koch's fluid', tuberculin, an extract from the culture of tubercule bacilli, brought him, finally, shame and reproach. If ever one man however can claim to have created, and over-inflated a science, it is Robert Koch.

C.J. Lawrence

Gesammelte werke von Robert Koch (2 vols, 1912). His classic work on anthrax has appeared in English, 'Die Aetiologie der Milzbrand-Krankheit begrundet auf die Entwicklungsgeschichte des Bacillus Anthracis', *Beiträge zur Biologie der Pflanzen*, 2, pp. 277–311 (1876), trans. as 'The Etiology of Anthrax based on the Ontogony of the Anthrax Bacillus', in *Medical Classics*, 2, pp, 787–820 (1937–8). See E. Metchnikoff, *The Founders of Modern Medicine: Pasteur, Koch, Lister* (1939).

252
KRASIŃSKI, Zygmunt, Count 1812–59

Polish poet and dramatist

During his lifetime Krasiński only published his writings anonymously. This unusual fact offers a revealing insight into a fundamental aspect of the poet's biography and psychology. Dominated and influenced by his father Wincenty Krasiński, a legitimist aristocrat, supporter of the tsarist regime, and enemy of Polish patriotic movements, Krasiński lacked the moral willpower to affront his parent with his nationalistic art. This pusillanimity and inability to act independently dominated his life and were the source of much spiritual torment. Ironically, in many of his writings Krasiński extols the virtues of action over thought. Further, whilst recent scholarship has downgraded the poet's artistic achievement in relation to that of Mickiewicz* and Słowacki, it is precisely the philosophic depth of his writing which is now considered his principal attainment.

Despite Krasiński's close association with the traditions of Polish national struggle, he was not a political exile. However, he spent the majority of his time abroad after 1829, when his father sent him to Geneva, where he deepened his knowledge of English Romanticism and came into contact with Henry Reeve and Henrietta Willan, who respectively had a deep intellectual and an emotional influence on the young man. His Romanticism, which had been earlier stimulated by a reading of Mickiewicz and by efforts to write historical romances à la Walter Scott*, was thus cemented.

The insurrection of 1830 aroused ambivalent feelings in Krasiński, which were to condition his subsequent outlook. Whilst attracted by the rebels' patriotic fervour, at the same time he began to move closer to his father's position, attacking the revolutionary and violent nature of the uprising. In the attitudes to class of the patriots, he perceived a threat to the aristocracy, which he considered the flower of the Polish nation. Similarly, the insurrection stimulated his historical interests, which he pursued through a reading of Herder and Hegel*, and contemporary French historians, developing a providential vision founded upon the belief that out of a future catastrophe would emerge a new order.

Krasiński's two dramatic masterpieces, *The Undivine Comedy* (*Nie-Boska Komedia*, Paris 1835, trans. 1924) and *Irydion* (Paris 1836, trans. 1927), the former written in 1833 and the latter planned even earlier, are born out of these turmoils. Both plays primarily propound the poet's historical theories, attacking political violence and exalting divine providence, although *The Undivine Comedy* also investigates through the central figure of Count Henry the limitations and dangers of an overdeveloped poetic imagination. Krasiński's lack of faith in the masses and his undermining of the figure of the poet are unusual Romantic perspectives. *The Undivine Comedy* with its overt Dantesque structuring, formal excellence and universalizing intentions is much superior to the structurally weak *Irydion*, which belongs rather to the traditions of Polish Messianism.

Emotional turmoils dominate these years of Krasiński's life until the early 1840s when his friendships with Delfina Potocka and the philosopher August Cieszkowski restored some equilibrium (a particularly impressive part of the poet's production is his prolific letter-writing to his friends, a pursuit which he continued throughout his life). This calmer phase finds expression in the more optimistic poem *Przedświt* ('The Hour Before Dawn', Paris, 1843) and the collection *Psalmy przyszłości* ('Psalms of the Future', Paris 1845). From 1846 until his death in Paris (which had also

been his birthplace), the poet became increasingly involved in political activities, whilst his emotional sufferings returned and continued.

Zygmunt G. Barański

The most complete editions of the poet's writings are *Pisma*, ed. J. Czubek (8 vols, 1912), and *Dzieła*, ed. L. Piwiński (13 vols, 1931). See: J. Kleiner, *Zygmunt Krasiński: Dzieje myśli* (2 vols, 1912); M.M. Gardner, *The Anonymous Poet of Poland: Zygmunt Krasiński* (1919); T. Pini, *Krasiński. Zycie i twórczość* (1928); M. Janion, *Zygmunt Krasiński – debiut i dojrzałość* (1962); *Zygmunt Krasiński. Romantic Universalist. An International Tribute*, ed. W. Lednicki (1964); Z. Sudolski, *Zygmunt Krasiński* (1974); Z. Sudolski, *Krasiński. Opowieść biograficzna* (1977).

253
KROPOTKIN, Petr Alekseyevich 1842–1921

Russian anarchist

Born in Moscow to a wealthy aristocratic family, Kropotkin's education in the Corps of Pages was intended to make him either a courtier or a soldier. His brief period as a page to Alexander II left him sceptical of the emperor's liberal reputation. From 1862 to 1867 Kropotkin served in the army in Siberia where he took a great interest in natural history and geology. He then studied mathematics at St Petersburg University and pursued his scientific investigations with such distinction that in 1871 he was invited to become secretary to the Imperial Geographical Society. He declined the post on the grounds that he had no right to such pleasures when others were struggling for a scrap of bread.

This was a crucial decision. Kropotkin now devoted himself to political activities and joined a socialist propaganda circle; he was duly imprisoned in 1874. After escaping to Switzerland in 1876 he won a reputation as the leading exponent of European anarchism. His activities led to expulsion from Switzerland and imprisonment in France. In 1886 he settled in England where he made a living by writing and speaking, principally on anarchism. Following the February Revolution of 1917 in Russia Kropotkin was able to return to his native land. Although on good terms with Kerensky, prime minister of the Provisional Government, Kropotkin declined a ministerial post on principle. After the October Revolution his relationship with Lenin's Communist dictatorship was distinctly uneasy until his death in 1921.

Kropotkin was unrelenting in his opposition to the power of the state. His own strength was as a peaceful propagandist, though he could have been more prompt to condemn bomb-throwing by other anarchists. The decision of 1871 was indeed crucial but it was not a turning-point. Kropotkin had been distressed for some time at the misery of others less distinguished and privileged than himself. He was influenced by Herzen*, Proudhon* and Bakunin*. Marx's* emphasis on conflict and his attempts to reduce human behaviour to pseudo-scientific laws had little appeal for Kropotkin who had an acute insight into the totalitarian potential of Marxism. To this extent he aligned himself with Bakunin against Marx; but Kropotkin's positive cast of mind distinguishes him from Bakunin, whose frivolous bellicosity led him to concentrate primarily on destruction.

Kropotkin's central doctrine was mutual aid, or a constructive refutation of sociological Darwinism. He respected Darwin* for his *Origin of Species* (1859) and did not deny that the struggle for existence was an element in evolution. However, he thought that some of Darwin's followers, notable T.H. Huxley* in the late 1880s, were excessively preoccupied with the struggle. Still more unsound, in Kropotkin's judgment, was the application of this evolutionary principle to society: as a counterbalance he cited the way in which animals protect each other and drew a sociological parallel with the cooperation amongst groups of peasants and tribesmen which he had observed in Siberia. Kropotkin was also strongly influenced on a visit to Switzerland by the craftsmen's guilds of the Jura watchmakers which he regarded as living proof of the possibility of cooperative activity without state intervention.

Private property would, in Kropotkin's system, be abolished so that both products and the means of production could be shared. Equal rewards for all would replace wages, regardless of the contribution to society made by the recipient. Although division of labour destroyed the human spirit, industrialization was to be welcomed: the machine would provide men with sufficient leisure to recoup their spiritual energies in agri-cultural exertions. It will come as no surprise in this context that Kropotkin was friendly with William Morris* and admired by Tolstoy*. The only form of organization envisaged by Kropotkin was the spontaneous federation of those directly involved to make practical arrangements for their work and daily life. These federations would collaborate with others to make larger groupings. The structure would start from the bottom and work upwards to avoid creating a state, socialist or otherwise, which would always intervene from on high in the individual's affairs.

Though neither a Marxist nor a Leninist, Kropotkin was a communist in his own way. If his trust in goodwill (doubtless stemming from his own benevolent nature) was naive and Utopian, his humane reflections are still a valuable corrective to the usual viciousness of Russian radical thought.

In his time Kropotkin was an important figure in European radical circles, though more on account of his character than his ideas. He was later to influence Gandhi and to enjoy something of a cult revival amongst youth movements of the Left in the 1960s and 1970s.

R.M. Davison

The bibliographical details of Kropotkin's writings are of immense complexity. The following list simply indicates the editions most easily accessible in English. By Kropotkin: *Memoirs of a Revolutionist* (1971); *Mutual Aid* (1972); *The Conquest of Bread* (1972); *Selected Writings on Anarchism and Revolution*, ed. Martin A. Miller (1970); *The Essential Kropotkin*, ed. Emile Capouya and Keitha Tompkins (1976). About Kropotkin: George Woodcock and Ivan Avakumović, *The Anarchist Prince* (1950); Martin A. Miller, *Kropotkin* (1976); P. Avrich, *The Russian Anarchists* (1967); Andrzej Walicki, *A History of Russian Thought from the Enlightenment to Marxism* (1980).

L

LAFORGUE, Jules 1860–87

French poet

Six years after Jules's birth in Montevideo, most of the Laforgue family moved to Tarbes in France and then returned to Uruguay in 1867. Jules and his older brother Émile stayed on in Tarbes, for their education at the *lycée* (these schooldays form the background of *Stéphane Vassiliew*, published 1946). The rest of the family were back in France in 1875 and settled in Paris the following year. Jules pursued his education at what is now the Lycée Condorcet, but never brought it to a successful conclusion, failing the *baccalauréat* three times and thus denying himself access to a professional career. Laforgue's mother, pregnant for the twelfth time, died in 1877, and Jules was left in Paris with his eldest sister, Marie, when his father returned to Tarbes in 1879. In these months of loneliness and poverty, Jules read widely in poetry and philosophy, in particular Schopenhauer* and Eduard von Hartmann's *Philosophy of the Unconscious* (French trans. from German, 1877), and made valuable personal contacts: Paul Bourget, Gustave Kahn, Charles Henry. 1881 found him attending the course in aesthetics given by Taine* at the École des Beaux Arts and in the employment of Charles Ephrussi, art-collector and later editor of the *Gazette des Beaux-Arts*, as a secretary, sharing his employer's enthusiasm for the Impressionists. Before the end of the year, Bourget and Ephrussi had secured for Laforgue the post of French reader to the Empress Augusta of Germany. For the next five years, Laforgue followed the empress in her annual progress, from Coblenz to Berlin to Baden-Baden, each year spending two months of the summer with his family in Tarbes. Laforgue's agenda of 1883 indicates an ill-defined affair with a member of the imperial entourage, R. His literary energies were devoted to art journalism and poetry – *Les Complaintes* appeared in 1885, as did *L'Imitation de Notre-Dame la Lune*. In 1886, Laforgue took English lessons in Berlin with Leah Lee, whom he married on 31 December. In the meantime, Kahn had founded a review, *La Vogue*, and was pleased to publish anything that Laforgue sent him; to be singled out among Laforgue's contributions are his translations of Walt Whitman* and his free-verse poems, arguably the first free verse in France, later collected as *Derniers*

Vers (1890). But Laforgue's health was rapidly deteriorating; he died on 20 August 1887, of tuberculosis, the illness that killed his wife the following year.

Although in sympathy with Taine's deterministic thinking, Laforgue could not consent to his aesthetic idealism, or to his belief in the moral utility of art. For Laforgue, the determining force is in part Schopenhauer's blind and aimless Will, the force of appetite, driving mankind pointlessly on to a pointless end; the only remedies are to be found in the contemplative equilibrium of Art or a life-denying asceticism that produces nirvana. Hartmann's Unconscious has nothing to do with Freudian notions – though Laforgue's submarine and foetal imagery moves in that direction – and is Schopenhauer's Will recast in fashionable physiological and neurological terms: a synthetic and relativized Absolute, individual and collective, a compound of unconscious idea and unconscious will. Aesthetically, the Unconscious had positive attractions for Laforgue, was an invitation to let himself go, to write associatively, capriciously, as the Unconscious 'dictated'; in practical terms, the Unconscious justified a nihilistic fatalism, reducing man to a set of reflexes, a plaything of pre-ordained patterns of instinct. The difficulty of Laforgue's relationships with women is ascribable to his fear of love's inevitable degradation to reproductive processes, and to his conviction that woman was the agent of sexual mindlessness, though he recognized that her enslaved condition was to blame for her sexual hypertrophy. He aspired to a more fraternal relationship with women, without ulterior motive or self-abandonment.

In a world in which sexuality and instinct are incurable illnesses, the sun, source of life and fertility, is shunned. Laforgue looks, rather, to the moon, the principle of sterility, total suspendedness, pure contemplation, the 'navel of Nothingness'. Anaemic and tubercular, the moon is a call to love which is a mockery of love. The spleen of the lunar nihilist is concentrated in Sunday, the idle day, the provincial day, dedicated to bourgeois ritual and complacent, illusory metaphysics, when the untouchable *communiantes* disguise their bodies in exercises of spiritual hygiene. These *communiantes* are the same girls who play the piano in suburban streets, practising their pieces to the metronome of their own existences. Laforgue's instrument is the barrel-organ, the Don Quixote and the fall-guy of music, the instrument of the *complainte*, mechanical enough to capture the metrical naiveties of popular song, but dissonant and uneven enough to be self-ironic. Not surprisingly, the two *personae* who dominate Laforgue's work are Hamlet and Pierrot. Hamlet, as he appears in the prose burlesques *Moral Tales from Jules Laforgue* (*Moralités légendaires* (1887, trans. 1928)), is the brother of Yorick, impulsive but undecided, never in possession of himself, finding in words all necessary evasions and yet a route, too, to transcendence, discouraging Ophelia from unavoidable self-depravation. Pierrot, masked beyond knowledge, is caught in the limbo between spurned day-to-dayness and ideals desired but not believed in, an acrobat in attitudes, a juggler with concepts; moon-lover, his expressionless floured face is a measure both of his ironic detachment and total vulnerability.

The kind of poetry that could cope with the beckonings of the Unconscious, with the succession of masks assumed by the hypertrophic dandy and dilettante, will-less, afloat in the fluid, ungraspable present, had to be peculiarly available, available to changes of tone and register, to sudden deviations, tangents, afterthoughts, and above all uncommitting, anticipating nothing. And yet it had also to be sufficiently poised, in a formal sense, to maintain its self-reflexive quality and to give leverage and discipline to its irresistible ironies. After the derivative, philosophical eloquence of the early poems of *Le Sanglot de la Terre* ('The Lament of the Earth', collected 1901), Laforgue moved into the multivocal, contrapuntal, heterostanzaic and heterosyllabic structures of *Les Complaintes*, oscillating, with their vocalic elisions, false liaisons, ungrammaticalness, often imparisyllabic lines, neologisms, exploration of savant vocabularies, between colloquial carelessness and learned meticulousness ('I possess my language in a more minute, more clownish way'). These are poems of monologue and dialogue, involving the reader as a potential interlocutor, so that processes of self-identification with the text are impossible for him. Instead, he is totally without privilege and *point de repère*, as subject to manipulation and textual double-cross as any *personae* within the text. Furthermore, because the text is ventriloquial, quotational, intertextual, it is already a metalanguage; there are no situations to penetrate through to, no person behind textual 'personality'; one can get only as far as the changing disguises, the shifts between different kinds of situation denoted by different kinds of text, in an infinitely recessive allusiveness. In the *Derniers Vers*, ('Last Poems') although the text is still highly allusive and wobbles between the urgency of exclamation and the shrugs of *points de suspension*, there is more tonal coherence, more consistency of stance. Laforgue's free verse is never far from regular structures and the attitudes embedded in them; it leans on the ready-made, the better to make it only approximate, vulnerable to corrosive innuendoes; and rhyme, now irregular and improvised, op-

erates both as the motor of association of ideas and as a constant cue to the text for merciless self-scrutiny.

If Laforgue has left his mark on the work of Apollinaire, Fargue, Toulet, Derème, Supervielle, it is the Anglo-American world that owes him most. In the 1928 Introduction to Pound's *Selected Poems*, Eliot speaks of Laforgue as 'if not quite the greatest poet after Baudelaire*, ... certainly the most important technical innovator', and admits that the free verse he began to write in 1908 or 1909 'was directly drawn from the study of Laforgue together with the later Elizabethan drama'. *Prufrock and Other Observations* (1917) abounds in Laforguian echoes, but most commentators on the connection find in Eliot a greater control, a greater ability to break out of the prison of personality, a greater sustainedness in the development of idea and utterance, less sheer verbalism, than in Laforgue. Pound claimed that Eliot's respect for Laforgue was less than his own. In his essay 'Irony, Laforgue and Some Satire' (1917), Pound praises Laforgue for being nine-tenths critic, for making a poetry out of literary poses and clichés which act, none the less, as vehicles for personal emotion. Elsewhere, he speaks of Laforgue's rediscovery of logopoeia, 'the dance of the intellect among words', a use of language which foregrounds usage and in which the meaning of words lies in the ideological assumptions of their habitual contexts. Textual borrowings are harder to trace, but the 'Hugh Selwyn Mauberley' cycle has many Laforguian turns. Laforgue's presence is also to be found in the poems of Aldous Huxley (*The Burning Wheel*, 1916), Edith Sitwell, Hart Crane and Wallace Stevens.

Clive Scott

See: M.Collie, *Jules Laforgue* (1977); J.-L.Debauve, *Laforgue en son temps* (1972); M.-J.Durry, *Jules Laforgue* (1952); E.J.H.Greene, *T.S.Eliot et la France* (1951); L.Guichard, *Jules Laforgue et ses poésies* (1950); W.Ramsey, *Laforgue and the Ironic Inheritance* (1953); D.Arkell, *Looking for Laforgue: An Informal Biography* (1979)

255
LAMARCK, Jean Baptiste Pierre Antoine de Monet de 1744–1829

French biologist

Born the eleventh son of a poor Picardy nobleman, Jean Baptiste de Lamarck was trained for the priesthood. On his father's death (1760), he began a military career that was, however, cut short by illness (1768). He became a medical student (1767–71), studying widely and acquiring dated chemical and physical ideas which discredited much of his later work. At the same time he devoted himself to botany, and came under the influence of Georges Louis de Buffon, one of the first scientists to notice the effect of environmental changes on organisms. Encouraged by Buffon and Rousseau, Lamarck published his *Flore françoise* ('French Flora', 1779) and was elected to the Academy of Sciences. After serving on a government commission that visited foreign gardens and museums, he became director of the herbarium at the Royal Gardens. During the tumult of the French Revolution these bodies were reorganized, and Lamarck emerged as professor of the 'zoology of lower animals' at the new National Museum of Natural History, an institution which he had urged the government to found. Although without any experience in invertebrate zoology, he was able to do some of his most valuable work in this field, beginning with his *Système des animaux sans vertèbres* ('Scheme of the Invertebrates', 1801), a major step in classifying invertebrates.

Lamarck married three or four times, and had eight children, most of whom died young. He was an eccentric, lacking in social graces, and remained poor all his life. As secretaries two of his daughters became indispensable, especially in his last ten years when he went blind. During his lifetime his great contribution to biology was not recognized, despite prolific writings on botany, anatomy, palaeontology, evolution, and invertebrate zoology. He died a pauper in Paris.

In Lamarck's work the heritage of eighteenth-century France left its mark, most notably in the concept of *progress* in contrast to a static view of life. The biological corollary of the latter was a belief in the fixity of species, as expounded by Georges Cuvier*, whereas the progress-idea allowed for the perfectibility of species by *transformation* over time.

This background, combined with acute observational powers, helped free Lamarck from many traditional views, at least in biology – a word which he himself coined in 1802. Thus in his *Flore*, a great descriptive botany, he reversed the assumption that classification should proceed from the complex or general to the simple. In this way observed characteristics of species provided the basis of his taxonomy rather than some dubious theoretical principle. As well, this book introduced a valuable dichotomous key for identifying plants.

Lamarck continued this work in a multi-volume systematic botany, *Dictionnaire de botanique* ('Dictionary of Botany', 1783–95), before moving into non-botanical fields. At the National Museum he produced great works on invertebrate taxonomy and morphology, beginning with the still valuable *Système*, a brilliant empirical classification based on Cuvier's anatomical work. In his *Recherches sur l'organisation des corps vivans* ('Researches into the Organization of Living Bodies', 1802) he studied animal structure. Combining his zoological ideas and numerous observations he continued

his classification and expounded his evolutionary hypothesis in *Zoological Philosophy* (*Philosophie zoologique*, 1809, trans. 1914), which he elaborated into the seven-volume *Histoire naturelle des animaux sans vertèbres* ('Natural History of Invertebrates', 1815–22), the climax of his research and thought. In this latter work he also established invertebrate palaeontology on the foundations of his extensive knowledge of fossils. Through this series of books Lamarck provides us with the basic divisions of the animal kingdom. He was the first to classify animals into vertebrates and invertebrates, and the latter into such fundamental groupings as crustacea, arachnida, etc.

During these years Lamarck also produced his *Hydrogeology* (*Hydrogéologie*, 1802, trans. 1964), in which he postulates a history of the earth based on a series of great floods which leave deposits that build up the continents. This is one of the first works recognizing the vast breadth of geological time.

Lamarck's interests ranged over a wide spectrum of science, which he viewed, as an eighteenth-century natural philosopher, as one whole linked by general principles. He was disturbed by the growing specialization and separation of the sciences, as exemplified by Antoine Lavoisier and the new chemistry, which made no attempt to fit into an overall view of nature. This Lamarck attacked in *Recherches sur les causes des principaux faits physiques* ('Researches into the Main Physical Causes', 1794) and in *Réfutation de la théorie pneumatique* ('A Refutation of the Pneumatic Theory', 1796). In these works he tried to resurrect the traditional four-element theory of chemistry in a revised form stressing the importance of 'fire'. He attempted to reunite all science by explaining chemical compounds and reactions, physical and chemical laws, and even life on this basis.

Lamarck's theoretical bend towards generalizing, however, proved most fruitful when it combined with his practical ability to gather and analyse data, for together they gave birth to 'transformism', the first carefully worked out theory of evolution.

Lamarck and others had recognized that there were similarities between some fossils and some living organisms. But this discovery raised the questions: what is the significance of these similarities, and why do only some fossils have living analogues? At the same time Lamarck was encountering difficulties in classifying some museum specimens of invertebrates which did not seem to isolate into distinct species. His solution to these problems was transformism: organisms change over time, one species leading into another; species are not created individually but are descended one from another. The first organisms arise by spontaneous generation and evolve because of a natural tendency to increasing complexity and because of a drive to perfection based on his four-element chemistry.

The mechanism of change is environmental.

Changes in habitat alter an organism's needs and habits. Organs which aid adaptation to this changed environment are strengthened; those which are detrimental or of no use atrophy and disappear. Thus environmental changes *directly* cause physical changes in organisms, and such acquired characteristics are then inherited. For example, in the distant past, the giraffe's environment changed so that browsing in trees became beneficial. To permit this habit, its neck and legs lengthened, and these changes were passed on to its offspring.

Lamarck's evolution theory has exerted a strong influence on later generations, even though aspects of it have been discredited. His motive force for evolution, the drive for perfection, is based on his unacceptable chemistry. As well he offers no explanation for the apparent immutability of some species over time. (He implies organisms should always respond to external change by useful modification.) Most renowned of the 'errors' of Lamarckism is the theory of inheritance of acquired characteristics, for which no unimpeachable and meaningful examples have been found. In fact, modern genetics makes it most likely that natural selection and DNA mediate and restrict the environment's impact on organisms, which thus becomes *indirect*.

In the oft-recurring controversy on the relative importance of environment and heredity in determining biological phenomena and especially human characteristics, Lamarck has been repeatedly summoned as principal witness for the cause of environment – by anti-Darwinian evolutionists, by Lysenko and Stalin, and by many other camps. Probably he would have seen nothing strange in this, as he always saw himself as a philosopher.

Michael Scherk

Other works include: *Illustration des genres* (1791–1800); *Mémoires sur les fossiles des environs de Paris* (1809); *Système analytique des connaissances positives de l'homme* (1820). Some texts are translated in *Lamarck to Darwin: Contributions to Evolutionary Biology*, 1809–1859, ed. H.L.McKinney (1971). See: The Open University, *The History and Social Relations of Genetics* (1976); H.G.Cannon, *Lamarck and Modern Genetics* (1959); H.G.Cannon, *Evolution of Living Things* (1958); Alpheus S.Packard, *Lamarck: The Founder of Evolution* (1901).

256
LAMARTINE, Alphonse-Marie-Louis de Prat de
1790–1869

French poet, diplomat and statesman

Lamartine was born at Mâcon (Saône-et-Loire), but spent most of his childhood at Milly where the family had a small country property. He was the eldest of six children, and the only son. He was educated for a short time at a boarding school at Lyons and then at the Jesuit college at Belley, leaving at the age of seventeen. Neither his Catholic education nor the strict piety with which his mother conducted the life of her household were able to give Lamartine any immediate direction to his life, and he was thirty before he settled to a regular career, taking up a post in the diplomatic service on his marriage in 1820 to an English girl, Maria Anna Elisa Birch. This is also the year in which his first volume of verse, *Méditations poétiques* ('Poetic Meditations') appeared. After ten years, spent mainly in Italy, Lamartine decided to go into politics, and after a slow start made a growing reputation in the Chamber of Deputies as an enlightened Republican. This reputation reached its zenith in 1848 when he was made head of the provisional government following the fall of Louis-Philippe, a precarious office which he lost in the aftermath of further insurrections. With the rise to popularity of Louis-Napoleon, who was elected president in the December of the same year, Lamartine's political career began to wane, and he returned to private life in 1851, burdened with huge debts. The last quarter of his life was spent in a bitter struggle to keep his head above water by the writing of commissioned books and articles, mostly historical and critical. His death in 1869 passed relatively unnoticed in the Parisian press.

Lamartine's original ambition was to make a reputation as a poet, and this he succeeded in doing from the moment of his first published work. These 'poetic meditations' had been carefully developed through practice and experiment in the years of apparent idleness before 1820. Lamartine found his point of departure in the elegy as it had emerged from the hands of Parny towards the end of the eighteenth century; later on, he also underlined the influence of Ossian. From Parny he took the device of concentrating two opposed themes within a single poem in order to strengthen the emotional impact; in Ossian he observed the appeal to the imagination of vaguely delineated landscapes. The first reactions to his poetry, all strongly favourable, were based on the fact that its readers saw the arrival of a new poet directly in touch with the outlook of the new period (which was Royalist and Catholic), respectful of poetic traditions and conventions, but capable of a lyrical intensity that gave fresh life to the accepted verse forms. Subsequently, Lamartine himself defined his contribution to French poetry as residing in the immediacy and naturalness with which he expressed both personal and philosophical themes. 'I am the first to have brought poetry down from Parnassus and given to what used to be called the muse, in place of a conventional seven-stringed lyre, the very fibres of man's heart'. The twenty-four poems of the first 'Poetic Meditations' cover a wide range of themes, dominant amongst which is the conflict between religious doubt and belief. The orthodox religious overtones cover grades of feeling and attitude ranging from the scepticism of despair to an inspired awareness of the nature of God. The most popular pieces, however, have been those of a personal and elegiac inspiration, particularly 'Le Lac' ('The Lake'), a finely constructed ode based on intuitions about time. But the circumstances reflected in the poem, a deep, spiritualized love affair with Julie Charles, married to a distinguished scientist and dying of tuberculosis, have clung to this and other pieces and given them a personal aura. Other heroines are present in Lamartine's poetry, however, and the figure to which he gives the name of Elvire in various pieces is a composite one.

Lamartine followed up his immensely successful début with a second volume, *Nouvelles Méditations poétiques* ('New Poetic Meditations', 1823), which broke little new ground and was not so enthusiastically received. In 1830, the year of his reception into the French Academy, he published a new collection of poems, *Harmonies poétiques et religieuses* ('Poetic and Religious Harmonies'), one of the great works of religious lyricism in French. Apart from the apparently effortless sequences of deeply reflective verse, the development of the lyrical imagination revealed in this book marks a further stage in Lamartine's mastery of certain techniques which will be of value to poets later in the century: the use of images and symbols to give an emotive charge to ideas and feelings, and of short, highly melodic pieces to give elegiac undertones to the themes of doubt and unease. His fourth and last lyrical collection, *Recueillements poétiques* ('Poems of Reflection', 1839), adds little to the development of his art.

Like many poets of the French nineteenth century, Lamartine aspired to the creation of a work of epic stature, the 'Great Poem', as he called it. Two long poems mark his incomplete attempt to write such an epic: *Jocelyn* (1836) and *La Chute d'un ange* ('The Fall of an Angel', 1838). *Jocelyn* is an 'episode' centred on the lives of two fugitives from the Revolution who come together in hiding in the mountains. One is a seminarist (Jocelyn), the other a girl (Laurence) who tries to keep up the male disguise she had adopted while escaping. Idyllic friendship, turning to the strongest love when Laurence's true identity is at length revealed, is thwarted by the vows of priesthood, and the two lives are condemned to separation, redeemed in the case of the priest by austere dedication to his calling, embittered, in the case of Laurence, by hopeless compromises which lead her into the world of the *demi-mondaine*. A death-bed scene in the mountainous and inhospitable region of Jocelyn's parish momentarily reunites the lovers. Laurence, on a pilgrimage to the scenes of her idealized happiness, taken ill and dying, recognizes the priest and is recognized. A long period still remains before the priest's death secures theoretical union for the soul-mates.

Jocelyn is developed over nine 'epochs', confined to a single life span. *La Chute d'un ange* is divided into fifteen 'visions', supposedly recounted by an ancient hermit during the poet's journey through Lebanon, a journey which formed part of a grand tour of the Middle East (1832–3), and which Lamartine described in his *Souvenirs, impressions, pensées et paysages pendant un voyage en Orient* ('Memories, Impressions, Thoughts and Landscapes during an Eastern Journey', 1835). The poem, again indicated as an 'episode' in the sub-title, takes as its scene the antediluvian world and as its subject the forbidden mingling of human beings and angels, a theme which had tempted the imaginations of other poets at this period, amongst them Byron* (*Heaven and Earth*, 1822) and Vigny* ('Le Déluge', 1829), but from which Lamartine aspired to the creation of a work whose scope was far beyond these fragments. The angel Cédar, through his love for Daïdha, a girl from a nomadic tribe, takes on human form in order to rescue her when she has been caught in a net and dragged off by marauders. Successive 'visions' recount the tragic destiny of the pair. Savagely handled by the nomadic tribe, subsequently trapped in the lethal machinations of the court of the tyrant Mephed, King of Baalbek, they escape from the monstrous prisons of the city, through the force of the fallen angel, but perish in the desert, Daïdha and their twin children from starvation and thirst, Cédar on a pyre of his own making. The scenes of barbaric violence are relieved, in the seventh and eighth 'visions', by the teaching of a prophet, who reveals to Cédar and Daïdha the fundamentals of a divine code set down, in the form of a revelation followed by commandments, in a 'fragment of the primitive Book'. The doctrine is a synopsis of Lamartine's own views, an amalgam of deism, idealism and an elevated form of rationalism designed to lead towards religious certitude.

Both poems, master works in their conception and through the imaginative power controlling them, are uneven and imperfect. *La Chute d'un ange* came in for especially harsh criticism when it was published, both for its faults of technique and construction and for the unorthodox religious attitude expressed. It is also unlikely that the public was aware of the link which Lamartine intended to establish between the two works. *La Chute d'un ange* was planned as an epic of redemption, with the spirit of Cédar passing through successive stages, each one a human life. *Jocelyn* was envisaged as the last of these stages. Both poems were condemned by the Roman Church, as had been the *Voyage en Orient*, and in these three works, as in the events and decisions in Lamartine's life during the 1830s, can be seen clear signs of crisis.

The death of his daughter Julia, at the age of ten, during the tour of the Middle East, heightened the tension between doubt and belief which had long disturbed him. Success in his political life resolved, after 1839, the conflict between the claims of poetry and those of public service. When he returned to writing during the 1840s, it was as a prose writer aiming to inform and edify as wide a public as possible. His *History of the Girondists* (*Histoire des Girondins*) published in Paris in 1847 and immediately translated into English (1847–8) encouraged him by its extraordinary success. After his fall from power, he continued, mainly for financial reasons, with historical works such as his *Histoire de la Turquie* in eight volumes (1854–5), with works of fiction, and with a long series of critical and reflective articles appearing monthly under the title of *Cours familier de Littérature* ('Literature for Everyman', 28 vols, 1856–69). Two books based on lightly disguised autobiographical episodes were written during the 1840s: *Graziella*, originally serialized in a Paris newspaper and published as a book in 1852, being an account of an early love affair with the daughter of an Italian fisherman, and *Raphaël* (1849), a romanticized version of the affair with Julie Charles.

Lamartine's life therefore comprises three careers, those of a nationally acclaimed poet, a diplomat and statesman, and a popular historian and critic. None of the three has yet been finally assessed, although progress has been made with the provision of modern critical editions of some of his poetry (notably the *Méditations*, ed. F.Letessier, 1968) and of a few important studies. The writings of his last period still merit much further consideration, while his political life and action could usefully be brought into much sharper association with the interpretation of his literary attitudes and achievements.

Clifford Ireson

Other works: *La Mort de Socrate* (1823), poem; *Dernier Chant du pèlerinage d'Harold* (1825), poem; *Sur la Politique rationnelle* (1831), short tract; *Des Destinées de la poésie* (1834), essay in *Revue des Deux Mondes*; *Histoire de la Révolution de 1848* (1849); *Toussaint Louverture* (play performed in Paris, 1849); *Geneviève, histoire d'une servante* (1850), novel; *Le Tailleur de pierres de Saint-Point* (1851), novel; *Histoire de la Russie* (2 vols, 1855); *Fior d'Aliza* (1866), novel; *Antoniella* (1867), novel. A complete works of Lamartine, under the editorship of the author, appeared between 1860 and 1863, in 40 volumes, a further volume appearing in 1866 (*Oeuvres complètes . . . publiées et inédites*). No more recent edition is available, and further works appeared after his death, notably a very incomplete edition of his letters: *Correspondance* (1873–4). The authoritative edition of his poetry is the *Oeuvres poétiques complètes*, ed. M.-F. Guyard, Bibliothèque de la Pléiade (1963). See: N. Araujo, *In Search of Eden: Lamartine's Symbols of Despair and Deliverance* (1976); J.C.Ireson, *Lamartine: A Revaluation* (1969);

C.M. Lombard, *Lamartine* (1973); H.R. Whitehouse, *The Life of Lamartine* (2 vols, 1918); H. Guillemin, *Lamartine, l'homme et l'oeuvre* (1940), general survey; H. Guillemin, *Lamartine en 1848* (1948). Translations include *Jocelyn: A Romance in Verse*, trans. H.P. Stuart (1954); *History of the French Revolution of 1848*, trans. F.A. Durivage and W.S. Chase (1973; first published 1854).

257
LAMB, Charles 1775–1834

British essayist

Charles Lamb was by birth and inclination a Londoner, and he remained an inhabitant of the city for most of his life. Born and reared in the Inner Temple, where his father served as clerk and personal attendant to one of the Benchers, he was educated at Christ's Hospital, through the patronage of his father's employer. The most formative experience of his seven school years was his friendship with a contemporary schoolfellow, Samuel Taylor Coleridge*. By 1789 Coleridge had left for Cambridge, and Lamb became a trading-company clerk, at the South Sea House originally, and subsequently, from 1792 until his retirement in 1825, at the East India House. But their friendship was maintained; during the winter evenings of 1794–5 the two met frequently, and under Coleridge's influence Lamb began to produce his first fragments of poetry. In September 1796 his sister Mary, ten years his senior, killed their mother in a sudden attack of violent frenzy. Charles took upon himself sole responsibility for the remaining members of the family, and committed himself particularly to care for his sister while she lived, thus procuring her release from permanent incarceration. This decision determined the shape of his future career: unlike the majority of his literary acquaintants who were more free to take the financial risk of living by the pen, Lamb's responsibilities kept him to his clerical desk. Mary's perpetual presence in his life, and the frequent recurrence of her illness, also debarred him from marriage.

The close bond thus formed between brother and sister proved to be in many respects a fruitful and happy alliance. Together they produced several volumes of tales and poems for children, one of which, their *Tales from Shakespear* (1807), was destined to become a classic. Motivated by the desire to encourage the imaginative potential of the child, these works demonstrate the Lambs' involvement with the characteristically Romantic glorification of childhood. But darker aspects of his identification with Mary also manifest themselves in Lamb's writing. A morbid strain, apparent in works such as his sentimental novel *Rosamund Gray* (1798) and his unsuccessful verse drama

John Woodvil (1802), betrays his need to exorcize through the medium of art the horror of the family tragedy. It has been suggested that Lamb's appreciation of the writings of the Elizabethan and Jacobean dramatists, and their ability to describe a horror starkly and yet without loss of aesthetic control, also originated in this concern. Whatever the forces behind his enthusiasm, its fruit, his *Specimens of English Dramatic Poets who lived about the time of Shakespeare* (1808), served to popularize the works of these playwrights at a time when they had generally been much neglected.

In his notes to the *Specimens* and in two of his 1811 essays, 'On the Tragedies of Shakespeare Considered with Reference to their Fitness for Stage Presentation' and 'On the Genius and Character of Hogarth', Lamb demonstrated qualities which have since marked him as an intrinsically Romantic critic. His method of appreciating art was to lay himself open emotionally before it and to extend an imaginative sympathy through which he re-created and captured in his own writing the essence of the work in question. This emphasis on subjective feeling and imaginative involvement also characterizes the literary criticisms of Coleridge and of William Hazlitt*, another personal friend of Lamb's. Through Coleridge he also became acquainted with William Wordsworth* and with Thomas De Quincey*. The Lambs' rooms became a general meeting-place for these writers on their visits to London. In his correspondence with them Lamb demonstrated and extended his critical and descriptive skills; his charming and witty letters often served as spring-boards for ideas later reworked in his periodical essays.

Lamb's fame, however, rests on the series of essays which he wrote for the *London Magazine* in the 1820s under the pseudonym of 'Elia'. Later collected and published as *The Essays of Elia* (1823) and *Last Essays of Elia* (1833), these pieces, both in form and content, furthered his popularization of certain Romantic tenets. Like Coleridge's conversation poems, the Elia essays develop organically; that is, they do not follow a logical pre-established structure, but are formed according to the immediate associations of the moment, and conclude when the emotional processes at work in the piece achieve resolution. Elia's familiar tone and his subjective, intimate approach have proved themselves to be attractive innovations in the development of the essay form, and his style was frequently imitated by subsequent nineteenth-century and twentieth-century essayists.

Jane Aaron

Other works: (with Mary Lamb) *Mrs Leicester's School* (1808), *Poetry for Children* (1809); *The Adventures of Ulysses* (1808); *Collected Works* (2 vols, 1818); *Album Verses* (1830). See: E.V. Lucas, *The Life of Charles Lamb* (2 vols, 1905); Walter Pater, in his *Appreciations* (1889); John Cowper Powys, in his *Visions and*

Revisions: A Book of Literary Devotions (1955); Geoffrey Tillotson, 'The Historical Importance of Certain *Essays of Elia*', in *Some British Romantics: A Collection of Essays*, ed. J.V. Logan, J.E. Jordan and N. Frye (1966); Fred V. Randel, *The World of Elia: Charles Lamb's Essayistic Romanticism* (1975).

258

LANDOR, Walter Savage 1775–1864

British writer

Walter Savage Landor was the son of a Staffordshire gentleman and a Warwickshire heiress. He was a precocious, irascible and opinionated youth – being withdrawn from his school (Rugby) and rusticated from his college (Trinity, Oxford). He brought out his first volume of poems, at his own expense, *The Poems of Walter Savage Landor* in 1795 when he was twenty. The volume was followed three years later by the blank verse *Gebir: A Poem in Seven Books* (the work was enthusiastically reviewed by Southey* who became one of Landor's closest friends), and in 1802 by *Poetry by the Author of Gebir*. In 1805, on the death of his father, he inherited the family estates; he bought Llanthony Abbey in Monmouthshire intending to live as a gentleman farmer – the project was a protracted failure. As a young man he had supported the French Revolution, but his antipathy towards all forms of monarchy or empire made him suspicious of Napoleon* and in 1808 he spent several months with the northern Spanish armies resisting French imperial expansion; he donated a considerable sum of money to the cause. In 1811 he married Julia Thuillier, a girl half his own age. By 1814 the debts incurred by the Monmouthshire venture forced Landor and his wife to move to Italy where they lived successively in Como, Pisa and Florence. During the 1820s and 1830s the extensive prose work *Imaginary Conversations* appeared. In 1835 Landor quarrelled with his wife and returned to England. Between 1838 and 1858 he lived mainly in Bath; during this period he frequented the Whig social and literary salon of Lady Blessington. Further volumes of verse followed: in 1846 and 1847 *Hellenics*, 1848 *The Italics*, 1853 *The Last Fruit off an Old Tree* and in 1863 *Heroic Idylls*. He returned to Italy in 1858 and died there, in Florence, in 1864.

Though his early *Gebir* in its exotic settings and revolutionary sentiments is clearly a poem of the Romantic movement, there is nevertheless an austerity about its language which owes much to classical models. Parts of the poem were indeed first written in Latin and then translated; a complete Latin version was published a year after the English edition. The publication of a Latin poem during the closing years of the eighteenth century indicates that Landor was not courting popular so much as educated approval.

Similarly, despite his support for revolutionary causes, his poetry frequently gives the impression of a disdainful contempt for vulgar opinion. The combination of revolutionary politics and *hauteur* reminds us of Byron*, whom Landor also resembled in his love of Italy which he presented as a place of sensuous delight in contrast to the rigours of life in northern Europe. The stereotype was learnt from Landor by Browning*, and through his representations is still with us.

Though Landor did not begin to write prose until middle-age it was his prose work *Imaginary Conversations* that seemed to nineteenth-century readers his major achievement. This records conversations between characters of all times from the classical up to the present, which vary in tone and subject from the satirical to the idyllic, the political to the literary. The most famous, and one of the longest, is *The Pentameron*, an extended conversation between Boccaccio and Petrarch mainly on Dante's poetry. The work was largely written at the Villa Gherardesca in Fiesole, the setting for Boccaccio's *Decameron*.

It is a paradox that though he produced such a vast quantity of work (to the above list must be added his closet dramas – *Count Julian*, 1812, and the trilogy *Andrea of Hungary*, *Giovana of Naples* and *Fra Rupert*, 1839–40) Landor is now best known as the author of such miniatures as 'I strove with none' and 'Rose Aylmer'. His favourite poets were classical – Sappho, Anacreon, Ovid and Catullus; as is evident from the *Imaginary Conversations*, he saw the essential experiences of humanity as constant throughout history. The belief naturally leads to epigram – the vast panorama of human activity can finally be reduced to a few constant truths – and it is his shortest and most delicately turned poems that succeed best. He attempted to define what is generally rather than what is locally true, and his admiration for splendid technique as an end in itself led him to impart to the surface of his poetry as high a polish as it would take. Such self-conscious care means that emotion in his poetry is more often reflective sentiment than immediate passion. The meaning is frequently commonplace when analysed; it is the formal delicacy of his best poetry that is its charm – despite the Latin translation of *Gebir* it is the kind of verse, like Campion's, which can evaporate almost completely in translation.

There is something wilful about Landor's work and career which has attracted passionate advocacy (from, for example, Swinburne* and Pound) but which has also repelled many readers; he wrote for a clerisy which seemed to be drawn largely from other authors – already dead or yet to be born. The attitude is apparent in his remark on his own future reputation: 'I shall dine late but the room will be well-lighted and the guests few but select'.

Dick Davis

action (like most of his work in celestial mechanics) has survived as the foundation of modern treatments. Equally enduring are his methods, notably the Laplace transform, for the solution of partial differential equations.

Despite its importance for specialists, the *Mécanique Céleste* was less widely read than his semi-popular digest of cosmology, the *Exposition du Système du Monde* (1796). Through this work, Laplace's name became associated with the 'nebular hypothesis', though his theory of the formation of planets by the contraction of the sun's atmosphere differs significantly from Kant's more familiar version. Laplace also addressed the general reading public in his *A Philosophical Essay on Probabilities* (*Essai Philosophique sur les Probabilités*), 1814, trans. 1902, a popularization of the mathematically forbidding *Théorie Analytique des Probabilités* (1812). His studies of the reliability of legal testimony and the probability of the correctness of a majority verdict became particularly well known.

In religion, Laplace was cautious. But in the nineteenth century he earned notoriety for his view of a universe which, unlike Newton's, would remain stable without divine intervention: according to this view, God became an admissible but unnecessary hypothesis. He was also frequently cited as a determinist. He argued that if an infinite mind could at one moment know the positions and motions of all the particles of matter, then the whole future course of the universe could be predicted. The vision was only finally shattered by Heisenberg's uncertainty principle (1926), which set a limit, in principle, to our capacity to know both position and velocity with complete precision.

Despite the interest which philosophers and religious writers have shown in his work, Laplace was essentially a scientist's scientist. He liked to regard himself as the Newton of his age, and he tackled many of Newton's unsolved problems. But he was a tidier-up of loose ends rather than a philosophical innovator. In that respect, he fell short of the master he revered.

Robert Fox

The first four volumes of the *Mécanique Céleste* were translated, under their original French title, by Nathaniel Bowditch (1829–39). The best general study of Laplace is the book-length article on him by Charles Coulston Gillispie in *Dictionary of Scientific Biography*, ed. C.C. Gillispie, vol. 15 (1978), but see also H.Andoyer, *L'oeuvre scientifique de Laplace* (1922). See: Robert Fox, 'The rise and fall of Laplacian physics', *Historical Studies in the Physical Sciences*, vol.4 (1974); Henry Guerlac, 'Chemistry as a branch of physics: Laplace's collaboration with Lavoisier', *Historical Studies in the Physical Sciences*, vol.7 (1976).

260

LARRA, Mariano José de 1809–37

Spanish Romantic essayist and critic

In 1828 Larra abandoned his studies and founded his first periodical *El Duende Satírico del Día*. Only five numbers appeared, but the best of them reveal extraordinary powers of observation and a particularly mordant humour in a boy of nineteen. The following year, also against parental opposition, he married. The marriage was a disastrous failure and the couple separated in 1834, the year, ironically, of Larra's only important play, *Macías*, with its exalted vision of the ideal of love. *Macías* stands as an early monument in Spain to romantic passion. In it Larra launched the great Romantic formula for drama: love, thwarted by fate, leading to death. Other Spanish Romantic dramatists developed it and it survives in Verdi's* *Il Trovatore* ('The Troubadour'), and *La forza del destino* ('The Force of Destiny'), both based on plays by Larra's immediate successors. After this seminal work and a historical novel *El doncel de don Enrique el doliente* ('The Squire of Don Henrique the Sad', 1834), Larra's major writings are constituted by the theatre criticism, literary and political satire and articles descriptive of Spanish life and behaviour which he published in his own papers, *El Duende Satírico del Día* and *El Pobrecito Hablador* (1832–3) and in half a dozen others. They show him to have been at once the most intellectually analytic and the most unhappy of the Spanish Romantics. He strove to believe in the triumph of truth over error, in the inevitability of human progress and in the resurgence of Spain from her long decline. But the consistent betrayal of liberal ideas by a succession of Liberal ministries in the 1830s left him bitter and disillusioned. This, combined with his innate scepticism, his failure to enter parliament and his break with his mistress, Dolores Armijo, led to his suicide.

The Romantics' interest in 'local colour' was the origin of modern literature of observation. The Spanish *costumbrista* writers produced pleasingly picturesque and amusing descriptions of Spanish manners and especially of those figures and customs which represented characteristic survivals from the past. Larra took over this kind of essay and developed it into something quite different, drawing brilliant satirical pictures of specific aspects of life in Madrid – cafés, housing, transport, private entertainments – or of Spanish social life in general – education, class-consciousness, the public services, and so on. Where others ramble, Larra passes swiftly to concrete illustrations; where others portray types, Larra depicts individuals. His own frequent participation and first-hand comments increase the impact of his criticisms. Observed detail, humorous dialogue and ironic asides combine with comic exaggeration to present recognizable people and familiar situations in a satirical light. The result is usually amusing and sometimes hilarious, but in many of Larra's most characteristic essays an undertone of despair is present in the end. As with Galdós* later, the picture he paints is of a corrupt, empty society, rotted by inefficiency, idleness and apathy.

In his political articles Larra's commitment to the revitalization of his country sometimes compromises his satirical manner. Beginning as a moderate, he became more radical with age. But he persisted in attacking attitudes of mind rather than social evils, seeing the remedy in education and enlightenment rather than in concrete reforms. In his literary articles, however, he asserted firmly a necessary connection between literature (which for him always meant literature of ideas) and the spirit of his own times. Thus he took his stand alongside Espronceda* as a representative of genuine Spanish Romanticism as against the medievalizing, 'historical' wing of the movement, which tried to preserve traditionalistic values.

What makes Larra a great writer is the personal involvement he always brought to his writing and his courageous discussion of the problem of Spain. For this reason he was at once recognized by the Generation of 1898 as their chief precursor, since like them he combined spiritual disquiet at the personal level and a deep preoccupation with the state of his country. In 1901 members of the Generation made a pilgrimage to his grave and commemorated him as the first modern writer dedicated to 'the Regeneration of Spain'.

D.L. Shaw

See his *Obras* (1960). There are numerous editions of his essays for English-speaking students of Spanish but no translations.

261
LARTET, Edouard Armand Isidore 1801–71

French palaeontologist and prehistoric archaeologist

Although in his early years Lartet made major contributions in palaeontology, some of which helped create the atmosphere for the acceptance of the antiquity of man, and while he continued to make contributions in the field until his death, it is for the role that he played, in the last ten years of his life, in the establishment of prehistoric archaeology that he is remembered. Born into relative affluence at St-Guiraud (Gers) he trained as a lawyer at Toulouse, where he moved in circles interested in natural history, and sympathetic to the search for 'fossil man', and at Paris, where he neglected the law for lectures at the Natural History Museum. Returning to Gers he established himself as a lawyer at Auch, giving with the generosity that was to mark his whole life free consultations to the poorer peasants.

These repaid him by bringing in curiosities from their fields amongst which were the fossil bones that led him to the discovery of the Miocene palaeontological site of Sansan.

In 1834 he gave up the law to excavate full time at Sansan. Here in 1837 he made a major discovery – the first find of a fossil primate, *Pliopithecus* (*Protopithecus*) *antiquus*. This contradicted the influential Cuvier*, who, in arguing against the existence of fossil man, had stated that no other fossil primates would be found either.

The find, published in the *Comptes rendus de l'Académie des Sciences* (t. 4, 1837, p.85), established Lartet as a palaeontologist, particularly of the late Tertiary and Quaternary. In 1851 he wrote his final account of Sansan, moving to Toulouse, and two years later to Paris. While he continued with palaeontological study and publication his early work had prepared him for the contribution he was to make to prehistoric archaeology.

Since the 1830s Boucher de Perthes had been arguing, with scant success, for the acceptance of worked flints from the river gravels of north France as the work of man and contemporary with the bones of extinct animals. In 1858 and 1859 visits by the Englishmen Falconer, Evans* and Prestwich brought general acceptance to the finds of de Perthes, and in 1859 Lartet joined forces with him to defend the finds in France.

While publishing his defences of de Perthes in Geneva and London, access to the *Comptes rendus de l'Académie des Sciences* being closed to him by his opponents, Lartet turned to the study of finds being reported from the caves of south-west France. In 1857 he had been sent details of excavations in the late Palaeolithic cave of Massat in the Pyrenees, which he presented via Geoffroy-Saint-Hilaire to the Academy in the same year, coupled with a tribute to the work of de Perthes. In 1860 he visited Massat where he recognized and established the Palaeolithic dating of the mobiliary art – engraved and decorated bones and tools – previously considered Celtic.

On his return he paused to excavate the cave of Aurignac, discovering important Palaeolithic material beneath Neolithic burials. He published the results in May 1861 in the *Annales des Sciences naturelles* (Zoologie, 4e série, t. 15, p. 177), stressing the role of human agency in the accumulation of cave sediments, and establishing the antiquity of the archaeological material, which he illuminated by comparisons with ethnographic material. Influential as a text, the paper became a manifesto, and the foundation stone of a new discipline – prehistoric archaeology.

In 1863, in association with Henry Christy, an English banker interested in American ethnography, he turned his attention to the Dordogne where the list of their excavations is a roll-call of famous sites: Le Moustier, Laugerie-Haute, La Madeleine, Gorge d'Enfer. The startlingly rich material recovered was published in 1864 in the *Revue Archéologique*, then in detail in the serial publication 'Reliquiae Aquitanicae', which appeared in London between 1865 and 1875, not being completed until after the deaths of both Christy (1865) and Lartet. Beside details of the excavations and an extensive iconography, further comparisons, to American ethnographic material, were made by Christy.

It was in the 1864 paper however that the major theoretical contributions were made. Here was propounded the first explanation for Stone Age art, the simple 'art for art's sake' theory that corresponded to contemporary opinion of all art; and also the sketch of the first scheme for subdivision of the Old Stone Age, a scheme established at the Paris Universal Exhibition of 1867. This suggested an 'Epoch of the Hippopotamus' representing the Lower Palaeolithic finds from the river gravels of northern France, and a 'Cave Bear and Mammoth Epoch' and 'Reindeer Age' covering four recognized divisions in the material from the caves of south-west France, and equivalent to the Mousterian, Aurignacian, Solutrean, and Magdalenian of later terminology. Although the palaeontological nomenclature was replaced by that of de Mortillet from 1869, and although Lartet himself was not clear about whether the divisions should be regarded as chronological, they do represent those that still provide the outline structure for Palaeolithic finds in Western Europe.

Although prehistoric archaeology entered a period of intellectual decline after the glorious decade 1860–70, the work of Lartet in discovery and observation, in the publication of finds, and in systematization, provided a solid foundation for the future, and marked out many paths that have only recently been taken up again.

Appointed a professor at the Natural History Museum at the age of sixty-nine, Lartet did not live to teach formally. Weighed down by the Prussian invasion, and by fears for the safety of his son Louis, he retired to Gers in 1870, where he died the following year.

Martin Hemingway

Background and biography: the best source on the period in France is Anette Laming-Emperaire, *Origines de l'archéologie préhistorique en France* (1964). No complete biography exists, but the early years are well dealt with by L.Meroc in 'Aurignac et l'Aurignacien', *Bulletin de la Société méridionale de Spéléologie et de Préhistoire*, vols. VI–IX (1956–9). Notices published after the death of Lartet were collected in *Vie et Travaux de Edouard Lartet* (1872), the most useful of which are those of E.Hamy (with bibliography) and J.Prestwich.

262

LAUTRÉAMONT, Comte de (Isidore-Lucien DUCASSE) 1846–70

French prose poet

Ducasse exerted no influence on the nineteenth century. His two books, the rambling *Les Chants de Maldoror* (1869) and the terse, polemical *Poésies* (1870, trans. 1978), were only scrappily published in his lifetime. He died at the age of twenty-four in a Paris hotel, from unknown causes and with no reputation. A freak offspring of the age of Berlioz* and Delacroix*, it took the convulsion of the Great War to make of his passionate, delinquent art something comprehensible to a wider sensibility. He was rediscovered, reprinted and extolled as a great precursor by André Breton who found the germ of Surrealism in *Les Chants* at the moment when the beauty of a boy is described as being like 'the chance meeting on a dissecting table of a sewing-machine and an umbrella!' From this was derived a literary theory of automatic writing and random imagery, a *reductio ad absurdum* – as Mario Praz pointed out in *The Romantic Agony* – of the idea of inspiration.

Born in Montevideo, the only child of a minor French diplomat, Ducasse was an outsider by birth as well as by temperament. His mother died in his second year. At thirteen he travelled to France and was educated at *lycées* in Gascony. Just one photograph exists, a fine angry face without self-pity. *Les Chants*, complete, was published in Brussels in 1869 at the author's expense and under the pseudonym 'Comte de Lautréamont' (a name by which he is still identified). One of only three contemporary notices describes it as 'a series of visions and reflections in bizarre style, a sort of Apocalypse whose meaning it would be futile to guess'.

This is a reasonable description of the strangest product of post-Byronism, a long quasi-autobiographical meditation from Maldoror-Ducasse which reconnoitres the twilit zone between the conscious and unconscious, wakefulness and sleep, sanity and lunacy, in pursuit of 'meaning', an enterprise that is doomed in this region of grotesque and mercurial apparitions where absolute meanings cannot apply. *Les Chants* is a prismatic text whose meanings depend largely on how it is turned and by whom, a prose poem of blasphemy, guilt, lyricism, and painful frustration. The form is rhapsodic but the texture is extremely self-conscious, full of parodies, puns, collages, thefts, jokes, abrupt shifts and personal interruptions, a style without kin until the twentieth century. For Ducasse the line between inspiration and self-intoxication has vanished. He has discovered a form for psychic explosion.

As a revolutionary delinquent, Ducasse is less successful than Rimbaud* (that is, more anarchic, less nourishing to read) because he is less certain of what he is doing. Rimbaud's attempt to endow his frustrations with significance succeeds through superior artistry and its powerful links with the mythic universe, whereas with Ducasse the same desire often reveals him as laying claim to a sophistication and experience he did not possess. Mercuriality can become chronic indecision, extravagance mere ostentation, the whole insufficiently realized even within its own outlandish terms. The extent to which his mystification is deliberate is always debatable. Thus *Les Chants* has become a labyrinth not so much of meanings as of motives.

Ducasse's alienation was social and sexual. The young man's failure to exorcize the father through financial independence, extending to a general revolt against prevailing values, seeks solace in the status of aristocrat. It is the perfect solution to his predicament, an elevation above the mass which confers the freedom to despise, yet without loss of social incorporation. More: the cult of transgression which in a poor clerk would be criminality or madness becomes in the case of the nobleman a glamorous experiment in personality. Ducasse's primary purpose in *Les Chants*, and in *Poésies* also, is not the manufacture of a work of art but the construction of an identity for himself. This narcissistic tendency for art to be the by-product of the artist's concern with his own identity has characterized much *avant-garde* art since Ducasse, except that what was self-dramatization in the nineteenth century became in the twentieth self-analysis.

The vehemence of his passion for words as texture, his incestuous intercourse with other authors (abductions from the Bible, Homer, Dante, Shakespeare, Baudelaire*, for example), the obsessional repetitions, his screams for attention, and lascivious addresses to the reader – a collection of mannerisms which resurfaces with a theory behind it in the books of William Burroughs – suggest that to an exceptional degree the character of his work derives from blocked sexuality. It is against this entrapment of his own flesh within words that he is fighting with such elaborate fury. Like all outsiders, Ducasse is churned by the tension between an animal, emotional yearning for acceptance, and an aristocratic and intellectual scorn of it. The first reaches out, the second twists the contact into a variety of perversions. Being a young man, he has neither detachment nor guile, and so the writing is sentimental and belligerent by turns. But Ducasse's youth gives this torture an exquisiteness which, when all the theoretical argument has fallen quiet, is his work's abiding beauty.

Duncan Fallowell

Oeuvres complètes, ed. Hubert Juin (1973). See: Peter Nesselroth, *Lautréamont's Imagery* (1969); Michel Philip, *Lectures de Lautréamont* (1971); Alex De Jonge, *Nightmare Culture* (1973); Claude Bouche, *Lautréamont due lieu commun à la parodie* (1974).

263
LAWRENCE, Sir Thomas 1769–1830

British artist

Saluted at the age of twenty-one by Reynolds with the words 'In you, Sir, the world will expect to see accomplished all that I have failed to achieve', Lawrence showed from his earliest youth an artistic talent which allowed him to rise from humble origins to become the portraitist of an emperor and a pope. It is perhaps this facility that explains the accusations – of superficiality and even vulgarity – levelled at him since his death. Though his painting is sometimes careless, such accusations fail to do justice to his gifts: the technical brilliance, the feeling for character, the daring inventiveness of pose and the sense of glamour which in his day made him the admired of Europe.

He was born in the West Country in 1769, the son of an innkeeper who realized the boy's precocious talent and inflicted it on every guest. By the age of eleven he was in Bath and in 1787 moved to London. Not for Lawrence slow success: in 1790 *Miss Farren* (Metropolitan Museum, New York) and *Queen Charlotte* (National Gallery) were the sensation of the Royal Academy, and the carriages of the fashionable blocked the street outside his studio. What the artist offered in these, and other, paintings of the 1790s was a new manner of portraiture still close to Reynolds, but sparkling and immediate. These portraits reflected his strong interest in his sitters, and created a sympathy between them and the spectator. He developed a novel style of presentation, in which the sitter is portrayed as hugely tall against a diminutive landscape, and often, as in *Miss Murray* (Kenwood), appears to be bursting out of the canvas. Thomas Campbell remarked: 'Lawrence's sitters seem to have got in a drawing room in the mansions of the blessed and to be looking at themselves in a mirror'. At their best, his pictures of the next two decades sustained his early promise, though sometimes the mannered quality to which he was prone, the contorted or extended limbs and the bizarre poses, become obtrusive, and the brilliant highlights shine meretriciously. The problem was his success. This was professional: he painted most of the leading figures of the Regency period – notably many portraits of George IV – and was so busy that his studio was full of half-executed canvases. It was also social: he was a lion, elegant, witty and urbane, who lamented the demands made by the fashionable world, but never ceased to attend its parties. He made a great deal of money but was constantly in debt, owing largely to his amassing of one of the greatest collections of old master drawings ever made. This was offered to the nation on his death, at a minimal price, and characteristically refused.

After Waterloo Lawrence was commissioned to execute a series of paintings of the monarchs and generals of Europe, to adorn the Waterloo Chamber of Windsor Castle. All of high quality, they include what is often considered his finest work, *Pope Pius VII*, a restless, sharp-eyed prelate in a setting of ambiguous splendour. In such a major work Lawrence shows not only his ravishing gifts as a painter of surfaces, but a delicate sensitivity to character and mood. His period abroad gave him confidence and in his last years he produced a number of spectacular works such as *Lady Peel* of 1827 (Frick Collection). He became President of the Royal Academy in 1820. Lawrence's abilities achieved almost for the first time an international reputation for English painting: the British painters whom Delacroix* and his associates extolled at the Salon of 1824 were Constable* and Lawrence. His style was much imitated in the early nineteenth century, by such artists as Phillips and Shee.

Giles Waterfield

See: K.Garlick, *Sir Thomas Lawrence* (1954); M.Levey, *Sir Thomas Lawrence* (National Portrait Gallery, 1979).

264
LEAR, Edward 1812–88

British draughtsman, illustrator, watercolourist, nonsense-writer

Lear's claim that his grandfather was Danish, and spelled his name Lør, is probably a piece of fanciful embroidery. On the other hand, his claim to remember (aged three and wrapped in a blanket) the illuminations that celebrated the victory of Waterloo may not be simply the work of an exceptionally vivid imagination. However, the fact that he was the twentieth child of Anne and Jeremiah Lear is not open to question, nor the fact that his general perception of himself was both acute and wryly self-deprecatory:

> How pleasant to know Mr.Lear!
> Who has written such volumes of stuff:
> Some think him ill-tempered and queer,
> But a few think him pleasant enough.
>
> His mind is concrete and fastidious,
> His nose is remarkably big;
> His visage is more or less hideous,
> His beard it resembles a wig.

If Lear was not endowed with good looks or good health (he suffered all his life from asthma, bronchitis and epilepsy), he had an extraordinary gift for making and keeping friends. But his congenial humanity seems to have excluded any passionate sexual love.

His affections concentrated on a number of men he admired, and on his cat Foss, with whom he shared seventeen years of faithful companionship. With children, in his happiest role of 'Adopty Duncle', he was at untrammelled ease – the endearing, slightly dotty, conspiratorial inventor of fantasy words and worlds, of amazing alphabets, limericks, puns and outrageous recipes.

The limerick was not Lear's original invention, but his impromptu private entertainments for children developed the form for a popular audience (his first *Book of Nonsense*, 1846, went into thirty editions during his lifetime), and also established it as a literary style.

From the age of eighteen, however, when he earned himself a reputation as an ornithological draughtsman, Lear's chosen career was that of artist. His industry was indefatigable, but his sales were occasional. Lear was no businessman, and throughout his life depended on private patronage. As a topographical watercolourist in perpetual pursuit of the picturesque, his nomadic travels took him from the comparatively civilized delights of the Mediterranean to more intrepid romantic views in Egypt, Albania, the Near East, and, at the age of sixty, on a physically debilitating trip to India and Ceylon. This last year-long journey was undertaken at the invitation of the then viceroy, Lord Northbrook, in exchange for one or two decorative scenes!

For the last thirty-five years of his life he nursed a project that would compliment and complement his friend Tennyson's* lyric 'genius for the perception of the beautiful in landscape'. But the planned series of 200 line and colour illustrations was never completed, and Tennyson did not particularly like what he saw.

Lear suffered more than his fair share of disappointments, but was able to transform his sense of gloom and isolation into triumphant comic absurdity in his writing. Sometimes the words remain uncompromisingly unintelligible, as in a letter to a friend which begins: 'Thrippy Pilliwinx-Inkly Tinksy pooblebookle abblesquabs? Flosky? beebul trimble flosky!'

But when sounds are made sense, as with his verse creations of creatures like the Quangle Wangle, the Jumblies, the Pobble and the Dong with a Luminous Nose, Lear combines surreal comedy with a haunting, underlying personal sadness. In these verses, a mix of quirky and commonplace vocabulary with hypnotic rhythms produce what Maurice Baring has praised extravagantly as 'architectonic music'. An inspired accompaniment was provided by the caricature 'doodles'. All the precise, painstaking draughtsmanship of his 'Landskip' work was jettisoned in favour of more crude, but 'spontegetatinous' imaginative design.

In his voluminous journals, Lear never refers to his comic writing and drawing. But of his landscapes he records every detail of progress, subjects, hours worked, prices, frames, exhibitions and even the comments of friends. Lear's place in the English watercolour school may be assured, but his immortality and true originality endure in his Nonsense.

Paul Sidey

Lear's works also include: *Journals of a Landscape Painter in Albania*, etc. (1851); *Journals of a Landscape Painter in Southern Calabria*, etc. (1852); *Journal of a Landscape Painter in Corsica* (1870); *Nonsense Songs, Stories, Botany and Alphabets* (1871); *More Nonsense, Pictures, Rhymes, Botany, etc.* (1872); *Laughable Lyrics* (1877). See: Angus Davidson, *Edward Lear: Landscape Painter and Nonsense Poet* (1938); Vivien Noakes, *Edward Lear: The Life of a Wanderer* (1968); John Lehmann, *Edward Lear and His World* (1977).

265
LE FANU, Joseph Thomas Sheridan 1814–73

Irish novelist

Brought up in a County Limerick parsonage during a period of bitter agrarian unrest, Le Fanu's education at Dublin University (Trinity College) brought him in contact with dissident Tories who expressed themselves in cultural terms through the *Dublin University Magazine* and in political terms through such groups as the Irish Metropolitan Conservative Association. By 1840 he was contributing actively to both, and by 1845 he had published his first novel, *The Cock and Anchor*, in which the influence of romantic nationalism is cautiously admitted. The rebellion of 1848, however, alarmed Le Fanu, and his story of that year 'Richard Marston' is a grim tale of self-betrayal and retribution.

Political reverses and marital unhappiness worked to keep Le Fanu's literary talents safely in the channels of anonymous journalism until 1863 when he resumed novel-writing with *The House by the Church-yard*. *Wylder's Hand* and *Uncle Silas*, the best of his so-called 'sensation' novels, followed in 1864. He continued to publish roughly a novel a year, together with some rather better tales, until his death. Much of this work appeared in the *Dublin University Magazine* which he owned and edited between 1861 and 1869.

The recurring theme of Le Fanu's work is guilt, usually portrayed in the repetition of past offences in the present. *Wylder's Hand* appears to offer a more harmonious vision of man, society and history, but its optimism is entirely cancelled in *Uncle Silas* where a tightly knit symmetrical structure extends the predestined fates of the characters virtually to a metaphysical level – Le Fanu's use of Swedenborgian symbolism anticipates Yeats in this respect. Though the novels from 1864 onwards are set in contemporary England, the real locus of energy is the Irish eighteenth century, the legacy of that proud Protestant hegemony being visited upon latter-day villain-victims. In the tales and short stories, Le Fanu effectively employs supernatural conventions to explore similar themes.

Pressed for money in a society where the middle class felt obliged to play the part of a dowdy aristocracy, Le Fanu wrote too much and on uncongenial terms. His work is very uneven, and with the exception of *Checkmate* (1871) none of the late novels deserves attention. The tales, however, are almost all marked in their style by an effective blend of tension and confidence: the most important collections are *Chronicles of Golden Friars* (1871), *In a Glass Darkly* (1872), together with some of the posthumously gathered *Purcell Papers* (1880).

Seen as precursor to the Anglo-Irish Revivalists, Sheridan Le Fanu must be ranked as their inferior. Yet his subversive challenge to the myth of a noble 'protestant ascendancy' in the Augustan Age had its influence on Yeats, while *The House by the Church-yard* was incorporated into the referential structure of Joyce's *Finnegans Wake*.

W.J.Mc Cormack

Uncle Silas is available in an annotated edition with an introduction by W.J. McCormack (1981). The short stories and tales have been comprehensively treated in two collections edited by E.F. Bleiler, *Best Ghost Stories* (1964) and *Ghost Stories and Mysteries* (1975). The standard biography is W.J.Mc Cormack, *Sheridan Le Fanu and Victorian Ireland* (1980).

266
LEO XIII 1810–1903

Pope

On 7 February 1878 Pope Pius IX died, bringing to an end the longest reign in the history of the papacy. His election in 1846, in succession to the ultra-conservative Gregory XVI, had provoked Metternich, the Austrian chancellor and guardian of the traditional order in Europe, into his well-known remark that he had 'allowed for everything except the accession of a liberal Pope'. By the time of his death, however, 'Pio Nono' had long lost his early radical reputation. The revolutionary events in Rome in 1848 and 1849 had convinced the pope that there could be no compromise between the Catholic Church and faith and the principles of the French Revolution, represented in Italy in their most uncompromising form by Mazzini*. The process of Italian unification further increased the distrust and distaste which he felt for the direction history was taking. The territory of the Papal States was steadily eroded by the aggression of the Piedmontese, whose king was determined to be the first monarch of a reborn Italian nation. By the time Rome itself was seized in 1870 the estrangement of Pius IX from the modern world, symbolized by the 1864 *Syllabus of Errors* which anathematized eighty propositions, seemed complete. Its ringing final condemnation denounced the idea that 'The Roman Pontiff can and ought to reconcile himself to, and agree with progress, liberalism and civilization as lately introduced'. As E.E.Y. Hales points out, the *Syllabus* can only be properly understood in the context of Italian politics – the liberalism of Mazzini was not that of Gladstone* or J.S. Mill* however fondly English radicals may have imagined it to be – but the general point remains. Not only was Pio Nono hostile to the political developments of his day but his positive contributions to the development of church doctrine, the proclamation of the dogmas of the immaculate conception of the Virgin Mary and of Papal Infallibility, though long implied in Catholic theology, seemed to fly in the face of the spirit of the age.

The election of Cardinal Pecci as Pope Leo XIII led to a fundamental change in the relationship between the church and the surrounding world. There is a widespread tendency to see Leo's reign, marked as it is by the revival of Catholic philosophy in its Thomist form and the great social encyclicals, *Rerum Novarum* (on the rights and duties of labour and capital, 1891) above all, as a creative reversal of the stands taken by his predecessor. This is at best a half truth and was certainly not the way contemporary Catholics saw matters. The denunciations and dogmatic pronouncements of Pius IX and the elaboration of a positive social doctrine by Leo XIII were part of the same process by which the Catholic Church, deprived in so many parts of Europe of the traditional support of Christian monarchies, found itself having to make explicit the concept of social order which had previously been inherent in its teaching. The reign of Pius IX marked an essential period of self-definition necessary before the enunciation of a positive programme of restoration. If Pio Nono had made it plain what Catholic thought was not, Leo XIII concerned himself with showing what it was and how relevant it was to the concerns of the modern world.

In the encyclical *Aeterni Patris* (1879), the new Pope recommended the study of the work of St Thomas Aquinas in Christian schools and universities. This was the beginning of the Thomist revival which was to exert a considerable influence on the development of European intellectual life. Catholic intellectuals, many of them converts, played a prominent part in the late nineteenth-century reaction against positivism and materialism and in this they were encouraged by a pope who was himself a noted scholar. But more significant still was the interest which Leo XIII took in social and economic affairs. The doctrine which he developed and the policies he recommended endorsed neither the unrestrained free-market policies of contemporary liberalism nor the revolutionary alternative of socialism. The doctrine of *Rerum Novarum*, carried

further in *Graves de Communi* (1901), set the discussion of economy and society in the context of a Christian conception of the duties owed by men to each other. It provided the inspiration for the policies of the new Christian democratic and trade union movements which were growing up in many parts of Europe, and stands at the beginning of the long line of social encyclicals which extends into the present day.

In contrast to his predecessor, Leo XIII, a skilled diplomat, encouraged the full participation of Catholics in the politics of liberal states. Anti-clericalism in France and Germany had to be fought on the battleground of parliamentary politics as well as by diplomatic pressure. It was this rather than any particular affinity for the republican form of government that led the pope to advise the predominantly monarchist Catholics of France to reconcile themselves to the republic. His attitude, as Philip Hughes has put it, was that 'Liberalism having come to stay, Catholics must be shown how to live in a Liberal world, and yet live by their Catholic principles; they must learn, not only how they could survive in such a world, but how to be active loyal citizens of the liberal states'. If Leo XIII is one of the greatest of the modern popes it is because, from the beleaguered and isolated throne to which he was called, he turned a tide that seemed to threaten the survival of the Catholic Church as an effective force in the world. He renewed Catholic confidence in philosophical thought as well as in social and political action. He left the Catholic Church with the strength to face the pressures of the new century in a positive spirit.

David J. Levy

Pope Leo XIII's major encyclicals are collected in *The Church speaks to the Modern World* ed. Etienne Gilson (1959). See also: *Leo XIII and the Modern World* ed. E.T. Gargan (1961); E. Soderini, *Il pontificato di Leone XIII* (3 vols, 1932–3). For Pius IX see: E.E.Y. Hales, *Pio Nono* (1954).

267
LEOPARDI, Giacomo 1798–1837

Italian poet

A critical battle has raged over Leopardi ever since he began writing. No one denies the beauty and power of his poetry; he is the finest Italian poet since the Renaissance. The fight was over whether he was a sickly, unhappy man whose personal misfortunes were expressed in a perversely pessimistic vision of existence, or whether he was the lucid critic who penetrated the bourgeois, liberal, Catholic ideology of the industrial revolution with its belief in progress and the eradicability of suffering, and who accurately articulated a

Romantic crisis of the Enlightenment tradition. There is truth in both descriptions; the first is of little use for an understanding of the poet and his work, the second overrates what was a seriously flawed and limited critique of the society in which he lived. A third approach to Leopardi was to take little notice of the intellectual structure of his thought, and to concentrate on the formal and sensual beauty of his poetry. Unfortunately, this meant ignoring large amounts of his artistic prose and verse which were primarily philosophical.

Born on 29 June 1798 into a pious and conservative aristocratic family in Recanati, a provincial town near Macerata in the Papal States, he was brought up as a precocious scholar, studying the classics in his father's remarkable library. Later, in his poetry, he would write with nostalgia of a childhood which had been denied him and sacrificed to study. He was often ill, developed a hunchback and suffered from afflictions to his eyesight. It was with great difficulty that he escaped from Recanati, and in 1822 went to Rome, was disillusioned with what he found there, and returned home the next year. He left again in 1825, lived in Bologna and Milan working for a publisher on anthologies of Italian literature; Pisa, the only place where he said he was truly happy; Florence, where he got to know the important progressive thinkers of the time and fell unhappily in love; and finally Naples with his close friend Antonio Ranieri, who nursed him till his death on 14 June 1837.

Leopardi asked that his ideas be judged on their merits rather than being attributed to the unhappy circumstances of his life. All his writings stem from a fairly unified system of thought in which the world is seen as purely material, human consciousness as deriving from sensation, and the force that keeps the individual alive as a ceaseless desire for pleasure. Nature (the force responsible for material existence, the *natura naturans* of the scholastics) has endowed man with desires which his reason tells him can never be satisfied. The imagination creates illusions of happiness and pleasure which are threatened by the truths that reason reveals. Rousseau's influence is strong in Leopardi's view of history as a progressive falling away from a primitive natural state (a state of harmony both with *natura naturans* and with *natura naturata*), into a condition in which man is no longer inspired by hopes and illusions to deeds of nobility and magnanimity, but rather has been led to inactivity, and a cowardly refuge in the foolish boast that he can solve the problem of evil by means of his reason and the machines it has created. The history of mankind has been a move from imagination to reason, illusion to truth, and this is the path the individual follows in his growth from childhood to manhood. Poetry can work in the realm of the illusions, 'deceiving the imagination' by evoking a world with hope, without definite limits, larger than what is 'known' (ideas akin to those of the 'sublime' in England). Since man's yearning is for infinite pleasure,

it can be soothed by pleasures that hint at infinity and stimulate the imagination: vague images of vast things. In his most famous poem (*L'infinito*, 'Infinity', 1819) Leopardi sits behind a hedge atop a hill and imagines infinity beyond the hedge, drowning his thought in its immensity.

While his theory of poetry was one of escape and consolation, his practice was often very different. He used rhetoric, irony, sarcasm and invective in didactic poems: attacking Italians for the humiliating conditions in which Italy lay under the oppression of foreign rulers, mocking liberal progressives for their belief in the perfectibility of human existence through the inventions of science, pouring disdain upon the superstitions which had men believe that while the hiccough of a volcano could exterminate them, nevertheless they were immortal and of prime importance to the creator of this suffering universe – superstitions that were doubly base because they were harboured by men who had inherited an 'enlightened' culture. He exhorted men to courage and noble deeds, to the integrity to face honestly the truth of the human condition, and to the dignity of solidarity and rebellion against the evil force which had brought about this suffering.

His work can be divided into three periods. First there are the patriotic *canzoni* on Italy's lowly state, rhetorical and noble in style, the first, *All'Italia* ('To Italy', 1818), ending with the magnificent oration of Simonides over the dead Spartans. In this period come also the tender, intimate lyrics called the 'first idylls', in which he contemplates natural scenery and reflects on his own unhappiness. Few educated Italians even today would be incapable of quoting from these poems. Their apparent simplicity conceals a great deal of labour and a technical mastery that is rivalled only by Petrarch. This first period also produced philosophical poems on the injustice of man's destiny, and the alienation from nature that followed the decline of pagan religions. After a poem addressed to the ideal woman of man's imagination, impossible and ethereal, he stops writing poetry in 1823 for a few years. In this hiatus, he writes the majority of his philosophical prose satires, the *Operette morali* ('Little Moral Exercises'), consisting of fables and allegories of human existence and satirical dialogues, often modelled on Lucian, ridiculing the anthropocentrism and optimism of his contemporaries' belief in progress. The stylized, classicizing, epigrammatic prose of the *Operette* was to be influential in Italian letters for the next hundred years.

He returned to poetry during his stay in Pisa in 1828, and in the next two years composed his 'great idylls'. In *A Silvia* ('To Silvia') he compared the death of a young girl to the way nature fulfils the hopes and promises of youth; in *Le ricordanze* ('Memories') he compares those hopes with the melancholy life of the present, devoid of sensation, through evocations of life at Recanati; in *La Quiete dopo la tempesta* ('The Quiet

After the Storm') he asserts that pleasure is nothing more than the cessation of pain, and compares this to the calm following a thunderstorm; in *Canto notturno di un pastore errante dell'Asia* ('Night Song of a Wandering Asian Shepherd') he affectionately asks the moon if she can explain what is the point of our futile journey from birth to death. There is a profound pessimism in these poems, expressed in an incantatory verse of simple intensity and musicality.

His stay in Florence in the early 1830s led to a cycle of poems arising out of his unrequited love for Fanny Targioni Tozzetti. At first a eulogy of the power of love, then a meditation on love and death, then a fantasy deathbed kiss, then an ironical critique of the lover's perspective, and a harsh and bitter rejection of love as a worn-out illusion and the assertion of the 'infinite worthlessness of everything'. He now turns against the illusions that had been his solace, and writes a satirical *Palinodia*, or 'Retraction', of all his beliefs, pouring sarcasm on the liberal progressives of his time. One of his last and finest poems combines the lyrical, intimate tone of tender address to the *Ginestra*, the 'Broom', that grows humbly on the slopes of Vesuvius, with the passionate oratory of a tirade against his fellow men for their foolish pride and cowardly religious superstition.

A characteristic of Italian literary culture is the organic unity that runs through its history. Leopardi builds on recognizably Petrarchan elements, particularly in the stylized, euphonious vocabulary he uses; even the free stanza-form of his *canzoni* derives its effect from the way it compares and contrasts with the Petrarchan form. He leads back to past centuries, but also forward to ours; Ungaretti and Montale, the two most important poets of the first half of this century, are full of the influence of Leopardi. Similarly, his critique of the progressive ideology of his times has been compared to positions held by Italian Marxists in the 1968 'movement' influenced by the work of the Frankfurt school.

Christopher Wagstaff

His major works are his collection of lyric poems, the *Canti* (1831, 1835, complete in 1845), the *Operette morali* (1826, 1827, 1834), *Paralipomeni della Batracomiomachial* (1842, trans. 1974), *Pensieri* (1845), *Discorso di un italiano intorno all poesia romantica* (written 1818), *Zibaldone di pensieri* (written 1817–32) – all to be found in *Tutte le opere* (1969). Translations: *The Poems of Leopardi*, trans. G.Bickersteth (1923); *Selected Prose and Poetry*, trans. Iris Origo and John Heath-Stubbs (1966); *Essays, Dialogues and Thoughts of Giacomo Leopardi*, trans. James Thomson (1905). Biography: Iris Origo, *Leopardi, A Study in Solitude* (1953). Criticism: Francesco De Sanctis, *Leopardi* (1960); Walter Binni, *La nuova poetica leopardiana* (1947), and *La protesta di Leopardi* (1973); C.

Galimberti, *Linguaggio del vero in Leopardi* (1959); S. Battaglia, *L'ideologia letteraria di Giacomo Leopardi* (1968); G. Singh, *Leopardi and the Theory of Poetry* (1964); G. Carsaniga, *Giacomo Leopardi* (1977).

268
LERMONTOV, Yuriy Mikhailovich 1814–41

Russian writer

Best known to Russians as one of their greatest lyric poets – conventionally regarded as the natural successor to Pushkin – Lermontov was an outstanding figure in late (i.e. post-Byronic) European Romanticism as a whole, and the author of one of the most astonishing works of prose-fiction (*Hero of Our Time, Geroy nashego vremeni*) in European literature.

He traced his family origins to George Learmont, a seventeenth-century soldier of fortune (descended traditionally from the medieval bard Thomas the Rhymer), and used this supposed Scottish ancestry as a powerful symbol for his sense of rootlessness and constriction in the early poem 'Zhelanie' ('Wish', 1831). His mother died in 1817, and his childhood was marred by acrimony between his father, a small landowner, and his wealthy maternal grandmother, who brought him up partly in Moscow, partly on her distant estate, but with visits for health reasons to the Caucasus (an area that left an indelible impression on him and was to become his second homeland).

In 1830 he entered Moscow University, but left without graduating in 1832. Already his striking personality – magnetic to some, abrasive to most of those who came into contact with him – was leading him into personal discord and brushes with authority, and he had embarked on a series of amorous entanglements that generally proved wounding or unsatisfactory for one or both parties (reflected variously in the lyric poetry and in *Hero of Our Time*). On leaving university he enrolled as an officer cadet at the Guards' school in St Petersburg.

Precociously gifted in music and art as well as literature, he turned early to poetry, and from 1828 onwards a mass of juvenilia, quantitatively far outweighing his mature work, survives. Amid the derivative Romantic pessimism and general attitudinizing there are some remarkably perfect short poems: for example 'Parus' ('The Sail', 1832), 'Chasha zhizni' ('Cup of Life', 1831) and, significantly, 'Net, ya ne Bayron, ya drugoy . . . ' ('No, I am not Byron, I am different . . . ', 1832). The impact of Byron*, whom he read in English from 1830, was overwhelming, yet there was anyhow a home-bred 'Byronic' element in his psychological make-up, in his way of life and in his early writing (absorbed perhaps through Pushkin). He perceived himself as a *déraciné* wanderer, his hopes, loves and aspirations prematurely disappointed.

Lermontov throughout his career wrote narrative as well as lyric verse, and both *Demon* (1829–41, many times reworked) and the later *Mtsyri* (1839) – each with romantic Caucasian settings – have an important place in his canon. In St Petersburg from 1832–7 his flow of lyric poetry slackened, and he produced his first uncompleted experiments in prose as well as a rather lurid, socially satirical verse-drama *Masquerade* (*Maskarad*), which he unsuccessfully tried to get through the censorship in 1835–6.

Despite his precocious fluency Lermontov was rigorously discriminating towards his own work, and published little until near the end of his short life. His quite extended poetic apprenticeship lasted until 1837; in January Pushkin (at the height of his powers) was mortally wounded in a duel, and Lermontov dashed off a rhetorical poetic assault on the court circles that had hounded the great writer to his doom, *Smert' poeta* ('Death of the Poet'), to which he soon added a particularly vituperative coda. This unpublishable tirade ('worse than criminal', according to the then chief of police), passing from hand to hand, assured Lermontov's fame, but also his banishment (by the tsar's order) to active service in the campaign against Caucasian tribesmen. Illness forced a stop at the spa of Pyatigorsk; this and other travels of that period were to be an important factor in the genesis of *Hero of Our Time*. At the end of the year however he was allowed to return to St Petersburg. 1838–9 were to be his only years of relatively settled life and mature literary endeavour: he prepared a collection of his poems and the first edition of *Hero of Our Time*. But a duel and other provocative activities early in 1840 resulted in further punitive posting to notoriously hazardous military operations against the Caucasian chieftain Shamil; Lermontov fought with great distinction, but the tsar refused to decorate him. Returning in 1841 from a brief leave, he stopped again at Pyatigorsk, threw himself into social life, and on 15 July was killed in a duel with a retired officer, Martynov, whom he had teased once too often (Tsar Nicholas's comment is known: 'A dog's death for a dog'). His end came at a particularly poignant moment in view of the achievement and promise of his last year: it saw the definitive version of *Hero of Our Time*, and a renewed flowering of lyric genius that produced most of the poems by which he is remembered, among them 'Rodina' ('Homeland'), 'Poslednee novosel'ye' ('Last Housewarming'), 'Son' ('Dream'), 'Vykhozhu odin ya na dorogu . . . ' ('I go out alone onto the road . . . '), and 'Prorok' ('Prophet'). He had been planning to resign from the army and devote himself to his writing.

Though noted for a passionate strain of confessional *Ich-Dichtung*, Lermontov's verse is in fact highly varied thematically and technically. Its tone ranges from the lofty to the bitingly epigrammatic, from the song-like to the conversational, from prolixity to terseness, from resignation to rebellion; most characteristic of his originality is the breathless rhetorical piling-up of epithets and visual images, far removed from the balance and sobriety of Pushkin, to whom he none the less owed much. However he is a poet not only of the self and the passions, but of nature (whether Russian or Caucasian) – in which the fragmented human personality might find wholeness – of society and of history; ethical and philosophical themes underlie his glittering or mellifluous poetic surface.

Lermontov's rebelliousness was ambiguous; in the repressive atmosphere of Nicholas I's Russia it was bound to have political implications, but fundamentally it was an existential stance taken up in defiance of malign and inexorable destiny. Such an attitude is most fully exemplified in Pechorin, the central character of *Hero of Our Time*. This remarkable work is usually called a novel, and indeed its impact on the subsequent 'classic' age of the Russian novel was considerable; however it is *sui generis*, and Lermontov's narrator more justly refers to it as his 'chain of tales'. With its two brief but important prefaces, the work consists of seven sections, dissimilar from each other in length, in kind, in mood, in narrative manner and in point of view, arranged unchronologically, linked together solely by the personality of Pechorin (who is incidentally 'killed off' less than halfway through). What began apparently as simple (naive, indeed) travel-notes of a journey through the Caucasus is transformed into a very much more difficult journey into the interior of a human heart. There can be no conclusion to this quest, save in the structural circularity that refers the book's end back to its beginning; philosophical questions of determinism and free will, that had been obtruding themselves more and more insistently upon Pechorin, remain unresolved (which itself gives him an answer of sorts). Pechorin's amoral, destructive (indeed consciously self-destructive) and petty adventures take on a cosmic, solipsistic significance that press-gangs the reluctant reader's sympathies; the author exploits the ironic possibilities of this particularly in his two strange, cajoling prefaces, and indeed in the work's very title, which carries multiple layers of meaning. Yet this *tour-de-force* of fictional technique is written in the most lucid, modern, 'unpoetic' prose, and Lermontov's gifts as a story-teller grip the reader from start to finish – so much so that individual episodes are often (somewhat misguidedly) anthologized as short stories.

Critics often write as if Lermontov 'overcame' Romanticism in his prose and some of his late poetry, supposedly advancing into realism: but the dichotomy is a false one, reflecting only the ironic self-distancing (or self-questioning) of his maturity. He belonged to an uneasy, questing, diverse literary generation (near-coevals include Büchner*, Dickens*, Goncharov*, Kierkegaard*, Wagner*) and his thought-world was instinctively Schopenhauerian* rather than Hegelian*; he sought for peace, for the sublimation of a powerful will in a hostile world, rather than for facile spiritual uplift and progress. His best poetry (more 'finished' than Byron's, less fugitive than Heine's*) achieves a tension between spontaneous expressiveness and controlled reflection that held fresh inspiration for the twentieth-century generation of Blok and Pasternak. But his greatest monument is *Hero of Our Time*: in its experimental verve it forms a 'bridge', almost unique in nineteenth-century fiction, between the narrative intricacies of the age of Sterne and those of the age of modernism; thematically it has claims to be the progenitor of the European 'psychological novel' from Dostoevsky* to Camus; and by anybody's standards it is a compellingly readable tale.

Robin Milner-Gulland

Lermontov, *Selected Works* (Moscow, 1976), poetry, prose and drama in translation; *A Hero of Our Time*, trans. P.Foote (1966), a fluent translation, with introduction. *The Penguin Book of Russian Verse*, ed. D.Obolensky (1962), contains a judicious selection of the poetry with English prose translations. See: J.Mersereau, *Mikhail Lermontov* (1962); L.Kelly, *Lermontov: Tragedy in the Caucasus* (1977); R.Milner-Gulland, 'Heroes of their Time'?, in *The Idea of Freedom*, ed. A. Ryan (1979); C.J.G. Turner, *Pechorin* (1978); R. Freeborn, *The Rise of the Russian Novel* (1973).

269
LEWES, George Henry 1817–78

British man of letters

Little is known of Lewes's early years, except that he was born in London, had an unconventional education in schools in London, Jersey and Brittany, and began the study of medicine, which he soon gave up in favour of a life of freelance writing and bohemianism. Like his grandfather, Charles Lee Lewes, a well-known comic actor in his day, Lewes was early attracted to the theatre. Throughout the 1840s he wrote, acted, and adapted from French several farces, and was for a time a member of Dickens's* Amateur Company. In 1841 Lewes married Agnes Jervis, by whom he had four sons. A fifth, Edmund, was born in 1850, fathered not by Lewes but by his friend Thornton Hunt, son of Leigh Hunt and co-founder and editor with Lewes of a weekly newspaper, the *Leader*. Lewes registered the child as his own, thus condoning the adultery, which did not violate his freethinking principles. By the time Lewes met George Eliot* (then Marian Evans) in Oc-

tober 1851, Agnes was pregnant with her second child by Hunt. Because he had condoned the adultery, Lewes was unable to divorce Agnes and marry George Eliot, with whom he lived from 1854 until his death.

Already the author of some precocious articles in Leigh Hunt's *Monthly Repository* in the late 1830s, Lewes first visited Germany in 1838. On his return he wrote some innovatory articles on the Germans, particularly on Hegel* and Goethe* (*British and Foreign Review*, 1842 and 1843 respectively) and on Lessing (*Edinburgh Review*, 1845). In 'Hegel's Aesthetics' (1842), which was the first English article on the subject, Lewes advocated the German view of criticism as a science, not as a mere 'branch of trade'. The influence of Goethe (and Carlyle*) is apparent in Lewes's early efforts at fiction. *Ranthorpe* (written in 1842, published in 1847) is a rambling novel of education borrowing much from *Wilhelm Meister's Apprenticeship* in its broadminded study of the apparently haphazard experiences, literary and social, of the budding artist-hero. His second novel, *Rose, Blanche, and Violet* (1848), though containing some witty dialogue, is badly plotted and lacking in structure. It was not as a novelist but as an appreciative critic of others – notably Jane Austen*, Charlotte Brontë*, George Sand*, and of course George Eliot, whose talent he recognized and encouraged – that Lewes claims our attention.

Also innovatory was Lewes's article on Spinoza, published in the *Westminster Review* in 1843 and subsequently sold as a pamphlet. Lewes recalled in a later article ('Spinoza', *Fortnightly Review*, 1866) that as a young man he had joined a metaphysical society which met in Red Lion Square, one member of which, a watchmaker named Cohn, had introduced the neglected philosopher to the group. Lewes's interest in philosophy led to his giving a set of lectures on which was based his influential work, *A Biographical History of Philosophy* (4 vols, 1845–6). An introductory guide to philosophy for the interested layman, the work went through several reprintings. According to Herbert Spencer*, it was Lewes's book which first aroused his own interest in philosophy and psychology. Written in a lucid and lively style, it was a simplified study of the main directions in philosophy from Bacon (important, according to Lewes, as the introducer of a scientific Method) to 'the Bacon of the nineteenth century', Comte*. Comte's contribution was the study of social conditions and the aim to make a new science, sociology, evolved from the other known sciences. To Lewes, Comte's positivism seemed the most exciting and promising step in modern philosophy. With John Stuart Mill*, he was among the first Englishmen to accept and popularize Comte's writings. In 1853 he published an introductory study, *Comte's Philosophy of the Sciences*. However, when Comte moved away from the empirical approach of his early works to 'assume the part of pontiff, arbitrarily arranging individual and social life according to his subjective conceptions', Lewes refused to follow him, though he remained 'a reverent heretic' ('Auguste Comte', *Fortnightly Review*, 1866).

Lewes and George Eliot met through Herbert Spencer and John Chapman, editor of the radical *Westminster Review*, to which both contributed regularly during the 1850s. Indeed, throughout his life Lewes was an industrious writer of articles on topics ranging from drama and philosophy to biology and psychology. Among the periodicals to which he contributed were the *Edinburgh Review*, *Blackwood's Magazine*, the *Cornhill Magazine*, and the *Fortnightly Review*, which he helped to found in 1865 on the model of the *Revue des Deux Mondes*. Under Lewes's editorship articles were signed and there was minimal editorial interference.

A controversial figure because of his unconventional domestic situation and his freethinking opinions, he was mistrusted by some contemporaries. Margaret Fuller* thought him 'a witty, French, flippant sort of man', to Mrs Carlyle he was 'the most amusing little fellow in the whole world – if you only look over his unparalleled *impudence*', and Meredith* dismissed him as 'a mercurial little showman'. Nevertheless, partly through his own work and partly through his association with George Eliot, Lewes moved increasingly in distinguished circles. His correspondence and diaries (which, with George Eliot's, form a large manuscript collection in Yale University Library) in the 1850s, 1860s and 1870s indicate his close relations, professional and personal, with such leading Victorian thinkers as Mill, Spencer, Darwin*, Huxley*, Tennyson*, Browning*, Trollope*, and Dickens. Relations with Dickens cooled in 1853 when Lewes objected in print to Dickens's flouting of scientific possibility in the episode of Krook's spontaneous combustion in *Bleak House*. 'My Dear Dickens', wrote Lewes in the *Leader*, 'What you write is read wherever the English language is read. This magnificent popularity carries with it a serious responsibility. A vulgar error countenanced by you becomes, thereby, formidable'.

Lewes is now known chiefly as the 'husband' and encourager of George Eliot. He did, indeed, act as her literary agent, negotiating on her behalf with her publisher Blackwood. But he deserves to be known on his own account. One work for which he was celebrated in his own day and which is still admired by experts is his *Life and Works of Goethe* (1855). Lewes felt an affinity with Goethe, as can be seen from his article 'Goethe as a Man of Science' (*Westminster Review*, 1852), later incorporated into the *Life*. Like Lewes himself, Goethe had interested himself in science, particularly anatomy and botany, but was sneered at by professional scientists. Lewes was able to give Goethe full credit for his discoveries in these fields, as he himself was at work during the 1850s on *Sea-Side Studies* (1858), *The Physiology of Common Life* (1859–60), and *Studies in*

Animal Life (1862). The *Life of Goethe* was Lewes's most important and influential work. Researched in Weimar and Berlin in 1854, with George Eliot's help, it was a masterpiece of lucid, analytical biography and criticism. As George Eliot wrote, Lewes's book was 'a *natural history*' of Goethe's works, showing 'how they were the outgrowth of his mind at different stages of its culture'. Though some German critics complained that Lewes's treatment of Goethe was not reverential enough and quibbled with some of his facts, the work was a success in England and Germany, selling 900 copies in the first six weeks. Lewes announced in the preface to the edition of 1863 that the *Life* had already sold 13,000 copies in the two countries. It was, as one critic wrote, 'the crowning achievement of his general literary activity' (James Sully, *New Quarterly Review*, 1879).

During the 1860s and 1870s Lewes's main interest was scientific. Although his works were coolly received by his fellow scientists in England, Pavlov* mentioned *The Physiology of Common Life* as influential on his own early interest in physiology. And it is certain that George Eliot's frequent use in her novels of metaphors from biology to illustrate social and personal characteristics stems from the interest she took in Lewes's studies of animal life. The great work of Lewes's last years was his not altogether successful attempt to construct an empirical metaphysics by applying physiological knowledge to psychology. Of this ambitious work, entitled *Problems of Life and Mind*, Lewes published the first series, *The Foundations of a Creed*, in 1874, and the second, *The Physical Basis of Mind*, in 1877. George Eliot completed the third, *The Study of Psychology*, after Lewes's death. She also set up, with the cooperation of scientists, the George Henry Lewes Studentship in Physiology at Cambridge.

Although he desired scientific fame, it was as an astute critic of his contemporaries, English and foreign, as a popularizer of philosophy and science, and as the biographer of Goethe that he is most important. With his many interests and talents, he is a fine representative of all that was progressive in Victorian criticism, philosophy, and science.

Rosemary Ashton

Among Lewes's best critical essays are: 'Balzac and George Sand' (*Foreign Quarterly Review*, 1844); 'Currer Bell's Shirley' (*Edinburgh Review*, 1850); 'The Lady Novelists' (*Westminster Review*, 1852); and 'The Novels of Jane Austen' (*Blackwood's Magazine*, 1859). There is no biography of Lewes, but much can be learnt about him from G.S. Haight, *George Eliot: A Biography* (1968), and *The George Eliot Letters*, ed. G.S.Haight (vols 1–7, 1954–6; vols 8 and 9, 1978). See also: Anna T. Kitchel, *George Lewes and George Eliot: A Review of Records* (1933); and Alice R. Kaminsky, *George Henry Lewes as Literary Critic* (1968).

270
LIEBIG, Justus von 1803–73

German chemist

In the first half of the nineteenth century Liebig came to hold a position of great influence in the world of chemistry. His father was a Darmstadt dealer in drugs and chemicals who encouraged his son's early interest in chemistry and apprenticed him to an apothecary. He went on to study chemistry at the Universities of Bonn, Erlangen and Paris. It was in Paris that the talented young Liebig came to the attention of A. von Humboldt* who persuaded the Giessen authorities to accept the nineteen-year-old prodigy as their new Professor of Chemistry.

Liebig is often credited with the invention, in his early Giessen period, of the modern analytical chemistry laboratory. It was a claim he certainly made for himself. 'At that time,' he commented, 'chemical laboratories in which instruction was given in analysis did not exist; what people called such were rather kitchens . . . nobody knew how to teach analysis.' Liebig certainly knew how for from his laboratory there emerged most of the leading analytic chemists of his day. To publish the results that poured out from the laboratory he founded in 1832 a new journal known, since 1840, as the *Annalen der chemie* – then, as now, one of the leading journals of organic chemistry.

It was, however, as an organic chemist that Liebig first established his reputation, working frequently in collaboration with Friedrich Wöhler of Göttingen. When Liebig began his career he was faced with the enormous difficulty of actually making quantitative organic analyses. Berzelius, for example, was reported to have taken eighteen months to complete the analysis of only seven compounds. To overcome this Liebig introduced his celebrated combustion apparatus, still in use today, with which the amount of hydrogen and carbon present in organic compounds could be determined in a simple and routine manner.

With the combustion apparatus Liebig and Wöhler could at last tackle what they termed the 'primeval forest' of organic chemistry. Their main achievement was to establish, in their classic 1832 paper on the benzoyl radical, the first coherent theory of the structure of organic compounds. This arose from their analysis of a number of organic compounds such as benzoyl bromide, benzoyl cyanide and benzoyl iodide which revealed that each of the compounds consisted of the same benzoyl radical ($C_6H_5.CO-$) combined with a bromide, cyanide and iodide group respectively.

On the basis of this analysis they termed the benzoyl molecule a 'compound radical' which they defined as a group of atoms which could be present in a series of compounds, could be replaced as a whole in those compounds and could also enter as a whole into other compounds. Organic chemistry then simply became the study of such organic compounds.

Their so-called 'compound radical' theory had a relatively short life. It was soon found to have only limited application and met with strong competition from the 'type' theory of Jean-Baptiste-André Dumas. Nevertheless, despite its falsity, the theory was important for what it promised rather than for its accomplishments. By showing that order and control of even a limited and transient kind could be imposed on the organic domain they demystified its chemistry. The question was no longer whether organic molecules could be treated systematically but rather which was the best system to adopt.

By the late 1830s Liebig had just about had enough of organic chemistry. It had been an exciting but demanding period. 'We worked from break of day until nightfall,' he later recollected. In any case, he commented, with the foundations of science laid, 'the edifice may . . . be built up by workmen. Masters are no longer needed.' He was not a modest man.

Instead, he claimed of chemistry that 'only the applications attract me', that he was tired of laboratory work and when, in 1852, he moved to Munich he did so on the understanding that there would be no laboratory teaching. Thus began the second, equally important, part of Liebig's career. Many chemists before him had seen the importance of chemistry in industry; indeed the heavy chemical industry with its production of sulphuric acid, soda and bleaches had been virtually created by chemists in the first decades of the nineteenth century. They however set out to produce and market chemicals; Liebig had a deeper vision; he wanted to sell and apply chemistry.

The first step in this campaign was the publication of his enormously influential *Die Organische Chemie in ihre Anwandung auf Agricultur und Physiologie* (1840), immediately translated into English as *Organic Chemistry in its application to Agriculture and Physiology* (1840) and some seven other languages by 1848. He began by attacking the view that the fertility of the soil lay in the decayed organic matter known as humus. He had no difficulty in showing that some plant crops actually increased the amount of carbon in the soil rather than using it up. The source of the plant's carbon he correctly identified as the atmosphere.

If the success of manure in promoting growth was not by its replacement of humus, where then did it lie? Liebig argued that plants also needed certain inorganic substances which could be found in the breakdown products of manure. The implications of this were profound. If the plant absorbs not the manure directly but its inorganic decay products, then it should be possible to provide such products directly without recourse to the limited sources of manure.

In other words, there could be such things as chemical or artificial fertilizers. Liebig's analysis of the nature of such fertilizers was inadequate and done much better by John Lawes and his Rothamstead colleagues; the initial insight, however, lay with Liebig.

Liebig also published *Animal Chemistry*, (*Die Thierchemie*, 1842, trans. 1842), in which he sought for 'points of intersection of chemistry with physiology'. Although Wöhler had shown in 1828 that the organic compound urea could be synthesized in a test tube as easily as any inorganic substance, Liebig remained a vitalist. While there may not be any unique, unanalysable substances in an organism he could still insist that vital forces are needed to control the growth and development of living forms.

Derek Gjertsen

No modern editions exist of Liebig's works on agriculture and physiology. The only comprehensive biography is J. Volhard, *Liebig* (Leipzig, 1909). Substantial accounts of his work are to be found in vol. 4 of J. Partington, *History of Chemistry*, and, mainly on his vitalism, in J. Goodfield, *Growth of Scientific Physiology* (1960).

271
LINCOLN, Abraham 1809–65

Sixteenth President of the United States

Born on 12 February 1809 in Kentucky, Lincoln arrived in Illinois at the age of twenty-one, having lived the previous fourteen years in Indiana. The northwest, and Illinois in particular, was growing more rapidly in population and in the means of producing wealth than was any other region in the United States. It was a good location for an able and ambitious man. Engaging in a variety of occupations before making his reputation as a lawyer, Lincoln entered politics as a Whig, that is, as a member of the political party most committed to the idea of a strong central government in a nation defined by its regional and sectional diversity. By the time he entered national politics in the 1840s it was sectionalism and its associated problem of slavery which dominated the national political scene and Lincoln's own political career was shaped by it and was ultimately dedicated to the search for a reconciliation between the needs of the nation and the diversity of its components.

After serving a single undistinguished term in Congress during the Mexican War Lincoln was thrust into the political wilderness by the partial eclipse of the Whig Party in Illinois. He returned to the fray with renewed enthusiasm in 1854 as a result of the Kansas-Nebraska crisis. Douglas's plan for the settlement of Kansas and Nebraska attempted to take the associated issue of the expansion of slavery out of national politics by making it a matter for local self-

determination. Pro– and anti-slavery forces hastened to confront each other in the new Territory and the continued turmoil in Kansas became a reference point for the emergence of a new set of political alignments. The Republican Party, opposed to the spread of slavery, replaced the Whig Party in the North whilst the Democratic Party, purged of its northern anti-slavery elements, and reinforced by southern Whigs, upheld the equal rights of slavery. Over the course of the next six years Lincoln emerged as the leader of the Republican Party and it was the positions he took which came to define the central ground within that party. Those positions will best be understood, perhaps, when contrasted with those of his principal opponent, Stephen A. Douglas.

Both Lincoln and Douglas were nationalists but their nationalism differed. Douglas equated nationalism with expansion and democracy; the latter he conceived of in terms of the spread of American democratic institutions and of popular sovereignty, that is, local self-determination. Lincoln was less expansionist because he recognized that in the context of the mid-nineteenth century it involved less the expansion of the nation than of its sections. His commitment to democracy was, moreover, more complex than that of Douglas. It was never for him merely a matter of majority rule and certainly not one of local majorities. It was the content of politics which mattered, not merely its operations. The American Union was defined for Lincoln by its commitment to certain goals and principles. These had been enshrined in the Declaration of Independence at the moment the nation was conceived. It was the moral content of American democracy which concerned Lincoln and at the centre of a web of moral propositions was the idea of equality. He refused to contemplate the implication of Douglas's position that slavery and freedom shared an equal moral status depending upon the whims of local majorities. He also refused to contemplate the abdication of the central government from a determination of national issues in the interest of political quiet. Lincoln's sense of the past, his insistence that the Constitution be read in the light cast upon it by the Declaration of Independence, was complemented by a sense of history as an ongoing process. American ideals were belied by American practice but Lincoln conceived of a nation in which they would converge.

The slavery issue was a crucial test of the national commitment to such a vision. Arguing that the Founding Fathers had been prepared to compromise their principles with respect to slavery only because they assumed its inevitable demise, Lincoln denied the possibility that the nation could survive on the basis of a permanent coexistence of slavery and freedom. Yet the course of events in the 1840s and 1850s pointed towards a commitment in the South to the permanence of slavery and, indeed, towards a vigorous promotion of its interests. Lincoln's response was to invoke the Declaration of Independence on behalf of black as well as white Americans. Equality was a universal right. His concept of the meaning of equality was narrow when compared to that prevailing in the late twentieth century, and even when compared to some radical spirits in his own day, but it was well in advance of the majority of his compatriots. His ability, after coming close to defeating Douglas in the 1858 senatorial contest, to make his own position that of the centre of his party testifies to his political skill. It was around his ideas that the Republican Party coalesced and fought and won the presidential contest in 1860 which sparked off the secession of the South from the Union. What Lincoln posited, in essence, was the interpendence of white and black freedom. Pressing Congress in 1862 to agree to his scheme of voluntary and compensated emancipation in the loyal states he insisted that 'in *giving* freedom to the slave, we *assure* freedom to the free.'

It was his recognition that the future of the Union, as he conceived it, and the future of slavery were inextricably linked that enabled Lincoln to embark upon a political course that always carried with it the risk of civil war. It was only because the Union contained a profound moral quality that the risk was worth taking. Lincoln clearly underestimated the risk, and he equally clearly had no conception of the cost of the struggle to preserve the Union, but even with greater foresight he might have been willing to pay the price to preserve the 'last, best hope of earth'.

Lincoln's extraordinary political skill was exhibited during the Civil War in his ability to maintain the integrity of his administration, and the commitment of his party to the war, in the face of fierce opposition and of continued and severe reverses on the battlefield. The eventual collapse of the Confederacy ensured the final abolition of slavery. Lincoln's assassination, only days after Lee's surrender, on Good Friday 1865, left the even more difficult task of reconstruction in other hands, but Lincoln's work was done. In great part through the force of his own character and determination he had preserved the Union thereby guaranteeing the unity and great power of a major part of the North American continent. He had played an important role in the release from servitude of some four million human beings. Above all, perhaps, his commitment to an American purpose, to the idea of the United States as embodying certain principles, had a decisive effect, if only because of its association with the Civil War, in moulding a continued sense of American idealism. Often crass, but sometimes noble, that commitment has had a profound effect upon subsequent world history.

Duncan MacLeod

The literature on Lincoln is enormous. Larger biographies include: Carl Sandburg, *Abraham Lincoln: The Prairie Years* (2 vols, 1926) and *The War Years* (4 vols, 1939); and James G. Randall, *Lincoln the President* (4 vols, 1945–55). The best one-volume biographies are: Benjamin Thomas, *Abraham Lincoln* (1952); and Stephen B. Oates, *With Malice Toward None: The Life of Abraham Lincoln* (1977). His speeches and letters can be found in Abraham Lincoln, *Collected Works*, ed. Roy P. Basler (9 vols, 1953–5).

272
LIST, Friedrich 1789–1846

German economist

Born into a large family in the town of Reutlingen, Duchy of Württemburg, Friedrich List was first apprenticed to his father's tannery before, at the age of seventeen, entering the state administration as a clerk. By 1816 he had risen to the position of chief examiner of accounts, and his support for reform and municipal self-government led to his appointment as professor for 'State Administration and Science' at Tübingen in 1817 despite his lack of formal academic training. His increasing activity on behalf of the movement for tariff reform in Germany led however first to his dismissal in 1819, and then in 1822 to a sentence of ten months' hard labour for sedition in his role of deputy for his home town. Fleeing on pronouncement of sentence, he was arrested in Stuttgart in 1824 and interned; his release in January 1825 was coupled with exile. With wife and family he emigrated to the United States, where he once again became involved in the movement for tariff reform, this time however for the creation of protective barriers. At the same time he planned and built one of the first operating railways in the United States, and became involved in the campaign for the presidency of Andrew Jackson. In 1830 he returned to Europe as an American consul, and during his period in Leipzig from 1834–7 he was instrumental in the construction of one of the first commercial German railway lines, from Leipzig to Dresden. While his promotion of tarriff reform and railway construction was in the 1830s clearly successful, he was discouraged and spent the latter part of the decade in Paris. It was here that he began work on the book for which he became famous, *The National System of Political Economy* (*Das Nationale System der Politischen Ökonomie*, 1841, trans. 1885 and 1916), which was published in Germany. However, his restless nature would not allow him to be satisfied with this; and discouraged by what he saw as the reverses in German economic union of the early 1840s, he committed suicide in 1846.

Friedrich List is known chiefly as the architect of the German railway system and the founder of the doctrine of *infant industries*, which proposes that protective measures should be taken during the period in which new industries are developing in specific countries. In Germany during the nineteenth century he was widely regarded as the economic theorist of Unification, but it would be more accurate to describe him as a committed economic publicist rather than a theorist. His repeated attacks on the theories of Adam Smith were for instance more relevant to English doctrines of free trade in the period following the Napoleonic Wars than to the actual teachings of Smith; and as a consequence English historians of economic thought have tended to dismiss his importance.

But while it may be true that List presented no great theoretical formulations, his emphasis on the national aspects of economic policy were of decisive importance. His period in America taught him that the opening up and creation of a new economic unity was internally reliant on rapid means of transport, and externally on a range of tariff controls that would enable a new economy to achieve a state of balance with established states. His earlier commitment to economic reform in Germany became by the 1830s a programme for 'economic nationality', in which the construction of a railway network was conceived as an important means for the creation of a coherent and united Germany. This is expressed in his essay 'On a Saxon Railway System as the Foundation of a German Railway System and especially on the Construction of a Railway from Leipzig to Dresden' ('Über ein sachsisches Eisenbahnsystem . . . ') of 1833, which while the most well-known of his writings on the subject was followed by many others, all of which re-emphasized the same line of argument.

Today List remains influential on the continent, where he is seen by many as the promoter of ideas of economic unification which lie at the basis of the European Economic Community. His emphasis on protection was however never a dogma, for he wrote in terms of equal trading relations between nations. In the Europe of his day the dominance of the English economy meant that the general adoption of free trade would have reduced many nations, including Germany, to British economic dependencies. It was for List a question of national survival, and not international supremacy, that led him to support a system of tariffs and quotas in world trading relations.

Keith Tribe

The only other substantial work in English is 'Outlines of American Political Economy' (1827), which appears in Margaret Hirst, *Life of Friedrich List and Selections from his Writings* (1909). His collected writings have been published under the title *Friedrich List: Schriften/Reden/Briefe* by the Friedrich List Gesellschaft (10 vols, 1927–35).

273
LISTER, Joseph 1827–1912

British surgeon

Lister came from a pious Quaker family and his life-long meticulousness, industriousness and self-questioning bear witness to his childhood. He remained devoted to his father, Joseph Jackson Lister, a wealthy wine merchant who contributed substantially to the perfection of the objective lens system of the microscope and who also fostered his son's early interest in science. In 1844 Lister registered at the only English university open to a Quaker, University College, London. In 1848 he suffered a nervous breakdown but eventually resumed his studies and received his MD degree and fellowship of the Royal College of Surgeons in 1852. Already by this time Lister was resolved to be a surgeon, and was pursuing microscopical researches in his spare time.

In 1853 Lister moved to Edinburgh. Here he was befriended by the famous surgeon James Syme. In 1854 he became Syme's house surgeon and the following year married Syme's eldest daughter Agnes. It was at this time, as worldly success began to come his way, he resigned his membership of the Society of Friends. By 1860 his lecturing and research on inflammation had brought sufficient reputation for him to be elected a fellow of the Royal Society. In 1860 he became Regius Professor of Surgery in Glasgow and entered into the most intellectually fruitful period of his life.

Victorian hospitals were essentially centres for the treatment of the poor. Cleanliness and nutrition were often inadequate and in surgical wards mortality could be very high. The main cause of death was 'hospitalism', the post-operative development of sepsis and gangrene in wounds. This problem had become particularly acute by the 1860s for anaesthesia had been introduced in the late 1840s and had resulted in a rise in the number of operations performed and an increase in operating time.

Lister, fascinated by the attendant question of inflammation, was also preoccupied by the theoretical and practical issues surrounding suppuration. Already by 1865 he was doubting the prevalent view propounded by Justus von Liebig* that putrefaction was simply a form of combustion occurring when moist organic substances make contact with oxygen. In the same year his attention was drawn to the claims of Louis Pasteur* that putrefaction was essentially a fermentative process produced by living organisms. Over the next two years Lister began using carbolic acid as an agent to protect accidental and surgical wounds against infection. The wound was both cleaned with the acid and covered with a dressing impregnated with it. His results were remarkable. In eleven cases of compound fracture, nearly always a fatal injury, nine patients recovered. The new technique and Lister's claims for its success were described in a series of reports in the *Lancet* (1867) – 'On a New Method of Treating Compound Fracture, Abscess, etc., With Observations on the Condition of Suppuration'.

Lister's ideas and methods were by no means immediately accepted by the medical profession. To begin with most surgeons had their own favoured methods of dealing with sepsis and secondly carbolic acid treatment was unpleasant for the surgeon and its action on the wound delayed healing. In the long term acceptance was eventually assured by the gradual establishment of the germ theory, associated with Robert Koch*, in the 1880s. The growth of antiseptic treatment was also closely associated with Lister's own personality. His indefatigable lecturing, research and European and American propagandizing helped convert the younger generation of surgeons.

Over the years he gradually extended his technique to cover all bacteriological exigencies. Innovations included a 'donkey engine' and then a 'steam spray' to atomize carbolic acid over the operative area. Eventually, however, he abandoned these. Towards the end of the century other surgeons began to advocate aseptic as opposed to antiseptic surgery. This technique involved scrupulous presterilization of the skin, the operating area, and all instruments in contact with the wound. It remains the basis of modern surgery. Lister, although he recognized the theoretical basis of the procedure, always doubted whether it was practically effective. Antiseptic surgery, however, had made such a concept possible.

For Lister himself the triumph of antiseptic surgery brought great personal fame, enormous wealth, and finally a baronetcy. It might be said that his contribution to the modern heroic mythology of the surgeon was as great as his achievement in surgical practice.

C.J. Lawrence

Lister's works are collected as *The Collected Papers of Joseph Baron Lister* (2 vols, 1909). See: Rickman J. Godlee, *Lord Lister* (1917); Richard Fisher, *Joseph Lister 1827–1912* (1977).

274
LISZT, Ferencz 1811–86

German-Hungarian composer and pianist

One of the foremost musicians of the Romantic period, Liszt was born into a German speaking family, being the son of a steward on the Esterhazy estate where Haydn had previously served as *kapellmeister*. As a youth he received piano tuition from Carl Czerny and composition lessons from Salieri, the teacher of Beethoven* and Schubert*. After his first public appearance at the age of eleven, which met with high critical acclaim, he gave up lessons and embarked on a course of self-instruction lasting five years. Afterwards he lived exclusively on his earnings as an international virtuoso pianist until early retirement in his mid-thirties. In 1823 he settled in Paris, though during the next decade he travelled extensively visiting Russia, Portugal and Turkey as well as England and the rest of Europe. In 1848, having abandoned most of his performing activities, he took up permanent residence at the court of Weimar as musical director. By now he had all but given up the concert stage and instead applied himself to the task of composing orchestral works and directing operatic music. His friendship with Wagner* at this time produced piano transcriptions of 'Tannhauser', 'Lohengrin' and new scores by Berlioz* whose music he had always championed. These performances realized a life-long ambition to publicize the many unrecognized compositions of his contemporaries; however, he eventually clashed with the court authorities and resigned his post in 1859. Soon afterwards Liszt moved to Rome where in 1865 he took up orders as a minor canon of the church. From then on until his death in 1886 his time was divided travelling between Rome, Weimar and Budapest where he spent his remaining years both as a teacher and promoter of new music.

Aptly described as a truly international artist Liszt's unique musical style reflects a vast interest in the literary eclecticism of the Romantic period: such philosophical inquiries were frequently expressed in the formal and harmonic experiments within his works. Though the composer himself wished to be thought of primarily as a Hungarian with strongly nationalistic traits, his early training in Vienna brought him in touch with more classical concepts via the music of Bach and Beethoven which during the 1820s was considered out of favour. However, his move to Paris added the new dimension of Romantic thought to the conception of his compositions and concert performances. This new exposure led him to meet not only the writers Victor Hugo*, Lamartine*, Sainte-Beuve* and George Sand*, but also the painter Delacroix* whose creations were the embodiment of Romantic imagery. Liszt's early interest in the church can be traced to this period when he was to study the spiritual writings of Lamennais and Saint-Simon* whose philosophies of Christian socialism and the advocation of art as a means of attaining moral perfection were to colour the composer's religious attitudes in later life. Such influences explain the strongly programmatic and spiritual elements in most of his output.

Besides these literary considerations, more musical influences must also be taken into account. Liszt's meeting with Berlioz, Chopin* and Paganini* in the early 1830s offered new opportunities for experiment in his many piano works of the period. The recent success of Berlioz's *Symphonie fantastique* caused Liszt to transcribe it for piano solo and also enabled him to champion the Frenchman's later works, many of which rarely met with the public's approval. The programmatic elements of Berlioz's scores together with their frequent use of a cyclic musical thread of *idée-fixe* did much to shape Liszt's own thinking in terms of a similar 'thematic metamorphosis' within his own larger compositions. It was Chopin who offered Liszt new approaches to the treatment of sonority and pianistic effect together with singing melodic lines derived from the lyrical operatic arias of Bellini*. Liszt assimilated these characteristics into his own style by further extending their emotional content via more rubato, dynamic range and rhythmic interest. The addition of folk rhythms from central Europe, advanced chords and particularly distant modulations to unrelated keys made him the most daring of composer-performers. During this period the development of orchestral instruments lagged far behind that of the piano and this is the main reason why Liszt preferred a medium over which he had total personal control. Probably the greatest contribution to his art was that of Paganini whose violin recitals he attended in Paris in 1831. Though much less a composer than performer, Paganini gave the young musician the impetus to study and perfect a kind of showmanship and extroversion unknown during this period and yet so typical of the Romantic spirit. Liszt was not only impressed with the violinist's daring performances but was determined to emulate this method of musical sorcery both with the inception of a new kind of pianistic virtuosity and by way of its presentation.

Liszt's composing life spanned seventy years and though a large proportion are original works for piano, he also made many transcriptions and arrangements of songs, orchestral works and symphonies for the medium. Added to this there are over a dozen symphonic poems, the programmatic *Faust* and *Dante* Symphonies (1856), concert pieces and two piano concertos (1856, 1861), together with many choral compositions and songs. The mature piano works are well represented in the *Études d'Exécution Transcendante* (1851), many of whose titles convey the particular technical device or mood to be exploited. Of less difficulty are the three sets of short pieces called the *Années de Pèlerinage* (vols 1 and 2, 1850; vol. 3, 1867–77) and reflect his impressions as a visitor to Switzerland and Italy. The brilliant Sonata in B minor (1853), an extended movement on four interrelated themes, exploits the process of thematic metamorphosis by subjecting the material to constant variation in tempo, texture and mood as it progresses on its journey: similar procedures are to be found in the piano concertos and in many of the symphonic poems. These descriptive works, though generally rather short, exploit a similar cyclic use and follow the train of thought in some work of poetry or painting that provided the creative inspiration: their essentially programmatic nature is displayed in such titles as *Les Préludes* (1848), *Mazeppa* (1851), *Hamlet* (1858) and many others which like *Hungaria* (1854) are strongly nationalistic. Similar preoccupations can be seen in the nineteen *Hungarian Rhapsodies* written between 1846 and 1886: these are again free in conception, taking the czardas as their formal basis and contrast many sections of tempo changes, melodic variations and virtuoso devices.

It is to be regretted that the vast output of Liszt's works has been unduly neglected in favour of those piano pieces which have either been exploited for their overt sentimentality or opportunities for mindless virtuosity. Only very recently, through the efforts of the composer Humphrey Searle and the pianist David Wilde, has a new aspect of Liszt's personality been revealed – initially at least by the discovery of material written in his old age. Though he gave up a virtuoso career at the age of thirty-five he continued to write for the piano until his death. These late works were only heard by a close circle of friends and pupils who appeared reluctant to reveal their existence. Their availability now shows that Liszt was constantly paring down his musical materials to a minimum and that his experiments were to be responsible for shaping the outlook of many composers at the beginning of this century. This process of economy invariably mixed with advanced chromatic treatment appears in the early *Années de Pèlerinage* and in the *Malédiction* for piano and strings sketched as early as 1830. Similar practice with roving harmonies and obscure key centres can be seen in the two great organ works *Fantasia and Fugue on Bach* (1855) and in his Meyerbeer* arrangement on the choral *Ad nos, ad salutarem undam* (1850): both works foreshadow the heavy chromaticism of Richard Strauss and Max Reger by nearly fifty years. Though the above mentioned are rather severe in style, many of the lighter piano pieces also look to the future as in the four *Valses Oubliées* (1881–6), the three *Mephisto Waltzes* (1860, 1881, 1883) and especially the *Fountains of the Villa d'Este* (1877) which strongly influenced the Russian school of pianists and the impressionist works of Debussy and Ravel. The majority of these late works reflects the composer's obsession with his own mortality though their melancholy feeling can often be explained by Liszt's increasing use of exotic scales derived from folksong: good examples of this effect can be seen in the *Czardas Obstiné* (1884), *Czardas Macabre* (1882) and the little known *Hungarian Portraits* (1885). The aphoristic style of these piano pieces together with the *Lugubre Gondola* (1882), *R.W. – Venezia* (1883) and *Am Grabe Richard Wagner's* (1883) memorial fragments were to be a major influence on the harmonic experiments of Busoni and Bartók. Many were just sketches conceived for optional performance as chamber music for solo strings with harmonium or piano accompaniment as can be seen in the enigmatically titled *Dark Star*, *Sleepless*, *Sinister* or *Grey Clouds*: their economy of melodic and rhythmic material may well convey the composer's spiritual disappointment and resignation to the 'idle uselessness that frets me'. Likewise, other strange essays of this period reflect a similar state of mind, the meditation *Via Crucis* for chorus and organ (1878) and the final symphonic poem, *From the Cradle to the Grave* (1881–2).

The position of Liszt as a composer of major importance went unrecognized in his own time and up until very recently Wagner was considered to be the sole prophet of new developments in twentieth-century music. Though both men were fully involved with a creative means of expression which encompassed traits of nationalism and Romanticism in the nineteenth century, it was left to Liszt to anticipate the importance of a later internationalism in music of the future. His enthusiasm knew no boundaries while the legacy of his performing and teaching has continued well into this century.

Michael Alexander

See: C. Wagner, *F. Liszt* (1911); E. Newman, *The Man Liszt* (1934); H. Searle, *The Music of Liszt* (1954); B. Szabolcsi, *The Twilight of Liszt* (1956); *Franz Liszt, the Man and his Music*, ed. Alan Walker (1970); A. Walker, *Liszt* (1974).

275
LIVINGSTONE, David 1813–73

British explorer

In the year of David Livingstone's death Florence Nightingale* referred to him as 'the greatest man of his generation'. He was a missionary who only made one convert, an impassioned opponent of the slave-trade who was often dependent for the necessities of life on the slavers, and an explorer whose discoveries were rendered worthless in his own eyes by their failure to live up to his expectations – the Zambesi was not God's Highway to Central Africa, Lakes Nyasa and Moero were not the sources of the Nile, the Victoria Falls were awesomely beautiful but inconvenient. But for all his failures he was intemperately loved and revered. His life-story is so incomprehensible in terms of worldly motivations that his contemporaries believed him to be a saint. It suited his sponsors, the Society of Missionaries and the Royal Geographical Society, and his would-be saviour H.M. Stanley*, to promote his legend, but the circumstances of his solitary explorations were enough to make him a figure of romance. He was a hero custom-made for Victorian Britain. Not only did he typify their most admired qualities, he provided them, before they even needed it, with a moral justification for imperialism.

He was born in 1813 at Blantyre, near Glasgow, and grew up in a room 10 feet by 14 in which he, his parents and his five siblings cooked, ate, read (those of them who could) and slept. At the age of ten he went to work as a cotton-piecer. His working hours were from six in the morning until eight at night, after which he went on to study for two hours at a local school and to teach himself Latin in the remaining hours of the night. His qualifying himself to enter, at the age of twenty, a medical training school for missionaries is one of the most impressive of all his remarkable feats. It was achieved at some cost. To study so intensely in that crowded room he had to learn to distance himself from those around him; he was never again fully at ease with the members of a white race.

He sailed to South Africa in 1840. Disappointed by the realities of missionary life he quarrelled with colleagues and took every opportunity to push further and further away from other settlements, 'to work beyond other men's lines'. He married the daughter of Robert Moffat, the leader of the South African missionaries, but in 1852 he sent her and their children back to England. He had already travelled further north into the interior than any European before him. Now, walking or riding an ox, he made his way across deserts, through rain-forests and past the territory of hostile tribes to the west coast at Luanda. Realizing that his own journey had been too fraught with danger and difficulty to be feasible for others but still determined to find a route through which the word of God and Western civilization could penetrate Central Africa, he retraced his steps and continued along the River Zambesi to the east coast. In four years of appalling hardship he had crossed Africa.

He returned to England a national hero. Queen Victoria* laughed at one of his ponderous jokes. He was invited to lecture and to write a book. He was eager to explain himself. He had been met at the mouth of the Zambesi by a letter from the Missionary Society pointing out that his wanderings had little bearing on his supposed calling. The criticism hurt; he had, as his journals show, already been considerably exercised to justify his actions.

He respected the tribal institutions of those among whom he had spent so many years. His experiences had shown him how contact with Europeans distorts and corrupts that organization. He knew that to Africans, who worked only to feed themselves and had no concept of capitalism, the industrial revolution had little to offer. Worst of all, he already guessed, and soon would know with certainty, that his explorations opened up new routes, not for missionaries but for slavers. Yet he was driven by a desire which went beyond reason to see Africa 'civilized'. To this end, he argued, explorers should open the way for traders. Commerce would rapidly destroy the generous cooperative responsibility which was the essential premise of tribal life. This was regrettable but necessary. The African, isolated by the erosion of familiar social structures, would more readily convert to Christianity. Meantime legitimate trade would make the native prosperous enough to resist the slavers. Trade was to be the underpinning of the new Africa, the winning of converts and the abolition of slavery its twin justifications.

Livingstone returned to Africa in 1860 as Her Majesty's Consul for Civilization and Commerce. The expedition was disastrous. His five European companions and the mission which, responding to his inspirational last lecture in Cambridge, followed them out suffered from famine, malaria, the hostility of slavers, and the dangers of tribal warfare. Watching Livingstone attempting to navigate unnavigable rivers and to settle forbiddingly hostile terrain, some of them concluded he was mad.

Recent biographers have agreed with them. Livingstone was probably a manic-depressive, the extremity of his moods being increased by his belief in divine providence. He believed that he was appointed to do God's work and that he was therefore invulnerable. When things went well he was fearless and fanatically energetic, but setbacks of any kind unnerved him. A sandbank was not just an annoyance, it was a sign that God had withdrawn his protection. At such times he would try to throw off his depression by means of violent physical exertion and he had no sympathy for other people's weaknesses. The Zambesi expedition ended inconclusively, leaving many, including Livingstone's wife and the man who was to have been the first bishop of Central Africa, dead.

He embarked on his last journey in 1866. His official purpose was to find the source of the Nile; his private justification for such an ungodly exercise was that it might provide him with opportunities at least to hinder the slave trade. For seven years he wandered, increasingly infirm and despondent. His geographical discoveries were momentous but they meant little to him. In all his travels he kept copious notes, recording details of flora and fauna and compiling vocabularies of tribal languages. His maps are almost unbelievably precise; he was once known to take over 2,000 sightings to establish one position. He was a gifted geographer and natural scientist but his conscience would not allow him to devote his life to the pursuit of mere knowledge.

He was now in almost constant pain from internal bleeding, ulcers and from the shoulder which, twenty years before, had been crushed by a lion. He had repeated attacks of malaria. His ready sympathy with any non-European made him tolerant of the slavers. He wrote that they should be judged 'by the standards of an East African Moslem, not by ours', but his frequent dependence on their charity demoralized him. In 1871 he witnessed the massacre of about 400 Africans by slavers at Nyangwe and after that he would accept no Arab kindness. By the time he was found by Stanley he was close to destitution but he refused to return to the coast.

By now the sources of the Nile had assumed a mystical significance for Livingstone. He yearned to find those twin fountains of which Herodotus and Ptolemy had written, to trace the river back to the Mountains of the Moon. He set off once again. His chronometer had been damaged; his miscalculations proved fatal. After wading for days through mud which sometimes reached their armpits the African porters woke up one day to find their leader dead.

Livingstone's life was not as fruitless as he despairingly imagined it to be. His account of the Nyangwe massacre provided the abolitionists with essential ammunition. Within two years of his death the slave-market at Zanzibar was closed and thereafter the East African slave-trade withered away. He had opened up vast tracts of previously uncharted territory. More profoundly, his equation – commerce and the attendant disruption of tribal life = civilization = Christianity and the end of slavery – was to give those who, in the subsequent generation, carved up Africa a high and holy excuse for doing so.

Lucy Hughes-Hallett

Livingstone wrote two books: *Missionary Travels and Researches in South Africa* (1857) and *Narrative of an Expedition to the Zambesi and its Tributaries* (1865). Other published writings include: *Some Letters From Livingstone 1840–1872*, ed. D. Chamberlain (1940); *Livingstone's African Journal 1853–1856*, ed. I. Schapera (1963); *The Last Journals of David Livingstone in Central Africa*, ed. H. Waller (1874). See: Tim Jeal, *Livingstone* (1973); Oliver Ransford, *David Livingstone* (1978).

276

LOBACHEVSKY, Nikolas Ivanovich 1793–1856

Russian mathematician

Some advances in our scientific understanding of the world not merely provoke the opposition of the entrenched establishment, but shock that establishment to the bone. To launch a theory with these characteristics on to the world requires an uncommonly brave spirit. Copernicus was such a man, challenging the most basic notions of Ptolemaic astronomy. Lobachevsky was another, challenging the even more sacrosanct assumptions of Euclidean geometry. Euclid had reigned supreme for more than two millennia. His geometry had been taught by venerable schoolmasters, and was accepted by the greatest scientists and philosophers as more certain than holy writ. Newton paid Euclid the highest compliment by writing his *Principia* in the Euclidean style and by using only Euclidean methods of argument. Kant roundly asserted that the truths of Euclidean geometry were transcendentally necessary, that is, he claimed that they underpinned the very possibility of rationality: deny Euclidean geometry and rationality would begin to disintegrate!

Gauss* was sufficiently astute to realize that Euclidean geometry was less secure than the homage of the scientists and the eloquence of the philosophers attested. It is quite likely that Gauss could have published the material in Lobachevsky's *Onachalaki geometrii* ('Principles of Geometry', 1829). But he did not. He knew what an outcry there would be: how every opinionated mathematical nobody in Europe might publish articles 'proving' him wrong. In a word, he would be 'jumped on' by the entire establishment of middle talent. Only the exceptionally able would see his point, but they would be vastly outnumbered by the outraged multitude.

Lobachevsky called his new geometry 'imaginary geometry', i.e., a system of description of space relationships as they *might* be. But this 'might be' was no mere flight of the imagination. Ordinary physical space might turn out to be more like Lobachevskian geometry than Euclidean over vast distances, and Lobachevsky himself later made an attempt to check this conjecture with astronomical observations. Today Lobachevskian geometry is generally known as 'hyperbolic geometry', and is contrasted with another type of non-Euclidean geometry discovered later in the century by Riemann*, 'elliptic geometry'. Riemann also conceptualized more general forms of non-Euclidean geometry ('Riemannian geometries') and it is to these later geometries that physicists, following Einstein, have turned to describe the physical space of the cosmos as a whole. So Lobachevsky, in asking the question whether cosmological space was non-Euclidean, was a century ahead of his time.

The model for Lobachevsky's new geometry was Gauss's discovery of imaginary (complex) numbers. Gauss had shown that there was a system of numbers which was logically consistent and extremely useful in technical ways inside mathematics, but which had no representation in ordinary experience. One never found $10i$ (where i is the imaginary unit, the square root of -1) coins in a purse, or $4i$ people in a boat, but, nevertheless, '$10i$' and '$4i$' were reputable mathematical entities. Lobachevsky posed to himself the question: could there be a similar phenomenon in geometry, i.e., geometries which are not actually exhibited in physical space, but which are none the less consistent systems-in-themselves?

The starting point for Lobachevsky's investigation was his awareness that there was a slight crack in the logical surface of Euclid's geometry. Euclid's fifth postulate said that if we have a line L in a plane and a point p, also in that plane but not contained in L, then

there is a line L', drawable through p, which never meets L and which is said to be *parallel* to L. Many mathematicians, from Euclid onwards, had felt that it ought to be possible to prove this postulate from the other postulates: but no proof was ever found. This was highly significant, because it seemed to establish that it would be possible consistently to deny the fifth postulate, whilst accepting the other Euclidean postulates. Lobachevsky's denial of the fifth postulate took the form of the conjecture that there might be more than one line through p which, however much it was extended, would never meet L. We may show this situation on a diagram: Suppose there were two such lines, pq, pr, which never met L: then there would also be an infinity of further lines passing through p between pr and pq.

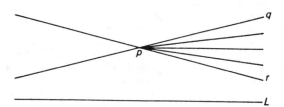

Lobachevsky called these new lines *ultra-parallels*, as opposed to the *parallels* pq and pr. Suppose the angle between pq and pr were a millionth of a degree! It would be virtually impossible to detect the presence of the ultra-parallels by physical methods, despite their remarkable numerousness.

On such foundations Lobachevsky built up an elaborate structure of definitions, configurations and theorems. He showed how trigonometric and algebraic methods could be used in the new geometry. In a word, he put into existence a structure of mathematical concepts which exhibited just the kind of logical argument, variety of form, and scope for future development, as we find in Euclidean geometry itself. Gauss learnt Russian in order to be able to read Lobachevsky's work, and he always treated Lobachevsky with the greatest respect, though he never actually said in public that he accepted the Lobachevskian system: perhaps it was too painful a concession for Gauss, knowing that he could have done it himself several years earlier. In 1832 Janos Bolyai published a similar body of results in Hungary, apparently unaware of Lobachevsky's work. The years 1828–32 were epoch-making years in mathematics, for it was also during this period, but completely unknown to Lobachevsky and Bolyai, that the young Evariste Galois* was taking the even bolder step to non-representational algebra.

Nikolas Lobachevsky was born on 2 November 1793 in Makarief, a district of Nijni Novgorod, into a poor family. His father died when he was seven, leaving his mother Praskovia Ivanovna and her two other sons quite without means of support. Praskovia moved to

Kazan, where she taught the boys herself, to such good effect that each in turn won a free place at the local *Gymnasium*. Nikolas progressed to the newly founded University of Kazan, where he studied under Martin Bartels, a friend of Gauss. By 1812 he had gained his master's degree, was Professor Extraordinary in 1814 and Professor Ordinarius in 1822. He was strongly imbued with the work ethic, and the University of Kazan took full advantage of his tireless energy. Twice he was dean of the department of physics and mathematics (1820–1, 1823–5), librarian to the university (1825–35) and finally he was appointed rector (vice-chancellor) in 1827, a post he held for nineteen years until he was unaccountably dismissed in 1846. In 1832 he married Lady Varvara Aleksivna Moisieva, a woman of means, but Lobachevsky's salary at the university was not high, and their large family of seven children meant that they were never rich. In 1837 he received a title: so finally he rose socially into the lower ranks of the aristocracy.

In some ways Lobachevsky may have benefited from his relatively obscure niche in Kazan. His endless work in setting the new university on a sound foundation protected him from local criticism, and his mathematical ideas were not sufficiently known in Europe to bring the mathematical establishment immediately on his head. Gradually, however, the word did spread. In 1832 Lobachevsky was ridiculed in a review by M.V. Ostrogradsky, the leading mathematician in the St Petersburg Academy. It is clear that Ostrogradsky completely failed to understand the significance of Lobachevsky's work. But he was not alone in this. As late as 1865 the leading English mathematician, Arthur Cayley, also failed to take the point. Only slowly did such pioneers as Weierstrasse and Poincaré* begin to propagate Lobachevsky's ideas. A major step forward occurred in 1858 when Beltrami showed that Lobachevskian geometry could be illustrated by the behaviour of geodesics on a pseudosphere. It was only towards the end of the century that Lobachevsky and Galois were finally recognized as the main architects of a totally new conception of mathematics: a study, not merely of actuality, as presented to the senses, but of the full range of self-consistent, formal possibility.

Christopher Ormell

The complete works may be found in *Polnoe sobranie sochinenii* (5 vols, 1946–51). The *Geometrische Untersuchungen zur Theorie der Parallellinien* (1840) was translated as *Geometrical Researches on the Theory of Parallels* (1891). His other works include *Pangéometrie* (1855), written in French. See: E.T. Bell, *Men of Mathematics* (1937); and H.S.M. Coxeter, *Non-Euclidean Geometry* (3rd edn 1957).

277
LONGFELLOW, Henry Wadsworth 1807–82

US poet

Few poets, nineteenth-century American or otherwise, can have enjoyed the quite stupendous esteem given by his age to Longfellow, or subsequently have suffered so decisive a reversal of critical favour. On both sides of the Atlantic popular taste eulogized him as America's national laureate, the poet of familiar and loved Victorian domestic themes and of the founding Puritan and Indian legends. His suitably genteel choices of subject, metrical virtuosity, and admired public demeanour suggested the very incarnation of the high-toned man of letters, an American equivalent of Tennyson* or Browning*. If there were dissenters, and Poe* was one of them, easily more typical was the praise which came from every hand establishing him as the pre-eminent of the New England 'Fireside Poets'.

Victor Hugo* spoke for many Europeans in judging him the epitome of New World eloquence. English Victorian stalwarts from Tennyson to Gladstone* to the Queen* herself fêted him. In 1869 Oxford and Cambridge both gave him honorary doctorates and in 1884 a bust was unveiled to him in Poets' Corner. To his fellow New England *literati* – Emerson*, Lowell*, Holmes*, Whittier*, Prescott* and others – he was additional testimony, if it were needed, to the hereditary cultural wealth of their Boston and Cambridge world. Like them he came to represent the Brahmin class, another educated voice of WASP New England and a Harvard professor and respected European linguist and translator. From the outset, perceptibly enough, he was not without his advantages – affluent American birth, the means to pursue extensive private European travel and study, early academic position, stunning acclaim and sales of his poetry, and an unaffected patrician ease of manner which apparently endeared him everywhere. In private, the evidence suggests, he was a more complex figure than his stately, benign general image, on occasion deeply self-doubting and no stranger to personal and family tragedy. At his funeral, it was appropriately Emerson, another ancestral New England voice and nearing death himself, who spoke for the almost universal fine regard in which Longfellow was held when he described him as 'a sweet and beautiful soul'.

By the starkest contrast, to a later vantage-point shaped by the modernism of Pound, Eliot, Stevens and William Carlos Williams and accustomed to thinking Whitman* and Emily Dickinson* the best of the nineteenth-century American poets, Longfellow seems almost painful, typically the mannered versifier of *Hiawatha* (1855). Where read at all, it tends to be as part of the history of taste, an exemplar of what Victorian Americans thought 'poetic'. Undoubtedly Longfellow was lavishly over-praised in his time, understood little of the central historical currents of America, and cannot now be thought other than minor. But he by no means deserves the usual instant obloquy. His claims are several: the few strong poems, his kindly literary encouragement of others, and his efforts in translating and teaching Dante, Goethe* and a range of important Spanish, German and other European poetry by which he hoped to widen American horizons. In this latter, if in no other respect, he especially deserves acknowledgment.

Born into a prosperous leading family of coastal Maine (the sea becomes a recurring allusion in his poetry), he attended Bowdoin College (1822–5), where Hawthorne*, and a future president, Franklin Pierce, were classmates; studied in Europe (1826–9), experiences recalled in his Irvingesque* Outre-Mer (1835), before returning to Bowdoin as Professor of Modern Languages (1829–35); and in 1831, married, with enormous happiness, a Portland, Maine, girl, Mary Storer Potter. Four years later, while again in Europe to prepare for the Harvard Chair of Languages he had been offered in 1835, Mary Longfellow died in Rotterdam of a miscarriage. Longfellow assuaged his grief in work, as a Harvard teacher, and in the writing which flowed from his pen – Hyperion (1839), a thinly veiled prose narrative about his love for Frances Appleton who, though at first offended, married him in 1843; Voices of the Night (1839), his first full-length book of poetry; Ballads and other Poems (1841), the collection which includes the best known of his early poems like 'A Psalm of Life', 'The Wreck of the Hesperus' and 'Excelsior'; Poems on Slavery (1842), tepid, abolitionist verse which lacks the commitment of Whittier's anti-slavery poems; The Spanish Student (1843), an ineffectual blank verse play based on Cervantes and Thomas Middleton; and his oddly lethargic anti-war poem 'The Arsenal at Springfield'. In all these, Longfellow's technical competence rarely is at fault, rather the poetry lacks committed imaginative life. Increasingly he now turned to longer verse narrative, each, it has to be recognized, a laboured metrical confection: Evangeline (1847), an allegorical history of America told in the form of the Acadian flight from Newfoundland to Louisiana; The Golden Legend (1851), a medieval fable to do with the quest for faith; the two New England compositions on which his reputation has seemingly come to rest, Hiawatha and The Courtship of Miles Standish (1858); and Tales of a Wayside Inn (1863), which includes the immensely popular 'Paul Revere's Ride' and poems like 'The Saga of King Olaf'. In these latter, Longfellow treats American history as if it were pageant of a sort, almost operatic chronicle. They also, Hiawatha especially, reflect to quite tiresome, and unintendedly comic, effect Longfellow's interest in trochaic and other metrical experiment, notably in the Finnish Kalevala and Scandinavian oral-formulaic verse. In 1849, he

attempted his only novel, Kavanagh: A Tale, which explores liberal Unitarian theology and the making of an American literature derived from European tradition.

Longfellow was also to suffer a further major family tragedy. In Craigie House, the gift of his second wife's father and with which he is habitually associated in later photographs and portraits, he witnessed Frances's death when her hair caught fire and she was engulfed in the flames. The event almost unhinged Longfellow. But he won through, eventually, turning more than ever to religion both in his life and poetry. He worked principally on his translation of The Divine Comedy, an assiduous but finally undistinguished rendering, which saw publication in 1867–70. The later poems include his attempted magnum opus, Christus: A Mystery (1872), a compendious, often top-heavy, verse sequence which includes earlier work like The Golden Legend and The New England Tragedies (1868), and in which he sought to depict Divine good intentions in epic form. The result is thin, cumbersome, hardly of a kind with his professed models in Dante, Milton and Goethe. In later life, Longfellow's achievement rests principally upon his sonnets, together with the series for which he served as editor, Poems of Places (1876–), work like Keramos and other Poems (1878), Ultima Thule (1880) and his last, reconciliatory volume, In the Harbor (1883). His posthumous fragment, Michael Angelo (1883), usefully recapitulates many of his views about art, poetry, the meaning of belief and the heritage of Dante.

A. Robert Lee

See: Lawrance Thompson, Young Longfellow (1807–1843) (1938); Edward Wagenknecht, Longfellow: A Full-Length Portrait (1955); Newton Arvin, Longfellow: His Life And Work (1963); Edward Hirsh, Henry Wadsworth Longfellow, University of Minnesota pamphlet (1964); Cecil B. Williams, Henry Wadsworth Longfellow (1964).

278
LORENTZ, Hendrik Antoon 1853–1928

Dutch physicist

Although Lorentz never lived outside of the Netherlands, he was a truly international figure, who was widely known both within and beyond the scientific community. Lorentz received his education at the University of Leiden, where he was awarded his doctoral degree in 1875. As early as 1878 he was appointed Professor of Theoretical Physics in Leiden and until his death he remained connected with the University of Leiden. Because of his outstanding contributions to physics he became a leader in his field to whom many physicists turned for help and advice. In recognition of his achievements Lorentz received many honours and prizes, the most important of which was the Nobel Prize (1902). During the first part of his career, Lorentz led a fairly secluded life, but after 1900 he travelled extensively, both inside and outside of Europe. Everyone who met him was impressed by his mild and well-balanced personality, his integrity and his concern for his fellow-men. Albert Einstein, who often visited Leiden and who became very attached to Lorentz, wrote in 1953: 'For me personally he meant more than all the others I have met on my life's journey.'

During and after the First World War Lorentz used his influence to promote the cause of peace and to re-establish the international scientific contacts that had been severely disrupted by the war. He gained much respect and recognition because of his activities towards this goal in several international organizations, in particular in the International Committee on Intellectual Cooperation of the League of Nations, of which he was first a member and later the chairman.

Nationally, Lorentz also played an important administrative role as a member of several government committees. He contributed to the reform of the Dutch university system and, on a more practical level, he almost single-handedly carried out the calculations for the enclosure of the Zuiderzee by a dike.

Although his fifty-year long career spanned equal periods in the nineteenth and twentieth centuries, Lorentz may be considered one of the last great representatives of 'classical' nineteenth-century physics. It is true that he also contributed to several of the revolutionary developments that took place in physics during the first two decades of the twentieth century (relativity theory, quantum theory), but his most important achievements date from before 1900. This does not mean that his work is no longer valuable for modern physics. In fact, one might say that his fundamental contributions prepared the way for the creation of modern physics. It is, of course, impossible to do full justice to Lorentz's work without going into considerable technical detail, but its essence may be summarized in the following way.

Around 1870, much confusion existed in the field of electromagnetic theory, the theory describing electric and magnetic phenomena. Concepts such as electricity were not used in a consistent way and opinions varied widely on the nature of the ether, the medium in which the electromagnetic phenomena presumably took place. Lorentz's fundamental contribution to this field consists of the idea that ether and matter should be considered separate entities. In a series of publications, the first of which was his thesis (1875), Lorentz applied this idea to electromagnetic theory, combining it with the atomistic view of matter. The resulting theory reached its final form in 1904 and is known as the 'electron theory'. According to Lorentz, electromagnetic phenomena are caused by charged particles – electrons – creating a condition of 'stress' in the ether.

This condition is propagated through the ether with the speed of light and causes the mutual interactions of charged particles such as the attractive forces between charges of opposite sign.

At first, the ether was treated by Lorentz as a material medium, but in the course of the development of the electron theory it lost most of its material properties. The one property it retained was the property of immobility, and, as a consequence, absolute motion, understood as motion with respect to the ether, remained a meaningful concept within the framework of the electron theory. This feature distinguishes the electron theory from Einstein's theory of relativity (1905), to which it is mathematically almost identical. By abandoning the notion of absolute motion Einstein had eliminated the ether altogether. Lorentz had never been able to take this step; until his death he clung to the concept of the ether. Nevertheless, his idea of a separation between ether and matter and his application of it to electromagnetic theory have been immensely fruitful and clarifying. The modern concept of the electromagnetic field as an entity distinct from, but caused by, charged matter, derives directly from Lorentz's work. The only difference is that today the field is not treated as a state of the ether, but as an independent entity.

A.J. Kox

Most of Lorentz's published writings are included in his *Collected Works* (9 vols. 1934–9). See: *H.A. Lorentz: Impressions of his Life and Work*, ed. G.L. de Haas-Lorentz (1957); R. McCormmach, 'Lorentz, Hendrik Antoon', in *Dictionary of Scientific Biography*, ed. C.C. Gillispie (vol. VIII, 1973).

279
LOWELL, James Russell 1819–91

US author and diplomat

'A New Englander . . . of acute discursive mind and deft literary fingering' – so William Rossetti, introducing a British popular edition of the collected poems, characterized Lowell. His account was at once shrewd and usefully to the point. Like the other 'Fireside Poets' with whom his name is associated – Bryant*, Longfellow*, Holmes* and Whittier* – Lowell was, before he was anything, a hereditary New Englander, another nineteenth-century high American Brahmin and scholar whose family had been eminent in the affairs of Boston and the eastern seaboard since the earliest years of the Puritan settlement. To contemporaries, both in America and across the Atlantic, he ranked as a major representative American figure, not only as poet, essayist, satirist, editor and Longfellow's successor in the Smith Professorship of Modern Languages

376 / LOWELL, JAMES RUSSELL

at Harvard, but as a seasoned diplomat and ambassador. Lowell's writing no longer commands any extensive readership, except perhaps for *The Biglow Papers* (1848, 1862–3) and 'A Fable For Critics' (1848), but it was rarely other than agile – 'deft' in Rossetti's terms – the expression of a versatile, well-stocked but ultimately limited mind. Henry James*, who met frequently with Lowell in Europe and developed a complex, almost filial, relationship with him, once revealingly spoke of him as the 'oddest' mixture of 'the infinitely clever and unspeakably simple'.

Born in Cambridge, Massachusetts, and educated at Harvard, Lowell first thought of a career in the law, but the verse he had been writing since boyhood convinced him that his was a literary vocation. By 1839–40 he was contributing poems to the *Dial*, Emerson's* Transcendentalist quarterly, and to the *Southern Literary Messenger*, which Poe* had briefly edited. In 1841, he published his first collection, *A Year's Life*, genteel lyric and occasionally ironic pieces, and from then on, his confidence established, wrote voluminously, appearing in a range of contemporary periodicals – among others, *Boston Miscellany*, *Graham's Magazine*, *Massachusetts Quarterly*, *Putnam's* and the *U.S. Magazine And Democratic Review*. In 1843, he founded his own magazine, the *Pioneer*, which, though it ran for only three issues, served notice of his editorial flair; in 1844, he married Maria White, a considerable minor versifier in her own right who eased him away from his instinctive political conservatism, especially toward abolitionism; and from 1848–52 he edited and contributed to the *National Anti-Slavery Standard* and the *Pennsylvania Freeman*, both leading anti-slavery periodicals. The climax of his editorial career came with his appointment as editor from 1857–61 of the *Atlantic Monthly*, where he built a deserved and widely influential reputation, and to the *North American Review*, which he co-edited with Charles Eliot Norton, founder of the *Nation* and a Harvard Professor of Fine Art. Lowell's work as an editor merits recognition. He had a genuine shaping role to play in the creation and dissemination of an American national literature through the journals, and in making available to his countrymen a tradition of European writing.

The two other principal phases of Lowell's career were his Harvard professorship and his diplomatic appointments. When he succeeded Longfellow in the Smith Chair, he turned increasingly to literary criticism, reading widely in European literature (he was a skilled linguist) which led to a run of worthy if uncontentious essay collections, *Fireside Travels* (1864), *Among My Books* (First and Second series, 1870, 1876), *My Study Windows* (1871), *Latest Literary Essays and Addresses* (1891) and *The Old English Dramatists* (1892), all, for the most part, informed, easily digested, introductory surveys and annotation. In 1877, although his Harvard appointment nominally continued, Lowell was appointed minister first to Madrid (1877–80), then to London (1880–5), by the conservative Hayes administration whose policies he felt drawn to (his *Political Essays*, 1888, are worth consulting), thereby continuing the American habit of rewarding men of letters with distinguished diplomatic office and in which he joined Irving*, Hawthorne* and Howells*. In his later years, with Longfellow, he was widely taken to represent the high spirit of literature in America, an international name and almost yearly visitor to Europe to whom Oxford and Cambridge gave honorary degrees. He knew, and was warmly respected by, almost every leading English writer of the age. In 1890, venerable, a voice from an earlier, patrician phase of New England and American literary life, he saw through the presses a ten-volume collection of his work.

Lowell's best poetry was written when young. Principally, his claims rest upon 'A Fable for Critics', no *Dunciad* to be sure but a gently satiric *jeu d'esprit* (Lowell's phrase) in couplet-form which shrewdly depicts the best known of his American fellow *literati* – Emerson, Bryant, Holmes, Hawthorne, Cooper*, Poe ('There comes Poe, with his raven, like Barnaby Rudge,/Three fifths of him genius, and two fifths sheer fudge') and Irving. From the five volumes of poetry he published, *A Year's Life*, *Miscellaneous Poems* (1843), *Poems: Second Series* (1848), *Under the Willows and Other Poems* (1868) and *Heartsease and Rue* (1888), and the poems he contributed to the journals, among the likeliest to endure are 'The Vision of St Launfal' (1848), an inventive retelling of the Grail legend; 'After the Burial' (1850), written in remembrance of the death of his second child; the 'Harvard Commemoration Ode' (1865), a eulogy to Lincoln* and to the university's dead and worthy in parts of comparision with Whitman's* 'When Lilacs in the Dooryard Bloom'd'; 'The Cathedral' (1869), his tribute to Chartres and a statement of his own religious feelings; and the 'Ode to Agazziz' (1874), a touching remembrance of the Swiss-born naturalist. Lowell's other claims lie with *The Biglow Papers* (first series, 1848; second series in the *Atlantic Monthly*, 1862–3), the dialect sayings and opinion in both prose and verse of Hosea Biglow, a wry Yankee farmer. Lowell's versatility was rarely more evident. In Biglow's voice he was able to take aim at the Mexican War, slavery, secession and the threat to the Union. Whether Lowell's own reputation has been secure or not, he has enjoyed a species of reflected glory in two later scions of the family, Amy Lowell, the pioneer imagist poet, and Robert Lowell, whose 'confessional' poetry perhaps most strikingly marks the difference between us and the American nineteenth-century genteel tradition.

A. Robert Lee

See: Leon Howard, *A Victorian Knight Errant: A Study of the Early Career Of James Russell Lowell* (1952);

Martin Duberman, *James Russell Lowell* (1966); Claire McGlinchee, *James Russell Lowell* (1967).

280
LUBBOCK, Sir John (created 1st Baron Avebury, 1900) 1834–1913

British prehistorian

Lubbock was the model late-Victorian 'Renaissance Man'. He was a member of a brilliant group of scientists, which included Huxley*, Lyell* and John Evans*, that formed the nucleus of the Royal Society in the mid-nineteenth century. The formative influence on his youth was Charles Darwin*, who lived only three miles from the Lubbock family home in Kent. Like many of his associates Lubbock was neither a university man nor a professional scientist: he joined the family bank at the age of fourteen and remained as a director all his life.

As an arch-Liberal politician Lubbock was responsible for much enlightened legislation, including parliamentary acts for the protection of wild birds and ancient monuments; as a zoologist and entomologist he made many scientific studies of a wide range of animals and insects; but it was as a prehistorian (perhaps the first archaeologist entitled to the name) that he made his greatest impact.

His *Prehistoric Times* (1865) was based on a series of regular visits to excavations in many parts of Europe. The entire sweep of European prehistory from earliest times until the Iron Age was included in the synopsis. The book brought before the notice of the English-speaking public the excavations of Danish burial mounds and coastal middens, the discoveries of the Swiss 'lake villages', and the cave explorations in the Dordogne. These discoveries provided a framework of West European prehistory that has remained substantially valid until the present day. Lubbock himself invented the terms 'Palaeolithic' and 'Neolithic'. The raw archaeological data were transmuted into prehistory by drawing on the accumulating studies of existing primitive peoples, such as those of Tylor*. This was the first extended use of ethnological evidence for the elucidation of the life of early man – a topic that was considered more fully in *The Origins of Civilisation* (1870).

Lubbock was a strong adherent of the doctrine of human progress, believing, like Spencer*, that progress had the inevitability of natural law. He rejected the idea of diffusionism, holding that identical discoveries had been made independently by many societies at different periods. He was also a strong opponent of the idea, popular in his time, that existing 'savages' were the degraded descendants of more civilized societies. He believed in the unity of mankind, but he had no

doubts about the superiority of the civilized condition over that of primitives, whom he saw as mentally and morally inferior, though inevitably moving forward towards the desirable state of being represented by late nineteenth-century England. 'If the past has been one of progress,' he wrote, 'we may fairly hope that the future will be so also, that the blessings of civilisation will not only be extended to other countries and other natures, but even in our own land they will be rendered more general and more equable.' The instrument of progress, and hence the greater happiness of mankind, was science.

Prehistoric Times remained in print until 1913, and had an enormous influence on the interpretation of archaeological remains until well into this century. Today Lubbock appears very much a man of his age. His was the easy optimism of the liberal middle classes, confident of the virtues of their own culture and determined that they should be enjoyed by all. Archaeology was a means by which the fundamental unity of all mankind and its progress towards greater happiness could be demonstrated. This was a humane (and Liberal) interpretation of Social Darwinism.

C.F.Hawke-Smith

See: H.G. Hutchinson, *The Life of Sir John Lubbock* (1914); Glyn Daniel, *One Hundred and Fifty Years of Archaeology* (1975).

281
LYELL, Charles 1797–1875

British geologist

Lyell was born in Scotland, but was brought up in Hampshire. He graduated from Exeter College, Oxford, in 1819. He trained and practised as a lawyer for a few years, but his interest in geology outstripped his interest in the law and he devoted the rest of his life to the science. He held only one academic appointment: from 1831 to 1833 he was Professor of Geology at the new King's College, London. Thereafter he was supported by private means and the income derived from his writing. His chief institutional allegiance was to the Geological Society of London, of which he was president from 1836–7 and from 1850–1. He lived in Harley Street, London, but travelled regularly and widely on geological expeditions.

Three aspects of his work can be distinguished: first, his ambition to establish what he believed to be the correct methodological principles for the science of geology; secondly, the content and impact of his most important book, *Principles of Geology*; thirdly, his views on evolution and his relationship with Charles Darwin*.

Lyell's fundamental methodological principle for the

construction of the history of the earth was what he called, informally, 'ordinary forces and time'. He argued that the geological forces that can presently be seen to be modifying the face of the earth – erosion, sedimentation, rivers, oceans, earthquakes, volcanoes, ice, etc. – are sufficient to have produced all the phenomena that the geologist investigates, provided that unlimited time has been available for their action. For example, no matter how old a stratum of rock, nor how cataclysmic and unique the forces that at first sight might seem to have been necessary to have produced its contorted appearance, geologists should frame explanations of the formation of that stratum in terms that require only the application, perhaps over millions of years, of forces precisely similar to those that are currently observable. Lyell's predecessors and contemporaries took a somewhat different view. They argued that the geological phenomena themselves, and especially the older rocks, dictated the conclusion that the forces that have shaped the earth certainly acted formerly with far greater intensity, and may even have no modern analogues at all. Lyell's views were dubbed 'uniformitarianism', and the views of his opponents 'catastrophism'. The terms achieved no standard currency during the nineteenth century and their resurrection by historians has not been very helpful, although the terms do succeed in giving something of the flavour of the alternative explanatory systems.

The methodological principle of 'ordinary forces and time' underlay Lyell's first and major work, *Principles of Geology* (3 vols, 1830–3). The book's subtitle expresses the principle more formally: *Being an attempt to explain the former changes of the earth's surface by reference to causes now in operation.* In the book, Lyell codified and anthologized all current geological knowledge, including palaeontology, meteorology, ecology and aspects of biology. The conception of earth-history that emerges from the book is one of endless time, during which a perfectly balanced set of forces has built mountains and eroded them away, has replaced land masses by oceans, hot climates by cold, jungles by deserts, all in a perpetual, recurring, directionless flux. This continuous, but immensely slow, change at the earth's surface has produced an endless succession of environments which have been stocked by the Creator with well-adapted species of plants and animals. Species' adaptations, however, are never flexible enough for them to survive the inevitable change in their environments. Eventually, each species gets out of step with its environment and goes extinct.

Principles of Geology was extremely successful and it ran to twelve editions in forty-five years. Keeping it up to date was Lyell's regular occupation. He included in it much original research, especially on the Tertiary period. Much of his research was accepted by the geological community, and, henceforth, geologists explored the potential of 'ordinary causes' with greater

zeal, but the book did not revolutionize practice in the science. Its impact was diffuse. The book influenced younger scientists like Robert Chambers, T.H. Huxley*, Herbert Spencer* and Charles Darwin. They accepted and rejected specific aspects of the book, but overall they saw in it a programme for the completely naturalistic explanation not only of earth history, which Lyell had intended, but also of the history of life, which Lyell had not. The book gained a wider, popular currency. It informs the reflections on time, change and extinction in Tennyson's* *In Memoriam*, and it lent force to the view that the biblical account of the history of the earth and of life had either to be discarded or radically re-interpreted. The controversy about Genesis was conducted largely outside the geological community: the literal, biblical account had already been discarded by most practising British geologists, even though many of them were clergymen. Parson-geologists aimed to show that while geology might not confirm the scriptures, it plainly exhibited the workings of providence in the natural order. Although Lyell was keen to turn geology into a quite secular activity, he felt, and expressed in his work, a providentialism as strong as that of his ordained colleagues.

Lyell became uneasy when naturalists started to use his work to support a conclusion that he had personally rejected, namely that species have not come from the hand of the Creator, but have evolved. He had helped the young Darwin to establish himself in London scientific society on his return from the *Beagle* voyage, and the two men kept up a productive association on geological matters. In 1858 Darwin confidently entrusted the first public airing of his theory of evolution by natural selection to Lyell, fully expecting his friend to endorse the theory completely. Darwin saw his own work in some measure as a completion of the project for a naturalistic explanation of earth history that Lyell had initiated, but Lyell was never able to give his full assent to Darwin's work. He had always felt deep private reservations about the implications of evolution theory for mankind's place in nature. He considered descent from the brutes to be incompatible with his conception of human dignity. Accordingly, the last fifteen years of Lyell's life are marked by equivocation whenever he dealt with problems that had an evolutionary aspect. This equivocation came out in his *Geological Evidences of the Antiquity of Man* (1863), and is poignantly recorded in the private journals he kept.

As a clearer understanding of the sophistication of the geological work of Lyell's contemporaries emerges, and as the idiosyncrasies of some of Lyell's own views are confronted, the simple notion that Lyell revolutionized geology fades, but Lyell must continue to be seen as the most famous geologist of his day, and as one who gave enormous imaginative and scientific force to the ideas that the earth is immensely old, and that, species creations excepted, no supernatural interventions have been necessary to modify its surface.

Michael Bartholomew

The standard Victorian biography is *Life, Letters and Journals of Sir Charles Lyell, Bart.*, ed. K.M. Lyell (2 vols, 1881). A good modern account can be found in D.R. Oldroyd, *Darwinian Impacts* (1980). Lyell's private journals have been published: *Sir Charles Lyell's Scientific Journals on the Species Question*, ed. L.G. Wilson (1972).

LYTTON, Lord: see under BULWER-LYTTON, Edward

M

MACAULAY, Thomas Babington, Baron Macaulay
1800–59

British historian

T.B. Macaulay was the eldest son of Zachary Macaulay, Scots philanthropist, West Africa merchant and campaigner against the slave trade, and Selina Mills, daughter of a Quaker Bristol bookseller. Nurtured in Dissent and 'Good Works', Macaulay grew up and remained a fervent Whig; he attempted a universal history when only seven, and, educated privately by an evangelical clergyman, avoided a public school: in 1818 he entered Trinity College, Cambridge, where he won a Craven scholarship and, in spite of the incapacity for mathematics of a born writer, was elected a Fellow in 1824. Though called to the Bar, he never practised, but soon won reputation by articles in the *Edinburgh Review* and by 1830 as MP for Calne he eloquently championed Reform. By 1833 secretary to the Board of Control of the East India Company, he was appointed in 1834 to the Supreme Council for India for five years at £10,000 a year; and his first major public decision was that British Indian education should be geared to English, rather than Indian, culture on the absurd claim that he would 'challenge any oriental to deny that a single shelf of good European Literature is worth the whole native literature of India or Arabia'. More successfully, in 1837, he devised a new criminal code for British India.

On his return to England, with substantial capital saved in India and a legacy from an uncle, which offset the collapse of his father's business, Macaulay in 1839 began his famous *History of England*, covering the period from 1688 to 1820, and, though briefly MP for Edinburgh and Secretary of War, wrote his immensely popular *Lays of Ancient Rome* (1842) and his vivid account of the *Trial of Warren Hastings*. In 1843 he published his brilliant *Essays*, reprinted from the *Edinburgh Review*, which confirmed his celebrity.

By 1848 the first two volumes of the *History* appeared and Macaulay woke up to find himself even more famous. His aim was then new for a historian: 'To supersede the last fashionable novel on the tables of young ladies.' Clarendon had written in depth of affairs of state, and Hume with analytic calm, but Macaulay, whose memory was phenomenal, dramatized history

with lucidity, detail and force. Though never in battle, he depicted it with headlong imaginative confidence, made his characters heroes or villains, and celebrated the triumph of the English establishment after 1688 for its mid-Victorian beneficiaries. In confidence and power of phrase he owed something to Gibbon, but where Gibbon combined superb writing with wit, irony, insight, and range, Macaulay's brassy public style is often the declamation of a politician; and while the sweep of his narrative compels attention and his apposite detail haunts the mind, compared with Gibbon, Thucydides, Tacitus or von Ranke*, he remains a brilliant if sometimes shallow provincial.

Yet his hard common sense, dislike of abstractions and limited range well suited his public, while his style and sense of place were hypnotic; as on the siege of Londonderry:

> It was the twenty eighth of July. The sun had set: the evening sermon in the Cathedral was over; and the heartbroken congregation had separated; when the sentinels on the tower saw the sails of three vessels coming up the Foyle. Soon there was a stir in the Irish camp. The besiegers were on the alert for miles along both shores. The ships were in extreme peril: for the river was low . . . . At length the little squadron came to the place of peril. Then the Mountjoy took the lead, and went right at the boom. The huge barricade cracked and gave way.

Readers brought up on Scott's* romantic novels were swept along by the pace and vigour of a pictorial narrative, and a robust and public style, spiced with the intimate and picturesque, appealed to readers who considered political events supremely important. And Macaulay took sides; as in describing Clive's exploit with a tiny force 'determined to put everything to the hazard' at Plassey, though reflecting 'against what odds, and for what a prize, he was in a few hours, to contend.' He also depicted character by appearance; as Warren Hastings, supposedly a 'culprit', who looked:

> Like a great man, and not like a bad man. A person small and emaciated, yet deriving dignity from a carriage which, while it indicated deference to the court, indicated also habitual self possession and self respect, a high and intellectual forehead, a brow

pensive, but not gloomy, a mouth of inflexible decision, a face pale and worn, but serene, on which was written, as legibly as under the picture in the council-chamber at Calcutta, *Mens aequa in arduis*.

Having created such vivid and obvious versions of public events and characters, Macaulay confirmed the prejudices of his readers and asserted his own authority by confident and apparently final judgments in the light of his belief in progress.

So, when in 1855, the third and fourth volumes of the *History* appeared, 26,500 copies sold in ten weeks and earned their author £20,000. Within ten years sales had reaches 140,000 in Great Britain alone, with equivalent sales in America, and on the continent of Europe. In 1857, on the recommendation of Palmerston, the historian was created Baron Macaulay; but by December 1859 he was dead of heart trouble, to be interred in Westminster Abbey.

Macaulay was short, stout, voluble and good company: a man of the world with a better political judgment than many academics. A confirmed bachelor who liked his comforts, he was a beloved uncle to the family of Sir Charles Trevelyan, an eminent official who had married Macaulay's sister, who herself edited the posthumous fifth volume of the *History* in 1861. An eight-volume edition was published in 1858–62 and one in four volumes in 1863–4; *Miscellaneous Writings* appearing in two volumes in 1860. The *Life and Letters of Lord Macaulay*, edited by Sir G.O. Trevelyan (two volumes) was published in 1876 (revised 1959).

Macaulay's influence was lasting and pervasive, particularly on the historian G.M. Trevelyan, on Sir Winston Churchill's *A History of the English Speaking Peoples*, and on many modern historians distinguished by their style. But this success and some of its imitators provoked reaction, especially as, following the outstanding success of scientific method, some historians were trying to make history a 'science', a sheer accumulation of facts presented with entire and unattainable impartiality. Hence the inept current distinction between 'literary' historians and 'researchers', irrelevant to history which is inevitably an art, and, if not literary, boring and even unintelligible. While Macaulay in depth and range was hardly of the first rank, he was a brilliant writer and the tradition he enriched is in the mainstream of historiography.

John Bowle

See: Sir Arthur Bryant, *Macaulay* (1932); and H.R. Trevor Roper, 'Macaulay and the Glorious Revolution', in *Historical Essays* (1957).

283
MACH, Ernst 1838–1916

Austrian scientist, historian and philosopher of science

Although Mach had wide-ranging scientific interests and contributed to various fields, especially sound and physiology of perception, these contributions were not perhaps of the first importance, and his lasting influence has been based largely on his work in the history and philosophy of science. This work was widely known in Vienna at the end of the nineteenth century and beginning of the twentieth (Mach spent the last six years of his working life at the University of Vienna) and his very strict positivist views undoubtedly strongly influenced Wittgenstein and the members of the Vienna Circle – indeed, the public organization formed by several members of the circle was given the name *Ernst Mach Verein* (the 'Ernst Mach Society').

Mach was born in 1838 in Chirlitz-Turas, near Brno, Morovia (now part of Czechoslovakia). His father played the central role in his early education, instilling in him a particular love of 'nature study'. Mach spent five years studying mathematics, physics and philosophy at the University of Vienna, obtaining his doctorate, with a dissertation on electrical discharge and induction, in 1860. The wide range of his scientific interests is to some degree reflected in the variety of his subsequent university titles. He was Professor of Mathematics and then of Physics at Graz (in fact he spent most of his time there working on 'psychophysics' – on what we would now call the psychology and physiology of perception). In 1867 he became Professor of Experimental Physics at Charles University, Prague. And finally he returned to Vienna as Professor of the History and Theory of the Inductive Sciences in 1895. He retired in 1901, becoming in that same year a member of the upper house of the Austrian parliament. He died in 1916.

His name is remembered in the theory of perception for the so-called 'Mach bands' which he studied and described, and in supersonics for the 'Mach numbers' (based on the ratio of the speed of an object to the speed of sound in the undisturbed medium in which the object is travelling).

The general philosophical position that he developed was an extreme version of empiricism, reminiscent in certain respect of Berkeley's view. Its fullest exposition appears in his book *The Analysis of Sensations* (*Die Analyse der Empfindungen und das Verhältnis des Physichen zum Psychischen*, 1886, 9th edition, trans. 1914). He insists that 'the world consists only of our sensations'. Talk of physical objects, independent of ourselves and causing these sensations, is not to be interpreted realistically. More generally, our scientific theories are not to be regarded as hypothesizing a reality hidden behind the phenomena – *only* the phenomena are real – the role of theories is simply to codify and schematize the phenomena in a convenient and economical way. The aim of theoretical science is not to explain, but to introduce 'economy of thought' through the construction of functional relationships between entities ultimately denoting the elements of sensation. His general philosophical position led Mach to the view that the barriers between the various sciences are purely artificial: there are no differences of subject matter – all the sciences study our sensations.

Although Mach's phenomenalism has been very influential, there are certain rather obvious difficulties with it (such as the problem of other minds, the fact that it flies in the face of the realist beliefs of the overwhelming majority of scientists, etc.) to which Mach produced no very convincing reply. And, indeed, although twentieth-century Anglo-Saxon philosophy has in the main tended towards a positivism of a more or less Machian kind (Russell's 'neutral monism', for example, owes much to Mach), there have been notable philosophers who have reacted strongly against this mainstream view, and have subjected Mach's position to attack. One famous attack was launched from the viewpoint of dialectical materialism by Lenin in his 1909 book *Materialism and Empirio-Criticism: Critical Comments on a Reactionary Philosophy*. More recently, Karl Popper has been a consistent critic of positivism in general and of Mach's position in particular.

Perhaps the most fundamental *internal* difficulty in Mach's views is this: on the one hand he taught that no concept was admissible in science unless it is firmly rooted in (definable in terms of) 'experience'; on the other hand, he saw the role of science as that of maximizing 'economy of thought'. What guarantee have we that these two ideas do not clash? Why may not the theory producing the most economical representation of the phenomena involve highly theoretical or metaphysical concepts which are *not* 'reducible' to experience? Mach's famous opposition to the atomic-kinetic theory (discussed below) highlights this difficulty.

The idea that the world consists only of our sensations was never very influential within science itself. But Mach's claim that concepts which cannot be 'reduced' to experience must be eliminated from science *was* widely discussed by scientists. Because of his vigorous advocacy of this claim, Mach is usually cast in the strange dual role of dogmatic reactionary concerning one scientific revolution, and visionary progenitor of another.

Not surprisingly, Mach was very much opposed to invisible atoms and molecules, and this translated itself into near life-long opposition to the atomic-kinetic theory of heat. Despite his opposition, this theory underwent a most fruitful revival during the second half of the nineteenth century. The theory, developed by Clausius*, Boltzmann*, Maxwell* and others, held that gases, for example, are made up of molecules moving around randomly at high velocities. Heating the gas gives a greater mean velocity to the molecules and in fact the temperature of the gas is a measure of the mean kinetic energy of its constituent molecules. Mach insisted that no good could come of hypothesizing such invisible entities and advocated that scientists stick more closely to the direct phenomena of heat – to so-called phenomenological thermodynamics. There were undoubtedly real difficulties in the kinetic theory to which Mach could point; but most scientists preferred to tackle these difficulties rather than reject the whole theory on dogmatic anti-atomist grounds. Their attitude was vindicated when the atomic-kinetic theory turned out to have new consequences which were dramatically confirmed experimentally.

It seems that Mach's insistence that all scientific concepts be experimentally definable and his consequent crusade against atoms at least partially blinded him to the possibility that the kinetic *theory* could be scientifically superior to its rivals. Indeed this superiority would be explained on Mach's own terms if the atomic theory turned out to classify more phenomena more 'economically' than other theories. This illustrates the main difficulty in Mach's views alluded to above.

Although his anti-atomism was very much out of tenor with mainstream scientific thought, Mach's similarly based opposition to certain mechanical notions is held by many commentators to have helped instigate the Einsteinian relativity revolution.

In many ways Mach's most impressive work was his *The Science of Mechanics: A Critical and Historical Account of its Development* (*Die Mechanik in Ihrer Entwicklung historisch-kritisch dargestellt*, 1883 trans. 1942). He there charts the history of mechanics – principally with a view to conceptual analysis of its foundations. Pursuing his overall objective to rid science of any concept not firmly rooted in experience, Mach strongly criticized Newton's notions of absolute time, space and motion. According to Newton there is, as well as motion relative to some more or less arbitrarily chosen 'fixed' point, *absolute* motion – motion 'relative' to space ('God's sensorium') itself. Moreover, according to Newton, there is no need to refer time to anything in our experience – time too is absolute, 'flowing uniformly without regard to anything external'.

Mach had no time for such metaphysical notions – for example, all motion is, for him, relative, because only if it is observed can it exist and motion can only be observed relative to some chosen coordinate system.

The most distinctive feature of the special theory of relativity which Einstein proposed in 1905 as a rival to, and replacement for, Newtonian mechanics, is its insistence that all motion is indeed relative to a frame of reference. Moreover, according to relativity theory, the time interval too is frame-dependent; two events which are simultaneous in one frame of reference may not be simultaneous in another frame moving relatively to the first. It is no surprise then that Mach is regarded as having played an important role in the genesis of relativity theory – especially as Einstein himself admitted that Mach had influenced his early thought.

Mach is also attributed a role in the development of *general* relativity theory, which yields Einstein's account of gravitation and which was proposed in 1914. In the *Science of Mechanics*, Mach had criticized not only Newton's treatment of motion but also his treatment of *mass*. Newton had characterized this as 'quantity of matter' – much too metaphysical an idea for Mach since it is not firmly grounded in experimental procedures. Mach proposed a different characterization of the mass of a body, which has, as a consequence, the proposition that a single body in an otherwise empty universe would exhibit no resistance to acceleration, i.e. have no mass. Einstein christened this proposition 'Mach's principle'. Its precise consequences and its role in the genesis of general relativity theory have ever since been matters of heated debate. (Although the principle could well have been suggestive for Einstein, it does *not* follow from his general theory as he eventually realized.)

We have Einstein's word for it that Mach's views influenced him, but whether these views played a really significant role in the relativity revolution is open to doubt. Certainly other factors (internal factors from within science itself) played a more important role; and certainly the idea that the relativity breakthrough consisted chiefly of ridding science of some excess metaphysical baggage is greatly exaggerated – relativity theory is, in its own way, just as 'absolutist' as its Newtonian predecessor. Einstein himself later came to realize the untenability of Mach's positivism; and, as for Mach, he always disclaimed any responsibility for relativity theory, which he *explicitly* rejected.

John Worrall

Other books by Mach include: Knowledge and Error (*Erkenntnis und Irrtum* 1905, trans. 1926, 1976); and two important historical works: *The Principles of Physical Optics* (*Die Principien der Physikalischen Optik. Historisch und Erkenntnis-psychologisch entwickelt*, 1921, trans. 1926) and *Die Principien der Wärmelehre: Historisch-kritisch entwickelt* (1896).

284
MACHADO DE ASSIS, Joaquim Maria 1839–1908

Brazilian writer

Unanimously reckoned as the foremost name in Brazilian literature and one of the very greatest masters of fiction in Portuguese, Joaquim Maria Machado de As-

sis was born a poor mulatto on a Rio hill, where his parents lived under the protection of the widow of an empire grandee. He was brought up by a kind stepmother, a negress. Still in his teens, the self-taught boy, who learnt French from the Gallic bakers of the Court district, S. Cristóvão, was helped by a Dickensian figure, the printer and bookseller Paula Brito, into entering the world of journalism and of the belated Latin-American Romanticism; he spent most of his twenties as a drama critic, a translator (notably of Hugo* and Dickens*) and a parliamentary reporter deeply attached to liberal causes. His status improved at thirty, when he became a government official, and when he married Carolina, the mature and learned sister of his friend, a minor Portuguese poet named Faustino Xavier de Novaes. A tough social climber, he turned his back on everything connected with his humble past, including his stepmother. Machado had suffered for long from epilepsy, though of a milder kind than Dostoevsky's*. Shortly before he was forty, a major crisis forced him to a protracted convalescence in a mountain resort near Rio. The result was a baffling transformation of the outlook of his work, issuing in the unique prose works which earned him his enduring glory. By the closing years of the century, he led, with the critic José Veríssimo, the group of the Revista Brasileira, cradle of the Brazilian Academy, whose chairmanship he was offered by general consensus. Remote as he was to everything smacking of edifying literature, he died as the living symbol of institutional fine letters, widely acclaimed yet scarcely understood. The subsequent heroic age of the *avant-garde* entailed further misunderstandings; the noisy Dionysiac nationalism of 'modernismo' was indeed a far cry from the subtle shadows of Machadian art.

Machado first reached consistent literary quality as a poet. In *Americanas* (1875) he added moral probing to the staple Romantic subject matter of *indianismo*; the *Ocidentais* (written *c*. 1880) yield philosophical musings in impeccable Parnassian technique. The beginnings of the story-teller were also romantic. Like the founder of Brazilian novel, José de Alencar (1829 – 77), who befriended him, Machado was alive to the dialectic of love, money and ambition in well-to-do urban settings of mid-century Brazil; on the other hand, he still sticks to the Victorian versions of values such as honesty, self-sacrifice and the work ethic. But he shows remarkable skill in drawing female characters and eventually, in his fourth novel, *Iaiá Garcia* (1878), eschews melodramatic language for the sake of natural dialogues and deeper psychological analysis.

Yet it was the short story that harboured his final break with Romanticism. The novelette 'The Alienist', a masterpiece where Swiftian humour is enhanced by anachronism, portrays the toils of Dr Simon Bacamarte, a paragon of moral and scientific integrity who, having started a thorough research on human folly as 'an island lost amidst the ocean of reason', fatally begins to suspect it is rather like a continent. Madness, and especially madness *qua* vice, is universal; man is most often a predatory animal, and men slaves to opinion. Coming back to one's senses actually means coming back to *other's* senses, says the story which theorizes about selfhood as the 'external soul'. The significance of Machado's later novels lies in their ability to project this wry cast of mind on the formal level. Thus *Epitaph of a Small Winner* (*Memórias póstumas de Brás Cubas*, 1881, trans. 1952), originally entitled 'Posthumous Memoirs of Brás Cubas', technically amounts to a wilful return from Flaubert* to Sterne – a Sterne purged of sentimentality. This odd book, written 'with a mocking pen and melancholy ink', re-enacts an old genre: the Menippean satire, the comic-fantastic brand of philosophical narrative. Machado is a modern Lucian who put the menippean within the crazy autobiographical framework of a 'dead author', Brás Cubas, a wealthy, selfish *fainéant* with a few amours and much spleen, who deems nature a plague and history a catastrophe. The background of his erratic memoirs discloses the misery and sadism of slave-owning elites ever hankering after lust and power. Machado writes as a disillusioned French moralist well acquainted with Schopenhauer*, who cannot help caricaturing philosophical optimism ('humanitism') as sheer nonsense. Nevertheless, unlike other late nineteenth-century pessimists, he is by no means a determinist, and does not seem to hold too tragic a view of mankind. Instead, he keeps a sense of *lusus naturae*, and defines man as 'a thinking erratum'. Most of Machado's later *contos* (short stories) are in keeping with this poetics of disillusion. Although he was also an excellent *conteur à la* Maupassant*, as well as a master of the apologue, Machado's favourite focus fell on the painting of characters in the La Bruyèrean sense: taken together, his *contos* present a magnificent moral pageant, rendered with a command of narrative technique unsurpassed in the Iberian countries until Borges. Machado's characters are not, like those of Naturalism (which he opposed), *described* – rather, they *betray* themselves, caught, as it were, in the net of nimble sentences fraught with witty, revealing tropes.

The *Epitaph*'s sequel, *Philosopher or Dog* (*Quincas Borba*, 1891, trans. 1954), is also told in short chapters, but in the third person and with the humorous authorial interventions made more organically related to the plot. The anti-hero, Rubião, far less eccentric than Cubas, is a humane fool, a *loco cuerdo* enriched by an inheritance and – as a victim of megalomania – an easy prey to the cupidity of those he helped or saved. With *Dom Casmurro* (1899, trans. 1953), Machado returned to the first person novel, but this time with fewer characters. Dom Casmurro – 'the Brazilian Othello', as an American critic described him – is an unsocial widower trying to relive the green paradise of youthful love. He is obsessed with Capitu, the sensuous brunette who embodies the 'life is treason' theme, not the least because their son grows into a startling resemblance of the couple's best friend. The 'impregnation' motive – the idea that a woman can lend her child the looks of her beloved even though the latter has not fathered it – was already present in Goethe's* *Elective Affinities* (1809) and at the centre of young Zola's* *Madeleine Férat* (1868); but Machado tackles it with a wonderful, truly Jamesian* impressionistic sensibility, particularly apt at grasping the feeling of time.

The novels of maturity are crowned by *Esau and Jacob* (1904, trans. 1966), again in the first person, but with a positively self-effacing narrator, the retired diplomat Ayres. Allegory prevails throughout, especially around Flora, a Botticellian beauty who proves foreign to the world of passion and appetite (and the rivalry of two brothers) because she is in love with the absolute. Since the action of *Epitaph for a Small Winner* harks back to pre-Independence Brazil, and *Esau and Jacob* comments on the first decade of the Republic, with a novel like *Iaià Garcia*, set in the days of the war with Paraguay, in the middle, one might say that Machado's chronicle of Brazilian life covers the whole of his century. In spite of his conscious avoidance of 'social' fiction, no other novelist provides more insight into the national mind of the age. In an oblique way, Machado often showed the huge gap between progressive bourgeois ideology and the grim realities of Brazilian class structure. His book-length farewell to fiction, *Counsellor Ayres' Memorial* (*Memorial de Aires*, 1908, trans. 1973), goes beyond misanthropy in the purest music of Machadian prose. Some see in his language – a faultless balance of high and low, old and new usage – his most precious bequest to Brazilian literature; its expressive powers also shine in a modest but most popular genre, the *cronica*, which was established by Machado. Perhaps the biggest paradox about Machado de Assis is that such a profound writer, in whose hands Brazilian letters outgrew the age of naive consciousness, should also be the least solemn of authors.

J.G. Merquior

For a selection of his short stories see *The Psychiatrist and Other Stories* (trans. 1963). Important studies include: Augusto Meyer, *Machado de Assis* (Rio, 1958); Eugenio Gomes, *Machado de Assis* (Rio, 1958); Helen Caldwell, *Machado de Assis: The Brazilian Master and his Novels* (1970); Dieter Woll, *Machado de Assis – die Entwicklung seines erzaehlerischen Werkes* (1972); Roberto Schwarz, *Ao Vencedor as Batatas* (São Paulo, 1977); R. Magalhães Jr, *Vida e Obra de Machado de Assis* (4 vols, 1981).

285

MAETERLINCK, Mauritius Polydorus Maria
Bernardus 1862–1949

French-Belgian dramatist and essayist

Bilingual in Flemish and French, Maurice Maeterlinck grew up in Ghent, later the centre of the Belgian Symbolist movement, to which he contributed along with his poet friends Charles van Lerberghe and Grégoire le Roy. After the Parisian stir occasioned by his first play *La Princesse Maleine* (published in 1890 but never staged), Maeterlinck became a controversial figure in his native country, where new departures in the arts were not encouraged. By 1897, he had moved to France, where he took up residence for the rest of his life in a succession of picturesque retreats, including a medieval abbey and a converted casino near Nice to which he gave the fairy-tale name of Orlamonde. Apart from an early liaison with the actress Georgette Leblanc, his later marriage, his wartime exile in the United States (1940–7) and the various literary honours that accrued to him, Maeterlinck's life was outwardly uneventful, being rather a series of adventures of the spirit pursued in a comfortable privacy.

Maeterlinck's first publication was a collection of Symbolist poems entitled *Serres chaudes* ('Hothouse Blooms', 1889). These comprise on the one hand poems in regular quatrains which sound a wistful and naively folkloric note; and on the other, several innovatory free-verse pieces. These evoke typically Symbolist moods of ennui or melancholy: their originality lies in the wilful strangeness of their oddly juxtaposed images, in which indeterminate references transmit connotations of unrest, doubt, poignant enigma. It is as though, imbibing the poetic influence of Whitman*, Poe* and Rimbaud*, Maeterlinck had made an intuitive leap into an idiom of hallucinatory landscaping which even anticipates some of the bizarre visions of Surrealism, as witness these lines from 'Cloche à plongeur' ('Diving-bell'):

Take heed! the shadows of great schooners are
    cruising over the dahlias in the forests beneath
    the sea!
And for a moment I fall in the shadow of whales
    as they head for the Pole!
At this very instant, the others are doubtless un-
    loading ships laden with snow in the harbour!
There was still a glacier left amid the July
    meadows!
They are swimming backwards in the green waters
    of the bay!
At noon they enter gloomy grottoes!
And breezes from the open sea are fanning the
    terraces!

Maeterlinck had hit on a formula for eliciting waves of indefinite yet powerful association by the oblique presentation of people doing simple yet unexplained things in strange and empty places. The essence of his Symbolist procedure lies in this poetic structuring of moods of uncertainty and foreboding, and it is out of this that he developed the successful style of his early dramatic work. *Les Aveugles* ('The Blind', 1890) is a one-act dialogue between thirteen blind people who stand in a grim Nordic forest scarcely lit by faltering moonlight, waiting with varying degrees of impatience for a nameless stranger, who never shows up. The play is entirely static, consisting merely of the speeches of these practically disembodied voices, which comment in hollow tones on the emptiness of life and the hopelessness of the human condition. Nothing happens or can happen: existence seems to have seized up. The play is a remarkable early manifestation of absurdist paralysis in the theatre, anticipating Beckett's *Waiting for Godot* (1955) by over six decades.

In comparison, *Pelléas et Mélisande* (1892, trans. 1894) resembles a colourful melodrama in its collation of extravagant themes, including adulterous passion, attempted and actual fratricide, and the heroine's final tragic death. Yet for all its essential Romanticism, Maeterlinck shapes the play in a decisively discrepant way, deliberately depriving the action of any colour or energy. The plot advances with scarcely any perceptible stress, the characters speaking abstractly *past* rather than *to* one another – or else speaking on one level while listening in on another. They give the impression of being 'somewhat deaf somnambulists who keep getting dragged out of a painful sleep', in the dramatist's own rather rueful words. As if caught in a cycle of hypnotic repetition, the characters enact another allegory of doomed waiting, borne down by a horrifying fatality that stifles all personality and initiative. *Pelléas et Mélisande* is a play which compulsively shies away from explanation. Who exactly is Mélisande? What are her true feelings towards Golaud? Why does she lose her wedding-ring in the fountain? How is it that Pelléas fails to realize he is falling in love with her? Does Golaud act consciously or in a state of maddened automatism when he kills Pelléas? Maeterlinck allows no answers: the texture of the action is all murmur and mystery, a drift into darkness. As such, the play's affinities lie less with drama proper than with the wordless suggestivity of music, and the play indeed inspired fine incidental music by Fauré* (1889) and Sibelius (1905), as well as Debussy's *drame lyrique Pelléas et Mélisande* (1902), where spellbound recitative and shimmering orchestral textures exactly match Maeterlinck's minimally accented portrayal of human helplessness.

'It should never be supposed that language ever serves as a true communication between people' is a disturbing aphorism from 'Le Silence', in Maeterlinck's first book of essays, *The Treasure of the Humble* (*Le Trésor des humbles*, 1896, trans. 1897). But what might at first be construed as a watchword of pessimism, the recognition of man's irreducible solipsism and consequent irredeemable solitude, soon emerges in more positive light as Maeterlinck, under the influence of Georgette Leblanc, goes on to speak of the intuitive non-verbal contact that links sensitive people together. Maeterlinck speaks of an 'active silence' through which man can divine his position within the unspeaking world of nature. And far from sticking to the bleak fatalism of the early plays, Maeterlinck will argue his way forward in a long cycle of major essays composed throughout the rest of his life, in search of a position of ultimate serenity, fascination and sense of belonging in the world. It is true, Maeterlinck contends, that we are unable to articulate the deeper meanings of existence, so that the world appears to lack final explanation. Yet we should not abandon hope, for our intuitive understanding of the ineffable mysteries is advancing all the while.

A sedulous observer of phenomena like sleeping and dreaming, and an ardent student of telepathy and other aspects of para-psychology, Maeterlinck adumbrates a poetic metaphysics which is as confident as it is ultimately unfalsifiable. In it he shows himself to be an heir to the mysticism of his countryman Ruysbroeck (whose *Adornment of Spiritual Marriage* he translated in 1889) and of the German Romantic Novalis (whom he translated in 1895), as well as to the occult tradition at large, which he surveyed in *Le Grand Secret* ('The Great Secret', 1921).

Though Maeterlinck had a keen interest in the natural sciences, it usually played second string to his poetic fancy. In *The Life of Space* (*La Vie de l'espace*, 1928, trans. 1928), he addresses himself to the poetic implications of the idea of a fourth dimension: 'The problem of the fourth dimension is not only a mathematical problem; it is a problem integral to real life.' The book is a highly speculative gloss on post-Einsteinian hypotheses, and is in some measure indebted to the ideas of Ouspensky. Maeterlinck's broad intention in his metaphysical essays is to reconcile the two ways of the spiritual and the material: 'It is probable that where there is matter, there is equally spirit, since they are in all likelihood two aspects of the same substance, matter ending with the beginning of spirit, and spirit beginning with the end of matter.'

The oracular lyricism of such propositions is balanced by a cycle of essays about observable natural phenomena – the life of insects and plants. In *The Life of the Ant* (*La Vie des fourmis*, 1930, trans. 1931), Maeterlinck describes with the patient delight of a Fabre the complex habits of the insect, while also allowing himself occasional divagations on such topics as the immortality of the ant, and the 'totemism' which he sees as underlying the religious structure of its collec-

tivized community. In *L'Araignée de verre* ('The Glass Spider', 1932), he reports in close detail his personal observations of the *Argyroneta aquatica*, the water-spider which creates its own under-water air supply, contenting himself here with the straightforward description of a marvel in order implicitly to underline the point that Nature is more inventive and mysteriously consistent than man normally recognizes. In *The Intelligence of Flowers* (*L'Intelligence des fleurs*, 1907, trans. 1907), he is at pains to list the incredible variety of plant forms, the subtleties of their smells, their many far-fetched modes of reproduction. The moral is again uplifting: if such a colourful exhibition of oddities and monstrosities can be shown to have purpose, then all creation must surely have meaning – there is no phenomenon which does not function in the universal teleology.

The essays are sometimes flawed by sententiousness and aphoristic glibness, as well as by sentimentality and a rather naive approach to themes like reincarnation and human immortality. Maeterlinck is manifestly a poet rather than a philosopher: even so, his essays on existence have a lingering charm, deriving mainly from his recourse to poetic analogy, and especially the notion of a harmony between inner and outer reality, wherein he manifests his fundamental kinship with nineteenth-century and specifically Romantic currents of thought.

Maeterlinck's reputation was at its peak in the 1890s, during the period of his first theatrical productions. It remained small but even through the next few decades when, withdrawn from public life, he released a steady stream of meditative essays to the world. But in a postwar period coloured by discussions of existentialism and political commitment, the quietistic colouring of his work could no longer have any impact. His death in 1949 passed unnoticed in France, and although in recent years his reputation has been assiduously promoted in his native Belgium, the 1911 recipient of the Nobel Prize for Literature is today practically unknown within European culture at large.

Roger Cardinal

Maeterlinck's other plays include: *La Mort de Tintagiles* (1894, trans. *The Death of Tintagiles*, 1899); *Ariadne et Barbe-bleue* ('Ariadne and Bluebeard', 1902); and the best-selling fairy-play *L'Oiseau bleu* (1908, trans. *The Blue Bird*, 1909). The early Symbolist plays (1889–1902) have been reissued as *Théâtre Complet* (1979). The two score volumes of his essays also include: *La Vie des abeilles* (1901, trans. *The Life of the Bee*, 1901); *Le Temple enseveli* ('The Buried Temple', 1902); and *La Grande Porte* ('The Great Doorway', 1939). There is also a volume of childhood reminiscences, *Bulles bleues* (1948, trans. *Blue Bubbles*, 1949). His poetry is collected in *Poésies complètes* (1965). English translations of Maeterlinck were a commonplace up until the thirties, but today very little remains in print. See: May Daniels, *The French Drama of the Unspoken* (1953); W.D. Halls, *Maurice Maeterlinck* (1960); *Maurice Maeterlinck 1862–1962*, ed. J. Hanse and R. Vivier (Brussels, 1962); Alex Pasquier, *Maurice Maeterlinck* (Brussels, 1963); Marcel Postic, *Maeterlinck et le symbolisme* (1970).

286
MAHLER, Gustav 1860–1911

Austrian composer

The second of fourteen children Mahler studied music at the Vienna Conservatoire under Robert Fuchs and Franz Krenn and at the University of Vienna with Anton Bruckner*. He began his career as a conductor at Linz in 1880 and returned to the Linz Opera as one of its two chief conductors in 1886, having spent the intervening years as conductor at the Cassel Opera, the Prague Opera and elsewhere. The First Symphony (1888), the *Lieder eines fahrended Gesellen* (1884) and *Das klagende Lied* (1880) belong to this early period of his creative career.

In 1888 Mahler was appointed director of the Budapest Opera and in 1891 the chief conductor of the Hamburg Opera. For the ten years from 1897 to 1907 Mahler was conductor and general director of the Vienna Opera and also occasional conductor of the Vienna Philharmonic. In 1901 he married Alma Schindler. During these years as conductor of the Vienna Staatsoper he composed Symphonies 4–8 and the *Rückert Songs*.

Following his resignation from the Vienna Opera in 1901 Mahler left Europe to take up a post in America as conductor of the Metropolitan Opera and the New York Philharmonic. He returned to Europe in the early months of 1911 and died in Vienna in May of that year.

Despite the bitter controversy surrounding his appointment and tenure of office as the director of the Vienna Staatsoper – a controversy which eventually led to his leaving Vienna – Mahler was generally acknowledged to be one of the finest conductors of his generation. Composing was almost entirely confined to the summer months, when the opera was closed, with what little free time was available during the rest of the year being devoted to copying and scoring the works.

Apart from a number of songs for voice and piano or voice and orchestra, Mahler's creative output consists entirely of symphonies. Mahler's symphonies can be conveniently divided into three chronological and stylistic groups: 1) the first four symphonies, all of which employ material from Mahler's settings of poems from the *Das Knaben Wunderhorn* collection of German folk poetry (Symphonies 2, 3 and 4) or from the *Lieder eines fahrenden Gesellen* song cycle (Symphony 1). With the exception of the First Symphony all the works in this group employ voices: a single soprano voice in the Fourth Symphony; soloists and a large chorus in Symphonies 2 and 3; 2) the three purely instrumental middle period symphonies (nos 5, 6 and 7); 3) the works of the final years including the vast Symphony no. 8, the so-called 'Symphony of a thousand' (the performance of which requires a double mixed chorus, a children's chorus and eight solo voices as well as a large orchestra), *Das Lied von der Erde*, a 'symphony' for tenor and alto soloists and orchestra, the instrumental Ninth Symphony and the unfinished Tenth Symphony.

In many respects Mahler's symphonies can be seen as the final products of the tradition of the Austro-German symphony during the Romantic period. Like most nineteenth-century German composers Mahler felt that Beethoven* had established the symphony as the supreme musical form and consequently regarded it as being the only form suited to the expression of sustained, serious musical-philosophical thought. Many of the characteristics of Mahler's musical style are a logical extension of the features to be found in the work of his immediate predecessors. Thus, for example, Mahler's time scale springs from that of the Wagnerian* music drama, his use of large choral and instrumental forces in a symphony from the example of Beethoven's Choral Symphony, his fondness for simple folk-like melodies and for folk dances such as the Ländler from Schubert* and Weber* and his discursive and frequently leisurely developmental technique from Schubert. On a less purely musical level many of those features that appear to be peculiarly Mahlerian – his love of the grotesque, the demoniacal and the sinister, his view of the artist as an individual isolated from society, his feeling for nature and for natural sounds and his occasional triumphant visions of the possibility of redemption – are equally typical of much of the artistic work and thought of the German Romantics. Although Mahler expanded both the time scale of the individual movements and the number of movements in a work, his formal designs are those traditionally employed in the German symphony, the weight of the musical argument being concentrated in the sonata form first movement and in the last movement of the work (which may also be a sonata form) with the central movements (often, in Mahler, a collection of three or four short movements) forming a lighter, more relaxed episode.

Alongside such traditional and characteristically late-romantic elements, however, can be found many techniques and an aesthetic outlook that now strike us as peculiarly modern and forward-looking. Like Berlioz*, the other great virtuoso composer-conductor of the nineteenth century, Mahler had an unerring ear for instrumental timbre. By employing his large forces less to create big 'massed' effects than as a means of obtaining a wide variety of instrumental colour, Mahler created a new 'unblended', chamber music-like texture (achieved by bringing together clearly differentiated solo timbres) that was to have a great influence on those composers who followed him. To some extent this handling of the orchestra was a result of Mahler's equally forward-looking conception of music as being essentially polyphonic, the harmonies resulting from the coming together of a number of separate melodic lines. In the Ninth and Tenth Symphonies the individuality of the parts, coupled with the large leaps and the extreme chromaticism that springs from the desire for maximum emotional expression, creates a harmonic structure that frequently borders on the edge of atonality.

Equally significant as a pointer to future musical developments are the aesthetic implications of Mahler's style. In Mahler's works intensely emotional and deeply felt passages exist alongside music which seems deliberately to question and undermine this emotional ardour; the folksongs give way to tortuous chromatic lines, the simple dance melodies to biting dissonance, the naive to the sardonic, the noble and elevated to the banal and trivial. The characteristically late-romantic yearning is, thus, coupled with a bitter acceptance of the impossibility of recapturing the tonal and moral innocence towards which much of the music seems to reach. It is this emotional ambiguity, the ironic detachment which enables Mahler to confront his own emotional response and his own illusions, that makes him such an influential figure in the development of the twentieth-century music. A typically Mahlerian use of the cheap and trivial can be found in works as different as Berg's *Wozzeck*, Britten's *Peter Grimes* and Vaughan Williams's Fourth Symphony as well as in much of the music of Shostakovich and Peter Maxwell Davies. To the extent that Mahler's irony is also a means of creating a music which questions its own premises – a means, that is, of creating a music about music – Mahler's work not only looks forward to the themes of such apparently antithetical works as Berg's *Lulu* and Stravinsky's *The Rake's Progress* but anticipates one of the basic concerns of much twentieth-century art.

Douglas Jarman

See: *Mahler, Memoirs and Letters*, to Alma Mahler, ed. Donald Mitchell (1973); *Selected Letters of Gustav Mahler*, ed. Knud Martner (1979); Bruno Walter, *Gustav Mahler* (1941); Donald Mutchell, *Gustav Mahler; The Early Years* (1958) and *Gustav Mahler; The Wunderhorn Years* (1975); Henry-Louis de la Grange, *Mahler* (vol. 1, 1974); Natalie Bauer-Lechner, *Recollections of Gustav Mahler* (1980).

287
MAINE DE BIRAN, Marie François Pierre Gontler 1766–1824

French philosopher and psychologist

For a man whose main aim was to reflect on the nature of his inner experience, Maine de Biran was, paradoxically, deeply involved in public affairs. Born in Bergerac (Dordogne), at eighteen he joined the Royal Lifeguards in Paris where he was slightly wounded whilst defending Louis XVI at Versailles in 1789. The changing political situation led to a period of retreat at the family home until 1795, when he became administrator of the Dordogne. A brief appointment as member of the Council of Five Hundred during the Directory ended with the *coup d'état* of Fructidor. Other administrative posts followed, including that of subprefect of the Dordogne. In 1812 he took up his seat on the Legislative Body and distinguished himself as a member of the Commission of Five. During most of the Restoration he was deputy for Bergerac and a member of the Council of State. His diary attests to the conscientious manner in which he carried out these duties and also to his tolerant although rather conservative political attitudes.

Alongside this active public career Maine de Biran led an intense inner life which is reflected in his philosophical diary. From 1794 to 1804 he was associated with the *Idéologues* who, inspired by Locke and Condillac's sensualism, attempted to refine these anti-metaphysical and empiricist philosophers. He was also attracted to Rousseau's projects to analyse the variable effects of the environment on human will. Very soon, however, he rejected the main ideas of the *Idéologues* and moved towards a belief that inner experience is different from the outward sensations that were so important to Condillac and the *Idéologues*.

In his first published work, *The Influence of Habit on the Faculty of Thought* (*L'Influence de l'habitude sur la faculté de pensée*, 1802, trans. 1929), Biran stressed the importance of the will and distinguished between, on the one hand, passively experienced sensations (*la sensibilité passive*), and, on the other, perceptions which depend on conscious inner effort (*L'activité motrice*) and which are capable of increased perfection (the acquiring of skills, for example). He summed up his thinking at this stage when he suggested that, 'There is in man an active force, which we must be careful not to confuse with the purely passive impressions we receive from our senses', and that, 'Effort, the immediate evidence of activity, is in its two terms (subject and resistance), the basis of personal consciousness, of knowledge, of the external world and of all intellectual operations.'

In subsequent works, particularly in *Mémoire sur la décomposition de la pensée* ('The Analysis of Thought', 1804) and in *Essai sur les fondements de la psychologie*

('Essay on the Foundations of Psychology', 1812), he reaffirmed these ideas and cemented the foundation of his psychology, which lies in the synthesis of this theory of effort, as a complex mental act, and the consciousness of resistance to this effort. Man's unity and identity stem from the inward awareness (*sens intime*) of this act.

Influenced by his renewed study of Pascal after 1815, his final works, especially the unfinished *Nouveaux essais d'anthropologie* ('New Essays on Anthropology', 1824), identify religious belief (*croyance*) as a further source of knowledge. There is in this idea an unresolved contradiction, for, unlike effort which depends on the active nature of the self, belief is passive and not concerned with natural knowledge. While less convincing, indeed the diary suggests an emotional need for religious consolation, this notion is clearly consistent with Biran's emphasis on inward experience.

In these essays he identified three stages in man's psychological development. 'Animal Life' is concerned with a purely passive self; in 'Human Life', effort and the notion of freedom play preponderant roles. The final stage is closer to pure religious experience and one cannot fail to notice the mystical tendencies in 'Spiritual Life', where the inward experience transcends humanity.

In spite of these later developments Biran was aware that his study of the human mind depended on a thorough scientific investigation. In his diary we find a vivid picture of unremitting self-examination in which we experience the hesitations and despairs of the philosopher and perceive the originality of this minute observation of his intellectual and emotional fluctuations. In this field, Biran can be seen as an important forerunner to such thinkers as Pierre Janet and Freud, who realized part of what had to be done and suggested an analytical method for its completion. In the essays he writes his own epitaph when he says, 'I have, for a long time now, been engaged in studying man, or rather myself; and, at the end of a long life, I can truthfully say that no man has seen himself or watched himself go by as much as I have.'

David Bryant

The most complete edition is *Oeuvres de Maine de Biran* (1920–1949), supplemented by: *Journal de Maine de Biran* (3 vols, 1954–7); *De l'existence* (1966); and *De l'aperception immédiate* (1969). See: H. Gouhier, *Les Conversions de Maine de Biran* (1947); A. Huxley, 'Variations on a Philosopher', in *Themes and Variations* (1950); P. Hallie, *Maine de Biran Reformer of Empiricism* (1959); and F.C.T. Moore, *The Psychology of Maine de Biran* (1970), which contains an excellent bibliography.

288
MALLARMÉ, Stéphane 1842–98

French Symbolist poet

Mallarmé trained as a teacher of English and settled in Paris in 1871, where he led a Jekyll and Hyde existence as a conscientious if unenthusiastic *lycée* teacher by day and, by night, a toiling insomniac passionately devoted to the construction of a revolutionary poetic language which remains his distinctive and monumental contribution to poetry. His uneventful public life was chequered only by four brief visits to England. Yet Mallarmé lived cocooned rather than secluded. He took seriously his role as the head of a family and valued greatly the company of the fellow-artists who came to pay him court at his famous Tuesday-evening gatherings in the rue de Rome. The rarefied and often ritualistic character of Mallarmé's social encounters (it is reported that he would allow the reading of poetry to begin only after the room was saturated with cigar smoke) perhaps represents a psychic compromise struck between a fear of loneliness and a Baudelairean abhorrence of 'real' life: 'The proper occupation of any self-respecting man is to contemplate the blue sky while dying of hunger.'

If this unlusty outlook needs an explanation more specific than that afforded by the general nature of poetic sensibility, then it is probably attributable to the series of bereavements and separations which punctuated Mallarmé's life. His mother died when he was a child, as did his beloved sister, Maria; and his own son died at the age of eight. But whatever their origins in his personal experience, the notions of 'nothingness' and death came to loom large in the mature poet's thinking about the creation and the mode of being of the poetic universe: 'I found nothingness, then I found beauty.' He held that the imitation of death in life was a prerequisite for the evocation of the spiritual realm to which poetry must aspire; and the conjuring up of this realm presupposes the linguistic destruction of the detail of the real world, in order that its 'pure notion' be released into the fall-out atmosphere of the world's 'vibratory disappearing', and sensed in or through the musical quasi-substantiality of the destructive language itself. Death, which 'speaks' in this language, is thereby defeated, by being not cancelled out but transvalued. Poetry redeems when it demonstrates that it is 'nothingness which is the truth': it is the brother who, as a living person, is in a deficient state of being relative to the dead sister, so that his biological death holds out hope of reunion with her in the truth of non-being, which for Mallarmé is not a void but the impersonal 'silent music' revealed and guaranteed by poetic language.

Mallarmé was never tempted to transpose this aesthetic credo into a religious faith, but the ease with which this could have been done attests to the literalness with which he believed, with Proust, that art alone effects salvation. His daily devotion to art, moreover, may be properly described as religious, for Mallarmé laboured endlessly and anxiously over a relatively small poetic output which, in a deathbed gesture of characteristic perfectionism, he instructed, unavailingly, to be burned.

The first phase of his output consists in poetry written in a lyrical-descriptive Parnassian vein between 1857 (the year of his sister's death) and 1862. These technically conventional juvenilia, in which the influence of Poe*, Banville and Gautier* is apparent, show a marked talent for the kind of lyrical composition which Mallarmé soon came to regard as facile, but which continued to tempt him throughout his later striving to develop the austere 'cerebral' poetry to which he owes his fame and influence. The first batch of this mature poetry appeared in the *Parnasse contemporain* of 1866, and thanks mainly to the publicizing efforts of Verlaine* and of Huysmans*, Mallarmé came to prominence in the mid-1880s as the leader of the Symbolist movement. By this time his *oeuvre* was becoming increasingly hermetic, a tendency which culminated in the seeming obscurantist hocus-pocus of his typographical poem *Un coup de dés jamais n'abolira le hasard*, which attempts to emulate the capacity of music to express meanings simultaneously rather than in the linear sequence enforced by typographical conventions.

This notorious hermeticism has two aspects. The first, which may be described as the 'obscurity' of the poetry, arises mainly from his philologically erudite use of words and, more bewilderingly, from a private symbolism, the origin and development of which is not made clear in its context of use, as it is in Proust. The words 'wing', 'window', 'glory', 'dream', among others, simply appear on the page bearing meanings that lie outside the fields of normal semantic connotation and even 'sophisticated' cultural association. It has been pointed out that the meanings attributed to those words in the complex poems may be made clear by studying their use in simpler contexts. Thus L.J. Austin says that 'the aim must be to make the utmost use of the documents available – earlier versions, parallel texts in prose, correspondence.' But it might well be felt that poetry loses its vitalizing cultural function when it becomes the preserve of scholars in possession of the necessary documents.

The other, more justifiable aspect of Mallarmé's hermeticism may be described as the 'difficulty' of the poetry, and this is distinct from its obscurity both in that it results from formal complexities and in that these largely do yield to sustained analytical and imaginative attention. For the most part, this difficulty is intrinsic in the new poetic language which Mallarmé spent his life developing. It is accordingly more pervasive and obstructive of easy understanding than the

elements of obscurity. The difficulty of this language is organically connected with its aesthetic productivity: it is contrived to yield to pressure and not to yield univocally. But what is new and exquisite is that the residual indeterminacy appears as the mystery of the reader's process of *creating* meaning rather than as a background of missing intelligibility against which assimilated meaning is set. The result is the 'bright darkness' of the poem, the glimpsing of the darkness that the process of dispelling darkness is for itself.

The purpose of Mallarmé's language was to express what he variously called his Dream, the Idea, the Ideal, or Literature, although it is perhaps his description of poetry as the 'musician of silence', or of reading it as a 'solitary silent concert', which best conveys the flavour of the aesthetic experience to which these abstractions refer. Language must be made to create or present a universe envisaged as a dynamic or musical system of analogic relations accessible to the imaginative intelligence rather than to the senses. For Mallarmé 'Poetry . . . is Musique *par excellence.*' Where for Baudelaire* the system of universal analogy was still material, and apprehended in synaesthesia, with Mallarmé it is refined into pure spiritual structure or 'silent' music. He was dogmatically convinced that this spiritual music can be played only by poetry, and that it is 'more divine', by reason of its silence and pure form, than the 'public or symphonic expression' given by the orchestra. 'It is not from the elementary sonorities of the brass, string or wood instruments, but from the intellectual word that . . . Music, as the totality of relations existing in the universe, must result.' The suggestion seems to be that it is the *propositional* structure of language, present in poetry as in prose but absent from music, which, suitably cast and effectively interacting with patterns of word-music (rhythm, assonance and alliteration), supplies the vital ingredient that makes poetry alone capable of expressing the music of the spheres.

Be this as it may, propositional meaning is an essential part of Mallarmé's poetic language. This fact is important, firstly because it implies that the syntax of the poems was meant to be and can be understood, although understanding here is usually a matter of winning from the syntax a dialectic of tentative proposals as opposed to a set of mutually confirming confident propositions. Secondly, the ballast given by ordinary propositional meaning prevents the aesthetic meaning of the poem from being monopolized by word-music, in the manner of some Surrealist poetry. His method is not to allow word-music to take over from propositional meaning, but to produce silent music by bringing the two into suggestive modes of contact through the 'artifice of dipping words by turn in sonority and in sense'. The sound-system, instead of being merely confirmatory, inflects, deflects and even contradicts the acquisitions of the propositional (syntactical) system; a word or phrase will change colour when 'dipped' in some dimension of the sound-system, an effect which acquires a special poignancy in a poetry that playfully treads the tightropes of philosophical dilemmas (do Platonic Ideas exist objectively or only in the imagination?) relevant to the nature and aspirations of literary creativity. Syntactical commitments entered into in the penultimate tercet of a sonnet condemn an anticipated object not to exist. Inexorably the syntax snakes its way down to the final line of the poem where it names and annihilates its victim: a rose indwelt by night. But the protective isolation in which this image is placed by the short octosyllabic line allowing room for it and for not a syllable more, reinforced by the self-sufficient beauty of the image, confers on the rose a kind of absolutism which liberates it from the control of the ambient negative forces that logically ought to destroy it. Audio-visual effects afford the fleeting illusion of the rose blossoming at the moment of its obliteration by syntax. The same sonnet begins with the title-line '*Surgi de la croupe et du bond*,' a literally meaningless phrase which strikes the reader as a garbled version of the more plausible *Surgi de la coupe et du fond*. But this is as Mallarmé intends: the printed line causes the reader to follow through with his mind's eye the movement of a vase springing into being, while the more plausible line implants spectral submeanings which later reveal their connections with the declared themes of the poem. This interplay of meaning-systems accounts for a pervasive and distinctive characteristic of Mallarmé's poetry: the disproportion between tininess of linguistic cause and colossalness of metaphysical effect.

The immediate obstacle confronting the reader of a Mallarmé poem is its contorted syntax, which is rich in suggestivity quite apart from its transactions with the sound-system. Without actually dislocating it, Mallarmé bends and twists syntax, pulls it out of true and recasts it with about the same degree of deviation from the norm as Cézanne* imposes on the contours of surfaces. Ambiguities are courted, expected affirmations tortuously deferred, linear developments give way to vertical imbrications of syntactical units, by means of long parentheses, contrapuntal contrivances and far-flung appositions. A given stretch of words often belongs to more than one syntactical pattern. The result is a multiplicity of meanings 'flickering' among themselves, and the emergence of the poem as an autonomous linguistic world in which meaning constantly makes and unmakes itself. The sound-system is contrived to the same end. Mallarmé likes to think of verbal sounds as facets of precious stones exchanging reflections and refractions. His use of words in oblique senses evoking strange but revealing associations is also a factor here. But for the main it is ordinary language which these techniques transform into a keyboard. The guiding intention is to ensure that the reader 'no longer receives the impression of anything external'; by their play of verbal mirrorings, words 'no longer appear to have their own colour, but to remain only as the transitions of a gamut.'

Mallarmé's syntactical convolutions have led many people to describe his poetry as 'intellectual'. Others, more impressed by its phonetic qualities, see it as pure musical substance. The first of these emphases is inadequate because it neglects the sensuous quality of the poetry, the second because it assumes that this sensuous quality consists in word-music alone. But it lies just as much in visual imagery imported from the real world. This imagery is 'poetic' in so far as it is 'unreal', and to purify it of real denotation is the function of the referential aspect of his language. The problem of reference, and so of sensuous imagery, may be stated as follows: on the one hand, the creation of a poetry in which the unworldly Dream might seem to be realized calls for a language where meaning is separated from existential reference, since this ties meaning to the real world: on the other hand, words which did not *somehow* refer to the real world would have no value as bearers of images, forming a trivial realm of analytical discourse. (What would absent flowers be without real flowers?) It follows, therefore, that the only relation which Mallarmé's language can tolerate with the world is one in which reference is restricted to distilling the spiritual structure of sensuous experience. Things are referred to (inevitably), but in a way which yields up their latent spiritual content by means of obscuring their real existence – a kind of verbal equivalent of Husserl's transcendental reduction. Poetry practises the art of suggestion when its language simultaneously combines these positive and negative functions. It must 'paint, not the thing but the effect it produces'. The negative condition of the poem's being able to capture the inwardness of things is that it should never name them. 'To name a thing is to destroy three-quarters of the pleasure of the poem.' And in order to suggest without naming, Mallarmé dispenses with titles, spins elaborate periphrases, besets his terms with privations and restructions, keeps his metaphors implicit, all of which adds to the difficulty of the poetry.

'My art is an impasse.' Mallarmé's prophetic words explain and correctly predict the scope of his influence. The limits of intelligibility had been reached. The literary contingent of the flock of artists who came to his 'Tuesdays' are today nearly all great names, including Proust, Gide, Verlaine*, Maeterlinck*, Claudel, yet wisely none of them attempted to emulate him. But his *ideas* on poetry have had a profound and far-reaching impact, immediately and personally through his illustrious friends and subsequently through the established position he now occupies in the theory of poetry. He was the major impetus behind the emergence of the short-lived Symbolist Theatre in France; however it is as a poet and poetic theorist that his international stature has steadily grown, casting its shadow over all future innovators. Perhaps the most revealing reflection on Mallarmé's existence is that Verlaine, his admiring fellow-poet, should have almost equalled him, with the sonorous joys of a new simplicity.

Roger McLure

Mallarmé's complete *oeuvre* is collected in the Bibliothèque de la Pléiade edition (1945), edited and annotated by Henri Mondor and G. Jean-Aubry. Most of Mallarmé's mature poems are collected in *Poésies* (1965). An English edition of *Poésies* in the original French, accompanied by translations, is A. Hartley, *Mallarmé* (1965). See: J. Seherer, *L'Expression littéraire dans l'oeuvre de Mallarmé* (1947); G. Davies, *Les Tombeaux de Mallarmé* (1950); G. Delfel, *L'Esthétique de Stéphane Mallarmé* (1951); L. Cellier, *Mallarmé et la Morte que parle* (1959); K.G. Kohn, *Towards the Poems of Mallarmé* (1965); Emilie Noulet, *Vingt Poèmes de Stéphane Mallarmé, Exégèses* (1967); M. Bowie, *Mallarmé and the Art of Being Difficult* (1978).

289
MALTHUS, Thomas Robert 1766–1834

British political economist

A rather remarkable father, David Malthus, entertained both David Hume and Jean-Jacques Rousseau as house guests when his second son was only three weeks old. That son was educated privately, in accordance with his father's Enlightenment ideas, before entering Jesus College, Cambridge, in 1784. There he read widely, won prizes for declamation, led a vigorous social and sporting life, but nevertheless went on to graduate as Ninth Wrangler – the only one from his college in his year. He took Holy Orders immediately, and in 1793 was elected a Fellow of Jesus College, a place which he had to resign on his marriage in 1804. It was as a curate at Albury near his father's home that he wrote, and published anonymously, *An Essay on the Principle of Population as it affects the future Improvement of Society, with Remarks on the Speculations of Mr. Godwin, M. Condorcet, and other Writers*.

This *First Essay* of 1798 was a long polemical pamphlet urging, against both those named and his own well-loved father, that all such utopian dreams are bound to be frustrated by the relentless pressures of population. How is any society to make good on its promise to provide 'to each according to their needs' when ever more takers come crowding in to demand their shares too? The publication of this pamphlet created an enormous stir, converting, among many others, William Paley, Jeremy Bentham* and the younger Pitt.

Malthus however was not satisfied, and made two study tours: in 1799 to Norway, Sweden, Finland and Russia; and in 1802 to France and Switzerland. The results appeared in 1803. This *Second Essay*, although it is always catalogued only as a second edition, is best – as the author says in the preface – 'considered as a new work'. The title of this treatise, nearly four times as long as the *First Essay*, is significantly less passive. It reads: *An Essay on the Principle of Population: or, a View of its Past and Present Effects on Human Happiness; with an Inquiry into our Prospects respecting the Future Removal or Mitigation of the Evils which it occasions*.

On the basis of the reputation earned by these two first publications Malthus was in 1805 appointed to the faculty of the new East India Company staff college at Haileybury. The Chair of Political Economy there, which he held till his death in 1834, was in fact the first in Britain. (Adam Smith at Glasgow in the previous century was Professor of Moral Philosophy.) Throughout his Haileybury years Malthus taught well, researched hard and published. He earned unchallenged status as, quite apart from the work on population, one of the British classical economists. Lord Keynes, perusing the twelve year long correspondence between Malthus and his friend David Ricardo lamented the influence of the latter: 'If only Malthus, instead of Ricardo, had been the parent stem from which nineteenth-century economics proceeded, what a much wiser and richer place the world would be today.'

For better or for worse, it was as the writer of a pamphlet and a treatise on population that Malthus became a maker of that century's culture and not of ours. Except for a peculiar notion of moral restraint introduced into the *Second Essay* the conceptual equipment remained from beginning to end the same. The first principle of population is an enormous power of multiplication. Offsetting, and always preventing anything like the full realization of this power, are various checks. Malthus, who had at Cambridge enjoyed an excellent grounding in the elements of Newtonian physics, was both well aware of and reasonably pleased with the parallelism between this theoretical scheme and that of the operation of the First Law of Motion circumscribed by several countervailing forces. So in the *First Essay* he systematically mistakes it that everything is the outcome of laws of nature, being determined by inexorable contingent necessities: no matter what we do population must be forever pressing to the limit of available resources.

Always Malthus contrasts the power of population to multiply in a geometrical progression – 1, 2, 4, 8, 16, 32, and so on – with what he offers as a very generous estimate of the limit to the possibilities of increasing the production of food and other resources required to sustain that population – an arithmetical progression starting 1, 2, 3, 4, 5, 6. This comparison of the ratios did a lot to persuade people that his conclusions had been proved mathematically.

When we make such comparisons it becomes obvious that checks must be operating (almost) everywhere and at (almost) all times. Like most aspiring social scientists Malthus was concerned not only with how things in fact are, and why, but also with how (he thought) they ought to be. So, without ever making this distinction explicit, he provides two methods of classifying checks. One is neutral and purely descriptive, dividing them into positive and preventive. These are – roughly – causes of death and causes of not being born. The other is committed and strongly prescriptive. In the *First Essay* there are only two recognized alternatives, vice or misery. But in the *Second Essay* and after moral restraint is admitted as the third.

In this technical usage the meaning of that expression is peculiarly restricted. Although a minister of the Church of England Malthus, like most of his peers, maintained the sexual norms traditionally associated with hardline Roman Catholicism: intercourse before or outside marriage is always illicit; and contraception is categorically vicious. The moral restraint recommended, therefore, is restraint from marriage until such time as you can reasonably expect to be able to raise as many children as you can then reasonably expect to have. To advocate contraception as a means of relieving population problems is not Malthusian but neo-Malthusian.

The full significance of the introduction of the concept of moral restraint seems never to have been grasped either by Malthus or by his critics. The crux is that this constitutes an admission of the inescapable reality of human choice: a genuine social science cannot come up with the conclusion that no one could have done anything other than they did, for that would imply that they were not free agents at all. In the *First Essay* the multiplicative power of population is construed as a natural power: given the appropriate conditions it cannot but be exercised. But in the *Second Essay* it ought to be interpreted as a human power: in certain conditions it may be overwhelmingly likely that the agents possessing this power will choose to use it; and yet it must always be in fact possible that they will not, and never contingently necessary that they will.

Malthus was surely wrong to argue in the *First Essay* that nothing can be done to defeat the over-population menace, and wrong too in the *Second Essay* to rule out any measures other than what could be embraced in his own stilted notion of moral restraint. Yet these are trifling faults to set against a massive achievement. On the scientific side he gave a huge impetus to population studies. Practically he forces everyone who really does intend the relief of man's estate to take account of the population implications of every policy proposed. There are to this day far too many professing reformers, and still more practising revolutionaries, who reveal

their fundamental bad faith by refusing or even denouncing all such attention. William Nassau Senior, another British classical economist, summed up the agreement reached in his own controversy with Malthus: 'no plan for social improvement can be complete unless it embraces the means both of increasing production, and of preventing population making a proportionate advance.'

Antony Flew

See: *An Essay on the Principle of Population*, ed. Antony Flew (1970). Other works include: *Principles of Political Economy Considered with a View to Their Practical Application* (1820). See also: J. Ronar, *Malthus and His Work* (1885, rev. 1924); K. Smith, *The Malthusian Controversy* (1951); D.E.C. Eversley, *Social Theories of Fertility and the Malthusian Debate* (1959).

290
MANET, Edouard 1832–83

French painter

Although he was a reluctant rebel, Manet played a leading role around the middle of the nineteenth century in formulating a new and modern style of painting in opposition to the outworn conventions of academic painting. He was a friend of Monet* and Degas*, but while his innovations were to have a decisive influence on the Impressionists he refused to be associated with the group and never contributed to their exhibitions. It was Manet's ambition to achieve success within the official art establishment, but ironically his work was repeatedly rejected by the Salon and castigated by the critics, even after he had established a reputation as the leader of the modern school.

Manet was the son of a magistrate and it was only after twice failing the entrance examinations to the Naval Academy that his father permitted him to enrol, in 1849, at the École des Beaux Arts, where he studied under Thomas Couture. From his master he imbibed a love of Venetian art and a vigorous painterly technique. But the pupil's methods were too radical for the teacher, and after quarrelling with Couture, Manet left his studio in 1856 to complete his education by copying in the Louvre and travelling in Italy, Germany and Holland. His first entry for the Salon, in 1856, *The Absinthe Drinker*, was rejected, in spite of Delacroix's* support, but in 1861 a portrait of his parents and *The Spanish Guitar Player* were shown at the Salon and he was at once hailed by young painters and progressive critics as a leader. During the next decade the pattern continued, with major works being rejected or creating scandal in the press, but with such writers as Astruc, Baudelaire* and Zola* rallying to his defence. At the Café Guerbois, artists and critics gathered to hear

Manet speak, and his Paris studio became a meeting place for artists. In Fantin-Latour's painting of 1870, *A Studio in the Batignolles*, Manet is shown surrounded by Renoir*, Monet, Bazille, Zola, Scholderer and Maître, at work on a portrait of Astruc.

Manet was surprised at the official response to his work since he regarded himself as a traditionalist. He greatly admired the Spanish masters, and his broad handling and rich, dark colouring, with a liberal use of black, are derived from Velazquez, Ribera and Goya. A number of his early works also treat Spanish themes, such as bullfights and Spanish dancers. His chief entry for the Salon of 1863, *Le Déjeuner sur l'herbe*, was rejected and created a scandal at the special Salon of rejected works – the so-called 'Salon des Refusés.' It derives its composition from an engraving by Marcantonio Raimondi after a lost Raphael painting, and transposes into a modern idiom the arcadian idyll of Titian's early *Fête Champêtre* in the Louvre. But critics were appalled by the sight of naked women beside men in contemporary dress, and, furthermore, attacked Manet's style. In looking back to the example of Velazquez, Manet rejected the detailed finish, polished surface and laborious modelling of academic painting for a rapid execution and bold colouring. In order to preserve the vitality of his visual impressions he simplified what he saw, encompassing figures in bold outlines and eliminating the carefully modulated halftones favoured by the academic masters.

Manet daringly applied this radical technique to contemporary themes. In 1863, at an exhibition of his work at the picture dealer, Martinet's, he showed a painting of fashionably dressed Parisians, amongst them his friends, parading in a park. *A Concert in the Tuileries Gardens* is a landmark because it treats modern life in a spontaneous style, in a composition that is apparently so unpremeditated as to be almost haphazard. At the Salon of 1865 Manet caused yet another scandal with his *Olympia*. The picture is a reinterpretation of Titian's *Venus of Urbino*, but the reclining female nude is defiantly modern, so much so that she outraged the public. The model, as in *Le Déjeuner sur l'herbe*, was Victorine Meurend, but here she is more abrasively erotic, brazenly staring at the spectator, naked except for a pair of slippers and a black velvet lace around her neck.

It is impossible to determine how much of the air of worldliness and vulgarity in *Olympia* is intentional. Manet denied that he intended to shock, but in transposing a Renaissance Venus into a nineteenth-century boudoir she became a prostitute, and Manet's intuition and honesty as an observer prevent him from denying the fact. He is the painter of modern life *malgré lui*, and it is precisely his keen sense of the flavour of modern life that earned him the admiration of Baudelaire and Zola.

Not until 1865 did Manet in fact visit Spain and encounter the work of Velazquez and Goya in quantity, and in 1867 he painted a large picture of *The Execution of the Emperor Maximilian*, inspired by Goya's *Third of May*. That same year he exhibited some fifty paintings at the Exposition Universelle but with little success. During the Franco-Prussian War he served as a staff officer in the National Guard, but under the Commune of 1871 he retired to the country with his family. He travelled in Holland in 1872 and *Le Bon Bock*, which was a great success at the Salon of 1873, shows the strong influence of Frans Hals.

The next phase of Manet's career shows him turning increasingly to modern themes, and even, under the influence of the Impressionists, painting out of doors. It was through Berthe Morisot, his pupil since 1868, and one of the models for *The Balcony* (Salon 1869), that he became intimate with Monet and Renoir. During the summer of 1874 he joined Monet at Argenteuil and painted river scenes and regattas in a lively Impressionist technique. Such pictures as *Boating* (1874) and *Monet painting in his Floating Studio* (1874) are more brilliant in colour and more loosely painted than his earlier work, but still retain some touches of the black of which he was so fond.

The association with the Impressionists did nothing for Manet's reputation, and he suffered more Salon rejections in 1876 and 1877. Nor did his paintings of modern life help. From the mid-1870s he began a dazzling series of pictures, close in spirit to the work of his friend, Degas, of bars, concert-halls and prostitutes which includes *Nana* (1877), *La Servante de Bocks* (1878, two versions), and culminates in the masterful *Bar at the Folies-Bergère* (1881). This late work, completed less than two years before his death, defines the type of the modern female, in her glance, her pose, her dress, and in her habitat, the brash, noisy and mysterious world of the café-concert reflected in the mirror behind her.

Manet first began to feel the effects of the illness (*locomotor ataxia*) that was to lead to his death in the summer of 1879. Over the next four years he retreated increasingly to the seclusion of the country around Paris, to Bellevue, Versailles and Rueil. In semi-retirement his work took on a lighter and more domestic character, with paintings of women sitting in his garden, and pastel portraits of such lady friends as the actress Méry Laurent. Even his chief Salon exhibits of these years, *In the Conservatory* (1879) and *At Père Lathuille's* (1880), are like vignettes of modern life, comedies of manners in a light, romantic vein. From this period also date many of Manet's still-lifes. It was above all in this genre, in small canvases of peonies or asparagus, that he displayed his keen colour sense and virtuoso brushwork.

Manet's influence in his own lifetime and since has been enormous. His early disciples included Monet, Berthe Morisot and Eva Gonzales, but his process of bold simplification of form was to determine the approach of most of the Post-Impressionists, as well as the early Picasso and Matisse. But he also created the genre of contemporary social themes which was taken up by Toulouse-Lautrec*, and also debased by many fashionable painters of the latter part of the century, such as Boldini, Carolus-Duran and Émile Blanche. The aspect of Manet's achievement that is most often neglected is his psychological insight. Because his understanding of the modern human animal is so much more subtle than Renoir's, for example, he avoids the latter's excesses of sentimentality. In his pictures of men and women meeting, conversing, at a bar or a ball, over lunch or dinner, he creates a drama which, though calculated understatement, evokes with great intensity the spirit of the era.

Michael Wilson

See: Julius Meier-Graefe, *Edouard Manet* (1912); Etienne Moreau-Nelaton, *Manet raconté par lui-même* (2 vols, 1926); George H. Hamilton, *Manet and His Critics* (1954); Pierre Courthion, *Manet* (trans. 1962); Anne Coffin Hansen, *Edouard Manet* (1967); Pierre Schneider, *The World of Manet* (1968).

291
MANNING, Henry Edward 1808–92

British churchman

At different points in his life Manning seemed set on courses which might have led him to either the prime ministership of the English State or the primacy of the English Church. Instead he became Archbishop of Westminster, and, perhaps, one of the few Englishmen to have had any chance of becoming pope.

Manning's father was an ambitious West India merchant and a Member of Parliament; during Henry's infancy he served a term as Governor of the Bank of England. He was sent to school at Harrow, and then to Balliol College, Oxford, where he became one of the luminaries of the newly founded Oxford Union, alongside Gladstone* and Samuel Wilberforce. His intended career in politics had to be abandoned when his father went bankrupt. He became a clerk in the Colonial Office; but under the zealous persuasion of Favell Lee Bevan (most remembered as the authoress of *Reading without Tears*, 1857), he decided to enter the Church, as his father had always hoped he would. He returned to Oxford as a fellow of Merton, within sight and sound of the Tractarian nest at Oriel, and identified himself with the Evangelical arm of the Church of England. In the course of one eventful year (1833) he became curate of Lavington, Sussex, succeeded his rector upon his death, and married the rector's daughter, thus becoming Samuel Wilberforce's brother-in-law. By 1841 he was Archdeacon of Chichester, and, having slowly

changed his posture, was regarded as one of the leaders of the Oxford Movement, although an outspokenly anti-papal one. Soon Wilberforce, by now Bishop of Oxford, was urging Manning's fitness for a bishopric. But the Gorham Case destroyed his faith in Anglicanism. (The relevant point about the case here is that final judgment was made by the Judicial Committee of the Privy Council, which seemed to imply that the Privy Council was the ultimate authority for Anglicans in matters of doctrine.) In 1851 he became a Roman Catholic. The death of his wife, childless, in 1837, meant that Manning was eligible for the priesthood of his new church, and he was ordained by Cardinal Wiseman almost immediately. After studying in Rome, where he became an intimate of Pope Pius IX, he was appointed Provost of the Westminster Metropolitan Chapter. In 1865 he succeeded Wiseman as Archbishop of Westminster, and was made a Cardinal in 1875.

Manning brought a unique range of qualities and experiences to the English Roman Catholic episcopate. Unlike his brother bishops he had not passed his life among an isolated minority, but much of it at the centre of a brilliant 'Establishment' generation; unlike them he was a sometime married man, who mourned his wife until the day of his death. In him some of the traditions of the Church of England ran ineradicably deep: 'the morning and evening prayers and the music of the English Bible,' he wrote of his time as an Anglican priest, 'for seventeen years became part of my soul.' His appointment as Archbishop of Westminster was not uncontroversial. Those who knew him best had not even included his name amongst those they submitted to Rome for consideration. Manning went to Westminster as Pius IX's personal, independent, nominee.

Before Emancipation in 1829 the Roman Catholic Church in England was not a missionary body. Manning had seen his church gain tolerance; it was his aim to see it gain popularity. An ardent Ultramontane, he increased the English church's dependence upon the authority of the Holy See; a staunch advocate of the idea of Papal Infallibility at the First Vatican Council (1869–70), once the idea had become doctrine he vowed to do more than his all to promulgate it. The church in England was thoroughly Italianized – the vestments, the pronunciation of the Latin of the liturgy, the music largely limited to the Gregorian chant – thus causing Catholics to lose more of whatever they may have had in common with Anglicans.

But to Manning, who by instinct was a thoroughly patriotic Englishman, this renewed separateness may have seemed to be an advantage. He saw a huge missionary field among the working classes, where Irish immigrants already formed a considerable Roman Catholic presence, among people to whom the Church of England, with its wealth, privilege and close entanglement with the state, must often look unsympathetic and sometimes phoney. 'They will trust you,' he told Herbert Vaughan who was to succeed him at Westminster, 'but not my brother Benson' (E.W. Benson, Archbishop of Canterbury, 1883–96) – a remark which recalled his successfully decisive role in the settlement of the London Dock strike of 1889 beside the unhappy intervention of Benson in the same dispute.

Manning was busy in all the favourite causes of Victorian reformers – education, housing, temperance – always with suitable emphasis on the needs of his own flock. His proselytizing zeal was matched by his concern for protecting Catholics from losing their faith, whether through despair at the conditions in which they lived or through subversion by intellectual influences. To this end he at one extreme secured legislation enabling children of Catholic parents in workhouses to be brought up as Catholics and to be visited by their priests, and at the other consistently opposed the admission of Catholics to Oxford and Cambridge.

Manning's Catholics were imbued with something of a *laager* mentality which would have been unfamiliar to their predecessors in the days of persecution but which was to be entirely familiar to their successors until the Second Vatican Council (1962–5). But he made the archbishopric of Westminster an office whose occupant would always have a national platform. He himself was at ease in fashionable drawing rooms and slums alike, and, though an ascetic, was liberally hospitable, especially to the denizens of the former. He never lost the autocratic manner which as a young man had earned the nickname 'The General'. As a Cardinal-Archbishop he had tremendous presence: 'As he entered the ante-room where one awaited his approach,' wrote G.W.E. Russell, 'the most Protestant knee instinctively bent.' His funeral, in an age by no means bereft of heroes, attracted wider demonstrations of popular respect than any since the Duke of Wellington's forty years before.

Timothy O'Sullivan

There is no satisfactory biography of Manning, but see: V.A. McClelland, *Cardinal Manning: His Public Life and Influence, 1865–92* (1962); D. Newsome, *The Parting of Friends: A Study of the Wilberforces and Henry Manning* (1966); J.McM. Rigg, in *The Dictionary of National Biography*. See also: G. Faber, *Oxford Apostles* (1933); K.S. Inglis, *Churches and the Working Classes in Victorian England* (1963).

292
MANZONI, Alessandro 1785–1873

Italian novelist, playwright and essayist

Manzoni was born in Milan of an aristocratic landowning family. Austrian-ruled Milan had been a lively centre of Enlightenment culture, and was to become the first and major centre of Italian Romanticism in the post-Napoleonic period. Manzoni was in many ways representative of the liberal Milanese intellectuals of his generation – relatively small in number in a society with a very high illiteracy rate, linked to the emerging land-owning and commercial bourgeoisie who had seen their interests and activities promoted by Napoleonic rule and then thwarted by the returning Austrians after the Congress of Vienna, cautiously progressive politically, patriotic and therefore anti-Austrian but suspicious and even fearful of popular initiative and mass action, they responded to the Austrian restoration at first through a cultural battle fought under the banner of Romanticism and then by supporting or actively participating in the unsuccessful *coups* of 1820–1. Milanese Romanticism consisted mainly in a keen awareness of the need to free literature from the rules and restrictions imposed on both form and content by the classicist tradition, and to promote instead a literature that could appeal to the wider reading public through the expression of more modern, relevant topics in an accessible language. Manzoni was reluctant to commit himself publicly to this cause: he declined the request to contribute to the weekly journal *Il Conciliatore*, and his only public utterance on the Romantic movement (*Lettera sul romanticismo*) appeared in 1823, when the Milanese group had already disbanded. But he shared their aims, both cultural and political – he had in fact not only a deeper knowledge of German, and French, Romanticism, but a more rigorous theoretical awareness of cultural issues. Crucial for Manzoni's intellectual development were his contacts with French culture and his commitment to Catholicism. The years spent in Paris (1805–10) enabled him to acquire a first hand knowledge of the French *encyclopédistes* and European Romantic culture – he also became thoroughly familiar with the seventeenth-century French Catholic moralists. In Paris around 1810 Manzoni underwent the religious crisis which was to lead him from religious indifference to a position of serious Catholicism; from then on all his writings bore the mark of his religious beliefs. His Catholicism never meant an uncritical acceptance of the dictates, theological and political, of the church establishment, nor a nostalgia for the *ancien régime*. It provided a theological framework for his rigorous search for truth; it always implied a severe judgment of the shortcomings of the church and a rejection of the Jesuit tradition. Politically, he was a progressive liberal Catholic. He opposed the continuing temporal power of the pope and consistently supported the annexation of Rome to the Italian state.

Manzoni's first creative writings after his return to Milan in 1810 were four *Inni sacri* (written 1812–15), concerned with major dates of the church calendar; these also marked his abandonment of the Neoclassical poetic style. He then progressed to drama, writing two historical tragedies in verse form: *Il Conte di Carmagnola* (written 1816–19, first performed 1828), on a Renaissance *condottiere*, and *Adelchi* (written 1820–2, first performed 1843), set at the time of the struggle between Longbards and Franks for the domination of Italy in the eighth century. Both tragedies follow Romantic canons: they disregard the Aristotelian units dear to the classicist theatre and include choruses having the role of providing comment on the action, as theorized by A.W. Schlegel*. *Adelchi* is the more interesting of the two. It was a direct result of the new perspectives on medieval history, and literature as exploration of historical reality, which Manzoni acquired through his renewed contacts with French cultural circles in 1819–20. Manzoni's stated aim in writing *Adelchi* was to throw light on the lives of the native Italians subjected to the Longbards, and to shift the focus from illustrious to ordinary people. In this respect *Adelchi* was a failure: the protagonists turned out to be the famous among the Longbards and the Franks; the indigenous masses only appeared as the object of comment in one of the choruses.

Manzoni's aim of highlighting the lives of ordinary people, frustrated by the medium of drama, found fulfilment in *The Betrothed* (*I promessi sposi*) which he began writing in 1821. His decision to attempt a historical novel was influenced by the enthusiastic belief of his French friends in the epistemological validity of this genre. *The Betrothed* is set in Spanish-dominated Lombardy at the time of the Thirty Years War. Against a background of famine, military invasion, and plague, it narrates the story of Lucia and Renzo, two peasants cum silk-spinners, whose impending marriage is prevented by the local feudal lord's designs on Lucia. Manzoni was convinced that a historical novel should portray historical characters, events and situations with total adherence to historical reality, whilst the invented elements must be consistent with historical verisimilitude. The writing of the novel was in fact preceded and accompanied by a huge amount of painstaking research into the most varied aspects of the history of seventeenth-century Lombardy. But Manzoni's historical concern extended beyond factual accuracy to an analysis of the moving forces behind facts and situations and a rigorous search for ethical judgment. What emerges is a severe critique of seventeenth-century society: this is seen as a society where the poor are oppressed by the rich and powerful, the state is unwilling to curb feudal lawlessness, the church indulges in corrupt practices and collusion with state and feudal power, political and ecclesiastical authorities display incompetence and wilful negligence in dealing with political problems and natural disasters, and most of the educated minority indulge in a futile culture concerned with trivialities, riddled with superstition, and expressed in a pompous ornate language.

This totally negative view of seventeenth-century society, which only allows for a few exceptional individuals inspired by a heroic Christian morality, is expressed through the use of ironical language, as well as through direct, explicit analysis and comments. The reader is constantly reminded of the presence of the author, who often interrupts the narration and intervenes directly to express judgments, offer his analysis of characters and events, suggest analogies with the present times, highlight his narrative technique.

Manzoni breaks with tradition by choosing two poor peasants as his protagonists and treating them as serious, not comic, characters. It is in fact by alternately following their respective itineraries ensuing from their forced separation that he comes to portray the political and social forces which control that society. The poor in the novel, though viewed on the whole sympathetically, retain however a decidedly subaltern role. When situations and problems are presented through their eyes, and their minds, the author usually intervenes to reorganize and often correct their analysis – the powerful are endowed with far greater psychological complexity – popular initiative in the face of famine is viewed as folly leading to distasteful mass violence, whilst it is suggested that the solution to social evils must rest with a rigorously ethical use of power by those to whom power is entrusted. Lucia and Renzo's private story is given a crucial turn towards its happy ending by the intervention of powerful individuals who are or have become good Christians. Indeed the eventful outcome of the story, with Renzo risen to the position of small entrepreneur, points to a solution of individual progress through the social hierarchy rather than advancement for a whole social class.

The Betrothed, written during the period of heaviest Austrian repression against the political and social initiatives of the liberal patriots, can also be read as a project for a society organized according to the principles of the liberal bourgeoisie – a society freed of the worst features of the *ancien régime* through the action of enlightened leaders and freed also of the dangers of popular initiative from below. Manzoni's attitude does not however fully coincide with that of other liberal intellectuals; his belief in the ultimately inscrutable working of divine providence precludes any indulgence in their often naive optimism. In Manzoni's view of things humans, especially those in positions of power, have the duty to follow a severe ethical code, but no historical project is guaranteed of success.

Manzoni's uncompromising attitude towards the duties of writers soon led him to abandon creative writing altogether, and after 1827 his writings consisted mainly of essays, on philosophy, history, politics and economics, literature, and language. In Manzoni's view literature must not merely provide entertainment nor does it contain its own justification; it has essentially a moral function. Its aim must be no less than truth, and it must appeal, in both form and content, to a readership beyond the restricted circle of professional writers. Throughout his literary career Manzoni struggled with a definition of truth in literature: in the sense of moral truth, which he ultimately identified in the divine realm, as well as factual truth. But whilst in 1823 he suggested that the problem of factual truth in a work of fiction could be solved through the notion of verisimilitude, he later came to the conclusion that only historiography, correctly undertaken, can fulfil the aim of providing a true interpretation of reality (*Del romanzo storico*, begun 1828, published 1850).

The first draft of the novel (*Fermo e Lucia*), finished in 1823, was never published – *The Betrothed* first appeared in 1827, extensively recast in its narrative structure and rewritten in what he hoped would be a supra-regional language based on Tuscan. The final edition (1840) was the result of further linguistic corrections undertaken with a more thorough knowledge of spoken Florentine. Manzoni sought to find a living idiom that could provide a norm for the written language. For historical reasons, Italy only possessed a common literary language, which was totally inadequate to express everyday life, while different regions had their own spoken idioms, often mutually incomprehensible and bearing little relationship to the language of the literary tradition. The problem of the language for Manzoni was not however confined to literature. He saw it as a fundamental aspect of the process of Italian unification, and discussed it in a series of published statements spanning the period 1845–68, as well as in numerous unpublished earlier writings. According to Manzoni the normative criterion for languages must be their living usage, and a language can only be considered such if it is possible to use it for communication at all levels, from the domestic to the scholarly and scientific. For him, spoken Florentine alone among Italian idioms fulfilled these criteria. In 1868, seven years after the unification of Italy, Manzoni chaired a parliamentary committee convened by a sympathetic Minister of Education with the aim of suggesting ways of spreading a common language among Italians of all regions and social classes. The resulting recommendations included the drafting of a dictionary of live spoken Florentine, the maximum use of Tuscan teachers in all schools, and the rewriting of text-books and catechisms by Tuscans. The new dictionary was completed in 1897, and the suggested educational policy was partly implemented for a while, but the continuing deficiencies and uneven development of the school system inevitably prevented any real achievement along Manzonian lines. Dialectual monolingualism was to remain for a long time the norm among the lower classes, and the linguistic unity gradually achieved among the cultured was to be the result of structural changes within Italian society. The

application of Manzoni's theories, such as it was, only produced a new form of purism and pedantry.

The Betrothed soon generated a school of novelists who tended to reproduce Manzonian themes, characters, situations, and linguistic devices, whilst the Italian novels that matter would follow different ways, often polemically opposed to a Manzonianism that had become an official institution. Nevertheless, echoes from the novel that generations of Italian schoolchildren have loved to hate are to be found in the most diverse products of Italian culture to this day and Manzoni remains the person who produced the most coherent and original expression of liberal culture in nineteenth-century Italy.

Verina Jones

A critical edition of Manzoni's complete works is being published by Mondadori of Milan (*Tutte le opere di Alessandro Manzoni*, 1957–; six out of the seven planned volumes have so far appeared). A. Manzoni, *I promessi sposi* (1971 published by Einaudi) contains the text of the first version of the novel, and an interlinear edition of the second and third. The most recent English translation of *The Betrothed* appeared in 1972. See: N. Sapegno, *Ritratto di Manzoni* (1961); A. Leone de Castris, *L'impegno del Manzoni* (1965); L. Caretti, *Manzoni, ideologia e stile* (1972); E. Raimondi, *Il romanzo senza idillio* (1974); S.S. Nigro, *Manzoni* (1978); B. Reynolds, *The Linguistic Writings of Alessandro Manzoni* (1950).

293
MARC, Franz 1880–1916

German painter

Marc was one of the leading painters of the German Expressionist movement. 'Expressionism' was a term coined by critics, not by artists, in an attempt to indicate that after a period when the French had led modern painting with their Impressionism, German art had taken the next step. Marc, whose mother was a native of Alsace, and who had been influenced, on visits to France, by Impressionist, Post-Impressionist and eventually by Cubist painting, did not subscribe to the nationalism which marked some German artists of the time, not least because his closest artistic contact was the Russian Kandinsky, with whom he created Der Blaue Reiter ('The Blue Rider') movement in Munich in 1911, a movement and grouping of artists with an international membership. Kandinsky himself later recalled this second Expressionist movement (after *Die Brücke*), for all those who participated in its exhibitions, in these terms: 'we were two'. French, Russian and Italian Futurist influences there were, but the international flavour of the modern movement had also to coexist with Marc's awareness of his own national identity. In a letter of 1915, written from the battle-field, he said:

> I am myself . . . so wholly German in the old sense, one from the land of German Dreamers, Poets, and Thinkers, the land of Kant and Bach of Schwind [a Romantic painter of whose work he was particularly fond], of Goethe*, Hölderlin* and Nietzsche* . . . [that I wonder uncomfortably] whether the Slavs, especially the Russians, won't soon take over the Spiritual leadership of the world, while Germany's spirit grows worse and worse, involved in business and war matters. But any thought always leads me back to my good little Deer!

Marc's idealist and religious spirit was present in the letter – he had begun a study of philosophy and theology – but the mention of deer leads us to the work for which he has always been best known – as a painter of animals. There were indeed many paintings of deer, some of which he liked to keep in his garden at Sindelsdorf to the south of Munich, but the painting for which he became most famous, and with which he conquered even conventional spirits, was called *Der Turm der blauen Pferde* ('The Tower of Blue Horses') of 1913. The painting has been lost, as have many modern works which were considered by the Nazis to represent what they called *entartete* ('degenerate') art, but photographs show a large painting, vertical in format, where four horses, their heads rising one above another, are set in a landscape whose forms, like those of the horses themselves, bear traces of geometrical simplification in a sub-Cubist manner close to that of Henri Le Fauconnier, one of whose works had been exhibited with *Die Blaue Reiter* and illustrated in their *Almanac* (1912). Marc's painting was provided with a summit – a rainbow – in neo-Romantic manner.

The Tower is a leading work from Marc's 'middle period', if such a term is applicable to a career which, juvenilia excepted, lasted a bare four years. He had studied at the Munich Academy from 1900 (his own father was a competent landscape painter working in the current tonal manner of Lenbach). His very first paintings were similarly naturalistic. But in 1910 he painted his well-known *Three Red Horses*, followed in 1911 by *The Large Blue Horses*. As can be seen from these titles, naturalism was now abandoned, partly encouraged by the Post-Impressionist works he had seen in Paris and in Munich and furthered by his own belief in the spiritual value of colour. He had no precise and consistent language of colour, nor even the synaesthetic beliefs of Kandinsky, but a belief that art should speak to the soul on an intuitive level. Another aspect of this style is evident in the linear rhythms created both by the horses themselves and in their relationship with their landscape setting. The curvi-

linear forms seem to owe something to *Jugendstil* (German Art Nouveau) and the holism implied here in morphological terms where horses and setting are seen in unified terms was soon, through the influence of Robert Delaunay, to be supplemented by a colouristic holism. Marc, with his friend the Rhenish painter August Macke, visited Delaunay in Paris in 1912. The Frenchman's 'Orphism' was a 'Pure Painting' (both terms were coined by Apollinaire) which dispensed with the object. This art, with Kandinsky's, was enough to encourage Marc and Macke to turn toward a non-objective art. Marc appreciated, too, Tolstoy's* belief that art should have a purpose, and reconciled this seemingly all too functional belief with his own spirituality by seeing the purpose of art not in social but in ontological terms. After a period of seeking the 'animalization' of painting (which was itself a substitute for the 'impurity' of the human form) this philosophical artist came eventually to find something 'hateful' in all nature and found the abstract form (though not wholly devoid of empathetic implications) to be a purer substitute in both moral and aesthetic terms. Thus in 1914 he painted his *Hot*, *Playing*, *Fighting* and *Fragmented Forms*.

This process seems to be summed up in an unintentionally ironically titled drawing (ironic because he was in the artillery) which he made while at the front and titled *Arsenal for a Creation*. Two of his most important works had been painted in 1914. These were *Tirol* and *The Fate of Animals* (*Tierschicksale*), which were both works which could be considered prophetic. *Tirol* was the successor to a painting of 1913 called *Armes Land Tirol* ('The unhappy land of Tirol'), a mountain landscape with a graveyard and some skinny horses. *Tirol* itself is far more abstract, and only with reference to its predecessor can a mountain landscape where the light of sunrise and darkness do battle be deduced. No animal is present, but Marc softened these jagged forms by adding as an afterthought a form based on that of a primitive Bavarian wood-carving of the Virgin. Marc had chosen *The Book of Creation* as his subject for a projected series of Bible illustrations, to be undertaken by himself, Paul Klee, Alfred Kubin, Erich Heckel of *Die Brücke* and Kokoschka. He was not himself a Catholic, but this Virgin seems to bless the darker side of the landscape. All 'Blue Rider' artists admired primitive art forms, many of which were illustrated in their *Almanac*. Marc himself made some experiments with the Bavarian technique of *Hinterglasmalerei* (painting behind glass). He also made some sculptures of his own, including a *Tiger* which is very powerful and expressive.

The Fate of Animals, which can now be seen in Berne, had an alternative title written on the back by Marc: *Und alles Sein ist flammend Leid* ('All Being is flaming suffering'), a quotation from the Vedas. Marc was said by Klee to have considered yet another title: 'The trees show their rings, the animals their veins.' The effect created is as of a forest fire from which beasts, not least deer, are fleeing. The painting was itself damaged by fire soon after execution and was carefully restored by Paul Klee. Its style is similar to *Tirol* but it is larger and may be considered Marc's masterpiece.

Marc was above all important as a painter whose work quickly became popular and which made 'modernism' accessible to a wide public. He cannot be said to have exerted a strong influence on the specific style of any other artist, but was important as one whose work demonstrated the viability of non-objective values in painting.

Brian Petrie

Some of Marc's letters have appeared in *Briefe 1914–1916 aus dem Felde* (1938) and *August Macke – Franz Marc Briefwechsel* (1964). His 'Aphorisms' can be found in *Franz Marc: Briefe, Aufzeichnungen und Aphorismen* (2 vols, 1920). Alois Schardt's catalogue of the works (1936) is now outdated, but has not been succeeded. See Klaus Lankheit, *Franz Marc* (Berlin, 1950).

294
MARCONI, Guglielmo 1874–1937

Italian technologist

Marconi was born in Bologna in 1874 and by the end of the century he was famous. A year later, in 1901, his name entered the history books; by 1909 he had won the Nobel Prize. It was a remarkable rise. Marconi subsequently lived to the threshold of the Second World War, an institution rather than a man. He sustained his success: he pushed the technology ahead with nerve and flair; his companies prospered whilst most of his rivals fell by the wayside. He became rich, fêted, friend of the grand and the powerful.

Marconi was the 'Father of Wireless Telegraphy'. It was Marconi who, against the most weighty scientific opinion of the day, showed first that the 'wireless' could work, second that it could become a reliable system, and third that it could broadcast to the world. Marconi was a single-minded technologist, who worked incessantly to perfect and to develop his wireless system. Marconi's early success was a product of his independence of mind, tenacity, imagination, thoroughness. That he became widely known was partly, no doubt, because his demonstrations *worked*; but also because the press found Marconi's exploits irresistible. The communicators were always interested in developments in communications; they were also interested in this unlikely figure: bi-lingual, Anglo-Italian, well-connected, handsome and a ladies' man. This was a far cry from the typical image of the boorish technol-

ogist/unkempt inventor. But Marconi *was* a dedicated technologist: he worked long hours and never shrank from working in conditions like heaving seas, the cabin awash with sea-water, whilst he kept going determinedly with his transmissions. It was Marconi, more than anyone else, who, by the exercise of imagination and will-power, technical dexterity and flair, practical and commercial judgment, turned the world into an electronic village.

To appreciate Marconi's achievement it is necessary to bear in mind the kind of world into which he was born and in which he grew up. It was a world of new-found communications. Telegraphy was triumphant, with lines criss-crossing Europe and a substantial number of underwater cables linking continents. In 1866 Brunel* had laid the transatlantic cable, a feat of olympian proportions. Everywhere messages were being carried on *wires* by the agency of this remarkable electricity.

It was in 1887 that Heinrich Hertz* discovered radio waves or 'Hertzian waves', as they were known at first; but they were little more than a laboratory trick. They were weak, indiscriminate in wavelength, and could only be detected at distances of a few metres. Physicists such as Hertz himself, Oliver Lodge, Bose in India, Righi in Bologna, found them interesting because they confirmed the theoretical predictions of James Clerk Maxwell*, but the interest was mainly in the phenomenon as a phenomenon, not in what it might be made to do.

Hertz **died** in 1894 and the young Marconi, then twenty, read an obituary notice about Hertz whilst holidaying in the Italian Alps. Suddenly the idea came to Marconi that it might be possible to use 'Hertzian waves' to convey messages around the world. He said later: 'in those mountains of Biellese I worked it out in my imagination.'

Suddenly Marconi, whose boyhood had been listless, divided and awkward – bullied at school in Florence, a failure in exams at Leghorn – saw his role in life. He had long been addicted to all things electrical and had infuriated his father with his constant experimenting with scientific toys. Now, however, he had an aim.

Back home at the Villa Grifone he set up his laboratory in the attic. He repeated the basic Hertzian experiments; he devised improvements; he lengthened the range, first to the door of the attic, then down the stairs, then on to the terrace, and finally out into the estate. By chance he discovered the efficacy of combining an aerial with an earth. He tried every permutation of arrangements, always searching for improved efficiency, and always using a minimum of theory. By 1895 his 'range' was over half a mile. He came to England with his talented Anglo-Irish mother to seek resources to go further. On Salisbury Plain his range was 4 miles, by 1897 nearly 9 miles, and in 1899 he sent messages across the Straits of Dover.

Then Marconi staked his reputation and that of his company on sending messages across the Atlantic. It was considered a preposterous idea by the scientific opinion of the day, for the Hertzian waves were like light and would surely travel in straight lines, passing far above Marconi's Newfoundland kite-carried aerials! When, in December 1901, Marconi finally heard the three dots of the morse 'S' faintly audible behind the crackle of transatlantic static, he knew it was the start of a new era. From this beginning it took Marconi several years to perfect his transatlantic service, but he stuck at it, and finally got it right.

When Marconi began on the research in 1894 there were three monumental reasons why his work *seemed* to be ill-advised: (a) it was not needed; telegraphy on wires was a proven, reliable, heavily capitalized system; (b) it was hard to see how 'wireless' could be financed; who would be induced to *pay* for information thrown indiscriminately to all and sundry?; (c) the range would be very short, at best a hundred miles or so.

Many years later the *Electrician* commented that Marconi had two pieces of striking luck: his talented, well-connected, doting mother, Annie Jameson, and the existence of the ionosphere! It was the ionosphere which bounced his transmissions back to earth and confounded the scientific opposition. It was his mother who kept him going during 1894 and 1895, when he was considered an eccentric fool and the foundations of his triumphs were being laid.

Christopher Ormell

See: Address by Marconi to the Institution of Electrical Engineers, *Journal of the Institution of Electrical Engineers*, vol. 28 (1899); Degna Marconi, *My Father Marconi* (1962); W.P. Jolly, *Marconi* (1972).

295
MARRYAT, Captain Frederick 1792–1848

British novelist

It is doubtful whether Frederick Marryat ever saw himself as a maker of nineteenth-century culture. He was far too honest and unpretentious to have taken his achievement so seriously. Yet a balanced understanding of the age is not complete without some appreciation of the way in which he contributed both to early Victorian patriotism and to the development of that singularly English literary genre, the popular adventure novel.

His father was a chairman of Lloyd's, the marine underwriters, and Member of Parliament for Sandwich, and the young Marryat was destined from the first to a seafaring career. In 1806, at the age of fourteen, he was posted as midshipman to the *Imperieuse*

under the command of Lord Cochrane, famous for his brilliance and dash; the boy's naval experience during a period in which the service was basking in the glories of Trafalgar was suitably exciting. In 1812 he became a lieutenant, and at the end of the Napoleonic Wars in 1815 he was promoted to a command.

Subsequent journeys took him to St Helena, and during the first Burmese War he was noted for his 'able, gallant and zealous co-operation at Rangoon'. He gained particular distinction as a saviour of lives – some of them by throwing himself overboard – and in 1818 he was awarded the Royal Humane Society's medal. A year later he was made a Fellow of the Royal Society for his work in advocating and publicizing Sir Hume Popham's signalling system for use in the mercantile marine.

It is not at all clear why he turned to writing novels. Retirement from the navy no doubt gave him the restlessness common to all sailors on land and his finances were seldom wholly sound. In any event *Frank Mildmay*, published in 1829, amateurish though it is in comparison with the classic *Peter Simple*, was a runaway bestseller, for whose first printing he got £400, and from then on he produced books at the rate of one per year from 1830 to 1842, taking on, in addition, the editorship of the *Metropolitan Magazine*. During the 1840s he turned to the increasing market for children's fiction, with comparable success. He had also written a discursive account of his travels on the continent, published as *Olla Podrida* in 1835. In 1847 he tried to reapply for service afloat. Rage at the admiralty's refusal induced a mild haemorrhage, from which he had barely recovered when the shock brought on by the news of his son's death finally killed him.

Marryat is not a great literary artist – few writers are, indeed, more candidly artless – but it is precisely this lack of affectation which gives his books their enduring charm. As a story-teller he is utterly irresistible, and for the sheer pulse and energy of its narrative his masterpiece, *Mr Midshipman Easy*, is unrivalled by anything in its decade save the work of the young Dickens*. Using the old-fashioned picaresque manner of the previous century he created an image of the seafaring Englishman as a bluff, open-hearted champion of the underdog, loyal to his flag, ready to obey orders, yet quick to challenge injustice, which not only set the tone for a whole series of distinguished analogues and imitations but drew genuine admiration from writers such as Joseph Conrad, certain of whose themes and character types are undoubtedly coloured by his enjoyment of Marryat, 'the enslaver of youth' as he memorably terms him.

It was the adventurous young of the Victorian era to whom Marryat most effectively spoke. A work like *The Children of the New Forest*, written during his years of retirement in Norfolk, celebrates the ideals of chivalrous conduct, magnanimity, bravery tempered by modesty, and sheer pluck, on which the ethics of the public schoolboy and the empire builder were to be based. If history has shown the truth to be somewhat otherwise, then that is hardly the novelist's fault.

Jonathan Keates

See: Florence Marryat, *The Life and Letters of Captain Marryat* (2 vols, 1872); Oliver Warner, *Captain Marryat: A Rediscovery* (1953).

296
MARTI, José 1853–1905

Cuban revolutionary

José Marti was born in Cuba in 1853, while the island was still a Spanish colony. Educated by free-thinking liberals, his attitude towards Spain was, from an early age, deeply critical. Thus he gave full support to those who declared the Cuban War of Independence in 1868. In 1869, his public support earned him a six-year sentence in a penal colony. This was later commuted to exile in Spain, where he continued to work actively with other Cuban exiles. Yet he took no part in the mass popular movement which led, in February 1873, to the foundation of the Spanish Republic. Then, as always, his sole and enduring concern was Cuban independence from Spain, whatever the nature of Spain's government.

By 1875, Marti was in Mexico, where an attempt at democratic reform under the presidency of Lerdo clearly impressed him. Its subsequent failure left him deeply embittered, and he left Mexico, returning eventually to Cuba. There, the War of Liberation had ended in 1878, with the Pact of Zanjon. A year later, however, Marti was implicated in another attempted rising and was again exiled to Spain. This time he stayed there only a few months, making his way to New York, which was to be his base until his final return to his native island in 1895.

Until 1895, Marti earned his living as a critic and journalist, and continued his work among the exiled Cuban community. Increasingly his work was with Cuban workers, particularly black Cuban workers in New York, and the migrant tobacco workers of Florida. This both reflected and influenced Marti's growing emphasis on class questions, and the class character of the Cuban liberation movement. For he grew more insistent that such a movement must speak as much for the 'wretched of the earth' as for the bourgeois nationalists of his country. The 1887 Manifesto, produced by Marti and others, emphasized the political nature of the new liberation war – and implicitly attacked the notion that a military victory over Spain was the sole objective of the independence struggle.

This did not mean that Marti felt that armed struggle was unnecessary. As a founder member of the Club Los Independientes, whose object was specifically to collect funds for arms, he made clear the link he saw between the military and the political. It is true that Marti was cautious about launching a premature liberation war – which earned him a defeatist label from some Cuban groups. Yet it was clear that his concern was not to hold back the struggle, but to ensure that it took place under the best possible conditions, and with the broadest possible support. In 1891, a new political crisis seemed imminent in Cuba, as the promised reforms that had ended the war of 1868–78 clearly came to nothing. Now, Marti felt, the issue of national liberation was again on the agenda.

For the migrant tobacco workers of Florida, Marti was the natural leader of such a movement, and he was called to Tampa, Florida, in November 1891 to address them. There, in two of his finest speeches ('With all and for the good of all' and 'The new pines'), Marti set out the bases of this new movement. He restated his conviction that only armed struggle could achieve independence, but insisted that the military wing must always be subject to the *political* leadership of the movement. And he laid out his concept of a 'sincerely democratic nation' developing in the context of a Latin America wholly free from imperialist domination, whether Spanish or North American.

In 1892, Marti formed the Cuban Revolutionary Party, which rapidly won support from Cuban exiles throughout the Americas. It provided the instrument for co-ordinating the revolutionary forces both inside and outside Cuba, so that, by late 1894, Marti clearly felt the time and the conditions were right to launch a second and definitive war of Cuban national liberation. The first attempt to provision and arm three ships to sail from the USA to Cuba (the Fernandina Plan) was a failure. Yet by February 1895 the Liberation War had begun. On 11 April Marti reached Cuba to assume the supreme leadership of the movement. Two weeks later he was dead – killed in action.

In 1898, Cuba won its independence and Spain lost its last American colony. By 1899 the United States, the newest imperialist power, had written the first Constitution of the new Cuba and taken effective control over its economy and society. That dominion would last until 1959. Marti (in his famous essay 'Our America') had warned that the United States was waiting in the wings. Yet the fate of the revolution he briefly led should not minimize his immense contribution to the Cuban national independence struggle.

The Cuban Revolution of 1868 had enjoyed the support of Cuba's patrician, landowning families, frustrated by the tight and limited control exercised by the Spanish colonial administration. It was these families that provided the military leadership and the political horizons of the movement. Slavery still existed in Cuba in 1868, and the blacks who joined the liberation

armies in pursuit of their own freedom found themselves under the command of men who had enjoyed
the fruits of slavery and were often ambiguous about
its abolition. The Pact of Zanjon ended the war and
brought certain reforms which permitted the rich landowning classes a greater degree of autonomy in local
government. Yet the slaves remained slaves.

It was Marti's most important contribution to the
continuing liberation struggle to ensure that the Liberation Army of 1895 should be an army of abolition,
whose objectives were far more radical than those of
1868. His work among black Cubans in New York and
migrant workers in Florida ensured that the coming
revolution would liberate Cuba in a global sense, not
only from external domination, but from the class
structure that colonialism had created in its own interest. This would be a war for national independence,
social justice, democracy and an end to slavery. The
leaders of 1868, Maceo and Gomez, were deeply hostile
to Marti, and distrusted his radicalism. At their first
meeting, in New York in 1884, Marti was struck by
Maceo's arrogance, his vision of the revolution as his
personal domain. Maceo was equally disenchanted.
From their meeting, Marti drew the central lesson that
the political leadership of any movement must predominate at every stage, and control its military wing; and
further that, if it is to be a popular war, it must speak
for all classes, and be committed to far-reaching social
change. To this end, Marti worked both with intellectuals of the middle class, like himself, and with the
nascent working-class organizations, to achieve the
broadest support for his movement. His success in
doing so allowed him to return to Maceo and Gomez
in 1892 and offer them the military leadership of the
revolutionary forces, secure in the knowledge that its
political direction would be determined by a civilian
political organization, the Cuban Revolutionary Party.
When Marti joined the rising in Cuba in 1895, Maceo
and Gomez acknowledged the central role he had
played in its creation, and accepted his nomination as
supreme commander of the revolution.

Marti's death did not undermine the deep-going nature of the second War of Liberation, nor dilute its
central commitment to the abolition of slavery, nor lose
the support of Cuban workers inside and outside the
country.

He did not live long enough to see the new colonialism replace the old, nor to see his advocacy of the
liberation struggle finally vindicated by the Cuban revolutionaries of 1959. But he left an epitaph contained
in one of the simplest and best known of his poems –
'Guantanamera': 'I shall cast in my lot with the
wretched of the earth.'

Mike Gonzalez

See: J. Mañach, Marti: *Apostle of Freedom* (1950); F.

Lizaso, *Marti: Martyr of Cuban Independence* (1953); *Our
America by José Marti*, ed. P.S. Foner (1977).

297
MARTIN, John 1789–1854

British painter

Martin was born near Haydon Bridge in the north-east
of England, the son of a usually unemployed labourer
and a religious mother ambitious for her sons. In 1803
he was apprenticed to a Newcastle coach-builder and
then became a pupil of the immigrant artist Boniface
Musso. In 1806 Martin travelled to London with
Musso and spent a number of years as an unsuccessful
china and glass painter. His first success came in 1812
with his apocalyptic landscape *Sadak in search of the
Waters of Oblivion*, which was bought by a governor of
the Bank of England. This picture bears similarities to
the work of De Loutherbourg and to the scenes found
in the popular dioramas in London. At this time Martin received patronage from Prince Leopold of Saxe-
Coburg. He produced a number of large and breathtaking historical canvases until the end of the 1820s,
notably *Joshua commanding the Sun to stand still* (1816),
The Fall of Babylon (1819), *Belshazzar's Feast* (1820), *The
Deluge* (1826), and *The Fall of Ninevah* (1829). Martin
would exhibit many of these separately (he was never
an RA) and charge admission fees as well as selling
prints of the picture to an eager public. He also produced illustrations to *Paradise Lost* (1825–7) and to the
Bible (1831–6) and designed a number of monuments
for London. During the 1830s Martin devoted most of
his time to plans for embankments, sewage systems,
railway termini, parks and ventilation schemes for
mines. Although often brilliant and prophetic, and despite the support of men like Faraday* and Godwin*,
all of these plans were unsuccessful and he became
virtually destitute by 1837. He resumed his large
romantic landscapes and in the 1840s he painted *The
Eve of the Deluge* and *The Assuaging of the Waters* (1840),
Pandemonium (1841), *The Last Man* (1849), *The Great Day
of His Wrath* (1852), and *The Plains of Heaven* (1853).
He died on the Isle of Man on 17 February 1854.

Martin had a radical social and religious vision
which he sought to express in his enormous paintings
dealing with ancient history. In their scale, their concern with huge natural forces of creation and destruction and their architectural splendour, Martin's
pictures combined his hopes for the reconstruction of
metropolises like London and his almost Spenglerian
sense of historical catastrophe. In the vast buildings
and piazzas of his legendary Babylon can also be seen
the raised water systems and wide spaces which Martin
hoped would end the frequent cholera epidemics and
appalling poverty which beset London. His art repre-

sents the last attempt at large-scale apocalyptic Romanticism in painting and foreshadows the cinematic splendour of works like D.W. Griffith's *Intolerance* (1916) and before that some of the sumptuous visions of mythology painted by Symbolists like Moreau*. His reputation has wavered considerably, from the praise of fellow artists in the 1820s to the mockery of Ruskin* and the sale of his Last Judgment canvases in 1935 for less than £7. D.G. Rossetti* and William Frith admired Martin's work for its 'perspective of feeling', dizzying spatial construction and minute detail; but at the same time they represented a reaction against this Romantic vision which Hazlitt* claimed showed 'a total want of imagination' in its very magnitude.

Richard Humphreys

See: T. Balston, *John Martin* (1947); W. Feaver, *The Art of John Martin* (1975).

298
MARTINEAU, Harriet 1802–76

British journalist, social commentator, feminist

Born in Norwich in 1802 into a middle-class family engaged in the textile business and practising the Unitarian religion, Harriet Martineau was largely self-educated, though she was encouraged to be reflective and intellectually disciplined and was sent to study with Unitarian pedagogue Lant Carpenter as a girl of her family's radical political-religious-philosophical persuasion might be. In spite of deafness and a high-strung temperament, she became one of the nineteenth-century England's major intellectuals, an important journalist, an interpreter of economic, social, and political theories coming to the fore in her day, among them political economy, positivistic philosophy, and agnosticism, an advocate of numerous radical causes of her time, among them abolition of American slavery, better working conditions for domestic, agricultural and factory labourers and the rights of women in every domain. She was one of the most famous women in her lifetime, becoming a celebrity in 1832 when she published a monthly series of didactic stories intended to popularize the new notions of political economy, the *Illustrations of Political Economy*, which by 1834 were selling 10,000 copies monthly.

She travelled in America during 1834–6, was fêted by such political leaders as Supreme Court Chief Justice John Marshall, Senators Daniel Webster and Henry Clay and two presidents, Andrew Jackson and James Madison. She met such literary figures as Margaret Fuller* and Ralph Waldo Emerson* and historian George Bancroft, but she lost some of her national honoured guest status when she joined the abolitionist group surrounding William Lloyd Garrison

and was outspoken in public meetings against slavery at their urging. Upon her return to England, she wrote *Society in America* (1837), a careful and thoroughgoing analysis of American social principles and practices judged against the American constitutional principle of democratic equality. Scholars of American society consider *Society in America* a classic study, a forerunner of the discipline of sociology, a parallel in time and value to Alexis de Tocqueville's* *Democracy in America* (1835), Tocqueville's work being from the point of view of a conservative French nobleman, Martineau's from the point of view of a British middle-class radical. Martineau had written a very fine methodological essay, *How to Observe Manners and Morals* (1838), on board ship as she was bound for America. She subsequently published a lighter travel account of her American journey, *Retrospect of Western Travels* (1838). She continued a life-long correspondence with her American abolitionist friends, Maria Weston Chapman among them being the literary executor to whom she entrusted her manuscript *Autobiography* to be published posthumously (1877).

A second enduring influence of Martineau's is in the area of what we today call feminism, 'the woman question' in her era. From the beginning to the end of her life, she wrote about and took up causes intended to improve the situation of women. Her first published piece, in the little Unitarian *Monthly Repository*, when she was nineteen, was on 'Female Writers of Practical Divinity' (1822). Her last writing effort was in support of the Ladies' Campaign against the Contagious Diseases Acts, most significant of which were three letters and a petition published in the *Daily News* in the last four days of 1869 at the launching of this Josephine Butler-led effort against generally woman-incriminating anti-prostitution laws, a campaign that was to put into effect organized women's rights efforts all over England. Between those years, in the *Daily News*, in books and journals such as the *Cornhill Magazine*, the *Edinburgh Review*, the *London and Westminster Review*, she advocated women's right to work, women's right to education, sensible dress and health measures for women, fairness to working women such as needlewomen, governesses, and domestic servants. She was an advocate for the establishment of the first colleges for women, Queen's College in Hartley Street in London (1848) and the Ladies' College in Bedford Square (1849), and wrote in support of Florence Nightingale's* school for nursing at St Thomas's Hospital in London in the late 1850s. She wrote for and about the women's rights conventions in America in the 1850s, devastating the conventional argument of influence versus office as the place for women. In the *Daily News* in London in the 1850s she wrote leaders that were influential in passing the Divorce and Matrimonial Causes Acts. She, unlike her nationally popular friend Florence Nightingale and Queen Victoria*, supported and signed the first petition for the vote for women that went to parliament sponsored by John Stuart Mill* (1866).

Just as she was typical of many Victorian writers in her allegiance to such ideas as *laissez faire* economics (she was a life-long defender of Adam Smith) and rationalistic morality (she was a necessarian, a Benthamite, abhorred unmarried sexual liaisons such as those between W.J. Fox and Eliza Flowers, and Harriet Taylor and John Stuart Mill), she was also typical of her time in espousing such eccentricities as mesmerism and phrenology. In the early 1840s, she had a mysterious illness for some years from which she claimed to be cured by mesmerism. This sequence of events and beliefs, travels in the Near East, and a relationship with Henry G. Atkinson, led her to the publication of a curious agnostic book, *Letters on the Laws of Man's Nature and Development* (1851), mostly Atkinson's work, but espousal of an intellectual stance toward religion which wrought a permanent breach with her once beloved brother, her closest childhood companion, the eminent Unitarian divine, James Martineau.

Less peculiar to a twentieth-century vantage point, but consistent with a rationalistic religious stance, was Martineau's achievement as a social critic and a proponent of what we today call social scientific method. In 1851 she read and translated into English Comte's* *Positive Philosophy* (1853). But before that she had written comparative studies of societies, and after that she wrote much on social causes and effects of human behaviours.

Perhaps Martineau's most outstanding exemplary contribution was as journalist. Though she wrote some bad fiction (*Deerbrook*, 1839; *The Hour and the Man*, 1841), and some good popular history (*The History of England during the Thirty Years' Peace 1816–1846*, 1849–50), it was as a reporter and commentator on national and international affairs that she achieved most. A voluminous writer, she published over 1,400 leaders in the *Daily News* between 1852 and 1866 and also published a great deal in leading journals of the period. Much of her work was collected into books or pamphlets as soon as it had been published in pieces: e.g. *Biographical Sketches, 1852–1875* (1877); *The Factory Controversy: A Warning against Meddling Legislation* (1855); *Household Education* (1848); *Health, Husbandry and Handicraft* (1861).

At the end of her life, quite characteristic of her, it was the obituary that she wrote for herself more than twenty years before when she thought she was dying that was probably most revealing of who she was. She said of herself:

She could sympathize in other people's views, and was too facile in doing so; and she could obtain and keep a firm grasp of her own, and, moreover, she could make them understood. The function of her

life was to do this, and, in as far as it was done diligently and honestly, her life was of use.

Gayle Graham Yates

See: T. Bosanquet, *Harriet Martineau* (1927); R.K. Webb, *Harriet Martineau: A Radical Victorian* (1960); Valerie Kossew Pichanick, *Harriet Martineau and her Work, 1802–1876* (1980).

299
MARX, Karl Heinrich 1818–83

German historian, economist and revolutionary

Marx was born in Trier on 5 May 1818, the son of a prosperous Jewish lawyer. He studied at the Universities of Bonn and Berlin between 1835 and 1841; in Berlin he associated with the 'Young Hegelians', who constituted the radical wing of Hegel's* followers. When the reactionary Friedrich Wilhelm IV came to the Prussian throne in 1840, the government became increasingly hostile to the Young Hegelians, and Marx had to give up all hope of an academic career. Instead, he turned to journalism, and in October 1843 he moved to Paris to take up the editorship of a new journal. His stay in Paris, which lasted until February 1845, was of great importance in his life. It was in Paris that he first met Friedrich Engels*, who was to become his life-long friend and fellow-worker; it was there, too, that he began a serious criticism of Hegel's philosophy. He was at first influenced in this respect by the German philosopher Ludwig Feuerbach*, but by 1845 he was criticizing Feuerbach too and was well on the way towards his own distinctive doctrines. Expelled from France in 1845, and later from Belgium and Germany, Marx arrived in London in August 1849. He continued to live in London until his death on 14 March 1883.

Marx's doctrines are of great range and power, and their influence has been enormous. But there have been, and still are, fierce disagreements about the exact nature of the Marxism of Marx. In recent years, argument has centred around the problem of whether one is to see his thought as an organic whole, developing in an orderly way, or whether there was a sharp break in his thought. However, there is no reasonable doubt that the main lines of Marx's thought were fixed by 1848, the year in which he and Engels published their *Manifesto of the Communist Party* (*Manifest der Kommunistischen Partei*). This is probably their most influential work, and is certainly a masterpiece of polemical literature – compact, wide-ranging and forcibly argued. Though *The Communist Manifesto*, as it is now commonly called, was a joint production, Engels insisted that its basic idea belonged to Marx alone. This basic idea, commonly known as historical materialism, is a thesis about human history, and according to Engels it did for the study of history what Darwin's* theory had done for the study of organic nature. Very briefly, it asserts the fundamental importance of class struggles, both in the present and in the past, and it claims to explain their nature and inevitability. Section I of *The Communist Manifesto* begins with the assertion, 'The history of all hitherto existing society is the history of class struggles.' This is important both for what it denies and for what it asserts. If you are to understand human history, says Marx, you must not see it as the story of great individuals; you must not even see it simply as the story of states and their conflicts. You must see it as the story of social classes and their struggles with each other. Social classes have changed in the course of time, but in the middle of the nineteenth century the most important classes, Marx argued, were the bourgeoisie and the proletariat. By 'the bourgeoisie' is meant the class of big capitalists, who own the factories and the raw materials which are processed in them. The members of the proletariat, on the other hand, are completely property-less. They do not even own hand-looms or their own small plots of land, as small-scale manufacturers used to do between the sixteenth and the eighteenth centuries. All that they have is their power to work, and this they sell to the bourgeoisie. These two classes are not merely different from each other, but also have opposite interests. Here we reach the heart of the Marxist position. The struggles between bourgeoisie and proletariat, and the struggles between classes which existed before them, are not a chance affair. They are necessary and, like the existence of the contending classes themselves, they can be explained.

In his explanation, Marx distinguishes between 'productive forces' and 'production relations'. Productive forces include not only tools and machines, but the human beings who make and use them; that is to say, human labour is a productive force. As to relations of production, Marx points out (*Wage Labour and Capital*, 1849) that production is a social matter. When human beings produce things they enter into relations with each other, and only in the context of these social relations does production take place. What is called a 'society' is these relations of production taken as a whole. So far, there have been three main types of society: ancient, feudal and bourgeois. These types of society involve social classes of distinctive sorts – e.g. slaves in ancient society, serfs in feudal society, the proletariat in bourgeois society – so the relations between classes belong to the relations of production. Marx adds that productive forces and production relations, besides being unable to exist in isolation from each other, also influence each other. In *Wage Labour and Capital*, Marx says that production relations 'will naturally vary according to the character of the means of production'. For example, on the introduction of

fire-arms – a new instrument of warfare – 'the whole internal organization of the army necessarily changed'. Again, as Marx said in *The Poverty of Philosophy* (*La Misère de la philosophie*, 1847), an attack on the French socialist Proudhon*, 'The hand-mill gives you society with the feudal lord; the steam-mill, society with the industrial capitalist'. But production relations can also influence the development of productive forces. For example, the bourgeoisie, in the early stages of its history, helped to develop productive forces, creating (as *The Communist Manifesto* puts it) 'more massive and more colossal productive forces than have all preceding generations together'.

We now reach a very important part of Marx's theory. Corresponding to productive forces of any given sort, Marx thinks, there is a set of production relations that fits those forces. More than this: these fitting production relations will come into existence. Feudalism provides an illustration. At a certain stage in the development of the means of production, feudal property relations ceased to be compatible with the productive forces that had already been developed. In the words of *The Communist Manifesto*: 'They had to be burst asunder; they were burst asunder.' According to Marx, there is a parallel situation in the nineteenth century, but now it is bourgeois society that provides the fetters, in that bourgeois production relations no longer fit the new and powerful forces of production. 'For many a decade past,' says *The Communist Manifesto*, 'the history of industry and commerce is but the history of the revolt of modern productive forces against modern conditions of production, against the property relations that are the conditions for the existence of the bourgeoisie and of its rule.' Marx argues that this revolt will have an inevitable outcome. Just as feudal society was burst asunder, bourgeois society will suffer the same fate.

The detailed defence of this thesis forms an important part of the first volume of Marx's chief work, *Capital* (*Das Kapital*; vol.1 was published by Marx in 1867; vols 2 and 3 were edited by Engels and published in 1885 and 1894). The bulk of this work concerns economics, and its two major principles are the labour theory of value and the theory of surplus value. The latter, according to Engels, was Marx's second great discovery, worthy to be set beside his new conception of history. Marx started from the thesis (which he derived from Adam Smith and David Ricardo*) that labour is the source of all value. He then asked how this can be reconciled with the fact that the workers receive only a part of the value that they create, and have to surrender the rest to the owners of the means of production. In other words, Marx set out to explain the exact nature of what he saw as the exploitation of workers by capitalists, and his theory of surplus value is central to this explanation. So much is clear; but whether Marx succeeded in his aim – whether, as he would claim, the labour theory of value and the theory of surplus value have the status of scientific laws – is far from clear. Certainly, these theories have not had the wide influence enjoyed by Marx's theory of history, and some Marxists go so far as to argue that Marxism can do without the labour theory of value. But the real power of *Capital* lies in the chapters of volume 1 that describe, with burning passion, the rise of capitalism, the misery that it creates, and its future downfall. These culminate in a famous passage, in which the clash between productive forces and production relations is clearly stated:

> The monopoly of capital becomes a fetter upon the mode of production, which has sprung up and flourished along with, and under it. Centralization of the means of production and socialization of labour at last reach a point where they become incompatible with their capitalist integument. This integument is burst asunder. The knell of capitalist private property sounds. The expropriators are expropriated (ch. 24, trans. Moore and Aveling).

To sum up: the relations between hitherto existing social classes – and these are hostile relations, struggles between classes – have to be seen in the light of the development of productive forces, and the way in which this is helped or hindered by the relations of production. But it is also Marx's view that history so far essentially *is* the story of class struggles. In the preface to his *A Contribution to the Critique of Political Economy* (*Zur Kritik der politischen Ökonomie*, 1859) Marx put his point in the form of a metaphor. The passage in question is very condensed, and its precise interpretation is disputed, but Marx's main point is usually taken to be this: that the material productive forces and the relations of production, which together constitute the 'mode of production of material life', form a 'basis', a 'real foundation', on which there arises a 'superstructure' of law, politics, religion, art and philosophy. Marx also asserted that this superstructure is 'determined by' the economic basis. 'It is not,' he says, 'the consciousness of men that determines their existence, but their social existence that determines their consciousness.' So the conflict between the forces of production and the relations of production is of fundamental importance for human history as a whole. Hegel, too, had (in his own way) recognized the importance of conflict within reality, and it may have been this aspect of Hegel's thought which Marx found attractive, and which led him to proclaim himself 'a disciple of that great thinker' (postscript to the second edition of *Capital*, 1873). Hegel, said Marx, had some idea of the true nature of dialectic – i.e. of the basically contradictory nature of reality – but he 'mystified' it by turning the thought process into an independent subject. But there is a rational kernel within the wrappings of mystifica-

tion, and this can be discovered if one turns Hegel's dialectic the right way up. This seems to mean that we should regard matter (in the shape of the economic basis) as prior to mind, instead of regarding matter as a form of mind, in the way that Hegel did. The extent of Marx's debt to Hegel is hotly disputed. Perhaps the truth is that the way in which Marx presented his views in *Capital* owed something to Hegel's philosophy; but it is unlikely that the *content* of his thought would have been fundamentally different if he had never read a word of Hegel.

Marx's theory of the relations between basis and superstructure, and between the components of the basis itself, is a form of historical determinism. Marx's version of determinism is sometimes called 'the economic interpretation of history'; here, attention is drawn to the determination of the superstructure by the basis as a whole. Sometimes it is called a technological determinism', where the emphasis is on the fundamental role played within the basis by the forces of production. But however it is described, Marx's determinism may seem to involve a paradox. On the one hand, Marx speaks of law, politics, etc. as being determined, i.e. necessitated; on the other, Marxists have always been extremely active politically, and behave as if the outcome of historical development were not a foregone conclusion. The problems of human freedom exercised Engels, but Marx seems to have paid little attention to them. An often-quoted remark from Marx's *The Eighteenth Brumaire of Louis Bonaparte* ('Der achtzehnte Brumaire des Louis Napoleon', 1852), a study of events in France leading up to the seizure of power by Louis Napoleon in 1851, states that 'Men make their own history, but they do not make it just as they please; they do not make it under circumstances chosen by themselves, but under circumstances directly encountered, given and transmitted from the past.' This seems to allow some freedom of action to human beings, but only within certain limits. The same view is presented in the preface to *Capital*, in which Marx says that the discovery of the laws of the movement of society cannot alter the necessary phases of development; it can at best shorten and lessen their birth-pangs. What is certain is that for Marx there can be no question of the proletariat sitting back and letting events take their course; the proletariat's struggle is itself a part of events, a factor in the historical process. Marx emphasizes, too, the practical importance of a comprehension of the nature of historical development. Such a comprehension is not a purely theoretical affair, restricted to a scholar's study; it is itself a factor in the transformation of society. Theory, Marx wrote in an early critique of Hegel (1843), 'becomes a material force as soon as it has gripped the masses'. Marx's term for theory-based revolutionary activity, a union of theory and practice, was 'revolutionary praxis'. The term 'praxis' has played an important part in recent

Western Marxism, where it often has a much vaguer sense than that which Marx gave it; for some modern Marxists it seems to mean no more than 'revolutionary activity'.

When he explains the nature of the superstructure in his preface to *The Critique of Political Economy*, Marx makes use of another important concept, that of ideology. He says that law, politics, etc. are so many 'ideological forms' in which men become conscious of the conflict within the basis and fight it out. Just as we do not assess individuals by what they think about themselves, so our judgement of a historical epoch ought not to be based on what it thinks about itself, i.e. on its consciousness of itself. Rather, we should explain this consciousness, which belongs to the superstructure, in the light of conflicts occurring within the economic basis. An ideology, then, is not just a set of ideas; it is not even just a set of false ideas. Rather, it is a set of ideas which mask their true dependence on the economic basis; ideas that involve (to use a phrase employed by Engels) a 'false consciousness'. The ideologist believes, falsely, that his thought is autonomous; he fails to recognize the real forces that impel him.

Marx's thesis about the dependence of the ideological superstructure on the economic basis is a sweeping generalization, the detailed justification of which is beyond the power of any single man. Many Marxists have tried to confirm this thesis in the realms of law, religion, art and philosophy; Marx himself, in his investigations of the dependence of the superstructure on the basis, paid most attention to politics. His account of the nature of the state may serve as an illustration of the character of his arguments, and is also important in its own right. The state, according to Marx, does not exist for the benefit of the community as a whole; it exists to serve a class interest. 'The executive of the modern state,' says *The Communist Manifesto*, 'is but a committee for managing the common affairs of the whole bourgeoisie', and more generally, 'Political power is merely the organized power of one class for oppressing another.' However, Marx has to qualify this. The theory expounded so far may be called 'instrumentalist', in the sense that it regards the state as just a means by which an exploiting class maintains itself in its dominant position. But Marx had to recognize that this was not always the case. In *The Eighteenth Brumaire of Louis Bonaparte* he described a situation in which there was a balance of social forces, which led to the emergence of a state which was relatively autonomous, in the sense that it was not in the service of any specific class-interest.

Marx's view of the state as a means of class oppression had, as he saw, important implications for the future. With the triumph of the proletariat and the disappearance of the bourgeoisie as a class, there will no longer be a class society, in the sense of a society in which one class opposes another. So the state, as an instrument for the oppression of one class by another, will cease to have a function and will disappear, as a useless part of the body disappears in the course of evolution. As Engels put it, in a famous phrase, 'The state is not "abolished", it withers away.' This does not mean that a future classless society will be without any organs of control. *The Communist Manifesto* says simply that 'the public power will lose its political character', which implies that a public power will still exist. But this power will be exercised by society as a whole and not by one social class over another.

But between the overthrow of the bourgeois state and the establishment of a classless society there will be an interim period. The transition to a classless society, Marx thought, was unlikely to be peaceful. He came to think that a peaceful transition is possible in some countries (England was one); in the main, however, he thought that the overthrow of bourgeois rule would be by means of violent revolution. This being so, there will be a period during which the victorious proletariat and the defeated and resentful bourgeoisie coexist, and during this period it will be necessary for the proletariat to maintain their dominant position by force. There must be, in other words, what Marx called a 'class dictatorship of the proletariat', as 'the necessary transit point to the abolition of class distinctions generally' (*The Class Struggles in France, Die Klassenkämpfe in Frankreich*, 1850). In his book *The State and Revolution*, written just before his seizure of power in 1917, Lenin laid great emphasis on this part of Marx's political theory. Lenin's 'dictatorship of the proletariat' turned out to be a dictatorship of the Communist Party, and writers on Marxism often point out that Marx and Engels did not have this in mind. According to *The Communist Manifesto*, the Communists are the most advanced section of the working-class parties of each country, but they do not form a separate party. This does not mean that Marx and Engels would have disapproved of Lenin's methods; he was operating under conditions that were very different from those envisaged in *The Communist Manifesto*. But they would not have regarded Lenin's idea of a separate, rigidly disciplined Communist Party as necessarily applicable to all epochs and all countries.

It is natural to ask, 'How did Marx envisage the future classless society?' The new society will of course be a communist one, but Marx refuses to speculate about its precise nature. In his view, the elaborate pictures of a new society painted by some socialists and communists, such as Fourier* and Robert Owen*, are mere Utopias. What is clear is that *The Communist Manifesto* emphasizes, not the abolition of private property as such, but the abolition of *bourgeois* property; it does so because such property is 'the final and most complete expression of the system of producing and appropriating products that is based on class antagonisms'. Earlier, in the so-called *Economic and Philosophic Manuscripts* ('Ökonomisch-philosophische Manuskripte aus dem Jahre 1844', written in Paris in 1844, but not published until 1932), Marx related his ideas about the abolition of private property to what he called 'alienation'. Marx recognizes no fewer than four kinds of alienation in capitalist society. First, the worker is alienated from his product, in that he sees the product as foreign to him, and indeed as dominating him. Second, the worker is alienated from himself; only when he is not working does he feel truly himself. Third (and more obscurely) the worker is alienated from man's 'species life'. Marx seems to start from the position that labour is fundamental to human beings, i.e. that man is by nature a producer. It follows that, to the extent that the produce of his labour is taken from him by the capitalist, the worker is less of a human being. Finally, in capitalist society man is alienated from man; that is, in a competitive society a man is set against other men. One might expect Marx to say that alienation is produced by private (or, more exactly, bourgeois) property. Curiously, he says that private property is initially the *product* of alienated labour; only later does private property become a cause of alienation. For Marx, the solution to the problem of alienation is communism. But not what he calls 'crude communism' – not, that is, a form of communism which is based on general envy and aims at a levelling-down. Communism of this kind still regards possession as the ultimate end; for Marx, on the other hand, communism is 'the real appropriation of the human essence by and for man'. One may take this to mean that communism is not concerned with what a man has; it is concerned with the fulfilment of his potentialities as a human (and that means as a *social*) being. Communism of this kind, says Marx, is humanism.

Although Marx's theory of alienation has had great influence on Western radical thought since the Second World War, Marxists disagree about its importance in Marx's thought as a whole. It is noteworthy that the term 'alienation' occurs most frequently in works that Marx himself did not publish – in the *Economic and Philosophic Manuscripts* of 1844, and in the so-called *Grundrisse*, a rough draft of *Capital* written in 1857–8. True, Marx always emphasized the miserable lot of the proletariat under capitalism, but the view of alienation that he expounded in 1844 covers much more than that. The dispute has been sharpened by the fact that the Marx of 1844 is often regarded as having a fundamentally different world-view from that of the later Marx. The early Marx, it is argued, saw communism as a moral ideal; the later Marx saw it as a scientific doctrine. Some Marxists see this as introducing a contrast where none exists. Marx, they argue, never drew a sharp distinction between fact and value, and so between the fields of science and morality. If this view

of Marx is correct, then the development of his thought from the 1844 manuscripts to the works of his maturity may be regarded as a unified whole. But it cannot yet be said that the problem has been resolved.

G.H.R. Parkinson

Although there have been very many editions and translations of the works of Marx and Engels, there is as yet no complete edition. Publication of the complete works in the original languages was begun in Moscow in 1927 but abandoned after 1932; a fresh start was made in 1975 (*Karl Marx/Friedrich Engels, Gesamtausgabe,* Berlin). In 1975 publication was also begun of a 50–volume edition in English of *Marx and Engels: Collected Works* (Moscow and London). The literature about Marx is enormous. The following books give lucid and critical accounts: Isaiah Berlin, *Karl Marx: His Life and Environment* (1st edn 1939, 4th edn 1978); D. McLellan, *Karl Marx: His Life and Thought* (1973); J. Plamenatz, *Karl Marx's Philosophy of Man* (1975); L. Kolakowski, *Main Currents of Marxism*, vol. 1, *The Founders* (1978). Of the many defences of Marx's doctrines, one of the most able is G.A. Cohen, *Karl Marx's Theory of History: A Defence* (1978).

300
MAUPASSANT, Henri René Albert Guy de
1850–93

French short-story writer and novelist

Born near Dieppe, at Fécamp or at the Château de Miromesnil, Maupassant's native Normandy and his family background both had a determining influence on his development as a writer. The failure of his parents' marriage and their separation when he was eleven created a feeling of instability in the household which was later reflected in the short stories. His mother, Laure, was the sister of Alfred Le Poittevin, the childhood friend of Flaubert* who was later to guide Maupassant's first literary efforts. Educated at the seminary of Yvetot and then at the *Lycée* in Rouen, he moved to Paris in 1869 to study law and lived briefly with his father. This was soon interrupted by the outbreak of the Franco-Prussian War in 1870.

1873–80 were crucial years for Maupassant. His job as an obscure civil servant in Paris and his passion for boating on the Seine provided first-hand material for his narratives. Above all, Flaubert continued to watch over his literary development and brought him into contact with such writers as Zola*, Goncourt*, Turgenev* and Henry James*. Maupassant was initially associated with the Naturalist movement and was one of six young Naturalists who met at the Trapp restaurant in April 1877 to discuss their admiration for

Flaubert, Goncourt and Zola. Three years later he contributed one of his finest short stories, 'Boule de suif', to Zola's Naturalist collection *Les soirés de Médan*, which enabled him to embark on an independent literary career.

During the following ten years Maupassant produced innumerable stories and novels, balancing a prolific output with an ever increasing enjoyment of the material comforts of life. His literary successes, however, which included 'La Maison Tellier' (1881), 'Mlle Fifi' (1883), 'Miss Harriet' (1884), 'M. Parent' (1885), 'Toine' (1886), 'Le Horla' (1887), and 'L'Inutile Beauté' (1890), could not compensate for the slow disintegration of his mental stability. It was only after 1891 that Maupassant suffered from hallucinations and madness that led to an attempted suicide in 1892 and finally to his premature death the following year in a Paris clinic. Yet, from his early twenties he had been aware that he was suffering from a form of syphilis that attacked the nervous system and in 1889 he witnessed the death from madness of his younger brother, Hervé, which suggested a hereditary connection. This knowledge and the intellectual energy expended between 1880 and 1890 explains his fascination with stories dealing with morbid mental states such as 'Lui?' and 'Le Horla'.

During the nineteenth century, an expanding reading public and the appearance of short stories in magazines and newspapers led to the increased popularity of short fiction, of which Maupassant was to become the most complete exponent. He wrote over 300 stories which mainly appeared in *Le Gil Blas* and *Le Gaulois*. They reflect the society of the period and deal with objectively observed everyday subjects situated in places familiar to Maupassant, such as Paris, Normandy and the Mediterranean. The subject matter shows his overriding concern with *l'humble vérité* and underlines his belief that the aesthetic value of literature depends on the artist's ability to penetrate reality. To this end, Maupassant limited his observation to such themes as prostitution ('La Maison Tellier'), the Franco-Prussian War ('Boule de suif'), Norman peasants ('La Ficelle'), struggling civil servants ('La Parure'), and, more generally, to themes concerning family relations ('Le Papa de Simon'), money ('Un Million') and affairs of the heart ('Miss Harriet').

Maupassant is a pessimist who portrays the world as contingent and man as the victim of circumstances. Although possessing a sense of humour which reveals a profound humanity, he tends to distance himself ironically from his world and deploys his acute observation to lay bare the foibles of human nature. The rapid tempo of his stories usually moves towards a striking conclusion that conveys a wry picture of an aspect of human experience. The inventive use of the narrator and the oral framework induces a feeling of authenticity whilst his style is classical and self-effac-

ing. Maupassant is a great story-teller whose major achievement was to have created a world which appears to mirror reality whilst at the same time masking the extraordinary artistic selection that makes all this possible.

The relative lack of status of the short story in France, even today, probably explains Maupassant's need to prove himself in the novel and why he is more readily appreciated as a short-story writer abroad. His first novel, *A Woman's Life* (*Une Vie* 1883, trans. 1965), suffers from the short story technique. *Bel-Ami* (1885, trans. 1961) is in many ways far more successful, in that the shallow psychology of the hero, Duroy, is adequately conveyed through action and the objective technique. *Mont-Oriol* (1887, trans. 1949) has little to recommend it but *Pierre and Jean*, *Pierre et Jean* (1888, trans. 1962) does show that Maupassant could adapt his objective manner to a more penetrating character study. His final novels, *The Master Passion* (*Fort comme la Mort*, 1889, trans. 1949) and *The Human Heart*, *Notre Coeur*, (1890, trans. 1929), show a change of direction in which he abandons his earlier techniques and moves towards the psychological novel, made popular by Bourget. Although these novels contain undoubted merit they take Maupassant into areas unsuited to his talents.

The influence of Maupassant on short fiction has been widespread throughout the present century and his views remain essentially modern; yet his technical orthodoxy and apparent ease of production have often provoked an intellectual reaction, particularly in France, that demotes him to the level of an efficient craftsman who lacks soul. In many ways, Maupassant has become the victim of his artistic sleight of hand and he leaves us with a picture of society that many secretly recognize but which few care to acknowledge.

David Bryant

The most recent edition is *Oeuvres complètes* (17 vols, 1969–71), to which should be added *Correspondance* (3 vols, 1973). For an excellent edition of the short stories consult *Contes et Nouvelles* (2 vols, 1974, 1979). For an English translation see M. Laurie, *The Works* (10 vols, 1923–9). Among numerous editions of the short stories in English, H. Sloman, *Boule de Suif and Other Stories* (1946) and *Miss Harriet and Other Stories* (1951) are recommended. See: C. Castella, *Structures romanesques et vision sociale chez Maupassant* (1972); A. Lanoux, *Maupassant le Bel-Ami* (1967); F. Steegmuller, *Maupassant* (1949); E. Sullivan, *Maupassant the Novelist* (1954) and *Maupassant, the short stories* (1962); and A. Vial, *Maupassant et l'art du roman* (1954).

301
MAXWELL, James Clerk 1831–79

British physicist

Apart from some periods of ill-health and some friction with his first childhood tutor, Maxwell's background was highly conducive to his progress towards becoming one of the most distinguished physicists of the nineteenth century. His father was laird of a modest Scottish estate and had the means to provide James with the education that suited his needs. During the latter years of his schooling in Edinburgh, the young Maxwell was able to accompany his father to meetings of the Edinburgh Society of Arts and the Royal Society of Edinburgh, both of which were active and thriving. When he was only fifteen, Maxwell made an analysis of the geometry of oval curves that was sufficiently original to be presented to the Royal Society and published in its proceedings. Maxwell received his university education mainly at the University of Cambridge. He was appointed to the Chair of Natural History at the University of Aberdeen in 1856 and moved to a similar position at King's College, London in 1860. For the last eight years of his life Maxwell filled the Chair of Experimental Physics at the University of Cambridge. He superintended the design and construction of the Cavendish Laboratory and directed the early years of its operation.

Maxwell's major achievement was his formulation of electromagnetic field theory, a theory which identified the passage of light with an electromagnetic wave and which was eventually to lead to the production of the first radio waves. By the end of the century this first 'field' theory had led to the undermining of a view widely held in the nineteenth century, namely, that all physical phenomena are mechanical phenomena explicable in terms of Newtonian mechanics.

Maxwell's innovations in electromagnetism stemmed from the researches of Michael Faraday*. Faraday pictured what Maxwell came to call electric and magnetic fields in terms of 'lines of force' emanating from the electrically charged bodies and magnets and circling the current carrying circuits that were their source. Aided by some mechanical analogies of William Thomson's (see Lord Kelvin*), Maxwell set out to put Faraday's results on a firmer theoretical foundation. In Maxwell's theory magnetic fields corresponded to vortices in the ether and electric fields to some kind of distortion of the ether. The first full version of Maxwell's theory was presented in 'A Dynamic Theory of the Electromagnetic Field' (1864) and was elaborated on in his *Treatise on Electricity and Magnetism* (2 vols, 1873). The feature of the electromagnetic theories of Faraday and Maxwell that makes it appropriate to label them *field* theories is the extent to which they explain electromagnetic phenomena in terms of what

goes on in the space surrounding charged bodies, magnets and electric currents. This contrasted with the approach taken by most continental theorists, such as W. Weber and G. Riemann*, who postulated electric fluids or particles residing in charged bodies and flowing through conducting circuits at the same time acting upon each other at a distance across empty space.

A spectacular success of the field approach in Maxwell's hands was the formulation of an electromagnetic theory of light. The general equations of Maxwell's theory yielded a wave equation representing transverse waves propagated through space with the velocity of light, and Maxwell was able to identify these with light. Maxwell's successors were able to show on the basis of his theory how radio waves, electromagnetic waves with a longer wavelength than that of visible light, could be produced. The first successfully to realize this possibility in the laboratory was the German physicist Heinrich Hertz* in 1888. Whilst Maxwell's theory certainly had its dramatic successes, it also had its weaknesses. One of these was the failure of Maxwell to make at all clear what 'electricity' was. To questions such as 'What is it that resides in electrically charged bodies?' and 'What happens in a wire when a current flows through it?' Maxwell's work offered no clear answer. Clear answers became possible when the Dutch physicist H.A. Lorentz* reconciled Maxwell's fields with some aspects of the continental 'action-at-a-distance theories.' The result, which had emerged by the final decade of the century, was the electron theory. From the viewpoint of that theory, bodies become charged by acquiring an excess or dearth of electrons whilst currents through conductors correspond to a flow of electrons. In addition, electrons give rise to fields in the medium surrounding them, the fields corresponding to those of Maxwell's theory.

Lorentz, like Maxwell, understood the electric and magnetic fields to represent mechanical states of an ether. By the beginning of the twentieth century, and particularly in the light of Einstein's theory, it had become clear that electromagnetic fields were elementary entities not reducible to the mechanical states of an ether. The nineteenth-century ideal of reducing all physical phenomena to Newtonian mechanics had collapsed. Einstein observed that 'the lion's share of this revolution was Maxwell's.' We thus have the ironical situation that Maxwell embarked on the project of reducing electromagnetic theory to mechanics, and in carrying it out he produced a theory that was to play a major part in undermining that very project.

Maxwell's other major contribution to physics was his work on the kinetic theory of gases, a theory in keeping with the general project of reducing all physical phenomena to Newtonian mechanics. According to the kinetic theory a gas is composed of molecules in random motion, colliding with each other and with the walls of the containing vessel. Prior to Maxwell's work elementary versions of the theory had been forward, for example by Bernoulli and Joule*, whilst Maxwell's contemporary, R. Clausius*, had already developed it well beyond its most simple form. As Maxwell realized, the kinetic theory was essentially a statistical one. The aim was to characterize not the motion of each individual molecule, but rather the net effect of the random motions of aggregates of molecules. Maxwell introduced statistical techniques capable of dealing with the random motion of aggregates of molecules and so founded what has since become known as statistical mechanics.

In order to stress the fundamentally statistical character of the theory, Maxwell employed the services of a hypothetical being that has become known as Maxwell's 'demon'. This 'very observant and neat-fingered being' was able to open and close a small frictionless trapdoor in a partition between two volumes of a gas initially at the same uniform temperature. It is supposed to be so adept at this task that it can open and close the door in such a way that only fast-moving molecules pass one way and only slow-moving molecules pass the other way. By concentrating the faster-moving molecules in one compartment and the slower-moving ones in the other in this way, the demon is able effortlessly to raise the temperature of one compartment with respect to the other. The net result, then, is that heat has been made to flow from a cold to a hot body without the expenditure of work, in violation of the second law of thermodynamics. The fact that this hypothetical occurrence is in conflict with thermodynamics but not with the laws of Newtonian mechanics indicated to Maxwell that the former cannot be simply a species of the latter. The kinetic theory of heat adds a fundamentally statistical component to Newtonian theory so that, in Maxwell's words, 'the second law of thermodynamics has the same degree of truth as the statement that if you throw a tumblerful of water into the sea, you cannot get the same tumblerful of water out again'.

Subsequent to Maxwell's efforts the statistical kinetic theory was further improved, especially by the Austrian, Ludwig Boltzmann*. Some of its deep-seated difficulties could only be removed with the advent of quantum mechanics and the replacement of classical statistics with quantum statistics. In this context, it is interesting to note that, in his very first paper on the kinetic theory, 'Illustrations of the Dynamical Theory of Gases' (1860), Maxwell noted that the kinetic theory clashed with known results concerning the relation between the principal specific heats of a gas and acknowledged that it 'could not possibly satisfy the known relation'. Since most of the productive development of the theory took place after 1860, we have a nice counter example to the view that a clash with the facts is a sufficient condition for abandoning a theory. The classical theory never did remove the difficulty highlighted

by Maxwell. Only when the theory was replaced by its quantum mechanical successor could specific heats be adequately accounted for.

Maxwell made other contributions to physics that were minor compared with those described above. He was productive in his studies of colour and colour vision, phenomenological thermodynamics and theories of elasticity. He also published a detailed study of possible accounts of the composition of Saturn's rings, a study which first won him general recognition by professional physicists. Maxwell's theoretical work was almost invariably accompanied by extensive experimental work designed to put his theories to the test.

Alan Chalmers

Most of Maxwell's scientific papers have been collected in *The Scientific Papers of James Clerk Maxwell*, ed. W.D. Niven (1965). Other works: *Theory of Heat* (1871); *Matter and Motion* (1877); *The Electrical Researches of the Honourable Henry Cavendish, F.R.S.* (1879); *An Elementary Treatise on Electricity* (1881). An early biography is L. Campbell and W. Garnett, *The Life of James Clerk Maxwell* (1882). A more recent one is C.W.F. Everitt, *James Clerk Maxwell: Physicist and Natural Philosopher* (1975)

302

MAZZINI, Giuseppe 1805–72

Italian nationalist

Mazzini the propagandist belongs, with Cavour the statesman and Garibaldi* the soldier, to that trio of Italians who led the drive towards national unification in the mid-nineteenth century. The main lines of his thinking were developed during that relatively innocent period in the history of European liberalism, between 1815 and 1848, when it was still possible to believe that the liaison with nationalism was more than a marriage of temporary convenience. At that time those who exercised authoritarian rule over such regions as Greece, Poland, and Italy itself were generally the same dynasts as those who refused to concede greater autonomy to the smaller nations of Europe. Thus it was easy for liberals like Mazzini to underrate the extent to which, under other circumstances, nationalism might be transformed into a foe of freedom.

Born at Genoa into a doctor's family, Mazzini studied law at the local university. By 1827, when he graduated, he was already immersed in the activities of the Carbonari secret society. This strove to liberate the Italian peninsula from its divided condition and from its subservience, whether direct or indirect, to Austria. In 1830 he was arrested as a subversive plotter by the Piedmontese authorities and, though acquitted, was driven into exile. During the following year he expressed his distrust of excessive French influence over the Carbonari by founding Young Italy, an organization of his own which had won by 1833 some 60,000 members. Its programme spurned federal solutions, and insisted that Italy's grand civilizing mission in the world at large could be fulfilled only on the basis of a unitary state possessing a republican constitution. His movement was more successful at education than at actual insurrection, and after a series of failed risings he withdrew in 1837 to London which remained thereafter his chief base of activity.

It was during the 1840s that Mazzini began work on the essays, finally collected as *The Duties of Man* (*Doveri dell'uomo*, 1860), for which he is best remembered. His text was directed most urgently to 'the Italian working class', and it hammered home the point that enjoyment of rights could follow only upon the fulfilment of obligations. Mazzini mapped out the way in which man's supreme duty to God (not defined in any specifically Christian terms) might be discharged through acting positively on a set of mutually compatible responsibilities imposed by Family, Nation, and Humanity. Thus, for example, the achievement of full Italian nationhood would be a step towards that greater 'moral unity' required for the continent at large, and so also towards the supra-national goal of an harmonious 'United States of Europe'. This was a vision which, as later events revealed, gravely underestimated the amount of antagonism that competing nationalisms could generate. None the less something of its spirit pervaded the proceedings of the 1919 Paris Peace Conference, and lingered as an influence upon proponents of 'the European idea' down to more recent times. Outstanding among those who, still farther afield, expressed a debt to the sheer generosity of Mazzinian ideals was the great Indian nationalist Mahatma Gandhi.

Mazzini's own most dramatic practical effort to realize his aims came in the revolutions of 1848–9, when he was active with Garibaldi first in the Milanese rising and then at Rome. Here he served as an efficient and tolerant triumvir in the short-lived Republic. After its downfall he resumed his life of exile in London, where he founded the Friends of Italy and did much to promote sympathy for his cause among influential British circles. His encouragement through the 1850s of various plans for revolutionary insurrection in the peninsula played a vital role in sustaining the nationalist enthusiasm of Italians. Equally, it made him an embarrassment to Cavour and the Piedmontese authorities who, since they were now pursuing their own monarchical scheme of unification through the channels of international diplomacy and war, feared that his radicalism might alienate potential allies and even condemned him to death in his absence. Mazzini's direct role in the heady events of 1859–60 was limited, though followers of his did help to launch the Sicilian revolt upon which Garibaldi capitalized so skilfully and

he himself did spend some time at liberated Naples before the South was handed over to Piedmont. He never took the seat to which he was elected in the parliament of the new Kingdom of Italy, remaining in exile even after his death sentence was revoked in 1866. His final eruption into Italian events came four years later, when he was arrested off the coast and briefly imprisoned for encouraging a republican revolt in Sicily.

By the time that Mazzini died in Pisa national unification looked, on one level, complete. Within that whole process, as Derek Beales comments, 'his significance as a symbol, as Italy incarnate, was immense. In his lifetime he was incomparably more effective than Marx' (*The Risorgimento and the Unification of Italy*, 1957). None the less he himself confessed to a sense of failure and disillusionment. He believed that the new Italy reflected less of his vision than that of 'the medley of opportunists and cowards and little Machiavellis' represented by Cavour and those who followed in government. The North's contemptuous and greedy treatment of the *mezzogiorno* was only the most obvious symptom of qualitative deficiencies in the kind of unity actually achieved. To this disappointment Mazzini had to add his recognition of the fact that, during his last years, the leadership of the wider internationalist cause was slipping from fellow-liberals into the hands of socialists about whose understanding of freedom he was deeply sceptical.

Michael Biddiss

Mazzini's works were brought together in the monumental 'National Edition' of the *Scritti editi ed inediti* (94 vols, 1906–43). His *Duties of Man* is most easily available in the Everyman's Library version (1907 and later printings). Among secondary studies, see: Bolton King, *Mazzini* (1903); Gaetano Salvemini, *Mazzini* (1956); and Gwilym O. Griffith, *Mazzini: Prophet of Modern Europe* (1932).

303
MELVILLE, Herman 1819–91

US writer

'I love all men who *dive*' – so, in part, runs Melville's reaction on hearing a lecture in Boston in 1849 by Ralph Waldo Emerson*. It was generous acclaim, for Melville thought Emerson's Transcendentalism largely a fraud, a well-meant but facile credo of optimism and spiritual good cheer which failed to acknowledge the tragic currents in man's condition, his especial vulnerability to pain, war, evil and illusion. But in designating Emerson a 'diver', Melville as aptly might have been speaking of himself. For in nearly all his fiction and poetry, and in his lively correspondence and several reviews, he confirms his own deep probing energies of mind, the writer-diver in search of the elusive, absolute condition of things. This irresistible 'diving' for truth, a life-long, unslackening curiosity which finds expression through the intelligent playfulness and vitality of his style, situates him, with Emerson, Hawthorne*, Whitman* and Thoreau*, at the centre not only of the mid-nineteenth-century 'American Renaissance' but the American literary tradition at large, a restive, major imagination whose powers come best into focus in his whaling epic, *Moby-Dick* (1851), stories like 'Bartleby, The Scrivener' (1853) and 'Benito Cereno' (1855), his 'Ship of Fools' allegory, *The Confidence Man* (1857), and the posthumous novella, *Billy Budd* (1888–91). The scale of Melville's 'curiosity' – his 'ontological heroics' as he describes matters in his correspondence – has rarely been better perceived than in the diary entry made in 1856 by Hawthorne, then American Consul in Liverpool, after he and Melville spent an afternoon in discussion on the Southport sands:

> Melville, as he always does, began to reason of Providence and futurity, and of everything that lies beyond human ken .... He can neither believe nor be comfortable in his unbelief; and he is too honest and courageous not to try to do one or the other.

The reputation that once attached to Melville, and which the revival of his critical fortunes begun in the 1920s still has not entirely dislodged – that of the compelling but artless teller of sea-stories – has nevertheless given way to a growing awareness of how layered his writing was from the outset. So, at least, from differing angles, fellow-authors like D.H. Lawrence, Cesare Pavese, Albert Camus and Charles Olson have born impressive witness. Paradoxically for a writer at one time thought only an American-Victorian purveyor of 'adventure', and whose career dissolved into obscurity after *Moby-Dick*, Melville has increasingly been taken for a prophet of 'modern' consciousness, a wary, sceptical, knowingly ironic voice of resistance to every manner of human ruling illusion. Whether recognized for his arts of narrative, or for the fine ambition of his thought, Melville has justly entered the American literary pantheon. Few of his writings are entirely free of fault, but his essential 'depths', as Hawthorne remarked of *Mardi* (1849), Melville's least gainly book, 'compel a man to swim for his life'.

Melville alleged that his life only 'began' when he wrote his engaging first work, *Typee* (1846). Yet his beginnings were auspicious, if not necessarily for a literary career. He came of two socially eminent American families, the Melvilles of Boston and the Dutch-descended Gansevoorts of Albany, New York. One grandfather, Major Thomas Melvill (sic), took a leading part in the Boston Tea Party; the other, Peter Gansevoort, fought as a general in the War of Independence. This patrician stock was an important source of pride in Melville, the basis of high personal expectations. He grew up, one of eight children, in a busy, well-connected and convivial home, in New York city. In *Redburn* (1849), *Pierre* (1852) and parables like 'Bartleby' and 'The Two Temples' (1854), Melville would reveal himself as a writer of the city as much as the sea. The unexpected bankruptcy, then delirium and death of his father, Allan Melville, an 'Importer of French Goods and Commission Merchant' and a seemingly prosperous member of New York's commercial middle class, in the recession of 1832, brought profound family reverses. For Melville it inflicted a trauma he would try to re-confront in the writing of *Pierre*. In the short-run, it made for a series of abrupt personal false starts.

First, in 1834–6, he clerked in an Albany bank, and in the summer of 1835 worked on his uncle's farm at Pittsfield. Fifteen years later, he himself bought a farm in Pittsfield, drafted the early versions of *Moby-Dick* and, following the publication of his essay, 'Hawthorne And His Mosses' (1850), discovered the author of *Mosses from an Old Manse* for his neighbour in nearby Lenox. In 1837, he tried teaching in a country school. The same year he made his writing début in the correspondence columns of a local paper, and then as the author of a two-part Gothic story fragment. In late 1838 he studied engineering in hopes of working on the Lake Erie canal system. In June 1839, he sailed down the Hudson to New York, and secured a place to Liverpool and back as a deckhand on the packetship, *St Lawrence*. His encounters with the brute equations of Victorian sailor and city life he portrays, in some irony, in *Redburn*. Once back in New York, and again jobless, he tried another spell of teaching, and in 1840 took off to Illinois, where he saw and travelled the Mississippi, experience put in store and re-worked in his canny 'metaphysical' satire, *The Confidence Man*.

In near desperation, in January 1841, appropriately the turn of a new year, he sailed out from New Bedford as a whalerman and harpooner aboard the *Acushnet*, the beginning of four years of Polynesian and whaling adventure. His journeys into the South Seas, on the *Acushnet* and two subsequent whalers, took him to a multitude of ports and sailor haunts, and specifically to the Marquesas, Tahiti and Honolulu. Later he would visit ocean outposts like the Galápagos, where he found the inspiration for his cycle of island portraits, 'The Encantadas', as Darwin* had for his *Origin of Species*. His litany of adventure includes jumping ship and his vaunted 'stay mong the cannibals' (which yielded *Typee*), a spell of detention in the local 'calaboose' and various intervals of beach-combing of which he makes use in *Omoo* (1847), even temporary managership of a bowling-alley, and his eventual return to Boston in 1844 via the Horn and Latin America as an enlisted seaman aboard the frigate, *United States*, on which his fifth book, *White-Jacket* (1850), is based. On his reunion with his family, he could look back to these years, life lived dangerously and at full throttle, as a seasoned ex-mariner, the one-time patrician for whom a whaler (as he testifies in *Moby-Dick*) had been his 'Harvard and Yale', and who knew from the inside the testing, male, enclosed ship-world of the common sailor, and that toughest of forcing-grounds, the Pacific whale-fisheries. It is this dense, energetic personal history, and more, that Melville gives imaginative expression to in the fiction which culminates in *Moby-Dick*.

His early writing, in sequence *Typee*, *Omoo*, *Mardi*, *Redburn* and *White-Jacket*, centres upon a young, usually ingenuous, 'isolato', a quester embarked for adventure, and even outright 'truth', whose eventual incarnation will be Ishmael in *Moby Dick*. Each narrative, thus, Melville conceives as a journey-out, a remembered diary of events either on land or aboard different types of ship. In *Typee*, Melville's setting is Nuku Hiva in the Marquesas, and a concealed inland 'cannibal' valley to which Tommo, the narrator, and his companion flee, only to become prisoner-guests, two fugitive consciousnesses from the West set down amid the arcana and totemic mysteries of Typee culture. Despite its surfaces as 'adventure', Melville, as he says, 'varnishes' his facts at every turn, playing one ambiguity off against another, and hinting of darker other worlds beneath the affable outward show of the valley. The zest of the telling, and the story's lavish, contrapuntal play of detail, make for an astonishing first effort. *Omoo* continues the saga, Melville's most free-wheeling volume, genuinely light of touch and funny, almost South Seas picaresque. With *Mardi*, he begins as before, another jumping from ship and the promise of Polynesian derring-do. Less than a third along, however, the story changes radically in temper, and for the worse. For into this third narrative, Melville poured an avalanche of recent reading, from Plato and Montaigne, Spenser and the Elizabethans, from the major European Romantics, and even from Victorian books of flower symbolism. The results are painful, a cluttered would-be 'philosophical' travelogue in which Taji, the hero, and his retinue, pursue an ethereal albino princess across a mythic archipelago of sixteen islands. *Mardi* with justice can be taken as a dummy-run for *Moby-Dick*, but one which outran Melville's control. Stung by the criticism aroused by *Mardi*, Melville spoke of returning to the 'cakes and ale' world in *Redburn*. Based on the Liverpool journey he made at eighteen, and a subtler effort than he allowed, it tells the rite-of-passage endured by Wellingborough Redburn, youthful confrontations glossed and teased by an older, far wiser head. The stark scenes of sailor DTs, death, malignity in the person of the sailor Jackson, and the observation of Liverpool penury and human suffering and of the plague which breaks out among emigrants

in steerage, make for vivid, dramatic narration. In *White-Jacket*, also told as first-person narrative, Melville depicts the hierarchic, man-of-war world of the frigate, a compendious account of American navy custom and life seen from his customary fo'c's'le stance. In the shedding of the narrator's emblematic white coat, as Redburn's before, Melville projects a sea-version of the fall from innocence, the awakening of a deeper, 'ocean' state of knowing.

By the time he published *Moby-Dick*, Melville had married (in 1847) Elizabeth Shaw, daughter of the Chief Justice of Massachusetts; read like a novice possessed the works of Shakespeare; and, having published in *The Literary World* (1850) his admiring account of *Mosses from an Old Manse*, met and began his astonishing correspondence with Nathaniel Hawthorne. His 'whale-book', large, striking in canvas and reach, represents him at full imaginative stretch. Ostensibly the story of the *Pequod*'s search for the definition-eluding white whale, it quickly yields many other levels of quest – for self-meaning, community, 'light', and again, overwhelmingly, 'truth'. Defined one way, then another – by Ahab as evil, by Starbuck as a 'dumb beast', by the Parsee counter-crew as a god, by Queequeg as a hieroglyphic mystery, the whale dominates the narrative, incapable of being 'caught' and fixed by any single meaning. Melville declares the organizing principle of *Moby-Dick* to be 'careful disorderliness', an appropriately flexible mode of narrative able to contain, and actually discipline, the book's abundance, both the cetology and the epic flights of speculation. Whether read as simple whale adventure, or metaphysics, or as 'modernist' self-reflexive narration, *Moby-Dick* offers Melville's central legacy, an essential landmark of American literary history.

With *Moby-Dick* behind him, Melville turned his imagination inland, and in *Pierre or The Ambiguities* attempted a portrait of a heroic 'Fool of Truth' ultimately entombed by his endeavour to redeem his father's abandonment of a mysterious, illegitimate daughter, the hero's half-sister. Within its apparent Gothic labyrinths lies a profound drama of sexual feeling, and Melville's own 'inside narrative' of the writer's life. Between 1853, when he tried to secure a consular appointment, and 1857, he turned to the short story, publishing in 1856 his *Piazza Tales*, five pieces (with an introduction) from the fourteen he had issued in *Putnam's Monthly Magazine* and *Harper's New Monthly Magazine*. These stories are now rightly taken to rank among his best efforts. In 'Bartleby' he tells a parable of Wall Street, an account of liberal capitalism's impact on the human spirit redolent of Kafka. In 'The Encantadas' he depicts a version of hell, a bleak landscape of island volcanic ruins to complement the saddest and worst of human isolation and loss. In 'Benito Cereno', a story almost Conradian in its hints of ineffable corruption, he makes an act of slave-insurrection his occasion, a bleak, violent portrait of the moral blindness slavery requires for its very existence. These, and his other stories of the 1850s, and *Israel Potter* (1855), a satire of American national heroes, prepared the way for his blackest chronicle of illusion, *The Confidence Man*. If literary kin could be claimed for *The Confidence Man*, it would include Dostoevsky's* *Notes from the Underground*, Mann's *Felix Krull* and Kafka's *The Castle*. A Mississippi river story, begun and ended on April Fool's Day aboard the steamer *Fidèle*, it sets about the gullibility and panacea-seeking of latterday American 'pilgrims' with Swiftian incision. The instrument is an apparent master confidence-man, a 'metaphysical scamp', whose different avatars mock and ensnare the unvigilant. Within its onslaught on different American shibboleths, it contains key clues to Melville's overall theories of fiction (especially chapters XIV, XXXIII and XLIV). Neither the tone, nor the precise direction of Melville's satire, can always easily be pinned down, but his idiom is never less than vigorous, brilliantly alert and inventive.

By 1856, Melville was approaching nervous collapse. He sailed for the Levant as an attempt at recuperation; visited Hawthorne in Liverpool; and in 1857, after his trip to the Holy Land, landed back in America a month after the publication of *The Confidence Man*. In 1858–60 he tried lecturing on the Lyceum circuit; sailed with his brother Tom to San Francisco in 1860; sold the Pittsfield farm in 1862–3 and, dismayingly for a man who had written *Moby-Dick*, in 1866 was obliged to take employment as a minor Customs Inspector in New York, a post he discharged with resigned diligence for nineteen years. His times saw little improvement. His volume of Civil War poems, *Battle-Pieces and Aspects of the War* (1866), and the later *Clarel* (1876), a massive Victorian work of doubt and faith longer than *Paradise Lost*, barely gained a readership. In 1867, his son Malcolm died, a probable suicide, to be followed in 1886 by the second Melville son, Stanwix. Only two further works were published in Melville's lifetime, both privately, the poems in *John Marr and Other Sailors* (1888) and *Timoleon* (1891). The work which first saw light in 1924, however, *Billy Budd*, after a confused textual history, has come to be recognized for Melville's final masterpiece. A fable of 'iniquity' and sacrificial innocence, it explores the triangulation of three 'phenomenal' men, Captain Vere, the master-at-arms John Claggart, and 'welkin-eyed' Billy Budd – hanged for alleged murder aboard a British warship during the Napoleonic Wars and in the wake of the risings at Nore and Spithead. Whether read as Melville's testament of 'acceptance', or 'rebellion', or as more complex dialectical drama, it underscores the enduring, radical strengths of his art. Melville ended his career as he began, an unyielding 'diver' for truth.

A. Robert Lee

See: F.O. Matthiessen, *American Renaissance: Art and Expression in the Age of Emerson and Whitman* (1941); Leon Howard, *Herman Melville: A Biography* (1951); Jay Leyda, *The Melville Log: A Documentary Life of Herman Melville, 1819–91* (2 vols, 1951); Newton Arvin, *Herman Melville* (1957); Charles Olson, *Call Me Ishmael* (1958); Warner Berthoff, *The Example of Melville* (1962); *Melville: A Collection of Critical Essays*, ed. Richard Chase (1962); Edgar A. Dryden, *Melville's Thematics of Form: The Great Art of Telling the Truth* (1968); *Studies in the Novel*, Herman Melville special number, vol. 1, no. 4 (Winter 1969); *New Perspectives on Melville*, ed. Faith Pullin (1978).

304
MENDEL, Gregor 1822–84

Austrian botanist, founder of genetics

As the son of a peasant in the Silesian village of Heinzendorf (Hynčice), Mendel showed promise at the village school and was selected for academic studies in Leipnik and Troppau. When he left the *Gymnasium* at Troppau in 1839 he entered the Philosophy Institute at Olmütz. There financial worries and overwork dogged his progress so that it was with relief that he entered the Augustinian Monastery at Brünn (Brno) in 1843. This was the centre of intellectual life in the area. Several of the monks taught in the local schools, as did Mendel from 1849 until he became abbot of the Monastery nineteen years later.

In addition to his work as teacher and cleric Mendel was an active member of the Natural Science Society (*Naturforschende Verein in Brünn*), he was on the central board of the local agricultural society (*K.K. Mährisch-schlesischen Gesellschaft zur Beförderung des Ackerbaues, der Natur– und Landeskunde*), and he was known locally as a plant breeder, apiculturist, and meteorologist.

Despite Mendel's academic ability and excellence as a teacher he twice failed to pass the teachers' examination in the natural sciences. The time which he spent at Vienna University (1851–3) preparing for re-examination proved invaluable for his subsequent researches into plant hybridization although it did not lead to success in the teachers' exam. Mendel's hybridization experiments – with the edible pea – lasted from 1856 to 1863. His study of the Hawkweed (*Hieracium*) was completed in 1871 by which time his duties as abbot took almost all his time. These latter years were marked by controversy over the new ecclesiastical tax on monastery property which Mendel obstinately refused to pay. His funeral in 1884 was a major event in Brünn, but it was another sixteen years before his researches in plant hybridization became generally known and identified as the foundation stone of the modern conception of heredity.

When Mendel studied science at Vienna University the subject of the fixity of species was under discussion. The adherents of *Naturphilosophie* had pictured life as developing progressively under the direction of an inherent, non-material agency of 'world soul'. Species therefore had been changed or transmuted, albeit gradually. The old dogma of the constancy of species had already come under attack in the eighteenth century and Linnaeus had weakened his hard line on the subject when he suggested that many species had originated from the hybridization of a few original types, the generic forms. This claim was greeted with scepticism. It was pointed out that hybrids were frequently sterile, and when they yielded progeny these tended to 'revert' to one or other of the originating species. Debate over this 'hybridization theory' of the origin of species, however, continued and prizes for essays on the subject were offered by the Dutch Academy of Sciences in 1830 and the Paris Academy in 1860.

Mendel recognized that the debate over the hybridization theory would only be settled when a systematic and extensive series of experiments had been carried out in which the transmission of each differing trait united in the hybrid had been followed through successive generations in a large population of its offspring. Between 1856 and 1863 Mendel raised some 28,000 plants, involving crosses between varieties differing in one, two, and three hereditary traits.

In all cases where the parents differed in one trait, such as seed shape – round or wrinkled – the seeds produced by the resulting hybrids were either round or wrinkled, never intermediate between the two forms. Moreover, the proportion of round to wrinkled seeds approximated to the ratio 3:1. This proved to be the case for all the seven traits he studied. Further studies revealed that the round seeds were of two types, one breeding true, the other yielding both round and wrinkled seeds. The latter were twice as numerous as the former, so the ratio of 3:1 was really 1:2:1, the middle term representing the hybrid forms, the first and last terms the true-breeding forms.

With his training in mathematics Mendel realized that the 1:2:1 ratio corrresponded with the terms of the binomial series: $(A + a)^2 = A^2 + 2Aa + a^2$). Mendel pictured the two letters in the binomial as representing the two contrasted forms brought together in the hybrid. The fact that the offspring yielded by sexual reproduction mirrored the binomial expansion in their statistical relations suggested to Mendel that sexual reproduction involved a process equivalent to the multiplication of the terms A and a. Evidently the forms A and a became separate from each other, then they united in all possible combinations with equal frequency. Since each fertilized egg cell was produced by the fertilization of one female germ cell by one pollen

grain it must be in the formation of these cells and grains that the separation of types A and a occurred. These gametes were hence either of type A or type a and their union in fertilization gave the forms A, Aa and a.

Mendel went on to show that where more than one pair of contrasted characters was involved the hereditary transmission of each was independent of the other. Thus in the case of two pairs of contrasted characters brought together in a hybrid the offspring showed all possible combinations between the two pairs. These combinatorial forms corresponded in their relative frequencies with the terms in the expansion of *two* binomial series. When dominance was involved the resulting ratio was 9:3:3:1.

These statistical regularities which have become known as Mendelian ratios were Mendel's empirical discovery. The explanatory hypothesis which he advanced to account for them is generally known as germinal or Mendelian segregation. Today these achievements tend to be regarded in terms of the light which they have thrown upon the nature of inheritance, a subject which lacked a sound theoretical foundation until Mendel's work became generally known. For Mendel, the significance of his work lay in a different direction. He had set out to throw some light upon the hybridization theory of the origin of species and the conflicting reports of plant hybridists thereon, and it was to their work that he devoted the concluding section of his paper. He urged that the unit of analysis was not the species but the hereditary characters. The results obtained by hybridists therefore depended upon the number of such characters which differed in the originating forms. According to the binomial theorem if this number was n then the number of different types of hybrid offspring would be $3n$. If n was 7 the reappearance of either of the originating types would be likely to occur only once in 16,000 hybrid offspring, whereas if n was 1 the expected frequency would be 1 in 4. That previous hybridists using different species arrived at different results was hardly surprising. Nor was it a matter for surprise that hybrids showed a wide range of variability, for this again was a function of the number of differing characters crossed. There was no need to postulate the existence of species or of characters with varying degrees of constancy. It sufficed to distinguish hybrids in which germinal segregation occurred, whose progeny followed the example of the edible pea, and those in which it did not occur, where permanent hybrids were formed which represented new combinations of characters from the originating species.

Although Mendel's papers were referred to a number of times in the nineteenth century their importance was not recognized. Thus the standard bibliographical review of W.O. Focke merely noted Mendel's numerous hybridization experiments and added somewhat sceptically that Mendel 'believed he had found constant numerical ratios between the hybrid types'. When in 1900 three botanists, Hugo de Vries, Erich von Tschermak and Carl Correns, rediscovered Mendelian ratios and read Mendel's paper the Mendelian theory was finally launched. Six years later the term 'genetics' was introduced for the subject whose theoretical foundation had been furnished by Mendel.

Robert Olby

The best biography of Mendel is still that of Hugo Iltis, *Life of Mendel* (trans. E. and C. Paul, 1932; reprinted 1966). A translation of Mendel's paper and associated documents will be found in C. Stern and R. Sherwood, *The Origin of Genetics: A Mendel Sourcebook* (1966). For a discussion of the context of Mendel's research see R.C. Olby, *Origins of Mendelism* (1966).

305

MENDELEYEV, Dmitry Ivanovitch 1834–1907

Russian Chemist

Mendeleyev was born in Tobolsk, in Siberia, where his father was a teacher. He was the fourteenth and last child of the family. When he was sixteen his mother took him to St Petersburg to be trained as a teacher; he did very well, but quarrelled with bureaucrats and was posted to the Crimea. In 1856 he returned to St Petersburg and took his Master's degree in chemistry, supporting the views of Charles Gerhardt who saw molecules as units rather than polar arrangements of diverse atoms, and who classified them into series which he called 'types'. In 1857 he became a *privatdocent* in the University of St Petersburg; and in 1859 he was sent for two years to Germany and France to study chemistry. He attended the Karlsruhe Conference, one of the first major international gatherings of scientists, called in 1860 to try to reach agreement on chemical formulae and atomic weights. In 1861 he became Professor of Chemistry in the St Petersburg Technological Institute, and retained throughout his life an interest in applied chemistry and in industry generally. In 1867 he was in addition made Professor of General Chemistry at the University of St Petersburg. He was a founder of the Russian Chemical Society in 1868.

Chemistry seemed in the 1860s a mass of facts and recipes without clear organizing principles. Students seemed to need to memorize great quantities of data, and the Karlsruhe Conference had only recently produced some agreement about even elementary questions such as whether water was HO or H_2O. Mendeleyev, on being appointed to the Chair of General Chemistry, determined to write a textbook which would bring order into the treatment of the various

chemical elements. He was fond of playing Patience, and the arranging of cards into sequences may have helped him in his great triumph of classifying the elements into families. He was not the first to do this, but his was the version which prevailed because he took into account the full range of chemical properties and not just the atomic weight, and because he predicted the existence of certain elements which were indeed soon afterwards isolated.

There were some sixty elements known in the 1860s, and classifying them might have seemed easier than arranging the countless species of insects; but it did not prove so. Some elements like chlorine, bromine and iodine clearly formed a family, but to establish an overall pattern proved very difficult. Following the Karlsruhe Conference, there was agreement on atomic weights; and various attempts were made, notably by J.A.R. Newlands in Britain, to arrange elements in order of increasing atomic weight but in rows of columns so that similar elements would come in a line. Newlands hit upon a 'law of octaves' according to which every eighth element was similar; but this did not work for all the elements, and sometimes two had to be put into the same square, and the result looked forced and artificial.

Mendeleyev in 1868 hit upon his more general 'periodic law', according to which when elements are placed in order of atomic weight then similar elements recur at regular intervals. In order to fit the elements in, Mendeleyev had to leave some gaps; to 'correct' some atomic weights, notably that of cerium; and to put iodine and tellurium out of order. These seemed like devices to make facts fit a theory, and when Mendeleyev published his law and the 'periodic table' based upon it in 1869, it was not received with enthusiasm. In 1871 he published his textbook, *Principles of Chemistry* (*Osnovy Khimii*, trans. 1891), which ultimately became a classic translated into many languages, and which was based upon his classification; but it was not until after 1875 that the fundamental importance of the periodic table was evident to all. In that year Lecoq de Boisbaudrom, who knew nothing of Mendeleyev's work, isolated a new element which he called gallium; this turned out to be what Mendeleyev had predicted as eka-aluminium, detailing its properties with great accuracy because he knew those of neighbouring elements in the periodic table. Contemporaries were astonished when they found that the theorist had known more about the element than the practical chemist who discovered it; and from then on the table began to assume the prominent place which it occupies in chemistry lecture-theatres.

In 1877 William Crookes drew attention to Mendeleyev's work in a long article on 'The Chemistry of the Future', and later published an English translation of Mendeleyev's long paper. Mendeleyev rapidly acquired a high reputation abroad, and was elected into foreign academies and awarded medals by them. At home, he became a Corresponding Member of the Academy of Sciences, but he was never elected to full membership. His first marriage had ended in divorce, and his remarriage was a social stigma; and he was still prone to disputes with officials, and quarrels with the Germans then prominent in Russian science. In 1890 he delivered a student petition to the Ministry of Education; the result was that his resignation was demanded. He had powerful friends as well as enemies, and gave up academic life to enter the Civil Service where he spent his latter years at the Ministry of Finance and the Board of Weights and Measures. He kept up with theoretical chemistry, but his own great contribution had been made; and at the end of his life he was doubtful about radioactivity and electrons, because he believed in unchanging elements which could be classified once and for all. There is an irony here, because Ernest Rutherford's atomic model, with its nucleus surrounded by electrons in quantized orbits, turned out to explain how the elements can be arranged in the periodic table. Mendeleyev's work thus not only brought order into chemistry, but proved to be one of the routes leading towards a theory of matter acceptable to both chemists and physicists.

D.M. Knight

Mendeleyev's *Principles of Chemistry* (1871) appeared in English translation in 1897, with later editions. On his work, see J.W. van Spronsen, *The Periodic System of Chemical Elements* (1969); and for a biography and bibliography, B.M. Kedrov, 'Mendeleyev', in *Dictionary of Scientific Biography*, vol. IX, ed. C.C. Gillispie (1974).

306

MENDELSSOHN-BARTHOLDY, Jakob Ludwig Felix 1809–47

German composer

For many years his family were practising Jews, his grandfather being Moses Mendelssohn the philosopher. His father Abraham was a banker, and his mother Leah brought up their children as Christians and adopted the surname Mendelssohn-Bartholdy. Felix and his elder sister Fanny showed their musical gifts early; Felix's overture to *A Midsummer Night's Dream*, composed at the age of seventeen is a brilliant and completely individual masterpiece, more striking than anything written by Mozart at that age. The hardly less fine Octet for strings, op. 10, came slightly earlier and had been preceded by several operas and many symphonies for strings. His teacher Zelter was a friend of Goethe* and arranged for Felix to pay a visit to the great poet in 1821; the two became firm friends. In addition to composition he was active as a concert pianist and conductor and in 1829 he conducted the first performance of J.S. Bach's *Passion according to St Matthew* since Bach's death. In the same year he paid his first visit to London and, with his very attractive personality, he soon made innumerable friends. A visit to Scotland gave him the initial inspiration of the *Hebrides* Overture (1832) and the 'Scottish' Symphony (1830–42); his appreciation of the beauty of Edinburgh is vividly expressed in his letters. Foreign travel played a great part in his life. In 1837 he married Cecile Jean-Renaud who came from a French Huguenot family; she appears to have been a gentle, perhaps rather shadowy figure.

One of his most deep-rooted traits was his devotion to his family, especially his father and his sister Fanny. His father was a benevolent autocrat who constantly urged Felix to write an oratorio; after his death, which was a terrible blow, his son's first impulse was to complete *St Paul* (1836) in his memory. Fanny, who married the painter Wilhelm Hensel, was a pianist and composer, and the shock of her sudden death in 1847 probably contributed to the apoplectic condition that led to his own death later in the same year. As a personality he had great charm and an almost superabundant vitality. Genial and equable when all was going well, he could easily be upset, especially during his unfortunate directorship at Düsseldorf. His youthful triumphs in Berlin led to a certain amount of jealousy, aggravated probably by anti-Semitism, and his associations with that city became increasingly unsympathetic in his later years. English society, including that of the royal family, he found very congenial, not always, perhaps, to the benefit of his composition. The performance of *Elijah* at Birmingham in 1846 was one of his greatest public successes.

For many years it was regarded, in England at least, as his masterpiece; viewed from a distance it reveals more inequalities, though much of it, especially the choruses, is still deeply impressive. Mendelssohn's imagination was certainly more fired by the dramatic Old Testament story than when writing *St Paul*. Apart from the music for *A Midsummer Night's Dream* (1842), written many years after the overture, his best work for the stage is the pleasant comic opera *Son and Stranger*, composed in 1830. His songs are full of characteristic tunefulness and occasionally something more, as in the very moving *Nachtlied* written shortly before his death. But Mendelssohn did not respond to words as vividly as Schubert* or Schumann* and the emotional range of his songs is more limited than theirs. The works for piano, less enterprising than those of Chopin* and Schumann, are on the whole underrated, though the *Variations Sérieuses* (1841), one of the best of them, is still quite often played. But there are others, such as the six *Preludes and Fugues*, the Fantasia in F sharp minor, and the Sonata in E, that are well worth attention. The *Songs Without Words* contain much that is genuinely touching and appealing, and some of them, such as the *Volkslied* from op. 53 and the *Funeral March* from op. 62, have remarkable power. The works for organ are on the whole less interesting though the sonatas contain fine things.

It is not suprising that Mendelssohn's best chamber work, the *Octet*, should be written for a medium that gives most scope for orchestral effects. The string quintets and quartets and the two piano trios may seem sometimes to strain their medium, but they all contain splendid and full-bodied music; most remarkable is the Quartet in F minor, op. 80. This was written shortly after Fanny's death and is in a startlingly sombre and passionate vein. But it is in the orchestral works that the greatest of Mendelssohn is to be found; his marvellous sense of colour can be felt in the opening bars of the *Midsummer Night's Dream* overture. Of the symphonies the 'Reformation' (no. 5), written in 1830, is, in its outer movements at least, rather laboured and self-conscious. The 'Italian' (no. 4, 1833) is brilliant and high-spirited, with touches of mystery behind its sparkling façade. The 'Scottish' (no. 3), which had been conceived many years before its completion, is more ambitious. There is some attractive local colour in the Scherzo and the first and last movements are full of picturesque and sometimes melancholy grandeur. The two Piano Concertos (1831 and 1837) are pleasant works, but have not the extraordinary charm of the much later Violin Concerto (1844), with its passionate first movement, serene and unsentimental Andante and sparkling Finale. Familiarity has sometimes blinded us to the wonderful freshness and originality of this work. Of the overtures three are outstanding, all inspired by the sea; although Mendelssohn was instinctively suspicious of extra-musical influences, he could on occasion respond to them vividly. *A Calmed Sea and a Prosperous Voyage* (1828–32) is brilliant and exhilarating, *Melusina* (1833) contrasts the gentle and formidable aspects of the sea, and the *Hebrides* is undoubtedly Mendelssohn's masterpiece, combining all his finest qualities with an added power and depth of imagination.

For many years he was, in England at any rate, admired first and foremost as a composer of choral music, and a successor to Handel. Now the fine qualities of *Elijah* are still appreciated, but some of the minor choral works such as the *Hymn of Praise* (1840), which was once thought noble and inspiring, now seem pompous and complacent, especially when put beside the vividly exciting pagan choruses in the *Walpurgisnacht* cantata. When attempting to emulate the solemnity and richness of a Beethoven* slow movement he usually failed; on the other hand among his scherzos there are many that behind a playful exterior show a strange, sometimes uncanny imaginativeness. In his last years his inspiration was more fitful, but it could

still produce works as dissimilar as the *Midsummer Night's Dream* music and the Quartet in F minor, both undoubted masterpieces. He had many accomplishments outside music: he painted, was a fluent and vivid letter-writer, and was very sociable. Had he been able to lead a less hectic life and withdraw more into himself, he might have been a still greater composer, but of the greatness of his best work there can be no doubt.

Philip Radcliffe

Other works include Concertos for two pianos, Sonatas for violin and piano and for cello and piano, many songs, part-songs and choral works, some of which are setting of Psalms, and the opera *The Wedding of Camacho* (1825). See: Sebastian Hensel, *Die Familie Mendelssohn* (English translation 1881); Rosamund Gotch, *Mendelssohn and his Friends in Kensington* (1934); Eric Werner, *Mendelssohn* (trans. 1963); Philip Radcliffe, *Mendelssohn* (1976).

307
MEREDITH, George 1828–1909

British author

The first decade of the twentieth century is distinguished by an incredible degree of self-regard among English men of letters in respect of their calling. This was the age of the literary essayist and the era of the 'little histories' of English literature designed to accompany thoughtful reading of those cheap editions of the classics issued by the more high-minded publishers. It was also the epoch *par excellence* of the literary pilgrimage, the reverent and admiring journey to the idol's shrine, so frequently culminating in tea and a signed copy. Southern England was indeed dotted with such places of worship, and on 12 February 1908 Flint Cottage near Dorking, Surrey, became the focus of an act of homage hardly paralleled in the annals of literary celebrity. The eightieth birthday of George Meredith drew congratulations not only from the national press, but from King Edward VII himself, and the Society of Authors sent Anthony Hope and Israel Zangwill bearing an address. Perhaps the most impressive tribute was a memorial of the occasion containing 250 signatures on vellum representing science, art, literature and public life.

He had made it, but it is nowadays increasingly hard for us to appreciate what all the fuss was about. In many ways the celebration of one of the most incomparably verbose of English writers embodies a characteristic Edwardian hunger for self-abasement in the presence of the artist. It also implies what we cannot ignore, that Meredith was considered by many of his contemporaries to be the greatest living novelist and the retailer of a philosophy profound to the point of almost total obfuscation.

George Meredith was the son of a Portsmouth naval outfitter and a tavern keeper's daughter, and his roots in the lower middle classes later provided him with excellent copy for one of his few enduringly readable novels, *Evan Harrington* (1861), which is also a subtle examination of Victorian snobbery. He was educated at the Moravian School at Neuwied on the Rhine, but never attended an English university, a fact which some have held significant in reviewing a literary style so patently unrestrained by a traditional education. At the age of twenty-one he married Mary Ellen Nicholls, a naval officer's widow and daughter of Thomas Love Peacock*: it was a generally disastrous union, ending in embittered separation in 1858, but the experience drove Meredith towards his finest achievement as a poet, the cycle of caudated sonnets (i.e. with additional lines), *Modern Love*, published four years afterwards.

Earlier poems had earned praise from Tennyson*, Kingsley* and Rossetti*, and George Eliot*. He had commended the oriental fantasy *The Shaving of Shagpat* (1856) as 'a work of genius, and of poetical genius'. Young Victorian England seized avidly on *The Ordeal of Richard Feverel* (1859) which, after an initial drop in sales following the *Spectator*'s condemnation of its low moral tone (Mudie's Library forthwith cancelled its order), became one of Meredith's most successful novels, an achievement magnificently followed up by *Evan Harrington*.

On the strength of such work Meredith was offered the post of literary adviser and reader to the publishers Chapman & Hall, as successor to John Forster, who had acted as their negotiator with Charles Dickens*. Though he occupied the post for nearly thirty years, he must have found the experience a chastening one; and it inevitably contributed towards even greater refinements of literary style than those he had already acquired. A natural fastidiousness led him to reject several works which were later best-sellers, including Mrs Henry Wood's *East Lynne*, Whyte Melville's *Market Harborough* and Samuel Butler's* *Erewhon*. Evelyn Waugh's father, a member of the firm, praised his 'extraordinary versatility in the post', spoke of the 'shining integrity of his literary ideals' and said that he 'was bound to support the claims of literature'.

Claims of another sort brought him a fortunate marriage to Marie Vulliamy, whose depth of suppressed emotion made Meredith describe her as 'my dumb poet'. In 1866 he was sent to Italy as correspondent for the *Morning Post* to cover the war with Austria which culminated in Victor Emmanuel's triumphal entry into Venice, and found himself in the distinguished company of G.A. Henty, the socialist reporter Robert Hyndman, and Matthew Arnold's* favourite target, George Augustus Sala of the *Daily Telegraph*, as well as meeting Leslie Stephen*. The result of all this was one

of his least popular but most interesting works, *Vittoria*, serialized in the *Fortnightly Review* in the same year.

The remainder of Meredith's long life was a sedate movement towards dignified apotheosis as one of the panjandrums of Victorian art, cultivated by those in search of the 'higher seriousness' and encouraged in their quest by his increasing incomprehensibility. Such a position was ultimately guaranteed by the appearance in 1879 of *The Egoist*, whose mature handling of comedy in its most sophisticated applications recalls Henry James*, on whom the writer was an obvious influence. Nothing Meredith did after this quite matched *The Egoist*'s verve and polish, and it was James himself, in respect of the turgid *Lord Ormont and his Aminta* (1894), who expressed what many have since felt when he wrote: 'Not a difficulty met, not a figure presented, not a scene constituted – not a dim shadow condensing once into audible or visible reality – making you hear for an instant the tap of its feet on the earth.' Nevertheless Meredith had become a cultural institution and was accordingly honoured (as indeed James was later to be) with the Order of Merit in 1905. His progress towards the grave was marked by the soft foot-prints of visiting Edwardians, and he died, after drinking a bottle of beer and smoking a cigar, in a distinct odour of literary sanctity.

It might have been expected that, like Trollope* and Scott*, he would soon afterwards pall in public estimation, but unlike these two he has never been successfully subjected to a critical salvage venture. The man whom the *Quarterly Review* called 'this Burne-Jones* of Victorian prose writers' has made only a partial recovery through the modest appraisal of his poetry which has taken place. Tennyson's admiration for *Love in a Valley* is now seen to be fully justified in the context of Meredith's undoubted skill as a fluent metrist, unrivalled (apart from Tennyson himself) by any other contemporary poet except Swinburne*, of whom Meredith was a life-long admirer. *Modern Love* takes its place beside the poems of Browning* and Hardy* in that intriguing dimension of Victorian poetry which probes the nature of emotional inadequacy in sexual relationships, and shorter pieces like *Juggling Jerry*, *The Old Chartist* and *Martin's Puzzle* make a good claim for Meredith's distinctive outlook within the verse medium.

His novels, representing the bulk of his output, offer a far greater challenge to the modern reader. Modern editions of *The Egoist*, *Beauchamp's Career* and *The Ordeal of Richard Feverel* testify to a modified respect for his achievement, but there has been comparatively little interest shown in questioning our neglect of it.

The decline in his reputation has a good deal to do with the daunting toughness of a prose style which seems so often to be trying to persuade us by over-writing and pomposity. A sentence like the following, from *Beauchamp's Career*, 'From his point of observation, and with the store of ideas and images his fiery yet reflective youth had gathered, he presented himself as it were saddled to that hard-riding force known as the logical impetus, which spying its quarry over precipices, across oceans and deserts, and through systems and webs, and into shops and cabinets of costliest china, will come at it, will not be refused, let the distances and breakages be what they may', effectively illustrates Siegfried Sassoon's description of Meredith's manner as 'an assault on the nervous system'. It is the style of a man not altogether certain either of himself or of his public and it was to grow worse with age.

Nevertheless the very same novel features descriptive moments of a haunting, visionary excellence and the minutely focused intensity of the Venetian scenes is worthy of George Eliot. A far greater consistency conditions *The Egoist*, whose brilliantly sustained comedy mitigates its author's unwillingness to let the reader relax. Meredith's boldest stroke as a novelist was to abandon vicissitude as an essential plot element in favour of moral and emotional nuance in character relationship. A careful and selective scrutiny of his best work brings us closer to an understanding of the high premium set on seriousness by the thoughtful Victorian reader.

Jonathan Keates

See: *The Works of George Meredith* (27 vols. 1909–11); *The Letters of George Meredith*, ed. C.L. Cline (3 vols, 1970). The standard biography is Lionel Stevenson, *The Ordeal of George Meredith* (1926); Siegfried Sassoon, *Meredith* (1948); V.S. Pritchett, *George Meredith and English Comedy* (1970).

308
MÉRIMÉE, Prosper 1803–70

French writer

Mérimée occupies an unusual place in the great flowering of French culture during the period 1820–50. He was a contemporary of the great figures of the era, Balzac*, Vigny*, Musset*, Hugo*, Lamartine*, Delacroix*, Berlioz*, and for a long time a close personal friend of the only significantly older figure, Stendhal*. Superficially at least he would seem to have had much in common with them in some of the details of his literary beginnings, his upbringing and early manhood in Paris. Yet Mérimée's contribution to French culture at this time, a contribution to the distinct if lesser literary genre of the short story, was achieved in many respects against the surging Romantic tide of the 1820s and 1830s. Unlike the vast majority of his literary contemporaries, Mérimée neither needed nor cared much to make a commercial impact on the reading public. For most of his career he was a secure, well-paid civil servant, notably from 1834 Inspector General of Historical Monuments (and as such commendably efficient and influential); in his mature years he devoted himself to historical writings and to foreign languages and literatures, mainly Spanish and then increasingly Russian (e.g. Pushkin*, Gogol*, and Turgenev*). He was a wit and notorious womanizer, and throughout his life a strong, wilful, ironic personality. It took such a person to withstand the seductive vogues of his early years: both the matter of Romanticism, idealized presentations of Christianity, women, democracy, the noble savage, the Middle Ages, etc., and the manner, grandiose abstraction and lyrical effusion.

Mérimée's first literary works were not in fact short stories. He was involved like his friend Stendhal in the struggle to foster a more Shakespearian type of theatre in France, and as early as 1822 he wrote a *Cromwell*, which has not survived. His first extant work, the *Theatre of Clara Gazul* (1825), was a highly eccentric contribution to the literature of the Romantic period. At this early stage of the movement's history in France and of his own personal development, Mérimée revealed a key feature of his personality, a fondness for *mystification*, (anti-) Romantic caricature, ironic distancing from some of the more preposterous attitudes struck by his contemporaries. In this elaborate hoax he assumed the identity of one Joseph L'Estrange, who had allegedly translated into French the plays of a Spanish actress, Clara Gazul. There were six of these tongue-in-cheek pastiches in 1825 and another two in 1830, including the only one which has been professionally performed with any degree of success, *The Coach of the Holy Sacrament* (*Le Carrosse du Saint Sacrement*). The hoax was backed up by a portrait of 'Clara Gazul' herself – in fact Mérimée in dress and mantilla. In between the two editions of the plays there was *La Guzla* (1827), the anagrammatic resonance of which title failed to alert many that this collection of Illyrian ballads by 'Hyacinthe Maglanovitch', a bard and virtuoso of the *guzla* was another hoax. The butt this time was the cult of local colour.

Still experimenting with form, Mérimée forsook the parodic mode and next presented two sombre studies of subjects which fascinated the Romantic imagination, thanks in France to the influence of Scott* and Shakespeare, medieval and Renaissance history. *La Jacquerie* (1828) was a series of 'feudal scenes' in dialogue form but not intended for performance, in which Mérimée interpreted the peasants' revolt – 'I have attempted to give an idea of the atrocious customs of the fourteenth century.' A far more important work, *La Chronique du Règne de Charles IX* (1829) is centred on a similarly gruesome event in French history, the St Bartholomew Massacre of 1572. It is a short, loosely structured novel which still has many admirers, and its significance is that Mérimée discovered in it his ideal medium, prose fiction. Thereafter he devoted himself to the short stories or tales, usually called *Nouvelles*, for which he is most remembered. The best known are *Mateo Falcone*, *The Storming of the Redoubt* (*L'Enlèvement de la Redoute*), *Tamango* (all 1829), *The Game of Backgammon* (*La Partie de Trictrac*) and *The Etruscan Vase* (*Le Vase Etrusque*) (both 1830), *The Double Misunderstanding* (*La Double Méprise*, 1833), *La Vénus d'Ille* (1837), *Colomba* (1840) and *Carmen* (1845). Mérimée's manner in these works is to treat highly dramatic subjects, revenge, murder, violence, even the supernatural in a laconic, unrhetorical way, pitching his narrative, like a French Classicist, at the peak of a human crisis. Mérimée's tales are somewhat uneven in quality, and disparate in length, form and subject matter. Yet the best of them are masterpieces of careful, restrained prose at the service of a (for the times) rare view of human frailty: a welcome achievement in an age when Balzac and Hugo were prolix and moralistic.

Ted Freeman

Théâtre de Clara Gazul, Romans et nouvelles, ed. Mallion and Salomon (1978); *La Guzla* (le Divan edn, 10 vols, 1927–31). Translations include: *Carmen and Colomba* (1965); *The Venus of Ille and Other Stories* (1966); *A Slight Misunderstanding* (1959). *Correspondance générale* (17 vols, 1941–64). See: F.P. Bowman, *Prosper Mérimée: Pessimism, and Irony* (1962): R.C. Dale, *The Poetics of Prosper Mérimée* (1966); M.A. Smith, *Prosper Mérimée* (1972); A.W. Raitt, *Prosper Mérimée* (1970), an excellent study with a very useful bibliography.

309
MEYERBEER, Giacomo 1791–1864

German composer

Meyerbeer is one of the most fascinating cases in the history of the arts during the nineteenth century. The range of his influence spread wider than that of any other composer between Beethoven* and Wagner* (whose early scores, especially *Rienzi*, are heavily Meyerbeeresque despite his subsequent denigration of the man and the style) and overshadows certain portions of the work of every major operatic master of the mid-century. Yet his music, thoughtful, ambitious, so nicely calculated, continuously fails to achieve a distinctive personality. The individual hardly ever emerges from behind the web of experiment and preparation, and the effect of listening to *Le Prophète* (1849) and *L'Africaine* (1865) is that of hearing not one, but at least five composers on the job. Mendelssohn's* description of *Robert de Diable* as 'heartless' is cruel but entirely accurate.

Like Mendelssohn Meyerbeer was born (as Jakob Liebmann Beer) into a family of emancipated Prussian Jews, but unlike his great contemporary never succeeded in making an adequate artistic capital from his cosmopolitanism. He too figured as a child prodigy in the salons of Berlin, appearing as a pianist at the age of nine, and receiving tuition from Clementi and, in company with Weber*, from the distinguished Abbé Vogler at Darmstadt. His first successful opera, *Ali Melek*, was given at Stuttgart in 1813, but it was only after its failure at Vienna that the advice of Salieri directed the young Meyerbeer to try his luck in Italy, and the piano was firmly abandoned for the stage with the triumphs there of *Emma di Resburgo* (1822) and *Il Crociato in Egitto* (1824).

Predictably, neither of these works was popular in Germany, and Meyerbeer, alert no doubt to the success of Auber's pioneering *La Muette de Portici* (1828) and Rossini's* enormously influential *Guillaume Tell* (1829), left Berlin for Paris in 1830, where he remained for the rest of his life. The patterns created by these two operas, themselves conditioned by a residual penchant for grandeur and spectacle remaining as a legacy from the ardent Neoclassicism of Napoleonic France, inspired Meyerbeer to design an operatic form which polished and developed their outlines in conformity with the tastes of contemporary Parisian society. His librettist was Eugène Scribe, whose attitude to text and drama was coldly and exclusively professional. Aided by the brilliant scene painters of the Paris Opéra, such as Cicéri, and by the commercial drawing power of the ballet, its dancers 'protected' by the capital's *jeunesse dorée*, Meyerbeer and Scribe devised a species of artistic package intended to pander to the most cherished fads and susceptibilities of the July Monarchy and the Second Empire.

Robert le Diable, with its allusions to Weber and Beethoven, was premiered in 1831 and given 330 times at the Opéra during the next twenty years (an average of sixteen performances a year). Five years later came *Les Huguenots*, one of the grandest operas of the nineteenth century, and arguably the most successful. Its enormous popularity was echoed in London and Berlin, to which, in 1842, Meyerbeer was able to make a triumphant return as *generalmusikdirector*. The success of *Ein Feldlager in Schlesien* in 1843, remodelled eight years later as *L'Étoile du Nord*, was due in part to its having provided a perfect frame for the talents of the young Swedish singing star Jenny Lind, a woman who, according to P.T. Barnum*, her American impresario, 'would have been adored if she had had the voice of a crow'.

Paris in 1849 saw the first performance of *Le Prophète*, a work of epic proportions based on the life of the sixteenth-century Anabaptist John of Leyden, and nowadays chiefly famous for its ballet music. Meyerbeer never lost an engaging fondness for a lighter and more lyrical vein, shown to advantage in *Ein Feldlager in Schlesien*, and developed this in *Dinorah, ou Le Pardon de Ploërmel*, a comedy with a Breton setting, given in

1859. The fact that Paris had had to wait ten years for a new opera from Meyerbeer is typical both of his meticulous attitude towards the preparation of his stage works, an attitude which had its effect of the young Wagner, and of the healthy state of his professional finances, over which he was comparably solicitous. He died while his last opera, *L'Africaine*, a lurid account of fabulous incidents in the life of Vasco di Gama, was still in production.

His influence had already made itself felt throughout European music. It can be seen working, not always favourably, on the Parisian operas of Donizetti*, on Verdi's* *Les Vêpres Siciliennes* and *Don Carlos*, and on Bizet's* *Ivan IV*, as well as, of course, on Wagner, Gounod* and Massenet. All these composers, both before and after his death, seem to have been impressed by his attempts to impose a greater homogeneity on the operatic score, thereby guaranteeing a stronger sense of dramatic unity and momentum, and by his invariably interesting manipulation of orchestral tone colour. We may add to this a positively encyclopedic capacity for dealing with every species of character and subject matter.

The best of his operas must inevitably be *Les Huguenots*, its crowded and vivid canvas displaying the perfect Dumas*-like French Romantic vision of the age of Catherine de Medici. It is the ideal 'singers' opera', achieving a splendid balance between solo and ensemble, and often, as in the massive duet between Raoul and Valentine, fascinatingly experimental. Significantly, most of Meyerbeer's work after this shows a gradual falling off, and *L'Africaine*, an opera of quite cynically formulaic construction, suggests an almost total loss of nerve. The flabby, shapeless quality of much of its music is essentially what has allowed Meyerbeer's reputation to slump so disastrously in our own century. Prestigious revivals of *Le Prophète* and star-studded recordings of *Les Huguenots* and *Dinorah* can do little to rehabilitate a composer whose obsessive eclecticism and stylistic refinement, wedded to a fatal inability to create really durable and sustained melodic lines, continuously stifle his moments of raw, spontaneous musical impulse. He remains both a figure of tremendous historical interest and significance for the development of modern European opera, and a composer whose memorable originalities of imaginative concept were all too easily suppressed by an ephemeral bombast.

Jonathan Keates

See: L. Dauriac, *Meyerbeer* (2nd edn 1930); Arthur Hervey, *Meyerbeer and his Music* (1913).

310
MICHELET, Jules 1798–1874

French historian

The only child of a small printer who made a precarious living under the empire, being imprisoned for debt and eventually losing the right to print, Michelet escaped from material hardship thanks to parental sacrifices and to his academic achievements and skills as teacher and writer. After completing doctoral theses on Plutarch and Locke he was instrumental in introducing the thought of Vico to France, translating the *Scienza Nuova*. In 1827 he was appointed Professor of History and Philosophy at the already prestigious École Normale Supérieure, and after the July Revolution he was chosen to be tutor to Louis-Philippe's daughter Clémentine. In the years that followed he deputized for Guizot in the Chair of Modern History at the Sorbonne, was given his own chair at the collège de France and, most importantly, became head of the National Archives, a post which gave a decisive direction to his historical vocation and helped shape his work on the Middle Ages.

Michelet's spectacular academic career was, however, brought to a premature end. Like his friend Edgar Quinet, with whom he wrote the polemical *Des Jésuites* (1843), Michelet was an anti-clerical republican. His *Du prêtre, de la femme et de la famille* (1845) was placed on the index, and in January 1848 Michelet's lectures (which, particularly in their view of the student as a source of social revolution, look forward to the debates of May 1968) were suspended by ministerial decree. Although Michelet (together with Quinet) returned in triumph to the Collège de France after the February Revolution, with the demise of the shortlived republic his lectures were once more suspended, this time permanently. After the *coup d'état* he refused to take the oath of allegiance to the empire and left the academic profession and his post at the National Archives. Less radical in his resistance to Louis-Napoleon than his fellow republicans Quinet and Hugo*, and less inclined to practical political commitment, he did not follow them into exile. Indeed, in one respect this period was one of personal fulfilment for Michelet, who had married the nearly thirty years younger Athénaïs Mialaret in 1849 and now began to preach the virtues of domestic contentment (the fascinating complexities of the couple's actual relationship as opposed to the idealized public version, can be traced in the disturbing and obsessive pages of Michelet's posthumous diaries). Under the Second Empire he continued work on his *History of France* (1833–69) and his *History of the French Revolution* which had begun to appear in 1847. He also produced a series of didactic books expressly directed at a wider audience than that reached by his histories – works of popular natural history, *L'Oiseau* (1856),

L'Insecte (1857), La Mer (1861), La Montagne (1868); celebrations of love and marriage, L'Amour (1858), La Femme (1859); hymns to progress and the power of education, La Bible de L'Humanité (1864), Nos Fils (1869), – all redolent of the lay piety that was to flourish among the reformist writers and educationists of the Third Republic. Yet although Michelet's religion of humanity, his faith in the harmony and benevolence of nature and his belief that social justice would be achieved peacefully simply by the power of love and enlightenment, constitutes the overt message of these works, what arrests the modern reader are the unresolved social, moral and sexual conflicts to which Michelet constantly gives oblique expression. This ambiguity together with Michelet's vigorously personal manner and stylistic virtuosity redeem these later non-historical works and justify the increased critical attention to which they have been subjected in recent years, in the wake of Roland Barthes's illuminating analyses of the network of myths and obsessions which structure all Michelet's writings, whether historical or not.

Nevertheless, his reputation today must still rest chiefly in the histories. He is above all the national historian of France. No other French historian has provided such a persuasively complete vision of his country's past: he seeks the meaning of society in its diet, dress, entertainments, in its scientific, artistic and intellectual productions, in its laws, superstitions and popular traditions. In his ambition for totality he resembles his Romantic contemporaries Hugo and Balzac*, and he uses to the full the literary resources of imagery, symbolism and eloquence to persuade us of the unity of his re-created world. Michelet's task, which he refers to as 'the total resurrection of the past', thus depends on the exercise of the imagination, but it remains anchored in the scrutiny of archives and the respect for fact. The combination of creative interpretation and critical attention to documentary evidence is particularly well exemplified in his short masterpiece on the significance of witches and their persecution, La Sorcière (1862).

In spite of the qualities which clearly distinguish Michelet's work from the more self-effacing productions of modern French historians – his intense patriotism, his belief in progress, his sense of the historian's heroic mission – he remains an exemplary figure for the Annales school with its price curves and statistical analyses. If historians like Braudel and Duby can invoke him with such enthusiasm it is not simply out of nostalgia for a form of history which is no longer possible but also because Michelet can be regarded as a precursor of their studies of civilization as a material and collective phenomenon. Michelet's history, for all its idealism, emphasizes the physicality of the human body and allows the constraints of climate, work and food an important role. Although personalities (Joan

of Arc, Marat, Saint-Just) emerge forcefully from his pages, the individual is not seen as the measure of history. Collective movements, in particular the emergence of popular self-awareness, are the historian's essential subject. In this respect Edmund Wilson's decision to begin his study of the origins of socialism, To the Finland Station, with an essay on Michelet (arguably the best introduction to the writer available) is a logical one. This does not mean, however, that Michelet can be regarded as a socialist. His conception of class relationships, expressed most thoroughly in Le Peuple (1846), is, from a Marxist* standpoint, naive and paternalistic, even though he makes a serious and well-informed attempt to describe the material conditions of working people in different categories of rural, industrial and commercial occupation. There is of course no critique by Michelet of his own class position – to expect one would be anachronistic – but he nevertheless sensed an inadequacy in his writing of and for the people. It is true that he saw the problem above all as one of expression – 'the people's language has been inaccessible to me. I have failed to make it (the people) speak' (Nos Fils) – but the fact that he acknowledges the limits of his comprehension of the people, into which he claims to have been born, deserves to be set against the petit-bourgeois simplifications and myths of social harmony which mar parts of his work.

Roger S. Huss

P. Viallaneix's excellent definitive edition of Michelet's Oeuvres complètes (20 vols, from 1971) is still in progress. Michelet's Journal can be consulted in a very good critical edition (4 vols, 1959–76). The best edition of Michelet's lecture course at the Collège de France (1847–8), known as L'étudiant, is that edited, with an introductory essay, by G. Picon (1970). See: R. Barthes, Michelet par lui-même (1954) and 'La Sorcière' in Essais Critiques (1964); P. Viallaneix, La voie royale: essai sur l'idée de peuple dans l'oeuvre de Michelet (1971).

311
MICKIEWICZ, Adam Bernard 1798–1855

Polish patriot, poet and essayist

The importance of Mickiewicz in Polish life goes beyond cultural boundaries. Characterized as the 'national' poet, his life and art (as is the case with his two great contemporaries Juliusz Słowacki and Zygmunt Krasiński*, and to a lesser extent, with the younger Cyprian Norwid*) can only be understood in relation to the vicissitudes and eccentricities of nineteenth-century Polish history; a history dominated by efforts to preserve the traditions and re-establish the reality of an independent Poland. After the three eighteenth-century Partitions of the Republic (1772, 1793, 1795), and the reimposition of Austrian, Prussian and Russian rule in 1815, it became the chief role of the intellectuals to maintain alive and develop the national heritage. Whilst studying at Vilna University, Mickiewicz was a leading member of a semi-clandestine student organization (the Philomaths) whose activities conformed to this aim. The separation between political action and art, therefore, became increasingly blurred; and although Polish Romanticism conventionally emerged as a reaction to Classicism – its beginnings are traditionally associated with the publication of Mickiewicz's poem 'Romantyczność' in 1822 – under the pressures of political realities and repression, it soon acquired its unique character of militancy. After the unsuccessful November 1830 Insurrection and the ensuing Great Emigration of Polish patriots, Paris became until about 1850 the chief centre of Polish cultural life and political debate. Despite deep and frequently bitter ideological divisions, all the factions fervently and, at times, fanatically clung to a belief in the sacrosanctity of 'Polishness', a belief which gave rise to the ideas of Polish Messianism. Emerging from Herder's ideas on the role of nations, this ideology posited for Poland the moral leadership of oppressed countries. Clearly not a logical system, it degenerated with the passing of years and the undermining of national hopes into mystical escapism and sentimental self-indulgence.

Mickiewicz was born near Nowogródek in Lithuania into the lesser landed nobility and died in Constantinople whilst trying to organize a Polish force to fight the Russians; these details of his biography point, as if emblematically, at the vagaries of his career. He was educated at Vilna University and during 1819–23 was a school teacher at Kowno. As a student he came under the influence of the classical philologist G.E. Groddeck and the eminent historian J. Lelewel, and the teachings of the French Enlightenment, a heritage which he never totally rejected. However, his increasing admiration for German and English Romanticism, his reading of Shakespeare, his unhappy love for Maryla Wereszczaka, and his fascination for his native folklore inevitably induced the young poet to try to write a poetry which was to be 'the apotheosis of sentiment, and reach the realms inaccessible to reason'. He collected this verse in the two volumes of *Poezje* ('Poems', Vilna, 1822, 1823). The texts contained in these collections constitute a radical realignment in Polish letters. Mickiewicz not only introduced contemporary European sensibilities, but also elevated the popular to the realm of poetry and experimented with new metrical and stylistic forms. Particularly, in *Forefather's Eve*, Parts II and IV (*Dziady*; Part I remained unpublished in a fragmentary form, whilst Part III was to be written almost ten years later), Mickiewicz blends with great originality in a dramatic structure folklore, investigations on love, and an analysis of individual suffering – the key themes of his youthful period. However, in the narrative poem *Grażyna*, Mickiewicz's historico-political preoccupations appear. The story of the princess's patriotic sacrifices in her struggles against the Teutonic Order had an obvious contemporary relevance.

After his arrest in 1823 for his political sympathies, Mickiewicz was sent in 1824 into exile in Russia. He never saw his native land again.

The five years the poet spent in Russia were of crucial importance in his artistic and intellectual development. A first-hand knowledge of tsarist power was counterbalanced by friendships amongst the Russian liberal intelligentsia, stays in St Petersburg and Moscow, the experiences of Salon life, and a memorable voyage to the Crimea. Two principal literary creations emerged from these experiences: the Petrarchan *Sonety* ('Sonnets', Moscow, 1826) charting sentimental moods and travel impressions and the highly influential political allegory *Konrad Wallenrod* (Moscow, 1828), in which the pseudo-historical story of the fanatical Lithuanian knight, who by treachery and self-sacrifice destroys the Teutonic Order from within, represented the poet's answer to the political realities he saw around him. Despite its banning by the Polish Congress, this poem, together with some of Mickiewicz's earlier compositions, became one of the chief spiritual stimuli to the generation which fought in the November Insurrection. Mickiewicz had become the voice of Polish patriotism.

Thanks to the intercessions of friends, the poet was allowed to leave Russia in 1829, and until 1832 he travelled extensively in Western Europe coming into contact with, amongst others, Hegel*, Goethe*, Schlegel*, and J.F. Cooper*. In Rome, under the influence of clerical friends and a reading of Lamennais, Mickiewicz began to temper his extreme patriotic solutions with religious beliefs: a fusion which was to become basic to his thought. With the outbreak of the insurrection in Poland, the poet, by inexplicably delaying his departure and then by the roundabout mode of his journeying, only reached the outskirts of Poland when the revolt had failed. Tormented by self-remorse, moved by the enthusiastic receptions granted to the Polish patriots by the inhabitants of Lower Saxony, and spurred on by quasi-mystical ideas as to his own mission, Mickiewicz composed in Dresden in 1831 one of his most powerful pieces, the visionary-historical drama *Dziady III* (Paris, 1833). Using the trials of the Philomaths in the 1820s as the background, the poet presented the sufferings of Poland as akin to Christ's; and although its messianic ideas dominated Mickiewicz's subsequent life, the real importance of *Dziady III* lies in its unique formal syntheses, multiplicity of tones, and dramatic originality. To this composition the poet appended his poetic cycle 'Ustęp' ('Episode'), in which he depicted in a more realistic manner his view of Russia.

As did many of his compatriots, Mickiewicz settled in Paris in 1832, where he published his *Księgi narodu polskiego i pielgrzymstwa polskiego* ('Books of the Polish Nation and of the Polish Pilgrimage', 1832), in which he tried to give a historical-moral vindication of his messianism. This work was translated into several languages and exerted some influence in the period leading to the events of 1848. Whilst Mickiewicz kept himself apart from the factionalism of his fellow Poles, he constantly reiterated his belief in the leading position of Poland in any wider revolutionary movement. His ideology, a blend of radicalism and mysticism, became even more extreme after his meeting with Towiański in 1841, which further isolated him from the other *émigrés*. Despite his awkward political position within the Polish community, Mickiewicz's international prestige increased. In 1838 he was appointed to the Chair of Latin at Lausanne, whilst between 1840 and 1844 he was Professor of Slavonic Language and Literature at the Collège de France. His lectures ('Course on Slav Literature', Paris, 1842–5), in which he propagated his historiosophic ideas, were attended by leading Parisian intellectual figures. After their suspension for political reasons, Mickiewicz in 1848 formed a Polish legion to fight with the Italians, was briefly editor in 1849 of *La Tribune des Peuples*, and from 1852 until his departure to the Crimea worked at the Arsenal as librarian.

From 1833 Mickiewicz's career was almost bereft of literary production, as he became increasingly embroiled in political matters. The one exception is his masterpiece *Pan Tadeusz* ('Master Thaddeus', Paris, 1834), which has exerted an influence ever since on Polish life and letters. Born in a moment of calm and nostalgia, it evokes the optimism of 1812 with the advance of the Napoleonic armies in the Lithuanian countryside. Everyday life in all its manifestations, a world where people live in harmony with their environment are described with great artistic skill and clarity. The myth of a changeless past, untouched by subsequent historical catastrophe, separates this work from the mainstream of Mickiewicz's committed art and from his ideas of change and renewal.

Despite Mickiewicz's incessant political work and his heroic stature in the Polish national memory, it is his art which is his greatest achievement. The originality and breadth of his poetic genius, occasionally marred by structural weaknesses, make him one of Europe's great writers, whose reputation has suffered because he wrote in a little known language and in an often misunderstood tradition.

Zygmunt G. Barański

The standard edition of Mickiewicz's writings is *Dzieła*, ed. L. Płoszewski (16 vols, 1948–55). Some

English translations are *Konrad Wallenrod and Other Writings of Adam Mickiewicz* (1925), *Poems by Adam Mickiewicz* (1944), *Pan Tadeusz* (1962 and 1964), and *Forefathers* (1968). See: W.Weintraub, *The Poetry of Adam Mickiewicz* (1954); *Adam Mickiewicz in World Literature*, ed. W. Lednicki (1956); D. Welsh, *Adam Mickiewicz* (1966).

312
MILL, James 1773–1836

British political thinker

It is easy to undervalue the role of James Mill in the early nineteenth-century British movement of 'philosophic radicalism'. He was fated to be overshadowed in reputation by his predecessor Jeremy Bentham* on the one hand, and by his successor and son John Stuart Mill* upon the other. However, during the critical decade prior to the Reform Act of 1832, it was the energy of the elder Mill as author and lobbyist which proved vital in giving force and direction to that political utilitarianism which all three, in their different ways, promoted.

James Mill was particularly fortunate to be born in Scotland – where, far more so than in late eighteenth-century England, any outstanding talent in a boy of humble origins had a chance of being appreciated and developed. Thus this shoemaker's son could proceed to Montrose Academy, and then in 1790 to the University of Edinburgh where he came under the influence of Dugald Stewart's philosophy and distinguished himself especially as a Greek scholar. After graduation Mill concentrated on Divinity, and in 1798 obtained a licence to preach within the Church of Scotland. He made no direct use of this, since he promptly lost his belief in God; instead, his abiding capacity for evangelical zeal was henceforth exercised through more secular channels. Work as a private tutor drew him into the family circle of Sir John Stuart of Fettercairn, who in 1802 brought him to London. Three years later Mill, now a rising journalist, married – and by 1806 he had a first son whom he named after his patron.

Around this time he embarked on the most monumental of his writing projects, *The History of British India*. This three-volume work, when it finally appeared in 1817, met with acclaim and secured for its author a post as Examiner of Correspondence with that same East India Company whose previous policies he had been reviewing so critically. Something of Mill's influence on subsequent changes in the East India Company's attitudes can be gauged from the fact that in 1830 he became head of the India House Office. By then his reputation had also been enhanced by such works as *Elements of Political Economy* (1821), a popularization of the teachings of his close associate David Ricardo*; *Essays reprinted from the Supplement to the Encyclopaedia Britannica* (*c.* 1825), based on material about political, educational and legal issues which had first appeared between 1816 and 1823; and his *Analysis of the Phenomena of the Human Mind* (1829), which developed certain aspects of the associationist psychology of David Hartley. Mill had also written regularly for periodicals, especially the *Westminster Review* in the years 1824–6. All these writings had contributed, most particularly, to establishing their author as a leader of those philosophic radicals who were building on the work of the now octogenarian Bentham.

The two men first met in 1808 and sustained a close association thereafter. For a great part of four years, between 1814 and 1817, the Mill family actually resided in Bentham's home at Ford Abbey. In temperament the older figure was the more relaxed, and one can see the intellectual corollary of this distinction in Mill's more puritanical approach to utilitarian hedonism: in essence, there should be no pursuit of pleasure that cannot somehow be associated with the pursuit of virtue. This was one of the chief themes which he hoped to substantiate through *British India.* The book eschewed anything like 'fieldwork' in our modern sense. It was, rather, an example of 'philosophical history', seeking to exemplify general principles of human nature and experience in a mode much influenced by models erected by William Robertson, Adam Ferguson, and other luminaries of the Scottish Enlightenment.

The aim of providing a general science of society, in terms of a suitably refined Benthamite theory of psychology and ethics, was something that Mill pursued most notably in the *Britannica* essays. Of these 'Education' and 'Government' are the best known. In the former he defined education as 'the best employment of all the means which can be made use of, by man, for rendering the human mind to the greatest possible degree the cause of human happiness'. Here Mill aimed to promote the common good both by convincing the informed minority that they had no valid grounds for resisting a much wider diffusion of knowledge across society and by making 'the many' more responsibly aware that happiness amounted to something deeper than instant gratification. One of the author's most impressive practical achievements in the educational sphere was his contribution to the establishment in 1828 of University College London. More mixed had been the outcome of his efforts in regard to the training of his eldest son; they were successful to the extent that John Stuart did indeed emerge from the pedagogic hot-house well equipped to take over the promotion of the broadly utilitarian message, and unsuccessful in so far as the process had much to do with that 'mental crisis' which the pupil had eventually to overcome before freeing himself from undue dependence upon an unusually desiccated version of parental authority.

Mill's essay on 'Government' confirmed that, whatever his pleas for greater access to education, there were limits to his political populism. He was clearer in condemning the tendency of all monarchical and aristocratic systems to abuse power than in delineating the precise nature of the compensating involvement which he envisaged for some wider political public. His indecisiveness about universal manhood suffrage led more extreme radicals to doubt his courage, while cautious Whigs (including, most resoundingly, Thomas Macaulay*) took him to task for his great naivety. It is certainly plain that Mill's willingness to advocate some wider franchise for Britain depended upon an extraordinarily generous view of the merits and restraining influence of the informed bourgeoisie:

> There can be no doubt that the middle rank, which gives to science, to art and to legislation itself, their most distinguished ornaments, and is the chief source of all that has exalted and refined human nature, is that portion of the community of which, if the basis of representation were ever so far extended, the opinion would ultimately decide. Of the people beneath them a vast majority would be sure to be guided by their advice and example.

The Reform Act of 1832 was thus something that Mill could support: the Charter, had he lived to see it, would have been a severer test of his precise judgement.

As the nineteenth century went on, Mill's certainty about the proper locus of political and moral authority being found within the class into which he himself had risen began to look increasingly over-optimistic. John Stuart was indeed left with the task of adapting philosophic radicalism to the circumstances of an epoch during which the relationship between democracy, freedom, and order would become ever more painfully confusing. In relation to the elder Mill himself, it was Bentham who had already gone to the heart of the matter by remarking that James's own brand of liberalism stemmed 'less from love of the many than from hatred of the few'.

Michael Biddiss

See: J.S. Mill, *Autobiography* (1873): Leslie Stephen, *The English Utilitarians* (3 vols, 1900); Elie Halévy, *The Growth of Philosophic Radicalism* (1928); and William Thomas, *The Philosophic Radicals* (1979), especially ch. 3.

313
MILL, John Stuart 1806–73

British thinker and essayist

Mill is a giant among modern thinkers. Nearly all subsequent political philosophers, economists, sociologists and writers on culture and society have started from Mill, whether following, amending or reacting against him. Any student can be taught to find contradictions in parts of him, but no thinker has surpassed him when taken as a whole. For a long time he was thought of as the very model of a fully systematic thinker (or at least an acceptable one: Bentham* with feelings). But recent studies of his whole output, made possible by the reprinting of his scattered major essays, reveal a more complex, contradictory but stimulating thinker than the 'Saint of rationalism', 'the prince of utilitarians' or the 'king of the philosophic radicals'. He always strove for conclusions relevant to policy or personal conduct, but finally the red thread running all through his life and works appears as a dedication to free-thinking or to the character-forming process of thinking freely itself: the 'free-spirit' outlasts the 'social-engineer'.

His father was James Mill*, a disciple and friend of Jeremy Bentham who, although employed by the East India Company, taught John Stuart himself, in the early mornings and evenings, using the Benthamite principle of didactically associating 'the good' with pleasure and evil with pain. He began Greek at three and by six was reading the great Latin authors. Walking with his father he was questioned ceaselessly on what he had read and prepared during the day. By fifteen, after massive doses of economics, history and philosophy, he was ready to be introduced to Bentham's works themselves: almost at once he understood them as a unifying principle to be applied to all political, social and moral life, the great 'Felicific Calculus', always to calculate the 'greatest happiness of the greatest number' according to 'our two sovereign masters, Pleasure and Pain'. As he wrote in his *Autobiography* (1873): 'I now had opinions; a creed, a doctrine, a philosophy; in one of the best senses of the word, a religion.' Rarely can a child, except in a strictly religious household (like his father's Calvinistic, Scottish youth), have been brought up so seriously, so ideologically, so solitary and so joyless. At seventeen he became a corresponding clerk with the East India Company, but very soon articles began to flow forth promoting the Benthamite cause, and he was active in forming discussion groups and debating societies with other talented young men, all advocates of reform and, in varying degrees, disciples or admirers of Bentham and James Mill.

In 1825 he performed an awesomely complex and taxing editorial labour for Bentham, reducing to one coherent book three early and varying manuscript versions of his great *Rationale of Judicial Evidence*. The following year he fell into a depression and became obsessed with the pointlessness of activity and the meaninglessness of life. Reading by chance a literary passage about the death of his father, tears flowed, natural feelings or sensibility began to return or to grow and he found that the poetry of Wordsworth* and the ideas of Coleridge* spoke to him, whom previously he had had to read as bad examples of the Benthamite 'fallacy of the feelings'. Articles at this time showed not repudiation, but a subtle and cautious modification of the utilitarian doctrine: there were true *higher* pleasures, such as poetry; ultimately it was better/happier to be 'Socrates unhappy than a pig happy'. In 1829 Macaulay* made a savage attack in the *Edinburgh Review* on James Mill's *Essay on Government*, and when John Stuart came to help his father compose a reply for the *Westminster Review* he dispassionately discovered that, apart from the tone, he was much in agreement with Macaulay: the sum total of self-interest did not add up to the general good or the social interest; good government did not always need an identity of interest between rulers and ruled, one could occasionally know what was best for other people; and the idea of model institutions derived from pure reason needed tempering to custom, culture, different levels of understanding and the relativity of circumstances. But only after Bentham's death in 1832 and the trauma of his father's death in 1835 did he openly attack the limitations of Benthamism in his famous essays on Bentham and on Coleridge which keep him still read by (in our far more culturally fragmented times) students of literature as well as by political philosophers. Mill did not abandon reason and the spirit of the French *philosophes*, rather he argued that Bentham and his father were wrong to look for a single principle from which rules of legislation and personal conduct could be deduced: there were many such principles of society compelling respect and understanding, and they all had to be adapted to circumstances sociologically and compromised together politically. For a period Mill became so unassertive, so unlike the young Benthamite missionary, that some people thought that he was turning Wordsworthian or Coleridgean Tory; and the myopic Carlyle* actually believed that Mill was becoming his disciple, simply because he listened and high-mindedly strove to find some truth in all that sage's early blather. But he also read Comte*, Saint-Simon* and Tocqueville* as well.

Tocqueville was especially congenial to Mill. His *Autobiography* admits that it was reading Tocqueville that made Mill understand that even democracy needs 'a necessary protection against its degenerating into the only despotism of which, in the modern world, there is real danger – the absolute rule of the head of the executive over a congregation of isolated individuals, all equal but all slaves.' Yet Saint-Simon's speculations on cooperativism and Comte's on necessary cultural stages of society also remained with him.

Amid so much mental change, small wonder that he found in this period 'a perfect friendship'; rather he fell desperately in love in 1830 with a married woman with three children. Harriet Taylor was the wife of a prosperous, radical merchant and her mind was forceful, bold, energetic but rather vain and mediocre. To Mill she was a perfected human type. In his *Autobiography* Mill wrote that 'it was years . . . before my acquaintance with her became at all intimate and confident.' He painted a picture of a high-minded Platonic friendship, a spiritual love which George Bernard Shaw was to take as a dramatic model and which some have seen as the forerunner of that alleged 'sacerdotal celibacy' that some of the first generation of married dons at Oxford professed to practise. But it was untrue. Whether or not there was actual sexual intercourse, their letters reveal that the twenty years before her husband's death were full of the most painful and romantic storm and stress, of which her tolerant husband quickly tired, setting her up on her own where Mill was free to visit her, indeed to take her and her children on holiday together while all the time pretending to live at home with his sisters.

His *A System of Logic* (1843) was his first book and the last uninfluenced by Harriet. It dominated British philosophy in the nineteenth century and Book 6, on the method of the social sciences, is of lasting value. While his insistence on inductive method is now generally rejected, as in Karl Popper's argument that science begins with hypotheses to be tested and refuted, not with observations made from a *tabula rasa* mind, Mill himself is surpassingly rich in fertile hypotheses, whether or not he thought they were derived from pure reason (deduction) or pure observation (induction). His *Principles of Political Economy* followed in 1853 and he claimed that the 'qualified socialism' of the last chapter on 'The Probable Futurity of the Working Classes' was 'entirely due to her'. Scholars once thought that these were the pietistic words of a besotted lover, but correspondence between them shows this to be all too true: his scepticism was swept away by her idealism and bullying, at the expense of flagrant contradictions in the text. It was the least successful of his major works. Apart from Harriet's socialism, he went back to what his father had taught him in the 1820s, ignoring twenty years of subsequent economic theory.

There is now no reason to doubt that *On Liberty* (1859) was a truly collaborative work, written together after his retirement from the East India Company. But this greatest work was fortunately on a theme on which they had both always basically agreed. He was to speak of the young Benthamites as having had 'an almost unbounded confidence in the efficacy of two things: representative government, and complete freedom of discussion'; only the young Benthamites would not have even appeared to value eccentricity for its own sake, or for example to conformists, but only if it led to the truth. And the essay does contain some criteria for limitations on liberty, which Mill inserted but which Harriet mercifully glossed over, not greatly stressed, but then a famous writer has some right to assume that people knew where he stood already: that there can be *utilitarian* grounds of public order for limiting individualism, but never absolute moral grounds. 'You may not do this because it is not convenient to most of us' at least leaves more in place than the absolute prohibition, 'That is wrong.'

If he enjoyed his great public fame, it must have been somewhat marred by Harriet's quarrelling with nearly all his celebrated friends during their seven years of marriage before she died unexpectedly in Avignon in 1859. Mill moved there with her daughter Helen, bought a house and installed in it the entire furniture and fittings of the hotel room in which she had died. The rationalist shared the Victorian cult of the dead. But gradually his old ways resumed, friendships and publications; and even three years in the House of Commons as Radical Liberal Member for Westminster, though unsuccessful in re-election because of his support on principle for the atheist Bradlaugh, a man he disliked personally. *Considerations on Representative Government* appeared in 1861, a subtle discussion of the relationship of the idea of democracy to types of institutions and circumstances. Democracy was universally possible, but only with universal compulsory education and, moreover, its forms would vary greatly. So strong was national feeling, for instance, that he doubted if representative government was possible in a multi-national state (a view that Lord Acton* regarded as 'uncivilized'). So an historical relativism had come to temper the old rationalism, and the idea of an open, educated, cultivated and rational elite (open to all eventually, but eventually) tempered the old Millite utilitarians of each actual opinion counting as one. He even advocated, somewhat tentatively, that while each person should have a vote, votes should be weighted according to education. But he noted that the politicians were, indeed, interested in a property not an educational franchise. So proportional representation became his last piece of Benthamite institutional advocacy.

The last years were extraordinarily fruitful. 1861 saw his final attempt, still intellectually impressive, to synthesize Bentham and Wordsworth, in *Utilitarianism*. During the American Civil War he attacked pro-Southern writers strongly and influentially. In 1871 came *The Subjection of Women*, an emancipatory tract in which, if Harriet's influence is obvious, he was also returning to his first serious criticisms of Bentham and his father, both of whom were somewhat half-hearted in their acceptance of women as equally mankind. He came to terms with his own intellectual development in his *Autobiography*, published in 1873 soon after his death. Though austere and solely concerned with the intellect, it is impressive and moving. Only a few pages were removed by Helen Taylor (now recovered). His last words were: 'You know that I have done my work.' An unseemly public controversy broke out as to whether such a great man who was a sceptic should or could be buried at Westminster Abbey. The wily Gladstone* hedged on the issue. But Mill had insisted on being interred alongside Harriet at Avignon. His bust appeared in secularist and Unitarian meeting houses until very recently, and every free-thinking intellectual until 1914 had his portrait on the study wall.

Bernard Crick

See: *Collected Works of J.S. Mill* (from 1963). A good modern selection from both the political and cultural essays is *Essays on Politics and Culture* ed. Gertrude Himmelfarb (1962). See also: F.A. Hayek, *John Stuart Mill and Harriet Taylor* (1951); Michael St John Packe, *The Life of John Stuart Mill* (1954): Joseph Hamburger, *Intellectuals in Politics: John Stuart Mill and the Philosophic Radicals* (1965); C.L. Ten, *Mill On Liberty* (1980).

314
MILLAIS, Sir John Everett 1829–96

British painter

Millais was a child prodigy; he was only eleven years old when he began his training at the Royal Academy Schools and the youngest student ever admitted. His career there was a model of success, culminating with the winning of a Gold Medal for *The Tribe of Benjamin Seizing the Daughters of Shiloh in the Vineyards*, a respectful exercise in the painterly, fleshy manner of the most highly regarded British painter of the day, William Etty. The picture with which he made his precocious début at the Royal Academy exhibition in 1846, *Pizarro Seizing the Inca of Peru*, is an equally routine piece of work, following in the decidedly undistinguished tradition of British romantic history-painting. Among Millais's fellow students by this time were William Holman Hunt* and Dante Gabriel Rossetti*, with whom he became friendly and began to have serious, subversive discussions about art. These led to the formation in 1848 of the Pre-Raphaelite Brotherhood – comprising seven members, of whom Millais, Hunt and Rossetti are by far the most important – and to the most drastic change of course in Millais's development as an artist.

The Pre-Raphaelites came to the view that painting had reached a state of advanced degeneration, the symptoms of which were free brushwork (which they

called 'slosh'), theatrical lighting and poses, idealization, and a general air of artificiality. The rot had set in with Raphael and other painters of the High Renaissance. As far as they could tell from the few works they had seen, earlier artists had painted in a more detailed style based on fresh observation and reverence for nature – and they would do likewise. The most important of the paintings Millais produced in the heat of the Pre-Raphaelite moment were *Isabella*, a subject from Keats*, and *Christ in the Carpenter's Shop*, which were exhibited at the Academy in 1849 and 1850 respectively. Both are executed with tiny brush-strokes in hard, bright colours; both are rich in the detailed symbolism to which such a detailed style lends itself; the figures in both are portraits of friends and relatives rather than beautiful professional models; their features are recorded unblinkingly and unflinchingly; and their gestures are untheatrical, even wilfully awkward. The realism of the latter work, in which Christ appears as a rather sickly-looking boy with lank red hair and Joseph has dirty finger-nails, struck many spectators of the time as outright blasphemy and brought Millais a notoriety he only shook off with the less controversial *Ophelia* and *A Huguenot*, which he showed at the Academy of 1852.

In the mid-1850s Millais began to grow impatient with the laboriousness of the Pre-Raphaelite style and to paint somewhat more loosely. More importantly, he also began to reduce the narrative content of his pictures, concerning himself more with the creation of mood than story-telling, and to reduce facial expression in favour of a look of impassive beauty. This is well illustrated by what is arguably his greatest work, *Autumn Leaves* (1855–6), a wistful, dream-like study of some girls building a bonfire at sunset. *Autumn Leaves* is a landmark in Millais's career, after which it seems less appropriate to speak of him as a Pre-Raphaelite than as the forerunner of painters of the 'Aesthetic Movement' such as Whistler* and Albert Moore. He maintained the same haunting intensity in *Spring* (1857–9) and *The Vale of Rest* (1858–9) but in disappointingly few of his subsequent pictures.

Millais's exceptional gifts as a draughtsman made him well suited to illustrative work. Establishing a reputation with the famous Moxon edition of Tennyson* (published 1857), he went on to contribute to a vast number of books and periodicals, becoming the most important figure in the remarkable flourishing of British illustration as a whole in the 1860s. His designs are generally faithful to the given text, varying subtly in style so that novels are treated naturalistically – figures are often cut by the edge of the image in a way that deliberately recalls photography – and poetry and the Scriptures in a gently stylized manner. Millais's best-known illustrations are to the Moxon Tennyson, *The Parables of Our Lord* (1864), the magazine *Once a Week* and various novels by Trollope*, including *Framley Parsonage (1860–1), Orley Farm (1861–2) and The Small House at Allington (1862–4).

In 1863 Millais was elected a Royal Academician. The work with which he chose to represent himself in the Academy's Diploma Gallery was his Souvenir of Velasquez of 1868, a simple study of a pretty girl in fancy dress. By this date, his painting technique had relaxed to a degree which in his Pre-Raphaelite days he would undoubtedly have condemned as 'sloshy'. Painters of the fifteenth century and before had been surpassed in his estimation by painterly masters of the Baroque, especially Frans Hals and, as the title of his diploma picture suggests, Velasquez. He even developed a liking for Sir Joshua Reynolds (whom the Pre-Raphaelites had called 'Sir Sloshua') and imitated him in a series of child-pictures with an eighteenth-century flavour, including Cherry Ripe (1879) and the infamous Bubbles (1885–6). Childhood is the favourite theme of Millais's later work and even his historical subjects, such as The Boyhood of Raleigh (1869–70) and The Princes in the Tower (1878), tend to feature children.

The great wealth that Millais accumulated in the 1870s, 1880s and 1890s was largely due to his popularity as a portraitist. Many of the most familiar likenesses of eminent Victorians, including Gladstone* (1878–9), Disraeli* (1881), Cardinal Newman* (1881), Tennyson* (1881), Henry Irving (1883) and Arthur Sullivan* (1888), are portraits by Millais. His male sitters he invests with a strong sense of 'character', conveyed through expression and pose, especially the placing of the hands, and enhanced by the sheer assurance of his technique. In female portraits such as Hearts are Trumps, which shows the three daughters of Sir William Armstrong playing cards (1871–2), the dresses and accessories provide an opportunity for exuberant displays of brushwork. The most remarkable of Millais's later works, however, are neither his child-pictures nor his portraits, but the large landscapes he painted during his annual sporting holidays in Scotland, beginning in 1870 with Chill October. Though painted in a fairly deadpan style, these bleak, often distinctly unpicturesque views seem somehow charged with human feeling – a quality that greatly impressed the young Van Gogh*.

Malcolm Warner

See: Marion H. Spielmann, Millais and His Works (1898); John Guille Millais, The Life and Letters of Sir John Everett Millais (1899); and Mary Bennett's catalogue to the exhibition Millais held at the Walker Art Gallery, Liverpool, and the Royal Academy in 1967.

315
MILLET, Jean François 1814–75

French painter

Born into a prosperous peasant family near Cherbourg, Millet studied in Paris under Delaroche. His early work consists mostly of portraits, interspersed with erotic scenes, executed in a florid late-Rococo manner. His first wife's death in 1844, after only three years of marriage, may have helped trigger the reconsideration from which his mature art emerged; these years also coincided with political and social disturbance. In 1849 he moved to the village of Barbizon near Fontainebleau, where landscape artists like Corot*, Diaz and Theodore Rousseau also worked. Throughout the 1850s a succession of large paintings on peasant themes brought him controversy, and eventually, in his final years, immense popular success.

Millet's essential contribution is to have created an enduring iconography of labour, sufficiently ambiguous to have fertilized a wide variety of later artists, and to have stood for many different creeds at different times. Its genesis remains mysterious; his figures owe something to his study of Brueghel, and also to Daumier*. Initially interpreted as protests against the plight of the peasant, Millet's chief works would become by the 1890s schoolroom texts for the dignity of labour. The Sower (1850) was the first of these archetypal images and exists in several variations; as Van Gogh* realized when making his own version, it carries unavoidable overtones of parable.

It is this aspect of Millet which the anarchist Pissarro* found unsympathetic – 'He was just a shade too biblical' – and his own use of Millet's Peasant Ploughing as a cover for Kropotkin's* 'The New Age' underlines this ambiguity; was Millet speaking of present ills or, rather, in praise of some timeless Golden Age? The Angelus (1855–7) shows two peasants working overtime in the fields; when they hear the sacred note, the woman bows devoutly, while the man dumbly, or perhaps sullenly, watches. Here as elsewhere the low viewpoint is important in creating monumentality; in Millet's own words: 'It is astonishing toward the approach of night, how grand everything on the plain appears, especially when we see figures thrown up against the sky. Then they look like giants.' Millet was too much a symbolist to be a radical; here the male figure could easily be retailored to become Puvis de Chavannes's* Pauvre Pêcheur, rapt in mystical acceptance of his lot.

The figures in The Gleaners (1857) are life-size, and in its magnificent rhythmic interval it remains Millet's formal masterpiece, epitomizing also his characteristic use of primary colours, softened by rounded modelling. Yet the contrast between the groaning harvest wagon behind, and the back-breaking labour of the foreground could be more telling; and it might be argued Millet's classic harmony dulls the edge of his protest (in contrast to the rougher music of his contemporary, Courbet*). The only work where Millet's radical sympathies emerge unclouded is the terrifying *Man with a Hoe* (1860) whose apocalyptic implications were immediately recognized.

All his life Millet was a peerless draughtsman, in pastel or in black crayon, and the vigorous studies of individual labourers have worn better than the more rhetorical 'machines'. His visionary landscapes are the masterpieces of the 1860s: *November*, the plough abandoned in the desolate crow-haunted field (an image widely known through Van Gogh's version); or *Spring*, from the *Four Seasons* (1865–73), where, amid astonishing light effects, winter is cast out by a rainbow and flowers burst from the glistening grass.

The unfinished *Brushwood Gatherers*, with its funereal bowed procession, can be viewed at Cardiff alongside another late masterpiece, the *Peasant Family*. 'Such works,' wrote Sickert* in 1912, 'are the ultimate works of art. There is only one way to paint and here it is.' Yet Millet's last and possibly greatest painting stands apart: the bizarre scene, recollected from childhood, of *Boys Clubbing Birds to Death by Torchlight* (1874). The lunging puppet figures, silhouetted against jagged bird-broken aureoles, seem like dancers in some primeval ritual; the resonance is of man's gratuitous and somnambulistic cruelty.

Millet's reputation has fluctuated more than any comparable master. *The Angelus*, originally purchased for 1,000 francs, was fetching 300,000 by the 1880s, and 800,000 ten years later. But over-exposure blurred the originality of his Epic Naturalism; many twentieth-century critics have re-echoed Delacroix's* early judgement: 'deep but pretentious feeling'. In France, Millet's influence extended through Degas's* pastels and Seurat's* twilight drawings, to Pissarro and Gauguin*, and to Van Gogh, who above all understood that 'in Millet everything is at once both reality and symbol', and whose art is unimaginable without that example. It has taken the current reassessment to recognize how pervasive Millet's iconography has remained, in Kathe Kollwitz, Constant Permecke, Josef Herman, and countless others, even to the present day.

Timothy Hyman

See: Robert L. Herbert, *Millet* (Arts Council Catalogue, 1976); Rosalyn Bacou, *Millet: One Hundred Drawings* (1975).

316
MOMMSEN, Theodor 1817–1903

German historian of Rome

Mommsen was born on 30 November 1817 at Garding in Schleswig, a duchy which has produced German-speaking scholars in profusion. He was the son of a poor pastor, educated at the University of Kiel between 1838 and 1843, where he took a degree in law. His most influential teacher and friend was Otto Jahn, musician, philologist, and archaeologist, who was dedicated to the idea of a systematic collection of Roman inscriptions. Mommsen's first work was on the Roman associations and tribes, but the three years from 1844 which he spent on a travelling fellowship from the Danish government in Italy were decisive in extending his classical interests beyond the Roman *urbs* to the provinces. He produced pioneering studies of Oscan and the lower Italian dialects of the pre-Roman period, and was encouraged by the Italian scholar Borgesi to make a start on the inscriptions of Samnium and the kingdom of Naples. The Berlin Academy had called on Jahn to start a project on Roman inscriptions similar to that of August Boeckh's *Corpus Inscriptionum Graecarum*. Jahn in his turn went to Mommsen for help, but he rejected the conditions laid down for the work by the Academy; the Academy did not come round to his topographical scheme for inscriptions until the publication of his *Inscriptiones Regni Neapolitani Latinae* in 1852, when he was invited to take charge of the *Corpus Inscriptionum Latinarum*, which was to be the *magnum opus* of a prolific scholarly career.

On his return from Italy, Mommsen had been caught up in the liberal and national politics of 1848, becoming editor of the *Schleswig-Holsteinisch Zeitung*, the organ of the provisional government of the duchy. The defeat of his cause in 1848 impelled his removal to a professorship of Roman law at Leipzig, where he taught alongside Jahn and Moritz Haupt. But the political arm of reaction reached them, and the three professors lost their posts in 1851. In 1852 Mommsen became Professor of Roman Law at Zurich, and in 1854 moved on to Breslau, his last staging-post before he made his home in Berlin. The Berlin Academy had summoned him as a member, and he was made Professor of Ancient History there. Publishers who had heard him lecture had already commissioned Mommsen to write a *History of Rome* (*Römische Geschichte*, trans. 1862–75), which appeared in four volumes from 1854 to 1856, taking the story up to the dictatorship of Caesar. This first complete survey of republican history was an instantaneous success in Germany, and rapidly won over scholars and general readers alike in England, France, and Italy. Its main advantages were its decisive tone and its energetic dramatization of the crisis of the republic in contemporary terms. Cicero emerged as an ineffectual liberal wind-bag; Caesar by contrast as a statesman with a realistic grasp of the imperatives of the moment. Mommsen was accused of a hero-worshipping Caesarism, but he always stressed that his interpretation rested on the political collapse of the republic's institutions rather than a glorification of empire. Caesar gave the quietus to the factious oligarchy of the republic, but Mommsen believed that the loss of free self-determination for the majority of the citizens outweighed all the benefits of imperial rule.

In 1858 Mommsen became editor of the *Corpus Inscriptionum Latinarum*, and the appearance of its volumes from 1868 steadily revolutionized the study of Roman history. Mommsen took within its scope all the inscriptions on stone, wood, metal or terracotta produced in the Roman provinces, and insisted on each being examined personally if possible. Apart from the first volume of the inscriptions of the republic, the remainder were arranged geographically and threw a new light on the Romans outside the city. Mommsen's own fifth volume of his *Roman History*, which appeared in 1885, was the first of a new generation of historical treatments which could do full justice to the Roman provinces (*Provinces of the Roman Empire from Caesar to Diocletian*). Of the sixteen volumes of the *Corpus Inscriptionum Latinarum* in folio, Mommsen was personally responsible for fourteen out of the forty-one parts into which they were divided. But alongside his historical work on inscriptions, he furthered his initial interest in Roman law. From 1870 to 1888 appeared the three volumes of the *Römisches Staatsrecht*, the first systematic treatment of Roman constitutional law. It was built up of a series of monographs on the different institutions, and it remains to this day the foundation stone of all studies of the subject. Mommsen's strength was his ability to bring together the widely scattered source materials, and work them up into a systematic structure; the evolution of institutions over time, and the external influences upon them, played necessarily a smaller role. One of the most significant historical insights to which it gave rise, despite these handicaps, was into the role of the Senate as a continuing source of *auctoritas* under the principate. A dyarchy persisted, in Mommsen's view, until the reign of Diocletian, when principate finally became empire. Mommsen was also the author of the standard work on Roman criminal law, his *Römisches Stafrecht* (1895). If this were not enough for one man, as secretary of the Berlin Academy from 1874 to 1895, Mommsen played an important part in sponsoring work in the new fields of prosopography, systematic archaeology, and papyrology. He had already published an important contribution to the study of Roman coinage, and in later life went on to edit several early medieval texts for the *Monumenta Germaniae Historica*.

Mommsen's role in maintaining Germany's lead in studies of ancient history after Niebuhr and Boeckh cannot be overestimated. As a teacher his lecturing technique was not impressive, but he compelled attention by his scholarship, dedication, and energy. Even beyond his own sphere of ancient history, Mommsen was legendary as the type of Germanic scholar, regarded with awe and veneration. The range of his scholarly output and its sheer quantity staggered the contemporary imagination, as it should stagger ours. A century later, the most substantial of his works still provides a starting point for study of the social, legal, and economic history of the Romans.

Peter Jones

A full list of Mommsen's books and articles, 1,513 titles in chronological order, is found in K. Zangemeister and E. Jacobs, *Theodor Mommsen als Schriftsteller: Ein Verzeichnis seiner Schriften* (1905). A very good selection appears in Mommsen's 8–volume *Gesammelte Schriften* (1905–13). See: Albert Wucher, *Theodor Mommsen, Geschichtschreibung und Politik* (1956); and L. Wickert, *Theodor Mommsen, Eine Biographie* (3 vols, 1959–80).

317
MONET, Claude 1840–1926

French artist

The most important member of the Impressionist group, Monet was born in Paris, the son of a wholesale grocer. At the age of five he moved with his family to Le Havre and lived there until adult. A physically strong and self-willed boy, Monet loved deeply the sea and its shore in all its moods: fierce, stormy or gentle and limpid. No doubt this continuing early fascination provided the basis for much of his art.

He was fortunate to have met in Le Havre by the age of eighteen the painter Boudin, among the first to realize that painting carried out in the open air in front of the depicted subject contained an immediacy and vitality lacking in studio work. Boudin's paintings have a delightful freshness and, although more than sketches, retain something of the sensuous excitement to be found in such preliminary work. Monet wrote later that after he had tried Boudin's method he continued to paint *en plein air*: 'It was as if a veil had suddenly been torn from my eyes. I understood. I grasped what painting was capable of.'

Whilst enduring a short term in the army Monet worked with the Dutchman Jongkind, a more dramatic painter than Boudin but one who also worked out of doors. By 1862 the young Monet was in Paris, shortly to study at Gleyre's studio and to see Manet's* exhibition at the Galerie Martinet, Salon des Refusés. Manet's paintings at this time were not acceptable to the official jury members. Monet was greatly impressed by Manet's work but was soon to diverge from the older man's view of painting, over the question of shadows.

In France during the nineteenth century a number of people were investigating the optical laws of vision and of colour. Chevreul had published *The Principles of Harmony and Contrast of Colours, and their Application to the Arts* in 1839. This book made clear the theory of negative after-images whereby a colour becomes surrounded faintly after a moment or two by its complement or opposite. This negative effect modifies the surrounding colour so that green which has a patch of yellow in its centre will appear slightly brown because of the mauve after-image superimposed upon it by the eye. Colour complements or oppositions of primary to secondary colours had been known before the nineteenth century. However, Chevreul also discovered that two small areas of colour close together will, when seen at a distance, merge and produce a neutralizing effect. Later the Post-Impressionists realized that by contrast, when the two complements are used in larger areas, they intensify each other.

The difference between the Impressionism of Monet and Manet lay largely in the treatment of shadows. Manet claimed that to paint sunlight there had to be a sudden change and strong contrast from light and dark. It is as though he imagined not only the artist's eye moving to survey sunshine and shade but the whole person walking into it and being surrounded by sudden shade. Monet took a more objective, distanced and less dramatic view so that the eye could move back and forth comparing and becoming aware of the effects of refraction and reflection within both light and shade. He sought not the oppositions but the similarities, thus unifying his painting.

When first exhibited, Impressionism seemed strange to the public. Not only was the work produced in the open air, it dealt with contemporary subject matter rather than historical myths or events which was the usual province of the painter until Courbet* broke with that tradition. He met Monet in 1865 when the younger man was already rapidly moving towards the finest period of Impressionism, that of the 1870s.

By 1869 Monet, his friends Renoir*, Pissarro* and Bazille were producing highly accomplished works in the new style and seeking a means of exhibiting them. A typical work of this period by Monet was *La Grenouillère* of 1869. It depicted his great love, water, a bathing and boating area of the River Seine on the outskirts of Paris. Manet and Monet painted a similar view of the same place and the comparison is instructive. Monet's version shows a small island connected by wooden planking to the river bank and to the bathing station. On it people sit or stand. A few bathers chest-deep in water look across to the far bank of the river where a mass of variegated yellow greens suggest a line of trees in sunlight. In the foreground the trees are painted in blue greens for they, like the people and boats, are all in the shade. The painting of the water is the most striking effect. Strong short strokes of various colours form the shadow side of lively curving ripples and almost pure white the crests. The work is brilliantly alight and alive and compared with Renoir's softer version of the same year is crisply and sharply seen. Manet's *River at Argenteuil* (1874) differentiates little between the greens in the foreground and on the far bank. Distance is emphasized by the controlled use of black bonnet ribbons near to, slightly less dark boats in the middle distance and a grey structure even further away.

It was *Impression: Sunrise* of 1872, produced whilst Monet was in England during the German attack upon Paris, that gave the Impressionist movement its name. The fogs of nineteenth-century industrial London afforded Monet great delight. They had the effect of both unifying the view and dissolving the forms of buildings and structures so that he is left with a mass of reflecting and refracting colour. The Thames was a major source for subject matter during these visits.

One work of 1878 by Monet called *Rue Montorgeuil Decked out with Flags* foreshadows Jackson Pollock's *Blue Poles* of 1953. The New York Abstract Expressionists of the gestural kind, such as Pollock, have admitted a great debt to Monet. Certainly the Monet scene with tricolours by the hundred fluttering in the quick morning air above an enormous crowd winding down the street is almost an abstraction of large and small strokes which express an immense hedonistic pleasure in being alive and part of the day's activities. However much Monet attempted to be no more than 'an eye', his sturdy temperament makes itself felt, sometimes with extreme sensitivity as in the painting of his dying and beloved wife Camille.

Gradually he came to realize along with many of his contemporaries, both writers and artists, that 'realism' as it was often termed was not in itself sufficient for great art. For Monet this meant a greater search for colour structure. He rejected Seurat's* Pointillisme of the 1880s because of its deliberate slow technique and static hieratic effect upon form. Monet, used to painting 'fleeting moments of time', understood movement and change.

He once more became interested in choosing an object and painting it several times under different lighting conditions. In 1891 he produced the *Haystacks* series and the *Poplar on the Epte* variations which he himself prized greatly. The Tate Gallery version shows a dramatic curve and counter-curve of dancing tree tops, from top right-hand corner of the work to bottom left-hand. The wide swinging brush strokes of leaf clusters follow the curve across the row of parallel thin trunks which are set against a brilliant blue sky with swirling small white clouds. It is a painting produced with confidence and panache.

Then follows the exquisite *Rouen Cathedral* series whilst Monet is building his water gardens at Giverny. The result of this endeavour are the glorious views of these gardens with bridge and water-lilies, works known as the *Nymphéas*.

In 1908 after an illness Monet visited Venice for the first time and whilst staying with a friend in a house on the Grand Canal painted views of that city, rising above and reflected in the waterways. The paintings are quieter in mood although intense but unified in colour.

Amongst his last works are the water-lily decorations (1916–23) in the Musée de l'orangerie, a small palace in Paris. Here, 'subject, sensation and pictorial object have all become identical.' By that Monet means that the picture is an equivalent sensation for that which the eye experiences; an eye, however, constantly on the move but rejecting an entirely intellectual or imaginative appraisal of the visual world.

Pat Turner

Other works include: *Westminster Bridge* (1871); *Gare St-Lazare* (1877). See: Daniel Wildenstein, *Monet* (Biography and Catalogue Raisonné, 3 vols, 1974–9); Joel Isaacson, *Claude Monet* (1978); John House, *Monet* (1981).

318
MOORE, George (Augustus) 1852–1933

Irish novelist

Moore made an important contribution to the emergence of realism and modern narrative techniques in the novel in English at the close of the century. His creative originality as well as his limitations were acknowledged by numerous modern writers, among whom the most notable were Arnold Bennett, D.H. Lawrence, Virginia Woolf, Roger Fry, Theodore Dreiser and James Joyce. Novelists writing in English from the late 1880s onwards were beneficiaries of his campaign to liberate fiction from the trammels of three-volume form and the control of publication by circulating libraries such as Mudie's and W.H. Smith. The success of Moore's campaign rested partly on his advocacy in the pamphlet *Literature as Nurse* (1885), which followed arguments made less forcefully by mid-Victorian admirers of Balzac* such as G.H. Lewes*, Thackeray* and Wilkie Collins*, but was principally due to his verve and delicacy in writing the novels which form his chief claim to fame.

Moore is best known for *Esther Waters* (1894), the first sympathetic exploration by a Victorian novelist of dilemmas facing the domestic servant class. As a single parent following her dismissal for pregnancy, Esther faces suffering and rejection, but she and her son are able to survive. This instance of a successful struggle for survival is presented without sentimentality or exaggeration from the woman's point of view; the avarice, hypocrisy and destructiveness of the social setting are presented with uncompromising clarity. Like the work of Dickens* and Zola*, and Hawthorne*, whose work came to his hands too late to influence his art, Moore's writing is inspired by a strong social conscience, but his fiction dispenses with the garishness and violence of his precursors. This novel was thought by Sir Arthur Quiller-Couch to be superior to *Tess of the D'Urbervilles*, to which it is a riposte; however, Moore's handling of the maternal instinct and its triumph over a harsh environment lacks the mythic dimension which permeates Hardy's* novel.

Rigorous abstention from the rhetoric of irony and detraction which marred the Victorian fictional treatment of women, combined with a sensuous evocation of provincial, Irish and domestic settings and the faithful outlining of subjective experience, are the hallmarks of Moore's technical and thematic advance on the work of his precursors. Among the latter, Thackeray and Miss Braddon* should be noted, as well as Hardy and George Eliot*. Novels such as *A Mummer's Wife* (1884), *A Drama in Muslin* (1886) and *Evelyn Innes* (1898) form the peaks in his large output of writing during the two decades of the major period, down to 1900. Moore's reputation suffered partly through changes in literary taste and, more significantly, through his having outlived his own creativity. Besides the novels, among which *Vain Fortune* (1891) in the 'new edition' (1895) was best admired by James Joyce, Moore excelled in short stories and *nouvelles*, of which two volumes appeared, *Celibates* (1895) and *The Untilled Field* (1903).

Other literary genres held Moore's attention with varying degrees of success. His plays reflect his championship of Ibsen* and Wagner*, and he contributed to the formation of two dramatic movements, the Stage Society and the Abbey Theatre. Judiciously he refrained from adding to the unpolished verses in styles borrowed from Swinburne* and Baudelaire*, which appeared in his earliest publications, *Flowers of Passion* (1879) and *Pagan Poems* (1881). Though *Confessions of a Young Man* (1888) falls short by the standards of rigour and elegance which were upheld by other autobiographical writers of the period, thus lacking the scrupulousness of true confession and the drama of *Bildungsroman*, it is nevertheless a good contribution to an important later Victorian genre. Later excursions in this field, notably *Hail and Farewell* (1911–14), did lasting damage to Moore's reputations as a writer. As a critic, however, Moore occupies an important position between Pater* (his principal literary model) and Arthur Symons. His championship of Whistler*, Manet* and Cézanne* in *Modern Painting* (1893) ensured the acceptance of Impressionism and Post-Impressionism in Edwardian times and the modernity of his criticism was acknowledged by Roger Fry. His essays on Balzac, Flaubert*, Rimbaud* and Turgenev*, most of which appeared in *Impressions and Opinions* (1891), are among the first and best of their kind in their period.

Born at Moore Hall on the shores of Lough Carra in County Mayo, George Moore was the eldest of three sons in a strongly literary and artistic Catholic household of the lesser Irish gentry. A combination of unsuitable educational facilities and his withdrawing temperament led to his failure in ordinary schooling, but the environment of the ateliers in Paris, where he studied painting, laid the foundation of his literary flowering. His contact with Manet and the Zola circle was the main formative influence of his youth. Moore's commitment to social issues, his endorsement of liberal Irish nationalism and his renunciation of the role of landlord in favour of the mirror of art are sketched in an important document which he never reissued and rarely referred to, *Parnell and his Island* (1887). By the time of the Irish civil war (1922–3), when Moore Hall was burned down, Moore was an elder statesman of the London literary households with little to offer beyond renewed reminiscences and revisions of debatable worth to his early works. In his last phase of substantial work, however, he embarked on the religious controversies which haunt the pages of his early writing, but he lacked the tenacity and research of modern giants such as Flaubert and Joyce. His novel *The Brook Kerith* (1907) and *The Apostle* (1911), a play, explore the role of Essenes in the formation of Christian tradition.

Though lacking the clarity and versatility of his greater compatriots Yeats and Joyce, Moore is nevertheless an important contributor to modern literary thought and to Irish letters. The complexity of his literary and autobiographical references has tended to obscure the originality of his reinterpretations of Victorian fictional themes and problems. A considerable body of critical and scholarly writing has formed around his work, and good television dramas have been based on *Esther Waters*.

Christopher Heywood

George Moore, *Letters 1895–1933 to Lady Cunard*, ed. Rupert Hart-Davis (1957); *George Moore in Transition: Letters to T. Fisher Unwin and Lena Milman, 1894–1910*, ed. Helmut E. Gerber (1968). See: Joseph Hone, *The Life of George Moore* (1936); Malcolm Brown, *George Moore: A Reconsideration* (1955); *George Moore's Mind and Art*, ed. Graham Owens (1968); Richard Cave, *George Moore* (1978).

319
MOREAU, Gustave 1826–98

French artist and teacher

Before attending the École des Beaux Arts in Paris from 1846 to 1850 the young Moreau studied painting in Italy. His knowledge of classical artists, of Greek myths and legends remained the core of subject matter for almost all his own art. However this interest in historical subject matter was synthesized with a number of other influences both from within and from outside art so that his work became highly original.

At the end of his college training Moreau met the painter Chassériau who became a close friend. This artist's style was based largely on that of Delacroix* and with his example in mind Moreau's work became more exotic. Later, stylistically, his painting has similarities with the more decorative aspects of the 'Decadence' and the 'Art for Art's Sake' movements. Included in these developments were considerations of neo-Platonic ideas. Gautier*, one of Chassériau's group of friends, wrote in 1856:

We believe in the autonomy of Art. Art for us is not the means but the end. Any artist who has in view anything but the beautiful is not an artist in our eyes; we have never been able to understand the separation of idea and form.

The cult of the beautiful was anti the Romantic 'sublime'. It sought sophisticated love and eroticism rather than natural storm and terror. It was a different type of subjectivity. In addition to his love of the beautiful, Moreau was contending with strong religious feelings, which led to the concept of the ideal and towards mysticism:

I believe only in Him. I don't believe either in that which I touch or that which I see. I believe only in that which I don't see and that which I sense. My brain, my reason, seem to me ephemeral and of doubtful reality. My inner sentiment alone seems to me eternal and incontestably certain.

These transcendent concerns are linked to Moreau's relationship with his mother, who was a musician with a strong mind, both adored and feared by her only son. The subjective side of his art drew strongly upon his subconscious neurotic conflicts with her and these, coupled with a vivid imagination and an excessively critical spirit, produced an art of considerable passion, wherein love, eroticism and death are symbolized by the legendary characters and objects of his subject matter.

Woman came from sensual nature, in Moreau's view. She was the inscrutable mindless force with which man had to battle in order to achieve his spiritual superiority, epitomized by the heroic artist. The first important painting in his *oeuvre* is *Oedipus and the Sphinx* (1864). In this work the beautiful young man approaches the half animal, dominating female, to ascertain the source of her inscrutability. Exhibited at the Paris Salon that year it was highly acclaimed and Moreau adulated by society, even to the extent of an invitation to Court.

Later work by the artist, however, becomes more obviously sadistic and *Prometheus* (1869), depicting an older man, alive but bound, whilst his flesh is viciously attacked by a predatory bird, was severely criticized. Female images also at times turned treacherous or vicious although retaining their sexual beauty.

One of these images is the Christian *Salome* (1876) who turns into the *femme fatale* so attractive to the 'Decadents'. In Moreau's series of works on the subject Salome is standing, half commanding, half afraid, before a vision of the bloody head of John the Baptist, which hovers in a vast dimly lit building, more suggestive of Buddhist than Judaic origins. Moreau's most exquisite version of his theme is celebrated by Huysmans*, an art critic and controversial author of the period. In his book *À Rebours* the dandy hero, Des Esseintes, adoringly owns the same Salome painting. No doubt Moreau's thought with regard to exoticism is exceedingly close to that of Flaubert* whose book *Salaambo* also contains a Salome theme, and to the 'Spleen' poems of Baudelaire*.

One of the concepts in art that affected Moreau deeply and endeared him to the Symbolist movement of the 1800s was that of a 'beautiful inertia'. If Delacroix was dynamic, rhythmic, fluent in his art, as in *Sardanapulas*, also a subject of rape and sadism, then Moreau was equally dramatic but with a strong sense of the hieratic, so that a scene, such as that in the *Suitors*, begun in 1852, left then finished toward the end of his life, where all the suitors for Penelope's hand are dying violent deaths upon the return of Odysseus, is transfixed into a state of dream-like timelessness and the horror of the moment obtains for ever.

Throughout his life Moreau's technique varied considerably. Not only did he make jewel-like sketches in water-colour which are pure abstractions of extreme beauty and markedly innovatory, but he also produced finished oil paintings that range from smooth purely tonal works to thickly encrusted surfaces containing brilliant colour. He says in his notes: 'Just as a dream is situated in a suitably coloured atmosphere, so a concept, when it becomes a composition, needs to move in a fittingly coloured setting. There is obviously one particular colour attributed to some part of the picture which becomes a key and governs the other parts.' For Moreau colour has a symbolic as well as a structuring role in the work. He continues: 'All the figures, their arrangement in relation to one another, the landscape

or interior, which serves them as a background or horizon, their clothes, everything about them in fact, must serve to illuminate the general idea and wear its original colour, its livery so to speak.' He is involved with the central 'general idea' in art which again brings him into the Symbolist aesthetic with its key concept of 'the Idea'.

It is possible that Wagnerian theory also affected Moreau. Wagner's* *Gesamtkunstwerk* concept of an art which embraces all the other arts is akin to that which gives the operatic qualities to Moreau's works. The architectural settings are magnificent yet convey little sense of an exact period, therefore the characters can act symbolically and universally and in an excessive manner. Through extremes of sensuality they can be immortalized by their deaths and transcend the earthly flesh. So it is that purity in the form of an expressionless woman can rise on the blood of martyrs. She is the *Mystic Flower* (1890) growing in a rocky canyon from the heart of a lily and raising to heaven a flaming cross over the horde of dead or dying saints.

Perhaps the most beautiful paintings by Moreau are the water colours forming the illustrations to the fables of La Fontaine. An artist such as Moreau who had spent long hours studying plants and animals from life would find these subjects most acceptable. One such illustration called *The Peacock Complaining to Juno* allows Moreau to indulge in his favourite pose for a woman. Juno's long lissom body follows an arabesque so that she leans to the left with arms outstretched to the right and head turned sharply again to the left so that it is in profile. She thus forms an undulating diagonal across the page, floating in a perfect sky over a jewelled bay with a star above and a gorgeously vivid emerald, blue and gold peacock at her knees. Partially naked, she is Helen, Galatea, Semele – all Moreau's beautiful and innocent heroines in one.

The nearest work in terms of beauty in oils is Moreau's late large scale oil of *Jupiter and Semele* in 1895. The paint is so thick it becomes almost a relief sculpture and the god fills the canvas with his presence which is felt as powerful and all embracing; Semele, small and delicate lies across his knee.

After the death of his mother in 1884 Moreau made a journey to Belgium and Holland to study the mystical realism of the early Flemish primitives. He was then elected to the Académie des Beaux Arts in 1888 and three years later asked to take up teaching at the École des Beaux Arts where he had himself once studied. As a teacher he was much liked and admired by his pupils, many of whom later achieved considerable fame. Perhaps his most important is Matisse. Although Matisse's work whilst a student with Moreau in no way reflect his master's, he was encouraged to experiment with technique, to study widely and to develop his own personal sense of direction so that his endeavours could attain increasing strength and originality. At times akin to the Englishman Burne-Jones*, particularly of *King Cophetua and the Beggar Maid*, Moreau's real inheritors are the North European Symbolists such as Khnopff, Klimt* and Böcklin*.

Pat Turner

See: J. Paladilhe, J. Pierre, *Gustave Moreau* (1972); P.-L. Mathieu, *Gustave Moreau* (trans. 1977). Catalogue Raisonné of finished works, J. Rewald, *Redon, Moreau, Bresdin* (1962).

320
MORELLI, Giovanni 1816–91

Italian connoisseur

Giovanni Morelli was a pioneer of one aspect of connoisseurship, that of attribution. His apparent insistence upon the scientific nature of his theories was much criticized in his lifetime but his method of identifying the personal style of an artist was to be used in modified form by many art historians, most notably by Bernard Berenson whose paraphrase of Morelli's methods is outlined in his essay *Rudiments of Connoisseurship* (1902).

Morelli was born in Verona but grew up in Bergamo where his choice collection of paintings may be seen today. As a Protestant he had to seek his education outside Italy. He studied natural science and medicine in Switzerland and at the University of Munich where he mastered German, the language of his subsequent publications. He was never to practise medicine. From 1848 he was closely connected with the struggle to unify and liberate Italy and turned to a study of his country's art as a solace during those difficult years. He visited the most obscure Italian villages as well as the principal European galleries. His demanding public life (from 1861 he was deputy for Bergamo in the first Italian parliament and in 1873 he was made a senator) left him little time to write up his researches. He interested himself in the conservation of Italy's art treasures but privately communicated his passion for North Italian painting to English collectors like Sir Charles Eastlake and Sir A.H. Layard, finding and selling them Brescian and Bergamesque works of art.

From 1874 Morelli published a series of articles on Italian Renaissance paintings in the Borghese and Doria-Pamfili galleries in the *Zeitschrift für Bildende Kunst* under the anagrammatical pseudonym of Ivan Lermolieff. This was followed by a study of Italian paintings in German galleries. Their scope was broad: he sought to establish the artistic personality of each painter he discussed. His reattributions were dramatic: he identified the Dresden *Sleeping Venus* (previously called a copy of Titian by Sassoferrato) as a Giorgione. He established the chronology of Correggio's early ca-

reer. Forty-six paintings were renamed in the Dresden Gallery alone.

The theory which lay behind his reattributions is outlined in these articles later republished as *Kunstkritische Studien über Italienische Malerei* (1890). In a startling first chapter, 'Principles and Methods' (written in the form of a dialogue between the author, supposedly a youthful Russian, and an elderly Italian patriot), Morelli attacked the vagueness of current methods of attribution. He had scant regard for documentary evidence and believed that identification should be made on the basis of stylistic comparison. He held that an artist's personal 'signature' was best revealed in the way in which he painted minor details particularly hands, feet, draperies and landscape. Because such details were painted routinely Morelli believed that they were invariably executed idiosyncratically.

His detractors mocked the simplicity of his method pointing out that his system would be useless if applied to copies. There can be little doubt that the spectacular accuracy of his attributions was due not to a rigid application of his methods but to an ability to associate with the spirit of a painter and his school through a profound knowledge of his *oeuvre*, both paintings and sketches. Thus it may be argued that he arrived at his results through intuition rather than science. Perhaps his real innovations lay in his use of photographs to make stylistic comparisons and his realization of the importance of drawings as means of understanding an artist's style.

Tanya Harrod

Morelli's works include: *Die Werke italienische Meister in den Galetien von München, Dresden und Berlin. Ein kritischer Versuch* (1880, trans. *A Critical Essay on the Italian Paintings in the Galleries of Munich – Dresden – Berlin*, 1883); *Kunstkritische Studien über Italienische Malerei die Galerian Borghese und Doria-Pamfili in Rom* (1890, trans. *Italian Painters: Critical Studies of their Works*, 1892–3). See: Bernard Berenson, *The Study and Criticism of Italian Art* (1902); Max J. Friedlander, *On Art and Connoisseurship* (1942); E. Wind, *Art and Anarchy* (1963); Richard Wollheim, *On Art and the Mind* (1973).

321
MORGAN, Lewis Henry 1818–81

US ethnologist

'Morgan created the science of Anthropology,' said his biographer, Carl Resek. Some historians would dispute this, but during the 1860s and 1870s he was praised by such famous American historians as Henry Schoolcraft, Henry Adams*, Francis Parkman*, and many prominent British and continental intellectuals, among them Karl Marx* and Friedrich Engels*, who modified some of their own theories after reading Morgan's major work, *Ancient Society* (1877). After becoming enshrined in Marxist eschatology, Morgan's works became subject to remarkably polarized interpretations. Yet he was really only a bourgeois lawyer, financially successful enough to retire in early middle-age and devote himself to his ethnological researches on the American Indians – and certainly no kind of socialist.

L.H. Morgan was born near Aurora, New York, graduated from Union College, and practised law in Rochester. In his spare time, he undertook to present to the US government and the public his scientific descriptions of the customs of the neighbouring Seneca Iroquois Indians. In 1858, during a business trip to Marquette, Michigan, Morgan became interested in the Ojibwa Indians there who, although belonging to a language family different from the Iroquois, had a mode of designating kinsmen that was identical to that of the Iroquois and very different from that of Europeans. This was a system which Morgan called 'classificatory' because father's brothers were also called 'father' by an individual ('Ego') and mother's sisters also were 'mother' and the children were all 'brother' and 'sister' to Ego, and their children all became 'son' and 'daughter'. The European terminology, which seemed to Morgan to be more accurately genealogical, he therefore called the 'descriptive system'. When he discovered that still other American Indians, without apparent exception, also used the classificatory system, Morgan felt that he had found a means to trace the provenience of the Indians, perhaps to Asia. After much correspondence with missionaries and colonial officials in remote parts of the world, Morgan found that the Tamil, a Dravidian-speaking people of south India, had a kinship system identical to that of the Iroquois. But he did not allow this discovery to end his researches. The enormous bulk of data on the world's kinship systems that he had acquired over the years was eventually published as *Systems of Consanguinity and Affinity of the Human Family* (1870).

Later Morgan published his *Ancient Society*, which contained his final thoughts on the grand evolution of human society. Essentially, Morgan was a monogenesist in the theological argument against polygenesism (the theory of separate origins of the human races), and against the 'degradation theory' of man's fall from grace. In short, he argued for a theory of evolutionary mental-moral human progress from a lowly origin in savagery to barbarism and finally to civilization. This progress was charted by Morgan in terms of 'inventions and discoveries', the 'idea' of government, the 'idea' of the family, and finally the 'idea' of property. But he paid only lip service to the material inventions and discoveries; by far the dominant concern of the book is with the growth of institutions through ideas, and in

particular the development of moral ideas that led humanity from original sexual promiscuity through a stage of 'group marriage' (which accounted for the surviving 'classificatory' kinship systems in the primitive world); and from lack of government to 'democratical' institutions; and from primitive 'communism' in property to a brief immoral stage of feudalistic entailed hereditary estates, toward a society which would 'rise to mastery over property, and define the relations of the state to the property it protects.'

It was this message about property, and how it created the hated principle of aristocracy and privilege, that so impressed Marx and Engels. After the death of Marx, Engels published his own version of their joint appreciation of Morgan as *The Origin of the Family, Private Property and the State* (*Der Ursprung der Familie, des Privatigenthums und des Staates*, 1884).

Morgan's theory of primitive kinship systems was severely criticized in his own time by the Scottish ethnologist, John C. McLennan, who considered classificatory kinship terminologies to be not of genealogical relevance at all, but as designating social status in general and therefore not directly related to such imaginary historical reconstructions as 'group marriage'.

Except among Marxists, Morgan's work hung fire until the advent of academic cultural anthropology in the USA in the twentieth century under the leadership of Franz Boas, an anti-evolutionist. Morgan was criticized thereafter by foremost students of Boas, A.L. Kroeber and particularly by Robert Lowie in his *Primitive Society* (1920). Finally, American, British and French ethnologists seem to have found little of intellectual value in Morgan, and little to be said favourably of any other theories of cultural or social evolution.

In more recent years, the American ethnologist Leslie A. White, in several works, has attempted to revitalize Morgan and cultural evolutionism, and the British social anthropologist leader, Meyer Fortes, has published a favourable appraisal of Morgan's scientific 'structuralism' in his *Kinship and the Social Order* (1969). In the USSR and other communist nations and among Marxists elsewhere, ethnologists have remained loyal to the spirit, if not always the letter, of Morgan's works. It is indeed a remarkable episode in the intellectual-scientific history of Western thought that such totally opposite interpretations should exist about a man who would have remained rather insignificant to us today but for the notice he received from Engels and Marx.

Elman Service

Morgan's other major works are *League of the Ho-de-no-sau-nee, or Iroquois* (1851) and *Houses and House Life of the American Aborigines* (1881). Morgan's main biography is Carl Resek, *Lewis Henry Morgan: American Scholar* (1960). See also Bernhard J. Stern, *Lewis Henry Morgan, Social Evolutionist* (1931), and Leslie A. White, *Pioneers in American Anthropology: The Bandelier-*

Morgan Letters, 1873–1883 (1940). The major criticisms of Morgan are by Lowie, as cited above and also in his *History of Ethnological Theory* (1937). McLennan's criticisms are best found in his collection of articles, *Studies in Ancient History* (1886).

322
MÖRIKE, Eduard 1804–74

German poet

A relatively slender literary output and an uneventful provincial life notwithstanding, Mörike is important as more than merely the author of texts set to music by Hugo Wolf*. Born in Ludwigsburg, near Stuttgart, he seldom moved beyond the confines of his native Swabia: after theological studies in Urach and Tübingen, he held a number of curateships in local villages (becoming known, eventually, as 'the oldest curate in Württemberg') and was finally appointed vicar of the small town of Cleversulzbach in 1834. Pastoral duties were not to his liking; ill health and lethargy afflicted him and he resigned his post after only nine years of service. Some years later (1851) he married and accepted a post as lecturer in literature at a girl's school in Stuttgart; but the marriage was in many ways unhappy and Mörike was in constant financial difficulties. He was not unknown during his lifetime: a number of distinguished contemporaries (including Turgenev*) admired his work and visited him; but his circumstances were too restricted for him to be able to participate in the broader movements of Nineteenth-century European culture.

Yet Mörike's poetry, limited though it be in thematic scope, cannot with any justice be described as escapist or even, indeed, as minor. In one of his best-known short poems, 'Gebet' ('Prayer'), the speaker prays that God grant him a state of emotional temperateness between the extremes of joy and sorrow: but in Mörike's best work, the reader is aware of the precariousness of this emotional balance. The poems concerned with love, for instance, dwell more readily on impermanence and pain than on requital; nature, whatever pleasure it may impart, tends to exclude the onlooker, gently impressing upon him the unhappy fact of his otherness, or, as in 'Die Schöne Buche' ('The lovely Beech-tree'), subduing his human awareness with sinister, panic silence; death and transience urge the fact of their inevitability even amidst the most harmless Biedermeier surroundings. A recurrent theme of Mörike's is that of transition: the opening poem in his collection *Gedichte* (1838, but frequently reprinted during his lifetime with additions and omissions) is entitled 'An einem Wintermorgen vor Sonnenaufgang' ('On a winter morning before dawn') and evokes that state of mental and emotional flux that accompanies the gradual coming of daylight. The poem moves, though not without detours and relapses, from passive introspection to active acceptance: and, early though it be (Mörike wrote it at the age of twenty-one), it stands appropriately as prelude to his poetic work as a whole in its combination of delicacy and assurance: the firm but undistorting registration of the subtle fluidity of consciousness.

Mörike's work ranges from folksong simplicity to the formal sophistication of the classical hexameter (he was well read in Greek and Latin poetry and a prolific translator). He admired Goethe* and Hölderlin*, but possessed neither the range of the one nor the lofty concentration of the other: to a greater extent than theirs, his poetry is rooted in the local, the immediate – rooted, but not confined. In one of his greatest poems, 'Auf eine Christblume' ('On a Christmas Rose', 1841), the discovery in a churchyard of the rare, winter-blooming flower occasions a meditation in which time, death, transcendence, Christian and pagan elements, presence and mystery are woven together in a verbal net which is delicate to the point of weightlessness, yet profoundly actual in a way that far removes it from any charge of preciosity. And this is true of all Mörike's finest poetry: that the gentle subtlety of his lyricism is continuous with, not opposed to, or removed from, the grain of living experience.

Mörike's prose writings, including the *Bildungsroman*, *Maler Nolten* ('Nolten the Painter', 1832, but extensively rewritten during the poet's latter years), are now, with one exception, little read except by specialists. The exception is the novella *Mozart's Journey to Prague* (*Mozart auf der Reise nach Prag*, 1856 trans. 1957). The plot of this work is slight: Mozart and his wife Constanze, on their way to Prague for the première of *Don Giovanni*, spend the day at the home of a sympathetic aristocratic family. The day passes in a happy (but authorially carefully structured) *mélange* of genial conversation, music and anecdote; but perceptible beneath the general cheerfulness is a sombre undercurrent which surfaces in the passage where Mozart plays to the assembled company the final scene of his new opera: the fateful interview between the implacable Commendatore and the defiantly unregenerate Don Giovanni. Next morning the composer and his wife depart; but the daughter of the house, filled with the melancholy conviction that the earth cannot sustain such genius for long, finds her mood confirmed by a poem (allegedly a Bohemian folksong) which she happens to find. Images of youth and fruition – a young fir-tree, a rose-branch, two grazing colts – unconsciously affirm the coming death (of Mozart and of all men) at whose ceremonies they will assist. The colts, when fully grown,

. . . werden schrittweis gehn
Mit deiner Leiche,

Vielleicht, vielleicht noch eh'
An ihren Hufen
Das Eisen los wird,
Das ich blitzen sehe.

(will go step by step/with your corpse;/perhaps, perhaps even before/from their hooves/the shoe is loosened/which I see flashing.)

Much of Mörike's work – and there is no denying the existence of stretches of whimsy or cosy rusticity – may, to modern taste, seem redundant, but the lyrical compression, the combination of lightness and inexorability in such poems as this retains its full power and ensures its permanence.

Corbet Stewart

See: Mörike, *Sämtliche Gedichte* (1975). See also: Benno von Wiese, *Eduard Mörike* (1950); Margaret Mare, *Eduard Mörike, the Man and the Poet* (1957).

323
MORRIS, William 1834–96

British writer and designer

As poet, translator, painter, designer, craftsman, socialist, Morris has rightly been described as a pivotal figure of his age. A rebel against his own time, he was yet deeply of his time, deeply Victorian, and this is only one of the many fertile paradoxes that make his manifold activity so fascinating.

Morris was born into a wealthy bourgeois family (enriched by speculation in copper) which ensured him a handsome private income. In 1853 he went up to Oxford and formed a lasting friendship with the future painter Burne-Jones*. Their High Church zeal was soon ousted by literature (Tennyson's* Arthurian legends, medieval chronicles and romances), then, after a visit to the gothic cathedrals of France and Belgium, by art and architecture. Deeply impressed by Carlyle* and Ruskin* – especially the latter's *Stones of Venice*, in which gothic architecture is presented as the supreme example of creative joy in labour under a harmonious, pre-commercial social order – they conceived the ideal of a quasi-medieval fraternity, only then to discover the existence of the nascent Pre-Raphaelite Brotherhood. In 1856 Morris began work for the architect G.E. Street, but was seduced away from architecture to painting by D.G. Rossetti*. In 1858 a first volume of verse, *The Defence of Guenevere*, was published. Morris's artistic interests extended further into the field of practical designing and in 1861 he founded the 'Firm' (Morris, Marshall, Faulkner & Co., later to become Morris & Co.) which, with help from Burne-Jones and others, would produce fine quality stained-glass, furniture, wallpaper, chintzes, tiles, carpets and tapestries, and in which Morris, with Philip Webb, was to take a major designing role.

1867 saw a first long epic poem, *The Life and Death of Jason*, followed in 1868 by the first volume of the massive *Earthly Paradise*. A period of pessimism – due in part to the failure of his marriage with the Pre-Raphaelite beauty Jane Burden – was countered by the discovery of Norse literature: Morris found its vigorous stoicism a good corrective to 'the maundering side of medievalism'. Not only did he publish 'translations' of Icelandic sagas but also his own *Sigurd the Volsung* (1876), probably his most effective epic.

In 1877 Morris, enraged by examples of inept restoration, founded 'Anti-Scrape' (Society for the Protection of Ancient Buildings); subsequently he was to help found the Art Workers' Guild and, through his lectures on the 'lesser arts' in the seventies and eighties, to inspire not only the Arts and Crafts movement but the socialist movement as well. For Morris was drawn increasingly into political activity as a necessary extension of his ethical-aesthetic vision. Disillusioned by the opportunism of the Liberals, he joined the Democratic Federation in 1883 but left the following year to found the Socialist League, dedicated to safeguarding the pure principles of socialism. He was to give generously of his income and his energy to the movement. Active in street demonstrations, he also edited the periodical *Commonweal* and published in 1885, after his *Chants for Socialists*, the political poem *The Pilgrims of Hope*. 1886 saw the historical prose romance *The Dream of John Ball*, based on the peasant revolt of 1381; 1888 the collection of lectures *Signs of Change*. The romance *The House of the Wolfings* (1888), like *The Roots of the Mountains* (1889), portrays struggles against tyranny in the fifth century, whilst the important utopian romance *News from Nowhere* (1890) embodies much of Morris's nostalgia, aspiration and vision in the dream of a harmonious, post-revolutionary but curiously neo-medieval England of the twenty-first century. That same year, Morris's Hammersmith Branch split off from the Socialist League, which had become dominated by anarchists. His final years were as creative as ever: in 1891 he founded the Kelmscott Press, to resurrect the art of fine printing, and subsequently published the unhistorical romances *The Wood beyond the World* (1894), *The Well at the World's End* (1896) and, posthumously, *The Water of the Wondrous Isle* and *The Sundering Flood* (1897).

If at first one is struck by the variety of Morris's activities, in the end it is the deeply felt moral unity beneath them that ensures his stature. A true Victorian rebel against commercial and industrial civilization in the lineage of Carlyle and Ruskin, he had a keener historical understanding than either. It is said that he sought to reconcile Ruskin and Marx*: certainly his vision begins with architecture and the vital question of the nature of work, and is completed and enriched by the insight into commercialism and the historical process he derived from his reading of *Capital*. This saved him from the repressive work-ethic of Carlyle and the equally repressive neo-feudal authoritarianism of Ruskin's late writings. His understanding is best expressed in the lectures on art and society: 'The Art of the People', 'How we live and how we might live', 'The Aims of Art', 'A Factory as it might be', etc. Always he returns to his ideal of art 'made by the people and for the people, a joy to the maker and the user' – something that can never be achieved in an inorganic society founded on competition and the search for profit.

Examining Morris's achievement in the individual spheres of his work, we realize that his greatness lies in no particular field *per se*: in each there are contradictions and inadequacies, though also evidence of his influence on succeeding generations. The activities of the Firm offer clear examples of paradox, not least that of a capitalist (albeit paternalistic) enterprise run by an ardent socialist. Morris's own designs, notably for wallpaper and textiles, have kept an astonishing freshness, but the fact remains that his gift was especially for repeating patterns which demanded of the printer a monotonous handwork remote from his ideal of joyous, creative labour. Ironically, these patterns are admirably suited to machine-production, whereas in theory Morris wanted to give precedence to handicrafts over industrial methods. While in his writings he railed against the division of labour, the Firm practised it, often separating designer and 'hand'. His ideal was 'simplicity of life begetting simplicity of taste', but he and his collaborators were, willy-nilly, under the influence of Victorian taste, and the Firm's interiors were rich and elaborate (though a development towards lightness and relative simplicity is apparent in later work).

Little of what the Firm practised was wholly original – the architect and designer Pugin* had preceded them in many fields, and the medieval revival was very much a feature of the age – but the overriding concern was for quality of design and execution. Throughout, the enemy is clear: 'It is a shoddy age. Shoddy is king. From the statesman to the shoemaker, all is shoddy.' But this gives rise to another paradox: quality of this order was expensive, and for all Morris's democratic principles, his products were available only to the privileged few.

Whilst he never designed a building, his influence on the approach to architecture and planning is real through his writings. He was a pioneer of environmentalism in his insistence on the need to clean the land of pollution, his concern for a more organic environment safeguarding the ideal of community. On industrial architecture and the whole concept of the workplace he had much of lasting importance to say, arguing the need for garden factories combining, in an ethical fusion vital for Morris, daily work with culture and education.

If Morris painted little, finding he had no gift for human figures (his genius in the visual arts was above all for the stylization of natural forms, their transformation into pattern), on the other hand he wrote at enormous length, and his poetry suffers from this prolixity. His verse lies firmly within the Romantic tradition, and is severely limited by it, even though as a thinker and activist he was able to step beyond Romanticism. This is especially apparent in late committed verse, *Chants for Socialists* and *The Pilgrims of Hope*, where the Romantic diction can conflict with the revolutionary subject-matter. His own literary tastes were inflexibly Romantic, and despite the blood and guts in some of his epics, his mode is not the realist one that dominated literature in the second half of the century. His first verse was promising: *The Defence of Guenevere* expresses, through the medieval subject, a sense of loss and nostalgia captured in the hesitant, flexible rhythm. This Keats*-like quality will later give way to the monotony of rhythmic competence; already in *The Earthly Paradise* the pessimistic nostalgia is diluted in verbiage. More positive in tone, *Sigurd* wields greater force with its stoic theme of steadfast courage in the face of eternal recurrence. The prose romances are also frequently hampered by ornamental archaic diction, the final ones being especially self-indulgent and largely forgotten, though an age that enthuses over Tolkien may well discover a taste for them. However, the best of the romances, *John Ball* and *News from Nowhere*, appear as something more than escapism into remote past or imagined future; for they embody a tension between reality and dream, thanks to the presence within the work of a narrator-dreamer who, belonging to the modern world, can movingly contrast with its inadequacies his vision of apocalyptic change or of the perfect community. Thus a work like *News* is not merely a charming fantasy but a deeply committed work which forces recognition of Morris's political importance generally. Though acknowledging that his work was 'the embodiment of dreams in one form or another', he was anxious that the new socialist theories should not be 'left adrift on the barren shore of Utopianism'. Yet he had little talent for politicking, and the intransigence of the Socialist League tended to cut it off from the 'wearisome shilly-shally of parliamentary politics'. He feared and denounced the tendency for socialism to sink into compromise and palliatory reform, offensive to his total ethical vision. Only in his final years, uncompromisingly styling himself a communist, did he come to accept the educative value of local struggles, whilst always insisting that these should be catalysts for total change. Engels* scorned Morris, yet in the end this is a judgement on Engels' own narrow, deterministic outlook. A socialism that can comprehend Morris – in all his variety and all his unity

– is more open and human than one that cannot. If vision is now recognized as 'the education of desire' then not only his best work in particular, but above all the example of the man's thought and activity as a whole, have almost unequalled force in this respect.

David Meakin

See: E.P. Thompson, *William Morris: Romantic to Revolutionary* (1967); P. Henderson, *William Morris: His Life, Work and Friends* (1967); P. Thompson, *The Life and Work of William Morris* (1967); I. Bradley, *William Morris and his World* (1978); R. Watkinson, *William Morris as Designer* (1967).

324

MORSE, Samuel Finlay Breese 1791–1872

US inventor and artist

Samuel Morse is an example of a fairly rare kind of man, a man who changed his career in his mid-forties. Up to that time Morse was known to his friends and acquaintances as a painter of miniatures and portraits; a painter in some demand, for he painted Lafayette, James Fenimore Cooper* and W.C. Bryant*. After that time Morse's energies were increasingly invested in his great project the 'electric telegraph', but it was not until 1844 – when Morse was fifty-three – that he became, in the eyes of the public, Morse 'the inventor'. Eventually Morse became extremely rich as a result of the invention which bears his name. He came to be a national institution, with a mansion at Poughkeepsie, and a generous disposition, – which led to donations to Vassar, Yale and many other worthy causes. He died at the age of eighty in his brownstone house, 5 West 22nd Street, New York.

Today 'Morse' is the name of a code, still in use in maritime communication, though no longer used in conveying telegrams. But his code was only one aspect of the system Morse devised: a system which, for fifty years, provided the world with a wealth of instant communications of a kind previous generations had hardly dreamt of. The transformation of the world from a community dependent on communicating painfully slowly by letter to a community in which information circulated instantaneously occurred as a result of Morse's work. Later the tele*phone* took over. It was more convenient, natural, expressive; but the instantaneity established by the telegraph was already an accepted expectation.

Morse was born on 27 April 1791 in Charlestown, Massachusetts. After attending Phillips College, Andover – where his academic record was none too good – he went to Yale College, graduating in 1810. Morse was an individualist, his interests highly selective: he was fascinated by painting, design, electricity, gadgets.

While at Yale he began to develop a distinctive talent in painting miniature portraits. This led to the proposal that he should accompany his tutor, Washington Allston, and his wife, on a trip to England. Morse stayed in England with the Allstons until 1815, and it was during this period that he began to make his name as a painter. His large canvases of classical themes, such as Jupiter and Hercules, attracted a good deal of admiration, but, back in the United States in 1815, Morse found that he could not sell such paintings to the American public. Morse's only means of livelihood in painting was to concentrate on portraits.

To gain commissions Morse had to travel from area to area, but his reputation grew, and after 1823 he was able to settle in New York. He did not spend all his time in the studio however – his fascination with gadgets developed too. In 1817 he patented (with his brother) a piston-pump for fire engines, and in 1823 it was discovered that a marble-cutting machine he had invented infringed a patent. About this time, also, Morse developed a theory of colour. In 1825 he founded a society, which became, in 1826, the National Academy of Design. Morse was its first president, a position which he held until 1845. Just as his life was settling down, Morse's family began to disintegrate: he lost his wife in 1825, his father in 1826 and his mother in 1828. In 1829 Morse set sail for Europe. It was the turning-point in his life. He left New York with a circle of influential, intellectual artistic and wealthy friends, a painter of rising reputation and connection. He returned to New York (in 1832) as a prospective inventor, consumed with the possibilities of an exciting design idea, that of sending messages by electricity.

Morse's conversion from artist to inventor occurred on the return voyage, on the *Sully*. Morse was present at a dinner conversation in which Dr Charles Jackson expounded some recent developments in electricity and in particular the phenomenon of the electromagnet, discovered by William Sturgeon in 1824. Afterwards Dr Jackson demonstrated apparatus. Suddenly Morse realized that the phenomenon of electromagnetism could be put to use in communications. He remarked, 'If the presence of electricity can be made visible in any part of the circuit, I see no reason why intelligence cannot be transmitted instantaneously by electricity.' In a state of high excitement Morse began sketching out a system based on the idea, and it is the notebook Morse filled on board the sailing ship *Sully* that finally establishes Morse's priority to the invention.

Morse was only one of many people who conceived the general idea of sending messages by means of electric current at about this time: indeed such an idea had already been mooted before 1800. The raw idea, however, was beset with major snags. First, the cost of wire was high. A lot of wire would be needed, and it had to be wire of a high degree of purity, in order to achieve a suitably low resistance. Furthermore, *two* wires seemed to be required, one to take the message to its distant destination, and the other to complete the circuit. Second, a very large source of electrical power seemed to be needed, to overcome the residual resistance of even the best wire. It was easy to send a message across a room, or even across a street, but when it came to sending messages for many miles, the power needed would be altogether a different matter. Third, the 'messages' which could be sent by means of the presence of current in a wire seemed to be limited to a single gesture, like the black sail of Greek legend, or the lighting of the Armada beacons. In each case the 'information content' of the message was what we call nowadays a single *bit*: the sail was black or white; the beacon was lit or unlit; the current was *on* or *off*.

Morse began by solving the second and third problems. The key to Morse's success was his invention of the electromagnetic *relay*. This was a delicately sprung switch which was operated by an electromagnet. When a weak current flowed through the electromagnet its magnetic 'pull' closed a switch – a switch in a different, independent circuit. This was crucial. It meant that a feeble current could be made to switch-in a fresh power source: thus, as it were, instantly replenishing the vigour of the message. Instead of using a single, massive power source at the end of the line, it was possible to incorporate a number of 'Relay Stations' along the line, each contributing only a modest power input. It was also possible to introduce branch lines.

The key to the problem of information content was the idea of signalling by means of short and long bursts of current, followed and spaced by gaps, to punctuate the message. Morse's first working model was probably completed in 1835, but it was not until 1837 that Morse gave a demonstration of his equipment at the City University of New York, where he was by now Professor of Painting and Sculpture.

Between 1837 and 1844 when Morse's system was finally triumphantly demonstrated, he had to put up with many vicissitudes. Congress at first refused to provide financial backing. Morse reduced himself almost to penury. Two design changes, however, sealed the success of Morse's system. He discovered that it was possible to use but a single wire, the 'Earth' being used to complete the circuit. (This was a discovery of Steinheil's in Europe.) His friend Joseph Henry suggested hanging the wire from poles, which solved at a stroke the troublesome problem of insulation. So it was that on 24 May 1844 Morse sent the first historic message from Washington to Baltimore, a distance of 37 miles: 'What God has wrought!'

Why Morse should have succeeded, so improbably, where others failed may need some explanation. Morse was a man of great ability, but he did not try to do it all himself: he used the ideas of others too. It was, in the end, however, the extraordinary range of Morse's social connection which made the difference. He had close contacts in the arts, in commerce, Congress, the universities. Morse was a multi-talented man whose final talent was to be able to mobilize a great circle of friends to give the invention the initial quantum of credibility which it needed to get it going.

Christopher Ormell

See: Carleton Mabee, *The American Leonardo: A life of Samuel F.B. Morse* (1943); Oliver W. Larkin, *Samuel F.B. Morse and American Democratic Art* (1954); Marshall B. Davidson, 'What Samuel Wrought', in *American Heritage* vol. 12, 12–31 (1961).

325
MOSCA, Gaetano 1858–1941

Italian political writer

Mosca was for a while a civil servant, taught constitutional law and history of political doctrines in Palermo, Turin and Rome, was a Liberal-Conservative member of parliament, 1908–18, under-secretary for the colonies, 1914–16, and, in 1918, was made a senator for life. He also wrote for newspapers but gradually gave it up towards the end of the 1920s when the Fascists were depriving the press of independence. Although he began as a critic of the democratic ideology and institutions, in his later years he came to regard the parliamentary government as the least defective. None the less, he made only one speech against Mussolini, and remained silent thereafter while retaining his seat in the senate. He never wrote anything either for or against the Fascists although he did insert incidental remarks on the virtues of representative government into his book and articles on the history of political ideas which were his only products during the Fascist era.

Mosca's first book (*Teorica dei Governi*, 'Theory of Government', 1887) was a kind of survey of world history and of the contemporary scene, the aim of which was to show that all states had or have a ruling class. Though in a more attenuated form than Vilfredo Pareto, he accepts the view of Marx* and Engels* about the ubiquity of divisions and conflicts between the classes but rejects their idea that these might be eliminated: a ruling class may be overthrown but will only be replaced by another. This is more or less the same idea as Pareto's theory of circulation of elites. There was a long dispute between them about priority, but it seems that they have arrived at very similar conclusions independently and more or less simultaneously. Mosca objected to the term 'elite' on the ground that it implies excellence or superiority whereas in reality many ruling classes were thoroughly incompetent or wicked. They agree that the fate of the nations depends above all on the quality of their ruling classes, but Pareto thinks that this quality depends on the selection of (presumably genetically determined) psychological types whereas Mosca gives greater weight to moral information.

Mosca looks at political systems as oscillating in two dimensions between two sets of polar alternatives which he called principles: one concerns the composition of the ruling class and the other the manner of governing. The composition of the ruling class may be based on inheritance (that is, 'the aristocratic principle' in his terminology) or on the open entry for talented individuals from the lower classes, which he calls 'the democratic principle'. The rulers may be inclined and obliged by the constitution to heed the wishes of the ruled or they may disregard and overrule them. In Mosca's terminology the first type of government is based on the liberal principle, while the second on the authoritarian principle. It must be noted that what he calls 'the liberal principle' is what most people nowadays would call 'the democratic principle'. Following Aristotle and Polybius, Mosca thinks that the best political system is a mixed one where none of the said principles is pushed to the extreme. However, they spoke only of a golden mean between democracy, oligarchy and monarchy – which Mosca reinterprets as a balance between the liberal and authoritarian principles. In addition, he extends the idea of balance to the composition of the ruling class. A hereditary closure of the ruling class produces ossification but a certain degree of closure may be beneficial according to him, because it dampens the intensity of the struggle for power and permits a transmission of traditions and skills which may have considerable value.

Another crucial point in Mosca's view of history and politics is his widening of Montesquieu's theory of the division of power between the independent legislative, executive and judicial authority as a condition of freedom. Mosca finds it too legalistic and likely to remain or become a mere piece of paper unless it rests upon a division of social forces. He does not define 'social forces' but from the examples he gives we can see that he is thinking of social classes as well as institutions like the church, the bureaucracy or the army. Even more important than the division indicated by Montesquieu is the division between the political, economic and spiritual powers. On the basis of this theory he made a remarkable prediction in 1902 (in the article 'Inchiesta sul Socialismo', reprinted in *Cio che la Storia Potrebbe Insegnare*, 'What History Could Teach Us') of the results of an application of the Marxist doctrine. Assuming that it would entail a fusion between the political, economic and spiritual powers, he was able to forecast the main features of Stalinism.

Mosca was completely uninterested in methodology and philosophy. He simply believed that by studying history and observing people we can discover regularities in social processes; and that this knowledge would enable us to explain many phenomena and understand what was possible and desirable. He arrives at his generalizations by rough and ready induction without attempting any systematic confrontation of the thesis with the data. Thus he never discusses the tricky question of the boundaries of the ruling class (or 'the political class' in his terminology) although he talks about it all the time. None the less, his main work, *Elementi de Scienza Politica* ('Elements of Political Science', vol. I, 1895, rev. 1923; vol. II, 1923), remains the most comprehensive treatise on politics, unsurpassed in the range of problems, subtlety and originality. For example, Mosca was the first writer to study civil-military relations from a comparative viewpoint. One of the many illuminating rule-of-thumb generalizations which he puts forth is his 'law of the alloy', according to which an ideology or doctrine can become a political force only if it appeals to the noble and the base motives at the same time.

Mosca can be described as either a realist or a pessimist. He believed that oppression and strife were the rule, while a higher civilization was very fragile. Extreme democracy and authoritarianism appeared to him as equally dangerous. Although he called himself a liberal, he thought that 'freedom' was a chimerical notion and that the only attainable ideal was 'juridical defence', by which he meant the rule of law and the checks on arbitrary exercise of power. His practical preoccupations are surprisingly topical today: he thought that the greatest dangers to the liberal political system stemmed from the growth of the power of the bureaucracy and of the unions – especially of the unions of public employees.

Both volumes of *Elementi de Scienza Politica* were reprinted in 1939 with a few additional footnotes by the author. *Teorica dei Governi* (an astoundingly erudite book for an author who was only twenty-five), together with various shorter works and the short reflections published posthumously, are reprinted in *Cio Che la Storia Potrebbe Insegnare* (1958). Other articles from journals are reprinted in the volume *Partiti e Sindicati Nella Crisi del Regime Parlamentare* ('Parties and Trade Unions in the Crises of Parliamentary Rule', 1949). Articles from newspapers are reprinted in the volume *Il Tramonto dello Stato Liberale* ('The Decline of the Liberal State', 1971), each with a useful introduction by Antonio Lombardo. *The Ruling Class* (1939) is a slightly abridged and rearranged translation of *Elementi* with a scholarly introduction by Arthur Livingstone. Mosca's last book was *Storia delle Dottrine Politiche*, ('History of Political Doctrines') based on his yearly lectures on history of political institutions and ideas at the University of Rome. It was published in 1933 and reprinted with a few footnotes in 1939. The last chapter, 'La Teoria della Classe Politica', is Mosca's summary of his own work. It is worth noting that Mussolini's censors did not veto the penultimate chapter which contains a refutation of the racist theories of history.

Stanislav Andreski

See: James H. Meisel, *Myth of the Ruling Class: Gaetano Mosca and the Elite* (1958).

326
MURRAY, Sir James 1837–1915

British lexicographer

Sir James Murray was the founding father of scientific lexicography. He established the principles and set in motion the prodigious labours that produced *The Oxford English Dictionary* (1884–1928) over fifty years. He did not live to see it completed, but more than half of it was produced under his personal editorship. The *Dictionary* is still the only comprehensive historical dictionary in the world; and many of the principles and methods invented by Murray are still followed by his epigoni.

Murray was born in 1837, the son of the village tailor of Denholm, near Hawick, in the Borders. He was a precocious boy, fascinated by the local dialects and all varieties of language. He left school when he was fourteen, and took casual jobs on neighbouring farms while continuing to educate himself. He was appointed an assistant master at Hawick United School, and became the Border Aristotle in pursuit of antiquities, phonetics and languages. He moved to London and took a job as a bank clerk in a vain attempt to save the health of his first wife.

He continued his studies in his spare time until he must have been the most learned bank clerk in history. Incredibly, in view of his lack of academic qualifications, he was invited to read papers to the Philological Society; he edited a volume for the Early English Text Society; and he published a treatise on the *Dialect of the Southern Counties of Scotland* (1873). He established his reputation as a professional philologist by his article on the English language in the *Encyclopaedia Britannica*.

To make more time for study he returned to schoolmastering, this time at Mill Hill. While there he was appointed editor of *The Oxford English Dictionary* in 1879. It was agreed that the work should take ten years. In fact it took fifty. Murray built a scriptorium at Mill Hill, which served as a model for the corrugated-iron shed he built in his back garden up the Banbury Road when he removed, slip and slippage, to Oxford. From these improbable cottage-industry erections, with a few assistants, mainly some of his eleven children with Anglo-Saxon names, he devised the great engine of research that published the greatest dictionary of modern times.

The idea of a completely new English dictionary was conceived and the collection of materials started in 1857. The purpose was to produce for the first time a dictionary that showed the history of words and families of words, and to record the changes of form and sense that words had historically passed through. The original title was *A New English Dictionary on Historical Principles*. Its first editors were Herbert Coleridge and Dr F.J. Furnivall, but their work consisted only of collection of illustrative quotations and other materials.

When Murray took over, that disorganized enthusiast Dr Furnivall sent him some ton and three-quarters of materials that had accumulated under his roof. Murray organized the material and procured much more; he maintained the enthusiam of more than 800 voluntary readers; and he set in motion the preparation of material for the press and its publication.

In addition to the innovation of tracing the history of words from their earliest appearance, the dictionary illustrated each change with dated quotations. It listed and defined all recorded English words from the seventh century to the twentieth. It gave etymologies and pronunciations for the first time determined professionally by modern scholarship. The *Dictionary* contains 414,825 headwords. There are 1,827,306 quotations to illustrate them. The apparently simple little word *set*, for example, was given more than twenty-two large pages of three columns each.

Although he was personally responsible for only half of the *Dictionary* (A-D, H-K, O, P, T) Murray was its chief creator, trained his successors, and laid down the plan and the scope. The first fascicle or section, *A-Ant*, was published in 1884; the other fascicles followed in majestic procession until *Wh-Wo* was the last published in 1928.

The labours were much greater than anyone had calculated. The remuneration was mean. Academic and national recognition came shamefully late: until Murray proved otherwise, lexicographers had been considered artisans, not scholars. The process that Murray invented of recording the history of a language in its words continues with *Supplements* to *The Oxford English Dictionary* and other historical dictionaries in other languages.

Philip Howard

See: Frederick James Furnivall, *A Volume of Personal Record* (1911); Lady Murray, *The Making of a Civil Servant* (Sir Oswyn Murray) (1940); K.M. Elizabeth Murray, *Caught in the Web of Words* (1977).

327
MUSSET, (Louis-Charles-) Alfred de 1810–57

French writer

It is tempting to see the life of Alfred de Musset as a chronicle of wasted opportunity and squandered talents; if once his works seemed to assure him a privileged place among French Romantic authors, criticism has in recent years tended more and more to question the validity of many of them. Of aristocratic stock, like Lamartine* and Vigny*, Musset was born in 1810. This meant that when, after a cosseted childhood and successful, if not particularly happy, schooldays, Musset first made his appearance in literary circles, he found himself in the company of a number of writers half a generation older who had already made something of a reputation and were conscious of their role in bringing Romanticism to the fore in France. Musset was made welcome in Charles Nodier's salon at the Bibliothèque de l'Arsenal, and though Hugo* was instinctively apprehensive about a potential rival, he too was glad to invite the young man to his receptions in his house in the rue Notre-Dame-des-Champs. A strikingly handsome figure, dandified and pleasure-loving, Musset created a great impression, and he appeared to all to possess the Romantic temperament to the full. He hastened to demonstrate that this was so. In 1828 he published a free translation of De Quincey's* *Confessions of an Opium Eater*, and early in 1830 appeared his *Tales from Spain and Italy* (*Contes d'Espagne et d'Italie*). This collection of tales and lyrics, which owes something to Byron* but more to Hugo, relishes its Romantic clichés as if they were newly coined. Even in its day it was not taken entirely seriously while the versification, which struck some as daring, seemed slack or absurd to others.

In 1831, again following in Hugo's footsteps, Musset thought of showing his paces in the theatre. But *The Venetian Night* (*La Nuit vénitienne*) was a resounding failure, and though Musset was to continue to write plays he did not again seek to have them performed. In June 1833 Musset first met George Sand*, a prolific novelist of tempestuous temperament. The relationship between them developed rapidly, the lovers spending some months together in Venice in the winter of 1833–4. Soon, however, the liaison broke up, despite various attempts at reconciliation. These events occupy a central position in any study of Musset. They appear to have been the experience which, though it certainly did not initiate Musset's tendency to temperamental instability, certainly confirmed it irrevocably, shaking his capacity to cope with life and exacerbating a habit of morbid self-pity. It was no doubt in an effort to exorcize the demon that Musset produced an account of his emotional life in *The Confession of a child of this century* (*La Confession d'un enfant du siècle*), first published

in its entirety in 1836. The writing of the book gave him, however, no real relief. The title with its overt attempt to generalize the problem and put the blame for personal difficulties on historical and social factors also points up Musset's own sense of his continuing immaturity.

Though Musset shrank from permitting performances of his works after the failure of *The Venetian Night*, dramatic expression still attracted him. Between 1832 and 1836 he wrote a number of plays in a variety of forms, and they have come to be appreciated as the most accomplished and the most poignant examples of French Romantic drama. As if to emphasize that these texts were intended for reading only, Musset chose for two volumes of his collected plays the title of *Armchair theatre* (*Un Spectacle dans un fauteuil*). The dramas of Hugo and Dumas *père** which stirred the theatre-going public in the 1820s and 1830s are full of boisterous melodramatic action, heavy local colour and ranting grandiloquence. By contrast, Musset, freed from the material considerations of stagecraft as understood in Paris in the earlier part of the nineteenth century, was able to devote all his attention to situation, character and dialogue, preferring supple prose to the Alexandrine as his medium. One of his dramatic modes is exemplified by *Love's no laughing matter* (*On ne badine pas avec l'amour*) of 1834. Ever since the seventeenth century there had been something of a social tradition of taking proverbs and illustrating them in amusing dramatic scenes. Musset adapts this fragile form and develops it, first adding a vein of rich humour, then presenting an affecting tragedy as the lovers part. In a setting as entrancingly artificial as any comedy of Marivaux's and often on the very verge of sentimentality, the impact of *Love's no laughing matter* is all the more powerful because in a work of this sort we are never quite prepared for great emotional intensity. Another facet of Musset's dramatic style is represented by *Lorenzaccio*, also of 1834. In it Musset transforms the youthful Lorenzo de Medici who longed to rid his beloved Florence of a vile despot, his cousin Alessandro, into an archetypal Romantic character. Possessed of talents for which he feels he can find no scope, torn by conflicting desires and sensing he has himself been contaminated by the corruption all around him, Lorenzaccio is an enigma, half-Musset and half-Hamlet. The dramatic technique too, with its swift movement and alternation of mood and with its genre scenes in the Renaissance city, recalls Shakespeare, the great exemplar of all the Romantic playwrights. That Musset had great and original dramatic gifts was clear, and a number of performances of various plays were given from the middle of the century onwards. But *Lorenzaccio* did not receive its première until 1896 when Sarah Bernhardt triumphed in the title role, and it has never become a standard item in the repertoire. A number of Musset's slighter plays are, however, regularly performed as curtain-raisers at the Comédie-Française.

Between 1835 and 1837 Musset also composed his most ambitious lyric poems, *The May Night, The December Night, The August Night* and *The October Night (La Nuit de mai, La Nuit de décembre, La Nuit d'août* and *La Nuit d'octobre)*. The nocturne is a favourite Romantic motif, and Musset uses it for impassioned dialogue with his Muse about the pangs of love. Certainly these four elegies count among the monuments of French Romanticism, and they remain before the public in the musical setting by Berlioz*, but the posturing and the rhetoric ring false now. A work of quite different character from this period is Musset's *Letters between Dupuis and Cotonet (Lettres de Dupuis et Cotonet)* of 1836–8. In the form of a correspondence between two worthies in the provinces anxious to learn all about the latest fashions in the capital, this presents in a hilarious light the literary squabbles of the day.

The final twenty years of Musset's life are a tale of successive mistresses and bouts of ill-health. He continued to write stories, lyrics and plays, but his creativity was gradually drying up. As time passed, he did, however, receive some marks of public recognition, becoming a Chevalier of the Legion of Honour in 1845 and gaining election to the Académie-Française in 1852, five years before his death.

C.N. Smith

The most convenient edition of Musset's works is *Oeuvres complètes*, ed. P. van Tieghem (1963). For translations of the plays, see George Graveley, *A Comedy and Two Proverbs* (1955). Margaret A. Rees's edition of the *Contes d'Espagne et d'Italie* (1973) contains a good introduction. For criticism and biography, see: M. Allem, *Alfred de Musset* (1948); P. van Tieghem, *Musset* (1957); H. Guillemin, *La Liaison Musset-Sand* (1972); J. Pommier, *Variétés sur Alfred de Musset et son théâtre* (1966); C. Affron, *A Stage for Poets: Studies in the Theatre of Hugo and Musset* (1971). Simon Jeune, *Musset et sa fortune littéraire* (1970), traces the evolution of critical appreciation of Musset.

328
MUSSORGSKY, Modest Petrovich 1839–81

Russian composer

The most original composer of the 'Mighty Handful' was educated privately and then at the Cadet School of the Guards in St Petersburg. He served in the Preobrazhensky Regiment of Guards and was later employed in the civil service. His interests shifted from the traditional pursuits of Guards officers to some of the most advanced ideas of the time. He claimed to have been drawn to music through folk art rather than art music, and despised the rules and conventions of the latter. In 1857 he encountered for the first time Balakirev*, Stasov and Dargomyzhsky. The first-named attempted to guide him along his customary musical path, Stasov eventually became a life-long friend, and Dargomyzhsky pioneered some of the ideas and techniques which Mussorgsky later embodied in his own compositions. From 1863 or so his music begins to show his deep interest in folk art and his attachment to truth rather than beauty as an artistic ideal. His projected opera *The Marriage* (1868) is the laboratory in which he experimented with modelling vocal lines on the inflections of (Russian) speech, an idea recently tried out in Dargomyzhsky's *The Stone Guest*. His avoidance of grandiose cosmopolitan subjects, his concentration on various aspects of Russian life, treated realistically, and his taste for caricature draw him close to the utilitarian ideas of the time and to the group of painters known as the 'Itinerants'. But his talent for vivid representation through highly unorthodox musical devices put his works beyond the comprehension of the majority of his contemporaries, even of many musicians sympathetically disposed to him. In his case bouts of alcoholism compounded the inability, characteristic of many Russian composers of this period, to bring projected compositions to completion, and his works were much altered after his death in the name of turning them into performable material.

Ever an enemy of routine and convention, Mussorgsky did not really try to make a successful career as a composer by the lights of the time. Particularly in its first version (1868–9), but to some extent also in the second (1871–2, performed in 1874), *Boris Godunov* was not tailored for immediate success. Its very subject made it liable to censorship troubles. It was deficient in opportunities for the expected vocal display and ballet, and it was short of love interest and comedy. Yet it is a masterly work, in its own terms, in which Mussorgsky's gift for characterization is brought to bear on the psychological development of Boris himself, and in which the stark and sombre music magnificently reflects and communicates the events and atmosphere of the time. The 'time of troubles' in the early seventeenth century which preceded the beginning of the Romanov dynasty's rule provided the composer with a serious subject from the Russian past which gave him scope for musical depiction of a wide variety of characters, including nobles, peasants, clergy, Polish aristocrats and Jesuits. His knowledge of Russian folk music determined the character of the greatest part of the Russian scenes. Rimsky-Korsakov's* version, which for long kept out Mussorgsky's original, has smoothed out and made 'grammatical' what in the original was more striking and novel, while its orchestration has often substituted conventional tinsel for what the composer had coloured with greater discrimination and sensitivity.

With *Khovanshchina*, on which Mussorgsky worked from 1872 until his death, it is more defensible to use Rimsky-Korsakov's version of 1883, given the incomplete and rather unsatisfactory state in which the composer left it. Once more the subject is a troubled period of Russian history – the 1680s, when the Princes Khovansky tried to overthrow the ruling Romanovs. The former personify the old feudal class and the latter more modern ideas. An important part is played by Old Believers, who remained faithful to details or Orthodox ritual after these had been changed by Patriarch Nikon in 1653. It is probable that Mussorgsky intended to close the opera (in good *grand opéra* style) with their mass suicide by fire. The precise course of the action was not worked out in advance, and the plot is sprawling and over-elaborate. Like *Boris*, it is concerned not so much with the interaction of individuals as with the unfolding of a national tragedy. There is much fine music in it.

Still less was written of *Sorochintsy Fair* on which the composer worked between 1874 and his death. This opera, based on a short story by Gogol*, was more humorous in tone but still allowed Mussorgsky to use his gift for graphic characterization. He was handicapped, however, by his failure to work out a scheme to begin with and by an inadequate immersion in the Ukrainian language and background of the proposed opera. *Pictures from an Exhibition* (1874) is a series of short piano pieces, each 'representing' a work by the artist Victor Hartmann, linked by a 'walking' theme ('Promenade'). Each is a brilliant miniature which seizes on some aspect of the picture's content and translates it into sound.

Mussorgsky's particular talent for characterization is made clear in his nearly fifty songs, plus three cycles. The vast range over which this talent extended, together with the development of the composer's style and technique, is also shown in the songs. 'Where are you, little star?' (1857) has strong references to the modes, harmony, cadences and ornamentation of folksong. *Kalistrat* (1864), *The Peasant Lullaby* (1865), *Hopak* (1866) and *Eryomushka's Lullaby* (1868, dedicated 'to the great teacher of musical truth, A.S. Dargomyzhsky') follow on from it in still more rigorous style.

Gathering Mushrooms (1867) and the first song of the *Nursery* cycle (1868–72) exemplify the composer's attempts to capture speech inflections while using a single note-value (the crotchet) for the vocal part. The cycle shows his ability to penetrate the thought processes of a child, and his readiness to encapsulate them in musical language of unprecedented empiricism.

In *Svetik Savishna* (1866) Mussorgsky depicts an unhappy idiot declaring his love for a girl while acknowledging that his condition deprives him of everything including love. The music is 'realistic' in the sense that it most cleverly reflects the manner of voice and gesture of the scene; from such songs we might well deduce that the composer was a mimic of considerable talent. *The Seminarist* (1866) shows a student learning Latin nouns and indulging simultaneously in amorous reflections. *The Classicist* (1867) is a lampoon of a critic who had attacked the 'modernism' of Rimsky-Korsakov's *Sadko*. A subjective lyrical vein and a more conventional handling of musical figures are revealed in the cycle *Sunless* (1874). The bold graphic quality of many other songs is here replaced by a degree of stylization. The *Songs and Dances of Death* (1875–7) sum up the most important features of Mussorgsky's songs. Vivid yet structured, inventive yet disciplined, speech-inflected yet generating lyrical melody – this cycle is one of the composer's best works. Each song shows the intervention of death in an area of human life – taking a sick child from its mother, serenading a sick girl, dancing with a drunken peasant, and on the battlefield – and treats each subject like a miniature *scena*.

When he had characters and dramatic situations to stimulate him, Mussorgsky could respond with music of wonderful truth and imagination. Song and opera offered greatest scope, and it is in these forms that Mussorgsky's splendid marriage of music with drama succeeded most consistently. His influence was felt most strongly after his lifetime – by Debussy, Stravinsky, Prokofiev and Shostakovitch.

Stuart Campbell

See: Jay Leyda and Sergei Bertensson, *The Mussorgsky Reader* (1974); M.D. Calvocoressi (completed and revised by Gerald Abraham), *Mussorgsky* (1974).

N

329
NAPOLEON BONAPARTE 1769–1821

Emperor of the French

The future Emperor of the French was born on the fringes of France, in the town of Ajaccio in Corsica, which had become part of France in the previous year. His family were poor minor nobility, whose sympathies for Pasquale Paoli, the apostle of Corsican independence, ensured that they found it difficult to achieve prosperity under French rule. Pale, undersized and unkempt, Napoleon experienced hostility and derision at the military academy of Brienne where he trained for an army career alongside the sons of important noble families from the mainland. He owed his rapid rise in the ranks of the French army after 1793 not only to his own talents, but also to the emigration from revolutionary France of most of the nobility who had formed the officer corps of the Ancien Régime. Without the collapse of the aristocracy he would have found it difficult to rise to any commanding military rank. The army which Napoleon led was also very different from that of the old order. A small, professional army including many foreign mercenaries was replaced, during the revolutionary wars, by a far larger, conscript army composed entirely of Frenchmen: it was the first modern, national army in French history. Such an army, officered largely by bourgeois or men risen from the ranks, was in a position to become an independent political force in a way that the old armies could not have been, and were not interested in becoming. This is the basic factor influencing Napoleon's early career and his seizure of power in 1799.

Napoleon first came to prominence by his action in 1793 which culminated in his recapture of the port of Toulon which had been seized by the British. He kept himself in the limelight by the promptitude with which he crushed an attempted Royalist rising in Paris in 1795. This action brought him valuable contacts, including the Director Barras, whose former mistress, Josephine Beauharnais, he married on 9 October 1796. Now a general, marriage gave him the social and political contacts to gain high command and in 1796 he was made commander-in-chief of the French army in Italy. His victories over the Austrians and Russians in Piedmont and Lombardy, opening with the battle of Lodi, put him into the position of being able to conduct

his negotiations with the defeated powers independently of the Directory. The loyalty of his army, whose supplies and pay he had ensured better than any other general, was a powerful factor in insuring him from recall by Paris. The Treaty of Campo Formio, which sold the Venetian Republic to Austria against the wishes of Paris, was the direct result of this political independence. It was therefore not surprising that Napoleon's next assignment was well away from the borders of France. His capture of Malta and Egypt in 1798 was succeeded by an advance into Syria in January 1799. However, by August he was back in Egypt, having been repulsed by the British at Acre late in May. Meanwhile, the armies of the French Republic had been suffering massive reverses on almost all fronts. Economically and politically, the government of the Directory seemed increasingly frail. Napoleon abandoned his army in Egypt on 22 August, reached Paris on 16 October, and seized power by the coup of 18–19 *brumaire* (9–10 November 1799). He was thirty.

But Napoleon's rise to power, romantic though it was, was far from being inevitable. His own military position in the Near East had reached stalemate. It was fortuitous that many other young and able generals equally able to size up the weaknesses of the Directory were killed very shortly before *brumaire*: Hoche died in 1797 in Germany and Joubert in Italy in 1799. As it was, in spite of the politicking made open to him by his contacts in the Directory, Napoleon in fact almost failed to secure endorsement from the legislative bodies in Paris, and in a state of collapse saw the position saved by the efforts of his younger brother, Lucien.

As First Consul, Napoleon's support came from the army, then overwhelmingly Republican, and from many Republicans in political life, who saw the weakness of the Directory as opening the way to Royalist counter-revolution, and therefore turned with relief to the young and usually victorious General Bonaparte to institute a strong régime in France. However, this support wavered when Napoleon's desire for supreme power for life began to appear too clearly. In 1802, by means of a carefully planned referendum, Napoleon managed to extend his term of office from ten years to life. In 1804, he crowned himself Emperor in Notre Dame.

There is not space here to give a detailed account of Napoleon's campaigns after 1804. Suffice it to say that the German campaign of 1805–6 humiliated Austria

452 / NAPOLEON BONAPARTE

and laid open the centre of Germany to France. A series of campaigns between 1805 and 1808 resulted in the subjugation of all the Italian states with the exceptions of the islands of Sicily and Sardinia. Sweden and Denmark fell in 1806, and Spain became nominally French two years later. In 1812, Napoleon began his famous and ill-starred attempt to invade Russia, from which the French army returned a shattered wreck. Defeated by a coalition of his enemies, Napoleon abdicated on 6 April 1814, and was exiled to Elba. Escaping from there, he landed in France at Fréjus on 1 March 1815, but was defeated at Waterloo on 18 June. Deported by the allies to St Helena in the Atlantic, he died there on 5 May 1821, after having dictated a series of memoirs which determined the future history of the Napoleonic legend and hence of much of the interpretation of the French Revolution itself.

Clearly, such a prodigious military effort could not have been produced without far-reaching changes in society and government. In spite of the rapidity with which his empire collapsed, it left permanent marks not only on France but also on Europe, at the institutional, the political and the ideological levels. In order to stabilize power after 1799, he took an immediate step away from the revolutionary principle of government by elected committees. In local government, these were replaced by the prefect and the *sous-préfet*, both appointed by the central government. This type of local administration has lasted in structure up to the present day. Napoleon took care that he should have control over all appointments, including most of those in the administration of justice. The representative assemblies such as the Senate and the Tribune were reduced to the position of being little more than debating chambers. They could no longer initiate legislation, or refuse their consent to decrees originating with the government. This remained the position in the French Chambers until the Fifth French Republic of 1958. Napoleon's governmental reforms thus centralized and concentrated his power. He also undertook a conscious policy of social engineering. He deliberately excluded from office extremists of any kind, whether Jacobin or Royalist, and made a policy of employing only moderates, often men who had begun their careers in the royal administration before the revolution, men such as Gaudin and Mollien, his two chief financial advisers. In this way he calmed the political conflicts which had rendered so unstable all previous governments. He also thereby helped to contribute to the great extent to which the personnel of the bureaucracy of the Ancien Régime survived into the Restoration. Napoleon also sought to make his peace with the aristocracy of the Old Régime. The laws against émigrés were gradually relaxed, and from about 1804 they returned to France in great numbers, and often found employment in the new Imperial Court which Napoleon and Josephine were creating. But the emperor also sought to create a new nobility of men personally loyal to himself, whose devotion to the empire was made even more secure by gifts of land and revenues from territories in the conquered provinces. Under the Restoration, the conflict between the old élite and the new was to form one of the dominant political themes. Napoleon also knew that in betraying the ideals of republicanism, he had lost support not only from the intellectuals but also from many sections of the lower middle class. He thus instituted a series of social legislation designed to capture the allegiance of the bourgeoisie proper. Laws against trades-union combinations were therefore succeeded by the Napoleonic law codes, still in force in France and in many of the subject states of the empire, such as Italy, which not only replaced the legal codes of the revolution but did so in a socially conservative direction. Divorce was made less easy; the financial powers of the head of the household over wives and children was increased, as were the legal powers of employers over workers. A special Commercial Code catered for the special needs of the financial and entrepreneurial strata of the bourgeoisie. The foundation of the Bank of France in 1801, and its reform in 1805–6, established government finance upon a modern footing. Napoleon also conciliated conservative opinion inside France by arranging a reconciliation of the French state with the Catholic Church by the Concordat of 1802. However, although he regarded religion as an important means of social control for the masses, he was also concerned not to lose ideological supremacy to the church. He therefore set up, in the Imperial University, the first state administration of all levels of education in France. The conflict between church and state in this field, embodied in the struggle between the Napoleonic *lycées* and the church's seminaries, was to remain a major political conflict in France for the rest of the nineteenth century.

Bonapartism remained a viable political force in France culminating in the election of Napoleon's nephew, Louis Napoleon, as President of France in 1850. He remained the symbol both of French greatness and of the romantic leader long into the Restoration as Stendhal's* novel *Le Rouge et le noir* makes clear. His regrouping of the Italian states into three major divisions foreshadowed many of the struggles for unification of the peninsula; in Germany, the reaction against his rule foreshadowed the same events. Above all, the rule of Napoleon meant that the Bourbons could not return to a situation which was a carbon copy of that of 1789: the existence of the Napoleonic alternative meant that their rule could never again be taken as the only possible one.

Dorinda Outram

Napoleon's memoirs exist as the edition by Las Casas, *Mémorial de Sainte-Hélène*. The classic though still incomplete edition of his correspondence and dispatches is the *Correspondance de l'Empéreur Napoléon Ier, publiée par ordre de Napoléon III* (28 vols, 1857–69). Studies of Napoleon are innumerable. Still the best review of the controversies surrounding his career is Pieter Geyl, *Napoleon, For and Against* (1949). Among the best biographies should be mentioned: J.M. Thompson, *Napoleon: His Rise and Fall* (1952); E. Tersen, *Napoléon* (1959); E. Tarlé, *Napoléon* (1937).

330
NASH, John 1752–1835

British architect

John Nash gave London its West End. His contemporaries, mocking his fondness for stucco, declared that he found London all brick and left it all plaster, and yet it was Nash who created for the disorganized eighteenth-century city a new coherence, in the central spine of Regent Street, and introduced to English individualism revolutionary ideas about town planning. As an architect he was often careless, and in Pugin's* eyes dishonest and trivial, but he created some of the most visually enjoyable buildings in Britain.

Nash was probably born in London, and at an early age entered the office of the architect Sir Robert Taylor. In the late 1770s he set up as a speculative builder-architect, but the business did not flourish and in 1783 he went bankrupt. A bankrupt's best refuge appeared to be Wales, and there he worked for the next thirteen years, designing utilitarian buildings such as gaols as well as country houses, and absorbing the ideas of Uvedale Price and Richard Payne Knight about the 'picturesque'. By 1796 he felt sufficiently secure to return to London, and with his appointment in 1806 as architect to the Department of Woods and Forests (ancestor of the Ministry of Works) his financial position was established. He worked assiduously as a builder of country houses of all sizes, at first in partnership with the landscape designer Humphrey Repton, and was a fine hand at the cheerful eclecticism expected of the Regency architect: his work included an Italianate villa at Cronkhill (1802), a castle for himself at East Cowes, Isle of Wight, in the approved picturesque manner (1798 onwards; demolished), a Gothic Tudor mansion at Longner Hall, Shropshire (1805), rustic cottages at Blaise Hamlet (1810–11), and, in the Indo-Chinese manner, the Royal Pavilion at Brighton (1815–21). He excelled as an architect of the picturesque, giving his buildings pleasingly irregular exteriors and ground plans and arranging them to best advantage in their landscape settings.

Nash's client at the Royal Pavilion was the Prince Regent, and it was George who proved his most rewarding patron. The prince was determined that London should possess a centre worthy of a world capital, and on the reversion to the Crown in 1811 of lands in Marylebone he resolved on the creation of a new park and ceremonial street. Nash was chosen to act as supervising architect and in addition as organizer and entrepreneur responsible for obtaining leases along the proposed route and for lighting and drainage. Though what was actually erected was on a grand scale, the original intention was for something even more imposing: a processional way leading from Carlton House, the Prince of Wales's residence in St James's Park, through Mayfair on one side and Soho on the other (a socially convenient division as was intended), up the existing Portland Place, and into the new Regent's Park. Here the prince was to have another palace, a *guinguette*, surrounded by the villas of the nobility, with superb terraces in a variety of styles around the borders. The Regent's Park development was planned as the Regency equivalent of a New Town, with provision for all social classes and needs: behind the terraces Nash built housing for working people, churches and barracks were provided, and the Regent's Canal supplied the new markets. Only about a fifth of the villas, and not all the terraces, were built, and there were serious difficulties over the design of the street itself, but the scheme was an outstanding achievement. It owed a great deal to Nash, for his organizing ability, his skill at theatrical effects and the ingenuity of his planning in the dashing sweep of the quadrant and the artfully placed All Souls, Langham Place. The street itself has been heavily rebuilt, but enough survives at the north end to convey Nash's talents, as Park Crescent throws open its arms to the park in the approved picturesque manner, ushering the promenader from town into country.

Nash's patron was an extremely unpopular man, and on his death in 1830 the architect's fortunes deteriorated. He had been involved from 1825 on rebuilding Buckingham House as Buckingham Palace, an enormously expensive enterprise which was incomplete on the king's death, and he had already been called before parliamentary committees for investigations into his financial dealings. Though exonerated, he had not emerged with credit. He was dismissed from his public office and the palace commission was removed from him. A year after his death his buildings were ripe for lampooning in Pugin's *Contrasts*: a new era had arrived in architectural morality.

Giles Waterfield

See: J. Summerson, *John Nash* (1935, rev. 1981); T. Davis, *John Nash* (1966).

331
NERVAL, Gérard de (Gérard Labrunie) 1808–55

French writer

Born Gérard Labrunie, Nerval lost his mother at an early age and was brought up by an uncle in a village outside Paris. A school friend of Gautier*, he participated fully in the Bohemian activities of the Romantic circle grouped around Hugo*. Like so many of his generation, he was enamoured of the theatre, and wrote a number of plays and operas, though none brought him lasting success. In keeping with the practice of his contemporaries, he also fell madly in love with an actress, Jenny Colon, and paid her extravagant homage, including writing for her the title part in an uncompleted opera, *The Queen of Sheba* (*La Reine de Saba*). This passion was unrequited, yet it obsessed him throughout his life, even after Jenny's death in 1842. Nerval's career as a man of letters was effectively one of irregular journalism: he contributed to upwards of sixty different journals, often pseudonymously. He also translated Goethe's* *Faust* and poetry by Bürger and Heine*, and wrote a series of biographies of obscure eccentrics, *The Illuminati* (*Les Illuminés*, 1852). But his reputation today rests on a relatively small number of prose works of an autobiographical cast, and a collection of sonnets, *Chimeras* (*Les Chimères* 1854).

That Nerval led an unsettled life, full of compulsive journeys abroad or within France, that he was desperately unhappy in love, and that, after a series of psychological crises, he eventually hanged himself in a dark alley in central Paris one winter's night, these are the bare facts around which the popular imagination, abetted by certain simplifying commentators such as Alexandre Dumas *père**, created a trite caricature of Nerval. Until comparatively recently, he was held to be only a minor figure, at best a naive though charming story-teller, at worst a Romantic lunatic whose last works defy logical comprehension. It has been the achievement of a number of painstaking critics in recent years to have demonstrated that Nerval's work is in fact both coherent and marvellously complex, the creation of a supreme literary artist who quite possibly rivals Hugo as the outstanding talent of French Romanticism.

Nerval makes no secret of the fact that he was 'one of those writers whose life is intimately linked to the works that have made their name'. But this is not to say that his writing was merely a passive record of things that happened to him. Rather it was a medium of self-discovery, in the sense that Nerval constantly made use of his experiences to illuminate facets of his sensibility, with a view to eventually 'seizing' himself as an integral being. If his actual life was one of chronic insecurity in all respects – professionally, emotionally, psychologically – then the literary act was a means of

restitution whereby the sorry autobiography of Gérard Labrunie could be transfigured and elevated into a purer and more permanent form thanks to the art of Gérard de Nerval.

It is true that much of Nerval's writing still bears the casual stamp of notes taken from life, diary entries without depth. A story may begin on the slenderest anecdotal pretext: a blonde girl met while swimming in the sea at Naples ('Octavie') or a curious book found on a market-stall in Frankfurt ('Angélique'). Yet such chance encounters are fraught with presentiment, for Nerval lives in a world of signs and omens which suggest to him an infinity of vibrant meanings. It is as though the world were packed with multiple analogues for his private preoccupations, so that outside appearances become so many mirrorings of his inner self. To be alive was thus to interrogate places, people and circumstances and to probe reality for those hidden correspondences which inform all things and which may illuminate him as both observer and, in a sense, architect of his experience.

Nerval's *Journey to the Orient* (*Voyage en Orient*, 1851) is a semi-fictionalized account of a journey through the Mediterranean to Egypt and Turkey, based on actual travels made in 1842–3. A compendium of colourful set-pieces – descriptions of Cairo streets, slave markets, dancing dervishes, Coptic weddings and other foreign customs – the book is, at a deeper level, a journey into Nerval's imagination. Intercalated into the traveller's narrative are tales about mythological heroes with whom Nerval clearly identifies: Adoniram, the frustrated lover of the beautiful Balkis, Queen of Sheba, or the Caliph Hakem, another unhappy lover, who encounters his double. Such identifications gave Nerval scope obliquely to explore the problems of his own personality and to elaborate the book at large as a kind of allegory of psychic self-construction. The many dualities in Nerval's nature are symbolically reconciled in a journey which balances the contrary principles of the Occident and the Orient, reality and myth, actuality and ideality, and is framed by visits to Konstanz and Constantinople, presented as twin cities and thus as affirmations of the principle of the equilibrium of opposites.

Though he frequently engaged on excursions to other foreign territories like Italy and Germany, Nerval returned time and again to two places which can be seen as focal regions in what he calls his 'magic geography': the streets of Paris and the landscape of his childhood, the Valois region north of the city. In typically casual fashion, he will describe, in works like *October Nights* (*Les Nuits d'octobre*, 1852) and *Rambles and Recollections* (*Promenades et souvenirs*, 1854), his wanderings through the labyrinth of the metropolis, and especially his experience of night-life and the fringes of society. Entirely unpugnacious by temperament, Nerval was none the less an outsider who loved nothing more than to spend the night with rough coachmen in outlandish cafés and to court the irritation of the police by carrying no papers. He frequently describes impulsive sorties into the countryside, the most memorable being that evoked in 'Sylvie' (1853), a nostalgic journey by night to Loisy, a village deep in the Valois where years before the narrator had known two attractive girls, the saintly Adrienne and the more earthly yet scarcely less elusive Sylvie. With great poignancy, the narrator uncovers, for himself as much as for the reader, a pattern of doomed amorous relationships, culminating in that with a Parisian actress, while tying these aching recollections to descriptions of a region he had known in his most tender years and from which he now feels himself to be fatefully exiled. In 'Sylvie', reminiscences from different stages of Nerval's personal past are superimposed upon recollections of local history and folklore, and across the whole tale floats a kind of dreamy pastoral mist thanks to which authentic memory and literary myth blend to form one of Nerval's most perfect works.

Nerval was a voracious and eclectic reader, and a whole industry of Nervalian scholarship has arisen to track down his multiple references to history, geography, mythology and literature, and above all the hermetic sciences of astrology, magic and alchemy, to which he had been introduced by his uncle. The late collection of enigmatic sonnets, *Chimeras*, is held to be a masterpiece of polyvalent allusion, the repository of a bristling array of references to the practices of the occult, and above all to their philosophical base in the notion of universal harmony, a notion to which Nerval was almost pathologically sensitive. He appears to have sincerely believed in his own ability to synthesize mystical beliefs from sources both pagan and Christian, and the sonnets sketch a ritualistic and visionary scenario in which the poet witnesses the triumphant resurrection of the lost religions of antiquity: 'They will return, those Gods for whom you still weep!/Time will restore the order of ancient days;/Already the earth has shaken with a prophetic tremor.'

Further clues to the syncretistic nature of Nerval's fantastic metaphysics are given in his last prose work, *Aurélia* (1855), where the figure of the unattainable beloved Aurélia (the literary transcription of Jenny Colon) modulates into a series of timeless images of the Eternal Feminine (echoing the Helena episode in *Faust*). This ideal woman is at once Nerval's lost mother, his desired Jenny, Adrienne, Balkis, Artemis and the radiant goddess Isis, who appears in a celestial vision to reassure him:

I am the same as the Virgin Mary, the same as your mother, the same one you have always loved in many different forms. With each of your trials, I have dropped one of the masks which veil my features, and soon you will see me as I truly am.

To this transcendental theme adheres a tragic personal story, for *Aurélia* is equally the candid account of that mental derangement which cast its shadow over Nerval's last years; the text was indeed composed at the suggestion of Nerval's psychiatrist as a kind of therapy. The 'descent into hell' of hallucination and delusion of reference is described in clinically authentic terms, while Nerval also provides a series of dream accounts full of potent archetypal imagery. Written in a manner which is as persuasive as it is visionary, *Aurélia* takes the reader into the most remote regions of Nerval's imagination, where reality commingles totally with dream-life and clear-sightedness veers giddily into a delirium at once fearful and exhilarating.

Nerval's gift for manipulating resources beyond the limits of normal consciousness lends his style a wonderful depth and resonance. He writes like an inspired dreamer whose images cross-refer and reverberate at levels beyond the reach of superficial scanning. His practice was in a sense simple: constantly to rework his material afresh. And almost all his works may be said to be variants on a basic set of personal themes, images and mythic references: the quest for security, for love, for understanding; the labyrinth, the guiding star, the double; Orpheus, Prometheus, and Horus, son of Isis. But the reworking of these familiar threads is handled with the utmost discretion and subtlety. While individual texts may seem disappointing and flat when read on their own, they gain immeasurably in impact the more one reads them in combination. Thus 'Octavie' will at first reading come across as little more than the tale of a casual flirtation, yet will acquire extra meaning almost line for line once the reader is attuned to the Nervalian code of allusions, becoming indeed a kind of hieroglyphic key to the *Chimères* cycle. The curious short story 'Pandora' was held back at the last moment from Nerval's last collection, *The Daughters of Fire* (*Les Filles du feu*, 1854): this may in part be explained by reference to the sensitive autobiographical material therein, which touches on Nerval's hapless affair with the pianist Marie Pleyel in Vienna; in part because Nerval felt the story to be too obscure and aesthetically unkempt. The disjunctive narrative, with its swift shifts of scene and chronology, is indeed disturbing at first; yet once it is set in the context of Nerval's other works (especially the 'Amours de Vienne' section of *Le Voyage en Orient*), the allusions begin to fall into place, and the reading experience is transformed from bewilderment into a queerly pleasurable, quasi-intuitive participation in the disclosure of meaning.

Nerval's reputation is still growing. Major critics have written impressively about him from a whole range of angles; biographical criticism, the erudite study of sources, thematic and phenomenological criticism, psychoanalysis and psycho-stylistics, structuralism and post-structuralism – all have something to say, and moreover nearly all manage to say something interesting! Within French literary history, Nerval seems to have assumed an increasingly magnetized position, as if all influences mysteriously passed through him. Certainly he did marshal impulses from Rousseau, Restif de la Bretonne, Cazotte and the German Romantics and relay them to the Symbolists, Barrès*, Proust, Alain-Fournier, Apollinaire, the Surrealists and others. Undoubtedly he was neglected for too long and unjustly relegated to the status of *petit romantique*. On the other hand, it must soon be time to take critical stock of the myriad analyses and commentaries which have emerged over the last decade or so, and it is possible that a final evaluation will be rather more modest. What is already established is that Nerval remains an indispensable exemplar of the Romantic artist – a *Romantic* in his unabashed admixture of passionate feeling into his writing, an *artist* in his supreme control of the resources of his medium.

Roger Cardinal

Works in print: *Oeuvres*, ed. A. Béguin and J. Richer (2 vols, 1952 and 1958); *Les Chimères*, ed. N. Rinsler (London, 1973). Translations: *Journey to the Orient* (1972); *Selected Writings* (1958). See: Jacques Geninasca, *Analyse structurale des 'Chimères' de Nerval* (1971); Raymond Jean, *Nerval par lui-même* (1966) and *La Poétique du désir* (1974); Jean-Pierre Richard, 'Géographie magique de Nerval', in *Poésie et profondeur* (1955); Jean Richer, *Nerval: Expérience et création* (1963); Norma Rinsler, *Gérard de Nerval* (London, 1973); Gerald Schaeffer, *Le Voyage en Orient de Nerval* (1967); Benn Sowerby, *The Disinherited: The Life of Gérard de Nerval* (1973); Dominique Tailleux, *L'Espace nervalien* (1975).

332
NEWMAN, John Henry, Cardinal 1801–90

British Roman Catholic churchman and theologian

Born in London, the son of a banker, on 21 February 1801, Newman's childhood and adolescence were spent there, and he was schooled privately in Ealing, where he proved himself to be a child of remarkable intellectual gifts, with a strong predilection for the Greek classics and the Greek New Testament. In the year 1816 he underwent a singularly profound experience of Christian 'conversion' which, it cannot be doubted, dominated the future course of his life and career, although the exact content of this conversion has for long been a matter of speculation and disagreement within the area of Newman scholarship, some contending that it was more or less a conventional 'evangelical-protestant' experience (based upon study of the Scriptures) while others have suggested that it

was more 'Catholic' and doctrinal in content and orientation.

In June 1817 Newman went up to Trinity College, Oxford, where, because of an infirm disposition and mental strain brought on by overwork, he was awarded a degree of a poor class towards the end of 1820. Despite this, he was successful in his attempt to win a fellowship at Oriel by examination in the following year. It was at this time that Newman, the raw young Evangelical, came under the theological influence of Richard Whately (1787–1863), later to be Archbishop of Dublin, and the High Churchman Edward Hawkins (1787–1863), later provost of Oriel. Although both men were later to be critical of the Tractarians, in the 1820s they did much to orient Newman into a more 'Anglo-Catholic' direction, as did a new fellow of Oriel, Edward Bouverie Pusey (1800–82), after 1841 to be the acknowledged leader of the Oxford Movement. At this period also, Newman's mind received an impetus towards a more metaphysical type of theology by reading Bishop Butler's *Analogy of Religion*. Newman was ordained to the diaconate in 1824, at about the time when he finally decided that he was called to live a celibate life, and when he was considering a life of missionary service abroad. But he accepted an invitation from Whately, the new principal of St Alban's Hall, to become its vice-principal, and he was ordained priest in May 1825. In the following year, Newman was appointed a tutor at Oriel, at about the same time when two new fellows were elected to Oriel, Robert Isaac Wilberforce (1802–57) and Richard Hurrell Froude (1803–36), the latter of whom soon became an intimate friend of Newman's.

With John Keble (1792–1866), who had been a fellow and tutor of Oriel from 1817 to 1823, the brilliant group which included Newman, Froude, Wilberforce, Pusey, Isaac Williams (1802–65), William Palmer (1803–85), J.B. Mozley (1813–78) and H.J. Rose (1795–1838), may be considered responsible for the so-called 'Oxford Movement' which aimed at a Catholic revival, in doctrine and practice, within the Church of England. The group became increasingly critical of the contemporary state of the Church of England, and in the year 1832–3 Newman and Froude made a tour of Mediterranean countries, which made Froude wax lyrical about the glories of Catholic Christendom, which in his view the Church of England had well-nigh lost through sinful and lukewarm apathy. The Oxford Movement may be said to have begun with the conference on church reform at Hadleigh Rectory (where Rose was the incumbent) on 25 July 1833, about ten days after the preaching of Keble's famous 'assize sermon' before the University of Oxford on 14 July, which Newman for the rest of his life celebrated as the very day when the Oxford Movement began. The sermon *began* as a protest against the attempt of the civil legislature, in the teeth of ecclesiastical opposition, to suppress ten Irish bishoprics, but it quickly developed into something else – the declaration that the entire nation was in 'apostasy', allowing, because of its profound and insidious apathy (clothed in the disguise of 'tolerance') to the supernatural life of grace enshrined within the Christian Church, a secular, even profane, civil authority to interfere in the affairs of a body which Christ had committed to his apostles and their successors alone. Keble's views and sentiments were enthusiastically shared by his colleagues, including Newman, who had since 1828 been vicar of St Mary's, the university church in Oxford. The most obvious consequence of these events was the beginning of the publication of the 'Tracts for the Times' and the formation of an Association of Friends of the Church. The scene was now set for a bitter conflict, with Newman and his sympathizers on the one side and their civil and ecclesiastical opponents on the other.

Newman had already begun a life of scholarship inspired by the writings of the early Fathers of the Church, which is available to us in his book *The Arians of the Fourth Century* (1833) and in his multi-volumed *Parochial and Plain Sermons* (1834–42). And this patristic orientation and inspiration is plain in the very first tract of the series, which came from Newman's pen, 'Thoughts on the Ministerial Commission Respectfully Addressed to the Clergy'. In this, one of the twenty-four tracts for which he was responsible, Newman argued that the episcopate and the priesthood do not at all derive from a civil, even profane, state, but from a commission of Christ alone, who set apart his apostles in a peculiar sense and gave them authority to hand down their powers and gifts through an 'apostolic succession', which has been preserved, miraculously, in the Church of England. Such a society, the Body of Christ (no less), is independent of and invulnerable against the degradations of a godless civil society. Throughout his own tracts Newman loyally defended what came to be known as the *via media anglicana* – the principle that the Church of England occupies the middle ground between the extreme of 'Popery' and 'Romanism' on the one hand and 'Dissent' (Reformed Protestantism) on the other. But, on the whole, the authors of the tracts (Newman included) set before themselves the aim of pushing the Church of England in the direction of Catholicism as represented by Rome – hence the stress of the Tractarians on the doctrine of the Real Presence of Christ in the Eucharist, on priestly celibacy, on the veneration of the saints, on monastic asceticism, on fasting, on auricular confession, on baptismal regeneration, on the apostolic succession, on the minutiae of the liturgy, and the like. It is not easy to characterize the spirit which motivated the Tractarians: certainly, the Oxford Movement was, partly unconsciously perhaps, an ideologically conservative reaction against the liberalism, toleration and rationalism unleashed in Europe by the 1789 Revolution in France and a philosophical reaction against the utilitarianism of Bentham*; equally it was a protest, in the name of metaphysical and supranaturalistic religion, against the alleged reductionistic naturalism and empiricism which were seen as the inevitable consequence of the *Aufklärung* in Germany (Rose had published at Cambridge in 1825 his grossly unfair and hostile discourses, *The State of the Protestant Religion in Germany*); doubtlessly, it was an understandable protest against the apathy, lethargy and over-comfortable moderation of many in the post-Enlightenment Church of England. Importantly, it was an unmistakable aspect of the European Romantic Revival pitted over against the severe, classical, cool, quasi-mathematical spirit of the Age of Reason, an aspect which found expression in the nineteenth-century preoccupation with the Middle Ages, in the speculations concerning angels and the doctrine of transubstantiation, and in the building of Gothic churches and railway stations.

No doubt Newman was the bearer of this spirit in most of these aspects, but there was something in him which separated him from most of the Tractarians. Most of them (with the notable exception of W.G. Ward, 1812–82, F.W. Faber, 1814–53, and Newman himself) shrank from pursuing their theological inquiries or from indulging in liturgical or devotional practices to that point which would carry them out of the Church of England or detach them permanently from the basic principle of the *via media*. But there was in Newman a pitiless logicality, an inability to do other than follow the truth (as he saw it) wheresoever it would lead him, even if this meant abandoning the church into which he had been born. In 1837 he published his *Lectures on the Prophetical Office of the Church* and in 1838 his *Lectures on Justification*, both of them still subtle defences of the Church of England's *via media*. But from around 1839, it is clear, he began to change his mind. Up to that point he believed that the Church of England approximated more or less to the true Church of Christ in its possession of holiness, catholicity and antiquity, and that it was still in essential unity with it. But the protestantism and 'insularity' firmly embedded in the *via media* worried him intensely and created in him the unshakable suspicion that the Church of England might not at all share in those ancient and unmistakable marks of the true Church of God which were clearly displayed for all to behold in the Church of Rome. The obvious outcome of his worry and uncertainty was the publication in 1840 of the notorious Tract No. 90, whose object was to demonstrate the compatibility of the Thirty-nine Articles of the Church of England with the post-Tridentine theology of the Roman Church, but whose consequence was the harsh accusation flung at Newman that in his subtle playing with familiar words he was clearly a deceitful trickster and a traitor. The argument that in condemning the Romish doctrine of Purgatory the framers of the Thirty-nine Articles did not intend to reject *the* doctrine of Purgatory, or in rejecting 'the sacrifices of masses' sixteenth-century Anglican Protestants did not intend to repudiate '*the* sacrifice of the Mass', proved to be the last straw for an outraged ecclesiastical establishment, and the teaching of Tract No. 90 was condemned out of hand by the university authorities at Oxford in 1841. What probably lay behind the writing of Tract No. 90 was the reading by Newman in 1839 of an article in the *Dublin Review* by Monsignor (later Cardinal) Wiseman, Superior of the English College in Rome, in which the latter compared the position of the Anglican communion, *vis-à-vis* Rome, to that of the heretical Donatist sect *vis-à-vis* Rome in the fourth century. At that very moment Newman happened to be intensely researching on the history of the heretical Monophysite sect in the fifth century, and he was struck by the parallel between Anglicanism's relation to Rome in the modern world and that of Monophysitism's relationship to Rome fourteen hundred years earlier, and his eventual inescapable conclusion was that if the Monophysites were heretics and schismatics, then so were the Anglicans.

In hindsight, it is beyond doubt that reflections like these set Newman on a slippery slope leading inevitably to one destination – submission to Rome. It was no longer merely a suspicion he entertained that the Church of England lacked the great defining marks of the true Church of God, catholicity and antiquity; between 1841 and 1845 the suspicion became a certainty. In 1842 he moved from Oxford to Littlemore; in 1843 he resigned the living of St Mary's. In 1845 he was received, as he later put it, 'into the Church of Christ' by Friar Dominic Barberi, a Passionist. By June 1847 Newman had been (conditionally) ordained priest by Cardinal Fransoni in St John Lateran in Rome.

The break had now been made. By 1849 Newman had founded the oratory at Birmingham, which was to be, except for the four abortive years 1854–8 trying to found a Catholic university in Ireland, Newman's home until his death in 1890. During his final years as an Anglican, it cannot be doubted that he had been restless, wrought with anxiety, bedevilled by uncertainty, accused of duplicity and disloyalty. Yet, following his conversion to Rome, it can also hardly be doubted that he failed somewhat to find peace and serenity; it is not going too far to say that for much of the remainder of his life he was harrowed by attacks and suspicions directed at him from both the Anglican and Roman fronts, and that he felt obliged again and again to justify himself in the face of these. In 1845, almost contemporaneous with his reception into Rome, Newman brought out *An Essay on the Development of Christian Doctrine*, partly in order to explain his own imminent assent to Roman dogma to his former Anglican colleagues. This is a subtle work of great erudition and brilliance, which J.M. Cameron has

compared to Augustine's *De Civitate Dei*, to Aquinas's *Summa* and Calvin's *Institutes* in its world-shaking power. In it Newman argued that everything taught by contemporary Catholicism was entailed explicitly or, more often than not, implicitly, in that of an earlier age, and that this implication can be traced backwards, so to speak, right to the Early Church and indeed to the Apostolic Church. The rather low estimate which such a theory accords to the age of the Reformation did not endear Newman to his Protestant contemporaries. But, on the other hand, the theory (and especially that ingredient in it which allocated a significant role to the rise and combating of heresy in the evolution of Roman dogma) was regarded as distinctly innovatory by certain extremely traditionalist Roman Catholics, some of whom, we may be certain, regarded the *Essay* as tainted by a certain Protestant apologetic rationalism which its author had brought with him to Rome. To put this another way, the author of the *Essay* could hardly be regarded as one who had just committed a suprarational *sacrificium intellectus* for the contemporary magisterium of the Roman communion, and it is beyond doubt that this is one of the grounds of those suspicious of him which began to be harboured in Rome, and which were to last for decades. There is abundant evidence that the freshly converted Newman did not quite understand the mentalities of his new co-religionists, and that this misunderstanding simply generated more suspicion of him in high ecclesiastical quarters: a good case in point is the astounding affair of Newman's abortive attempt to found a Catholic university for the education of the laity in Dublin. It is impossible today to read an account of this and not conclude that Newman simply did not, because he could not, comprehend that in the last analysis the Roman Catholic hierarchy did not want a laity which had been educated in a university, whether a Catholic one or not. It is to this period, the 1850s, that Newman's important work *The Idea of a University* belongs. And it was a period which frustrated and confused and saddened him.

But it was not only his fellow Catholics who saddened him. In 1864 the Anglican divine and novelist Charles Kingsley* published a most distasteful remark about Newman while reviewing J.A. Froude's* *History of England* in the January 1864 issue of *Macmillan's Magazine*: Kingsley remarked: 'Truth, for its own sake, had never been a virtue with the Roman clergy. Father Newman informs us that it need not, and on the whole ought not to be; that cunning is the weapon which heaven has given to the Saints.' The final outcome of the controversy was the publication in 1864 of Newman's classic *Apologia Pro Vita Sua*, one of the great autobiographies in the English language, which takes the form of a history of the Oxford Movement and of Newman's part in it, and lays bare the motives which led Newman and his colleagues to write and act as they did, and which led him in 1845 to break with the Anglican communion in favour of Rome. It is an intensely moving work, rich in pathos, and filled with spiritual honesty and insight. Its closing passage is said to have moved even George Eliot* to tears, and the *Apologia* as a whole led the sceptical Lytton Strachey to remark that 'Kingsley could no more understand Newman than a subaltern in a line regiment can understand a Brahmin of Benares.'

Newman's troubles were still not over. His plans to establish an oratory in Oxford were quashed, an event which helped to alienate him from the newly appointed (1865) Archbishop of Westminster, Henry Edward Manning*, a former fellow Tractarian in the Church of England. In the period leading up to the promulgation of papal infallibility in 1870, the fact that Newman was an 'Inopportunist' (see Döllinger*) brought him into further conflict both with the ultramontane Manning and Pius IX's powerful personal secretary, Monsignor Talbot. They were both suspicious of and hostile to Newman's expressed fears about the pope's temporal claims, his desire to see the laity of the Catholic Church consulted in matters of doctrine, and his ambition for Catholics to seek entrance to the universities, especially Oxford. The year 1870 saw the publication of what is probably Newman's most profoundly intellectual work, his *Essay in Aid of a Grammar of Assent*, which is devoted roughly to the areas of metaphysics and epistemology, with special reference to man's knowledge of God. Its argument is remarkable in its differences from the metaphysical proofs found in the schoolmen of the Middle Ages, and the classical theistic demonstrations we find in the English rationalists of the seventeenth and eighteenth centuries, whose defence was still undertaken in Newman's time by Whately of Oriel. Newman gives a prominent place to conscience and the facts of moral experience in the starting-point of his argument. He reserves a unique place for the will as a motive for knowing the divine existence. Finally, the argument is made to turn upon man's possession and use of his 'illative sense' which, in the words of one of his distinguished interpreters, 'signifies the capacity of our intellect to undertake an informal inference in order to discern a unified pattern of evidence in a group of independent but converging arguments' (James Collins, *God in Modern Philosophy*, 1960).

The last decade or so of Newman's life witnessed his longed-for rehabilitation in certain Roman and Anglican circles. In 1877 he was elected to an honorary fellowship by his old Oxford college, Trinity, which gave him much pleasure. In 1879, due partly to the happy intervention in Rome of prominent and influential members of the English Catholic aristocracy, he was created a Cardinal Deacon by Pius IX's successor, Leo XIII*. He died in August 1890, in his ninetieth year, one of the most famous and influential Englishmen of the nineteenth century.

It is not easy to indicate in brief compass the kind of estimate accorded to Newman today. Catholic Anglicans remain grateful to him for beginning a movement which did so much to enrich and revive the life, teaching, worship and witness of the modern Church of England, even if they have been unprepared to follow him in a Rome-ward direction. Indeed, British Protestantism as a whole could be said to have benefited from impulses and movements traceable back to Newman. In certain Roman Catholic circles, he is hailed as the great nineteenth-century prophet, anticipator and luminary of the twentieth-century Second Vatican Council. And it is not surprising that, on the grounds of his scholarship, his contributions to spirituality (he was the author of *The Dream of Gerontius*, and of the hymns 'Lead Kindly Light' and 'Praise to the Holiest in the Height'), his long life of Christian witness and faithful endurance under affliction, his influence which overflowed denominational boundaries, there has existed for some time in certain international Catholic circles a considerable movement whose aim is his canonization by Rome. Of course, this business of Newman appraisal has not been independent of subjective conviction, principle and stance. Without doubting his greatness and integrity in the least, there have been liberal theologians, especially those who have been well-informed of German developments, who were forced to the reluctant conclusions that there was something impoverishingly defective and philosophically narrow in his lifelong 'anti-liberal' convictions and antipathies; that if much modern religious thought has consisted largely in rich and varied epistemological and logical responses to forces, difficulties and challenges released by the eighteenth-century Enlightenment, it is to be regretted that the overall thrust of Newman and his sympathizers was to push Christian theology into excessively 'churchy', supranaturalistic, antiquarian and dogmatically authoritarian channels. It can be argued that it is cruelly ironical that one who pleaded so vehemently for monarchical ecclesiastical authority, rooted in the traditions of antiquity, should have suffered so severely, and so long, at its hands.

James Richmond

Newman's other works include *Certain Difficulties Felt by Anglicans in Catholic Teaching* (1876). See: Sir Samuel Hall, *A Short History of the Oxford Movement* (1906); Wilfrid Ward, *The Life of John Henry Cardinal Newman* (1927); G.C. Faber, *Oxford Apostles* (1933); Louis Bouyer, *Newman: His Life and Spirituality* (1958); James C. Livingston, *Modern Christian Thought* (1971); Roderick Strange, *Newman and the Gospel of Christ* (1981).

333
NIETZSCHE, Friedrich 1844–1900

German philosopher

Nietzsche was born in 1844 in Saxony, then a part of Prussia. His life-long intellectual war with Christianity was tied to his having come from a male line of Lutheran pastors and his father having died when Nietzsche was only four, a traumatic event for the young boy, who thereafter grew up in a household of women. At the extraordinarily young age of twenty-four Nietzsche was appointed to the Chair of Classical Philology in Basel, a position he held for ten years until failing health forced his resignation. From the age of twenty-seven his life was to be a persistent struggle with torturing migraine, stomach complaints, and various other illnesses. Commentators have related his poor health to syphilis which he may have caught as a university student. The one strong influence on Nietzsche's thought had both an intellectual and a personal side. For most of the Basel years he was a close friend of Richard Wagner*, to the point that he virtually became a member of the family. Through Wagner he was also influenced at this time by Schopenhauer's* work.

From 1879 when he left Basel Nietzsche spent ten years travelling alone, from single room to single room, from Genoa to Sils Mania to Turin, living out of one suitcase, reading little, rarely meeting friends and then briefly, his notebooks his only steady companions. No philosopher has ever lived in such intimate contact with his work – these years saw him write virtually all of his important work, above all *The Gay Science* (*Die Fröhliche Wissenschaft*, 1882, trans. 1974), *Thus Spake Zarathustra* (*Also Sprach Zarathustra*, 1883–5, trans. 1954), *Beyond Good and Evil* (*Jenseits von Gut und Böse*, 1886, trans. 1968) and *The Genealogy of Morals* (*Zur Genealogie der Moral*, 1887, trans. 1968). In Turin in 1889, after running across a square to protect a horse that was being cruelly whipped, Nietzsche collapsed into madness. He lived until 1900 in an increasingly catatonic state, mainly in the care of his mother.

Nietzsche's importance is first and foremost as a psychologist, as the first psychologist in the sense that we who live after Freud now use that term. He was the first man to go intensively and across a broad frontier into the question of motives, of why people do what they do. There are thousands of Nietzsche's aphorisms that explore the complicated relations between impulses and desires, fantasies and rationalizations – and how they influence what we do. Typical of the content and style of his aphorisms is: '"I have done that," says my memory. "I cannot have done that," says my pride, and remains inexorable. Eventually, memory yields.'

The focus of Nietzsche's psychologizing is over morality. His starting point is the query as to whether morality itself does not present the greatest danger to human society. Perhaps what has hitherto been praised as 'good' is 'a seduction, a poison, a narcotic, through which the present was possibly living at the expense of the future'. According to Nietzsche's history of morality there was originally an aristocratic age in which the terms 'good' and 'bad' were employed to describe noble, high-spirited, self-affirming action, and alternatively that which was plebeian, uninspired, and utilitarian. Only late in human history did the relationship of the noble to the common become moralized. Simultaneously the egoist-altruist dichotomy took possession of human consciousness. The early product of, and in turn catalyst for, this transition was the priest; with him emerged the reactive type, he who, in the absence of spontaneous passions to direct his actions, applies his intellect to create a network of moral, religious, and metaphysical rules to guide his conduct. The reactive emotions – pity, compassion and humility – are endowed with supreme virtue; altruism is established as the moral yardstick for social interaction. Finally, a second type of reactive emotion – vengeance, envy and resentment – takes root at a deeper level, and erodes the remaining capacities for impulsive, expressive action: 'the slave revolt in morals begins by "resentment" turning creative and giving birth to values.'

Nietzsche maintains that it was in a desperate attempt to avoid pain, to evade the cruelty and hostility of his neighbour, that man was driven to sharpen his wits, to extend his memory – to think. But this same struggle to reduce tension also gave birth to morality; thereby it provided community with its most powerful nexus, its most resilient self-preserving bond. Nietzsche is led finally to differentiate the universe of human action into two broad classes: the one aristocratic, powerful, hedonistically vital, later egoistic, creative, irreligious, and a-social; the other structured and rationalized according to a strict moral code, Christian, utilitarian, reactive emotionally, and community-centred.

However, the history of morality is not simply a malign one. European culture, and with it the highest achievements of civilization, have been nurtured in the same soil, that of the slave's attempt to master his hostile environment: the priest with his evil introduced the seeds out of which man grew 'interesting', 'complex', and 'deep'. The quality of a philosopher's thought, for instance, is directly related to the levels of instinctual repression under whose burden he struggles. Ultimately Nietzsche does not criticize the slave morality itself, but a society in which the priest has gained too much power, where the creative forces of the master are in danger of becoming completely repressed. It is this advance of the naive conception that morality and social constraint, and the instinctual renunciation that they enforce, are fully ameliorable that prepares the way for Freud's insights into the psychological nature and necessities of civilization. Nietzsche's analysis here provides the supreme example of psychological ambivalence at work.

Nietzsche's life-long wrestling with the problem of morality drove him ultimately to choose the beautiful rather than the good. Thus it is that his central socio-historical concern is with *Kultur*; thus it is that he scorns ethical commitment to individual happiness and social melioration; and thus it is that he singles out the politically optimistic philosophies of liberalism and socialism as mutilating human reality through their ideals. Nietzsche's qualms about humanist ethics stem from his fatalist conviction that man does not have the power, by means of conscious choice or application, to improve the quality of his life. 'Quality' is an aesthetic concept, and the 'beautiful', whether in the form of a human creation or of an exemplary individual, is supra-historical – it can neither be predicted nor prepared for. Man is more than an animal only in that he finds expression for the beautiful. Additionally, it is significant merely that he may recognize and praise that beauty which moves him. The ugliness of the ideological and the political lies in their legitimating the pursuit of the trivial: they have no rapport with the essence of beauty, nor with its elusive origins.

In terms of the status of philosophy and knowledge Nietzsche was a sceptic. He argues that philosophers have placed an unwarranted trust in concepts, they have absurdly overestimated consciousness. He poses the question again and again of whether the whole of conscious life is not a reflected image, of whether thought and belief bear any relation to active life other than that of providing it with an *ex post* signature.

This querying of *homo sapiens'* cardinal assumption about himself intensifies Hegel's* reflection that the owl of Minerva takes flight at dusk, that the time for philosophy is when the action is over. Nietzsche's sounding of knowledge is potentially far more radical, and self-annihilating, than Marx's* contention that hitherto philosophy had failed to change the world. Nietzsche, in addition, questions the very assumptions of our thinking, calling the principle of causality at best a useful fiction.

Nietzsche identifies philosophy as being like tragedy, one of the high arts of living. At its best, philosophy is the means used by one type of exceptional man to represent himself, to tell his tale with the uncompromising honesty which renders it hauntingly beautiful. The reflective process is in this case vindicated:

Gradually it has become clear to me what every great philosophy so far has been: namely, the personal confession of its author and a kind of involuntary and unconscious memoir; also that the moral (or immoral) intentions in every philosophy constituted the real germ of life from which the whole plant had grown.

Nietzsche implies that the search for knowledge conducted on any other basis, for example that of positivist science, is not fundamentally serious.

Nietzsche called himself the philosopher with a hammer. His psychology and his scepticism fuse in his model for philosophy, or thinking. All modern men are infected with slave morality, and as a result bad conscience and half-heartedness. Zarathustra mimics the modern decadent: 'One has one's little pleasure for the day and one's little pleasure for the night: but one has a regard for health. "We have invented happiness," say the last men, and they blink.' The slave morality's leading symptom is idealism, the fact that men need to tell themselves what they *ought* to do, and whom they *ought* to be. Nietzsche sets up his philosophy as a method of self-criticism, of the individual putting his own ideals into question. 'Self-overcoming' is the first task of thinking. Nietzsche describes himself as taking a tuning fork to the ideals of the time, including his own, and tapping them to hear how hollow they sound.

Nietzsche is famous for his proclaiming the 'death of God'. He meant to command and to warn, for once God is truly removed there are no moral markers left to tell men what to do. Only those with an undertow of driving, Dionysiac instincts will survive, if there are such men left. With characteristic ambivalence Nietzsche places nihilism as the cardinal modern disease, and at the same time advocates a mode of thinking guaranteed to make men less confident in their moral attachments.

The Anglo-Saxon world in particular has often damned Nietzsche as one of the founders of Nazi ideology. In fact Nietzsche was no anti-Semite and the Nazi movement itself would have appalled him. Nevertheless there are parts of his political philosophy, and his ideal of the 'superman', that have close affinities with the later ideas of Nazism. But essentially Nietzsche was an unpolitical man: as Thomas Mann suggested, his political views are the fantasies of an inexperienced child, anticipating rather than creating fascist ideology. It is more important to recognize in conclusion that much of Nietzsche's own life, like his politics, was disturbed. To take him at his own instruction, to judge the work in terms of the man, should make us wary of his philosophy, and perhaps turn to his great French precursor, La Rochefoucauld, an utterly sane and engagingly urbane character who produced a similar psychology, and also in the form of maxims. However that would be to deny the sheer brilliance of Nietzsche's insights, the uncanny accuracy and pungency of much of his prophecy; all of which makes him one of the handful of great thinkers of the nineteenth century. Freud several times said of Nietzsche that he had a more penetrating knowledge of himself than any other man who ever lived or was ever likely to live.

John Carroll

Other important works by Nietzsche include: *Die Geburt der Tragödie* (1872, trans. *The Birth of Tragedy*, 1968); *Unzeitgemässe Betrachlungen* (4 vols 1873–6, trans. *Thoughts Out of Season*, 2 vols 1909); *Menschliches Allzumenschliches* (1878, trans. *Human All-Too-Human*, 1911); *Götzendammerung* (1889, trans. *Twilight of the Idols*, 1968); *Der Antichrist* (1895, trans. *The Antichrist*, 1968); *Nietzsche Contra Wagner* (1895, trans. 1954); *Ecce Homo* (1908, trans. 1968). See: Arthur C. Danto, *Nietzsche as Philosopher* (1965); Karl Jaspers, *Nietzsche* (1965); R.J. Hollingdale, *Nietzsche: The Man and his Philosophy* (1965); Walter Kaufman, *Nietzsche: Philosopher, Psychologist, Antichrist* (1968).

334

NIGHTINGALE, Florence 1820–1910

British founder of modern nursing

The second daughter of a wealthy and cultivated country squire, Florence Nightingale was educated at home by her father. She studied classical and modern languages, history and philosophy. Florence proved an excellent scholar but early on grew restless in the confines of the drawing-room. When she was not yet seventeen she wrote that God had called her to his service.

She was twenty-four when she decided that nursing was to be her vocation but the shocked disapproval of her family prevented her from entering a hospital. Instead she prepared herself by studying official publications on public health and hospitals. She also visited hospitals in England and on the continent whenever she could. In 1851 she trained for four months as a nurse at the Kaiserswerth Institution for Deaconesses in Germany.

In 1853 she took up her first post as superintendent of an institution for sick gentlewomen in distressed circumstances in London, successfully reorganizing the administration and accounts of the establishment.

In March the following year England and France declared war on Russia. By the autumn the British public had grown indignant at the appalling suffering of the casualties in the Crimea publicized by *The Times*. A call for Englishwomen to nurse the troops was made in the newspaper.

Florence Nightingale's letter volunteering her services crossed with an invitation from Sidney Herbert, the Secretary at War, asking her to introduce female nurses into hospitals in the British Army. She was appointed officially as 'Superintendent of the Female Nursing Establishment of the English General Hospitals in Turkey'.

In November 1854 Miss Nightingale and her party of thirty-eight nurses arrived at the huge barracks hospital at Scutari on the shores of the Bosphorus. She found the converted Turkish barracks verminous and filthy, desperately short of medical supplies, food, clothing, bedding and furniture. At first the doctors, furious at the 'unwise indulgence' of allowing women to nurse soldiers, ignored Miss Nightingale and the supplies that she had brought with her.

A few days after her party arrived, hundreds of fresh casualties from the battle of Inkerman were brought into a hospital totally unprepared to receive them. There were no operating tables, bandages, pillows or blankets. The army method for supplying the hospital was confused and antiquated and it broke down completely under the strain of overcrowding. The only person with money and the authority to spend it was Florence Nightingale. She had about £30,000, through funds raised by *The Times* and public money, and became, in effect, purveyor to the hospital.

The first requisition she made was for 200 scrubbing brushes. Sanitation was non-existent. The privies were overflowing, the water-pipes blocked up and dysentery cases were dying at the rate of one in two.

Through her organizational ability and iron will she cut through the army's red tape. Extra diet kitchens were set up, wards were cleaned, repaired and equipped, sewers were flushed and walls lime-washed. By the spring of 1855 the mortality rate had dropped dramatically and Miss Nightingale had established an orderly, hygienic base hospital.

Army officials still obstructed her, but she had saved the lives of hundreds of the troops and they adored her. She alone on the British side emerged from the Crimean War with a high reputation.

The government offered a man-of-war to take her home in state after the war but she slipped back into England incognito. On her return she campaigned for army reform, determined that the costly chaos of the Crimea should never recur. On her insistence and with the support of Queen Victoria*, a Royal Commission on the Health of the Army was set up, with Florence Nightingale approving the selection of the commissioners and advising them at every turn. Her long and detailed evidence was held to be conclusive. As a result, the diet and living conditions of the soldier were improved in peace and war and the design, administration and equipment of military hospitals were reformed. Careful statistical records of illness and disease were also kept.

The Indian Mutiny of 1857 drew her attention to army conditions in India and she painstakingly collated a record of the health of the troops in every Indian army station although she had never visited India. Successive viceroys consulted her on questions of public health and through her intervention a sanitary department was set up in the India Office.

Her influence spread to civilian hospitals where preventive medicine was no less necessary to reverse the high mortality rate. After her book *Notes on Hospitals* was published in 1859 she was constantly asked for her advice on hospital construction. In 1860 she opened the Nightingale Training School for Nurses at St Thomas's Hospital, with the proceeds of a fund raised in her honour. She was organizer and patron of the school, which was designed to produce nurses of a high calibre, capable of training others. She was also instrumental in establishing a school for midwives and for reforming conditions and nursing in the workhouses in the course of a long and extraordinarily industrious life.

Yet she lived as an invalid and a recluse after her return from the Crimea, without any official position, directing operations from her sofa where ministers of state, doctors and civil servants called daily.

She exploited her 'illness' in order to devote herself to work and she drove her collaborators beyond their endurance. Yet she was ruthless with herself too and she detested the sentimental image of 'the Lady with the Lamp' so cherished by the public. In 1907, when she was nearly ninety, she was the first woman to receive the Order of Merit. Her personal influence raised the status of nursing from a menial occupation to an honourable profession and improved the standard of public health in Britain and abroad.

June Rose

Florence Nightingale's other writings include: *Notes on Matters Affecting the Health, Efficiency and Hospital Administration of the British Army* (1858); *Notes on Nursing* (1860); *Observations on the Evidence contained in the Stational Reports submitted to the Royal Commission on the Sanitary State of India* (1863). The standard biography is Cecil Woodham-Smith, *Florence Nightingale* (1950). See also Lytton Strachey's debunking essay in *Eminent Victorians* (1918).

335
NOBEL, Alfred Bernhard 1833–96

Swedish industrialist and philanthropist

Nobel was brought up in Stockholm and, from 1842, St Petersburg where his father, a failed architect, moved in 1837 after being declared bankrupt in Sweden. He was tutored privately and before joining his father's munitions business in 1853 travelled widely in Europe and the United States. A further bankruptcy in 1859 forced the family back to Sweden.

Success appeared to have come to Nobel's father at last when, in 1862, he appeared to have worked out a reasonably secure method for the large-scale production of nitroglycerine. This powerful explosive was discovered by the Italian chemist A. Sobrero in 1846 by nitrating glycerine but, despite the attempts of several chemists to develop its commercial potential, it had proved far too unstable to handle in any quantity. In 1864 the family factory, starkly called Nitroglycerin Inc., was opened at Heleneborg outside Stockholm. Hardly had production begun when a serious explosion destroyed much of the factory and killed Nobel's brother Emil. Clearly much more needed to be done.

It was Alfred Nobel three years later who made the crucial step permitting the full commercial development of the new explosive. He mixed the oily nitroglycerine with an inert earth known as kieselguhr able to absorb some three to four times its own weight. Exploded by the mercury fulminate detonator developed by Nobel in 1863 the new explosive, known as dynamite, became one of the great forces of change, allowing feats of construction to be executed which would not have been even considered earlier in the century.

Dynamite, patented by 1867 in Sweden, America and Britain, used throughout the world by the civil engineer rather than the military, was the basis for Nobel's vast fortune. A further advance was made in 1875 when he developed blasting gelatine. More powerful, less sensitive to shock and with greater resistance to moisture, the new explosive opened up additional markets, including the safe cracker, under the more familiar name of gelignite.

Despite his fortune Nobel's life was far from idyllic. His offer of marriage to his secretary Bertha Kinsky was rejected and in later life he suffered from angina. He wrote of himself: 'When at the age of 54 one is left so alone in this world, and a paid servant is the only person who has so far showed one the most kindness, then come heavy thoughts, heavier than most people imagine.' There were also business disputes and legal battles in his later years which added to his general gloom.

In his will Nobel left most of his fortune of 33 million kroner, equivalent to about £50 million at 1980 prices, to set up a fund, the income of which would be used to award annually five prizes. Specifically prizes were to be awarded in the fields of physics, chemistry, medicine and physiology for 'the most important discoveries or inventions made during the previous year', in literature for 'the most outstanding work . . . of idealistic tendency' and the peace prize for 'the best work for fraternity among nations'.

The prizes were first awarded in 1901 and have since continued, despite several minor crises of confidence, to hold an unchallenged esteem in both the popular imagination and the world of learning. The conjunction of peace prize and explosives manufacturer added precisely the right degree of paradox to guarantee its uniqueness.

Derek Gjertsen

Nobel wrote one book, *On Modern Blasting Agents* (1875). There are two biographies: E. Bergengren, *A. Nobel, the man and his work* (1962); and H. Schück and R. Sohlman, *The Life of A. Nobel* (1929). Details of the Nobel Foundation and its operations can be found in *Nobel, the Man and the Prizes* (1962), edited by the Foundation itself, and sociological aspects of the prizes are dealt with in H. Zuckermann, *Scientific Elite* (1977).

336

NORWID, Cyprian Kamil 1821–83

Polish poet and artist

Norwid's influence has been predominantly on twentieth-century Polish letters, growing more important with each new literary generation. Until his rediscovery by Zenon Przesmycki-Miriam at the turn of the century, the poet had been generally shunned by the Polish reading public. Although his philosophic views found few supporters, it was principally on account of Norwid's formal experimentation and obscurity that his art was denigrated and dismissed by his contemporaries. However, the poet's achievement is considerable. Metrical and strophic innovations are coupled with a formidable lexical eclecticism and syntactic flexibility. These elements are further integrated into an allusive, ironic, parabolic structure. The cycle of poems in *Vade-mecum*, written principally in the early 1860s, although the majority of the texts were published between 1901 and 1956, is as crucial an event in the development of the Polish poetic tradition as the appearance of Baudelaire's* *Les Fleurs du mal* in the West European one. And although certain similarities exist between Norwid's work and that of the Symbolists, the Pole does not appear to have been influenced by the French poets.

Norwid was a highly reserved man, whose isolation within and differences from the *émigré* Polish community marked most of his career. Essentially self-taught, in 1842 he left Poland to continue his art studies abroad. The contact with Mediterranean culture was fundamental in shaping his philosophy based on an investigation of the relationship between man and history and in stimulating his fascination, closely related to this ideology, with biblical and classical antiquity. Although welcomed during the 1840s by the older *émigrés*, particularly as his youthful more conventional verse published in Poland had been well received and as he had also acquired a reputation as a patriot, his orthodox Catholicism distanced him from Mickiewicz*, whilst his age inevitably separated him from the members of the Great Emigration. Norwid, however, participated in the debates of this period, expressing views clearly influenced by Krasiński*, which he presented in poetic compositions such as *Wigilia (Legenda dla przyjaciól)* ('The Eve. – A Legend for Friends', Paris, 1848) and *Jeszcze słowo* ('One More Word', Paris, 1849). However, after 1848 Norwid began to take up positions which were closer to those of the utopian European Left. In his important allegorical poetic drama *Zwolon* (Posen, 1851, but written in 1848–9), he attacked Romantic ideas of revenge and violent action, and presented the homeland not as an extreme emotional concept, but as a practical Christian question of human community and responsibility. He developed these ideas in his great poetic synthesis *Promethidion* (Paris, 1851), in which he fused folklore, aesthetics and historiosophy. In this work, a dialogue inspired by Platonic and neo-Platonic ideas, Norwid presented art as a practical phenomenon, akin to work. Through a reconciliation of these two activities, whereby the artist elevates the national to the universal, progress will be achieved and suffering alleviated. It was from the publication of these difficult works that the attacks upon Norwid began, although throughout his life the poet defended the validity of his experience. In 1852 he left for America but, disillusioned, he returned to Paris in 1855, which was his home until his death. Increasingly ignored, his work unpublished, Norwid also suffered extreme material hardships. However, the range of his literary skills did not diminish. He wrote social, erotic, philosophical, satirical, celebratory verse, parabolic short stories, letters on many subjects, a tragi-comedy, and historical drama. The most important pieces of this second period are the dramatic poem *Quidam* (Leipzig, 1862, although principally written in 1855), which is the fullest expression of Norwid's historiosophy, and *Fortepian Szopena* ('Chopin's Piano', Paris, 1865), his reaction to the Polish insurrection of 1863.

Norwid's art was both an attempt to find an adequate medium of expression for his complex ideology and a means to establish his own poetic identity in relation to the 'Big Three', Mickiewicz, Słowacki and Krasiński. Yet, despite his originality and rejection of Romantic modes, his debt to these is significant.

Zygmunt G. Barański

The critical edition of Norwid's work is *Pisma wszystkie*, ed. J.W. Gomulicki (10 vols, 1971–3). See: K. Wyka, *Cyprian Norwid, poeta i sztukmistrz* (1948); W. Borowy, *O Norwidzie* (1960); T.F. Domaradzki, *Le Symbolisme et l'universalisme de C.K. Norwid: l'homme, le langage et l'art* (1974); G. Gömöri, *Cyprian Norwid* (1974); R. Jakobson, '"Czuosc" C. Norwida', in *For Wiktor Weintraub*, ed. V. Erlich (1975), pp. 227–37; J.W. Gomulicki, *Cyprian Norwid. Przewodnik po życiu i twórczości* (1976).

O

OFFENBACH, Jacques (Jacob) 1819–80

French composer

At the age of fourteen Offenbach left his home-town of Cologne and went to Paris to pursue his musical studies and make a career. His father rightly took the view that France offered better prospects to a musician of Jewish extraction than did Germany in the illiberal days of the first half of the nineteenth century. All places at the Conservatoire were normally reserved for French pupils, but Cherubini* was so impressed by Offenbach's promise as a cellist that he stretched the regulations and admitted him. Within a year, however, the lad parted company with his teachers and began making a precarious living as a soloist and orchestral player. He rapidly gained a reputation as a virtuoso, sometimes performing his own compositions. Far more important in the development of his interest in music for the stage was the experience he gained in the orchestra pit, first at the Ambigu Comique, then at the Opéra Comique. He was also fortunate to serve as musical director of the Comédie-Française for five years from 1850, despite the frustrations of working in a theatre that persisted in treating music as a mere adjunct to the spoken word in drama.

In 1855, the year of the great International Exhibition in Paris, Offenbach decided to make a bid for independence. So far he had had scant success in interesting theatre managers in his operettas. Now, with crowds of tourists expected and every prospect of a brilliant season, he judged the time had come to found a company of his own to perform his works. With financial backing from Henri de Villemessant, founder of Le Figaro, he leased a tiny theatre in the Champs-Elysées. Under the name Les Bouffes-Parisiens, the new company was an immediate success. In the autumn, when the exhibition closed, Offenbach looked for more central premises, and the company moved into the Théâtre des Jeunes-Élèves in the fashionable Passage Choiseul. Police regulations at the time stipulated that no more than four characters should appear in productions in the minor Parisian theatres, and Offenbach's operettas from this period are marred by this unnatural limitation. Generally they are in a single act, three separate works making up an evening's entertainment. The plots are simple and either hackneyed

or the working out of just one fresh idea. Light in tone, sometimes sentimental or else spiced with a certain topicality, these operettas were extremely popular in their day. Some of the credit is due to the librettists, Henri Meilhac (1831–97) and Ludovic Halévy (1834–1908). But Offenbach was the driving force behind Les Bouffes-Parisiens, and it was his gift for catchy tunes and bright orchestration that gave life to these trifles.

Orpheus in the Underworld (Orphée aux enfers) was first performed in 1858. It was in two acts, and this longer form allowed Offenbach to develop his delight in uproarious travesty and irreverent parody, sparing neither Homer nor Gluck. Six years later, Offenbach surpassed this triumph with Fair Helen (La Belle Hélène). In 1866 he transformed a hoary horror story into farce in Bluebeard (Barbe-bleue). That same year he also pretended to treat contemporary life in the French capital in La Vie parisienne, only to show a succession of hilarious escapades. La Grande-Duchesse de Gerolstein (1867) is set in a petty German state, complete with minuscule army and haughty aristocrats. The basic attitude, however, remains the same, as the Grand Duchess pursues her amours with reckless abandon, like the inhabitants of Offenbach's Olympus. Many critics emphasize satiric qualities in these operettas, seeing in them sharp criticism of the hollow vanity of the Second Empire with its parvenu aristocracy and thinly veneered immorality. But it could be more useful to think rather of festive comedy, in which, for a short while, the jester is at liberty to make mock of all that is held sacred. Napoleon III dealt harshly with any subversive force, yet he enjoyed the operettas, while Offenbach, who acquired French citizenship thanks to the emperor's intervention when his application for naturalization was under consideration, became something of an establishment figure. Cheeky, irreverent, always ready to see the funny side of everybody who took himself seriously, an inveterate parodist of everything that was pretentious, Offenbach was too joyous to be a satirist. In his great creative phase, Offenbach owed much to the artistes he employed, especially the ever-popular Hortense Schneider, and Meilhac and Halévy continued to supply him with deftly constructed (if poorly worded) librettos. But these operettas would not be remembered today, were it not for Offenbach's gifts as a melodist and orchestrator.

Offenbach's success waned with the collapse of the Second Empire, though he went on writing for the theatre, providing, for instance, incidental music for Sardou's* spectacular melodrama *Hatred* (*La Haine*) in 1874. He died in 1880 before completing *The Tales of Hoffmann* (*Les Contes d'Hoffmann*); it is a fine score by an accomplished musician and reveals a more profound vein than the operettas.

C.N. Smith

Offenbach's own account of a moderately successful visit to America in 1873 has been translated by Lander MacClintock under the title *Orpheus in America* (1958). See: Alexander Faris, *Jacques Offenbach* (London, 1980); J. Harding, *Jacques Offenbach* (1980); and, in French, A. Decaux, *Offenbach, roi du Second Empire* (1958); and Jacques Brindejont-Offenbach, *Offenbach, mon grandpère* (1940). See also: Gervase Hughes, *Composers of operetta* (1962).

338

O'GRADY, Standish James 1846–1928

Irish miscellaneous writer

Born in County Cork in 1846, the son of a well-born Church of Ireland clergyman, O'Grady was educated at Tipperary Grammar School and Dublin University (Trinity College). Called to the Irish bar in 1872, he adopted journalism as a career, writing leaders for the (Dublin) *Daily Express*. As a young man he came by chance on a copy of Sylvester O'Halloran's *General History of Ireland* (1774), and thereafter devoted himself to the emulation of the great Irish past in the less encouraging conditions of the late nineteenth and early twentieth century. In this regard, he was faithful unto death.

His historical writings in the years 1878–81 have little value as history, but by highlighting the figure of Cuchulain they contributed much to the mythic material of the Anglo-Irish renaissance. *The Crisis in Ireland* (1882) is the first of several polemical works on landlordism and democracy, in which the (conflicting) influences of Thomas Carlyle* and Karl Marx* are discernible. Between 1889 and 1902 he wrote several historical romances, but his edition of the Elizabethan war chronicle *Pacata Hibernica* (1896) is arguably of more lasting value. In 1898, he took control of the *Kilkenny Moderator* thinking to exhort the local aristocracy to emulate Cuchulain and the heroes of the Tudor period: instead he became embroiled in a ludicrous scandal in which the Church Lads' Brigade were harangued on the Roman virtues. The *All Ireland Review* (1900–7) was a more successful contribution to journalism and cultural revival.

O'Grady's literary attitudes may be gauged from a manuscript note he added to a copy of his *The Bog of Stars* (1893) – 'All the tales in this book may be read

as History except the first . . . ' – while an annotation to his *Story of Ireland* (1894) reads: 'I wrote this outline of Irish history rapidly, in less than a month! Looking up no authority during its composition except for the Battle of the Boyne.' Of the fiction, little deserves re-reading, though the polemical works remain vigorous and stylish: *Selected Essays and Passages* (c. 1918) is representative.

Essentially a radical Tory, O'Grady's political achievement paradoxically was to reveal the fraudulence of Anglo-Irish 'ascendancy' pretensions, and to suggest with less artistic achievement a mythology suited to that demoralized class.

W.J. Mc Cormack

See: Hugh Art O'Grady, *Standish James O'Grady: the Man and the Work* (1929); Phillip L. Marcus, *Standish O'Grady* (1970); Vivian Mercier, 'Standish James O'Grady', *Colby Library Quarterly*, series IV, no. 16 (November 1958).

339

OWEN, Robert 1771–1857

British manufacturer, factory reformer, social theorist

Robert Owen was born at Welshpool, Montgomeryshire (Powys), the son of a saddler. He left school at the age of nine and took various jobs in England connected with drapery and cotton. As a young man in his twenties he was established as a mill manager in Manchester. Business remained his preoccupation, though he interested himself in science, health and education generally. In 1799 he bought the New Lanark mills in Scotland which, in conjunction with various partners, he ran at a considerable profit for thirty years. What distinguished him was a concern for 'improvements of the living machinery'. New Lanark was run as a closed community. In the village he provided improved houses, streets and sanitation, food and drink. An Institution for the Formation of Character supplied social activities. Corporal punishment and swearing were both banned. If 'enlightened' in his practices, it is likely that his wages were lower than those paid in other mills in central Scotland. The enterprise remained firmly under Owen's control. The factory was closely supervised – though workers had a distinctive right of appeal. Education seemed to Owen the key to progress and his schools at New Lanark, if not unique in Scotland, looked advanced from an English perspective. His *New View of Society* (1813) expanded on the notion that the character of any community could be shaped by the appropriate educational provision. The process should begin with nursery schools and the possibility of making children happy should not be excluded. Men would be so impressed by his principles and system that the errors which had afflicted previous generations could be eliminated. Universal love and benevolence would prevail. Previous religions had become corrupted and what he offered in his *Address to the Inhabitants of New Lanark* (1816) was a religion of charity, unconnected with faith. The mental liberty of man being secured, he would become a reasonable and consequently a superior being. The vision that Owen proclaimed and the language in which it was couched partakes of the same mood as contemporary millenarianism.

The prophet brought his word to London as his promise to 'let prosperity loose upon the country' excited both radicals and established political figures concerned about the conditions of life in the new factory systems. His vision, on closer inspection, alarmed as much by its naivety as by its thoroughness. His suggestion that if the cotton trade could not reform itself it had better cease did not appeal. Although invited to present proposals for a factory bill the 1819 measure was so emasculated by the time it reached the statute book that Owen, in turn, became disillusioned with politicians and the reception given his ideas. Radicals criticized Owen's autocratic conduct and Cobbett* accused him of creating 'parallelograms of paupers'. Undeterred, Owen was prepared to spend his own money in propagating his cause both in Britain and Europe. He found the ministers of despotic powers well disposed to the 'new system of society' which he proposed, though he was later forced to admit that his own ideas and the European systems of government were incompatible.

It was in these circumstances that Owen's mind turned again to schemes for the future as in his *Report to the County of Lanark* (1820). About the same time, he heard of various religious communities in the United States. In October 1824 he sailed across the Atlantic to complete the purchase of an area of 20,000 acres and to establish there a new community, New Har-

mony. It would attract scientists and working men in a grand co-operative enterprise. Inevitably, it also attracted many who were neither as well. By 1827, New Harmony had failed, due, Owen argued, to the continuing strength of the individualist superstition. Failure, however, lost the prophet prestige and money, although various new communal experiments were started in America, Britain and Europe, all of which claimed Owen as an inspiration. Back in England in the early 1830s Owen turned to the formation of the Grand National Consolidated Trades Union which would include every trade and craft and abolish the distinction between masters and men. Once again, the organization was a failure in practice. As an individual, Owen became more and more difficult to deal with. New Lanark was in fact his only completed experiment. Always ready with a lofty vision, he showed an increasing inability to consider practical conclusions. If his business sense had once been acute, it deserted him. His behaviour became more and more unpredictable as he travelled the world declaring the principles of a rational society. Nowhere quite matched his expectations. Visiting the United States as an old man he found there more 'mental slavery' than existed in England. Always ready to offer guidance on paper to any unknown inquirer, the guidance and support he gave to his own family was never very conspicuous. Towards the end of his life he became a spiritualist. If, therefore, it is difficult to point to any specific legacy left by Owen, his views lived on in a variety of socialist, labour and communitarian groups.

Keith Robbins

See: M. Cole, *Robert Owen of New Lanark* (1953); J.F.C. Harrison, *Robert Owen and the Owenites in Britain and America* (1969); *Robert Owen, Prince of Cotton Spinners*, ed. J. Butt (1971); S. Pollard and J. Salt, *Robert Owen* (1971).

P

PAGANINI, Niccolo 1782–1840

Italian instrumentalist and composer

The Romantic cult of the self inevitably found a reflection in the increasing popularity of the solo performer. Such acclaim was not restricted to singers. As technical modifications and the demands of the composer increased the scope of the solo instrumentalist, he found himself flung into bolder relief, so that an entire concerto literature of the early nineteenth century exists in which the orchestra plays little part other than as the punctuator of a series of acrobatic displays by the soloist. Among violinists the greatest exemplar of Romantic solo performance as an art in itself was undoubtedly Niccolo Paganini, a figure whose legendary bravura provided the model for a type still not wholly eclipsed in our own day, when concert audiences are notionally more discriminating.

Born into the family of an impoverished Genoese shipping clerk, Paganini was taught by a music-loving father and by the leading theatre violinists of his native city, but his ambitions as a performer were initially fired by hearing the Polish virtuoso Duranowski, then on a concert tour. Taken by his father to Parma to study with Alessandro Rolla (who was later to teach Verdi*) Paganini found the composer ill in bed and while waiting in an ante-room took up a newly written concerto lying on the table and played it through at sight. Rolla was sufficiently impressed as to send him directly to Ferdinando Paer, then the doyen of younger Italian musicians, with whom he studied for a year.

In 1801 Paganini went to Lucca as leader and conductor of the orchestra at the court of Napoleon's* sister Elisa Baciocchi, Queen of Tuscany. This was a particularly favourable and fertile period in his career, during which he not only established his primacy among Italian violinists, but gave evidence of his serious concern with the standards of orchestral playing and performance. He left Lucca in 1809, when the orchestra was replaced by a string quartet, and embarked on the life of a wandering soloist which was to occupy him for some thirty years.

His Italian successes led to engagements abroad, and his fourteen concerts in Vienna in 1828 introduced Austrian musicians to a new violin style. An equally triumphant visit to Prague was marred by an operation on his jaw which demanded the removal of all his teeth. In the following year he visited Berlin, where his broadly emotional style captivated the musical public of a city notorious for its hitherto cold and detached attitude to foreign artists. Though Goethe* and Spohr* (himself a noted violinist and no doubt chary of a brilliant rival) were resolutely unimpressed, Paganini's manner, and an absolute mastery of his instrument to an extent which appeared diabolical, caught the imagination of the poet Heinrich Heine* and the young Robert Schumann*, who was later to adapt his solo caprices for piano.

In 1831 he appeared in Paris, where a characteristic enthusiasm among the younger Parisian Romantics was alloyed by a press campaign against Paganini, emphasizing his supposed meanness. His most uncritically appreciative audiences awaited him in London, where he became a concert favourite during the early 1830s and made the considerable sum of £10,000 from his first eighteen concerts. Dogged by continuing accusations of parsimony (for which no evidence exists) and exhausted by the rigours of concert touring he abandoned his journeyings altogether in 1834.

The following year he was appointed *intendant* of the prestigious court opera at Parma, but his admirable thoroughness in the execution of his duties and his sweeping plans for improving the quality of the orchestra were frustrated by intrigue and pettiness among the ducal officials. His health had begun to deteriorate and his last years were spent in quiet Italian retirement. Refusing to see a priest, he died at Nice (then in Piedmontese territory) in 1840 but was not given burial until, five years later, the Duchess of Parma allowed his body to be returned there.

Paganini's effect upon the audiences of his day was as powerful as his influence on the whole nature of violin-playing, especially in the French and Belgian traditions typified by Vieuxtemps and Ysaye. He was a dramatic performer, whose appearance and platform manner, coupled with his seamless virtuosity of execution, gave rise to a host of legends, centring on the hoary musical cliché of a pact with the devil. It was these qualities which so haunted the imagination of other musicians, including Liszt*, Chopin* (who composed *Souvenirs de Paganini* in homage to him), Berlioz*, from whom he commissioned the viola symphony *Harold in Italy* in 1833 and Rachmaninov.

As a composer in his own right he developed a

unique and unmistakable idiom, which finds its sharpest delineation in the twenty-four Caprices published in 1820, and in the six violin concertos, in which the musical language seems the perfect instrumental counterpart of *bel canto* opera. Above all, his music reflects his passionate concern with the nature of his chosen instrument in all its moods. He gave to violin-playing the cachet of solitary romance which it has never since entirely forsaken.

Jonathan Keates

See: Lillian Day, *Paganini of Genoa* (1929); Jeffrey Pulver, *Paganini: The Romantic Virtuoso* (2nd edn 1969); Geraldine I.C. de Courcy, *Paganini the Genoese* (2 vols, 1957).

341
PALMER, Samuel 1805–81

British painter

Palmer's present reputation rests overwhelmingly on the works he produced between 1825 and 1832 at Shoreham, Kent, some of which are amongst the finest jewels of English landscape painting.

He was born and brought up on the still rural edges of London and Kent. Although his parents were Baptists, Palmer's liking for tradition and ritual led him to join the Church of England. He acquired very early a love for poetry, his favourites being Virgil and Milton, both of whom could endow familiar country scenes with spiritual significance. His older friend John Linnell perceptively steered him away from contemporary landscape painting, which had little to offer him, towards the early Italian, Flemish and German old masters, especially Dürer. In 1824, Linnell introduced him to William Blake, whose ideas on art, poetry and religion were to be crucial to Palmer throughout his life; and it was in the same year that he first visited Shoreham. From 1825 dates a series of works in sepia, including *The Valley Thick with Corn*, which depict nature in all its fecundity and possess an almost hallucinatory intensity. Palmer went to live in Shoreham, which he called the 'Valley of Vision', in 1826 and was joined there by a circle of like-minded friends calling themselves the 'Ancients', who were united by their admiration for Blake.

Palmer's Shoreham paintings combine an accuracy of detail with an extraordinary imaginative freedom. The compositions make use of a somewhat flattened, Gothic perspective and a high horizon line, above which a large moon sometimes dominates, as in *Coming from Evening Church* (1830); there is always a 'mystic glimmer behind the hills'. The hills, which are rounded and breast-like, are complemented by trees and church spires and, although Palmer would have been shocked by a sexual interpretation of his symbols, it seems to modern eyes that they may well derive part of their power from this source; nevertheless, the erotic charge is doubtless the greater for not being explicit. In typically Romantic fashion, his landscapes usually (but not always) contain at least one person, which aids the viewer's participation in the scene: such is the role of the figure walking through the twilight with his large staff in *Cornfield by Moonlight with the Evening Star* (c. 1830). If the contemplative mood of this picture is tinged with melancholy the same, though less obviously, is true of nearly all Palmer's many depictions of harvest, even though they are first and foremost celebrations of God's plenty. For his love of the harvest was linked to his High Church and Tory love of tradition: an appreciation of things that have come to glorious fruition, made more poignant by the knowledge that their passing away is imminent. Although the Shoreham years were the most fulfilled of Palmer's life, he was never even then free from bouts of despair; these had first been brought on by his mother's death when he was thirteen and were later to become worse with the early death of two of his three children. This disposition to a pessimistic view of life fuelled his horror at the unpoetic and secular quality of advancing industrialism; a horror which accounted for his semi-feudal views and his tendency, somewhat corrected later in life, to romanticize the condition of the rural poor, with whom at Shoreham he was on amicable but never intimate terms. No doubt this made it easier for him to paint, as he did, in the pastoral tradition. His paintings, many of which depict shepherds and/or shepherdesses with their flocks or similarly tranquil bucolic scenes, re-create an earthly paradise. But, if his aims were not realistic, nor were they idealizing in the manner of Claude. Suffused with emotion and the desire for redemption, Palmer's Shoreham landscapes fulfilled his ambition of revealing the divine behind the natural.

In 1834, partly, for financial reasons and partly from personal disappointments, Palmer returned to London. The vision faded. Several tours in the British Isles produced work which was little more than topographical. In 1837 he married Linnell's daughter and toured Italy with her for two years. It is true that in a sense this experience broadened his art but it also diluted it, robbing it of almost everything that had made it special. Financially dependent as he was on his increasingly tyrannical father-in-law, Palmer fell ever more victim to the mediocrity which the Linnells in practice forced on him, even to the extent of living in a vulgarly mock-Tudor villa in Redhill, Surrey, the antithesis of everything in which he believed. His art never recovered to the level of the Shoreham period but he did master a new medium, that of etching, in which in the last years of his life he produced some outstanding work. In 1865, he began a series of etchings illustrating Milton, of which *The Lonely Tower* and *The Bellman* are particularly fine examples. From 1872 he worked on a series of etchings illustrating Virgil, although these were less successful – doubtless because Palmer's genius and feeling for landscape were firmly anchored in the North European tradition, a fact which he did himself a great disservice by ignoring so often. His influence was not felt until the twentieth century and then, characteristically, it surfaced in the work of two thoroughly English painters: Paul Nash and Graham Sutherland.

Gray Watson

See: Geoffrey Grigson, *Samuel Palmer: The Visionary Years* (1947); Carlos Peacock, *Samuel Palmer: Shoreham and After* (1968); David Cecil, *Visionary and Dreamer* (1969); James Sellars, *Samuel Palmer* (1974).

342
PARKMAN, Francis 1823–93

American historian

Born in Boston, Massachusetts, Francis Parkman was descended from a New England family of wealth and social standing. Even as a child, and more obviously as a student at Harvard during the early 1840s, Parkman showed a consuming interest in the geographical explorations made by the earliest American settlers. Throughout his youth he journeyed into areas of wilderness and in 1845 published accounts of his adventures.

By 1846, Parkman seems to have formed a clear plan of his life's work. In April he embarked on his 'Oregon Trail' from St Louis with the twofold aim of studying the Indians and improving his health which had begun to deteriorate at Harvard. The first aim was successfully achieved: he became intimately acquainted with the conditions of life at the edges of European culture. But his health broke down completely, and during his convalescence he wrote the still popular *Oregon Trail* (1849).

In 1848 he began his *History of the Conspiracy of Pontiac*, the first volume of his monumental work depicting the struggle between France and England for possession of the continent, eventually to be called *France and England in North America*. Labouring under the immense difficulties of nervous and physical disorders, Parkman completed the book three years later. After the death of his wife and son, he suffered a further nervous crisis in 1858. But in 1865 appeared *Pioneers of France in the New World*, a remarkable achievement of will and determination, which secured his reputation as a historian. Between 1867 and 1877 there followed *The Jesuits in North America*, *La Salle and the Discovery of the Great West* (1869), *The Old Régime in Canada* (1874) and *Count Frontenac and New France under Louis XIV*

(1877). Fearing the approach of a final collapse, Parkman broke the chronological sequence to write its conclusion which was published in 1884 as *Montcalm and Wolfe* (2 vols). In 1892 he completed the series with *A Half-Century of Conflict* (2 vols). Shortly afterwards he contracted pleurisy and died less than a year later.

It is as both a historian and as a literary artist that Parkman's lasting reputation has been established. As a historian, Parkman combines the subjectively interpretative approach of the nineteenth century with the modern Germanic devotion to precise and scrupulous examination of empirical evidence. His work not only charts the chronological progress of the Anglo-French struggle in America, but portrays too the landscapes in which this conflict was enacted and the psychology of its protagonists. Parkman's unique blending of history and geography, narrative and drama, sustains the dominant theme of his historical writings: the contest between two highly developed civilizations for control of an emerging continent of wilderness and savagery. His imagination is occupied in re-creating the challenge of geographical expansion so that his colonizers and frontiersmen embody the heroic virtues of self-reliance and endurance. Hence, Parkman's writing possesses a quality of grandeur as he celebrates the spirit of conquest.

Whilst Parkman's episodic approach may now seem simplistic, his documentary researches were exhaustive, and he gathered together manuscript material which, in its field, has not been entirely superseded. His research also included a personal familiarity with the conditions and life-styles of the early explorers. There is much that his work does not take into account, and it inevitably lacks the philosophical sophistication of recent historical writing. Nevertheless, Parkman does undertake some sort of comparison between the social and political organizations of the rival civilizations in order to suggest a fundamental reason for the final outcome.

It is no accident that Parkman responded imaginatively to embodiments of indomitable resolve for his own task was achieved during a lifetime blighted by severe physical and nervous disorders. Yet the enormous strength of will required to continue his work is belied by the elegant clarity and urbane ease of his prose. At least one writer in the twentieth century has paid tribute to Parkman's literary qualities: Donald Davie's lengthy poem, *A Sequence for Francis Parkman* (1961), draws its inspiration from Parkman's prose and celebrates a man whose intense suffering and resolute determination never obscured his humanity.

Andrew Swarbrick

Collected editions of Parkman's work: *The Works of Francis Parkman* (20 vols, 1897–8) and *Francis Parkman's Works* (12 vols, 1901–3). Biographical studies include C.H. Farnham, *A Life of Francis*

Parkman (1900), and H.D. Sedgwick, *Francis Parkman* (1904). Amongst more recent studies are: R.L. Gale, *Francis Parkman* (1973); D. Levin, *History as Romantic Art* (1959); O. Pease, *Parkman's History: The Historian as Literary Artist* (1953); M. Wade, *Francis Parkman: Heroic Historian* (1942).

343
PARNELL, Charles Stewart 1846–91

Irish statesman

The son of an Anglo-Irish landowner and an American mother, Parnell had a lonely childhood and adolescence, culminating in rustication from Magdalene College, Cambridge, in 1869. He returned to Ireland and associated himself with the parliamentary group led by Isaac Butt which petitioned for Irish Home Rule. In 1875 he entered the House of Commons, but soon adopted radical attitudes which won him the support of the militant nationalists (Fenians). From 1877 onwards he adopted a highly successful obstructionist policy in the Commons which brought Ireland to the centre of political debate. His tactic of allying himself to extra-parliamentary forces was extended when he became president of the National Land League of Ireland and chairman of the Home Rule party in the Commons in 1880. During the next decade, he was one of the most influential figures in British politics: his conversion of W.E. Gladstone* to a Home Rule policy marks one level of his power; the Land Acts of 1881 and 1885 (and after) mark another. This meteoric career had its obverse side, of course: Parnell was accused of sympathy with political assassination following *The Times'* publication of letters of his which were finally proved to be forgeries, and his private life increasingly affected his political behaviour in the latter half of the decade. Having embarked upon an affair with the wife of one of his followers (Captain William O'Shea) with the evident connivance of the husband, Parnell was cited as co-respondent in O'Shea's divorce in 1890. His refusal to offer a denial or a defence led to revulsion among Gladstone's liberals, despite Gladstone's knowledge of the affair and his use of Mrs O'Shea as an intermediary. The Irish party, at first loyal to their leader, but soon stimulated by fears of abandonment by the liberals in Westminster, fears of clerical censure at home in Ireland, and by the vituperative wit of Tim Healey among their number, voted to unseat Parnell in adopting once more a radical stance, though without any electoral success in Ireland. In June 1891 he married Katherine O'Shea, and on 6 October he died in Brighton of inflammation of the lungs.

Parnell's significance may be measured politically. He ensured the viability of a parliamentary politics for the ultimately independent Ireland, and greatly assisted the transfer of land ownership to the occupiers, thus creating the petit-bourgeois electorate of modern Ireland. Paradoxically, he is more often assessed in literary terms: both James Joyce and W.B. Yeats incorporated Parnell into their work. Yeats's notion of him as a tragic aristocratic figure dragged down by the mob, and Joyce's fondness for the image of *l'homme moyen sensuel* are complementary portraits. The intensity of feeling, and resonance of implication, may be gauged in the Christmas dinner scene of Joyce's *A Portrait of the Artist as a Young Man*. Objectively considered, Parnell's historical legacy could hardly have gratified the politics of either the poet or the novelist who preferred to create a mythological figure instead.

W.J. Mc Cormack

The standard biography is F.S.L. Lyons, *Charles Stewart Parnell* (1977). See also: R.F. Foster, *Charles Stewart Parnell: The Man and his Family* (1979); Herbert Howarth, *The Irish Writers 1880–1940; Literature Under Parnell's Star* (1958); Peter Bew, *Parnell* (1980).

344
PARRY, Charles Hubert Hastings 1848–1918

British composer

The received photographic image of a rubicund, mustachioed country squire, a few well-meant but unconsidered revivals of his weaker works, and three generations of ill-informed criticism have left Hubert Parry one of the disaster areas of British music. Paid lip-service as a pioneer of the late nineteenth-century musical revival, chiefly as a teacher, he is generally considered an academic conservative; his huge compositional output has, until recently, only been remembered by the fine choral setting of Milton's *Blest Pair of Sirens* (1887), a grandiose coronation anthem for Edward VII, and 'Jerusalem' (1916) – which, unaccountably enough, just happens to be one of the great tunes of all time. That in itself suggests the reputation is obscuring a more complex reality.

Parry was ideally placed by talent, social station and personality to be a leader. He was the only major English composer from the aristocracy – his father, the painter Thomas Gambier Parry, was squire of Highnam Court in Gloucestershire, and Hubert married Lady Maude Herbert, sister of the Earl of Pembroke. Educated at Malvern, Twyfold, Eton, and Oxford, he displayed musical gifts from an early age, and after three years working for Lloyds Shipping House he devoted himself entirely to music. His mentors and teachers had included S.S. Wesley, Sterndale Bennett and (in Stuttgart) Hugo Pierson; but in London he was particularly encouraged by Edward Dannreuther, a protégé of Liszt* and champion of Wagner*. The

1870s saw his principal output of chamber and instrumental music, culminating in the Piano Quartet (1879), perhaps the finest chamber work an Englishman had produced since the beginning of the century. But 1880 was the year in which he first gained widespread recognition: indeed the première of *Scenes from Shelley's 'Prometheus Unbound'* for soli, chorus and orchestra at the Gloucester Festival is still generally considered to mark the beginning of the 'English Musical Renaissance'.

The work was not in fact a success, and now sounds heavily derivative of Mendelssohn*, Schumann* and early Wagner. But the choice of Shelley* rather than a religious text, the robustly idiomatic setting of the English language, and the composer's unusual skill in the sonorous handling of large choral forces, did indeed bespeak a new spirit which ultimately would wrest British music from the grasp of Victorian conventionality and the domination of the cathedral festivals. Parry was none the less obliged to produce a series of large-scale works for them in the next twenty years. Three oratorios – *Job* (1892) is sometimes misguidedly revived – went against his grain and are largely dead wood; but various pieces to secular texts show increasing individuality and mastery, and the exercise of a keen literary as well as musical intelligence: especially *Blest Pair of Sirens, The Lotos-Eaters* (1892), *Invocation to Music* (1895), and *A Song of Darkness and Light* (1898) – the latter two being collaborations with the poet Robert Bridges* which display Parry's growing philosophical bent. At the same time he was setting new standards for English word-setting with the first four volumes of his *English Lyrics* for voice and piano; and attempting to win equal recognition for orchestral music. In his Third Symphony, the 'English' (1889), he produced a work worthy to stand with the symphonic achievements of his German contemporaries, and the Fourth Symphony (1889) and Symphonic Variations (1897) consolidated an instrumental style that reached back through Brahms* to Handel (and in the choral works was to go further back, to Schütz). Yet already in the remarkable *Concertstück* for orchestra (*c.* 1884, not performed till 1981) he had discovered pronounced 'modernist' tendencies, a grasp of later Wagner and late Liszt astonishing for the period.

The same twenty years saw the burgeoning of the educative and administrative gifts that were to make Parry the teacher of an entire generation of distinguished composers. He joined the staff of the Royal College of Music in 1883 and became Choragus at Oxford in the same year. In 1894 he succeeded Sir George Grove as director of the Royal College of Music, a post he retained till his death, and from 1900 to 1908 he combined it with the professorship of music at Oxford. His personal concern for his students' welfare was legendary. He had assisted Grove with the first edition of the latter's famous *Dictionary of Music and Musicians*, and went on to produce several important books, in addition to much extra conducting and examining. Never conventional in his views (his political radicalism had provoked a long and bitter separation from his father), Parry, though outwardly bluff, was highly emotional, with a pronounced depressive streak. It may well be that the strain of many years' overwork, combined with his own and his wife's frequent ill-health, is sufficient explanation of the striking unevenness of an output that was now largely composed to order as and when he could find the time.

In the early 1900s he attempted to replace the outmoded oratorio form with a series of choral works to broadly agnostic philosophical texts, often from his own pen. These 'ethical cantatas' or *sinfoniae sacrae* are generally disappointing, but they include one major breakthrough in *The Soul's Ransom* (1906), an inspired and tough-minded 'Psalm for the Poor' which represents his most successful fusion of his earlier 'radical' tendencies with the English choral tradition: it is probably the most important work in that tradition between Elgar's *The Dream of Gerontius* and Vaughan Williams's *Sea Symphony*.

The works of Parry's last decade – by which time he was widely regarded as a spent force, a judgment the next generation was to take as axiomatic in its rejection of the Germanic component in English music – constitute his finest achievements: the highly original one-movement Fifth Symphony (1912) and the symphonic poem *From Death to Life* (1914) both fulfil the stylistic promises of the early *Concertstück*; the radiant and festive setting of Dunbar's *Nativity Ode* (1912) is his choral-orchestral masterpiece. These, together with the introspective *God is our Hope* (1913) and the noble series of unaccompanied motets, *Songs of Farewell* (1916–18) that were his testament, are only now beginning to attract attention.

Parry was a greatly gifted musician, a man of high moral and artistic integrity, a visionary, a practical idealist, and a mind of great intellectual breadth. However, as his advice to Vaughan Williams ('Write choral music, as befits an Englishman and a democrat') suggests, he was not an uncompromising Romantic revolutionary in the Berlioz*-Wagner mould, a fact which eased his assimilation and partial neutralization by the late-Victorian establishment. These conflicting aspects were crucial for the early development, and problems, of the English Musical Renaissance. If Elgar and Vaughan Williams were greater geniuses, Parry's role cannot be diminished to that of a mere forerunner. He was the most considerable creative personality on the English musical scene since Handel, and their achievement would have been impossible without his example.

Malcolm MacDonald

Parry's many other works include: the opera *Guinevere* (1885–6, full score lost); Ode to St. Cecilia's Day

(1889) and *The Pied Piper of Hamelin* (1905) for chorus and orchestra; the orchestral *Elegy for Brahms* (1897); Theme and Variations for piano (1878–85). Principal writings: *Studies of Great Composers* (1886); *The Art of Music* (1893); *Johann Sebastian Bach, the Study of a Great Personality* (1909); *Style in Musical Art* (1911). There is no adequate modern study of Parry's life, music, or significance, but see: C.L. Graves, *Hubert Parry* (1926); and Frank Howes, *The English Musical Renaissance* (1966).

345
PASCOLI, Giovanni 1855–1912

Italian poet

The happiness of Pascoli's early childhood in the countryside of Romagna was shattered by the unsolved murder of his father in 1867, soon to be followed by the death of his eldest sister, his mother and two brothers. He was to assume responsibility for his surviving sisters, nurture the myth of the cruel destruction of his family 'nest' and develop the obsessive memorial cult which largely accounts for the major themes of death and human suffering characteristic of his poetry, and possibly for some of his rebellious postures. As a university student at Bologna, he took part in anarchical activity culminating in his being sentenced to almost four months' imprisonment in 1879. On his release, he abandoned active politics and for the rest of his life was a teacher in various parts of Italy, finally succeeding Carducci* to the Chair of Italian Literature at Bologna. In his later years, he drew great comfort from the long periods he spent in his country villa at Castelvecchio di Barga where he found the inspiration for many of his better known poems.

Pascoli is recognized as the most original figure in the so-called Decadent movement and is emerging as the most interesting Italian poet of the second half of his century. While his ingenuousness and spontaneity are reminiscent of the Romantics and he showed a certain spiritual and affective affinity with the rustic and nostalgic (rather than the polemical and satirical) compositions of Carducci, the dominant poet of the day, his technical innovations were a rejection of the latter's adherence to traditional structures and opened new horizons for Italian poetry.

His major collections are *Myricae* ('Tamarisks', 1891–1903) which contains rapid, impressionistic country sketches alongside representations of his personal family tragedy and a dark, painful vision of life; *Primi poemetti* ('First Short Poems', 1897) – and later *Nuovi poemetti* ('New Short Poems', 1909) – in which a long, initial georgic composition contrasts with others that dwell on the unfathomable mystery of the universe and the sad condition of humanity. Again, *Canti di Castelvecchio* ('Songs of Castelvecchio', 1903) are in a sense a continuation of his first collection, drawing their inspiration from the countryside and memories of his dead relatives, and *Poemi conviviali* ('Convivial Poems', 1904) offer an ideal, subjective interpretation of the classical age in which the figures of antiquity become symbols of the artist's own feelings. He was also the leading poet of his generation writing in Latin, and his much admired *Carmina* ('Songs', 1887–1911) reflect his life-long cult of the ancient world.

Pascoli's most enlightening prose writing is *Il Fanciullino* ('The Little Child', 1903) in which he expounds the principle of the irrational and intuitive nature of art and his poetics of objectivity (the concept that poetry is not invented but pre-exists and can be discovered in things themselves). The poet, like the little child in the heart of all men, perceives the marvel and mystery of life through isolated images and impressions, so that all poetry depends on the intensity of the moment rather than the intellectual, ordering process. Feeling and vision are thus infinitely more important than any mode of expression. In this sense, his poetry is probably at its purest and least 'contaminated' in *Myricae* where this new sensibility imparts unity to the fragmented impression of individual compositions, and in *Canti di Castelvecchio* where, in some poems, we also find a musical transcription of sensory experiences, correspondences and analogies that could be called symbolist. When, however, he steps outside the world of the 'little child', his intellect and erudition tend to destroy his mysticism and imagination: his historical poetry degenerates into a type of chronicle; his patriotic socialism results in grandiloquence; his classical culture can lead to preciosity; his preaching on the brotherhood of men transforms his new symbolism into didactic allegory; and, in general, his expressive originality often gives way to stylistic artifice. Yet it has been argued that even in his 'authentic' poetry he somehow fails to satisfy, that he impresses more through his potential than the result he actually achieves. Indeed, it is difficult to discount entirely Croce's harsh assertion that Pascoli is 'a strange mixture of spontaneity and artifice: a great-little poet who . . . lingers in a sphere of semi-poetry'.

He undoubtedly remains significant, however, in so far as both his poetic temperament, with its tendency to give images an obscure symbolic value, and his spiritual sense of bereavement prompt him to break with tradition. The apparent humbleness of his themes and simplicity of his techniques brought about the disintegration of established form. Almost instinctively, he was anti-rhetorical and all but anti-literary in his efforts to isolate the emotive significance of single images, and above all, stands out as the creator of a new type of language which tried to abolish the normal distinction between the grammatical and evocative use of words. In his search for an instrument capable of expressing and deepening the implicit poetic nature of reality, he had recourse to a technical and select vocabulary, colloquialisms, dialect and onomatopoeia, yet his poetry remains more sensitive and suggestive than realistic. Moreover, certain characteristics, such as the obsessive presence of the dead and the mystical aura surrounding his verse, reveal him as a precursor of the Hermetic poets such as Montale, Ungaretti and Quasimodo and anticipate a modern aesthetic trend.

R.D. Catani

Pascoli's complete works (*Opere complete*) were published by Mondadori, Milan, from 1939 onwards. See: B. Croce, *G. Pascoli* (1920); W. Binni, *La poetica del Decadentismo* ('The Poetics of Decadentism', 1936); *Studi per il Centenario della nascita di G. Pascoli*, ed. R. Spongano (3 vols, 1961). M. Biagini, *Il poeta solitario* ('The Solitary Poet', 1963), is the most recent biography, while selections, under the title *Poems*, have been translated by E. Stein (1923) and A.M. Abbot (1927).

346

PASTEUR, Louis 1822–95

French chemist and microbiologist

As one of the greatest scientists of the nineteenth century Pasteur provides a striking example of social promotion from provincial obscurity to the rank of a national hero on the basis of a career in scientific research. The son of a tanner from the Franche-Comté region of France, Louis was born in Dole but spent most of his young life in nearby Arbois. In 1838 his father was persuaded to send him to M. Barbet's school in Paris with the intention that he should go on to the École Normale. Unfortunately the young Pasteur did not settle and was returned to Arbois. Although he continued his education at Arbois and Besançon he was forced eventually to return to M. Barbet's school before he passed to the École Normale. His three years there as a student (1843–6) and two as *préparateur* in, chemistry were followed by two provincial professorships in chemistry, first at Strasburg (1849–52), then at Lille (1854–7) where he was also dean of the faculty of sciences. Despite the undoubted success of his work in Lille University, when the call came to return to the École Normale he accepted. Apart from the seven years he spent as Professor of Chemistry at the Sorbonne Pasteur remained at the École Normale until he became director of the new Institut Pasteur in 1888.

In his life Pasteur exemplified the industrious, upright and independent qualities which marked his family. An admirer of authority and leadership his political inclinations were towards the Second Empire of Louis Napoleon. He was intensely patriotic and so keenly did

he feel the defeat of France in 1871 that he returned the honorary degree conferred on him by the University of Bonn, requesting that his name be effaced from the archives of the medical faculty. It was during the Franco-Prussian War that Pasteur took up the subject of brewing with the intention of laying the foundation for an improved French product that would rival and supersede the beers of Germany so popular in Paris cafés.

Like Galileo, Pasteur was combative and self-confident. Despite the pleading of his elders he could never refrain from responding to criticism, and opponents were demolished without mercy. One such victim challenged him to a duel. Another, the famous Robert Koch*, was forced to concede ground. If Pasteur's claims were questioned he would issue a challenge as he did to the Turin Veterinary School over the effectiveness of his anthrax vaccine, to Charles Bastian over spontaneous generation, and to Liebig* on acetic acid fermentation. Added to his qualities as debater and experimentalist Pasteur was an excellent organizer and he attracted support for his researches which by French standards was exceptional. For the Pasteur Institut alone two million francs were collected.

Pasteur first made his reputation in the field of crystallography. It was known that substances with different crystal forms affected polarized light differently. Some rotated the plane of polarization to the right, others to the left, and yet others were optically inactive. Against this general rule two substances which had the same chemical composition and allegedly the same crystalline form – tartaric acid and paratartaric or racemic acid – affected light differently. The former rotated the plane of polarization to the right while the latter was optically inactive. Pasteur studied the tartrates and paratartrates and revealed the presence of facets on certain corners of the crystals which rendered them asymmetric and hemihedral. All the crystals of the tartrates showed the same hemihedra, but those of the paratartrates were either symmetrical or in the sodium-ammonium salt they were of two kinds – right-handed and left-handed hemihedra. Their separate solutions affected light differently, one rotating the plane of polarization to the right, the other to the left. Together, as in the paratartrate, the solution was optically inactive. Pasteur advanced his law of hemihedral correlation with much boldness; only later under the pressure of exceptions did he place more emphasis upon the relation between optical activity and molecular structure rather than with crystal structure.

This very simple and striking work constituted a major foundation to the growing subject of stereochemistry. To Pasteur it seemed rather to open a route to the experimental study of another great problem – that of life itself – for he was convinced that all optically active organic compounds were the products of living organisms and could not be synthesized in the laboratory. Only in living things were the requisite asymmetric forces at work which would yield such asymmetric molecules. Needless to say, his own attempts to stimulate such forces in the laboratory were fruitless.

Pasteur's move to the industrial town of Lille brought him into contact with the manufacturers of alcohol from beetroot by fermentation. Another product of fermentation, amyl alcohol, which must have been available in the town was of special interest to Pasteur because of its optical activity. Clearly for Pasteur its synthesis required the presence of living organisms, and since it was a product of fermentation it was natural that Pasteur should side with those who claimed that fermentation was a vital process rather than a mere chemical process as the chemists Liebig and Berzelius maintained. Pasteur realized that fermentation was no simple chemical disintegration but a complex process in which a variety of products resulted. In addition to alcohol these included glycerin, succinic acid, amyl alcohol and lactic acid. Just as his predecessors had shown the invariable presence of yeast wherever alcoholic fermentation occurred so Pasteur demonstrated the presence of a fine grey deposit of another yeast-like substance where lactic fermentation took place.

From these and succeeding studies Pasteur was able to correlate a whole range of different fermentations with different micro-organisms. The simple chemical theory was not designed to cope with such diversity. Moreover it required the presence of organic nitrogenous matter in the process of disintegration, for this was held to be the agent of fermentation. In 1858 Pasteur succeeded in bringing about fermentation in the absence of organic nitrogen, thus destroying the central feature of the chemical theory. He concluded that the different fermentations were due to the activity of different micro-organisms. Their germs were present in ordinary air and water; they contaminated the surfaces of vessels, corks, hands, etc. Depending upon the environment one or another of these micro-organisms would reproduce in the medium – grape juice, malt, beet sugar – bringing about its particular type of fermentation. Some, like the butyric ferment, could only live in the absence of oxygen others like yeast could exist with or without oxygen; yet others, like the *Mycoderma asceti*, required oxygen for its fermentation to yield vinegar.

In 1860 a prize was offered for experiments on the subject of spontaneous generation. Pasteur decided to compete. All his experiments, some very ingenious, were designed to show that such generation of living organisms only occurs in a sterile organic medium if it becomes contaminated with microscopic germs from outside. As in the study of fermentation, so in this study he contructed his programme upon his faith in the existence of microscopic germs. Believing that their distribution would vary according to location and altitude he broke and resealed a series of flasks containing a sterile medium at his laboratory and in the vaults of the Observatory, then at the foot of the Jura and at 2,000 metres on the Mer de Glace. Only one of the twenty flasks at 2,000 metres showed microbial growth. In 1862 Pasteur was awarded the prize.

Meanwhile, Felix Pouchet, whose experiments with spontaneous generation of hay infusions had caused the revival of interest in the subject, decided to expose such infusions at an even greater height than Pasteur. With Nicolas Jolet and Charles Musset he exposed eight flasks at 3,000 metres in the Pyrenees, all of which showed spontaneous generation. In 1864 the Académie set up a commission to decide between Pasteur and Pouchet. In the event Pouchet withdrew from the contest, leaving the field to Pasteur. Thirteen years later Charles Bastian also decided not to repeat his experiments on spontaneous generation before the commission set up to judge between him and Pasteur. Both these opponents of Pasteur had demonstrated spontaneous generation in sterile conditions because, unknown to them, the hay infusions they employed contained bacterial spores resistant to boiling. Had they persisted in their challenge the two commissions would have been forced to accept their results.

The implications of the germ theory of fermentation for surgery were appreciated by Joseph Lister* whose introduction of antisepsis was made in the 1860s. The suggestion that contagious diseases were, like fermentation, due to microbes gained support only slowly. In his first study of animal diseases – the *pébrine* and *flacherie* of silkworms – Pasteur proved curiously resistant to the microbial or germ theory. By 1867 his attitude had changed. He went on to contribute to the microbiology of anthrax, fowl cholera, swine erysipelas, and rabies. His greatest achievement was to show that weakened or 'attenuated' forms of these diseases could be produced by serial culture which, like Jenner's cowpox vaccinations, rarely caused the disease, but conferred resistance to the virulent strain, thus protecting or immunizing the host. Pasteur gave dramatic demonstration of the effectiveness of his vaccines in the case of anthrax at Pouilly-le-Fort in 1881 and in the case of rabies when he vaccinated Joseph Meister in 1885. In the ensuing decade some 20,000 people bitten by rabid animals were given the vaccine and less than one half of one per cent died. These achievements established the germ theory decisively in medicine as the basis for treatment of contagious diseases.

It had required three attempts before Pasteur was elected to the mineralogy section of the Académie in 1862, six years after the Royal Society had awarded him the Rumford Medal. In the 1880s honours were heaped upon him. His death was a national event marked by a state funeral at Notre Dame.

Robert Olby

All Pasteur's publications and a large part of his correspondence have been published in *Oeuvres de Pasteur* (7 vols, 1922–39) and *Correspondance* (4 vols, 1940–51). For an account of Pasteur's early life see René Vallery-Radot, *The Life of Pasteur* (trans. 1928), although the treatment of his later scientific career is hagiographic. The best scientific rather than historical analysis of Pasteur's work is Emile Duclaux, *Pasteur: The History of a Mind* (trans. 1920).

347
PATER, Walter Horatio 1839–94

British writer

Walter Pater was born in Stepney, London. His father was a surgeon in a predominantly slumland area. After his death in 1842 the family moved to Enfield. In 1853 Walter went to King's School, Canterbury, and in 1858 entered Queen's College, Oxford, as an exhibitioner in classics. He attended Matthew Arnold's* lectures and received private tuition from the influential classicist, Benjamin Jowett*. His earliest interests had been poetry and religion, and as a boy he had determined to become a priest. At Oxford, however, he became sceptical of church dogma and retained only an aesthetic interest in the liturgy. Amidst a general atmosphere of theological uncertainty he turned increasingly to painting and literature as objects of spiritual devotion. In part this reflects an interest in Hegelian* philosophy and Arnold's concept of culture, and in part a temperamental predisposition to satisfy the desires of a reclusive and intuitive sensibility. Both Arnold's 'Hellenism' and the Oxford Hegelians had seen a conscious certainty of the 'self' as attainable through an intense concentration on one's own impressions, in response to the disruptive flux scientific thought had made an apparently dangerous fact of existence. Such a dedication to the imagination and sensibility was, furthermore, a healthy balancing factor against the unduly pragmatic and provincial cast of Victorian morality. With these abstract interests Pater combined a quite radical interest in modern French authors like Gautier*, Flaubert* and Baudelaire*, a passion for Renaissance painting and a rather obsessive concern with mortality.

In 1864 Pater was elected a fellow of Brasenose College, Oxford, and quickly developed a close friendship with a pupil, C.L. Shadwell, with whom he travelled in Italy in 1865. Pater was suspected of being a homosexual throughout his adult life, but although his name was twice mentioned during Oscar Wilde's* trial in 1895, no firm proof of his sexual tendencies was ever discovered. His other friends at Oxford included the 'scandalous' Simeon Solomon, a painter later convicted for his homosexuality, and the poet Swindurne*. During the late 1860s Pater became something of a cult figure among undergraduates for his supposedly immoral and 'pagan' opinions and at this time published a number of articles including important pieces on Coleridge* and Winckelmann. In both these men Pater found sympathetic figures, dedicated to the pursuit of the highest aesthetic experience and also both clergy *manqués*. It was in 1873, however, that he first attained widespread notoriety with the publication of his *Studies in the History of the Renaissance*. This was a collection of not especially scholarly essays on, amongst others, Pico della Mirandola, Du Bellay and Leonardo da Vinci. In the latter's *Mona Lisa* Pater finds the mysteries of history in a single image. 'The picture summed up a thousand experiences . . . and . . . all modes of thought and life'. In his essay on Botticelli he rediscovered a great Italian painter. It was in Pater's 'Conclusion' to the *Renaissance* that his ideas were fully expressed. Each individual mind is a 'narrow chamber' receiving fleeting impressions and its main activity must be to attain sharp and eager observation. 'To burn always with this gem-like flame, to maintain this ecstasy, is success in life. Failure is to form habits; for habit is relative to a stereotyped world.' Pater renounced the claims of abstract philosophy or fixed morality and thereby shocked the orthodox opinions of most of his academic colleagues. 'Of this wisdom, the poetic passion, the desire of beauty, the love of art for art's sake has most; for art comes to you professing frankly to give nothing but the highest quality to your moments as they pass, and simply for those moments' sake.' This almost existential sense of passing instants of awareness was seen as a direct threat to notions of an after-life posited in an idealized future and perhaps more dangerously, as an exhortation to discover an excess of natural and not-so-natural physical pleasures. On more than one occasion the Bishop of Oxford used Pater's text to warn his congregation of the dangers of the new pagan sensibility arising in an age of uncertainty.

Pater published nothing more, in fact, until 1885 when his imaginary portrait of *Marius the Epicurean* appeared, telling the story of a Roman in the times of Marcus Aurelius who moves from paganism to Christianity. When Flavian, Marius's early friend, is killed off by disease and Cornelius, the Christian, wins his affection, Pater symbolically recounts his gradual withdrawal to his desire as a young man to find a more substantial philosophy than that he actually propounded in the *Renaissance*.

After the publication of *Appreciations* in 1889 Pater became a national celebrity and won the admiration of men like Wilde, Lionel Johnson, Arthur Symons and Aubrey Beardsley*. He was flattered by the attention of these rising stars but embarrassed by his reputation as a sort of demonic and anglicized Baudelaire. (He had repressed the 'Conclusion' in the second edition of the *Renaissance* to avoid further accusations of being a corrupter of youth.) As a close examination of his writings on art, literature, history and ideas shows, the reduction of his thought to a purely 'sensationalist' bias is inaccurate and distorts his full idea of 'style' which he presented in an essay of the same title in 1888. In this piece he asserts that it is finally the matter that determines whether a work of art is of significance or otherwise and not merely the form. Thus 'true and noble' ideas are the hallmarks of the great geniuses like Dante and Goethe*. The artist must search for concrete expression of ideas which further the cause of peace and humanity as well as startling the mind to heightened apprehensions of beauty in the present. In his essay on Wordsworth* Pater declared, 'That the end of life is not action but contemplation – being as distinct from *doing* – a certain disposition of the mind: is, in some shape or other, the principle of all the higher morality.'

Pater's thought stands somewhere between Arnold's, which emphasizes the need for strict canons of taste and ascertainable standards in art, and Wilde's, which largely saw the artist's and critic's task as presenting subjective impressions only. Pater touches on all the vexing intellectual issues that concerned the later Victorians and is alert to subtleties of culture and morality as well as to those of his own passing appetites and perceptions. It is his prose style which has perhaps withstood best the test of time, fittingly, with its beautifully wrought images and cadences and its capacity to inspire the closest scrutiny of the individual work. This, naturally, has tended to place him firmly in the camp of the aesthetes and decadents and has obscured the real complexity of his outlook and personality.

Richard Humphreys

See: A. Ward, *The Idea in Nature* (1966); Iain Fletcher, *Walter Pater* (1971); S. Wright, *A Bibliography of the writings of W. Pater* (1975); *W. Pater: The Critical Heritage*, ed. R.M. Seiler (1980).

348
PAVLOV, Ivan Petrovich 1849–1936

Russian physiologist

As the eldest of ten children, the family of Pyotr Dmitrievich, a member of the lowest priesthood in the provincial town of Ryazan, Pavlov knew poverty and unremitting toil. Following in his father's footsteps he entered the Theological Seminary in Ryazan where contact with scientific and philosophical literature kindled in him an enthusiasm for science. George Lewes's* *The Physiology of Everyday Life* (Russian translation 1861) and I.M. Sechenov's *Refleksy golovonogo mozga* (1863) left a deep impression upon him. These authors who expounded the empiricist stance and experimental

method in physiology, and championed mechanism and objectives as against vitalism and subjectivism, found a ready disciple in Pavlov. The popular writings of the radical intellectual, Dmitri Pisarev – his conviction of the progressive character of natural science – and especially his enthusiastic account of Darwin* also influenced the young Pavlov.

Although no revolutionary activist Pavlov had hopes for the ameliorating impact of science upon society. Leaving the Ryazan seminary before completion of his studies he enrolled in the natural science section of the faculty of physics and mathematics at St Petersburg (now Leningrad) University. By 1874 he had made physiology his major subject. The next year M.I. Afanasiev and he were awarded a gold medal for their study of the enervation of the pancreas. Physiology was but a young science in Pavlov's student days; those who had fought for its status as an experimental science belonged to the nineteenth century. Russia, though considered backward in relation to other European countries, had a galaxy of outstanding scientists in St Petersburg, the physiologists I.M. Sechenov and E.F. Cyon, the clinician S.P. Botkin, and the chemists Mendeleyev* and Butlerov. Sechenov had founded Russia's first school of physiology at St Petersburg before he resigned his post there in 1870. In 1890 Pavlov wisely chose to stay in St Petersburg and accept the Chair of Pharmacology offered him by the Military-Medical Academy rather than go to the new University of Tomsk in Siberia. He remained in or near St Petersburg for the rest of his life.

Pavlov's researches can be divided into three phases: his study of blood circulation between 1874 and 1888, his research into the physiology of digestion from 1879 to 1902 for which he was awarded the Nobel Prize in physiology and medicine in 1904, and his investigations into the conditioned reflex and higher nervous activity from 1902 to the end of his life. All this work was marked by a conscious concern over method. When he moved on to the higher mental processes thus entering the field of psychology and psychiatry he remained true to his physiological upbringing and relied upon the objective methods of that science. Like a later generation of behaviourists in America Pavlov described in his Nobel lecture how he and his co-workers tried to discipline their thought and speech 'in order to completely ignore the mental state of the animal'. Unlike the behaviourists, however, they 'desired to remain physiologists instead of becoming psychologists'. All three phases of Pavlov's work were also marked by recognition of the leading part played by the central nervous system in all physiological processes. This was Botkin's doctrine of 'nervism'. It was a recognition of the integration of physiological processes by the centripetal nerves and of the action of the *whole* organism in relation to its surrounding environment. This relation was subtle and adaptive, and to investigate it successfully called for great care in surgical treatment so that the animal remained healthy and normal. Both in his studies of physiological and of psychical secretion he developed chronic as opposed to acute surgical treatment which left the animal functioning normally and with a reasonable life expectancy. Some of the greatest achievements of nineteenth-century physiology were in the field of digestion. Beginning with the studies of an open-stomach wound described by William Beaumont in 1833 physiologists used surgery to produce a duct or 'fistula' from the digestive glands to the exterior. Glandular secretion could then be studied. Unfortunately such fistulas tended to close up, or the normal pattern of secretion disappeared; often the animal died soon after the operation. After a period of study under Rudolf Heidenhain, hitherto the most successful practitioner of the fistula, Pavlov and his co-workers overcame these problems by modifications of technique and skilful surgery. Pavlov described these problems and his solutions to them in his famous *Lectures on the Work of the Principal Digestive Glands* (*Lektsii o rabote glavnukh pishchevaritelnykn zhelez*), publication of which in 1897 brought their author international recognition.

Pavlov's studies of the digestive glands had impressed him with the remarkable powers of adaptation of the organism to changes in its diet. On a carbohydrate diet the intestinal digestive juices were weak in proteolytic enzymes but strong in such enzymes for a protein-rich diet. Likewise, a dry diet stimulated a copious secretion of saliva, a moist diet only a slight secretion. Also striking was the power of the stomach to start secretion after the animal had been 'sham-fed', i.e. food from the mouth was diverted by surgical modification from the stomach. Evidently it was not the direct contact with food that caused gastric secretion but a more remote 'signalling' system. Likewise salivary secretion was stimulated by the sight or smell of food before the food made contact with the lining of the mouth. Pavlov referred to this production as 'appetite juice' or 'psychical secretion'. In his address to the International Congress of Medicine in Madrid in 1903 Pavlov recalled how he and his co-workers 'had honestly endeavoured to explain our results by fancying the subjective condition of the animal. But nothing came of it except unsuccessful controversies'. Rejecting subjective explanations, Pavlov turned instead to the physiological theory of the reflex. The result, he told his audience, was the opening of 'a second immense part of the physiology of the nervous system'. The first part had concerned the relations within the organism, the second concerned its relations with the surrounding world.

In that there was a definite stimulus or signal and a response, psychic secretion did not differ from physiological secretion. The difference lay in the distance of the stimulus and the 'unessential' even accidental property of the stimulus. In a physiological reflex the property of the stimulus was 'essential', i.e. intimately connected with the physiological role of the glandular secretion. Furthermore, he noted a striking contrast between the constancy or *unconditioned* nature of physiological secretion and the inconstancy and apparent capriciousness of psychic secretion. The latter he therefore called a *conditioned* reflex. Its performance was conditional upon its association with the stimulus to the unconditioned reflex. The more frequently this association was made the stronger the conditioned reflex became. It was in his Madrid lecture that Pavlov described his efforts to discover the laws governing conditioned reflexes based upon the experiments on the dog carried out by his co-worker, F. Tolochinov. To the English-speaking world he gave a more developed version of the subject in his Thomas Huxley* lecture in London in 1906. Not until the translation of his *Lectures on Conditioned Reflexes* in 1929 by his American co-worker, W. Horsley Gantt, however, did the riches of the Pavlovian experimental programme become fully appreciated in the Western world.

In the first phase of these studies Pavlov had used 'natural' conditioned reflexes – those formed by the 'natural association' between, for example, the sight of food and eating it. Later work concentrated on 'unnatural' conditioned reflexes, such as the sound of a bell before presenting food. Such reflexes could be rendered exact, were easily controlled and varied, and they opened up a vast field for research. Both types of conditioned reflex showed law-like behaviour. Repeated without the unconditioned stimulus – e.g. food – the conditioned stimulus evoked progressively less response until it was completely extinguished. Left unstimulated for a few hours the animal's conditioned response was spontaneously restored. Restoration was also achieved by presentation of the conditioned stimulus with the unconditioned stimulus. Such a procedure could be repeated to reinforce it, but coupling the unconditioned stimulus with another signal inhibited the original conditioned response. It was the temporary nature of these reflexes which allowed the organism to be delicately adapted to its changing environment.

Further studies showed that the power to make conditioned reflexes was associated with the cerebral hemispheres, and stimuli could only be effective if the centre in the cerebral cortex to which the sense organ in question was connected remained intact. Pavlov looked upon these centres and their associated sense organs as 'analysers'. They acted as a signalling system since they gave the animal signals for its needs. The number of potentially significant signals for food were legion, but with repeated presentation of a given stimulus with food the conditioning became more narrowly limited to this signal. This was possible because the analysers decomposed the mass of signals from the animal's surroundings. In 1932 Pavlov suggested that in addition to this first signal system there was in man a second signal system which generalized and analysed the multitude of signals from the first system. The most important signals for this second system were those from the kinesthetic stimulations of the speech organs; its functions were abstraction and speech. It marked 'the very last attainment in the evolutionary process'.

In the earlier phase of his study of conditioned reflexes Pavlov was distinctly hostile to psychologists. When he became familiar with the work of Thorndike and later with those of the early behaviourists he modified his position but he criticized E.R. Guthrie and K. Lashley. To the school of Gestalt psychology he was vehemently opposed. Köhler especially he viewed as a serious threat to objective research, and in one of his 'Wednesday' meetings he declared 'We are at war with him. This is a serious struggle against psychologists.' Pavlov was not a crude materialist but he believed in the need for objective methods and denigrated what he considered were the subjective methods of psychology. Yet he looked forward to a time when 'the physiological and the psychological, the objective and the subjective will really merge, when the painful contradiction between our mind and our body . . . will either *actually* be solved or [will] disappear in a natural way.'

The theory of the conditioned reflex had a considerable impact upon psychology. In the nineteenth century the reflex had been a prominent element in Herbert Spencer's* psychology and it was the dominant element in I.M. Sechenov's treatment of higher mental processes, but it was the incorporation of the *conditioned* reflex into behaviourist literature around 1915 that introduced it to the mainstream of twentieth-century psychology. Many of the numerous instincts attributed to animals in the literature of comparative psychology were then banished and their place taken by conditioned reflexes. Shorn of the special surgical difficulties associated with Pavlov's fistula technique conditioning experiments became a major feature of behaviourist research.

Robert Olby

The best collection of extracts from Pavlov's writing is *I.P. Pavlov: Selected Works*, ed. K.S. Koshtoyants, trans. from Russian by S. Belsky (1955); his best-known work is the *Lectures on Conditioned Reflexes* (2 vols, 1928 and 1941). There are many biographies, the most readily available of which is E.A. Asratyan, *Ivan Petrovitch Pavlov, Work* (1953, latest edn 1979). See also: Jeffrey A. Gray, *Pavlov* (1979).

349
PAXTON, Sir Joseph 1803–65

British gardener and architect

Joseph Paxton personifies many ideals of English nineteenth-century society. He was from humble origins; he rose through his own efforts, albeit under the protection of a trusting patron, to be recognized and accepted in the highest society. His home life was a model of cooperative domesticity and his energies were diverse and gigantic, applied in turn to gardening, horticulture, new methods of building, railway management, commerce and architecture. For eleven years he was an active Member of Parliament involved in the issues of the day, both at home and abroad. His life, therefore, also forms a bridge between two ages and two societies, between the age when talent depended upon private patronage, to the age of the public man.

He was born in Milton Bryam in Bedfordshire on 3 August 1803. After early experience as a garden boy at Battlesden Park he moved in 1823 to the newly established garden of the Horticultural Society at Chiswick, west London. This garden adjoined Chiswick House, which was owned by the Duke of Devonshire. The gardener and the Duke met and struck up an acquaintanceship so that when in 1826 a new head gardener was needed at the duke's great estate at Chatsworth in Derbyshire, the job was offered to Paxton. Whether through intuition or impulse, the offer was inspired: his work at Chatsworth was to make Paxton nationally famous and was in no small measure to increase the duke's reputation. Paxton was then twenty-three years of age. He arrived in Derbyshire on 9 May 1826 at 4.30 in the morning. By breakfast at 9.00am he had inspected the grounds, set men to work, had the famous water works demonstrated, met and fallen in love with his future wife, and by his own account, she with him. Thus from this one day can be seen to spring the two major relationships of his life. His wife was Sarah Brown, niece of the housekeeper at Chatsworth. She was later to prove invaluable in his burgeoning career, as a shrewd and wholehearted manager of his affairs. She also bore him six daughters and one son.

Paxton's relationship with his employer, William Spenser Cavendish, sixth Duke of Devonshire, was to mutate from employee to closest friend and confidant. His early work at the estate and a later characteristic of all his undertakings was to organize effectively the army of gardeners under his command and to establish extremely efficient procedures for work. This achieved, he was able, with the duke's support, to give greater range to his powerful intelligence. In his alternate role as chief forester, he transported fully grown trees into the estate, once moving palm trees (one weighing 12 tons) from the south of England to Chatsworth in the north. It was from his interest in horticulture that his involvement with building a series of glass conservatories started. There is a symbiotic relationship between his developing double skills as a horticulturalist and as a constructor of transparent buildings. He devised a ridge and furrow structure for rigidity but also to face the sheets of glass square to the sun, associating with it a bearing member with integral guttering. In 1840 the largest conservatory in the world, 272 feet long and 123 feet broad, rising to 67 feet, was completed, but the culmination of these intertwined pursuits followed in 1849 with the construction of the new Lily House.

Kew Gardens had acquired from the Amazon in 1836 a great water lily, named at that time Victoria Regia, which could not be persuaded to flower. Paxton acquired a sample, built a special tank within his most refined glasshouse and was able to bring it into bloom. The synchronicity between the structure of the great leaves and the building which housed it has often been commented upon. This triumph immediately acquired the stature of a public event of the new Victorian age and Paxton travelled to Windsor to present a bud and a leaf to Victoria* herself. He had by now become a public figure. The Lily House, being built of iron and glass and being rectilinear, was the prototype for his most famous work, the building to house the Great Exhibition of 1851 in Hyde Park, London.

His other activities while head gardener included numerous other building work in the grounds, the most notable being Edensor, the estate village, a picturesque ruined aqueduct, the Emperor fountain and associated reservoir and a curiosity, a fountain in the form of a small tree. At the same time he was busy with private commissions for the design of parks, notably Prince's Park, Liverpool, in 1842 and Birkenhead Park in 1843. Despite his enormous energies it must be said that his work never rose above the level of a landscape gardener. All his endeavours, including those at Chatsworth, fail to achieve the level of a work of art, and they mark a further decline from the great tradition of landscape architecture established in the seventeenth and eighteenth centuries, following the trivializations of Repton and his version of the Picturesque. Paxton's work in the laying out of these urban public parks, however, had a regrettably pervasive influence over nearly all of the new municipal parks of the newly public-conscious industrial towns throughout England.

From 1831 Paxton also pursued a career as journalist and author, publishing periodicals and books, including in 1838 a very successful 'Practical Treatise on the Cultivation of the Dahlia'. In 1845 he, with three others, launched a national daily paper, the Daily News, engaging Charles Dickens* as editor. His editorship lasted three weeks and Paxton's active involvement was also shortlived. This diversity of energy is perhaps one of the clearest indications of his character.

At this time the railway industry was booming. Very much with the guidance of his wife Sarah, Paxton had begun to invest in the railways. Through her cool judgment and prudence, Paxton was able to escape wealthy and unscathed from the collapse of speculation in 1845. Through this involvement he met the later notorious George Hudson, 'The Railway King', and probably from him he acquired what was to become possibly the most fervent preoccupation of his later years, that of pursuing commercial enterprises. From the 1840s onwards his outside commitments caused him to lead a hectic life which more and more took him from his wife and family, undermining their relationship and placing a considerable strain on his health.

His most famous achievement came about in an almost accidental way, made possible only by the enterprising quickness of his mind, and the corresponding vigour of the age. The idea for a 'Great Exhibition of the Works of All Nations' had been put forward by Prince Albert* and Henry Cole in 1845. A site in Hyde Park was chosen, a Royal Commission established in January 1850 and the project went ahead financed by private subscription. An unsuccessful competition was organized for the design of the exhibition building, and the Building Committee was forced to produce its own design. This met with considerable public hostility and the whole project threatened to end in fiasco. Paxton visited the site at the height of the controversy in July and, on seeing Henry Cole, promised a design and a price within nine days.

The sketch for the structure, an elevation and a section, was doodled on a blotter during a Midland Railway Committee meeting, of which Paxton was a director. During the following week he produced through his office at Chatsworth detailed plans which he took to London. With the support of the two eminent engineers on the Building Committee, I.K. Brunel* and Robert Stephenson, and through his own publicizing of the proposal through the Illustrated London News, the design was accepted, nine months before the exhibition's planned opening, The building was to be a huge rectilinear construction of glass and iron, which Punch magazine promptly named the Crystal Palace.

The speed with which the building was erected astonished the world then, and seems equally incredible today. The success depended upon the resolving of the building into standard components, their accurate manufacture in factories remote from the site and a precise timing and organization of their assembly on site, the first and perhaps finest example of industrialized building and co-ordination. The site boundary fence was designed to be fitted into the building as the flooring on the completion. The role of the railway engineers, Messrs Fox & Henderson, who took over Paxton's Chatsworth drawings and prepared the final design and were the contractors, is often underestimated. The true triumph of the building was that it was built with the syncopation of a railway. Just as the Crystal Palace represented the finest manifestation of what had been learnt in the first industrialized age, so the monument to its remarkable patron, Prince Albert, created near the exhibition site in the next decade represented the emptiness of later Victorian taste, and the loss of clarity and vigour. Thus the whole enterprise can be seen as a high water mark, from which, some would argue, we have never ceased to retreat. More truthfully it marked the last time when certain illusions concerning the machine and the mechanization of society were still just tenable, the final point where, on the one hand, the desperate misery of the new industrial centres could be ignored, and on the other, the romance that art and the machine were happily wedded could be sustained.

Later the Crystal Palace was to be considered by architectural historians as a seminal work for the new architecture of the twentieth century, although there is little evidence that its author in his later career as an architect drew any inspiration from it.

The final fourteen years of Paxton's life were given over to his work as a Member of Parliament, having been elected for Coventry in 1854, the re-erection and enlargement of the Crystal Palace at Sydenham in south London and the laying out of the surrounding park and the expansion of his architectural practice in association with G.H. Stokes. From 1850 all his major activities were centred in London, his wife remaining at Chatsworth. The most well-known of his later buildings is Mentmore, for Baron Mayer Rothschild, a lifeless imitation of a great Elizabethan house.

Joseph Paxton died at Sydenham in 1865 and was entombed in the village churchyard at Edensor, Chatsworth. His vast and various achievements are possibly secondary to what he came to represent, the self-made, undoubting, energetic and inventive public hero of the high Victorian age.

Frederick Scott

See: Charles Downes, *The Building Erected for the Great Exhibition in Hyde Park 1851* (1852; facsimile 1971); Violet Markham, *Paxton and the Bachelor Duke* (1934); Yvonne ffrench, *The Great Exhibition 1851* (1950); G.F. Chadwick, *The Works of Sir Joseph Paxton* (1961).

350
PEACOCK, Thomas Love 1785–1866

British novelist

Peacock was born in comfortable circumstances and educated himself thoroughly in the classics in his early years. He began writing poetry as a child and contin-

ued it throughout his life, but found a distinctive voice only in the seven alert and intelligent novels which he began publishing in 1815. Peacock was at this time a close friend of the poet Shelley*, by whom his literary tastes and ambitions were certainly quickened. The novels were well received, but Peacock was forced to find a securer livelihood when he wished to marry. So, in 1819, he joined the East India Company, which he served with exemplary efficiency and in increasingly senior positions until his retirement in 1856. After the brief headiness of his days with Shelley, Peacock seems to have lived quietly and in some seclusion. Generally, he spent his weekdays in London, but weekends with his family at Lower Halliford, by the Thames, reading widely, listening to music and giving a good deal of attention to his dinner-table and wine-cellar.

From *Headlong Hall*, the first of Peacock's novels, to the last, the calm, accomplished *Gryll Grange* (1860), we are aware of the author's originality and eclecticism. With the exception of the two ironic medieval romances, *Maid Marian* (1821) and *The Misfortunes of Elphin* (1829), Peacock's fiction is composed of novels of conversation, largely set in country houses, and marked by their playfulness, their clever debates on questions of polemical interest, their mocking wit, and the slightness of their plots and characterization. They bear few resemblances to the works of Peacock's contemporaries and are very far from naturalism. Their mode is fresh: influences can be traced from Roman satirists such as Petronius, and from Aristophanes and Rabelais, but the Peacockian novel is a unique creation for which no single ancestor can be found. Equally, though much admired, it has had no worthy successors: works such as Aldous Huxley's *Crome Yellow* are only pallid imitations of the real thing.

Peacock has been unfairly presented as a serene bystander whose brittle art simply applies the cool standards of the Augustans to the absurdities of the Romantic period. In fact, everything about him is intimately bound up with the stresses of the age in which he lived. Social and political upheavals, the growth of a radical new literature and the erosion of certainties involved in a time of fundamental change all affected him as nearly, if not as directly, as his peers. A note of fracture and unease is constant in Peacock's work, though it rarely subdues the brilliance of his comic invention and is usually countered, with more or less vigour, by a romantic trust in the value of certain basic human strengths which have especially to do with love and physical enjoyment. The result of this is that the novels are far from settlement or triviality: they are jokey and often festive, but they are not mere Epicurean *jeux d'esprit*. Their stratagem is that of debate and they emanate risk and dialectic, working tensely and with sharp, sceptical intelligence towards achieving some accommodation of optimism and pessimism and coping with the strains and dilemmas of a world from which the author was acutely disaffected. In addition, Peacock's books show a revulsion not just from the political oppressiveness, hypocrisy and fashionable petty-mindedness of his own society, but also from all societies, and operate both on a level of immediate satire and as disenchanted, lucid consolations for an existence in which he can see little that is dependable or conducive to happiness (and nothing at all in the public sphere). In spite of their sophisticated irony, there is a pastoral turn to these novels, and this is important to their encouragement of feelings of joy and hopefulness: a firm basis in the countryside provides Peacock with a secure starting-point from which to deal with problems and assert truths which in his time (and in all times) must always be under threat.

The aim of Peacock's works, therefore, is clarification and compensation: they move us to understanding and equilibrium. And, in an age so full of pretentiousness and misdirection, there is no shortage of targets at which he can direct the barrage of his witty subversion. A principal means by which he conducts his campaign is through 'crotcheteers', whom he first devised for *Headlong Hall* but developed to perfection in his attack on the fancifulness of Romantic literature in *Nightmare Abbey* (1818). These crotcheteers are comic obsessives, creatures of a single all-consuming interest, perhaps craniology or Kantian metaphysics, around which they try to organize the whole of their experience of the world about them: they are reductionists, replacing the variety and freedom that Peacock valued with the rigidity of system and authority. Generally, these characters are portrayed with a striking contemporary colouring: their hobby-horses may derive from the fashionable controversies of Peacock's day, or they may draw material from figures like Shelley or Coleridge* who happened to be appositely in the writer's eye while he was composing his novel. In the past, the crotcheteers were mostly taken as simple, parodic transpositions from life into literature, but this is only rarely true. More often, they put together elements cunningly annexed from different sources, and rearrange them sharply in the interests of artistic vivacity rather than convincing, authentic commentary. As a technique, crotcheteering is in Peacock's hands uniquely and extraordinarily successful: it permits both comedy and qualification, and sometimes, as in the case of the languid Hon. Mr Listless in *Nightmare Abbey*, attains a kind of poetic heightening that was afterwards only realized again in Dickens*.

When we look at Peacock's targets, we see that his opposition to the rule of prescriptive theories and smothering institutions, and his resulting trust in the holiness of the heart's affections and the restorative effects of barons of beef and good burgundy, show themselves throughout his novels. In argument, his scepticism is manifest in the deliberate irresolution and undercutting which attend each discussion of the crotcheteers, though this diminishes after the romances and is subdued to a more normal, conversational repartee in *Crotchet Castle* (1831) and *Gryll Grange*. It is only in Peacock that argument so consistently gets nowhere, and that its procedures seem so comically futile by contrast with the bodily pleasures to which they are opposed. Socially, Peacock's disapproval of constricting values which lead man away from fulfilment, instead of towards it, is evident in his attacks on purely fashionable criteria of literary worth or personal behaviour. He is always aware of basic qualities and unavoidable needs, and he sees these betrayed by the thoughtless pursuit of transient standards whose aim is frivolous effect and not real satisfaction. Thus in art he condemns trickeries of ornament and affectation, and endorses the nature and simplicity which he finds best embodied in the music of Mozart and the literature of the Greeks, and in conduct he assails the regimen of status, wealth and *bon ton* which for too many of his characters impedes a proper expression of honest emotions. In politics, Peacock repudiates all the institutions of the modern state, together with the complex apparatus of self-seeking and corruption by which they are supported. This radical theme is unchanging from Peacock's earliest novel to his last, and is upheld in his sharply turned reviews and poetry as well as in his fiction. It was stimulated by discussion with Shelley, and reaches its apogee in *Melincourt* (1817), the committed, politically disillusioned book which was the poet's favourite and which mounts a strident, large-scale offensive against the entire English political system with its bribery, false representation and sectarian interest.

The enduring attractiveness of Peacock's work lies in the wit and tautness of its approach: something serious and deeply felt is attempted, but with a pragmatism and urbanity which seldom allow either sermons or crude jeremiads, and where there coexist a sense of mankind's fundamental strength and decency and a determined resistance to the forces which are threatening to swamp these qualities. Peacock is always a critic, forcing us to see clearly, to judge and be aware, forbidding unthinking acceptance in the interests of preserving the values of love and freedom from constraint to which he was most attached.

Bryan Burns

The standard edition is *The Works of Thomas Love Peacock*, ed. H.F.B. Brett-Smith and C.E. Jones (10 vols, 1924–34). The central critical work remains Jean-Jacques Mayoux, *Un Epicurien anglais: Thomas Love Peacock* (Paris, 1933), though Marilyn Butler, *Peacock Displayed* (1979), is excellent on the background and *Peacock: The Satirical Novels*, ed. Lorna Sage (1976), reprints some of the best shorter studies.

351
PEARSON, Karl 1857–1936

British mathematician

Karl Pearson is associated with the emergence of statistics as a distinct subject, with the journal *Biometrika* which he edited for thirty-five years, and with a particular statistical method, the chi-squared test. He also wrote a powerful and influential philosophical work, *The Grammar of Science* (1892), which conveyed a feeling of the strength, sense and coherence of the scientific point of view. In many ways Pearson may be compared with John Stuart Mill*: a thoroughgoing empiricist, feminist, socialist and logician of science. But if *The Grammar of Science* is less eloquent than Mill's *Logic*, there is still the feeling that Pearson knew what he was talking about, that behind the words on the page there is a veritable wealth of background experience. It is particularly in his handling of philosophical arguments that Pearson's unique style comes through. He shows his confidence and firmness of step by his aim, by going straight to the centre of a difficulty. Another figure against whom one may measure Pearson is Henri Poincaré*. Both were mathematicians first, polymaths of formidable power second, logicians of science third. It should be said at once that Pearson could not match Poincaré's sheer mathematical brilliance and creativity; nor are Pearson's thoughts on the logic of science quite as luminous and penetrating as Poincaré's. But when we turn to the experimental and common sense basis of science, Pearson, with his grip on details and empirical facts, with his practicality of view, makes a stronger impression than the evanescent Frenchman. Pearson also displayed considerable incidental imagination and foresight into the future, predicting minor technological developments like stone-grading machines, the 'telephone exchange' view of the human brain, and the polarization of politics into individualistic versus socialistic positions.

Karl's father, William Pearson, was a barrister of the Inner Temple. His son was educated at home until the age of nine, after which he attended University College School in London. In 1875 Karl won a scholarship to King's College, Cambridge. He read for the mathematical tripos and emerged as Third Wrangler in 1879.

On leaving Cambridge Pearson continued his studies at Heidelberg, where he read such authors as Dante, Rousseau and Goethe* in addition to scientific texts. It was during this period that he adopted the Christian name 'Karl' in preference to the 'Carl' of his early years. On returning to England he spent the three years 1881–4 in law practice, though he found time to take on temporary work as a lecturer in mathematics at London University. He also gave extensive lectures on 'Heat' during the period 1880–4, and was active in

radical politics. At this time too he wrote two literary works, *The New Werther* (1880) and *The Trinity: A Nineteenth Century Passion Play* (1882). It was only in 1884 that he fully settled down to the mathematical work which occupied him for most of the rest of his life. In that year he was appointed Professor of Applied Mathematics and Mechanics at University College, London. Subsequently he held two other chairs in the University of London: in 1891 he became Gresham Professor of Geometry and in 1911 Galton Professor of Eugenics.

In 1893 Pearson began a monumental series of eighteen articles entitled 'Mathematical Contributions to the Theory of Evolution' which lasted until 1912. It was a vehicle for many of his innovations in statistics, including his celebrated work on the chi-squared test. Pearson was stimulated by the work of Francis Galton* and W.F.R. Weldon on heredity, and quickly perceived that many of the controversies in this area could only be tackled satisfactorily from the statistical point of view. In fact what was needed was a refinement of statistical technique to the point where one could extract the greatest possible degree of probability from the mass of evidence available.

Once Pearson had settled into his chosen field of study (statistics), his output of work was, by any standard, prodigious. He worked on correlation, the 'Pearson Curves', and many other statistical topics. In addition to the series of articles mentioned above, he sent thirty-five communications to the Royal Society on statistical matters, and he wrote about seventy other papers on related themes.

Pearson was co-founder (with Galton and Weldon) of the journal *Biometrika*, and he used it successfully for many years to provide a platform for the idea that mathematics – not merely statistics – could be usefully applied to biology. Today we take it for granted that mathematics can be applied to the biological sciences, and modern sixth-form biologists are required to learn, among other statistical methods, Pearson's chi-squared test. But this acceptance of the role of mathematics in biology is a comparatively new phenomenon. It did not come easily: it had to be won against the dialectical fire-power of an entrenched establishment. Biology was, many held, a characteristically descriptive and non-mathematical science; and the very idea of bringing mathematical techniques systematically to bear on it was one which aroused much temperamental opposition. In this fight *Biometrika* was the flagship, Pearson the admiral on the bridge.

Pearson's chi-squared test was essentially a way of computing the probability that a set of experimental values of a variate would differ from the expected values by the margins which were actually found. It made a big difference if one were studying any empirical situation whether this probability was 0.1 or 0.001. The former value meant that one's expectations (the expected values used in the calculation) were reasonable: the latter value showed that what one had observed could only be expected about once in a thousand times if one's expectations were correct. This was said to be 'significant' in the sense that it threw doubt on the reasonableness of one's original expectations.

The test consists in the computation by means of a fairly straightforward formula of the statistic α^2. One then compares this computed value with a table of values and their probabilities and reads off the probability from the table. It must be remembered that the table had to be worked out from a theoretical analysis of the α^2 distribution and each entry had to be calculated laboriously one at a time. Pearson's contribution lay in conceptualizing the problem, the statistic and its distribution: and then, by means of classical analysis, deriving the theoretical distribution. Even then the table of values required computation, and this was no mean feat in the pre-computer age.

In *The Grammar of Science* Pearson clearly envisages the role of a science which he calls 'Bio-Physics': in other words, biology studied in the manner of a physical science. He comments: 'This science does not appear to have advanced very far at present, but it not improbably has an important future.' It is a sobering thought that the promise of the early idea of applying mathematics (and the methods of the physical sciences) to biology has not yet been fully kept. A mass of specific applications has been established, but great strategic generalizations comparable with the laws of physics still seem to have eluded us. Molecular biology is, however, at last beginning to achieve the kind of results which vindicate Pearson's optimism of ninety years ago. He would have been pleased to learn that the tradition he created led eventually to the double helix and the structure of insulin, and that biologists did indeed have to turn in the end to mathematics in order to crack these baffling codes.

Christopher Ormell

Pearson's other works include: *The Ethic of Free Thought* (1888); *The Chances of Death and other Studies in Evolution* (1897); *The Life, Letters and Labours of Francis Galton* (1914); *Tables for Statisticians and Biometricians* (1914, 1931); *Tables of the Incomplete Gamma Function* (1922); *Tables of the Incomplete Beta Function* (1934).

352
PEIRCE, Charles Sanders 1839–1914

US philosopher and logician

One of the most original and versatile thinkers America has produced, C.S. Peirce was born in Cambridge, Massachusetts, the son of the leading American mathematician of his times, Benjamin Peirce, Perkins Professor of Mathematics and Astronomy at Harvard

University. After reading mathematics, physics and chemistry at Harvard, he joined the US Coast Survey in 1861. He made significant contributions not only to the survey but also to the theory and techniques of measurement in physics. Resigning his post in 1891, he retired to the seclusion of a farm near Milford, Pennsylvania, where, in poverty, he pursued his research in philosophy and logic. Twice married, he had no children.

Deeply influenced by Kant as an undergraduate, Peirce sought to create a systematic philosophy closely in tune with the methods of modern science. To this end he proposed a theory of meaning which he called 'pragmatism', according to which the cognitive meaning of a concept lies solely in its conceivable bearing on the conduct of life. Our idea of an object consists entirely in our conception of those effects of it which have a conceivable bearing on our action. Since observable effects have the most conspicuous influence on our actions, these must play the most prominent role in our idea of the object. In calling a substance 'hard', for example, what we mean is that it will not easily be scratched by many other substances. This theory was first proposed in the article 'How to Make Our Ideas Clear' (*Popular Science Monthly*, January 1878). It was taken up and elaborated by William James*, whose version of it Peirce rejected on the grounds that it was too phenomenalist and subjectivist.

Pragmatism was the main tool with which Peirce constructed his theory of knowledge. He argued that just as our ideas concern those characteristics of things which bear upon action, so our beliefs constitute rules or habits of acting, for what we believe partly determines how we act. Belief is preferable to doubt, for, unlike doubt, it generally makes for appropriate action. It is the purpose of inquiry to secure stable beliefs and remove doubt. Science provides the best method of inquiry, for its method is the best means for fixing belief. All other methods, such as intuition and authority, produce beliefs which readily fall prey to doubt. No scientific belief, however, is certain, and any may be mistaken, for science consists in reasoning on the basis of experience, and the experience can never attain absolute exactness or universality. Nevertheless the scientific method provides a definite means for settling doubt whenever it arises. Moreover, as the method is pursued indefinitely, the beliefs it leads to become more and more fixed. But why should we value fixed beliefs? Because, Peirce replies, absolute fixity is indistinguishable from truth: the truth is what would be believed ultimately if the scientific method were pursued *in infinitum*. As science progresses, it approximates asymptotically towards the whole truth; but at any finite time it is never certain.

The essential point of this doctrine, which Peirce called 'fallibilism', is that although scientific method is fallible, it is self-correcting. Science proposes explanatory hypotheses which are tested by observing whether or not their empirical consequences occur. For example, a general hypothesis of the form 'The proportion of As that are B is x/y' is tested by observing what proportion of As are B among a numerous random sample of As. If the observed proportion differs from that hypothesized, then the hypothesis can be corrected by further sampling, which is bound to lead to a closer and closer approximation to the correct ratio. This is the method of induction. Its validity, Peirce argued, does not depend upon a metaphysical principle of the uniformity of nature; it depends solely on the fact that if pursued indefinitely, its results will necessarily approximate to the facts. Consequently, the rationality of science presupposes a commitment to a cooperative, never-ending quest.

In his metaphysics Peirce was a realist in one sense, for he rejected the idealist view that to be is to be perceived, holding instead that reality is what exists independently of what any individual mind thinks or perceives. Following Duns Scotus, he held that properties (universals), laws (universal facts), and possibilities are real – a view he called 'scholastic realism'. The hardness of a diamond, for example, is a real potentiality – an ability to resist scratching – which may never be realized: a diamond that never has been, or ever will be, scratched, is none the less hard. Peirce classified real entities into three fundamental categories: under 'firstness' come properties and possibilities; under 'secondness' come things and actualities; and under 'thirdness' come thoughts and laws.

In another sense Peirce was not a realist, but rather an 'objective idealist', for he held that reality, as what corresponds to true beliefs, is the object of the beliefs at which scientific inquiry, pursued in infinitum, would ultimately settle. A concept of reality as wholly independent of thought is meaningless from the pragmatist point of view. Peirce's objective idealism bears a certain similarity to Kant's transcendental idealism.

Peirce's most substantive metaphysical thesis – 'synechism' – is that there are real continuities, such as space, time, matter, and consciousness. These are continuous in the sense that between any two distinct parts, or successive intervals, of them there is a third part or interval. He regarded this as an explanatory and heuristic hypothesis that gave coherence and direction to scientific inquiry. Synechism implies fallibilism: since absolutely exact values of continuous quantities can never be observed, laws of nature can never be absolutely exact; hence our knowledge always swims, as it were, 'in a continuum of uncertainty and indeterminacy'. Laws of nature, moreover, are not absolutely strict or deterministic, but probabilistic, for there are chance departures from them. They express the general propensities or habits of things. This hypothesis – 'tychism' – he thought was required to explain the growing diversification of the universe. Strict

law can explain the regularity in the universe; only absolute chance can account for its variety. The very laws of nature are evolving, from a chaos of irregularity in the infinitely distant past towards a harmony of absolute regularity in the infinitely far-off future. Yet there will always be, at any finite time in the future, chance aberrations from strict law. There is a corresponding evolution of mind into matter: 'Matter is effete mind, inveterate habits becoming physical laws.'

A logician of extraordinary originality, Peirce largely founded the theory of relations and the theory of signs, discovered quantification theory (independently of Frege*) and the truth-value method of proving logical theorems, as well as making important contributions to Boolean algebra (see Boole*) and set theory.

Although he had a great influence on William James and John Dewey and later American thinkers such as W.V.O. Quine, he received little recognition during his lifetime, largely because his philosophical writings were published in diverse journals and ·because he never held a permanent academic position, though he gave some lectures on logic at Harvard and Johns Hopkins. Besides, his thinking was very *avant-garde*: ideas like fallibilism and indeterminacy had little appeal to an age whose faith in classical physics was at its highest pitch; they had to await more propitious times, when they were re-introduced by thinkers such as Popper and Heisenberg respectively.

D.R. Murdoch

See *The Collected Papers of Charles Sanders Peirce*, ed. C. Harshorne, P. Weiss and A.W. Burks (8 vols, 1931–58). Useful collections are *Philosophical Writings of Peirce*, ed. Justus Buchler (1955), and *Charles S. Peirce: The Essential Writings*, ed. Edward C. Moore (1972).

353
PÉREZ GALDÓS, Benito 1843–1920

Spanish novelist and dramatist

The most important single Spanish writer between the Romantics and the Generation of 1898. After abandoning his law studies in the University of Madrid, he devoted his life exclusively to writing, except for brief forays into politics on the Liberal-Progressive side, and to extensive travel both in Spain and abroad. He remained a bachelor, but was far from being a celibate. Elected to the Spanish Academy in 1889 he was a candidate for the Nobel Prize in 1912.

Essentially a realist writer, Balzac* and Dickens* (whose *Pickwick Papers* he translated, from the French, in 1868) were his acknowledged masters. Before 1870, when he published his first (historical) novel, *La Fontana de Oro* ('The Fountain of Gold'), Spanish fiction had been in a phase of decline. The Revolution of 1868 and the loosening of censorship produced a recovery. Until 1875 Galdós continued to produce historical novels, including a first set of *Episodios nacionales*, exploring systematically Spain's past since 1807 with the basic intention of tracing the living forces, social and political, which were still at work in his own day. He went on producing historical *Episodios* (which were excellent money-spinners) until well into the twentieth century, discreetly advocating political moderation and civic responsibility. Eventually they ran into thirty-four volumes. But disillusion with his own middle class and its betrayal of the ideals of 1868 in the end led him to disenchantment and to sympathy with the Republican-Socialist opposition.

Already in 1876, after the restoration of the Bourbons to the throne had begun to offset the achievements of 1868, Galdós had turned to contemporary Spain with one of his most famous works, *Doña Perfecta*, a head-on attack against religious fanaticism, followed by *Gloria* (1876–7) and *La familia de León Roch* (1878) in similar vein. These are novels of dramatic conflict rather than psychological studies, but their heavy emphasis on theme does not preclude an adequately balanced presentation of the clash of traditionalist and progressive outlooks. In 1881, with *La desheredada*, ('The Disinherited'), the central phase of Galdós's fictional work opened. Leaning slightly more towards naturalism, with its emphasis on the uglier aspects of social and psychological reality and on hereditary and environmental determinism, Galdós now abandoned fictional settings for his novels and emerged as the classic novelist of nineteenth-century Madrid. Emphasis on social mobility replaces a static vision of a closed society, characterization becomes less ideological and more subtly ambiguous, dialogue becomes more realistic. Galdós's interest in the religious question now merges into deeper and more widely perceptive social criticism and satire. In *El amigo Manso* (1882), *El doctor Centeno* (1883), *Torment, Tormento* (1884, trans. 1952), *The Spendthrifts* (*La de Bringas*, 1884, trans. 1951), and *Lo prohibido* ('The Forbidden', 1884–5), Galdós uses Balzac's techniques of reappearing characters and the interlacing of national events with private life-stories to depict a Spain which is hollow, squalid, devoid of ideals, peopled by fools, rogues and mediocrities, and dominated by self-deception, hypocrisy, immorality, administrative inefficiency and the cult of appearances.

1886–7 brought plenitude and Galdós's masterpiece *Fortunata and Jacinta*, (*Fortunata y Jacinta*, trans. 1973). The chronicle of two family groups in Madrid, its story concerns the illicit relationship between the middle-class Juanito Santa Cruz and his working-class mistress Fortunata, together with their respective legal marriages. The inner theme is the struggle between natural instinct and social conventions. Both marriages, though sanctified by the church are unsuitable and sterile; the liaison is fulfilling and produces children.

At the end, for almost the only time in Galdós's major works, harmony and equilibrium triumph as Fortunata is vicariously accepted into the bourgeois family of her lover when she gives up her child to the childless Jacinta, Juanito's wife. Although technically the novel belongs to Henry James's* category of 'loose, baggy monsters', we recognize in it one of the lasting achievements of nineteenth-century realism.

With *Miau* (*Miau*, 1888, trans. 1963) Galdós entered his final phase, in which he began to move away from realism towards the exploration of abnormal states of mind and behaviour, though no longer as in *Lo prohibido* in a specifically social perspective. The note of spiritual preoccupation, never far from Galdós's mind, begins to sound strongly once more, but not as in his early aggressive novels of thesis. Thus God appears as a speaking voice in *Miau*, the story of the suicide of a redundant civil servant. *La incógnita* ('The Unknown', 1888–9) and *Realidad* ('Reality', 1889) explore the loneliness of ethical superiority in a rotting, bourgeois society. *Angel Guerra* ('Angel War' 1890–1) and a series of four novels published between 1889 and 1895 whose central figure is Torquemada, a grasping moneylender, develop the bifurcation between social and spiritual reality already prominent in *Miau*. Finally in *Nazarín* (1895), which has been successfully filmed by Buñuel, *Halma* (1895) and *Misericordia* (1897) Galdós studies varieties of saintliness. Benina in *Misericordia* is Galdós's most memorable heroine, a supreme example of practical Christian charity, though founded on small-scale fraud. In the same ironic way both Christ and the mad Don Quixote serve as models for the creation of Nazarín. Galdós's last major novel, *El abuelo* ('The Grandfather' 1904), proposes the theme of tradition and renewal which links Galdós to the Generation of 1898.

The great speed at which Galdós wrote did not preclude skilful construction and considerable technical originality. A number of the earlier novels especially show great dramatic ability combined with a fine sense of narrative tempo and economy of method. Later, in *El amigo Manso* for example, Galdós was able to portend some of the techniques of Unamuno in the twentieth century and to blend observation, humour and fantasy in a strikingly innovatory way. But his fondness for symbolic names, novelesque contrivances and proliferation of characters are of his time.

As a dramatist Galdós produced more than twenty original plays and adaptations of his novels. These were staged chiefly in two periods: 1892–6 and 1901–5. They included four striking successes: *La de San Quintín* (1894), *Doña Perfecta* (1896), *Electra* (1901) and *El abuelo* (1904). *Electra*, once more on the theme of misguided religious zeal, was the greatest theatrical sensation of its time in Spain, sold 20,000 copies in a matter of days and was a major factor in bringing about the fall of the government. In general Galdós's plays represent an isolated attempt to revitalize Spanish drama, which was dominated by debased post-Romantic theatricality. But Galdós did not possess the technical skill to achieve his aims consistently, his audiences were unready to accept his innovations of form and content, and he failed to create a lasting movement.

Galdós's influence was enormous. Later novelists in Spain, such as Baroja and Pérez de Ayala, confessed it eloquently. In Latin America it is clearly visible in novelists up to and including Carlos Fuentes and in some pre-Second World War dramatists. Frequent cheap re-editions of his major novels attest their popularity and critical interest has been so great that a journal, *Anales Galdosianos*, has been devoted exclusively to his work.

D.L. Shaw

W.T. Pattison, *Benito Pérez Galdós* (New York, 1975), is a handy general study. More specific and critical are: S.H. Eoff, *The Novels of Pérez Galdós* (St Louis, 1954); and the critical guides to *Miau* by E. Rodgers (London, 1978) and to *Fortunata y Jacinta* by G. Ribbans (London, 1977).

354
PETRIE, Sir William Matthew Flinders 1853–1942

British archaeologist and Egyptologist

The individual style of Petrie's work owed much to youthful isolation. The only child of an energetic middle-class professional family, he was brought up largely in the company of adults, and given very little formal education. Earnest self-improvement took its place. He collected Greek coins, studied his mother's collection of minerals, and taught himself mathematics and surveying. As a young man he took to making long, solitary walking trips in the south of England, surveying earthworks and stone circles, intending to publish the results in a series of volumes. One on Stonehenge rapidly appeared, as did a precocious treatise on the whole subject of ancient metrology. These works display an obsession with measurements and numbers, and led, through a family interest, to his undertaking a private survey of the Giza Pyramids in Egypt, with great and lasting success. It was during this visit that he developed an urge to excavate, partly as a reaction to the rapid destruction of ancient sites which he witnessed, and partly from an emerging ambition: to establish with precision the full spectrum of changes in ancient fashions so that artefacts from any point within ancient Egyptian history could be dated to within a few reigns. These twin motives remained to guide Petrie through a long career as an archaeologist, and go far in explaining the pattern of

his work. Thenceforth he managed an almost annual expedition to Egypt or to Palestine, apart from the years of the First World War, which he used as an opportunity for preparing catalogue volumes of the extensive collections he built up at University College, London. In the early years he worked partly with private backing and partly on behalf of the Egypt Exploration Fund, with which body his relations were often strained.

The exploration of ancient Egypt had already witnessed a number of meticulous surveys of standing ruins, but excavation was crude and undisciplined. Petrie's principal innovation was a concern for pottery and other small finds, even when broken, which he saw as an essential part of the full picture of Egyptian civilization which he wished to build up. His first major success was in the discovery and excavation of the Greek colony of Naukratis in the western Nile Delta, made in 1884–5. In addition to rescuing an outline plan from a site already badly plundered he provided a schematic section to illustrate the vertical distribution of finds at one part of the site, and illustrated in his report a mass of pottery and fragmentary artefacts. In 1890 he carried out a single season of excavation in Palestine on the mound of Tell el-Hesy (Eglon or Lachish). Again, by means of schematic vertical recording of finds and study and publication of selection of pottery, he established an outline history of the site, and with it an archaeological framework for Palestine from pre-Biblical to Roman times. Many of his later excavations were on cemeteries in Egypt, and at Nagada in 1895 he cleared with some care the largest predynastic (Neolithic) cemetery ever to be found in Egypt. From the results he constructed a relative chronology of the predynastic period which stands as an important early application of statistical methods to archaeology. Five years later, at Abydos, by sifting carefully the debris from a recent French excavation, he was able to salvage a coherent record of the tombs of Egypt's earliest kings, those of the First Dynasty (*c.* 3000BC).

Petrie's worthy scientific motives, however, were becoming the means for expressing a pronounced restlessness. Most years had to see a new site started, and in retrospect it is clear that many of his excavations were only limited soundings, though a flair for locating the most productive areas gave him constant success. By hard work and a practised short-hand form of publication he managed to maintain a flow of excavation memoirs such as few, if any, other archaeologists have ever achieved. They are often characterized by a kind of instant scholarship made possible by a retentive memory, yet frequently highly selective in its scope, and unresponsive to current scholarship. This characteristic enabled him, at the same time, to range with confidence over a wide field of subjects: the formation of the alphabet, prehistoric hill figures of England, the growth of the Gospels, to name but a few.

488 / PISSARRO, CAMILLE

A useful division in Petrie's long career can be made at 1905. He had, since 1892, been Professor of Egyptology at University College London and had collected a number of honorary degrees. Now came a manual on excavation, *Methods and Aims in Archaeology*, his thirty-third book. At the same time his intolerant attitude towards colleagues who did not share his dedication to archaeology as a serious, full-time pursuit led him to break, for the second time, with the Egypt Exploration Fund. As a support for his future work he set up a rival organization, the British School of Archaeology in Egypt, based at University College. This enabled him to continue field work in Egypt and, after 1926, in Palestine. But the style of his work remained in the same mould as that of his early days, sometimes with less attention to detail.

As a nineteenth-century figure Petrie has the heroic stature of the largely unaided outsider who became an innovator and moulder of attitudes in a new discipline. His contribution to Egyptology by virtue of the quantity of material found and published is considerable and lasting. But to the modern archaeologist, who may prefer to see as the founding figure of his subject the leisurely and painstaking figure of General Pitt Rivers*, Petrie commands only passing attention. The great flaw in Petrie's approach lay in the disparity between the scale of the work attempted and the amount of archaeological skill available. On any dig one archaeologist can cope with only a very restricted area of ground. For Petrie, with limited resources, results which satisfied appetites whetted by half a century of treasure-hunting in Egypt required the directing of enormous energy not just at the skilled tasks of recording, but at controlling a labour force of Egyptian peasants. Petrie's writings have much to say on this topic. The terrible lure of quick and arresting results caught Petrie, as it has continued to catch others, in the trap of trying to apply a scientifically objective eye to a way and to a scale of digging which is inherently crude.

Barry J. Kemp

A comprehensive bibliography of Petrie, comprising 1,024 items, is in the *Journal of Near Eastern Studies*, Vol. 31 (1972), pp. 356–79; *Seventy years in Archaeology* (1931) is his autobiography. See also W.R. Dawson and E.P. Uphill, *Who was who in Egyptology* (2nd edn, 1972).

355
PISSARRO, Camille 1831–1903

French painter

A prolific though essentially modest painter, Pissarro is remembered for his close friendships with Claude Monet* and Paul Cézanne* and for his lasting commitment to the aims of French Impressionism. Initially influenced by Corot* and the painters of Barbizon, he exhibited regularly at the Paris Salon though was considered sufficiently progressive to be the only artist to show his work in all eight Impressionist exhibitions from 1874 to 1886. The admiration for Corot was readily acknowledged and the early work has all the clarity of detail that we associate with the painter of orderly landscapes set under clear southern skies. But the Impressionists were more concerned with the systematic study of particular effects of light and the absolute necessity for working out of doors face to face with the motif to ensure the authenticity of their vision. Here Corot was of little help and a less precise method was needed. The robust palette-knife of Courbet* was a possible answer and Pissarro had much sympathy for the older man's Socialist principles, but it was the fruitful working relationship with Claude Monet whom he met at the Académie Suisse in 1859 that helped to mould the style of his middle years. The two men worked together and evolved a less exacting technique better suited to capturing the fleeting effects of sudden movement, though as late as 1865 Pissarro still exhibited at the Salon as a 'pupil of Corot'. In 1870 both men were in London avoiding the threat and disruptions of the Franco-Prussian War and there is little doubt that they were impressed by the works of the English landscape painters, in particular the vivid atmospheric effects and seemingly spontaneous compositions of J.M.W. Turner*, though there is no evidence that they were able to see the countless watercolour sketches we now see as his most 'impressionist' works. Less impressed by the damp mist and London fog, Pissarro moved to the outer suburbs and the paintings made there have a delicacy and deftness of touch quite unlike anything he had painted in France. The friendship with Paul Cézanne dates from 1861 and the two men worked closely together. Pissarro encouraged Cézanne to move away from the turgid, melodramatic and often erotic subject matter of his early years and he began to produce works in the Impressionist manner. In turn Pissarro's work shows a firmer grasp of pictorial structure in which the angled brush-strokes reflect the surface of the canvas as much as any specific natural phenomena. Both men relished the opportunity to work directly from nature and to be strictly objective in their vision. For a time Pissarro flirted with the optical-mixtures of Seurat*, but soon returned to his now settled descriptive style in which what he saw as the truth of the matter was the essence of his art. Ironically like Monet his eyesight failed and towards the very end of his life he was forced indoors and the paintings seen from the studio window inevitably have an unwanted distance that weakens the normally perceptive way of seeing. There is a sad *Self Portrait* (Tate Gallery, London) painted in 1903, the year of his death, which sums up his life-long achievement. The near blind man sits with his back to the window from which he has been working, the face with the thin spectacles is little more than a delicate impression, and the beard a lightly applied multi-coloured mixture of small brush-strokes. In sharp contrast the silhouetted dark hat and coat show an awareness of the need for controlled formal organization. Pale sunlight filters into the room from the street outside. It is a small picture of no great importance. Pissarro left no masterpieces but his contribution to the more revolutionary art of his friends and his simple uncomplicated eye enable us to see clearly why he was so well loved by those who changed the course of nineteenth-century art.

John Furse

Camille Pissarro, *Letters to His Son* (trans. 1943). See also: L.R. Pissarro and L. Venturi, *Camille Pissarro. son art, son oeuvre* (12 vols 1939); John Rewald, *The History of Impressionism* (1961); John Rewald, *Camille Pissarro* (1963).

356
PITT RIVERS, Augustus Lane Fox 1827–1900

British archaeologist

Augustus Lane Fox, as he was known until 1880, was born into an upper-class military family. Although he became a professional soldier, serving with distinction in the Crimean War and ultimately attaining the rank of major-general, army life does not seem to have been altogether congenial to him. Most of his military career was spent in non-combatant roles and he was especially concerned with the development of the modern rifle. He became a collector of fire-arms and other weapons from every part of the world and this stimulated his interest both in primitive peoples and in the history of weaponry. He believed that the key to the history of weaponry, and other artefacts, lay in their *typology* – a term he was the first to use in its modern archaeological sense. He became convinced that there was a precise analogy between the way types of artefact developed in complexity and Darwinian* evolution. Accordingly, the progress of human societies, as revealed by their material culture, was to be investigated in just the same way as the phenomena of the natural world.

Lane Fox's vision of a science of the 'evolution of culture' was set out forcibly in a lecture under that name delivered to the Royal Institution in 1875. This lecture rejected outright the idealistic and Romantic view that the human mind and spirit will always resist scientific inquiry: history could not claim exemption from the logic of evolution, whose understanding constituted the highest form of knowledge. 'Human ideas', he argued, 'as represented by the products of human industry, are capable of classification into genera,

species and varieties in the same manner as the products of the animal and vegetable kingdoms, and in their development from the homogeneous to the heterogeneous they obey the same laws. . . . History is but another name for evolution.' A society was successful to the extent that it was a vehicle of those ideas that proved 'fittest' and hence survived in the long term. For Lane Fox this was proved by the progress of technology, whose products were seen as symbols of the human mind.

Lane Fox's fortunes were transfigured in 1880 when he inherited the vast estates of his distant relative, Lord Rivers, at Cranborne Chase in Wiltshire. As Pitt Rivers, he now dedicated himself to the twin tasks of promoting evolutionary concepts in the popular mind and the scientific investigation of archaeological sites. He was a forerunner of many twentieth-century aristocrats in opening up his estates to the masses and erecting a public museum and zoo. His motives, however, were not commercial (entry was free), but purely instructive. For several years he served as the first Inspector of Ancient Monuments under the act introduced in Parliament by his son-in-law, Sir John Lubbock*, and travelled to all parts of Britain. Most of his excavations, however, were undertaken on unspectacular sites within his own grounds. He learnt something from Canon Greenwell, the excavator of Yorkshire barrows, but his techniques were really the product of his own systematic experimentation. Under his hands excavation was transformed into a science, as exacting in its way as clinical dissection. Technically his methods fell only a little short of those followed in the best excavations at the present day.

Pitt Rivers's apocalyptic evolutionism, though an ascendant faith in his time, now seems overblown and inapposite. His typological studies still have some value, but his most lasting contribution to the sum of human knowledge was his demonstration that archaeology could not attempt to be a substitute history: it has its own special kind of data. He taught that archaeology's most valuable documents were the evidences for the lives of ordinary people: the commonplace objects of everyday existence were richer in meaning than the rare 'art' pieces. In this, as in his excavation methods, Pitt Rivers stands out as a pioneer of modern archaeology, in contrast to his contemporaries, like Schliemann* and even Sir Arthur Evans*. The Pitt Rivers Museum in Oxford was formed around nucleus collections made by Pitt Rivers and the whole is arranged according to his typological principles.

C.F. Hawke-Smith

M.V. Thompson, *General Pitt-Rivers* (1977) is the only biography. This contains a reprint of the 1875 lecture, *On the Evolution of Culture*. For Pitt-Rivers's archaeological achievement see Glyn Daniel, *One Hundred and Fifty Years of Archaeology* (1975).

357

POE, Edgar Allan 1809–49

US poet, short-story writer and critic

Edgar Allan Poe was born in Boston and brought up by foster-parents in Richmond, Virginia, and in England. He spent a year at the University of Virginia, two in the US Army and a short time at West Point. Early volumes of poetry attracted little money and scant critical attention. Poe busied himself with producing short stories – largely humorous satires on contemporary literary taste. The course of his career changed decisively only in 1835, when he joined the staff of the *Southern Literary Messenger*, to which he had previously contributed tales and book reviews. Thereafter, he spent most of his life as a literary journalist and editor, working for various magazines in Baltimore, Philadelphia and New York. Many of his best-known stories first appeared in these publications.

Poe won early notoriety as an abrasive and controversial critic. But, when twenty-five of his stories finally appeared in book form, in 1839, as *Tales of the Grotesque and Arabesque*, reviews were complimentary but sales were small. Poe became a celebrity only in 1845, with the publication of the poem 'The Raven'. As serious acclaim seemed imminent, however, Poe involved himself in fierce and acrimonious exchanges with the literary establishment in New York. Success came his way again in 1845, with the publication of a selection of *Tales*. But Poe's attacks on others continued to provoke counter-attacks, and he became engaged in a 'War of the Literati'. Rivals and enemies assailed his literary reputation, and his personal reputation was damaged by gossip and slander. Poe still found time, however, for serious literature. *Eureka*, a prose poem attempting to relate scientific thought to poetic intuition, was published in 1848, and some of Poe's finest poems were composed in the last three years of his life. Poe died in Baltimore, in circumstances which have remained mysterious.

The defamation of Poe continued after his death, and the Poe legend came into being – the myth of a morbid and deranged man, addicted to melancholy, drink and drugs, whose personal conduct, family and sexual history were all open to suspicion. Poe was often identified with the madmen he had created, and his character and morals impugned. Defenders of Poe, however, proved to be as ardent as his detractors, and he was also exalted as a rebel-hero, in solitary revolt against a crass and materialistic America. Both conceptions of Poe have some foundation in fact. But modern scholars have sought to strike a balance, emphasizing the essentially normal sides to Poe, his ability and diligence as a journalist, his keenly logical mind.

In his time, Poe was best known as a critic, and his achievements in the field of criticism should not be underestimated. He was quick, for instance, to recognize Hawthorne's* talent, and he wrote perceptively about the weaknesses of Longfellow's* poetry. Poe's criticism is important partly because he himself took it so seriously. He argued for a criticism independent of other disciplines, and concerned with texts rather than extraneous material. He saw discrimination and evaluation as the critic's duties, and thought that the critic should identify canons for sound judgment. He himself tried to base his criticism on a coherent set of principles. Hostile to didacticism, he elaborated a theory of the autonomy of art, anticipating the doctrine of 'art for art's sake' that was later to become so popular in Europe. He emphasized the freedom of the imagination. For Poe, realism, fidelity to fact, to literal truth, were no part of the artist's responsibilities. He saw the writer as at liberty to create his own universe. Poe attacked the literary nationalism so prevalent in early nineteenth-century America. But he also insisted that American writers should beware of imitating European models. Though he saw the poetic faculty as essentially intuitive, he also argued that the writer should be principally a craftsman, and stressed the importance of precise attention to technical detail.

As a young poet, Poe was much influenced by Byron*, Coleridge*, Shelley* and Keats*. He saw poetry as the rhythmical creation of beauty, an art concerned with the ideal whose purpose was to elevate the soul. Favourite themes were the unattainability of the ideal, and death – particularly the death of beautiful women. (His cousin, and wife, Virginia, whom he had married when she was a mere thirteen years old, doubtless served as a model for some of the female wraiths that flit through his world.) Poe was frequently concerned to evoke the indescribable by indirection and recondite symbolism. In choosing words, he was inclined to pay more regard to their associations and overtones than their actual meaning. Critics have praised his poetry for its profundity. But others have attacked it for its vagueness, the very 'indefinitiveness' Poe claimed he wished to achieve. Poe was a clever metrist. But his effects have often been condemned as vulgar and meretricious. That he tended to subordinate sense to sound is indisputable. His poetry is perhaps of most interest as a bridge between the work of the Romantics and the Symbolist movement, particularly in France. French poets who admired and were indebted to Poe include Baudelaire*, Mallarmé* and Valéry. Symbolist aesthetics and Symbolist practice owe much to Poe's example.

It is Poe's short stories, however, that are his major achievement. He was intimately in touch with the American mass market, and catered to it with his own brand of the Gothic horror story. Influenced, like Hawthorne, by Tieck and E.T.A. Hoffmann*, he excelled in his handling of morbid and dismal subjects: death, insanity, crime, disease, the collapse of personality. He was skilled in the creation of fraught and maddened characters. His protagonists are often burdened with obsessions and guilts, goaded into action by perverse impulses, torn between opposing desires, capable of reason but bereft of ordinary humanity and common sense. Inclined to Gothic excess, Poe was also aware of its absurdity. A number of his stories are burlesques of the Gothic mode. Poe's tales include trenchant satires, adventure stories and romantic and idealistic fantasies. Some pieces perpetrate elaborate hoaxes. Others expose them. The master of horror and terror also wrote *Tales of Ratiocination*, and invented the detective story. The curious combination of a cool and calculating intelligence with the most bizarre irrationalities is perhaps what is chiefly responsible for the singular appeal and the peculiar variousness of Poe's tales.

Poe's was a strange and complex personality, and his writing and thought are correspondingly complex. Poe was, at one and the same time, a romantic poet and a shrewd journalist and critic. He was assiduous in giving the public what it wanted. But he scorned it as he did so. A worshipper of the ideal, he mourned the death of poetic legends at the hands of science. But, in *Eureka*, he showed a sound grasp of contemporary scientific thought, and an eager interest in scientific method. He denied the logical principle of contradiction, and yet he defended consistency. He exalted the power of intuition but professed a cult of reason and lucidity. He revelled in mystery and was obsessed with solving it. He dreamt up the most gruesome horrors and laughed them to scorn. He invented maniacs who are logical in their lunacy, and logicians who take logic to lunatic extremes. He delighted in imbalance and incongruity: minds in which certain faculties are prodigiously developed at the expense of others; characters who swing abruptly from one mood or attitude to another; stories which lurch from melodrama to burlesque, from parody to solemnity. A foe to allegory, Poe wrote stories that encourage an allegorical reading. Yet the hunt for symbols and significance, so common in Poe criticism, often deadens the work and ignores the pleasures it offers. Poe was adept at the calculated effect, the artful trick. The horror and humour often depend on cunning contrivance. Endowed with a murky, ghoulish imagination, Poe was also gifted with the skills of a literary engineer. His methods are worth as much study as his meaning.

Poe's influence has been as complicated and as various as his writing itself. It had been detected in the work of writers as diverse as H.P. Lovecraft and Robert Frost, Tennyson* and Graham Greene, Swinburne* and Dostoevsky*, Robert Louis Stevenson* and Gide, Joyce and Borges. Poe's horror stories and detective stories have influenced many subsequent practitioners in these genres, notably Conan Doyle*. He is a central figure in the tradition of American Gothic writing that

runs from Philip Freneau to William Faulkner. His influence on European poetry in the later nineteenth century has already been remarked on. His impact on other arts has been widely recognized. Magritte and Debussy are among the painters and musicians who have acknowledged his influence. As a writer of American fiction, Poe lacks the sophistication of a Hawthorne, or the imaginative range and intellectual seriousness of a Melville*. As a poet, he is entirely without the passionate intelligence of the Baudelaire who so esteemed him. His achievements as a critic are ultimately dwarfed by those of a Coleridge. But his importance as a pioneer and seminal figure remains unquestionable.

Andrew Gibson

Works: The following were published in volume form during Poe's lifetime: *Tamerlane and Other Poems* (1827); *El Aaraaf, Tamerlane and Other Poems* (1829); *Poems* (1831); *The Narrative of Arthur Gordon Pym* (1838); *Tales of the Grotesque and Arabesque* (1839); *The Prose Romances of Edgar A. Poe* (1843); *Tales* (1845); *The Raven and Other Poems* (1845); *Eureka* (1848). See: E. H. Davidson, *Poe: A Critical Study*, (1957); P. F. Quinn, *The French Face of Edgar Poe* (1957); V. Buranelli, *Edgar Allan Poe* (1961); E. W. Carlson (ed.), *The Recognition of Edgar Allan Poe* (1966); D. G. Hoffmann, *Poe, Poe, Poe, Poe, Poe, Poe, Poe, Poe* (1973); J. G. Symons, *The Tell-Tale Heart: The Life and Work of Edgar Allan Poe* (1978).

358
POINCARÉ, Henri 1854–1912

French mathematician

In Henri Poincaré France produced a mathematical giant who subsequently became a philosophical and literary giant. This is not a common transition, and one must turn to Bertrand Russell and Alfred North Whitehead for figures of similar power and breadth in recent times. But there is a difference between the two Englishmen and the Frenchman they admired: Poincaré began as a creative mathematician of astonishing originality and punch, whereas the Englishmen were primarily mathematical logicians and systematizers in their early years.

Poincaré is often called the 'Father' or 'Founder' of the mathematical science of topology. One can hardly expect exact scientific accuracy in such a claim: it is, rather, an expression of the way in which he saw, as a whole and as a potential unity, a mass of questions which, before his day, had been dealt with under various heads. Poincaré was to topology as Gilbert was to magnetism: the man whose name is indelibly linked with the new knowledge, because it was he (Poincaré) who saw its inter-connectedness, its significance as an attempt to answer a small set of fundamentally similar questions.

Poincaré was born in Nancy in 1854. His father was Professor of Medicine at the university, his mother a warm, intelligent, cultivated woman, who set about to educate her precocious, but frail, son at home – at least until he was able to enter the local *lycée*. Henri's progress at the Nancy *lycée* left his contemporaries standing, but there was one Achilles heel – Poincaré was poorly co-ordinated and, as a result of this, could never draw to the standard expected of an outstandingly clever boy. When he subsequently sat the examination for the École Polytechnique his mark for drawing was actually zero! (In spite of this the examiners made an exception and let him in.)

The École Polytechnique led to the School of Mines and, in 1879 at the age of twenty-five, Poincaré received his doctorate in mathematical science at the University of Paris. After two years on the faculty at Caen, he moved to Paris in 1881, first to be Maître de Conférences, and later (in 1886) to be Professor of Mathematical Physics and Probability.

From the time when he received his doctorate onwards Poincaré maintained a prodigious output of books and papers. During his life he published nearly 500 memoirs on mathematical topics, more than thirty books on mathematical physics and astronomy, and six books on more general themes.

Poincaré's recognition of the importance of topology is all of a piece with his poor drawing skill, because a poorly drawn but complete figure and a well drawn figure have this in common: they are topologically equal. Topology is concerned only with the question whether two points p and q are joined by a continuous line or curve, not with the shape of the curve nor straightness of the line. Later popularizers have called topology 'rubber sheet geometry' because it is about those properties of spatial relationships which remain intact when the figures, drawn on a rubber sheet, are pulled around, i.e. deformed, but not cut or torn.

Poincaré's work on topology, entitled *Analysis situ*, was published in 1895. With this event mathematicians began to recognize the existence of a major new research area – a comparatively rare event in the history of mathematics. The new science could be applied to many things besides plane figures: to space as a whole (general relativity), to tangles (knot theory), and to spatial permutation (combinatorial topology). Yet none of these applications has quite justified the feeling of intellectual pregnancy associated with topology for more than eighty years. Throughout this period it has captured the interest of many of the most creative research mathematicians and has been widely seen as the modern branch of mathematics *par excellence*. There is a direct link with Thom's later 'Catastrophe Theory'. But the subject has yet to generate the kind of sub-

stantial body of intellectually important applications which it has seemed to promise. The prime target for such applications must be the biological topic of morphology, but the breakthrough to a neat, intellectually elegant treatment of this area still eludes us.

Poincaré's greatest technical achievement in mathematics was his theory of automorphic functions. These were functions which remained unchanged when one changed their 'arguments' in certain ways. (The argument of a function is the variable to which one applies the function: for example 'x' is the argument of the function log (x).) The simplest elementary example of an automorphic function is sin (θ), which obviously remains unchanged when one adds 360 to its 'argument' θ – having turned through a complete circle, one is left pointing in the same direction. It was this theory (of automorphic functions) which led Poincaré to non-Euclidean geometry and topology, to new ways of solving differential equations, and to the solution of other technical problems in mathematics. Poincaré also did important work on the classical 'three body problem', leading to the new methods of 'asymptotic expansions' and 'integral invariants'. Poincaré did not solve the problem – which is about the mutual effects of three or more bodies attracting each other gravitationally in space – but he did make enough progress to qualify for the prize given by the King of Sweden for work in this area.

In astronomy Poincaré showed that a rotating gravitational fluid mass subject to the influence of a steady torque would gradually become pear shaped and would finally throw off a moon.

In philosophy of science Poincaré's name is associated with a view often described as 'conventionality'. He pointed out, for example, that it is possible to describe space using non-Euclidean geometries (see Lobachevsky*, Riemann*), so that there is a certain degree of conventionality in our normal use of the Euclidean concept of space to describe the world around us. Nevertheless there is a reason for adopting one convention rather than another; namely, that the Euclidean point of view is 'simpler', 'more convenient' or 'advantageous'. 'Geometry', he says in *Science and Method* (*Science et Méthode*, 1908, trans.1914), 'is not true, it is advantageous.' Poincaré applied this view of conceptual frameworks to other examples, such as time, rotation, and the laws of mechanics.

The nineteenth century produced a crop of individuals of astonishing intellectual power whose influence came to fruition after 1900: men like Babbage*, Mendel*, Peirce*, and Pearson*. Even in this select company Poincaré stands out. It is a triumph of mind over matter that Poincaré, who was physically myopic, developed intellectually into a figure exceptionally long, and exceptionally broad, sighted. But unlike the thinkers mentioned above, he was not neglected in his day. He won almost every honour, prize, medal or fellowship for which he was eligible. His books were widely read. He wrote to be understood, and he was understood.

Christopher Ormell

Poincaré's works: *Oeuvres de Henri Poincaré*, Académie des Sciences de Paris (10 vols, 1916–54); *The Foundations of Science*, trans. G.B. Halsted (1913); *Dernières Pensées* (1913), trans. *Mathematics and Science: Last Essays* (1963). See: E.T. Bell, *Men of Mathematics*, ch. 28 (1937). An interesting obituary notice may be found in *Proceedings of the Royal Society*, Series A, 91, 5–16 (1915).

359
PRESCOTT, William Hickling 1796–1859

US historian

William Hickling Prescott was born in Salem, Massachusetts, where his father Judge William Prescott was a successful lawyer of patrician background. The family's prosperity enabled Prescott to have a privileged education in local private schools before going to Harvard in 1811. His record at Harvard was solid, if undistinguished, and on graduating in 1814 he intended to follow his father into a career in law. During his junior year, however, Prescott's left eye was injured irreparably by a hard crust of bread thrown in a college mêlée; some two years later his right eye was affected by rheumatic inflammation and with seriously impaired vision in both eyes he was forced to abandon his legal studies. On a trip to London in 1816 Prescott purchased a noctograph, a device made for the blind which made it possible for him to write without the aid of an amanuensis. He married in 1820 and his wife, Susan Amory, and a series of faithful secretaries and readers became the 'eyes' which were to guide him through the extensive and demanding historical research of his later life.

On giving up his plans to study law Prescott's predilection was for a career in literary journalism. He read widely in the literatures of Western Europe, especially those of England, France, Italy and Germany, and throughout the 1820s and early 1830s he produced a steady stream of articles and reviews for established journals such as the *North American Review* and the *United States Literary Gazette*. His eclectic interests and meticulous researching enabled him to write, with some authority, on Byron*, medieval romance, Molière, Italian narrative poetry, Scottish ballads, and, as if not seeming to ignore a nascent American literature, the novelist Charles Brockden Brown. (The 'Life of Charles Brockden Brown' was first published in Jared Sparks's *The Library of American Biography*, 1834, and it remains, to this day, a lucid and informative account.)

Reviewing, however, became increasingly for Prescott a training ground for the more arduous demands of historical writing and research, and it was after some four years of freelance journalism that he turned his attention, with the guidance of his friend George Ticknor, to the history of imperial Spain. By amassing a large personal library of Spanish materials and by training his secretaries to pronounce Castilian 'in a manner suited . . . much more to my ear than that of a Spaniard' Prescott began the eleven years of research that were to result in the three-volume *History of the Reign of Ferdinand and Isabella, the Catholic* (1837). This was followed by the *History of the Conquest of Mexico* (3 vols, 1843), *A History of the Conquest of Peru* (2 vols, 1847) and the *History of the Reign of Philip the Second, King of Spain* (3 vols, 1855–8) – the last was left incomplete at Prescott's death in January 1859.

With the publication of the *History of the Reign of Ferdinand and Isabella, the Catholic* Prescott established himself not only as a respectable historian but also an immensely popular one; this popularity was reinforced by the *History of the Conquest of Mexico* which endures as the most readable and successful of his histories. Modern scholarship has, of course, considerably amplified Prescott's portrait of imperial Spain and he has been justly criticized for the rationalistic and republican bias that he brings to his accounts of ancient civilizations, but historians agree that his use of primary sources and the narrative energy of his writing are exemplary.

Prescott is often linked with other nineteenth-century American historians such as Francis Parkman* and George Bancroft as subscribing to a romantic model of historical writing where emphasis is laid on great individuals as the makers of history, where political and constitutional issues are accorded only cursory treatment, and where vivid characterization and epical rhetoric seem to overwhelm disinterested observation. Prescott, however, was himself more inclined to an eighteenth-century view of history: he thought its purpose was to edify and instruct and he followed Gibbon in holding to the belief that the writing of history should serve some moral utility. But he did not discount the place of entertainment, and it was from Voltaire and Sir Walter Scott* that he drew the method of constructing his histories around an individual figure or dramatic event and then building up scenes in a tableau-like, rather than chronological, fashion. The fact that Prescott remains the most accessible of all Anglo-American historians of the Hispanic world is ample testimony to his mastery of this method of historical narration.

Henry Claridge

W.H. Monroe, *The Works of W.H. Prescott* (22 vols, 1904), is the standard edition of Prescott's writings; C. Harvey Gardiner, *William Hickling Prescott: A Biography* (1969), is the best biography. Gardiner has also edited *The Papers of William Hickling Prescott* (1964). Prescott's work is discussed in: *The Cambridge History of American Literature*, vol. 2 (1918); Van Wyck Brooks, *The Flowering of New England* (1936); and David Levin, *History as Romantic Art: Bancroft, Prescott, Motley and Parkman* (1959).

360
PROUDHON, Pierre-Joseph 1809–65

French Socialist and anarchist

Proudhon was born at Besançon in the Franche-Comté, his father a notably honest brewer who refused to make a profit, so that the family was raised in poverty. Proudhon attended the Collège de Besançon, but was primarily self-educated at the town's public library. Later a forceful polemicist – he is best known for the phrases 'property is theft' and 'God is evil' – Proudhon established anarchism as a major force in French, and later European, political life, primarily through a critique of authority. His books are usually a disorganized but exhilarating combination of angry polemics, philosophical reasoning and political analysis, dealing with a multitude of subjects. He remained strongly attached to his peasant origins, though his work mainly influenced the new urban working class then becoming established in France. His origins may account for the unexpected survival of a strand of anti-feminism in his thought.

He was apprenticed as a printer, and his earliest contact with radical thought occurred in 1829 when he supervised the printing of *Le Nouveau monde industriel et sociétaire* ('The New Industrial and Cooperative World') by Charles Fourier*; Fourier's proposals for cooperatives were an early influence, later rejected. Proudhon's most important early work was *What is Property?* (*Qu'est-ce que la propriété?*, 1840, trans. 1969), which attacks the injustices caused by property, but does not deny the need for possessions. In 1843 his contact with the Lyons Mutualists, a secret society of working men, led to an interest in the question of association. This developed into a theory of organization, later called 'Mutualism', in which members of small units worked together, and credit was to be reformed through a People's Bank.

From the revolution of 1848 onwards Proudhon's thought developed in direct response to political events. During the Second Republic he wrote for or edited four Paris newspapers between April 1848 and October 1850. These were *Le Représentant du peuple* (1848), *Le Peuple* (1848–9), *La Voix du peuple* (1849–50), and the short-lived *Le Peuple de 1850* (1850). His intention was to provide the ideas which he believed the revolution lacked. Proudhon's journalism is remarkable for its perceptive critiques of events; he also correctly anticipated that Louis-Napoleon Bonaparte would become president of the republic and later emperor. He attracted considerable support among the Parisian working class after other socialists were discredited or imprisoned, but in accordance with his theories firmly refused to head a party or political group. His attacks on Louis-Napoleon led to his imprisonment in 1849, though under conditions which allowed him to continue as editor and author.

Proudhon's *Confessions d'un Révolutionnaire* ('Confessions of a Revolutionary', 1849) is indispensable for an understanding of the events of 1848, but the major theoretical work to emerge from this period is the *General Idea of the Revolution in the Nineteenth Century*, (*Idée générale de la révolution au XIXe siècle*, 1851, trans. 1923). Proudhon had been elected to the National Assembly in 1848, but found himself cut off from events and from the people he represented; further, the extended franchise had led to the election of a reactionary assembly and a bourgeois president. The *General Idea* therefore criticizes representative democracy, objecting that even when the people are supposedly sovereign actual political authority is exercised by only a small number of people. Arguing for individual liberty, Proudhon proposes a network of contracts between individuals: 'The producer deals with the consumer, the member with his society, the farmer with his township, the township with the province, the province with the State.' In this way the citizen and the state were to be equalized.

In 1854 he survived an attack of cholera which caused him increasing ill-health as well as difficulty in writing, until his death in 1865. A scurrilous attack by a Roman Catholic priest provoked the composition of his greatest work, *De la Justice dans la révolution et dans l'Église*, ('Justice in the Revolution and in the Church', 1858), described by George Woodcock as 'one of the noblest works of social thought of the nineteenth century'. Justice is put forward as a moral concept based on a recognition of human dignity. It is the basis of the relations between people, and consequently of their social and economic relations. Men most naturally cooperate in work, and groups of working men would form the basis of the revolutionary movement. Proudhon's arguments, here as elsewhere, proceed by identifying related opposites or antinomies, setting them in conflict and proposing the establishment between them of a dynamic equilibrium. This dynamism would ensure the vitality of any society applying such ideas. *Principle of Federation* (*Du principe fédératif*, 1863, trans. 1980) sets out clearly Proudhon's mature federalist theory of the relations between individuals, larger groups and states.

Proudhon's debate with Marx* had important consequences for the development of nineteenth-century revolutionary politics. Proudhon's identification of Marx's latent authoritarianism ('Do not let us become the leaders of a new intolerance ... Let us accumulate and encourage protest [against our own ideas]' in a letter of 1846 ended direct relations between the two men. In response to Proudhon's *System of Economic Contradictions* (*Système des contradictions économiques, ou philosophie de la misère*, 1846, trans. 1972), Marx wrote his attack *The Poverty of Philosophy* (*Misère de la philosophie*, 1847, trans. 1936). In 1864 the International Working Men's Association (the First International) was founded, in which Proudhon's followers were Marx's most powerful opponents. Proudhon's primary influence was upon the libertarian socialist movement in nineteenth-century France, which was opposed to the authoritarian Marxist tradition which eventually triumphed because of its greater relevance to industrial societies. In the anarchist tradition Mikhail Bakunin* and Petr Kropotkin* most effectively continued Proudhon's ideas, particularly his federalism; though Bakunin, unlike Proudhon, believed in the necessity of violent revolution. In the 1870s Proudhon's ideas spread through Pi y Margall to Spain; and through Alexander Herzen* and Leo Tolstoy* to Russia. He influenced Georges Sorel* and in England Wyndham Lewis. Proudhon was less influential on the anarcho-syndicalist movement at the turn of the century, and in recent decades his direct influence has been almost non-existent; but spontaneous revolts, such as that in Paris in 1968, are anticipated in his writings as an appropriate form of revolutionary activity.

Alan Munton

Complete works: *Oeuvres complètes*, ed. C. Bouglé and H. Moysset (19 vols,1923–59). Not completed. *Correspondance* (14 vols, 1875); *Carnets* ('Diaries'), ed. P. Haubtmann (from 1960). Other works: *De la Capacité politique des classes ouvrières* (1865); *La Guerre et la Paix* (1970); *La pornocratie, ou les femmes dans les temps modernes* (1865). Selections in English: *Selected Writings*, ed. S. Edwards (1969). See: Edward Hyams, *Pierre-Joseph Proudhon: His Revolutionary Life, Mind and Works* (1979). See also: Robert L. Hoffman, *Revolutionary Justice: The Social and Political Theory of P.-J. Proudhon* (1972); J. Hampden Jackson, *Marx, Proudhon and European Socialism* (1958); Henri de Lubac, *Proudhon et le Christianisme* (1945; trans. *The Un-Marxian Socialist: A Study of Proudhon*, 1948); Alan Ritter, *The Political Thought of Pierre-Joseph Proudhon* (1969).

361
PUCCINI, Giacomo 1858–1924

Italian composer

Puccini was born into a family whose musical tradition stretched back several generations and included com-

posers of sacred as well as secular music. His early training in Lucca was primarily as a church musician, but in 1876 a performance of Verdi's* *Aida* persuaded him to pursue an operatic career. He moved to Milan to study composition with Amilcare Ponchielli, and it was there, in 1884, that his first opera, *Le villi*, was produced. *Edgar* (1889), his next work, was less successful with the public, but *Manon Lescaut* (1893) brought him an international reputation, in spite of inevitable comparisons with Jules Massenet's opera of the same title.

This success was consolidated with the next three works, all of which remain firmly in the operatic repertoire. *La Bohème* (1896) depicts a tragic love affair against the background of bohemian artistic life in Paris; the sentimentality of the plot, and its blending of comic and serious elements, have led many to consider it the opera in which subject matter is most convincingly matched with Puccini's particular musico-dramatic gifts. However, *Tosca* (1900) marked a sharp change in direction. The violence and cruelty of the plot did not prevent Puccini from including several lyrical scenes, but it did perhaps encourage him to experiment with various 'modernistic' musical devices, in particular with harmony based on the whole-tone scale. *Madama Butterfly* (1904) again attempted to break new ground, this time with an exotic, oriental setting and, at least on the surface, a more refined orchestral sonority.

After *Butterfly* the pace of Puccini's creative output slowed considerably. From his published letters it seems that the major problem was that of finding suitable operatic subjects. As we can see from the last three operas discussed, he clearly disliked repeating himself in his choice of dramatic setting, presumably because the background of a work produced the initial stimulus towards composition. In every respect the comparison with Verdi's relatively unproductive period (from *Aida* to *Otello*) is striking and relevant, and can tell us much about the composers' creative processes. The breakthrough finally occurred when Puccini discovered a story set in the Californian gold-rush of 1849. *La fanciulla del West* (1910) was, in the violence and austerity of its plot, somewhat akin to *Tosca*, but it noticeably lacked the earlier opera's sections of sustained lyricism and perhaps for this reason has tended to be less popular with the opera-going public.

La rondine (1917) has been even less frequently revived, but the next work, *Il trittico* (1918), showed many interesting innovations. Three contrasting one-act operas make up the evening: a sinister melodrama (*Il tabarro*); a sentimental tragedy, entirely for female voices (*Suor Angelica*); and a pure comic opera, set in thirteenth-century Florence (*Gianni Schicchi*). Though rarely seen as a complete evening, these operas (particularly the first and third) are important documents in the development of Puccini's musical personality. The new orchestral refinements of *Il tabarro* show that the composer was less indifferent to the music of his more radical contemporaries, Debussy in particular, than is sometimes suggested (we might also remember that he was an attentive listener at one of the earliest performances of Schoenberg's *Pierrot Lunaire*). On the other hand, *Gianni Schicchi* places in the clearest possible context Puccini's debt to Verdi, and to that composer's last opera, *Falstaff*, in particular.

Puccini's final work, *Turandot* (first performed 1926), represented yet another change in dramatic direction. The fairy-tale atmosphere of the plot, and its bold mixture of various dramatic genres, initially struck the composer as a source of limitless possibilities, as a chance to supersede all his previous work; but ultimately the complicated dramatic structure created severe problems of musical continuity, and the work remained unfinished at the composer's death. It is performed today in a completed version by Franco Alfano.

In spite (perhaps, in some circles, because) of Puccini's vast popular success, he has frequently been the target of academic/critical abuse, both on the dramatic and the musical level. Joseph Kerman, for example, describes the musical texture of *Tosca* as 'consistently, throughout, of café-music banality', and eventually identifies the 'failure, or, more correctly, the triviality of [Puccini's] attempt to invent genuine musical drama'. But perhaps today we are beginning to see signs of a less jaundiced approach to the composer. It must be admitted that, in spite of his obviously sincere attempts to search for new areas of dramatic expression, his mature musical language (from *La Bohème* onwards) changed little and was only marginally affected by contemporary developments. However, most sympathetic commentators argue that Puccini was above all a master of the theatrical situation – that his operas can be assessed realistically only in the opera house itself. There the almost fanatical precision with which he judged the pace of the drama always seems to justify itself magnificently, and even in some cases to transcend the limitations of his musical language.

Roger Parker

All Puccini's operas have been mentioned above. He also wrote a number of songs, some religious music and a few choral, orchestral and chamber works, the vast majority of them during the 1880s. Source writings: *Epistolario*, ed. Giuseppe Adami (1928, trans. Ena Makin, *Letters of Giacomo Puccini*, 1931); and *Carteggi Pucciniani*, ed. Eugenio Gara (1958). Mosco Carner, *Puccini: A Critical Biography* (2nd edn 1974), covers all the works in detail and includes a full biography.

362

PUGIN, Augustus Welby Northmore 1812–52

British architect and designer

The Gothic style and the Catholic faith were the two passions which dominated Pugin's brief life. His interest in Gothic architecture was communicated to him by his father Augustus Charles Pugin, a refugee from the French Revolution who worked as a draughtsman for John Nash* and for several publishers of topographical engravings. The younger Pugin assisted in some of his father's publications on medieval architecture and furniture, and after his father's death he continued to publish volumes of plates illustrating Gothic detail.

In 1836, stimulated by his recent conversion to Catholicism, Pugin attracted the notice of the public with a provocative book, *Contrasts, or A Parallel Between The Noble Edifices of the Fourteenth and Fifteenth Centuries, and Similar Buildings of The Present Day, Shewing The Present Decay of Taste*. Here bleak or incongruous views of Georgian institutions were set beside idealized evocations of their medieval equivalents, complete with benevolent bishops and orderly citizens. No less influential was *True Principles of Pointed or Christian Architecture* (1841), in which Pugin prescribed:

> 1st, that there should be no features about a building which are not necessary for convenience, construction or propriety; 2nd, that all ornament should consist of enrichment of the essential construction of the building . . . In pure architecture the smallest detail should have a meaning or serve a purpose.

Although forcefully phrased, these principles were scarcely original, for similar prescriptions had been set forward by several German and British theorists in the preceding decade, and by French writers in the preceding century. Nor should Pugin's words be interpreted as a call to 'functionalism', since all kinds of elaborate ornament, unnecessary to the structure, could be introduced in the name of 'propriety' or 'meaning'. Indeed, it was the very ambiguity of these principles which recommended them to many Victorian architects, who quoted them in justification of their multifarious creations.

As an architect Pugin won a number of ecclesiastical commissions, of which the most important were St Chad's Roman Catholic Cathedral in Birmingham, Killarney Cathedral, Eire, and St Giles's Church, Cheadle, Staffordshire. He supplied additions and alterations to a series of country houses, notably Scarsbrick Hall, Lancashire, and Alton Towers, Staffordshire. In general his architectural ambitions outstripped his patrons' purses, and the results were individual in style but seldom outstanding. The great exception, and Pugin's supreme achievement, was the new Houses of Parliament in London, designed in collaboration with Sir Charles Barry* in 1835 and still unfinished at Pugin's death. Pugin was responsible for devising the copious details and furnishings – Gothic, but distinctively Victorian style – and for organizing these into a coherent pattern. Much of the success of this immense project must be attributed to the close relationhip which he established with certain firms of specialized craftsmen, led by George Myers (masonry and wood-carving), John Hardman (metalwork), John Gregory Crace (fabrics, furniture and wallpaper) and Herbert Minton (encaustic tiles). With their aid Pugin was able to offer his patrons a complete and consistent scheme of design.

Pugin's ecclesiastical ornament was admired by a large audience at the Great Exhibition of 1851, whose Medieval Court was arranged by himself and displayed his own work. By now, however, he was showing signs of the mental illness which led to his death in the following year.

Pugin was a collector of rare books and medieval antiquities, as had been several of the eighteenth-century connoisseurs who had initiated the Gothic Revival in Britain. But whereas the earlier generation had employed Gothic motifs largely as vehicles of diffuse romantic association, Pugin's medievalism was altogether less frivolous, paying close attention to historical precedent and to Christian iconography. His polemical writings marked the start of a particularly combative era in British architecture. After Pugin, architectural debate was no longer a pastime for the armchair aesthete; it became a battleground in which were deployed the emotive weapons of religious, moral and social criticism.

Patrick Conner

The principal biography is still *Recollections of A.W.N. Pugin*, by Pugin's friend and fellow-architect Benjamin Ferrey (1861; reprinted 1978, with an introduction by Clive Wainwright). See also: Michael Trappes-Lomax, *Pugin, A Medieval Victorian* (1932); and Phoebe Stanton, *Pugin* (1971).

363
PUSHKIN, Aleksandre 1799–1837

Russian writer

In Russian literature Pushkin occupies a position analogous to Goethe's* in German, in that both figures are regarded in their own countries almost as the *fons et origo* of all that came after them; and like Goethe he also belongs, but more ambiguously, to world literature. He partook of a generation that reacted, at times vehemently, against French culture influences after Napoleon's* abortive march on Moscow in 1812. But if the nationalistic tendency is strong in Pushkin's work, it yet retains a deliberate 'European' compass; and among the great Romantic writers of the early nineteenth century Pushkin is outstanding for his versatility of form (he left no genre untouched) and for his command of an astonishing range of mood and voice.

Pushkin was born into the minor aristocracy of Moscow in 1799. His uncle, Vasili Pushkin, was a poet; and on his mother's side his great grandfather, Abram Hannibal, was reputedly an Abyssinian prince. Visits to his grandmother's estate outside Moscow, and the influence of a nanny, nurtured an early, and abiding, love of Russian folk history and folk tale. In 1811 he entered the Imperial Lyceum at Taarskoye Selo, and by the time he left to take up a post in the Foreign Office in St Petersburg in 1817 he had already gained a reputation as a poet: indeed, the verse romance *Russian and Lyudmilla* (1820), which marked a radical departure from classicist traditions, was begun while Pushkin was still at college.

In May 1820 Pushkin was banished from St Petersburg for the writing of two unpublished political poems, 'Volnost' and 'Derevynya'. Thereafter, although he was pardoned by Nicholas I in 1826, his life was never entirely free from surveillance by government agencies. Poetically however his exile in southern Russia was of the utmost benefit. During his travels in the Caucasus and the Crimea, reading and absorbing Byron*, Pushkin greatly extended his understanding of 'Russian' themes, completing *The Gypsies (Tsygane)* in 1824. At the same time he began *Yevgeny Onegin* (1833), the verse novel with a contemporary setting which, as well as being an undisputed masterpiece, is generally acknowledged as the inspiration for the realist school of Goncharov*, Turgenev* and Tolstoy*. A third major work of this period, written on his parents' estate at Mikhaylovskoye in 1824–5, was the historical tragedy *Boris Godunov* (1833), a verse and prose drama that employs Shakespearian models to present a revolutionary critique of court life during the reign of Ivan the Terrible.

When the freedom that Pushkin enjoyed during the years of his exile was replaced by the blighting touch of official pardon (Tsar Nicholas even appointed himself Pushkin's 'personal censor'), his output diminished sharply. From 1826 until 1829 the only important work to be completed was the epic poem *Poltava*. But then, after a short stint with the army on the Turkish front in 1830, a visit to Nizhny Novgorod (now the city of Gorky) rekindled his genius. Although from 1831 he once more lived in St Petersburg, the last seven years of his life saw a steady flow of valued creations, beginning with the four tragedies *Skupoy rytsar* ('The Covetous Knight', 1836), *Mozart and Salieri* (1831), *Kammeny Gost* ('The Stone Guest', 1839) and *Pir vo vremyachumy*

('Feast in Time of the Plague', 1832), and continuing with the two novels *Dubrovsky* (1841) and *The Captain's Daughter* (*Kapitanskaya dochka*, 1836). During this period Pushkin endeavoured, as much as possible, to avoid public life; but his marriage in 1831 to Natalia Goncharova, a woman of more indiscretion than charm, led ultimately to his being obliged to challenge Baron George d'Anthés, an officer in the Horse Guards, to a duel. He died from wounds received on 10 February 1837, at the age of thirty-seven.

The central problem with Pushkin is one of translation. The normal 'impossibilities' of translating poetry, which in differing ways apply to every poet, to Dante, to Homer, Shakespeare, Horace, Virgil or Byron, are in some way compounded. The trouble, at its simplest level, is that Pushkin is not generally saying anything that compels an immediate response from the reader when it is put before him in familiar words. Whereas the architecture of Milton's and Dante's creations compel attention and admiration in any form, even prose, whereas the axiomatic precision of Horace is easily communicable, or whereas the crude vitality of Byron's *Childe Harold* or *The Corsair* transfers into other languages just because it has no home of its own, with Pushkin it is different. How different is tacitly shown by the fact that the *Oxford Book of Verse in English Translation* (1980), chosen by the poet Charles Tomlinson, has not a single mention of him. '*Il est plat, votre poète*,' said Flaubert* to Turgenev, in honest puzzlement when the Russian recited bits of Pushkin to him in French. And Flaubert was quite right: in this form the finest things in Pushkin *are* flat, irresolvably and inescapably. So it is natural enough that even the experienced scanner of literature should be sceptical, for what is in question is something other than poetic 'simplicity'. A very simple effect in great poetry often retains its force in translation because it can be seen to be the focus or still centre of a whole human situation. It is moving when Dryden's Antony in *All for Love* says to Cleopatra, 'We are both unhappy.' It is moving when Homer's old men on the walls of Troy see Helen go by and utter sentiments to the effect that such a woman is worth all the trouble. Such an effect is of course in the wide sense dramatic, but it is not exclusively so, nor does it seem a deliberate summation by the poet. It is rather a sudden depth of meaning, an impression of depth transferable from one language to another.

Simplicity, or 'flatness', in Pushkin has no such justification. It justifies itself by exhibiting language as poetry, as if language, like a sleeping beauty, had suddenly been brought to life — a comparison suited to Pushkin because his poetry itself delights in magic and fairy tale. In a different linguistic context however the fairy princess is not awakened. Any attempt to jazz up the simplicity of Pushkin results in a kind of poeticity more hideous than any degree of flatness. But in Russian Pushkin has only to say 'I am not that sort of man' (*The Gypsies*), or 'He is too old' (*Poltava*), or 'The sea, where ships were running' ('The Covetous Knight'), or 'Mine will be a sad tale' ('The Bronze Horseman') for the words to appear like the finest poetry. There is something of the miraculous in it, as if the Russians, like Moliere's Monsieur Jourdain who did not know he was speaking grammar, had not realized that the poetry of their language resided in such phrases until Pushkin uttered them.

The genuineness of the miracle is vouched for by the fact that the foreign reader who has acquired a little Russian can suddenly see what it means. If he has experience of poetry the thing bursts upon him. It does so even upon one who knows the language, and whose language is close to it. But as the Polish poet and 1980 Nobel prize-winner Milosz has testified in his autobiography *Native Realm*, a principal ingredient of reading Pushkin is a sense of 'otherness', and even of danger. Pushkin's poetry as language, his poetry as nation, are set apart, and this to the outsider is both a powerful source of attraction and also of distrust. The wholly uninstructed western reader registers this dual response only as a kind of baffled exasperation, an awareness of strongly atavistic feelings which he has no means of sharing. This is indeed no recipe for the kind of instinctive understanding and intellectual reciprocity which give a poet a reputation throughout Europe and the world. There is a queer connection between the attraction of the Russian language as poetic 'otherness', and of Russian as the source of the vital forces of revolution. Milosz says that for him the revolution was personified not by Lenin but by Mayakovsky, the direct descendant of Pushkin, but a poet 'who welded revolutionary theory with the old dream Russians had of themselves as the chosen nation'. It may be that an obvious irony – the internationalism of the revolutionary ideal, and its actual implementation as Russian chauvinistic messianism – bears some relation to the paradox of Russian poetry: the strong attraction of its otherness to outsiders who have learnt to admire it, and the tradition of its own profound and primitive linguistic exclusiveness.

Such generalizations are bound to be misleading. Pushkin's poetry is not of one kind. Its gaiety, effervescence and vivacity are as marked, and in a sense more deliberate, than its untranslatable magic. Pushkin is often determined to be Byronic, to be Horatian, to be Romantic, even above all to be French; and the economy and agility of his thought and expression can be as sophisticated as anything in European literature. His most internationally famous poem, *Yevgeny Onegin*, has all these qualities, and the difficulty in translating it, just as great as that of rendering the Pushkinian 'simple' line, is of a different kind: no foreign syntax can possibly keep up with the natural brio of Pushkin's. He is being in one sense more comprehensively European in this work than any other European poet, more *Mozartian* than any of them. Some Russian poets of this century – Mandelstam, Akhmatova, Brodsky – have all demonstrated in various ways this 'super-European' quality. But under it none the less lies the ancient power of the language, its deep natural exclusiveness, more marked than in any other European tongue, and his personification of this ineluctable poetic nationalism is properly felt to be the 'real' Pushkin.

Even so cosmopolitan a figure as Prince Mirsky, author of *A History of Russian Literature*, suggests that the essence of Pushkin is to be found not in *Yevgeny Onegin*, but in the 'magic' tales like *Ruslan and Lyudmilla*, the *skaski* and in the unfinished dramatic poem *Rusalka*. Such an idea of the 'real' poet, however chimerical, has none the less something revealing about it. We do not talk about the real Shakespeare or Goethe or Dante, but with Pushkin we feel compelled to. Consider for example a famous line of Racine from *Iphigènie*: '*Et tout dort, et l'armée, et les vents, et Neptune*'; and then compare it with a line from *Rusalka*:

Ostalsya
Odin v lesu ma beregu Dmepra
('He has remained alone in the forests by the banks of the Dnieper').

The simplicity of Racine's description is not only euphonious; it sums up a situation familiar to all European readers: the Greek fleet becalmed before its fateful setting out for Troy, and the soothsayer's prophecy for the need of sacrifice. The line effortlessly balances all the stresses of a traditional reference. Pushkin's line on the other hand conveys no such populous traditional resonance. It seems instead, in the original, to disappear into unknown and unvoiced experience, into primeval darkness and silence. Of course, it has a local dramatic reference – the prince, now married, is mourning the girl he was false to, now drowned and become a *rusalka*; but the metonymic power is local and comparatively feeble, almost irrelevant by comparison with the elemental power of Pushkin's line language.

Pushkin's place in world literature – not an edifying term but one difficult to avoid – is thus one that has no real precedent, in that it remains both unique and esoteric. Dostoevsky* insisted upon it, as have many other Russian writers and critics, both in Tsarist and Soviet times, claiming that no writer, not even Shakespeare, was so 'universal' as Pushkin, in his subjects, his scope, his sense and understanding of life. Excellent reasons can be found for this, and the enthusiasts have proceeded to discover and elaborate on them, but in all their analyses and explications there is something decidedly factitious. The truth is the ideas and significances, plot structures and meanings in Pushkin's poetry, however much they may possess a suggestiveness

and economy upon which devotees can build and fantasize, are not in themselves more impressive in an overall translation than are the lines and verses which it is acknowledged that no translator can come anywhere near doing justice to.

What they do possess, however, is a remarkable power to show the way and to inspire; to indicate to the epigoni in a manner that often seemed Delphic and mysterious the way that Russian literature should go. Pushkin as a historian, as a writer of historical romances – *Dubrovsky* and *The Captain's Daughter* – as a writer of short stories, did not produce in any of these genres any of their greatest examples. But to the writers who followed him – Gogol*, Turgenev, Dostoevsky, Tolstoy – these works are infinitely suggestive. Pushkin showed them the Russian way to do things. And they are still being done that way. Everyone is familiar with the deliberately Pushkinesque opening of *Anna Karenina*. But even in our own time, when a writer such as the former Gulag inmate Varlaam Shalamov opens one of his 'Kolyma Tales' with the sentence 'They were playing cards in the hut of Narumushkin, the convict who looks after the mine horses', we must look to *The Queen of Spades* for the original: 'They were playing cards at Narumov's, the Horse Guards officer.' For the Russian reader the echo would carry a terse and pervasive message of irony.

The conclusion must be that Pushkin's stature as a writer must always be involved with the idea of 'initiation'. To the bulk of his fellow-countrymen he is a symbol not only of national pride but of a national paradox: Russian exclusiveness and Russian messianism.

John Bayley

Many translations of *Eugene Onegin*, including one by Vladimir Mabokov (4 vols 1964). See also the *Complete Prose Tales* trans. Gillon R. Aitken (1966) and *The Letters of Alexander Pushkin* ed. J. T. Shaw (3 vols 1964). See: D. S. Mirsky, *Pushkin* (1926); Janko Lavrin, *Pushkin and Russian Literature* (1947); David Magarshak, *Pushkin: A Biography* (1967); Henry Troyat, *Pushkin* (trans. 1970); John Bayley, *Pushkin: A Comparative Commentary* (1971).

364
PUVIS DE CHAVANNES, Pierre 1824–98

French artist

Puvis de Chavannes appears to have been a man of sanguine temperament, simple tastes and liked by almost everyone. No other painter of the period seems to have avoided the strife and confusions of the art world in mid-nineteenth-century France as well as Puvis. Serenely he designed and carried out large scale decorations which after exhibition at the official salons were then placed in the major public buildings for which they were intended in cities throughout France. It seems likely that Puvis avoided conflict mainly because his paintings were not easel paintaings and commissioned for the most part by the state. Consequently he was not competing in the same field for recognition as the Realists and Naturalists who were at times critical of his work.

Born in Lyons, son of a civil engineer, Puvis was sent to study law in Paris but transferred his attentions to the ateliers of art. Having twice visited Italy he was taught first by Henry Scheffer, briefly by Delacroix*, and finally settled to study with Couture, himself a pupil of Ingres*. Here Puvis found an education more in tune with his inclinations for his studies were of classicism and it was the Italian old masters whom he admired most, in particular the grace and delicacy of Piero della Francesca, and later the idealism of the French Poussin.

His first Salon appearance was of a religious subject, a *Pietà* of 1850, in which a group comprising three figures crouch, mourning in an imaginary landscape. This liking for nature, idealized and made beautiful, provides a perfect setting for the saints and allegorical figures which Puvis used to portray all the virtues of both the Bible and Ancient Greece. Puvis made it the source for a kind of primitive Golden age in which groups of figures are for the most part shown as children of nature, thus making architecture an unimportant part of the designs. For the most part where architecture does appear it takes the form of rough shelters or screens and only occasionally a simple building from the early Renaissance.

In 1865 Puvis received a commission from Amiens, in 1869 from Marseilles, then Poitiers in 1874. By 1880 his reputation was established and attacks by such supporters of Realism as Castagnary ceased. Impressionism itself was now the target for adverse comment and taste in art was moving towards a more imaginative literary as well as painterly style, that of Symbolism. It was here that Puvis found his greatest support.

Besides mural decorations the artist had produced and regularly exhibited a number of smaller easel paintings. Amongst these were the famous *The Poor Fisherman* (1881), the *Prodigal Son* (c. 1879) and *Hope* (c. 1871), all symbolic figures projecting delicate nuances of mood and painted in a simple manner. They convey a dream-like quality that endeared Puvis to all the Symbolists, poets such as Mallarme* and Rimbaud*, as well as painters like Gauguin* and his followers, the Nabis.

Porcelain (1891), a later painting and part of Puvis's decoration for the gallery at Rouen, is of two women in Victorian dress and unusual in that it relinquishes the classical for the contemporary. The two women carry a dish and an urn along a path between decorative flower beds which border simple square buildings. The tipping forward of the straight pathway so that it appears flattened on to the surface of the canvas at right angles to a transverse path echoes the severity of the buildings. This reduction and flattening of form contrasts with the fluent shapes of the women and the decorative plant forms. In subject matter, composition and style the work is markedly similar to Maurice Denis's treble portrait of Mademoiselle Yvonne Lerolle (1896–7). Equally when viewing the section entitled *Pottery* one is irresistibly reminded of Holman Hunt's* early sagas such as *A Converted British Family, sheltering a Christian Priest from the Persecution of the Druids* (1899–50). Indeed Puvis's development seems strongly to parallel that of the Pre-Raphaelites in some respects. The influence of early Italian Quattrocento art, the symbolism, the simplicity of form synthesized with flower decoration, the increasing richness of colour are all factors. However the insistence upon 'truth to appearances' in Pre-Raphaelite thought is contrary to Puvis's idealizing search for essential beauty.

He was to write that 'Simplicity means an untrammelled idea, the simplest conception will be found to be the most beautiful', and again 'It is necessary to cut away from nature everything that is ineffective and accidental, everything that for the moment is without force.' Perhaps Puvis's two most famous decorative series are those for the Panthéon in Paris, depicting the life of Sainte Geneviève, started in 1876 and finished the year of his death, and those for the Hôtel de Ville in Paris, entitled *Summer* and *Winter* (1890 and 1893).

Finally it is of interest to compare Puvis de Chavannes's work with that of Gustave Moreau*. Both artists were working at the same period; both were concerned with classical and Christian mythology; both idealized and generalized. However, whereas Puvis reduced his forms in such a way that they begin to look forward to expressive abstraction, Moreau complicated his and made addition upon addition to his surface. Further, where Moreau's art is violent and often sadistic, Puvis's is gentle and mildly melancholic. It can be said that of the two styles, Puvis's, in its primitivism, its reduction of form and intensification of mood, must have been the more progressive art for its time.

Pat Turner

See: André Michel *Puvis de Chavannas: A Biographical and Critical Study* (trans. 1912); Rene Jean, *Puvis de Chavannes* (2nd edn, 1933); Brian Petrie, *Puvis de Chavannes* (1981).

R

365
RACHMANINOV, Sergei 1873–1943

Russian composer and pianist

Born into the lesser Russian nobility at a time when the family fortunes were waning, Rachmaninov had an insecure home life, though his musical ability was recognized and encouraged from an early age. A continuation of these reduced circumstances caused the family to split up and move to a much humbler home in St Petersburg. This emotional turmoil, together with the loss of his younger sister, did much to fashion the composer's life-long feelings of emotional insecurity and fear of death shielded by a rather subdued temperament. In 1882 he attended the local conservatoire where he received piano lessons together with a general education. Lack of self-motivation promoted a move to the Moscow Conservatoire where tuition under the pedagogue and disciplinarian Nikolai Zverev caused him to show immediate improvement by way of a concentrated work programme involving a study of the classics and the virtuoso piano tradition of Liszt* and contemporaries. Living in at the Zverev household he was to meet the greatest musicians of his day including the pianist Anton Rubinstein, the composers Arensky and Taniev who were soon to become his teachers and above all Tchaikovsky*, whom he idolized. By 1890 Rachmaninov had sketched his First Piano Concerto and was also promoting other compositions via many public concerts. His graduation exercise, the opera *Aleko* from Pushkin*, won him the conservatoire's Great Gold Medal in 1893 and the approval of Tchaikovsky, though a later performance at the Bolshoi Ballet was only moderately successful. By 1895 he had completed the First Symphony but a disastrous première under the baton of the popular Glazunov plunged him into the depths of despair: he withdrew the work and sought the help of a psychiatrist. Under this successful treatment he produced the famous Second Piano Concerto (1901) and its companion piece, the Second Suite for Two Pianos (1901) which has become equally popular. His marriage to his cousin in 1902 brought great stability into his life and soon afterwards he released his first book of Piano Preludes, op. 23 (1903) and another Pushkin opera entitled *The Miserly Knight* (1905). During the early years of this century he took up various conducting posts, starting at the

Bolshoi Opera where his own works were premièred, though he soon moved to Dresden where he began the beautifully lyrical Second Symphony (1906). At this time he also wrote one of his most haunting works, the symphonic poem *The Isle of the Dead* (1909) based on a Symbolist painting by Böcklin*. The same year an offer to tour America resulted in the exceedingly difficult Third Piano Concerto which won him new audiences both for his piano playing and conducting of Russian music. On his return to Europe he once more sought emotional security and purchased a large estate called 'Ivanovka' where he could work in seclusion. Indeed this was one of Rachmaninov's most fertile composing periods for he was to pen the choral *Liturgy of St Chrysostom* (1910) and two more sets of piano pieces, the Preludes, op. 32 and the *Études Tableaux*, op. 33. The continuation of some conducting work did not prevent him occasionally from going abroad and it was on a trip to Rome in 1913 that he wrote his choral symphony *The Bells*, though the outbreak of war led to the cancellation of its projected performance in England.

The crisis of world events and the fact that Rachmaninov was a member of the landed gentry put him in a precarious position. Accordingly he decided to leave Russia on the pretext of a concert tour of Scandinavia. Now finding himself an exile, he emigrated to the USA setting up home in San Francisco in 1919 and signing important contracts with recording companies. Throughout the 1920s he travelled extensively around Europe, though very few compositions were produced during this period. The poor reception of the Fourth Piano Concerto (1926), which was criticized for its lack of melodic interest, once more plunged him into a depressive state. As a result he moved first to Paris and then to Lucerne where he wrote the highly inventive *Rhapsody on a Theme of Paganini* (1934), to be followed by the Third Symphony (1935). The final decade of Rachmaninov's life brought him international success not only because of his extensive concert tours but also because of a collaboration with the Philadelphia Orchestra which recorded most of his major works under the leadership of Eugene Ormandy. These performances, together with those of solo repertoire, are both superb documents of creative insight and remarkably modern in interpretation. Already the strain of such a busy life-style was beginning to take its toll, though the composer, after rejecting many requests for film scores, did produce his last and probably most nostalgic Russian work, the *Three Symphonic Dances* (1940). Indeed these are the summation of a whole life's work and incorporate all the influences on his mature style while adding yet a new dimension of chamber scoring to the often ethereal textures of the piece. By 1942 Rachmaninov was already very ill with cancer and after the cancellation of an important concert tour he was to die the following year at the age of sixty-nine.

Rachmaninov is generally thought of as a composer in the late Romantic tradition who followed in the footsteps of Tchaikovsky. Though this is true, unlike his predecessor's, most of his compositions were conceived in terms of keyboard figuration whether in the songs, where the vocal lines are often woven within the piano counterpoint, or in the orchestral works which were initially sketched at the piano. Like Tchaikovsky his output contains a strong vein of lyricism, melancholy tone and rhapsodic expansiveness of a kind rarely seen in the more nationalist works of Borodin* and Rimsky-Korsakov*. The orchestral scoring is more weighty than that of his contemporaries, being influenced by the fuller textures of Brahms* and the German school. To this Rachmaninov adds thematic -material which is exclusively Russian with melodies reminiscent of Orthodox chant and modal folksong often gravitating around one note. An early interest in Symbolist art with its dream and death imagery pervades many of his pieces: this obsession often takes the shape of the 'Dies Irae' which is hinted at in the symphonic slow movements and in the *Isle of the Dead*. Throughout his busy life as pianist, composer and conductor there was the inevitable conflict caused by an inability to fulfil all his ambitions at once. The failure of his early works may explain why he experimented little over forty creative years. Having lost all his possessions as an exile, he was often faced with financial problems which drove him on to the concert platform all too frequently, though his recitals always met with great success especially when he played popular transcriptions of his own songs and instrumental compositions by Bach, Mendelssohn* and Fritz Kreisler. Such appearances invariably detracted from the appreciation of his larger orchestral and choral compositions, as did the wholesale plagiarism of his Romantic style by Hollywood film composers. Fortunately the recent revival of interest in large-scale symphonic writing, the availability once more of Rachmaninov's expert recordings and the unbiased assessment of his music by a younger generation have shown that his performances were remarkably up-to-date in conception, thereby having ensured him a place in musical history as the finest pianist of his day and a composer whose music is expertly crafted and full of emotional sincerity.

Michael Alexander

See: V.I. Seroff, *Rachmaninov* (1951); S. Bertensson and J. Leyda, *Sergei Rachmaninov: A Lifetime in Music* (1965); R. Threlfall, *Sergei Rachmaninov* (1973); P. Piggott, *Rachmaninov's Orchestral Music* (1974); G. Norris, *Rachmaninov* (1976); P. Piggott, *Rachmaninov* (1978).

366
RANKE, Leopold von 1795–1885

German historian

The greatest German historian of his time, Leopold von Ranke developed a systematic historical method of establishing what he termed 'the solid ground of history', which would impartially reconstruct 'how things actually were'. He was both a great writer and a great teacher, devising 'seminars' with all their consequences, for good or ill, in Germany and beyond, and he pioneered the ordering, classification and critical editing of documents. He set standards to which most of a now professional academic world aspire and long directed the bias of historical studies strongly towards politics and diplomacy.

Born in Thuringia in Saxony, the son of a Lutheran pastor, he was early and strictly grounded in classics at Leipzig, where he also studied theology, and this classical and godly discipline remained fundamental to his mind. By 1818 he was teaching at the *Gymnasium* at Frankfurt-on-Oder, lecturing on Herodotus, Thucydides and Livy, and already influenced by Niebuhr's *History of Rome* with its original and intuitive insight into origins. Niebuhr also early interested him in medieval history.

In 1824 Ranke published his *History of the Latin and Teutonic Peoples 1494–1535* (*Geschichten der romanischen und germanischen Völker*, 1494–1535, trans. 1887). In 1825 he was rewarded by a call to the University of Berlin as assistant professor, where by 1834 he became full professor, a post he held for fifty years.

He declared that 'the door to his true life had opened'; and soon, in Berlin, he found forty-seven volumes of the dispatches of the Venetian ambassadors of the sixteenth and seventeenth centuries which transformed his view of European politics by their cool dispassionate objectivity. On this evidence, in 1826, he wrote his next work on *The Ottomans and the Spanish Monarchy of the Sixteenth and Seventeenth Centuries* (*Die Osmanen und die Spanische Monarchie*, trans. 1843) which included a detailed survey of the Spanish empire. Following up a series on *The Princes and Peoples of Southern Europe*, Ranke in 1827 made his first travels abroad to Vienna and Italy, a major epoch in his life.

In Vienna he became interested in the Slav struggle against the Turks and wrote the *History of the Revolution in Serbia* (*Die serbische Revolution*, 1829, trans. 1847), up to the establishment of the Principate of Miloš I Obrenovich in 1814; but the pioneer work was less important than the fruits of Ranke's study of the Viennese archives which he followed up in Venice and Rome, and which led him in 1834–6 to his great work *The History of the Popes, Church and State (Die römischen Päpste, irhe Kirche, und irhe staat*, trans. 1840). Though a Lutheran and denied access to Vatican archives, Ranke wrote objectively of the papacy as a great European influence, and marshalled a fascinating amount of detail, extending from the early Middle Ages to the papal states and the Counter-Reformation, and including vivid portraits of personalities. He saw and depicted a pattern of divinely guided fate, and his work annoyed only the extremists of both sides, who considered his lofty and far-ranging tolerance tame.

Ranke's next major work was written in the light of his quasi-religious concept of the state. Although he had come to maturity in the climax of the Romantic Age, and was deeply influenced by Herder's cult of the *Volk* as a broad basis of national history, his Lutheran faith and neo-Platonic belief in a transcendental order made him impervious to the heady influence of Hegel*, who had looked down on him in Berlin as a junior professor; but he firmly and confidently interpreted modern European history in terms of the rise of great states. Like most Germans of his time, he, indeed, made a cult of the state as an 'ethical being', and for him the most important state was of course Prussia, operating within a state system regulated by an apparently harmonious European balance of power.

So Ranke now concentrated on the rise of the great European modern states and nations. First in *German History in the Reformation Era (Deutsche Geschichte im Zeitalter der Reformation* 1839–47, trans. 1839–47); then in *Nine Books of Prussian History (Neun Bücher preussische Geschichte* 1847–8, trans. 1849); then in *Französische Geschichte* (1852–61); and, finally, in *Englische Geschichte* (1859–68), Ranke surveyed the political development of the great powers. His flair for the essentials of English seventeenth-century history in the light of continental events is particularly striking, his calm olympian view refreshing to anyone steeped in the controversies of the age.

Ranke can hardly be said to have been impartial in his glorification of Luther, though his *German History* is impressive in range; but his strong Protestant and patriotic stance brought him vast popularity in Germany and in 1841 he was appointed historiographer to the Prussian State.

The *French History* was based on Parisian archives hitherto rather neglected, and, coming from a German, it was singularly objective. Beginning in the sixteenth century, the book culminates in the age of Louis XIV, and was highly critical of the memoirs on which most French history had hitherto been written, though some French critics alleged that his own use of their archives

had been superficial. The *English History* begins properly with Henry VIII, whom he rightly depicts as having 'no sympathy with any living man' and using men as 'instruments'; a monarch for whom we feel at once admiration and dislike. He is too hard on James I, who at least fended off trouble, and overrates Charles I's political skill, though not his religious sincerity, and grossly overrates Pym. The best part of the book is the treatment of the policies of William III in terms of the king's continental designs.

Ranke thus summed up the essentials of the development of the three greatest central and western European states; but in considering this development as providential and relatively harmonious, he undermined with his great authority the cosmopolitan eighteenth-century humanist view of European civilization accepted by Voltaire and Gibbon, and clothed the ugly lineaments of emerging national sovereignty with a deceptive mystical glamour, thus intellectually, if indirectly, contributing to the catastrophe of 1914–18.

In 1858, at the request of Maximilian II of Bavaria, Ranke founded the Historical Commission for the Bavarian Academy of Sciences and in 1865 he was ennobled by the King of Prussia.

In his eighties, saying 'it was impossible to live without work', he gallantly undertook to write his *World History (Weltgeschichte*, 7 vols, 1881–5), in which, although he now had to dictate through secretaries, he reverted to his youthful interest in antiquity and the *Volkerwanderung*, but had to conclude with the death of the Emperor Heinrich IV in 1106. The work combines accounts of 'deep tumultuous movements' with evocations of the personalities of Alexander, Constantine, Charlemagne and Otto the Great. Concluding when it did, the *World History*, in spite of its title, was confined to central and western Europe, and left out the history of the British Empire, the United States and, in spite of Russian impact on central Europe, even that of Russia. It remains, for all its faults, an extraordinary achievement.

Ranke in old age dominated the German historical profession, placing his pupils in most of the key positions, and his influence extended widely over Great Britain, France and the United States. It was a conservative influence, taking the social order for granted and with little appreciation of the vast social and economic changes following the Industrial Revolution in an Age of the Oceans. The elaborate method of German historical research was admired and imitated, particularly by Freeman and Stubbs at Oxford and by Lord Acton* and J.B. Bury at Cambridge, sometimes to paralysing effect. But on balance, and in spite of over-concentration of politics and diplomacy, Ranke's influence was salutary. 'I found by comparison,' he had written in 1824, after comparing Walter Scott* with Commines, 'that truth is more interesting and beautiful than romance. I turned away from it and resolved to avoid all imagination and invention . . . and stick to the facts.' 'History,' he wrote in the preface to the *History of the Popes*, 'has had assigned to it the task of judging the past, of instructing the present for the benefit of ages to come. To such lofty functions this work does not aspire. Its aim is merely to show how things actually were – *wie es eigentlich gewesen.*'

This objective need not, as some of Ranke's followers believed, imply an awesome and arid professionalism dedicated to 'production' in 'workshops' by 'division of labour', or a pseudo-science which excludes imagination and style, and scorns 'literary' historians when any effective historian needs literary skill. Ranke, a charming man, happily married, who greatly enjoyed his research and celebrity, and who was much liked in court circles in Berlin and much valued the affection of his many pupils, would hardly have sanctioned historiography becoming a prestigious but boring and sometimes pointless accumulation of facts by professionals attempting to create a 'science' out of something inevitably an art. Though they need training, historians are born, not made.

John Bowle

Ranke's works are collected in *Sämmtliche Werke*, 54 vols (1867–90); the *Weltgeschichte*, in nine parts, was posthumously completed from notes in 1881–8. See: Theodore H. von Laue, *Leopold Ranke, the Formative Years* (1950); R. Vierhaus, *Ranke und die soziale Welt* (1957), which lists English translations; and, the best introduction in English, G.P. Gooch, *History and Historians on the Nineteenth Century* (1913).

367
REDON, Odilon 1840–1916

French artist

Redon belonged to the generation of the Impressionists and shared many of their attitudes and experiences. Like them, he explored the expressive force of texture and colour in an individualistic style that was independent of state institutions and of conservative orthodoxy in the arts. But he differed radically from the Impressionists in his understanding of the basic aim of art. He called them 'parasites of the object' and reproached them for neglecting what he considered to be the true subject of art: nature transformed by the imagination. He became a leading figure in French Symbolism, regarded during his lifetime and since as the Mallarmé* of painting.

Redon's early opposition to both conservative art and progressive Impressionism isolated him from groupings of artists until Decadents and Symbolists became a coherent force in Paris in the 1880s and 1890s. The teaching establishments of the Second Em-

pire were anathema to him; when young he failed as a student of architecture and as a pupil of the acadamic painter Gérôme in Paris. He turned for guidance to individualist artists who were developing aspects of Romanticism towards new possibilities, such as Corot* and Fromentin, and was profoundly influenced by Delacroix*. He also turned away from Paris, usually the goal of the aspiring painter, to the provincial context of his home region around Bordeaux, where a small group of mentors provided him with help and advice. The minor painter Stanislas Gorin discussed with him the implications of Romantic art. The botanist Armand Clavaud introduced him to contemporary literature, including Baudelaire*, and made him familiar with the mysterious aspects of plant life. The etcher and lithographer Rodolphe Bresdin was an encouraging example to him there both of the isolated artist and of one who transformed nature through fantasy; Redon shared with Bresdin a life-long passion for the engravings of Rembrandt and Dürer. The Bordeaux region, above all, offered Redon the physical setting that he came to regard as an essential source of his art: Peyrelebade, the family estate in the bleak and lonely Médoc where Redon spent his childhood. Throughout his life, Redon would divide his time between Paris and the Bordeaux region, the public and private poles of his existence. One of the few events of his life, remarkable for its lack of incident, was the enforced sale of Peyrelebade in 1897.

Until about 1870, Redon produced works that were exploratory and often derivative. After the Franco-Prussian War, he began to produce mature works in quantity, chiefly charcoal drawings that he called his *Noirs* ('Blacks'). The medium of charcoal suited him firstly because of the richness of its textures, and secondly because restriction to black and white takes the spectator away from objective perceptions towards subjective experiences. In these *Noirs* temporal and spatial dimensions become ambiguous or unidentifiable. Landscapes are deliberately imprecise or are inhabited by disconcerting and bizarre figures. These figures suggest areas of subject matter but deny particularization. They sometimes relate to legends or myths, such as Orpheus or Faust, but in an opaque and plurivalent manner that cannot be reduced to a scenario or allegory. Hybrid creatures are formed by the conjunction of normally unassociated details of the perceived world, such as a smiling spider (*L'Araignée Souriante*, 1881), and chimerical beasts of Antiquity, such as Pegasus, are given a new significance. Animal and plant forms fuse. Disembodied floating heads form striking geometric structures. Redon referred to this sombre domain as 'the dark world of the indeterminate'. Its purpose was to express indefinite but intense states of mind, generally pessimistic in tone. The strength of its imagery stems from its relationship with observed nature, as Redon himself pointed out: 'All my originality therefore consists of making unreal beings live humanly according to the laws of the real, by putting, as far as possible, the logic of the visible at the service of the invisible.'

The small scale and originality of such works made effective exhibiting of them difficult, and they remained virtually unknown until Decadents and Symbolists in Paris after 1880 saw in them all that they aspired to in art. Even then, it was writers rather than fellow painters who praised Redon. He was seized upon by the literary *avant-garde*, becoming the friend and ally of Huysmans*, Mallarmé and others. This success was prompted partly by two exhibitions Redon held in Paris in 1881 and 1882, but far more by his adoption of lithography at the very time that Symbolism was becoming a force in Paris. Lithographs, unlike drawings, could be disseminated in quantity, and Redon added to this advantage a technical virtuosity that made lithography more than the equal of charcoal. Between 1879 and 1899 Redon published twelve lithograph albums that spearheaded his reputation in France and abroad. Although still neglected by the public at large, he became influential amongst writers and artists in Paris and in Brussels, and contributed to the foundation of the Société des Artistes Indépendants in Paris in 1884. The literary orientation of his career in turn influenced his own style, notably in lithograph albums that bore literary titles and captions, as in *A Edgar Poe* (1882) or were inspired by literary texts, as in the three albums (1888, 1889 and 1896) based upon descriptive passages from Flaubert's* *Tentation de Saint Antoine*. Some critics have seen this literary dimension as a weakness of Redon's style, but interaction between images and words was a feature of a general interpenetration of art forms that, stimulated partly by Wagner*, was a rich aspect of French Symbolism. Like other Symbolists, Redon was attracted by the notion of the unity of the arts, and constantly compared the effect of his works to that of music. Like Gauguin*, he was a skilful writer. Towards the end of his life, he began to collect his writings into a book that was published posthumously as *A Soi-Même* ('To oneself', 1922).

Throughout these years Redon had used colour, but only for studies and occasional works. From 1890 onwards, he began to give colour a more central place in his output (e.g. *Les Yeux Clos, Closed Eyes*, 1890) and some ten years later he abandoned black and white altogether. Charcoal gave way to pastel; oil, watercolour and gouache were all adapted to his use of suggestive texture. Some changes in subject matter occurred; nightmarish scenes were succeeded by sumptuously lyrical flower pictures and large scale decorative works, such as his murals (1910–11) at Fontfroide Abbey in southern France. Serenity and optimism replaced pessimism. This slow and complex change was occasioned partly by personal circumstances, such as the birth of

his son Arï in 1889, and the sale of Peyrelebade in 1897, a physical break with a primary source of the *Noirs*. But it was also part of a change of artistic climate in France, involving the demise of Symbolism and the emergence of Fauvism. Redon knew and was admired by Bonnard, Matisse, van Dongen and other young colourists. His colour works contributed to new developments in French painting until the advent of Cubism.

Since his death, Redon's late colour pictures have been more admired than his *Noirs* and have even been considered to be quite different in style from them. This view fails to perceive the underlying unity that binds all these works together. Despite a shift of emphasis in later years from dark nightmare to light flowers, all Redon's works are concerned with a relationship between nature and the mind, between observation and imagination, between experience and meditation. The *Noirs* take their cue, directly or indirectly, from nature; the late flower pictures suggest states of mind. Although he was not concerned with ideas, Redon is making assumptions about the functioning of the human mind that belong to nineteenth-century idealist philosophy. This separates him from the Surrealists, to whom he is sometimes compared, as well as from Impressionism. Redon's form of art has never won wide understanding from the public; today his achievements are often ignored or distorted. But young artists at the turn of the century, including Marcel Duchamp as well as the Nabis and the Fauves, unhesitatingly saw in him both an original style and a liberating force, comparable in importance to them to the art of Cézanne*.

Richard Hobbs

The standard catalogue of Redon's prints is in André Mellerio, *Odilon Redon* (1913, reprint. 1968). See also Alfred Werner, *The Graphic Works of Odilon Redon* (1969). The chief studies of Redon are: André Mellerio, *Odilon Redon, peintre, dessinateur et graveur* (1923); Sven Sandström, *Le Monde imaginaire d'Odilon Redon* (1955); Roseline Bacou, *Odilon Redon* (1956); Klaus Berger, *Odilon Redon, Phantasie und Farbe* (1964, trans. *Odilon Redon, Fantasy and Colour*, no date); Jean Cassou, *Odilon Redon* (1972); and Richard Hobbs, *Odilon Redon* (1977).

368
RENAN, Joseph-Ernest 1823–92

French religious historian, critic and philologist

A mariner's son born in Tréguier, Brittany, Renan's relatively humble background and Celtic origins both have a significant bearing on the character of his thought. After the death of his father in 1828, he was cared for by his mother and his sister, Henriette, who was responsible for securing for him a scholarship to Paris where he began preparing for a career in the priesthood. He studied philosophy and theology during the period 1841–5, but found himself unable to accept the final step into Holy Orders and left the seminary of Saint-Sulpice in October 1845 to begin a lay career. The promise of his work in Semitic languages was recognized as early as 1847 by the award of the Volney Prize and it was in this field that he was later appointed professor at the Collège de France. During 1848, the same year in which he received his *agrégation de philosophie*, Renan began work on *The Future of Science* (*L'Avenir de la science*, 1890, trans. 1891) in which he gave expression to his vision of a new religion of learning and reason to take the place of his former faith. Renan did not, however, publish his book until 1890, two years before his death, and, even by the autumn of 1849 when he left Paris on a learned mission to Italy in the wake of the French expeditionary force, it is clear that his own mood was changing to a less rigorous view of the spiritual needs of humanity.

In line with the disillusionment felt by many writers of his generation, Renan's break with his own youthful idealism is in part a response to the outcome of the Revolution of 1848, which had initially fostered it, and takes the form of a cult of artistic purity and detachment to the exclusion of personal or dogmatic opinion. Renan was not a philosopher in the strict sense of the term: his thought is always matched by a sense of the wistful and the poetic which may be attributed to his Breton heritage. But he progressively developed a manner of thinking, ironical, parenthetical, deliberately inconclusive, which became the hallmark of his mature style and would leave its imprint on the intellectual climate of nineteenth-century France.

It was in 1863, after an expedition to Syria and the Holy Land, that Renan published the work that enjoyed a notoriety probably unequalled by any other in the age. His *Life of Jesus* (*Vie de Jésus*, 1863, trans. 1955), the first book of the seven-volume *Origins of Christianity* (*Les Origines du Christianisme*, 1863–82, trans. 1897–1904), went through ten editions within the year and had been translated into a dozen languages by 1864. Ever since his years at the seminary, Renan had been fascinated by the character of Jesus as the focus of his rational doubts and his own sentimental and moral longings. He set out now to portray a Jesus whose miracles could be explained away as legends or embellished natural events and whose divine and tragic role was progressively imposed upon him by enthusiastic disciples. The personal charm of this mortal Jesus remains, however, no less magnetic and his moral teaching and all-pervasive idealism no less exemplary. This ambivalence is sustained in Renan's language in a work which is not so much a history or even a biography as a novel in a great age of novels; that is

to say, a work of art having its own internal logic and released thereby from the decisiveness of theological pronouncement. Not only does his *Life of Jesus* reflect the spirit of a generation which, having dispensed with religion, remained attracted to religiousness, but, even while undermining traditional christology, it touches on the recognition, which constitutes one facet of the mature Renan's thinking, that certain fictions may be necessary to a mankind which finds hard truths insupportable.

Following the controversy which his *Life of Jesus* provoked, Renan was expelled from the professorial chair which he had held since 1862 and was not reinstated until the fall of the Second Empire in 1870. In 1869, he had a brief flirtation with politics, standing unsuccessfully for the National Assembly on a programme for constitutional monarchy, a line of thought which the events of the war hardened into a call for authoritarian reconstruction preached in his *La Réforme intellectuelle et morale* ('Intellectual and Moral Reform', 1871). In 1878, he was elected a member of the French Academy and, by 1883, when he published *Recollections of My Youth* (*Souvenirs d'enfance et de jeunesse*, trans. 1883), he was certainly one of the most celebrated figures in French intellectual life.

The *Origins of Christianity* were concluded by the beautiful study of Marcus-Aurelius (*Marc-Aurèle et la fin du monde antique*, 1882), a volume which reflects much of the climate of disintegration that Renan sensed around him in acknowledging his temperamental and intellectual affinity with the great emperor. Before this, Renan had published a series of dialogues *Philosophical Dialogues and Fragments* (*Dialogues philosophiques*, 1876, trans. 1883) which constitute, both in form and content, a summary of the range of his own political and philosophical attitudes. Renan divides the dialogue into 'certainties', 'probabilities' and 'dreams', caricaturing in the last something of his own intellectual elitism, but conceding in the first a philosophy of stoical resignation to a natural purpose which transcends human knowledge. The dialogue form itself, latent in much of Renan's writing and finding further expression in the later *Drames philosophiques* ('Philosophical Dramas', 1888), mirrors the persistent polarities in his mind and his conception of the right of the thinker to indulge in the free-ranging play of ideas.

Towards the end of his life, Renan began work on a *History of the People of Israel* (*Histoire du peuple d'Israël*, 1887–93, trans. 1895) which may be seen as a companion and parallel work to the earlier *Origins*, with Jesus as the central pivot, the meeting point of Jewish and classical cultures. Though not a racist in any modern sense, Renan had been interested from his earliest published writings in cultural and linguistic distinctions, seeing Western civilization as the product of the interaction of Semitic and Hellenic characteristics. His own intellectual allegiances owe much to this dichotomy in that the moral and religious instinct which never leaves him and which he associates with Semitic monotheism is balanced by the aesthetic and intellectual detachment of the Graeco-Roman. Here again, the sense of antithesis in a writer whom Professor D.G. Charlton appropriately terms 'a creature of dialogue' is fully apparent as is Renan's readiness, evident in his *Life of Jesus*, to account for the past in the light of his own personality.

The tendency to treat ideas as the matter for intellectual games or refined and sceptical speculation led Renan, during the years of religious and moral revival in France at the end of the nineteenth century, to become the subject of attack from those who considered him a dilettante or even a debilitating influence on the nation. Judged against *Intellectual and Moral Reform*, the charge was unjust, but some of his late work, notably the *Philosophical Dramas*, encouraged the claim and it may be that he published the youthful essay *The Future of Science* as a testimony of his underlying seriousness. But the legend has persisted and, apart from universal recognition of his incomparable prose style, Renan is neglected by a new century which has come to value commitment and action and which regards as alien both his sophisticated ironies and the anti-democratic spirit which pervades his political writings. He deserves to be better appreciated as a major historian concerned to confront the irrational forces shaping modern civilization and equally for his sense of the intellectual and moral dilemmas faced by mass, post-Christian societies.

David Lee

Oeuvres complètes, ed. Henriette Psichari (1947–61). See: I Babbitt, *Masters of Modern French Criticism* (1912); L.F. Mott, *Ernest Renan* (1921); J. Pommier, *Renan d'après des documents inédits* (1923); Albert Schweitzer, *The Quest of the Historical Jesus* (1948); R.M. Chadbourne, *Ernest Renan as an Essayist* (1957); D.G. Charlton, *Positivist Thought in France during the Second Empire, 1852–70* (1959); H.W. Wardman, *Ernest Renan: A Critical Biography* (1964); R.M. Chadbourne, *Ernest Renan* (1968).

369

RENOIR, Pierre-Auguste 1841–1919

French painter

Although he is always chiefly regarded as one of the leaders of the Impressionist group, Renoir's career extends into the twentieth century, well beyond the Impressionist years, and his art embraces other styles and other subjects than the sunlit landscapes with which Impressionism is often associated. After the initial years of struggle and hardship, he achieved success

at the Salon and found himself sought after by society as a portraitist. His output was enormous, and the greater proportion of his work dates from the last thirty years of his life, when, his reputation established, he devoted himself above all to his family, painting countless pictures of his wife, his sons, his servants and the models that posed for him at his country house near Cagnes.

However, there are consistent strands which link together his life's work. Renoir was not an intellectual painter and he was not an eager revolutionary. He was little concerned with theories of perception, and of the analysis of light, and was gratified by public recognition when it came. Even while participating in the Impressionist group exhibitions, he continued to submit works to the Salon, and of all the Impressionists he had most success in official circles. He was the first of the major artists of the group to grow disillusioned with its aims and return to a more traditional idiom, and unlike Monet* and Pissarro* he had no interest in politics or social concerns. All this is reflected in his work, in the sustained note of charm and gaiety that permeates it. Renoir was always attracted by people and even his landscapes are seldom without a strong human element. As an unrepentant hedonist, he gave free expression to the pleasure he found in beautiful women and pretty children. He wanted no further pretence for a picture than a lovely face or a seductive figure. When his master, the academic painter Gleyre, remarked to him 'one does not paint for amusement', Renoir is said to have replied, 'If it didn't amuse me, I wouldn't paint', words which neatly sum up his approach to painting.

It would be wrong, though, to think of Renoir as a mere dabbler, a kitten playing with coloured wool, as Degas* spoke of him. His origins were working class. He was born in Limoges, the son of a tailor, and in Paris, where he came as a child, he was trained as a porcelain painter. His ambition was to be an artist, and he graduated to it through painting china, fans and decorative blinds. But through this arduous apprenticeship, he developed a strong belief in the importance of craftsmanship, and a sense of pride in something well done. Throughout his life he applied himself to painting in long and regular sessions, like an artisan rigorously carrying out his obligations.

In 1862 Renoir enrolled at the École des Beaux Arts and took tuition at the studio of Gleyre, where he befriended Monet, Bazille and Sisley*, his fellow pupils. It was in their company that he began to study landscape painting, working in the open in the forest of Fontainebleau, and with them he shared an admiration for Courbet* and Corot*. It is the influence of Courbet above all that dominates his early works, such as *At the Inn of Mother Anthony, Marlotte* (1866), *Lise* (1867), *Diana* (1867) and *Alfred Sisley and his Wife* (1868). These pictures are firmly modelled, sombre in colouring and show Renoir striving towards an official manner. He had some success, exhibiting at the Salon in 1864, 1865, 1868, 1869 and 1870, but only at the expense of suppressing his own personality. Diaz had advised him to use more colour, and the effect of his advice shows in his more private work. He formed a strong friendship with Monet and the two of them painted together at the popular bathing and boating place of La Grenouillère on the Seine near Bougival, in the summer of 1869. Renoir's paintings of the scene are light in tone and abound with life. His experience as a porcelain painter reveals itself in the high-keyed colour and delicate touch. He painted alongside Monet, but the difference in their characters already shows, in Monet's concentration on effects of light and in Renoir's delight in the holidaymakers. People are given peremptory treatment by Monet; Renoir focuses his attention on them, so that their light-hearted mood permeates the pictures. As described by Maupassant* some years later, La Grenouillère was a vulgar and sordid place, but, as one of the bourgeoisie, Renoir shares in the frivolity and his paintings have more the air of an eighteenth-century *fête galante* than a nineteenth-century resort. As a porcelain painter, Renoir had copied Watteau and Boucher, and it is their spirit which infuses his scenes of modern life.

The Franco-Prussian War of 1870, in which he fought, interrupted Renoir's artistic development, but back in Paris afterwards he worked again with Sisley, and in search of inspiration undertook some free imitations of Delacroix* – costume pieces with models posing as Algerians. But he was at last finding his own idiom, and the decade of the 1870s saw some of his finest productions. He maintained the light tone of the La Grenouillère pictures and applied it to a series of paintings which are modern in subject and personal in feeling – that is, they express his sense of pleasure in the sights and experiences of modern life. Amongst the earliest and most famous is La Loge, which he exhibited in 1874 at the first Impressionist exhibition, a picture which is charming, and richly evocative of the spirit of the time. It is also more technically accomplished than anything Renoir had yet painted – subtle in colour, confident in its modelling, and yet using softly merged paintwork to give the effect of life captured in a fleeting impression. He also strove to capture the light and atmosphere of the open air. Not such a fervent apostle of *plein air* as Monet, he confined himself to subjects he loved, couples, women and children enjoying themselves in the sunshine. He could see no point in painting snow scenes or unpopulated landscapes. *The Swing* (1876) is typical of this genre. The filtering of light through trees and the colouring of the shadows are brilliantly caught, but their effect is above all to add charm to the image of the woman at a swing in the alley of a garden, a subject that might be taken from Fragonard. As indeed might the subject of one of Renoir's chief works of the seventies, *The Ball at the Moulin de la Galette* (1876). Manet* had treated a similar theme in his *Concert in the Tuileries Gardens* in 1860, and thereby opened the door to paintings of modern-day entertainments, light-hearted pictures without story or moral. But Renoir's fondness for his theme makes his treatment more *galante*, in an eighteenth-century sense, than Manet's. Although the dancers are only the artists and shop-girls of Montmartre, in Renoir's eyes they are elegant and beautiful. It means that he misses the more profound aspects of the life he depicts, that note of tragi-comedy that Manet hints at in his café scenes. Renoir's people are always charming, rarely interesting or moving. But the sincerity of his vision does mean that his charm is authentic, and in the nineteenth century this is a rare commodity. His women and children are robust, healthy and endowed with a well-being which is as deep and refreshing as Renoir's own.

In spite of this, Renoir, like the other Impressionists, had difficulty in selling his works and was attacked by the more conservative elements of the press. Albert Wolff, the critic of the *Figaro* and one of the fiercest opponents of Impressionism, wrote of his *Torso of a Woman in the Sun* (1876), 'Try to explain to M. Renoir that the body of a woman is not a mass of decomposing flesh, with the green and purple spots that denote the entire putrefication of a corpse.' Like his friends, Renoir sold works to Père Martin and Père Tanguy for small sums and the dealer Paul Durand-Ruel courageously bought his pictures knowing he had little chance of selling them. But gradually Renoir built up a small circle of patrons, amongst them a civil servant, Victor Chocquet (who shared with him a passionate admiration for Delacroix and whom Renoir introduced to Cézanne*), and Georges Charpentier, the publisher, and his wife. Chocquet was a highly sensitive man (as can be seen in Renoir's touching portrait of him in the Reinhart Collection, Winterthur) and greatly appreciated Renoir's painterly art, but it was the Charpentiers who 'made' the artist. At Madame Charpentier's *Salon* he became known to visitors and intellectuals, and his large portrait of her with her daughters was a great success at the Salon of 1879.

The commissions he received from the Charpentiers released Renoir from financial constraint and for the first time in his life he was able to travel. In 1880 he visited Algiers and in 1881, after his marriage, he travelled in Italy where he discovered Raphael and the Roman frescoes at Pompeii. His Italian experience coincided with a developing discontentment with his own work and the methods of Impressionism. He confessed that he did not know how to paint, and set out to introduce greater structure and discipline into his work. There is a new clarity in his pictures of couples dancing (1883), and *The Umbrellas*, which was painted over a period of years and completed around 1884, clearly shows the change in style. The women and children on the right are painted in his earlier 'soft' manner; the girl on the left and the umbrellas in a new, linear style. Renoir stayed at l'Estaque with Cézanne too at this time and may well have derived something of this austere manner – his *manière aigre* – from the Provençal painter. The pictures of this period are more laboriously worked-up than hitherto, consciously assembled in the studio, and sometimes, like the *Grandes Baigneuses* of 1885, they are based on traditional prototypes. Renoir borrowed the composition for this work from a bas-relief at Versailles by the sculptor Girardon. The painting itself is linear and sculptural, and the colour (little more than tinting) no longer conveys the light and atmosphere of the open air.

Renoir was temperamentally unsuited to such a chaste and academic approach, and by 1890 he had reverted again to soft contours, merging colour and swelling forms. But the work of his last years is far from the naturalism of early Impressionism. His figures and landscapes are robust, warmly coloured and simply modelled, an evocation of physical well-being, an imagined golden age. The onset of arthritis caused him from about 1902 to move south to Cagnes, and there he centred his attentions increasingly on his family: his wife, his sons Pierre, Jean and Claude, and their servant Gabrielle, all of whom regularly appear in his paintings. In Cagnes the family lived prosperously. Renoir had many commissions for portraits, bathers and decorative panels, and the dealers Durand-Ruel and, from 1894, Vollard had no difficulty placing his work. Success was accompanied by official acclaim. In 1896 six of his works, included in the Caillebotte bequest, were finally hung in the Luxembourg Museum and in 1900 he was awarded the Legion of Honour. Only the outbreak of war in 1914, when the two eldest sons were called to the front, disturbed the calm tenor of life at Cagnes, and Renoir died there in 1919, finally crippled by arthritis. But he continued to paint up to his death, in a wheel-chair with brushes strapped to his hand. And he also directed an assistant to model sculptures, the three-dimensional counterparts of his painted figures. The last paintings are broad in treatment, lacking in all detail, yet rich in colour and of extraordinary amplitude, with no less a sense of the pleasure of life than the great Impressionist pictures of forty years earlier.

Michael Wilson

See: *Catalogue raisonné de L'oeuvre peint* ed. François Daulte (4 vols from 1971); John Rewald, *Renoir: Drawings* (1946). See also: Albert C. Barnes and Violette de Mazia, *The Art of Renoir* (1935); Jean Renoir, *Renoir, My Father* (trans. 1962); William Gaunt, *Renoir* (1962); Lawrence Hanson, *Renoir, The Man, The Painter and His World* (1968); Parker Taylor, *Renoir* (1969).

370
RIBOT, Théodule-Armand 1839–1916

French scientist and intellectual

Ribot, sometimes dubbed the stepson of Taine* and Renan*, was a scientific pioneer and *animateur* of the highest order. Born in Guingamp, Brittany, and educated at the local lycée, Ribot subsequently took the *Agrégation* in philosophy at the École Normale. A well-known experimental psychologist, he was also a devotee of contemporary English and German philosophy, publishing an influential study of Schopenhauer* in 1874. Thus, with his friend, F. Alcan, he founded the *Revue philosophique de la France et de l'étranger*, an imaginative interdisciplinary journal with a positivist prejudice against abstract, metaphysical thinking. In the 1880s his epoch-making studies on memory, personality and will brought him national and international recognition. After giving classes in experimental psychology at the Sorbonne, he graduated, in 1888, to a new chair of experimental and comparative psychology at the Collège de France, created at Renan's instigation. He then produced numerous studies of affective states, notably *The Psychology of the Emotions* (*La psychologie des sentiments*, 1896, trans. 1897), *Essay on the Creative Imagination* (*Essai sur l'imagination créatrice*, 1900, trans. 1906), and *La Vie inconsciente* ('The Life of the Unconscious', 1914).

In the tradition of the positivists Ribot sought to place philosophy and psychology on a sound experimental basis. His own intellectual masters were the French ideologues, Destutt de Tracy, Condillac and Maine de Biran*, the English empiricists, especially Spencer* and Bain, and the German quantitative psychologist, Wundt*. Synthesizing this wide-ranging material and following the scientific method of Claude Bernard*, Ribot revolutionized the study of human behaviour with a method based on experimentation and precise measurement, the histology of the nervous system and, finally, the study of pathological cases. However, in his aim to define mental and psychic phenomena in terms of organic processes and the mechanisms linking subconscious and conscious reflexes, Ribot stopped short of the excessively mechanistic explanations of the German School.

His influence was considerable and spread into many fields. He launched the vogue for Schopenhauer, whose ideas were to mark the generation of Barrès* and the Symbolists. Later, his collaboration with Alcan bore fruit again in the general series *Bibliothèque de la philosophie contemporaine* which contained dozens of studies in the diverse fields of aesthetics, moral philosophy, psychology and scientific inquiry and which patronized a number of *fin de siècle* intellectuals – from the revolutionary Georges Sorel* to the philosopher Henri Bergson. Ribot's interest in Spencer and Darwin* was to inspire the new science of sociology in the writings of Tarde, Espinas and, above all, Durkheim.

Essentially he was an academic scientist whose general interests put him in touch with many emergent disciplines and new developments. While in France he is seen as the founder of the science of psychology, perhaps his lasting achievement was to forge links with philosophers, writers, biologists and clinical doctors, like Charcot, thus creating the atmosphere in which Janet and Freud produced their work on neurotic and subconscious states. And in America his experimental method, through the work of William James*, influenced the whole functional movement from which Gestalt psychology and behaviourism developed.

Christopher Bettinson

Other works by Ribot in English translation: *English Psychology* (1873); *Heredity: A Psychological Study . . .* (1875); *Diseases of Memory* (1882); *German Psychology of Today* (1886); *The Psychology of Attention* (1890); *The Evolution of General Ideas* (1899). See: Th. Ribot, 'Philosophy in France', *Mind*, vol 2 (1877); and Th. Ribot, *Choix de textes et études sur l'oeuvre par G. Lamarque* (1926).

371
RICARDO, David 1772–1823

British political economist

In both the popular imagination, and in the mainstream of academic histories of economics, the founding figure of Classical economic theory is usually seen as Adam Smith, his central text being *The Wealth of Nations*. Yet in many ways a far better claim to pride of place among the founders of classical political economy could be made – and indeed has been made – on behalf of David Ricardo. Through his *Principles of Political Economy and Taxation*, and via his pamphlets and extensive correspondence, Ricardo exerted an enormous influence on nineteenth-century economic thinking, both among those – such as J.S. Mill* and Karl Marx* – who directly and indirectly drew upon his ideas, as well as among those who rejected his views: to a significant extent, innovations in mid- and late-nineteenth-century economic thought can be categorized as a 'reaction against Ricardo'. Perhaps more than any other theorist of the Classical period, his work remains influential in modern economics, and serious academic battles are still being fought over the precise character and importance of his contribution to economic discourse, and over its modern relevance.

David Ricardo was born in 1772, the son of a Portuguese-Jewish stockbroker who had moved to London after having been part of the Amsterdam financial community. He began work with his father at the age of fourteen, and seven years later, following a rift with his family caused by his marriage to a Gentile, was in business for himself on the Stock Exchange, where within five years he became a wealthy and well-known figure. In his early thirties he became a not-very-hard-faced man who did well out of the Napoleonic Wars: the exigencies of war finance generated a sharp expansion of government borrowing, which was organized through loan contractors, of whom Ricardo was one. In consequence, his hitherto respectable fortune became, by the time of Waterloo, a very substantial one (he was worth about three-quarters of a million pounds on his death in 1823). He moved his fortune subsequently into landed property, which included buying a fine house, Gatcomb Park, in which to retire to the life of a country gentleman. In 1819 he became a Member of Parliament.

Ricardo became interested in political economy at about the turn of the century, though his first really important writing did not come until 1815 when he published a pamphlet called *An Essay of the Influence of a Low Price of Corn on the Profits of Stock*. Essentially this was an attack on the Corn Laws (which protected domestic grain production with tariffs against imported corn), though an attack of a peculiar, perhaps epoch-making kind; this is because the piece argued for a particular political measure on the basis of a quite new kind of abstract, rigorous theoretical model of the operation of a capitalist economy. Ricardo sought to demonstrate, through a logical theoretical sequence, that protection of the grain market led to an extension of domestic grain production, which had the effect of raising agricultural rents, which had as its counterpart a lower rate of profit in both agriculture and industry, which in turn implied a constraint on capital accumulation; conversely, free trade in grain would generate higher profits and greater accumulation. It is perhaps worth emphasizing that, influential though these ideas became, the long-term significance of this text may lie less in the argument than in the method by which that argument is set up, namely through a conceptually coherent model of capitalist economic functioning.

Ricardo was a close friend of James Mill*, who encouraged him ('pressured' might not be too inappropriate a term) to expand the theoretical innovations of the *Essay* into a full-scale work. Despite an almost neurotic sense of his own inadequacy for the task, Ricardo did so: the result, *Principles of Political Economy and Taxation*, was first published in 1817.

The *Principles* was, and remains, a major work. It contains, among treatment of many other topics, a labour theory of value freed from the ambiguities present in Adam Smith's work; a full-scale theory of income distribution; an account of the relationship between income distribution and price formation, the ideas of which have played a part in one of the most important debates in modern economics (the 'capital theory controversy'); a treatment – in the third edition – of the relationship between mechanization and what might be called 'technological unemployment'; an extensive discussion of tax theory; and a theory of international trade. This last, the theory of foreign trade, has today a practically unique status among economic concepts since, as Arghiri Emmanuel has ironically put it:

in a branch of learning in which hardly anyone agrees with anyone else, either in space or in time; in which practically nothing is generally accepted . . . in which everything is various and contradictory, up to and including the categories and concepts employed . . . David Ricardo's famous proposition (on comparative costs) emerges from the fray as a truth that is unshakeable, if not in its applicability and scope, then at least in its foundations.

In all of these areas, Ricardo's ideas remain part of the currency of modern economic debate. Arguably the most important recent impact of his ideas is via the writings of the editor of Ricardo's *Collected Works*, Piero Sraffa. Sraffa's rather deceptively straightforward book *Production of Commodities by Means of Commodities* (1970) develops and systematizes certain Ricardian ideas into what is claimed by Sraffa's adherents to be nothing less than a destruction of the logical foundations of modern Neoclassical economics.

Assessments of Ricardo's achievements, at least by economists, are various and conflicting. Keynes, for example, referred to Ricardo as 'the most distinguished mind that had found economics worthy of its powers', while also taking the view that the emphasis placed, in the course of the development of British economics, on Ricardo's views at the expense of those of Malthus*, was deeply unfortunate. Disagreement continues, however, not just on the correctness of Ricardo's ideas, but on what the central thrust of his work actually is. In recent years, for example, it has been claimed on the basis of scholarly research that Ricardo is: (a) essentially a theorist of an agrarian capitalist system whose work breaks down when the problems of an industrial capitalist economy are confronted (in Keith Tribe, *Land, Labour and Economic Discourse*, 1978); (b) a theorist, on the contrary, whose ideas are founded on the problems faced by a mechanized capitalist economy undergoing technical change (in Maxine Berg, *The Machinery Question and the Making of Political Economy*, 1980); and (c) neither of the above, but rather a precursor of modern general equilibrium theory (in Samuel Hollander, *The Economics of David Ricardo*, 1980). This writer inclines to the first of these interpretations, but since it is plainly the case that none of them is definitive, it can safely be said that we will be hearing more of David Ricardo.

Keith Smith

See: *The Works and Correspondence of David Ricardo*, ed. Piero Sraffa with the collaboration of Maurice Dobb (10 vols, 1951–5). See also: Mark Blaug, *Ricardian Economics* (1958) and *Economic Theory in Retrospect* (1979).

372
RICHARDSON, Henry Hobson 1838–86

US architect

There is only one idea of America: it is that of the New World, that of not a Utopia, but of a Paradise. The American Constitution is a programme for realizing this. Her heroes are those that have this idea central in their being; her traitors are those who attempt to emulate the values and styles of the Old World. Thus it may often appear that the most cultured are the most philistine. The condition only becomes apparent at times of cultural crisis. The true American artist retains his nation's vision through a primitive quality in his work, and this he finds by descent.

Henry Hobson Richardson was born on a plantation of English ancestry in 1838, in Louisiana, studied at Harvard, and received his architectural training at the École des Beaux Arts in Paris, the second American ever to do so, during the Civil War years, which delayed his return. He arrived back in New York in 1865 at the second beginning of the American Nation after the end of the Civil War, marrying his fiancée Julia Gordon Hayden from Cambridge, Massachusetts, and settling in Staten Island, the island on which were landing the waves of immigrants from the Old World.

The war effectively finished the reign of the Neoclassical 'colonial' style of architecture over American buildings. On his return, Richardson found two contesting and essentially illusory styles dominating, one with English and one with French origins, the styles of Ruskinesque* Gothic and of the Deuxième Empire. They were however the mirror of his own experience, of his Beaux Arts training and of his travels and interest in England.

He established his practice with buildings in both styles, building to begin with two churches from 1866–9 which, except for a certain wildness about the openings, would appear unremarkable in an English Victorian suburb. In 1869 he completed the Western Railway Offices at Springfield, which from above the ground floor was an equally unremarkable exercise in the Neo-Renaissance style. The lower level however was handled with signs of a startling vigour, the symmetrical composition formed using roughly hewn stone, more primitive than any European rustication. The dichotomy of style reached a crisis with the building of the Worcester High School in 1871, a hugely unsuccessful attempt to work in the flux between the Classic and the Gothic. He attempted to resolve the difficulty of his task and of his path to an authentic American architecture in two important church commissions, built within sight of one another in Boston, by reversion to a working of a round-arched Romanesque style. This style had been propounded earlier as appropriate for the emergent Great Society, intuitively, perhaps attempting to avoid de Tocqueville's* censure, to sustain civilization between barbarism and the decadence that great wealth and freedom constantly offer.

The first building, the Brattle Square Church of 1872, shows a new found ease of composition using simpler, more elemental forms and openings particularly in the design of the tower. Between this and the second church, he worked on a large lunatic asylum in Buffalo, which had an increasing assurance at elevating Beaux Arts rational planning into an early Gothic form.

Trinity Church, built as a result of his winning a limited competition, is often considered one of his masterworks, but is better seen as a summation of his achievements up to that time. The plan has a wonderful, rigorous resolution which was a tribute to his Beaux Arts training and the massing as shown in the competition drawings was as picturesque as any English Gothicist, and greater than anything he would attempt again. As is typical of the artist's progress, he learnt here not what he would have expected, which would have been some attitude to prevalent styles, but that the architecture could be changed and fully realized during the building, that the form might have a will to be independent of the drawings. This deeply absorbed illumination was crucial to his emergence.

The tower of Trinity Church as shown in the drawings caused many dissatisfactions and difficulties in the building. The story goes that he was sent a photograph of the Cathedral at Salamanca which he handed to his assistant Stanford White, who brilliantly adapted the form of the Romanesque tower for the new church. In the task of adapting the half-finished building he began a close lifelong association with his builders, the Norcross brothers. From this time onwards he increasingly distrusted drawings, except for in the solving of the plan, and increasingly worked with a Southern engagement, his fine mind in a powerful body, competing, to shape his creations as they emerged from the Arcadian earth. It has been said that often neither his assistant, clients, nor builders, and perhaps not himself, could see what he was driving at until the building was finished. He required consequently, a considerable indulgence from all parties, and, being adored, he was allowed this on enough of his major projects.

Richardson came to believe that the architect's primary responsibility was, if he saw how to improve a building, to change it even as it approached completion. Such an approach necessarily depended upon a soundness of the plan.

Building Trinity prompted him to move home to be near it. He rented a house near Boston in a landscape of rolling hills, punctuated with rock outcrops, carefully landscaped in an untamed romantic manner, thinly populated by the cultured rich and influential. From these surroundings he was to draw out his most important clients, collaborators and friends. The most important was F.L. Olmsted, who lived within, for such large men, a stone's throw of the Richardson house, who was an established landscape designer of great vision, a man who thought in terms of whole regions, deeply concerned as he was, after Rousseau and Thoreau*, for democratic man's place in nature. Brookline, as the estate where they lived is called, was described then, and could be now, as containing the most impressive pieces of real estate in an area of rare loveliness.

Olmsted collaborated on many projects, but more importantly he by proxy provided Richardson with the theoretical basis for his work that the architect himself never wished to articulate, but which is the essential of all great architecture, and with the image of a social programme that at least all architecture since the eighteenth century has needed.

Richardson's maturity of work and life, the two symbiotically linked, began with his move to Brookline. Adjoining the house he added studios within which he grew an intimacy wtih his assistants that was essential to his art, and his library, being a great lover of books, and of much else.

Fittingly many of his finest buildings are libraries. In particular the Crane library of 1883 at Quincy, Massachusetts, and the Ames Memorial library at North Easton of 1879 are both convincing examples of his mature work, of how he made the Romanesque style strange and new. Although nearly literal in many of their details, in their massing, in the organization and form of the openings, doors and windows and in the wild surface of the stone, they are completely American and his own. However massive and simple the form, in the savage treatment of the surface and the originality of the composition, the buildings have an urgent freedom about them, as if the Romanesque style had been received from books found in a cave or washed up on the shore in this other Eden.

The entrances to both libraries were huge, engulfing arches of pure geometry and rough stone. This motif he was to work repeatedly in other buildings, reaching its most elemental in the Ames Memorial Gatehouse. As Warren Chalk has said, this motif was to recur and will recur again, in the work of all the finest American architects after him. Although he made an important contribution to what was to be called by Vincent Scully the Shingle Style with the Stoughton House of 1883 in Cambridge, Massachusetts, quintessentially his material was stone. The question remains if the shingle style can only make large private houses, if this is the true American style, is this then the adequate and appropriate programme?

Richardson built many of his finest works for Harvard University, notably the Austin Hall Law School, completed in 1883. His most impressive assemblage is the Allegheny County Court House and Jail of 1884 and his most charming small buildings are the commuter railway stations on the Boston and Albany Railway.

During the 1880s, the decade of his greatest successes and declining health, he undoubtedly undertook too many commissions, and the varied quality of many of the works that carry his name bears witness to this. Of all his achievements, in the end he drew pride from the Pittsburgh Court House and the Marshall Field building in Chicago, of 1887. The Field building was to be a large commerical building, what was then a new programme in a new city, with new pressures of space and money, and as such a crucial test for his art. Considered by many to be his opus, the building is in many ways away from the body of his other best work, at an extreme of his favoured methods of working. The façade for instance was obviously resolved through drawing. It cannot be said that in this engagement between the new programmes and an ancient art a complete harmony was achieved. The conflict was between the pressure of the utilitarian volume within the building and the use of stone for the walls. The depth of the plan required extensive daylighting and the increasing height of such buildings depended upon a sophistication of structure that only metal could fulfil, all of which served to stretch and dilute the power of his beloved rock.

Richardson was a difficult architect to follow. His two most brilliant ex-assistants, White and McKim, working in partnership, in reaction emulated the Beaux Arts style in their most important works, and he remains today, like his contemporary Frank Furness, peculiarly undigested by American architectural thought and practice. In the grotesque refinements of the European Modern movement practised by many current American architects, purged of social relevance, there is no inheritance. The question remains, apart from the large private house and the office block, what is the appropriate programme that will revive a true American architecture, to which Richardson first gave expression?

Frederick Scott

See: Henry Russell Hitcock, *The Architecture of H.H. Richardson and his Times* (1966); M.G. Van Rensselaer, *Henry Hobson Richardson* (1969); James F. O'Gorman, *H.H. Richardson and his Office* (1974).

373
RIEMANN, Georg Friedrich Bernhard 1826–66

German mathematician

Bernhard Riemann was born in 1826, the second of six children of a Lutheran pastor. He lived only to the age of thirty-nine, and his life was composed largely of poverty and family tragedy. His mother and a sister died early on of consumption, which disease later accounted for the lives of two more sisters and a brother. In addition his father long opposed Bernhard's mathematical vocation, intending him for the ministry. And yet by every account his exceptional mathematical talent exhibited itself from the earliest age. At ten he was far ahead of his first teacher, Schulz, himself a reasonable mathematician. At fourteen, Riemann attended the Lyceum, a gymnasium in Hanover, where he stayed with his grandmother. When she died two years later, he returned to his home town, Quickborn, and attended another gymnasium in nearby Luneburg. There he read Legendre's *Théorie des Nombres* in six days and it was this early reading which probably led to his interest in prime numbers and so eventually to the conceptualization of the 'Riemann Hypothesis'.

In 1846 Riemann was enrolled at the University of Göttingen, but soon moved to the mathematically more stimulating University of Berlin. He returned in 1849 to Göttingen to prepare for his doctorate. In 1851 he submitted his thesis, which was warmly praised by Gauss*. Staying at Göttingen, he was admitted as a *privatdozent* in 1854, and appointed professor extraordinarius in 1857. It was not until he became a full professor in 1859 however that he gained adequate remuneration, by which time his reputation as Gauss's true successor had already begun to spread. Now honoured and fêted by learned societies in Berlin, London and Paris, Riemann was not long to enjoy his success. A month after his marriage to Elise Koch in 1862 he contracted pleurisy, which in turn led to tuberculosis. Despite travels in Italy and Switzerland there was no lasting remission, and he died in 1866 at Selasca on Lake Maggiore.

If his health had been stronger, Riemann might have surpassed Gauss to become the nineteenth century's leading mathematician. As it is, he is justly famous for his work in non-Euclidean geometry, taking on from where Lobachevsky* and János Bolyai had left off. He discovered the second great branch of non-Euclidean geometry ('elliptic geometry') which still retains many Euclidean features. He also discovered more general varieties, thus providing the basic material for Einstein's General Theory of Relativity, given to the world fifty years after Riemann's death.

Euclid had maintained, in his celebrated Fifth Postulate, that, when we are given a line L and a point p, not belonging to L, there is one and only one line through p which never meets L however far it is produced. Lobachevsky showed that one could consistently postulate more than one such line, and that this immediately entailed that there would be an infinite number of such lines. Riemann realized that there was another case: there might be *no* such line through p. And it was by replacing the Fifth Postulate of Euclid with the postulate that no such line existed – together with some other, minor changes – that he was led to form a system of elliptic geometry. This was not so spectacular a discovery as that of Lobachevsky and Bolyai, because the principle had already been established that non-Euclidean geometries were possible; but it led Riemann to general forms of geometry which turned out to be even more significant in the long run.

The key to these new geometries was Riemann's analysis of three fundamental concepts: distance, curvature and manifold. Taking the last first, Riemann discovered that one could get a kind of abstract 'space' by forming sets of co-ordinates of any respectable mathematical kind, including things like imaginary numbers or elements of Galois* fields. Riemann then showed how these abstract co-ordinates could be used to define a kind of 'distance', or *metric* in modern terminology. Finally, he showed that it was possible to define the degree of curvature of the 'space' under consideration without any reference to another space enclosing it. This final point is of immense significance, as it allowed physicists to postulate that physical space was 'curved' without committing them to assert the existence of an unknowable containing space within which it was curved. In principle he showed how one could determine the 'curvature' of space entirely by means of measurements made within that space; and this meant it was possible to talk about the curvature of space without resorting to metaphysics. That Riemann was fully conscious of the direction in which his work was moving is manifest from his comment at the end of the famous paper of 1854, in which he developed the theory: 'This leads us into the domain of another science, that of physics, into which the object of this work does not allow us to go today.'

Riemann is known to students of mathematics as the author of a variety of integration, of several functions, of 'Riemann surfaces' and of the celebrated 'Riemann Hypothesis', which is still an unsolved problem. Like Gauss, he is a mathematician's mathematician. But unlike Gauss he was much less prepared to undertake mammoth feats of symbolic manipulation. Rather, he achieved his results by searching pre-mathematical thought, by careful selection of question, and careful selection of method. The revolution in the core concepts of mathematics that earlier in the century had emerged from the work of Gauss, Lobachevsky and Galois found its flowering in Riemann, who was the first complete master of the modern style. Of those who

followed, perhaps only Poincaré* could match the depth and profundity of Riemann's thought.

Christopher Ormell

The *Collected Works*, ed. H. Weber with the assistance of R. Dedekind (1876), were first translated in 1953. See: H. Freudenthal, 'Riemann', in *The Dictionary of Scientific Biography* (vol. XI, 1975); E.T. Bell, 'Anima Candida', *Men of Mathematics* (1937, 1953).

374
RIMBAUD, Arthur 1854–91

French poet

At a superficial level Rimbaud has attracted worldwide attention as a quasi-mythical figure, the archetypal rebel, the poet prodigy who abandoned poetry at the age of twenty, and eventually became a trader in Abyssinia. More significantly for modern culture, his actual work places him at the source of modernism, exercising its influence throughout the whole of this century right up to the present day.

Born in 1854 in Charleville in the Ardennes, he had, by the age of fifteen, gone through the stages first of pastiche and then of parody of poets such as Hugo*, Leconte de Lisle and Banville, and was writing poetry which though still traditional in form was already intensely personal. Characteristically it swings between the two poles of idealism and revolt, the idealism taking the form of a passionate desire for freedom and adventure, for a oneness of body and soul, and a sublimation of eroticism into an ecstatic communion with nature: the revolt is against all constraints, in particular those of bourgeois society and religious hypocrisy. God and Napoleon III also come in for their fair share of opprobrium; but the intense disgust seems to apply to all the limitations of the human condition generally.

The best-known poems of this period are 'Dormeur du Val', 'Ma Bohème', 'Premières Communions', 'Les Assis'. He was also at this time developing ideas which have their sources in the social illuminism of earlier nineteenth-century thinkers like de Maistre* and Fourier*, and which unite a belief in social revolution and possibilities of a new fraternity with a mystical desire to fuse with the one dynamic, spiritual force uniforming the universe. Rimbaud's practical hopes for social change were dashed after a brief disillusioning experience of the actuality of revolution in Paris just before the tragic experience of the Commune, and with characteristic intransigence and ambition he then turned all his energies to his vocation as poet and *voyant*. The aim was nothing less than to '*changer la vie*' (the phrase that, taken out of its context, has done more than anything to make him typify the revolutionary stance). The task of the poet as *voyant* is to attain, to 'see' the spiritual unknown, and then to express his visions in a form which will inculcate in his fellows a new sense of harmony and splendour and lead them forward to social progress. The means of attaining these visions of the unknown were to be found through the famous '*dérèglement de tous les sens*', the abuse of the body through alcohol, fasting, drugs, perversions of all kinds, in order to extend consciousness, even if these experiments might lead the *voyant* to the point of death. These theories, first expressed in May 1871 in two short letters to a schoolteacher and to a schoolfriend, were put into practice in the deservedly famous 'Le Bateau ivre' where the dazzling imagery, the powerful rhythms, the poignant intensity of tone go some way to justifying the pretensions of the ambitious young *voyant*. This was the poem with which he hoped to take Paris by storm. With admirable generosity a group of writers headed by Verlaine* had invited him to join them there, but Rimbaud's scandalous behaviour and in particular his passionate affair with the recently married Verlaine, eventually tried even the patience of those who admired his genius and he was sent back to the Ardennes in the summer of 1872. There he produced a fascinating, still enigmatic collection of poems, *Derniers Vers*, very much under the influence of Verlaine. Indeed these delicate, tenuous poems expressing in simple folk-melodies not only his tortured love but also the extreme states of mystical experience engendered by the physical deprivations which were leading him close to madness and even death, can also be read as part of a dialogue perhaps unique in literature, a *réplique* and already a critique of Verlaine and his *Romances sans Paroles*.

In September the anguish turned to euphoria as Verlaine decided to leave his wife and go with Rimbaud first to Belgium and then to London. It was there during the winter of 1872–3 that Rimbaud began to write his extraordinary collection of prose-poems: *Les Illuminations*, which best show his revolutionary attempts to translate his visions of the 'unknown' into a form which will be organic and no longer preordained. True to their title these visions, whether of the unknown or of a childish, primitive world of fantasy and wish-fulfilment, are brilliant, dynamic, theatrical, as vivid and sometimes as frightening as hallucinations. They manage to create a total imaginary universe, with its own mythology, its own new god-like beings, its landscape and its fabulous new towns which may have something to do with London but more with Rimbaud's own New Jerusalem. Rimbaud's avowed aim as poet-voyant had been to find a language which would appeal to all the senses so as to attract the reader into his vision magnetically. Through the associative powers of the imagery, the dense musical patterns, and the hypnotic rhythms, these brilliant, breathless fragments indeed show an innovatory use of language which has been immensely fertile in its influence on the development of French poetry.

The affair with Verlaine ended abruptly and tragically. In the summer of 1873 Verlaine left Rimbaud, who, however, followed him to Brussels. Tried beyond his endurance, he actually shot at Rimbaud wounding him slightly. The ensuing case against Verlaine was influenced by the revelation about his homosexuality and he was sentenced to three years in prison. The effect on Rimbaud was traumatic. In the autumn he completed a short prose work, *Une Saison en enfer*, which, although written out of the personal hell of a guilt-ridden and unhappy passion as well as the failure of an over-ambitious aesthetic, has also wider significance in the way in which it works through the idea of hell itself as fostered by Christianity towards a new and still ill-defined humanism, inspired by the characteristic ideas of fraternity (as opposed to dependence on a debilitating sexual passion), of a new and proud love (as opposed to Christian charity and guilt due to original sin) and a transcendence of the age-old dualism between the flesh and the spirit. Each short prose piece condenses in highly dramatic and often ironical form a stage in this rapid evolution. The progress is via a dialectic; the pull of the past, of superstition and human weakness, relived through brief, bright images, works against the visionary fragments of an impossible idealism in order to produce a third, more realistic stance, that of the sane, the independent, the possible. It is a unique work: in highly condensed form an exemplar of a whole spiritual crisis in Western society.

Rimbaud had claimed that his fate depended on this book. It was in fact not published until much later. Whether this marked the end of his literary endeavour, or whether he continued to add to the *Illuminations* during the following year when he came back to England with Germain Nouveau has been a subject of critical discussion for many years. Certainly from 1875, that is at the age of twenty-one, he showed no further sign of interest in a literary career and embarked on a quite different life of travel and adventures, eventually setting up in 1880 as a trader in Harrar, Abyssinia. He died of cancer in a hospital in Marseilles in 1891. It was due finally to Verlaine that most of the *Illuminations* were published for the first time in *La Vogue*, in 1886.

The ambivalence implicit in his life and work has continued in the nature of his influence. The topicality of problems raised by his '*dérèglement de tous les sens*' is too obvious to be stressed. Claudel is said to have been converted to Christianity after reading Rimbaud. The Surrealists used his '*changer la vie*' as their device for revolution and yet could not forgive him for having sold out. However, it is through them, and their recognition that he had found a language fit to explore and express the urges and desires of the unconscious, that his influence has been fostered. Few living French poets would deny if not a positive influence at least a deep admiration.

Margaret Davies

For Rimbaud's complete works see *Oeuvres complètes* (1972). For poetry in translation see: *A Season in Hell, The Illuminations*, by Enid Rhodes Peschel (1973); *Complete Works*, by Paul Schmidt (1967). The most useful critical works in English are: Wallace Fowlie, *Rimbaud* (1965); C.A. Hackett, *Rimbaud*; *A Critical Introduction* (1981); N. Osmond, introduction and notes to his edition of *The Illuminations* (1979). The best biographical work in English is Enid Starkie, *Rimbaud* (1949).

375
RIMSKY-KORSAKOV, Nikolay Andreyevich
1844–1908

Russian composer

It was into an aristocratic family with a tradition of service to the state that the composer was born. His earliest years were spent in the provinces where folk music and the gorgeous ritual of a nearby monastery made a profound impression on him. The Corps of Naval Cadets in St Petersburg provided his education from 1856 to 1862, and the musical life of that city introduced him to a wider musical world. Until 1873 he served in the navy, both aboard ship and ashore; as with many such appointments in the Russian public service, duties were not at all onerous. In 1871 he was appointed to a professorship at the St Petersburg Conservatoire, where he remained on the staff (with a brief interruption, for political reasons, in 1905) until his death. He was also at various times Inspector of Naval Bands, director of the Free School of Music, and assistant musical director in the Imperial Chapel. His career encompassed teaching, conducting, editing or completing the works of others (including Dargomyzhsky, Borodin* and Mussorgsky*), authorship and folksong collecting as well as composition.

The single most important event in his musical development occurred when he met Balakirev* in 1861. He thus was introduced to the circle of dilettante musicians drawn 'as if by magnetism' by the power of Balakirev's personality. He exchanged ideas with like-minded young composers (Borodin, Cui, Mussorgsky) and under Balakirev's tutelage the compositional activity of all of them was given direction and purpose. Their mentor persuaded his disciples to undertake works on a scale they would never have attempted without him, and thus they progressed from talented dabblers to serious composers. With his Conservatoire appointment, however, Rimsky-Korsakov felt an obligation to study systematically the elements of music ('practical composition and instrumentation' initially) which he was employed to teach, and he went on, by self-instruction, to acquire a greater mastery of the technical aspects of music than any of these associates ever possessed. In completing or preparing for publication the works of Mussorgsky, he at times substituted more conventional treatment for the boldly original ideas of the composer; this is notoriously the case with *Boris Godunov*. Though now regretted, Rimsky-Korsakov's work did begin to acquaint the public with that and other masterpieces.

Rimsky-Korsakov began to compose with the example of Glinka* before him. Mendelssohn*, Schumann*, Berlioz* and especially Liszt* also served as models, but the composer was primarily animated by the idea of writing Russian music. In the subject matter of his operas and orchestral music, Russian material predominates. History and folklore supply the majority of subjects, sometimes viewed through the works of Russian writers. His treatment inclines to the objective, avoids emotional excess and eschews the extremes of experiment of, for instance, Mussorgsky. He regarded opera as 'primarily a musical phenomenon', and had no sympathy with Wagner's* ideas about musical drama. He completed fifteen operas, and some of these are his most important works.

His orchestral music is noteworthy for the brilliance of its orchestration. Acquaintance with much of it reveals a restricted melodic invention and a paucity of constructional resource. The finest works are *Sheherazade* and the Russian Easter Festival Overture (both 1888). The influence of the composer's orchestration may be felt not only in the work of his Russian pupils, who include Lyadov, Glazunov, Stravinsky and Prokofiev, but also in orchestral music by Debussy, Ravel and other composers.

Serious historical topics and fantastic tales involving the supernatural are the main areas for operatic subjects. Convincing characters are conspicuous by their rarity, and the composer is happier with a ritualistic enactment of historical events or imaginary, fairy-tale figures. The real world of his own time never impinges, unless *The Golden Cockerel* (1906–7) is viewed as a burlesque of the Russo-Japanese War of 1904 and Russian government; this is a debatable interpretation, though there was no doubt at the time that the opera was near the bone. The musical representation of good and evil, or 'real' and fantastic is achieved in this opera (as in many other works) by the use of diatonic music for the former and chromatic music for the latter; this distinction, familiar from Weber's* *Der Freischütz*, is exploited in Glinka's *Ruslan* and later in Stravinsky's *The Firebird*. Rimsky-Korsakov takes it further by contriving fresh arrangements of notes in non-diatonic scale patterns.

The outstanding example of an opera using folk motives is *The Snow Maiden* (1880–1). This incorporates elements from folk wedding celebrations and the Shrovetide festival, and is full of folk-like melodies and instrumental effects. The method of treating brief tunes of narrow melodic range, relying on ostinatos and pedals, is distinctive. *The Maid of Pskov* (1868–72, 1876–7 and 1891–2) is perhaps the best example of a historical opera by this composer. It deals with Ivan the Terrible's campaign of 1570, in which the inhabitants of Pskov are menaced by the same cruel treatment the tsar has just meted out to Novgorod. This fate is prevented by the tsar's discovery in Pskov of one who is his own daughter. Her lover, though, wishes to kill the tsar and rescue the 'maid of Pskov' from him. She is accidentally killed in the ensuing fight.

Stuart Campbell

Other works include: Symphony no 2 (*Antar*, 1868, 1875, 1897); *Musical Picture – Sadko* (1869, rev. 1892); *Capriccio espagnol* (1887). Operas: *May Night* (1878–9); *Christmas Eve* (1894–5); *Sadko* (1894–6); *The Tsar's Bride* (1898–9); *The Tale of Tsar Saltan* (1899–1900); *The Legend of the Invisible City of Kitezh and the Maid Fevroniya* (1903–5). *Forty Folksongs*, a collection compiled in 1875; *Collection of 100 Russian Folksongs*, compiled in 1875–6. Rimsky-Korsakov's *Chronicle of my Musical Life* is available in a translation by J.A. Joffe (1942); his *Principles of Orchestration*, ed. M.O. Shteynberg, has also been published in English (2nd edn, 1964). See: Gerald Abraham, *Rimsky-Korsakov – A Short Biography* (1945).

376
RITSCHL, Albrecht Benjamin 1822–89

German Lutheran theologian

Born in Berlin in 1822, the son of a superintendent in the Prussian Church in Pomerania, Ritschl was educated in the universities of Bonn, Heidelberg (where he was influenced by the theologian Richard Rothe), Halle (where he absorbed the message for Christianity of the eighteenth-century *Aufklärung*), and Tübingen, where he was successively pupil of and then collaborator with the celebrated German New Testament scholar and historian Ferdinand Christian Baur*. Ritschl began his teaching career at Bonn (1851–64), and from 1864 until his death was Ordinarius Professor of Systematic Theology at Göttingen.

In his early days at Tübingen, while under the supervision of Baur, Ritschl accepted the Baurian thesis that the evolution of the New Testament canon and the history of primitive Christianity must be understood in terms of a 'conflict' between Jewish Petrinism and universalist Paulinism which was resolved (*aufgehoben*) in quasi-Hegelian fashion in the emergence of the 'old-catholic' Church of the second century, a the-

ory which is reflected in the first edition of Ritschl's published dissertation, *Die Entstehung der altkatholischen Kirche* (1850). But Ritschl swiftly became disillusioned with and highly critical of Baur's thesis, coming to believe that the emergence of the 'old-catholic' Church must rather be understood in terms of a 'hellenization' of genuine, primitive, Galilean, ethico-spiritual, practical Christianity by its insertion into the cultural milieu of the Graeco-Roman world, a hellenization which can be identified in the emergence of philosophical theology, asceticism, mysticism, a hierarchical church order, and firmly defined liturgical rites. This latter Ritschlian thesis is reflected in the much altered second edition of his *Die Entstehung der altkatholischen Kirche* (1857). Thereafter Ritschl's theological programme followed a distinctly anti-Baurian and anti-Hegelian course, although in recent and contemporary Ritschl scholarship it is widely conceded that Ritschl gravely misunderstood the nature of Baur's 'Hegelianism', believing that Baur insensitively imposed a Hegelian threefold dialectical scheme upon his literary materials, and failed to grasp the extent to which Baur's historical reconstructions were achieved independently of the respect for Hegel* which he undoubtedly entertained. Consequently, many recent Ritschl scholars have judged that Ritschl's excessive anti-Hegelian bias somewhat impoverished his own work, imparting to it an alarming antiphilosophical flavour, and a distorting and harmful confusion of the 'metaphysical' with the 'ontological'.

At Göttingen, from 1864, Ritschl was urged by his philosophical colleague Rudolf Herman Lotze (1817–81) to return to Kant for philosophical guidance in the construction of his theological system. Under Kantian and Lotzean influence, Ritschl elaborated his celebrated epistemology of 'value-judgments': declaring that Christian theology has nothing to do with 'theoretical judgments' (as found, e.g., in the sciences, metaphysics, cosmology), he confined all genuine theological statements to value-judgments which express the 'value' or 'worth' (*Werth*) which religious realities (God, Christ, grace) have for the ego struggling to extricate itself from and to dominate the 'world' of blind, impersonal nature (as portrayed by late nineteenth-century naturalism and materialism) and of harsh, dispassionate, and impersonal society. But Ritschl, as a Christian theologian, was adamant that the ego thrusting for such value can only find itself satisfied by the revelation of God in Christ witnessed to in the New Testament scriptures, a revelation entertained, nourished and proclaimed contemporaneously by the Christian community. Accordingly, in his christology, Ritschl portrayed Christ as a world-transcending and world-dominating figure, who loftily ignored or overcame all opposing 'worldly' forces (temptations, enemies, treachery) in fulfilling his divinely given vocation to proclaim and found the Kingdom of God, understood by Ritschl as God's *Summum Bonum* for both man and the world, the eventual moral reunification of men under the Lordship (*Herrschaft*) of God. But Ritschl's treatment of the divinity of Christ has been judged to be defective: his unreflective anti-ontological bias motivated him to reduce Christ's divinity to his salvific value for the component members of the Christian community, at the expense of the ontological status of Christ's person; and his excessive anti-metaphysical stance rendered him incapable of dealing with the pre-existence of Christ (interpreted as the notional or ideational pre-existence of Christ in the mind of God), or the heavenly exaltation of Christ (interpreted as the contemporary prolongation of the posthumous *beneficia Christi* mediated through the contemporary Christian community). No alleged activity of the contemporary Christ can be entertained which cannot be guaranteed by reference to the historical Jesus – hence the charge of 'historical positivism' widely brought against Ritschl.

Nevertheless, the contribution of Ritschl to social ethics was impressive. He argued that each justified Christian was obliged to work for the common good in whatever place and station he found himself by divine providence. Over and against post-Reformation protestant mystical pietism and late medieval Catholic monasticism, he urged in Lutheran vein that the truly justified Christian served God by dutifulness in his civic vocation, whether that of home, market-place, school, government or church. Justification (rendered by God's free forgiveness of the sinner by grace) must issue in reconciliation, in which the justified Christian strives for God's kingdom in church and state. Such teachings evoked from Karl Barth and his followers in the twentieth century the accusation that Ritschl and his disciples had expounded an 'anthropocentric' or 'Kantian' or 'moralistic' theology, an accusation that was countered by the assertion that Ritschl had but achieved a long overdue correlation of faith and works, a problem bequeathed to modernity by the Reformation and post-Reformation periods.

Ritschl's theology is important not merely intrinsically: it is arguably the link between the theology of the first half of the nineteenth century and the first half of the twentieth; many maintain that a Ritschlian type of theology inspired the 'social gospel' of American theological thinking before and after the First World War; in recent Ritschl scholarship it has been argued that Ritschlian theology, in its christocentric, bibliospheric and pistobasic aspects, has significantly anticipated many twentieth-century Christian theological trends; its stress on the 'value of Christ for the soul' mediated, through Ritschl's disciple Herrmann to Herrmann's pupil Bultmann, the emphasis on Christ's 'existential significance for the self' in modern existentialist theologies. It has even been argued that a renewed reflection on Ritschl's notion of the Kingdom of God, partly realizable within history, would make a salutary contribution to modern theologies of hope and liberation. But Ritschl is also deservedly famous as the founder of the Ritschlian theological school, whose members included W. Herrmann, A. v. Harnack*, J. Kaftan, F. Kattenbusch, F. Loofs and Th. v. Haering. A renewed interest in Ritschl's work has been discernible since about 1950, when scholars began to reinvestigate the leading nineteenth-century German Protestant theologians independently of the rather hostile accounts of their work which had been for several generations produced by neo-orthodox theologians influenced by the viewpoint of Karl Barth's neo-orthodoxy.

James Richmond

Translations: *A Critical History of the Christian Doctrine of Justification and Reconciliation* (1872); *The Christian Doctrine of Justification and Reconciliation* (1900); *A. Ritschl: Three Essays* (1972). See: A.E. Garvie, *The Ritschlian Theology* (1899); James Orr, *The Ritschlian Theology and the Evangelical Faith* (1897); J.K. Mozley, *Ritschlianism* (1909); Paul Wrzecionko, *Die philosophischen Wurzeln der Theologie Albrecht Ritschls* (1964); Philip Hefner, *Faith and the Vitalities of History* (1966); D.L. Mueller, *An Introduction to the Theology of Albrecht Ritschl* (1969); David W. Lotz, *Ritschl and Luther* (1974); James Richmond, *Ritschl: A Reappraisal* (1981).

377
ROBERTSON, John Mackinnon 1856–1933

British historian and sociologist

Born in a Scottish village, Robertson left school at thirteen but acquired astounding erudition in several languages, and wrote 103 books and thousands of articles and reviews. While working as a clerk, he began writing for periodicals and newspapers, became a journalist in his late twenties, and later (though intermittently) an editor and publisher. He was very active in the rationalist movement and the Liberal Party, was a Member of Parliament from 1906 to 1908, and a parliamentary secretary from 1911 to 1915. He was an indefatigable speaker at public meetings and adult education classes. He married at thirty-six and had one daughter. Though never rich and often on the edge of poverty, he amassed a library of over 20,000 volumes.

In his historico-sociological works, Robertson was a continuator of Thomas Henry Buckle*, interested principally in the same question of social conditions of intellectual progress. He was the only outstanding British writer in the field of comparative sociology since Herbert Spencer*, superior in the range of knowledge, clarity of thought and sureness of judgment to a number of much better remembered continental and American authors.

Although his sociological explanations of historical processes have the most lasting value, they constitute only a small part of his writings which cover a wide range of subjects from politics, economics and ethics to biography and literary criticism. His bulkiest tomes are devoted to rationalist criticism of theological interpretations of the Bible and the history of free thought. In *The Fallacy of Saving* (1892) he anticipated Keynes's theory of unemployment.

In many of his books, more than half of the space is devoted to polemics with various upholders of theological, racist, irrationalist and anti-sociological approaches to history. Robertson was always right but the butts of his criticism, though famous at the time, are little known today, which now detracts from the interest of his works. Because a large part of his positive contributions to knowledge – the sociological explanations of historical processes, especially of changes in religion – are dispersed among polemical writings of lesser interest today, he does not receive the attention warranted by his intellectual merit.

Robertson's most important work is *The Evolution of States* (1912) where he treats a number of states from various eras as case studies of progress or decadence, which he tries to explain in terms of interaction of the factors which he discusses in the theoretical chapters. The other most substantial explanatory analyses of history can be found in *The Saxon and the Celt* (1897) – where, after refuting various racist and jingoist interpretations, he gives his own historical explanation of the peculiarities of the Irish situation. In 'A Short History of Christianity' he gives explanations of the growth of the early church and the course of the Reformation, the English form of which is likewise treated in 'Dynamics of Religion', which might have been welcomed by the Marxists, had Robertson not been an opponent of all dogmas. *Pagan Christs* and *Christianity and Mythology* are massive comparative studies of belief and ritual with a large ingredient of sociological explanation.

Robertson addressed many of his polemics against militarism, protectionism which he linked with imperialism, the selfishness of the wealthy classes which he identified with Toryism, and all religious beliefs. He was a moralist but of a humanistic and rationalist kind. 'There is but one way,' he wrote, 'in which a whole community can be raised and bettered from within, and that way begins in the free play of new thoughts against the old.'

Stanislav Andreski

Robertson's other works include: *Buckle and his Critics* (1895); *Essays in Sociology* (2 vols, 1904); *The Meaning of Liberalism* (1912); *A Short History of Christianity* (2nd edn, 1913); *The Dynamics of Religion* (2nd edn, 1926);

A History of Freethought in the Nineteenth Century (2 vols, 1929); *A History of Freethought Ancient and Modern to the Period of the French Revolution* (4th edn, 2 vols, 1936). See: S.L. Andreski, 'A forgotten genius: John Mackinnon Robertson', in *Question*, April 1979.

ROCHE, Martin: see under HOLABIRD and ROCHE

378
RODIN, François-Auguste-René 1840–1917

French sculptor

Rodin's early life was marred by two failures. Firstly, after a period at the 'Petite École' (École Spéciale de Dessin et de Mathématiques) under Horace Lecoq de Boisbaudran, he was refused by the 'Grande École' (École des Beaux Arts). Secondly, when he submitted a bust to the Paris Salon in 1864 it was rejected. Meanwhile he earned a living by taking various craftsmanly jobs, working for jewellers, stonecutters, architectural decorators and the Sèvres porcelain factory. Only by the early 1880s were financial conditions less straitened. By that time Rodin's sculptural career had begun.

In his first full-length work, *The Age of Bronze* (1876), a gesture of anguish was transformed to one of awakening – not into erotic self-awareness, like Michelangelo's *Bound Slave*, seen six months before on a visit to Italy – but into a realm of pure thought. Accustomed only to Salon suavity, his audience accused him of working from casts of his model, Auguste Neyt. *St John the Baptist Preaching* (1878–80), another full-length bronze, this time of an Italian named Pignatelli, was less stable and coolly modelled. It displayed what Rodin himself called 'progressive development of movement'; the man, speaking as he walked, had been captured in the process of shifting his weight from foot to foot. Physically, it was a study in mobility, emotionally an impression of the way a powerfully felt message could conquer hardship and derision, historically a meditation on transition, announcement, a bridge from one era to another. Both figures have the air of a manifesto; they speak of the blindness of the present and the gigantic effort needed to transcend it. Both have the qualities of all of Rodin's work – a tension between idealization, nobility, a desire to elevate the audience, and a counterbalancing appeal to reality, the hard facts of day-to-day experience. Both figures are taken beyond their merely physical existence by thought, inspiration or faith. One reviewer compared the man in *The Age of Bronze* to a sleep-walker. Indeed, thought has provided the only escape route possible. St. John concerns himself with more public issues, yet lacks any evidence whatsoever. Only his fervour can sustain him. One key issue in Rodin's art is the passionate desire to express spiritual values simply by means of physical gesture, to combine the spiritual and aesthetic. Like St. John, he descended into an arena of action.

In 1880 the French Government Fine Arts Committee commissioned him to make a door. At his death *The Gates of Hell* remained unfinished. For thirty-seven years he altered over 180 figures which filled the double portal. They became an anthology of his most poignant themes and the faces and gestures he returned to most often in his life. The theme was religious, yet vital to his entire conception was a reading of Charles Baudelaire's* *Les Fleurs du Mal*, which he illustrated. Surmounting the hosts of the damned is not God but simply a man thinking, a miniature version of his *Thinker* (1880). Of the figure he said, 'He is no longer dreamer, he is creator', an indication that once again he wished to challenge the theme of thought as an escape from the world of action. By transferring the whole of Dante into the mind of the artist he was dramatizing the divisions which most concerned him as an artist – between interiority and superficies, spirit and musculature, mind and matter – but also, perhaps, seeking vainly to heal the breach between these oppositions. The Gothic sculptors he so respected recognized no such dichotomies. Between their time and the nineteenth century some Eliotean 'dissociation of sensibility' had occurred, or rather some undermining caused by the 'death of God'. Rodin's religious views are obscure and possibly irrelevant. He had, however, been a member of a religious order, taking the name Brother Auguste. In his art he concerned himself with every kind of physical existence, from sanctity to high eroticism. There is an almost dogged desire to run whatever gamut the flesh could offer. Could this have concealed some search for an enabling philosophy?

The Burghers of Calais was commissioned in 1884. Taken from an incident in Froissart's *Chronicles*, it showed the sacrifice of six Calais citizens who had surrendered to Edward III during the Hundred Years' War in exchange for his ceasing an eleven-month siege of their city. One of Rodin's original plans was to fix his six statues one behind the other on the stones of the *place* outside the Calais town hall, so that they would seem to be wending their way toward Edward's camp. 'And the people of Calais of today, almost elbowing them, would have felt more deeply the tradition of solidarity which unites them to the heroes.' That proposal was rejected. Instead, the figures moved in a circle, at differing speeds and with various degrees of visible distress, united in passivity by the concordant diagonal sweep of their procession, most clearly seen from behind. As with *The Gates of Hell*, Rodin researched each of the figures fully before beginning, worked from models and made nude maquettes before

clothing his characters. In *The Gates of Hell* Rodin had accepted no programme; he would work, he said, simply from his imagination. In *The Burghers of Calais* he was operating in a definable historical mode. Perhaps the need to establish and authenticate some sense of historical otherness – in Dante, in Froissart – is a familiar result of artistic estrangement in the nineteenth century. Paradoxically, if this can be seen most easily in Rodin's public, monumental pieces, it could be possible to interpret it as the indication of a deeply felt private doubt. George Bernard Shaw reported that as he watched his own portrait being sculpted, Rodin took it through Byzantine, Mannerist and classical phases before allowing it to congeal into some final likeness. In his description we sense at once the international 'modernist' of the twentieth century, adrift in time and space. If the thinking man at the top of *The Gates of Hell* is Dante, he is also Baudelaire watching Paris being rebuilt, Tiresias or H.C. Earwicker dreaming their respective masterpieces. Are his eyes open or closed? Is he locked into history or is the whole of time his domain?

The easiest way to answer the question is by examining Rodin's greatest achievement, his *Balzac*. Honoré de Balzac* had died when Rodin was ten. Working from caricatures, photographs, details remembered by acquaintances, even tailors' records, he reconstructed the figure of the paunchy, gap-toothed writer. Even at the outset it was evident that the research methods of the two men bore striking resemblances; Rodin visited the district where Balzac was born in order to study facial types. After several full-scale experiments in which his subject stood nude, he eventually hit on the idea of radical simplification; the entire body would be covered by the Dominican friar's habit he wore when writing. 'I had to show Balzac in his study, breathless, hair in disorder, eyes lost in a dream, a genius who in his little room reconstructs piece by piece all of society in order to bring it to tumultuous life before his contemporaries and generations to come.' The press pilloried the final version of *Balzac*. And, indeed, the way the great writer had been captured almost invites such treatment; the portrait is a vivid and immediate presence such as every satirist yearns to convey. Yet it is only registered, not pushed to satirical ends. The sheer arrogance of the creative mind unaware of anything except its own imaginative process is an ultimate Romantic solution. Yet for a sculptor the means of conveying the dialogue between the self and the other differs fundamentally from that of the writer. When he made a portrait of Baudelaire Rodin refused to create anything but a head, polished until it shone, eyes glazed, inviting ambiguous responses without providing any keys to unlock them. He defended his decision to dispense entirely with the body. 'With him the head is everything,' he replied. Balzac seems all body, and his body, as critics have since pointed out, is a man-size column reminiscent of a phallus; in his sheer fecundity Balzac has been transformed into an instrument of reproduction. Yet we cannot *see* writers in the act of creation. By some lateral legerdemain the spectator reads 'mind' for 'body', takes assertion for truth, interprets narcissism as genius. Rosalind Krauss, who has pointed out that the mature career of Rodin coincides with that of Husserl, has suggested that their attitudes may have a lot in common. The idea that meaning is synchronous with experience, the notion that if self is private and inaccessible then each of us would be two people – one to ourselves and another to others – can be paralleled in Rodin. Absence of premeditation and foreknowledge, best and most obviously proposed in an examination of the act of creation, and a total emotional dependence on the external gesture reveal Rodin's religion as a kind of paganism, total truth achieved by a realization that the self is what is manifested to others. 'Truth to materials' in his work takes the form of a record of the procedure by which the goal was accomplished. On the surface is the whole story of the bronze, its handling and casting. Rodin did not devise a solution to the problems raised by all of the dichotomies which beset him. But he did lodge himself securely between the poles of each, and *Balzac* reveals how brilliant a device that was.

After a century of academic dullness in sculpture, Rodin came and, as Brancusi said, 'succeeded in transforming everything'. Honoured and abused during his lifetime, he was seldom ignored. Private affairs were publicized, his technical prowess became legendary, and his work was fiercely attacked. Half a century later he remains an enigma. Rooted in academic models, he persisted in applying mythological and literary titles to his sculpture despite an uncanny grasp of modernist abstraction. Obsessed with the rehabilitation of monumental sculpture, his approach probably hastened its decline. Instrumental in encouraging Degas* to experiment, he himself drew back from the course he may have advocated. Rodin's use of the fragment alone ensures him a place as a proto-modern. Yet as the Rodin expert, Albert Elsen, has written:

Like the biblical Moses, he lived only long enough to look on the Promised Land. Not his death, however, but his steadfast adherence to naturalism and certain of its traditions prevented Rodin from entering into the new territories that were being surveyed and colonized by younger sculptors.

Stuart Morgan

See: Albert Elsen, *Rodin's Gates of Hell* (1960) and *Rodin* (1963); *Rodin, Readings on his Life and Work*, ed. A. Elsen (1965); Robert Descharnes and J.F. Chabrun, *Auguste Rodin* (1967); *The Drawings of Rodin*, ed. A. Elsen and K. Varnedoe (1972); *Rodin and Balzac*, ed. A. Elsen, S. McGough and S. Wander (1973); Victoria Thorseon, *Rodin Graphics* (1975); Monique Laurent, *The Rodin Museum of Paris* (1977).

379
RODÓ, José Enrique 1872–1917

Uruguayan essayist and philosopher

Rodó was the originator of *arielismo*, an important movement in Latin American thought which attempted to counteract the positivistic materialism and imitation of the North American way of life characteristic of the middle and upper classes in South America in the late nineteenth century. Compelled to leave university by the death of his father, he turned to literary criticism and helped to found the *Revista Nacional de Literatura y Ciencias Sociales* ('National Review of Literature and Social Sciences', 1895) whose appearance marked a turning point in the developing culture of the River Plate region. Influenced by classical authors such as Marcus Aurelius and by modern writers such as Macaulay*, Sainte-Beuve* and (especially) Renan*, he published a trilogy of long essays: *El que vendrá* (1896), *Rubén Darío* (1899) and his most famous work *Ariel* (1900, trans. F.J. Stimson, *Ariel*, 1922). In the first two of these he emerged as a powerful critic of late nineteenth-century literary and artistic trends and a leading advocate of the movement towards conscious aestheticism and a certain neo-paganism which, led by Darío, came to be known in Spanish America and Spain as *modernismo*. A later work, *El mirador de Próspero* ('The Gallery of Prospero', 1913), contained more literary criticism.

Positivism, with its strong emphasis on materialism and 'scientific' method, its rejection of metaphysics and its tinge of social Darwinism, was the first fully fledged philosophy to strike Latin America in the post-Independence period. It became a cult and in places acquired the status of a lay religion. At the same time admiration and envy of the economic, social and political progress of the United States were widespread, especially after the impact made by the works of Sarmiento*. In *Ariel* Rodó set out to withdraw the allegiance of his readers from what he saw as the 'utilitarian' values preached by positivists and adulators of North America, as well as from egalitarian interpretations of democracy and from the spiritually damaging effects which he believed sprang from these. Believing that Anglo-Saxon civilization was in danger of decay because of its growing indifference to higher values, Rodó saw in Latin America a still uncorrupted repository of spiritual ideals, though he did not associate these specifically with the sub-continent's Roman Catholic religious tradition. Rather he saw the answer in a fusion of the Christian spirit of love with the 'elegance' of classical humanism.

Ariel is not an argument, but a moving exhortation to the young to free their souls from the taint of materialism (i.e. from the influence of Caliban; hence the title) and to purge society, and especially politics, from the preponderance of the peaceful hordes of the ad-mass, which Rodó regarded as worse than those of Attila. He accused the United States of worshipping materialist vulgarity and of having failed to evolve the right methods of democratic selection of its political leadership. He asserted passionately that social progress could only come from acceptance by a growing number of individuals that the classic triad of goodness, beauty and truth existed objectively and constituted a life-directing pattern of absolutes. Cleaving to these values would he believed, 'preserve the integrity of the spirit' and, in the end, produce an élite, an aristocratic minority characterized by its moral stature and its culture. This would permit Latin America to seize the torch of human progress as it fell from the hand of the Anglo-Saxons.

Essentially Rodó's system of thought combined voluntarism with elements of classical and modern humanism to provide what he thought was a panacea both for the spiritual ills of the individual and for the wider problems of social and political progress. The weaknesses of his outlook were that he confused democracy (at that time comparatively undeveloped) with democratism, and that he tended to regard love of beauty as inseparably allied to love of virtue and truth, and hence saw it as a source of moral improvement. Despite these misconceptions Rodó's ideas had an immense impact on Latin Americans, who were anxious to be reassured that their racial heritage was qualitatively better than that of their powerful Anglo-Saxon neighbours and that cultural reformism rather than violent social upheaval was the solution to their problems.

A characteristic of Rodó's élite minority was their pronounced sense of vocation. In *The Motives of Proteus* (*Los motivos de Proteo*, 1909, trans. A. Flores, 1928) he analysed the origin and nature of individual vocations, relating them to his belief in ideals as dynamic forces. He built up a theory of vocation which culminated in the concept of the hero as the man of universal vocation. The example for Latin America was, of course, Bolivar*.

For decades Rodó's *arielismo* and Sarmiento's earlier approach to the Latin American problem as one of innate barbarity struggled for preponderance, with the former influencing a succession of writers about Latin American culture, especially in Argentina and Mexico. More recently, Marxist-orientated interpretations have tended to eclipse them.

D.L. Shaw

See: Rodó's *Obras completas* (1967); *Ariel*, ed. G.

Brotherston (1967); and C. Pereda, *Rodó's Main Sources* (1948).

380

ROLFE, Frederick William 1860–1913

British novelist

Rolfe was born near St Paul's Cathedral in the City of London into a family of Dissenting piano-makers and, according to his brother Herbert, was 'eccentric from early youth'. At the age of fourteen he had his breast tattooed with a cross and soon after experienced a profound vocation for the priesthood which, thwarted as it was by his own exasperating temperament, was to shadow the rest of his life.

He left school at fifteen and the lack of formal education explains an ostentatious display of learning in his works. While still in his teens he managed to become a schoolmaster, a task at which he excelled since his interest in boys went beyond obligation. But in 1886 he was received into the Roman Catholic Church and had consequently to surrender his post at Grantham Grammar School. The following year he went to study for the priesthood at St Mary's College, Oscott, where he pursued his interest in poetry, painting and photography at the expense of his devotions, and was obliged to leave.

In 1889 under the sponsorhip of the Roman Catholic Archbishop of Edinburgh – another surprising contrivance – he entered the Scots College, Rome. Again he caused widespread offence and after six months had to be physically removed from the premises by the college servants. Now began his life of drifting, sponging, and wild vituperation.

Rolfe took refuge with an Englishwoman, the Duchess of Sforza-Cesarini, spending the summer at her house in the Alban Hills where he met a young Italian peasant called Toto and confirmed the love for Italy which forms the background to most of his work. He reappeared in England calling himself Baron Corvo, a title he claimed the Duchess had given him, and worked as an itinerant artist, photographer and journalist, propelled round the country by debts and violent rows with friends.

As 'Corvo' he began to contribute his Toto stories to the *Yellow Book* in 1895. This led to two collections, *Stories Toto told me* (1898) and *In His Own Image* (1901), in which his favourite themes of Catholicism, paganism and pederasty are blended with a dry humour. He continued to employ the pseudonym for his lurid history *Chronicles of the House of Borgia* (1901), and his translation of the *Rubaiyat of Umar Khaiyam* (1903) from the French. But even Rolfe seems eventually to have found the title onerous, because hereafter he prefers to mislead in another way – as 'Fr. Rolfe'. Besides, as

Baron Corvo, his pathetic pretensions had already beeen exposed in well-researched detail by a newspaper in Aberdeen (where he had once resided). The author was never ascertained but to the Catholic Church's spiritual humiliation was now added social disgrace, underlined when soon after Rolfe was forced to seek shelter in a Welsh workhouse. These painful experiences fed the strains of paranoia and megalomania in his personality.

In 1899 he took an attic in Hampstead where he worked on his most famous book, *Hadrian the Seventh* (1904), whose opening pages contain a frank and vivid self-portrait. Rolfe was well able to regard himself objectively, but on the whole he preferred a far more romantic, aggressive outlook, often insufferable for others. The book is both strongly autobiographical and a dream of wish-fulfilment, a tragi-comic extravaganza of great beauty and intensity, full of thinly disguised portraits of contemporaries he wished to revile, and at the centre Rolfe as the hero George Rose, scourged by the church which, seeing itself in error, apologizes by asking him to become pope. Self-obsessed, driven inwards by loneliness and poverty, embittered by lack of recognition as an artist, lack of love as a man, Rolfe corrected it all in this baroque climax to nineteenth-century England's love-hate affair with Roman Catholicism. Just as Rolfe was a natural and gifted writer who often referred to the 'loathsome occupation of writing', so he was a devout Catholic who detested the church. *Hadrian* earned him no money but it brought him the admiration of the few, especially of the Catholic convert R.H. Benson, son of the Archbishop of Canterbury. Benson expressed his delight that Rolfe was a 'proper pagan', adding 'All sound Catholics must be that'.

Don Tarquinio, a Kataleptic Phantasmatic Romance was published in 1905, an account in voluptuous language of one crucial day in 1495 in the life of a young Roman aristocrat and outlaw. After this, nothing. Rolfe continued to write, as he put it, 'profusely and with difficulty', but he had pledged so much of his future income against loans that he came to prefer no publication at all than that someone other than himself should gain from it. His energies were bled further by the pointless literary partnerships with nonentities into which he went in search of 'the Divine Friend'. All of them, including one with Benson, disintegrated in acrimony.

In the summer of 1908 Professor R.M.Dawkins took Rolfe on holiday to Venice. He never left it. Despite enormous hardship in which he had to be increasingly grateful for his robust constitution, Rolfe found an emotional refuge there and in return added to its legends. His letters to Charles Masson Fox, published as *The Venice Letters* (ed. Cecil Woolf, 1972), were appeals for money via detailed and exuberant homosexual depictions of lagoon life. Before his death in the Palazzo Marcello from heart failure, Rolfe found a generous patron in the Reverend Justus Serjeant whose allowances briefly enabled Rolfe to indulge his fantasies for the first time. He became a tourist attraction by parading on the waters in an outrageously caparisoned boat, reclining on a leopard skin, and rowed by his boy lovers in livery.

Rolfe's 'Romance of Modern Venice', *The Desire and Pursuit of the Whole*, was not published until 1934, the same year as the book to which he owes his resurrection, A.J.A. Symons's *The Quest for Corvo*. Two other important novels were published posthumously, *Nicholas Crabbe, or the One and the Many* (1958), a picture of London literary life which stands between *Hadrian* and *The Desire* in the autobiographical trilogy wherein Rolfe recast his adult life; and *Don Renato, or an Ideal Content* (1963), the diary of a priest attached to Don Tarquinio's family in the early sixteenth century – Rolfe had suppressed it on the verge of publication in 1909.

In these large fantastic books with their love of richness and careful exaggeration, Rolfe provides an unexpected link between the works of Charles Dickens* and Mervyn Peake. Bitter and crazed though he was, there is something truly heroic in his life, and in his writings a conviction and artistry which endure.

Despite the pedantry and the religiosity, Rolfe is an authentic sensualist, guiltless and spirited. His fascination with surface, his love of language, verbal invention, and the tactility of prose, the brilliance of his imagery, express a joy in physical existence whose presiding deity was of the Toto type: direct, beautiful, animal, warm. Rolfe's Catholicism was a wholesome flight to the senses in a world of Victorian inhibition. His love of the Italian Renaissance grew from his vigorous distaste for English puritanism. It was in the tradition of Pater's* and Symonds's preoccupation with pagan Greece and Rome, but it was sharper, more open, and much more modern.

Duncan Fallowell

See: Donald Weeks, *Corvo* (1971); Miriam J. Benkovitz, *Frederick Rolfe: Baron Corvo* (1977).

381
ROSSETTI, Christina Georgina 1830–94

British poet

The nineteenth century is full of examples of lives which imitate and fulfil the principles and intentions of art, and among the most interesting of these in terms both of personality and career is that of the subdued and somewhat enigmatic figure of Christina Georgina Rossetti. The innumerable likenesses of her by painters and photographers (notably her brother Dante Gabriel Rossetti* and that most distinguished of amateurs Lewis Carroll* testify to her remarkable ability to represent, better perhaps than a professional model, a prevailing artistic idea of form and intelligence towards which the more thoughtful Victorians could stretch out. As the Virgin in her brother's superb treatment of the Annunciation, *Ecce Ancilla Domini* (though she was merely one among several types studied for the figure), she contributed, not only through her facial features but through a characteristic expression of sombre intuitiveness, to a species of womanhood far removed from the mixture of upholstery and 'accomplishments' which constituted the orthodox mid-century ideal of femininity. Yet she was not, in any declared sense, a feminist, and her life was well characterized by her brother William Michael as 'replete with the spirit of self-postponement'.

Her upbringing and childhood world were as ordinary as being the daughter of a free-thinking Neapolitan *improvvisatore* and an Anglican schoolmistress, whose Italian father had written a successful horror story before committing suicide, would allow. In the atmosphere of the Rossetti household, noisy with 'fleshy good-natured Neapolitans, keen Tuscans, emphatic Romans' and the *enragé* painter friends of her brothers (including Millais* and Holman Hunt*, with whom they banded together as the Pre-Raphaelite group) Christina herself was a shrewd and tranquil presence, partly owing, as contemporaries were aware, to a natural vein of indolence, and partly to a love of solitude and retirement which made many of her acquaintance wonder why she shrank from joining any of the contemplative religious societies which Tractarianism and the reviving interest in Romanism had made popular.

Certainly her concerns were more frankly devotional than those of either William Michael, who substantially supported his family on the earnings of a civil service clerk, or Dante Gabriel, for whom religious subjects were simply the fuel to a tumid visual imagination. Christian faith played a large part in her rejection of two suitors, to both of whom she was nevertheless deeply attached. In deference to her scruples the Catholic painter James Collinson converted to Anglicanism, but a deep pang of conscience sent him back to Catholicism and lost him Christina. Religious issues were again involved in her estrangement from Charles Bagot-Cayley, though she continued to love and esteem him. She seems, indeed, to have meditated entering a convent on various occasions, but the thoughts which finally gave her pause are powerfully conveyed in her poem 'The Convent Threshold'.

Much of her later life had, in any case, those qualities of retirement built into it for which she most craved. It is impossible to view her role as an affectionate daughter and sister and a long-suffering invalid without relating these to her evident desire to distance herself from a world whose more trivial realities meant less and less to her. The preoccupation of the Pre-Raphaelite circle with a romantically envisaged medieval past, linked as this obsession was with ideas which, voiced by Ruskin* and Morris*, were to create a marked and enduring strain in modern English liberal culture, found a ready echo in Christina's poetry, some of the very best written in the century's later decades and only recently starting to earn a reappraisal. Her diction is correspondingly touched with moments of High Art quaintness, and like Morris, Jean Ingelow and others of her generation, she is heavily influenced by the form, rhythm and vocabulary of the early English ballads.

The themes of her poems reflect her concern with retirement, not simply from the life around her, but from existence iteself. She is arguably the most morbid of all the Victorian poets, in an age which invested death with a unique quality of melodrama. Yet her treatment of dying and burial is calm, reflective and wholly lacking in sentimentality or hysteria. Her imagination is of a type which builds upon the positive aspects of worldly renunciation without gloom or regret, and in certain of her shorter pieces she comes curiously close, both in mood and in the assurance of her technique, to the writers of the seventeenth-century meditative tradition which was being rediscovered in the years immediately before her death in 1894.

Like her brother Dante Gabriel she was an accomplished sonneteer, with a firm grasp of the medium's more flexible and immediate qualities which relates works such as her 'Monna Innominata' (from *A Pageant and Other Poems*, 1881) to Mrs Browning's* influential 'Sonnets from the Portuguese' and distinguishes Christina from the jewelled preciosity of some of her male imitators of the 1890s. Of her longer poems the finest are unquestionably the allegorical *Prince's Progress* of 1866 and the almost insidiously subtle *Goblin Market* of 1862, a tale of sin and redemption which, both in overtones and undertones, held a powerful appeal for her contemporaries. Hers is a quiet, authoritative voice, not obviously linked with any literary trend except those she created for herself, and her work, after the inevitable period of rejection, now commands an increasing critical interest.

Jonathan Keates

Works: *Poetical Works of Christina Rossetti* (1904) and *The Family Letters of Christina Georgina Rossetti* (1908), both ed. William M. Rossetti. See: Margaret Sawtell, *Christina Rossetti: Her Life and Religion* (1955); Lona Mosk Packer, *Christina Rossetti* (1963); Georgina Battiscombe, *Christina Rossetti* (1965).

382

ROSSETTI, Dante Gabriel (Gabriel Charles Dante Rossetti) 1828–82

British painter and poet

More than that of most creative men, Rossetti's was a divided nature. At its simplest this is reflected in his Anglo-Italian background out of which came the translations from Dante (who was always an obsession, hence the transposition of his Christian names, and who was drawn, like most of Rossetti's iconography, from a not wholly imaginary time when the Renaissance overlapped the Middle Ages) and the early Italian poets (1861, revised as *Dante and his Circle*, 1874). At its deepest was an impossible conflict between the spiritual and the sensual which he attempted to overcome by transferring to art much that had previously belonged to religion and to sexual love, hence the charge of fleshliness made in poetry by Robert Buchanan (*The Fleshly School of Poetry*, 1871) and in painting by Holman Hunt*, who in a letter as early as 1860 said that Rossetti's picture *Bocca Baciata* was 'remarkable for gross sensuality of a revolting kind'. The assertion of the flesh was of course an urgent need in Rossetti's day although it is typical of his neurosis that he was never comfortable with the nude.

The ambivalence of his origins, aggravated by a patchy education in London (where he was born and where, on the whole, he lived) made Rossetti both pugnacious and socially sensitive. He was a natural leader but his confidence and powers of application were constantly undermined by an excess of self-questioning. He was lazy and brooding, and therefore came to venerate inspiration – always a woman. He was extremely vulnerable to criticism and suffered from periods of persecution mania. He disliked showing in public and stopped doing so as soon as his reputation was made, retaining the copyright of his pictures to prevent their unauthorized exhibition. He was an exaggerated Romantic, not a Decadent, because in him remorse was pitched as high as passion and he vibrated helplessly between these two points of command. The only possibility for blunting this conflict was the horrible descent into melancholy. His work is dominated by the autumnal mode, but never was this mode more vehement.

In the heyday of bohemianism in London and Paris, when the writings of Ruskin* and Baudelaire* had revived the romance of the artistic life, Rossetti's was as artistic as any. His was the originating genius of the Pre-Raphaelite movement. He and Elizabeth Siddal (known as 'Guggums') were the classic Pre-Raphaelite couple, imprisoned by guilt, anxiety and death. She took to veronal, gave birth to a dead child, and within two years of their marriage killed herself. Stricken by a bad conscience, Rossetti buried a manuscript of poems with her. But in 1869, seven years later, at the prompting of Charles Howell who supervised the macabre operation, the manuscript was exhumed and published as *Poems* (1870) – naturally to great acclaim. In that year Rossetti also completed his portrait of Elizabeth, *Beata Beatrix*, perhaps his greatest picture. Yet he was unable to exorcize her – on the contrary, he attempted to make contact through seances. Buchanan's attack precipitated a collapse in 1872 and Rossetti tried to commit suicide by swallowing a bottle of laudanum: his morbidity had been made insufferable by an obsession for William Morris's* wife, Jane. But the tortured dreamer was also a hard-headed man of business. He derived a large income from the *nouveau riche* magnates of the north of England (*Astarte Syriaca*, his most ambitious portrait of Jane Morris, was commissioned by Clarence Fry for two thousand guineas) and was tough in his dealings with clients. Many of his finest pictures are now to be found in the public galleries of Manchester and Liverpool. Rossetti became addicted to chloral, taken originally for insomnia, and was helped through his last years by Watts-Dunton and finally Hall Caine.

It is understandable that a man for whom art was simply a more vivid form of life should extend his activity into literature and aesthetics generally. His poetry provides a link in the strain of mysticism which passes between Blake and Yeats, although in Rossetti's case this is usually expressed as 'yearning'. But it is the distinctive intensity of his visual imagination which continues to be fascinating, especially in his portraits of women where his sexuality is made ferocious by denial. The Rossetti woman was such an extreme type that she came to be fixed in the popular mind as the Art Woman, to be replaced eventually not by Isadora Duncan but by the attenuated figures of Edith Sitwell and Virginia Woolf. Heavy, fecund, the embodiment of a lust made drowsy with the weight of accumulated delay, but capable, when aroused by the inflictions of sado-masochism, of an overwhelming congress, she is empress-like in scale, but whether one sees her as an Amazon or a cow depends on mood because she is both (Rossetti's menagerie at Tudor House in Chelsea included a Brahmin bull because he said its eyes reminded him of Jane Morris's). These female figures, like Michelangelo's male nudes on the Sistine ceiling, border on the grotesque, even on the comic, but the laughter is uneasy and they remain very powerful presences, unlike anything else in art.

Rossetti liked to play up his English aspect but it was the infusion of his warm Mediterranean blood into the English artistic world which supplied the audacity which the other Pre-Raphaelites required in order to fulfil themselves; because the Pre-Raphaelite movement, even when it thought otherwise, was fundamentally dedicated to a reawakening of the senses in a society dulled by habits of prudery and obligation.

Millais* was technically more accomplished, Holman Hunt more moral, and Burne-Jones* a purer master, but it is the art of Rossetti which expresses fully that crucial moment in nineteenth-century culture when the challenge to decorum is held in a paralysis of tragic passion.

Duncan Fallowell

See: Max Beerbohm, *Rossetti and his Circle* (1922); Evelyn Waugh, *A Life of Rossetti* (1928); Oswald Doughty, *A Victorian Romantic* (1949); Christopher Wood, *The Pre-Raphaelites* (1981).

383

ROSSINI, Gioachino 1792–1868

Italian composer

In 1829, the year Rossini's *Guillaume Tell* ('William Tell') was produced at the Paris Opéra, the 37 year-old composer was at the height of his brilliant career. Almost universally recognized as the greatest living Italian composer, he had left his homeland after producing a stream of successful repertoire pieces, both comic and serious. Now, with a smaller number of carefully worked scores which gestured towards (and in some senses altered) the French tradition, he had conquered Paris and the notoriously conservative Opéra. On every side impresarios and nobility clamoured for his services, both as an opera composer and an enormously well paid salon performer. Rossini's answer was to do what he had threatened for some time: he retired. During his remaining thirty-nine years he wrote no more operas and indeed produced only two major works. This artistic renunciation, unprecedented in the history of composition, has been taken by some to indicate Rossini's essential triviality; but to others it stems, at least in part, from the composer's profoundly innovative musical personality.

Gioachino Rossini was born in Pesaro in February 1792. Both his parents earned a sporadic income from music – his father as a horn player, his mother as a singer of secondary operatic roles – and as a consequence much of his early life was spent in a theatrical environment. The earliest operas, including *La cambiale di matrimonio* ('The Bill of Marriage', 1810) and *La scala di seta* ('The Silken Ladder', 1812), inevitable reflect the current fashion in Italian opera, in particular the operas of Paisiello, Cimarosa and, perhaps most significantly and long-lastingly, Mozart. Rossini's first substantial success came with *La pietra del paragone* ('The Touchstone'), peformed at La Scala, Milan, in September 1812. By the time of *Tancredi* and *L'italiana in Algeri* (both 1813) the composer (perhaps with the help of other, less well-known contemporaries) had established various set forms which were to remain

with Italian opera for the next forty or so years. Basically these were expansions of eighteenth-century set pieces: the solo aria being divided into two contrasting sections, the slow *cantabile* and the faster *cabaletta*, often with a dramatic interlude for chorus or secondary character; the duet and finale evolving similar, though more complex, articulated structures. These expanded forms had the advantage of allowing composers to inject more musico-dramatic impetus into the static, 'number opera' format, but also quickly became formulae – unthinkingly applied whatever the dramatic context.

After consolidating his North Italian success with several further operas, Rossini moved to Naples in 1815. Here, partly owing to the influence of the famous soprano Isabella Colbran, he wrote mostly serious operas, although he did find time to produce in Rome two of his most famous comedies, *Il barbiere di Siviglia* ('The Barber of Seville', 1816) and *La Cenerentola* ('Cinderella', 1817). In order to prevent singers from adding tasteless decorations, his vocal lines during this period became increasingly florid, while musico-dramatic continuity was (at least notionally) improved by using the orchestra to accompany all recitative passages. The later operas of this period, in particular *Semiramide* (1823), show a concern to develop the dramatic potential of the chorus, possibly with a view to the French tradition. In fact, *Semiramide* was the last major work Rossini was to write for Italy. In thirteen years of frenetic activity he had composed thirty-four operas; exhausted but still ambitious for the wider European stage, he moved the centre of his operations to Paris.

In France, partly through force of circumstance, partly through increasing financial security, Rossini's operatic output slowed considerably. He made a thorough study of French prosody before committing himself to the highly critical French audience, in the meantime presenting new productions of some of his most recent Italian works. Two of these, *Maometto II* and *Mosè in Egitto* ('Moses in Egypt'), underwent substantial revision and appeared in French translation (as *Le Siège de Corinthe* and *Moïse*) at the Paris Opéra. Rossini's final two operas were composed especially for Paris. *Le Comte Ory* (1828) is a comedy partly culled from earlier music, while *Guillaume Tell* (1829), based on Schiller's play, is a highly innovative grand opera. *Tell* is the culmination of the composer's French manner in its testing of the singers (particularly the tenor Arnold) with forceful, declamatory lines and its employment of the chorus and scenic effect as an essential ingredient of the drama.

As mentioned earlier, Rossini's reasons for retirement after *Tell* are not easily explained. Certainly his rapidly deteriorating health and his firm financial position were important factors. But perhaps more fundamental was his gradual realization that, after twenty years of innovation, time was beginning to overtake him. The Paris of 1830 saw Meyerbeer* as the rising star whose grand operas (proceeding in part from Rossini's example) pushed vocal declamation and grandiose scenic effect further than the sensitive Italian would ever have countenanced; in Italy, Donizetti* and Bellini* (both again profoundly influenced by Rossinian formal devices) were becoming famous through their new, more directly expressive vocal lines. Whatever the explanation, only two major works appeared after 1829, both of them religious: the *Stabat Mater* (partly composed in 1832) was first performed in Paris in 1842, and the *Petite messe solennelle*, for twelve soloists, two pianos and harmonium, in 1864. The composer's inscription on the autograph of the *Petite messe solennelle* describes the piece as scored for 'twelve singers of three sexes – men, women and castrati' and though this is the number of the apostles, Rossini swears 'that there will be no Judas at my supper and that mine will sing properly and *con amore* Thy praises and this little composition, which is, alas, the last mortal sin of my old age.' This delicate sense of irony mixed with deep religious devotion is a perfect preparation for the pieces themselves, which, in their skilful adaptation of operatic language and avoidance of operatic formulae, show that Rossini's dignified silence did not mean that he had ceased to respond as a creative musician. Towards the end of his life, the composer produced an extensive series of salon pieces (entitled *Péchés de vieillesse* – 'Sins of Old Age') which were mostly performed in musical evenings at his Paris home. Rossini died near Paris in November 1868.

Roger Parker

Other Rossini operas include: *Il Signor Bruschino* (1813); *Otello* (1816); *La gazza ladra* (1817); and *La donna del lago* (1819). About Rossini: Stendhal, *Vie de Rossini* (1824, trans. Richard N. Coe, *Life of Rossini*, (1970), is entertaining but highly unreliable; H. Weinstock, *Rossini: A Biography* (1968), is the most reliable modern biography in English.

384
ROSTAND, Edmond 1868–1918

French poet and dramatist

Edmond Rostand was born in Marseilles into a prosperous family on 1 April 1868. He studied, but never practised, law, and devoted most of his life to the theatre. His plays were interpreted by some of the most famous actors and actresses of the day: Coquelin, Sarah Bernhardt (for whom the Duc de Reichstadt in *L'Aiglon*, verse drama, 1900, was written), Lucien Guitry, de Max, and many others. Except in his last two plays he achieved an overwhelming popular success. The last twenty years or so of his life he lived principally in

Arnaga, his estate in the South of France. He died in 1918.

Rostand is obviously not today a popular dramatist, nor is he favourably treated by those few critics who bother to mention him at all. Yet *Cyrano de Bergerac* (verse heroic comedy, 1897) is widely read and fairly frequently revived, if only because it provides a spectacular 'vehicle' in Coquelin's old role of Cyrano. *L'Aiglon* too is read and acted in France and was revived on British television some years ago, though it is too lachrymose and chauvinistic for modern taste.

The popularity of the plays in their own day largely depended on their defiant patriotism, their colourful, self-indulgent lyricism, their wit and astounding verbal acrobatics and their uninhibited Romantic challenge to the grim Naturalism of European literature of their time. The Dreyfus scandal may also have helped to give French audiences a taste for romantic entertainment, and particularly for such a self-congratulatory image of France as Rostand's plays provided. He himself came out strongly in support of Dreyfus in the controversy, which was at its height when *Cyrano de Bergerac* was produced.

Rostand's greatest debt is clearly to Victor Hugo's* dramas and dramatic theories about the mixture of the sublime and the grotesque. He follows Hugo in his elaborate plots, his combination of lyricism and melodrama – though in Rostand the lyricism is more strained and the melodrama less portentous heavy-handed. The characters too are for the most part taken from the Romantic stock, where an unpromising physique is almost a guarantee of a heart of gold, and where boundless if rather simple-minded ambitions are thwarted by the heroes' incapacity for ordinary action. But, whereas Hugo's heroes live in an unambiguous, if improbable, world of virtue and misconduct – Lucrèce Borgia knows she's a bad lot – Rostand's *La Princesse Lointaine* (1895) and *L'Aiglon* for example breathe a far more sentimental and decadent air: the moral worlds of these plays are far more ambiguous.

Though *La Princesse Lointaine* suffers from its echoes of *Phèdre* and *Tristan und Isolde* and though Rostand's sensibility makes *L'Aiglon* almost unendurably mawkish, his main virtue is an unerring, if somewhat extravagant, sense of what goes in the theatre. The poetry is too lush, the verbal tricks and clever rhymes become an irritating mannerism, and his habit of endlessly embroidering a verbal effect can be tiring; but he has a wonderful skill in painting a scene, managing intricate crowd conversation and movement, and developing an argument, – qualities that all but triumph over his obvious weaknesses. His dialogue is sparkling and varied. Above all, he has a sense of humour and an eye for the absurd: despite his models, his plays are rarely unintentionally funny. In fact, it is as a writer of comedy that he excels: if *La Princesse Lointaine*, *La Samaritaine* (biblical verse drama, 1897) and even

L'Aiglon are for one reason or another virtually unreadable today, there is still life in *Les Romanesques* (verse comedy, 1894) despite the pawkiness of this little Romeo and Juliet-inspired comedy, while the atmospheric and ingenious *La Dernière Nuit de Don Juan* (dramatic poem, posthumous) is in its way masterly, and *Chantecler* (verse play, 1910) though difficult to imagine in the theatre, and again much too long-winded, has moments of real beauty and inspiration.

If Rostand is a flawed dramatist in general, *Cyrano de Bergerac* is a triumph. It has been criticized for being improbable – which it is; psychologically inconsistent – which it is; historically inaccurate, and many uncomplimentary things (all in their way true) besides. But here in this one play Rostand has created a masterpiece, almost despite himself. His sentimentality, his ingenuity, his verbosity, his skill in the direction of crowd scenes, his outrageous rhymes, even his exaggerated and schematic characterization; above all the sheer energy – the famous *panache* – carry the audience along. The very theatricality of the play saves it from the fate of much Romantic drama: it has the courage of its own artificiality. Whereas Hugo's heroes demand – impossibly – to be taken seriously, Rostand's hero is protected by the irony with which he is presented: he is sublime *because* he is absurd. The play's artificiality and excess allow the spectator to enter imaginatively into a purely theatrical context, where improbability ceases to be an obstacle to our acceptance of the hero. The nineteenth-century Romantic heroes generally fail to convince because we are aware that for all their 'historical' authenticity they belong in the property-box. Cyrano lives only in the imagination: Rostand has invented a folk-hero whom we can accept on much the same terms as we accept Bluebeard or Baron Munchhausen. We can forget that Rostand was at best a derivative minor poet: *Cyrano de Bergerac* may not have the literary quality of Musset's* *Lorenzaccio*, but between them they show that Romantic tragedy and heroic comedy should not necessarily be despised.

Joseph Bain

For a translation of the plays see *Plays of Edmond Rostand*, trans. Henderson D. Norman (2 vols, 1921). See: Jean Suberville, *Le Théâtre d'Edmond Rostand* (1919); R. Gerard, *Edmond Rostand* (1935); Hobart Ryland, *The Sources of the Play Cyrano de Bergerac* (1936).

385
ROUSSEAU, Henri (known as Le Douanier)
1844–1910

French painter

After a period in the French army, Henri Rousseau worked for some years as a minor official in the Paris toll-gate service, whence the grandiose nickname he later received: 'Le Douanier', the Customs Officer. He was in his forties before he began to paint, but he at once found his idiom and gave up his job to devote himself to art, making a living from occasional private lessons in painting and music. From 1886 onwards he regularly exhibited in Paris at the annual Salon des Indépendants, his intention clearly being to gain recognition as an artist among other artists; this aim he pursued with dignity and total dedication, even though many considered his entries to be a standing joke. His reputation grew as sponsorship came from a succession of writers and artists, whose attitude seems to have evolved from tongue-in-cheek patronage to genuine, somewhat startled enthusiasm. The poets Alfred Jarry* and, later, Guillaume Apollinaire had their portraits painted by Rousseau; Robert Delaunay became a sincere admirer and friend, while Picasso began collecting his pictures in the same spirit as he collected African tribal art – seeing in them a significant formal stimulus and a demonstration of the power of innocent vision. Half figure of fun, half aesthetic innovator, Rousseau was to emerge as both mascot and exemplar for the *avant-garde* of Fauvism and Cubism; his mixture of naivety and skill fulfilled a necessary myth of spontaneity, of inventive design liberated from academic constraints.

Almost entirely an autodidact, Rousseau kept to a narrow range of favourite subjects: principally portraits, cityscapes and exotic landscapes. The portraits, usually of neighbours and their children, give the clearest indication of his untutored hand: sitters are portrayed as monumental figures with stereotyped features standing woodenly in decorative parkland. Rousseau's cityscapes record picturesque aspects of Paris and environs, often showing bourgeois families out for a Sunday stroll in the public gardens or along the river; they are characterized by the naive artist's affection for the telling detail: the distant Eiffel Tower, an ostentatiously posed fisherman, an airship as if pinned up on the sky. The impression of whimsicality mingled with painstaking literalness modulates into something more compelling when Rousseau turns to imaginary exotic landscapes; it is indeed these which have most contributed to his reputation as a naive who somehow transcends his naivety.

Rousseau's art is certainly 'naive' in the sense that it falls short of the standards of traditional mimesis to which, it appears, he nevertheless diligently sought to conform. His figures look frozen stiff rather than simply immobile; his sense of scale is aberrant, his grasp of perspective faulty. But undismayed by such deficiencies (if indeed he ever recognized them as such), Rousseau was able to compile a repertoire of compensatory virtues. His sharply outlined and flattened figures can have a strange formal seductiveness: a chestnut-tree or a standing woman take on an emblematic radiance once placed within a scene. And the meticulous rendering of detail, the insistent patterning of such repeated elements as foliage, the concern for nuances of colouring, the compulsive brushing-in of each last square inch of canvas – these symptoms of over-earnestness, of the naive's desire to produce 'the professional look' at all costs, do end up creating an idiom of intensity which has a coherence and an allurement all of its own.

Rousseau's most powerful effect – a kind of hypnotic translucency of finish – is nowhere more memorably achieved than in the series of paintings of wild beasts in exotic settings. In *The Sleeping Gypsy* (*La Bohémienne endormie*, 1897), a lion is shown nuzzling a sleeping woman beneath a desert moon. The woman, black-skinned and massive, wears a dress patterned in bright multicoloured stripes which echo the design on her pillow and the parallels of the strings on the nearby mandoline. The contrast between this visual dazzlement and the stark simplicity of the surrounding sand, hills and sky creates an effect of visual consternation and a queer mood of suspense. In *The Snake Charmer* (*La Charmeuse de serpents*, 1907), a naked negress plays her flute by the river bank. As snakes sway towards her out of the jungle, she herself remains in shadow, an inexplicable silhouette set against the gleaming water and sky: we discern only two staring eyes within the illegible blackness of her form. The impression is of hidden depths, an enigma equally suggestive of unspoken ferocity and utopian tenderness.

Several jungle paintings exploit the incongruity of setting a lady in splendid town clothes down in the middle of a profusion of tropical vegetation. Such a juxtaposition of the familiar and the extraordinary is a favourite device, and may be seen as translating Rousseau's basic project of offering us windows through which we can perceive the world in an adventurous new way. However it cannot be claimed that the jungle pictures, with their rampant beasts of prey, eccentric birds and tropical storms, are at all naturalistic. The animals are frequently derived from such sources as illustrations in popular encylopaedias; the plants are thought to be largely inspired by Rousseau's visits to the tropical section of the botanical gardens in Paris, the Jardin des Plantes. And whole pictures have been shown to be the result of simplified copying from undistinguished engravings. Yet by a curious reversal, Rousseau's images are at their most compelling to the extent that they are manifestly unrealistic and thus most overtly fantastical. His most sophisticated performances arise from a fine balance between the theatrics of his jungle tableaux, where leaping jaguars and flamboyant orchids appear almost to be snipped out from cardboard, and the sheer resplendence and depth of his colours – he once boasted that he had used twenty-two variants of green in a single canvas – and

no less a colourist than Gauguin* is said to have envied him his command of black tones.

Elevated by the *avant-garde* into a kind of cult hero for Modernism, Rousseau has a claim to being seen as a central figure in the development of twentieth-century art. His influence has been traced to Surrealism and the work of De Chirico, and to the current of Magical Realism in Germany and Austria. As a naive, Rousseau also takes his place in the specific history of neo-primitive painting. Promoted in the twenties by collectors such as Wilhelm Uhde, who placed him with other naives like Séraphine Louis and Camille Bombois, he has since been universally acknowledged as the grand master of naive art in this century. Meanwhile, seen within a more academically respectable perspective, his work has been considered worthy of representation in the Louvre and the National Gallery in London.

How then should Rousseau finally be evaluated? It has to be said quite bluntly that some of his pictures reveal the untutored hand at its worst; they are downright incompetent, and lack any saving grace in terms of impetuous colouring or artless design. Again, several paintings have that fussy prettiness which is one of the less stimulating characteristics of naive art. But above these loom the true masterpieces, from *A Carnival Evening* (*Un Soir de Carnaval* c. 1886) to *The Dream* (*Le Rêve* 1910), a series of works which remain marvellously authoritative and consistently appealing. These are paintings whose subject matter may be palpably ridiculous or else merely trivial, yet whose technical execution lifts everything on to an entirely fresh expressive plane. In them, Rousseau is able to transcend all the ready-made categories and to assert his originality as the creator of an inimitable personal style.

Roger Cardinal

See: Ronald Alley, *Portrait of a Primitive: The Art of Henri Rousseau* (1978); Adolphe Basler, *Henri Rousseau* (Paris, 1927); Roger Shattuck, *The Banquet Years* (1969); Wilhelm Uhde, *Henri Rousseau* (Dresden, 1921); Dora Vallier, *Henri Rousseau* (Cologne, 1961).

386
ROY, Ram Mohun 1772–1833

Hindu social reformer

A Hindu religious and social reformer, Ram Mohun Roy is regarded by some as the father of modern India. Born into a wealthy rural family in the Burdwan district of West Bengal in 1772, he spent the first thirty years of his life mastering Sanskrit, Farsi (Persian), Arabic, Hebrew, Greek, and English. He combined a study of the scriptures of major religions in the original with widespread travelling. At the age of thirty-one he began a successful career with the (British) East India Company: it lasted twelve years. After retiring in 1815, he moved to Calcutta.

Here he engaged himself in religious, social and political work. He founded Atimaya Sabha (Spiritual Association) and used it *inter alia* as a vehicle for propagating his reformist views on Hinduism. During the period 1815–19 he published a Bengali translation of the *Upanishadas*: Hindu scriptures in Sanskrit which deal primarily with metaphysics and subjective analysis (*atman*). He also published his ideas on Hindu theism. In his *Precepts of Jesus* (1820), he rejected the theology of Christianity but accepted its humanitarian and ethical teachings.

In 1823 he appealed to Lord Amherst, the governor-general of British India (with its capital in Calcutta), to introduce scientific and English teaching into Indian schools which, run along traditional lines, limited themselves to teaching classical subjects, primarily Sanskrit. At the same time, as a champion of political reform, he campaigned for the repeal of the repressive Press Ordinance of 1823. He established newspapers in Bengali, Farsi (the official language of the Moghul empire administered from Delhi) and English. He also founded secondary schools where modern subjects were included in the curriculum.

In 1828, Roy transformed Atimaya Sabha into Brahmo Samaj (Society of God). Influenced by Christianity and Islam, Brahmo Samaj members denounced polytheism and expressed belief in only one Hindu deity: Brahma, the Creator. They were opposed to what they considered medieval practices of Hinduism: animal sacrifice, idol worship, polygamy and the caste system. Advocating a return to the basic principles of Hinduism, as outlined in the *Upanishadas*, they stressed rationalism rather than faith. The Brahmo Samaj movement won many converts among upper caste professionals and intellectuals in Bengal, and prepared the ground which, a century later, yielded a rich crop of Marxists and radical nationalists.

Roy's campaign against *suttee* – the practice of immolation of a widow on the funeral pyre of her dead husband – succeeded in 1829: Lord Bentick, the British governor-general, banned the practice. The next year Roy left India for London to plead the case of the Moghul emperor before the British government. In this he was only marginally successful. Following a long illness, he died in Bristol in September 1833.

Dilip Hiro

See: Upendr Nath Bala, *Biography of Ram Mohun Roy* (1933); Iqbal Singh, *Ram Mohun Roy: A Biographical Inquiry into the Making of Modern India* (1956).

387
RUSKIN, John 1819–1900

British writer on art and critic of society

John Ruskin was the only man of his century whose writings on painting and architecture were widely read outside specialist circles; and the extent of his influence in artistic matters has never been matched. He achieved this pre-eminence, however, without publicizing the trivial or immediately appealing aspects of art. On the contrary, he subjected his readers to a stern re-examination of the fundamental principles of art, and its connections with human personality and social behaviour.

The only child of a wealthy sherry importer, John Ruskin was educated privately in south London, but the seclusion of his childhood was relieved by annual tours with his parents, in Britain and abroad. By the age of twenty he had published scholarly essays on geographical phenomena, and a book-length series of articles entitled *The Poetry of Architecture*. At Oxford University he gained a reputation as a skilful water-colourist and amateur geologist. In 1843, as 'A Graduate of Oxford', he published the first volume of *Modern Painters*, boldly proclaiming 'the superiority of the modern painters to the old ones', and eulogizing above all the art of J.M.W. Turner*. Ruskin was scathing in his analysis of many of the established masters of the seventeenth-century painting, but won respect nevertheless for his acute observation of nature and for his lyrical evocations of Turner's art.

In 1845, on a momentous visit to Italy, Ruskin 'discovered' the work of the fourteenth- and fifteenth-century artists of Pisa, Florence and Venice. It was these artists, together with Tintoretto, who were the heroes of the second volume of *Modern Painters* (1846). Ruskin commended the sense of calm devotion which he discerned in the painting of the early Italian masters, contrasting this quality with the insipidity and self-absorption which he found in the work of Raphael and his successors of the 'High Renaissance'. These sentiments were largely shared by a group of young British artists, led by William Holman Hunt*, John Millais*, and Dante Gabriel Rossetti*, who formed the Pre-Raphaelite Brotherhood in 1848; and when in 1851 the Pre-Raphaelites were fiercely criticized, Ruskin defended them in the columns of *The Times*, and initiated a revival of their fortunes.

By this time Ruskin was preoccupied with architecture. In *Seven Lamps of Architecture* (1849) and *The Stones of Venice* (1851–3), he drew the attention of the public to the merits of pre-Renaissance Italian architecture, and thereby broadened the scope of the Gothic Revival in Britain; substantial evidence of his persuasive powers can still be seen in the Anglo-Venetian capitals and arches of many an English suburb – as Ruskin himself observed, and regretted, in later life. These books also exerted a more fundamental influence on Victorian attitudes to architecture. *Seven Lamps* put forward, a little clumsily, the notion of architecture as a manifestation of such moral qualities as 'truth', 'life' and 'sacrifice'. Then *The Stones of Venice*, Ruskin's *tour de force*, fully exemplified his conception that a work of art reflects the personality of its creator – and in the case of architecture, a collective personality or age-spirit, whose growth, health and decay could be traced even in the smallest details of architectural decoration.

Ruskin espoused architecture, however, at the expense of his wife, who left him in 1854. Their marriage, which in six years had not been consummated, was annulled, and she married Millais in the following year. Meanwhile Ruskin began to patronize Rossetti, and his writing proved an inspiration to William Morris* and Edward Burne-Jones*, whose enthusiasm carried Pre-Raphaelite principles into many branches of the decorative arts. They inherited from Ruskin a hostility to classical and Renaissance culture which extended to the arts and design of their own time. Ruskin and his followers believed that the nineteenth century was still afflicted by a demand for mass-production and standardization which had been initiated in the sixteenth century or even earlier. They opposed themselves to mechanized production, meaningless ornament and anonymous architecture of cast iron and plate glass – all symbolized in the Great Exhibition and Crystal Palace of 1851.

Towards the end of the 1850s Ruskin's message was significantly redirected. As he lost his faith in the Protestant Christianity of his youth, he became less confident in the correlation of artistic merit with purity of soul, and found a new respect for the 'magnificent animality' of Titian, Giorgione and Veronese. He taught drawing at the Working Men's College, and became concerned increasingly with the economic and social aspects of art. In his Manchester lectures of 1857, on 'The Political Economy of Art' (republished as *A Joy for Ever*), he emerged as an articulate opponent of capitalism and the ideology of *laissez-faire*. The pursuit of profit, he maintained, condemned the working man to an inhuman existence of mindless routine. Proclaiming that the principle of cooperation was superior to that of competition, he called for a return to the guild system of craftsmanship, the manufacture of articles of lasting value, and a steady wage guaranteed by a strong, paternal government.

These proposals were unacceptable to many of Ruskin's contemporaries; the fury aroused by a series of articles written by Ruskin for the *Cornhill Magazine*, attacking the libertarian principles of Ricardo* and J.S. Mill*, prompted its editor, Thackeray*, to cut short the series. But in the succeeding decades these articles, reprinted as *Unto this Last*, reached a wide audience; such diverse figures as Tolstoy*, Mahatma

Gandhi and the early leaders of the British Labour movement acknowledged the powerful influence of *Unto this Last* on their own philosophy.

Conversely, those works of Ruskin's which were most popular at the time of publication – *Sesame and Lilies* (1864) and *The Ethics of the Dust* (1866) – have appealed much less to subsequent generations. These offered advice to young men and women on their proper roles in life, with (in the second work) elaborate geological and botanical allegories. Ruskin continued to revel in controversy, however, lecturing to the cadets of Woolwich Academy on the glories of war, and advising the citizens of Bradford to decorate their new town hall with pendant purses in honour of their presiding deity, the 'Goddess of Getting-on' (*The Crown of Wild Olive*, 1866).

The last decades of his life were occupied with short-lived philanthropic ventures, unrequited love for young girls, lectures delivered as Slade Professor of Fine Art at Oxford University, and debilitating bouts of mental illness, whose effects are often evident in his monthly publication commenced in 1871, *Fors Clavigera*. In these 'Letters to the Workmen and Labourers of Great Britain' he pronounced erratically on art, literature, mythology and political economy. In an early issue he launched 'The St George's Guild', a form of rural commune financed principally by himself, on which there were to be 'no steam engines . . . no untended creatures . . . no liberty'. The Guild gained few Companions, but much of its museum still survives.

In a later issue of *Fors* Ruskin criticized a painting by Whistler*, *Nocturne in Black and Gold: The Falling Rocket*: 'I never expected to hear a coxcomb ask two hundred guineas for flinging a pot of paint in the public's face.' Whistler sued for libel, won a farthing's damages without costs, and was bankrupted. Ruskin was perhaps seen as the moral victor, but in retrospect this celebrated lawsuit of 1878 has come to symbolize the clash between the traditional but outmoded values of figurative art and the daring innovations of the modern movement – an ironic reversal of roles in the case of Ruskin, once the champion of the *avant-garde*.

Ruskin spent most of his final fifteen years as an invalid at Brantwood, near Coniston, but managed to produce one last major work: his unfinished autobiography *Praeterita*, which, although unreliable in matters of fact, is as compellingly lucid as any of the works of his prime.

Patrick Conner

Most of Ruskin's works have been reprinted individually since 1970. The standard collection remains *The Works of John Ruskin*, ed. E.T. Cook and A. Wedderburn (39 vols, 1903–12), whose massive index volume is the single most valuable aid to the study of Ruskin. Since that compilation, however, many volumes of Ruskin's letters and diaries have

been published, notably *The Diaries of John Ruskin*, ed.
Joan Evans and John H. Whitehouse (3 vols, 1956–
9): these are listed in *Ruskin, a Bibliography 1900–1974*,
ed. H. Kirk Beetz (1977), which supplements
*Bibliography of the Writings in Prose and Verse of John
Ruskin*, ed. J. Wise (Dawson reprint, 1964). Recent
studies include: Quentin Bell, *Ruskin* (1963); Robert
Hewison, *John Ruskin: The Argument of the Eye* (1976);
John D. Unrau, *Looking at Architecture with Ruskin*
(1978); Patrick Conner, *Savage Ruskin* (1979); Joan
Abse, *John Ruskin: The Passionate Moralist* (1980); John
Dixon Hunt, *The Wider Sea: A Life of John Ruskin*
(1982). Ruskin's artistic output is examined in Paul
Walton, *The Drawings of John Ruskin* (1972).

S

388

SAIGŌ TAKAMORI 1828–77

Japanese hero, rebel and government member

Saigō was born to a minor official in the Satsuma fief, which was in the far south of Japan and had long cherished a spirit of independence and reluctant subservience to central government authority. He was reportedly blessed with an enormous frame and an amiable disposition and these factors helped him acquire a certain prominence within the fief, where he was associated with the anti-government side in the years leading up to the Meiji Restoration of 1868. Under the patronage of the *daimyo* of the fief he took part in a number of delicate political intrigues in the capital and elsewhere, but upon the latter's death in 1858 Saigō was caught up in a purge of anti-government elements and spent some five years in internal exile. It was also at this time that he made an abortive suicide attempt: his failure seems to have nurtured in him something of a death-wish and it may well have exerted the influence on his future conduct it is often supposed to have done.

Once he had been released from his place of exile, he threw himself once again into anti-government activities and was instrumental in organizing the coalition of southern fiefs whose concerted action sealed the fate of the Tokugawa government and ushered in the Meiji Restoration, whereby power was nominally restored to the emperor after centuries of military rule. Saigō also played a leading role in some of the military operations accompanying the Restoration, but was noted for his attempts to minimize the bloodshed. He was subsequently offered high honours by the new government in recognition of his services, but he declined them, although he did in 1871 yield to requests that he join the government: he was made a counsellor of state, thereby participating in the governance of Japan, and the following year he was given command of all the armed forces in the land. However, he was soon disturbed by the indulgence of his colleagues in the trappings and personal perquisites of office, all of which he disdained, and by the pace of the centralization and westernization being carried out by the government to which he belonged.

During 1872–3 many members of the government were overseas on the Iwakura mission to Europe and America, which reminded Japanese government leaders forcefully of Japan's relative backwardness and the fragility of her international position. Saigō, however, stayed at home and became embroiled in a diplomatic dispute with Korea. Japanese efforts in 1872 to have Korea open its doors to trade had been rebuffed and the emperor's dignity had been impugned. Saigō and others were in favour of a punitive mission and Saigō proposed that he be sent to Korea as an ambassador, fully expecting that he would be killed there, in which event an invasion would be justified. Amongst his motives for favouring an invasion was the desire to provide opportunities for the Samurai class, which by then had been dispossessed by the Meiji government and which in Saigō's opinion had been shamefully treated. However, the returned members of the Iwakura mission were convinced that the priorities were to develop Japan's economic and military strength and not to indulge in costly overseas adventures that might arouse the antagonism of the European powers, and they managed to scotch Saigō's plan. Saigō thereupon left the government, as did a number of his supporters, and withdrew to Satsuma where he poured his resources into educational establishments specializing in agriculture, the military arts and moral training. And he refused several offers from his former government colleagues, who wished him to return to their circles.

In 1874 and subsequent years there was a number of minor rebellions of former Samurai in various parts of the country. The leaders of some of these had been associated with Saigō, so the government became anxious about a possible uprising in Satsuma and attempted to move arms and ammunition by boat from the largest city in the province to a safer location. However, as soon as they heard of the attempt, some of Saigō's younger followers launched an attack, thereby forestalling the move as well as translating hostility into open rebellion. Saigō was aware that he could not hope to be successful against the forces the government had at its disposal but nevertheless he took up leadership of the rebellion and declared that his quarrel was not with the emperor but with his malicious and wrong-headed advisers, a formula that has often been resorted to in Japanese history. The army ranged against Saigō and his adherents was vastly superior in both numbers and supplies. The campaign lasted seven months and cost many casualties, but the new army of peasant conscripts proved itself in combat against Saigō's Samurai army and thus put an end to the military supremacy of the Samurai. When the end was near Saigō disembowelled himself, and most of his followers did the same or were killed.

In spite of the rebellion and his official disgrace, Saigō has remained a popular and respected figure. In 1890 he was posthumously pardoned and restored to his former ranks. He had been one of the key figures in the Restoration movement and one of the Meiji leaders, but his political influence was never great and the reasons for his lasting popularity must be sought elsewhere. Thus Saigō could easily be seen as the representative of all those who were feeling left behind by the rapid changes Japan was going through. He was one of the few government members who had never visited the West, his tastes were simple in the extreme and untouched by the tide of westernization, and he remained attached to his provincial origins in the midst of the Tokyo-centred world of Meiji Japan. So he could be and was admired both by nationalists, for his defence of traditional Japanese values, and by radicals, for the anti-Establishment strand in his life.

Peter Kornicki

See: I. Morris, *The Nobility of Failure* (1975); and H. Borton, *Japan's Modern Century* (2nd edn, 1970).

389
SAINTE-BEUVE, Charles Augustin 1804–69

French writer and critic

Born at Boulogne-sur-mer, he was educated in that town and in Paris where, after studying medicine, he devoted himself entirely to literature. Friendship with the young Romantics, especially Victor Hugo*, led him to defend the new movement in his *Tableau historique et critique de la poésie française au XVI⁴ siècle* ('Historical and Critical Outline of French Poetry in the Sixteenth Century', 1828) which related Romanticism to the older French tradition of Ronsard and the Pléiade. In 1829 he produced a volume of elegiac verse, *Vie, poésies et pensées de Joseph Delorme* ('The Life, Poetry and Thought of Joseph Delorme'), followed by the *Consolations* (1830) and *Pensées d'août* ('August Thoughts', 1837). In 1834 he published an intimate semi-autobiographical novel *Volupté*. His achievement in creative writing was very modest and never equalled that of the major Romantic authors, even though it provides interesting evidence of the moral crisis he was undergoing at this period. He was soon to show that his real vocation lay elsewhere, for lectures he gave at Lausanne in 1838 resulted in his remarkable study of Jansenism, *Port-Royal* (1840–59). Meanwhile, he had begun to write articles for reviews, eventually collecting them into volumes of 'portraits': *Portraits littéraires*

(1832–9), *Portraits de femmes* (1844) and *Portraits contemporains* (1846). From 1848 onwards he contributed weekly articles to the *Constitutionnel, Le Moniteur* and *Le Temps* with the title of *Causeries du Lundi* ('Monday Talks', 1851–62) and *Nouveaux Lundis* ('New Monday Talks', 1863–70). A short-term professorship at Liège led to the important *Chateaubriand et son groupe littéraire sous l'empire* ('Chateaubriand* and his Circle', 1861) which was much more critical of Romanticism than his earlier studies. Appointed in 1854 to the Chair of Latin poetry at the Collège de France he resigned because of the students' hostility. He also lectured on French literature at the École Normale Supérieure. He entered the French Academy in 1844 and was appointed to the Senate in 1865.

Sainte-Beuve has been described as 'the father of modern literary criticism' not only because of his seriousness and sense of vocation but also for having given criticism a new and distinctive status: repudiating the dogmatism of earlier critics who based their judgments on absolute standards, he replaced the idea of a rigid critical system by a more flexible method. His primary aim was not to judge the authors he read but to understand them and, to do this, he carefully documented himself on their lives, character and background. His criticism was of a semi-scientific nature, for although he was – largely through jealousy or rancour – often unjust to his contemporaries, he usually made a genuine effort to be objective, trying to produce what he called the 'natural history' which would lead to the 'classification of minds'; he described himself as 'a kind of naturalist trying to understand and describe as many groups as possible'.

His objective approach to literature was combined with a wide-ranging curiosity, considerable psychological insight and a highly developed sensitivity. He insisted that he was not interested in erudition for its own sake but only in 'an erudition controlled by judgment and organized by taste'. His criticism, therefore, contained a markedly intuitive and even impressionistic element as he strove to penetrate the 'soul' of the author and period he was studying. Since he believed that it was difficult to understand a work without an adequate knowledge of the author, his criticism often had a strongly moral emphasis. Moreover, he did not limit himself to great writers but also studied minor ones as a means of understanding the psychology of their age. In the course of a long career as critic he tended to abandon his early enthusiasm for Romanticism for a great admiration for the classical era, but his classicism always remained liberal and remarkably free from dogmatism.

Sainte-Beuve affirmed that every critic should have a poetic side to him, in order to be able to appreciate beauty and at the same time to unite sensitivity to intelligence. Since he himself brought to his writing a remarkable literary gift, he not only imparted a creative quality to literary criticism but helped to make it a genre that was valid in its own right. He anticipated various aspects of modern criticism – the scientific, scholarly and impressionistic – without being completely identified with any of them. He himself summed up the function of criticism when he defined the critic as 'a man who knows how to read and teaches others how to read'.

Ronald Grimsley

In addition to the works of Sainte-Beuve already mentioned there is an important edition of his correspondence, *Correspondance Générale*, ed. J. and A. Bonnerot (1935–77), and a personal volume, *Mes Poisons*, ed. V. Giraud (1926). See also: H. Nicolson, *Sainte-Beuve* (1957); M. Regard, *Sainte-Beuve* (1959); A.G. Lehmann, *Sainte-Beuve: A Portrait of the Critic, 1804–42* (1962); P. Moreau, *La Critique selon Sainte-Beuve* (1964).

390
SAINT-SAËNS, (Charles) Camille 1835–1921

French composer

From his earliest years Camille Saint-Saëns demonstrated an astonishing facility both as composer and performer. For about eighty years he composed prolifically, and his enormous output encompasses all the nineteenth-century categories of music. Besides all this, he left a great deal of writing about music, expressing clear and strongly-held views on all aspects of his art. In composition his very facility worked against him: it all came so easily and rapidly that there seemed to be little time for self-criticism and discernment of musical quality. In consequence, only a small number of his works have withstood the test of time. He believed that a composer produces music 'as naturally as an apple-tree produces apples'. Like Stravinsky, he set little store by inspiration and the expression of emotion in his composing; the important things were clarity of style, purity of line, satisfying form. Steeped in the Viennese models of sonatas, symphonies, concertos, and strongly influenced by Mozart, Bach, Mendelssohn*, and Schumann*, Saint-Saëns pursued an art of assimilation, basically conservative, in which Austrian, German and French traditions were blended. But there were many other ingredients – the French dance forms of the seventeenth century, Spanish influences, oriental colouring – all was grist to the Saint-Saëns mill. The result is a kind of stylelessness, or rather a multitude of styles, in his works, with many saving graces – a spontaneous lyrical gift, a colourful imagination, a sense of humour and much good-humour; and always an infallible craftsmanship.

Saint-Saëns started learning the piano from his great-aunt when he was two and a half years old; and his first piano piece was written at the age of three. Eventually, he entered the Paris Conservatoire when he was thirteen; and at sixteen, his *Ode à Sainte-Cécile* (for voices and orchestra) won a prize awarded by the Société de Sainte-Cécile in Paris, and it was given a performance. He was only twenty-two when he obtained the important appointment of organist of the Madeleine. Liszt*, who became a close and lasting friend, was a strong influence in his development. Saint-Saëns began to write symphonies. For four years he taught music at the École Niedermeyer – his only teaching appointment – and among his pupils were Messager and Fauré* (another lasting friendship). Meanwhile, he had acquired a formidable reputation as a pianist and organist.

All fields, in fact, were there to be conquered. The five piano concertos, which extend over a period of about thirty years, were a showcase for Saint-Saëns to appear in the Lisztian combination of composer and virtuoso-pianist, which he did with enormous success. The second, fourth and fifth retain a popularity today – especially the fourth, in C minor, which is one of the composer's most unified and satisfying works. The fifth is known as the 'Egyptian' Concerto because it was composed in Luxor in 1895 and makes use of some oriental flavouring.

Saint-Saëns was indeed an inveterate traveller – in Europe, Africa, Indo-China, South America, and the USA – sometimes as soloist, sometimes as conductor. And he frequently visited England, where he was always warmly received – the first time in 1871, when he gave some organ recitals at London's Albert Hall. Cambridge University made him an honorary Doctor of Music in 1893.

With Romain Bussini, in 1871, Saint-Saëns founded the Société Nationale de Musique. Its motto, *Ars gallica*, emphasized its purpose, which was the encouragement and performance of new French music – particularly orchestral and other instrumental music. Important works by Franck*, d'Indy*, Chausson, Fauré and others were first heard under the Société's auspices, and some extremely interesting symphonic poems by Saint-Saëns himself. It might be thought that with his views on 'pure' music, anything resembling a descriptive 'programme' would have been anathema to him. But his stipulation was that it should always be justifiable in itself as music, whatever the initial conception may have been. To this category belong Saint-Saëns's *Le Rouet d'Omphale*, *Phaéton* and *Danse macabre* – all of which are still heard today – and, of course, *Le Carnaval des Animaux*. The last-named was written as a private joke, caricaturing music by many other composers – and his own *Danse macabre*. The composer disliked the *Carnaval* and forbade performances of it during his lifetime; it is now, ironically, his most popular work.

Of the symphonies of Saint-Saëns, the one most frequently heard today is no. 3, the so-called 'Organ' Symphony (because of its important part for organ). Dedicated to the memory of Liszt, this was first performed in 1886 in London, at a concert of the (now Royal) Philharmonic Society.

Although Saint-Saëns devoted a good deal of his energy to writing music for the theatre, his immense gifts did not include the ability to portray drama and character really convincingly through music. It is significant that his most successful opera, *Samson et Dalila*, dating from the 1870s, was originally conceived as an oratorio; and the work in its final form is a series of tableaux rather than a developing musical drama.

In musical terms the range and variety of Saint-Saëns's output is enormous. Besides operas and other stage works, symphonies, concertos and concert-pieces for various instruments, overtures, symphonic poems, the list of his chamber music is formidable; likewise, there is a large amount of vocal music, with and without orchestra, and innumerable solo songs with piano. Curiously, for a renowned keyboard exponent, the solo piano and organ compositions are the least interesting side of his output. Saint-Saëns was a man of wide culture, and in his literary works he vividly expresses the viewpoint of one who believes in 'art for art's sake' – very different from the widely held nineteenth-century Romantic viewpoint. His work as a whole, with its clarity, wit and craftsmanship, provided a powerful example and stimulus to many other French composers, including Fauré and Ravel.

David Cox

The composer's memoirs, *École buissonnière*, were published in 1913. See: Arthur Hervey, *Saint-Saëns* (1921); James Harding, *Saint-Saëns and his Circle* (1965).

391
SAINT-SIMON, Claude-Henri de Rouvroy, Comte de 1760–1825

French social thinker

Saint-Simon has become best known for his influence on the development of early nineteenth-century socialism. Yet he has an equally significant claim on our attention by virtue of his insistence that science and industrialization would be the dominant forces of the future, and that matching principles of a positivistic kind must henceforth provide the guiding compass for all efforts at social understanding.

Born in Paris, Saint-Simon belonged to the impoverished younger branch of that noble family which, eighty-five years before, had also nurtured the great chronicler of court life at Louis XIV's Versailles. He was privately educated, counting among his tutors the *encyclopédiste* D'Alembert. Having joined the French army in 1777, he saw action in the American War of Independence and distinguished himself at Yorktown. During the 1780s he was much concerned with unsuccessful attempts to promote various canal projects in Mexico and Spain. When the French Revolution occurred he expressed sympathy with its objectives, renounced his title, and for a time assumed the name of Citizen Bonhomme. His motives were however far from altruistic, as he soon exploited the market in cheap land made available by the confiscation of clerical and *émigré* properties. Towards the beginning of the Terror he was arrested by mistake (November 1793), and not released from gaol until nine months later. Saint-Simon's material fortunes were at their peak under the Directory (1795–9), when the profits from his land speculation enabled him to finance a lavish Parisian salon for politicians, men of letters, and scientists, especially from the new École Polytechnique. By the end of the Consulate (1804) his brief marriage had foundered and his coffers were virtually empty. It was in more straitened circumstances, and with dependence on the generosity of friends, that he pursued most of his new career as a writer on social reform over the last twenty years or so of his life. His limited means, and his failure to make greater impact with ideas which he himself took to be the product of self-evident genius, led to bouts of depression. Indeed, two years before his death, he failed only narrowly in an attempt at suicide.

Underpinning all of Saint-Simon's writings is a broad philosophy of history that postulates gradual alternation between 'critical' and 'organic' phases in civilization. The medieval epoch, for example, was deemed to represent one of the latter, when social and political institutions were harmoniously geared to man's requirements as these were then understood. But this concordance had subsequently faded due to the great rise in science, commerce, and industrialization, all of which were taken as being at odds with the traditional emphasis on 'feudal' military, clerical and landowning power. The French Revolution amply confirmed just how far Europe had moved into a condition of 'critical' disequilibrium. The heroes of 1789 had done much to destroy the old structures, but by that very same process they had threatened to create a dangerous vacuum in which 'all the existing relations between the members of a nation become precarious, and anarchy, the greatest of all scourges, rages unchecked'. Thus the most urgent challenge was now to build up a new condition of organic wholeness, concordant with the recent and prospective achievements of scientists and captains of commerce and industry.

Saint-Simon's most important early works were the *Letters of a Genevan to His Contemporaries* (*Lettres d'un habitant de Genève à ses contemporains*, 1802); the *Introduction to the Work of Science in the 19th Century* (*Introduction*

aux travaux scientifiques du XIXe siècle, 1807); and the
Memoir on the Science of Man (*Mémoire sur la science de
l'homme*, 1813). These were all concerned in some way
with clarifying the intellectual basis for reconstruction.
Particular stress was laid on the transition from
polytheism to theism, and thence to truly scientific
understanding, according to a historical progression
which August Comte* was soon to tidy up as 'the law
of three stages'. Following the habits of the Enlightenment, Saint-Simon looked to Newtonian gravitation as
the great model of systematic comprehension and of
ultimate unity in every branch of knowledge. Towards
the end of the Napoleonic Wars, when the Congress of
Vienna was assembling, he published a widely read
pamphlet titled *De la Réorganisation de la société euro-
péenne* ('On the Reorganization of European Society',
1814) which dealt with some of the international implications of the quest for organic equilibrium. The
next phase of activity focused on a succession of short-
lived periodicals which appeared intermittently under
his own editorship: *L'Industrie* (1816–18); *La Politique*
(1819); *L'Organisateur* (1819–20); and *Du Système industriel* (1821–2). Here Saint-Simon addressed himself directly to that industrial and commercial bourgeoisie in
whose wisdom and initiative he had such faith. The
essays of this period were much influenced by his close
association with Comte, who served as his secretary
from 1817 until 1824, in which year a bitter quarrel
divided them. In his final book, *Le Nouveau Christianisme*
('The New Christianity', 1825), Saint-Simon turned to
the role that religion (or some secular imitation of
religion as hitherto understood) should play in future
society. His 'New Christianity' had precious little to
do with theology or metaphysics, being directed rather
towards the provision of such ethical values as might
properly be held in common by those who accepted
the supremacy of scientific truth.

These texts contain little that is unequivocally socialist in tone. The need for a planned economy is fully
stressed, and the fact of transition from a feudal to a
bourgeois order is clearly stated. Yet little enthusiasm
emerges for radical social equalization or for any further shift of political authority into the hands of the
working class. According to Saint-Simon, capital and
labour must be treated as potentially complementary
forces having, in a well organized community, a shared
commitment to the success of the productive process.
Only by harnessing the guiding talents of an educated
elite could society assure the well-being of proletarian
or peasant. Central administration should be conducted within a framework of three chambers: one
body made up of engineers and artists to propose plans,
a second comprising scientists charged with assessing
such projects, and a third drawn from the ranks of
industrialists whose task would be that of implementing the resulting schemes according to the interest of
the whole community. Administered in this way and

further fortified by the consensual ethos of the 'New
Christianity', societies would no longer have need of
their coercive machinery, and government in the conventional sense would dwindle to the most residual
functions.

The linkage between Saint-Simon's name and early
socialism was due less directly to him than to the band
of disciples, many trained at the École Polytechnique,
who radicalized his ideas in the years immediately after
his death. Especially notable here were Olindes Rodriguez (who financed the master's last phase of work),
Armand Bazard and Barthélemy-Prosper Enfantin.
The views of their group, given collective expression in
L'Exposition de la doctrine saint-simonienne (1830), constituted a threat to existing property rights. Inheritance,
above all, was now deemed incompatible with the
attainment of Saint-Simon's goals. While not precisely
abolishing private ownership, the state should assume
responsibility for redistributing capital according to
capacity and need, and thus convert property (in
George Lichtheim's words) 'from an absolute right into
a social function alterable at will'. The Saint-Simonian
group had no real hand in the February Revolution of
1830, but in the unsettled condition of French and
European politics around that time they attracted
widespread interest. Their impact would doubtless
have been more sustained had they not succumbed to
divisive quarrels, especially over the religious aspects
of their programme. The Parisian 'community'
founded in 1829 under the 'supreme fathers' Bazard
and Enfantin was soon rent by schism, and in 1831 the
latter figure moved off to establish a shortlived rival
establishment at Ménilmontant in the suburbs. This
became quaintly notorious for its symbolic costumes,
for rumours of free love, and for its leader's efforts to
supply himself with a 'female Messiah', and the authorities soon forced it to close as an offence to public
decency.

Even though the movement had little future in this
tightly organized sense, Saint-Simonianism did manage to exert a more diffuse influence on French political
debate. Together with selected Fourierist* insights, it
helped to inspire the most important socialist tract of
the Orleanist period, Louis Blanc's *Organisation du travail* ('The Organization of Labour', 1839). Equally, the
great economic expansion of the Second Empire owed
much to financiers and industrialists who in their
younger days had warmed to Saint-Simon's vision of
their particular destiny within the epoch of heroic materialism. Abroad, he influenced figures as diverse as
Carlyle* and J.S. Mill*, Herzen* and Dostoevsky*.
Not least, he was read across the Rhine by the so-
called Left Hegelians. Utopian he may have seemed to
Marx* and his circle, yet they learned much from the
sheer breadth of Saint-Simon's historical treatment of
the transformation from feudal to bourgeois society. It
was indeed Engels* who alleged that this Frenchman

2222222

possessed, alongside Hegel*, 'the most encyclopaedic mind of his age'.

Michael Biddiss

The Anthropos edition of the *Oeuvres de Claude-Henri de Saint-Simon* (6 vols, 1966) assembles his writings. A brief English sampling, well chosen with an exceptionally helpful introduction, is *Saint-Simon: Selected Writings* ed. Felix Markham (1952). See: Sebastien Charléty, *Histoire du Saint-Simonisme* (1896); M.M.Dondo, *The French Faust, Henri de Saint-Simon* (1955); Émile Durkheim, *Socialism and Saint-Simon* (1958); Frank E. Manuel, *The New World of Henri de Saint-Simon* (1956); and J.P. Plamenatz, *Man and Society* (1963), vol. 2, ch. 2.

392

SAND, George (Amantine-Aurore-Lucile Dupin) 1804–76

French novelist

All her life George Sand was conscious of the clashing loyalties of her mixed heredity. The death of her father when she was only four meant that, though she was brought up by her aristocratic grandmother, she yearned for her plebeian mother. Aurore's education was largely conducted at Nohant, in Berry, by her father's old tutor, supplemented by her own wide reading and a couple of important adolescent years at the fashionable English convent school in Paris. There she was given a respite from the emotional tug-of-war of her two 'mothers' and underwent a sudden conversion; even when later she turned away from formal religion her genuine streak of mysticism remained.

When her grandmother died Aurore was left, at the age of seventeen, mistress of a small estate and of independent means. But pressured by her mother and conscious of her isolation, she made, the next year, the incompatible marriage to Casimir Dudevant which was to affect the rest of her life. The birth of their son, Maurice, in 1823, satisfied for a time her strong maternal instinct but Casimir was incapable of understanding his wife's intellectual or emotional needs and she of tolerating his traditional squire pursuits of shooting and drinking. His infidelities encouraged her to look elsewhere for happiness and in 1830 she made an extraordinary agreement with him, by which she spent half the year in Paris on a small allowance, and half at Nohant. Thus partially liberated she set about her career as a novelist, first in collaboration with her young lover, Jules Sandeau, and then on her own, as George Sand. From then, till her death forty-five years later, she was a professional woman of letters, writing on average two books a year.

It is difficult, and perhaps unnecessary, to separate the different phases of George Sand's literary career from her successive lovers. On the other hand, too much should not be made of her indebtedness to them; she always gave as much as she took. Her early romantic novels owe as much to Rousseau, Byron* and Madame de Staël* as to Sandeau or Musset*, while the elements of revolt, passion and feminism stem from her own personal awareness of the iniquities of repressive marriage laws and of woman's inferior role in society. Her first novel, *Indiana* (1832), in which a young wife speaks up for her sex against marital slavery, created a furore and was hailed by Balzac* as 'a modern novel'. And those that followed, *Valentine* (1832), *Lélia* (1833, the most complex, questioning and 'shocking' of her works), *Jacques* (1834) and *Mauprat* (1837), combined with rumours of her scandalous life to make her 'the most talked of woman in Europe'. Her stay in Venice with Musset was personally disastrous but professionally an unequivocal good for it led to her using the theme of Italy and the artist for many of her novels and to writing the extraordinarily rich and varied *Lettres d'un Voyageur* (1834–6), for the *Revue des Deux Mondes*.

By 1836 she had survived the punishing notoriety of a lawsuit and was legally separated from Casimir, who received the income from her other property while she retained Nohant. Now, prompted by her latest lover, the advocate Michel de Bourges, she turned her attention outwards, away from her own emotional life to the sufferings of society. Her imagination was seized by the gospel of humanity as preached by Pierre Leroux, with its blend of meliorism and mysticism, pantheism and feminism – and many very different novels bear its mark: *Spiridion* (1839); *Le Compagnon du Tour de France* (1840); *Consuelo* (1842); *Jeanne* (1844); *Le Meunier d'Angibault* (1845). One important aspect of most of the novels of this period is a hero or heroine drawn from the people; although her novels are still not short of aristocrats, they are made to express democratic sentiments. *Consuelo*, the work which best reveals her deep love and understanding of music, was written in this period of, for the most part, tranquil happiness of her relationship with Chopin*, which was shattered in 1847 by a painful quarrel unscrupulously engineered by her daughter, Solange. But even that grief was to provide George Sand with copy for self-justification in her later novels. She was as deft at making shreds of experience work for her as in transforming scraps of material into marvellous costumes for the puppet theatre at Nohant.

The next year she eagerly seized the opportunity to play an active part in Paris in the 1848 Revolution as editor of the *Bulletin de la République*, for the few hectic months in which the future of the country seemed genuinely in question. But with the cause of the Socialist Republic lost she returned to Nohant and continued to write in the gentle, pastoral strain which she had begun with *La Mare au Diable* (1845) and *François le Champi* (1847). Now there followed *La Petite Fadette* (1849) and *Les Maîtres Sonneurs* (1853), stories which, in their truthful country detail and background were written as a deliberate riposte to what she felt was Balzac's cynical presentation of the peasant mentality. These 'bergeries' have been much loved for their simplicity and idealism and (in Proust's words) the 'generosity and moral distinction' of the prose.

By now, in her middle age, she had attained fame and respectability. She wrote indefatigably on: many plays, mainly stage versions of her books; many more very long novels, well described by Henry James* as 'charming, improbable romances for initiated persons of the optimistic class'; quite a number of essays and one fine, if not dependable, 'autobiography', *Histoire de ma Vie* (1855), in which she gave lively portraits of her parents and grandmother and memorably re-created her own youth. For the most part she wrote for money, to support her large Nohant establishment, professionally but effortlessly, 'much as another person might garden,' she said – but, alas, without a thought of pruning. No trace of her earlier passion remained; the rebel, George Sand, had become La Bonne Dame de Nohant.

It is as a remarkable personality, extraordinarily gifted, independent, fascinating, a woman far ahead of her time in the example she set of sexual and social daring, that George Sand has remained in the consciousness of many who have never read a word of her fiction. It is only of late years that she has been rediscovered as a writer whose influence upon other literary men and women was both great and enduring. She was read in translation but also in the original (for her French is very easy to follow) all over Europe and in America. Avowed disciples and admirers included Arnold*, Clough*, Charlotte Brontë*, George Eliot*, Elizabeth Barrett Browning*, Mazzini*, Dostoevsky*, Turgenev*, Belinski, Herzen*, Heine*, Emerson*, Whitman*, Poe* and James – but even such a mixed bag does not convey the magical element of her appeal which often bore very little relation to the quality of the work which inspired it. She was not incapable of control and brevity as is evident from such a small masterpiece as *Les Maîtres Mosaistes* (1834), an imaginative re-creation of fifteenth-century Venice; but she remained unconvinced by Flaubert*, the friend of her last decade, of the importance for the artist of impersonality. Indeed the novels which seemed to have the greatest liberating effect on the hearts and imaginations of her readers were those in which they felt closest to her in her fluid self-revelations.

In her moods of despair, *ennui*, passion, stoicism, humiliation, and optimism she voiced many of the unspoken thoughts, feelings and aspirations of her more inhibited contemporaries. Renan's* fine image of her as 'the Aeolian harp of our time' was a well-chosen

tribute – for it stresses not only her Romantic inheritance, as found in her wonderful descriptions of nature and the musical cadences of her prose, but her sensitive response to every passing breeze of social and intellectual change.

Patricia Thomson

For French texts with scholarly introductions see (novels) Classiques Garnier; (autobiographical works) the Pléiade edition (ed. Georges Lubin, 1971); (letters) *Correspondance*, ed. G. Lubin (14 vols so far, 1964–). The Sand-Flaubert letters were translated in 1922 by A.L. Mackenzie. Biographies are very numerous and include: André Maurois, *Lélia* (trans. G. Hopkins, 1953); Curtis Cate, *George Sand* (1975); Joseph Barry, *Infamous Woman* (1977). Critical: Henry James, *French Poets and Novelists* (1884); *Henry James, Literary Reviews and Essays*, ed. Albert Mordell (1957); Ellen Moers, *Literary Women* (1976); Patricia Thomson, *George Sand and the Victorians* (1977).

393
SARDOU, Victorien 1831–1908

French playwright

A prolific and successful writer, Sardou is identified by posterity with the formula of the 'well-made play' which he inherited from Eugène Scribe (1791–1861), who dominated the popular theatre in France from the 1820s to his death. The well-made play (whose plot is constructed according to a tight logic, not according to the looser, less predictable dictates of character; character being subordinated to plot, and plot conceived in terms of preparation, crisis and dénouement, with a series of contrived climaxes to create suspense) perfectly suited the 'comédie-vaudeville' of the middle of the nineteenth century. However, when the same mechanical construction, turning characters into puppets controlled by chance, was applied (by Sardou and others) to more serious social dramas and problem plays, the limitations of the formula became very evident. Sardou, who frequently wrote for Sarah Bernhardt, to whom the success of many of his plays in Paris was due, was also much played in the London theatres from the 1860s to the end of the century, and Bernard Shaw became his most forceful critic. Shaw coined the term 'Sardoodledom' to devalue the empty craftsmanship of melodramas like *Fedora* (1882); and his scornful denunciation of Sardou's contrivances ('the two Sardovian servants . . . their pretended function being to expound the plot, their real one to bore the audience sufficiently to make the principals doubly welcome when they arrive') and coincidences ('the postal arrangements, the telegraphic arrangements, the police arrangements, the names and addresses, the hours and seasons, the tables of consanguinity, the railway and shipping time-tables, the arrivals and departures, the whole welter of Bradshaw and Baedeker, Court Guide and Post Office Directory ... make up an entertainment too Bedlamite for many with settled wits to preconceive') makes very amusing reading. In fact Sardou had a remarkably wide range. The genres in which he achieved his best-known successes – those of social drama or melodrama (*La Famille Benoiton*, 1865; *Rabagas*, 1872) or historical melodrama (*Madame Sans-gêne*, 1893; *La Tosca*, 1887, which was adapted by Giacosa and Illica in the libretto for Puccini's* opera) – show his dramaturgy at its most mechanical and least inspired; and he was capable of writing both with a lighter touch and in a more genuinely serious vein. For instance, the widespread public interest in the projected divorce legislation (passed in 1883) gave rise to two very different plays on this topical subject: in *Divorçons* (1880) Sardou adopted the manner of the vaudeville, producing a lively farce in the style of Labiche or Feydeau* (in which the proliferation of coincidences is of course an asset), whereas in *Daniel Rochat* (1880) a clash of attitudes towards marriage produces a serious, even a moving, study in credible terms of the relationship of a young couple. One hallmark of a Sardou play, whether on a modern or a historical subject, was a punctilious attention to detailed realism of setting – an inheritance from the 'couleur locale' which had so preoccupied Dumas *père*, for instance, in his historical dramas, just as much as from the realist theatre of the Second Empire. In Sardou's case, there is a tendency for such stage 'business' at times to conceal a certain absence of more weighty or more memorable qualities. Not invariably, by any means: the subject of *Thermidor* (1891), for instance, was capable of provoking a near-riot in the Comédie-Française by left-wing students objecting to Sardou's condemnation of Robespierre and the Terror; the banning of the play by the Minister of the Interior was upheld by Clemenceau after a stormy Cabinet meeting.

Despite his great success in his lifetime both on Parisian stages and abroad, Sardou is now forgotten except by the specialist. Like Scribe before him, he was the servant of the theatrical public, ready to exploit whatever dramatic form seemed assured of popular success. He lacked the higher ambition to guide and direct public taste, and was largely content to follow it.

W.D. Howarth

See: *Théâtre complet* (15 vols, 1934–61); R. Doumic, *De Scribe à Ibsen* (1912); J.A. Hart, *Sardou and the Sardou Plays* (1913).

394

SARGENT, John Singer 1856–1925

US painter

Sargent always retained his American nationality, although he was born in Florence and trailed all over Europe as a child by his peripatetic parents, studied art in Paris and spent most of his career in London. The mentor of his early life as an artist was the fashionable Parisian portraitist Charles-Émile-Auguste Carolus-Duran, whose studio he entered in 1874 at the age of eighteen. The corner-stones of Carolus-Duran's teaching were bold brushwork, modelling by means of strong tonal contrasts and painting *au premier coup*, without preparatory sketches or underpainting. Keenly observant and gifted with extraordinary manual dexterity, Sargent became a star pupil. He left to set up his own studio in 1879. In the same year he visited Madrid and in 1880 Haarlem, where his education in the painterly manner was filled out by a study of Velasquez and Frans Hals. Sargent had a life-long fascination with travel and the exotic, and the most important of his early subject-pictures, El Jaleo (1882), was inspired by a flamboyant Andalucian dance he witnessed in Spain.

The influence of Carolus-Duran, Velasquez and Hals was augmented in the later 1880s by that of the French Impressionist painters. Curiously, it was not in France that Sargent painted his first pictures to show an assimilation of Impressionism, but England, during summer visits to the Cotswold villages of Broadway and Fladbury. Indebted above all to Monet*, whom he knew and visited at least once at Giverny, Sargent began to show a new delight in broken brushwork, bright colour and transient effects of light. Nowhere is this more in evidence than in the masterpiece of this part of his career, *Carnation, Lily, Lily, Rose* (1885–6), a study of the two daughters of his artist friend Frederick Barnard lighting Chinese lanterns in a garden at twilight; and yet, with its relatively careful drawing, wistful mood and latent symbolism, *Carnation, Lily, Lily, Rose* stops short of the extreme objectivity and dissolution of form to which Impressionist ideas led Monet. Impressionism extended Sargent's range as a painter but, perhaps because the human figure was always his first interest, it never wholly claimed him. The most Impressionist works of his mature career were to be the oil and watercolour landscape sketches he made in large numbers, and purely for his own pleasure, on his long summer holidays abroad.

In 1886, still smarting from the ridicule levelled at his portrait of the society beauty *Madame Gautreau* when it was shown at the Paris Salon of 1884, and having found a circle of artistic friends in England far warmer and more sympathetic than anyone he knew in France (they included Henry James* and Edmund Gosse* as well as the painters Frederick Barnard and Alfred Parsons), Sargent decided to move to London; he lived in Tite Street, Chelsea, for the rest of his life. *Madame Gautreau* had been the culmination of an impressive series of portraits painted in Paris and Sargent had hoped it would establish his reputation specifically as a portraitist. In London his reputation in this field grew with almost startling ease and rapidity. By 1894, when he was elected an Associate of the Royal Academy (he became a full Academician in 1897), he was more or less universally recognized as the leading portraitist in England; and he only gave up this position at his own wish, virtually abandoning his practice around 1907 except for quick head-and-shoulders sketches in charcoal. Dubbed by Rodin* 'the Van Dyck of our times', he enjoyed the patronage of both aristocracy and *nouveaux riches*, investing such sitters as the Duke and Duchess of Marlborough with the appropriate pomp and superiority but clearly more at home with the family of Asher Wertheimer, a Bond Street art dealer of unashamed affluence, whom he painted in a series of portraits, most of which are now at the Tate Gallery.

Sargent's technique, always the most fascinating aspect of his work, becomes ever more dashing in his London portraits, ever more that of the supremely confident virtuoso; brushwork which at the proper distance denotes some accessory or part of a dress becomes quite meaningless, though often ravishingly beautiful as a purely abstract design, when seen close to. Sitters were struck by his way of charging at the canvas from a distance, armed with a loaded brush and muttering strange oaths, rapidly painting in an area and then retiring to contemplate the result. At his best, moreover, Sargent shows just as much flair for overall design as for brushwork, taking idiosyncratic viewpoints, inventing brilliantly original poses and, in the case of portraits including more than one sitter, groupings that suggest complex psychological relationships. He was a worthy heir to the great tradition of portraiture in Britain stretching back to Van Dyck via Reynolds, Gainsborough and Lawrence* – a tradition that had languished for most of the Victorian period and has languished ever since.

In the work on a monumental scale that Sargent carried on from 1890 onwards in the form of his murals in the Public Library and the Museum of Fine Arts in Boston, he is hardly recognizable as the same artist. Tackling an elaborate symbolical programme describing the development of religious thought from paganism to Christianity in the first, and various classical themes in the second, he replaces painterly bravura with a rather routine decorative style derived largely from Italian Renaissance models. More successful than any of the murals is the large-scale figure composition entitled simply *Gassed* (1918–19), which Sargent painted to a commission from the War Artists Committee. The feeling of authenticity about *Gassed* is undeniably powerful, but set against the work of younger war artists such as Paul Nash, its realism looks just as undeniably antediluvian.

Since his death, Sargent's reputation has suffered unjustly from the tendency of art history to pass over artists who are not of the *avant-garde*, from the too easy equation of facility with superficiality and, perhaps most of all, from the fact that his work is so closely bound up with wealth and class. The balance has begun to be righted in recent years, largely by Richard Ormond's book *John Singer Sargent* (1970) and the exhibition *John Singer Sargent and the Edwardian Age* held at Lotherton Hall in Leeds, the National Portrait Gallery in London and the Detroit Institute of Arts in 1979 (catalogue by James Lomax and Richard Ormond).

Malcolm Warner

395
SARMIENTO, Domingo Faustino 1811–88

Argentine writer and statesman

Born in San Juan, in the then primitive far west of Argentina, Sarmiento was largely self-taught. Many years of his life after 1831 were spent in exile in Chile, where he published *El General Fray Felix Aldao* (1845) and his most famous work *Facundo* (1845, trans. Mrs Horace Mann, *Life in the Argentine Republic in the Days of the Tyrants*, 1868, 6th edn, 1976), to be followed twenty years later by *El Chacho*. The theme of these works was the struggle between the forces of civilization and those of barbarism in Argentina and by extension in Latin America. After his return to Argentina in 1855, Sarmiento held ministerial and diplomatic posts, including that of Ambassador to the United States (1865–8) and in 1868 became the first civilian president of his country. After his term of office ended in 1874 he devoted himself chiefly to educational projects. His other literary works (cf. the *Obras completas* 1885–1914, originally in fifty-five volumes, now in their sixth edition) include *Recuerdos de provincia* ('Memoirs of Provincial Life', 1850), *Campaña del Ejército Grande* ('Campaign of the Grand Army', 1852), *Conflicto y armonía de las razas en América* ('Racial Conflict and Harmony in South America', 1883), the moving *Vida de Dominguito* (1886) after the death in battle of his adopted son, and *Condición del extranjero en América* ('The Foreigner in South America', 1888), as well as travel books (*Viajes*, 1854; trans. I. Muñoz, 1963), a life of Lincoln* and numerous educational tracts.

In *Facundo*, of which there are innumerable editions and two adaptations for English-speaking students of Spanish, Sarmiento wrote the most important single work of Spanish American nineteenth-century literature. Using a heavily 'slanted' biography of a well-known Federal guerilla leader, Facundo Quiroga, to illustrate his theory of geographical and historical determinism (pre-dating that of Taine* in Europe) he produced an interpretation of the 'problem of Latin America' which influenced Latin Americans' image of themselves as a racial group from the nineteenth century to the advent of Marxism*. Facundo and the dictator Rosas were presented as incarnations of the barbarism of the Latin American national character, a barbarism rooted in the emptiness of the vast interior of the sub-continent as well as in the racial heritage and the historical conditions left behind by the Spanish. But as a staunch believer in the inevitability of progress, Sarmiento saw barbarism and civilization as successive stages of development and advocated the deliberate imitation of Europe and North America (though not uncritically) as a means of eradicating the violence and destruction which followed the Latin American Wars of Independence.

His solutions were: legislation, immigration (preferably by white, Protestant, Northern Europeans) and education, together with the improvement of communications with the interior. In practice legislation proved ineffective; the flood of immigrants into Argentina came chiefly from southern Europe and brought their own problems with them; educational systems are now seen as reflecting the value-systems of the society they serve as much as modifying them, while improved communications have assisted dictators to preserve their grip on their countries. Most of all Sarmiento overlooked the economic forces which contribute to Latin America's social and political instability. Nevertheless, his view of the problem of Latin America primarily in cultural terms (with a certain racist tinge, more apparent in *Conflicto y armonía* . . .) provided Latin American literature with what for a century was its central theme and one which survives vigorously in, for example, the essays of Octavio Paz. *Facundo* is a hybrid production which mixes myth with history and resolutely over-simplifies a complex set of historical forces and events. But it was the first in-depth attempt by a native writer to come to terms with Latin American conditions. It marks the first realization in the sub-continent that political solutions lack foundation if social reality is not intensively analysed.

In his other works Sarmiento emerges as the leading advocate in his time of Panamericanism, popular education, religious tolerance and feminine emancipation. Finally, his *Recuerdos de provincia* are the most readable memoirs to have appeared in Latin America in the nineteenth century.

D.L. Shaw

See: A. Bunkley, *The Life of Sarmiento* (1952); and S.E. Grummon and A. Bunkley, *A Sarmiento Anthology* (1948).

396
SCHELLING, Friedrich Wilhelm Joseph 1775–1854

German philosopher

Within the remarkable constellation of contemporaries who came together at the Protestant theological college in Tübingen near the turn of the eighteenth/nineteenth century three luminaries excelled: Schelling, Hegel* and Hölderlin*. Of these, Schelling, who was the youngest, became famous first. His road to fame might easily have been blocked by authority even before it had begun. The Duke of Würtemberg nearly had the young Schelling rusticated when it was discovered that he and a fellow student had translated the 'Marseillaise'. Schelling, born in Leonberg – then a stronghold of middle-class industry and pietistic theology – had been accepted in the college at Tübingen, a ducal foundation, at the age of fifteen by special dispensation. The normal age of entry was seventeen. Schelling began his studies in 1790. Despite the duke's strict regime at the college, the ideas of the French Revolution poured in irresistibly. Secretly the boarders read Rousseau, Schiller's revolutionary play *Die Räuber* (1781), poems by Schubart and hymns by Klopstock, and Spinoza's writings.

Schelling's first writings, going back to his time as a college student, are concerned with the historical exegesis of the Bible. Myth, religious legend and early philosophical tales came under a new type of hermeneutic scrutiny which had its roots in Enlightenment thought: a rationalist historicism which undertook to explain mythical and early philosophical documents in terms of an evolutionary stage in the dawning of human consciousness. At the age of seventeen Schelling wrote a master's dissertation on Genesis III, a critical investigation of how the teaching of mankind's involvement with evil arose. At the age of eighteen he wrote an essay on the distinction between historical myths and philosophical tales. At the age of nineteen Schelling ventured into an essay 'On the possibility of a design of philosophy in general' (*Über die Möglichkeit einer Form der Philosophie überhaupt*) and in the following year he wrote his dissertation on Marcion, a heretic, which he submitted as part of his final examination at Tübingen. In the same year (1795) he wrote *Vom Ich als Princip der Philosophie oder über das Unbedingte im menschlichen Wissen* ('Concerning the Self as the principle of philosophy or the absolute in human knowledge'). In other words, at the age of twenty Schelling was an accomplished philosopher. After a period as tutor to a group of young aristocrats at the University of Leipzig he was offered a chair at the University of Jena, where he joined Fichte* (1798).

In *Vom Ich* . . . , which is deeply indebted to Fichte's *Foundations of the Entire Science of Knowledge*, Schelling heralds the necessity of a revolution in and through philosophy. While all philosophy had hitherto been in pursuit of a fundamentally epistemological principle to find out the truth about objects, it now had to be put on a different footing in order to free man from his preoccupation with objects and enable him to gain the full theoretical stature of human awareness. Philosophy was to be developed as the prime instrument to overcome all petty restriction of thought by the world of objects, so that it would cease to be subdivided into so many different disciplines and begin to evolve as a unitary system of mind. This was how mankind could discover the true nature of its being, which was anchored solely in the laws of freedom. 'The beginning and the end of all philosophy is – freedom!' he declares enthusiastically. A year later, in 1796, when he was still a private tutor, he jotted down on a few sides what was to prove the embryonic substance of his entire philosophy. This document, with all its speculative flair and its speculative obscurity, with its revolutionary boldness and its covert accommodation with irrationalism, now known as the first programme of the system of philosophy ('das älteste Systemprogramm'), only came to light in 1914. Here are some of its major assertions: 'The foremost idea is obviously the idea of myself as an absolutely free being'; 'Simultaneously with the self-aware being a whole world appears from nothingness'; 'Only when philosophy provides the ideas, when experience provides the data shall we arrive at the kind of grand physics which I expect of the coming age'; 'Only the substantiality of freedom can be called idea'; 'I intend to show that there is no idea of the state, because the state is something mechanical'; and 'The state must treat free men as wheels in a mechanism; this it should not do; hence it must cease to exist.' He proposes to analyse the whole of history, 'to strip it to the bones' of any impediment to freedom, like state, constitution, government, the law, church, parsons, etc., however deeply the latter may have camouflaged themselves with principles of enlightened reason. Finally he promises to let the idea of beauty shine forth, for he believes that the highest act of reason is to marry the good and the true in the beautiful. Philosophy must become poetic, aesthetic, mythological and mythology must become philosophical in order for the people to be able to accept and understand the ideas of philosophers and for the philosophers to learn to express themselves in the ideas of the people. He speaks of the necessity for a new philosophical religion.

Such thoughts may be idealistic, highflown and not a little confused, but they indicated a boundless, anarchic desire for freedom from the shackles both of the obscurantist government of the feudal-absolutist petty princes in Germany and from that of orthodox religion and theology. They also encapsulated, albeit in fragmentary form, the extraordinary breadth of a philosophical project whose execution, not surprisingly,

earned its author the dubious epithet of a 'philosophical Proteus'. It is as a result of the extraordinary energy and all-encompassing vision of his objective idealism that he briefly outshone Fichte in the ensuing years, only to be outshone in turn – irrevocably it seems – by Hegel, his older friend from Tübingen who at first had contributed considerably to the augmentation of his fame. In his *Difference between Fichte's and Schelling's System of Philosophy* of 1801 Hegel had clearly come down in favour of Schelling but distanced himself later. There is no agreement amongst historians of ideas and, in particular, amongst Schelling specialists, how many fundamental turns his philosophy underwent. There certainly are a number of distinct phases in Schelling's philosophical development. All of them can be regarded as different aspects of his fragment on a system of philosophy gaining ascendancy to dominate a particular phase of his thinking. There is first the philosophy of the absolute self in the footsteps of Fichte; then the philosophy of nature, which is followed by the philosophy of absolute idealism and the philosophy of identity. From about 1804 onwards a more irrationalist and politically acquiescent philosophy of mythology and a positive philosophy take over.

While Schelling's beginnings are strongly influenced by Kant and Fichte, he soon became dissatisfied with the former's cautions on the possibility of objective knowledge and with the subjectivism of the latter. Instead, Schelling, following Spinoza's *deus sive natura* and Leibnitz, attempted to deduce the whole sequence of things in the outer world from ideas that arise in the mind as an activity of the mind. Philosophy, he said, was only the physics of the mind. From there he progressed to a concept which would have been anathema to Kant: that of intellectual perception (*intellektuelle Anschauung*), i.e. the perception of objects as a result of intellectual activity. While Kant insisted on the necessity of sense perception, Schelling rejected it as an impurity that might determine the mind from outside. The objective world had to be shown as a determining result of the mind. Schelling transformed Leibniz into dialectics: objects are as much the product of a delimiting, intellectual activity as they are themselves intelligent being. Hence his preference for Spinoza. It cannot be surprising that for a philosophy which attempted to transgress all division of pure reason and sense perception, of nature and mind, of subject and object into the point of their fusion in the absolute, beauty, the shining forth of truth in finite mode, accessible to the senses, should become the focal point of its thinking preoccupation. After he had explained nature as unconscious activity in continuous evolutionary development and man's activity springing from conscious volition, he searched for the point where nature, fettered by immutable laws, and intellect, as the movement of freedom, came together in inextricable synthesis. This was in the production of artistic objects.

Art, for Schelling, signalled total mastery of nature by man, subjugation of nature without destroying it, the conscious appropriation of nature's unconscious evolutionary processes. Art could therefore be defined by him as 'the synthesis of nature and freedom' (*System of Transcendental Idealism*, 1800). Object and subject formed a unity in it and both changed in dialectical interaction because of their effect one upon the other. Art is the paradigm of all practical action in that it brings together nature and history, matter and spirit, the world of appearance and the world of reason. It is therefore the actualization of the absolute, the transition to perfection, the mythology of eternity, the anticipation of paradise. It is the critical fomentation of this world of aesthetic culture against that of mean political pragmatism which may yet prove to be Schelling's most valuable contribution to the development of Western philosophy.

Schelling's aesthetic theory brought him to the brink of his philosophy of identity, which he worked out between 1801 and 1803, when he left Jena. There can be little doubt that at that time this little town had the most progressive university, attracting the most scintillating minds, such as Reinhold, Fichte, Schiller, Goethe*, Hegel, the brothers Schlegel* and Caroline Schlegel, whom Schelling married after a long affair in 1803. It was also the centre of publication for some of the most important literary and philosophical journals (e.g. *Philosophisches Journal, Allgemeine Literaturzeitung*). It was as much rumour and gossip in Jena that drove him away as an invitation to the reformed University of Würzburg that attracted him. Here Schelling reached the peak of his fame, amongst students of medicine and the sciences as well as amongst those of theology and philosophy. Nature was now a divine, structured organism. It was God articulated in a manifold totality. Spinoza's *deus sive natura* had taken over and Schelling, although at the height of his fame, was slowly but surely moving from the ground of Enlightenment rationality and emancipatory intellectual battle to ethereal, super-human perspectives of a philosophy of the absolute which Hegel, in the introduction to his *Phenomenology of the Spirit* (1807), compared with the 'depth of night in which all cows are black'. Schelling, hovering between the writers of early German Romanticism (Schlegel, Tieck, Novalis) and those of German Classicism (Goethe and Schiller, with the latter tied to him by close bonds of friendship), finally succumbed to a fascination with mythology, spirituality and Romantic irrationality which amounted to a betrayal of the practical revolutionary propositions he had set out in his early fragment on the possibility of a systematic philosophy. At that time he could say: 'Man does not have a predetermined history, he can and should make his own history; for this is the essential character of man.' Now he teaches that time is but the history of the realization or real revelation of God. Philosophy is now defined as the 'history of the *res gestae Dei*'. Schelling went to Munich and then, after Hegel's death, was called as his successor to the Chair of Philosophy at the university in Berlin. What could have been his greatest triumph turned out to be an embarrassing fiasco. The stature of his predecessor was too large, his memory was too strong and Schelling's lectures too obscure for him to hold his students for long. And yet, Schelling's preoccupation with divine revelation veiled his partial renunciation of objective idealism and his turning toward history. He called this his conversion from negative philosophy (the philosophy of the absolute spirit) to positive philosophy. Absolute idealism had wrongly subordinated the 'logic of matter to the matter of logic'. The implicit critique of idealism by one of its major proponents is packed with ironies. Politically, Schelling was on the side of conservatism in 1830 and again in 1848; philosophically he was trying to beat a path into real history, but ideologically he was fettered by the language of religious metaphor.

Wilfried van der Will

F.W.J. Schelling, *Sämmtliche Werke*, ed. Karl Friedrich August Schelling (14 vols, 1856–61), and *Briefe und Dokumente*, ed. Horst Fuhrmans (3 vols, 1962–75). See: F. Copleston, *A History of Philosophy*, vol. VII (1962); Paul Collins Hayner, *Reason and Existence, Schelling's Philosophy of History* (Leiden, 1967).

397

SCHINKEL, Carl Friedrich 1781–1841

German architect

Schinkel was an architect of diverse styles who was the major figure of German Neoclassicism, and of its development Romantic classicism. Neoclassicism in architecture is associated with the revolutionary social reforms of the eighteenth and nineteenth centuries. Winckelmann, from his studies of the antique, had concluded that only liberty could bring art to perfection, and thus the revival of the assumed principles of Greek architecture was consciously associated with the progressive politics of the time. If the previous Baroque style was worked through some excited sensual conspiracy among the artists, this new style of revived ancient virtues was coolly and objectively developed to represent by its architectonic clarity the unquestionable rightness of the new rule of reason. From its earliest representation in the paintings of Poussin, the style was concerned with abstract qualities of pure form and geometry, and thus from the beginning acquired a certain remoteness, an objective detachment. In seeking to develop an architecture to house the perfect society that would result from progressive thought,

Neoclassicism was as dependent on theory and unbuilt projects as it was on built examples. In its search for perfect exemplars the style was strictly demanding, requiring architects of great ability to realize its fullness. The shared sensuality of the Baroque which it replaced becomes in Neoclassicism a cerebral eroticism, an exposed idealization of a machine-like severity; this being the price of an ordered unimpassioned calm to which all aspects of the style aspire. Many of the themes were later adopted and developed by the International Modern Movement in the twentieth century. The philosophy of the style can be heard echoed in Le Corbusier's statement that architecture is the masterly, correct and magnificent play of primary forms brought together in light.

Carl Friedrich Schinkel's early training was with the Berlin architects David Gilly and his son Friedrich, whom he joined in 1798 at the age of sixteen. The father and son in their separate approaches to architecture embodied the two distinct tendancies in post-revolutionary French Neoclassicism, respectively the rational encyclopaedic classification of Durand, and the visionary Utopian architecture of L. E. Boullée and C. N. Ledoux. Schinkel was to wait some seventeen years until after the defeat of Napoleon* and the return of the Prussian king from exile before his career as an architect began. During this time, he worked as a scenery designer, a painter and a creator of immense panoramas of cities. The latter were produced annually, were exhibited in a special building with animated lighting effects, were immensely popular with the Berlin public, and the main source of his early fame. His paintings were highly proficient works first in the style of Poussin, and later in the Gothic Romantic style of Caspar David Friedrich*.

The unifying characteristic of his tripartite early vocation was a fascination with a correctness of the rules of depiction, with scientific perspective. This interest in the effect of buildings as separate forms set in free space, seen obliquely as if moving among them, was to be a major influence on his later urban work, and on the design of several country villas.

In 1815 Karl Friedrich Wilhelm III commissioned from Schinkel what was to be his first and one of his finest major buildings. The Neue Wache at the eastern end of Unter den Linden was built in a true Neoclassical style, the double rank of Doric columns emerging from the pure block of the building with all the forthright clarity expected of this neo-primitivism, of this return to supposed truthful ancient virtues.

At this time the Gothic style was increasingly associated with a growing German nationalism, and the classic with the international, intellectually more rigorous theories concerning the appropriate style for a progressive society, supported in particular by the writings of Schinkel's friend, von Humboldt*. Schinkel was to use this quite small beautifully proportioned build-

ing as the fulcrum for his major urban planning work in the re-organization and siting of new buildings within the area between Unter den Linden and the Schloss standing on the island in the Spree. Within this quarter he built the majority of his finest works, including the Schauspielhaus, the Alte Museum, the Neue Packhof quayside development, and the Bauakademie. Both the theatre and the architectural academy contain important seeds of the later modernity.

In the treatment of the façade of the theatre the windows are unframed and suppressed, integrated within the overall composition, thus losing their ancient anthropomorphic associations to become abstract parts of the rational totality. A similar approach, using different materials, was to produce the curtain walling of modern buildings. The academy was built after Schinkel's visit to England in 1826 where he had studied industrial buildings, particularly in Manchester. The building was an elegant iron-framed structure, using industrialized products for its construction and for its furnishings, an early and successful effort to create an architecture from the new means of production.

In his role as State Architect to the Prussian Court, he also built several country residencies for various members of the royal family. The most notable was the Schloss Charlottenhof designed in 1826 for the Crown Prince at Potsdam It is an extremely skilful asymmetrical arrangement of internal and external spaces using devices such as loggias to introduce an ambiguity into the relationship between interior and exterior. The vocabulary of the buildings is Neoclassical, but the composition, as shown in his engravings, is picturesque. The complex, in the purity of its forms, the asymmetry of its overall plan and the continuities between interior and exterior space was to be a major influence on Mies van de Rohe in the seminal design for a brick country house one hundred years later.

There are two late unbuilt projects for royal residencies on hilltop sites. The first, for the German King of Greece, was boldly sited on the Acropolis, brazenly incorporating the famous remains. The second, Schloss Orianda, for the German Czarina of Russia, is for a site overlooking the Black Sea. For this he deserted his usual clearly delineated evenly-lit drawing style and produced a remarkable set of coloured lithographs. Although the buildings use Neoclassical elements, and the plan has a strict symmetry, the lithographs represent an attempt to work together his two early contradictory influences of the classic and the eerie Romanticism of Caspar Friedrich. There is a quality in the design that points towards the fantastic palaces of the mad melancholy Ludwig of Bavaria. As Mario Praz has commented in a different connection, in this late stage of Neoclassicism there creeps in an air of caricature of the ancient order, where classicism becomes romantically the material of dreams, when reason sleeps.

Neoclassicism in its adoption in France and the United States was associated with ideas of liberty and republicanism. In working almost exclusively for an autocratic royal family, Schinkel would seem to contradict by his work this relationship between style and society. However, the Prussian court was one where Hegel's* influence was pervasive. The style was powerfully appropriate, not to ideas of liberty, but to the idea of the supremacy of the state and the centralization of power. Each building, treated as an objective exemplar of abstract qualities of truthfulness and pure form, needed necessarily to be sited separately, surrounded by amorphous space, ideally infinite in extent, rationalized through the use of the grid. In its application to city planning, Neoclassicism eroded the intimacy and enclosing sense of place of the historic cities, formed largely by continuous co-joined buildings, cooperatively renewed as with a living body. Instead the style proposed for the city homogenous public space which belongs to everyone and to no one and thus is necessarily the domain of some overall authority. There is a delicacy of proportion and scale in even Schinkel's most monumental building, the Alte Museum, a quality that is lost in the gross proposals of the twentieth century which otherwise stem from Neoclassicism, and from his work in particular. It is notable by its absence in both the Radiant City project of Le Corbusier, and in the Third Reich projects of Albert Speer.

In his final years, Schinkel was increasingly plagued by migraine attacks. He finally collapsed into an intermittent coma in September 1840, and died in October of the following year. It is perhaps historically appropriate that the part of Berlin where his influence can still be discerned, at the eastern end of Unter den Linden, should now lie within the realm of an all-powerful, post-revolutionary state, and perhaps also an inevitability of history that the continuous public space that is an essential of his urban style is now curtailed by the most impenetrable of walls. Berlin remains today like a split brain, the cool virtues of rationality kept strictly separate from the sensuality of experience.

Frederick Scott

See: Hermann G. Pundt, *Schinkel's Berlin* (1972); Mario Praz, *On Neo-Classicism* (trans. 1969); and H. R. Hitchcock, *Architecture: 19th & 20th Centuries* (3rd ed. 1968).

398
SCHLEGEL, August Wilhelm (von) 1767–1845

German literary historian, critic, translator and philologist

The elder of the Schlegel brothers is remembered principally for two achievements: the definitive translation into German of the majority of Shakespeare's plays; and the course of lectures he delivered in Vienna in 1808, in which he summarized and publicized the literary theories evolved by the Early Romantics in Germany a decade earlier.

Whilst studying classical philology in Göttingen (1786–91) Schlegel had begun work on a translation of *A Midsummer Night's Dream* in collaboration with his literary mentor, the poet Bürger. In 1797 he published excerpts from a translation of *Romeo and Juliet* and an essay defending the dramatic structure of the play. Schlegel here initiated the reception of Shakespeare in Germany in Romantic terms, interpreting Shakespeare's use of contrast and variety as a conscious artistic principle, not the eccentric formlessness of a wild genius.

Another essay at this time, 'Etwas über William Shakespeare bei Gelegenheit Wilhelm Meisters' ('Some Thoughts on William Shakespeare on the Occasion of Wilhelm Meister'), published in Schiller's *Die Horen* (1796), contained a series of conjectures about a new translation of Shakespeare which would be more accurate and yet more poetic than the previous versions by Wieland and by Eschenburg. Schlegel maintains that the translation should be in blank verse, since it would allow the audacity and licence in handling language which marks Shakespeare's own style. Such a translation would not iron out the 'displeasing peculiarities of his style' in order to reduce the vigour of Shakespeare's language to a weak prose paraphrase; it would demand 'the boldest use of our language in its whole range', regardless of the objections of grammarians. These principles inform the translations of sixteen plays which Schlegel published between 1797 and 1801, including *Hamlet, The Merchant of Venice* and *As You Like It*.

Schlegel lectured on aesthetics and literature at the University of Jena in 1798 and again in Berlin between 1801 and 1804, but the Vienna *Vorlesungen über dramatische Kunst und Literatur* (1809/11; trans. *A Course of Lectures on Dramatic Art and Literature* by John Black, 1815) were the first to be published. These lectures draw a fundamental distinction between the art of antiquity and romantic art (not synonymous with modern art, since some modern works, notably in French Classicism, have imitated the ancients). Greek art in particular is marked by joyful and harmonious experience of the physical and sensuous 'within the confines of the finite'. Romantic art, beginning in the Middle Ages and reaching a peak with Shakespeare and Lope de Vega, is decisively conditioned by Christian belief in immortality and is torn between adherence to the physical and wistful attempts to attain the infinite. Greek art could fulfil its limited aims to perfection; romantic art 'can satisfy its striving towards the infinite only by approximation'.

Schlegel argues for the equal validity of these two basic types of art, seeing them as historical and not normative categories, and rejecting Neoclassical insistence on the ancients as the sole model. Each type is 'great and miraculous of its kind'; there can be no 'despotism of taste', 'no monopoly of poetry for particular ages or nations'. The Vienna lectures express some of the main tenets of German Romantic thought: the affirmation of movement and change; the devotion to dynamic confusion rather than static order, the attraction to what Schlegel here calls 'the chaos which ceaselessly struggles to produce new and miraculous births'; the belief in an artistic form which evolves organically by 'true growth', not by mechanical intervention and imposition of rules; the sanctification of art as the means by which ineffable mysteries are conveyed in symbolic form.

These ideas had been previously set down in aphoristic and often obscure form by Schlegel's brother Friedrich* and other Early Romantics, and it is not difficult to show a general dependence on Herder and Schiller; but the achievement of the Vienna lectures lies in presenting these theories in systematic form and in relaying them to a wider European public. A French translation appeared in 1813 and exercised an important influence on Hugo*, especially on his programmatic Préface de Cromwell (1827). Coleridge* read the lectures in the original in 1811 and was deeply impressed by Schlegel's distinction between organic and mechanical form. Following the publication of the English translation, an appreciative review by Hazlitt* appeared in the Edinburgh Review, and the lectures were also read by Walter Scott*, Southey* and De Quincey*. The historian James Mackintosh wrote to Schlegel: 'I know of no book so generally read and followed or opposed as your Lectures on Dramatic Poetry. You are become our National Critic.'

Schlegel's years in Jena (1796–1801) had also been the period of his passionless but intellectually stimulating marriage to Caroline Böhmer (née Michaelis), who after their divorce in 1803 married the philosopher Schelling*, himself a member of the Jena cénacle. Around 1799 the Schlegels' home in Jena became the focal point for the German Early Romantics, including Friedrich Schlegel, Novalis and Tieck. The principal journal in which this group published, Das Athenäum (1798–1800), was co-edited by the Schlegel brothers. Schlegel's subsequent period in Berlin ended in 1804, when he was adopted by Madame de Staël*, whom he served as literary adviser, intermittent lover and companion on her travels throughout Europe until her death in 1817. Between 1812 and 1814, under the influence of Count Bernadotte in Sweden, he became involved in diplomatic intrigues against France, publishing a number of essays on political issues. In 1818 he accepted a chair at the University of Bonn and held this post until his death. Amongst the students attending his lectures in Bonn was the young Heine*; his The Romantic School (Die Romantische Schule, 1835) cruelly satirizes the ageing Schlegel's personal vanity and political conservatism, but remains deeply indebted to his analysis of the distinction between Greek and romantic art.

During his Jena period Schlegel had also been extremely active as a critic, and amongst his hundreds of reviews there are perceptive pieces on Goethe's* Hermann und Dorothea (1797) and his Römische Elegien (1795). Schlegel's reviews are characterized by a rejection of 'judicial' criticism, assessment in accordance with a predetermined set of rules, and he prefers to interpret each individual work in its own terms, applying what he calls in the Vienna lectures 'the versatility or universality of the true critic'. His translations were not confined to Shakespeare: in 1803 he published an anthology of Italian, Spanish and Portuguese poetry (Dante, Petrarch, Camões, Cervantes) and a selection of translations from Calderón. In general he sought to enrich German culture by introducing his own public to foreign literatures. Between 1815 and 1818 he researched and published on Provençal literature, and in the 1820s he produced philological studies of Sanskrit and editions of such Indian works as the Bhagavad-Gita (1823). Bearing in mind also the panoramic surveys of European literature in his lectures, it is not unreasonable to regard August Wilhelm Schlegel as the founder of Comparative Literature.

Richard Littlejohns

Brief but characteristic extracts from John Black's translation of the Vienna lectures were published with annotations in Romantic Criticism, ed. R.A. Foakes (1968). See: M.E. Atkinson, August Wilhelm Schlegel as a Translator of Shakespeare (1958) and the introduction to R. Pascal, Shakespeare in Germany (1937); R. Wellek, A History of Modern Criticism 1750–1830, vol. 2, The Romantic Age (1955); R.W. Ewton, The Literary Theories of A.W. Schlegel (1972); G.T. Hughes, Romantic German Literature (1979).

399

SCHLEGEL, (Carl Wilhelm) Friedrich (von)
1772–1829

German literary theorist and critic, philologist and
cultural historian

Friedrich Schlegel's conversion to Catholicism in 1808
has often been regarded as a volte-face and the turning
point of his career. In fact it was a predictable expression of a lifelong impulse. At nineteen he wrote to his
brother August Wilhelm Schlegel* of his 'consuming
desire for activity or, as I would prefer to call it, the
longing for the infinite'; and this quest for an all-embracing totality transcending the crisis of fragmented
modern civilization recurs in his youthful idealization
of Greek Antiquity, in his excursions into Pantheism
around 1800 and in the eccentric Catholic theologizing
of the period immediately before his death. In his last
twenty years, based in Vienna, he had also been an
energetic publicist for the Metternich regime; served
as an Austrian delegate at the German Federal Diet;
and acted as a philosophical apologist for the Restoration monarchies, being the leading figure amongst
the reactionary 'Vienna Romantics' and the editor of
their journal, *Concordia*. His enduring influence on
European culture is to be found, however, in his earlier
achievements: the innovations in aesthetic and literary
theory which he conceived whilst at the centre of the
Early Romantic group of writers, moving between Berlin and Jena (1797–1801); and the researches into Indic
language and culture and into medieval art begun in
Paris in 1802, continued in Cologne from 1804 to 1808
and tailing off with his lectures on literary history in
Vienna in 1812.

Schlegel studied Law in Göttingen and Leipzig, but
after moving to Dresden in 1794 he became obsessively
interested in Greek and Roman culture. His resulting
familiarity with the social and political institutions of
Antiquity merged with his enthusiasm at this stage for
the French Revolution to give rise to his *Versuch über
den Begriff des Republikanismus* ('Essay on the Concept
of Republicanism', 1796), in which he argued against
Kant that a republic is feasible only on the basis of the
will of the majority. Yet the main aim of his classical
studies was consciously to do for literature what
Winckelmann had done for the plastic arts: to provide
a normative system of aesthetics based on the model
of the Ancients. The most important essay to emerge
from this preoccupation, *Über das Studium der grie-
chischen Poesie* ('On the Study of Greek Poetry', written
in 1795), argues that Greek poetry is characterized by
'objectivity', whilst modern literature is distinguished
by 'interest', in a Kantian sense, i.e. involving the
'interested' subjectivity of the author.

The decisive development in Schlegel's aesthetics
occurred between 1795 and 1797, partly under the
influence of Schiller's *On Naive and Sentimental Poetry*:
the analysis of modern literature was unchanged, but
Schlegel now allowed it, in a reversal of evaluation, a
status equal if not superior to the literature of the
Ancients. The pejorative designation 'interested' was
thus rendered inappropriate, and Schlegel hit instead
– fatefully – on the term 'romantic'. The exposition of
his new commitment to romantic literature occurs most
prominently in the journal *Das Athenäum*, which he
co-edited with his brother between 1798 and 1800.

Schlegel found a novel form of expression in his
collections of polemical or paradoxical aphorisms. The
'Fragments', as he called them, were to be as stimu-
latingly prickly 'as hedgehogs', demonstrating 'elasticity' of thought and an associative procedure he called
'combinatory art'; Goethe* aptly described them as a
'wasps' nest', into which the mediocrity of his contemporaries might stumble. The first such series of aphorisms in the *Athenäum* is called simply 'Fragments'
(1798) and contains Schlegel's celebrated definition of
romantic poetry as 'a progressive universal poetry'. By
'progressive' poetry he means literature in a form
which is open-ended, eschewing classical perfection
and finality; its essential feature is that it is 'still becoming', perpetually evolving in its efforts to encompass necessarily elusive totality. The ceaseless
extension towards perception of the infinite can only
be achieved in a work if the author remains conscious
that all finite pronouncements have only relative value,
if he appreciates – as Schlegel remarks in another
'Fragment' – the 'impossibility and necessity of a complete statement'. This insight forms the basis of Schlegel's theory of irony, worked out at a number of points
in the *Athenäum* and elsewhere, in which he also breaks
new ground. Irony involves 'a constant alternation between self-creation and self-destruction', in which the
work is 'raised to a higher power' when the author
reflects critically on his own conceptions as they are
conceived.

For Schlegel the connections between the term 'romantic' and the German word 'Roman' (novel) are not
merely etymological. He suggested that any specimen
of romantic literature is a novel in his sense, and for
him romantic literature includes Shakespeare, Cervantes and a whole tradition deriving from the Middle
Ages (but not, for example, the lachrymose narratives
of eighteenth-century sensibility). This leads to an ingenious and prescient theory of the novel, summarized
in his 'Brief über den Roman' ('Letter on the Novel')
which forms part of the 'Gespräch über die Poesie'
('Dialogue on Poetry'), also published in the *Athenäum*, (1800). The novel, as he defined it, should not be
confined to narrative; it may include verse, dialogue
and other non-epic elements. In structure it can abandon linear narration in favour of whimsical juxtaposition and digression (the models include Diderot and
Sterne), for its unity is not dependent on plot but on

an 'intellectual focal point' located in the imagination of the author. These theories were tested out in Schlegel's novel *Lucinde* (1799), but the formal experiment went largely unnoticed amidst the moral strictures heaped on the book, which expresses audacious opinions on sex and marriage. This semi-autobiographical work portrays, with perhaps excessive candour, the relationship between Schlegel and Dorothea Veit, the married woman with whom he had lived for a year and whom he later married.

Another section of the 'Dialogue', entitled 'Discourse on Mythology', refers with veneration to Spinoza and insists on what Schlegel calls the 'infinite abundance' of eternally mutating Nature, an idea which also echoes through *Lucinde*. Man will only evolve a new mythology to give symbolic expression to this dynamism and animation in the universe when he suspends 'rationally thinking reason' and reverts 'to the beautiful confusion of the imagination, to the primeval chaos of human nature'.

A passing remark in the 'Discourse' names the Orient as the most promising source of the new romantic mythology, and it was partly the Persian and Indian manuscripts in the Bibliothèque Nationale which attracted Schlegel to Paris after the break-up of the Early Romantic *cénacle*. Here he undertook a systematic study of Sanskrit, writing to Ludwig Tieck in 1803 that it was 'the source of all languages, all thoughts and poems of the human spirit'. He came to believe that Europe was irrevocably divided and incapable of its own salvation; his persistent longing for an ideal of wholeness was now directed towards the East, in the culture of which he claimed to find 'everything in One'. The product of these ideas and studies was his treatise *Über die Sprache und Weisheit der Indier* ('On the Language and Wisdom of India', 1808), a pioneering work in which he laid the foundations for comparative philology and for the Sanskrit scholarship of his brother and others in the 1820s.

In Paris Schlegel also founded and edited another journal, *Europa*. The first issue contained his 'Nachricht von den Gemälden in Paris' ('Information on the Paintings in Paris', 1803), which was supplemented by later instalments; these articles give enthusiastic accounts of medieval Christian art in the Louvre, emphasizing in particular the merits of the 'Old German' school and the Italian primitives. Supported by the assertion that the purpose of these paintings is 'to glorify religion', Schlegel's descriptions served to undermine Neoclassicism in contemporary German art and to legitimize the 'new-German religious-patriotic art', as it was later dubbed with Goethe's approval, which evolved in the first decades of the nineteenth century, particularly the work of the Nazarene school of painters, whose themes were almost exclusively religious and medieval. The Boisserée brothers had also aroused Schlegel's interest in Gothic architecture, and

in 1806 he published an essay which did much to encourage the taste in Germany for Neo-Gothic buildings which was to reach its culmination in the work of Schinkel*.

These new interests are clear symptoms of Schlegel's drift towards Catholicism, and by 1808 he could write off the speculative quasi-religion of his *Athenäum* period as 'aesthetic daydreaming, this unmanly pantheistic fraud'. His Catholic beliefs underlay his *Lectures on the History of Literature: Ancient and Modern* (*Geschichte der alten und neuen Literatur*, 1815, trans. J.G. Lockhart, 1818), which were delivered in Vienna in 1812. Here Schlegel extolled the Catholic art of the Middle Ages as the highest expression of romantic poetry, and therefore of all poetry. He rejects modern literature as too closely attached to 'real life' and advocates instead a poetry centred on history and legend. The lectures thus represent the logical conclusion of his literary theories, but also their reduction to conservative conformity.

These lectures had some international impact, but in general Schlegel's influence on cultural history was indirect. Through the communal 'symphilosophizing', as he termed it, between himself and Novalis, the theologian Schleiermacher* and Tieck, through his guidance of the younger poets Brentano and Eichendorff*, but above all through the popularization of his theories in the lectures given in Vienna in 1808 by his brother, Friedrich Schlegel determined not only the definition of Romanticism *vis-à-vis* Classicism but the whole course of European Romanticism and the development of modern aesthetics.

Richard Littlejohns

Some of Schlegel's more important early writings have appeared in two modern translations: *Dialogue on Poetry and Literary Aphorisms*, trans. E. Behler and R. Struc (1968); and *Lucinde and the Fragments*, trans. P. Firchow (1971). Translated extracts from the 'Dialogue on Poetry' and from the aphorisms are included in *European Romanticism: Self-Definition*, ed. Lilian R. Furst (1980). H. Eichner, *Friedrich Schlegel* (1970), offers an illuminating introduction to Schlegel's work and contains a list of translations published in the nineteenth century. See also: R. Wellek, *A History of Modern Criticism 1750–1830*, vol. 2, *The Romantic Age* (1955); M. Stoljar, *Athenäum: A Critical Commentary* (1973); G.T. Hughes, *Romantic German Literature* (1979); V. Lange, 'Friedrich Schlegel's Literary Criticism', *Comparative Literature*, vol. VII (1955).

400

SCHLEIERMACHER, Friedrich 1768–1834

German Protestant theologian

Universally known as 'the Father of Modern Protestantism', Schleiermacher was indubitably the greatest and most influential Protestant thinker, both within and without Germany, of the nineteenth century, his influence enduring right up to the outbreak of the First World War in 1914. Born into a family of Moravian Pietist persuasion in Breslau in 1768, he was educated first at Moravian institutions in Niesky and Barby, and then at the University of Halle (from 1787), which was in Schleiermacher's day in intellectual turmoil and ferment over Kant's criticisms of continental rationalism, with special reference to his rejection of the possibility of metaphysics and metaphysical theology. In 1794 Schleiermacher was ordained to the ministry of the Reformed Church, and his first ecclesiastical appointment (1796) was as chaplain to the Charité Hospital in Berlin. During this (first) Berlin period, he became intimately involved in that circle of young Romantics (including the brothers A.W. von Schlegel* and F. von Schlegel*, and Henriette Herz) who were on aesthetic grounds heavily criticizing the sterility and aridity of much *Aufklärung* thought. His first, and extremely important, book, *On Religion: Speeches to its Cultured Despisers* (*Über die Religion: Reden an die Gebildeten unter ihren Verächtern*, 1799, trans. 1958), was addressed to the young 'cultured despisers' of religion such as those with whom he consorted in Berlin Romantic circles. (The third edition of 1806 was one of the most significant contributions in the spheres of the phenomenology and philosophy of religion during that century.) In 1800 appeared a contribution to ethics, his *Soliloquies* (*Monologen*, trans. 1957). After several years' pastoral work in Pomerania, he was appointed Professor of Theology in his old university at Halle (1804), but the dissolution of the university brought about by the Napoleonic invasion occasioned his move to Berlin (1807), where he was appointed pastor of the Holy Trinity Church (Dreifältigkeitskirche) from whose pulpit he exerted a considerable influence during the rest of his life. In 1810, upon the reconstitution of the (Humboldt) University of Berlin, he was appointed Professor of Theology and the first dean of the theological faculty. His beautifully moving dialogue on the Incarnation, *Christmas Eve: Dialogue on the Incarnation* (*Die Weihnachtsfeier*, trans. 1967), had already appeared in 1806. From 1818 until 1831 Schleiermacher's colleague in the philosophical chair at the university was G.W.F. Hegel*, with whom he had a somewhat strained and unsympathetic relationship. Schleiermacher's life's work was his *The Christian Faith* (*Glaubenslehre*, 1821–2, trans. 1928), possibly the greatest work in Protestant dogmatics of the nineteenth century, profoundly influencing generation upon generation of students down to the first decade of the present century.

Schleiermacher was vividly aware of the dismissal of Christianity by the intelligentsia of his time; he was implacably hostile to the deistic, rationalistic and unemotional religion of the *Aufklärung*; he was horrified by the eighteenth-century conception of the Deity understood as 'First Cause' or 'Cosmic Designer' located behind, above, alongside or before the world; he was revolted by the notion of God as some kind of suprarational hypothesis filling the gaps in man's understanding of nature. At Halle he had read and digested most thoroughly the writings of Kant: he assented to the validity of Kant's critique of metaphysical theism, and accordingly deplored any attempt whatsoever to make religion derivative from or parasitic upon metaphysics or the natural sciences; but he came to deplore just as vehemently the attempt of Kant (in his *Critique of Practical Reason*) to make religion derivative from ethics. A prerequisite for understanding Schleiermacher is to appreciate his conviction that religion had lost its independence and surrendered its autonomy, and that *the* theological task of the day was to demonstrate the *sui generis* character of religion and the intellectual autonomy of theological science.

In the *Speeches*, Schleiermacher expresses his solidarity with the 'young despisers' of religion who have only impatience for religion misunderstood as metaphysics, ethics, systems, commentaries, apologies and the like; with them, he expresses profound distaste for that post-Reformation bickering over creed, authority and dogma, which in the previous several centuries had led to intolerance, persecution, inter-sectarian hatred and even war. But he warns them not to confuse *genuine* religion with these deplorable trappings in which it had become entangled! For, surely, the essence of true religion is 'the immediate consciousness of the universal existence of all finite things in and through the infinite, and of all temporal things in and through the eternal'. In this celebrated definition there are three very important key-terms: by 'immediate' Schleiermacher intended the conviction that religion is not *mediated* to us by, say, metaphysical or scientific reflection; his term 'consciousness' indicates that his entire theological life's work is to be centred on consciousness; his twofold use of the word 'all' is indicative of the function of concepts like 'all things', 'the All', 'the Whole', throughout much of his later work. It is a mistake to think of religion as being in the first instance knowledge, for it is primarily 'an affection, a revelation of the Infinite in the finite, God being seen in it and it in God'. Nor is it primarily ethics, which he understands as a science of action (human doing, producing, manipulating, and the like): essential to religion is a certain passivity, for 'piety (i.e., genuine religion) appears as a surrender, a submission to be moved by the Whole which stands over against man', so that religion must be closely linked with a certain form of contemplation. There is no more famous definition of religion in the *Speeches* than this: 'True religion is sense and taste for the Infinite.'

At the very heart of the *Speeches* lies Schleiermacher's teaching that what stands over against man is *not* a passive, inert, inactive, dead system of objects (as in *Aufklärung* cosmology and physics), but rather something active, moving, dynamic, even living, which takes the initiative and *moves* ineluctably towards man, creating within and evoking from him a certain response. Hence he writes that religion 'arises when the Whole approaches and touches the individual', and that in genuine religion man 'is stimulated and determined by that which stands outside of him', and that our feeling (*Gefühl*) 'is piety in so far as it is the result of the operation of God in you by means of the operation of the world upon you', or that true religion 'comes about by means of sensations and the influence of all that lives and moves around, which accompanies and conditions them'. The religious response, in Schleiermacher's view, is 'raised above all error and misunderstanding', which means that the truly religious experience is primal, more fundamental than rational reflection and criticism. The genuinely religious man attributes unity to what moves him and produces holy feeling within him, which is a unity of the Infinite permeating and penetrating his finite life.

Schleiermacher's phenomenological description of piety leads him to a key-conception – the 'Spirit of the All', the 'World-Spirit' (*Weltgeist*), immanent not merely in nature but in all that exists and moves around man, stimulating and evoking from him holy feeling. This operation is apparent within the human aspect of man's environment (e.g., family and church), but the sphere of history is also a significant source of enrichment for the development of the individual. The sketch he gives of human development allows him to develop what was to become the cardinal concept for his life's work – that of dependence (*Abhängigkeit*). The child is dependent upon parents and home; home is dependent upon wider society, which in turn depends upon the world, and so on, in ever-widening circles. And in genuine religious experience man has an 'active presentiment' of something higher than humanity and world which bounds and lies beyond them; but this comes to man not as an argument but as a vision which can be enjoyed only from the standpoint of pious feeling. The essence therefore of religion is 'the feeling of absolute dependence' (*das Gefühl der schlechthinigen Abhängigkeit*). But what of religious dogmas, ideas and principles? A superficial reading of the *Speeches* might convince us of their implacable hostility to all such – as Schleiermacher says, 'ideas and propositions are all foreign to religion'. But this is not really so, for in the work there is a new and revolutionary place for dogma and idea. For the religious subject can become an

object to himself and of his own inquiry, contemplating, spelling out, describing and analysing his own religious feelings, and all such analyses and descriptions are indeed religious ideas and principles. But Schleiermacher immediately qualifies his position: theology is *not* religion, but is the mere offspring of religion; the description (i.e., the dogma) 'cannot be equal to the thing described', which greatly transcends the powers and scope of human language; and, most importantly, a man's use of theological principles and conceptions must be referrable back to his own experience and he must be capable of demonstration of their origin in himself. Religion 'cannot and will not originate in the pure impulse to know', i.e., in the metaphysical quest for knowledge of the ultimate constitution of things.

The structure of Schleiermacher's magisterial *Glaubenslehre* was controversially revolutionary, breaking with the tradition of both pre- and post-Reformation dogmatics, all of which took the divine existence, nature and works as their starting point, and working towards man, salvation, church, sacraments and eschatology. Schleiermacher's method was daringly different: the theologian begins with an empirical study of the activity and consciousness of the actually existing Christian community; he must relate this systematically to the fundamental organizing principle (the feeling of absolute dependence), and in so doing relate his materials to his own religious consciousness; he controls and checks his procedure by appealing to confessional documents behind which stand the New Testament scriptures themselves; but, and this is emphatically significant, he must render his theology essentially systematic by exhibiting the homogeneity of each proposition 'with other propositions already recognized'. (It has been argued by German historians of theology that we see here the genesis of the modern science of systematic theology.) Although Christianity is by no means the only religion, but one of the 'positive historical religions' (each of which is an expression of the feeling of absolute dependence), it is the highest, as a potentially world-universal form of ethical monotheism. The genesis of Christianity as a positive historical religion is incomprehensible apart from the person of its founder Jesus of Nazareth, for Schleiermacher the 'Ideal Representative of Religion', the 'Archetype and Founder' of the Christian religion, the 'Second Adam' (Paul). In contradistinction to everyone else in history, the *consciousness* of Jesus was absolutely saturated by awareness of God. Since empirical man lacks God-consciousness, or depends for his existence on that which is less than God so that flesh is superior to spirit, the work of Jesus consists in renewing and bringing to fulfilment the God-consciousness of sinful man. Christians may be defined as those whose feeling of absolute dependence upon God has been renewed through the work of Christ, and it is this intersubjective God-consciousness of Christians which binds them into and constitutes the historic Christian Church.

The question of Schleiermacher's fundamental philosophical presuppositions has proved to be highly contentious. While it is hard to substantiate the widespread criticism that he was a pantheist (in spite of his explicit admiration for the work of Spinoza) or a panentheist, there can be little doubt that he adhered to some form of philosophical monism: the view that ultimately reality is one (Greek *monos*), designated by him as 'the World', 'the All', 'the Universe', within which God (the World-Spirit, the Spirit of the World) is almost wholly immanent, and about whose transcendence over it the theologian can say precious little. Defenders of this view have pointed to those passages in the *Speeches* where he comes close to using religious language of nature (e.g., that we must commit ourselves into the hands of nature, or accept all that happens to us *vis-à-vis* nature as the working out of nature's eternal laws), or to those passages in *The Christian Faith* where he comes within a hair's breadth of identifying the will of God with causal necessity in nature, or where he is highly critical of New Testament conceptions of the devil and of the dualistic strand in Hebrew-Christian religion. They have also directed attention to his contention in the *Speeches* that God does not need to be conceived as one distinct object beyond the world.

It was inevitable that a theological system so wide-ranging and deeply original as Schleiermacher's should evoke varied and widespread criticism. Much of this emanated, predictably, from the neo-orthodox school associated with the name of Karl Barth (although Barth, who fully conceded Schleiermacher's creative genius, dissociated himself from some of the wilder and more undisciplined comments of some of his adherents). Barth personally regretted that Schleiermacher initiated a century of Protestant theology which took man rather than God as its starting point, producing anthropocentric rather than theocentric or christocentric Christian thought. In the area of Schleiermacher criticism, there was one highly unfair and regrettable charge laid against him: namely, that he had subjectively psychologized or emotionalized the Christian faith (see, e.g., Emil Brunner's *Die Mystik und das Wort*, 1924). Too many of Schleiermacher's wilder critics quite overlooked the extent to which he had made it clear that the terms used to characterize man's response to the divine, 'intuition' (*Auschauung*) and 'feeling' (*Gefühl*), were responses of the 'whole man', and not just of the emotive or aesthetic sides of human nature, a defence of him which has been adequately clarified for us by twentieth-century thinkers such as Rudolf Otto and Paul Tillich. Hence, the uniquely valuable contribution of Schleiermacher to the twentieth-century discipline of the phenomenology of religion should not be overlooked. On the rather more negative side, it is undeniable that Schleiermacher bequeathed several highly intractable problems to his disciples and interpreters, two of which deserve mention. First, it is beyond question that he failed to ask at the outset if there are indispensable *nonexperiential* elements or themes within the total fabric of the Christian religion. The most pointed example is that of 'everlasting life', of which both in the *Speeches* and in *The Christian Faith* he provided extremely unsatisfactory treatments. Second, his unprecedented stress on the referral of doctrines back to the individual or on the derivation of doctrines from the empirical Christian community at any given point in time led to a certain regrettable devaluation in his thought of the historico-communal element in the formation of doctrine, whose genesis is incomprehensible if we forget that much of it derives from the experience, reflection and testing of theologians, saints, councils, synods and communities over extremely long periods of time, an element which figures prominently of course in Catholic and Orthodox theology. But the existence of such problems cannot deprive Schleiermacher of his status as one of the theological giants of post-Reformation Protestantism.

James Richmond

Other works by Schleiermacher include *Kurze Darstellung des theologischen Studiums* (1811, trans. *Brief Outline on the Study of Theology*, 1966). See: Wilhelm Dilthey, *Schleiermachers Leben* (1870); Richard R. Niebuhr, *Schleiermacher on Christ and Religion* (1964); Paul Tillich, *Perspectives on 19th and 20th Century Protestant Theology* (1967); Stephen Sykes, *Friedrich Schleiermacher* (1971); James C. Livingston, *Modern Christian Thought: From the Enlightenment to Vatican II* (1971); Karl Barth, *Protestant Theology in the Nineteenth Century* (1972); Claude Welch, *Protestant Thought in the Nineteenth Century*, vol. I, 1799–1870 (1972); Martin Redeker, *Schleiermacher: Life and Thought* (1973).

401
SCHLIEMANN, Heinrich 1822–90

German archaeologist

Schliemann, the son of a clergyman, was compelled to break off his formal education at the age of fourteen to serve a five-year apprenticeship as a grocer. At the end of this he set out from Germany to make his fortune in Venezuela but was shipwrecked just off the Dutch coast. He abandoned his South American scheme and took a job as a clerk in Holland, learning several languages in his spare time, including Russian. In 1846 he was sent to St Petersburg as the agent of an export firm and soon began trading on his own account, exploiting the circumstances of the Crimean War to win huge profits handling chemicals. The next twelve years were devoted to expanding his business and at the end of that period Schliemann had amassed a vast fortune. He then wound up his business so that he could spend the rest of his life realizing a childhood ambition – the excavation of the ruins of Homeric Greece.

At this period the world of classical learning was divided between those who regarded the *Iliad* and the *Odyssey* as pure fiction, and those who believed that they contained a kernel of historical truth. In general the German school was hostile to historical interpretation, whose greatest support came from amateur classical scholars in England, like Gladstone*. Schliemann, however, seems originally to have taken the extreme view that the Homeric poems could be read straightforwardly as historical documents. It was by acting on the detailed geographical evidence provided by the poems – the subject of his doctoral dissertation in 1869 – that he located Troy where he did.

The site, at Hissarlik in western Anatolia, was a huge artificial mound or 'tell', which Schliemann tackled by cutting a wide trench across from north to south. The results of the first three seasons, in which he was assisted by his young Greek wife, were disappointing. His technical competence was far in arrear of his enthusiasm: he did not appreciate the complex stratigraphy of the site, which reflected the collapse of successive settlements of clay brick dwellings over a period of some 2,000 years. The later layers, including those belonging to the city now believed to have been Homeric Troy (Troy VI), were simply hacked away with the object of reaching solid stone walls. The sort of success Schliemann was looking for came in 1873 with the discovery of fortress walls and above all a mass of gold, silver and copper vessels and weapons. These are now assigned to a city of the Early Bronze Age (Troy II) *c.* 2300 BC. At the time these finds were greeted by the scholarly world mainly with amused scepticism.

Schliemann had then to break off his Trojan enterprise because of the offence he had caused by smuggling out the entire Trojan 'treasure', one half of which had been promised to the Turks. He turned his attention in 1874 to the Homeric cities of Greece itself, and here his successes were more immediate and sensational. Great quantities of gold, silver and bronze items were unearthed from a series of cist burials, known as the Shaft Graves. The best known of these is the beaten gold mask that Schliemann christened the 'head of Agamemnon'. These excavations were the subject of enormous fascination to the European public at all levels, though many scholars refused to believe that they belonged to the Homeric age, preferring to attribute them to the Medieval Dark Ages.

When Schliemann returned to Hissarlik in 1879, and again in 1882–3 and 1889–90, he was assisted by ex-

perts in classical archaeology. Techniques were improving rapidly, and the fruits of these years have considerably more scientific value. In the intervening years he dug at Orchomenos, Tiryns and Ithaka. All these excavations were promptly and comprehensively written up and published.

Perhaps only a Schliemann with the amateur scholar's naivety and the self-made millionaire's assurance and initiative could have accomplished so much in the space of two decades. The popular mind was excited by the sheer brilliance of the treasures he had unearthed. This had an impact far in excess of any other archaeological discoveries before, and perhaps since. He did not only prove (though not in the way he imagined) the historical foundation of the Homeric poems; he also proved that the past is recoverable by techniques other than the study of the written word. It was archaeology's first public triumph.

C.F. Hawke-Smith

Leo Denel, *Memoirs of Heinrich Schliemann* (1978) is based on Schliemann's own writings. The standard biography of Schliemann is by Emil Ludwig (1931); a more recent popular biography is Robert Payne, *The Gold of Troy* (1959). See: C. Schuchhardt, *Schliemann's Discoveries of the Ancient World* (1891, reprinted 1979); C.W. Ceram, *The World of Archaeology* (1966); Glyn Daniel, *One Hundred and Fifty Years of Archaeology* (1975).

402
SCHOPENHAUER, Arthur 1788–1860

German philosopher

When he spoke he looked like Voltaire and when he was silent his head, save for his scintillating eyes, looked not unlike Beethoven's*. This external appearance, reported by contemporaries, seemed the perfect expression of his philosophical stance: enlightened pessimism and a deep fascination with music, the direct voice of the 'will to live'.

Schopenhauer was born in Danzig (Gdansk), the son of a wealthy and cultured merchant and of a mother who, after her husband's sudden death – almost certainly by suicide – in April 1805, settled in Weimar where she entertained a literary salon. She became the authoress of novels, essays and travelogues and her salon was frequented by such illustrious literati as Goethe*, Wieland, Bettina von Brentano, Savigny and the brothers Schlegel*. Although Schopenhauer benefited from the acquaintance with his mother's friends – he published an essay *On Seeing and Colours* in 1816 as a direct result of his discussions with Goethe on this subject – he regarded her conduct as flippant. It would not be unreasonable to assume that some of his extreme views on the necessity for male domination over woman, particularly in his incidental observations published in 1851 under the title *Parerga und Paralipomena* (trans. *Parerga and Paralipomena*, 2 vols, 1974), were influenced by his disapproval of his mother's way of life. It was his father for whom he retained a lifelong respect, although Heinrich Floris Schopenhauer had very nearly succeeded in forcing his son to become a merchant like himself. This project was undone only by his father's suicide. Schopenhauer's share of his father's inheritance was enough to allow him a materially carefree life; he needed to knuckle under to no one and could formulate his thoughts in complete freedom. He expressed gratitude to his father for this in his curriculum vitae for the faculty of arts at Berlin University in 1819. Furthermore, he was indebted to his father for a cosmopolitan, specifically anglophile, education and also for a critical attitude to authority, including the authority of the state, which he regarded merely as a necessary collective egoism curbing individual egoism. However, he was wary of democracy as is evident from his negative attitude to the Frankfurt Parliament and to the events of 1848. He clearly did not inherit the fierce republicanism which had motivated his father to leave Danzig, at considerable material cost to himself, when it was annexed by Prussia in 1793. The family had then moved to the free city of Hamburg.

In his application for a doctorate in philosophy at the University of Jena in 1813 – after studies at the Universities of Göttingen and Berlin – the young Schopenhauer confessed that his patriotism was not confined to Germany, a bold statement at a time when German nationalistic fervour against foreign occupation by the Napoleonic armies was rife. Schopenhauer's cosmopolitanism was no doubt a contributory factor in his disregard of day-to-day politics and his scorn for history. History cannot be the basis of a science, he asserted, although he allowed that it may be the object of much knowledge. However, in contradistinction to philosophical knowledge which seeks the general in the multitude of particulars and the permanent and unchangeable idea behind the confusing screen of its many appearances, history is but a confluence or an extended stream of singular events, different individuals, endless particularities. While history may make us believe that at different times different things happened, philosophy gives us insight into past, present and future as mere variations of the same.

Schopenhauer was out of tune with the main tenor of German philosophy in the first half of the nineteenth century. While his great philosopher contemporaries – Fichte*, Schelling* and Hegel* – sought to encompass history by philosophical theory, Schopenhauer, influenced by Vedic thought, saw it as *maya*, as a delusion of variety where in truth there was but an eternal revolution of the same. The great German philosophers

who held sway at the universities were concerned with questions of philosophical and historical dialectics. Schopenhauer defined dialectics simply as the art of discourse directed at the discovery of the truth. Consequently he had little to say on the subject, except that dialectics demanded a theory explaining the technique of conducting that discourse. From the remunerated small holdings of their university chairs the great philosophers, whom he derided as sophists and philistines, were holding out visions of progress, of the improvement of life in general and mankind in particular. Schopenhauer turned his back on such optimistic naivety and stoically defended the position that history has no goal, that there is neither natural nor historical progression – although he did not rule out the biological and ethical improvement of mankind – and that this whole colourful becoming and decaying of matter, organic and inorganic, 'this our world, which is so real, with all its suns and milky ways' is 'nothing'. Perhaps Schopenhauer's philosophy might best be understood as the reverse of an optimistic Romantic idealism which dominated the age, but which was shot through with dark forebodings of a world in the grip of luciferic forces (E.T.A. Hoffmann*), facing apocalyptic disaster (Joseph von Eichendorff*) and revealing its ontological nihilism once it was no longer enhanced by religious faith (Schopenhauer).

Schopenhauer's doctoral dissertation, *The Fourfold Root of the Principle of Sufficient Reason* (*Über die vierfache Wurzel des Satzes vom zureichenden Grunde*, written 1812–13, trans. 1974), argued that there were four, and only four, conditions of sufficient reason, because there were four, and only four, kinds of cognitive objects: becoming, knowing, being and acting. These are governed respectively by the principle of causality, of reason and truth, of time (arithmetic) and space (geometry), and of will and motivation. This work remained the epistemological basis for the rest of Schopenhauer's philosophical project. For its further elaboration he continued to draw heavily, as he had done up until then, on Plato's notion of immutable transcendent ideas and on Kant's notion of the 'thing-in-itself'.

Schopenhauer's thinking became informed by a simple thesis ('*simplicitas sigillum veritatis*' was one of his favourite sayings), namely that the world was 'will and idea' (*Die Welt als Wille und Vorstellung*, 1819; first published in English as *The World as Will and Idea*, 3 vols, 1883). His major work was subdivided into two main strands of thought, with a bifurcation in each: first the objects of intellectual representation as governed by the thesis of sufficient reason (Book I) and as objects of art (Book III); second the will in its various stages and gradations of objectification (Book II) and the will negated by the cognitive subject (Book IV). This, the most famous of his works, begins with the statement: 'The world is my idea.' It would be facile to suppose that Schopenhauer meant to say that the external world was not actually real or that, if real, it was nevertheless only a creation of the thinking subject. His frequently quoted opening sentence means that inasmuch as there is a perceived world it is the product of intellectual representation (*Vorstellung*, which might otherwise be rendered as 'idea', 'mental image', 'notion', 'concept' – there is no one satisfactory translation). The prime facility of this human faculty is understanding, that is the comprehension both of causes in space and time, and of the origin and purpose of intellect itself. Schopenhauer begins with this human faculty although it is but a tertiary phenomenon, a tool of the will. But it is through this tool that we can have knowledge of the will. It is through intellectual representation that we understand all being as a relationship between subject and object, and all representation as anchored in the will to live. Take the human body (Schopenhauer's own example): it is an object of cognition just like any other; yet at the same time we know that there is operative within it a life force, a will that urges the body on to go beyond itself, to procreate and not to rest content until it has achieved this. And so with all bodies. They are but materializations of the will. Intellect is the handmaiden of the will. The will is operative in all beings, it is the condition of all existence, sentient and insentient, organic and inorganic, darkly in the forces that hold together the stone, and distinctly in the gender-divided species. Man is the highest and most complex 'objectification' of the will. Its prime instruments in man and woman are the human genitalia. They encapsulate the will's eternal craving for more life, for more materialization, for more individual forms. Schopenhauer reveals himself as a true son of nineteenth-century West European society when he assigns to woman the role of servant for the species being. 'Woman,' he says, 'as is evident from her shape', is the vessel of will (man). It is one of the quirkier moments of the masculine aspects of this philosophy when Schopenhauer declared that the child inherits the will force, i.e. its character, from the father and its intellect, i.e. the servant faculty of the will, from the mother. Will, then, is the source of and the force operative in all particular beings. By itself it is undivided, immaterial, the thing-in-itself, the perfect idea. It is only in time and space that will unfolds and elaborates itself in so many myriads of striving forms, each containing the will in its entirety, but each limited by a definite space and a definite time and thus driven by an urge to be infinite. The higher individuals swallow the lower, the more powerful the weaker. Will is a disgusting force, forever wanting new life, forever dissatisfied with what it is, forever hankering after futures of more being, more birth, a senseless vortex of pullulating, engendering multitudes. Man, endowed with a 'metaphysical urge', searches for the meaning of being behind its appearances in an age when religious faith is beginning to crumble and he finds only the enormity of the will indefatigably, inexorably rushing into life, drawing in its wake pain, misery and death. But this vortex has two escape hatches: art and ethics.

In the aesthetic moment man reaches a stage of 'will-less perception' in which all desire to increase, to multiply, to consume, all craving and wanting is suspended in the recognition of beauty. This is possible through the sense of sight which does not affect us so directly with sensations of pleasure or pain as do the other senses. In other words, it is not intertwined with the will and hence is capable of distance, objectivity, reflection. It is the sense which enables man to reach a state of contemplation, removed from the whirl of the will, bringing about oblivion of our contingent individuality and allowing in us the emanation of pure subjectivity. It is in this state that cognition according to the principle of sufficient reason, causality, i.e. scientific cognition, is abandoned and a higher, artistic form of cognition is reached. The intellectual subject, no longer fettered by the step-by-step discovery of relations between things – as in the natural sciences, which are engaged in the service of the will – attains the vision of the things in themselves, mirroring the idea of their species being through their manifold individual appearances. Architecture, landscape gardening, sculpture, painting, poetry and drama are all concerned with the representation not of incidental individuals but of ideas, above all that of mankind in all its moral and amoral, base and sublime, noble and ignoble possibilities. The creative genius in imitating nature surpasses it by evolving its inherent idea. Schopenhauer insists, however, that the aesthetic moment, because of its essentially passive and contemplative character, can basically be attained by everyone, no matter whether in the confines of a prison cell or the expanse of a palace.

The highest art, music, is not concerned with the representation of ideas, but with that of the will, the metaphysical principle itself. While the other arts – according to Schopenhauer – can discover that principle only indirectly, namely in its ideational differentiations into a plurality of species, music is a direct materialization of the will, an 'unconscious exercise in metaphysics in which the mind does not know that it is philosophizing'.

If in art the will-to-live reaches a state of self-reflection, it goes on to a state of self-negation in ethics. Suffering, particularly his own, prompts man to see through the *principium individuationis*, i.e. through the differentiation of the will into many life forms. It enables him to recognize the suffering of others as his own, as the suffering of the species being. Hence man, identifying with the species, is capable of compassion, capable of transcending the inborn egoism of the individual. Suffering is like a purifying fire which produces the 'silver vision of the negation of the will-to-live'. The most admirable moral stance is one of conscious mortification of the will, denying it pleasure and satisfaction: the life of an ascetic, a monk, a saint.

Schopenhauer was an immensely influential thinker in the second half of the nineteenth and in the early twentieth century. His breakthrough to fame began with an article by John Oxenford in the *Westminster Review* in 1853. The composers, writers and thinkers who came under his influence include Richard Wagner*, Hans Pfitzner, Hauptmann*, Wedekind*, Wilhelm Busch, Thomas Mann, Eduard von Hartmann, Dilthey*, Bergson, Burckhardt*, Nietzsche* and it extends to C.G. Jung, Freud, Max Scheler and Merleau-Ponty. Ironically his influence waned as the mass horrors of the world wars approached. His philosophy, which allowed only for the sporadic negation of the will by individual men, could never conceive of the possibility of the will preparing the means for total self-destruction of mankind by scientifically developed weapons of global effectiveness.

Wilfried van der Will

Collected works: *Arthur Schopenhauer: Sämtliche Werke*, Arthur Hübscher (ed.), (16 vols, from 1937). Other translations include *The World as Will and Representation* (2 vols, 1958). *Essays and Aphorisms* (1970) is a selection from *Parerga und Paralipomena*. See: F.C. Copleston, *Arthur Schopenhauer: Philosopher of Pessimism* (1947); P.L. Gardiner, *Schopenhauer* (1963); *Schopenhauer: His Philosophical Achievement*, M. Fox (ed.), (1980), with essays by, amongst others, Thomas Mann, Max Horkheimer, Georg Lukács; D.W. Hamlyn, *Schopenhauer* (1980).

403
SCHREINER, Olive 1855–1920

South African writer

Born in the mission station of Wittebergen in Basutoland (Lesotho), where her father, Gottlob Schreiner, was a London-trained missionary working for the London Missionary Society, Olive Schreiner was educated principally from her father's stock of books and by her Cornish mother. As the author of her best-known work, *The Story of an African Farm*, which was published under her shortlived pseudonym 'Ralph Iron' on George Meredith's* recommendation by Chapman and Hall in 1883, she emerged as an important London literary figure of the 1880s. Her novel was striking for its simplicity of construction and thematic power; it had a significant impact on the formation of subsequent Victorian and Edwardian fiction. Its advanced thinking stemmed from her critical admiration for Goethe*, George Sand*, John Stuart

Mill*, Herbert Spencer* and George Eliot*. The long list of writers and public figures who have admired her runs from W.E. Gladstone* to Vera Brittain and includes Charles Wentworth Dilke, Havelock Ellis, Edward Carpenter, D.H. Lawrence and Arnold Bennett. All southern African writers are in some measure indebted to the example of this founder of their tradition.

The Story of an African Farm is set in the Cradock district of the eastern Karoo. The central figures are Waldo Farber, whose will is sapped by his intense sympathy with the exterminated San ('Bushman') population of the region, and Lyndall, whose pregnancy, death, and potent expressions of dissent are the negation of Europe-oriented settler aspirations. The drifting population of the farm, a patchwork of Afrikaner, Irish, English, German and assimilated Khoi ('Hottentot') elements, expresses in microcosm the author's abrasive view of colonial achievements. Few novelists writing subsequently escaped the appeal of this work, which encapsulated central and strongly felt doubts about the entire organization of imperialist social and political ambitions, yet fused them with a haunting earnestness about the role of women in modern society.

The twin elements of this radical vision reappeared separately in subsequent works by Olive Schreiner. The ambivalent presentation of settler *mores* and the energetic focus on the oppression of women in marriage stemmed partly from the Godwin* tradition in Victorian literature. In the allegorical *Trooper Peter Halket of Mashonaland* (1897), protest is directed against British military action in Rhodesia (Zimbabwe). In *Woman and Labour* (1911), women, their work and values, are presented as a neglected but integral part of modern industrial society. Posthumous works include *Thoughts on South Africa* (1923) and the novel *From Man to Man* (1926), an uncompleted work which had occupied most of her working years.

As the wife of Samuel Cronwright Schreiner, a senator in the South African government, and as a fearless opponent of Cecil John Rhodes in the later years of his work in South Africa, Olive Schreiner occupied a central position in the formation of the protest tradition in South African literature. Small in stature, yet intense in presence, she has played a significant role in the formation of modern literature and thought.

Christopher Heywood

Letters, ed. S.C. Cronwright Schreiner (1924). See: Vera Buchanan-Gould, *Not Without Honour: The Life and Writings of Olive Schreiner* (1948); C. Heywood, *Aspects of South African Literature* (1976); Kenneth Parker, *The South African Novel in English* (1980); Anne Scott and Ruth First, *Olive Schreiner* (1980).

404

SCHUBERT, Franz 1797–1828

Austrian composer

Both Schubert's parents were of peasant stock, but his father, thanks to Joseph II's educational reforms, became a schoolteacher in Vienna where he married (not long before the birth of their first child) Maria Vietz, seven years older than her husband and in service as a cook in the city. Franz, twelfth child of what seems to have been a happy union, was born in a two-roomed tenement in one of Vienna's poorer districts. In 1801 the parents with the four surviving children were able to move to somewhat better quarters – the schoolhouse where they remained until 1818. By this time Franz Schubert senior had been promoted and his sons Ignaz and Franz became his assistants. He had married, a year after his wife's death in 1812, a merchant's daughter twenty years his junior. (Schubert formed and maintained a loving relationship with his stepmother.) Both professionally and socially his status improved until, in 1826, he was honoured by the municipal council for long service and work for charity. Whatever may have been the insecurity and occasional penury of Schubert's chosen way of life, he never forfeited the care and affection of his devout and *bien-pensant* father. Believers in the neurosis of creative genius will find no support in Schubert.

The boy's first instruction in music came from his father – a capable practitioner like many of his profession in the empire – and from his elder brother Ignaz who, finding him already in his eighth year in need of more advanced tuition, sent him to Michael Holzer, choir-master of the parish church, who taught him singing, organ playing and the rudiments of harmony and counterpoint. Piano and violin he continued to learn at home. In 1808 the already highly accomplished boy won a place in the Convikt, the choir-school of the Imperial Chapel, run by monks. Here Schubert completed his education, studying with Wenzel Ruziczka (an excellent musician and dedicated teacher) and playing in the school orchestra, which he later conducted.

If compared with the juvenilia of Mozart, Beethoven* or Mendelssohn*, Schubert's earliest compositions show much imagination, but limited power in organizing his ideas. The first string quartet and the diffuse vocal works (*Hagar's Klage*, *Eine Leichenfantasie*, *Der Vatermörder*) are not without rhetorical force and vehement expression but scarcely hint at the intuitive organizing faculty of prospective genius. The boy's healthy appetite for sombre, even lurid subjects led him to set (with extensive revisions) Schiller's *Der Taucher*; the poet's depiction of the whirlpool and its monsters from the deep inspired harmonic adventures that would have seemed intemperate to the young

Brahms* a generation or more later. In the same year, 1813, the first Schubert symphony, dedicated to the star pupil's headmaster, revealed an easy conformism and a prodigious ability to manage themes derived from the works played by the school orchestra. The second and third symphonies (1815) are also essays in the lighter classical manner, abundant in charm and orchestrated with accuracy and practical skill. In chamber music a higher degree of originality had hindered formal control. In the summer of 1812 Schubert had become a pupil of Salieri, who, even if he recognized the flashes of unpredictable genius, must have doubted his gift for extended composition. Yet by the end of 1815 the symphonies, two masses, operas, and, above all, nearly two hundred songs had revealed a young master of scarcely comparable inventiveness and facility.

As for his stature, an assessment based on the orchestral works, church music and pieces for the stage would have forecast a brilliant career as a favourite of the Austrian bourgeoisie that found in music a refuge from the prosiness and boredom of life under the rule of the oppressively paternal Leopold. If the forms of these compositions were of classical derivation their themes and harmonic language showed the softening influence of the well-established Romanticism dismissed by Goethe* as early as 1804, besides the engaging Italian style with which Rossini* conquered Vienna at the end of 1816. None of this made a fit inheritance for the young artist whose imagination and understanding made him the only true successor to Beethoven. The basis for this claim, than which none could be higher, lies, up to the time mentioned, in a handful of songs, beginning with 'Gretchen am Spinnrade' (October 1814). This song is more than a marvel of intuitive understanding of the heart, though such it is; the seventeen-year-old Schubert grasped the deepest truths of tonal harmony – they are not conventions but resemble the truths of poetry – with a clairvoyant certainty denied to all but the greatest composers. Once the gift is bestowed nothing can cancel it, but though the numerous songs of the wonderful years after 1814 show enough perfect examples to make Schubert already music's finest lyrical poet, much also betrays a too ready response to facile sentiment, a weakness from which scarcely any of even his most sublime achievements is altogether free. The Beethovenian power and impetus of 'Der Erlkönig', 'Rastlose Liebe' (both 1815) or 'An Schwager Kronos' (1816) were slow to find a way into the instrumental music, where for most of the time Schubert luxuriates as innocently as the Keats* of *Endymion*.

These are not the only qualities to be valued and Schubert's too numerous songs contain perfect lyrics ('An die Musik') together with much that does not really rise far above the plangency of the Byron* of the lyrics – or Tom Moore. Again one thinks of Keats who, also born to scale the mind's mountains (to borrow a phrase from Hopkins*), had to contend with a not less innate fluency in a second-rate style. The gifted young people who made Schubert the centre of their circle (that their symposia were called Schubertiades testifies to his intellectual ascendancy) warmed him with their devotion, but could only encourage a too easy ability to please, when what he needed was to be understood (and criticized) as a supremely gifted artist almost submerged in mediocrity. Apart from songs and the Neo-classically perfect Fifth Symphony (1816) nothing before the 'Unfinished' Eighth Symphony in B minor (1822) reveals beyond mistaking 'the vision and the faculty divine'. This is not to deny the pervasiveness of genius in Schubert's too abundant output, but its manifestations are sporadic and often obscured by trivial contexts; the 'Unfinished' could have been written only by a master symphonist and certain things – the beginning of the first movement's development – touch the utmost height of the art. A large work of this period, the Mass in A flat, has splendid moments with others either pretentious or sentimental. In 1827 a friend wrote in a letter to Schubert, 'Credo in unum Deum. Du nicht, das weiss ich wohl' ('I believe in one God. You, I know well, don't'). Wittgenstein described him as 'irreligious and melancholy'. When God is mentioned little of value appears; Schubert's profound sense of religious awe and wonder responds to non-Christian texts as in Auflosüng, Nachthymne, and, above all, the long, marvellously sustained Im Walde (F. W. Schlegel*). The unfinished Lazarus (1820) had foreshadowed with vivid inventiveness the emotional excesses to come in the Romantic era.

By the end of 1822 the venereal infection dating back perhaps to 1818 or earlier returned as an illness from which there was to be no lasting recovery (though it was not directly connected with Schubert's death). Some verses (Mein Gebet), written in May 1823, reveal deep distress; a year later he wrote to Leopold Kupelwieser, 'Imagine someone whose health will never be sound again, and who through despair over this acts in ways that make his state worse rather than better.' Disappointed hopes of success in opera and the need to return to the parental home combined with the breakdown in health to provoke a personal crisis that left little trace in the music, Die schöne Müllerin and the bad opera Fierrabras being written between May and the end of the year. The song-cycle, innovatory in design and (for the first time since Symphony no. 5) faultlessly consistent in tone, transcends the poems' sentimental excesses thanks to Schubert's integrity of feeling, though the deathly sweet final song ought to be heard in some unfamiliar language. A few weeks after completing the cycle Schubert took one of the most moving things in it, 'Trockne Blumen', as the theme for a set of brilliant and tawdry Variations for flute and piano, ending with a jaunty march. He has

been reproached with insensitivity over this, but was he not repudiating with a rude gesture the exaltation of low spirits implicit in the sequence of these wonderful songs?

1824 was to be a year of recuperation; this strongminded artist was not much in love with easeful death and rapidly composed a part-masterpiece – the A minor quartet – and the Octet, a prime example, like the 'Trout' Piano Quintet of 1819, of the superlative second-best Schubert. A second stay in Hungary produced two works for piano duet in which, as in the first and third movements of the A minor quartet, the profound thinker of the 'Unfinished' can be discerned, though not consistently. In November one devoted friend (Schwind) wrote to another (Schober), 'Schubert is here [in Vienna] healthy and divinely frivolous (leichtsinnig), rejuvenated by bliss and sorrow and an easy life.'

Although the last years of a life more brief even than Mozart's saw the composition of his greatest works, Schubert's development shows no consistent pattern. In 1825 he wrote some of his finest piano music (Sonatas in A minor, D 845, and C major, D 840) followed by the Sonata in D major which moves from the grandiose to the near-trivial.

The D minor quartet ('Death and the Maiden') was completed early in 1826, not without delays and revisions; its scarcely less great and even more original successor in G (D 887) was composed in less than a fortnight; it is sadly diminished by a garrulous and at moments almost nugatory finale. The following spring Joseph von Spaun was summoned to hear some 'terrible songs' (schauerliche Lieder), i.e. the first group of Die Winterreise. Notions of the romantic artist would readily account for these by relating them to Schubert's unremitting disappointments in his career and the renewed attacks of his incurable illness that drove him out of the consoling circle of friends, but this was also the time of the Piano Trio in B flat, social music full of gaiety and unserious passion. The second Trio, op. 100, is more aware of its responsibilities, but the stroke of genius that brings back the theme of the Andante in the finale cannot save that movement from its vain repetitions and empty chatter.

That Schubert's last year was the richest in creative activity since 1815 should not be seen as the result of any premonition. Publishers were beginning to show some interest and a concert in March brought a profit. He finished in March the Symphony in C (no. 9), a work that, especially in its outer movements, meets as an equal the greatest things in abstract music.

Uniquely in all Schubert, the themes are reducible to formal patterns derived from the most elemental harmonic procedures; free from all hint of expressiveness these can be repeated to build vast designs sustained by the nuclear force of tonality. The other large-scale works of 1828 – the String Quintet and three Piano Sonatas – are full of marvels but cannot conceal the inability of lyrical, often elegiac or plangent melodies to function as stress-bearers. In the symphony Schubert, like Siegmund claiming the sword, shows he possesses the heroic strength to be the heir of Beethoven. It has been his posthumous misfortune to suffer the popularity of his weaker compositions among 'music-lovers' from whom the true nature of this inexhaustibly great artist would be as remote as it was from most of his contemporaries.

Basil Lam

Franz Schubert's Letters and other Writings, ed. Deutsch (1974). See: Otto E. Deutsch, *Schubert: A documentary Biography* (trans. 1946); Alfred Einstein, *Schubert* (1951); Harry Goldschmidt, *Franz Schubert. Ein Lebensbild* (1954); Maurice J.E. Brown, *Schubert: A Critical Biography* (1958). See also: D.F. Tovey, *Essays and Lectures on Music* (1949).

405
SCHUMANN, Robert Alexander 1810–56

German composer

Being the fifth and youngest child of a bookseller and publisher in Zwickau, Saxony, Schumann grew up surrounded by books and with a taste for literary expression manifested in his childhood as strongly as his gift for music. As a boy he was for ever compiling stories, verses and translations and sharing his literary enthusiasms with school friends. His musical education was in the hands of a local organist, Kuntzsch, and in 1819 the boy was taken by his father to Carlsbad to hear the celebrated virtuoso Moscheles. The new brand of piano virtuosity then sweeping Europe intoxicated the young Schumann who quickly developed a remarkable technique. In 1828 he matriculated as a law student at Leipzig University but devoted his time there to literary efforts and to a series of early compositions, mainly songs and piano pieces. He also began to take piano lessons with the celebrated teacher Friedrich Wieck. His second year of law studies was spent at Heidelberg, but he then returned in 1830 to Leipzig, where he remained for fourteen years. Musical and literary composition preoccupied him more and more, especially after his career as a virtuoso was cut short by persistent weakness in his right hand, an infirmity often attributed to his use of a mechanical practising device but more probably caused by mercury poisoning, mercury being then prescribed as treatment for syphilis.

Although he attempted orchestral music and had part of a symphony in G minor performed in 1832, his main output was for the piano, each piece taking on an unmistakably personal profile. The op. 5 *Impromptus*

were based on a theme by Wieck's twelve-year-old daughter Clara; *Carnaval*, op. 9, was based on the letters ASCH, which spelled the town where lived a fellow-pupil Ernestine von Fricken with whom Schumann was then in love. The music also refers to his secret society, the *Davidsbund*, dedicated to war against the 'Philistines'. In the same cause he was the moving agent in the foundation of a new periodical, the *Neue Zeitschrift für Musik*. He was principal editor and contributor for the first ten years of its (still continuing) existence, and in it appeared many of his most characteristic writings, often polemical or fantastic in tone.

In 1835 there began the love affair with Clara Wieck, then aged fifteen, which was to culminate in their marriage five years later after a prolonged and bitter struggle with her father, whose previous generosity evaporated as soon as he felt his paternal possession threatened. Clara being already a well-known pianist, Wieck took her away on tour as much to remove her from contact with Schumann as to display her gifts. Despite periods of bleak despair, during which Schumann resigned himself to her loss and even contemplated suicide, they set themselves to win permission to marry. This was awarded by the Leipzig courts in 1840 after Wieck had attempted every legal (and some unscrupulous) means to block it.

Although composing in many media, Schumann had hitherto published only piano music. In 1840, however, he returned to song with new creative vigour and composed his finest cycles, the two *Liederkreis*, *Myrthen*, *Frauenliebe und -leben*, *Dichterliebe*, and many individual songs, a prodigious outpouring of lyrical genius which at once placed him on a par with his adored Schubert*.

Clara's influence may be detected in his turning next to orchestral composition, a field which she believed would best kindle his imagination. The *Spring Symphony*, no. 1, the *Overture, Scherzo and Finale*, the first movement of the Piano Concerto, and another symphony (eventually labelled no. 4) were all completed in 1841. Chamber and choral works followed in some profusion. Already fully stretched by the editorship of the *Neue Zeitschrift* and obliged to accompany Clara on her tours (a task he found by no means congenial), the signs of physical and psychological breakdown were already felt. In 1844, despite a show of reconciliation from Wieck, the couple decided to move to Dresden. There he continued to compose at a feverish pace, including the choral *Faust-Szenen*, the opera *Genoveva*, Symphony no 2 and some music for Byron's* *Manfred*. Alongside these were many smaller pieces for piano and organ, songs and chamber works. Disturbed by revolutionary events in 1849 and their failure to establish roots in Dresden, Schumann and his wife moved in 1850 to Düsseldorf, where he succeeded his friend Hiller as the city's musical director, the only permanent post he ever held. The engagement was not a success. His shortcomings as a conductor were soon observed and his precarious health deteriorated rapidly. His hearing was badly impaired and by 1853 it was clear he could not continue. In February 1854 he attempted to drown himself in the Rhine and was soon thereafter confined to an asylum near Bonn where he spent the remaining two years of his life. Clara was not permitted to see him during these years and was only reunited with her husband two days before his death on 29 July 1856.

Schumann's music represents many facets of German Romanticism, a movement to which he also contributed much as a writer. Although he attempted all genres of composition, it is his piano music and songs which best epitomize his refined Romantic sentiment and his individuality. But his symphonic and chamber works are rightly admired in the tradition that links Beethoven* to Brahms*. It was Schumann's deliberate aim to emulate Bach and Beethoven in particular, and thus he became more and more preoccupied with contrapuntal technique and symphonic form, two elements of which his earliest and most impulsive music is relatively free. His larger compositions, especially *Genoveva* and the choral music, suffer from a ponderous mode of utterance and from unimaginative orchestration, although his laudable aim was to dignify the best traditions of German music by blending Romantic feeling with solid technical craftsmanship. His four symphonies have found a wider public, since feeling and form are there in fine balance, and the Piano Quintet, the Piano Quartet, the Piano Trios and the String Quartets deserve the same recognition. It is not true, as often asserted, that his late music is all of inferior quality, but his output is uneven, like that of his friend Mendelssohn*, passing from a brilliant youth to more staid middle years.

His most characteristic music antedates his marriage in 1840. His op. 1, a set of variations in the fashionable *brillante* style of 1830, shows him aping the piano virtuosi of his day. After the impact of Paganini* and Chopin* his style moved not towards a copy of either of theirs but to a marked individuality and freedom of its own. His private world, dwelling on fantasies drawn from Jean-Paul, Hoffmann* and others, provided a theatre for musical invention, revolving around persistent symbols like butterflies, moths, masks, cryptic letters, the harlequinade, and so on. In *Carnaval* (1833–5), the *Phantasiestücke* (1837), *Kreisleriana* (1838), or the *Noveletten* (1838) these and other images (often unexplained and inexplicable) inspire sometimes very brief pieces loosely attached in groupings of various size. Their lack of formal rigour intensifies an impression of ideas seized in dreams or moments of inspirational lucidity. At the same time Schumann devoted much energy to larger-scale forms in, for example, the two published sonatas in F sharp minor and G minor, also in the *Études symphoniques* (1834–7), a curious title given to a set of variations which he felt to be orchestral in character.

In two spheres his great gift for miniature forms and for deft imagery showed itself superbly. One was in music for children, the *Kinderszenen* (1838) being thirteen brief but sharply characterized pieces evoking the child's world; *Album für die Jugend*, ten years later, contained forty-three such pieces. The other was his mastery as a song-writer. To the *Lieder* tradition Schumann contributed many ballads and strophic songs of a well-tried type, but he also developed a new relationship between the voice and the piano which no longer treated the latter simply as an accompanist. Thoughts left unsaid by the singer could be subtly voiced in the piano's interludes and postludes. He also borrowed from Beethoven, rather than Schubert, the notion of a song-cycle as a work unified by its music as well as by its verses. It is much harder to extract individual songs from the *Dichterliebe* or *Liederkreis* than from Schubert's cycles. His favourite poets were Heine* and Goethe*, the evocative imagery and simplicity of their lyrics being especially suited to his needs. He composed some three hundred songs in all. There are also over seventy part-songs, much neglected today, but representing an important part of his output, often close in spirit to the solo songs.

His music is never free from a tendency for lyrical expression, nor from the shapes and idiom of piano-writing. He expanded the harmonic language of his day, as Chopin and Liszt* did, with yearning appoggiaturas and touches of expressive chromatic colour, and he made frequent use of imitative treatment of parts in quasi-fugal or quasi-canonic textures. Some ideas he borrowed unashamedly from Bach or Beethoven (for example, the link into the last movement of the Piano Concerto from Beethoven's 'Emperor' Concerto) and he had much in common with Mendelssohn. His prophetic admiration for the young Brahms in 1853 reflected a spiritual kinship which Brahms was only too happy to acknowledge.

A perception of talent in other composers and strong views about healthy and unhealthy trends are noticeable in his work as a critic. His recognition of Brahms had been anticipated by similarly far-sighted articles on Chopin in 1831 and Berlioz* in 1836. He warmly praised Sterndale Bennett. At the same time he was ruthlessly entrenched against Italian music and against Meyerbeer*, and his writings reveal vagaries of judgment which posterity has not endorsed. They are intimately related to his music in his fondness for aphorism and allusive imagery. Criticism and fiction are interwoven so that a fanciful story bears a musical message, or a review of new music is couched in elaborate fictional dress. The invented characters of his imagined brotherhood make frequent appearances: Florestan and Eusebius representing polarized projections of his own character, Meister Raro an occasional arbitrator, and many more.

Schumann's standing as a leading figure of German

Romanticism was fostered by Brahms and by his widow Clara and has never been challenged despite the evident failings of some of his larger works. Modern criticism has attempted to belittle the impulsive side of his nature by tracing long-range thematic similarities in the piano collections and song cycles, although the conclusions are far from convincing. Eric Sams has also demonstrated widespread use of cyphers and letter-codes in Schumann's themes, it being well recognized that Schumann was absorbed by word-games and cryptic language throughout his life. Yet in no composer's work is artifice so well concealed as in Schumann's music of the 1830s, a monument to the purest forms of Romantic inspiration. Ultimately he forged strong links with the mainstream of German classical music but he would still command our admir-·ation if he had never felt impelled to do so.

Hugh Macdonald

Schumann's letters and critical writings have long been available to English readers, the latter in two volumes entitled *Music and Musicians* published in 1877. A first volume of his diaries has recently been published (*Tagebücher*, vol. 1, 1971), covering the years 1827–38. General coverage is best provided by two symposia, the first edited by Gerald Abraham (*Schumann: A Symposium*, 1952), the second by Alan Walker (*Robert Schumann: The Man and his Music*, 1972, rev. 1976). See also: Robert Haven Schauffler, *Florestan: The Life and Work of Robert Schumann* (1945); Joan Chissell, *Schumann* (1948, rev. 1967); and the admirable summary by Gerald Abraham in *The New Grove Dictionary of Music*, vol. 16 (1980).

406
SCOTT, George Gilbert 1811–78

British architect

Gilbert Scott was born, the son of a clergyman, into a household without any special claims to artistry, in 1811. His grandfather was the noted theologian Thomas Scott, 1747–1821. Scott's professional life as an architect began twenty-four years later when, in 1835, he formed a partnership (lasting until 1846) with W.B. Moffatt, following his apprenticeship in several architects' offices, including those of Sir John Smirke and Henry Roberts. His first works were mainly workhouses and asylums, and Reading Gaol (1842–4, where Oscar Wilde* was later imprisoned), but he rapidly progressed to ecclesiastical architecture under the influence of Pugin* and the assertions of the *Ecclesiologist* magazine. Indeed, it was ecclesiastical work that provided most of Scott's (eventually enormous) office's livelihood, the acceptable basis for his style, and his first major foreign commission – Hamburg's Nikolai-

kirche. This he won in competition in 1844 (although it was not completed until 1860), the design of which was specially commended for its appropriate style, reflecting Scott's belief, expressed in his 1857 book *Remarks on Secular and Domestic Architecture*, in, above all, the Gothic of northern Italy, the Low Countries and Germany. Several large-scale church commissions followed, including St John's Cathedral, Newfoundland (1847–8), St John's Col! ₂ge Chapel, Cambridge (1836–72), and the Episcopalian Cathedral, Edinburgh (1874–9).

Scott's ecclesiastical work also extended to considerable restoration work, of which Ely (begun 1847) and Lichfield (begun 1857) Cathedrals are notable examples – but which were particularly disliked by Ruskin* – together with Hereford, Salisbury, Ripon and Westminster Abbey. By restoration the Victorians did not mean what we mean by conservation today. The Victorian Gothicists actually believed their medieval originals to be defective – the result of an incomplete understanding and too slow working methods – and they felt it their duty to correct the consequent flaws in the originals. Hence the feeling often engendered today that their restoration work is insensitive, inappropriate, even gross. Scott, through his restoration work, was nevertheless jointly responsible for the founding of the Society for the Protection of Ancient Buildings.

Established as the major star in the Gothic firmament, following Pugin's early death (1852), promoting a style seen as truly (and ironically, in view of his book's concerns) British and symbolic of a national revival, Scott, in 1856, entered the two competitions for the Foreign and Home Offices in Whitehall – the first ever competitions for offices – with designs in the stipulated Gothic style. In spite of winning neither, he was eventually commissioned to create both in a unified Government Office design: a typical outcome of the wheeling and dealing, compromise and lobbying that characterized the immensely important competitions of the time. However, Palmerston, after his election as prime minister, insisted on a change in style to a sixteenth-century interpretation of the Byzantine. Scott compromised and agreed to change style rather than lose a large and significant commission, to the annoyance of his former apprentices, such as the eventual winner of the Law Courts competition, G.E. Street, who came to believe they and not Scott were sporting the true Gothic banner. Thus it came about that political dictates concerning style caused the two outstanding governmental buildings of the mid-Victorian era to be built by architects in the 'wrong' style: Scott's classical Government Offices and Barry's* Gothic Palace of Westminster.

Scott built many other secular buildings in Gothic. Of these, the Albert Memorial (1863–72) is interesting as both a social document (public testament to Albert*, focus of a Victorian urban development, and demonstrative of the Victorians' evaluation of great forms and figures of the past) and in reflecting Scott's own interpretation of Victorian architecture. The architects represented on its famous frieze of worthies are Cockerell, Barry, Pugin and (in the background) Scott himself. The idea for the memorial is, however, strongly influenced by two unrepresented architects, Thomas Worthington (the Albert Memorial in Manchester, 1862–7) and Meikle Kemp (the Scott Memorial, 1840–4, in Edinburgh). But probably Scott's greatest secular achievement is the Midland Grand Hotel at St Pancras (1868–74). Here, on an awkward London site, he erected the most splendid of London's railway hotels, complete with vast galleries, staircases and the celebrated dining-room. The building sweeps round and up to the elevated height of the platforms behind. The elevation is crowned by a clock tower clearly based on Barry's and Pugin's Big Ben clock tower at the Palace of Westminster. But perhaps more remarkable than the building itself is the contrast between the hotel and the station behind, covered by its wonderful single span arch (W.H. Barlow and R.M. Ordish, 1863–5). Here the difference in attitude to architecture and engineering and their uses becomes absolutely apparent: architecture reflecting in the decoration of the various styles the pomp and self-esteem of the age, fronting the real, wealth-creating achievements of the engineers.

Scott's office produced, in his working life, over 1,000 designs – an enormous output – including several housing estates and country houses. Like Barry and also Alfred Waterhouse he founded a family architectural dynasty, and like Barry he was outstripped by the stylistic developments of his time (a development in stylism of which Thomas Hardy*, himself trained as an architect, writes so scathingly in 'A Laodicean') – Barry by the supremacy of Gothic, Scott by changing understandings of that same Gothic. Nevertheless he was held in continuing respect, being knighted in 1872 and becoming an early president of the Royal Institute of British Architects (1873–5), whose Gold Medal he also won.

Ranulph Glanville

See: J. Summerson, *Victorian Architecture in England: Four Studies in Evaluation* (1970); R. Dixon and S. Muthesius, *Victorian Architecture* (1978).

407
SCOTT, Sir Walter 1771–1832

Scottish poet and novelist

In a lifetime of sixty-one years, Sir Walter Scott fulfilled more careers than most men have early ambitions. By the time he was forty-three he had been called to the Bar, helped form a Volunteer Regiment, been appointed Sheriff of Selkirkshire, become a clerk to the Court of Session, founded the publishing house of Ballantyne & Co., fathered four children (Sophia, Walter, Anne, Charles: in that order), purchased his own Border estate of Abbotsford – and still had time to attain such popular success as a poet that he had been offered the Poet Laureateship (which he refused). To most people the spectacle, let alone the exertion, of so much energy would have been enough. But in 1814, with the publication of the anonymous novel *Waverley*, Scott was only beginning a new career that would establish him as a classic: the perfection of what was virtually his own invention, the historical novel. In the remaining eighteen years of his life Scott not only wrote twenty-seven more novels but continued his other multifarious activities.

Walter Scott was born in Edinburgh on 15 August 1771, the ninth of twelve children born to Walter Scott – a Writer to the Signet – and his wife Anne. As a child Walter lost the power of his right leg due to polio and was sent, for the sake of his health (which improved and left him with a limp) to his grandfather's farmhouse in Roxburghshire. Thus Scott's 'first consciousness of existence' was the Border country, not the city. Back in Edinburgh he was sent to the high school and then to the university where he earned the nickname of 'Greek Blockhead' because of his inability to learn the language. In 1785 he was apprenticed to his father as Writer to the Signet and later decided to qualify as an advocate (the Scottish equivalent of a barrister). In 1792 he and his friend William Clerk were called to the Scottish Bar and Scott was, as he wrote in an autobiographical essay, 'a gentleman, and so welcome anywhere'.

In 1795 Scott wrote a passionate love letter to Williamina Belsches, an heiress whose father Sir John had squandered his own inheritance and was several thousand pounds in debt. The following year Scott published, anonymously, his first book: *The Chase, and William and Helen*, two translations from the German of Bürger. Williamina was impressed by the little book but decided, for financial reasons, to marry the son of a rich banker so her family's financial problems would be solved. Scott was shattered, 'broken-hearted for two years . . . but the crack will remain till my dying day'. On the rebound Scott married a French girl, Charlotte Charpentier, and embarked on thirty-nine years of marriage which might (he told a correspondent) have fallen 'something short of love in all its fervour' but was nevertheless a good working relationship.

The first book published under Scott's name was *Goetz of Berlichingen* (1799), a translation of Goethe's* drama. It made little impact. However, Scott was turning to the indigenous culture of Scotland; as Sheriff-Deputy of Selkirkshire he had the time to collect great traditional ballads which were still in oral circulation (and to tamper with the texts). The result was the publication, in three volumes, of the *Minstrelsy of the Scottish Border* (1802–3). This was a critical and commercial success and, encouraged by the attention paid to the ballads, Scott thought he might create something to appeal specifically to antiquarian interests. Borrowing Coleridge's* 'Christabel' metre and using (at the suggestion of the Countess of Dalkeith) the legend of Gilpin Horner, Scott wrote his first major poetic work *The Lay of the Last Minstrel* (1805). It combined metrical fluency with a strong narrative gift and tapped the public's interest in nostalgia. Throughout his life Scott regarded literature more as a source of income than as an aesthetic necessity and the triumph of *Minstrel* convinced him of his own financial potential. Constable, the publisher, paid 1,000 guineas for an unseen narrative poem *Marmion* (1808); for *The Lady of the Lake* (1810) Scott took a 2,000 guinea fee and a share of the profits.

'I determined that literature should be my staff but not my crutch,' said Scott and his motive for completing *Rokeby* (1813) was frankly mercenary. In 1811 Scott decided to buy Cartley Hole Farmhouse on the Tweed and raised half of the 4,000 guinea purchase price on the promise of *Rokeby*. He moved in, renamed the farmhouse Abbotsford, and proceeded (at colossal expense) to transform it into a baronial mansion; Abbotsford, where he could act out his own fantasies, was the real love of Scott's life. *Rokeby* was not the success Scott hoped it would be and the reason for this was the appearance of a formidable rival: Lord Byron* who 'awoke and found myself famous' after the publication of *Childe Harold* (1812). Scott was outwritten and knew he would never again have a monopoly of the market for narrative poetry. Scott was more an accomplished versifier than a poet; that is, his approach was purely functional and he eschewed euphony and imagery in the interests of a solid narrative pace. His octosyllabic couplets – predictable in rhythm and rhyme – tend to wear down the modern reader. Here, from *The Lord of the Isles* (1815), are some typical lines:

> Avenger of thy country's shame,
> Restorer of her injured fame,
> Bless'd in thy sceptre and thy sword,
> De Bruce, fair Scotland's rightful Lord,
> Bless'd in thy deeds and in thy fame
> What lengthen'd honours wait thy name!

In later life Scott always maintained that he gave up poetry because 'Byron beat me' but business acumen must have played an important part in his decision. In 1805 Scott had thought of attempting a prose narrative and accordingly 'threw together about one-third part of the first volume of *Waverley*'. Somehow a 'critical friend' discouraged the publication of the novel and, rather than risk his reputation as a poet by a sudden adventure into prose, Scott put the manuscript into an old writing desk which was eventually stored in a lumber garret at Abbotsford. The lost manuscript was recovered in 1813 and Scott, still sensitive about his poetic reputation, decided against putting his name to a work which might fail. *Waverley* was published anonymously, in three volumes, on 7 July 1814, and so indifferent was Scott to his reception as a novelist that he, literally, left the book behind him and went on a two-month tour of the Scottish islands. In his absence *Waverley* took off on an astonishing journey to international celebrity; by the end of the year 5,000 copies had been sold at a profit of more than £2,000. 'I have seldom,' Scott said, 'felt more satisfaction.' He had every reason to be satisfied. Here was a way he could finance his increasingly ambitious plans for Abbotsford; that he had developed a new literary genre was by the way.

Scott's most telling literary innovation was to present the past so vividly that readers felt they were actually participating in historical events. To Scott the past was a meaningful experience, not an escapist fantasy or a Gothic extravaganza. However romantically inclined the central figure might be, the historical panorama was conveyed with accuracy and artistic integrity. In the first chapter of *Waverley* Scott explained his method: 'I would have my readers understand, that they will meet in the following pages neither a romance of chivalry, nor a tale of modern manners . . . the object of my tale is more a description of men than manners.' Scott was the first novelist to make fictional history believable and to integrate his invented characters completely with real people. In choosing to set his first novel at the time of the 1745 Jacobite uprising he was asking his readers to re-examine the basis of their own time, to wonder at what was lost (idealism, blind loyalty) and what was gained (prosperity, stability). Although Scott has been caricatured as an incurable romantic this label does not relate to his finest work. *Waverley* shows the reality of Jacobitism and the horrors of war. As Edward Waverley moves through Scotland, after hearing of the defeat of the clans at Culloden, he sees clearly the consequences of conflict: 'As he advanced northward, the traces of war became visible. Broken carriages, dead horses, unroofed cottages, trees felled for palisades, and bridges destroyed or only partially repaired, – all indicated the movements of hostile armies.' In such passages Scott anticipates the documentary fiction of Solzhenitsyn.

After *Waverley* Scott saw that writing novels could enable him to live in luxury. His second novel *Guy Mannering* (1815) – which contains the colourful spaewife Meg Merrilies – was written in six weeks and the first edition of 2,000 copies sold out in a day. Scott preserved his anonymity partly because it was good for business (as the public speculated on the identity of the Great Unknown) and partly because he cherished his life as the Laird of Abbotsford. He wrote out of the public gaze, beginning at 5 a.m. and finishing his writing by breakfast so he could spend his day with colleagues, family and friends. There can be little doubt that the aristocratic life-style meant more to Scott than his reputation as poet and novelist. We have it on Lockhart's authority that 'at the highest elevation of his literary renown – when princes bowed to his name, and nations thrilled at it – he would have considered losing all that at a change of the wind, as nothing, compared to parting with his place as the Cadet of Harden and Clansman of Buccleuch.'

Scott's fascination with the aristocracy went hand-in-glove with his reactionary Tory politics and he cultivated the rich and influential who, in turn, deferred to his intellect. In 1820, as well as publishing three novels (*Ivanhoe*, *The Monastery*, *The Abbot*) he was created a baronet by George IV; two years later he personally stage-managed the king's visit to Scotland. Despite the physical pain he had to endure, from gall-stones, he seemed to lead a charmed life up until the fall of 1826. In 1824 he completed work on Abbotsford and published *Redgauntlet* which is probably his most subtle and deeply felt fictional achievement, a creative refutation of those critics who accuse Scott of superficiality and dullness. The characterization in *Redgauntlet* is rich, the narrative modes diverse. It is set *c.* 1766 with the House of Hanover securely established and the catastrophe of Culloden a painful memory to all but a few Jacobite fanatics like Redgauntlet.

Scott's cast of characters includes ordinary people involved in extraordinary events and, in creating them, he drew deeply on personal experiences. Alan Fairford, the conscientious lawyer, is Scott himself; Darsie Latimer, the impetuous kinsman of Redgauntlet, is modelled partly on Scott's friend Will Clerk and partly on the romantic side of Scott's own nature; Mr. Fairford (with his 'anxious, devoted and unremitting affection') is a portrait of Scott's father; and Green Mantle is a tribute to Scott's first love Williamina Belsches. As befits a novel that explores the persistence of the past *Redgauntlet* begins, in the eighteenth-century manner, with an epistolary exchange between Alan and Darsie. About one-third of the way through the book Scott suddenly abandons the 'advantage of laying before the reader, in the words of the actors themselves, the adventures which we must otherwise have narrated in our own'. Henceforth the novel uses third-personal narration and first-personal extracts from Darsie's journal. Scott, usually so relentlessly consistent, thus sustains several stylistic levels in the book: the familiar tone of the letters, the urgency of Darsie's journal, the elegance of Scott's best prose. And he incorporates in the novel two of the greatest moments he ever achieved in fiction.

First is the vernacular *tour de force*, 'Wandering Willie's Tale', which appears in Letter XI from Darsie to Alan. Darsie has met the blind fiddler who entertains him with a chilling tale that is drawn from Scott's immense knowledge of the oral tradition:

> Men thought [Sir Robert Redgauntlet] had a direct compact with Satan – that he was proof against steel – and that bullets happed aff his buff-coat like hailstanes from a hearth – that he had a mear that would turn a hare on the side of Carrifra-gawns – and muckle to the same purpose of whilk mair anon.

The second moment of artistic supremacy comprises the powerful and poignant finale of the novel. Redgauntlet and other dedicated Jacobites have persuaded Charles Edward Stuart (no longer a Bonnie Prince but a weary *de jure* king) to stage another uprising. Jacobitism, though, is a spent force and – as Redgauntlet has to acknowledge – 'the cause is lost for ever'. Scott has realistically come to terms with a legend and his description of Charles Edward in distress contains both dignity and historical insight.

As a writer Scott was a phenomenon: a graphomaniac who was a master of English prose and Scottish speech-rhythms and who combined them in a vision of Scotland as a country haunted by the past and reluctant to prepare for the future. The last period of Scott's life demonstrated his own heroism. In 1826 Scott's printers and publishers collapsed and he was faced with debts of almost £117,000 (including private debts of around £20,000). The Duke of Buccleuch and other rich friends offered to help but Scott said, 'No! this right hand shall work it all off!' He entered a furious period of productivity: his *Life of Buonaparte* was published in 1827 and in 1828 he published *The Fair Maid of Perth* and the first series of *Tales of a Grandfather*. He also began his *magnum opus*, a complete annotated edition of his novels. By the end of 1828 he had earned £40,000 for his creditors and by the end of 1831 he had cleared all his debts ('I could never have slept straight in my coffin till I had satisfied every claim against me'). The end of his life was not without its pathetic moments. In 1831 Scott decided to appear in Jedburgh on behalf of the Tory candidate; as Scott's carriage passed a group of radical weavers it was stoned and his attempt to make a speech drowned out in abuse. Scott left Jedburgh to a hail of stones and cries of 'Burke Sir Walter' (a reference to William Burke hanged in 1829 on the evidence of his fellow bodysnatcher William Hare). Ironically, given his political views, Scott died in the year of the great Reform Act; on his deathbed he was heard muttering the phrase 'Burke Sir Walter'.

Alan Bold

The classic biography is *Memoirs of the Life of Sir Walter Scott* (7 vols, 1837–8) by J.G. Lockhart; a Marxist view of Scott is contained in Georg Lukács,

The Historical Novel (1962), and a fine critical study of Scott is Edgar Johnson, *Walter Scott: The Great Unknown* (2 vols, 1970).

408
SCRIABIN, Aleksandr Nikolayevich 1872–1915
(also SKRYABIN, SCRIABINE, SKRJABIN)

Russian pianist and composer

Scriabin came from an aristocratic Moscow family and was brought up not by his parents but by doting female relatives who may be responsible for his highly fastidious and egocentric behaviour in later years. His musical gifts were nourished by Konyus, Zverev and Taneyev, and in 1888 he entered the Moscow Conservatoire where Rachmaninov was a fellow-pupil. He was soon launched on a career as a pianist and his early compositions, heavily influenced by the music of Chopin*, appeared in rapid succession in the 1890s from the houses of Jurgenson and Belyayev, the latter of whom extended his bountiful patronage to Scriabin, sending him on a European tour in 1895–6 and providing financial support.

From about 1902 until his early death in 1915 Scriabin displayed an increasing preoccupation with philosophical and mystical ideas, and at the same time his musical style developed so startlingly that he was soon heralded, along with Schoenberg and Richard Strauss, as one of the most advanced composers of his time. After the abandonment of his marriage he travelled widely in Europe and America, only returning to Russia for any extended period in the last few years.

His compositions are almost exclusively for the piano and for orchestra. He had no feeling for vocal music and gave up plans for a 'philosophical opera'. The ten piano sonatas and the five large orchestral works span his brief career, with numerous smaller piano pieces – mostly entitled 'prelude' or 'poem' – and some early orchestral pieces to complete his output. The charming manner of the early preludes and mazurkas (the titles betray their debt to Chopin) was replaced first by a more massive, Lisztian* style, then by a dynamic, sensuous style derived from extended chromatic harmony and decorated with poetic titles and instructions. The first two symphonies were untitled, but the third was the *Divine Poem* of 1902–4, for large orchestra, which explored areas of voluptuous and dramatic ecstasy new to symphonic thought. The *Poem of Ecstasy* (1905–8) took this process considerably further with a feverish concentration of lush orchestral sound in a single movement. Scriabin published a long poem to accompany the music, revealing his obsession with the dream-like, semi-mystical images that filled his notebooks at this time. Originally drawn to Nietzsche*, he transferred his obsessive devotions to theosophy and the teaching of Madame Blavatsky, with a growing conviction that he himself was the god-like centre of the cosmos, dominating all things with his creativity. This egomania lies behind his last orchestral work, *Prometheus, Poem of Fire* (1908–10), which, despite this background, is a work of supreme originality and craftsmanship composed in an advanced post-tonal style Scriabin had both invented and perfected in a very short period. It introduced a 'colour-organ' to give an extra dimension to the music.

His gradual emancipation from tonal mannerisms is more clearly traced in the piano music. He relished the sonorous, non-functional identity of chords, as did Debussy, and built up extensions of dominant sevenths over little or no rhythmic pulse, creating a languid, timeless sound-world. The last five sonatas (1911–13) form an astonishing group of exploratory works, each in one movement, each individually characterized in harmonic colour and form. The very last pieces, of 1914, took him even further into atonal territory.

Scriabin's best work, of all periods, is highly concentrated, imaginative in technique and carefully balanced in structure. The dazzling progress from early to late music may be attributed to his unswerving consciousness of his own genius, backed up by a characteristically Russian obsession with an idea, pursued beyond what to more moderate minds would seem reasonable limits. After 1920 his reputation quickly subsided and his excesses were easily decried. In recent years his music has been reappraised and is now more fairly classed among the most cogent and progressive of its time.

Hugh Macdonald

Faubion Bowers, *Scriabin* (2 vols, Tokyo, 1969), provides a very full biography drawn from Russian sources, especially his letters. The most searching exploration of Scriabin's ideas and their infusion in his music is found in Manfred Kelkel, *Alexandre Scriabine* (Paris, 1978), and there are numerous analytical studies of the music by, for example: C.C. von Gleich, *Die sinfonischen Werke von Alexander Skrjabin* (1963); V. Dernova, *Garmoniya Skryabina* (1968); Hanns Steger, *Der Weg der Klaviersonaten bei Alexander Skrjabin* (1972); Dietrich Mast, *Struktur und Form bei Alexander N. Skrjabin* (1981). A general introduction to the music is found in Hugh Macdonald, *Skryabin* (1978).

409
SEURAT, Georges Pierre 1859–91

French painter

Georges Seurat was born in Paris, the youngest child of a bailiff. He was a pupil of Henri Lehmann, a disciple of Ingres*, at the École des Beaux Arts, 1878–9. He studied antique sculpture, the Renaissance masters and the drawing of Ingres. While on military service at Brest, 1879–80, he began to paint landscapes. On his return to Paris he became interested in urban social subject matter and began to develop the distinctive drawing style for which he is famous, using soft conté crayon on heavily textured paper. These studies with their monumental forms devoid of hard outline were prototypes for his painted figures. While working at drawing and painting Seurat read the works of Charles Blanc and Michel-Eugène Chevreul on colour contrast and harmony and Hermann von Helmholtz* on physiological optics. His painting style during this period was close to that of Barbizon and Impressionist artists. In the autumn of 1884 he showed his celebrated large canvas Une Baignade à Asnières (1883–4), which had been refused by the Salon, at the first exhibition of the Société des Artistes Indépendants, which he had founded with Signac, Redon* and other radical artists. In 1886 he exhibited the other very large canvas for which he is renowned, La Grande Jatte (1883–5), at the last Impressionist exhibition. This was his first major attempt at what became known as 'pointillism' or 'neo-Impressionism'. A number of Symbolist writers and critics, like Felix Fénéon and Gustave Kahn, rallied round Seurat and also Paul Signac, in defence of their art and theories. Painters like Cross, Angrand, Lucien Pissarro and Luce became 'neo-Impressionists' and Van Gogh*, who met Seurat this year, incorporated some of the latter's ideas into his own work. Seurat died quite suddenly of infectious angina in 1891. He produced seven large canvases, sixty small ones, 160 very small wood panel studies and nearly 500 drawings.

Seurat's art, developed in a little over ten years, grew from a number of 'scientific researches' into physiological optics, colour theory and the affective qualities of colours, lines and forms, as well as from a scrupulous technique and a great deal of study of earlier masters. His earliest researches into the simultaneous contrast of colours, based on a reading of Blanc and Chevreul, and a study of Delacroix's* use of colour, led to Une Baignade on which he worked for over a year and reworked in 1887. Seurat made thirteen preparatory oil sketches and numerous drawings for this work which, with its elemental composition, its monumental figures and banal industrial suburb for background, seems to be a secular reworking of Piero della Francesca's art. It certainly bears a relationship to the work of Seurat's Symbolist contemporary Puvis de Chavannes*. Although the work is based on firmly moulded forms and a geometrical composition, the first traces of the pointillist technique can be discerned in the grass in the foreground. All the hues have a luminosity and intensity which derives from the use of pure and largely unmixed colours. It was La Grande Jatte,

showing Parisians relaxing on a Sunday afternoon, which was the first extreme example of pointillism and fully reveals the influence of scientific ideas on his work. All the colour is applied in small dots and strokes which, at a certain distance, are 'optically mixed' by the spectator's eye. Around the edge of this and future canvases is a thin border or 'false frame', which contrasts with adjacent colours. The figures are still and hieratic, as if seen in an atmospheric frieze, and the first traces of an elegant 'art nouveau' line can be traced in some of the forms. As with most of Seurat's major works La Grande Jatte was carefully composed over a long period from a large number of studies. After 1886, under the influence of the scientist and aesthetician Charles Henry, Seurat's work often deals with movement and he developed in his last years a complex linear style which was meant directly to affect the beholder's emotions by its formal arrangement. The emotional tones of pictures like Le Chahut (1889–90) and Le Cirque (1890–1) show the considerable impact of Henry's ideas concerning the relationships obtained between linear directions by measuring their angles with a Rapporteur Esthétique, a sort of aesthete's protractor. Seurat's own formulation of these theories was made in a letter to a friend, the writer Maurice Beaubourg, in August 1890, in which he stated, 'Art is Harmony. Harmony is the analogy of contrary and similar qualities in tone, colour and line, considered with reference to a Dominant and under the influence of a scheme of lighting in cheerful, calm or sad combinations.' These ideas had a major impact on later Symbolist and abstractionist theories of art and, in revising the tenets of Impressionism, led to the creation of more conceptual and schematic art forms than either Impressionism or traditional varieties of realism had offered. The Italian 'Divisionists', in particular Boccioni and Balla, were to develop these ideas into Futurism. Similar experiments in Germany by Kandinsky and Klee were to lay some of the foundations of a formally non-objective art. Like Degas* and Cézanne*, Seurat tried to reinvent the classical elements of structure and over-all design in painting without sacrificing the mainly scientific advances that had been made since the advent of Impressionism. Seurat, in his scientific studies and researches, revived the image of the artist-philosopher in the tradition of Poussin and, before him, Leonardo.

Richard Humphreys

See: H. Dorra and J. Rewald, Seurat (Paris, 1960); Seurat's Drawings, ed. R.L. Herbert (1963); W.I. Homer, Seurat and the Science of Painting (1964); J. Russell, Seurat (1965); J. Arguelles, Charles Henry and the formation of a Psychological Aesthetic (1972).

410
SHAW, Richard Norman 1831–1912

British architect

Norman Shaw is one of the most important domestic architects of the late Victorian period. Works most associated with his name are those designed in the Old English styles and that of the Queen Anne revival, and yet his manner and sources remained diverse, sometimes looking to vernacular cottages in Sussex, at other times to the Scottish baronial (New Scotland Yard). He was, in part, responsible for the move away from the severity of High Victorian Gothic designs to a more 'homely' and habitable style, today seen vulgarized in the semi-detached suburban house.

Born in Edinburgh, he came to London when young and began his architectural apprenticeship in 1849 under William Burn. In 1856 he was articled to Salvin in whose office he met W.E. Nesfield with whom he formed a partnership from 1863–6. Though each worked independently a cross influence of styles was inevitable. It was working in G.E. Street's office, as principal assistant, following Philip Webb, that was the most decisive influence during his training. It was there, so he said, that he learnt everything he knew about architecture. Street's influence can be seen most especially in Shaw's High Victorian church architecture such as Holy Trinity, Bingley, Yorkshire (1866–7).

At this period Shaw was considering a career in ecclesiastical architecture – a field that had been so securely occupied by A.W. Pugin*, W. Butterfield and Street. It is this interest which is shown in his first publication, *Architectural Sketches from the Continent* (1858). The one hundred lithographs consist mainly of Gothic cathedrals and monuments, after sketches he had made while touring Italy, France and Germany in 1854–6, a tour made possible by his winning the Royal Academy Travelling Scholarship award in 1854.

It was not until 1862, on a visit to Sussex with Nesfield that Shaw shifted his interests from church designs towards domestic, an area where there seemed greater opportunity for commissions. His sketches of that date show an interest in vernacular buildings, an example of one such being Sedlescomb, East Sussex, of *c.* 1611, and this research was important for the development of Shaw's Old English style, a term loosely covering borrowings from the Gothic and Tudor periods.

Shaw's first significant commission was the extending of a Georgian house at Willesley, for John Calcott Horsley RA. Shaw imposes an irregularity on the existing eighteenth-century house which is not altogether successful, and much of the rustic decoration is amateurish. Yet the inclusion of a medieval hall was to become a regular feature of his large country houses, a characteristic that was later taken up by Baillie Scott.

Glen Andred (1868), Leyswood (1870) and Hillside (1870–1) are the major works in the Old English style, and in their imposing settings they appear as descendants of the aesthetic of the picturesque movement.

The 'fortress-like' Leyswood, one of Shaw's most influential buildings, both in England and America, announced the vocabulary of his mature Old English style, in its use of tile hanging, half-timbering, lofty gables and massive ribbed chimney stacks. The clarity of the blocks and firmness of the individual detail show an assurance in part indebted to Street, that escapes nostalgic references and muddled planning of so many Victorian houses.

In the towns where Old English was felt to be inappropriate it was the Queen Anne style that caught on, taking the place of Italianate stuccoed façades. Nesfield had already experimented with this style in his Kew Lodge (1867), but it was Shaw who was responsible for its popularity. The label, again inappropriate, refers to takings from English and Dutch red brick architecture of the seventeenth and eighteenth centuries with some French and Flemish details.

In 1872, a year after he started his London career, he was commissioned to build Lowther Lodge, a town 'country' house near Hyde Park, using as a model the seventeenth-century Kew palace. Queen Anne elements introduced here become more prominent in other works of this decade, such as New Zealand Chambers (1871–3), Swan House (1875–7), the Albert Hall Mansions, and the many houses he designed in Cadogan Square, Queen's Gate and along the Chelsea Embankment.

In later years Shaw increasingly turned toward the classical style, the two most ambitious projects being Bryanston (1889–94) and his additions to Chesters (1891–3), the latter in a free classical style with a baroque vocabulary, that he later employed in the Piccadilly Hotel (1905–8).

Shaw's achievement lies in his revolutionary contribution to country house design. His influence, continued through his pupils, Lethaby, Prior and Newton, was not only felt in England but, through publications, contributed to the development of the 'Shingle' style in America.

Calan Lewis

Other works include: Cragside (enlargement of shooting lodge into a country house, 1869–86); Convent of Sisters of Bethany, Bournemouth (1873–5 and 1878–80); 196 Queen's Gate, London (1874–6); Cheyne House (1875–7); Clock House, Chelsea Embankment (1878–80); All Saints' Church, Compton, Leek (1884–7). See: Andrew Saint, *Richard Norman Shaw* (1976).

411

SHELLEY, Mary 1797–1851

British novelist

Mary Shelley was the daughter of Mary Wollstonecraft and William Godwin*. Authors and radicals, both disapproved of marriage but were legally joined in time to legitimize Mary who was born late in 1797. Mary's mother died shortly after the birth and the girl grew up in effect an orphan as her remarried father treated her with a detached benignity. In 1814 she met Shelley* and eloped with him to the continent, returning after a few weeks to a debt-haunted existence in London. In 1816, more secure financially, they returned to Europe and it was while the party was holidaying with Byron* by Lake Geneva that the story of *Frankenstein* (1818) was conceived. Back in England Shelley and Mary were eventually married after the suicide of the poet's first wife. In the year of *Frankenstein's* publication Shelley and his entourage went into what was, for him, a perpetual exile: he was drowned in the Bay of Spezia in 1822. Mary and her one surviving son, the more anxiously tended because he was her living link with a revered husband, came back to their native country. Shelley was obliquely commemorated in several of the novels Mary wrote after the poet's death; something of her sense of isolation is perhaps indicated in the apocalyptic work *The Last Man* (1826). She later produced the first edition of his poems (1839), although the durable hostility of Shelley's father to his son's memory had to be overcome. Mary Shelley died in 1851.

Her books, such as *Lodore* (1835) and *Falkner* (1837), have a strong autobiographical aspect, as does her only work of real significance, *Frankenstein*. The account of its inception is familiar: '"We will each write a ghost story," said Lord Byron, and his proposition was acceded to' (from the author's introduction). Mary claimed that the essence of the story came in reverie – 'My imagination, unbidden, possessed and guided me' – underlining the romantic primacy given to the non-rational area of the mind by Shelley and his circle. The framework of the novel is provided by a series of letters written home by Walton, an Arctic explorer and himself an echo of the ambitious visionary Frankenstein. His ship ice-bound, he rescues the scientist who is in pursuit of the artificial monster (it is never given a name). The bulk of the book is Frankenstein's account to Walton of how he came to create the 'being of a gigantic stature', how he turned away in loathing from what he had made and how the monster revenged itself on his family and friends. Rejecting the monster's plea that the scientist should make a mate for it, Frankenstein tries to destroy what he has made. He dies before accomplishing this; the narrator-explorer confronts the monster who returns to lament his creator and last victim and who shows a capacity for remorse and pity never apparent in its maker. Finally it leaps on to an ice raft and is 'borne away by the waves and lost in darkness and distance'.

This extraordinary novel invites interpretation on several levels: as a Gothic extravaganza; as a projection of elements in Mary's life at the time of composition (there are affinities between the characters of Shelley and Frankenstein); as a modern reworking of the Promethean myth, a man's hubris in trying to create life like a god being punished by the recoil of his daring; as one of the earliest and direst warnings against scientific discovery and development unchecked by moral restraint. *Frankenstein* can also be understood in psychoanalytic terms as a metaphor for the unacknowledgeable connection between the conscious and the subconscious mind. The monster made by a man is too repulsive to be looked at directly but the author's attitude towards it is ambivalent. There are episodes of considerable poignancy, for example where it stretches a hand towards its creator after its 'birth'. The monster educates itself in isolation by eavesdropping outside a peasants' cottage from the inhabitants of which it requires only 'compassion and friendship'. Only after it is rejected does the monster become destructive: 'I am malicious because I am miserable.' Mary adopted the views of Godwin and Shelley that the inequity of society makes for individual corruption and vindictiveness, but the multiple ambiguities of *Frankenstein* do not really allow such a comfortable and simple resolution. It is the final and paradoxical achievement of this novel written by a nineteen-year-old girl that the monster acquires the most 'human' status of any character in it.

Philip Gooden

For Mary Shelley's life see Jane Dunn, *Moon in Eclipse* (1978); for an extended and illuminating treatment of *Frankenstein* and its sources see Christopher Small, *Ariel Like a Harpy* (1972).

412

SHELLEY, Percy Bysshe 1792–1822

British poet

Any bald account of Shelley, whose phantasmagoric idealism, in his progress through life, left a trail of forlorn women, dead babies, and suicides bobbing in its wake, can scarcely avoid depicting him as a sort of Ur-hippy. Matthew Arnold* was being kind when he called Shelley 'an ineffectual angel'. He may have been ineffectual; he was also ruthless – though out of blindness rather than insensitivity or set intent.

Percy Bysshe Shelley was born in 1792 at Field Place near Lewes in Sussex, the scion of a socially *arriviste*

Whig family whose money derived from a series of wealthy marriages made by his American-born grandfather, Bysshe Shelley, who became a baronet in 1806. Shelley was given a typically upper-class education, first at Syon House, where two of his enthusiasms were scientific experimentations (the headmaster was a friend of Joseph Priestley) and the reading of Gothic horror novels – both of which continued to the end of his life. Thence he went to Eton, where he was bullied and miserable, but kept up his interest in chemistry and Gothic novels (he published one while still at school) and began to absorb the ideas of the radical but by then somewhat *passé* philosopher and novelist, William Godwin*, whose *Political Justice* (1793) based its argument against property, marriage, and the evils of government upon the supremacy of reason and the perfectibility of man. Poetry began to attract him, and in 1810, just after leaving school, he published his first collection of juvenilia. In the same year he entered Oxford, from which he was expelled with his friend T.J. Hogg (1792–1862) less than six months later, for refusing to disavow a provocative pamphlet called *The Necessity of Atheism* (1811) which he distributed among bishops and the heads of colleges.

Shortly after leaving Oxford he eloped with a fifteen-year-old schoolgirl, Harriet Westbrook – according to Shelley, he did so in order to save her from her father's tyrannic behaviour (it seems that Mr Westbrook was bent on forcing his daughter to go to school against her will). The pair made a Scotch marriage in Edinburgh, where Hogg accompanied them. But after Hogg attempted to seduce Harriet while Shelley was in London arguing with his father about his allowance, the Shelleys broke with him and fled to Keswick in the Lake District. Here Shelley began an uneasy friendship with Southey* (they were to quarrel later; unluckily for him he did not meet either Wordsworth* or Coleridge*) and, more importantly, a correspondence with his hero and mentor, William Godwin.

Shelley never stayed long in any one place. The beginning of 1812 found him in Dublin, engaged in a futile campaign for Catholic emancipation and the liberation of Ireland. He returned to England in April and, after some wanderings, settled in Wales. In 1813 he published his first notable poem, *Queen Mab*, which in his lifetime was the best known of his works, from the notoriety of the atheistical and revolutionary ideas adumbrated in the notes to the poem. In the same year Harriet gave birth to his first child, which was followed by another in 1814.

But by then Shelley had met and fallen in love with the sixteen-year-old Mary Godwin (Mary Shelley*), Godwin's daughter by his first wife, the pioneer feminist, Mary Wollstonecraft (1759–97). To Godwin's horror – albeit he was an advocate of free love – they eloped to the continent, accompanied by Mary's half-sister Claire Clairmont, who was to prove something

of a succubus. Shelley's grandfather died the following year, leaving him the eventual heir to a fortune of £200,000 (more than twenty times that figure in today's money). Henceforth his financial position was considerably easier, though he remained unreconciled to his father, whom he delighted to shock, and at whose conventionalism most of Shelley's rebellious attitudinizings were aimed. The crucial year for Shelley, however, was 1816: it saw the publication of *Alastor*, his encounter with Byron* (through Claire Clairmont, who had become Byron's temporary mistress), the suicides of Mary's other half-sister Fanny Imlay and of his wife Harriet, who was found drowned and pregnant in the Serpentine; almost immediately afterwards, Shelley married Mary Godwin. The meeting between Byron and Shelley, who had in common their aristocratic upbringings and comparatively lavish incomes but were otherwise opposites, resulted in a mutually valuable creative friendship. Byron's realism tempered Shelley's idealism, and vice versa; both benefited. All Shelley's major poems, beginning with the *Hymn to Intellectual Beauty* (1817), were written after this meeting.

Partly because of his failure to get the custody of his children by Harriet, and partly because of poor health, Shelley finally left England in 1818, never to return. Accompanied by his wife and child, and Claire with her daughter by Byron, for the next two years he wandered over Italy, from Venice to Rome, Naples and Florence, finally settling at Pisa in 1820. Two of his infant children died in the course of these wanderings, which led to a coldness between him and Mary. But at Pisa he became the magnet that drew together a group of English expatriates – half-pay officers, remittance men, dilettante artists, their mistresses and wives – which became known as 'The Pisan Circle' and eventually included Byron and the Cornish adventurer Edward Trelawny* whose *Recollections of the Last Days of Shelley and Byron* (1868) gave powerful impetus to Shelley's posthumous reputation. It was during the Italian years that Shelley's major works were produced: *Prometheus Unbound* (1820); *The Cenci* (1820, a play in Shakespearian blank verse); *The Mask of Anarchy* (1832); *Peter Bell the Third* (1839); *Ode to the West Wind* (1820); *Adonais* (1821); *The Defence of Poetry* (1840); and the unfinished *Triumph of Life* (1824), which he was still writing at the time of his death by drowning in the Bay of Lerici on 8 July 1822, a month before his thirtieth birthday.

Like Byron's, Shelley's life was a spectacular mix of marital tragedy, sexual adventure and romantic action, quite unlike the comparatively dull lives of Blake, Wordsworth, Keats*, or Clare*, to name some of their Romantic contemporaries. Like Byron's, Shelley's life was in some sort a part of his *oeuvre*, for the myth of Shelley the free spirit, the idealistic revolutionary, the iconoclast and the doomed youth, is an element in the impact of his poetry. Ideas and emotions were more real to Shelley than things; the quotidian world was of no interest to him. Thus most of his poetry – and in his short life he wrote an immense amount – rests on no solid basis of observation or experience, but depends upon a peculiar intensification of the emotions he evoked or derived from ideas and abstract concepts. Yet as T.S. Eliot says, he did not have a metaphysical or philosophical mind: 'his mind was in some ways a very confused one: he was able to be at once and with the same enthusiasm an eighteenth-century rationalist and a cloudy Platonist.' It is not surprising that music should be the inspiration or subject of Shelley's finest lyrics, and of his most striking metaphors. Yet as Claire Tomalin remarked in her excellent short life of Shelley (*Shelley and His World*, 1980) 'how supremely well he wrote when tied to the real world and actual experience.' Instances are the *Letter to Maria Gisborne* (1824) and the superb *Julian and Maddalo* (1824), which is largely a record and re-creation of his conversations with Byron in Venice.

The intense feeling that Shelley could bring to abstract concepts lent an edge and incandescence to his political and satirical poems like *The Mask of Anarchy*, *Peter Bell the Third* and *Similes for Two Political Characters of 1819* (1832), where in philosophical and didactic poems like *Prometheus Unbound* and *Epipsychidion* (1821) it tended to produce diffusiveness and blurring. None of Shelley's best political poems were published till after his death – they were felt to be too dangerous, even by radical editors like Hunt – or he might have found the audience and the public he so desperately wanted in his lifetime. Shelley's fame and influence were almost entirely posthumous, enhanced by his early and romantic death. He became a cult figure, not only with the young and radical – James Thomson, Robert Browning*, Thomas Hardy*, Swinburne*, Yeats, and almost every poet up to Wilfrid Owen and Edward Thomas* were influenced by him – but even with respectable Victorians who admired the superb euphonius rhetoric of poems like *Adonais* – that elegy supposedly for Keats but really about himself – and *To a Skylark* (1820) almost as much as they deplored his principles and behaviour. His reputation has waned since. Eliot dismissed enthusiasm for Shelley as 'an affair of adolescence'; and his verse has earned black marks from influential critics like F.R. Leavis and Allen Tate. But recent studies by Richard Holmes (*Shelley: The Pursuit*, 1974) and Claire Tomalin indicate that Shelley may again be returning to favour. Certainly, when he has his ideas and emotions in control, and his eye on the object, there is hardly a more exquisite lyric poet than the author of *Stanzas Written in Dejection, near Naples* (1824), *The Aziola* (1829), *The Question* (1822), and *To Edward Williams* (1834).

David Wright

Editions: *Shelley: Poetical Works*, ed. Thomas Hutchinson (1968); *Complete Poetical Works*, ed. Neville Rogers (1972; two out of four volumes published); *Complete Works of Shelley*, ed. Roger Ingpen and Walter Peck (10 vols, 1965); *Collected Prose of Shelley*, ed. E.B. Murray and Timothy Webb (1982); *Letters of P.B. Shelley*, ed. F.L. Jones (1974). See: T.J. Hogg, *Life of Percy Bysshe Shelley* (1858); Newman Ivey White, *Shelley* (1947); Richard Holmes, *Shelley: The Pursuit* (1974); Claire Tomalin, *Shelley and His World* (1980). Criticism: Matthew Arnold, *Essays in Criticism* (2nd series, 1888); T.S. Eliot, *The Use of Poetry and the Use of Criticism* (1933); F.R. Leavis, *Revaluations* (1936); Stephen Spender, *Shelley* (1952); Donald Davie, *Purity of Diction in English Verse* (1952); Graham Hough, *The Romantic Poets* (1953).

413
SICKERT, Walter Richard 1860–1942

British artist

Walter Sickert was born in Munich on 31 May 1860, of Danish descent. Both his father and his grandfather had been distinguished painters, and his mother, who was English, had been on the stage. The family settled in England in 1868 and, after attending various schools in London, Sickert himself went into the theatre in 1877, playing in numerous companies including that of Henry Irving, an experience he made much of in later life. In 1881 he enrolled at the Slade, but left soon afterwards to become a studio assistant to Whistler*, whom he had first met in 1879. He was strongly influenced by the older artist, and through him became acquainted with many of the leading figures in the London and Paris *avant-garde*, meeting Degas* in 1883, who was to become the major single influence on his later work and beliefs.

Like Whistler, Sickert fused elements of both British and French art in his own painting, but he looked to very different examples in both cultures, preferring the British illustrative tradition of Cruikshank*, Rowlandson and Charles Keene, and the starker, more painterly realism of Degas and the Nabis. This led to an inevitable break with Whistler, who was unable to tolerate evidence of independence amongst his immediate acolytes. In the nineties Sickert was generally associated with the *Yellow Book* circle in London, contributing illustrations to the magazine in 1894 and 1895. He was also a prime mover in the establishment of the London Impressionist group, a secessionary breakaway group from the increasingly conservative New English Art Club, writing the catalogue preface for the group's first exhibition in 1889. Having been divorced by his first wife in 1899, he spent several years living and working in Europe, spending long periods in Dieppe, Paris and

Venice. He returned to London in 1905 at the age of forty-five, convinced that a younger generation of painters would be more receptive to his own strong missionary sense of what constituted the correct modern tradition. To this end he formed the Fitzroy Street Group in 1907, with a number of painters who had recently left the Slade, including Harold Gilman and Spencer Gore. This was in a sense another attempt to capture the lead of the British *avant-garde*, which he had failed to do in 1889, but it was also the first of many groups which Sickert formed as informal alliances over the next twenty years, meeting regularly 'at home' in order to discuss painting and to sell directly to clients from the artist's studio.

The most celebrated of these groups was the Camden Town Group, which was founded in 1911 in response to the tremendous success of Roger Fry's Post-Impressionist exhibitions. The bulk of Sickert's followers joined forces with those of Fry to form the London Group in 1914, following the premature death of Spencer Gore, but Sickert remained outside this group in protest at the presence of such figures as Jacob Epstein and Wyndham Lewis. It is characteristic of Sickert that he resigned from the Royal Academy in 1935 to protest at the then president's refusal to sign an appeal for the preservation of Epstein's sculptures on the BMA building in the Strand. He continued to work prolifically, and to exhibit regularly in London and Paris, moving from London to Thanet in Kent in 1934, and finally to Bathampton in 1938, where he died four years later, the grand old man of British painting. He was survived by his third wife, the artist Thérèse Lessore, until her death in 1945.

In 1900 Sickert was almost exactly halfway through his life. His career cannot however simply be divided in two. As a young painter and etcher he had been completely overwhelmed by the presence of Whistler, just as he was later to become overwhelmed by Degas. His own prickly, eccentric and somewhat autocratic personality comprised a bulwark of mannerisms which he slowly accreted in self-defence against his tendency to hero-worship. In a similar way he had to dig very deeply into his own social and cultural roots in order to establish his uniquely complex identity as a painter. Hence the highly personal iconography of much of his work, and his constant references to working-class life and popular culture in such titles as *Off To The Pub, What Shall We Do For The Rent?*, and so on, as well as his ironic use of classical titles. Sickert was possessed by his sense of the history of painting and believed, like Roger Fry, that it was up to him to guarantee the survival of a particular kind of artistic cultural practice. Hence his rejection of Whistler, whose technique of lowering all tonal values in a lacquer-like manner seemed increasingly incompatible with the qualities of direct painting in careful stages from drawings which he most admired in certain British and French trad-

itions. Indeed, it might be said that he tended to apply the lessons of 'La Peinture' to the example of British draughtsmanship.

At the same time it should be noted that Sickert's best work invariably proceeded from his own psychological conflicts and complexity. Highly reticent about his private life, he poured his fantasies and obsessions into his subject matter – claustrophobic images of sexual tension and domestic stress, as well as random memories of popular prints, places, music-hall scenes and so on, which he returned to again and again, with a rare trust in the intrinsic value of whatever he personally found fascinating. But Sickert's lasting achievement lay in his ability to match such highly varied themes with painting techniques approximating to their significance, ranging from the extraordinarily violent painting of many early nudes and interiors to the subtle *contre-jour* effects of his Camden Town Group period and the raw surface qualities of his later work, most of which derived from photographs or Victorian graphic sources. Sickert almost always worked by a process of indirection in order to control his responses to the actual motif, just as he preferred to leave a considerable period of time, often many years, between the initial blocking in of a canvas and its eventual completion. Unlike most of his contemporaries, he never settled into a formulaic relation between subject matter and style. Hence the range and alertness of his work, right up to old age. He was also a considerable critic, and the posthumous collection of his writings, *A Free House! Or The Artist As Craftsman* (1947), edited by Sir Oswald Sitwell, remains one of the handful of necessary books of twentieth-century art theory.

Simon Watney

The most important authority on Sickert's work is Dr Wendy Baron, whose 1973 catalogue, *Sickert*, for the Fine Art Society, London, is the best introduction. Her monumental study of his career is *Sickert* (1973). The standard biography remains Robert Emmons, *The Life And Opinions Of Walter Richard Sickert* (1941). See also: Marjorie Lilly, *Sickert: The Painter And His Circle* (1971); Simon Watney, *English Post-Impressionism* (1980).

414
SIDGWICK, Henry 1838–1900

British philosopher

Born at Skipton in Yorkshire, Henry Sidgwick was educated at Rugby School and Trinity College, Cambridge, where he had a brilliant career, first as an undergraduate and later as a fellow and lecturer. He was Knightsbridge Professor of Moral Philosophy from 1883 till 1900. With his wife, Eleanor Balfour, he took an active interest in the cause of higher education for women.

Sidgwick's influence as a thinker was due largely to his classic, *The Methods of Ethics* (1874), a work of rare breadth, subtlety and rigour. As a defence of utilitarianism it surpassed anything written before. Sidgwick sought a general theory that would comprehend our ordinary moral judgments in terms of a few basic principles. He gave a careful and detailed analysis of what he took to be the three main candidates for such a theory: intuitionism, egoism and utilitarianism.

The intuitionist holds that moral judgment rests upon self-evident axioms that are known by intuition: we clearly see that certain kinds of action are right or binding regardless of their consequences. Intuitionism, Sidgwick held, coheres with our commonsense view of morality to some extent, but it has two major shortcomings. First, very few moral rules are axiomatic, for they lack the essential properties of axioms, being neither clear and precise, nor genuinely self-evident, nor mutually consistent, nor universally accepted. The few principles that are self-evident are uninformative tautologies. Second, the rational end of all action is the good; hence the consequences of an act must be relevant to the question of its moral worth.

This point is recognized by the egoist, or egoistic hedonist, who holds that the ultimate good is happiness – a pleasant state of consciousness – and that whether or not an act is right depends solely on its having pleasant or painful consequences for me. Sidgwick accepted the hedonistic definition of the good, but he thought that egoism has two major drawbacks. First, it does not cohere with our commonsense view of morality as altruistic, with the conviction that doing our duty sometimes requires us to put the happiness of someone else before our own. Attempts to show that one's happiness is best secured by following the dictates of duty are unconvincing. There is nevertheless a tension within practical reason between two disparate, but equally rational, demands, the demand of morality and the demand of prudence – a tension he saw no sure way of resolving. Second, it is difficult to justify the thesis that the happiness of one particular person, namely oneself, is morally preferable to that of any other.

The utilitarian, or universalistic hedonist, holds that the rightness of an action is determined by the pleasantness of its consequences, not just for me, but for everyone affected by them. This view, Sidgwick argued, follows from two fundamental self-evident principles: 'I am bound to aim at good generally' and 'The good of any one individual is of no more importance, from the point of view of the universe, than the good of any other.' Utilitarianism combines the merits of intuitionism and egoism, while lacking their defects, recognizing, with the one, the intuitive basis of morality and, with the other, the importance of consequences. More-

over, it largely coheres with commonsense morality: the utilitarian basis of many duties is obvious – though with some it is not; and where ordinary moral rules are vague or conflicting, appeal is generally made to considerations of utility.

Sidgwick did not advocate the creation of a new, utilitarian ethics to replace commonsense morality which, however imperfectly utilitarian, provides nevertheless the most practicable rules for realizing the general happiness. Utilitarianism, rather, should have a regulative role, helping us continually to sharpen our moral awareness.

D.R. Murdoch

Sidgwick's other works include *Principles of Political Economy* (1883) and *Elements of Politics* (1891). See also J.B. Schneewind, *Sidgwick's Ethics and Victorian Moral Philosophy* (1977).

415
SISLEY, Alfred 1839–99

French painter

Alone among the major Impressionist painters, Sisley's fame and popularity, in his own lifetime and since, have been eclipsed by the movement of which he was a part. In spite of the freshness of his work, he has not been esteemed as he deserved, and he remains overshadowed by Manet*, Renoir* and Pissarro*.

Sisley was born in Paris of wealthy English parents, and except for brief visits to England and Wales, lived and worked all his life in France, chiefly in the countryside around Paris. As a youth he was sent to London for four years (1857–61) to learn the language and prepare for a career in commerce. He returned to France, however, intent on becoming a painter, and in 1862 entered the studio of Gleyre at the École des Beaux Arts where he befriended Monet*, Renoir and Bazille. In 1863 they worked together in the open, at Chailly near Fontainebleau, and in the following years Sisley continued to paint with Renoir in the region. He had some success at the Salon but in 1870 fled France, and war, for London. The Franco-Prussian War brought financial ruin to his father, and what had been for Sisley a diverting occupation became an earnest struggle. In the succeeding years he endured extreme poverty, and even when his friends began to find buyers for their works and to become more popular, Sisley's paintings sold, if at all, for derisive sums.

Early in the 1870s Sisley habitually worked in those places around Paris that Impressionism has made famous: Louveciennes, Argenteuil, Marly, Bougival and Pontoise, and in 1874 he spent the summer in London with one of the rare patrons of the Impressionists, the singer Faure, painting at Hampton Court. In 1877 he moved to Sèvres, working at Meudon and Saint-Cloud, then in 1879 to Moret, and in 1882 to Moret-sur-Loing where he finally settled.

Sisley exhibited five landscapes at the first Impressionist Exhibition in 1874 and contributed to three of the subsequent shows (1876, 1877 and 1882). In 1883 Durand-Ruel gave him a one-man show, which had little success, and Sisley remained neglected until only a few weeks before his death, when a series of articles by Gustave Geffroy stimulated interest in his work.

It is hard to understand why Sisley should have been ignored, since his work has an obvious charm, and does not in either style or subject matter openly challenge convention to the extent of Monet's, for example. He was almost exclusively a painter of landscape, and the influence of Courbet*, Corot* and Daubigny is not hard to discern. His predilection for secluded rural scenery and the villages and the country-towns of the Île de France bind him strongly to the earlier *plein air* painters, and throughout his life he, alone among the Impressionists, continued to treat the same subjects – river banks, country lanes, orchards, kitchen gardens – in a direct, uncomplicated manner. Sisley was a quiet, retiring man, and his character is reflected in his pictures, which invariably show peaceful corners of the countryside, with only the occasional passer-by. It is probably this reticence, the lack of variation in his themes, and the absence of large canvases and boisterous figure-subjects, that account for his neglect.

The quiet tenor of Sisley's paintings is deceptive. On to a basis of careful observation inherited from Corot, Sisley, from about 1870, grafted a clear, light-toned palette and a vigorous technique of quick, broken touches of colour, gleaned from Monet. Such paintings as *The Foot-Bridge at Argenteuil* (1872), *View of the Sèvres Road* (1873) and *Louveciennes, Hilltops at Marly* (1873), all in the Musée du Jeu de Paume, Paris, display a freedom and a sureness of touch unparalleled by any but Monet. With extraordinary speed, Sisley grasped the basic tenets of Impressionism as discovered by Monet on the eve of the Franco-Prussian War. His shadows are richly coloured, his surfaces vibrate with broken lines, and, above all, his skies and waters are limpid and luminous. His colour is never muddy, never false, and the quick, sure touches of liquid paint which make up his pictures always convey light, air and space with breathtaking freshness. Although he is relegated, mistakenly, to the second rank, Sisley's paintings in the 1870s epitomize Impressionism. With tenacity and, as his pictures prove, penetrating vision, Sisley explored every effect of light through all times of day and all seasons. There are snow-scenes, like *Snow at Louveciennes* (1878), views of flooding, where the water reflects dazzling winter sunlight (*Boat in the Flood at Port-Marly*, 1876), autumnal scenes of mist in cottage gardens (*Fog*, 1874), and countless summer landscapes. Amongst a simple repertoire of rural themes Sisley seems for ever to find untried viewpoints, fresh and arresting effects of light, and new insights into nature. His inventiveness, while disguised by the simplicity of his themes, is apparent in his constant avoidance of hackneyed and formularized effects.

In continuing up to his death with the same range of subjects Sisley was regrettably unable to maintain the inspired freshness of his early work. His technique grew looser and his observation less sharp. With the acuteness of his vision dimmed, his pictures lose interest. Nevertheless, while he was unable to halt this decline, he retained the luminosity and sensitivity of touch which are the hallmarks of his work.

Michael Wilson

See: George Besson, *Sisley* (1946); François Daulte, *Sisley: Landscapes* (1963). See also: John Rewald, *History of Impressionism* (rev. edn. 1961).

416
SISMONDI, Jean Charles Léonard Simonde de
1773–1842

Swiss economist and historian

The form of industrial capitalism which dominated nineteenth-century European economic growth found in Sismondi one of its earliest and most acute critics. Born into a prosperous Genevan family of remote Italian ancestry, he was encouraged by his father, a Protestant clergyman, to embark upon a commercial career. Thus the sixteen-year-old Sismondi was already at work in a Lyons bank when the French Revolution erupted. That upheaval prompted the family to beat a prudent retreat to England. In 1794 they made a brief return to Geneva before commencing a second period of exile during which they ran a farm in Tuscany. In 1800 Sismondi came back again to his native city, which thereafter remained his base for a new career as a writer. He soon became a member of the talented circle with which Madame de Staël* surrounded herself at nearby Coppet, and he was part of the entourage that she took on journeys to Italy in 1804–5 and to Germany and Austria in 1807–8. Though he gave occasional lecture courses, Sismondi's success as an author was eventually such as to allow him to decline offers of regular academic employment. His reputation even brought him favourably to the notice of the Emperor Napoleon*, and in 1815 Sismondi surprised fellow-republicans by emerging as a propagandist for the reform programme that accompanied Bonaparte's ill-fated return from Elba. Thereafter the course of the Genevan author's life was largely uneventful, and it is rather to his works that we must turn for an understanding of his importance.

Amongst contemporaries Sismondi was known as

much for his historical as for his economic writings. Between 1809 and 1818 he published in Paris a sixteen-volume *History of the Italian Republics in the Middle Ages* (*Histoire des républiques italiennes du moyen âge*, trans. 1831), in which he sought to rescue at least one facet of medieval civilization from the supercilious disdain which characterized so much of the Enlightenment's approach to the epoch. As Italian nationalism developed during the nineteenth-century Risorgimento this celebration of pioneering republican spirit became one of the literary sources of inspiration for Mazzini* and his followers. During the last decades of his life Sismondi directed is energies towards an even more monumental *Histoire des Français* ('History of the French', 31 vols, 1821–44), which had reached the reign of Louis XV by the time of its author's death. This work broke new ground in the extent of its reliance upon original sources. However, like the earlier historical project, it was marred by an excess of anachronistic moral judgment; and, as a presentation of French national history, it was to be overshadowed in popularity by the more vivid writing of Augustin Thierry and Jules Michelet*. On a somewhat smaller scale, Sismondi also published an 'Historical View of the Literature of the South of Europe', (*De la Littérature du midi de l'Europe*, 4 vols, 1813), which is especially notable as an early effort to establish the social and political influences that had affected works produced chiefly in the Romance languages.

It was, however, as a commentator upon economic issues that Sismondi made his most lasting impact. His first treatise, the *Tableau de l'agriculture toscane* ('Description of Tuscan Agriculture', 1801), capitalized upon his experiences of the 1790s in exile, and it was quickly followed by *De la Richesse commerciale* ('On Commercial Wealth', 2 vols, 1803). In these works Sismondi accepted the conventional wisdom of eighteenth-century classical economics as propounded most famously by Adam Smith, with its emphasis upon *laissez-faire* principles. Central to an eventual change of mind about certain major aspects of this consensus was the second visit that Sismondi paid to England, the most advanced industrial country of his day. Here in 1818 he saw at first hand the commercial crisis that ensued after the ending of the Napoleonic Wars, when many commodities were still flooding on to the market despite the unwillingness or sheer inability of potential consumers to purchase them, and where he noted also the lack of relevant response from the government itself. All this led Sismondi to question whether in an economy increasingly geared to factory production, and thus to a distinctively industrial form of capitalism, one could continue to rely upon the self-equilibrating mechanisms postulated by Smith, by 'Say's Law' about the balance of market forces, and by David Ricardo's* recent *Principles of Political Economy* (1818).

Such doubts lay at the heart of Sismondi's most famous book, which challengingly echoed the very title of Ricardo's work. In the *Political Economy and the Philosophy of Government* (*Nouveaux principes d'économie politique*, 2 vols, 1819, trans. 1847) Sismondi stressed the need for a greater awareness of the possibility – and even the inevitability – of chronic underconsumption and cumulative disequilibrium. He also put forward, albeit somewhat vaguely, the case for greater intervention by government 'to regulate the progress of wealth'. According to him, *laissez-faire* principles might well help to increase aggregate production, and yet there were moral as well as quantitative economic issues to be considered. Unless the resulting wealth was well distributed there could be no guarantee at all of any concomitant enhancement in human happiness and welfare. Sismondi envisaged, indeed, that the continuation of current trends would bring only an increasingly conflictal polarization between richer capitalists and ever more impoverished workers. This was a view which influenced Thomas Malthus* during the final drafting of his own *Principles of Political Economy* (1820), as well as prompting the significant section 'On Machinery' which was added to the 1821 edition of the previously mentioned work by Ricardo.

It is easy to see why the *Political Economy* should find a prominent place in every history of early nineteenth-century socialist thought. But this is not to say that Sismondi himself ought to be regarded as a socialist, as opposed, say, to a left-wing liberal. He was more trenchant as a negative critic of current socioeconomic trends than radical in positive recommendations as to what might improve them. As was revealed by a later political work, the *Études sur les constitutions des peuples libres* ('Studies on the Constitutions of Free Peoples', 1836), Sismondi was distrustful of extensive democracy and inclined to advocate that ruling authority be placed in the hands of intellectuals and other categories of the urban bourgeoisie. Possibly because of his own background and life-style, he proved incapable of envisaging anything more than an adaptation – indeed, a rather backward-looking one – within the framework of a still fundamentally capitalist system. 'His ideal,' commented G.D.H. Cole,

> was a stable population of peasants cultivating the land by intensive methods, serving and served by a sufficient body of urban craftsmen and traders, and governed politically by an educated class of bourgeois merchants, administrators, and intellectuals who would identify their own interest with that of the poor.

Sismondi's attitude towards land and capital as things possessed upon trust – that is, as objects to be enjoyed only so long as they were used so as to yield a wider benefit to society as a whole – was one that appealed, for instance, to moderate Saint-Simonians (see Saint-

Simon*). When Marx* and Engels* in *The Communist Manifesto* of 1848 categorized their forerunners, they treated Sismondi as being both for France and England the chief figure within the school of 'petty-bourgeois socialism', a version astute in much of its diagnosis of the imminent crisis of industrial capitalism but 'reactionary and Utopian' in its failure to make a thoroughgoing break with the old property relations. This was an opinion echoed by Lenin when in 1896 he attacked Russia's own latter-day 'Sismondists' for what he derided as their 'economic romanticism'. Though socialist thinkers at large have often tended to underrate his pioneering perceptiveness, it is entirely fitting that Sismondi should have been better treated by economists of more liberal disposition. In particular, within the twentieth century his merits have been recognized above all by many advocates of a Keynesianism whose own career of intellectual hegemony began as a response to much the same kind of general and cumulative economic dysfunction as the Swiss observer had predicted more than a hundred years before.

Michael Biddiss

Among other works of Sismondi, note the *Études sur l'économie politique* (*Studies on Political Economy*, 2 vols, 1837–8). Secondary studies include: Henryk Grossman, *Sismondi et ses théories économiques* (1924); Jean R. de Salis, *Sismondi: La vie et l'oeuvre d'un cosmopolite philosophe* (1932); Georges Sotiroff, *Ricardo und Sismondi* (1945); and Alfred Amonn, *Sismondi als Nationalökonom* (2 vols, 1945–9). See also: Maxime Leroy, *Histoire des Idées sociales en France*, vol. 2 (1962); and Eric Roll, *A History of Economic Thought* (4th edn, 1973).

417
SMETANA, Bedřich 1824–84

Bohemian composer

Smetana was born in Litomyšl in eastern Bohemia, then part of the Austro-Hungarian Empire, but unlike other musicians from the Austrian provinces he spent most of his working life on home territory. Not only that, he associated himself with the nationalist cause and is justly regarded as the founder of a specifically Czech music. In 1848 he even took part in the unsuccessful rising in Prague, where he had been living since 1843, working as a private teacher and eventually setting up his own music school (it was also during this time that he struck up a friendship with Liszt*).

For several years from 1856 he was away from Bohemia, first taking a conducting post at Göteborg in Sweden, then touring as a concert pianist, and it was during this period that he composed his first notable works, three symphonic poems based on Liszt's model:

Richard III (1857), *Wallenstein's Camp* (1859–60) and *Hakon Jarl* (1861). Then in 1863 he returned to Prague and spent the rest of his life there. And now his nationalist feelings began to gain expression in his music, first and most freshly in his opera *Prodaná nevěsta* (*The Bartered Bride*, 1864, revised 1870). Smetana had been brought up German-speaking and he had difficulty in setting Czech words, but despite this he contrived to create a score which, while using few actual folk melodies, appealed strongly to national instincts in its alternately joyous and sentimental portrayal of the Bohemian peasantry.

He followed up his success with a more serious opera, *Dalibor* (1867), which, however, was criticized for its Wagnerism, though in fact Smetana's technique here still owes much more to Liszt than to Wagner*. Then came *Libuše* (1868–72), not so much an opera as a festival pageant, ending with a prophecy of the Czechs' glorious future. Its première was delayed until it could be used to inaugurate the National Theatre in Prague in 1881, by which time Smetana had composed three more operas: *Dvě vdovy* (*The Two Widows*, 1873–4), *Hubička* (*The Kiss*, 1875) and *Tajemství* (*The Secret*, 1877). When *Libuše* was produced it proved a great success, and Smetana was encouraged to finish another opera, *Čertova Stěna* (*The Devil's Wall*, 1879–82). This, however, was a failure, and he made only slow progress on his last, unfinished opera, *Viola* (begun 1881), based on *Twelfth Night*.

Throughout the last ten years of his life Smetana was totally deaf, and yet it is to this period that many of his greatest works belong, including not only the operas mentioned above but also his two string quartets and his cycle of symphonic poems *Má vlast* (*My Country*). This is a set of six separate works, composed between 1874 and 1879, and suggestive of various aspects of Bohemia's history and landscape: *Vyšehrad* (*The High Citadel*), *Vltava* (the river, better known by its German name of Moldau), *Šárka* (leader of the Bohemian Amazons), *Z českých luhů a hájů* (*From Bohemia's Fields and Woods*), *Tabor* (the Hussite stronghold), and *Blánik* (a mountain, the Hussite Valhalla).

If *Má vlast* was Smetana's finest tribute to his country, in the quartets he looked into himself, both of them having the title *Z mého života* (*From my Life*), though this is now normally reserved for the first, in E minor (1876). Here he looks back on a youth of love, art and dancing, and then, in the fourth movement, turns to his joy in creating national music, a joy destroyed by the piercing high E that was constantly in his ears as deafness approached. The second quartet, in D minor (1883), continues the autobiography, containing, as he said, 'the whirlpool of music in a man who has lost his hearing'. Smetana's example, in combining illustrative content with classical chamber-musical form, was not lost on later composers, including Tchaikovsky* and Schoenberg, while his discovery of a Czech musical idiom, particularly in *The Bartered Bride* and *Má vlast*, was a vital stimulus to musicians in his own country.

Paul Griffiths

See: Brian Large, *Smetana* (1970); John Clapham, *Smetana* (1972).

418
SMILES, Samuel 1812–1904

British author

No other British nineteenth-century background – childhood, education, entrance on a career – left such a distinctive mark on those who shared it as that of the Scottish small-town boy, university graduate, and penurious professional man. Smiles did more than anyone to articulate the values and aspirations of those who shared this upbringing, and to ensure that others had the chance to share them at second hand, not only in England, but in every industrializing nation in the world. His own progress was archetypal. Born at Haddington near Edinburgh in 1812, one of eleven children of a general merchant, he was enabled to study medicine at Edinburgh University by family thrift. His father's death in 1832 made this dearly bought education still more strenuous, and once he had qualified with a diploma from Surgeons Hall, Smiles found medical practice in Haddington in competition with eight others almost as severe. While there Smiles was able however to profit from the libraries, evening classes, and self-improving societies, which contributed so much to the ethos of Scottish provincial life at this time. The three elements of hostility to leisured elites, rejection of unthinking materialism, and belief in the individual's capacity to mould his own personality by effort alone, which ran through all his works, can best be appreciated by allowing this background its full weight in the development of Smiles's philosophy.

In 1838 Smiles moved to Leeds, and became editor of the *Leeds Times*, a radical newspaper – but even more important threw himself into the running of mechanics' institutes and other forms of adult education. Smiles was an enthusiastic supporter of the cause of workers' cooperation, though not of trade unions or political demonstrations. Leeds in the 1840s was the anvil on which the ideas of *Self-Help* were hammered out, though the book was not published until 1859 when Smiles had moved to London. The anecdotal illustrations were first given as lectures to about a hundred young working men who had set up an evening school for 'mutual improvement'. So the 'gospel of work' was not the self-congratulatory rationalization of competition for the successful bourgeois, but an attempt to capture the essence of working-class self-improvement in an environment of mutual help. Nor were many of

Smiles's ideas original; even the use of biographical case studies owed much to the evangelicals' celebration of the Christian life. Smiles acknowledged explicitly the inspiration of Thomas Carlyle*, in his concern for work and the hero. Behind Carlyle, Smiles harked back, perhaps unwittingly, still further to another Scot, Adam Smith. Smith's *Wealth of Nations*, Book V, argued for an education which would mitigate the consequences of the division of labour, supply the deficiencies of a wholly material culture, and compensate for the loss of rural community and independence.

Self-Help (1859) provided patterns of thrift and industry for the aspiring working man, and, as Smiles was keen to point out in later life, those patterns were not guarantees of material success but a means of self-fulfilment. Smiles's exemplars *did* rise in society, but this rise was an outward sign of this fulfilment, not its substance. The fundamental economic virtue that Smiles preached was thrift, which could enable an individual, no matter how small his income, to accumulate gradually and create capital (ultimately, in Smiles's view, capital was always created by thrift). It was the accumulation of capital in this way that Smiles admired, not its deployment; it followed that Smiles found no cause for celebration in the prosperity of Britain in the 1850s and 1860s: he reminded his readers that fluctuations in the trade cycle were inevitable, and that it behoved the wise man to store away his substance in expectation of the lean years to come. As well as finding the contemporary worship of economic success sterile and stultifying, Smiles was ready to attack *laissez-faire* attitudes in the face of social evils. Towards the end of *Thrift* (1875) comes a stinging attack on 'Nobody', who is to blame for food adulteration, poisonous drink, undrained towns, overcrowded jails: 'Nobody has a theory too – a dreadful theory. It is embodied in the words: laissez-faire – let alone'. There is a negative, critical side to Smiles, as well as the well-known optimistic, celebratory side.

Self-Help was a runaway success, selling 20,000 copies in the first year, and achieving sales of over a quarter of a million copies by 1905 (outselling the great novelists). But still more surprising perhaps was its popularity all over the world in translation. Italy and Japan were particularly receptive to the 'gospel of work', regarding Smiles as a principal benefactor of mankind. *Character* (1871), *Thrift* and *Duty* (1887) were all respectable bestsellers in the same vein, relying on moral exhortation interspersed with anecdotal illustrations. But Smiles was also a founding father of the history of engineering and technology. *Lives of the Engineers* (1861–2), *Lives of Boulton and Watt* (1865) and *Industrial Biography* (1863) were in fact not so different from Smiles's self-help books, varying only in the proportion of biographical detail to moral exhortation. But Smiles did invest a considerable amount of research in the careers of his engineers and industrial entrepreneurs, and succeeded in capturing vividly what it must have been like to participate in the heroic age of Victorian engineering. These books suffer as history from an over-reliance on the familiar mechanisms of thrift and perseverance as explanations for success, and are biased towards transport and steam (not surprisingly, since Smiles was for a time secretary to various railway companies), rather than industrial engineering. But for the modern reader they have more appeal than the self-help books, and deserve their recent reprinting as classics of the genre.

Smiles's later life was bedevilled by ill-health and a growing sense of resentment at misinterpretation of his message, emphasis on the material at the expense of the moral and spiritual. By the time of his death in 1904, he may well have felt that he was living in a hostile age, but the facile mockery of the 'gospel of work' has proved evanescent in its turn.

Peter Jones

In addition to the works mentioned above, Smiles compiled lives of other exemplary individuals, including George Stephenson, James Nasmyth, George Moore, and Robert Dick. His own life story is told in *The Autobiography of Samuel Smiles*, ed. Thomas Mackay (1905), and there is a modern biography by Aileen Smiles, *Samuel Smiles and his Surroundings* (1956).

419
SMITH, Joseph 1805–44

US religious leader

Born in Vermont on 23 December 1805, Joseph Smith grew up in upstate New York at a time when that region was being swept by waves of intense religious revivalism. Praying for guidance as between the claims of competing sects, Smith experienced in 1820 a vision of God and of Jesus Christ. Three years later he was informed in another vision of the existence of ancient texts respecting the Israelitish origins of some American Indians and of the record of a colony in the western hemisphere which survived from about 600 BC to about AD 400. In 1827 the texts, engraved upon golden plates, were delivered into Smith's hands; with divine help he was enabled to translate them and in 1830 the *Book of Mormon* was published in Palmyra, New York. In April of that year the Church of Jesus Christ of Latter Day Saints was organized.

The early years of the church's history, up to and beyond the death of Smith himself, were beset by hardship and persecution. Smith led a migration of church members into Kirtland, Ohio, in 1831, but further revelations indicated Jackson County, Missouri, as the new Zion and purchases of land there and consequent migrations were commenced immediately. New Englanders in origin the Mormons were mostly anti-slavery in their political views. Their intrusion into the pro-slavery environment of Missouri generated tensions culminating in their being driven out of Jackson County in 1833. Settling after 1836 in Caldwell County they were joined by the remnants of the Kirtland community which had been undermined by financial problems. Again experiencing persecution they moved to Illinois and established the city of Nauvoo which received influxes of European migrants converted in Europe by missionaries sent over in the 1830s. In 1844 Smith determined to enter the national presidential contest on a fairly liberal ticket. But he did so at a time when political tensions between the Mormons and their neighbours were again rising. In his capacity as mayor of Nauvoo Smith ordered the destruction of an opposition press and eventually was jailed. A mob stormed the jail and Smith, along with fellow Mormons, was murdered.

Thus the great exodus westward and the settlement of the desert regions in and around Utah was left to his successor Brigham Young. Much of later Mormon culture can, however, be traced back to the ideas and teaching of Joseph Smith. Moreover, his own fate was greatly to enhance the tendency within the Mormon community to look back to the era of migrations and exodus as of immense importance in their evolution. The exodus marked the beginnings of a great growth in the membership of the Church of Latter Day Saints. The initial settlement of from 10,000 to 15,000 was followed by subsequent waves, including approximately 100,000 European converts. By 1925 church membership was reported to be about 575,000, since when it has more than doubled each quarter of a century: to 1.9 million in 1952 and about 4 million in 1977. Of the latter figure about 2.7 million are to be found outside the southwest region of the United States, although the direction of the world church still emanates largely from Utah as does the most significant missionary activity.

Smith left his mark upon the course of the church's history in various ways. His most important contributions were undoubtedly the *Book of Mormon* and the various revelations he received. The spiritual authority recognized by the church includes the Bible, the *Book of Mormon*, the revelations to the presidents of the church, notably Smith, and for individuals the revelations to which they personally have been privy. But the organization of the church was replicated in many ways in the organization of the society and here Smith's influence was also considerable. In the southwest of the United States towns were set out from which farmers farmed the surrounding countryside. New England and some Spanish settlements apart, this was an unusual arrangement for North America; it encouraged a sense of community, something of great importance to Smith and to his followers since. Within the community a network of mutual assistance programmes exists and the arrangement represents a very real attempt to marry Judaic-Christian precepts to the goals of prosperity and happiness. Within the community the family is of vital significance and the early existence of polygamy within the church probably represented as much as anything the desire to draw within family communities those who might otherwise have been spinsters or widows. Within the church there is an insistence upon the priesthood of all the worthy, upon clean living, and upon the fundamental importance of education without which God's truth cannot be learned.

Duncan MacLeod

See: James B. Allen and Glen M. Leonard, *The Story of the Latter-Day Saints* (1976); Donna Hill, *Joseph Smith: The First Mormon* (1977); Leonard J. Arrington and Davis Bitton, *The Mormon Experience: A History of the Latter-Day Saints* (1979). See also: *The Book of Mormon* and, for further references, *A Mormon Bibliography, 1830–1930*, ed. Chad J. Flake.

420

SMITH, William Robertson 1846–94

British biblical and Semitic scholar, editor, librarian

W. Robertson Smith was one of the most famous Semitic scholars of the nineteenth century, whose influence extended far beyond biblical and Arabic studies to affect the foundation of the sociological study of religion and later anthropological research in the social organization of preliterate peoples. In addition, Smith edited the great ninth edition of the *Encyclopaedia Britannica* which popularized the scholarly breakthroughs of that period. He also served as chief librarian of the University of Cambridge during its modernization.

Smith was educated at home, mainly due to ill health. His father, a minister in the Free Church of Scotland, provided an extraordinarily intensive education allowing Smith to enter Aberdeen University on a scholarship at the age of fifteen, where he distinguished himself in physics, mathematics, languages and religious studies. Graduating from Aberdeen (1865), Smith entered New College, University of Edinburgh, which he left the year he was ordained (1870) to take up a chair in Hebrew and Old Testament studies at the Free Church College at Aberdeen. Earlier (1868, 1869) he studied intermittently at Bonn and Göttingen where he absorbed the new biblical criticisms pioneered by German and Dutch scholars.

At Aberdeen Smith began contributing essays on biblical topics to the new *Encyclopaedia Britannica* which he presented in terms of the new criticism. These in-

cited violent criticism from the conservative Free Church culminating in a much publicized trial and dismissal from his post (1880). The case consumed nearly five years during which Smith toured the Near East, lectured in his defence and published further encyclopaedia essays which only exacerbated his difficulties. In defence of his position he published *The Old Testament and the Jewish Church* (1881) and *The Prophets of Isreal* (1882). After his dismissal, he was made a co-editor of the *Encyclopaedia Britannica* and soon became chief editor, eventually writing over two hundred entries. In this capacity he exerted immense influence on popular understanding of modern biblical studies. In 1883 Smith was appointed reader in Arabic at the University of Cambridge (Trinity College) and in 1885 became a fellow of Christ's College where he remained until his death. In 1885 he published *Kinship and Marriage in Early Arabia*. In 1888 he was fêted by international scholars assembled at Cambridge to celebrate the completion of the *Encyclopaedia*. In 1888–9 Smith delivered the Burnett lectures at the University of Aberdeen, covering the very topics that had led to his earlier disgrace in that city. These were published as *Lectures on the Religion of the Semites* (1889), his most influential work. That same year Smith was appointed to the Chair of Arabic at Cambridge. By then Smith was seriously ill; apparently always tubercular, he died prematurely, in large part due to overwork. A collection of his most important essays was published posthumously (*Lectures and Essays of William Robertson Smith*, ed. J.S. Black and G. Chrystal, 1912).

Unlike most biblical scholars Smith made repeated visits to the Near East to improve his spoken Arabic and to gain a better feel for the region. He toured the remoter areas of the Arabian peninsula and visited Fayum oasis with Sir Richard Burton* (1879).

Smith believed that the Bible could best be understood within the context of the society in which it was written. Consequently he argued that apparent discrepancies in it were in large part due to the differences in understanding and needs which various writers held on account of the varying social conditions when they wrote. Each addressed himself to his own time. This was grounded both in a form of social relativism in which meaning and values reflected particular social situations and, given the nature of Christian belief, in a more universalistic, evolutionary scheme whereby primitive Old Testament belief slowly culminated in Christianity. The first set of ideas led Smith to develop a sociology of religion where beliefs reflected society, while the second led to a developmental analysis which sought to isolate essential or core ideas from which more elaborate and 'higher' beliefs and conditions evolved. Smith's study of early Arab kinship was an attempt to grasp the most basic aspects of Semitic society thereby paving the way for understanding its primal beliefs. Such an approach is now discredited, but this study provided anthropologists with the first clear analysis of how preliterate societies could be politically organized through kinship, feud and warfare without formal institutions of government.

Smith's study of religion emphasizes social action (ritual) over belief (myth), centring his work on the study of sacrifice which he saw as a commensal rather than a piacular rite. This view is now in decline among biblical scholars but in different forms profoundly influenced important social thinkers such as Durkheim and Freud. Durkheim's *Elementary Forms of the Religious Life* was deeply influenced by Smith's communal theory of ritual. A less fortunate but influential aspect of Smith's work was his promotion of his friend J.F. McLennan's theories about the origin of religion in totemic beliefs, culminating in Smith's relating biblical sacrifice to totemic propitiation. Not only was this approach taken up by Durkheim but widely elaborated in Freud's *Totem and Taboo*. To support these theories Smith encouraged his student, Sir James Frazer*, to write *Totemism* (1887) which led in turn to *The Golden Bough* (1890).

Despite inevitable inaccuracies when measured against current scholarly findings, many of Smith's arguments remain vigorous and are permanently reflected in the fact that no scholar would now attempt meaningful analysis of religious beliefs outside the context of the social fabric in which these were produced and developed.

T.O. Beidelman

The most comprehensive biographical study remains J.S. Black and G. Chrystal, *The Life of William Robertson Smith* (1912). The basic current evaluation of his work and definitive bibliography of his publications and those of his critics is T.O. Beidelman, *W. Robertson Smith and the Sociological Study of Religion* (1974).

421
SOANE, Sir John 1753–1837

British architect

Architect of the Bank of England and creator of the first architectural museum in Britain, Soane was one of the most original architects of the nineteenth century in Europe. Unlike many more conventional contemporary works, his buildings have suffered severely from destruction and alterations, so that his achievement can now only be fully appreciated from plans and drawings.

Soane worked at a period when in Britain an architect was expected to turn his hand to any style. He accordingly worked in the classical modes, sometimes reinterpreting antique buildings, such as the Temple

of Vesta in the Tivoli Corner at the Bank of England, and less willingly produced Gothic paraphrases, but he excelled in originality. He believed that architects should be learned in the buildings of the past – hence his museum – but that this knowledge should equip them to create an architecture fitted to their own age. His striving for a 'modern' style is apparent in his more personal buildings, which to his contemporaries could appear unfamiliar and even barbarous, but which have survived as some of the most notable achievements of the age.

'The ruling passion of my life', Soane once remarked, 'is to be distinguished as an architect'. In 1768 he entered the office of George Dance the Younger – whose atmospheric buildings such as Newgate Prison strongly influenced him – and later that of Henry Holland. He became a student at the Royal Academy Schools, where he won the Gold Medal for Architecture, and in 1778 set out with a Travelling Studentship for Rome, where he engaged in the earnest study of classical buildings. From Rome he was seduced back to Britain by the Earl-Bishop of Bristol and Derry with the promise of magnificent commissions, but when Soane expectantly returned in 1780 the commissions did not materialize. The 1780s were spent on various minor jobs, especially in East Anglia, but in 1788, through the influence of William Pitt, he was appointed surveyor to the Bank of England, and became established professionally. Although his country house work continued, with such commissions as the alterations to Wimpole Hall, Cambridgeshire, of 1791–3, and Tyringham Hall, Buckinghamshire, of 1793–1800, he concentrated increasingly on official work. His accumulation of official positions, such as the Clerkship of the Works at Whitehall, Westminster, and St James's, gave him the opportunity to design, alter or restore many national buildings: the Bank of England, from 1788 to 1833, the Board of Trade and Privy Council Offices, Whitehall (1824–6, remodelled 1845–6), additions to the House of Lords (1822–7, burnt 1832), and the refacing of the Whitehall Banqueting House. He also executed for the Waterloo Commissioners a group of London churches, notably Holy Trinity, Marylebone (1826–7). His work received due recognition: he became an RA in 1802 and a knight in 1832, and at the end of his life his continuous efforts to establish architecture as a regular profession led the new Institute of British Architects to offer him its presidency.

As Sir John Summerson has pointed out, Soane's range of motifs was comparatively small. He could when necessary design classical buildings on a grand scale, as in the screen wall of the Bank of England, a dignified and appropriate solution for the building's façades. His most memorable exteriors are less splendid but more peculiarly his: structures like the Dulwich College Picture Gallery of 1811–13, or the stables at

Chelsea Hospital (1809–17). In these he abandons classical orders: working in his favourite material, London stock brick, he creates elevations in a 'primitive' vein, manipulating surface and scale through a series of receding blank arches, and restricting his ornament to thin incised lines. These buildings show his concern to give his architecture an atmosphere appropriate to its function, an interest that has earned his work the label of 'Romantic Classicism'.

His interiors are even more remarkable. Soane's vocabulary of thin pillars or pilasters, shallow domes lit by clerestories and minimal linear decoration is combined with a strongly imaginative sense of planning and space. His feeling for scale was such that he could use the same devices in the sublime halls of the Bank of England – all demolished – in the library at Wimpole and, in miniature, in the breakfast room of his own house. It is not easy architecture, neither decorative nor comfortable. He had little in common with the Greek Revivalists of his day, Wilkins and Smirke, who were content to imitate antique buildings as far as possible; his name is more satisfactorily coupled with that of Schinkel*. He was an individualist, and his style died with him.

The most evocative remaining building by Soane is his museum and house in Lincoln's Inn Fields, developed by him from 1792 until his death. In this claustrophobic and neurotic interior – which reflects his difficult character – the visitor is both exhilarated and oppressed by the accumulation of architectural drawings, fragments of classical buildings, paintings and sculpture; by the breakfast room with its dozens of small convex mirrors, and the museum room, a celebration of death, the walls stacked with funerary urns around an Egyptian sarcophagus; and by the sheets and sheets of architectural schemes, for palaces and parliaments, gargantuan and unexecuted.

Giles Waterfield

See: A.T. Bolton, *The Works of Sir John Soane* (1924) and *The Portrait of Sir John Soane* (1927); Sir John Summerson, *Sir John Soane* (1952); D. Stroud, *The Architecture of Sir John Soane* (1961).

422
SOREL, Georges 1847–1922

French social thinker

The first forty years or so of Sorel's life gave little forewarning of the excited confusion that was to characterize much of his new career as writer over the subsequent three decades, during which time he expressed with passionate vigour a series of ideas that would call into question every conventional scheme of political labelling and allegiance. Born at Cherbourg into the family of an unsuccessful businessman, he trained in Paris at the École Polytechnique where he excelled at mathematics and qualified as an engineer. He then pursued this profession until 1892, making very respectable progress within the government department of roads and bridges. At that point, fortified with a modest legacy from his mother, he simply resigned. Three years earlier he had brought out in Paris his first two works, the *Contribution à l'étude profane de la Bible* ('Contribution to the Secular Study of the Bible') and *Le Procès de Socrate* ('The Trial of Socrates'). Now he was determined to devote his full attention to further study and publication in the broad field of social and political affairs. The rest of his career seemed devoted to shocking a bourgeoisie whose notions of respectability still influenced his own private life, even to the point where he would not legitimize his 'marriage' with a servant-girl whose humble status made her unacceptable to his relations.

Much of Sorel's writing appeared first in newspapers and journals, and usually constituted a response to some problem of the moment. The lasting repute that he eventually won rested more on the penetrative power of particular insights than on any possible claim to systematic theoretical coherence, and the record of his own volatile political loyalties serves to confirm the untidiness in his thinking. During the mid-1890s Sorel put aside his earlier faith in the value of liberal conservatism and moved into a phase of full Marxist enthusiasm. This coincided with a period of similar sentiment on the part of the idealist philosopher Benedetto Croce, and for a time the two were closely associated in spreading the communist message amongst an Italian public. Dissatisfaction with the deterministic scientism of Friedrich Engels* and Karl Kautsky soon drove Sorel from the camp of the self-styled 'orthodox' – a departure illuminated by a work of 1902 published at Palermo, the *Saggi di critica del marxismo* ('Critical Essays on Marxism'). Even so, there was no cessation of his sympathetic engagement with issues raised by Marx* himself, such as the nature and significance of class warfare. By the end of the 1890s Sorel was moving towards the reformist social-democratic position defended by Eduard Bernstein and the 'revisionists'. Though he counted himself among the supporters of Captain Dreyfus, Sorel was so deeply disgusted by the manner in which other sympathizers – most notably Jean Jaurès – had exploited the great affair for immediate political advantage that he never returned again to any advocacy of parliamentary democracy. His interests now shifted in the direction of revolutionary syndicalism which, especially in France and Italy, linked anarchist inspirations with the organizational potential of the trade unions. He believed for a time that this at last offered to the proletariat an opportunity of implementing the creative tasks which now fell upon it as the one morally uncompromised class within contemporary society.

By 1910 Sorel was again changing his ground, having become disillusioned by the way in which even the anarchosyndicalists were showing compromising reformist tendencies. Increasingly indebted to Henri Bergson's vitalist philosophy, he was now enthusing over the nationalistic mysticism represented by the rhetoric of *la terre et les morts* ('the soil and the dead') found in Maurice Barrès* and the Action Française. The French war-effort of 1914–18 appalled him, however, in so far as it was characterized as a defence of liberal-democratic values. After the Great War he felt able not only to praise the new Bolshevik regime but also to show sympathy for the nascent Italian Fascist movement which then attained power shortly after his death. While Lenin ignored him, Mussolini showed that he was in greater need of intellectual fig-leaves. Thus the Duce declared: 'I owe much to Georges Sorel. This master of syndicalism by his rough theories of revolutionary tactics has contributed most to form the discipline, energy, and power of the Fascist cohorts.' Even our mere summary of Sorel's career indicates that here was a mind refusing to be constrained by customary categories and labels. But beneath the swirl of inconsistency there did flow certain steadier currents. In particular, Sorelian thought was marked by three more constant themes: a revolt against the bourgeois world's acquisitiveness and its search for passive contentment, a dialogue with Marx's legacy, and an exploration of the realms of creative violent energy.

These features were at their clearest during Sorel's phase of association with French syndicalism. His immediate influence on the movement was small. But its journal, *Le Mouvement Socialiste*, provided an organ for the essays making up his best-known works, *The Illusions of Progress* (*Les Illusions du progrès*, trans. 1969) and the *Reflections on Violence* (*Réflexions sur la violence*, trans. 1916), both published as books in Paris in 1908. Especially in the latter study, Sorel made his own major contribution to that 'revolt against positivism' which Stuart Hughes (in *Consciousness and Society: The Reorientation of European Social Thought, 1890–1930*, 1959) has encouraged us to regard as the pivotal characteristic of cultural and intellectual history at this epoch. The *Reflections* advocated the deflation of rationalistic presumptuousness, not least amongst socialists themselves, and treated Bergson's *élan vital*, or 'life force', as a conception concordant with Sorel's own belief that human fulfilment depended upon an energetic creativity which had to be appreciated emotionally rather than scientifically. The bourgeois world could be overthrown only by a form of socialism founded not upon scientism but upon 'social poetry' – by a Marxism less concerned with the material than with the moral order and thus by a creed which had converted itself into an elite-inspired 'myth'. The efficacy of myth as an instrument of social change was not to be correlated with the extent of its accuracy as a representation of reality. Its ability to generate activity and thereby to mould the future was related, rather, to its capacity for mobilizing the will and channelling the emotions. At the time of the *Reflections*, Sorel believed that the anarcho-syndicalist weapon of a totally uncompromising general strike provided the most promising basis for a myth of this kind. Labour would there be withdrawn not in order to improve conditions within a corrupt system but in order utterly to shatter the system itself – and, above all, its dehumanizing attitude towards workers as mere objects of profit.

Even when he went on to embrace mystical nationalism, Sorel was consistent in searching still for whatever would foster an epic state of mind as pre-condition for social, and indeed moral, regeneration. 'Violence', he declared, 'is an intellectual doctrine, the will of powerful minds who know what they are doing.' Sorel, like the anarchist Peter Kropotkin*, wished to distinguish between this liberating violence and the repression stemming from the employment of mere force. None the less, we can easily see what hostages he left to fortune, especially in its Fascist version. In the final analysis, he must be included within the ranks of those whose achievement was more impressive in its negative than in its positive aspects. Yet, like his contemporary Friedrich Nietzsche*, he cannot be dismissed simply on that account. Most particularly, Sorel remains worthy of attention because his corrosive criticism and his concern with the non-rational springs of human action touched upon so many of the major points of agenda confronting those writers, such as Émile Durkheim, Max Weber, and Vilfredo Pareto, who were at the same epoch engaged, in a less eccentric and untidy manner, upon establishing the foundations for twentieth-century academic social science as we now know it.

Michael Biddiss

Among Sorel's other works note especially: *Introduction à l'économie moderne* (*Introduction to the Modern Economy*, 1903); *La Décomposition du marxisme* (*The Decomposition of Marxism*, 1908); and *La Révolution dreyfusienne* (*The Dreyfusard Revolution*, 1909). See also: J.H. Meisel, *The Genesis of Georges Sorel* (1951); Richard D. Humphrey, *Georges Sorel, Prophet with Honour: A Study in Anti-Intellectualism* (1951); Irving L. Horowitz, *Radicalism and the Revolt Against Reason: The Social Theories of Georges Sorel* (1961); and Isaiah Berlin, 'George Sorel', in *Against the Current: Essays in the History of Ideas* (1979), pp. 296–332.

423
SOUTHEY, Robert 1774–1843

British writer

Southey is a difficult person to categorize, the more so if we observe a critical purism that demands a separation of life and work. We have to respond to him as a whole: as poet, prose-writer, political commentator, reviewer, editor, letter-writer extraordinary – and all this in the context of a life that takes him from early radicalism in Bristol (where he was born) to the rampant conservatism of his established middle age. The outward events of his life are not as important as the mirror he provides for an age of turbulence, although there are various crucial sign-posts.

In his rebellious youth at Westminster School he was passionately committed to Godwin's* rationalism, to Goethe's* romantic hero *Werther*, and to the optimism of Rousseau; he applauded the French Revolution, he abhorred Pitt, he supported Paine. In 1794, when he was at Balliol College, Oxford (he left without a degree), he met Coleridge*, and together they formed the Utopian plan known as 'Pantisocracy': a select group of men and women would establish a self-supporting community on the banks of the Susquehanna in America. This came to nothing (apart from marriage, for both men, to a pair of sisters), and as the war with France encouraged a strong nationalism to overrule any other considerations, Southey became identified with the conservative views he had at one time violently opposed. Many saw his acceptance of the Poet Laureateship in 1813 (at Scott's* suggestion) as the final straw in a career characterized by naivety and opportunism.

His contemporaries viewed him with ambivalence: even his harshest opponents found warm things to say about him in spite of everything. But what was seen as his apostasy seemed, especially to the younger generation, an exaggerated version of the general drift towards high Toryism of former heroes like Wordsworth* and Coleridge. Southey was a convenient scapegoat. He was always in the public eye, and everyone could vent their spleen on him. He did not mind appearing foolish, and gave his opponents ample opportunity to ridicule him mercilessly. If he distrusted theory (and all his social commentaries, often philanthropic to a degree, concern themselves essentially with practical matters), he was not much better at conducting a pragmatic campaign. The fiasco over his early dramatic poem *Wat Tyler* illustrates all his weaknesses: just as he was advocating, in 1816 and 1817, with hubristic extravagance, doctrines for the swift suppression of democratic reforms, his youthful work celebrating the radicalism of his ancestor was published by his opponents. Southey made matters worse by offering an apologia that paled beside the invective of his outraged critics.

Southey believed that there was nothing wrong with changing his mind; but from the demise of the Pantisocratic scheme onwards he did it to such an alarming extent that it could only be seen as a culpable innocence, especially when he persisted in his role as spokesman, in journals such as the *Edinburgh Annual Register* and the *Quarterly Review*, for the *status quo*, in terms of increasing paranoia. His early radicalism he either disowned as ignorance, or totally denied. As early as 1796 he was quite happy that the republican sentiments of his *Joan of Arc* should not rock the ship of state, and managed to persuade himself that by writing for the *Quarterly Review* he was not subscribing to their ministerial views, but that their 'influence' would give 'currency and weight' to his own opinions. Small wonder that few could forgive his greatest absurdity, 'A Vision of Judgement' (1821), a poem in hexameters devoted to the supposed arrival of George III in heaven. In a preface to the poem he attacked Byron* and the 'Satanic school' of poetry, but Byron's devastating answer (in the form of a poem of the same name) did not deter Southey from including poem and preface in his *Collected Works* (1829).

In a moment of generosity, Byron described Southey as 'the only existing entire man of letters', and that is perhaps how we must see him. He wrote, basically, for money, for survival. He was honest enough (though not necessarily right) to admit that he was 'ill-fitted for writing'; but the other careers open to him – the church, law, medicine – held few attractions. His life was one of constant, regulated scribbling. The list of what he wrote is daunting in its length and scope: depressing, ultimately, in its remorselessness. He wrote long and thoughtful reviews for the major journals of the day (he should not be remembered only for his savaging of the *Lyrical Ballads* in 1798). He wrote an immense *History of Brazil* (1810, 1817, 1819); he translated endlessly from the Spanish and Portuguese; his *Letters from England by Don Manuel Alvarez Espriella* (1807) and *Colloquies on the Progress and Prospects of Society* (1829) formed a substantial critique of his age (later answered by Macaulay*). He was an industrious editor of other men's works, notably Cowper's (1835–7). His lives of Nelson (1813) and John Wesley (1820) were exemplary pieces of popularization and condensation: the Wesley biography showed, too, his capacity for open inquiry, even if later his basic aversion to Methodism (never as strong as that to Roman Catholicism) came to the surface to buttress his diatribes against democracy. He produced that curious gallimaufry *The Doctor* (1834–47), where we stumble across the story of 'The Three Bears' amongst calculations of how many languages you could learn in the time you spent shaving during an average life. He developed a prose style of remarkable clarity and strength, admired by a critic as hostile as Hazlitt*: many would argue that his prose was his greatest legacy. He was certainly one of the best letter-writers of the period. There is something impressive about such a record.

The paradox was that Southey really wanted to escape altogether from the society he wrote about (in practical terms he did, living with the Coleridges at Greta Hall in Keswick from 1803 onwards). He was a thinker who ended up bewildered and confused, an 'unfit man', he said, 'to mingle with the world'. His professional prose writing was an escape from the terrors of poetry, from the emotion he feared. People spoke of his coldness, and typically the portrait of the author at the front of *The Doctor* showed merely the back of his head. Just as in his prose he tried to create elaborate fictional masks, so he would try to lose himself in long epic romances (*Madoc, Thalaba, Roderick, The Curse of Kehama*), whereas his real virtues as a poet came out in the dramatic, sardonic, violent ballads, such as 'God's Judgement on a Wicked Bishop', or in shyly personal poems like 'To a Spider', 'The Holly Tree' or in the lines to his cousin, Margaret Hill.

Books were his defence against life, against the turbulence that poetry induced; he preferred them to people as the 'only safe attachment'. His lyric 'My Days among the Dead are passed' is the sad summation of his life. Three years before his death, his mind had gone, and Wordsworth visited him. After a brief flash of recogniton Southey sank back into a torpor, 'patting with both hands his books affectionately, like a child'.

Mark Storey

Selected Poems, ed. M.H. Fitzgerald (1909); *Selected Letters*, ed. M.H. Fitzgerald (1912); *New Letters*, ed. Kenneth Curry (2 vols, 1965); *Selected Prose*, ed. Jacob Zeitlin (1916). About Southey: William Haller, *The Early Life of Robert Southey* (1917); Jack Simmons, *Southey* (1945); Geoffrey Carnall, *Robert Southey and his Age* (1960); Lionel Madden, *Southey: The Critical Heritage* (1972); Kenneth Curry, *Southey* (1975).

424
SPENCER Herbert 1820–1903

British philosopher

Outside the fields of the natural sciences and technology on one side and the artistic literature on the other, Herbert Spencer appears as the dominant intellectual figure of the later part of the nineteenth century. In particular his concept of evolution presided over the thinking in the nascent studies of sociology and anthropology, and permeated the view of the world held by educated Europeans and Americans. The later success of this concept was due to Darwin* and Wallace*, but it was Spencer who gave it currency. Darwin gave

a causal explanation of the processes through which species are modified and eventually transformed, whereas Spencer's concept of evolution (which means 'unfolding') suggests a predetermined goal or plan guiding the general trend. Spencer believed that there was a universal movement from the simple to the complex, the criterion of complexity being differentiation of the parts and their integration, that is mutual dependence.

There is some overlap between him and Darwin, according to whom the more complex organisms have come into existence by gradual modifications of the simpler and, therefore, appeared later in time. But Darwin does not say that the simple organisms are likely to disappear, and postulates no all-embracing trend throughout the animate nature, whereas Spencer sees it not only there and in the socio-cultural realm, which he calls 'superorganic' but in inanimate nature as well. His 'evolution' could be described as a cosmic anti-entropic trend. Although he tries to back it with references to astronomy, physics and chemistry, his diagnosis goes far beyond what could have been inferred from these sciences. It is even less tenable now, as modern physics postulates entropy – that is the tendency towards an equal distribution of energy throughout the universe – and sees a movement in the contrary direction as possible only in restricted parts of the universe. As a cosmological principle, however, entropy is perhaps even less tenable than Spencer's evolution because how can anything be undergoing a process of dispersion without having previously undergone a process of concentration?

Although he did not believe in a personalized God, and explained the origins of religion in terms of experience of dreaming, Spencer could be classified as a deist on the ground that he believed he knew the fundamental principle presiding over all the changes in the universe. There is some contradiction between his definition of God as 'the Great Unknown' and his claim to know the ultimate goal of the cosmos. The infusion of this metaphysical element enabled Spencer to build a system of ethics on the tacit assumption that since evolution – that is the trend from the simple to the complex – is universal, it must be good, from which follows that whatever promotes this trend is good, while whatever impedes it is bad. Almost needless to say, this involves a jump over Hume's barrier between what is the case and what ought to be the case. It may be worth noting that if we tried to make an analogous jump and build a system of ethics on the physics of today, then the principle of entropy would lead us to advocacy of nihilistic destructiveness.

Spencer was influenced by Auguste Comte* but disapproved of his scheme for a new society and wanted to improve upon his theories. They were the only authors in recent times who imitated Aristotle in covering all branches of knowledge, although Spencer only briefly refers to mathematics, physics and chemistry in his *The First Principles* (1862), while Comte devotes the first half of his six volume *Cours de la philosophie positive* to an exposition of their most general ideas. Spencer, however, deals at greater length with biology where his master key is more useful. Nevertheless though admired for the remarkable wealth of his knowledge by the few who have read *The Principles of Biology* (2 vols, 1864 and 1867), Spencer is not regarded as important by the historians of biology. *The Principles of Psychology* (1855; 2nd edn, 2 vols, 1870 and 1872) also had little influence on the development of its subject. Perhaps it was too early for such a book to be written as neither systematic or clinical observation nor experimentation had yet begun, and so there was no knowledge, going beyond introspection and common sense, to be synthesized.

Undoubtedly the most permanent bequest of Spencer lies in sociology and anthropology, which were dominated by 'evolutionism' until the early part of the present century. What made it possible was the better fit between Spencer's concept of evolution and the facts in these fields, and the bridge which it provided between these and Darwinian biology. In the realm of the superorganic, the more complex forms have displaced the less complex which (unlike the microorganisms) are disappearing. We can see here, to use another of Spencer's terms, a general 'advance of organization'. Dealing with social evolution he not only diagnoses correctly the general trend but also offers a convincing explanation: in the struggle for survival between groups the larger and more highly organized invariably win when the difference on these scores is big enough. A large state can never be defeated by small tribes of hunters, whereas a mammal can be killed by bacteria and is powerless against insects. Spencer's expression 'survival of the fittest' is circular in biology, where fitness is measured by survival, but in sociology it can be interpreted as meaning that the more highly organized groups tend to survive. Marx's* Law of Industrial Concentration can be subsumed under this evolutionary principle.

The primeval form of struggle for survival is war, and Spencer correctly sees in it a prime agent of social evolution which, through conquests and alliances for defence, has led to the emergence of large polities where a more advanced differentiation and integration of parts is possible.

In *The Principles of Sociology* (3 vols, 1876–96), Spencer deals in turn with various institutions – religious beliefs, the family, ceremonies, professions, economic (or, as he calls them, industrial) and political organizations – showing the origins of the more recent and complex forms in the simpler. His treatment is of the most lasting value where his master key fits best – that is, where the process of differentiation and integration can be discerned most clearly – which is in the political and economic structures. Best of all is his treatment of the political and military institutions on the level of the transition from tribes to states because here we can see in its purest form the mechanism which he regards as the cause of evolution: namely the struggle for survival and the elimination of the simpler formations by the more complex. His treatment of the family, religion and art is so much less illuminating, because in these spheres no clear trend from the simple to the complex can be ascertained, and it is not clear what the struggle for survival means in this context. Indeed, the structures of kinship are much simpler in ours than in the primitive societies. Although there are more words in the languages of contemporary nations (which, however, does not mean that the average individual knows more words), the grammatical structures of languages spoken by minute tribes can be very complex. Furthermore, the complex economic and political institutions are relatively recent; and there are many cases of their emergence recorded in documents. We also have reliable and detailed descriptions of stateless societies without division of labour beyond that between the sexes and with very little trade, if any. So we have some data which throw light on the questions of the origins of the state, market economy, professional armies or bureaucracies. In contrast, it is impossible to reconstruct the stages in the evolution of language between the simple simian forms and the (structurally more or less equally complex) known human languages. Likewise, we can never know what were the prehistoric forms of the family or religion. Evolutionism fell into disrepute largely because of its exponents' concern with the latter domains where they could not go beyond completely unverifiable conjectures.

Although Spencer coined the term 'comparative sociology', he did not practise comparative analysis of the kind which we can find in Durkheim's *Le Suicide*, or in Otto Hintze's essay on the conditions of emergence of representative governments, where they try to unravel causal links with the aid of comparisons which approximately fit Mill's* methods of induction. Spencer compares mainly to classify or illustrate the stages of evolution, giving an astounding number of examples from all epochs and parts of the globe but going into none of them in great detail; in contrast, for example, to T.H. Buckle* who compares only four countries of Europe but employs a mass of factual data to unravel the constellations of forces which have propelled these countries in different directions. Spencer's evolutionary classification of societies is just as good (if not better) than any other which has been proposed but classifying must be a dead end unless it is supplemented by studies of causation. True, some of Spencer's propositions assert causal links, but he is only interested in the most general factors of evolution: he explains, for instance, polygyny as an adaptation to warfare which has a great survival value on the tribal level, but (in contrast to, for example, John Mackinnon Robertson*) he says nothing which would help us to understand why evolution went on faster in one place or era than another: why for example, science developed in Europe rather than India or why the industrial revolution occurred in Britain rather than Spain.

The other part of Spencer's heritage is known as 'organicism', the essence of which is the focus on analogies between organisms and societies and searches for homologous structures and functions. Thus, for instance, trade and transportation are likened to the circulation of the blood, and the nervous system to the administrative machinery of the state. This approach was a valuable step towards a full appreciation of the enormous complexity of social differentiation, integration and self-regulation. However, especially in the hands of Spencer's less subtle followers, it soon degenerated into an unfruitful game of listing superficial analogies. Although he followed Spencer very closely in his first major book, *De la Division de travail social* (1893), Emile Durkheim initiated a new departure by insisting on more detailed study of facts of social life and a deeper analysis of social causation. Later, A.R. Radcliffe-Brown, who was a keen student of Spencer and Durkheim, transmitted the concern with the concepts of structure, function and their integration to the 'functionalist school' of anthropology, of which he was a co-founder. The functionalists abandoned all interest in evolution and (with the exception of Radcliffe-Brown) in comparative analysis, concentrating on intensive studies of individual primitive societies, which was the very opposite of Spencer's classificatory schemes. But they took from Spencer the idea of mutual interdependence of structures and functions, and ordered the data of their field work from this viewpoint, often discovering connections undreamt of by Spencer.

More recently, Spencer's idea that all self-regulating systems have common characteristics has been revived in the new form of general systems theory, although it is possible that its exponents did not get their inspiration from Spencer, as they never mention him. None the less, he was their forerunner. Anyone who has read Spencer and reads J.G. Miller's *Living Systems* (1978) will see that it is pure Spencerianism brought up to date.

Until the rise of machine industry, political (and especially military) structures were much more complex than the industrial; and they grew in complexity through the raw struggle for survival. After the industrial revolution the growth in complexity occurred mainly in the economic institutions. Commercial competition can be regarded as the new propellant of evolution which brings forth ever larger and more complex entities, while the smaller and weaker are eliminated. Spencer hovered on the brink of such an interpretation, which would have brought him to Marx's Law of Industrial Concentration. Such a con-

clusion, however, would have clashed with his commitment to fundamentalist liberalism, which he never abandoned despite its incompatibility with organicism which is more consistent with authoritarian collectivism because the growth of complexity of organisms is accompanied by an increase in the control of all parts of the body by the brain. Consequently, the idea of survival of the fittest was only used (especially by his followers) to justify the position of individual victors in commercial competition. This use – known as Social Darwinism – was based on the mistake of confusing social with biological success, the only measure of which is the number of offspring who survive and reproduce. Unlike Comte and Marx, who condemned the societies in which they lived and entertained visions of a better order, Spencer was a mildly reformist conservative who saw in the Victorian liberal order – which only needed to be purged of the remnants of militarism, Toryism and bureaucracy – the end product of evolution. This view was connected with the idea which he got from Saint-Simon* that militarism (or, as he puts it, militancy) was being displaced by industrialism, that is an orientation towards peaceful production instead of war. Industrialism, according to this view, also entailed a transition from coercion to cooperation. Since he paid so much attention to the role of war as the motor of evolution, and believed that this motor was due to stop, it is not perhaps surprising that he could not envisage evolution going far beyond the Britain of his time.

Despite its inconsistency with his sociological theory, Spencer's advocacy of ultra liberalism brought him widespread reverence, usually given to able apologists of the dominant social forces. Though widely applauded, his eloquent tirades against governmental regulation had little relevance to the ills of the Victorian Britain which (together with the United States of that era) was the most unbureaucratic large-scale society which ever existed. In contrast, Marx – bitter enemy of ill-treatment of the sellers of labour by the owners of capital – died almost in obscurity. With the decline of the businessman and the rise of the bureaucrat, Spencer was pushed into the shade, while Marx – whose theories condemn the capitalist and exonerate the bureaucrat – was posthumously brought into the limelight, just as the ills against which he thundered lost their acuteness while those which Spencer attacked acquired gravity which they did not have when he was writing.

In his life and character, Spencer typifies the greatness and the oddities of Victorian Britain. An abstemious and puritanical hypochondriac, he put all his energies into intellectual endeavour. An amateur belonging to no university, he was free from the academic routine and ritual and the temptations and pressures of petty politics. Having been taught by relatives in a highly individual manner, he was never subjected to scholastic standardization. He did, however, have to submit to the discipline of work because, as a son of a private tutor, he had to earn his living early and qualified as an engineer on the railways at the age of seventeen. He made a couple of minor mechanical inventions but soon began to be involved in reformist and political activities, and to write for provincial periodicals, At twenty-eight he got a job as a sub-editor on *The Economist*, moved to London and entered into contacts with the intellectual circles. Some years later he received an inheritance which gave him the means to devote himself to scholarly pursuits provided he did not have a family to support. He chose not to marry. With extraordinary persistence he went on with his project of a synthetic philosophy which he completed with *The Principles of Ethics* (2 vols, 1879 and 1893) when he was seventy-six. Always eccentric, in his later years he often put plugs into his ears in order not to have to listen to nonsense.

Though optimistic for a long time about the final victory of pure liberalism, he became pessimistic in old age and began to expect a recrudescence of militarism and statism. The link between the two was stipulated by one of his many theoretical propositions arrived at by a combination of deductive reasoning and a rule-of-thumb inductive survey. These propositions vary greatly in the degree to which they are connected with his most fundamental and general ideas discussed above, but all are interesting and cogently formulated. In the light of the knowledge available today, most of them appear plausible and many can be accepted as substantially correct.

Stanislav Andreski

Spencer's other works include: *Social Statics or the Conditions essential to Human Happiness specified, and the First of them Developed* (1850); *Education: Intellectual, Moral and Physical* (1861); *The Study of Sociology* (1873); *Descriptive Sociology* (1874 – compiled by others on principles laid down by Spencer, and continued after his death); *The Man versus the State* (1884); *An Autobiography* (1904). See also: *Structure, Function and Evolution*, ed. S.L. Andreski (1971); Y.D.Y. Peel, *Herbert Spencer, Evolution of a Sociologist* (1971).

425
SPOHR, Louis 1784–1859

German composer

Certain composers typify their age in a manner wholly disproportionate to their subsequent reputation, their acknowledged gifts or the general quality of their work. It would be unfair and inaccurate to dismiss Louis Spohr as a *petit-maître* or to ignore his significance in the development of central trends in nineteenth-cen-

tury German music, but his interest for us today lies as much in the authenticity of his 'period' voice as in the nature of his individual works.

Born in Brunswick, the son of a music-loving doctor, he was trained as a violinist and managed to impress Duke Karl Wilhelm Ferdinand sufficiently for him to be engaged at court. It was here that he made his first acquaintance with the music of Mozart, whose influence is so strongly reflected in his own compositions, and met the violinist Franz Eck, who took him on a concert tour to Russia and re-educated him as a soloist. A successful return to the Brunswick court in 1803 was followed by a series of concerts throughout Germany which brought him fame not only as a performer but also as a composer and conductor. With his wife Dorette Scheidler, a virtuoso harpist whom he married in 1806, he extended his musical travels to England, France, Italy and Austria and became one of the most celebrated artists of the era. While at Vienna, during two years spent directing the orchestra at the Theater an der Wien, he met and responded to the influence of Beethoven*, and at Frankfurt he attempted serious improvements in artistic standards during his brief tenure as director of the Opera.

It was in Kassel however, where he was appointed court *kapellmeister* in 1821, that he was given adequate leisure to develop his various roles as conductor (notable for his advocacy of the baton to increase orchestral precision), violin teacher (pupils included Hubert Ries and Ferdinand David) and concert promoter, a seminal figure in the Bach revival pioneered elsewhere by Mendelssohn* and responsible for early performances of Wagner's* *Tannhauser* and *Der Fliegende Hollander*. Despite financial difficulties connected with Kassel's internal politics, he was substantially consoled by his increasing reputation abroad, especially in England, where his popularity rivalled Mendelssohn's during the 1840s and 1850s. He died in an atmosphere of mellow respect, best embodied by Wagner's description, 'an old man worthy of the highest honour . . . whose youthful spirit is still directly illuminated by the radiant sunlight of Mozart.'

He composed in a wide variety of musical genres, ranging from virtuoso *pièces d'occasion* designed for his concert tours to oratorios such as *Das jungste Gericht*, a favourite with English choral societies as 'Spohr's Last Judgement', and his work as an operatic composer forms an important chapter in the development of German Romantic musical drama. The best of his operas, *Jessonda* (1822), is more interesting for its formal layout, involving a free use of the through-composition techniques of which he was an advocate, than for its rather pallid dramatic elements and unrewarding vocal lines.

His most important achievements, in which we hear the true voice of Biedermeyer Romanticism, are nearly all in the field of instrumental music. He was an accomplished master of the concerto form, leaving four superb examples for clarinet, and perfecting the violin concerto as a harbinger of the great virtuoso works of the succeeding generation of Vieuxtemps and Wieniawski. Perhaps the most imaginatively personal of all his compositions is the Violin Concerto no. 8 *'in modo di scena cantante'*, written in 1816 and clearly appealing to the rage for the newest type of Italian operatic vocal display in its unabashed and flamboyantly lyrical solo line uniting a single rhapsodic movement.

Spohr is best known today, however, for two chamber works of consummate charm, evidently inspired by Mozart and Beethoven and worthy rivals of Schubert* and Weber*. The delightful Octet for clarinet, two horns and strings, written in 1814, felicitously introduces a set of variations on Handel's 'Harmonious Blacksmith' theme, and the Nonet in F, published in Vienna the following year but actually composed earlier, distils a quality of wistful elegance which shows Spohr at his best, mingling the science and subtlety of his eighteenth-century inheritance with an expressive idiom which is strongly, indeed unmistakably, of its period.

Jonathan Keates

See: Dorothy Moulton Mayer, *Forgotten Master: The Life and Times of Louis Spohr* (1959).

426
STAËL, Anne Louise Germaine (Madame de)
1766–1817

French writer

Madame de Staël's life and writings substantially contributed to introducing new modes of thinking and feeling in France. Born in Paris, the daughter of Jacques Necker, the Swiss banker who became Louis XVI's finance minister, her excessive affection for her father was counterbalanced by a strained relationship with her mother, whose influential salon introduced her to such thinkers as d'Alembert, Diderot and Buffon. Her precocious talent revealed a predilection for the Enlightenment and her first successful work was *Lettres sur les ouvrages et le caractère de J.-J. Rousseau* ('Letters on the Works and Character of J.-J. Rousseau', 1788). Her marriage in 1786 to the Swedish Ambassador, Eric de Staël-Holstein, like many of her liaisons, subsequently ended in separation.

She openly welcomed the French Revolution and her salon became a political and artistic meeting-place. Her politics, however, later influenced by her stormy relationship with Benjamin Constant*, soon made her suspect to the government and after a trip to England (1792) and a period at Coppet, in Switzerland, she published *De l'influence des passions sur le bonheur des individus et des nations* ('Treatise on the Influence of the Passions on the Happiness of Individuals and Nations', 1796), which revealed strong pre-Romantic tendencies.

In 1798, she first suggested cooperation with Napoleon Bonaparte*, but given his conventional views on woman's place in society, this had little chance of being accepted. Furthermore, *The Influence of Literature upon Society* (*De la littérature considérée dans ses rapports avec les institutions sociales*, 1800, trans. 1812) argued for the superiority of northern cultures over those of the south and singled out English and German literature as models to be followed. Important for introducing to France the idea that literature is the vital expression of a nation's ethos, it guided both the Romantics and Taine*. *Delphine* (1802, trans. 1803) gives a magnified picture of the debates on women in post-revolutionary France and of the author's own challenging personality. It contains a strong plea for women's rights but as a novel is verbose, sentimental and derivative.

In 1803, Napoleon took measures to suppress the liberal resistance spear-headed by de Staël and Constant* and she was banished from Paris. Her struggle with Napoleon is graphically chronicled in *Ten Years' Exile* (*Dix années d'exil*, 1821, trans. 1821). The immediate consequence was a journey that opened her mind to German culture. At Weimar, she met Goethe* and Schiller and, in Berlin, August Wilhelm Schlegel*, who became a faithful friend and interpreter of German manners. After her father's death in April 1804, Coppet became her permanent base as well as a cross-roads of European intellectual life and symbol of resistance to Napoleon.

Her Italian trip (1805) inspired her second novel, *Corinna, or Italy* (*Corinne, ou l'Italie*, 1807, trans. 1807), which expands the debates in *Delphine*. De Staël asserts her independence as woman and artist and champions Italy as the embodiment of aesthetic freedom. *Corinne* had profound influence on the Romantic generation who echoed her belief in artistic inspiration and unfettered enthusiasm. Her second trip to Germany crystallized her ideas for *Germany* (*De l'Allemagne*, 1813, trans. 1813), which provides a wide-ranging discussion of German culture. Although distorted, it has the singular merit of introducing France to German influences and presents a vision of the artist as an inquiring free spirit. Publication was planned for 1810, but Napoleon, irritated by this admiring portrait of an alien culture, ordered the book's seizure and it was published during her London trip in 1813.

In 1814, after Napoleon's defeat, she returned to Paris where she re-opened her salon and worked on her *Considérations sur la Révolution française* ('Considerations on the French Revolution', 1818), which extols the English political system. A glorious interlude at Coppet in 1816, with a glittering intellectual gathering including Byron*, and marriage to Jean Rocca, her lover since 1811, could not compensate for her declining health. She died in Paris, appropriately on 14 July

1817. Her personality and writings inspired a new generation of writers such as Hugo*, Lamartine* and Michelet*. Today she is remembered in the History of Ideas for her struggle for the recognition of women's talents and her belief that societies cannot remain isolated, either politically or culturally.

David Bryant

For the complete works see *Oeuvres complètes* (17 vols, 1820–1), supplemented by *Oeuvres inédites* (3 vols, 1821). See also *Correspondance générale* (4 vols, 1962 onwards); and *Madame de Staël on Politics, Literature and National Character* (1964). On de Staël: R. Escarpit, *L'Angleterre dans l'oeuvre de Madame de Staël* (1954); J.C. Herold, *Mistress to an Age* (1959); W. Andrews, *Germaine* (1964); M. Gutwirth, *Madame de Staël, novelist* (1978); and S. Balayé, *Madame de Staël, lumières et liberté* (1979).

427
STANFORD, Sir Charles Villiers 1852–1924

Irish composer, conductor and teacher

Stanford was an important figure in what might be called the spade-work of the English musical renaissance which took place in the latter part of the nineteenth century: Stanford, Parry*, Mackenzie (Irish, English, Scottish respectively) each helped to lay a foundation for the upsurge of creative activity in the careers of Elgar, Vaughan Williams, John Ireland, Herbert Howells, Bliss, and many more. Stanford's influence came mainly through example (composition as a natural but disciplined everyday activity) and by a rigorous and challenging method of teaching which sorted out the real composers from the rest.

Cambridge University played an important part in Stanford's career. At eighteen he went there as a choral scholar – to Queen's College, where he read classics. Three years later, after graduating, he was appointed organist of Trinity College, and became conductor of the Cambridge University Madrigal Society. He was already composing regularly, in a style which owed much to Schumann* and Brahms* – symphonies, concertos, chamber music; also, at the author's suggestion, he wrote incidental music for a production of Tennyson's* *Queen Mary* in 1876. To broaden his scope, he was going frequently to Germany for tuition between 1874 and 1876. His first opera, *The Veiled Prophet of Khorassan*, was originally produced in Hamburg (1881); then in London at Covent Garden (1883). First Oxford University, then Cambridge conferred on him the honorary degree of Doctor of Music. He was appointed Professor of Music at Cambridge in 1887 – a post which he held until his death. With all this, he increased his activities as a conductor by taking over the

London Bach Choir and later the Leeds Triennial Festival. And when, in London, the Royal College of Music opened in 1883, Stanford became Professor of Composition, and it was there that his enormous influence as a teacher was to be established.

But however much his conducting and teaching made demands upon his time, he always set aside a number of hours each day for what he considered to be a very important activity – composing. His output extended to all categories – operas, symphonies, other orchestral works, chamber music, church and organ music, numerous choral works and songs; also a good deal of incidental music for plays. Stanford's capacity for work seemed to be limitless, and most critics would now probably agree that a high proportion of his large-scale compositions – operas, symphonies, choral works – were the result of industry rather than inspiration; admirable and skilful works within the accepted academic conventions of the time, but difficult to revive today. There are, however, notable exceptions: *The Revenge* (1886), a cantata to words by Tennyson, still lives as a powerful lyrical and dramatic work; the opera *Shamus O'Brien* (1896) achieved world-wide fame and is a fine, vital example of Stanford's Irish-coloured style; of large-scale choral works, the *Requiem* (1897) and *Stabat Mater* (1907) are profound and committed utterances which deserve regular performance. Some of the songs and much of the church music can be heard regularly – and this is likely to continue. Other works which should not be forgotten are the Variations on *Down among the Dead Men* for piano and orchestra, which over many years was a popular item at the Henry Wood 'Proms', and the Irish Rhapsodies and Irish Dances, in which Stanford's individuality finds clear and satisfying expression. The Clarinet Sonata (op. 129) is perhaps his best-known chamber-music work: it has a beautiful and characteristic second movement entitled *Caoine* (an Irish lament).

Stanford's music, however, never had as much influence as his teaching, the effect of which seems to be shown by the distinguished careers of many of his composer-pupils – Frank Bridge, Vaughan Williams, Herbert Howells, John Ireland, Eugene Goossens (to mention but a few).

David Cox

See: biographies by John F. Porte (1921) and Harry Plunket Greene (1935); J. A. Fuller-Maitland, *The Music of Parry and Stanford* (1935).

428
STANLEY, Henry Morton 1841–1904

British/US journalist and explorer

When Henry Morton Stanley encountered David Livingstone* on the shores of Lake Tanganyika in 1872 the age of African exploration's innocence was over. Stanley was the product of a new world, greedier, more pragmatic, less romantic than that from which Livingstone sprung. It was hard on Stanley that the more perfectly he embodied the new order and the more scrupulously he lived up to its standards, the more society felt it imperative that it should be seen to reject its creation.

By the time he met Livingstone, at the age of thirty, he had escaped from the Welsh workhouse in which he received what formal education he possessed, crossed the Atlantic as a deckhand, run a store in the backlands of Arkansas, fought for the Southern cause in the American Civil War, turned his coat to escape from a prisoner of war camp, served aboard several merchant ships and with the American navy, escaped death at the hands of Turkish bandits, and made himself the *New York Herald's* ace reporter. His first assignment was to cover General Sherman's Peace Commission, whose function was to persuade Indians to go quietly to reservations, leaving the way free for the railroad, an exercise which foreshadowed much of Stanley's subsequent work in Africa. His second was to follow the British army to Abyssinia, where, giving early evidence of his administrative genius, he contrived to get his report of the fall of Magdala back to the *Herald* several days before even the Foreign Secretary had been informed it had taken place.

Stanley set about his African expeditions with ruthless efficiency. He did what he was asked, whether it was to contact Livingstone, locate the sources of the Nile, rescue Emin Pasha or lay the foundations of a Congo Free State. He was extravagant with money and, more seriously, with men, but he always got results. Over and over again he was to be naively surprised at the unpopularity he won for doing what he thought was wanted.

His finding of Livingstone made him a celebrity but there was unspoken feeling in English scientific and aristocratic circles that in making the saintly doctor the subject of a sensational newspaper story he had defiled the whole high-minded business of African exploration and missionary work. He was even accused of forging the letters he brought back from Livingstone.

When, five years later, he returned from the astonishingly successful voyage of discovery during which he finally sorted out, in truly horrific conditions, the whole question of the sources of the Nile and Congo and followed the latter right across Africa, he was met again with apathy. He called the western nations to establish commerce, Christianity and civilization in the vast area he had opened up. The statesmen of Europe were embarrassed by his blunt invitation to colonize. From 1880 he served King Leopold of the Belgians in the Congo but his ostensible employer was the Association Internationale Africaine, a philanthropic front for Belgium's imperial ambitions. Between 1880 and 1884 he established a chain of trading stations in the inhospitable jungle. His ability to get roads built through unpromising terrain earned him the name Bula Matari, the Breaker of Rocks. He negotiated 450 separate treaties with tribal chiefs, thus making possible the creation of a unified Congo Free State. It was an astonishing achievement, but Leopold was as unappreciative as posterity, which still remembers Stanley chiefly for the pomposity with which he greeted Livingstone.

In 1887 Stanley led a mission to rescue Emin Pasha, a German-born Muslim who, as one of General Gordon's lieutenants, had been cut off in equatorial Africa after the fall of Khartoum. The journey was successful but traumatic. Stanley returned, for once, to an enthusiastic welcome. But the rapture wore off once the cost of the expedition had been counted. Stanley was a tough leader. To maintain discipline he once hanged two of his porters. When he encountered hostile tribes he bought them off where he could and where he could not he fought his way through their territory. In 1875, in a brutal and foolish act of vengeance, he fired on the inhabitants of Bumbiri, an island in Lake Victoria. His record with his own men was poor. Of the 356 men who accompanied him on his first Congo expedition 241 were to die *en route*, including all three of his white companions. For Emin Pasha's rescue he divided his party into two. He led the advance party, of whom 173 out of 384 reached Lake Albert. When, having contacted Emin, he returned to discover the fate of the rear column he found only 60 out of 271 left alive.

Men who ventured into uncharted jungle with the inadequate medicines of the time were exposing themselves to grave physical risk. Those who attempted to settle an already inhabited land would eventually fall foul of the natives. Geographical expeditions involving several hundred people, the majority of whom felt no personal loyalty to their leader or ideological commitment to his aims, could only be kept moving by dint of stern discipline. These unpalatable truths distressed Victorian Britain.

After the Berlin Conference of 1884 Britain, France, Germany, Belgium and Holland set about dividing up Africa, but the imperialists liked to have as their predecessors martyrs and chivalric warriors. Stanley, the shy and often boorish boy from the workhouse, who once embarrassed Leopold by openly admitting that the French and Belgians, ostensibly joint benefactors of the Africans, were in competition in the Congo basin, antagonized the colonial masters by showing them the truth about themselves. After a short and undistinguished career as an MP he retired from public life. His last wish, to be buried in Westminster Abbey next to Livingstone, was not granted.

Lucy Hughes-Hallett

See: *How I Found Livingstone* (1872); *The Autobiography*

of Sir Henry Morton Stanley, ed. D. Stanley (1909); R. Hall, *Stanley, An Adventurer Explored* (1974).

429
STANTON, Elizabeth Cady 1815–1902

US feminist

The woman honoured as the principal thinker of nineteenth-century feminism should properly be the woman who took the word 'obey' out of her own marriage service in 1840 and asked her correspondents to address her mail to her in her own name by 1848 rather than to 'Mrs Henry B. Stanton' and thus obscure her identity in that of her husband. Elizabeth Cady Stanton's intelligence and theoretical far-sightedness combined with the activism she and her partner in the women's rights struggle in America, Susan B. Anthony*, shared to give justly the two of them credit as the central co-founders of American feminism.

Stanton's personality was gracious and relaxed, warm and endearing; Anthony's was resolute and driving. Stanton was beautiful; Anthony was plain. Anthony was a splendid organizer; Stanton a better theorist and rhetorician. Stanton was an anxious public speaker; Anthony quick on her feet with words. Anthony was single; Stanton, married and the mother of seven children. After their fateful meeting in 1851, they formed one of the best fitting and mutually beneficial political partnerships and friendships in American history. In their lifetimes Stanton was more popular than Anthony, though Anthony has subsequently been given more credit for the work toward which each made her contribution.

Stanton was born in Johnstown, New York, to Margaret Livingston Cady and Daniel Cady. Daniel Cady was a successful lawyer, legislator and eventually a New York supreme court judge. Elizabeth's childhood biography yields three crucial shaping events for her feminist future. She was distressed as a child around her father's law offices when she saw examples of the deprivation of women under the law of their property and their children. At the time of her only brother's death, when she was eleven years old, her father said to her in his grief, 'Oh, my daughter, I wish you were a boy!' She resolved to prove to him that a daughter was just as valuable, a resolve that she was to make abundantly clear to the world and future generations, but there is no evidence her father (or her husband) learned this from her. She was also restrained as a child by her family's Calvinistic Presbyterian religion, a restraint against which she made radical rebellion years later.

In 1840 she married Henry Stanton, a well-known abolitionist ten years older than she. They left at once from their wedding for London where Henry was to be a delegate to the World's Anti-Slavery Convention. At that convention, there was a protest about the refusal to seat women delegates and Elizabeth joined the dissent and spent many hours with the Philadelphia Quaker minister, Lucretia Mott, with whom she vowed to hold a women's rights convention when they returned to America.

Between 1840 and 1848, the Stantons lived in Johnstown where Henry studied law with Elizabeth's father and Elizabeth had the first of their children. They then moved to Boston and had a lively life among Boston's liberals where Elizabeth was active in pressing legislators for a married women's property bill. Then they moved to Seneca Falls in western New York where Henry was to practise law. Small Seneca Falls was dull compared to Boston, and Elizabeth resented the restrictions of her five children and household responsibility. In 1848 Lucretia Mott visited the locality, and the two women, joined by Jane Hunt, Mary McClintock and Martha C. Wright, called the first women's rights convention to be held in America. The Seneca Falls Convention of 1848 was held in the Wesleyan Chapel and was presided over by Mott's husband, James Mott (Henry Stanton was out of town, probably deliberately). Elizabeth presented the women's 'Declaration of Sentiments', a document of profound historic importance.

The 'Declaration of Sentiments' was patterned after the American Declaration of Independence. Insisting that 'men and women are created equal', the declaration decried legal, moral and educational neglect and abuse of women and called for the vote for women the first time in a public proclamation in America. It was a rallying document for women for decades.

The Seneca Falls Convention, the long campaign for women's rights and woman suffrage, its documentation in the first three of the six-volume *History of Woman Suffrage* (1882, 1882, 1886), and *The Woman's Bible* were Elizabeth Cady Stanton's dominant contributions to history. The suffrage campaign she shared particularly with Susan B. Anthony.

The two women set up women's rights conventions together, travelled to make speeches together, wrote and organized petitions together, established the newspaper the *Revolution* in 1868 and ran it for a year and a half, and organized the National Woman Suffrage Association in 1869 over which Stanton presided for twenty-one years. Suffrage was their overriding theme. Though they had other goals, they did believe at times that the gaining of the vote would be the completion of women's equal rights with men. Anthony believed this more than Stanton, writing to Stanton on her last birthday in 1902:

We little believed when we began this contest, optimistic with the hope and buoyancy of youth, that half a century later we would be compelled to leave the finish of the battle to another generation of women. But our hearts are filled with joy to know that they enter upon this task equipped with a college education, business experience, the right to speak in public – all of which were denied to women fifty years ago. They have practically all but one point to gain – the suffrage: we had all.

Stanton's open-mindedness increased and she became more radicalized as she grew older. While her children were young, she clearly resented the care they took, though she grew mellow about joyful motherhood in her elder years. She wrote with great pride about the naturalness of her own physical child-bearing and wrote advocating healthy child-bearing in a natural way in her later life, as well as recommending general good health for women that included wearing sensible clothing and doing exercise such as bicycling.

She and her husband were never close, he not being supportive of her work, but they remained together throughout his life. Still, she was impassioned in her arguments for the right to divorce for women, suggesting something from her own experience fed the intensity of her arguments. Her radicalism was most evident in a late project of her life, undertaken in 1895, *The Woman's Bible*, an interpretation of Scripture and religious thought that she and some other women published. The aftermath of its publication was an enormous controversy, and she lost some of her popularity in the women's movement as well as in the public at that time.

In 1898, her husband having been dead twelve years, she published her memoirs, *Eighty Years and More*. She died four years before Susan B. Anthony and eighteen years before the passage of the woman's suffrage amendment to the American Constitution.

Gayle Graham Yates

See: *Elizabeth Cady Stanton as Revealed in Her Letters, Diary, and Reminiscences*, ed. Theodore Stanton and Harriot Stanton Blatch (2 vols, 1922); Alma Lutz, *Created Equal: A Biography of Elizabeth Cady Stanton* (1940); Eleanor Flexner, *Century of Struggle* (1968); *The Feminist Papers*, ed. Alice S. Rossi (1973); *The Concise History of Woman Suffrage*, ed. Paul and Mari Jo Buhle (1978); Lois W. Banner, *Elizabeth Cady Stanton: A Radical for Women's Rights* (1980); Zillah Eisenstein, *The Radical Future of Liberal Feminism* (1981).

430
STENDHAL (pseudonym of Marie-Henri BEYLE)
1783–1842

French novelist

Marie-Henri Beyle used some 170 pseudonyms during his life; 'Stendhal' was the one under which he published his most famous works, and under which he is now known as one of the three great nineteenth-century French novelists (Balzac* and Flaubert* being the other two).

Three major facts of his childhood probably influenced him considerably. First, social: he was born into a bourgeois Grenoble family, and during the rest of his life was to find material for satire in the provinces and in the middle class. Second, emotional: he lost his intensely loved mother at the age of seven, grew increasingly to loathe the father and aunt who then took care of him, and was always to retain a keen interest in the extremes of tenderness and hatred that can co-exist in the same personality. Third, political: the French Revolution took place when he was six, and even as a young child (if we are to believe his later writings) he was imaginatively involved with, and excited by, a wide range of its consequences, social upheavals and cruel executions alike.

As he grew up, he read broadly in the classics, in English literature, and in eighteenth-century French thinkers; he drew further stimulus from the part he played, in his youth, in Napoleon's* campaigns.

Stendhal wrote a huge amount: drama, literary criticism, art criticism, biography, autobiography, traveller's impressions of France and Italy that are part 'tourism', part social commentary. But the works he is most famous for are the two novels *Scarlet and Black* (*Le Rouge et le noir*, 1830) and *The Charterhouse of Parma* (*La Chartreuse de Parme*, 1839). There has been a strong tendency amongst Stendhal critics to explain the power of these novels in biographical terms: viz. that as a lonely imaginative man he created worlds of wish-fulfilment, peopled by heroes more attractive than he, yet who always represented sides of himself. Apart from the fact that this is probably true of many authors' creations, it is also a gross over-simplification of Stendhal's narrative talent, social percipience, and imaginative brilliance, none of which can even begin to be explained by the facts of his biography.

Stendhal's unique – and perhaps most pleasing – gift as a story-teller is his gift for rapid narrative pace. Many facets of his writing contribute to this: the extraordinary speed with which events often succeed each other in his works; their 'adventure-story' sides, about which the author is just quizzical enough to allow the sophisticated reader to lend his adherence; the wit of a narrator who intervenes with raconteur's asides that keep the narrative, paradoxically, both controlled and unpredictable; the apparently casual sentence-structure that seems urgent and yet keeps the reader waiting in suspense for important information; the frequent impression that such information is actually being omitted, which whets the appetite still further; and the discreet but persistent use of exaggerated vocabulary (ranging from semi-conventional superlatives to 'emphasizers' like 'he was the unhappiest man in the world', and including words and phrases conveying some state of extreme excitement, which one critic has found to recur every two pages in the two major novels).

Stendhal's other talents as a novelist all, of course, contribute to the 'good stories' he tells, and his narrative style, in turn, synthesizes these talents; but it is also helpful to look at them separately, and to consider Stendhal the historian, Stendhal the psychologist and humorist, and what one might call 'Stendhal the poet'.

It is one of Stendhal's achievements to have made the novel historical, not in any vague or romantic sense, but in a stringently political mode. He, as much as Balzac, changed the French novel by directly linking his fictional characters and circumstances to the historical events that had supposedly given rise to them. Indeed, the outstanding critic Auerbach, in his *Mimesis*, goes so far as to claim that 'modern consciousness of reality began to find literary form for the first time ... in Henri Beyle of Grenoble', and that some of Stendhal's key scenes would be 'almost incomprehensible without a most accurate and detailed knowledge of the political situation, the social stratification, and the economic circumstances of a perfectly definite historical moment'. This is to overstate; Stendhal is a fine enough novelist to have, constantly interplaying, many events that are entirely comprehensible to any moderately sensitive reader; besides which, there is a strong drive in his novels to *inform* his reader of shifts in social psychology, and to let that reader know his, Stendhal's, own diagnosis of the ills of the time. Yet it is the case that Stendhal evidently expects his reader to know his history, and will actually make a date the subject of a sentence: when he writes, as he does in *Scarlet and Black*, '1815 made him Mayor of Verrières', he simply assumes his reader will know that in 1815 Napoleon was defeated and replaced once more by the constitutional monarch and a new right-wing bureaucracy. And it is also the case that one of the two major love-affairs in *Scarlet and Black* is shown to be profoundly affected by its historical situation, even to spring from that situation: Mathilde, the young noblewoman, would not be so drawn to Julien the plebeian if she were less bored by her family's salon – this boredom itself deriving from the stagnation of the intellectual life of the aristocracy after the fears generated by the revolution; nor would she be able to attach so many glamorous and violent fantasies to this proletarian if she had met him before the revolution. Julien too

might not have had the same mixture of hatred for, and fascination with, the aristocracy either before the revolution or during Napoleon's reign.

The major novels are rich in such social analyses, whether overt or implicit; these treat many topics – religion, fashion, the role of the press. Some of the analyses are quirky, some repetitive, but most show at work an outstandingly original social observer whose insights into different types of power, and the force of stasis, remain biting and radical.

As a psychologist, Stendhal is perhaps most famous for the theory of love expounded in his *Love* (*De l'amour*, 1822). He suggests that love depends as much on our subjective state of feeling as on the qualities of the beloved; first, on our state of 'emptiness' before the potential partner comes into view; next, on the series of misunderstandings or obstacles which attach our feelings to the person concerned. He gives this process the name 'crystallization', comparing it to the magical enhancement taken on by a twig in salt-mines where the salt-crystals cling to, and eventually transform, this very ordinary twig – an object which was simply brought into the right atmosphere, like the love-objects in his novels. Stendhal is also much interested in the relativism of psychology according to geographical as well as historical circumstance, showing himself here a disciple of the eighteenth-century thinker Montesquieu; for example, he says he sees the French as predominantly vain and calculating, the Italians as predominantly passionate and spontaneous (although his actual fictional creations often belie these over-simple categories).

Discussions of Stendhal's novels too often ignore their humour. Some of this is created by the tongue-in-cheek narrative style mentioned earlier, some by litotes and understatement, some by the fading-out of a narrator who presents ludicrous facts in a deadpan manner. Butts of humour are numerous, ranging from riders who fall from their horses and muddy their clothes, to – on a less physical level – the bore. Stendhal constantly curtails his characters' lengthy monologues with mock apologies to the reader, or with comments about another character's impatience. *Lucien Leuwen* (posthumously published in 1855), Stendhal's other great, but unfinished, novel, is particularly rich in such brutal closures; its pages are sprinkled with quotations or speeches ending in 'etc., etc.'. Stendhal's enjoyment of over-lengthy communications spills over into enjoyment of difficulties in understanding at all levels, whether linguistic, as at the beginning of *The Charterhouse of Parma*, or psychological, as throughout *Scarlet and Black*, where the emotional lives of the characters will go through comical see-sawing effects – sometimes bedroom-farce effects – simply because of a misapprehension of the situation. As well as all this, Stendhal shows a greater penchant for malicious physical caricature than do many novelists; an ability to poke gentle fun at the adolescent 'crush'; a deflation (at varying pitches of virulence) of pride, pomposity and greed; and – perhaps what most effectively gives Stendhal's novels their sophistication – a consistently witty exposure of muddled thinking on many different levels.

As well as acerbic political and psychological insights, Stendhal's fictional works have exquisite scenes of affection, of exaltation, and of reflective purposefulness; it may be the generosity and tenderness of these scenes that have led some critics to rank him more highly than Flaubert and Balzac. Here, Stendhal finds an allusive and metaphorical style that still retains the vigour of his faster scenes, whilst suggesting the limitless power of the imagination. This ability to be allusive is apparent too in Stendhal's choice of titles for his two major novels, less attached to main names or situations than those of most nineteenth-century novels; in his subtle use of structure, with, for instance, consistent links made between prisons, high places, and the ability to withdraw into oneself away from the world of ambition; and in his concise evocation of highly sensuous details to convey erotic responses.

It is, of course, possible to fit Stendhal's novels into a 'pattern' followed by other nineteenth-century French novels. Like many such works, they describe the young man making his way in the world, and like these others they show an interest in the relationship between energy and enforced immobilization. Yet some critics have felt that Stendhal is in certain ways superior even to his great French contemporaries. He has a consistent lightness of touch, and a subtlety, that Balzac can lack; and in an oblique way, he opens a vast range of experience, bringing his reader up against the differences between violent death and peaceful death, between intemperate love and real tenderness, between despair and absorption in happiness. Above all, Stendhal reiterates the 'lesson' of many other great novelists – that the human character is capable not just of contradiction, but also of change.

Alison Finch

Stendhal's other works include: *Armance* (1827); *Vie de Henry Brulard* (posthumous, 1890); *Lamiel* (posthumous, 1889). See: Alain, *Stendhal* (1948); M. Bardèche, *Stendhal romancier* ('Stendhal the Novelist', 1960); F. Hemmings, *Stendhal: A Study of His Novels* (1964); J. Prévost, *La Création chez Stendhal* ('Stendhal's Artistry', 1951). Important essays are: E. Auerbach, 'In the Hôtel de la Mole', ch. 18, *Mimesis* (1946); J.-P. Richard, 'Connaissance et tendresse chez Stendhal' ('Knowledge and Tenderness in Stendhal'), in *Littérature et Sensation* (1954).

431

STEPHEN, James Fitzjames 1829–94

British jurist and moralist

The second son of Sir James Stephen and elder brother of Leslie* was educated at Eton and King's College, London before proceeding, in 1847, to Trinity College, Cambridge. His academic career was undistinguished and, having twice failed to win a scholarship, he contented himself with an ordinary or Pass degree. After leaving his university, Fitzjames decided to follow a legal career and was called to the Bar in 1854. The briefs, however, did not come 'trooping gaily' and in 1855 Stephen (who had married earlier in the year) began to supplement his income by writing for the *Saturday Review*, to which he quickly became one of the most prominent contributors, producing two hundred articles for the journal between 1855 and 1868. In 1869 he became the legal member of the Governor-General's council in India, and spent the next three years working on the codification of Indian law, a task which he performed with more energy than precision. After his return to England in 1872 he became deeply interested in codifying English law, publishing digests of the law of evidence in 1876 and of criminal law in 1877. Although the codification project was frustrated by a change of government, Stephen was raised to the bench in 1879. As a judge he was at his best in criminal cases, having little patience with the nice technicalities of legal argument, but the rigours of his judicial office and the labour of compiling his monumental *History of the Criminal Law of England* (1883) combined to produce a marked deterioration of his intellectual powers. His erratic behaviour at the celebrated trial of Florence Maybrick provoked criticism in the newspapers and in 1891 he was persuaded to resign from the bench. Even the award of a baronetcy could not arrest his mental decay and Stephen died in a private asylum in 1894.

As might be expected of a friend of Carlyle* and a passionate admirer of Hobbes' *Leviathan* ('one of the greatest of all books') Fitzjames Stephen was not enraptured by J.S. Mill's* essay on *On Liberty*. As he travelled home from India, Stephen composed a robust rejoinder to Mill, *Liberty, Equality, Fraternity* (1873), in which he argued that it was force and not freedom that governed the maintenance of human society. The ultimate sanction of Christian morality is Hell, but in a world in which the Christian faith is fast losing its authority its place must be taken by the Law. It follows that the punishment accorded to a criminal is to be conceived of not as a deterrent to potential wrongdoers, but as a justified act of vengeance expressing the degree of hatred with which society views any given offence. Men must be coerced into decency by the fear of furious reprisals. Predictably, some of Stephen's most vehement journalism was prompted by his opposition to proposals for the abolition of capital punishment ('no other way of disposing of great criminals is equally effectual, appropriate, and cheap'), and he advocated strenuously an increase both in the quantity of flogging and in its quality ('at present it is little . . . more serious than a birching at a public school'). Stephen, as his enthusiasm for retributive justice suggests, was not sanguine about mankind's capacity for bettering itself. While many other Victorian thinkers were busily projecting the glorious future progress of humanity, he was engaged in noting that 'the great characteristic danger of our days is the growth of a quiet, ignoble littleness of character and spirit', and in adopting a posture of stoic fortitude: 'What must we do? "Be strong and of a good courage"'. Act for the best, hope for the best, and take what comes'. Let us, he wrote, face death 'with no sophistry in our mouths and no masks on our faces'.

Stephen, no doubt, would have regarded himself as a sturdy realist (his favourite novel was that practical textbook of self-help, *Robinson Crusoe*) but in one thing his faith never wavered. The English Common Law constituted for him a gospel of undisputed authenticity, and it is fitting that he should be best remembered as its greatest and most zealous codifier and as its first serious historian.

R.J.Dingley

Stephen's other works include: *Essays by a Barrister* (1862); *A General View of the Criminal Law of England* (1863); *A Digest of the Law of Evidence* (1876); *A Digest of the Law of Criminal Procedure in Indictable Offences* (1883); *The Story of Nuncomar and the Impeachment of Sir Elijah Impey* (1885); *Horae Sabbaticae* (3 series, 1892). See: Leslie Stephen, *The Life of Sir James Fitzjames Stephen* (1895); Noel Annan, *Leslie Stephen: His Thought and Character in Relation to his Time* (1951); B.E. Lippincott, *Victorian Critics of Democracy* (1938); Leon Radzinowicz, *Sir James Fitzjames Stephen 1829–1894 and his Contribution to the Development of Criminal Law* (Selden Society Lecture, 1957); R.J.White, introduction to *Liberty, Equality, Fraternity* (1967).

432
STEPHEN, Leslie 1832–1904

British moralist and critic

The fourth child of a prominent Evangelical civil servant, Leslie Stephen was educated at Eton, King's College, London and Trinity Hall, Cambridge, of which he was elected a fellow in 1854. For the next decade he set himself to embody the ideals of muscular Christianity, coaching rowing-crews, competing in athletic events, and generally exemplifying his own injunction to 'fear God and walk a thousand miles in a

thousand hours'. The muscularity was to remain (in later years he achieved notable successes as an Alpinist), but in 1862 he abandoned Christianity and two years later he left Cambridge for London to pursue a new career in periodical journalism. His path was smoothed by his brother Fitzjames*, a leading contributor to the *Saturday Review*, and Stephen's articles were soon appearing regularly in that journal and others, among them the *Cornhill*, previously edited by Thackeray*, whose daughter Minny he married in 1867. In 1871 Stephen became editor of the *Cornhill*, an appointment that enabled him to devote more time to his *magnum opus*, a *History of English Thought in the Eighteenth Century* (1876). His first wife died in 1875 and Stephen's grief was for a time so acute that he became a virtual recluse, but in 1878 he married Julia Duckworth, an old friend, with whom he lived in occasionally precarious harmony until her death in 1895. Although Stephen continued to write extensively, much of his time after 1882 was occupied by the editorship of the *Dictionary of National Biography*, a massive undertaking to which he himself contributed almost four hundred entries and which so undermined his health that he was compelled to resign in 1891. Generally recognized as one of the leading intellectuals of his day, Stephen in his later years was showered with honours and in 1902 he was knighted by Edward VII. He died on February 22nd, 1904.

There can be no doubt that the most significant event in Stephen's mental life was his loss of religious belief. Confronted with Darwin's* evolutionary hypothesis, Stephen discovered quite simply that historical fact was now irreconcilable with Christian dogma, and his logical mind could entertain no alternative to an abandonment of the latter. Doubtless his decision was accompanied by a certain amount of intellectual disquiet, but there seems to have been for him none of the agonized soul-searching, the traumatic introspection, that characterized so many of his contemporaries when faced by the same problems. For Stephen had never possessed, and was never able really to understand, a faith based upon absolute personal commitment. For him, Christianity was rather a provisional system of thought which must be jettisoned in the light of new and contrary evidence. Besides, the agnosticism he subsequently espoused (and he espoused it with all the passionate fervour that had marked his Evangelical forbears) proved a congenial substitute for dogma. It left man intellectually self-reliant, stoically pursuing truth in the certainty only that no truth was absolute, and facing the unseen with rugged fortitude. It need occasion no surprise that the classic statement of Stephen's position occurs in an essay called 'A Bad Five Minutes in the Alps' in which he imagines himself hanging at the edge of a mountain precipice and inquiring into the meaning of existence. His solution is what might be expected from a dedicated sportsman:

'The effort to maintain my grasp on the rock became to me the one absorbing thought; this fag end of the game should be fairly played out, come what might, and whatever reasons might be given for it.'

Once God is removed or rendered problematic, the maintenance of moral standards becomes an issue of central importance. 'I now believe in nothing,' wrote Stephen in 1865, 'but I do not the less believe in morality. . . . I mean to live and die like a gentleman if possible'. In his *The Science of Ethics* (1882) Stephen recruited Darwinian principles to the defence of morality, arguing that those standards of behaviour are evolved by the social organism which conduce to its greatest happiness. This proposition is unsatisfactory in its failure to come to grips with the role of the individual conscience, but it at least serves to illuminate two constant preoccupations in Stephen's work. The first, and more positive, is his awareness of society as a conditioning factor in human affairs. This perception underlies Stephen's most original contribution to criticism. Literature, he pointed out, was 'the noise made by the wheels as they go round' and his pioneering book on the effect of social change on literary culture, *English Literature and Society in the Eighteenth Century* (1904) remains an important landmark in intellectual history. On the other hand, Stephen had little interest in purely aesthetic questions and his critical judgments are generally conditioned by his assessment of an author's moral worth. Naturally enough, the standards he sets up tend to be those which governed his own life, so that manliness and a dedication to 'noble ends' (of which Stephen's supreme exemplar was Wordsworth*) are preferred to displays of unbridled sensitivity ('Sensitive . . . is a polite word for morbid,' he observed in dealing with Pope). A conviction that 'the highest poetry . . . is the product of a thoroughly healthy mind' is too often permitted to obscure Stephen's fine awareness of the intractable complexity of individual personalities, and acute insights remain unexplored lest they should complicate the business of judicial discrimination.

Stephen's daughter, Virginia Woolf, portrayed her father as Mr Ramsay in *To the Lighthouse* and, although her picture is coloured by personal feeling, she offers a judgment of Stephen's intellectual status which neatly encapsulates both his great ability and his profound limitations. Ranging knowledge according to the twenty-six letters of the alphabet, 'his splendid mind had no sort of difficulty in running over those letters one by one, firmly and accurately, until it had reached, say, the letter Q. He reached Q. Very few people in the whole of England ever reach Q . . . But after Q? . . . R was beyond him. He would never reach R. . . .'

R.J. Dingley

Stephen's other works include: *Essays on Freethinking and Plainspeaking* (1873): *The Playground of Europe*
(1871; revised 1874); *Samuel Johnson* (1878); *Alexander Pope* (1880); *Swift* (1882); *An Agnostic's Apology and Other Essays* (1893); *The English Utilitarians* (1900); *Studies of a Biographer* (1898–1902); *George Eliot* (1902); *Hobbes* (1904); *Hours in a Library* (1907); see also: *Men, Books, and Mountains: Essays by Leslie Stephen*, ed. S.O.A. Ullmann (1956); *Sir Leslie Stephen's Mausoleum Book*, ed. Alan Bell (1977); *Selected Writings in British Intellectual History*, ed. Noel Annan (1979). On Stephen: F.W. Maitland, *The Life and Letters of Leslie Stephen* (1906); Noel Annan, *Leslie Stephen: His Thought and Character in Relation to his Time* (1951); Q.D. Leavis, 'Leslie Stephen: Cambridge Critic', in *Scrutiny*, vol. 7, pp. 404–15 (1939); Gertrude Himmelfarb, *Victorian Minds* (1968); John Gross, *The Rise and Fall of the Man of Letters* (1969).

433

STEPHENSON, George 1781–1848

British engineer

Father of Railways? Not quite! Guided transport went back to the Middle East in remote time. Father of the locomotive? Again, no! Richard Trevithick had produced a steam railway locomotive in 1804. But George Stephenson was to show that such things were *viable*, to make some men rich, benefiting many more by availability for freight and passengers in a world hitherto bound to roads and coastwise shipping.

George Stephenson was born on 9 June 1781 beside a railway (a simple horse-worked colliery tramroad) at Wylam, Northumbria, in a two-up, two-down tenement cottage. His father was fireman on the pit-engine at Wylam Colliery. With those, young George grew up; he was helping his father at thirteen. Needing to be literate, he managed about puberty, with a penny-schoolmaster. He took to mathematics as if born with them, observed everything from natural history to applied mechanics, and early developed a strong business sense. There were Scots antecedents. He was always about the colliery with its pumping engine.

Hitherto, from about 1712, steam engines had been of Thomas Newcomen's atmospheric sort, so-called because natural pressure did the real work after steam had been condensed to cause a vacuum below the vertical piston. James Watt's invention of a separate condenser improved the principle, but Richard Trevithick's invention of the high-pressure steam engine was revolutionary. Young Geordie *watched*. In 1802, Trevithick made, and drove from mid-Cornwall to Plymouth, a road steam-carriage. Two years later, he produced, and drove with a considerable train in South Wales, the world's first steam railway locomotive.

A Trevithick locomotive found its way to the north-east in 1805. Blackett's and Hedley's locomotive

Puffing Billy (1813) appropriately appeared on Stephenson's native Wylam Colliery Railway (with some early teething troubles, though ultimately working until 1862). A young man named Timothy Hackworth, later one of Stephenson's rivals and successful contemporaries, helped considerably

Ere that, steam locomotion had moved in with the Middleton Colliery Railway near Leeds, using Blenkinsop's rack-and-pinion idea ultimately to be very useful on steep-grade mountain railways. Stephenson was already, mentally, *improving* things. By now enginewright to a colliery at less than £2 a week (not bad, at that time!), he produced his first locomotive in 1814. *It worked*, on the Killingworth Colliery Railway.

Crude and imitative were the beginnings, even down to his surviving engine *Locomotion* of 1825 for the Stockton and Darlington Railway, promoted by the Pease family (wealthy north-eastern Quakers). But the mechanical engineers had been rising from mine and mill, ready for steam locomotion and navigation. In the case of the Stephensons, there was good fortune in George having begotten, through Fanny Henderson, their son Robert, to whom he gave academic advantage at Edinburgh University as well as practical experience. Both excelled as mechanical and civil engineers; indeed old George really *arrived* by surveying and building the new Liverpool and Manchester Railway across the supposedly bottomless Chat Moss, then showing (1829) that it could be worked by steam locomotive traction.

Opposition had been very severe.

Promoted by strong Liverpool interests, it was the first public railway, as later generations were to understand the term, with up– and down-roads, proper stations, some sort of signalling, and steam traction for all traffic. Its Sankey Viaduct, its tunnelling and its vast cut through Olive Mount into Liverpool were new wonders. As to locomotives, the Stephenson's *Rocket* (1829) had won in fair competition. They had produced the infant modern engine, not without the help of Henry Booth, while Marc Seguin in France doubtless had something to do with the *Rocket's* fire-tube boiler. The *Rocket* class was followed by the *Planet*, still in 1830 when the line was opened. The *Planets* were followed by the six-wheeled *Patentee*, and so it went on to the end of the steam reciprocating locomotive about a century and a quarter later.

So the Victorian railway system became Big Business, not all of it good. But a lot of it still, very properly, sticks. George Stephenson died in 1848, ere that telling a young man that, more remotely, electric power was to be the great one of the world. An improver, or an original inventor? He certainly invented the miner's safety lamp (the 'Geordie', to the great annoyance of Sir Humphry Davy*, who improved it).

C. Hamilton Ellis

See: Samuel Smiles, *The Life of George Stephenson*

(1857), C.F.D. Marshall, *A History of the Railway Locomotive* (1953); John Rowland, *George Stephenson* (1954).

434

STEVENSON, Robert Louis (Robert Lewis Balfour Stevenson) 1850–94

British novelist, essayist, poet, dramatist and short-story writer

It is the fate of many artists to be remembered for the wrong reasons. Such is the case with Robert Louis Stevenson. Two of his novels – *Treasure Island* (1883) and *Kidnapped* (1886) – are amongst the most widely read in the English language, and as a result Stevenson has come to be classed alongside Henty and Ballantyne as a writer of 'boys' stories'. It tends to be forgotten that his talents were highly praised by, amongst others, Henry James*, and that Stevenson was considered, in his day, to be 'a man of letters'. Born in Edinburgh, he was the son of Margaret Balfour and Thomas Stevenson, and heir to a famous family of engineers. As a child Stevenson suffered from chest complaints, and during long periods of confinement developed a deep love for literature. At the age of fifteen he wrote an imaginative account of the Pentland Rising of 1666, which his father published privately. When illness allowed, Stevenson attended a number of schools, including Edinburgh Academy. He then entered Edinburgh University to read engineering, but was an indifferent student, devoting his energies instead to writing. When he was twenty he told his father that he had no intention of becoming an engineer, and wished to be a writer. Thomas Stevenson reluctantly accepted the first point, but not the second; writing was not the profession of a gentleman, and he insisted that his son read law. This he did, but with no more application than he had previously studied engineering. Stevenson was called to the Bar in 1875, but was by then becoming estranged from his father.

Stevenson was a regular visitor to France, and in 1876, at Fontainebleau, he met Fanny Osbourne, an American eleven years older than himself who was separated from her husband. They fell in love, to the horror of his father, and in 1879 Stevenson followed her to America, arriving in California penniless and ill, but with the material for several books. They married early in 1880, and their honeymoon formed the basis of *The Silverado Squatters* (1883). Following a letter from his father, Stevenson, his wife and two step-children returned to Scotland, where he was reconciled with his family.

Stevenson had by now developed tuberculosis, but in spite of this began work on *Treasure Island* in 1881. The following year he visited the Highlands, and wrote some of his finest short stories, including 'Thrawn Janet'. But he also experienced several lung haemorrhages, and was forced to move with Fanny to the south of France. They then set up residence in Bournemouth, where Stevenson wrote *Kidnapped* and *The Strange Case of Dr. Jekyll and Mr. Hyde* (1886). However, the British climate proved intolerable to him, and in 1887 he sailed with his family to America. In 1888 he chartered a ship for an excursion to the South Seas. Wandering from island to island, Stevenson became fascinated by the local inhabitants and their environment, and his books on the region are remarkable pieces of journalism. He finally settled with his wife on the island of Samoa, where he died, without warning, of a cerebral haemorrhage.

Stevenson applied his literary talents in a variety of ways. His essays, particularly those in *Virginibus Pueresque* (1881), are stylish, though rarely profound, and with a tendency towards melancholy. He privately published a number of plays, and his *Child's Garden of Verses* (1885) contains some of the finest poetry ever written specifically for young children. But it is undoubtedly as a novelist that Stevenson merits his place in literary history. He had an austere Calvinist upbringing, and this fact has been used to explain the moral ambiguity which pervades much of his fiction. It is certainly true that Predestination – the belief that all who have not been marked for Redemption at birth are eternally damned – held a fascination for him, and that several of his novels seem intent on disproving the doctrine. In *Jekyll and Hyde* 'good' and 'evil' are revealed as facets of a single personality. Elsewhere, Stevenson refused automatically to couple heroic actions with conventional moral goodness. In *The Master of Ballantrae* (1889), the ruthless Master is nevertheless allowed a kind of heroism, while his unexceptional brother is shown to be morally degenerate under pressure. Perhaps the archetypal hero-villain is Long John Silver, the complex and charismatic central figure of *Treasure Island*. Squire Trelawny and his fellow treasure-hunters are presented by Stevenson as little better than Silver, and ultimately they survive more by luck than by virtue of any superior morality.

Stevenson was only forty-four when he died, and the novel left unfinished at his death would clearly have marked a turning-point in his career. *The Weir of Hermiston* (1895), although only a fragment, is Stevenson's finest achievement in the art of story-telling, at which he always excelled. Opposed to literary 'realism', he was none the less able to create a convincing world within each of his novels, through a concentration upon the development of character and action, against the background of a carefully observed landscape. *The Weir of Hermiston* is colourful and exciting, every word apparently chosen for a specific effect, and Stevenson utilizes Scottish dialect with consummate skill. Compared to the previous generation of English novelists, Steven-

son's was a minor talent, perhaps. But academic snobbery continues to undervalue his work and its simple narrative form.

Paul Nicholls

Stevenson's other works include: *An Inland Voyage* (1878); *Travels with a Donkey* (1879); *New Arabian Nights* (1882); *Prince Otto* (1885); *The Wrong Box* (1889; written with his stepson, Lloyd Osbourne); *Across the Plains* (1892); *Catriona* (1893; US title: *David Balfour*); *The Ebb-Tide* (1894); *St. Ives* (1896; unfinished). The best biographies are: D. Daiches, *Robert Louis Stevenson* (1947); and J.C. Furnas, *Voyage to Windward* (1951). See also: D. Daiches, *Stevenson and the Art of Fiction* (1951); *Robert Louis Stevenson: The Critical Heritage* ed. Paul Maixner (1981).

435
STIFTER, Adalbert 1805–68

Austrian novelist and narrator

Stifter was a country-boy, born in Bohemia and educated at the Benedictine monastery of Kremsmünster. He came to Vienna in 1826 as a law student but never qualified and in 1837 married an uneducated girl of doubtful respectability. To Stifter's sorrow they had no children and their efforts to adopt various young relatives ended on at least two occasions in tragedy. Stifter was a private tutor (of Metternich's sons, among others) and a school inspector from 1849. He was briefly involved in the political events of 1848 but the revolution itself so horrified him that he withdrew from politics for the rest of his life. Ill and depressed he cut his throat with a razor in January 1868.

He did not begin to write seriously until he was in his thirties and then wrote only prose, mostly fiction. His first published story *Der Condor* ('The Condor') appeared in 1840 in a Viennese periodical. Throughout the forties and early fifties he continued to publish stories in this way – all of them lengthy novellas for the fashionable periodicals of the day. Almost immediately they appeared he began to rewrite them extensively. The revised versions of thirteen stories were collected under the title *Studien* ('Studies', 1842–50) and five more, with the addition of one new one, appeared as a volume ostensibly for children called *Bunte Steine* ('Coloured Stones', 1853).

Many of Stifter's stories are set in his native region of forests and mountains, and the landscape itself often plays a central role in the story, as for instance in many of the *Studien* and most of the *Bunte Steine* stories. Yet some of the finest are set in countries Stifter had never visited, e.g., *Abdias* in the North African desert and *Brigitta* in Hungary. Two themes in particular run through all of Stifter's stories. The first is that of Fate, the arbitrary destiny which seems to strike at man like a bolt of lightning and then move on. According to Stifter this interpretation of Fate is false. All is cause and effect, guilt and punishment, could we but see it, and what appears accidental to us is linked into one great scheme under the so-called 'gentle law' of causality (*das sanfte Gesetz*). The second theme is that of the development of man as a member of a family or dynasty. At the simplest level this can be seen in the importance attached to father-son relationships, whether the son is real or adopted. It is carried much further in those stories which portray a dynasty and show the individual as the product of generations. In several stories, including *Die Mappe meines Urgrossvaters* ('My Great-Grandfather's Notebook'), of which Stifter produced not two but four versions and which he was still working on at his death, we have the extreme form of this when previous generations in a family write their memoirs, enjoining their heirs to read them and write theirs in their turn. Whatever the theme or setting, one should not be deceived into concentrating on the sometimes harmless-seeming surface of Stifter's stories and thereby missing the fact that he is far ahead of his time in portraying the diseased subconscious and the influence that the earliest years have on a person's development.

With his two novels *Der Nachsommer* ('The Indian Summer', 1857) and *Witiko* (1865-7), Stifter's writing moves into a new phase. *Der Nachsommer* is not so much a novel one reads as an experience one gives oneself up to. It centres around a young man, Heinrich Drendorf, whose development is largely determined by his encounter with Risach, the owner of a Utopian country estate where all is quiet harmony, and a love of art and the cultivation of the soil are the chief elements. The slow-moving pace of the novel, the minute depiction of the ritual of daily life, the loose plot, the absence of social realism and the measured style make this one of the strangest and yet most hypnotically compelling of all nineteenth-century novels. The unfinished *Witiko* (called after its hero), set in twelfth-century Bohemia, is even more lengthy and slow-moving. For all its grand design and at times vivid execution, one is compelled to admit that it is a failure, carrying the ideas of the earlier novel beyond the bounds of readability. Stifter's achievement must ultimately rest on the dozen or so of his best stories and on *Der Nachsommer*. It is these which make him in the words of Thomas Mann 'one of the most remarkable, one of the subtlest, one of the secretly most daring and most strangely gripping narrators in world literature'.

Helen Watanabe-O'Kelly

Very few of Stifter's works are available in English, even in nineteenth-century translations. Two of the very few translations undertaken in this century are *Rock Crystal: A Christmas Tale* (*Bergkristall*, rendered into English by Elizabeth Mayer and Marianne Moore, 1945) and *The Recluse* (*Der Hagestolz*, trans. David Luke, 1960). See Eric A. Blackall, *Adalbert Stifter: A Critical Study* (1948).

436
STOWE, Harriet Beecher 1811–96

US author and reformer

The absence of credible historical evidence for believing that Abraham Lincoln* did in fact attribute the outbreak of the American Civil War to Mrs Stowe's *Uncle Tom's Cabin* (1851-2) makes her no less remarkable a nineteenth-century phenomenon. She became, on the basis of her story of Uncle Tom, Little Eva and Simon Legree, a figure of international myth, an anti-slavery colossus in the mould of William Wilberforce* or William Lloyd Garrison, who enjoyed a trans-Atlantic reputation unequalled by any other American woman of her time. Although, then as now, her name is identified with the cause of abolition, a dutiful, unerring New England voice of reform, she was not actually a straightforward abolitionist, however malign she thought slavery. Nor, paradoxically given the notoriety it achieved, was *Uncle Tom's Cabin* her best work, or even a major work when measured against the American writing which appeared in the same decade like Emerson's* essays, the 'hidden' poems of Emily Dickinson*, *The Scarlet Letter* (1850), *Moby-Dick* (1851), *Walden* (1854) and *Leaves of Grass* (1855). Nevertheless, it was with *Uncle Tom's Cabin* that she caught the conscience of the Western world, a landmark Christian indictment of slavery which was at once subtler than its fervent admirers wholly acknowledged yet a weaker literary performance than its reputation suggests.

Behind the Mrs Stowe of received myth, the reductive picture of her as simply a righteous crusader, as behind *Uncle Tom's Cabin* itself, resides a more complex, more tentative and hence more interesting, personality. She was born into stern Calvinist stock in Connecticut, where she was raised in the shadow of her male siblings and stepmother, having lost her own mother at five in 1816, where the talk was frequently of sin, damnation and the hallelujahs of redemption, and which was unabashedly male-dominated and directed. Her father was no less than Lyman Beecher, a true Calvinist believer and apostle of the teachings of the eighteenth-century fundamentalist Jonathan Edwards and as acclaimed and unbending an orthodox Congregationalist as any in New England. Her brother, Henry Ward Beecher, similarly, won a massive following as the leading pulpit orator of the day. In 1836, after a girlhood in which she struggled to reconcile this ancestral Calvinism with the belief in a gentler Jesus of love and reconciliation (she eventually became an Episcopalian), she married another celebrated minister, Calvin Stowe, who, though a traditional New England protestant divine, did encourage her literary inclinations. Despite this difficult unbringing and an immediate family of her own, seven children in all which included twins, a long stint in provincial, plague-torn Cincinnati (1832–50) – she lost a child to cholera in 1849 – and her frequently admitted sense of household weariness and harassment, she consolidated the career which eventually yielded nearly thirty full-length volumes and a vast miscellany of pamphlets and essays.

In 1850, she returned to New England when Calvin Stowe was appointed to the faculty at Bowdoin College, Maine, then to a professorship at Andover Theological Seminary in Massachusetts in 1852. In 1853, 1856 and 1859, riding the crest of her success with *Uncle Tom's Cabin*, she made three rapturous visits to England and Europe, welcomed by Queen Victoria* and others, but also courting English disaffection by her intrusion into the controversy over Lord Byron* (in *Lady Byron Vindicated*, 1870 and earlier magazine pieces she alleged that Byron committed incest). She lost her eldest son in a drowning accident in 1857 for which she sought consolation in spiritualism. Another son, Frederick, was badly wounded in the Civil War. In 1868 she bought and wintered at a converted mansion in Florida, about which she wrote *Palmetto Leaves* (1873) and where she continued her work on behalf of Negro Americans. In 1873, she acquired a house in Hartford, Connecticut, close to Mark Twain's* home, a return to family roots. By her later years she had declined into a slightly senile, anachronistic presence, manifesting the mild eccentricity which had always threatened. If, to the public gaze, a figure of great apparent public success, she also lived a life beset with inner conflicts, the struggle of a talented Victorian-American and New England woman to achieve an identity of her own making.

The inspiration of *Uncle Tom's Cabin*, her second book, came while she was at prayer in Brunswick, Maine, in the form of a vision of an aged, white-haired slave being flogged, and from the Fugitive Slave Bill of 1850. Published first as a serial in 1851-2, in *The National Era*, then as a novel in its own right, it immediately became a stupendous bestseller and caused controversy and outrage everywhere, not least in Kentucky and the Southern slave states where Mrs Stowe had done meticulous research. Acclaim was frequent, from fellow reformers, and from writers like Tolstoy*, Heine*, George Sand* and Macaulay*. In America it aroused especially fierce debate, about abolition, miscegenation, the truth of its portraiture, and the claims and counter-claims of Yankee and Southerner. Within its plantation and river plot-line, *Uncle Tom's Cabin* brings into play a formidable variety of ingredients – slavery not only as racial but sexual exploitation, the Victorian cult of the child (Eva and Topsy), the com-

plicity of both Northerner and Southerner in slaveholding (Legree is a Yankee), the gory reality of floggings, slave-sales, the break-up of families, and the intricate layers of caste within both black and white slave culture. In Uncle Tom himself the novel's anti-slavery readers saw a saintly Christian martyr, even though to a later age his name is synonymous with fawning racial subservience, a label of contempt. *Uncle Tom's Cabin* can be inept and mawkish, yet as Edmund Wilson testifies, also simply 'startling' in its understanding of the whole edifice of slave ownership. It continues to impress, not only because of the energetic fulness with which the novel's world is given, but because of the deep fund of historic moral outrage behind it and which Mrs Stowe shared with every reform-minded Victorian. For doubters who thought her story too lurid, all exaggeration and melodrama, and for the slave-holding lobby which reviled her, Mrs Stowe corroborated the detail of her indictments with *A Key To Uncle Tom's Cabin* (1853), in which she offered case-histories and documentation like that of Father Josiah Hendon, an ex-slave, to whose story she wrote a preface in 1858. In this respect her novel usefully compares with other great ex-slave narratives like Frederick Douglass's* *Narrative* (1845) or Booker T. Washington's* *Up from Slavery* (1901). Whether James Baldwin is right in judging Mrs Stowe 'not so much a novelist as an impassioned pamphleteer', she assuredly had at least part of the measure of her achievement when she spoke of *Uncle Tom's Cabin* as 'incendiary', an attack on the 'peculiar institution' of slavery for which her Puritan heritage of Christian conscience and mission had given her a singularly appropriate preparation.

In serving as her centre-piece, *Uncle Tom's Cabin* has had the effect of eclipsing her other literary work, both the lesser efforts and her deserving novels of New England life. Among the occasional books should be included *The Mayflower, Or, Sketches of Scenes and Character among the Descendants of the Pilgrims* (1843), an encomium to Puritan history; *Sunny Memories of Foreign Lands* (1854), based on her European visits; her three autobiographical and family reminiscences, *Our Charley and What to Do with Him* (1858), *My Wife and I* (1871) and *We and Our Neighbours* (1875); *Religious Poems* (1867), a useful guide to the nature of Mrs Stowe's Christianity; and the local and children's writing she did under the pen name of Christopher Crowfield. The best of her other fiction undoubtedly requires mention: *Dred: A Tale of the Great Dismal Swamp* (1856), a tale of slave escape and religious fanticism which argues the moral deterioration brought on by slavery, and her sequence of New England novels: *The Minister's Wooing* (1859), a slightly arch adventure and love story set in late eighteenth-century Rhode Island which makes use of an abundance of regional detail; *The Pearl of Orr's Island* (1862), a moral tale of marital duty given an Atlantic seaboard context; *Oldtown Folks* (1869), Mrs Stowe's most impressive novel which offers her shrewd, knowledgeable analysis of New England social custom and the legacy of Calvinism; *Sam Lawson's Oldtown Fireside Stories* (1872), fifteen local-colour sketches reprinted from the *Atlantic Monthly*; and *Poganuc People* (1878), a deeply autobiographical fiction based on her early, and not wholly enchanted, childhood in the Beecher household. None of Mrs Stowe's novels is without flaw. She frequently veers into melodrama. Her style never completely frees itself of awkwardness. But she is both better and worse than her legend has allowed and she deserves to be read as the historic begetter not only of *Uncle Tom's Cabin* but of a considerable literary *oeuvre*, a complex, interesting nineteenth-century literary woman and Christian New Englander.

A. Robert Lee

See: Constance M. Rourke, *Trumpets of Jubilee* (1921); Charles H. Foster, *The Rungless Ladder: Harriet Beecher Stowe and New England Puritanism* (1954); Edmund Wilson, *Patriotic Gore* (1962); John R Adams, *Harriet Beecher Stowe* (1963); Edward Waggenknecht, *Harriet Beecher Stowe: The Known and The Unknown* (1965); Alice C. Crozier, *The Novels of Harriet Beecher Stowe* (1970).

437
STRAUSS, David Friedrich 1808–74

German theologian and New Testament critic

Born in Ludwigsburg, Strauss was a member (1821–5) of the brilliant group of students who sat at the feet of Baur* at Blaubeuren theological seminary. He continued his studies under Baur at Tübingen when the latter received a chair there in 1826, and also attended the classes of the two biblical 'supernaturalists' Steudel and Bengel. His admiration for the work of Schleiermacher* and Hegel* attracted him to Berlin from 1831 to 1832, although Hegel died shortly after Strauss's arrival there. From 1832 to 1835 he was a *Repetent* (occasional lecturer) at the Stift (theological seminary) at Tübingen, although suspicion of this theological position obliged him to teach mainly in the area of philosophy, which he did from an unambiguously Hegelian standpoint. The appearance in 1835 of his first and greatest work *The Life of Jesus Critically Examined* (*Das Leben Jesu Kritisch Bearbeitet*, trans. 1892), it has been said, simultaneously procured for Strauss not only fame but academic and ecclesiastical ruin, in that he was immediately dismissed from his teaching post at the Stift by Steudel, its president. Until around 1840 repeated attempts by Strauss to rehabilitate himself with his opponents failed, and the successful attempt to procure for him the Chair of Dogmatics at Zürich came to nothing, since conservative opposition to his position prevented him ever from occupying the chair, whose stipend he was thereafter paid in the form of a pension. His two-volumed *Christliche Glaubenslehre* (Christian faith, 2 vols, 1840–1) is a hostile account of the development of Christian doctrine down to his own day, and finally ruined any residual chance of reconciliation with the academic and ecclesiastical establishment. The remainder of Strauss's life was negative and sad: he involved himself in jouralism and biography (writing on Ulrich von Hutten and H.S. Reimarus); he contracted an unhappy marriage (with Agnese Schebest, the opera singer); he became embittered and cynical. His popular version of the life of Jesus (1864) did not affect his reputation one way or the other. His final book *The Old Faith and the New* (*Der alte und der neue Glaube*, 1872, trans. 1873) was notable for its rejection, on the grounds of Hegelianism and of the fashionable materialistic metaphysics of the day, of personal human immortality. On his death in 1874, Strauss was buried, on the explicit conditions laid down in his will of 1864, without any religious rites whatever.

Of all the possible descriptions of Strauss's theological position, that of 'radical' (or 'left-wing') Hegelianism does not wildly or unjustly distort it. In approaching the Gospel accounts of Jesus's life, Strauss importantly identified an impasse between two traditional, but mutually exclusive and incompatible positions: first, a 'naturalism' (rooted in the scepticism of the *Aufklärung*) that affirmed, dogmatically and *a priori*, the impossibility of the Gospel stories of the miraculous and the supernatural, and arguing that absolutely natural (i.e., scientifically intelligible) explanations must be sought for all such; and second, a 'supernaturalism' (as defended by his academic superior Steudel) which affirmed, according to Strauss, just as dogmatically and *a priori*, that, since at the heart of the Gospel narratives we find the coming into of flesh of none less than the Son of God, we have no logical right to make predictions (or to form hypotheses) about the wordly consequences of this *vis-à-vis* the everyday causal structure of experience, so that scepticism about allegations of miraculous and supernatural events in the Gospels is not only inappropriate, but intellectually arrogant, approximating to blasphemy.

The persistence of such an impasse meant for Strauss a dead end for biblical studies, and it was towards resolving this impasse that his historico-critical research may be said to have been directed. He did so by positing his celebrated theory that the problematic elements in the life of Jesus (miraculous, supernatural, apocalyptic, cosmic) should be classified and treated as 'myth' (German, *Mythus, Mythos*). He was aware that he was not the first modern scholar to do so, and that the term had been used by Eichhorn, Gabler (both Old Testament scholars), Hegel, Semler, de Wette and

Paulus. But he was dissatisfied with their piecemeal and partial application of the category; much attention had been directed to the myth of the Creation, or to the Birth and Resurrection narratives in the New Testament, and Hegel had been much preoccupied with the myth of the Fall in Genesis 3. Strauss now proposed the scientific and consistent application of the category to the Gospel materials as a whole.

At the heart of Strauss's theory (as expounded and applied in the opening section of his *magnum opus, Das Leben Jesu*) lies the incalculably important distinction between 'idea' and 'fact' (or, as we might now say, 'significance' and 'history'), and his interpretation of the relationship between the two. The key to understanding Strauss's book is his conviction that the 'idea', in Hegelian terms, is incomparably the more significant of the two, and possessed ontological, temporal and significative priority over historical 'fact' or 'facts'. Indeed, it is 'ideas', 'interpretative motifs' which form or determine so-called 'historical' factual complexes or patterns. Also close to the heart of his theory is his important analysis of historical religious community as essentially a 'myth-making' entity. If we combine these two notions of Strauss, we see that his fundamental thesis is that before, long before, the historical advent of Jesus, the religious community of Israel had been generating a considerable corpus of Messianic-soteriological-eschatological ideas in its 'corporate mind', with which in due season it crowned the historical person of Jesus of Nazareth. But the 'ideas' pre-date and indeed determine and constitute the so-called historical fact. Not that Strauss denied that there is a certain, if rather indeterminate, substratum of fact in the Jesus story: that Jesus was a Galilean who was baptized by John and indeed preached in Galilee; that he threw down the gauntlet to much contemporary Jewish belief and practice, an act which led to his trial and judicial crucifixion shortly after AD 30. But interwoven into this rather meagre historical outline is much that is, as sheer factual history, problematically unacceptable: the Virgin Birth narratives, the supernatural motifs of the baptism, the temptations, the miracles, the transfiguration, highly specific predictions by Jesus of his death, resurrection and second coming, and finally, the resurrection and ascension themselves. These latter must be interpreted in terms of ideas, expectations and motifs already existing in the corporate consciousness of the community as applicable to the 'Coming One'. An excellent example of what Strauss means by 'pure' myth is the transfiguration story (Mark 9, 2–8; *cf.* Matthew 17, 1–8, and Luke 9, 28–36): in the foreground are portrayed enduring religious 'ideas'; the high and holy mountain, the glistening white clothing of the messianic figure, the supernatural appearance of Moses and Elijah as respresenting the Law and the Prophets, the 'cloud of the presence', the heavenly voice, and the rest; the

character and historical concreteness of Jesus fade into relative insignificance. (Apart from 'pure' myth, Strauss conceded the existence of 'historical' myths, whose existence may have been generated by some historical event or other in the career of Jesus, although the precise nature of such events is now quite inaccessible to us.)

Of truly outstanding importance in Strauss's book is the set of criteria he offers by which myth may be readily identified – the irreconcilability of certain Gospel narratives with universally acknowledged laws of science, of natural succession, of human psychology (for the knowledge of which Strauss was clearly indebted to the critical philosophy of the *Aufklärung*). Of possibly equal importance is Strauss's breaking down of the Gospel narrative into 'blocks' and his demonstration of historical inconsistencies between them, work which contributed valuably to the modern science of 'synoptic' criticism. Myth may also be recognized by *form* (e.g. poetry) and *content* (e.g. Jewish legend, genealogy and prediction).

Now that the ecclesiastical and academic dust that was thrown up by the case of the 'alienated theologian' has long settled, it is possible to reach a balanced and judicious estimate of Strauss's significance and work. On the positive side, mention has already been made of his contribution to synoptic criticism; in the famous words of Albert Schweitzer, Strauss's subdivision of the Gospel materials 'marked out the ground which is now occupied by modern critical research', and ensured his place as a pioneer in this science. Again, he broke new ground in the study of biblical myth and stimulated much modern research in this area, and his research could be said to provide an important link between the theological scholars of the *Aufklärung* and the important twentieth-century 'demythologizing' proposals of Rudolf Bultmann (there is more Strauss in Bultmann than is generally realized).

However, on the negative side, two large and grave questions still loom large over Strauss's work. First, was not Strauss's unmistakable Hegelianism, with its stress on eternally valid but ahistorical 'ideas' developing and achieving configurations within the corporate consciousness of the religious community (Mind or *Geist* achieving self-consciousness in the human spirit) not every bit as dogmatically *a priori* as the dogmatic rationalism or supernaturalism which Strauss strove so valiantly to overcome? Did not Strauss approach Scripture with a pre-formed set of hermeneutical and philosophical presuppositions which determined well in advance what Scripture was allowed to say?

Second, and possibly more importantly, there is one huge question that Strauss did not, and, on his restrictive philosophical presuppositions, could not, answer. Given that there was, in the religious consciousness of Israel, a considerable corpus of Messianic, apocalyptic and eschatological motifs and expectations, why were these heaped upon such a vague, nebulous and insubstantial character as Strauss's Jesus? According to Karl Barth, Strauss's Jesus was 'shrouded in a veil of myth', and according to H.R. Mackintosh Strauss's view was that the primitive Christian community 'wove a wreath of adoration round the Master's head by worshipping fancy'. But why *this* man, rather than some other? What was there about *this* particular *historical* man that invited such treatment from his followers, who founded upon *his* person and work a world-wide church? Strauss's inability to give plausible answers to such questions explains partly at least the excessively harsh and unforgiving treatment meted out to him by the establishment of his day. But his work, by focusing critical attention upon such questions and answers, contributed vastly to historico-critical research into the life of Jesus during the following century.

James Richmond

See: D.F.Strauss, *The Life of Jesus Critically Examined*, edited with a long introduction by Peter C. Hodgson (1973); Van A. Harvey, 'The Alienated Theologian', in *McCormick Quarterly*, Vol. 23, pp. 234–65 (May 1970); Karl Barth, *Protestant Theology in the Nineteenth Century* (1972); Claude Welch, *Protestant Thought in the Ninteenth Century*, Vol. I, 1799–1870 (1972); Otto Pfleiderer, *The Development of Theology in Germany since Kant* (1890); James C. Livingston, *Modern Christian Thought: From the Enlightenment to Vatican II* (1971).

438
STRAUSS, Johann 1825–99

Austrian composer

Johann Strauss was the most celebrated member of a distinguished Viennese family of musicians who made their names directing and composing for their own dance orchestras. His father, the elder Johann Strauss (1804–49), had begun the family tradition, gaining acclaim during the second quarter of the nineteenth century not only in Vienna but also on extensive tours that included Britain in Queen Victoria's* coronation season. Though nowadays remembered for his *Radetzky March* (1848), it was largely through the elder Strauss that the waltz became established not only as the principal attraction of elegant society balls but also as music worth playing and hearing for its own sake.

The father opposed his sons following in his footsteps, so that the younger Johann was at first intended for a banking career. However, with his mother's encouragement he had taken violin lessons from a member of his father's orchestra and subsequently studied theory with Joseph Drechsler (1782–1852). In October 1844 he made his début with his own small orchestra at a *Soirée dansante* and soon began to establish himself

as his father's most serious rival – a rivalry heightened when the two supported opposing factions in the Revolution of 1848.

After the father's death the younger Johann continued to extend the family reputation both in Vienna and further afield – eventually inheriting from his father the accolade of 'Waltz King'. In 1863 he was appointed to the official position of Music Director of the Court Balls. With the demand for his services increasing, he was fortunate to be able to enlist the services of his brothers Josef (1827–70) and Eduard (1835–1916). Now the orchestra could be split, to enable it to fulfil simultaneous engagements during Vienna's Carnival time (January/February) or to enable one portion to remain in Vienna while another went on tour. Johann himself conducted summer concerts at Pavlovsk in Russia annually from 1856 to 1865 and visited Paris and London in 1867 and Boston and New York in 1872.

By 1870, however, Strauss was increasingly recoiling from incessant public adulation. Simultaneously Viennese impresarios, alarmed at the dominance of the Viennese musical theatre by the imported works of Offenbach*, sought to enlist Strauss's services. He accepted, resigned his position as Music Director of the Court Balls and, with Josef now dead, left the direction of the family orchestra to Eduard. He continued to compose operettas for the rest of his life, whilst contriving to continue to provide new material for the ballroom by adapting themes from his operettas, as well as composing the occasional dance for special occasions. In the late 1880s his attention turned to the composition of a genuine opera, but the resulting *Ritter Pázmán* (Vienna Court Opera, 1 January 1892) enjoyed no more than a *succès d'estime*.

Besides his fifteen operettas, one opera and one ballet, Strauss's compositions number some 170 waltzes, 150 polkas, 30 polka-mazurkas, over 70 quadrilles and nearly 50 marches. His finest waltzes mostly date from the 1860s: *Accelerationen* ('Accelerations', 1860), *Morgenblätter* ('Morning Papers', 1864), *An der schönen blauen Donau* ('By the Beautiful Blue Danube', 1867), *Künsterleben* ('Artist's Life', 1867), *Geschichten aus dem Wienerwald* ('Tales from the Vienna Woods', 1868), and *Wein, Weib und Gesang* ('Wine, Woman and Song', 1869). Later examples include *Wiener Blut* ('Vienna Blood', 1873), *Rosen aus dem Süden* ('Roses from the South', 1880), the coloratura soprano showpiece *Frühlingsstimmen* ('Voices of Spring', 1883), and the *Kaiser-Walzer* ('Emperor Waltz', 1889). His most famous polkas include the *Annen-Polka* ('Anna Polka', 1852), the *Tritsch-Tratsch-Polka* ('Chit-Chat Polka', 1858), *Unter Donner und Blitz* ('In Thunder and Lightning', 1868), and the *Pizzicato Polka* (1869) composed jointly with Josef.

In assessing the stature of Johann Strauss's dance music one should not isolate his name from that of his brother Josef. Certainly Johann produced the more immediately striking and therefore more widely popular melodies. Josef, however, was perhaps the more cultivated musician, adding an extra sense of tenderness or emotional tension that leads many to consider his the greater talent. Between them, at any rate, they produced dance music unequalled by any of their many rivals, music which reflects the glamour and brilliance of the Habsburg monarchy at its height and which transcends the constraints of dance rhythms as never before or since. To the regular beat of the polka they added a unique range of picturesque invention, whilst always using with discretion the special effects that were often added to give a piece individuality. It was, however, in the rhythm of the waltz that they had the finest vehicle for their talents.

The standard pattern of the waltz had already been established in the works of the elder Strauss, with a sequence of simple waltz themes preceded by an introductory section and rounded off by a coda recapitulating the main themes. His sons developed the structure by building up the introductions into miniature tone poems, lengthening the span of the waltz melodies and extending their range of expression. None of their imitators ever approached their consistent freshness of invention, their ability to build upon a striking main theme and renew attention throughout, or the utterly natural way in which they integrated the various contrasted waltz sections. The refined shading of their orchestration has always been especially admired.

For the composition of operettas Strauss was far less well suited. He never became a good judge of a libretto and never acquired a taste for setting lyrics to music. Some of the best music came when, in possession of no more than an outline of the action, he built up an appropriately atmospheric sequence of melodies to which words were then fitted by his lyricist Richard Genée (1825–95). It was his prodigious melodic invention that enabled him to overcome his natural shortcomings and create the distinctive Viennese operetta based on the waltz – a form successfully developed in the twentieth century by such composers as Franz Lehár (1870–1948). Of Strauss's fifteen operettas three are acknowledged masterpieces, each with its own distinctive style – the sparkling *Die Fledermaus* ('The Bat', 1874), the graceful *Eine Nacht in Venedig* ('A Night in Venice', 1883) and the more solid *Der Zigeunerbaron* ('The Gipsy Baron', 1885).

In his time Strauss used the popularity of his orchestra to introduce new music to a wider public – introducing themes from Wagner's* *Tristan und Isolde* to Vienna for the first time and giving the première of an early Tchaikovsky* composition in Pavlovsk. In return he enjoyed the admiration of many of the greatest musicians, including Brahms* who was a close personal friend. In our own time, too, his music continues to be performed around the world by the greatest

orchestras, opera companies, conductors and singers to a degree enjoyed by no other composer of music for the ballroom and popular musical theatre.

Andrew Lamb

There is an excellent and extensive literature in German e.g. Marcel Prawy, *Johann Strauss: Weltgeschichte im Walzertakt* (1975). Biographies in English include Joseph Wechsberg, *The Waltz Emperors* (1973), but the best assessment is the article (including list of works and bibliography) by Mosco Carner and Max Schönherr in *The New Grove Dictionary of Music and Musicians* (1980).

439
STRINDBERG, Johan August 1849–1912

Swedish playwright and author

Strindberg's father was a steamship agent, who married his housekeeper in 1847, after she had already borne him three children. Her death when he was twelve left Strindberg feeling deprived. He was married three times to women who all put their own careers first, and did not want to mother him. He had a pietistic upbringing which marked him for life, and he was never at ease without God. Before he discovered his vocation as a writer Strindberg tried a number of occupations: student, doctor, actor, and journalist. He wrote his first masterpiece *Master Olof* (*Mäster Olof*) in 1872, a play about the Lutheran reformer of the sixteenth century, Olaus Petri, but, in spite of its deep psychological insight and brilliant dialogue, it had to wait nine years for printing and performance. This was to be the pattern of Strindberg's career as a dramatist in Sweden. He never had more than brief periods of success, chiefly because he was always in advance of his times.

Fortunately for him he could write other things than plays. His seventy dramatic pieces are contained in only seventeen of the fifty-five volumes of his collected works. The rest contain poetry, novels, history, essays, pseudo-scientific and alchemistic writings. He made his breakthrough in Sweden with a novel, *The Red Room* (*Röda rummet*, 1879), a biting but light-hearted satire, written in sparkling Swedish, about his experiences in Stockholm. His first really successful play, *Lucky Peter's Travels* (*Lycko Pers resor*, 1882), was also a satire about the folly of illusions, a favourite theme in his later plays. This was preceded and followed by works that made him so unpopular in Sweden that he went to live abroad. In Switzerland, hoping to reinstate himself, he wrote *Getting Married* (*Giftas*, I-II, 1884–5), two volumes of short stories about sex and married life. But the first volume precipitated a trial for blasphemy, engineered, as he thought, by the feminists whom,

though he was acquitted, he attacked with great bitterness in the preface, and in some of the stories of the
second volume. 'The Breadwinner', the last story in
the book, was seen as a slur on his first wife, the
would-be actress, Siri von Essen, and only served to
increase his unpopularity. This was the first serious
crisis in his life, mental and physical. Theatres were
afraid to perform his plays, publishers to print his
books. The second volume also established his reputation as a misogynist, later confirmed by the so-called
'naturalistic' plays, the only works by which he is
widely known in this country. But though for a period
Strindberg was fiercely anti-feminist, he was no misogynist. 'I love women and I adore children and, as a
divorced man, I recommend marriage as the only commerce between the sexes,' he wrote in a letter of 1892.
In many of his later dramas, including his historical
plays, there is little trace of the woman-hater.

Strindberg was an omnivorous reader. Kierkegaard*, Brandes, Mill*, Darwin*, and Spencer* were
on his bookshelves before 1886; then, in order to understand the working of his own mind, and the minds
of others, he turned with enthusiasm to psychology and
pathology, and studied among others the Frenchmen,
Jacoby, Ribot* and Garnier, and the Englishman,
Maudsley, in whose book *The Pathology of Mind* he
found a complete diagnosis of himself. It is difficult to
say how far this reading coloured the self-portrait in
his autobiographical work *The Son of a Servant* (*Tjäns-
tekvinnans son*, 1886). He was an inveterate role-player,
and what he says about himself must not be taken at
its face value. He used his new knowledge to good
effect when he wrote the three powerful plays which,
in course of time, brought him international fame: *The
Father* (*Fadren*, 1887), *Miss Julie* (*Fröken Julie*, 1888)
and *Creditors* (*Fordringsägare*, 1889). These plays are
called naturalistic, though they in no way resemble
Zola's* photographic naturalism. In his preface to *Miss
Julie* Strindberg says: 'I believe I have observed that
for modern people the psychological development is
what most interests them, and that our inquiring minds
are not satisfied with seeing something happen, we
want to know why it happens.' *The Father* is a study of
the effects of doubt and female oppression on a pre-
cariously balanced mind. The construction of the play
is conventional but, in its three acts, every aspect of
mental torture is portrayed, what Strindberg called
'psychic murder'. *Miss Julie* is another case history, a
piece of brilliant analysis, acted in one continuous
scene 'to maintain the author's magnetic hold over the
audience'. This is not psychic murder. It is true that
Jean and the absent father exercise a hypnotic influence
at the end, but Julie commits suicide because she cannot face disgrace. In *Creditors*, another one-act play,
Strindberg has introduced Max Nordau's idea that
suggestion may be in dumb show: Gustav acts an epileptic fit, and Adolf has one and dies. Recognition of

the greatness of these plays was slow to come everywhere except Paris and Berlin.

During this same period Strindberg wrote two of his
most famous prose works: *A Madman's Defence* (*Le Plai-
doyer d'un fou*, 1888) and *The People of Hemsö* (Hem-
söborna, 1887). The first, written in French, and not
meant for publication, is the vindictive story of his
marriage to Siri; the second an amusing account of life
in the Stockholm archipelago. In both the theme of
sexual jealousy is prominent. Back in Stockholm he
produced another important prose work *By the Open
Sea* (*I havsbandet*, 1890), a story about the disintegration
of a human being when isolated from his intellectual
equals, and persecuted by the masses. It was written
during the period of his uneasy atheism, but is shot
through with a longing for God. In 1892 he wrote seven
plays, none of which were performed in Sweden though
one, *Playing with Fire* (*Leka med elden*), has since gained
international recognition. After this set-back, and his
divorce from Siri, which entailed the loss of his children, Strindberg again went into exile, first in Berlin,
then in Paris. For the next six years he abandoned
literature and turned to his own brand of science. His
great plan was to write a work which would enable
him to understand how the universe was governed. But
he was no ordinary scientist. He was an artist, who
believed in intuition, and though he did make some
experiments he distrusted them. He was retreating into
that inner world which became so real to him. This is
the world of his novel *Inferno* (*Inferno*, 1897), the book
that has always been taken as the clearest indication
that he was mad. It is in fact a highly coloured account
of what he called his 'occult' experiences in Paris from
1894 to 1896, the period known as his 'Inferno Crisis',
though then, as always, Strindberg knew perfectly well
what he was about. It is true that he experimented
with madness, as he did with other things, but he never
crossed the border line.

He emerged from this period a changed man. Swedenborg had revealed to him the meaning of his self-
induced, but often terrifying, experiences: they were a
punishment for sins committed in a previous existence.
From being an atheist he became a believer. He knew
this belief was a subjective matter. He needed God and
so he believed, but in a very individual way. In this
spirit he wrote one of his greatest dramas, *To Damascus*
I-II-III (*Till Damaskus*, 1898–1901). These plays were
quite unlike anything that had gone before. The technique was expressionistic, symbolism was freely used,
and the dramatic unities were not observed. *To Damascus* is a journey, in the Kierkegaardian sense of
Stages on Life's Way, in search of the self and of God.
Both frequently elude the Unknown One, the protagonist of the play, but he persists for, as he comes to
realize, if you cannot know you must believe. Like most
of what Strindberg wrote, *To Damascus* was before its
time in Sweden, both in content and scenically. It was

a precursor of the German expressionist movement of 1912.

The years from 1898 to 1903 were enormously productive. He wrote over twenty plays, some of them among his best. His cycle of historical dramas is the most effective dramatization of history since Shakespeare. The most popular of these is *Erik XIV* (1899), the Hamlet-like character, whom Strindberg himself called characterless. With *The Dance of Death* (*Dödsdansen*, 1901) Strindberg appears to be taking a step backwards to naturalism, but this is an illusion. The characters in this play are not men and women, they are types, elemental personifications of evil. As with many of Strindberg's dramas, episodes in his own life had fired his imagination, but it is the use he made of his source, not the source itself, that is important. As Ollén has pointed out: 'the details may correspond with uncanny precision . . . but the whole is fantasy . . . . By magnifying, distorting, and freely associating ideas, he has created characters who live a fantasy life entirely independent of their origins.'

For Strindberg the climax of his work came with *A Dream Play* (*Ett Drömspel*, 1902). Like *To Damascus* it is a journey of the soul towards disillusionment and release. As illusions are burnt in the flames of the Growing Castle, the symbol of human life, the bud that crowns it bursts into bloom as the world did when Buddha ascended into nothingness. The action of the play takes place in an inconsequent dream world where anything may happen, but the dialogue is often very matter of fact:

The Daughter: People are pitiable
The Father: They are indeed. And it is a riddle to me what they live on. They marry on an income of four hundred pounds, when they need eight.

In 1907 Strindberg wrote some one-act chamber plays for his own Intimate Theatre, among them *The Ghost Sonata* (*Spöksonaten*). It is often considered to be obscure; in fact it is a beautifully constructed play and demonstrates clearly that Strindberg knew exactly what he wanted to convey. The contending forces of good and evil are visually defined in the first scene, in the second the full extent of evil is revealed, both in the dialogue and in the setting, while in the third, in spite of the bright room in which it is set, darkness triumphs. The end is death, as it is in all but one of the chamber plays.

Strindberg was a great innovator; he had no more use for the well-made character than he had for the well-made play. 'Where is the self,' he wrote in 1886, 'which is supposed to be the character? It is neither in one place nor in the other, it is in both. The ego is not one unit; it is a multiplicity of reflexes, a complex of impulses, of demands, some suppressed at one moment, others let loose at another.' He showed that this complex self is more interesting than the straightforward character and, in his later plays, that the journey of the soul can be dramatically effective. He employed scenery in novel ways, and revolutionized dialogue by using everyday speech. His whole life was pilgrimage in search of himself. From the depths of his own experience he fashioned a new form of drama that gave expression to an inner world of trial and struggle, and his influence has been immense. Perhaps Eugene O'Neill springs most readily to mind, but there have been many others who could say with Strindberg: 'I find the joy of life in its fierce, cruel struggles, and my delight is in knowing something, in learning something.' People who can adopt this attitude will not find his plays depressing.

Mary Sandbach

Recommended translations: *The Plays*, vols I and II (trans. Michael Meyer, 1964–75); *The Vasa Trilogy* (trans. W. Johnson, 1950); *The Chamber Plays* (trans. E. Sprinchorn, 1962); *Twelve Plays* (trans. E. Sprigge, 1963); *The Red Room* (trans. E. Sprigge, 1967); *The Son of a Servant* (trans. E. Sprinchorn, 1967); *A Madman's Defence* (trans. E. Sprinchorn, 1968); *Getting Married* (trans. M. Sandbach, 1972); *Inferno and From an Occult Diary* (trans. M. Sandbach, 1979). See: Mortensen and Downs, *Strindberg, his Life and Work* (1949); Gunnar Ollén, *August Strindberg* (1972); G. Brandell, *Strindberg in Inferno* (trans. 1974); W. Johnson, *Strindberg's Historical Dramas* (1962); M. Lamm, *August Strindberg* (trans. 1971). John Ward, *The Religious and Social Plays of August Strindberg* (1980), has an excellent bibliography.

440
SULLIVAN, Sir Arthur 1842–1900

British composer

Sullivan has been one of the more conspicuous victims of English musical snobbery during the last hundred years. Those who lavish praises on the operettas of Offenbach*, Lehar and Strauss* are given to wrinkling their nostrils at the suggestion, amply borne out by an examination of the scores, that the Savoy Operas display a far subtler and more varied musical palette than any of these masters of the lighter genre. Such, however, is undoubtedly the case: Sullivan's exceptional early gifts, excellent training and professional dedication, linked with a cosmopolitanism unique among otherwise heavily parochial Victorian musicians, make him the most interesting English talent between Arne and Elgar.

Some of this catholicity and eclecticism derived from his family background. His father was a well-travelled Irish military bandmaster and his mother, Maria Clementina Coghlan, was half Italian. The boy Arthur, as a Chapel Royal chorister, gave rapid evidence of considerable promise, and went on to win the Royal Academy's first Mendelssohn scholarship to enable him to study at the Leipzig Conservatorium, then the finest in Europe. Out of this came the symphonic incidental music to Shakespeare's *The Tempest*, first performed in England at one of August Manns's enterprising Crystal Palace concerts in 1862, when the composer was only twenty.

The Tempest was followed three years later by Sullivan's only symphony, the 'Irish' (from its use of folk melodies in the scherzo), the most accomplished English symphony before Elgar's in A flat (1908) and a perfect example of its composer's ability to dilute the Mendelssohn* and Schumann* of his Leipzig days with touches of the Italian and French operatic manner for which he had such an abiding affection. Greater popularity, however, was to be gained in England by the production of those large-scale choral works which provided the staple fodder of Victorian music festivals and which, with one or two notable exceptions (Parry's* *Blest Pair of Sirens* and the three major examples by Elgar), are now totally forgotten. In producing works such as *The Prodigal Son* (Worcester, 1869) and *The Light of the World* (Birmingham, 1873) Sullivan established a reputation as the most enterprising and distinctive of the younger English composers, enhanced by his sterling abilities as a conductor and his notable grasp of every aspect of practical music-making. He was especially respected for his enthusiasm in promoting the teaching of music and for his encouragement of younger musicians, including Elgar, several of whose early works he conducted and whose style bears traces of his influence.

Witty and convivial, his talents as a raconteur and his fondness for 'fast' living brought Sullivan a smart and influential circle of friends, including the Prince and Princess of Wales and members of the aristocracy. As the doyen of late Victorian musicians he made the acquaintance of Liszt*, Gounod*, Dvořák and Saint-Saëns*. He was much in demand as a composer of effective incidental music, his best scores being prepared for *Macbeth* (with its eerily Wagnerian* prelude) and *The Merchant of Venice*. The sparkle and verve of the latter shows the authentic vein of comedy he was to develop after his meeting with W.S. Gilbert* in 1871.

Their subsequent collaboration lasted some fifteen years (ending with *The Grand Duke*, 1896) and wholly altered the pattern of Sullivan's professional life. In the eyes of many he was failing to fulfil his obligations as a serious composer, and Queen Victoria* herself suggested that he turn to grand opera, a suggestion which produced *Ivanhoe* (1891, to a dismal libretto by Julian Sturgis), a fascinatingly over-ambitious project. There is no doubt, however, that he had found his true *métier* and a close collaboration with the almost neurotically

painstaking Gilbert enabled Sullivan to demonstrate a kaleidoscopic range of moods and styles. The enormous success of the Savoy Operas, due in part to an inspired impresario Richard D'Oyley Carte, was alloyed by a serious quarrel between Sullivan and Gilbert, which broke the series for four years between 1889 and 1893, and by Sullivan's failing health. An immense crowd attended his funeral in St Paul's Cathedral, but perhaps the most impressive single tribute was Gilbert's, paid several years after his collaborator's death: his mournful response to the hint that he should find another composer was 'What use is Gilbert without a Sullivan?'

The charm and strength of the Savoy Operas (so called from D'Oyley Carte's theatre specially designed to house them) lies not only in the dazzling variety of Sullivan's polyglot style, but in his unique gift for affectionate parody. *Iolanthe* (1882), for example, is heavily marked by reminiscences of a visit to Bayreuth, with allusions to *Das Rheingold* and use of Wagnerian motifs. *Trial by Jury* (1875, the first collaboration with Gilbert) features, in the ensemble 'A nice dilemma we have here', what is in effect a brilliant reconstruction of the sextet 'D'un pensiero' in Bellini's* *La Sonnambula*. An enduring fondness for Italian opera irradiates the score of *H.M.S. Pinafore* (1878), and the whole of the second act of *The Pirates of Penzance* (1879) can be seen as a sustained homage to Verdi*. Notable also are Sullivan's attempts, in such numbers as 'Prithee, pretty maiden' in *Patience* and 'Brightly dawns our wedding day' in *The Mikado*, to imitate native English folk and madrigal styles.

As an orchestrator, armed with a practical performer's knowledge of most instruments, Sullivan stands comparison with Berlioz* and Rimsky-Korsakov*. Following his discovery, with Sir George Grove in Vienna in 1867, of Schubert's* lost *Rosamunde* music, he reflected a markedly Schubertian quality in the lightness and delicacy of his scoring. His most personal utterances are to be heard in the five works which best display the fluctuations of his rapport with Gilbert. *Patience* (1881), an inspired spoof of the Aesthetic craze spearheaded by Wilde*, Swinburne* and Morris*, and *Iolanthe*, satirizing the House of Lords and the legal establishment, show a mature command of musical form in their handling of ensemble and grandiose through-composed first act finales. *Princess Ida* (1884), a burlesque version of Tennyson's* *The Princess*, triumphs over Gilbert's ungainly blank verse text by virtue of the music's extraordinary refinement and seriousness of intention: its second act is perhaps the best demonstration of Sullivan's artistic powers. *The Yeoman of the Guard* (1888) once again subdues the banalities of its libretto, an appalling study in mock-Tudor, in what is unquestionably the finest English dramatic music of the nineteenth century. *The Gondoliers* (1889) represents, in terms symbolized by the nature of its comedy, an attempt by its creators to reconcile their differences, and stands as the perfect collaboration, welding Gilbert's inimitable wit to Sullivan's effervescently Italianate and often hauntingly romantic score.

As a serious composer Sullivan never overcame his self-consciousness in the face of contemporary English preference and prejudice, and works such as *The Golden Legend* and *The Martyr of Antioch* show the lack of conviction essential to his ultimate failure in this guise. His real talent, which finds its parallel not in the operettas of Offenbach and Strauss, but in the Italian *opera buffa* of Rossini* and Donizetti*, lay in his genius for applying his innate gifts as a melodist and an assured grasp of the techniques of serious music to the creation of a species of sophisticated comedy which has numbered among its innumerable devotees such apparently unlikely figures as Nietzsche* and Stravinsky.

Jonathan Keates

See: Herbert Sullivan and Newman Flower, *Sir Arthur Sullivan: His Life, Letters and Diaries* (1927); Hesketh Pearson, *Gilbert and Sullivan: A Biography* (1935); Gervase Hughes, *The Music of Arthur Sullivan* (1960).

441
SULLIVAN Louis Henry 1856–1924

US architect

Louis Sullivan's career rose with the evolution of the tall metal framed commercial buildings, during the last decades of the nineteenth century. Through his talents, he showed that such structures could be artistically considered, and thus brought them within the realm of architecture. His efforts in bringing a new order and grace to this type of building were parallel with those of such as Walt Whitman* and Mark Twain*, who equally were searching for a true American voice, and to free their creative production from European influences. Born in Boston in 1856 of Irish and Swiss parents, both musical, Louis Sullivan's early architectural experience and training were restless and varied. He spent a short time at the École des Beaux Arts in Paris, and worked in many architects' offices, including the office of Frank Furness in Philadelphia. He arrived in Chicago in the 1870s, during the city's first great building boom. Shortly after arriving, Sullivan met and sufficiently impressed Dankmar Adler to be offered a partnership in the latter's established practice. Adler was to act as technician and trusted friend during the major part of Sullivan's career, from 1881 onwards.

Their early work was much influenced by the buildings of H.H. Richardson*, particularly the exterior of their first major building, the Auditorium in Chicago of 1886. The interior, in its use of elemental geometry to organize the major spaces, was similarly influenced; the surfaces within, however, were extensively decorated, much of the decoration being remarkably inventive, derived from a combined use of geometry and natural form. Ornament in architecture was to be the most lasting theme in Sullivan's work. His use of it was organizational and metaphoric, to represent his deepest conviction in a natural law of form relating to function. Hating the Beaux Arts style, representing to him, as it did, Europe's tired decadence, he rejected the Beaux Arts principle of the dominance of the plan and its ancient role in carrying the meaning of the building and consequently his work became increasingly elevational, to concentrate on the façade, the plans within seemingly wilfully indifferent. The finest examples of his ideas as applied to the new tall building form were the Wainwright Building of 1890–1 in St Louis and the Guaranty Building of 1894–5 in Buffalo. Sullivan's increasing facility with ornament can be traced developing through a series of tombs, the best of which, the Getty Tomb in Chicago of 1890 and the Wainwright Tomb in St Louis of 1892, are composed of sombre pure forms set alive by the application of running, vibrating decoration.

In his famous essay of 1896, 'The tall office buildings artistically considered', he expounded his theories of the idea of the natural law as a basis of architecture. In doing this he was extending to buildings theories concerning fitness to purpose expounded earlier by Horatio Greenough, the American expatriate sculptor, and more generally, extending the essentially puritan New England natural Transcendentalism of Thoreau* and Emerson*. In so doing Sullivan was attempting to root this quintessential American spirit in the centres of the new booming cities. His conviction was that functionalism was a natural law, and that through a careful, ritualistic analysis of the needs that the building was to fulfill, by 'using nature's own machinery', the form would naturally emerge, like a plant from the earth. This belief allowed him to begin to form an architecture free from the wilful European formalism of the time. The poetry and potency of the idea is susceptible, however, to two major linked weaknesses. First, in its inability to recognize any conflict of interest, and in its dependance upon an intense spirituality for its fullness, the theory, through its workings as a conscious re-examination of the minutiae of requirement, could quickly decay into an unquestioning acceptance of the client's requirements, and a blindness to the larger social issues regarding, for instance, the relationship between the public and the private realms. It is, however, one of Sullivan's most lasting memorials that after him, the style of the American skyscraper remains to create public space within the building, adjacent to the street.

The second weakness revolves around the difficulty

of defining any function clearly. One might confidently say of a bread knife what its purpose is, but such a straightforward implement might find itself being used purposefully, in, for instance, the hands of a murderer. Thus in the complexity of engagement with the living, where the rule of natural order should be most vivid, the idea of clarity of function becomes most endangered. With the less easily defined functions that the simplest building must accommodate, the idea tends to useless generalities, without some other, perhaps unspoken, controlling intention. One might feel some confidence in defining the functions of an office building, but what of a house? And yet, Sullivan's edict that form follows function, together with Le Corbusier's claim that the house was a machine for living in were to become the two major beliefs of the International Modern Movement in the early twentieth century, paradoxically because of the dependence of the central concept.

Clarity of function depends upon the larger idea of propriety of use, and its antithesis, abuse. In architecture, the idea becomes a concern with the correct use of space and this in turn depends upon a concern for the correctness of human behaviour. Thus a creed that would pretend to be essentially amoral, is built upon and requires a necessarily determined morality. Thus functionalism is the unimpassioned mask of moral intentions and thus it was that the progressive European architects of the early twentieth century were able to engage with the idea of social programme, and in so doing, created their plain white taut façades to contain the workings of an essentially nineteenth century movement for social reform.

The hidden contradictions in Sullivan's thought concerning the programme for the tall commercial building has meant that the skyscraper remains enigmatic and challenging to American architects, unabsorbed as it is by either current theories, relating to the shingle style or the loosely termed post-modernist. The World Columbian Exposition, held in Chicago in 1893 represented a rejection by his adopted city of his thoughts and life's work. Apart from his own Transportation building, the predominant style was that of the Beaux Arts. Chicago had decided to appear, to represent its burgeoning wealth, as a *fin-de-siècle* mid-European city. Two years later, Adler withdrew from the partnership. This heavy double blow compounded his natural solitariness, resolved his path as that of the prophet alone, and ushered in the final phase of his life.

Sullivan's finest later works were a series of banks in small mid-west towns, notably in Owatoma, Minnesota, in Grinnell, Iowa and in Sidney, Ohio, in which there is the finest realization of his style of ornament related to building. Despite the vagaries of available commissions, during a time of depression, which this was, it is difficult not to read in these late works a retreat from and disillusion with the city. During this period up to his death in 1924 he concentrated much effort on writing, exploring, notably in *Kindergarten Chats* (1901–2) and *Autobiography of an Idea* (1924), his deep concern for the relationship between democracy and the practice of his art.

In 1924 a series of large drawings under the title *A System of Architectural Ornament According with a Philosophy of Man's Powers* were published, which are the most beautiful accomplished exposition of his genius for marrying geometry and plant form. These undertakings, carried out in a period of apparent decline, represent his finest work, and upon which, increasingly, his reputation will safely stand. It is a measure of his influence that his most brilliant assistant, Frank Lloyd Wright, would, in his mature work, carry further the major themes of Sullivan's life and work, the search for a democratic architecture, the relationship between ornament and building, and finally also, the retreat from the city.

Frederick Scott

Sullivan's major essays are included in *Kindergarten Chats and Other Writings* (re. 1918). See also: Hugh Morrison, *Louis Sullivan: Prophet of Modern Architecture* (1935); Willard Connely, *Louis Sullivan as He Lived* (1960).

442
SWINBURNE, Algernon Charles 1837–1909

British poet

Swinburne was born into an aristocratic naval family and brought up largely on the Isle of Wight and in Northumberland where he developed a passion for the sea and coastal landscape. He completed his education neither at Eton, where his latent algolagnia was elicited by the flogging block, nor at Balliol where he studied classics under Jowett* who later became a friend. In 1857, before leaving Oxford for unspecified reasons, he met the Pre-Raphaelites (William Morris*, Edward Burne-Jones* and D.G. Rossetti*) who were decorating the Union building with frescoes on subjects from the *Morte d'Arthur*, and thereafter became associated with them. Notably important was the worldly influence of Rossetti with whom he shared a *ménage* in Chelsea in the early 1860s. Together they comprise 'the Fleshly School of Poetry'.

But more vital to Swinburne's growth as an artist was his discovery at Oxford of Gautier's* *Mademoiselle de Maupin* and, several years later in France, of Baudelaire's* *Les Fleurs du mal* which he reviewed for the *Spectator* in 1862. In the preface to Gautier's novel the idea of 'art for art's sake' makes its first appearance, and Swinburne's review of Baudelaire is the first declamation of this doctrine in England. Briefly, it held that since any subject might be redeemed by art, all subjects were therefore available to it. This ran counter to the prevailing belief, typified by Ruskin*, that art was in the service of morality. The redemption of sin through incorporation in art soon became an obligation for the Decadent artist. By legitimizing the forbidden, Baudelaire taught Swinburne how to express in poetry the fundamental sado-masochism of his nature.

On the occasion of Baudelaire's death in 1867 Swinburne wrote one of his finest poems, 'Ave Atque Vale', published in *Poems and Ballads Second Series* (1878), a volume which also contains the beautiful Villon translations. But what was spiritual torment in Baudelaire became in Swinburne a Dionysiac paganism so pure that it lacked the capacity for growth. Yet Baudelaire's confrontation with the modern world was uncompromising, whereas Swinburne's narrower improprieties were couched, as such things always were in Victorian England, in classical and medieval myths.

His first important book was *Atalanta in Calydon* (1865). Of it Ruskin wrote, 'It is the grandest thing ever done by a youth, though he is a demonic youth.' Nothing comparable had appeared in England since Shelley's* *Prometheus Unbound*. Its leaping anapaests and dactyls were quite unexpected (Tennyson's* *Enoch Arden* had appeared the previous year) and its success was immediate. In style *Atalanta* is as close as English literature has come to the Greek tragedy, but this is the Greek world overshadowed by the Marquis de Sade. Swinburne had been introduced to his works, then difficult to obtain, by Lord Houghton who owned an erotic library of European reputation.

Poems and Ballads (1866), dedicated to Edward Burne-Jones, turned fame into notoriety. These two books represent Swinburne's significance, though not his entire worth, as a poet. Without warning, bestiality, cannibalism, necrophilia, hermaphroditism, sapphism, homosexuality, blasphemy, republicanism and, above all, sado-masochism had been released into the Victorian drawing-room in spectral and elusive but fully conscious forms. For a kiss to become 'the lips intertwisted and bitten/Till the foam has a savour of blood' was new and very alarming. In consequence Carlyle* is said to have described the poet as 'a man standing up to his neck in a cesspool and adding to its contents'. R.W. Emerson called him 'a perfect leper and a mere sodomite', although there is no evidence of sodomy in his life and he preferred to be whipped by women.

Swinburne is the poet of sensual intoxication and sexual pathology, of passion in its original sense of suffering, and of youth. No poet is more characterized by his physical constitution. He was very small, with steeply sloping shoulders and a large head, and his limbs jerked a great deal due to an excess of 'electric vitality'. So sensitive was he to stimuli that pleasure and pain, in the intensity of their registration, became indistinguishable in the overall afflatus. Sometimes, to

the consternation of his family and friends, this extreme excitability led to clinical fits, especially when he drank brandy.

In making explicit the masochism inherent in the Romantic view of man as the victim of Nature, Swinburne created his presiding goddess from La Belle Dame Sans Merci and thus transmitted the *femme fatale* to the European psyche as a whole, just as through him flagellation came to be known as *le vice anglais*. But he was composed of self-abasement and revolt in about equal measure, so that there is nothing simpering or affected in his work and his aggressive, hooligan joy was constrained only by a classical education. His rhythms are stressed heavily and become the rhythms of coition. Specific meaning in the poems is secondary to the erotic abrasion they supply. They are incantations for a secret ceremony, designed to arouse the senses and overwhelm the mind. There is no economy in Swinburne, no shortage of time, and few shocks of the intellectual sort.

Caught in a spasm of endless adolescence, he was rescued from an engulfing alcoholism in 1879 by Theodore Watts-Dunton who supervised the last thirty years of Swinburne's life at their house in Putney. As the lust left it, his poetry degenerated into Wordsworthian* pantheism and Turneresque* swirl but the nature of his original power was not forgotten and it is not surprising that he was passed over for the Laureateship on the death of Tennyson. He was the first English Decadent. His influence on Pater*, Wilde* and their followers was enormous. D'Annunzio said that in Swinburne 'there seems to live again, with incredible violence, the criminal sensuality which fills primitive dramas with wild cries and desperate slaughters'. His celebration of physical things comes with a glorious, screaming, swooning freakishness into High Victorian literature.

Duncan Fallowell

The Complete Works of Algernon Charles Swinburne, ed. E. Gosse and T.J. Wise (20 vols, 1925–7); *The Swinburne Letters*, ed. C.Y. Lang (1959–62); *Lesbia Brandon*, ed. R. Hughes (1952), a novel, his most candid algolagniac work. See: George Lafourcade, *La Jeunesse de Swinburne* (1928); *Swinburne: The Critical Heritage*, ed. Clyde K. Hyder (1970); Philip Henderson, *Swinburne* (1974).

443
SYNGE, John Millington 1871–1909

Irish dramatist and prose writer

Synge was born into an old Anglo-Irish family recently passed from the status of landowners to that of middle-class professionals, and inclined in religion to low-church zeal. These transformations occurring in the generation immediately before his have both coloured his achievement and obscured a proper assessment of it. He was educated haphazardly at Trinity College, Dublin, but pursued independently his studies in natural history, music, European literature and philosophy. His journeys to the Aran Islands (County Galway) from 1898 onwards provided a setting for a great transformative prose work, *The Aran Islands* (1907), in which romantic philosophy, aesthetics, politics, and self-scrutiny converge. Other important 'travel' writings have been collected as *In Wicklow and West Kerry*.

Synge is best known as a dramatist of the 'peasant' mode, but this is the result of a crudely 'naturalist' reception in part encouraged by W.B. Yeats for propagandist purposes in Ireland. Synge's debt to the architectonics of classical French tragedy is evident in *In the Shadow of the Glen* (1903), and his reading of Marx* and Nietzsche* informs *Riders to the Sea* (1904). *The Well of the Saints* (1905) is an important play in its portrayal of language as creative mediation, a direct assault on the naturalism of Synge's later enthusiasts. His best-known play, *The Playboy of the Western World* (1907), is moving towards self-parody and an exposure of the 'play' element in human identity.

Such a summary omits two less than completed plays, *When the Moon Has Set* (1901 onwards) and *Deirdre of the Sorrows* (1907 onwards). An intensive analysis of the interaction of the first play's Ibsenism* and the last play's mythic tapestries would reveal much of the underlying *Tod und Verklarung* ('Death and Transfiguration') motif in Synge's cultural politics. A comprehensive assessment of Synge has been frustrated by Yeat's deployment of him as a peasant dramatist sacrificed to a riotous and philistine petty bourgeoisie, by Marxist neglect, and by delay in the full presentation of his *oeuvre* to the world. The four-volume *Collected Works* goes some way towards rectifying this aspect of things.

W.J. Mc Cormack

Collected Works, ed. Robin Skelton and Ann Saddlemyer (1962–8). *Letters to Molly*; *John Millington Synge to Maire O'Neill* (1971) are essential reading. No satisfactory biography exists, but Synge's nephew Edward Stephens left a voluminous memoir-cum-study which Andrew Carpenter has admirably edited, *My Uncle John* (1974). See also: Nicholas Grene, *Synge: A Critical Study of the Plays* (1975); Declan Kiberd, *Synge and the Irish Language* (1979); W.J. Mc Cormack, *John Synge and the Genesis of Art* (1983).

T

TAINE, Hippolyte-Adolphe 1828–93

French philosopher, critic and historian

Taine was born in the Ardennes. His father, a country lawyer, died when he was twelve. The family moved to Paris and in 1848 Taine was admitted to the École Normale Supérieure. There, attempting to compensate for the loss of his religious faith, he immersed himself in metaphysics – Spinoza and, later, Hegel*. His 'pantheistic' views brought him into conflict with the contemporary philosophical and educational establishment which, especially after 1852, was clerical and reactionary.

After a brief period of school-teaching he abandoned this career and settled in Paris, publishing critical articles on a wide range of subjects. Collected, recast and prefaced, these became a series of influential books: *Les Philosophes français du XIXe siècle* (1857), an iconoclastic attack on the dominant *spiritualiste* philosophy and on Victor Cousin in particular; the *Essais de critique et d'histoire* (1858) and the *Nouveaux Essais* (1865) in which he championed Balzac* and Stendhal*; and the *History of English Literature* (*Histoire de la littérature anglaise*, 1864, trans. 1872), an attempt to understand the English character through literature. He also published his thesis on La Fontaine (1853) and a book on Livy (1856).

1862 was a year of crisis, described in a rare diary entry published in the richly informative *Life and Letters of H. Taine* (*Vie et correspondance*, 1902–7, trans. 1902–8). At thirty-four he was the leading critic of his generation. But he still had unrealized ambitions as a philosopher and he now discovered a vocation as a creative writer; he had a liaison with the mysterious novelist, Camille Selden; he was convinced that greatness comes only from the imagination. But he chose reason rather than risk. He broke with Camille Selden, abandoned his novel (the fragment, *Étienne Mayran*, was published in 1910) and, in 1868, married into a wealthy family.

The Commune of 1871 may have been responsible for the anti-Revolutionary emphasis of his major work, *The Origins of Contemporary France* (*Les Origines de La France contemporaine*, 1875–93, trans. 1885–94), but the decision to become a historian is the resolution of his 1862 conflict, a means of reconciling risk-free exposition and dangerous imagination or, to use the symbolical figures he himself created, of being in an attenuated form, both orator and poet.

The Origins which occupied the rest of his life is, as a result of this tension, a unique work, brilliantly combining narrative and philosophical history. It is an attempt to explain the whole development of modern France, a history which for the first time recognizes the importance of the provinces and which, in a highly contemporary way, describes the power of ideology.

His philosophy found expression in a treatise on psychology, *On Intelligence* (*De l'Intelligence*, 1870, trans. 1889), and he also produced *Lectures on Art* (*La Philosophie de l'Art*, 1880, trans. 1896), based on lectures he gave at the École des Beaux Arts.

Taine was the spokesman for the new positivist, determinist, anti-clerical, anti-Romantic philosophy which was to influence Zola* so much. John Stuart Mill* played a role but it was the impact of contemporary scientific achievement which led Taine to his basic belief, expressed powerfully in his article on Byron*: scientific method should no longer be applied only to the physical world; there should be a science of man – of literature, of art, of society.

Contemporaries saw him as a dogmatic positivist. Not until the publication of the correspondence and the early manuscript material was the Romantic, the metaphysician, the follower of Spinoza recognized and given full weight. Taine is relevant today because of the way he lived out the contradictions of science. His insistence on the need for limited, detailed observation, his concern for the individual, was in conflict with a heroic commitment to system, theory, law. His explanatory concepts are frequently obscure or inadequate, as when he claims to explain a writer or a society by three forces, 'race', 'milieu' and 'moment' and by 'contrariété' and 'concordance'. But his unremitting struggle to meet the simultaneous demands of dispassionate observation and of articulated understanding over a vast area of subject matter is what makes him one of the precursors of modern historiography, critical theory and social science. He is a remarkable example of a thinker who strove to reconcile a rationalist, continental outlook with Anglo-Saxon empiricism, who believed in the value of data collection and objectivity but nevertheless recognized the primacy of the structuring imagination and of subjectivity.

Colin Evans

Leo Weinstein, *Hippolyte Taine* (1972), contains a list of works translated into English. See: Colin Evans, *Taine, Essai de biographie intérieure* (1975); Colin Evans, 'Taine and his fate', in *Nineteenth Century French Studies*, Vol. VI, 1–2 (1977–78).

445
TAKIZAWA BAKIN 1767–1848

Japanese writer

Bakin was born to a Samurai family that during his childhood was stricken with illness and acute financial problems. His mother's dying wish was that he restore the family fortunes but his attempts to do so as a Samurai were no more successful than his forays into the professional world of the doctor, the Confucian scholar and the comedian, and it was through the poorly regarded trade of a novelist that he finally achieved fame. His first literary efforts were chapbooks, in which he added scholarly and didactic touches to the light humour that was customary in the genre. In these and later works he managed to avoid the trouble with the censors that few of his contemporaries escaped by eschewing political satire and lubricity. Shortly after the turn of the century he began to concentrate his efforts on the long romances known as *yomihon* and gradually forsook the bohemian society of writers for the company of scholars. He achieved unprecedented commercial success and it is almost entirely for his *yomihon* that he was revered in his day and is remembered now. His stout Confucian didacticism, his learning and familiarity with the Japanese and Chinese classics, his use of historical sources, and the appreciation of the romance of place he derived from his travels all contributed to the popularity of his *yomihon* with educated readers.

His chief work is the monumental *Hakkenden* ('Biographies of Eight Dogs', 1814–42). Like most of his *yomihon*, it was set before 1600 and is not without anachronistic references to contemporary life that have been seen as a pointer to the contemporary moral messages of his works. It tells the epic tale of the struggle for the restoration of the Satomi house during the wars of the fifteenth century. The family is aided in its conflict with local tyrants and usurpers of the imperial prerogative by eight heroes who each represent one of the Confucian virtues and is honoured by the emperor once supremacy has been won.

Although little read today, Bakin's works were immensely popular in the nineteenth century, even after the Meiji Restoration of 1868 and the subsequent introduction of Western literature and decline in the popularity of the historical romance. And even fifty years after his death he was being given credit for the overthrow of the Tokugawa government and the nom-inal restoration of authority to the emperor in 1868. Although this smacks of hagiolatry, there can be no doubt that he imparted to several generations a nationalistic fervour for Japanese history and an awareness of the rule of the emperor in times past. So he can be said to have laid some of the groundwork for the consciousness of emperor and nation that was to grow rapidly after his death.

Peter Kornicki

See L.M. Zolbrod, *Takizawa Bakin* (Twayne's World Authors no. 20, 1967).

446
TCHAIKOVSKY, Peter Ilich 1840–93

Russian composer

One of the most celebrated composers of the late Romantic musical period, Tchaikovsky was born at Votkinsk in central Russia where his father held a prominent position as a mining engineer. From an early age he showed great musical interest and was encouraged to learn the piano by his mother to whom he had become neurotically attached. Her death when he was only eleven set the seal on an idealized view of women for the rest of his life. In 1855 the family moved to St Petersburg and the youth was sent to the prestigious School of Law where he later graduated with honours. Accordingly he obtained a post in the Ministry of Justice where he remained for four years. However, the pull of music became so strong that he decided to enrol at the Conservatoire. Here he pursued full-time studies under Anton Rubinstein who had a high opinion of his composition exercises. Tchaikovsky's relinquishing of regular employment, just as he had become accustomed to a rather flamboyant life-style, meant a drastic drop in his living standards. He had to survive by giving lessons and acting as an accompanist for singers while writing his first compositions. Success in this field brought him a professorship of harmony at the new Moscow Conservatoire under Nikolai Rubinstein in 1866, and this enabled him greatly to increase his creative output. Compositions of this particularly fruitful period include the first three symphonies, the first piano concerto, three operas as well as *Romeo and Juliet* and the ballet *Swan Lake*; in addition, he was to produce articles for periodicals and become acquainted with many artistic contemporaries.

By his mid-thirties Tchaikovsky had met with enough acclaim both at home and abroad to fulfil short concert tours in Europe and purchase a house in the country for both rest and solitude. It is at this time that a curious correspondence was started with his new patroness Nadejda von Meck who over the thirteen years of their communications never made personal contact with the composer, though she did contribute greatly to his material needs. This, in contrast to his disastrous and shortlived marriage at the time, was to provide both platonic companionship and a secure income. In 1877 after recovering from a nervous breakdown and pathetic suicide attempt he embarked on a travel programme which took him to Switzerland and Italy. Dissatisfied with his position at the Moscow Conservatoire he resigned in the following year and devoted more time to writing. New works soon to appear were three orchestral suites, two symphonies, the second piano concerto, the violin concerto, *Sleeping Beauty*, the symphonic poems *Manfred,, Hamlet* and *Voyevode*, together with four more operas. Tchaikovsky spent his remaining five years touring Europe and promoting performances of his new scores. By the time that von Meck had terminated her friendship with the composer he had directed concerts in Paris, Geneva, London, Leipzig, Berlin, Cologne, Hamburg and Prague. In 1891 he went to America and conducted concerts in New York, Baltimore and Philadelphia. A final move to a country house at Klin enabled him to complete the sixth symphony, subtitled 'Pathétique'. The award of an honorary doctorate by the University of Cambridge in 1893 was made immediately before the mysterious circumstances of his death which occurred in St Petersburg. His death from cholera has only very recently been disputed by the appearance of Russian sources which give the impression that he was directed to take his own life because of a homosexual affair with the relative of a high member of state.

Although Tchaikovsky's musical fame rests upon relatively few works, his output was of sizeable proportions and embraced most forms of the late nineteenth-century period. Compared with his colleagues in 'The Five' (Balakirev*, Cui, Borodin*, Mussorgsky* and Rimsky-Korsakov*), who chose to write strongly nationalistic works, Tchaikovsky's style was designed to appeal to international audiences. Inevitably such influences do appear, as can be heard in his frequent use of long modal melodies and sequential repetitions reminiscent of folksong and Orthodox Chant. However, the fact that the infections of French and Italian cantilena figure strongly in his style and also that he adored the operatic works of Mozart, Rossini* and Verdi* contributes much to an understanding of his melodic characteristics. A great admirer of Bizet's* *Carmen* and the ballets of Delibes, Tchaikovsky drew upon these models and injecting his own personal brand of hysteria evolved a style which placed much less emphasis on the constraints of traditional architectural form. Though his most famous compositions have a tendency to be theatrical, he had no interest in the romanticism of Beethoven* or Wagner* despite the fact that his contemporaries Bruckner* and Brahms* drew extensively from such influences for their symphonic writing.

Tchaikovsky's orchestral works can be divided into two groups: those with a definite programme and mostly cast as single movements, and the symphonies based on more traditional forms. In this first group can be placed the tone-poems *Romeo and Juliet* (1869), *The Tempest* (1875), *Francesca da Rimini* (1876) and *Hamlet* (1888). Taking *Romeo and Juliet* as reasonably representative of the composer's formal layout we can see that he invariably commences a work with a slow introduction and follows with a fast sonata section of two contrasted themes; these are treated freely both within the exposition and development sections. Again in this tone-poem, three stylistic elements are evident: the first theme is vigorous and frequently agitated while the second is mournful but eloquent. The whole is held together with extended running passages of a forceful nature. The second category includes the abstract works, namely the mature works for solo instrument with orchestra and the three late symphonies. Here the composer's first movements again employ much developmental material within the expositions and frequently introductory themes recur in later movements also. In this procedure the over-emphasis of the same thematic materials tends to wear rather thin in long movements. However, the use of rhythmic devices such as syncopation or alternatively adept instrumental colouring frequently minimize any formal miscalculations on the part of the composer. Though the three early symphonies, no. 1 in G minor ('Winter Daydreams', Op. 13, 1866), no. 2 in C minor ('Little Russian', Op. 17, 1872) and no. 3 in D major ('Polish', Op. 29, 1875), show him grappling with just these problems, they are worthy predecessors to the more mature worrks. Much of their colourful orchestration is derived from Mendelssohn* and Schumann* who, like Tchaikovsky, were inspired by country scenes and local village dancing. Symphony no. 4 in F minor (Op. 36, 1877), which was written soon after his abortive marriage and dedicated to his new found friend von Meck, represents a new depth of expression with its 'fate' motive on fanfare brass and melancholic waltz theme: the whole work could be termed as autobiographical though the composer had no wish to be explicitly programmatic. The Symphony no. 5 in E minor (Op. 64, 1888) is more philosophical in its emotional attitude: the first three movements are Tchaikovsky at his best while any formal weaknesses in the finale are mollified by the work's universal popularity. The same can be said for the sixth symphony in B minor (Op. 74, 1893), the 'Pathétique'. Written close to his death, this work shows him both to have transcended the difficulties of form as well as present programmatic elements which bring the 'fate' theme to a convincing conclusion. Once again he draws from his palette feelings of utter despair as in the outer movements and contrasts these with a balletic *valse à cinq temps* as the centrepiece. Recently much more acclaim has been given to the lengthy and programmatic *Manfred* Symphony (Op. 58, 1885), based on the life of Lord Byron*: the composer was ambivalent towards this symphony for it presented him with the problem of providing themes capable of thematic transformation similar to those of Berlioz* and Liszt*.

Though there are several works for solo instrument with orchestra, only the first piano concerto in B flat minor (Op. 23, 1875) and the violin concerto in D major (Op. 35, 1878) have had any great following. Such works follow a narrower expressive range than the symphonies, though the latter is one of the finest written for the instrument since the death of Beethoven. Mention here must also be made of the light-hearted *Variations on a Rococo Theme* (1876) for cello and orchestra which show an interest in pastiche later to be taken up in the opera *The Queen of Spades* (1890) and *Mozartiana* (1887).

Tchaikovsky's three ballets, *Swan Lake* (1877), *The Sleeping Beauty* (1890) and *The Nutcracker* (1892), provided the Russian Ballet with a new kind of musical material from which to work. Prior to this audiences had to make do with French style *Divertissements* written by second rate musicians who had been used to providing light-weight dance scores for operatic interludes or pageants for high society. Tchaikovsky built on this tradition by adding symphonic materials to the well-known folk forms of the polonaise, mazurka and minuet as well as drawing upon foreign dances like the tarantella and bolero. Within the first two ballets these, together with the concert waltz, are subjected to extensive development. His expertise in the portrayal of fairy tales via the use of scintillating orchestration can best be seen in the vignette-like miniatures of *The Nutcracker* which owes a great deal to Delibes's *Sylvia* and *Coppelia* of twenty years earlier.

Of the dozen or so operas that Tchaikovsky wrote only the Pushkin*-inspired *Eugen Onegin* (1878) and the later *Queen of Spades* receive regular performances. The former is a masterpiece written at the time of crisis and owes more to the tragic lyricism of Bizet's *Carmen* than to the nationalist works of Glinka*. The latter, with its biting satire and rococo style, can be traced to Mozart's treatment of the medium, though here the composer adds his own chromatic spice to the rather formal proceedings while ideally balancing lyricism and dramatic expressiveness.

A reappraisal of Tchaikovsky's complete *oeuvre* is long overdue and it is to be regretted that the inflated popularity of a mere handful of orchestral compositions has detracted from the beauty of the early quartets, many songs and piano pieces. Indeed these chamber works often achieve artistic greatness in their Slavonic individualism. Perhaps it is this lighter side which has been taken up by his successors Glazunov (1865–1936) and Miaskovsky (1881–1950): whether by way of *déjà-entendu* in Rachmaninov's* symphonies or in the

made-to-order 'socialist realism' of Shostakovich's ballets, the lilt of the Tchaikovsky concert waltz is instantly recognizable. Like many Romantic composers of this period, his music contains many characteristic traits that have been copied. If the unstable side of his temperament frequently outweighs thematic and formal considerations, the humanity and sincerity of Tchaikovsky's artistry shines through.

Michael Alexander

See: R. Newmarch, *Tchaikovsky* (1907); H. Weinstock, *Tchaikovsky* (1943); Gerald Abraham, *The Music of Tchaikovsky* (1945); E. Evans, *Tchaikovsky* (1966); John Warrack, *Tchaikovsky Symphonies and Concertos* (1974); Vladimir Volkoff, *Tchaikovsky* (1975); John Warrack, *Tchaikovsky Ballet Music* (1979).

447
TELFORD, Thomas 1757–1834

British engineer

Father of modern civil engineering, and of roads as we have known them, Thomas Telford was born in an Esk Valley croft, south-west Scotland, on 9 August 1757, as son of a shepherd who died soon after, leaving the mother to cope with misfortune, helped out by some kind neighbours. He was to complete his life on 2 September 1834, so he cannot be called a Victorian. But the Victorian era was to inherit his great national road system, his splendid bridges, and his no less important work on harbours and canals. Ere that, the rail was emerging from its centuries-long infancy while the roads had degenerated since the Romans departed. Telford saved Britain's roads at long last.

Under adverse conditions, Telford was apprenticed to a stonemason in Lochmaben near Dumfries, but ran away in fear and dismay to complete his time with another at Langholm (still in Dumfriesshire). There he was befriended by a benevolent Miss Pasley, who lent him books and had some influence while he worked as a journeyman-mason at 8 pence a day on Langholm Bridge. Thus he learned the elements of bridge-building.

By 1780, Telford was in Edinburgh, where the New Town was going up. He further studied construction and, in 1782, went to London on a horse (to be delivered there) where he worked at once on Somerset House, thanks to Miss Pasley's brother John. Already a good draughtsman, he never stopped working. During 1784–6 he was on Portsmouth Dockyard work, and already executive. Such was the advance, through tireless work, love of calling, and often extreme frugality, of Laughing Tom (an early nickname).

The next phase began in Shrewsbury, with surveys and repairs of roads and bridges, with guidance and advance from a Mr Pulteney. St Chad's Tower had collapsed, offering plenty of reconstructive scope. Telford – still keeping his mother – became County Surveyor of Shropshire. There was plenty of church-building and restoration around. Briefly in trouble for radical opinions, French excesses shocked him out of Jacobinism. His first original bridge-building was small, near Shrewsbury in 1792.

Telford went back to London, then to Oxford and again to Shrewsbury. In 1793 – out of the blue – he was made engineer of the Ellesmere Canal (112 miles of inland waterway, under an act of that year). With no experience of canals, he was certainly helped by William Jessop, a pioneer of iron railways. The very hilly country involved mighty works. There were nineteen locks, rising 132 feet in 16 miles between Nantwich and Whitchurch. Chirk Aqueduct (1796–1801) came to ten 40–foot arches with canal water level 70 feet above the Ceiriog running to Dee, and that of Pont Cysylltan over the latter came to 127 feet between water courses, 1,007 feet long with nineteen arches (1795–1805). Telford used cast-iron troughs for the elevated canal parts.

Iron bridges had begun in 1777, with that still extant above the modern town of Telford. Thomas Telford's first iron bridge was between Bridgnorth and Shrewsbury. In 1802, however, he returned to make a survey of his native land, which had not known much of civil engineering since the work of General Wade in the way of pacifying the fiercely intransigent Highlanders by rapid movement of horse, foot and guns. Now harbour improvement was important, notably at Wick, Peterhead and Banff. There was work on the Caledonian Canal (connection of east and west coasts through three lochs down the Great Glen of Scotland from Inverness to the fjord called Loch Linnhe near Fort William). This canal work caused the King of Sweden to call in Telford as consultant on the Göta Canal (1808).

Now we chiefly remember Telford by his beautiful bridges. That over the Menai Strait remains superb. Built under an act of 1819, its single suspended span of 556 feet 16 chains connects great masonry piers 153 feet high; total length, 1710 feet. It was opened by passage of the Holyhead Mail on 30 January 1826. At Conway a smaller suspension bridge had, by its towers, to 'harmonize' with Conway Castle. As beautiful as any is the modest iron bow over the Spey at Craigellachie, Banffshire.

Thomas Telford was buried in the nave of Westminster Abbey in 1834. A stone, and those bridges, are his monuments.

C. Hamilton Ellis

See: Samuel Smiles, *The Life of Thomas Telford* (1867); L.T.C. Rolt, *Thomas Telford* (1958).

448
TENNYSON, Alfred, Lord 1809–92

British poet

Alfred Tennyson, first Baron Tennyson, was born in Somersby, Lincolnshire. His father was an emphatically gloomy country rector from whom the poet inherited a temperamental melancholy and from whom he received his early education, the rectory being well stocked with books. He began to write when he was eight years old. When he was eighteen, he and his brother issued *Poems by Two Brothers*. The next year Tennyson went to Trinity College, Cambridge, where he met Arthur Hallam. His discussions with the extremely clear-minded and sympathetic Hallam helped Tennyson to clarify his ideas about the nature of form in poetry and about poetic language. *Poems Chiefly Lyrical* (1830) and *Poems* (1833) established Tennyson in the eyes of Leigh Hunt, who had 'discovered' Keats*, Shelley* and Byron* and set about promoting Tennyson. Hallam's death in 1833 marked Tennyson's life and affected his development as a poet. His most original and distinctive work was in a sense produced out of his dialogue with Hallam. He never had such another reader or friend. For nine years he published very little but was writing *In Memoriam* (published in 1850). *Poems* (1842) included earlier work but also 'Locksley Hall', 'Ulysses', 'Morte d'Arthur' (a prototype for the *Idylls of the King*) and other important work. *The Princess: A Medley* (1847) includes some of his best lyrics in a rather dull blank-verse flow from which they can fortunately be rescued to stand alone.

Fame was – for one of his temperament – a necessary burden. *Maud: A Monodrama* (1855) and the first four *Idylls* (1859) brought him much fame. *Enoch Arden* (1864) marked a decisive falling-off – not that Tennyson wrote badly after that date, only that he wrote dully, with a few vigorous exceptions. He became Poet Laureate in 1850 and held the post for forty-two years. His poetic 'working life' was among the longest in English literature – sixty-five years. His excursions into verse drama, as into narrative, were unconvincing, though he devoted his later years to them. His later collections were *Ballads and Other Poems* (1880), *Tiresias and Other Poems* (1885), *Demeter and Other Poems* (1889) and *The Death of Oenone* (1892). The 1885 collection took its title from an early poem he recovered and revised for publication.

His virtues as a lyric poet are essentially prosodic rather than conceptual. His narrative and dramatic limitations are clear from *Maud*, with its immediately memorable local passages and its eminently forgettable and sometimes absurd larger designs. Tennyson bases his dramatic procedure in the plays on what he takes to be Shakespeare's, but he is unable to give distinctive dictions to his speakers. His mimetic talents do not include the kind of self-effacement required of a dramtist nor the sense of thrift and pace which Shakespeare might have taught a brisker poet. Tennyson will talk through his characters: they reveal general states of feeling, not states of mind in specific context. The characters do not speak *in* character.

Even excluding the plays, Tennyson's output is huge. The good poems rise to the surface far more readily than they do in the work of a more integrated imagination – Hardy's* for instance – or of a more artificial one – for instance Browning's*. Tennyson had the desire and compulsion to write, but what he wrote did not always have the additional compulsion of emotional or psychological necessity. We distinguish the poems of feeling from the poems of conventional sentiment, but even they have prosodic merits. In some poems he thinks; in some he adopts, unimaginatively, other people's thoughts or the liberal sentiments of the age. As the 'Representative Voice', his politics and his religion are rooted in an idealizing memory of the past and a fear of the future.

Matthew Arnold* discerned in 1860 that the Laureate, despite his vast accomplishments, 'is deficient in intellectual power'. This, of course, is one reason for the power of his lyric poems: they are not governed by ideas but by exquisitely held and apprehended feelings of a kind that 'intellectual power' might distrust, discard, or ironize (as was the case with Browning, who – though one would hardly call him intellectually powerful – was no doubt clever, too clever to be seen to be sincere). Tennyson's poetic weakness is the narrowness of his register. He was technically omnicompetent; but he is truly accomplished only in a small area of his competence. His was a refining style which, when he tried to escape it, produced such disastrous work as 'Dora'.

Part of Tennyson's originality is in his mimetic conception of poetic language: sound and syntax could create, he believed, equivalents to motion and image, as 'The Palace of Art' and 'The Lotus Eaters' very differently demonstrate.

His idealization of the past provides him with epic and legendary figures, the best of them old men (whom he fleshed out in his youthful poems) – Tithonus and Ulysses especially. Those poems express – or seem to – through the vehicle of a *persona*, Tennyson's deepest feelings and resolutions. The mask was for Browning a way of escaping the 'self'; for Tennyson it was a means of approach which suitably generalized the experience presented. No young poet has ever more effectively donned the mask of age.

His best long poem, *In Memoriam*, succeeds in part because it is an anthology of short poems arranged to follow the cycles of years and the gradual transformation of grief at the death of a friend into a kind of forced spiritual optimism. The lyrics – especially the melancholy ones – stand up well to reading out of

context, as do the lyrics from *The Princess*. Organic units have been marshalled by Tennyson into mechanical structures. It is no wonder the structures do not hold; but the units retain unique force, the sum of the parts exceeding the whole. The language of *In Memoriam* is, for the most part, plain and direct with that refinement of sincerity which rejects the evasions of irony on the one hand and those of exaggeration in 'contextualizing' on the other.

The success of *In Memoriam* is its fragmentariness. Each section is an elegiac idyll. As one critic said, the faith is flimsy while the doubt is potent poetry. Tennyson was 'the voice of his age' in various ways – not least in a kind of nostalgic and intransitive eloquence, pure of designs on the reader beyond the design to pleasure and to move him – but not to impel him to action, rather to reflection. It is a poetry that – at its best – cannot be used, can only be valued.

One of the most rewarding contexts in which to set Tennyson's work is that of the first and second generation French Symbolists. The analogies are numerous and underline the freshness of his poetic intelligence and original imagination, his prosodic resourcefulness, whatever may have been the limitations of his more cognitive intellect.

Michael Schmidt

Poems: *The Poems of Tennyson*, ed. Christopher Ricks (1969). See: Sir Charles Tennyson, *Alfred Tennyson* (1949); *Critical Essays on the Poetry of Tennyson*, ed. John Killham (1960); *Tennyson: The Critical Heritage*, ed. John D. Jump (1967).

449
THACKERAY, William Makepeace 1811–63

British writer

Literary history offers few more obvious examples of the writer *malgré lui* than William Makepeace Thackeray. His entire career can be viewed, on at least one significant level, as a continuing attempt to thwart the natural instincts of his genius on behalf of a nagging desire to be taken for a gentleman, as opposed to an author, and it is no accident that the bulk of his work is preoccupied with themes of imposture, make-believe and performance. English literature never produced a Balzac* – perhaps, indeed, it never needed to – but of all Victorian fiction writers it is Thackeray who comes closest in spirit (and sometimes in personal character) to the merciless Parisian annalist.

'Victorian' is, in certain sense, a misnomer for an artist whose roots lie so deeply in the louche, gaudy, reach-me-down world of the years between the battle of Waterloo (1815) and Victoria's* accession (1837). Born in Calcutta, he was sent to England at the age of six and educated at Charterhouse, the school which, with its adjacent almshouse, figures so notably in *The Newcomes*. In 1828 he went to Trinity College, Cambridge, where his contemporaries included Tennyson*, Edward FitzGerald* and Richard Monckton Milnes, all of whom became lifelong friends. A wealthy idler at Trinity, he left without taking his degree and went to Germany, visiting Weimar and meeting Goethe*, and in 1831 he entered the Middle Temple in a half-hearted attempt to practise as a lawyer. Financial crises in his family circle, however, put paid to a life of indolent dandyism on the Disraeli*–Bulwer Lytton* model, and he was forced to turn to journalism to earn his living.

Thackeray never quite reconciled himself to the business of earning money by the pen, and the portraits of journalists and literary men in his novels are distinctly ambivalent in presentation. The dominant irony of all this is that he should have emerged as undoubtedly the most brilliant of English nineteenth-century journalists, equalling Dickens* in passion and fecundity and wholly surpassing him in his mastery of the short forms dictated by the magazines and newspapers for which he wrote. Shrewd, witty, economical in resource, unsparing in attack, his contributions to the *Morning Chronicle*, the *National Standard*, the *Constitutional* and other relatively shortlived London papers are spiced with a species of racy bitterness particular to their author and strongly reminiscent of the eighteenth-century satirists whom he so admired.

The summit of his achievement as an essayist and social observer was reached during the ten years 1837 to 1847 in his work for *Fraser's Magazine* and *Punch*. In pieces such as *The Yellowplush Papers* (1837–8), sardonic glimpses of dandy decay and post-Byronic* follies through the eyes of a flunkey, and *The Second Funeral of Napoleon* and *The Irish Sketch Book* (both 1843), he discloses an eye for vivid detail and an almost daunting sense of the absurd, which reached a peak in *The Book of Snobs* (1846–7), where his cynicism is given its freest rein in a hilarious exposé of early Victorian social ambitions.

A natural result of such a marked concentration of interests was a drift towards more extended fictional forms, dictated as much as anything else by a need for money. His marriage to Isabella Shawe in 1836 had been effectively brought to an end by her decline into madness four years later, and though his later life was sweetened by the presence of a mistress, he was left with three children to bring up, besides having to maintain his wife. He had already written three short novels before completing *Barry Lyndon* (1844), a conscious attempt to revive the eighteenth-century picaresque but (despite the success of a recent filmed version) not a work which has won popularity with either critics or the general reader.

Thus the publication, during 1847–8, in the approved serial form, of *Vanity Fair* may seem surprising in its context, and its imaginative novelty of approach placed Thackeray justifiably among the giants of Victorian letters, admired by writers as disparate as Dickens and Mrs Gaskell*, recipient of a dedication from Charlotte Brontë* and an acknowledged model for the fledgling talent of Anthony Trollope*. The need to follow up *Vanity Fair*'s success brought *Pendennis* in 1848–50 and *Henry Esmond* in 1852, novels which, though they consolidated Thackeray's reputation as a writer with serious intentions, were seen here and there as lacking something of the verve and bite which had so obviously gone into the making of *Vanity Fair*. Something of a recovery was made in *The Newcomes* (1853–5), but none of the later fictions, *The Virginians* (1857–9), *Lovel The Widower* (1860) and *Philip* (1861–2), suggests that their author would ever have regained his hold on the satirical energy initially bequeathed to him through the valuable experience of journalism.

Perhaps he never wanted to. The hunger for respectability which drove Millais* to paint *Bubbles* and Sullivan* to compose *The Martyr of Antioch* turned Thackeray into a sentimental clubman, charming the queen's ladies-in-waiting with his decorous lectures on the Augustans while privately wincing under the twinges of a urethral stricture, the venereal legacy of a Parisian indiscretion. The hypocrisy and affectation he had so triumphantly pierced during the 1830s and 1840s he substantially underpinned during the 1850s in his *The English Humourists* and *The Four Georges*, two lecture series designed to flatter the Victorian notion that the nineteenth century was altogether more wholesome than its predecessor. So successful, indeed, was the latter group that it is only during the last decade that its overwhelming cliché of the Hanoverian royal family as a collection of boorish, lecherous semi-imbeciles has been successfully erased in English popular consciousness. Death at the early age of fifty-two removed Thackeray from the responsibility of having to maintain a role as posturing as that of his own Becky Sharp at her charity bazaars.

His reputation underwent a signal decline during the early twentieth century, and the reappraisal taking place in recent decades has resulted in the rehabilitation of the articles, essays, sketches and parodies at the expense of much of the longer fiction. *Pendennis*, for example, though it still finds its apologists, has suffered considerably in the light of the evidence of Thackeray's desperation to meet the deadlines on its various instalments. Even without such wisdom after the event, the book emerges as heavily flawed, especially in its latter stages, during which the hero is apparently reclaimed for mid-Victorian propriety by the operation of the humourless and priggish Laura Bell, the least endurable of those paradigms of virtue with whose creation nineteenth-century novelists ministered in public to their private embarrassments. The promise of the early chapters and the wealth of authentic inventiveness in such characters as Blanche, the Major and Captain Costigan go a long way towards excusing their author's subsequent failures of endeavour.

Esmond offers problems of a different kind. Critics are united in praising the intensiveness of research underlying Thackeray's presentation of figures and episodes from the reign of Queen Anne, a period in which his sympathies were so deeply engaged that he contrived not only to live in Kensington, historically associated with Augustan court life, but to design his house along neo-Georgian lines. Yet, for all his ready invocation of the shades of Addison, Swift and 'honest Dick Steele' and bravura duels and battle scenes, Thackeray's historical sense is consistently betrayed by his over-the-shoulder glances in the direction of his bourgeois readership. The world of Esmond and Lady Castlewood, sober, detached and mildly censorious, is so obviously not that of the flesh-and-blood historical characters who appear, just as it is far removed from the moral cut-and-thrust of the Fielding and Smollett whom the novelist furtively but fervently admired.

Far safer ground was reached in *The Newcomes*, which has not yet had the degree of analysis and commendation it richly deserves. It is undeniably prolix, muddled in its plotting, vague in its direction, inadequate in resolution, but a good deal more of the true Thackerayan vigour, the snarling grin of the mature satirist, is to be found here than in any of the other novels after *Vanity Fair*. Few other writers of the period (perhaps only Dickens in *Dombey and Son*) confront the conventional responses of English society with so coldly relentless a gaze. Barnes, Ethel, Rosy and the Colonel all contribute memorable metaphors to the book's composite vision of greed and sacrifice, closer, perhaps, than anything else of Thackeray's to the Balzacian world by which he was inevitably touched.

Only in *Vanity Fair*, however, did the novelist make his form work as he wished it to, and a contributory factor to this sense of overall control and sureness of aim was undoubtedly his undivided commitment to the nature of his subject. Like several other great nineteenth-century English novels, such as *Middlemarch* and *Great Expectations*, the book enjoys a carefully worked out historical perspective in a past which could be easily recalled by Thackeray's older readers, and part of its theme is an exploration of the Regency atmosphere which will mingle a wistful nostalgia with a shudder of retrospective cynicism. Thus, while figures like Sir Pitt Crawley and Lord Steyne are made positively grotesque and satanic, the character of Becky Sharp herself is held up to our ironic admiration precisely through those qualities of guile, resilience and resourcefulness which place her outside the preserve of the traditional Victorian heroine.

Such a heroine is both offered and withdrawn in the person of Amelia Sadley, whose virtue finally (at any rate by implication) wearies the very man who has suffered most for her during the course of the book, the gawky and indomitably decent Dobbin, Thackeray's generally successful attempt at sketching a gentlemanly anti-type to Becky. It is through such contrasts, indeed, and through its entire machinery of paradox and irony that the novel continually tugs and gnaws at the clichés and assumptions of the nineteenth-century novel and questions the values which sanctify the scapegrace George Osborne, a posthumous hero at Waterloo, as much as the vapid, clinging Amelia.

It is, most of all, in its vast comprehensive view of shifting ideals and the swiftness of social change that *Vanity Fair* stands alone among nineteenth-century English novels, an isolated concentration of those energies so magnificently diffused in the earlier journalism. In the progressive rediscovery of his shorter works, we come face to face with an absorbingly complex and bizarre personality, whose promise was destined to an incomplete fulfilment.

Jonathan Keates

Works: *Centenary Biographical Edition of the Works of Thackeray*, ed. A.T. Ritchie and Leslie Stephen (26 vols, 1910–11); *The Letters and Private Papers of William Makepeace Thackeray*, ed. Gordon N. Ray (4 vols, 1945–6). See: Gordon N. Ray, *Thackeray: The Uses of Adversity 1811–1846* (1955) and *Thackeray: The Age of Wisdom 1847–1863* (1958). See also: Lambert Ennis, *Thackeray: The Sentimental Cynic* (1950); *Thackeray: The Critical Heritage* ed. Geoffrey Tillotson (1968); John Sutherland, *Thackeray at Work* (1974); John Carey, *Thackeray* (1977).

450
THOMAS, Philip Edward 1878–1917

British poet

Edward Thomas was born on 3 March 1878 in Lambeth and, although he was to make his reputation as a writer concerned chiefly with the countryside, he spent most of his early life in London. Occasional holidays, however, were taken with relatives near Swindon, and these encouraged his admiration for Richard Jefferies, who had lived nearby. Jefferies's work and personality were to exercise a strong influence on his own. While a schoolboy at St Paul's Thomas's early essays brought him to the attention of the critic James Ashcroft Noble, who arranged for several of them to be published in the *Speaker* and the *New Age*. Others were included in his first book *The Woodland Life* which was published in 1897, and when Thomas went up to Oxford as a non-collegiate student later the same year he was already considering a career as a writer. He had also fallen in love with Noble's daughter Helen. In 1898 he won a history scholarship to Lincoln College, Oxford, where he continued to produce journalism and essays – now in a style much influenced by Walter Pater*. It was one of the most carefree periods of his often unhappy life, but its freedoms were restricted when Helen found she was pregnant. In spite of their professedly Shelleyean* attitude to their relationship, the couple were quickly married and their son was born in January 1900. That summer Thomas disappointed himself and his friends by gaining only a second class degree.

In spite of his father's advice to join the Civil Service, Thomas remained firm in his decision to live by his pen. His tenacity cost him increasingly dear. Before his death in April 1917 he was to introduce sixteen editions and anthologies, produce over a million and a half words of review, and write thirty volumes of topography, biography, criticism and belles-lettres. Many of these were on uncongenial topics, nearly all had to be produced very quickly, and their effect was almost literally soul-destroying. Between 1901 and 1916 he and his family (two more children were born in 1902 and 1910) moved house seven times in attempts to create a new start. But although he came to regard himself as a 'doomed hack', and although the quality of his prose work is uneven, its large bulk describes a sustained attempt at self-discovery. In a broader perspective, it may be seen as the struggle of a distinctly modern sensibility to emerge from the constraints of the nineteenth century. Thomas's prose is written in a gradually simplifying style and the best of it – his life of Jefferies, for instance, or his topographical books *The Icknield Way* and *In Pursuit of Spring* – combines clear judgment with close observation. In several cases, though, its chief interest lies in the fact that it anticipates the scenes, preoccupations and sometimes even phrasing of his poems.

At various times a number of Thomas's friends had tried to persuade him to write poetry – to no avail. But Robert Frost, whom Thomas met in 1913, slowly wore down his resistance, partly by force of personality and partly by sympathetic example. Frost's verse theories were extraordinarily similar to those Thomas himself had evolved independently in his reviews and criticism. Where Frost spoke of 'the sound of sense' Thomas used the phrase 'thought moments' to describe the rhythmical plain speech he admired. This quality is evident in his own poems, the first of which, 'Up in the Wind', was written on 3 December 1914. It is important to stress that all Thomas's poems were written after the outbreak of war. The conflict sharpened his (always keen) feelings of dignified, organic patriotism and – more practically – the long periods of training which followed his enlistment in 1915 gave him time to write. In the twenty-five months between finishing 'Up in the Wind' and his death in the battle of Arras he produced 142 poems. The war is openly mentioned in relatively few of these – 'As the team's head brass' is a notable

exception – but its pressures and dangers helped to shape them all. Characteristically, they describe a cautious search for a sense of Englishness which, if found at all, can only be glimpsed fleetingly. In this they recall the work of several earlier Romantic writers, Wordsworth* pre-eminently, but the fastidious pausing rhythms and intent particularity of his pastoralism are entirely individual. The natural world is always unsentimentally seen for what it is, as well as being used to contain and enact his pursuit of stable identity. The war, the decay of the old rural order, and his own melancholic self-doubt continually threaten his quest, and the result is poetry of much greater formal interest and emotional complexity than that written by the Georgian contemporaries with whom he is sometimes bracketed. Other more recent poets seem not to have overlooked this, if his influence on the young W.H. Auden and the mature Philip Larkin is taken as evidence. But more popular acclaim has been slower to come. It is only a century or so after his birth that he has become widely admired for using what one of his critics called 'the minor modes' to write poetry of 'major psychological subtlety'.

Andrew Motion

Works: *The Collected Poems of Edward Thomas*, ed. R. George Thomas (1978). Selections from the prose: *Edward Thomas on the Countryside*, selected by Roland Gant (1977); *The Selected Prose of Edward Thomas*, ed. Edna Longley (1981); *Edward Thomas: Selected Poems and Prose*, ed. David Wright (1981). Biography: Helen Thomas, *As It Was and World Without End* (1956); Eleanor Farjeon, *Edward Thomas: The Last Four Years* (1958); John Moore, *The Life and Letters of Edward Thomas* (1939). Letters: *Letters from Edward Thomas to Gordon Bottomeley*, ed. R. George Thomas (1968). Criticism: William Cooke, *Edward Thomas: A Critical Biography* (1970); *Edward Thomas: Poems and Last Poems*, ed. Edna Longley (1973); Andrew Motion, *The Poetry of Edward Thomas* (1980).

451
THOREAU, Henry David 1817–62

US author

Where Thoreau was known at all during his brief New England lifetime, it was essentially as an oddity, a figure of quirks and eccentric opinion. To many fellow New Englanders, in Boston and the surrounding townships of Cambridge and his birth-place, Concord, he seemed the very reverse of the gainful, purposive Yankee. He was a Harvard graduate, but had settled to no recognizable occupation, as minister, lawyer, or businessman. Though perceived as a minor ripple in the larger Transcendentalist current, he was none the less literally closer than any to the master, Emerson's* personal friend and protégé, and later a boarder and general handyman with the family. Then, despite the apparent outward severity of his character, a trait commented on not only by Emerson ('Henry is with difficulty sweet') but by Hawthorne*, Thoreau's one-time neighbour in Concord, he was a committed family man, but as the life-long bachelor who was a favourite uncle and loved brother. Though indubitably 'literary' in interests, he was also an alert and eloquent naturalist. No one knew better, or more first-hand, the topographies of New England, its geology and Indian relics, the farms, ponds, flora and fauna. Above all, Thoreau confirmed his supposed oddness when he refused to pay his poll tax in protest at the unjust foreign war he believed his country was conducting in Mexico, having taken up residence in the summer of 1845 in the hut he built by Walden Pond, on land owned by Emerson, and stayed there for nearly two years, the action of a man who, apparently in earnest, talked of 'significant living'.

Given a reputation which, true to Thoreau's contrary style, now exceeds that of Emerson, his Transcendentalist mentor, perhaps the saddest paradox is that his age barely noticed him for the two full-length works published in his lifetime, *A Week on the Concord and Merrimack Rivers* (1849) and *Walden* (1854), or for the essays which have subsequently become classics in the literature of political dissent, 'On the Duty of Civil Disobedience' (1849) and 'A Plea for Captain John Brown' (1860). Yet these writings, *Walden* most especially, were no less than cornerstones in the American Renaissance, the mid-nineteenth-century efflorescence which includes Melville*, Whitman*, Hawthorne and a run of minor Transcendentalists, and which Emerson heralded in *Nature* (1836) and 'The American Scholar' (1837). Further, if Thoreau's published output looks scant, he was also the author of nearly forty journal-notebooks, extraordinary notations of a mind taking cognizance of its own inclinations and powers, and of a number of posthumous 'travel' books. As befits a writer who sought to hone down existence to 'essence', or as he puts it in *Walden* 'to drive life into a corner and reduce it to its lowest terms', Thoreau also evolved a literary idiom of rare distinction, aphoristic, wonderfully spare, layered with congenial Yankee wryness and wit.

Something of Thoreau's contrariness was recognized by George Eliot* when she reviewed *Walden* for the *Westminster Review* in 1856. She saw his lakeside sojourn as 'a bit of pure American life', but retold 'through the medium of a deep poetic sensibility'. She testified to his 'unworldliness' yet also to his tempering 'sturdy sense'. Not unexpectedly, one of the most revealing estimates of Thoreau was offered by Emerson in the obituary essay he published in *Atlantic Monthly* in 1862. He emphasized, no doubt as much from personal

knowledge of the daily routines of his so-called 'practical disciple' as of his writing, the obdurate, Spartan, and as he termed it 'military' element in Thoreau, making reference to his 'inexorable demand on all for exact truth'. Emerson thought him 'a born protestant', who 'chose to be rich by making his wants few, and supplying them himself'. This radical self-sufficiency, which lies behind Thoreau's politics, and behind his wish to dissent from the prevailing orders of American capitalism and 'society', is everywhere reflected in his writing. Thoreau, according to *Walden*, wanted 'the flower and fruit of man', but only if seen and tested for himself. His bid for 'simplicity' thus was always highly complex, self-reliance not in the interests of conventionally defined rewards – material profit, possessions, social esteem – but as the path to higher 'essential' truths. Emerson was equally right to detect the 'transcendental' ends to which Thoreau put his naturalism, the habit of seeing in nature's fine detail abiding spiritual meanings.

Born of English Channel Island and New England store-keeper stock which had gone bankrupt, Thoreau was educated at Concord Academy (1829–33), then Harvard (1833–7), where he read widely. After a brief interlude in Concord's public schools, he set up a school venture of his own with his brother John (1838–41), with whom also he travelled the Concord and Merrimack rivers in 1839. In 1840, he had his first essays and poems published in the Transcendentalist journal the *Dial*; moved in with the Emerson family (1841–3); did some tutoring on Staten Island (1843); and on 4 July 1845, an 'Independence Day' dramatically different in kind from that celebrated by the majority of his compatriots, moved to Walden Pond and his self-constructed hut. In the interim, like his brother John, he had been turned down in marriage by Ellen Sewall; perfected a graphite process for his father's one-time lead pencil enterprise; acted as messenger and handyman for various of the townships, and begun his all-important notebooks. But by Walden Pond, where he had gone 'to transact some private business' and where, among other things, he wrote *A Week on the Concord and Merrimack Rivers*, he began the most significant act of his life, his two-year experiment as a 'community of one'. In 1846, he was arrested and kept in prison overnight for non-payment of the poll tax (the tax, to his annoyance, was paid by 'friends'). He travelled in 1846 to the Maine Woods; lived again with the Emerson family in 1847–8; lectured on 'Civil Disobedience' (1848), a year before *A Week on the Concord and Merrimack Rivers* was published; made a sequence of trips to Cape Cod (in 1850 with his great friend and first biographer, the poet Ellery Channing); visited Walt Whitman in Brooklyn in 1856 (he called the second edition of *Leaves of Grass* 'an alarum or trumpet-note ringing through the American camp'); and in 1859 lectured on 'A Plea for Captain John

Brown'. In 1860, during a camping trip, he caught cold, which exacerbated his hitherto dormant tuberculosis. Despite an excursion to Minnesota with Horace Mann Jr in hopes of recuperation, he died in Concord on 6 May 1862.

Ostensibly, *A Week on the Concord and Merrimack Rivers* re-creates the canoe journey Thoreau made with his brother into New Hampshire's White Mountains in 1839. Under his transforming design, however, it becomes also the transcript of another dimension of journeying, a diary of contemplation and thought and of Thoreau's testimony to nature as the repository of Emersonian-Transcendental spiritual 'laws'. He explains the metaphoric implications of his up-river, seven-day travel thus: 'True and sincere travelling is no pastime, but is as serious as the grave or any part of the human journey, and it requires a long probation to be broken into it.' This notion of figurative travel anticipates Thoreau's later, equally equivocal and teasing utterance, 'I have travelled much in Concord.' His 'week', in fact, is his version of the Genesis week, the Creation, as it were, retold in terms of a New England river expedition. The geography of the two rivers, and of the surrounding banks and ecology, not only yields a vivid, engaging portrait of nature itself, it acts for Thoreau as the means to his search for higher, ultimate meanings. *A Week* offers journey-narrative, thus, of a profoundly double kind, travel both outward and inward, into which Thoreau imports not only precise natural observations, but a range of learning ancient and modern, different vignettes, maxims and aphorisms ('The traveller must be born again on the road, and earn a passport from the elements, the principal powers that be for him'), and various illustrative poems, including his own notable 'I am a parcel of vain strivings'. Beginning from the Saturday and departure from river-source, each separate day is annotated in full, until the brothers re-arrive at the stiller waters of the port of Concord, home-coming as a time for retrospection and reflection. A line of comparable 'philosophic' nature writing might include John Aubrey's *Natural History*, or Gilbert White's *Natural History and Antiquities of Selborne*, or, closer to Thoreau's own time, Wordsworth's* Lake poems.

As he used the emblematic span of the Genesis week for his first book, so in his masterpiece, *Walden*, Thoreau refashions the actual time he spent at Walden Pond into a cyclic representative year, another chronicle of 'awakening' which occurs to the rhythm of the seasons, summer, autumn, winter and the rebirth of spring. The heart of his endeavour is given in chapter 2, 'Where I Lived, And What I Lived For':

I went to the woods because I wished to live deliberately, to front only the essential facts of life, and see if I could not learn what it had to teach, and not, when I came to die, discover that I had not lived.

I did not wish to live what was not life, living is so dear; nor did I wish to practise resignation, unless it was quite necessary I wanted to live deep and suck out all the marrow of life ... to drive life into a corner, and reduce it to its lowest terms.

By this Thoreau intended no hermit-like avoidance of the world, but an exemplary act of self-realization, the individual life seeking to fulfil its best, most encompassing, possibilities. The attacks on the 'cost' of insignificant work, on mere money profit, and on the unneeded intrusions of state and society, Thoreau makes as the authentic anarch, a preserver and defender of self-acquired values. As the pond and its associated natural life turn, so Thoreau documents the turns of his own evolving consciousness, the self as a separate but complementary world. Most aspects of the pond – its changing seasonal colours, patterns and temperature, even its herbiage and fish – suggest to him analogies with basic human growth and change. And just as he develops, even more surely than in *A Week*, a magnificent account of nature, he insists on the need to be 'expert in home-cosmography', the scholar of the inner individual human landscape. The culminating point of his 'experiment', having taken his plumb-line to measure the pond and by clear implication his own being, lies in the arrival of the spring: 'As every season seems best to us in turn, so the coming in of the Spring is like the Creation of Cosmos out of Chaos and the realization of the Golden Age.' As nature awakens in springtime, so each self, to Thoreau's perception, can awaken from past dormancy. Throughout *Walden*, and *A Week*, and in prose always subtly dual in angle, Thoreau adapts his observations of nature – and of 'economy' and 'profit' – to ends which are both moral and deeply existential. Typically, he writes at the conclusion of *Walden*: 'Let every one mind his own business, and endeavour to be what he was made.'

Thoreau's insistence upon the imperatives of unfettered selfhood equally marks out his essays. In 'Civil Disobedience', to which Gandhi, the pioneers of the British labour movement and a line of political 'resisters' have paid handsome acknowledgment, the ostensible object of attack is American slavery – but slavery not only as an actual historic and unconscionable indignity, but as the wider expression of how government always 'enslaves' its citizenry. Thoreau's spirited polemic seems to indict all statist systems, almost all imposed curbs on the claims of human liberty. Counter-arguments can, of course, be made. But the passion and controlling clarity of Thoreau's style make for one of the great, memorable formulations of dissent. Equally, Thoreau's espousal of John Brown in his famous 'Plea' is the argument of a philosophical radical to whom emancipation can, as at Harper's Ferry, justify murder. The other essays, and Thoreau's posthumous 'travel' pieces – *Excursions* (1863), *The Maine Woods* (1864), *Cape Cod* (1865) and *A Yankee in Canada* (1866) – have not had the currency of the earlier work, but they again underline his acute observational power and his principled insistence on individualism, the need for distinct, separate spheres of human consciousness.

Thoreau's 'eccentricity' is far less the expression of a man simply out of joint with his age, or with the American State and his inherited culture, but rather of a pragmatic, wholly undeferential, seeker after his own 'earned' truths. For him life was nothing if not lived in the particular, weighed and measured by individual inspection. The danger was always of solipsism, the self as all. But Thoreau's informed, radical respect for nature, and for the order of things as seen in his beloved New England forests and landscape, kept him mostly free of that impasse. Like Emerson he sought a 'transcendental' dimension, but only if gained through careful, meticulous personal experience. Here, as in almost every aspect of his life, he was the truest of Yankees, listening always, and never without irony, to his own drummer, the call of his own mind and conscience.

A. Robert Lee

See: Ellery Channing, *Thoreau: The Poet Naturalist* (1902); F.O. Mathiessen, *American Renaissance: Art and Expression in the Age of Emerson and Whitman* (1941); Joseph Wood Krutch, *Henry David Thoreau* (1948); *Thoreau: A Century of Criticism*, ed. Walter Harding (1954); R.W.B. Lewis, *The American Adam: Innocence, Tradition and Tragedy in the Nineteenth Century* (1955); J. Lyndon Shanley, *The Making of Walden, with the Text of the First Edition* (1957); Sherman Paul, *The Shores of America: Thoreau's Inward Exploration* (1958); *Thoreau: A Collection of Critical Essays*, ed. Sherman Paul (1962); *Twentieth Century Interpretations of Walden: A Collection of Critical Essays*, ed. Richard Ruland (1968); *The Recognition of Henry David Thoreau: Selected Criticism since 1848*, ed. Wendel Glick (1969).

452

TOCQUEVILLE, Alexis de 1805–59

French political sociologist

Tocqueville, politically liberal, temperamentally conservative, was born in Normandy of aristocratic family, but through all his writings sought to persuade his fellow aristocrats to accept the legacy of the French Revolution, to accept that a growing equality was inevitable but to study how liberty could be preserved in an egalitarian age. A contemporary described him as like 'pious Aeneas setting forth to found Rome though still weeping for abandoned Dido, "*Mens immota manet, lacrymae volvunter inanes*"' – the mind held firm but the

tears flowed down. 'Despotism,' he was to write, 'appears to me peculiarly to be dreaded in democratic times. I should have loved freedom, I believe at all times, but in the time in which we live I am ready to worship it.'

In 1831 he and a friend, Gustave de Beaumont, accepted a commission from the French Government to visit the United States and to write a report on reformed prison systems. From this resulted a published report in 1832 but also Tocqueville's great two volumes, *Democracy in America* (1835 and 1840). We now know that the broad idea was in his mind before going to America, indeed was largely the reason why he went: 'I confess that in America I saw more than America. I sought there the image of democracy itself, in order to learn what we have to fear or hope from its progress.' Moreover the main themes of his equally great and long laboured work, *L'ancien régime et la Révolution* (1856), were also forming. The two works must be seen as part of a single grand design: to establish how the old aristocratic order came to collapse; to persuade people of the inevitability of democracy (by which he meant equality of condition); and by studying actual democracy, the United States, where these tendencies had gone furthest, to see, as it were by comparative method, the future of Europe and learn how to safeguard its liberties against the unfinished work of the French Revolution. 'The nations of our time cannot prevent,' he concluded the first book of the *Democracy*, 'the conditions of men from becoming equal, but it depends upon themselves whether the principle of equality is to lead them to servitude or freedom, to knowledge or barbarism, to prosperity or wretchedness.'

In his *Recollections* (*Souvenirs*, 1893, trans. 1896), Tocqueville was to mock both the view of the politicians that all great events occur through 'the pulling of strings' and that of the philosophers that events can be traced to 'great first causes'. He spoke of tendencies rather than 'iron laws' and said that nothing occurs other than in the context of these tendencies, but that however ripe the time, nothing occurs by itself without the free actions of particular men. Thus he steers between determinism and voluntarism. There is an inevitable historical tendency towards equality, but the form it will take depends on unpredictable human action; but the success of such actions depends on understanding historical tendencies and sociological circumstances, although no amount of understanding can replace (rather than guide) political action. Thus Tocqueville can appear to strike an almost perfect balance between sociological and political explanation, neither giving too much nor too little to the influence of abstract ideas on historical events; but some have said that his examples are picked to suit his argument, rather than that the argument follows from the evidence. Certainly his America is an abstract model, full of brilliant hypotheses and theories relevant to all modern societies, rather than an empirical investigation of a particular country; but equally certainly the archival research that went into *L'ancien régime* was not merely original and impressive, but is still of great value.

From work in provincial archives he was able to formulate theories of lasting importance: that the actual revolution only speeded up a process of centralization long under way; that the time of maximum danger to an old order is when it tries to reform itself, and that the revolution occurred at a time of economic improvement, not at a time of peculiarly great hardship. He summed up the last two propositions by saying that men suffer hopelessly under despotism; they only stir when there are grounds for hope and signs of improvement.

Basic to both his great works is a distinction between liberty and democracy. He uses democracy in the classic sense as simply the rule of the majority which in turn implies an ever-increasing equality of social condition (he treated America as if it was a kind of middle-class classless society). Democracies may or may not encourage freedom of expression and individual choice in political action. Tocqueville thought that they could lead to greater liberty than ever before, both for general reasons that he states in *Democracy in America* and because of some institutions peculiar to America; but on the other hand many things in democracy uniquely threaten freedom and individualism: 'the tyranny of the majority', the intolerance of public opinion and the worship of uniformity and mediocrity, the distrust of eccentricity and excellence. Reading Tocqueville convinced John Stuart Mill* that the main danger to liberty in our times would come from democracy, not from (they both optimistically believed) rapidly fading autocracy. Tocqueville feared the emergence of a wholly new form of government that he called 'democratic despotism', the rule of a small executive over a vast number of equal but isolated individuals, removed from all intermediary institutions which create (as well as inequities and anomalies) structures for political action. This has often been glibly read as a prophecy of twentieth-century totalitarianism, but it is more like a Conservative's view of the modern welfare state: he speaks of a 'benign and tutelary despotism' that will do everything for the physical well-being of people, so long as they sacrifice their freedom. Louis Napoleon seemed to embody many of Tocqueville's fears: the deliberate corruption of a nation rather than naked terror.

Two things could prevent 'democratic despotism'. First, intermediary institutions between the state and the individual must be preserved, indeed pressure groups of all kinds tolerated and positively encouraged: Hobbes, Rousseau and Bentham* had all denounced such groups as 'worms within the entrails', 'divisive of the General Will' and 'sinister interests' respectively;

but Tocqueville argued that freedom was too great a price to pay for rationalizing away all such traditional or commercial inequities and anomalies. Secondly, beyond questions of social structure, the individual must act like a free citizen, even if the odds of the moment are against such actions – as Jack Lively has written: 'he posed the essentially classical idea of the free man as an active participant in communal affairs.'

Tocqueville was internationally famous in his day and elected a member of the French Academy. He was elected from his own district in Normandy to serve in the Chamber of Deputies from 1839 to the *coup d'état* of 1851. His *Recollections* covers the political events of those days, but he was a better author and theorist than politician, finding it hard to mix with the bourgeois politicians whose emergence on the historical scene he regarded as inevitable and on the whole salutary. Daumier*, in a memorable cartoon, gave him an intelligent but aloof and cynical face, showed him carrying many papers but clearly impatient with the Assembly and eager to be off. After the *coup* he worked in retirement on *L'ancien régime* and the *Recollections* and travelled in England and Ireland. After his early death, his beloved but pious wife claimed him as a good Catholic while French radicals elevated him to the secularist pantheon: even his silences were read both ways. Indeed his explicit views were generally honoured, rarely attacked but often expropriated by almost all different camps in French politics, except the socialists. Liberals saw him as anti-aristocratic and as taking the best from the French Revolution without the excesses; and Conservatives saw his doubts about democracy as repudiation of the principle itself. Both his doctrines and his methods have been more often praised than understood. The first English translation of 1835 for instance, by Henry Reeve, was a fine piece of prose, but the Tory journalist heightened all Tocqueville's fears for democracy and America and toned down his hopes. None the less, his influence on subsequent sociology and political theory has been immense. He can now be seen to stand as the greatest figure, as Raymond Aron has claimed, in a distinctively French school of political sociology which from the time of Montesquieu to a modern exponent like Aron himself has blended sociology with history in a comparative perspective with an openly moral concern both to understand and preserve free institutions.

Bernard Crick

Oeuvres complètes d'Alexis de Tocqueville (1860–5), ed. Mme de Tocqueville and Gustave de Beaumont; *Oeuvres, papiers et correspondances* (from 1951), ed. J.P. Mayer; there is much valuable biographical matter in *Democracy in America*, the Henry Reeve text as revised by Francis Bowen and corrected and edited by Phillips Bradley (1948). See also: George W. Pierson, *Tocqueville and Beaumont in America* (1938); J.P. Mayer,

Alexis de Tocqueville (1960); Jack Lively, *The Social and Political Thought of Alexis de Tocqueville* (1962); Raymond Aron, *Main Current in Sociological Thought*, vol. I (1965); Robert E. Nisbet, *The Sociological Tradition* (1967).

453

TOENNIES, Ferdinand 1855–1936

German sociologist

Ferdinand Toennies was born in Eiderstedt in Schleswig-Holstein. His father was a prosperous farmer and his mother came from a long line of Protestant ministers. Throughout his life Toennies remained deeply attached to the region of his birth and the small rural and urban communities among which he was raised. As a young man he studied a wide range of subjects at a succession of German universities. His PhD from Tübingen was in classical philology and in later life he was to hold chairs in both sociology and economics. His influence and reputation rest upon his first great book, *Community and Association* (*Gemeinschaft und Gesellschaft*, 1887), but he was a prolific writer and noted scholar in several fields. His work on Thomas Hobbes in particular enjoyed international renown. Toennies was an unusual figure in the German intellectual life of his day, a countryman, a liberal with strong socialist sympathies whose political outlook was neither nationalist nor cosmopolitan. His was not the liberalism of the great cities but based in respect for the humanity which he found exemplified in the farms and small towns of his homeland. He was jealous of his political independence but joined the Social Democrats in 1932 in the face of the rising Nazi tide. When Hitler came to power a few months later Toennies, who had written several anti-Nazi articles, was dismissed from his post. Three years later he died at the age of eighty. Such a life and such attachments make it unfortunate that some commentators – Ralf Dahrendorf in particular – have seen Toennies's work as having contributed to the Nazi ethos with its idealization of racially based community. There is little truth in this view. Nazi ideology needed no aid from scholars like Toennies though the affection for pre-industrial forms of life which he undoubtedly felt might in a lesser mind have weakened resistance to the siren calls to a new *Volksgemeinschaft*.

The impact of the industrial revolution made it inevitable that the nature of human community should be at the centre of sociological interest throughout the nineteenth century. Toennies could draw on a considerable literature which included the ambitious theoretical constructions of such men as Comte*, Spencer* and Marx*. *Community and Association* stands out from these earlier works. Where his precursors had treated the transformation of human community as a dependent variable, the result of the growth of knowledge or of changes in the mode of production, Toennies gave it central importance. He treated it as cause more than effect. He distinguished two fundamental forms of society, *Gemeinschaft* which is based upon kinship and neighbourhood, and *Gesellschaft* founded upon individual interest and contractual obligations. European history shows a steady transformation of the first into the second. The argument which Toennies builds upon this simple typology is anything but simplistic. He provides a powerful and distinctly sociological account not only of the rise of individualism and capitalism but of the growth of state power. Toennies envisaged the power of the state as the sole ultimate guarantor of order once the old bonds of *Gemeinschaft* have broken down. The influence of Hobbes is apparent in this but the Englishman's theory of the Leviathan state, to which men turn as an alternative to the state of nature where the war of all against all prevails, is placed in a historical context. It is, Toennies suggests, not the origins but the destiny of social order which Hobbes described.

Toennies's book made an immediate impact on his contemporaries. Max Weber and Émile Durkheim were among its early admirers. To many of his readers Toennies seemed to have given scientific expression to a fundamental change in the nature of human society which was widely felt. *Community and Association* was one of the books which heralded the late nineteenth-century break with the spirit of confident optimism characteristic of the mid-century. Comte, Spencer and Marx had seen in history itself the solution to the problems of their time. Typically they saw social problems as problems of transition awaiting resolution in a new order. Toennies belongs to a later, less enchanted generation. He spoke of the cost of change and voiced the awareness that emerging forms of social organization bring with them new, no less intractable problems. In recent years the continuing appeal of his first book has drawn readers to Toennies's other works but *Community and Association* remains his major legacy to posterity.

David J. Levy

Toennies's other works translated into English include *Custom* and *On Social Ideas and Ideologies* (1974). There is also a fine anthology in the University of Chicago Press's series 'The Heritage of Sociology': *Ferdinand Toennies: On Sociology, Pure, Applied and Empirical*, ed. Werner J. Cahnman and Rudolf Heberle (1971).

454

TOLSTOY, Lev Nikolaevich (Count) 1828–1910

Russian writer

Born in Yasnaya Polyana, near Tula, he was the fourth son of an aristocratic family of five children who were orphaned early by the death of their mother when Tolstoy was only two years of age. Given over to the guardianship of their Aunt Tatyana and their paternal grandmother, the children formed a close-knit group with their own nursery lore of an Ant Brotherhood and the legend of a little green stick on which the secret of happiness was written. The close intuitive understanding born of such relationships and the closed, protected world of Yasnaya Polyana itself, an estate supported by 800 or so serfs, were to influence profoundly Tolstoy's view of the world by leading to his insistence on the importance of the family as the basis of the social contract and the moral superiority of the country to the city, of the rural peasantry to the urban masses. The death of his father when Tolstoy was only eight contributed to the family's desire to close ranks, but Tolstoy's own curiosity about life, brilliantly conveyed in his first semi-autobiographical work *Childhood* (*Detstvo*, 1852), was unorthodox in its directness and clarity. The conventional education by tutors offered him little, just as his years at the University of Kazan (1844–7) ended without his completing the course. His own rich inner life impelled him into making encyclopedic plans for self-education, while his passionate masculine nature led to successive fruitless attempts at moral self-improvement, as his diaries testify. By the time he was twenty he was living the typically licentious life of a young Russian nobleman.

In 1849 he moved to St Petersburg with the intention of entering the university, but at the time of the arrests in connection with the Petrashevsky affair he appears to have returned hastily to Yasnaya Polyana. A superficially aimless life-style was soon interrupted when, in 1851, Tolstoy accompanied his brother Nikolay to the Caucasus and found himself involved in the Russian colonial wars against the hill tribesmen. The effect on him was of incalculable significance. It not only spurred him to write, but it also forced him to examine the nature of human motivation in war, the meaning of courage and the role of vanity in determining behaviour even at the limits of endurance. Such studies of Caucasian military life as *The Raid* (*Nabeg*, 1852) and *The Woodfelling* (*Rubka lesa*, 1855) supplied the groundwork for his masterly examination of war at its most brutal and senseless in his *Sevastopol Sketches* (*Sevastopol' v dekabre*, 1855; *Sevastopol v avguste*, 1856). Experience of the Crimean campaign in 1854–5 taught him that war was never glamorous, but that its only hero 'is he whom I love with all the strength of my spirit, whom I have striven to depict in all his beauty and who

always was, is and will be beautiful – truth.' Simultaneously he was completing the remaining parts of his autobiographical trilogy, *Boyhood* (*Otrochestvo*, 1854) and *Youth* (*Yunost'*, 1856).

By the end of the Crimean War he had become famous and he was lionized in the salons of St Petersburg during the winter of 1855–6, being cultivated particularly by Turgenev*. It was with Turgenev as his companion for part of the time that he went to Europe in 1857. A public guillotining which he witnessed in Paris and the vulgar behaviour of English tourists in Lucerne (which gave rise to the first of his philosophical works *Lucerne*, 1857) reinforced both his distaste for European standards and his sense of moral outrage. Upon his return to Russia, though he published *A Landowner's Morning* (*Utro pomeshchika*), *Three Deaths* (*Tri smerti*), *Albert* and the novella *Family Happiness* (*Semeynoye schast'ye*) during the following three years, he was gradually being drawn towards an interest in peasant education. The dilemma of conscience which faced so many members of the Russian nobility as the emancipation of the serfs approached (February 1861) took the form in Tolstoy's case of a desire to be of practical assistance to the peasants on his estate. This interest took him abroad again for the second and last time in his life between July 1860 and April 1861 when he studied educational practice in many European countries, visiting London, for example, where he attended a reading by Dickens* and is supposed to have met Matthew Arnold*. Back in Russia, he threw himself into the work of the peasant school which he established at Yasnaya Polyana and produced a dozen issues of an educational journal. Yet, at the age of thirty-four in 1862, he suddenly altered the pattern of his life by marrying Sonya Bers, sixteen years his junior, and settling down to raise a family.

In the following years the need for money obliged him to complete and publish *Polikushka*, his powerful study of peasant life, and his longest work to date, *The Cossacks* (*Kazaki*), which had been ten years in the writing. Probably during the summer or autumn of the same year he began writing the monumental work about the Napoleonic invasion of Russia upon which his reputation still principally rests, though it was originally known simply as *1805* or *All's Well that Ends Well*. *War and Peace* was written over a period of seven years and was completed late in 1869. The immense effort involved may have brought him close to a nervous breakdown, for it is thought that he experienced a horrific vision of death while staying in a hotel in Arzamas at this time (described in *Notes of a Madman*, *Zapiski sumasshedshego*, 1897). In the ensuing decade his thinking, like his writing, showed a growing preoccupation with the the purpose of life and ways to combat the apparent meaninglessness of death. Whether through his ABC book for schoolchildren, or the writing of his great novel *Anna Karenina* (1873–7), he aimed to show the universal moral norms at work in society and the need for the educated and privileged to learn the true meaning of goodness from the peasantry.

The last pages of *Anna Karenina* point the way to the religious conversion which Tolstoy described in his *Confession* (*Ispoved'*, 1882). For the remaining three decades of his life he devoted himself chiefly to writing tracts which expounded the fundamental tenets of his religious philosophy. This philosophy, while outwardly concerned with non-resistance to evil by violence, the virtues of work, vegetarianism and abstinence from alcohol and sex, was basically a prolonged attempt by Tolstoy to reconcile through religious precept the gulf between rich and poor, especially the gulf between the intelligentsia and the peasantry, which divided Russian society. His outspoken attacks upon the church and the state undoubtedly brought him enormous moral authority, but also led to his excommunication by the Holy Synod in 1901. He also placed his immense powers as a writer at the service of his philosophy and, apart from writing a great many simple, edifying tales for the people, he turned such fine works as *The Death of Ivan Ilyich* (*Smert Ivan Il'yicha*, 1886), *The Kreutzer Sonata* (*Kreytserova sonata*, 1889) and *Resurrection* (*Voskreseniye*, 1899) into illustrative tracts. In the 1880s he also began writing for the theatre with his sombre study of peasant greed and murder *The Power of Darkness* (*Vlast' t'my*, 1886) and his comedy about spiritualism and peasant guile *The Fruits of Enlightenment* (*Plody prosveshcheniya*, 1889), though probably his most original work for the stage was *The Living Corpse* (*Zhivoy trup*, 1900). In his last years two works demand special mention, his treatise on art, *What is Art?* (*Chto takoye iskusstvo?*, 1897), in which a case is made for the idea that art is a kind of emotional infection, and his remarkable short novel drawn from his early experience of war in the Caucasus, *Hadji Murat* (completed 1904, published posthumously).

The contrast between his high-minded advocacy of a religious life and the fact that he remained in the relatively comfortable circumstances of Yasnaya Polyana naturally caused tension between himself and his family, especially his wife. She was concerned for the future security of his nine surviving children and less eager than her husband to renounce all earthly wealth. There was the added complication that she felt she had been replaced in his affections by the Tolstoyanists or cult followers surrounding him, with the result that their relations became clouded by suspicion, enmity and open feuding. In despair Tolstoy finally left home in November 1910 and was taken ill at the railway halt of Astapovo on the Ryazan-Ural railroad where he died, aged eighty-two.

If Tolstoy's later renown as the founder of Tolstoyanism and an arbiter of morals for his time has faded to vanishing point since his death, his fame as a novelist has steadily increased. The reason for this is due largely to the fact that his religious and philosophical views were outdated even for the nineteenth century, deriving so clearly from an oversimplified, Enlightenment view of human capabilities and purposes, whereas his supreme gift as a writer was an outstanding clarity and freshness of viewpoint in depicting the world. His writer's vision had the straightforward, illustrative quality of photography, and he tended to represent life with all the kinetic vitality of the cinema. He deliberately avoided such artifices as plot-structure, narrated biographies of character or the domination of fiction by a single central portrayal, preferring to evoke the multiplicity of experience by offering successive and varied viewpoints through a multiplication of central figures with whom the reader can identify. Deliberately concealing his own authorial role in the fiction for the greater part, he dared to assume that fiction could represent life pictorially, always governed by a strict chronology, and that human nature changed with the passage of time and even discovered means to self-improvement. Probably the most daring of his achievements in this respect was his depiction of history and historical characters in *War and Peace* as relating to the same dimension as his fictional creations, so that the historical Kutuzov, the Russian commander, can be seen to know the fictional Pierre Bezukhov's wife, for example, and we as readers can appraise and appreciate Kutuzov through Pierre's eyes. Fiction and history here coalesce into a Tolstoyan truth which seems manifestly more real than the historian's.

For all the apparent breadth of vision and olympian skill with which Tolstoy moves us from a St Petersburg salon to the battlefields of Austerlitz or Borodino, from Pierre Bezukhov's world to the family world of the Rostovs, there are always certain limits of viewpoint and manner circumscribing the fiction and certain moralistic limitations or norms. In *War and Peace* the historical motivation imposes its own fatalism upon the lives of historical and fictional characters alike. Just as Napoleon* is shown to be no more than a puppet of dynamic processes over which he can exert no real power, so Prince Andrey Bolkonsky can be seen to be predestined to act the role of doomed hero. There is perhaps a similar element of predestination about the evolution of the delightful Natasha Rostov into the matronly figure of the first epilogue. But the greatness of the fiction lies not in such fatalism, nor in the theory of history that turns its final pages (of the second epilogue) into a rather bullying tract; it lies in the assertion of the vital and positive ideas permeating the characters' lives. The role of the family, for instance, as exemplified by the Rostovs, is one that suggests stability, shared love and an instinctive hostility to all that threatens such an ethos, meaning chiefly the French invaders. Similarly, it is a search for a positive meaning in life that inspires Andrey Bolkonsky to replace his Napoleonic ideal by a faith in the boundlessness of love and equate such love with a divine force, or makes Pierre Bezukhov seek in freemasonry and numerology an answer to life's purpose that is finally revealed to him, in a simple equation of God with life, by the peasant Platon Karatayev. The epic size of *War and Peace* is therefore assessable both in terms of its enormous range of characters, its variety of locales and its time-span, and in terms of the profundity of the religious and philosophical ideas which concern the central characters.

Anna Karenina, though less ambitious in its scope, is no less daring as a novel in its portrayal of Anna herself – one of the most remarkable female characterizations ever achieved by a male author – and in its exploration of the manifold pressures in Russian society of the 1870s. A novel about marriage, female emancipation, the contrast between urban and rural life, between reason and faith, between suicide and religious purpose, *Anna Karenina* presupposes that there are certain norms, as rigid perhaps after their fashion as the railway lines which bring Anna into the fiction at the beginning and kill her at the end (of part VII), and these norms point the way, so Tolstoy seems to be saying, either to personal fulfilment or to futility and suicide. Though a tragic mechanism may perhaps determine Anna's decision to leave her husband and son and give herself to Vronsky, the processes are so gradual and so subtle that her vitality seems always to outpace them. The extinguishing of the vital candle of her life is an act of immolation that indicts all the pretensions, hypocrisies and falsehoods of the society to which she has fallen victim. In compensation for her tragedy the parallel story of Konstantin Levin's marriage to Kitty and final discovery of an intuitive law of right and wrong known only to the peasantry is magnificent in its own right, but it scarcely prevails in its optimistic message against the darkness that finally engulfs Anna herself.

Tolstoy's realism is of a controlled richness in its detail, with emphasis always upon appearance and action, but at its heart is an awareness of both the physicality of experience, the sense, in short, that his characters inhabit bodies, and of the rational processes by which they may discover for themselves new truths and beliefs. However seriously he may have taken himself (and his work is not noteworthy for its humour), he was by nature the least pompous of men, and the gleam which shines from his eyes in so many of his portraits bespeaks a man who enjoyed life's peculiarities while recognizing its sinfulness and its grandeur.

Richard Freeborn

Other works (available in The World's Classics): *Twenty-Three Tales; What Then Must We Do?; On Life and Essays on Religion: Recollections and Essays; Tales of Army Life; The Kingdom of God and Peace Essays; The Snow Storm and Other Stories;* etc. A selection of his

letters translated by R.F. Christian has recently been published in two volumes (London, 1978). About Tolstoy: the two-volume biography by A. Maude, *The Life of Tolstoy* (1930), has been largely superseded by E.J. Simmons, *Leo Tolstoy* (1960), and H. Troyat, *Tolstoy* (1968). Recent critical works on Tolstoy (in alphabetical order) include an excellent work by J. Bayley, *Tolstoy and the Novel* (1966); the famous study of Tolstoy's theory of history by I. Berlin, *The Hedgehog and the Fox* (1953); T.G.S. Cain, *Tolstoy* (1977); R.F. Christian's 'critical introduction' to Tolstoy's work, *Tolstoy* (1969); a chapter devoted to *War and Peace* in R. Freeborn, *The Rise of the Russian Novel* (1973); E.B. Greenwood, *Tolstoy: The Comprehensive Vision* (1975); F.R. Leavis, *Anna Karenina and Other Essays* (1967); G.W. Spence's study of the dualism in Tolstoy's thought, *Tolstoy the Ascetic* (1967); E. Stenbock-Fermor's valuable, if eccentric, *The Architecture of 'Anna Karenina'* (1975); and E. Wasiolek's opinionated, but stimulating, *Tolstoy's Major Fiction* (1978). Two recent collections of critical essays on Tolstoy should also be mentioned: *Leo Tolstoy: A Critical Anthology*, ed. H. Gifford; and *New Essays on Tolstoy*, ed. M. Jones.

TÖNNIES, Ferdinand: see TOENNIES, Ferdinand

455
TOULOUSE-LAUTREC, Henri de 1864–1901

French artist

Born near Albi in the south-west of France into one of the most aristocratic of families, Toulouse-Lautrec's full physical growth was retarded as a result of injuries to his legs. He remained permanently self-conscious with regard to his handicap until his death from alcoholism in 1901.

His artistic career started formally in Paris, first at the studio of Bonnat and then at that of Cormon where he met Émil Bernard, Vincent Van Gogh* and Louis Anquetin with whom he remained on friendly terms for many years, painting their portraits and corresponding when he or they left Paris.

Lautrec's work developed starting with influence from Bastien Lepage, then from the Impressionism of Pissarro*, finally to his own personal style which took its main impetus from subtle and direct line drawing. This he, at times, adapted for the purposes of lithography. His subject matter remained almost entirely that of people.

In 1884 Lautrec set up his studio in Montmartre where he spent hours in cafés and cabarets drawing the people who worked there and the patrons who gave

628 / TOUSSAINT-LOUVERTURE, FRANÇOIS DOMINIQUE

them their living. At first he drew mostly those who came to Aristide Bruant's café cabaret, Le Mirliton, opened in 1885. Bruant wrote and sang many of the ballads performed at Le Mirliton himself. Before 1885 when he worked in a more expensive quarter of Paris his songs were light-hearted, at times amusing. Montmartre had the effect of providing more tragic themes. It was these later ballads, based on the lives of the people in the locale of Le Mirliton – prostitutes, pimps, dancers, actresses the homeless, forlorn or drunken – that provided Lautrec with subjects. Many of his paintings of the middle and late 1880s have titles taken from Bruant's ballads. *At Montrouge, Rosa la Rouge*, a single portrait of a girl of 1888, is a case in point.

It was at this time that Lautrec also adopted something of Degas's* style and subject matter, painting ballet girls with a light directional brush-stroke and achieving some acclaim for the work he exhibited. The brushwork then became less even and more open in handling and line began to separate itself from and dominate the colour areas. These portraits he carried out quickly but only after knowing and observing the person well. Generally he worked from memory and only rarely for commissions over which he was immensely conscientious, asking the sitter to pose dozens of times.

By the 1890s much of Lautrec's effort was directed toward lithography, in particular poster design. The most famous posters of this era must be those of La Goulu, can-can dancer at the Moulin Rouge.

In 1896 Lautrec painted and made lithographs entitled *Alone*. A prostitute is sympathetically portrayed resting on a bed. Other such pictures show moments of intimacy, of women combing their hair, tightening their corsets or waiting in a salon for customers.

Shortly before his death whilst spending the summer as usual in Bordeaux, Lautrec became enchanted by opera as well as operettas and some of his last works are evocations of the mood of moments from *Messaline* or *La Belle Hélène*.

Lautrec's very early drawings as a child show a liking for caricature. Later in life this preference takes the form of feeling for character so that the essential elements not only of an individual's personal appearance, but also the objects that suggest his or her personal tastes and role or profession in life are included.

Often Lautrec's view is cynical, but frequently it is also compassionate as he surveys the difficulties with which the most vulnerable in Parisian society had to cope.

Many later artists, such as those of the German and Belgian Expressionist movement, owed as much to Lautrec as to Van Gogh. One can see La Goulu in Felicien Rops's skeletal women; fat clients of the brothel houses more sharply criticized by George Grosz in scenes of corruption in Berlin. The decadence of the 'Gay Nineties' then becomes the despair of the early

twenties and Lautrec's cynicism the paramount attitude.

Pat Turner

See: Jean Adhémar, *Henri de Toulouse-Lautrec: Complete Lithographs and Drypoints* (1965); Eduouard Julien, *The Posters of Toulouse-Lautrec* (1966); M.G. Dortu and J.A. Méric, *Toulouse-Lautrec: The Complete Painting* (1981). See also: Henri Perruchot, *Toulouse-Lautrec: A Definitive Biography* (trans. 1969); André Fermigier, *Toulouse-Lautrec* (trans. 1969); and Douglas Cooper, *Henri de Toulouse-Lautrec* (1981).

456

TOUSSAINT-LOUVERTURE, François Dominique 1746–1803

Haitian revolutionary

When the independent black republic of Haiti was declared on the last day of 1803, Toussaint-Louverture was dead. Yet it was he who had led the black slaves into rebellion, through a ten-year war and finally to the threshold of independence.

Toussaint was born in 1746, son of a chief from Dahomey who had been brought in chains to the French island colony of Sainte Domingue to become a slave on its sugar plantations. The 42,000 whites of the colony (towards the end of the eighteenth century) deeply feared their 500,000 black slaves and maintained their domination with hideous cruelty. The mulattos, people of mixed race, many of whom were free, occupied an intermediate position in a society whose classes were racially defined.

The French Revolution of 1789 obviously had echoes in the rich sugar colony of Sainte Domingue. The talk of liberty and equality reached the educated mulattos, and fuelled the hatred and resentment of a black population which had already fruitlessly rebelled several times. It was the mulattos who rose first, however under Oge. They were quickly crushed; yet two years later, the French government granted the mulattos citizenship. This change of heart was not the result of the agitation of the liberal Amis des Noirs in Paris, but of French fears that the mulattos would join the rebellious blacks, who in 1791 had risen under the Jamaican Boukman. In the struggle that followed neither whites nor blacks gave any quarter, as the bitterness of centuries erupted.

Toussaint at this time was coachman on the Breda plantation. He had learned to read and write, and his quiet disposition had earned him a privileged position in the house. He did not join the rebellion immediately, taking his master's family to safety before he entered the ragged and undisciplined liberation army of the slaves.

He began to organize it into an efficient guerrilla army; his skill and diplomacy quickly won him a position of command. Together with commander-in-chief Jean François, it was he who negotiated with three French commissioners late in 1791. Nothing came of their discussions, for the colonists would not yield and the concessions made to the mulattos had only confirmed Toussaint in his most central conviction – that the abolition of slavery was not negotiable. Yet this determination was coupled with an unshaken faith in revolutionary France. Toussaint was a Jacobin, a child of the Declaration of Human Rights. For him, France was still the home of liberty and equality. Further, he believed that the island's economic future would depend on a continuing association with France. It is this that explains Toussaint's reluctance to seek independence, and why he continued to negotiate with the representatives of France. It explains, too, why this most astute of political leaders allowed himself to be taken to France to die.

Yet Toussaint was not blind to the realities of world politics. He continued the people's war against the colonists; when, in 1792, French troops came to suppress the rising, Toussaint and his army joined the Spaniards in the other half of the divided island. He was never deluded into believing that any colonial power had black interests at heart; he knew that Spanish, French or British support stemmed only from their desire to enlist his aid in their battle for control of the sugar-rich Caribbean.

In 1794 France approved the abolition of slavery and Toussaint returned to the colony; his army participated in the suppression of the white planters. In return, the French named him assistant governor and his generals were appointed full generals in the French army. But their objective, as Toussaint knew, was to use him to hold back restless mulattos in curious alliance with the white planters. As always, Toussaint trod the thin line between internal and external pressures. In France, the shifts of power were reflected in changing attitudes towards slavery and towards the planters in the colony. The fall of Robespierre, for example, brought a counter-revolution in France whose leaders demanded the restoration of slavery and the defeat of the black army. Internally, Toussaint's army barely contained the rivalries of ambitious generals and the class conflict between mulattos and blacks. Maintaining the balance became an increasingly difficult manoeuvre, and required a spreading network of informants and spies.

Toussaint's relationship with the new French commissioner, Sonthonax, was ambivalent. The Frenchman was committed to colonial independence, and envisaged a black republic with himself at its head. Toussaint stood in his way, and he began to plot against him. The General of the Slaves rapidly despatched him back to Paris, sending two of his children at the same time as a gesture of goodwill. Sonthonax, back in Paris, reported Toussaint's growing power on the island, and his replacement was given a clear brief to undermine the influence of 'this gilded African'.

Their assessment of Toussaint's unchallenged leadership of Sainte Domingue at this time was correct. The British had been defeated in their bid for control, and Toussaint had marked his triumph with a march across the whole island. The mulatto rebellion under Rigaud had also been defeated and the last French commissioner had been ignominiously repatriated. And despite Toussaint's resistance to the idea of independence, he had begun direct negotiations with both the USA and Britain.

In 1801, Toussaint began to face the problems of reconstruction. He refused to break up the old estates into small plots, and imposed a strict but scrupulously fair labour discipline. Thus by 1802 agricultural production had reached two-thirds of its pre-1791 level. A new simplified tax system cut bureaucracy to a minimum, and the new administration sent blacks and mulattos to France to be educated. Yet in France itself, Napoleon* had made clear his commitment to the restoration of slavery. And on the island, the younger generals expressed growing frustration with Toussaint's apparent willingness to give whites powerful positions in the bureaucracy, and with his new constitution, which accepted continuing colonial status. In December 1801, 20,000 French troops set out to crush Toussaint and restore slavery. Toussaint himself ruthlessly silenced his own detractors, yet continued to negotiate with Napoleon. He would realize his error too late. For the moment, however, he displayed again the old military skill; the hostile terrain, Toussaint's scorched earth policy, and the bravery of the commanders of the siege at Crête-à-Pierrot, who held out for five months, brought the French to the brink of defeat. At this point, Toussaint offered peace terms to Napoleon, which the French commander Leclerc was quick to exploit. One by one, Leclerc persuaded the black generals to lay down their arms, and finally convinced Toussaint that peace would come – and negotiation – if he would only retire. He had little time to spend on his farm, however, before he was arrested, transported to France, and imprisoned at Fort-de-Joux, in the Jura mountains. Inadequately fed, humiliated and alone, Toussaint died there on 7 April 1803.

In Haiti itself, the younger generals went beyond the limits set by Toussaint. His growing remoteness from the base of his army, his willingness to surround himself with white and mulatto advisers and to conciliate Napoleon, had ultimately undermined his power over his own people. By the end of 1803, Haiti was an independent black state where the colony of Sainte Domingue had once been.

Toussaint-Louverture led the first revolution on the Latin American continent, and he led it with vision and skill. At the core of his beliefs lay the immovable conviction that no man must ever be enslaved again. His refusal to assume total independence was rooted both in his perception of France as the highest representative of progressive thinking in his age, and in the knowledge that for three centuries France had taken the fruit of Haiti's land and its labour – without which Haiti could not survive or progress. It was a lesson that the rising revolutionary leaders of Latin America would have to learn again many times. And on the island he liberated, Haiti, the human freedom he fought and died for has yet to be won.

Mike Gonzalez

See: R. Korngold, *Citizen Toussaint* (1939); Paul Foot, 'Toussaint Louverture' (cassette, 1979); C.L.R. James, *The Black Jacobins* (1980); Wanda Parkinson, *This Gilded African* (1980).

457

TRELAWNY, Edward John 1792–1881

British writer

'Trelawny's contribution to the Romantic Revolution is Trelawny.' Or, put another way, his contribution to nineteenth-century culture was his own life. The poorly educated son of an old and respected Cornish family, Trelawny was, during his eighty-nine years, a sailor, adventurer, businessman, and dabbler in politics; he was also a womanizer. But, more important than any of this, Trelawny was, for a few brief months, a close acquaintance of Byron* and Shelley*, the two greatest poets of his day.

Trelawny's father, a lieutenant-colonel in the army, had little affection for his son, placing him in the navy at the age of thirteen. Discharged in 1812, he married for the first time a year later, but the marriage ended in divorce in 1819. With a modest private income, Trelawny toured Europe, and although only semi-literate, took an increasing interest in contemporary poetry, especially the work of Byron and Shelley, whose radical attitudes appealed to his own atheist and republican tendencies. In 1822, on the pretext of a friendship with a cousin of Shelley, Trelawny arrived in Pisa, where the poets had gathered around them a circle of writers and intellectuals. He was disappointed with Byron, whom he found a singularly unromantic figure, but fascinated by the charismatic Shelley, in whom he saw a reflection of himself. Six months later he helped cremate Shelley's body on the beach near Viareggio, after he and a companion had drowned in a boat designed by – Trelawny.

The following year Trelawny accompanied Byron on his expedition to the Greek War of Independence. The poet died of a chill in 1824, by which time Trelawny had become involved with the revolutionary leader Odysseus Androutzos, marrying his thirteen-year-old half-sister Tesitza, by whom he had a daughter, Zella. Surviving an assassination attempt in 1825, Trelawny fled Greece, spending two years in the Ionian islands, and returning to England in 1828. From there he sailed to Florence, where Walter Savage Landor* persuaded him to write an autobiography. The result was *Adventures of a Younger Son* (1831). Trelawny's description of his youth, at home and in the navy, is extremely vivid, although he is a veritable Munchausen in his capacity for expanding the truth. Implausible as autobiography, it is nevertheless an engrossing story, and a remarkable piece of literary eccentricity. Each chapter is prefaced by a quotation from Byron, Shelley or Keats*, and in this way Trelawny sought to place his book firmly in the Romantic tradition. To Mary Shelley* he wrote that his 'first three volumes are principally adapted to sailors'. There is certainly a somewhat over-assertive masculinity in the tone of the *Adventures*, and Trelawny would seem to have taken to heart Shelley's maxim, 'Man, who man would be,/Must rule the empire of himself.'

In 1833 Trelawny sailed for America where, amongst other things, he attempted to swim the rapids below Niagara. In 1839 he eloped with Augusta Goring; she and Trelawny married two years later, following her divorce. They parted in 1858, and from 1869 until his death, Trelawny lived with a Miss Taylor whom he described as his 'niece'.

In 1858 Trelawny published a volume entitled *Recollections of the Last Days of Byron and Shelley*, a collection of letters and reminiscences dealing with his months in Italy and Greece with the two poets. Less fanciful than his *Adventures*, the *Recollections* are still untrustworthy, particularly where details of Byron's last days are concerned. Twenty years later Trelawny revised and enlarged the book, re-titling it *Records of Shelley, Byron and the Author*. This is a significant alteration, since Trelawny's own personality lies at the heart of everything he wrote. By perpetuating myths concerning his two friends, and creating others, he fuelled his own image of himself as the personification of their Romantic ideals. After his death in 1881, Trelawny's body was cremated, and the ashes buried next to those of Shelley, in a grave he had bought for himself over half a century earlier. This was his final act of homage to the writer whose reputation he helped to build, and as whose friend he is remembered today.

Paul Nicholls

See: H. Buxton Forman, *Letters of Edward John Trelawny* (1910); H.J.Massingham, *The Friend of Shelley* (1930); Ann Hill, *Trelawny's Family Background and Naval Career* (Keats-Shelley Journal, 1956).

458

TROELTSCH, Ernst 1865–1923

German systematic theologian and philosopher

Troeltsch was educated at the University of Göttingen, where he was a pupil of Albrecht Ritschl* and Paul Anton de Lagarde (1827–91), philologist, religious thinker and Pangermanic theoretician. Troeltsch was a lecturer at Göttingen from 1891–2 and was promoted *ausserordentlicher* professor at Bonn in 1892; he was called to Heidelberg in 1894, and in 1908 his appointment to a theology chair at Berlin was blocked by the theological faculty there, which was opposed to his view of the Christian religion. But in 1914 he was successfully appointed to a philosophy chair at Berlin, and this move from one faculty to another has always been regarded as significantly symbolic of a profound change in his intellectual stance. He remained in the philosophical faculty in Berlin until his death in 1923.

Troeltsch's name has always been closely linked with the so-called *Religionsgeschichtlicheschule* of German theologians, whose members included Hermann Gunkel (1862–1932), Wilhelm Heitmüller (1869–1925), H. Gressmann (1877–1927) and Wilhelm Bousset (1865–1920). Troeltsch is widely regarded as being both the leader and the most distinguished member of the school, many of whose members, like Troeltsch himself, had been pupils of Ritschl, and of whose views on Christianity it became sharply critical. In particular, they objected to the way in which Ritschl (whose theological standpoint has been described as 'bibliocentric', 'pistobasic' and 'christocentric') had directed Christianity into impossibly narrow doctrinal channels, and had treated it as though it were an absolutely unique phenomenon, uninfluenced in its genesis by the contemporary thought-world of antiquity in which it first saw the light of day. Accordingly, members of the school did research into those elements common to Christianity on the one hand and Judaism, Hellenistic philosophy and mystery-religions and even Babylonian thought-systems on the other. Possibly one of the best-known publications from within the school was Bousset's *Kurios Christos* (*Christ the Lord*) in which he claimed that the title 'Lord' applied to Christ had strong parallels in the Greek mystery-religions prior to and contemporaneous with primitive Christianity. Others claimed that Baptism and the Eucharist possessed significant non-Jewish parallels.

It is against the background of the doctrines of this 'History of Religions' school that Troeltsch's leading ideas should be understood, with special reference to his insistence that Christianity must be located and studied within the general *milieu* of the history of religion, culture, ideas and philosophy. Troeltsch derived from his mentor, the German philosopher of history Wilhelm Dilthey*, the concept of 're-experiencing'

(*nacherleben*): we must attempt to 'relive' history by sympathetically entering into the events, movements and experience of the past. But to do so we must utilize certain techniques or laws. One of these is criticism, which had been developed throughout the nineteenth century: but such criticism can furnish at the best probability, or moral certainty; the assertion that such-and-such events really happened (e.g., the events recorded in the Gospel narratives) could never attain to the certainty or necessity we find in scientific or mathematical propositions. Another is analogy, which leads us to presuppose that the events of the past are roughly similar to those of the present, and that the experience of past men was not altogether different from human experience today; and research demonstrates that notions and doctrines claimed by Christianity find their analogous counterparts in the non-Christian religions. One significant casualty of the employment of the principle of analogy is miracle in the New Testament sense, for these are not commonly encountered in contemporary experience. Other principles are those of correlation and relativity: events in history must be capable of being correlated with all other events; the implication of this is that *all* events without exception are qualitatively the same, that they interact intelligibly with each other, and that however startling or distinctive an event, or series of events, may appear, it may not be regarded as miraculous or as transcending the causal nexus of all reality, which comprehends the sphere of history just as completely as it does the spheres of religion or art or science or politics. If these rules or principles are adhered to consistently, history as a whole becomes in principle intelligible.

Accordingly, Christianity is seen by Troeltsch as one distinctive historical phenomenon among others, as one distinctive religion among others: but it cannot be said to possess *absoluteness* over the others. According to the laws or principles outlined above, Christianity cannot be regarded as founded upon miraculous or unparalleled events, or upon the alleged irruption of God into the natural and historical orders. Christianity is to be regarded *as one expression amongst others* of what Troeltsch, against his background in philosophical idealism from Kant through Schleiermacher* to Dilthey, called man's 'religious a priori'; man is *homo religiosus*, with an inbuilt predisposition or taste for or affinity with the holy or the sacred, which underlies and calls into being *all religions* as such. While this appears to deprive Christianity of absoluteness, it does not at all mean that Christianity does not contain a distinctively great truth, or that it is not to be taken seriously, or that there is no obligation upon man to express his devotion within Christian worship. Truth is many-faceted and Christianity is one facet among others. There occurs in Troeltsch's writings a most significant phrase, 'for us'. Christianity is the true religion 'for us'; Christianity really is the revelation of God 'for us', and really is God's salvation and redemption 'for us'. By 'us' Troeltsch is expressing his strong Europeanism: the researches of the school to which he belonged had revealed that Christianity is an amalgam of Judaism, Graeco-Roman philosophy and law, Stoic ethics and much else besides; Christianity is inalienably and essentially European (and, therefore, also American). (It is interesting to recall that in the years prior to the First World War Troeltsch had a flirtation with his old teacher Paul de Lagarde's programme for an exclusively Germanic and somewhat anti-Semitic type of Christianity for the German-speaking peoples.) European *homo religiosus* then has no option but to be religious in a Christian sense. It is very possible that here Troeltsch retained the view of Ritschl, who had found it impossible to conceive of the occurrence of Christianity apart from and outside of the cultural ethos and the educational and social institutions of Europe. Be that as it may, all of this is emphatically not to deny that there may be other racial or ethnic or cultural groups, each with its own distinctive history, set of ideas and cultural predispositions, which apprehend the Holy, achieve redemption, and attain to authenticity of life in ways which are quite different from those prevailing within the Christianity of the West.

If so, the implications for, say, the missionary endeavours of the church are clear: there can be for Troeltsch no question of Christianity aiming at the 'conversion of the heathen'; rather, there can only be the mutual exchange of information and ideas, with the aim of identifying common doctrines, areas of co-operation and the like. And, indeed, Troeltsch presided over a special liberal missionary society whose policy was the interpretation of the great world religions. So far as the distinctive history of Christianity is concerned Troeltsch's main contribution is his book *The Social Teachings of the Christian Churches*, in which he investigated the social matrix of ecclesiastical doctrines: while agreeing with, say, Marx* that social conditions and movements decisively influence the formation of such doctrines, he agrees with Max Weber against Marx that such conditions do not create the doctrines; indeed, as Weber argued in *The Protestant Ethic and the Spirit of Capitalism*, occasionally religious doctrinal systems (e.g. Calvinism) themselves heavily influence social systems and structures (e.g. capitalism). And Troeltsch's sociological distinction between types of religious institutions (e.g. the 'church-type' as contrasted with the 'sect-type') continues to be interestingly debated in sociological and theological circles. Of continuing interest is Troeltsch's argument that the sixteenth-century Reformation did *not* bring the medieval era to an end; the Middle Ages were really ended by the *Aufklärung* of the seventeenth and eighteenth centuries.

It was perhaps inevitable that the neo-orthodox protestant revolution (which may be said to have begun four years before Troeltsch's death by the publication of Karl Barth's *Römerbrief* in 1919) was sharply critical of the relativism and historicism explicit in Troeltsch's teachings. Indeed, it is arguable that the affirmation of the neo-orthodox protestant theologians that at the heart of Christianity is an absolute, infallible, necessary, complete and exclusive revelation of God in Christ (the *locus classicus* of the affirmation is Barth's paper 'The Christian Understanding of Revelation' in *Against the Stream: Shorter Post-War Writings 1946–52*, trans. 1954) was in the first place directed against the position maintained so strenuously by Troeltsch and his colleagues. In the inter-war period, when Barthian theologians relentlessly attacked so-called nineteenth-century 'liberal theology', allegedly beginning with Schleiermacher and ending with the *Religionsgeschichtlicheschule*, Troeltsch and his colleagues were singled out for extremely harsh treatment. Consequently, during the second, third and fourth decades of this century, the names of Troeltsch and his colleagues were assigned to undeserved oblivion. But the heyday of neo-orthodoxy is over, partly at least because it ignored the issue of the relation of Christianity to the great world religions, an issue so thoroughly and scientifically investigated by Troeltsch. And today, in a rapidly shrinking world where contact and communication between ethnic groups with widely differing religious and cultural traditions are not merely possible but unavoidable, the issue simply cannot be ignored. Consequently, in the last decade or so there has occurred a remarkable resurgence of interest in the work of Troeltsch, and his texts and theories are once more being thoroughly and seriously examined.

James Richmond

Translated works include: *Writings on Theology and Religion*, trans. and ed. Robert Morgan and Michael Pye (1977); *Christian Thought: Its History and Application*, ed. and introduced by Baron F. von Hügel (1957); *Protestantism and Progress*, trans. W. Montgomery (1912); *The Absoluteness of Christianity and the History of Religions*, trans. David Reid (1972); *The Social Teaching of the Christian Churches*, trans. Olive Wyon (1960). See: *Ernst Troeltsch and the Future of Theology*, ed. John P. Clayton (1976). See also: John Macquarrie, *Twentieth-Century Religious Thought* (1963); Paul Tillich, *Perspectives on 19th and 20th Century Theology* (1967); James C. Livingston, *Modern Christian Thought* (1971).

459
TROLLOPE, Anthony 1815–82

British novelist

All authors may take courage from the extraordinary fortunes of Anthony Trollope, who enjoys arguably even greater respect a century after his death than ever he did at the height of his Victorian success. His eminence is the more remarkable as resulting from a critical recovery after nearly half a century of contemptuous neglect, exacerbated at the outset by the publication, a year after his death, of his extremely blunt and straightforward *Autobiography* (1883), a plain statement of his aims and achievements as a man of letters and a professional employee of the Civil Service. Such frankness on the part of an artist was intolerable to an age which cherished artifice and performance: indeed, it was scarcely admissible that Trollope was an artist at all. His novels became swiftly relegated to the ranks of those relished rather guiltily by readers in search of a comfortable nostalgia. A work like *Framley Parsonage* (1861), fourth in the famous 'Barchester' series, was enjoyed almost solely for its superb characterization and neatly arranged plot, while its profounder and more abstract issues, dramatized to such ironic effect in the marital manoeuvres of Lucy Robarts, Griselda Grantly and Miss Dunstable, were totally ignored.

Writing was an inalienable part of the Trollope family heritage. Anthony's elder brother Tom produced a long and turgid set of works on Italian subjects and their father, a hopelessly unsuccessful barrister, made several attempts as a historian. The miserable childhood of the Trollope children, reared in an atmosphere of shabby gentility and feckless Micawberish optimism, was somewhat lightened by their indomitable mother, Frances, who gained considerable fame as a novelist dealing with social questions of the day and produced, after an unsuccessful attempt to carry culture to Cincinnati, the amusing and highly readable *Domestic Manners of the Americans* (1832).

Trollope was educated at Harrow and Winchester, and was eventually pushed into a Post Office clerkship at the age of nineteen. His careful cultivation of a bluff, even boorish exterior manner seems to have been designed to mask the acute sensitivity developed in him during his unhappy adolescence, and we can find traces of such characteristics in the awkward, gangling protagonists of certain of the novels. He appears to have put much of himself, for example, into Johnny Eames, of *The Small House at Allington* (1864), and into Josiah Crawley, the gloomy curate hero of *The Last Chronicle of Barset* (1867).

The turn of his fortunes occurred in 1841 when he was transferred to Ireland to supervise postal operations in the central district. Here he was able to show a truly Victorian capacity for hard work and initiative, by which he soon won the respect of his superiors and sufficient funds to enable him to marry Rose Heseltine, the daughter of a Rotherham bank manager. He is almost exceptional among nineteenth-century novelists in having made a happy and successful marriage.

Ireland, its people and its problems offered him the material for his first and last novels, *The Macdermots of Ballycloran* (1847) and *The Landleaguers*, left unfinished at his death, and provided subject matter elsewhere in his work. He returned to England to maintain the two careers in tandem throughout the 1850s and 1860s, fuelling each with the prodigious physical and mental energy which allowed him to indulge his other consuming enthusiasm, hunting. Thus his fiction is permeated throughout with an exactness of topographical detail acquired from journeyings across England on Post Office business, and several of his finest stretches of writing, notably in *Phineas Redux* (1874), *The Eustace Diamonds* (1873) and *The American Senator* (1877), are concerned with scenes in the hunting field.

His private and professional life was never marked by any especially dramatic events. As a thoroughly dependable official, despite a certain tendency to quarrelsomeness wherever he felt he was being overborne by bureaucracy, he was sent to Egypt, the Caribbean and the Pacific on postal assignments, and wrote an interesting account of post-Civil War America after visits to the principal eastern cities. It was on his last voyage to New York that he was seen by Henry James*, whose account of the man and his work in *Partial Portraits* is one of the best of contemporary treatments. Trollope had a wide and loyal circle of friends, including George Eliot*, Browning* and the popular journalist George Augustus Sala, and died in the guise of a respected, if distinctly conservative, mainstay of the circulating library three-decker novel readership.

Few writers have been more honest in their assessments of personal achievement and few have done themselves a greater disservice by being so. Only during the last thirty years has the literary public recovered sufficiently from being told by Trollope himself that he made £68,939 17s 5d from his novels and that it is not necessary to wait for inspiration before writing, and distanced itself enough from the Victorian era for us to have begun a wholesale and much-needed reappraisal of his work. Such a revaluation has brought him the attention of committed scholarship and placed him very high indeed among the English novelists of his age. Instead of viewing him as a mildly entertaining chronicler of clerical indiscretions in an English country town, we have been taught to see him as the quietly complex and admirably tolerant analyst of the strains imposed upon quintessentially normal people and societies by the conventions they accept. He is never, in any of his books, hysterical, dogmatic or pompous, and it is by virtue of what Henry James called his 'complete apprehension of the usual' that he so frequently triumphs.

His transcendent humanity prompts him to invoke our compassion for even the most transparently duplicit of his characters: the ironic solution which drives us to sympathize with Ferdinand Lopez, in *The Prime Minister* (1876), with the impossible Lizzie Eustace in *The Eustace Diamonds*, with the unregenerate *fin-de-ligne* Sowerby of *Framley Parsonage*, or with gold-digging Arabella Trefoil as she prepares to marry Mounser Green in *The American Senator*, is always wholly acceptable. By the same method, other characters are made antipathetic by their unscrupulous cultivation of social orthodoxy: few are more chilling than the glacially correct and heartless Griselda Grantly of the Barchester novels or the monomaniacal Mr Kennedy in *Phineas Redux*, an offshoot of that profounder study of marital obsession, Louis Trevelyan in *He Knew He Was Right* (1869).

Pessimism, neurosis and the nightmare of social disgrace are always splendidly handled by the mature Trollope. His most perceptive treatment of these themes appears in *The Last Chronicle of Barset* and *The Way We Live Now* (1875). The first of these is, despite formal imperfections owing to an otiose sub-plot, an acknowledged masterpiece, in which the comic creations of the earlier Barchester novels are fleshed out with an impressively tragic dignity. The Lear-like figure of Josiah Crawley, learning survival through rejection and adversity, is cleverly opposed by the almost demonically self-destructive Mrs Proudie, the circumstances leading to whose death give the event a convincing pathos rarely equalled elsewhere in Victorian fiction. The second, the most ambitious work Trollope ever attempted, a mercilessly satirical indictment of debased values in the society of the 1870s, creates a comparable balance to the earlier book in counterpointing the buccaneering financier Melmotte with the pillar of antique squirearchical virtue Roger Carbury.

Trollope does not wholly underwrite Carbury's standpoint and, as if in acknowledgment that his exalted moral standards are too lofty for most of us, makes the heroine Hetta reject him in favour of the far more doubtful but ultimately more full-blooded Paul Montague. There is no doubt, however, that Roger Carbury speaks for much of what Trollope admired, and a succession of the novels creates for us a consistent view of the English gentleman culminating in the fascinating figure of Plantagenet Palliser, whose appearances with his wife Glencora serve to link together a series of six books beginning with *Can You Forgive Her?* (1864) and concluding with *The Duke's Children* (1880) some sixteen years later.

Just as the Barchester series dealt in detail with the manners and trials of rural clergy and landowners, so the Palliser novels, with an equally sharp scrutiny, approach the world of politics and government. Though there is no evidence to suggest that Trollope

planned either set through from start to finish, it is noteworthy that each is governed by the aura of a moral human presence – in the first case, that of Septimus Harding, hero of *The Warden* (1855), whose death in *The Last Chronicle of Barset* seems to ordain the sense of finality in the book rather than be ordained by it; in the second, those of Plantagenet and Glencora. The latter, by a master-stroke, is made to die before *The Duke's Children* opens, and the power of her often anarchic influence is felt through the behaviour of her children.

As a stylist Trollope is among the plainest of Victorian writers. His handling of dialogue has been admired to the point of declaring it the best among nineteenth-century novelists and his comprehensive and refreshingly unsentimental treatment of female characters contrasts favourably with most of the other male fiction writers of the age. In his early work the influence of Thackeray* can be felt too heavily, especially in the tiresome invocations to the reader in novels such as *Barchester Towers* (1857) and *The Three Clerks* (1858), and several of his later novels, such as *Kept In the Dark* (1882) and *The Fixed Period* (1882), show how fallacious was his reliance on a daily quota of written words. He is nearly always, however, a master of plotting, a talent displayed at its best in *The Eustace Diamonds* (though the structure has also been criticized for relying too heavily on sensationalism), the exuberantly comic *Ayala's Angel* (1881) and the nowadays critically lauded *Mr Scarborough's Family* (1883).

Unlike Dickens*, Hardy* and George Eliot*, Trollope seldom attempts to write within a consciously historical perspective, though, like each of them, he attempted a historical romance and, as in each case, it is not considered the equal of his other books. Whereas works such as *Great Expectations*, *Middlemarch* and *The Mayor of Casterbridge* rely for their effect on our awareness of the tensions between a recently vanished world and our vivid memories of its existence, novels such as *Orley Farm* (1862), *Phineas Finn* (1869) and *John Caldigate* (1879) rely on our sense of them as taking place within the ordinary world of the mid-Victorian reader. It was Trollope's achievement to have dissected that world within its own frame of reference, in a manner often severe but invariably humane. Recognition of this achievement has been belated but wholly sincere. Yet perhaps the best tribute ever paid to him by another writer was in the form of a note written by Tolstoy* during the composition of *Anna Karenina*, with its many Trollopian features: 'Trollope kills me, kills me with his excellence!'

Jonathan Keates

See: Michael Sadleir, *Trollope: A Commentary* (1928, rev. 1945); A.O.J. Cockshut, *Anthony Trollope: A Critical Study* (1955); P.D. Edwards, *Anthony Trollope* (1968); *Trollope: The Critical Heritage*, ed. Donald

Smalley (1969); R.H. Super, *Trollope and the Post Office* (1981).

460

TURGENEV, Ivan Sergeyevich 1818–83

Russian writer

Born in Oryol, he was brought up on his mother's estate of Spasskoye-Lutovinovo. His parents were cultured members of the Russian nobility, but his mother was the richer and more domineering; his charming and accomplished father remained aloof from the family commitments (as Turgenev's portrayal of him in *First Love, Pervaya lyubov'*, (1860) demonstrates so brilliantly). The growing boy received frequent beatings at his mother's hands and a generally tyrannical atmosphere in domestic affairs contrasted with a Frenchified, cultured taste in books and pretensions to elegance which prevailed at Spasskoye. The young Turgenev early realized the disparity between his privileged status and the servile conditon of the peasantry. He was later to swear what he called 'a Hannibal's oath' against serfdom. Educated by ineffectual tutors, he was to grow into a giant of a man, both physically and intellectually, and was to attend the Universities of Moscow and St Petersburg before, in 1838, aged twenty, he was to go abroad to complete his education at the University of Berlin. In Germany he first formulated his ideas on the need for Russia to learn from the West and grew to realize how important and precious was his own generation of young Russians who were to comprise the first generation of the Russian intelligentsia. When he returned to his homeland in 1841 he made attempts to gain a university chair and worked for a time in government service, but in 1843 his future seemed to be decided for him through the publication of a long poem *Parasha* which met with critical success and through his meeting with the famous singer Pauline Viardot. After his fashion he was to remain devoted both to Pauline Viardot and to literature for the rest of his life, though he never became completely wedded to either.

In the mid-1840s, to a great extent under the influence of V.G. Belinsky, the critic, he turned from imitative poetry to the writing of prose sketches of rural Russian life whose originality lay in their portrayal of peasant types. These *Sketches from a Hunter's Album* (*Zapiski okhotnika*) began appearing in the *Contemporary* in 1847 and first appeared in a separate edition in 1852. Although mostly written while Turgenev had been abroad, he had returned to Russia for their publication in a separate edition and largely on their account, though also due to an obituary notice he had written on Gogol*, he was arrested, imprisoned for a month and then exiled to his estate.

The enforced isolation made him take stock of his career. His efforts to become a playwright had ended with the banning of his only full-length play *A Month in the Country* (*Mesyats v derevne*, 1850), and though he wrote such famous stories as *The Diary of a Superfluous Man* (*Dnevnik lishnego cheloveka*, 1850) and *Mumu* (1854) at this time, he was beginning to feel his way towards the larger form of the short novel. At the height of the Crimean War he wrote his first novel *Rudin* (published 1856) in recognition of the need both to expose the weaknesses of his own generation and to justify its role in face of the mounting criticism from a younger generation. The same concerns dictated the elegiac tone of his second novel *Home of the Gentry* (*Dvoryanskoye gnezdo*, 1859), but with the approach of the emancipation of the serfs he acknowledged that the younger generation's desire for change was more assertive and radical and he portrayed it in Yelena's rejection of her past (in his third novel, *On the Eve, Nakanune*, 1860). His refusal to depict a Russian revolutionary in this novel (the hero is Bulgarian) caused a critical storm in the radical press. He responded by offering his own objective diagnosis of the nihilism of the period in the masterly portrait of Bazarov, the hero of his fourth and finest novel *Fathers and Children* (*Ottsy i deti*, 1862). The result was a further critical uproar which produced grave misinterpretations of the novel and persuaded Turgenev to turn his back on Russia.

For the rest of his life he chose to reside abroad, returning to his own country only for periodic visits. During the 1860s he lived in Baden-Baden, close to Pauline Viardot's retirement home. His attitude to Russia became one of resentment and pity, expressed in his extremely caustic picture of the Russian intelligentsia in his fifth novel *Smoke* (*Dym*, 1867). He also tended to develop themes concerned with superstition, the supernatural and the occult in 'tales of mystery' which he wrote in the final two decades of his life. At the time of the Franco-Prussian War he and the Viardots moved temporarily to London and then later settled in Paris. He had by now achieved an international reputation and was so closely identified with the French literary scene through friendships with Flaubert*, the Goncourts* and Zola* that he was regarded by the young Henry James*, who met him in Paris, as a writer to be included under the heading of 'French Poets and Novelists'. He had become more highly esteemed in Europe than he was among the younger generation of Russians. His last novel *Virgin Soil* (*Nov'*, 1877) was a bold attempt to win the sympathy of the revolutionary young in his own country, though his own liberalism and his scepticism about the revolutionary potential of the peasantry led him to suggest in his novel that the revolutionary movement in Russia was doomed. However, recognition of his services to Russia came from other quarters, notably from the University of Oxford which awarded him an honorary doctorate of civil law in 1879, much to his delight. Serious illness, which turned out to be cancer of the spine, afflicted him towards the end of his life. His last works took the form of 'mystery' tales like *The Song of Triumphant Love* (*Pesn' torzhestvuyushchey lyubvi*, 1881) and *Klara Milich* (1883) as well as a large cycle of *Poems in Prose* (*Stikhotvoreniya v proze*, 1882 and posthumously) which, if of uneven quality, offered a recapitulation in miniature of many of his favourite themes. He died in Bourgival in 1883.

Generally acknowledged to have been the first Russian writer to have achieved a major international reputation, nowadays he is thought of as a novelist who stands somewhat in the shade of his great contemporaries, Dostoevsky* and Tolstoy*. By temperament and talent Turgenev felt at home with such less extensive prose forms as the sketch, short story and short novel. In his studies of peasant Russia he created masterpieces of condensed, poetic description which conjured into brilliant and fleeting life types ranging from the practical, self-made Khor and the sensitive Kalinych (of his first *Sketch*) to the freedom-loving Kasyan, the inspired singer Yakov or the saintly Lukeria stricken by paralysis. His sardonic portrayals of Russian landowners revealed by their attention to detail and their scrupulous observation where the true evil of serfdom lay. He was similarly penetrating in his examination of the Hamletism and pretentiousness of the Russian intelligentsia. His early short stories and sketches are dotted with acute insights into the social and psychological aberrations in Russian life, though the urbanity and deftness of his style, accommodating both lyrical nature description and naturalistic dialogue, may seem on occasion to outshine all else in his work.

In his novels, upon which his fame now chiefly rests, he blended his expertise as a master of the love story with his capacity for social-psychological portraiture. His novels consequently became realistic appraisals of the evolution of the Russian intelligentsia in the 1840s, 1850s and 1860s. Always very sensitive to the changing political atmosphere in Russia and in Europe, he believed none the less that life enshrined certain permanencies – the permanency of nature and eternity, for example – and that man's role was at best ephemeral, that his hope of happiness was slight save through love and that when love failed his only destiny was a decent death. His recognition of the conflict between head and heart which so crippled his own generation of the intelligentsia led him to divide humanity into Hamlets and Don Quixotes (in his lecture of 1860 'Hamlet and Don Quixote'), the tragic egoism of the former being balanced against the comic altruism of the latter. His greatest fictional creation, the portrait of the nihilist Bazarov in *Fathers and Children*, can arguably demonstrate how the hero's Quixotic desire to serve the people is flawed and perhaps tragically foredoomed by

the Hamlet-like weakness, the introspection and romanticism, which he discovers in his own nature.

Turgenev differs from Dostoevsky and Tolstoy in his rejection of all religious solutions to life's problems. An agnostic, he viewed life realistically and with faintly amused detachment, representing it most successfully in the confined, theatrical form he chose for his novels, but there is no doubt that as he grew older his pessimism became more marked and he seemed to seek answers in the exploration of psychic themes. Probably his most memorable writing is to be found in his love stories, particularly *Asya* (1858) and *First Love* (1860), both of which have an autobiographical basis and depend for their effectiveness on romanticized nostalgia for a poignant but lost happiness. His evocative lyricism in depicting summertime and young love is unequalled.

As a man he was unpunctual, often hypochondriac, depressive, linguistically of outstanding gifts, a delightful conversationalist, an indefatigable letter-writer and, above all, charming. He charmed many of the leading celebrities of his day throughout Europe and it is his appreciative understanding of European sensibilities, preserved for posterity in his letters and numerous memoirs about him, that has greatly contributed to his enduring popularity.

Richard Freeborn

Other works: of recent translations Leonard Schapiro, *Turgenev's Spring Torrents* (1972), and Marion Mainwaring, *Youth and Age* (1968, containing 'Punin and Baburin', 'The Inn' and 'The Watch'), are noteworthy. Most of his other shorter works are available in Constance Garnett translations, though not generally outside libraries. About Turgenev: the recent biography, L. Schapiro, *Turgenev, His Life and Times* (1978), must now take precedence over earlier works by Yarmolinsky and Magarshack because it makes use of much new material, mostly letters, which has only become available in the last decade. Of recent critical studies relating to Turgenev the following are valuable (in alphabetical order): I. Berlin, *Fathers and Children* (1972), a study of Bazarov's Jacobinism; R. Freeborn, *Turgenev, The Novelist's Novelist* (1978), a study of Turgenev's novels; E. Kagan-Kans, *Hamlet and Don Quixote: Turgenev's Ambivalent Vision* (1975); V.S. Pritchett, *The Gentle Barbarian* (1977). A. FitzLyon, *The Price of Genius* (1964), is a biography of Pauline Viardot which pays particular attention to Turgenev's relations with her; and two detailed studies by Patrick Waddington illuminate aspects of Turgenev's relations with the West: *Turgenev and England* (1980) and *Turgenev and George Sand: An Improbable Entente* (1981).

461

TURNER, Joseph Mallord William 1775–1851

British painter

Turner was born in Covent Garden, London, the son of a barber. He received little education although his father encouraged his interest in drawing. In 1789 he studied at the Schools of the Royal Academy and at this time received tuition from the architectural draughtsman Thomas Malton. Turner's first exhibit at the Royal Academy, in 1790, was the *Archbishop's Palace, Lambeth* and shows the influence of the watercolourists Cozens and Sandby. During the nineties Turner became a prolific topographical artist, receiving many commissions and making a number of sketching tours throughout Britain. He worked at Dr Monro's 'Academy' with Thomas Girtin as a copyist and his style at this time is very similar to Girtin's. His first oil painting shown at the Royal Academy was *Fishermen at Sea* (1796) and is executed in the manner of the Van de Veldes.

Turner was receptive to the styles of many painters and in particular, during his early career, those of Claude, Poussin and Wilson. In 1800 he exhibited *The Fifth Plague of Egypt*, bought by William Beckford, which shows his first major attempt at a romantic historical landscape. The painting had considerable influence on the apocalyptic landscapes of Martin* and Danby. Turner was made a full RA in 1802, a title he was always very proud of despite his disputes with the art establishment. Taking advantage of the Peace of Amiens in 1802 Turner made his first tour of France and Switzerland, filling six sketchbooks and finding particular fascination in the Alpine scenery. In Paris he visited the Louvre to study some of Napoleon's* enormous collection of plundered paintings, and made notes and sketches especially of Titian, Correggio and Domenichino. In 1804 Turner opened his own gallery at premises in Harley Street creating a precedent in the exhibition of British art. In 1806, in emulation of Claude's *Liber Veritatis*, produced to prevent dissimulation and false attribution, Turner began the *Liber Studiorum*, a series of engravings, continued until 1819, recording seventy-one of his major works. In 1806 he also exhibited *The Goddess of Discord choosing the Apple of Contention in the Garden of the Hesperides* and as John Gage has shown this is one of the first works that reveals Turner's deep interest in occult and alchemical literature which remained with him throughout his career and informs much of his colour theory and choice of subject matter. In 1810 his *Fall of an Avalanche in the Grisons*, influenced by De Loutherbourg, transformed the elder painter's often facile impact into a romantically powerful and realistic one. Turner put some lines of his own verse to the picture, a convention he was to employ often to underline the deep relationship he felt between literature and painting and which he emphasized in his lectures at the Royal Academy as Professor of Perspective, begun in 1811. This year he began a sketching tour of the west country as preparation for the *Picturesque Views of the Southern Coast of England*, published between 1814 and 1826, and which earned him both popularity and a considerable income.

During this period Turner had a house built in Twickenham where he lived until the end of the 1830s. His oils of the 1810s and 1820s, such as *Snowstorm: Hannibal crossing the Alps* (1812), *Dido Building Carthage* (1815), *England: Richmond Hill* (1819), *The Bay of Baiae, with Apollo and the Sibyl* (1823), *The Harbour of Dieppe* (1825), and *Ulysses deriding Polyphemus* (1829), shows his immense range of interests and talent, his ambition to out-paint all rivals and his determination, in response to Reynolds's negative criticism of historical landscape painting, to make the genre the basis of a new English school. Turner made tours of the Rhine (1817 and 1825), Italy (1819–20), France (1826 and 1829) and continued to tour Britain. He produced a great amount of work including sketches, oils, watercolours and engravings. During these years his oil painting became more concerned with light and colour (or 'light as colour') and with adapting the experiments in watercolour and gouache, known as 'Colour Beginnings', which anticipate the abstract works of twentieth-century artists in their almost entirely formal concerns. With his famous landscapes and interiors painted at Petworth House, the home of his patron Lord Egremont, in the late 1820s and 1830s, Turner's work began to express a completely original sense of light with blinding yellows and deep reds which seem to dissolve objects in a phosphorescent mist. The major oil paintings of the thirties and forties, with their often unconventional subject matter, composition and colour, lost him much of his earlier wide popularity. *Staffa: Fingal's Cave* (1832), *The Fighting Téméraire tugged to her last berth* (1839), *Shade and Darkness* and *Light and Colour (Goethe's Theory*, 1843), *Rain, Steam and Speed* (1844) and his long series of Venetian paintings used techniques to implement a vision that few of his contemporaries could follow. Even Ruskin*, who defended Turner so strongly in *Modern Painters*, preferred his topographical work and played down the significance of his more experimental painting. Turner, renowned for his curious manners and coarse appearance, his egotism and love of money, his extraordinary energy and often great intellectual confusion, died in his Chelsea home on 19 December 1851, bequeathing his work to the nation and his wealth to the foundation of a home for poor painters. His will has only partially been fulfilled.

One of Turner's patron's sons, Hawkesworth Fawkes, described the painter's execution of a watercolour, *A First Rate taking in Stores* (1818), between breakfast and lunch, at the family home in Farnley:

[Turner] took a piece of blank paper – outlined his ships, finished the drawing in three hours and went out to shoot .... He began by pouring wet paint onto the paper until it was saturated, he tore, he scratched, he scrubbed it in a kind of frenzy and the whole thing was chaos – but gradually and as if by magic the lovely ship, with all its exquisite minutiae came into being.

This record, along with others of Turner's almost manic activity in bringing virtually stained canvases up to finished ones on the few 'Varnishing days' before Royal Academy shows, tells us a great deal about Turner the romantic artist. His work was frequently the result of observation, gestation and finally creation out of initial chaos. Turner's ideas on art which were so clumsily and elliptically expressed in his lectures found perfect expression in his painting, as if for all the immense literary, psychological, philosophical and historical knowledge he had stored up there was always a formal or colouristic equivalent. Turner's aesthetic was based upon a general theory of colour values both optical and emotional, unlike, for instance, that of his contemporary, Constable*, whose interests lay more in the specific attributes of particular natural forms. Turner, as Graham Reynolds has written, 'was conscious of an analogy between musical modes and the gamut of colour', and conceived of an overall colour structure almost divorced from empirical observation. His reading of Eastlake's translation of Goethe's* *Farbenlehre* clarified his already well-developed ideas in this area of investigation and directly influenced the production of the complementary canvases, *Light and Colour (Goethe's Theory), Morning of the Deluge – Moses Writing the Book of Genesis* and *Shade and Darkness – the Evening of the Deluge*, both of 1843. These employ Turner's favourite 'vortex' composition and reduce all the forms to the merest shadows and suggestions. In these and in other related canvases like *Snowstorm – Steam-boat off a Harbour's mouth* (1842) Turner anticipates the compositional devices of the Futurist painters of the early twentieth century. Upon close analysis many of Turner's paintings can be seen as subtle 'metaphysical contraptions' which try to embody in their own pictorial dynamism and colour-play complex and esoteric notions of art, nature, time, being and death.

Turner saw before any other European painter the very startling and revolutionary conclusions to be drawn from Romantic aesthetic theory and even perhaps, in his obsession with the contradictory positive and negative powers of yellow and blue, the end of painting. His pictures of the Great Western Railway, of Napoleon in exile (*War*, 1842) and David Wilkie's funeral at sea (*Peace*, 1842) echo the pessimistic tone of his ongoing epic poem *Fallacies of Hope*, a dialogue with Campbell's *Pleasures of Hope*, and convey his Faust-like sense of energy finally extinguished in a

death of its own making. These paintings provoke and sustain meditation on the abstractions of light and darkness, as they are meant to, and, most explicitly in *Angel Standing in the Sun* (1846), summon up a biblical apprehension of irrevocable Apocalypse that haunted Turner in the last decade of his life. To the apparently optimistic *Light and Colour* Turner appended his own lines:

The ark stood firm on Ararat; the returning sun
Reflected her lost forms, each in prismatic guise
Hope's harbinger, ephemeral as the summer fly
Which rises, flits, expands and dies.

Turner's influence on his near-contemporaries was important but only in so far as painters like Cox, Cotman, Stanfield, Eastlake and others followed his earlier style. His impact upon Delacroix*, partly through the mediation of Bonington, and then upon the Impressionists is difficult to assess and is again most probably confined to his more naturalistic work and his reinterpretation of aspects of earlier colouristic painters. Perhaps the greatest influence came in the 1890s when French painters like Monet*, Moreau* and Signac became fascinated by Turner's later work. Signac, an artist deeply interested in the science and symbolism of colour, found in the work after 1834 'colour for colour's sake' and in the *Deluge* pictures 'aggregations of colours . . . painting in the most beautiful sense of the word'.

Richard Humphreys

See: John Ruskin, *Modern Painters* (5 vols, 1843–60); A.J. Finberg, *The Life of J.M.W. Turner* (1939); J. Lindsay, *J.M.W. Turner: His Life and Work* (1966); J. Gage, *Colour in Turner: Poetry and Truth* (1969); G. Reynolds, *Turner* (1969); M. Butlin and E. Joll, *The Paintings of Turner* (2 vols. 1977).

462
TWAIN, Mark (Samuel Langhorne Clemens)
1835–1910

US novelist and essayist

When Twain was five the family moved within Missouri to Hannibal, the rich cultural location of his Tom Sawyer and Huckleberry Finn fictions. Brief schooling ended in apprenticeship on the Missouri *Courier*. In 1853 he worked his way east to New York and Philadelphia and back west to Iowa as journeyman printer. In 1857 he exchanged that life for apprentice and journeyman Mississippi riverboat pilot, vividly described in *Life on the Mississippi* (1883). Twain here has one of his very few cultural heroes without serious blemish, Horace Bixby, the dandy master pilot, the only acceptable heroic authority Twain acknowledged, and juxtaposes him with the bogus glories of 'the absolute South', with its aristocratic humbug and grotesque belief in itself as a civilization. But the Civil War closed the river. For about two weeks Clemens became second lieutenant in the Confederate army – his family were confirmed Unionists – and was then released for vague 'disabilities' (the affair is parodied in 'The Private History of a Campaign that Failed'). Discovering that being secretary to his brother Orion, secretary to Nevada State, entailed no work and no pay, he unsuccessfully tried prospecting, turned to reporting, and in 1862 became city editor on the Virginia City (Nevada) *Enterprise*, using for the first time his pseudonym (a fathom call on the Mississippi boats but curiously indicative of the future schism in his character).

After an absurd duel (personal journalism proving a liability) he worked for newspapers in San Francisco, where he met Bret Harte* and published 'The Celebrated Jumping Frog of Calaveras County', the just about funny story which made him famous and which he rightly did not value highly. The Sacramento *Union* assigned him travel reports in Hawaii, the Mediterranean and Palestine; the resulting *Innocents Abroad* (1869) combines the brash superiorities of the confident American tourist with a certain wariness of time and decay in monuments prior to America, largely brought on by the Sphinx gazing at Twain. The later tensions are already latent here: the overwhelming sense of time and eternity reducing men to transient data. With popular success and the editing of the Buffalo *Express*, he could marry Olivia, and their combined finances enabled him to buy a place in Hartford, Connecticut. His impulsive impracticality lost him a fortune in a typesetting machine already out of date, and in a publishing house which profited from General Grant's memoirs and then went bankrupt within ten years. Twain then wrote and lectured to pay debts and restore his finances. But inside national and international fame – between 1872 and 1900 he produced twenty-five books at least – private tragedy undermined him. A beloved daughter died, his only son died in infancy, his wife died in 1904 and another daughter in 1909. University honours were laid thickly upon him but, as he said, 'I take the same childish delight in a new degree that an Indian takes in a fresh scalp.' He finally left Hartford for Redding – still in Connecticut – and, having anticipated he would die with the return of Halley's comet, which had appeared at his birth, did so, of *angina pectoris*.

Twain's wit and humour constitute a balancing act, a controlled hysteria in the face of a contradictory and violent world, an edging towards the void of hopeless behaviourism and dehumanized determinism. Inside a witticism that the symbol of man ought to be an axe since 'every human being has one concealed about him somewhere, and is always seeking the opportunity to grind it', lies a sense of possible unbridled rapacity.

The genteel fears of bourgeois society forced him to costume criticism and pain in ironic comedy, satire that excoriated cruelty, ignorance and hypocrisy, and farce resulting from the gap between established moral standards and the truth. *The Gilded Age* (1874), written in collaboration with Charles D. Warner, contains the exemplary figure of Colonel Beriah Sellers, epitome of the success ethic operating in the speculative corruptions of Washington, where his energies become a danger to youth by perpetuating a myth beyond practicality.

Shocks of recognition come through as nervous hilarity. His finest works retain an astonishing balance between buoyancy and despair. *The Adventures of Huckleberry Finn* (1884) is a pattern of duplicity and disguise, with a twelve-year-old boy, technically dead, discovering the adult hypocrisy of slavery, feuding Southern aristocrats in full stupidity, the confidence trickster who exemplifies capitalist fraud, the parent who exploits his child to extinction, and the training of another boy (Tom Sawyer) to believe in the competitive aggressions and romantic violence of the age. Huck's revolt against Christian society and the Fugitive Slave Law is one of the most moving and valuable moments in literature, a beacon of sense in a darkness of characteristic apologetics. But the brief days he and Nigger Jim spend on a piece of broken raft on the Mississippi cannot constitute a possible society, however idyllic and educative. Huck learns to respect a Negro and reject the shore societies, but can only then 'light out for the Territory', get clear of American lies by heading West. His inventive, explorative language – Twain created a rich vehicle from his memories of Hannibal – carries him to articulate understanding which is useless in 'sivilized' America. In *A Connecticut Yankee at King Arthur's Court* (1889) the technology that Hank Morgan brings from the Colt factory to medieval feudalism, in order to transform serfdom, the chivalric order and a bigoted church into a reasonably humanitarian technocracy, turns to a violence which reflects American Civil War weaponry and the technological potentialities for aggression in the Philadelphia Exposition of 1876. A factory-colony is to turn 'groping and grubbing automata into men'. The revolution 'must *begin*, in blood, whatever may answer afterward. If history teaches anything, it teaches that.' Training is 'all there is *to* a person'. But the novel concludes with the nineteenth-century American mechanic roasting an army of knights on an electrified wire defence system. *Pudd'nhead Wilson* (1894) is one of the most savage and accurate exposures of racism and slavery ever written, but Twain also incorporates an analysis of American subservient snobbery before European aristocrats, the ruin of a young lawyer whose first mild joke is mistaken for stupidity by a stupid townspeople, and the lawyer's rehabilitation as a detective – a figure that will obsess American fiction in the following century and which

Twain neatly mocked a few years later in *The Double Barrelled Detective Story* (1902). In 'The Man that Corrupted Hadleyburg' (1898) derision is the response to a town's untested reputation for honesty, or vanity disguised as self-righteous uprightness, the classic Christian social sin. Wealth attacks a society which believes that all things are ordered, including corruption; it is left praying: 'Lead us into temptation!'

These masterpieces manage, as works of art, to exhilarate the reader with wit, humour, skilled plots and critical vision, while impregnating him with recognitions of human cruelty and stupidity. But increasingly the famous novelist and much demanded after-dinner speaker began to lock manuscripts away from public scrutiny, in order to retain fame and fortune, to be honest with himself while entertaining the public who, as usual, demanded what it approved of. Mr Clemens divided from Mark Twain; the humorist's art could not fulfil the embittered conscience; the well-meaning censorship of his wife, W.D. Howells* and others only exacerbated the schizoid life. The white-clothed public figure concealed the dark final phase of his genius. *What Is Man?* (1906) yields the creative impulse to mere training, behaviourism, and a cynical equation of Shakespeare and a machine or a rat. Human nature is always content with its condition 'no matter what its religion is, whether its master be tiger or house-cat'. 'Everything has been tried, without success', so do not waste feeling on the possibility of social change. In 1878, Twain wrote that 'To man all things are possible but one – he cannot have a hole in the seat of his breeches and keep his fingers out of it.' The later work explores the impulsive and irrational to the point where Twain can say, 'Fleas can be taught anything a Congressman can.' Man's boasted '*intellectual* superiority' to the contrary, 'the fact that he can *do* wrong proves his *moral* inferiority to any creature that cannot.' In *The Mysterious Stranger* (1916) the archangel Satan visits medieval Austria to reassure young Theodor that human history accurately reflects the vileness of mankind, especially in wars which religion and philosophy support. The rest is void: 'There is no God, no universe, no human race, no earthly life, no heaven, no hell. It is all a dream. Nothing exists but you. And you are but a thought, a useless thought, a homeless thought, wandering forlorn among the empty eternities!' Twain, like his contemporary Henry Adams*, is a sceptical index of the twentieth century, prophetic of its state of continuous emergency and creedless hypocrisy. 'Two or three centuries from now it will be recognized that all the competent killers are Christians; then the pagan world will go to school to the Christian – not to acquire his religion, but his guns': such is the chilling message to the modern world in *The Mysterious Stranger*. Angels, Satan adds, can only love each other; if they loved the human race, that love 'would consume its object like ashes. No, we cannot love men, but we can be harmlessly indifferent; we can also like them sometimes.' *Letters from the Earth* (1942) ridicules the inconsistencies and authoritarianism of Old Testament lore: 'The Biblical law says: "Thou shalt not kill". The law of God, planted in the heart of man at his birth, says: "Thou shalt kill".' Twain opened the way to American 'black' humour of the 1960s and the comedian of despair, Lenny Bruce.

Eric Mottram

Works: *The Writings of Mark Twain*, ed. Albert Bigelow Paine (37 vols, 1922–5); *Letters from the Earth*, ed. Bernard de Voto (1942); *The Complete Humorous Sketches and Tales*, ed. Charles Neider (1961); *Notebooks and Journal of Mark Twain*, ed. Frederick Anderson, Michael B. Frank and Kenneth M. Sanderson (2 vols, 1976); *Mark Twain and the Damned Human Race*, ed. Janet Smith (1962). See: Walter Blair, *Mark Twain and Huck Finn* (1960); Henry Nash Smith, *Mark Twain: The Development of A Writer* (1962); Justin Kaplan, *Mr Clemens and Mark Twain* (1966); J.M. Cox, *Mark Twain: The Facts of Humour* (1967).

463

TYLOR, Sir Edward Burnett 1832–1917

British anthropologist

Tylor was the dominant figure in anthropology in Britain for at least thirty years after the publication of his *Primitive Culture* in 1871. Today his position within the subject can only be assessed historically, but 'for his period he had remarkably few philosophical, religious or racial obsessions; and as the first great synthesizer and sifter of ethnological knowledge it was he who largely created the universe of discourse inherited, through Frazer* and Malinowski, by the senior living generation of British anthropologists' (Lienhardt, 1969). How Tylor attained this position is both interesting of itself and also illuminates the characteristics of anthropology as it developed in the second half of the nineteenth century.

Tylor was the third son of a Camberwell brass founder, and, as a Quaker, was educated until he was sixteen at a Nonconformist school at Tottenham. He then joined the family business until consumptive symptoms compelled his resignation four years later. Thereafter he possessed sufficient means to concentrate on his scholarly interests as a member of an intellectual group emerging from successful Nonconformist and Evangelical families.

In 1856, while on an American tour, he met Henry Christy, a banker, fellow Quaker, and archaeologist, 'in an omnibus at Havana', as Tylor somewhat romantically described it in his first book, *Anahuac: or Mexico and the Mexicans ancient and modern* (1861). Their four-month visit to Mexico followed, which set in train the process whereby Tylor became an anthropologist. Although primarily a travel book, *Anahuac* portrayed the author's interest in Mexican culture for its own sake. However, it was the intellectual history of the late 1850s and 1860s which profoundly influenced Tylor's anthropological attitudes, demonstrated in his books *Researches Into the Early History of Mankind* (1865) and *Primitive Culture*. The latter was his most important work, and led to his election as a Fellow of the Royal Society in the year of its publication. His last book was *Anthropology* (1881), an introductory text, and his only major subsequent publication was the paper 'On a Method of Investigating the Development of Institutions: Applied to Laws of Marriage and Descent' (*Journal of the anthropological Institute*, vol. 18, 1888).

Tylor did not enter academic life until 1883, when he was appointed Keeper of the University Museum, Oxford, in order to lecture on the subjects embraced by the collection given to the University by General A.H. Pitt Rivers*. Tylor became Reader the next year and a titular professor in 1896. He lectured regularly until his retirement in 1909, and was knighted in 1912. During his Oxford years he devoted much time to the organizational aspects of anthropology. Twice president of the Anthropological Institute, he was also the first president of the Anthropology Section of the British Association for the Advancement of Science. Ironically, despite Tylor's sustained efforts, Oxford refused to accept his proposals for a degree examination in anthropology.

Tylor was primarily a cultural evolutionist with a rather generalized view of human progress. According to a recent study by Joan Leopold, the *Early History* and *Primitive Culture* show influences extending from the Enlightenment and positivism to the German historical school and the Humboldtians. She has identified the themes in these works: (1) the interpretation of evolution, (2) the explanation of similarities by independent invention, inheritance and diffusion with the assumption of psychological and environmental unity, (3) the analysis of 'survivals', (4) methodology, and (5) the concept of culture.

From these elements Tylor developed a view of culture as an entity, embracing the past as well as the present:

> Culture or Civilization, taken in its wide ethnographic sense, is that complex whole which includes knowledge, belief, art, morals, law, custom and any other capabilities and habits acquired by man as a member of society. The condition of culture among the various societies of mankind, in so far as it is capable of being investigated on general principles, is a subject apt for the study of laws of human thought and action (*Primitive Culture*, p. 1).

Tylor saw the history of culture as one not of degeneration but of a general gradual progression from a natural condition. Although there were local, and explicable, retardations, it was possible to reconstruct scientifically the details of this progress, where it lay beyond historical facts, by means of the comparative method. Contemporary human institutions could be arranged sequentially in terms of their likeness or otherwise to the society of his day.

Aside from his stress on the study of culture, Tylor became famous for his interest in 'survivals' and his elaboration of the theory of animism. For example, magical belief was a 'survival', itself resulting from the very simple mental law whereby primitive man confused external phenomena with his own perception of them. Therefore animism was a primitive universal belief in the existence of spiritual beings, which provided a common basis to all religions, and so a means of comparing them. Methodologically, 'survivals' were as much vestigial clues to past attitudes and practices as were prehistoric artefacts. It was consistent with these views that Tylor saw anthropology as 'a reformer's science' (as he wrote at the end of *Primitive Culture*) in that one of its roles was to expose as irrelevant those remains of ancient thought which impeded the development of society.

Tylor's breadth of vision and rational attitude towards all forms of evidence have helped his influence to survive. His definition of culture retains a modern ring, as does his interest in words apart from their etymology. Certainly his concept of culture lacked theoretical integration and his evolutionism implied an attitude of racial superiority. But his insistence that anthropology was fit to help tackle the analysis of the great moral and social issues of his time is still significant.

Peter Gathercole

Anthropological Essays presented to Edward Burnett Tylor in Honour of his 75th Birthday, October 2nd, 1907 ed. N.W. Thomas (1907) contains a bibliography of Tylor's works. See also: R.R. Marett, *Tylor* (1936); George W. Stocking, 'Tylor, Edward Burnett', *International Encyclopedia of the Social Sciences*, vol. XVI (1968); Godfrey Lienhardt, 'Edward Tylor', in *The Founding Fathers of Social Science* ed. Timothy Raison (1969); Joan Leopold, *Culture in Comparative and Evolutionary Perspective: E.B. Tylor and the Making of 'Primitive Culture'* (1980).

U

464

UTRILLO, Maurice 1883–1955

French artist

Born in Paris in 1883, Utrillo celebrated the city in his art throughout his life. The son of the painter Suzanne Valadon, Maurice Utrillo inherited the rich traditions of Impressionist and Post-Impressionist painting, yet his attitude to painting was personal and idiosyncratic in the extreme.

His early years were difficult and by the age of eighteen he was an alcoholic. In the beginning, painting was a therapeutic exercise and through this he discovered a commitment and talent that were born into him. He underwent no formal art education but emerged fully fledged with a mode of painting inspired by the Impressionist painter Pissarro*, but which came naturally to him and which varied comparatively little throughout his life.

Utrillo's work presents an enigma for it is a unique combination of the sophisticated and the naive. He has often been referred to as a naive artist, yet his cityscapes, views of Parisian streets and buildings, show great competence and integrity. They are finely resolved works with no suggestion of slightness, incompetence or incompleteness. On the other hand Utrillo's subjects and style scarcely develop and on occasions he would paint from postcards. His technique was direct and decisive and his pigments sometimes thickened with plaster.

In 1905 Utrillo found support from the dealer Sagot and his recognition began. He was increasingly respected until his final years when taste moved away from his art somewhat. He exhibited at the Salon d'Automne in 1909 and four years later had his first one-man show. The apogee of his public recognition came in 1950 when he was chosen to represent France at the Venice Biennale. He died at Le Vesinet in 1955.

The Basilica of St Denis (1909) exemplifies the dense matted texture of his most powerful portraits of areas central or peripheral to Paris. Whilst the frontal composition may derive from a postcard, Utrillo has given the image a gravity and grandeur appropriate to the subject; it is solemn, asymmetrical and decisive.

John Milner

See: A. Tabarant, *Utrillo* (Paris, 1926); P. MacOrlan, *Utrillo* (1952); P. Pétrides, *Maurice Utrillo: L'Oeuvre Complète* (1959–62); W. George, *Utrillo* (1960).

V

465
VALLÈS, Jules Louis Joseph 1832–85

French socialist agitator, journalist and novelist

Born in Le Puy, the son of a schoolteacher of modest means, Vallès was a drop-out and rebel, contradictory in his life and in his work. A student activist in Nantes and Paris during the Second Republic, interned briefly in an asylum in 1852, he spent the years of the Second Empire in a variety of guises: law student, literary hack, municipal clerk, political journalist and aspiring politician. He was an early opponent of Thiers's provisional government in 1870–1, edited a Communard newspaper, was elected deputy for the fifteenth *arrondissement* and finally, on the repression of the Commune, was exiled in London until 1880. Constantly engaged on political journalism, social campaigns and autobiographical novels, Vallès wrote in favour of anarchists like Kropotkin* and against the educational and judicial systems, as well as the evils of colonial expansion.

Vallès was a rebellious misfit rather than a revolutionary, preferring Proudhon* to Marx* and emotional gestures and diatribe to consistent collective action. In newspaper articles and novels he lambasted the whole social order, rejecting all forms of bourgeois establishment thinking in politics, in literature and in education, in favour of a more spontaneous and passionate defence of the victims of urban blight – ragmen, buskers, madmen and other marginal figures whom he dubbed 'réfractaires' or social rebels. His *bêtes noires* were establishment liberals like Michelet* and Jules Simon, the classical educationists of the Sorbonne, the grandiloquent Hugo* and the cynical Baudelaire*, the Goncourts* with their fashionable realism, Zola* and the Naturalists with their illusory 'objectivity'. His heroes were Proudhon for his intelligence and conviction, the doomed leaders of the Commune, Dickens* for his compassion and comic genius, Champfleury and Courbet* for their directness and accurate depiction of poverty and alienation.

This sharp-shooting 'guerilla' of the fourth estate looked to literature, and in particular to the novel, to express his revolt against society and his sense of identity with the oppressed people of Paris. Aiming to be the chronicler of the generation which suffered under the Second Empire, rebelled as Communards and were crushed in 1871, Vallès created a hybrid form, somewhere between autobiographical memoirs and the impersonal social novel. Apart from several embryonic or unfinished political novels, his three-volume *Jacques Vingtras* stands out as an interesting attempt to fuse self-portrait and social document into a revolutionary whole. *The Child* (*L'Enfant*, 1878–1880) champions the rights of the minor against the repressive influence of the mother whose action is reinforced by school and by society at large. Distinctive in its verbal violence and caricatural verve, this novel brilliantly exposes the comic paradox and contradictions of social life. The seeds of alienation sown in childhood develop further in *The Student* (*Le Bachelier*, 1879–1881) in which the hero denounces society in all its manifestations in tones of rage and, often, self-pity. In the final novel, *The Insurrectionist* (*L'Insurgé*, 1882–6), Vallès creates an impressive amalgam of humour, caricature, dramatic reportage and ironic self-analysis as the petty bourgeois drop-out comes of age and seeks to fuse his identity with that of the Parisian proletariat in 1871. In fact, this is the first French novel to explore the relationship between the left-wing intellectual and revolutionary movements.

The trilogy is seen often as very uneven and lacking in overall purpose. Vallès reveals himself as the master of the short vignette, the cutting or humorous sketch, the incisive or bludgeoning allusion. Stylistically he anticipates Céline, Queneau and Hervé Bazin, whereas in narrative technique, his impressionistic style, composed of a succession of dramatic fragments, fleeting images and lively dialogue, heralds many twentieth-century innovations. Criticized in his day for his tasteless irreverence and uncompromising violence of expression, this militant liberal, as he has been called, illustrates in his work the artistic potential of committed literature in the modern sense of the term.

Christopher Bettinson

Further reading: Vallès's complete works have been published both by the *Éditeurs français réunis* (from 1951) and by the Livre-Club Diderot (1969–79). See: M.-C. Bancquart, *Jules Vallès* (1971); V. Brombert, 'Vallès and the Pathos of Rebellion', *The Intellectual Hero . . .* (1960); G. Gille, *Jules Vallès, 1832–1885 . . .* (1941); W.D. Redfern, Introduction to *Le Bachelier* (1972). In addition, consult the special volumes of *Europe* devoted to Vallès, vols 144 (1957) and 470–2 (1968).

466

VAN GOGH, Vincent 1853–90

Dutch artist

Son of a pastor, the young Van Gogh was placed in 1869 in the Dutch branch of the art dealers' firm, Goupil and Co., in The Hague. During the next seven years he journeyed variously to Paris and London carrying out his duties until finally dismissed for rudeness to his employers.

If Van Gogh was a man of sorrows it was because the abnormalities of his behaviour rendered him by turn violently excitable and then melancholically withdrawn. Those people who befriended him had extreme difficulty in maintaining their relationship so that the painter constantly found himself to be a social outcast. It is thought that the cause of his unacceptably intense moods derived from a lesion in the brain occurring at his birth. As his life progressed the problems became more acute until at the age of thirty-five he suffered his first attack of insanity.

Highly intelligent, an avid reader with a good command of four languages including English, Van Gogh had decided prior to his dismissal by Goupil that he would follow a higher calling, similar to that of his father. In 1877 he entered a small Evangelical College in Brussels, completing his training the following year but, because of his peculiar personality, failing the course. Of his own initiative he settled in that bleak part of Belgium known as the Borinage. In this coal-mining area reminiscent of that in Zola's* book *Germinal*, Van Gogh became a lay preacher. At the same time he began frequently to make drawings of the people in the area. He was much influenced in this activity by his collection of engravings cut from contemporary English magazines, such as the *Graphic*, which commented upon the social problems of the working poor in industrial areas of Britain. Soon after, in 1882, whilst at Nuenen, Van Gogh painted the famous *Potato Eaters* which portrays a poor family at the meal table. The dramatic contrasts of light and dark required only a low colour key and there is no hint of the colourist that the painter was to become.

By this time Van Gogh had realized his lack of aptitude for divine counselling and that he was better suited to the life of an artist. He left the church and settled for a time in Antwerp where he studied, amongst other works, those of Rubens. The appeal of these Baroque works probably lay in their warm colouring and lively movement. A further pleasure for the painter was his discovery of Japanese prints which he began to collect whilst at Antwerp. Their grace of line and simplicity of composition were as important to Van Gogh as they were to Gauguin*.

It was not until the following year, 1886, when Van Gogh joined his brother Theo in Paris, that he finally met not only Gauguin, but Cézanne*, Bernard, Anguetin and Pissarro* as well. Whilst studying at Cormon's studio, Van Gogh, undergoing an immensely stimulating year, became interested in the flower paintings of Adolphe Monticelli, a Marseilles artist. Van Gogh experimented with flower pieces himself at this time, setting blues against complements of orange and playing with other such oppositions. These in conjunction with the use of an impasto technique strongly suggest a Monticelli influence. During the winter, however, Impressionism finally became apparent to the Dutchman who, in the spring of 1887, lightened and unified his palette whilst working out of doors with Bernard on the banks of the Seine at Asnières.

None the less, Van Gogh still had the idea of starting a society of painters with a life-style he imagined to be like that of the Japanese, simple, homogeneous, warm and gracious. He travelled south in February looking for a suitable place and decided upon Arles in Provence. Here he painted some glorious spring pictures of orchards whilst he prepared a small house for the arrival of Gauguin. He had hopes that the master of the school of artists in Brittany could be induced to set up a similar arrangement in the south. Throughout the summer he corresponded with Gauguin urging upon him all the good reasons for complying with his request. At the same time he painted some remarkable pictures, arriving at expressive solutions with non-naturalistic colour as an important poetic element. He wrote of his interior *The All-Night Café* (1888) that he had 'tried to express the idea that the café is a place where one can ruin oneself, go mad or commit a crime'. The use of powerful reds, assertive blue greens and hot orange yellows gives the work an almost painful intensity. It was also during the summer that Van Gogh painted a series of views of the public gardens at Arles. He said he felt there the presence, along with that of other famous figures of the past, of Petrarch, who had lived not far away at Avignon. These paintings called the *Poets' Garden* were to hang in Gauguin's own room to express the idea of the master of today meeting in Arles with the masters from history.

Short of money, induced by the funds provided by Theo Van Gogh and perhaps preferring to winter in a warmer climate, Gauguin consented to Vincent's proposal and arrived in Arles in October. However, the relationship between Vincent and Gauguin proved no happier than previous ones and in December Gauguin acknowledged that he would have to go north again. At this point the Dutchman's sanity finally gave way and he entered the asylum at St Rémy. Between bouts of manic violence he continued to paint with acute control of colour and tone but with an increasing wildness of shape and form. Rolling mountains, waving cypress and olive repeat the whirling of sun and stars. The whole of nature, seen through the ferment of Van Gogh's temperament, takes on a tumultuous aspect.

To be nearer the ever comforting Theo, his new wife and small baby, also named Vincent, the painter entered another hospital, near Paris, at Auvers. Here he painted and wrote as long as he could. His last important painting was of black crows flying against a strip of sky, so dark in its blueness that it is almost black. It lowers heavily over a cornfield the colour of bile. The work expresses not only a psychological state of being but also the physical sensations resulting from extreme anxiety. At the same time Van Gogh felt it to be a projection of the energy of nature. A short while later, after these terrifying hours, Van Gogh wrote a letter to Theo stating that 'painters themselves are fighting more and more with their backs to the wall.' He finally could no longer face the notion of continued insanity and, according to a letter found in his pocket after his suicide, had come to accept the inevitable end with comparative tranquillity of mind. He shot himself in the chest, dying later from the wound on 29 July 1890.

Pat Turner

Van Gogh's works include: *Le Pont de Langlois* (1888); *Pink Peach Trees* (1888); *Café at Night Arles* (1888); *The Postman Roulin* (1888); *Van Gogh's Chair* (1888–9); *Sun Flowers* (1888); *Starry Night* (1889); *Yellow Cornfield* (1889). See: *The complete Letters of Van Gogh*, trans. Goch-Bouger and De Dood (1958); Meyer Schapiro, *Vincent Van Gogh* (1950); A.M. Hammacher, *Vincent Van Gogh* (1961); *Selected Letters of Van Gogh*, ed. Mark Roskill (1963); J. Meier Graefe, *Vincent Van Gogh: A Biographical Study* (trans. J. Reece, 2 vols, Nagera, *Vincent Van Gogh*: A psychological study (1967).

467
VERDI, Giuseppe 1813–1901

Italian composer

The son of an innkeeper and a spinner, born in the tiny hamlet of Le Roncole, near Busseto in Parma, Verdi always stressed his humble origins, sometimes at the expense of the truth: the humbler his birth, the more dramatic would seem his ascent to spectacular success. He also insisted throughout his life that he had enjoyed no regular education. In actual fact he received a basic humanistic training at the Busseto *ginnasio*, formerly the local Jesuit school, which re-opened in the year of Verdi's enrolment (1823); the teaching of the humanities was entrusted to canon Pietro Seletti, who was also an amateur musician. Verdi was taught the rudiments of music, and organ playing, in his native village but regular music lessons began only in the autumn of 1822 with Ferdinando Provesi, a leading figure in Busseto's musical life. Soon Verdi was able to assist and deputize for his teacher

in his various capacities as organist and head of the local Philharmonic Society (founded in 1816 jointly by Provesi and Antonio Barezzi, a rich Bussetan merchant). For this institution Verdi composed vocal pieces (arias, duets, trios), *sinfonie* (in the Italian sense of that term), virtuoso piano pieces and, on his own (perhaps somewhat mocking) later admission, 'marches for brass band by the hundred'. Also from this period came various pieces of church music, including a *Stabat Mater*.

By 1830 it was clear that the young musician's talent required further, less provincial teaching. An application to the Milan Conservatory was rejected, mainly on the grounds that Verdi was over-age and not a citizen of the Lombardo-Veneto kingdom, although the examiners' report bears witness to his talent for composition. But with financial support from Barezzi – who had in the meantime become Verdi's benefactor – private lessons were begun with Vincenzo Lavigna, former *maestro al cembalo* at La Scala, Milan. These, according to Verdi, consisted mostly of exercises in strict contrapuntal writing, although we learn from contemporary documents that *composizione ideale* (free composition) was also part of the training. At the same time Verdi established connections with a group of amateur musicians, mostly from the Milanese nobility, called the Philharmonic Society. Pietro Massini, who taught singing and was director of the society, soon detected talent in the young man, and under his guidance Verdi prepared performances of Haydn's *Creation* (April 1834) and Rossini's* *Cenerentola* (April 1835). In July 1835 Verdi returned to Busseto to become, the following March, the town's music master, a job which was alien to his temperament and inclinations, now decidedly turned towards opera.

Between January and September 1836 Verdi wrote an operatic work, originally entitled *Rocester*, which after various revisions was eventually performed at La Scala in 1839 under the title *Oberto, conte di San Bonifacio*. This first opera reveals the various models (Donizetti*, Mercadante, especially perhaps Bellini*) to which the composer had been exposed during the – relatively long – period of composition and reworking. The moderate success of *Oberto* encouraged Bartolomeo Merelli, the impresario of La Scala, to offer Verdi a contract for two other operas, the first of which happened, of necessity, to be a comic one: *Un giorno di regno* (1840), based on the revision of an old libretto by Felice Romani, was one of Verdi's rare fiascos, and he returned to the comic vein only much later in his career.

But the next opera, based on a new libretto by Temistocle Solera, marked the beginning of Verdi's triumphant ascent. *Nabucco* (1842), realized through a few elementary contrasts and with an important role for the chorus, owes its success to a perfect match between the dramatic conception – a vast biblical fresco – and the musical language in which this is expressed. The next opera, *I Lombardi alla prima crociata* (1843), is based on the same pattern (though with a different plot articulation) and, not by chance, is also on a Solera libretto and first performed at La Scala. For the smaller, more intimate theatre of La Fenice, Venice, Verdi composed *Ernani* (1844), his first encounter with a Victor Hugo* play. Here the drama centres on the conflicts between three male voices (tenor, baritone and bass) fighting for possession of a soprano; the 'abstract' quality of the characters and the action, developed almost exclusively through solo and ensemble set numbers, is emphasized by the absolute pre-eminence of the vocal writing.

With these operas Verdi established the basic patterns around which he worked in the following years. The immediate, enormous success of *Nabucco* and *Ernani* brought him to the forefront of the international operatic scene, and obliged him to fulfil demands for new scores from many of the most important theatres of Italy and abroad. In a period of about six years, from 1844 to 1850, he composed – or reworked – no less than twelve operas, gradually becoming aware of the necessity to realize a dramatic unity by musical means, of establishing relationships at the musical level between dramatically significant points in the action. He soon concluded that a motif announcing the appearance on stage of a major character (as in *I due Foscari*, 1845) was too simple and basically inarticulate; it was only on his encounter with Shakespeare, in the setting of *Macbeth* (1847), that we see the first successful attempt at solving the problem. From *Luisa Miller* (1849) until the end of his career, Verdi adopted a compositional procedure totally unknown in Italian tradition: he sketched the entire score on a small number of staves, notating only the vocal line(s), bass part and essential instrumental connective tissue. This 'continuity draft' helped him to establish musical connections between the various moments of the drama; in this way the set numbers, instead of being the basic dramatic unity (as they had been in previous Italian opera), became the means of establishing the duration of a section, a necessary tassel, outside of which, or even within which, the fundamental elements of the musical language were employed as powerful vehicles of dramatic conflicts.

Thus *Rigoletto* (1851) and *La traviata* (1853), based respectively on Hugo's *Le Roi s'amuse* and Dumas *fils*'s* *La Dame aux camélias*, are directional music dramas in which the action evolves mainly through the characters' development, and particularly through their conflicts; set pieces (mostly duets) and freer musical structures (*arioso*, recitative and *scene*, variously articulated) alternate in equal proportions, forming a balanced, tensely poised whole. In *Il trovatore* (1853), on the other hand, Verdi for the last time builds his score almost exclusively through set pieces, a structure fully in accordance with the elusive nature of the plot and the characters' lack of development; structural symmetries and correspondences therefore dominate.

The central period of Verdi's output bears two distinct features: the relationships of his musical theatre to French *grand opéra* and the pre-eminence of political themes. (Concerning the latter, the development of political content in the operas parallels the composer's position in his country. The early works provided several choruses of a very 'singable' character which gained immense popularity and became vehicles of Italian patriotic feeling. As Verdi became an emblematic figure – as well as a member of the first Italian parliament, at Cavour's request – so political themes as such became central to his plots.) *Les Vêpres siciliennes* (1855) is a full-scale (though not altogether satisfactory) experiment with the French genre; *Simon Boccanegra* (1857; thoroughly reworked in 1881) is an opera where the amorous element has a decidedly secondary role, the plot being built on conflicts between classes and personalities struggling for power – hence the necessity to experiment with new kinds of musical language and, especially, new methods of structural articulation. *Un ballo in maschera* (1859), on a revised libretto by the famous French dramatist Eugène Scribe, combines and blends a basically Italian organization with certain essentially French characteristics and musical features; unity is achieved mainly through a masterful handling of the overall structure of the score, and through the composer's developing skill in fusing light and serious musical elements. *La forza del destino*, written for the Imperial Theatre of St Petersburg in 1862 and revised for La Scala in 1869, exploits a tendency – typical of *grand opéra* – for small, isolated episodes: the opera contains, among other things, the first entirely comic character in Verdi's mature theatre, the monk Fra Melitone. Yet again *La forza* invents new types of musical organization for the set numbers, in particular employing articulation in the orchestral part rather than the voices. In *Don Carlos* (based on Schiller's play), written for the Paris Opéra in 1867 and much revised later, Verdi once again places the dramatic emphasis on conflicts of power and of political conception, the one influencing and eventually determining the other, thus creating the most complex of his dramatic structures. *Aida* (first performed at Cairo's newly opened opera house in 1871) is in fact an 'Italianization' of the *grand opéra* structure, a fusion of personal conflict and scenic display: the clash between individuals and power structures is again the unifying factor in the drama, and is matched at the musical level by an equally well measured organization.

After *Aida* Verdi's increasing pessimism over the Italian musical scene, the influence of German music and consequent lack of national musical integrity, as well as his despair over the distortions which conventional performance practice caused to his precise view of music theatre, caused a halt in operatic composition.

In 1874, however, came the *Messa di requiem*, composed to celebrate the first anniversary of the death of Alessandro Manzoni*. In this work Verdi's pessimistic vision of man in relation to his fellow beings is transferred to the problem of death and the hereafter. The *Requiem*'s remarkable blend of various influences (from Berlioz's* *Grande Messe des morts* to 'classical' polyphonic forms such as the fugue) creates a uniquely coherent conception which should not be underestimated: for many the *Requiem* contains some of Verdi's very greatest music.

A deepening contact with Arrigo Boito, encouraged by the publisher Giulio Ricordi, eventually gave rise to Verdi's final two Shakespearian masterpieces. In Boito, the composer at last found a collaborator with the perfect blend of musical awareness, theatrical understanding and ability to adapt (though not always passively) to his dramatic intuitions. After some intensive work together on the revision of *Simon Boccanegra*, the way was clear for *Otello* (first performed at La Scala in 1887). In comparison with the previous operas, *Otello* displays a simplified plot structure – although the decorative elements (basically the choral interventions) still perhaps lie rather uneasily in relation to the whole. But the force of the drama lies in the power with which the basic centres of attraction, the 'good' of Desdemona, the 'evil' of Iago, revolve around the protagonist as he inexorably plays out his tragedy. One of the many delights of *Falstaff* (also La Scala, 1893) is that the composer is summing up, consciously and ironically, the experiences of his operatic career. The opera, which begins with a pseudo sonata form and ends with a fugue sung by all the characters, is a constant, magnificent parody of the dramatic structures and problems of musical organization which Verdi had confronted during his long career. Verdi's final compositions were a series of religious choral pieces, the *Quattro pezzi sacri*, written between 1890 and 1896.

What mattered above all to Verdi was the creation of a musical object whose perfection of workmanship gave it a guarantee of contact, of direct relationship with the public; and in this he succeeded: the operas from *Nabucco* onwards have never left the repertoire of Italian theatres, and many of them are mainstays of the major opera houses of the world. Their extraordinary vitality comes primarily from their force as dramatic facts realized through the most suitable musical means, from the perfect functionality of the composer's musico-dramatic intuitions. It is this which explains the substantial unity of Verdi's *oeuvre*, from which many have learnt, but which none has attempted to imitate.

Pierluigi Petrobelli

Other operas include: *Giovanna d'arco* (1845); *Alzira* (1845); *Attila* (1846); *I masnadieri* (1847); *Il corsaro* (1848); *La battaglia di Legnano* (1849); and *Stiffelio*

(1850). See: Frank Walker, *The Man Verdi* (1962); Julian Budden, *The Operas of Verdi* (3 vols, 1973, 1978 and 1981).

468
VERGA, Giovanni 1840–1922

Italian novelist

The dubious benefits of fictional realism came rather late to Italy, owing in part to the fragmented nature of its culture and society in the decades before the final achievement of nationhood in 1870, but when it did arrive it was avidly seized upon. Nowadays it is customary to regard the whole realistic trend in the Italian novel, a movement represented at its best by writers such as Luigi Capuana in *Il Marchese di Roccaverdina* and Vittorio Imbriani in *Dio ne scampi dagli Orsenigo*, as a species of melodramatic aberration culminating in the disastrous advent of Gabriele D'Annunzio, a figure as much invented as genuine. Yet, amid numerous second-rate imitations of Flaubert*, Daudet* and the Russians, Italy produced a single master of the genre, whose style and treatment of theme established a tradition which has received striking renewals during the twentieth century.

As with Luigi Pirandello and Giuseppe Lampedusa, his being Sicilian is crucial to our estimation of Giovanni Verga. He was born into a society still based upon feudal ideals dating from the days of the Arabs and the Normans, and into a world which, at the same time, had committed itself fervently to the cause of unification. The fact that Italy meant little to Sicily and that life after the Garibaldian* liberation campaigns of 1860, during which Verga was a patriotic student in Catania, went on in much the same atmosphere of remote and inchoate corruption as it had before is reflected in many of his later stories and in his novel *I Malavoglia* (when the news of the Battle of Lissa, at which Luca Malavoglia dies, is brought to the village, it is reported as 'a battle between our men and the enemy, but nobody knew who that was').

Verga's upbringing was typical of the education of a child of the upper bourgeoisie in the mid-nineteenth century. Liberal ideals implanted by revolutionary preceptors inspired a first novel, the almost unreadable four-decker *I carbonari della montagna*, published in Catania in 1861, which earned Verga a favourable notice in a Florentine newspaper. His heart set on a literary career, he left Sicily for Florence in 1865 and for the next fifteen years lived mostly in northern Italy, earning money as a journalist and reviewer, writing the overblown and sentimental *Storia di una capinera* (1873), *Eva* (1874) and *Tigre Reale* (1875) – novels based on his observation of upper-class life in Sicily and Milan and heavily tinged with Balzacian* influences.

A return to Catania in 1876 marked the beginning of a gradual withdrawal from the brilliant world of Milanese salons, centred upon the circle of Countess Maffei, friend of Verdi* and Manzoni*, where Verga's youthful reputation had been established. During the early 1880s, while still based in Milan, he turned towards the creation of the series of tales and sketches of Sicilian peasant life, exemplified in *Vita dei Campi* (1880), *I Malvoglia* (1881, trans. Eric Mosbadier as *The House of the Medlar Tree*, 1953) and *Novelle rusticane* (1883), upon which his subsequent fame has been largely founded.

Much as Verga was admired as the leader of the Italian *veristi*, *I Malavoglia* met with a generally lukewarm reception, but notwithstanding this, the author pressed ahead, in *Mastro-don Gesualdo* (1888, trans. D.H. Lawrence, 1928), with his idea for a set of novels, in Zola's* *Rougon-Macquart* style, embodying the aspirations of *i vinti*, the conquered, those who, within a rigidly stratified society such as Sicily's, attempt to better their condition and ultimately fail. His thesis in this connection is set out at the beginning of *I Malavoglia* itself, though it was not destined to full accomplishment. A kind of meridional indolence seems to have overcome Verga in his later years, and a tendency to repeat characters, situations and backgrounds marks the stories in *Vagabondaggio* (1887) and *Don Candeloro e compagni* (1894). During the last two decades of his life, in which he successfully assumed the pose of the distinguished man of letters, an established figure in Catania society, he composed practically nothing, and though honoured with an official funeral and the usual tributes paid to literary panjandrums, he was soon afterwards, for an interval at least, ignored.

The revival of interest in Verga during recent years, much of it owing to the spate of cheap reissues of his work, has brought his sterling qualities firmly to our attention, and he can now be seen as, at the best, a splendidly unsentimental, yet tender and sympathetic chronicler of life among the Sicilian poor. It is precisely this quality of compassion which distances him from Zola, who, after meeting Verga, rejected him as a disciple because of his unwillingness to embrace the French novelist's credo to the full extent of its more absurdly 'scientific' reaches. In this respect Verga more resembles Thomas Hardy*, whose *Tess of the D'Urbervilles* has a coincidental similarity of intention to several of the *Novelle rusticane* in its treatment of a character struggling against destiny.

In his stories, Verga rejects Zolaesque determinism, based on studies of environment and heredity, in favour of a quality of fatalistic resignation which is not simply Sicilian but quintessentially Italian in feeling. His famous objectivity, branching out into an extraordinary exactitude of detail with regard to background and location (the setting of his celebrated *Cavalleria rusticana*, 1884, source of Mascagni's opera, matters almost

as much as the characters), is not so much an artistic cult as a natural gift for dispassionate observation. The essential superiority of his art to that of practically every other European realist (we may perhaps except Eça de Queiroz* and Pérez Galdós*) lies in the sincerity of its indulgence towards the weak, oppressed, erring figures it delights to portray.

Jonathan Keates

Other translations include *Little Novels of Sicily* (1925) and *Cavalleria Rusticana and Other Tales* (1928), both by D.H. Lawrence. See: T.G. Bergin, *Giovanni Verga* (1931); Alfred Alexander, *Giovanni Verga* (1972).

469
VERLAINE, Paul 1844–96

French poet

Verlaine was inevitably an over-indulged child: his parents had been married for twelve years before his birth and his mother had suffered three miscarriages; there were no further children. The emotional intensity of his relationship with his mother helps explain his subsequent homosexuality. In 1851, Verlaine's father, an army officer in the engineers, resigned his commission and the family moved to Paris. Verlaine's education here proceeded with a rapid loss of application, attrition of will, flirtation with illicit literature. Nascent alcoholism can be traced to 1862, the year he passed his *baccalauréat*. His father tried to draw him back to an ordered life and, in 1864, insisted that he take a job as a clerk, first in an insurance company and then in the Hôtel de Ville. Throughout this period, his literary interests and contacts had developed and 1866 saw the appearance of his first collection, *Poèmes saturniens*. The opening, in 1867, of the Salle Lacaze at the Louvre, with its collection of eighteenth-century canvases (Watteau, Fragonard, Boucher, Lancret) is one of the clues to Verlaine's second volume, *Fêtes galantes* (1869). It was in 1869, too, that he met the sixteen-year-old Mathilde Mauté whom he married the following year and to whom were addressed the poems of his third collection, *La Bonne Chanson* (1870).

His undiminished drinking habits intermittently led Verlaine to brutal treatment of both his mother and his wife. The early months of this marriage were further strained by the Franco-Prussian War, the Siege of Paris and the ensuing Commune; Verlaine's sympathies with the Communards lost him his job and made him something of a fugitive. His attempt to re-install himself in the world of bourgeois respectability was dealt a final blow by Rimbaud's* arrival in Paris in September 1871, a month before the birth of Verlaine's son, Georges. In July 1872, after more violence to his wife and son, Verlaine left with Rimbaud, first for Brussels and then for London. The months of wandering which followed and during which Verlaine sought both to reconcile himself with Mathilde and to keep Rimbaud came to an end on 10 July 1873, in Brussels, with Verlaine shooting Rimbaud in the wrist. Sentenced to two years' imprisonment, spent at Mons, Verlaine was converted to the faith in 1874, the year of the publication of *Romances sans paroles* and of Mathilde's legal separation from him.

Released from prison in January 1875, he returned to England to teach French and drawing at Stickney (Lincolnshire) and in 1876–7 was teaching French at Bournemouth. In October 1877, he returned to France and took up a teaching post at Rethel, where he struck up a relationship with one of his pupils, Lucien Létinois, a relationship which lasted through another visit to England, an abortive farming project at Juniville and until Lucien's death from typhoid in April 1883. In the meantime, *Sagesse*, containing the poems of his conversion, had appeared (December 1880). Having failed to be reinstated as a municipal employee, and after another short spell in prison, for drunken attacks on his mother, Verlaine finally settled in Paris, in poverty and squalor. The last decade of his life, which, ironically, saw the steady growth of his poetic reputation, was a sequence of seedy lodgings, hospitals, bouts of drink, homosexual liaisons (principally with the artist Frédéric-Auguste Cazals) and affairs with prostitutes (particularly with Eugénie Krantz and Philomène Boudin). Lecture tours in Holland, Belgium and England, his election as Prince of Poets on the death of Leconte de Lisle (1894), the publication of more verse-collections of diminishing quality, preceded his death from bronchial pneumonia in January 1896.

Verlaine's finest poetry belongs to *Fêtes galantes*, poems using the *personae* of the *commedia dell'arte* and the pastoral tradition, in eighteenth-century park settings and inspired by the work of Watteau and others, and to *Romances sans paroles*, poems growing out of the Rimbaud adventure, caught between Rimbaud and Mathilde, backed by the cityscapes of Brussels and London. The *Poèmes saturniens* contain adumbrations of this flowering, but are given over largely to Parnassian and Baudelairian* derivations. The early poems of *Sagesse* are also of the best vein; those of the conversion are more laboured and conventional.

Verlaine's is the poetry of a floating sensibility which operates in an ill-defined space between sensation and sentiment, self-surrender and anxious interrogation. His vocabulary is a vocabulary of etiolation (*blême, pâle, gris, vague, doux, incertain*), half-measure (*quasi, à peine, un peu*), of infantile diminutives, of locational uncertainty (*parmi, par, vers*), of oscillating or circular movement, pacifying and often mindless (*bercer, balancer, circuler, tourbillonner*). His is a world subject to reflexive or intransitive action, frequently evanescent (*s'évaporer, s'effacer, se noyer, se mêler*), a world of un-controllable autonomies and apparently directionless motivations. All sense of causality is submerged, and the connections between things, between subject and object are scrambled by intervening barriers (mist, foliage, indeterminate noise). It is, then, a poetry of responses, of the almost imperceptible creations and transformations of temperamental conditions. It would be misleading to speak of feelings, in any Romantic sense of the word; the Romantics have confidence in the value of feeling and in their possession of feeling; they feel with purpose, because feeling is self-projection and self-assertion, born not of sensation, but of ideology and moral imperative. With Verlaine, feelings are absorbed back into the more primitive state of sentience and a sentience peculiarly divorced from a sentient being. And repetition, so recurrent a habit in his work, situates the poem in a realm where obsession, hauntedness, ennui, self-hypnosis, formal self-consciousness cannot be put asunder. It is Verlaine's ability to capture the unfocused, almost undifferentiated ripplings of consciousness at its lower levels, the kinetics of the psyche, the flickering modulations of affective reaction, which gives his poetry its distinction. And the pleasure provided by his poetry is a pleasure in the act of reading rather than in subsequent reflection, a pleasure in the infinite resourcefulness and polymorphousness of his verse-art.

Verlaine's 'Art poétique', written in April 1874, appeared in *Jadis et naguère* (1884). Here he calls for music, an art that liberates response in a pure form and re-articulates the elements of semi-consciousness. This enterprise is aided by the use of the imparisyllabic line, which does not let verse-utterance settle, keeps it unstable, volatile, nervous, a safeguard against the portentous. He asks, too, that words be chosen with a certain carelessness, grammatical and semantic, so that precision and imprecision constantly shade into each other. The poet should prefer the nuance to the unambiguous colour, because nuance allows an unhindered trafficking between different kinds of dream, between different 'sonorities', the wistful and the resonant. He rejects satiric verse and the conceit, though the *Fêtes galantes* are given their peculiar alertness and textural crackle by a restless ironic undertone. Next, he attacks eloquence and rhyme. His own verse, with its familiar locutions, unfussy syntax, sudden changes of direction, never loses touch with common speech. What he faults in rhyme is its privilege, the way it monopolizes structural and semantic function, its exemplary conclusiveness. Verlaine seeks to reduce rhyme's prominence, to cast in doubt what it foregrounds, frequently by resorting to bold *enjambement*, by disregarding the traditional rules of rhyming (particularly the alternation of masculine and feminine rhyme-pairs, thus, paradoxically, liberating the expressive potentialities of rhyme gender), by reducing rhyme to assonance and by increasing line-internal music (alliteration, assonance, internal rhyme). Thus the way in which the reader locks into the verse is not rigorously coded; his attention is more uniformly and continuously engaged in a more uniform and continuous diversity. Verlaine's *vers libéré* is not however *vers libre*; whatever liberties he took, he stoutly refused to do away with rhyme and syllabic regularity, and mocked the *verslibristes* for doing so. Traditional prosodic structure, however masked, was a necessary anchorage (moral? psychological? aesthetic?); it acted as a verse-consciousness which could be constantly sunk in, and salvaged from, a highly mobile, hesitant, somnambulistic verse-texture.

Jadis et naguère is the uncomfortable miscellany of poems previously laid aside and new poems that Verlaine's unimpressive late collections often are. It was his intention to follow through the two fundamental strains of his experience, the spiritual and the orgiastic, in parallel volumes. *Sagesse* was succeeded by *Amour* (1888), *Bonheur* (1891) and *Liturgies intimes* (1892). Simultaneously, the erotic thread was taken up by *Parallèlement* (1889), *Chansons pour Elle* (1891), *Odes en son honneur* (1893), *Élégies* (1893), *Dans les limbes* (1894) and *Chair* (1896). But these collections are without momentum, falling back on the sentimental, the anecdotal, the rhetorical. Verlaine's poetry in these later years leaves his weaknesses untransformed: the infantile need for refuge, for the total passivity of naive belief or the oblivion of sensual self-immersion, and a mechanical reliance on poetic techniques now too conveniently a part of his growing reputation. There are also volumes of occasional verse: *Dédicaces* (1890), *Épigrammes* (1894), *Invectives* (1896).

If, in his earlier verse, Verlaine is a Symbolist, it is not because his poetry involves itself with metaphysical curiosity – though there is existential inquiry – or with essentialism, or with any excavation of idea from object. It is because his poems present, through sensory encounter, the shifting, polyvalent facets of a mood which is inhabitable but not definable; the poem unifies mood by harmonizing its multiplicity, not by resolving it into singleness. And if these earlier collections can be called Impressionist, it is because they cast anthropocentricity in doubt with their impersonal constructions, because they provide no dominant and stable perspective, because they relativize experience, because they totally subject concept to perception in a world of effects without causes, because they give peculiar substantiality to the half-realities of shadow and reflection, because they depict the mutual interpenetration of objects and surrounding space, because they pursue fugitivity in the free handling of their medium.

Verlaine's influence was marked but shortlived. In France, the Verlainian mode, that kind of poetry which veers between the most delicately musical tone and the prosy, which weds lyric indulgence in evanescent moods of disquiet and vague loss, moods often teased by erotic impulses, with a quizzical, often ironic, vigilance, leads through Laforgue* to Apollinaire, but not beyond. Some critics have found a Verlainian transparency in Éluard's verse, but Éluard's verse is altogether firmer; where Verlaine's poems are so often self-consolatory chantings, *berceuses* by nature, Éluard's poems exude a confidence in their own public efficacy and his utterance is more lapidary. The Surrealists looked to Rimbaud, at Verlaine's expense: 'the over-valuation of Verlaine was the great mistake of the Symbolist school' (Breton).

In the Anglo-American world, Verlaine enjoyed a cult among the Nineties poets, before slipping from sight with the Imagists. It was the neurasthenic strain in Verlaine which caught the fancy of the Nineties poets, the attractions of an experience governed by an atrophied will, by the subdued vyings of the sensual and the mystical, animated by the almost inaudible pulse of the subtlest and most transient sensations. Verlaine was translated (and copied) by Ernest Dowson, John Gray, Arthur Symons and others. In sending his poem 'Vanitas' to Victor Plarr (1891), for example, Dowson wrote: 'It's an attempt at mere sound verse, with scarcely the shadow of a sense in it: or hardly that so much as a vague, Verlainesque emotion.' Yeats had most of his familiarity with Verlaine's verse through Symons, and though he was unable to measure the extent of his debt, he indicated Verlaine's presence in *The Wind Among the Reeds* (1899); perhaps his pursuit of 'those wavering, meditative rhythms, which are the embodiment of the imagination, that neither desires nor hates' ('The Symbolism of Poetry', 1900) had something to do with Verlaine. But Pound found Verlaine to be of no pedagogic use, because he had not taken poetic art forward, as Gautier* and Gourmont had done (letter to Harriet Monroe, 1913), an opinion hard to endorse.

Clive Scott

Prose works: (a) criticism: *Les Poètes maudits* (1888), contributions to the series *Les Hommes d'aujourd'hui* (1885–93); (b) fiction: *Louise Leclercq* (1886), *Les Mémoires d'un veuf* (1886); (c) autobiography: *Mes Hôpitaux* (1891), *Mes Prisons* (1893), *Confessions* (1895). Poetry: *Verlaine: Selected Poems*, ed. J. Richardson (1974). See: C. Chadwick, *Verlaine* (1973); C. Cuénot, *Le Style de Paul Verlaine* (1963); O. Nadal, *Verlaine* (1961); N. Osmond, 'Verlaine', in *French Literature and its Background*, ed. Cruickshank, vol. 5 (1969); J.-P. Richard, 'Fadeur de Verlaine', in *Poésie et profondeur* (1955); E. Zimmermann, *Magies de Verlaine* (1967).

470
VERNE, Jules 1828–1905

French novelist

The reputation of this prolific, popular writer of adventure stories, a pioneer of science fiction, has undergone some startling fluctuations. The 'New Criticism' in France has recently inaugurated a stimulating rediscovery of works that had become scorned as mere edifying children's literature.

The son of a lawyer, Verne resisted pressure to follow the paternal example, preferring, in the 1850s, to write light-weight plays for the popular stage. In 1863, with the tale *Five Weeks in a Balloon* (*Cinq semaines en ballon*) he began publication of his *Extraordinary Journeys in Known and Unknown Worlds*, whose aim was described by the didactic publisher Hetzel as 'to summarize all geographical, geological, physical, astronomical knowledge amassed by modern science'. The *Extraordinary Journeys* were to total a hundred volumes, constituting sixty-two novels, produced at the rate of two per annum. In a sense, they may be seen as imaginary compensation for Verne's own settled existence. The only science in which he had any expertise was geography: a member of the Société de Géographie, he worked on an *Illustrated Geography of France and her Colonies* (1867–8). He also found time to act as municipal councillor in Amiens from 1884; despite the ambiguous suggestion of anarchist sympathies in novels such as *20,000 Leagues under the Sea* (*20,000 lieues sous les mers*, 1870), he followed a moderate, anti-radical line.

Verne's work may be said to belong to a tradition of imaginary journeys, for all the addition of nineteenth-century scientism. Indeed, the element of fantasy is supremely important. Verne criticism long took the form of 'prediction-spotting', but his science, we now know, was second-hand, culled from vulgarized sources; what we find in his work is not so much science as a mythology of science. 'Known worlds' shade disconcertingly into 'unknown worlds', science acts as threshold to myth. Overriding the paraphernalia of factual information are powerful recurrent images of mythic force, constituting what Michel Butor has described as the essence of Verne's naive genius, 'the prodigious power to make us dream'.

A frequent theme is the quest for uncharted locations – the source of the Nile, the Pole (*Adventures of Captain Hatteras*, *Voyages et aventures du capitaine Hatteras*, 1866), the centre of the earth (*Journey to the Centre of the Earth*, *Voyage au centre de la terre*, 1864) – that take on quasi-mythical significance, suggesting to the modern reader something akin to the Surrealists' *point suprême* where all contradictions are resolved. In Verne's poetically powerful vision of the Pole ('that unknown point where all meridians cross'), snow and fire are united: Hatteras discovers a volcano there, and goes mad in the attempt,

Empedocles-like, to enter it. Repeatedly the volcano is associated (unscientifically!) with initiation: it is through an extinct volcano that the protagonists of the mythologically rich *Journey to the Centre of the Earth* begin their descent into the underworld, and it is through a live volcano that they are expelled out of the earth's innards in a fascinating transcription of the trauma of birth. Fire is a recurrent theme, often refined and purified in electricity, 'soul of the industrial world', as in *Clipper of the Clouds* (*Robur le conquérant*, 1886). Electricity is even curiously united with the trappings of Gothic horror in *Carpathian Castle* (*Le Château des Carpathes*, 1892). Verne's fascination with caverns, volcanoes, labyrinths and islands attains its finest synthesis in *The Mysterious Island* (*L'Île mystérieuse*, 1874–5). It is clear that much in his work can be read in terms of Jungian archetypes. Equally clear is the predominance of the initiation-pattern, together with a taste for cryptograms and word-play: the quest of *Journey to the Centre* begins from a coded message left by an Icelandic alchemist. Verne's imagination has much in common with the alchemical tradition, itself poised between science and mythology – gold and fire are suggestively united in *The Golden Volcano* (*Le Volcan d'or*, 1906).

Not surprisingly, characterization in these tales is rudimentary and largely reduced to standard types: eccentric scientists, young novices, initiates, mysterious holders of knowledge and power (Captain Nemo), humorous servants. The element of humour, to be found in most of his works, no doubt played a large part in the success of *Around the World in 80 Days* (*Le Tour du monde en 80 jours*, 1873). In a sense, humour acts as a check on the initiatory scope of these works, for Verne holds back from 'excessive' initiation. Transgressors, such as Hatteras, are punished, whereas in general the characters return to a settled bourgeois life after a hint, a vicarious thrill of revelation. Roland Barthes has commented (in *Mythologies*, 1957) on the bourgeois aspect of Verne's work: a cult of enclosedness, the desire to reconstruct, with the help of science, a comfortable universe in microcosm, whether submarine, island or lighthouse.

However, Verne is not simply a representative of the optimistic nineteenth-century ideology of science. His later novels show increasing doubts about progress – *Master of the World* (*Maître du monde*, 1904), *The Survivors of the 'Jonathan'* (*Les Naufragés du 'Jonathan'*, 1909). A final story, *The Eternal Adam* (*L'Éternel Adam*, 1910), completes the development into pessimism: human history now appears as absurdly cyclical. Having expressed the nineteenth century's dream of science, its mythology, Verne finally, on the threshold of a more sceptical age, passes judgment on that dream.

David Meakin

Other important novels: *From the Earth to the Moon* (*De la Terre à la lune*, 1865); *The Children of Captain*

Grant (*Les Enfants du capitaine Grant*, 1868); *Black Diamonds* (*Les Indes noires*, 1877); *The Begum's Fortune* (*Les Cinq cents millions de la Bégum*, 1879); *Mathias Sandorf* (1885). See: M. Butor, *Répertoire I* (1960); I.O. Evans, *Jules Verne and his Work* (1965); M. Moré, *Le très curieux Jules Verne* (1960); S. Vierne, *Jules Verne et le roman initiatique* (1973).

471
VICTORIA and ALBERT 1819–1901 and 1819–61

Queen and Prince Consort

Queen Victoria, who ascended the British throne in 1837 and married Prince Albert of Saxe-Coburg-Gotha in 1840, is the only monarch who has given her name not only to an adjective, 'Victorian', but to a noun, 'Victorianism'. The adjective, apparently first used in 1851, has been applied to people, tastes, styles, institutions and values: the noun, apparently first used after her long reign was over, has usually been applied to a cluster of values, individual and social. Both usages frequently involve misconceptions. The very length of Victoria's reign meant that it saw many cultural changes, so that to apply the same adjective to all the shorter periods within it can be confusing: in addition, however, there was always a great variety of Victorian voices in any given period and it is impossible to select a number of them and treat them as typical of the whole. The noun, pointing to shared moral codes as well as shared convictions (e.g. belief in the gospel of work, in self-help, thrift, duty and character), was coined not by Victorians but by their successors, re-acting against what were felt to be obsolete and restrictive rules and conventions, not to speak of cant and hypocrisy: already, indeed, in the last decades of her reign such reactions can be traced. Yet later generations reacted in their turn against the first rebels, and there have been many subsequent swings of fashion, both in interpretations of 'Victorian' and 'Victorianism' and in the acquisition of Victorian objects ('Victoriana') and the conservation of Victorian buildings.

Victoria herself had no sense that she was a culture-bearer, though she had strong tastes of her own, for example an early passion for opera and a more persistent interest in painting, and held firmly also that after the reigns of the four Georges and William IV she had an obligation to set a moral example. It was a personal tragedy for her that her devoted husband, who was a dedicated culture-bearer, died so early in her reign. Albert was deeply interested both in the arts and the sciences and in the relationship of both to social morality. As early as 1841 he was appointed chairman of a royal commission concerned with the promotion and encouragement of the fine arts in Britain, and ten years later he was personally re-

sponsible for much of the success of the Great Universal Exhibition, held in the newly built Crystal Palace. Through such activities, which were part of a pattern which also included concern for social reform, Albert was brought into close touch with a number of people inside and outside political circles, who were interested in what has come to be thought of as 'Victorian culture', the culture of the middle years of the Queen's reign: they included Charles Eastlake, Henry Cole, Lyon Playfair, and from overseas Felix Mendelssohn* and Gustav Waagen. It was a non-specialist culture with provincial as well as international ramifications, and with a built-in recognition of market forces as well as patronage. Albert commanded respect within it less because of his position as Prince Consort than because of his personal abilities and interests. Yet he had to face considerable political and social opposition and was often the target of the Press. His most lasting contribution to posterity, apart from the controversial Albert Memorial, built to commemorate him, was the South Kensington complex of educational, artistic and scientific institutions, financed from the Great Exhibition surplus. Outside London the royal homes at Balmoral and Osborne were very much of his own conception: he also made significant changes at Windsor Castle.

Victoria was desolate when Albert died and spent years of her reign in deep mourning. Yet there was a final Victorian fling in the two royal jubilees of 1887 and 1897. Between the two jubilees an area of land forty times the size of Great Britain was added to Victoria's empire, of which India, over which she was declared empress in 1876, had been described as the brightest jewel in the crown. This overseas commitment ensured that Victorian tastes and styles are in evidence throughout the whole world: indeed, some of the most characteristic Victorian buildings can be seen in Bombay, Melbourne and Toronto. The adjective and the *ism* have also been used in relation to the United States.

The historian G.M. Young, whose *Victorian England, Portrait of an Age* (1934) marked the beginning of a change in attitudes to the Victorians, pushed further soon afterwards in relation to the visual arts by John Betjeman, insisted that the awkward terms 'Victorian' and 'Victorianism' should be applied, if they were to be applied at all, to other non-English-speaking societies also, where the terms have not usually found root. Down-grading the influence of Victoria, though not of Albert, he argued forcefully that ways and habits, fashions and prejudices, doctrines, ideas and even phrases which we think of as typically Victorian are really part of a general European cultural pattern. Albert, whose German education led him to Italy, was strongly European in his sympathies and aspirations, and Victoria, through her relatives, was closely linked to European courts. It was from the industrial north of England, however, that an address to Albert in 1857 thanked him for introducing a popular dimension into high culture: it spoke of Albert's 'encouragement . . . to whatever tends to promote the material comfort of the people or to foster in them a taste for intellectual pleasure'.

Asa Briggs

See: John Steegman, *Consort of Taste* (1950); Elizabeth Longford, *Queen Victoria* (1964); Winslow Ames, *Prince Albert and Victorian Taste* (1967). For contemporary colouring – and restraint – see the official *The Life of the Prince Consort*, ed. Sir Theodore Martin (5 vols, 1875–80), and *The Letters of Queen Victoria* (3 vols, 1908).

472
VIGNY, Alfred-Victor de 1797–1863

French poet, dramatist and novelist

Vigny was born at Loches (Touraine), from where the family moved to Paris in 1799. His father, Léon-Pierre de Vigny, a former captain in Louis XV's army and severely wounded in the Seven Years' War, played little part in his son's early upbringing, which was given a firm basis of piety by Madame de Vigny. At seventeen, Vigny was at the lycée Bonaparte (now Condorcet), preparing the examinations for the national military academy (École polytechnique), but on the fall of Napoleon* was able to take a commission for a time in a household regiment serving Louis XVIII, being later transferred to an infantry regiment of the Royal Guard (1816). Service in the army, although a tradition of his family, proved in many respects disappointing and uncongenial to Vigny. The ending of the Napoleonic Wars deprived him of the active service he had originally hoped for, and the qualities required for advancement in peace time did not come easily to a reserved and contemplative disposition such as his. He continued his military career none the less until 1827, when he was given a discharge on grounds of ill-health, and later looked back with some gratitude on this period which had afforded him the leisure and the incentive to think and write.

As a member of the aristocracy, hard hit by the revolution, he had no doubt nourished hopes of repairing his fortunes by an advantageous marriage, but his wedding, in 1825, to Lydia Bunbury, the daughter of an English colonial family, provided little in the way of dowry and, as events turned out, burdened him for over thirty years with an invalid wife, whom he sustained and nursed with devotion. Success in his work as a poet, and more particularly as a dramatist, brought him into contact with the main literary and social figures of the time and precipitated a liaison with the actress Marie Dorval, which lasted from 1831 to 1838. Like Lamartine* and Hugo*, he was drawn towards public life, not only by personal ambition, but also by a strong sense of the responsibility of the writer in the development of social and political values. His personal career proved difficult. His play, *Chatterton*, performed at the Comédie-Française in Paris in 1835, was the pinnacle of his immediate success. Later he stood unsuccessfully for election to the French Academy five times before being admitted in 1845. He was a supporter of the Revolution of 1848, having moved steadily from his original defence of the restored Bourbon monarchy towards ideas more in line with those behind the constitution of the American Republic, but two attempts to get himself elected to a seat in the Chamber of Deputies (1848 and 1849) proved fruitless. A brief acquaintance with Louis-Napoléon, in London in 1839 and in France (Angoulême, 1852), predisposed him to some extent in favour of the Second Empire, but his attempts at active involvement in politics were at an end, and despite indications of favour from the emperor, the last decade of his life was spent in relative seclusion, in which Vigny continued to write and to reflect on the values which had preoccupied him.

Poetry was for him, as for most writers of his generation, the first of the literary arts, and it was with a series of poems, which slowly formed themselves into his first major volume of verse, that his reputation began to be made. This is his *Poèmes antiques et modernes* ('Poems Ancient and Modern', 1837), various stages of which had appeared in 1822, 1826 and 1829. The 1837 edition contains twenty poems, arranged in three books ('Livre mystique'; 'Livre antique'; 'Livre moderne'), the individual pieces forming fragments of a vision of the development of human consciousness, spiritual and moral, from mythological times to the modern world. Two main ideas run through these poems, those of fatality and responsibility: the fatality of divinely ordained events, the powerlessness of Christianity to shift the burden of pre-ordained evil from human life; responsibility seen in its two forms, as part of a heavy destiny that weighs upon those born to command, and as a force capable of raising human life to remarkable heights of heroism. The ideas are for the most part not expressed directly, but are conveyed through narrative and through dramatic dialogue representing the actions and thoughts of symbolic figures. Most of the pieces are in the form which Vigny called the *poème*, which was originally a short epic, and an epic quality is retained in Vigny's verse, together with an attempt to preserve some basis of authenticity in the imaginative presentation of an episode ('Moïse', 'Moses', 'La Femme adultère', 'The adulteress', are interpretations of biblical passages; 'Le Cor', 'The Horn', is based on the *Chanson de Roland*). But there are also two 'Mysteries' ('Eloa' and 'Le Deluge') which owe something to Byron's* *Heaven and Earth* and *Cain*.

These use supernatural figures to represent ideas about the human predicament. 'Eloa', a long poem about the angel of pity, the victim of Satan and doomed to a relatively powerless role in fallen creation, was admired in its own time for the beauty and elevation with which the idea is projected. '*Élévation*' is the word which Vigny used for a third form of poem in this collection, a poem capable of dealing in lyrical terms with themes from contemporary life. 'Paris' is the most important example, the city viewed by night affording a basis for speculations about the new religious and political ideas, those of Lamennais, Fourier* and Saint-Simon*, which no longer seemed to Vigny to hold any part of the key to the future.

He also tried his hand at the historical novel, *Cinq-Mars. Une Conjuration sous Louis XIII* ('Cinq-Mars. A Conspiracy under Louis XIII') appearing in 1826, five years before Hugo's *Notre-Dame de Paris*. It is based on the plot against Cardinal Richelieu headed by the Marquis de Cinq-Mars and François-Victor de Thou. Vigny claimed that his personal contribution to the historical novel was in the use of real characters as protagonists in a narrative work, the main aim of which was to present ideas on a period of French history, in this case a period when the country was moving out of feudalism towards the status of a dominant power, and when conflicting values of justice and superstition bedevilled the structures of government. Though well received, *Cinq-Mars* was not entirely successful because of the liberties taken with historical detail and background, and Vigny did not persevere with this genre.

His second major novel, on the subjugation imposed by military service, *The Military Condition* (*Servitude et Grandeur militaires*, 1835, trans. 1964), is a stronger work, stamped with the authenticity of Vigny's own military background. Three officers, representing the conditions of service under three recent regimes are depicted, each in a tragic episode. The 'servitude' is the obedience of the soldier to the orders of the regime. The 'grandeur' is the code of honour and courage by which the best soldiers manage to live.

In the theatre, Vigny's success began with adaptations and translations of Shakespeare at a time of enthusiasm for the formula of the Shakespearian stage, and *The Moor of Venice* (*Le More de Venise*) was staged at the Comédie-Française in 1829. But his most important dramatic achievement was *Chatterton*, a prose drama in three acts produced in 1835 and running for five months as part of the repertory of the Comédie-Française. In this play, Vigny uses the suicide of the young English poet in order to construct a dramatic tableau representing in strongly sentimental terms the position of the genuine artist in modern societies. The drama is intensified by an imaginary episode of tragic and unavowed love between Chatterton and Kitty, the wife of the domineering John Bell in whose house he lodges.

Chatterton is used by Vigny as a symbol, in much the same way as the figures of his poems are used. He is the victim of the social order, a 'modern pariah' in Vigny's term, since the true poet cannot compromise with the requirements of society. The poet is thus associated in Vigny's thought with the soldier, both performing important acts for a society which ignores or exploits them.

A prose work, *Stello: A Session with Doctor Noir*, (*Stello*, 1832, trans. 1963), is a series of three episodes on the tragic lives of three poets (Chatterton, Gilbert and Chenier), treated with some imaginative freedom, but designed as a background to the more intensively developed thesis of *Chatterton*. It forms an obvious parallel with the three episodes of *The Military Condition*. Stello embodies the poetic, intuitive and idealist faculties in human nature. His companion, the enigmatically named Doctor 'Black' ('Docteur Noir': the word 'black' can be taken either as a name or a quality) represents reason at its most disabused and penetrative. The episodes recounted are a part of a 'treatment' of Stello's neurasthenic disorders. The Platonic nature of these 'consultations' offered a form sympathetic to Vigny's temperament, and he planned a second series under the title of *Daphné*, which was not published in his lifetime.

Daphné was set down in its present form in 1837. It is an elaboration of Vigny's view of the modern period, which he saw as still dominated by a failed religion, with only bankrupt systems of thought bidding to take its place. He looked back with admiration to the period of the Emperor Julian (the Apostate) who attempted the impossible task of reanimating the dying pagan cults in the face of advancing Christianity. Daphné is the name of a place of retreat occupied by the pagan Libanius, Julian's spiritual master, and the central episodes of the book are set here. Apparently contrasted, yet joined with them, are scenes in Paris witnessed by Stello and Docteur Noir in the aftermath of the 1830 Revolution, which refer them back to Daphné.

From this time (1837) Vigny published no more books – indeed, he saw his *Complete Works* through the press between 1839 and 1847 (seven volumes) – but continued to write poems. Eleven completed pieces, a number of which had appeared in the *Revue des Deux Mondes*, were collected after his death to form his second main volume, *Les Destinées* ('The Fates', 1864). Two apparently opposed attitudes emerge from these products of Vigny's most mature years, despair and measured confidence. No contradiction is involved. Two poems of religious despair re-create the sombre picture of the human condition as Vigny saw it. 'Le Mont des Oliviers' ('The Mount of Olives') presents a humanized Christ figure at Gethsemane questioning his incompleted mission which leaves unanswered all the universal enigmas facing man in his life in the world. 'Les Destinées', from which the volume takes its title, is an epic vision of the same event, the inconclusive passage of Christ in the world, which has substituted divine Grace for the pagan notion of fate.

Despite these poems, and the bleak or bitter messages of other pieces such as 'La Mort du Loup' ('The Death of the Wolf') and 'La Colère de Samson' ('The Rage of Samson'), Vigny's main aim in his later years is to establish a synthesis of modern values. He celebrates the colonizing of North America in 'La Sauvage' ('The Red Indian Girl'), underlines the excesses of parliamentary as well as of despotic governments ('Les Oracles', 'The Oracles', and 'Wanda, Histoire russe', 'Wanda, a Russian Tale'), and in two great poems combines images of discovery and technology with symbols of the responsibility of the artist in the modern world. These are 'La Bouteille à la mer' ('The Bottle in the Sea') and 'La Maison du Berger' ('The Shepherd's Caravan'). The first evokes an ill-fated voyage of exploration west of Tierra del Fuego, from which only a bottle containing information useful for navigation in those latitudes is preserved and finally reaches land in Europe. The second is a long meditative piece on the poet's need for freedom, for the companionship of woman and for conditions conducive to the concentration of ideas by art. The middle section gives a cautious reception to the technological age, symbolized by the railway train. Both poems deal with the expression of ideas, 'La Bouteille à la mer' stressing the power of art to preserve the message of the thinker, 'La Maison du Berger' reminding an age indifferent to poetry of the beauty and brilliance this form can give to thought, symbolizing these qualities by the pearl, the flame and the diamond.

From the evidence of his last poem, 'L'Esprit pur' ('Immaterial Mind'), Vigny appeared to believe that the values expressed in his work would gather power as time went on and the minds of new generations were drawn to them. But it was rather the techniques of his art, particularly his poetry, which gained in influence after his death. His use of symbols, and especially those drawn from objects and substances, as in his *Destinées*, suggested already some of the techniques of Symbolist poetry later in the century, while his dense, prismatic verse anticipated the art of the Parnassians in the period of the Second Empire. These are also the qualities of his work that have been prized by critics and scholars in the recent period. However, new editions of works such as *Daphné* and *Stello* and detailed commentaries on *Les Destinées* are providing a fresh view of the complexity of his thought and the religious and historical insights it affords.

Clifford Ireson

Other works: *La Maréchale d'Ancre* (1831); *Quitte pour la peur* (1833), plays; *Le Journal d'un Poète* (1867), private journal, much augmented in recent editions of his complete works. See *Oeuvres complètes*,

Bibliothèque de la Pléiade (2 vols, 1964–5). On Vigny: J. Doolittle, *Alfred de Vigny* (1967); P.-G. Castex, *Vigny: L'Homme et l'oeuvre* (1942); B. de la Salle, *Alfred de Vigny* (1963), general surveys; F. Germain, *L'Imagination d'Alfred de Vigny* (1961), detailed literary study.

473

VIOLLET-LE-DUC, Eugène 1814–79

French architect, historian, engineer and teacher

Viollet-le-Duc, a man with a deep understanding of French Gothic architecture, was a highly influential figure in the development of late nineteenth-century and early twentieth-century building, not only in his own country but throughout Europe and America. His importance is as a theorist and writer rather than as a practising architect and his ideas can usefully be seen in the context of the English Gothic revival led by A. Pugin*. The English movement had a different motivation and reached higher standards than the French.

Born in France in 1814, le-Duc became a pupil of A.F. Leclere, himself a student of Durand. Therefore le-Duc was thoroughly grounded in methods of construction and use of materials as well as knowledge of Greek, Roman and Renaissance style. His thought arose from a rationalist functionalist background and only after these aspects had been fully absorbed was he encouraged, through his association with Labrouste, a brilliant innovator, to produce imaginative ideas. Labrouste, in one of his most famous buildings, the library of Sainte-Geneviève, Paris (1840), used, in the interior, exposed iron work structures. This factor was important for the theories of le-Duc.

Despite time as a student in Greece, Rome and Sicily, it was finally to French Gothic that le-Duc was drawn. He studied with immense care not only its style but also the methods used for its construction. By 1854 he was able to publish the first of ten volumes forming the *Dictionnaire Raisonné de l'Architecture Française* (eleventh to sixteenth centuries). The final volume appeared in 1868 and the whole was translated into several languages; consequently it was read widely and became influential throughout Europe and America.

The significance of these books was in part that they encapsulated much which architects interested in revival were laboriously seeking by travelling to the sources. The main thrust of revival came from England where a Catholic religious movement was making itself strongly felt in intellectual circles in the 1840s. This necessitated the building of churches, not simply in imitation of Gothic but in the true spirit of the original French Catholic Gothic. This aspect became an important emotional element for those revivalist architects such as Pugin, himself a Catholic. The passion with which these men reinterpreted the early builders gave their work an authority and brilliance, lacking for the most part in France, where revival was in new church building largely an empirical matter.

Le-Duc, in spite of his many commissions to restore and at times reconstruct old cathedrals, such as those at Carcassonne and Vezelay, none the less was interested in contemporary developments in industrial technology, more especially in the use of iron. There is little evidence of this knowledge in his Paris building though. From 1846 to 1848 he built a block of flats in the rue de Liège and circa 1860 he built another in the rue de Douai. Both buildings are adjoined on either side by others, and each adapts to them, retaining a traditional, even slightly dour quality with evenly spaced long windows. The development in those years between the two blocks is slight. Le-Duc leaves out the shutters in the Douai block and, instead of recessing one small balcony with straight iron railings, projects one full width at the top, a smaller one lower down and faces them both with decorated iron railings in an organic rather than geometric style.

During the latter 1850s le-Duc, with his friend Lassus, was restoring and refurbishing Notre Dame in Paris. Whilst engaged upon this immense task Lassus died and the year after, in 1858, le-Duc allowed himself his only High Gothic extravaganza, the decorations for the tomb of the Duc de Morny.

Already famous for his *Dictionnaire*, le-Duc assured his continuing success by publishing his *Entretiens sur l'Architecture* in 1863 with plates appearing by 1872. In these volumes he makes clear his theoretical position with regard to the architecture of the future. One illustration suggests a church interior wherein the roof is supported by rectangular girders resting on thin rounded metal columns. These iron supports project diagonally upwards from the walls, as a type of buttress or large bracket. The effect is ungainly but later designers incorporated this type of structure into a more satisfying aesthetic.

Hector Guimard, the architect of many Art Nouveau domestic dwellings as well as Paris Métro stations, undoubtedly took up le-Duc's ideas. The sloping metal pillars appear as supports for overhanging façades and the charming decorative metal plant designs appear on houses and stations alike.

Le-Duc wrote that architects should find 'resources furnished by manufacturing skill' and that they ought to be 'making use of these means with a view to the adoption of architectural forms adapted to our times'. By this he meant that metal could be used not only for ornament but as structure, either as free-standing supports or as verticals and horizontals between infilling of masonry and glass.

In England these ideas were anathema to those who supported Ruskin* and Morris* in their condemnation of industry as immoral, through its degradation of la-bour. Nevertheless, in America le-Duc's proposals made rapid progress. In *Discourses on Architecture*, published in Boston in 1875, he wrote: 'A practical architect might not unnaturally conceive the idea of erecting a vast edifice whose frame should be entirely of iron, enclosing that frame and preserving it by means of a casing.' One Chicago architect, William Jenney, did exactly that and completed in 1885 the first skyscraper, ten storeys high. It took the invention of the Bessemer light-weight steel beam, unknown in le-Duc's lifetime, to make the top four storeys possible, but it was essentially le-Duc's proposition.

In England, despite lack of interest in his modern ideas, le-Duc received considerable recognition for his restoration work, as well as some criticism. He was invited to write for the *Ecclesiologist* and to visit Britain to tour Gothic buildings. When he came he pronounced the Houses of Parliament a 'frightful monstrosity', but later commended the work of the architect Burges. The RIBA saw fit to award him their Gold Medal although the École des Beaux Arts, of which le-Duc was Professor of Art and Aesthetics, caused him to resign as a result of its reaction to his ideas in *Entretiens*.

He continued to practise his architectural designing none the less and built some new churches, including by 1867 one at St Denis on the Seine, which is a pleasant, sturdy, traditional Gothic building with vaulted ceilings throughout, a tower minus a spire and some delicate decoration.

It was left however to the future architects to make le-Duc's dreams materialize. The brilliant engineer Contamin was to build the Halle des Machines for the Paris International Exhibition of 1889. This huge building with wall and roof in one was made of exposed metal ribs infilled almost entirely with glass. The same engineer was to provide the metal structure for the first ferro-concrete building of modern design, the Church of Saint Jean-de-Montmartre, built between 1897 and 1904 and designed by J. de Baudot.

The new materials introduced into building at this period made possible architecture with a more simple design. This knowledge, together with the understanding of basic structures inherent in early large scale historic buildings, was an important factor in the development of twentieth-century International style architecture. In this respect Viollet-le-Duc can be considered one of its most important progenitors.

Pat Turner

See: *From the Classicists to the Impressionists: Art and Architecture in the Nineteenth Century*, ed. E. Gilmore Holt (1966); N. Pevsner, *Pioneers of Modern Design* (1970); H.R. Hitchcock, *Architecture: Nineteenth and Twentieth Centuries* (1971).

474

VUILLARD, Edouard 1868–1940

French painter

A painter of intimate interiors and decorative panels Vuillard is essentially nineteenth-century in both spirit and method. Content to reflect the ordered and comfortable life of the Parisian bourgeoisie he was in no way seduced by the coming of the new technology or the rapid stylistic innovations of the Modern movement. His manner stems partly from Paul Gauguin* and the Symbolists and partly from French Impressionism but the greatest influence on his work dates back to the early years at home in the claustrophobic clutter of his mother's workroom. Surrounded by the rich textures and colourful patterns of the dressmaker he saw in the printed material the flat areas of pure colour that later meant so much to the Symbolists and realized that the quick brush-strokes of Impressionism were unsuited for what he had in mind. A modest man – devoted to his mother – he had many friends and though never committed to any one particular group was nevertheless involved briefly with both the Nabis and the poet Stéphane Mallarmé*. His designs for the Théâtre Libre and the Théâtre de l'Oeuvre for the actor-manager Lugne-Poe were well received and the two men – together with the painters Maurice Denis and Pierre Bonnard – shared a studio. Bonnard and Vuillard have much in common – their subject matter is often similar – but they are too readily linked. Vuillard lacks Bonnard's flair for colour for its own sake and on his own admission regarded himself as little more than a 'spectator' but for all the admitted limitations there is a keen eye for detail and the slow methodical technique is well able to cope with the undramatic events that fascinated him. Whether in the early simple groupings or the deliberately stylized works where Gauguin's influence is most obvious there is little affectation and few risks are taken. Posed they certainly are and often set in artificial light but a deft sense of composition sees him through and there is a touching sense of intimacy in many of the obvious family scenes. Vuillard used a camera and in a way a parallel can be drawn with the 'family snapshot' which can catch people unawares in acts of private contemplation or withdrawal.

The series of four large panels painted for his friend Dr Vaquez are finely observed with an almost glut of decoration cleverly contrasted with the simple outline of a door or mirror or perhaps with the white simplicity of a folded skirt or crumpled newspaper. Flowers in a painted vase flit lightly across the regular patterned wallpaper and there are cushions strewn across the floor. The people who live in the rooms are dwarfed by the sheer exuberance of the overall richness of the colour, though there are delicate – often tender – touches as a mother plays with a young child or tugs at her caught skirt. Vuillard notices such things and he is certainly no innocent. The frequent use of mirrors to extend our field of vision is knowing and a little extra daylight is let into an otherwise oppressive interior as a result. Outside he is less happy, though there is the occasional empty landscape but somewhat ironically when he leaves the living room and ventures out into the open air he becomes contrived and there is more often than not a hint of the stage set. He is happiest at home in a situation he knows well where his mother sits carefully stitching and little is seen that disturbs the day to day routine. Unlike many of his friends he felt no desire for change and he paints without comment. Gauguin did make him think and so too did his friend Mallarmé and he enjoyed the one night stands for Lugne-Poe, but what really excited him was what he saw around him and the way people lived and particularly what they wore and used to cover their walls. In his simple unaffected manner he shows us exactly how it was. We see the comfortable bourgeois way of life with its pleasantly mundane trappings and the need for decoration. The people seem to be less colourful but they are content and so too is Vuillard who leaves the trials and tribulations of the twentieth century to others more able to cope.

John Furse

See: A. Ritchie, *Edouard Vuillard* (1969); J. Russell, *Vuillard* (1971).

W

475

WAGNER, Richard 1813–83

German music dramatist

Wagner's work has often been described in terms of its paradoxes. And the fact that these paradoxes reveal so much about the sensibility of the nineteenth century is due to Wagner's having been as much a dramatist as a composer. He championed a socialist Utopia, free from financial cares, where the pursuit of art could be held as the highest ideal: yet subtly he reinforced the Christian-bourgeois morality of his day. He was an idealist and, for the most part, an optimist, yet death cast the longest shadow over his work. He unleashed in his music a liberating new sensuality and energy, whilst arguing dramatically that redemption could be achieved only through sublimation, renunciation and self-sacrifice. He worked on a massive scale, but was celebrated for his unprecedented sensitivity to expressive detail. As an artist, he was particular to the point of pedantry, but used his art to preach anti-intellectualism and a recognition of nature as the teacher of spontaneity. And whilst his operatic reforms and innovations were radical and international in their influence, they were, at the same time, rooted in a vast learning, and in mythic sources that were conspicuously German. Nowadays these opposites may readily be understood as necessary preconditions of each other. But earlier judgments of Wagner have, not surprisingly, been characterized by significant contradictions: he has been seen both as the high priest of love, and as a dangerous, even malevolent, theatrical wizard.

Something of this critical perplexity owes to a further apparent dichotomy: between the high seriousness and tenacity of his work on the one hand, and the rash impetuosity he showed in his personal and financial affairs on the other. This became evident even at an early stage of his life. Born in 1813, he matriculated from Leipzig University as a music student in 1831, at which time he studied composition privately with Theodore Weinlig (lessons recalled, perhaps, in *Die Meistersinger*). It was the epiphanies of this time, in drama (the plays of Shakespeare) and music (Beethoven's* Ninth Symphony, Weber's* *Der Freischütz*, Wilhelmine Schröder-Devrient singing Leonora in *Fidelio*) that were to lead in due course to the synthesis of the two arts into a 'higher' form. Also no less important

for the development of his impeccable sense of theatre and stagecraft was the early and extensive first-hand knowledge he gained of the operatic repertoire as music director in Riga (1837) and Dresden (1843), and as a resident in Paris (1840). As a consequence, his first three operas showed diverse influences: *Die Feen* (1833), *Das Liebesverbot* (1836), and the highly successful *Rienzi* (1840) owe as much to the examples of Bellini*, Mehul, Auber, Meyerbeer* and Spontini as they do to those of his German contemporaries. But these were also turbulent years privately. In 1836, he married Minna Planer, whose early, but brief, elopement with a Koenigsberg merchant boded ill for the couple's future. In 1839, debts compelled him to flee Riga. After travels to Russia and England he settled in Paris, where his extravagance landed him for a short time in debtor's prison.

There was a similar pattern to the next decade. With *Der Fliegende Holländer* (*The Flying Dutchman*, 1841), *Tannhäuser* (1847) and *Lohengrin* (1848), he found his own voice, took Romantic opera to its peak, uncovered most of his later dramatic concerns and provided a vital transition from sectionalized opera to operas where entire acts were unfolded as unbroken musical textures. Yet his participation in the Dresden uprisings of 1848–9 forced him to flee Saxony (Bakunin* said he was too much of an idealist to be an effective revolutionary), and in the following financially unstable years he derived his income from concert-giving (he later wrote a monograph on conducting), which entailed further travels to Italy, England and France (his pamphlet deploring the Jewish influence on music appears to have been occasioned by Meyerbeer's refusal to promote his work).

In the 1850s, the affairs with Jessie Laussot and Mathilde Wesendonck that led eventually to Wagner's separation from Minna were evidently bound up with the great effort of gestation demanded by the music drama format that engaged him for the rest of his life. At this time his principal sources were Grimm's* *German Mythology* and Greek drama (Aeschylus especially), sources central to his attempt to restore to the theatre a lost communal consciousness (the argument was further developed in *The Birth of Tragedy* by Wagner's protégé, the philosopher Friedrich Nietzsche*); and in *The Artwork of the Future* (*Das Kunstwerk der Zukunft*, 1849) and *Opera and Drama* (*Oper und Drama*, 1851) he undertook a comprehensive survey in order to describe how traditional technical features would in future have to be newly balanced and blended in order that music at all times could illumine the drama, and not vice versa (this is what is meant by *Gesamtkunstwerk*, the work in which all arts were synthesized).

The main fruit of this undertaking was *Der Ring des Nibelungen*, a music drama in three evenings (*Die Walküre*, *Siegfried* and *Götterdämmerung*) preceded by an introductory evening, *Das Rheingold*. The libretto was begun in 1848, the music completed in 1874, and the whole performed in 1876. In the meantime, he composed two other works motivated to a greater or lesser extent by biographical concerns. Of *Tristan und Isolde* (1859) he had written to his lifelong friend Franz Liszt*: 'As I have never in life felt the real bliss of love, I must erect a monument to the most beautiful of my dreams ... Tristan and Isolde.' And the extent to which he had absorbed the exotic nihilism of Schopenhauer's* *The World as Will and Representation* emerges from his remark that 'freedom from all our dreams' – in other words, extinction – 'is our only salvation.' In the comedy *Die Meistersinger* (1867), however, he offered through the words of Hans Sachs a defence of his own position as a German artist, and projected his aesthetic attitudes to the nature and function of high art.

But the end of the 1860s saw Wagner in changed circumstances. The publication of the poem of *Der Ring* had been prefaced by an appeal to an enlightened patron. In 1864, the young King of Bavaria, Ludwig II, declared himself ready and willing to respond. He eased Wagner's debts, promised him a regular income, and supported his projects – albeit intermittently – for the rest of his life. In 1861, Wagner had seen Minna for the last time (she died five years later); and two years after he settled in Villa Tribschen near Lucerne, he was joined permanently by Cosima Liszt, at the time the wife of the conductor Hans von Bülow, and daughter of the composer (according to whom she revered Wagner with a Senta-like devotion). Her diaries were to furnish biographical information for Wagner's later years, following on from his autobiography, which extended only as far as the mid-sixties. In 1871 he moved to Bayreuth, and the last twelve years of his life were devoted to founding a specially designed festival theatre (which opened in 1876), to building his own house (Wahnfried, 1874), to composing and producing his final music drama *Parsifal* (in part an idealization of Ludwig II), and to writing extensively on practical, musical and philosophical issues of the day. The organizational strain aggravated a heart condition (angina), and he died in Venice in 1883.

Although Wagner's art evolved extraordinarily during his lifetime, most of the main issues are essentially present in his first three mature works. In his transformation of Heine's* account of the *Flying Dutchman* legend, Wagner laid a special emphasis on the role of Senta. It is her self-sacrifice that redeems the Dutchman, who had been destined to wander the seas eternally in punishment for his Promethean defiance of divinity. In the ballad that forms the kernel of the work, she reveals (with what Thomas Mann described as the 'lofty hysteria' of all Wagner's heroines) not merely love, but a deep, abnormal bonding with the more-than-human, timeless hero. On the other hand, his love for her is both a yearning for redemption and a longing for death (without her love, he is tragically doomed 'never to die'): her sacrifice is part of his self-fulfilment. But through it, they are both transfigured, and in a conclusion that reveals an essentially Christian morality, love emerges triumphant. Musically, although the work is organized into discontinuous groups of scenes (Wagner soon came to prefer unbroken continuities in each act), it is powerfully homogeneous from a harmonic point of view – a feature of all Wagner's subsequent works.

If the Dutchman's quest for Senta represented part of the nineteenth century's (and Wagner's) quest for Goethe's* *ewig Weibliche* (eternal womanhood), then the examination in *Tannhäuser* (a significant conflation of two sources from *Das Knaben Wunderhorn*) of carnality (the court of Venus) and sublime purity (the Wartburg, the Minnesingers, Elizabeth and the pilgrims) established two poles important for Wagner's work generally. Their musical treatment through unstable harmony on the one hand, and pseudo-archaisms on the other, were to lead to the most characteristic sounds of *Tristan* and *Parsifal*. In the libretto, the two worlds are to a certain extent interdependent. Tannhäuser, a singer (with whom Wagner identified closely), recognizes that through Venus 'every sweet wonder stems', but nevertheless proclaims 'in the midst of joy, I crave pain'. On the other hand, the gravity of the saintly Elizabeth is at least partially sexually achieved: he has awoken in her 'emotions I had never experienced, longings I had never known'. Yet in its first version, the music (as with Senta's in the *Dutchman*) had not fully realized the feminine aspect of the text (Venus especially): and the post-*Tristan* revisions that developed the work's latent eroticism also unbalanced it stylistically. At the end of his life it remained the one work with which Wagner was still dissatisfied.

On the other hand, *Lohengrin* (derived from Wolfram von Eschenbach) is consummately achieved within its own terms. Here, humanity itself is put on trial, with only the divine and the superhuman exalted. Wagner saw in Lohengrin, a fearless emissary from the holy land of the Grail, a symbol of the artist, demanding unquestioning adherence to, and love for, his visions. Lohengrin agrees to defend and marry Elsa as long as she asks neither his name nor his origin. Inevitably, she is set upon by doubters, and, after the wedding ceremony, presses the forbidden question (why can't he trust her with his secret? she asks rather persuasively; how can love be ideal if she can't even address him?). Sadly, Lohengrin returns to the Grail, Elsa dies of shock and disappointment, and the moral is to be drawn – as Gustav Mahler* put it – that 'the capacity for trust is masculine, suspicion is feminine'.

But however two-edged Lohengrin's authoritarianism may be, there were three striking musical developments here: the impressive tableaux that portray an idealized medieval community are skilfully woven into a newly continuous texture; the music has a fresh synaesthetic splendour (the silvery sheen especially of the Lohengrin-Grail music); and the art of slow transition from one dramatic extreme (in Act III, festivity and private joy) to another (rupture, desolation and death) is effected by large-scale control of harmony that adds new dimensions to the meaning of words.

Indeed, Wagner's theorizing in the early fifties led to a reconsidered interdependence of word and music. Whereas previously, large-scale operatic continuity had been in part achieved by the use of 'reminiscence motives' – thematic entities that recurred with the effect of self-conscious quotations – Wagner now developed a constantly evolving orchestral web of thematic fragments, themselves significantly interrelated, which were symphonically developed in an 'unending' melodic flow, according to dramatic circumstances. Over these *leitmotives* (the term employed by Hans von Wolzogen) the voice part sang in a heightened recitative (*Sprechgesang*), occasionally taking up the orchestral fragments to give them definitive articulation. This practice was also extended through new uses of harmony and versification. The orchestra thus assumed a narrative role similar to that of the chorus in Greek tragedy: the humans seem the playthings of gods, and gods appear subject to the inexorable forces of destiny.

These new techniques are central to *The Ring*, whose quasi-Shakespearian complexity has given rise to so much critical debate. The work opens with the depiction of original sin: the dwarf Alberich's seizure of power (symbolized by a ring) through the renunciation of love. He cruelly exploits his fellow dwarfs and places the curse of death on all the ring's future owners (the capitalist analogies here are what fascinated G.B. Shaw). Conversely, it is the dread of loss of power that motivates Wotan, the ageing head of the gods (a paradox that humanizes him), to build Valhalla as a 'fortress against fear'. The cycle shows his fight against impending death, his acquiescence in it, and finally his combustion as flames sweep Valhalla.

Importantly, however, there are two aspects to Wotan's personality, as there were to Faust's. The male, mortal side schemes to perpetuate his power through the creation of a perfect hero, who, whilst being independent of himself, would represent a new and higher breed of being, capable of winning and guarding the ring (being fearless, he would be exempt from the curse). *Die Walküre* shows the failure of the hero's prototype, Siegmund; *Siegfried* shows the eponymous

hero's schooling (from nature, not from received learning), and his winning of the highest prize, his bride Brunnhilde. *Götterdämmerung* reveals the truth of the comment made in *Das Rheingold* by Wotan's wife Fricka (who is also the goddess of marriage and symbol of a legalistic, repressive society) that the god's eugenic plans are mere dreams: the 'tragic' destruction of Siegfried by Hagen (Alberich's son) is inevitable in a loveless world.

On the other hand, Wotan has a feminine, immortal side, shown in two ways: first, in relation to Erda (the earth goddess), who represents the wisdom of the universe, and his own deepest conscience. She reminds him of the inexorability of destiny, and her decline matches his. Secondly, in relation to his daughter by Erda, the Valkyrie Brunnhilde. As his 'wish-child', she guards his deepest interests and intuitions. When the incensed Fricka insists that Wotan destroy his illegitimate child Siegmund (who is the lover of his own sister, herself the wife of another man), Brunnhilde refuses to execute the command, as being contrary to Wotan's inner desires, and a denial of the love Siegmund feels for Sieglinde. Wotan's punishment – he strips her of her divinity – gives her the independence to perform the Senta-like 'world-redeeming' act of self-sacrifice, which atones for the sins committed against Siegfried, by casting herself on to the hero's funeral pyre. This act, together with the return of the ring to its guardians, the Rhinemaidens, forms the basis for the musical optimism with which the work ends (the conclusion, in fact, gave Wagner much trouble): the spirit of love remains if all else has perished.

What is so striking about this vast undertaking is the imaginative richness of its surface, especially in its use of the mythic, the elemental, the supernatural and the dynastic; in the complexity of its psychological situations (notably in *Die Walküre*); in the force of its dramatic parallelisms; and not least in the invention and variety of the music, on both the epic and the intimate scale.

In *Tristan und Isolde*, an essentially private 'action', extinction is seen as the only true consummation of love: as Carl Dahlhaus observes, the love-potion which the maidservant substitutes for the intended poison, is, in a poetic sense, also a death-potion. But this nihilistic stance is not all that Wagner learnt from Schopenhauer. The life-enhancing eroticism of the music, so pre-eminent in Act II, derived its impetus from the analogy drawn by the philosopher between the quality of music and the quality of the 'Will'. For he describes the 'Will' as the dynamic essence of things, the motivating energy of life before it has been refracted through, and tempered by, consciousness. The merging of the identities of the lovers in the duets is thus a shared return to the well-springs of nature, a rediscovery of what is usually found only in the night-time world of dreams. On the other hand, Wagner was too much of a moralist not to invest the day-time world of social contracts, embodied in the figure of King Marke, with its own dignity (Tristan appears to break honour in his love for Isolde); and the unification of the lovers in death – rather than in life – also offers a social answer to an illicit love (Marke's post-mortem absolution of Tristan and Isolde begs all kinds of questions). Technically, the work is notable for two reasons: first, Wagner's principle of *Stabreim* finds its *locus classicus* here (the principle establishes poetic continuity through the incantatory use of internal alliteration rather than end-rhyme); and secondly, the music derives new, complex and revolutionary means for obscuring its traditional tonal anchors, as a way of mirroring the language of the 'Will'.

Just as *Tristan* offers an interpretation of human energy in erotic terms, so does *Die Meistersinger* see the justification of art in the need to sublimate aggression, and to hold the pursuit of art for its own sake as the highest activity. In this work – a comic appendage to *Tannhäuser* – the central figure is no longer the impetuous young knight (in this case Walther), but the cobbler Hans Sachs (Wagner) who declines to play King Marke to Eva's Isolde. He is seen to offer advice that is mellow and wise: art, he says, must be rooted in dreams, not rules (his teaching Walther how to compose *Stollen*, stanzas, has nothing to do with the impotent criticism of Beckmesser: he merely tames the socially disruptive aspects of Walther's earlier song); the older artist must learn to re-create the impulsive spontaneity of youth; and new art must build on the achievement of the old (here, the German masters). And the musical language of not just the trial song, but of the entire opera does just this: its 'archaic' harmonies, its newly clarified tonality, its transparently articulated form, and the precision of its details have all benefited from Wagner's earlier innovations.

Wagner's final work, the 'sacred festival play' *Parsifal*, provoked a virulent attack from the estranged Nietzsche. The denial and sublimation of sexuality into Christian ritual (shown at its most theatrical), the covert misogyny, the obsession with the purity of blood (at this time Wagner cast doubt on Christ's Jewishness), the particular form of anti-intellectualism (*Parsifal* means 'so-pure-a-fool'), and the fringe crankiness (the Knights' protection of animals reflects the composer's vegetarianism), all contributed to what Nietzsche saw as a denial of the important elements in the earlier music dramas. Certainly, its winnowing, enervate sexuality is that of an older man, and its central premise – that redemption may be won through pity (for Wagner, the highest love; for Nietzsche, a form of contempt) – was indeed new. But for all that Nietzsche's Zarathustran ideals (as presented, for example, in the *Genealogy of Morals*) were, in part, founded on a self-conscious refutation of the Parsifal philosophy,

the criticisms represented only a half-truth. For in this work, as in *The Ring*, the kinship relations touch extraordinary depths (especially the Oedipal temptation of Parsifal by Kundry), and the music (orchestrated with a wonderful diffused light) is no less resourceful than that of *Tristan* in pursuit of new extremes of expression. Moreover, Wagner was reviewing here the worlds of Tannhäuser and Lohengrin, albeit with a Sachsian mellowness.

While the refutation of *Parsifal* contributed to the emergence of existentialism and the exploration of the consequences of 'the Death of God', both Nietzsche and Wagner were seen by Thomas Mann as part of a chain of German thinking that extended back through Mann's own novels and the writings of Freud to Schopenhauer and Kant. It was this tradition that also provided a foundation for so much of the thought in the writings of D.H. Lawrence. In France, on the other hand, it was chiefly the musical and synaesthetic effects of the music dramas that exerted so powerful an effect upon composers (Debussy, and later Messiaen), painters (Renoir* and Cézanne*) and writers (Baudelaire*, who wrote an important defence of *Tannhäuser*, Mallarmé* and Proust). James Joyce argued that the 'musical effects' of his Sirens chapter from *Ulysses* were superior to those of *Die Walküre*, and in Molly's final monologue he created a literary equivalent for the perorations of Isolde and Brunnhilde, albeit cast in a demotic language. Indeed, female protagonists are also central to the immediately post-Wagnerian German operas which pursue psycho-sexual disorders to their extremes: Schoenberg's *Erwartung* (1909), Richard Strauss's *Salome* (1905) and *Elektra* (1909), and Berg's *Lulu* (1928–35). The technical innovations in harmony, melody and instrumentation introduced in these and other works derived their impetus directly from the most advanced, rootless aspects of the music in *Tristan* and *Parsifal*, and led in due course to the formulation by Schoenberg of the twelve-tone system. This system, and the line of development supporting it, did not pass unchallenged, though the challenges (as with Nietzsche) derived strength from their opposition: even Stravinsky's neoclassicism was rooted in a refutation of the Wagnerian aesthetic.

In the years since the Second World War, the main effort has been to disassociate Wagner's name from the use to which it was put by Houston Stewart Chamberlain* and the leaders of the Third Reich (though even in the 1980s performances in Israel of Wagner's music arouse the strongest indignation). In the tendencies of his work and polemical writings, Wagner was not blameless. Yet, ironically, even the darkest side of his influence pays testimony to the extent to which his art explored the deepest and most powerful instincts of life.

Christopher Wintle

The prose writings were translated by W.A. Ellis as *Richard Wagner's Prose Works* (8 vols, 1892–1900), though a selection is available by A. Goldman and E. Sprinchhorn as *Wagner on Music and Drama* (1970). Still the best biography is Ernest Newman, *The Life of Richard Wagner* (4 vols, 1933–47), though Robert Gutman, *Richard Wagner, the Man, his Mind and his Music* (1968), is stimulating. A full list of critical writings is offered in the Wagner entry in *The New Grove Dictionary of Music and Musicians*, ed. Stanley Sadie, vol. 20 (1980). G.B. Shaw, *The Perfect Wagnerite* (1922), is a classic study, and Robert Donnington, *Wagner's Ring and its Symbols* (1960), is intriguing in its application of Jungian ideas. Carl Dahlhaus, *Richard Wagner's Music Dramas* (1971, trans. 1979), is the most thoughtful recent introduction to the works.

476
WALLACE, Alfred Russel 1823–1913

British biologist

A.R. Wallace was born into a poor English family residing in Usk, Monmouthshire. Receiving little formal education, he read voraciously and, after moving to London (1837), attended public lectures which led to his becoming an agnostic. He began to collect plants while working as a surveyor (1838–43) and a teacher (1844–45), and turned increasingly to the sciences, especially the works of T.R. Malthus*, Charles Lyell*, and Robert Chambers. It was Chambers's *Vestiges of the Natural History of Creation* that convinced Wallace that species had evolved and had not been created.

In pursuit of proof for this belief Wallace and a friend set off for the Amazon to assemble evidence. He collected specimens and made notes for four years, but on his return to England (1852) lost almost everything in a shipwreck. None the less he was able to publish *A Narrative of Travels on the Amazon and Rio Negro* (1853).

Wallace then spent eight years (1854–62) in the Malay Archipelago, exploring, studying and assembling a collection of over 125,000 biological specimens. He wrote to Darwin* about his views on the mechanism of evolution, and on 1 July 1858 the latter presented a joint paper to the Linnaean Society outlining the conclusion each had reached independently – that evolution proceeded by *natural selection*.

On returning to England Wallace studied his collections and wrote and lectured profusely. He married in 1866 and had three children. In the 1860s he became a spiritualist and later adopted other unpopular causes, such as women's rights and socialism, which he promulgated as eagerly as his scientific ideas. He died in 1913 in Dorset.

Wallace wrote about twenty books and four hundred articles and reviews which established him as a major

figure in natural history. Of special fame is his work on evolution, which he concluded was demonstrated in the geographical distribution of species, as he stated in an important essay of 1855. But that left him with the problem of *how* species evolve.

Like Darwin, Wallace had observed the wide range of variation among individuals of the same species and had seen that many of their distinctive traits were inherited by their offspring. In 1858, while suffering a severe fever in the East, he remembered Malthus's essay on population and his doctrine of the 'survival of the fittest'. With this in mind Wallace concluded that evolution proceeded by *natural selection* of the fittest from this pool of variations – those individuals most able to compete for a limited food supply – whose beneficial characteristics were then passed on to their offspring. This was also Darwin's conclusion and the argument of the joint paper presented to the Linnean Society in London in 1858.

In *Contributions to the Theory of Natural Selection* (1870), Wallace reprinted these essays along with others elaborating his views, including those few points on which he differed from Darwin. Wallace laid more emphasis on protective resemblance; for example, the physical resemblance of one species of fly to a dangerous wasp. More important, however, was his view of man, whom Darwin had placed at the pinnacle of evolution. Wallace, by now a spiritualist, argued that at a certain point in time the human body had ceased to evolve; the brain and mind now started to evolve independently of any physical evolution, making man a creature quite different from the animals. This mental evolution required a mechanism beyond natural selection. In other words, Wallace attempted to reconcile evolution with the existence of a higher being. With his later *Darwinism* (1889) we encounter one of the best nineteenth-century accounts of evolution by natural selection, a work which – unlike Darwin's *The Origin of Species* – firmly rejects Lamarck's* theory of the inheritance of acquired characteristics.

At least as important, however, is Wallace's work on zoogeography, which he greatly promoted through his classic *The Malay Archipelago* (1869), *The Geographical Distribution of Animals* (1876), and *Island Life* (1880). These books present the field work and deductions on which his evolution theory was based. As well, they define 'Wallace's Line', which he discovered – the boundary between the Australian and Asiatic zoogeographical zones, which runs through the Malay Archipelago.

Though overshadowed by Darwin, Wallace too was a formidable controversialist who deserves to be remembered for his fundamental contributions to modern biology.

Michael Scherk

Other works include: *Palm Trees of the Amazon and*

Their Uses (1853); The Scientific Aspect of the Supernatural (1866); Tropical Nature, and other Essays (1878); Natural Selection and Tropical Nature: Essays on Descriptive and Theoretical Biology (1891); Vaccination a Delusion, Its Penal Enforcement a Crime: Proved by the Official Evidence in the Reports of the Royal Commission (1898); The Wonderful Century: Its Successes and Its Failures (1898); Studies Scientific and Social (1900); Man's Place in the Universe: A Study of the Results of Scientific Research in Relation to the Unity or Plurality of Worlds (1903); My Life, A Record of Events and Opinions (1905); Alfred Russel Wallace; Letters and Reminiscences, ed. James Marchant (1916). Lamarck to Darwin: Contributions to Evolutionary Biology, 1809–1859, ed. H.L. McKinney (1971), includes Wallace's major articles on evolution. About Wallace: H.L. McKinney, Wallace and Natural Selection (1972); Wilma B. George, Biologist Philosopher: A Study of the Life and Writings of Alfred Russel Wallace (1964); Loren C. Eiseley, Darwin's Century (1958).

477
WARD, Mary Augusta (Mrs Humphry Ward)
1851–1920

British novelist and social worker

Though Mrs Humphry Ward wrote twenty-five novels, she earns her place here by the celebrity and influence of one work: Robert Elsmere (1888). If Carlyle's* Sartor Resartus (1833–4) was the first great Victorian fictionalization of religous doubt and J.A. Froude's* The Nemesis of Faith (1849) the most scandalous example of the genre, Robert Elsmere was the most complete literary document of the various shades of Victorian faith and doubt. As Sir Arthur Conan Doyle* commented, 'Trollope* and Mrs. Ward have the whole Victorian civilization dissected and preserved.'

The granddaughter of Dr Thomas Arnold* of Rugby and niece of Matthew Arnold*, Mary Ward inherited their moral earnestness. Her father, Thomas Arnold, was an inspector of schools in Tasmania, where she was born, the eldest of eight children, in 1851. He gave up his job in 1856 on becoming a Roman Catholic. The family returned to England, where the girls were sent away to be unhappy at Protestant boarding schools by their embittered mother, while the boys were reared as Roman Catholics. Thomas Arnold was reconverted to Anglicanism in 1865, and the joyfully reconciled family settled in Oxford. Here Mary married a don at Brasenose College, Thomas Humphry Ward, in 1872. To the family's horror, her father rejoined the Church of Rome in 1876, on the eve of taking up an Oxford professorship. He later became Professor of English Literature at University College, Dublin. Mary herself read biblical criticism and re-

jected the miraculous element of Christian dogma, retaining a quasi-Christian theism and stressing the need for ethical social action. Her interest in religious questions is reflected in most of her novels.

Robert Elsmere analyses at length, but with skill and a sympathetic insight born of her family experience, the strains of a marriage in which the partners differ about religion. It is also a remarkable documentary of the life of conscientious intellectuals in Oxford during the mid-nineteenth century, when Tractarianism, Newmanism*, Broad Churchism, and atheism were the alternatives facing those whose faith in the established church was being undermined by biblical criticism, geological and evolutionary studies. Though not a roman à clef, Robert Elsmere contains portraits of intellectual types who resemble Walter Pater*, Mark Pattison, T.H. Green, all of whom Mary Ward knew well during her life in Oxford. Robert Elsmere is a clergyman whose thirst for knowledge leads him to reject traditional Christianity. Tensions arise in his marriage to a staunchly Evangelical woman who has no intellectual curiosity. Elsmere resigns his orders, but practises a kind of Christian Socialism in a centre for the education of the working class in the East End of London.

Within three years the novel had sold 70,000 copies in Britain. According to Henry James*, it was 'not merely an extraordinarily successful novel; it was, as reflected in contemporary conversation, a momentous public event' (1892). Even Gladstone* reviewed it, calling it 'eminently an offspring of its time'. Robert Elsmere is an intellectual novel, but it also shows something of the descriptive power and imaginative sympathy of George Eliot's* fiction.

During the 1870s Mrs Ward supported the movement for the higher education of women, becoming the first secretary of Somerville College. Paradoxically, she later campaigned against women's suffrage, insisting on the importance of female influence in the home rather than in public life. Yet she herself was a notable public figure. In 1890 she helped found an unsuccessful establishment for popular Bible-teaching (not unlike Elsmere's centre) at University Hall in London. During the 1914–18 war she published two propagandist works, England's Effort: Six Letters to an American Friend, with a preface by the Earl of Rosebery (1916), and Fields of Victory, letters based on a journey through the battlefields of France (1919).

Mrs Humphry Ward was a representative late Victorian – learned, earnest, less than Christian but more than agnostic – who encapsulated in a fine imaginative work the representative spiritual problems of the earlier Victorian generation.

Rosemary Ashton

Works: The Writings of Mrs. Humphry Ward (16 vols, 1911–12). After Robert Elsmere Mrs Ward's best novel is *Helbeck of Bannisdale* (1898). Biography: Janet Penrose Trevelyan, *The Life of Mrs. Humphry Ward* (1923). Criticism: William S. Peterson, *Victorian Heretic: Mrs. Humphry Ward's Robert Elsmere* (1976); and Robert Lee Wolff, *Gains and Losses: Novels of Faith and Doubt in Victorian England* (1977).

478

WASHINGTON, Booker Taliaferro 1856–1915

US educator and racial leader

Born into slavery in Virginia shortly before the Civil War, Booker T. Washington grew up in an age of unbridled capitalism, rapid economic expansion, and 'self-made' men. Washington entered this competitive environment with few assets; his mother was a slave, his father an unknown white man. After emancipation, he walked with his mother, brother and sister to join his stepfather who was employed in a West Virginia salt furnace. Booker and his brother soon began working in order to supplement the family's meagre income. Opportunities for the personal advancement of a poor black boy were few. Less than forty years later, however, Booker T. Washington was being applauded by political leaders and entertained by some of the world's wealthiest men. President Theodore Roosevelt invited him to dinner at the White House, Andrew Carnegie* welcomed him as a guest at Skibo castle, and Queen Victoria* invited him to tea during one of his two trips to Europe.

Washington's climb from slavery to celebrity involved the coincidence of his personal and racial philosophy with that of the controlling white society. One of Booker's earliest memories was 'an intense longing to learn to read', and he pursued every avenue in his small West Virginia town that might further his education. He learned that pleasing important whites would open the doors of opportunity, and he impressed everyone with his self-discipline and willingness to work long hours to achieve his goals. In 1872, at the age of seventeen, Washington returned to his native Virginia to attend Hampton Institute. No one at the school knew that he was coming; he had almost no money; and he had to walk a good part of the five hundred mile journey. Booker's entrance examination involved sweeping and dusting a recitation room, and the New England Lady Principal was so impressed with his thoroughness that she admitted him to classes, although he had no money for tuition and the school year had already begun. At Hampton, Washington met the most influential person in his career. As principal at this industrial training school for coloured youth, Samuel Chapman Armstrong combined a sense of white missionary paternalism with a Puritan's devotion to clean living, discipline, and individual responsibility.

He represented that class of elite whites who felt it 'knew' what was best for the former slaves and who could help them most in their climb from the depths of depravity and ignorance.

Booker T. Washington internalized the Hampton message. His experiences as a youth affirmed Armstrong's views, and when Washington graduated in 1875 he was a disciple. He taught at a school in his home town for three years and spent a year at a Baptist seminary before returning to Hampton in 1879 as a night school teacher and secretary to Armstrong. In 1881 Armstrong recommended Washington as principal of a new normal school for blacks in Tuskegee, Alabama. Washington took the position with every intention of establishing a Hampton colony in the deep South. Beginning, as he later described it, 'with forty students in a dilapidated shanty near the coloured Methodist Church', Booker T. Washington built Tuskegee Institute into the best-known black school in the United States. At the time of his death the school had an extensive industrial training programme in addition to the normal curriculum, more than fifteen hundred students, and an endowment of almost two million dollars. Washington's international fame, however, arose from a ten minute speech he gave in 1895 before the Cotton States and International Exposition in Atlanta, Georgia.

The Exposition was a highly publicized event, but its timing had much to do with the appeal of Washington's message. On the one hand, the South was openly seeking to diversify its stagnant agricultural economy by attracting northern industrial investment. On the other hand, race relations were tense and black citizenship rights were eroding seriously under a torrent of hostile legislation. Washington made a simple recommendation for both of these situations, and for blacks and whites alike: 'Cast down your buckets where you are.' Americans should concentrate upon their nation's abundance and the opportunity for self-advancement. Ideally, blacks should look to whites for jobs and leadership, and whites should look to blacks for loyal and competent labour. Washington felt that racial tension impeded economic progress, and he advised blacks to be patient, to exercise discipline and self-control, and to avoid agitation in the face of lynching, segregation, and disfranchisement. Furthermore, Washington urged blacks to seek friendships with conservative white philanthropists, to reject labour unions, and to allow racial differences to work themselves out over time.

Blacks generally greeted Washington's message with restrained support, but the public white response was overwhelming praise. The young black educator offered them a relatively painless solution to the 'Negro Problem' by placing most of the burden upon his own people. He advocated a safe approach and his efforts earned white assistance. Very quickly, Washington became a powerful man among black Americans. Although a growing black minority, headed by W.E.B. DuBois, criticized Washington for his 'Atlanta Compromise' of their civil rights, whites invested him with considerable influence. He became an adviser to presidents, philanthropists and editors. Black politicians and college presidents awaited his signal to their white benefactors. As a black leader, Booker T. Washington was sincerely respected by his own people, and most publicly supported his 'go slow' policies. Black support came partly because Washington produced some modest results, but perhaps more importantly, his policies offered a natural course along the lines of least resistance. When he published his autobiography, *Up From Slavery*, in 1901, he presented his own life as an example of the success of his racial philosophy. It won him further acclaim at home and abroad.

Washington worked hard to implement his views. In 1900 he founded the National Negro Business League in order to promote pride in black businesses and to encourage economic independence. Most obviously, however, Washington used Tuskegee Institute as a model for industrial training and character building. His graduates represented the success of his conservative philosophy to the public, and faculty members such as the noted scientist George Washington Carver* regularly conducted workshops at farmers' conferences and other black gatherings in the South. Booker T. Washington rejected the more aggressive demands for full equality by the National Association for the Advancement of Colored People as impractical and dangerous. Instead, he accepted 'half a loaf' as a step 'toward obtaining the whole loaf later'.

When Washington died in 1915 he left his widow and three children by two previous marriages. His legacy also included a conservative approach to race relations which dominated American thinking until the civil rights upheavals of the 1950's.

Lester C. Lamon

Washington's other works include: *The Future of the American Negro* (1899) and *My Larger Education* (1911). Major works about Washington include: Samuel R. Spencer Jr, *Booker T. Washington and the Negro's Place in American Life* (1955); *Booker T. Washington and His Critics: The Problem of Negro Leadership*, ed. Hugh Hawkins (1962); Louis R. Harlan, *Booker T. Washington: The Making of a Black Leader, 1856–1901* (1972).

479
WEBER, Carl Maria Friedrich Ernst von 1786–1826

German composer

Though his whole life was contained within that of Beethoven*, Weber pursued a quite different kind of

music: more colourful, more illustrative of atmosphere and feeling, less bound by the logic of classical musical discourse. He was, in short, one of the founders of German musical Romanticism, and as such he had an influence on orchestration, piano writing and opera reaching forward to Schumann*, Wagner* and even Stravinsky.

Weber was born into a family whose business was music and the theatre: at the time of his birth his father ran a touring company, and only four years earlier his first cousin Constanze had married Mozart. He was thus encouraged in a musical direction from early childhood, and though his formal education in music was sporadic (he had lessons for short periods with, among others, Michael Haydn in Salzburg and the Abbé Vogler in Munich), by the time he was eighteen he had written three operas and numerous piano pieces. There followed appointments in Breslau (1804–6) and Carlsruhe (1806–7), where he composed his two symphonies, both in C major: the fact that he never returned to this form is indicative of his distance from the mainstream classical tradition and of his inclination towards more overtly theatrical genres, principally opera and concerto.

His next appointment took him to Salzburg, where he wrote the opera *Silvana* (1808–10) and incidental music for *Turandot* (1809). After this came a restless period of wandering. He stayed briefly in various German cities; he also visited Switzerland. And all the time he was gathering impressions from nature, from fellow musicians and from writers: he met E.T.A. Hoffmann* in Bamberg in 1811. He was also composing, and much more freely and individually than hitherto. For the stage he wrote the Singspiel (opera with spoken dialogue) *Abu Hassan* (1810–11), and there was a stream of songs and of works for soloist and orchestra: the two piano concertos, in C major (1810) and E flat major (1812), a Clarinet Concertino (1811) and two concertos for the same instrument, in F minor (1811) and E flat major (also 1811), and the Bassoon Concerto (again 1811).

In January 1813 he arrived in Prague and was persuaded to accept the directorship of the opera. While there he composed relatively little on a large scale, apart from the cantata *Kampf und Sieg* (1815) in celebration of the victory of Waterloo, but he had the opportunity through performance to acquaint himself thoroughly with the new kind of romantic opera being produced in Paris by Spontini, Cherubini*, Méhul and others. He also wrote his two most important chamber works, the Clarinet Quintet (1815) and the *Grand duo concertant* for clarinet and piano (1815–16), where again the presence of the clarinet as romantic soloist is significant.

After four years in Prague he moved on to Dresden to take charge of the German opera there, and he soon set about realizing a long cherished project: an opera in German, on a German subject, in tune with the literary romanticism of the day. This was *Der Freischütz*, which was completed in 1821 and staged that year, with immense success, in Berlin. In Dresden, however, Weber was the victim of rivalry and intrigue: he was unable to present *Der Freischütz* there until the following year, and prevented from finishing his next opera, the comedy *Die drei Pintos* (1820–1; this was eventually completed in 1888 by Mahler*).

Nevertheless, *Der Freischütz* established his international reputation. He received commissions to write operas for Vienna (*Euryanthe*, 1822–3) and Covent Garden (*Oberon*, 1825–6), but by this stage his health was in decline. During the last five years of his life he wrote almost nothing apart from these two operas, and he died in London eight weeks after conducting the première of *Oberon*. His remains were returned to Dresden in 1844, thanks to the intervention of Wagner, who had taken up his old post there the previous year.

Weber's great difficulty was that he was born to revive German opera before there had been any revival in the German libretto, and though his own literary works, including an unfinished novel and a quantity of criticism, suggest he could well have followed the course taken by his great successor, in fact he preferred to work with a librettist, however ill-equipped. *Der Freischütz*, which has all the freshness and excitement of a pioneer undertaking, remains a masterpiece, if only because it is so much a work of musical fantasy that the fantastic plot becomes quite secondary: the 'Wolf's Glen' scene, concerned with spectral apparitions, was quickly recognized as a working treatise in evocative orchestration. But both the medieval romance *Euryanthe* and the fairy pageant *Oberon* are so difficult to accept dramatically that they can barely hold the stage, despite their musical sophistication (*Euryanthe* has a *leitmotif* technique looking forward to Wagner) and the presence of many powerful numbers.

The highly imaginative orchestration of Weber's operas is also a feature of his orchestral works, where he plays with unusual groupings of strings or exploits the characterfulness of wind tone (this particularly, of course, in the pieces for clarinet and bassoon). The last of his concertos, the *Konzertstück* for piano and orchestra (1821), is remarkable for its single-movement design and for its association with a poetic programme by the composer, though the poetry of Weber's piano music – indeed, of his music in general – is such that it is better off without words.

Paul Griffiths

See: *Carl Maria von Weber: Writings on Music*, trans. Martin Cooper, ed. John Warrack (1981); John Warrack, *Carl Maria von Weber* (1968, 2nd edn 1976).

480
WEBSTER, Noah 1758–1843

US educator and lexicographer

Noah Webster fought alongside his father in the Continental Army, against General Bourgoyne, took a degree at Yale in 1778, and taught singing and classics in Connecticut, New York and Philadelphia. Called to the Bar in 1781, and being a believer in firm central government, he combined his fervours in polemics for national union – for example, in *Sketches of American Policy* (1785). He edited the daily *American Minerva* and its weekly selection in the *Herald* from 1793, strongly supporting Washington and Adams. His passionate Americanism also took the form of *Dissertations upon the English Language* (1789): 'As an independent nation, our honour requires us to have a system of our own, in language as well as in government.' His *Grammatical Institute of the English Language* (1783–5) demanded a language American in spelling, grammar and 'rules of reading and speaking'. Part One, published separately as *The American Speller*, became a bestseller, reaching sixty million copies by 1890, and popularly known as the 'blue backed speller' and considered a decided contribution to national cultural unity. Webster's spelling reformism, his interests in gardening and experimental science, his writings on literature and politics, his editing of *Winthrop's Journal*, his revised version of the Bible, his work as committee man and councilman, county court judge, director of a Bible society, vice-president of an agricultural society, and his wide travel in the United States and studies in Paris and London, all contributed to the lively sense of language meanings that poured into *An American Dictionary of the English Language*, completed in 1825 and published in 1828 (preceded by his *Compendious Dictionary of the English Language* in 1806). In 1840 Webster issued his corrected and enlarged edition – 70,000 words against the original 38,000 – and in 1843 G. and C. Merriam Company obtained the rights to produce further revisions of this linguistic masterpiece, based on the principle that American experience should be 'as independent in *literature* as [it] is in politics – as famous for *arts* as for *arms*'. Webster's fight to obtain a copyright for his work drew him into politics as a Federalist advocate of strong central government which could control the kind of legislation he needed. His versatility continued in *A Brief History of Epidemic and Pestilential Diseases*, *Experiments Respecting Dew*, statistical reports, and many other energetic projects. He was also a member of the Friendly Club, which included William Dunlap and Charles Brockden Brown.

Eric Mottram

Ervin C. Shoemaker, *Noah Webster, Pioneer of Learning*

(1936); Harry R. Warfel, *Noah Webster: Schoolmaster to America* (1936).

481
WEDEKIND, Benjamin Franklin (Frank)
1864–1918

German dramatist and performer

Wedekind was born in Hanover, the second of six children, on the return from the USA of his parents, Dr Friedrich Wilhelm Wedekind, physician, former man of 1848 and pillar of San Francisco society, and his wife Emilie, once an emigrant singer. Rejecting Bismarck's* Germany, Dr Wedekind moved his family in 1872 to the castle of Lenzburg in Aargau, Switzerland. Frank showed an early talent for light satirical verse-making after the manner of Heine*, and moved on to study French and, at his father's wish, law, at the Universities of Lausanne and Munich. But devotion to literature and gaiety led to a grand quarrel with his father and an interim earning a precarious living, partly in the advertising office of Maggi in Zürich, publishing his first essays and short stories in the *Neue Zürcher Zeitung*. Most of these are far too confident and accomplished to be regarded as journeyman work. Two essays of this period, 'Zirkusgedanken' ('Circus Thoughts') and 'Der Witz und seine Sippe' ('Wit and its relations', 1887), can be regarded as programmatic for his subsequent work in drama.

Reconciliation with his father, and soon afterwards his father's death, gave him a modest inheritance which enabled him to spend the next six years travelling, writing, becoming the literary Bohemian of his reputation. His first dramas included *Children and Fools* (*Kinder und Narren*, 1891) which already broached what was to become his theme: the forms imposed on women's erotic lives by social pressure. It contained an attack on Gerhart Hauptmann* both impersonal and personal, rejecting Naturalism as a dramatic mode, and denouncing the man who had drawn on Wedekind's private confession of his family tensions for material for his own play *Das Friedensfest*. There followed Wedekind's first major play, *Spring Awakening: A tragedy of childhood* (*Frühlings Erwachen: eine Kindertragödie*, 1891), which rapidly gained him the reputation of an important new talent. But it had to be published in Switzerland on account of difficulties with censorship in Germany, and was not performed until 1906, when Max Reinhardt put it on, heavily cut, at the Berlin Kammerspiel. It presented a generation of the young, variously maimed by the inadequacy of timid, authoritarian, hypocritical parents and teachers to help them into a sexually adult world. It was as innovatory in style, or styles, as in subject matter: open-ended, episodic, moving by way of juxtaposition of scenes

rather than by plotted sequence of acts; confronting the lyrical mode with the grotesque, the realist with the surrealist, it inaugurated a line of epic tragi-comedy which had progeny as various as the dramas of Dürrenmatt and Brecht.

The next four years Wedekind spent in Paris, with an interval of six months in London. His experiences there of Cabaret, Variétés, Music Hall, popular boulevard drama, Grand Guignol, the circus gave sharper focus to his dissatisfaction with the confining imitativeness of Naturalist drama, and to his wish to recover the flamboyant theatricality of popular entertainment. His encounters with the metropolitan half-world, the easy sexuality of the grisette, the friendships of circus strong-man (Willi Rudinoff) and financial manipulator (Willi Grétor, whose secretary he was for a while), reinforced his outsider's criticism of the precarious stabilities of bourgeois values.

His next major work, the 'monster tragedy' he worked on for a number of years, was to emerge after many revisions, some as late as 1911 and 1913, as the dual drama *Earth Spirit* (*Erdgeist*, 1895) and *Pandora's Box* (*Die Büchse der Pandora*, 1902). This amalgam of farce, myth and Grand Guignol, perhaps his greatest achievement, presents the rise and fall of Lulu, the courtesan from the gutter – or from before the world began – in an exploitative social world: the ambivalent eternal-feminine, joyful, destructive, changing, immutable, her sexual delight finally destroyed by sexual brutality. A famous performance was the private one-night stand in 1905 at the Trianon-Theater, Vienna, organized by Karl Kraus, in which Kraus played the minor part of Kungo Poti, Wedekind himself Jack the Ripper, and Tilly Newes, who was to become his wife, Lulu.

On his return to Munich in 1896 he became a regular contributor to Albert Langen's recently founded satirical weekly *Simplicissimus*, under the pseudonym Hieronymus Jobs. His satirical poems on political issues of the day brought fame – and trouble. Two of them – on Wilhelm II's journey to the Holy Land – provoked a prosecution for *lèse-majesté*, for Wedekind's pseudonym had been mysteriously broken, by Langen, he was convinced. At work on *Der Marquis von Keith* (1900, first performed 1901), Wedekind fled to Zürich. Once the drama was finished, he returned to face six months in prison. After the experimental forms of *Spring Awakening* and the Lulu-dramas, he adopted the classic conversation-piece for this presentation of the charlatan outwitted. The tables are ultimately turned on the extravagant imagination and enterprise of the swindling Marquis precisely by the philistine bourgeois whom he had set out to exploit. His vitality and sheer gusto, the theatrical version of the Nietzschean* life-force, represent a major theme in Wedekind's dramas. So, increasingly, does its defeat. But: 'life is a fairground slide,' concludes the Marquis, as he decides in the last line to live, rather than shoot himself.

Out of prison, Wedekind began a new career as performer, mainly to publicize his dramas, which audiences still looked at askance. He turned cabaret artist, reciting his own monologues, singing his songs to his own accompaniment on the guitar, joining the largely amateur group known as the Eleven Hangmen. Cabaret, the satirical bohemian import from France, was only just beginning in Berlin and Munich, and Wedekind was an innovator in a genre which has become a permanent feature of German fringe theatre. At the same time Wedekind turned actor. The sharpness of his dialogue, the *ad absurdum* extremity of his situations, the abstract caricature of his figures was something unfamiliar to actors and producers as well as to audiences. By taking on his own major roles, his powerful presence overwhelming his lack of professional skill, Wedekind was able to show the theatre what was required by way of intensity, energy, hardness. At various times he played The Ringmaster, Dr Schön, Jack in the Lulu-dramas, the title role in *The Opera Singer* (*Der Kammersänger*, 1899), Casti-Piani in *Dance of Death* (*Totentanz*, 1905), Buridan in *Censorship* (*Die Zensur*, 1908), Tschamper in *Schloss Wetterstein* (1910). After his marriage in 1906 to a first-class professional actress, he and his wife toured performing cycles of his works so successfully that, allowing for battles with local censors, his reputation as an abrasive, disturbing dramatist was established. His society had caught up with him, and he had found a role to play in it.

After *Keith*, a more argumentative, ideological note enters his dramas. Where Lulu is powerful as image – her richness lies in her ultimate irreducibility to ideology – later works are explicit, overt in their treatment of their themes: marriage, the battle between the sexes, the position of women, censorship: sometimes all at once. The situations are increasingly extreme and absurd, the comedy blacker, the figures and their relationships increasingly exemplifications of a case. There is general agreement on a decline in talent with an increase in stridency. Perhaps the Shavian *Hidalla* (1904) is the most successful. In it Wedekind puts into the mouth of the central figure, Karl Hetmann, his own attack on the 'feudalism of love': the prostitute for purchase, the virgin-bride for sale, the suffragette who denied her sexuality were all distortions of the true vocation of woman. In the final scene the grotesque visionary is seen as fit only for a job as a circus clown, and so destroys himself. It makes a dark comment on Wedekind's own fate as a truth-teller acceptable only as an entertainer – especially as Hetmann was Wedekind's most successful acting role. He frequently uses events and figures from his own life in these later plays, less for self-expression than to exemplify a general issue by means of his own situation, though the distinction

is not always clear. In *Hidalla*, Langen's betrayal of Wedekind is turned into the entrepreneur's betrayal of the intellectual. In *Censorship* Wedekind's own life-long battle with the authorities is stylized into the protests of the serious moralist against the bland paternalism of the highly placed priest, but the same play steers closer to the private wind when it also presents the tensions in the marriage between a controversial dramatist and an accomplished actress. In the one case the private issue is successfully generalized; not so in the other.

Wedekind critized his world not in political but in social and human terms, and the attitude to sexuality was the touchstone. In his time the terror of the bourgeoisie, he became, as perhaps he was bound to, a Good Liberal Cause, the literary opposition in Germany never failing to rally to his defence. He was the definitive pioneer of twentieth-century developments in non-realistic drama: not only did he break taboos of subject matter, but his drama was sensationally and self-consciously theatrical. Dürrenmatt has recognized his debt to Wedekind's tragi-comic absurdism; Brecht to his didactic buffoonery and 'alienation-effects'; the open form, the grotesque concentration, the dramatic subjectivity can be found again in the later Strindberg*; the comic abstraction of his situations – and some of his targets – can be traced in the expressionist comedy of Carl Sternheim. His parodistic use of established dramatic genres, and his rediscovery of the popular spectacle of circus and music hall have become widely diffused tricks in the modern dramatist's repertory. The power of the Lulu-dramas is perpetuated in Alban Berg's opera *Lulu* (1937, completed 1979). His cabaret chansons virtually founded the genre in Germany.

Joyce Crick

Collected works: *Gesammelte Werke*, ed. Artur Kutscher and Joachim Friedenthal (9 vols, 1912–21); a good selection, including additional unpublished material, is *Werke*, selected and introduced by Manfred Hahn (3 vols, 1954). Letters: *Gesammelte Briefe*, ed. Fritz Strich (2 vols, 1924). Biography: Artur Kutscher, *Frank Wedekind: Sein Leben und seine Werke* (3 vols, 1922–31); Günter Seehaus, *Wedekind* (1974). Secondary works: Klaus Völker, *Frank Wedekind* (1965); Sol Gittleman, *Wedekind* (1969); Alan Best, *Wedekind* (1975). Other dramas: *The Lightning Artist* (*Der Schnellmaler*, 1889); *That's Life* (*So ist das Leben*, (1902); *Musik* (1908); *Franziska* (1912); *Bismarck* (1916). Ballet scenarios: *The Fleas* (*Die Flöhe*, 1892); *The Empress of Newfoundland* (*Die Kaiserin von Neufundland*, 1897). Prose: *Minne-Haha oder Über die körperliche Erziehung der jungen Mädchen* (Minne-haha, or On the physial education of young girls, 1901). Translations: *Five Tragedies of Sex*, trans. Frances Fawcett and Stephen Spender (1952, containing *Spring's Awakening, Earth-Spirit, Pandora's Box, Death and Devil, Castle Wetterstein*).

482

WHISTLER, James Abbot McNeill 1834–1903

US artist

James Abbot Whistler was born in 1834 in Lowell, Massachusetts, USA. In later life he replaced Abbot with his mother's maiden name, McNeill. Much of his childhood was spent in Russia, where his father was employed as an engineer. Having spent three years as a cadet at the prestigious West Point Military Academy, he left the United States for Paris in 1855, entering the studio of Charles Gleyre as a student of painting. He mixed widely in Paris with young British and French contemporaries, and was himself profoundly influenced by the work of Gustave Courbet*, whose manifesto of Realism had been published in the year of Whistler's arrival in Europe. Having friends and relatives in London, he frequently visited England, where he gradually settled in the late 1850s. He met Rossetti* and the members of his entourage in 1862, and for many years his name was associated with the declining Pre-Raphaelite movement. In England in the 1860s he moved away from his earlier Realist style in favour of an increasingly economic version of the prevailing climate of Symbolist painting, with its rejection of analytic Naturalism. He worked closely with Albert Moore in the late 1860s, and was also largely responsible for the revival of British etching.

Following a visit to South America in 1866 he commenced his series of *Nocturnes*, employing a musical as opposed to a literary metaphor in order to describe his pictures, a practice which was very much in keeping with the Aesthetic movement, of which he was a leading representative. In 1878 he sued the critic John Ruskin* for libel, after the latter's momentously foolish remark that he had heard of cockney impudence, 'but never expected to hear a coxcomb ask two hundred guineas for flinging a pot of paint in the public's face'. Whistler was awarded only a farthing in damages and was in consequence bankrupted. Ruskin was discredited. Whistler's work in the 1880s became increasingly abstract. He was also active as an interior decorator, and published a number of highly polemical articles and essays which were eventually anthologized in 1890 under the title of *The Gentle Art of Making Enemies*. He continued to exhibit in England and France throughout the 1890s, his work being purchased by numerous state institutions. Whistler also sustained a high, and lucrative, reputation as a fashionable portrait painter. He was very badly affected by the premature death of his wife Beatrix in 1896, dying six years later, shortly after receiving *in absentia* an Honorary Degree of Law from Glasgow University, which possesses many of his finest paintings. He was buried at Chiswick cemetery.

The very ease with which Whistler moved between the *avant-garde* communities of London and Paris reveals the fundamental unity of concerns within the European Art For Art's Sake movement of the 1880s, and it is as a major international impresario and spokesman for Aestheticism that he will be best remembered. His reputation fell victim to Roger Fry's dogmatic Anglophobia, and his wildly over-simplified picture of the supposed relations between English and French art in the late nineteenth century, and has only been partially recuperated as the force and influence of that picture have gradually relaxed. For it was Whistler who stood between the historical figures of Baudelaire* and Oscar Wilde*, Whistler who reveals the shared cultural assumptions which lay beyond such ostensibly disparate tendencies as the influence of Japanese art and the Hellenism of the nineties. A highly serious painter and art theorist, Whistler's entire career after his removal to England constituted an eloquent and provocative denial of the middle-class assumption that painting was a mere appendage to literature and morality, an attitude which was quite as prevalent in France as it was in England. As he argued in the Ten O'Clock Lecture of 1885, 'to say to the painter, that Nature is to be taken as She is, is to say to the player, that he may sit on the piano'. For such uncompromising attitudes he was not widely loved, and his subsequent reputation for maliciousness and personal animosity was perhaps the inevitable result of his uncomfortable historical position *vis-à-vis* the official art establishments of his day. Thus he was fated to be condemned as a 'Decadent' by many of his contemporaries, and those Post-Impressionists who, a few years later, were to repeat many of his arguments in defence of such painters as Picasso and Matisse. Whistler is undoubtedly a difficult figure to come to terms with in the late twentieth century. In his obsessive insistence on the quality of paint itself he clearly anticipated one major strand of Modernism, yet the very emphasis on close tonal values and his attendant vocabulary of 'daintiness' and the 'exquisite' sound as generally off-putting today as they did in 1914.

Whistler represents the *ne plus ultra* of what was a necessary response to the total epistemological confusion of late nineteenth-century aesthetics. His role in painting was strictly analogous to that of his friend Mallarmé* in poetry, both men insisting on the specificity of the media in which they worked. He should also be regarded as a key figure in the genealogy of Romanticism across the threshold of Victorianism and into the twentieth century, with his absolute denial of any social role for art, and his insistence on supposedly timeless and universal criteria for aesthetic evaluation and pleasure. In this respect his position was not unlike that of his near exact contemporary Cézanne*, although the narrowness of concerns in his own painting, and the tendency to miniaturism in his later work, ensured that he exhausted the potential possibilites for developing his own style in his own lifetime. It was his lapidary wit more than his much vaunted 'valeurs gris' which has sustained his influence. Yet just as he struck an exemplary dandy's pose between the courts of Baudelaire and Wilde, so, faced by Ruskin at the Old Bailey, he continues to represent the dignity and independence of the visual artist, albeit an independence which he himself embodied ambiguously, and not without irony, in his studied persona as 'The Butterfly', the matinée idol of Aestheticism.

Simon Watney

The fullest account of Whistler's life remains Elizabeth R. and Joseph Pennell, *The Life of James McNeill Whistler* (2 vols, 1908). The best general introduction to his work and times is Robin Spencer, *The Aesthetic Movement* (1972). The most recent and exhaustive account of his career as an artist is Hilary Taylor, *James McNeill Whistler* (1978).

483
WHITMAN, Walt 1819–92

US poet

Long Island – 'fish-shape Paumanock' – nourished Whitman's earliest childhood, and the old port of Brooklyn his young manhood: landscape and the sea, and the urban commerce of America, are the main spheres of his poetry. Following a short schooling he apprenticed at fourteen to a printer, beginning his career in printing, editing and newspapers, broken only by intermittent years of school-teaching – 'one of my best experiences and deepest lessons in human nature'. His journalism exposed the rough condition of New York society, the social unrest of the times, and the dirt of politics. His early poetry was as conventional and sentimental as his temperance novel *Franklin Evans* (1842); but he began to read philosophy and the literary classics, and practised as a well-known speaker for the Democrats. With these bases he moved into a seminal period for his maturity. New York newspaper jobs began to irritate him; reformism and the theatre preoccupied him; he knew nothing of the vast expanse of America. Discharged from the Brooklyn *Eagle*, partly for political reasons, in 1848 he obtained a job on the New Orleans *Crescent*, and the journey south, with his brother Jeff, opened up his American experience, taking him into the Mississippi heartlands. (Myths of Whitman's children – six in New Orleans, twins in Brooklyn, a silent-movie actor calling himself Walt Whitman and looking like him – develop from this period; but his deeper sensual interests were restricted to a few young men – in particular Peter Doyle, a streetcar conductor in Washington – and to himself.) He quarrelled with *Crescent*'s editor, and back in New York decided to cut a dandy figure – clothes, a cane, the theatre, Bohemian cafés – and edited the *Brooklyn Times*, helping to support his family and buying real estate. He practised his rhetorical abilities, wrote angry poems on liberty, and lectured on art theory. Important for his later poetry, he absorbed the *bel canto* lines of opera and the exhibition of the world's arts and crafts at the World's Fair of 1853. Then in 1855 he printed and published the first small edition of the eleven accumulative editions of *Leaves of Grass*. The title page carries no poet's name (it appears in the copyright) but a frontispiece shows the image of the new bard, self-named Walt, the persona of the twelve untitled poems within – a deliberately undignified pose in worker's dress, dark hat on cocked head, one hand in pocket and the other on his hip, open-necked shirt showing a dark vest (the engraver said it was red). The myth proclaimed itself: 'an American, one of the roughs, a kosmos,/Disorderly fleshy and sensual . . . eating drinking and breeding', and not at all what he later called the tea-drinking British poet the American genteel copied. The persona enabled him to transcend his social and personal self into an ideal inquirer, on the road, looking for a sharing companion – 'I was the man, I suffered, I was there.' The book is his manifesto – 'who touches this touches a man' – and touch became a key word for his sensuous sociality. To the *Boston Post* the poems were 'foul and rank leaves of the poison-plant of egoism, irreverence and lust'; as Whitman said, 'I expected hell, and I got it'. But Emerson* found the book 'fortifying & encouraging', although he, too, hedged at the sexuality of later editions. Undoubtedly, the long-breathed paragraphic lines, the personal punctuation, the *bel canto* freedom of the basically dactylic measures, the passionate rhetorical mode, the unveiled presence of love and death, the unashamed exhilaration and reverence in the self was an offensive pattern to those who wished simply to be confirmed in the narrowness and timidity. *Leaves of Grass* is a democratic book in its invitation to share openness to the mental and physical opportunity to expand and break with the sets of convention. It refuses the authoritarian impositions of fixed metrics and dominant heterosexuality.

Whitman's working man's dress became a necessity when the depression of 1857 made him poor. But he continued. The 1860–1 third edition contained 'Out of the Cradle Endlessly Rocking', a more personal poem than the persona celebrations of 'Song of Myself'. The Long Island boy experiences his first intuitions of love and death through the loves of two mocking birds; the adult poet recognizes the main instigation of his poetic life as a 'singer solitary, singing by yourself, projecting me .... Never more the cries of unsatisfied love be absent from me'. The tension with Walt increased: 'before all my arrogant poems the real Me stands yet untouch'd, untold, altogether unreach'd'. The third edition contained poems on sex ('Enfans d'Adam') which, when Emerson wanted to introduce Whitman to the famous Saturday Club, caused Longfellow*, Oliver Wendell Holmes* and others to refuse to meet him.

The frontispiece image of the great 1860 edition shows the poet now in bardic Byronic* pose – large collar and large floppy cravat, curly hair, trimmed beard, jacket. But the double theme is still 'to make a song of These States' and to generate 'the evangel-poem of comrades and of love'. In Whitman's nation-alist poems ('Chants Democratic') the poet accepts his responsibilty for fusing the people into 'the compact organism of one nation'. In the love poems he speaks of 'my limbs, and the quivering fire that ever plays through them, for reasons, most wondrous'. He pur-sued this double fecundity as a myth of resources necessary to make the nation positive and powerful – a new moral and social standard. In the 'Calamus' poems, focused on a phallic-shaped flag growing in the eastern states, the sense of lonely longing 'adhesive-ness', his peculiar word for the total bonding of man to man, is therefore both personal and social in its vision. The Civil War shattered that American dream. Photographs of Whitman in his forties show him changing into a prematurely old man under the on-slaught of his experiences as a wound-dresser in hos-pitals where more young men died than on the battlefields. His journals contain a remarkable account of these terrible years and of his exemplary ability to look after the men, some of whom never forgot his kindness. In his wartime poems, *Drum-Taps* (1865), he included the great elegy for Lincoln*, 'When lilacs last in the dooryard bloom'd', one of his most formally accomplished poems.

His job as Department of the Interior clerk ended when the Secretary of the Interior discovered *Leaves of Grass*. The Attorney General's office took him on, but the sacking was a sign of the public reception he could still expect. Whitman turned his attention to the heal-ing of the split nation and a vision of universal peace under political and technological progress: 'My spirit has pass'd in compassion and determination around the whole earth,/I have look'd for equals and lovers and found them ready for me in all lands,/I think some divine rapport has equalized me with them.' Living still in an unheated room, still managing to publish his work, surprising recognition came from William Mi-chael Rossetti in the 1867 London *Chronicle*, and, such was American genteel snobbery, this impressed local critics. And this year, the fourth edition of *Leaves of Grass* introduced him to Germany. He wrote articles – primarily in reponse to Carlyle's* predictions that

American democracy would destroy civilization – which became *Democratic Vistas* (1871), one of the few intelligent texts on the philosophy of democracy. Now magazines began to pay him for work. Swinburne* praised the Lincoln elegy and compared him to Blake. A correspondence with Mrs Anne Gilchrist, widow of Blake's biographer, developed to the point where she proposed marriage in 1871. Whitman replied: 'I too send you my love .... My book is my best letter, my response, my truest explanation of all. In it I have put my body and spirit.' And later: 'Let me warn you about myself and yourself also.'

In 1871 the fifth *Leaves of Grass* appeared, reprinted in 1872 with 'Passage to India', a major visionary poem on the expansion of democracy westwards from America, across the Pacific into Asia, and so encircling the globe back to 'These States' (the poem is unaware of a possible imperialist interpretation of such an ac-tion). Now, through ill-health, emotional strain and a certain quarrelsomeness retained from his youth, Whit-man declined. In 1873 he suffered a paralytic stroke. He left Washington for Camden, New Jersey, to live with his brother George. Bored and lonely, he turned to Columbus as a stubborn visionary hero with whom in part to identify ('Let the old timbers part – I will not part!') and the figure of exploration ('anthems in new tongues I hear saluting me'). The subscription list for the Centennial Edition of *Leaves of Grass* included Tennyson*, the Rossettis*, George Saintsbury and many other famous names: the old man had made it. Mrs Gilchrist arrived in America; the romance did not develop. Whitman visited Colorado and St Louis (to see his brother Jeff), lectured in Boston (the distin-guished audience included W.D. Howells*), and had the seventh edition published by a prestigious Boston publisher (1881–2). Oscar Wilde* visited him in 1887 ('like a great big, splendid boy.' Whitman told a re-porter). In 1884 he could afford a small house in Camden, where he held court and, on his deathbed, held the 1891 *Leaves of Grass*.

The preface to an early edition announced the es-sential image: the frontier poet – 'here are the roughs and beards and space and ruggedness and nonchalance that the soul loves', replacing 'old theories and forms' with fresh compositions opposed to European elitism: 'the attitude of great poets is to cheer up slaves and horrify despots'. The poetry therefore fuses the ideal body with an ideal society through the actualities of life in a huge space where the reader is invited to move freely as a rational and sexual creative being. 'What-ever satisfies the soul is truth' – 'One's self I sing, a simple separate person,/yet utter the word Democratic, the word En-Masse' – 'The moth and the fish-eggs are in their place;/The suns I see, and the suns I cannot see, are in their place' – these are the bases of Whit-man's poetic faith, his vision of 'the procreant urge of the world', a vision which encompasses a confrontation with death, in 'The Sleepers', as well as 'the song of Sex and Amativeness, and even Animality' (1888). It includes an ability to let the body merge into nature which no other nineteenth-century poet possesses – 'Something I cannot see puts upward libidinous prongs;/ Seas of bright juice suffuse heaven' – and a willingness to present national events, for example, 'Song of the Exposition', for the Philadelphia Centennial show. He invented and endlessly developed a major and still influential verse method which demonstrates the controlled freedom of measure which best suits the form-making body. Whitman remains an inspiration to twentieth-century American poets in his forms, his fresh sexuality and his buoyant futurity in the face of pressing catastrophe: 'Solitary, singing in the West, I strike up for a New World.'

Eric Mottram

The Complete Writings of Walt Whitman, ed. R.M. Buckle and others (10 vols, 1902–68); The Collected Writings of Walt Whitman, ed. Gay Wilson Allen and E. Sculley Bradley (from 1961). See: Gay Wilson Allen, The Solitary Singer (1955, rev. 1967); Roger Asselineau, The Evolution of Walt Whitman (2 vols, trans. 1960 and 1962).

484
WHITNEY, Eli 1765–1825

US inventor and manufacturer

Whitney began his technological skills and business acumen on the home farm in Westborough, Massachusetts, as a youngster making nails during the revolutionary war which caused a shortage. The business flourished; he hired a man, and he still made a profit. Such skills financed him through Yale, where he graduated in law in 1792. Moving south to Georgia, he lived with the widow of General Nathaniel Greene, who gave him contacts with cotton plantation gentlemen: they needed Whitney's skills to make them wealthy. The metal projections of his 1793 'gin' (curtailed from 'engine') pulled cotton fibres free from the seeds, so that one machine could produce 50 lbs a day. Cotton became big industry. In one year after his invention, the United States cotton crop increased from 5 million lbs to 8 million lbs, in 1800 to 35 million lbs. In the year of his death, it was 225,000,000 lbs. Slave labour increased on the plantations; the owners began to project a Southern 'civilization', including the protection of the 'peculiar institution' of necessary slavery. The Civil War, partly fought to protect cotton, could therefore be due to Whitney's gin.

Whitney took his 50,000 dollar award from South Carolina's legislature back to New England, manufactured his gin in New Haven, and spent a fortune trying

to protect it from universal piracy. He failed; the principle of the machine was too simple. In 1798, after a fire in which he lost virtually everything, he went into government musketry and launched his second technological revolution: mass weapons manufacture. Applying technological analysis, he manufactured guns from identical parts made in large numbers. Parts could be replaced rather than the whole article remade. Labour could be semi-skilled or unskilled. Machine efficiency replaced craft skill. The worker did not have to know the making of the whole product. Manufacture became foolproof. Whitney's jigs and clamps largely eliminated hand-and-eye guesswork. This was the beginning of assembly-line cheap goods, the immediate antecedent of 'the American method' of Ford and Taylor, recommended by Lenin for Russia in a famous Pravda article, and excoriated by Gramsci. In 1801 Whitney convinced Jefferson that independence depended on independent manufacture on these lines. Americans had to invent to replace British patents and tools and make up for the national shortage of manpower. This time he made a fortune from his patent and organized his factories for division of labour in classic fashion. He became one of the first in a long and powerful line of American engineer-manufacturers, those men of control Veblen investigated in The Engineers and the Price System in 1921.

Eric Mottram

Jeanette Mirsky and Allan Nevins, The World of Eli Whitney (1952); C.M. Green, Eli Whitney and the Birth of American Technology (1956).

485
WHITTIER, John Greenleaf 1807–92

US poet and abolitionist

Whittier himself did not doubt that his imaginative powers were other than modest. 'I am not one of the master singers,' he wrote towards the end of his career, '& don't pose as one.' Yet in his own lifetime, most notably on the basis of 'Snow-Bound' (1866), the poem memorized by generations of American schoolchildren and by which he is deservedly still best remembered, he commanded a considerable reputation – though never one to equal that of Longfellow*, the most preeminent of the 'Fireside Poets', he was always misleadingly thought to resemble. In part, Whittier's self-disparagement came from believing abolition his principal vocation, in part from genuine native modesty. Whittier not only deserves honour for his fierce, principled stand on abolition, but as an editor, journalist and essayist of some note and as the author, besides 'Snow-Bound', of a handful of considerable minor verse.

Whatever his merits as a poet, and history continues to judge them slight, his contemporaries saw in Whittier the man first and indissolubly a representative New Englander. This New England heritage, marked by its ancestral Puritan sense of 'mission' and deep regard for region, shows in almost every aspect of Whittier's life: in the kindly but often difficult conservativism of his personal manner (like Thoreau* he remained a life-long, slightly askew, bachelor), in the pride he took in his Quaker ancestors who had stood brave and firmly against the prevailing Calvinist ascendancy, and in the choice of commonplace pastoral and religious themes and Quaker plain style of many of his poems. Though at no time an untroubled or a simple-minded believer, and an activist in whom politics blended sometimes uneasily with faith, he was ever, by common acknowledgment, an exemplary, good, dutiful Quaker Christian who acted true to his Inner Light, the very expression of the 'public' New Englander. As Walt Whitman* – the sexual emphases of whose poetry caused Whittier to throw Leaves of Grass into the flames – rightly detected, however, behind the Quaker libertarian and pacifist manner lay no less than 'the zeal, the moral energy that founded New England'.

Born and raised in a staunchly independent but narrow yeoman farming family in East Haverhill, Massachusetts, Whittier's early literary leanings were nourished on the Bible, Quaker luminaries like William Penn and John Woolman, the English Romantics, and the poet whose voice he tried initially to emulate, Robert Burns. A first poem, 'The Exile's Departure' (1826), brought him to the attention of William Lloyd Garrison, then a young abolitionist, who converted Whittier to the cause and helped him get the beginnings of a wider education. Largely through Garrison, also, Whittier began his career as a journalist, first as editor of the pro-Clay newspaper, American Manufacturer (he signally failed to grasp the changing current of American history heralded in the rise of Andrew Jackson), then, as editor or contributor to, among others, the Haverhill Gazette, New England Weekly Review, the Amesbury Village Transcript, National Era (to which in 1849 he contributed in serial form Margaret Smith's Journal, an excellent, often wry, re-creation of a young English girl's year in seventeenth-century New England), and Lowell's* – and later William Dean Howells's* – Atlantic Monthly. In many of the poems he published first in these journals his characteristic faults show through, the inertness of his language, the fastidious metrical self-display, the vague romantic moods of longing and his faux-naïf efforts at colloquialism. Further, in his first published full-length work, Legends of New England (1831), which blends prose with poetry, unlike say Irving* or Hawthorne*, he uses the American past to no significant mythic or psychological purpose but almost as historical decoration.

In John Greenleaf Whittier, An Appraisal and A Selection (1971), Robert Penn Warren intelligently calls attention to how Whittier's belief in abolition as his life cause paradoxically released in him his best poetic strengths. He enlisted at the outset as a propagandist and speech-maker; in 1831 published Justice and Expediency, his first written indictment of slavery; in 1835 served briefly in the Massachusetts Legislature; and in 1837 lobbied in New York for abolition and began contributing to the anti-slavery Democratic Review. Despite bouts of illness and collapse (most of them psychosomatic in origin), his various flirtations which came to nothing, and the deaths of his mother in 1857 and his adored sister Elizabeth in 1864, he established himself surely and progressively and often to considerable personal abuse, as a leading abolitionist force. At the same time his poetry grew in range and confidence. Between his first book of verse, Moll Pitcher (1840), a New England long narrative poem, and his Complete Poems and Prose Works (1888), he published overall nearly a dozen volumes of poetry, including Poems Written During the Progress of the Abolition Question in the United States (1837); Lays Of My Home And Other Poems (1843); Voices Of Freedom (1846); Old Portraits And Modern Sketches (1850); Home Ballads, Poems And Lyrics (1860); his impassioned Civil War poetry, In War Time And Other Poems (1863); Snow-Bound (1866); Ballads Of New England (1870); and a last collection, At Sundown (1890). By his death he had become a national institution, a legendary national voice of abolition, an admired versifier, and the incarnation of an earlier New Englandism of reform and high moral duty.

The best of Whittier's poetry properly includes 'Snow-Bound', which he once termed his 'Flemish picture', a Breughel-like invocation of past New England rural existence, nostalgia finely disciplined by its quiet patient language and dignified use of memory. To 'Snow-Bound', as Warren suggests, should be added poems like 'Massachusetts to Virginia' (1843), a vision of coming secession projected in the emblematic escape of a slave; 'Ichabod' (1847), an elegy to the death of the abolitionist statesman, Daniel Webster; 'The Panorama' (1856), American history seen as stained by slavery; 'Telling The Bees' (1858), a domestic poem of death and ritual exorcism which might compare favourably with Sylvia Plath's bee sequence in Ariel (1965); and 'In School-Days' (1870), Whittier's meditation on youthful time past. In these, unlike the lesser work which constitutes the majority of his poetic output, Whittier lays claim to being judged more than simpliste, the poet of mere New England pastoralism. Yet, like his fellow Massachusetts poet, Emily Dickinson*, it was in seeing 'New Englandly' that he discovered the centre both of his art and his life. However minor his poetry he remains an American figure of serious, deserving historical import.

A. Robert Lee

See: Lewis Leary, *John Greenleaf Whittier* (1961); John B. Pickard, *John Greenleaf Whittier: An Introduction And Interpretation* (1961); Edward Wagenknecht, *John Greenleaf Whittier: A Portrait In Paradox* (1967).

486

WILBERFORCE, William 1759–1833

British politician, social reformer and evangelical Christian

William Wilberforce was born in Hull, the son of a wealthy merchant. Educated initially at Hull Grammar School, he then went to London on the death of his father before returning to Pocklington in Yorkshire to complete his schooling. In 1776 he went up to St John's College, Cambridge. Although as a boy he was attracted to Methodism, his family had weaned him away from its influence and he considered himself to have led a life of pleasure at Cambridge, though already bent on a political career. Elected, at not inconsiderable expense, for Hull in 1780 and in subsequent years one of the county members for Yorkshire, his youth, wealth and charm of manner and speech soon brought him a circle of influential friends. Pitt became one of his closest companions, although they did not agree in every particular. Wilberforce could have been expected to follow a conventional ministerial career and might well have done had it not been for his conversion to evangelical Christianity in 1785 when on a journey to the Mediterranean with Isaac Milner, a Cambridge clergyman. Evangelical religion was already in the family – his uncle had married the sister of John Thornton of Clapham, a leading figure in the circle of devout Christians described as the 'Clapham Sect'. Wilberforce now no longer despised the 'enthusiasm' of his Thornton relatives and wrestled with his future plans. Although he resigned from fashionable clubs and set himself against mere self-advancement, he decided to remain in parliament in the belief, as he put it in 1787, that God had set before him two great objects – the suppression of the slave trade and the reformation of manners. Wilberforce's objectives were not easily achieved but his life was now built upon prayer and meditation and a scrupulous attention to his parliamentary duties. That did not mean he lost his power of persuasion, though he soon attracted criticism and derision. He and his associates received the collective nickname of the 'Saints'.

The Committee for the Abolition of the Slave Trade had been founded in 1787, made up largely of Quakers with little public reputation. Criticism of the trade had been steadily growing from the 1770s. Wilberforce himself claimed to have been sufficiently interested in the problem in 1780 to ask a friend to investigate conditions in Antigua, though he did nothing thereafter. In 1787, however, he did consent to become parliamentary spokesman for the committee. Although some wished to seek to abolish both the slave trade and the institution of slavery, the majority believed that success would be easier if they concentrated on one of these evils. To attack the trade seemed more likely to be acceptable than to launch a direct attack on the institution – which would raise difficult questions of property rights in general. The immediate task was to collect full information on the topic. A serious illness took Wilberforce out of the campaign for a short while but then he threw himself into mastering the indictment against the trade in its full complexity. Success seemed possible, at least as evidenced in the support of the leading parliamentary orators, Pitt, Fox, Burke and Sheridan, but rapid advance was halted by two events. The French Revolution induced a general mood of anxiety and caution. It was not the time to initiate change. Then there was a slave rebellion in St Domingue in 1791 which was used not as an argument for abandoning the trade and treating slaves better but as a reason for maintaining and strengthening the *status quo*. Wilberforce now found himself in a difficulty. Abolitionists, some of whom were by no means hostile, at least at the outset, to the French Revolution, advocated agitation in the country in a way that was alien to Wilberforce. In his general political views he remained strongly conservative, approving of the repressive measures taken against revolutionary sympathizers. So despondent had Wilberforce become that in 1799 he did not table what, until then, had been his annual motion in favour of abolition. After the turn of the century, however, the mood changed. When Pitt returned to office in 1804 abolition was acceptable to a majority in the Commons but he was not prepared to risk upsetting his government by championing the cause himself. Wilberforce, in turn, was not willing to use the votes of the 'Saints' to push the government into adopting abolition. After Pitt's death, Fox, Grenville and Grey gave government support to the abolition bill and in February 1807 it was passed – having been introduced into the Lords. Wilberforce's tract *A Letter on the Abolition of the Slave Trade* . . . summarized all the arguments used against the trade since he had first taken the matter up twenty years earlier. The campaign against slavery itself largely fell into other hands. Wilberforce retired from the Commons in 1824.

Wilberforce could also claim to have played a major part in the change of manners and morals amongst contemporaries of his own social class. The message of his *Practical View of the Prevailing Religious System* . . . *contrasted with Real Christianity* (1797) was that only the latter could bring about the necessary seriousness and earnestness in the government of the country. That appeal (which was not without self-interest) to the higher and middle classes met with considerable success. Practical piety of this stamp, whether finding expression in the Society for Bettering Conditions and Increasing the Comforts of the Poor or the Society for the Prevention of Cruelty to Animals, played a very important part in moulding the outlook and culture of influential sections of the English aristocracy and middle class in the opening decades of the century. It has no more attractive exemplar than Wilberforce.

Keith Robbins

See: Robin Furneaux, *William Wilberforce* (1974); John Pollock, *Wilberforce* (1977).

487
WILDE, Oscar Fingal O'Flahertie Wills 1854–1900

Anglo-Irish writer and wit

Oscar Wilde was born in Dublin, the son of Sir William Wilde the eye surgeon and Lady Wilde who wrote Irish nationalist verses under the name 'Speranza'. A godson of the King of Sweden, he possessed immense curiosity and a remarkable memory and was from the outset the opposite of the 'ghetto' or 'partisan' type. He always tended to the wider world, to the universal, and so gravitated naturally towards a study of the classics. After the Portora Royal School and Trinity College, Dublin, where he won the Berkeley Gold Medal for Greek, he went on to Magdalen College, Oxford, in 1874, eventually taking a double first in Mods and Greats. In the long vacation of 1877 he travelled to Italy and Greece and subsequently wrote the poem *Ravenna* which won the Newdigate Prize in 1878. At Oxford, despite his gregarious manner and bulky physique, he gained notoriety as an aesthete, became the disciple of Ruskin* and Pater*, Swinburne*, Rossetti* and Baudelaire*, and was excited by the glamour as well as the substance of art.

In 1879 Wilde moved to London and with a vigour that was characteristically Victorian achieved metropolitan celebrity by caricaturing – and so detaching himself from – his early influences. This capacity for detachment was one of his greatest strengths because Wilde sought to occupy in relation to the impulses of his personality the position of ringmaster and thereby acquire an individual gravitas sufficient, when married to his sense of purpose, to reconstitute his environment. This he increasingly managed to do but was finally dislodged from the creation of his own destiny by his love for Lord Alfred Douglas which in Nietzschean style he interprets in *De Profundis* (the full text of this long letter to Douglas from prison was not published until 1962) as a failure of will. But Wilde himself set in motion the sequence of legal actions which led to his downfall and when events were taken out of his

hands he had established all the preconditions for the completion of his life as a perfect drama.

In 1881 Wilde published his first collection of poems which are significant not so much as poetry as for the efficiency of Wilde's cannibalizing of his mentors. In 1882 he went on a year-long tour of the USA to lecture the Americans on beauty in connection with the performances there of Gilbert* and Sullivan's* *Patience*. This operetta, which had opened in London the previous year, was designed as a skit on Rossetti and Swinburne but typically Wilde had turned it into an advertisement for himself. In 1883 he made the first of many visits to Paris where he astonished and instructed its salons and leading literary figures. His pedagogic instinct, which repeatedly turned into parable, also operated in reverse. He parodied the teacher in himself and in this way he created a mask, as well as a vehicle, for his serious intentions.

In his espousal of a cause, from his preaching the doctrines of Aestheticism in the early 1880s onwards, high seriousness and high comedy always clash and flirt with each other. Wilde used ideas in motion, not at rest. That is to say, his relationship to his theories was always strategic, the very opposite of art for art's sake, and his method suggests the conceptual gymnastics of a Zen adept. Wilde's genius for contradiction permitted for example his hyperactive propagation of the cult of inaction; or the fervent individualism of a man who could function only in symbiosis (when, after his conviction for homosexual offences in 1895, he lost his audience, he lost also his motivation, writing nothing after his release from prison except *The Ballad of Reading Gaol*, 1898). This ambivalence disconcerted other artists, especially Whistler*, and they resented the familiarity with which Wilde sometimes treated them. But society was fascinated by the brilliant talker who entertained with his epigrams and hypnotized with his stories.

In 1884 his travels and burlesque postures were curtailed by his marriage to Constance Lloyd. They moved into a house in Tite Street, Chelsea, and immediately had two sons (Cyril, 1885; Vyvyan, 1886). At the age of thirty he settled down to consolidate his position through journalism. This is Wilde at his most straightforward, the editor of *Woman's World* (1887–9), eliciting contributions from Marie Corelli, Sarah Bernhardt, and the Queen of Roumania. At home he wrote for inspiration at a desk which had belonged to Carlyle*, publishing short stories, essays, reviews and poems, but only one book, *The Happy Prince* (1888). These fairy-tales catch something of Wilde's charm, mercuriality and freedom from malice, which Graham Robertson called an 'almost child-like love of fun' and Wilson Knight 'a boyish immaturity often difficult to distinguish from the integration of a seer'. In this he resembled Byron*, as he did also in his androgynous nature and appearance.

Marriage organized Wilde but it also crystallized the deep conflict between social acceptance and self-betrayal, classical restraint and romantic passion, love of others and love of self. From this derive his most important works beginning in 1891 with the publication of *Intentions* ('The Decay of Lying', 'Pen, Pencil and Poison', 'The Critic as Artist', 'The Truth of Masks', previously published essays much revised here), *Lord Arthur Savile's Crime and Other Stories, The Picture of Dorian Gray* (published the previous year in *Lippincott's Magazine* in a slightly less moral version), and a second volume of fairy-tales *A House of Pomegranates*. These books – indeed Wilde's entire *oeuvre* – are a complex and dangerous act of brinkmanship in which he attempts to subvert an entrenched world view without sacrificing his place in it. That is, he wished to affect humanity at large and not merely some convertible coterie. Hereafter, until his imprisonment and apart from a few poems and prose poems, he conducted his campaign exclusively in the theatre and in the real world.

Pater, in his essay on Coleridge*, wrote 'Modern thought is distinguished from ancient by its cultivation of the "relative" spirit in place of the "absolute".' Wilde was the first man to enact this as well as think it, which exposed him to charges of shallowness but increased his range enormously. So on the one hand there is the voluptuous Byzantine Wilde of *Salomé* (written in French and first published in 1893), romantic in style but modern in content, in which all is flux and dispute and no one speaks with authority; on the other, the streamlined Mozartian Wilde of *The Importance of Being Ernest* (first performance 1895), classical in style, modern in content. The characters of this play well understand the provisional nature of a statement, the techniques of role playing and image games, governable only by a transcendental ego. *Salomé* is dark and tragic, steeped in superstition; *Ernest* is light and humorous in the realm of the sublime. Neither can provide an exhaustive truth. Both are facets of reality. For a nineteenth-century mind already made dizzy by Darwinism*, Wilde made the vertiginous trauma of relativity tolerable by converting it into play: spectacle and symbol, insincerity and lying. This is why he wished to detach his message from conventional morality. But he knew that a prerequisite of lying (except for the insane) is an apprehension of the truth. So in his system insincerity becomes the opposite of delusion.

By 1895 Wilde's success was very great and the world as it stood offered no challenge. The too-integrated personality can separate itself from life and float off like a balloon – this was Nietzsche's* fate. Wilde rejected self-enclosure and plunged low to reconnect and stay sane (Alfred Douglas was both a poet and the most beautiful male aristocrat in the kingdom and therefore worthy of symbolic behaviour). The spiritual effect of Wilde's downfall, which was to preserve and

intensify his power, was the opposite of the social one. This was his final triumphant paradox: disaster rehumanizes him at the same time as it immortalizes him in myth.

He told Gide:

Understand that there are two worlds: the one that *is* without one's speaking about it; it is called the *real world* because there's no need to talk about it in order to see it. And the other is the world of art; that's the one which has to be talked about because it would not exist otherwise.

This is Wilde's challenge to entropy and takes us beyond Nietzsche into the regions of Gurdjieff, Aleister Crowley, Castaneda's Don Juan. Wilde belongs here too in that his ultimate concern is not with art but with power and transformation. But he scorned occultism and ridiculed it in the emblem of the green carnation.

Wilde was the last Romantic in his special claims for the artist in pursuit of ecstasy, and the first Modern in his knowledge of the relative manifestation of absolute being. In him these two opposed rotations are housed. As the first was overcome by the second, the capacity of Wilde's intellect and Wilde's sympathies enabled him – and only him – to hold them for a moment in dynamic balance, to accommodate both Salomé and Ernest in a weightless reciprocity of opposites – then it is gone, and we are in the twentieth century.

Duncan Fallowell

The kinetic nature of Wilde's thought and personality still disorientates scholars. There is no definitive biography or academic edition of his works. *The Collected Works of Oscar Wilde*, ed. G.F. Maine (1952), is convenient but untidy. See also *Letters*, ed. Rupert Hart-Davis (1962); Phillipe Jullian, *Oscar Wilde* (trans. 1969); Robert Hichens, *The Green Carnation* (1895); H. Montgomery Hyde, *The Trials of Oscar Wilde* (1948) and *Oscar Wilde: The Aftermath* (1963); Karl Beckson, *Oscar Wilde: The Critical Heritage* (1970).

488
WISTER, Owen 1860–1938

US writer

Owen Wister, one of the leading exponents of the romance and nobility of the American West in the second half of the nineteenth century, was born on 14 July 1860 in Germantown, a then well-to-do suburb of Philadelphia, and never saw the West until he was twenty-five. His paternal ancestors were successful doctors and merchants while his maternal ones included the actress and author Fanny Kemble, and Pierce Butler who served at the Constitutional Convention. Henry James* was a visitor in the home of Wister's youth. Wister attended a boarding school in Hofwyl, Switzerland, Germantown Academy, and graduated from St Paul's School in Concord in 1878. He then went to Harvard where he majored in music, graduating *summa cum laude* in 1882. There he made friends with Theodore Roosevelt, William Dean Howells*, Henry Lee Higginson, and Oliver Wendell Holmes*. After graduation Wister made the obligatory trip to Europe, but he carried letters of introduction to the likes of Franz Liszt* who much admired one of his compositions. Unfortunately, upon return there was nothing but the drab reality of a position computing interest at Union Safe Deposit Vaults in Boston. Only membership in the rather literary Tavern Club sustained him at this time. In 1885, his family and biographer agree, Wister made the most important trip of his life, a journey west to Wyoming for his health. As he wrote in his journal, 'I don't wonder a man never comes back after he has once been here for a few years.' But first he enrolled in Harvard Law School in the fall of 1885, graduating in 1888 and moving to Philadelphia where he was admitted to the Bar in 1890.

But the trips west continued and finally they became the reality and the law practice merely a sideline. In order to, as Wister put it, 'save the sagebrush' he began to write tales of the West he knew before it disappeared. His first stories 'Hank's Women' and 'How Lin McLean Went East' were published in *Harper's* in 1892. By 1894 his writing had become his main profession with eight pieces in *Harper's* alone and in 1895 his first collection of Western tales, *Red Men and White*, was published. Further collections followed in 1897 and 1900. Meanwhile in 1898 he married Mary Channing, who gave him six children before dying in childbirth in 1913.

During this period he wrote his first and most famous novel, *The Virginian*, published in 1902 and dedicated to Theodore Roosevelt. Subtitled 'A Horseman of the Plains'. the novel told the now familiar story of a handsome, daring, and rather chivalric cowboy known only as 'the Virginian' in the rough and tumble days of the 1870s and 1880s as he wooed the young Vermont schoolteacher Molly and upheld justice and virtue in the days before civilization arrived. In his introduction Wister called his hero 'the cowpuncher, the last romantic figure upon our soil'. In pointed criticism of the trends of the day and capturing the heart of the bourgeois American dreamer Wister continued, 'The cowpuncher's ungoverned hours did not unman him. If he gave his word, he kept it; Wall Street would have found him behind the times. Nor did he talk lewdly to women; Newport would have thought him old-fashioned.' Wister here has forsaken the realism of Howells's *The Rise of Silas Lapham* invoked in the novel's introduction. The

'horseman of the plains' is idealized into a chivalric knight who courts the schoolmarm leisurely and nobly and invokes knightly codes of battle with his enemies when he is not reading Shakespeare and Jane Austen* or investing in land. In fact, the Virginian often evokes the Alger* dream of self-help – 'The world did not beget you. I reckon man helps them that helps themselves.' The Virginian is both the rugged individualist, however, and the decorous gentleman who knows how to treat a lady. This knightly cowpuncher rises in the course of the novel from cowboy to foreman to ranchowner while still maintaining his heroic status by demonstrating his Western skill with horses and gun against rustlers and his long time opponent Trampas. At the same time, unlike many other Western heroes in literature, the Virginian demonstrates his ability to survive and thrive in the twentieth century by courting the East embodied in New Englander Molly Wood's learning, ancestry and manners.

The Virginian unified many of the American myths for the American public; the Buffalo Bill-anglo-frontiersman, the Horatio Alger upwardly-mobile poor, the virtues of the natural life, and the moral righteousness of Roosevelt's bully pulpit. And for sixty years Americans relived the story from Dustin Farnum's stage version, through four motion pictures, and a long-running television series. Although Wister would continue to write, it was *The Virginian* alone that achieved the cultural and mythic influence that makes him such a summation of late nineteenth-century dreams: the aristocrat as outdoorsman, joining Roosevelt and Frederic Remington as the great popularizers of an idealized West where virtue, nature and manliness were inextricably linked.

Charles Gregory

Other works include: *Philosophy Four* (1903); *When West Was West* (1928); *Lady Baltimore* (1906); *Roosevelt: The Story of a Friendship 1880–1919* (1930). See: Edward G. White, *The Eastern Establishment and the Western Experience: The West of Frederic Remington, Theodore Roosevelt, and Owen Wister* (1968); Joe B. Frantz and Julian Ernest Choate Jr, *The American Cowboy: The Myth and the Reality* (1955); Frances K.W. Stokes, *My Father, Owen Wister, and Ten Letters Written by Owen Wister to his Mother during his First Trip to Wyoming in 1885* (1952); Richard Etulain, *Owen Wister* (1973).

489
WOLF, Hugo 1860–1903

Austrian composer

Wolf was born in Windischgraz, lower Styria (now part of Yugoslavia), the son of a tanner. He studied at the Vienna Conservatoire, where one of his fellow students was Mahler*, with whom he later shared a room. His first important songs date from 1878; he had already composed piano and choral music. On leaving the conservatoire he supported himself mainly by teaching; a conducting post in Salzburg was abandoned after only three months. From 1884 to 1887 he was music critic of a fashionable Vienna weekly, the *Salonblatt*, where his outspoken criticisms made him notorious.

In 1888 he produced two of the great song-books on which his reputation rests; a third was begun in the same year. From now on he enjoyed increasing public success. His wish to write opera led to the composition of *Der Corregidor* (1895), his one completed work in that genre; a Hugo Wolf Society was established in 1897. But the same year saw a dramatic breakdown in his health, undermined by syphilis; insanity and paralysis followed; and he died in 1903.

Wolf is conventionally regarded, and rightly, as a major figure in the German *lieder* tradition; perhaps the last who is worthy of comparison with Schubert*, Schumann* and Brahms*. Schubert and Schumann he venerated, so much so that he avoided setting poems already set to music by them. Brahms he detested with the passion of a true Wagnerian, though Brahms's influence can be heard in some of his very early songs. Wolf had come under the spell of Wagner* in 1875, and had never escaped it; indeed his greatest contribution to the *lied* may be the way he brings a Wagnerian intensity of emotion, and a Wagnerian harmonic language, to this miniature form. Other important influences were Berlioz*, Liszt* and Chopin*.

Wolf's first great song-book was *Gedichte von Eduard Mörike* ('Poems of Eduard Mörike, for voice and piano, set to music by Hugo Wolf' – the emphasis on the poet is characteristic). The song entitled 'Lebewohl' is typical on several counts: its brevity (only twenty bars), its extreme dynamic range (from *pp* to *ff* and down again), its declamatory vocal writing (another Wagnerian trait), its chromatic texture (with a nod to Hans Sachs in bar 7), and its 'progressive tonality' (it ends in the dominant). The concept of the song-book, or collection, devoted to the work of a single poet seems to have evolved partly from the great speed with which Wolf always composed; one song followed another as if by chain reaction. It led to an idealization of the poet on the composer's part: at times Mörike* himself seems to be the subject of the song-book.

Wolf's *Eichendorff* song-book was conceived as a companion-piece to Schumann's Eichendorff* *Liederkreis*, concentrating on the humorous figures which Schumann had ignored. This delight in musical characterization, much admired by Reger, is seen again in Wolf's *Goethe* song-book, especially in his settings of poems from *Wilhelm Meister*, where he tried to realize in music the characters of the novel. Wolf's fourth major song-book, the *Spanisches Liederbuch* (1889–90),

sets translations of Spanish poems from the sixteenth and seventeenth centuries. It is in two sections, 'Sacred' and 'Profane', and the erotic/religious imagery inspires some of his most daring harmony; the piano writing, too, tends to be harsher than before, some of the sonorities anticipating Bartók. By contrast Wolf's final collection, the *Italienisches Liederbuch* (two volumes, 1890–1 and 1896: settings of Italian poems in translation), returns to a suaver, more lyrical style; here the vocal writing is perhaps his subtlest. Wolf himself said that many of the songs in the volume could be played equally well by a string quartet, and it is no coincidence that his most successful instrumental work, the Serenade in G (1887), is for this medium: it was later orchestrated as *Italienische Serenade*. Wolf's last songs are three to poems by *Michelangelo* (1897), in which the linear tendency combines with a bleak dissonance reminiscent of some of the Goethe* songs.

Der Corregidor, based on Alarcón's *The Three-Cornered Hat*, is notable for its Spanish subject – a more substantial Mediterraneanizing of music than that found in *Carmen*. Its 'song-book' style has caused it to be critized as undramatic, but this very lyricism, the containedness of the set numbers, gives it a Neoclassical quality far in advance of its time. Wolf told a friend that in his next opera (*Manuel Venegas*, left unfinished at his death) he would orchestrate like Mozart; this remark may be a surer indication of his future development than the style of the Michelangelo songs.

Wolf's achievement lies in his mastery of a single medium, the *lied*, rather than in his versatility. His concern for truth of expression led to a style of declamation whose aims, at least, had something in common with those of Mussorgsky* – and later with those of Fauré*, Debussy and Janáček. At the same time the motivic concentration of his work – a predominantly German characteristic – links it with that of his detested Brahms. His influence has naturally been felt most strongly by other song-writers: by Schoenberg, Webern, and Schoeck among the 'Austro-Germans', but also by a younger, English composer such as Robin Holloway. That one of Stravinsky's last creative acts was to orchestrate two Wolf songs suggests that this influence is not exhausted yet.

Derrick Puffett

Other works include: String Quartet in D minor (1878–84); *Penthesilea*, symphonic poem for orchestra (1883–5); *Christnacht* for soli, chorus and orchestra (1886–9). Wolf's works are published by the International Hugo Wolf Society under the editorship of Hans Jancik (Vienna). See: Frank Walker, *Hugo Wolf: A Biography* (2nd edn, 1968); Eric Sams, *The Songs of Hugo Wolf* (2nd edn, 1982), and 'Hugo Wolf', in *The New Grove Dictionary of Music and Musicians* (1981). See also: *The Music Criticism of Hugo Wolf*, trans. and ed. Henry Pleasants (1979).

490
WORDSWORTH, William 1770–1850

British poet

William Wordsworth was born at Cockermouth in Cumberland in 1770. His mother is on record as having called him a 'stiff, moody and violent child'; she died when Wordsworth was eight, and this loss was followed, when he was thirteen, by the death of his father. Dorothy Wordsworth, the poet's junior by a year, wrote later of the privation and unhappiness suffered by the orphaned family, and this belies the selective picture of his childhood which Wordsworth presented in *The Prelude*. The early loss of his parents is clearly significant when we consider two of his most characteristic themes, the vivifying security and innocence of family life in its influence on a child's development, and the necessity for that lonely and stoical endurance which circumstances so often demand of the characters in his poems.

He was educated at Hawkshead Grammar School and St John's College, Cambridge. He felt out of place in Cambridge and made little attempt to study seriously for his degree. In 1790 he visited France and Italy, crossing the Alps on foot. In 1791, having left Cambridge with little notion of how he was to make his living, he revisited France and became caught up in the revolution. He made the acquaintance of Michel Beaupuy, whose revolutionary ardour and idealism inspired in him an answering enthusiasm, and Annette Vallon with whom he fell in love. Though she bore him a child the two did not marry; the remorse this episode provoked in him, together with the destruction of his early political hopes as the revolution developed into the nightmare of the terror, clouded his mind with pessimism during much of the 1790s.

In 1793 *An Evening Walk*, a rather conventional exercise in heroic couplets, and the more adventurous *Descriptive Sketches*, which incorporated some of the Rousseauist notions that had drawn him to the revolution, were published. During 1795–6 he worked on a verse tragedy, *The Borderers*, in which he attempted to explore the near despair about the human condition which then gripped him.

His precarious financial circumstances began to improve – first by the payment of a debt owed to his family by his father's former employer, and then, in 1795, by a legacy of £900 left to him by his friend Raisley Calvert. In the same year Wordsworth met Coleridge* and the two became neighbours in Somerset, first at Alfoxden and then at Nether Stowey. In 1798 the two poets, together with Wordsworth's sister Dorothy, visited Germany, wintering at Goslar where many of Wordsworth's finest short poems (including the enigmatic 'Lucy' group) were written. The first book of *The Prelude* was also begun at this period; the

poem was originally written as a lengthy verse epistle to Coleridge (who is the frequently apostrophized 'friend'), though this structure was partly obscured when Wordsworth came to revise the work in his old age.

In 1798 Wordsworth and Coleridge issued *Lyrical Ballads*; in 1800 an enlarged edition with Wordsworth's 'Observations' added was printed, and in 1802 a further edition with an appendix by Wordsworth on poetic diction appeared. In 1799 he returned to the Lake District of his childhood, settling, with his sister Dorothy, at Grasmere; for the rest of his life his home was within five miles of Grasmere.

In 1802 he married Mary Hutchinson. By 1805 the first version of *The Prelude* had been completed; in the same year the death of his brother John and the physical decline of Coleridge contributed to the gradual sobering of Wordsworth's outlook. In 1807 the *Ode on the Intimations of Immortality from Recollections of Early Childhood* was published, together with *Miscellaneous Sonnets* and *Sonnets Dedicated to Liberty*; the date marks the end of his major period as a poet – he wrote little after 1807 that can compare in intensity of vision with the earlier work.

In 1813 he was appointed 'Distributor of Stamps to the County of Westmorland', a virtual sinecure that paid £400 per annum. *The Excursion*, a blank verse poem in nine books, was published in 1814 though its finest section, 'The Story of Margaret', had been written in 1797 and was one of Wordsworth's earliest attempts at blank verse. Though the publication of *The Excursion* preceded that of *The Prelude* (published, in a heavily revised version, in 1850) by more than thirty-five years, it was originally meant as a sequel to that poem; there was to have been a third part – which was never written – the whole work to be called *The Recluse*. The scheme was Coleridge's; the recluse of the title was to be Wordsworth himself in his role as contemplative observer of human life.

The relative failure of inspiration which is apparent in such later poetry as *Ecclesiastical Sonnets* was matched by a gradual rejection of his earlier political and philosophical concerns. He became an admirer of Burke (inserting a panegyric to him into *The Prelude*), that most compelling voice of political conservatism, and his sense of the numinous as a presence immanent in the natural world (and, in privileged 'spots of time', discernible) gave way to the defence of Anglican orthodoxy. Though the change was regretted by many (Browning* called him 'The Lost Leader'), it was not altogether surprising. Much of Wordsworth's finest poetry is concerned with a loss of the sense of the numinous and the necessity for stoical endurance in a world apparently bereft of immediate meaning; it is perhaps inevitable that such an apprehension of reality should seek solace in duty and orthodoxy, that a mind which saw humanity as largely estranged from its true sources of morality should insist on external control as a substitute for a lost innate moral sympathy between man and nature. Nevertheless a list of the causes against which Wordsworth in his old age campaigned makes depressing reading – it includes the abolition of slavery, the emancipation of Irish Catholics, the abolition of capital punishment, parliamentary reform and even a bill to make cruelty to animals illegal.

His religious and political conservatism turned the young radical into a prop of established society; in 1842 he was awarded a civil list pension, and in 1843 he succeeded Southey* as Poet Laureate. He died in 1850.

Though Wordsworth is regarded as a poet of nature, he rarely presents us with the visible details of the natural world in the way that, for example, Clare* or even Crabbe* do. His concern is with a more elusive reality which he discerns *through* rather than *in* nature; it is nature as manifestation of immanent truth, rather than the specifics of the natural world, which engages his attention. He links this dimly apprehended presence with his own mental state and implies a quasi-mystical identity between internal and external 'modes of being'. Though this intuition underlies many of his finest passages Wordsworth is aware that he is attempting to articulate a virtually ineffable apprehension, and the language is typically inspecific at moments of crucial intensity, for example the '*something* far more deeply interfused' of 'Tintern Abbey', or

but in the main
It lies far hidden from the reach of words

from *The Prelude*.

The 'spots of time' in which Wordsworth felt this identity of his own spirit with that of external reality diminished in frequency and intensity as he grew older, and much of his best-known poetry (e.g. 'Tintern Abbey', 'Ode on the Intimations of Immortality from Recollections of Early Childhood') both records the loss and attempts to suggest a consolatory wisdom born of understanding rather than intensity of vision. That the consolation was at best fitful can be gauged from the tenor of much of the poetry written after 1807 – *The Excursion*, for example, has been called 'a long sermon against pessimism' (Legouis – in 1964).

In his notorious phrase (from the Preface to *Lyrical Ballads*) describing the origin of poetry as 'emotion recollected in tranquillity' the most significant word is 'recollected'. Wordsworth's imagination worked almost entirely through and with his memory (how far this is true is immediately apparent when one examines *The Prelude*, a poem wholly built up from personal recollections); it is the memory of his earliest childhood (in which he felt he was at one with the natural world) and of the diminishing 'spots of time' (in which that identity was fleetingly recaptured) that forms the op-

timistic basis of his poetry. The desolation he experienced when cut off from this sympathy (it is tempting to see the prototype for this emotion in the early loss of his mother) and the remedies he sought against such feelings are the motive for his many poems on solitary figures who endure betrayal, penury or exile with more or less stoicism. Such figures are hinted at in the vagrant women of so early a poem as 'An Evening Walk', and in the gipsy of its companion piece *Descriptive Sketches*; Margaret (of *The Excursion*), the leech gatherer (of *Resolution and Independence*), the old soldier in Book IV of *The Prelude*, 'The Old Cumberland Beggar' and Emily (of *The White Doe of Rylstone*) are examples of the type. Such emblematic figures are like the parables of a sermon exhorting author and reader to endurance in the face of despair. Wordsworth is at his best in describing the ways in which man accommodates himself to his privation, spiritual or physical.

Wordsworth uses memory for two basic purposes: in order to draw a vivifying strength from past glimpses of an underlying identity between the human spirit and a hidden truth of nature. and secondly to maintain before his mind the admonitory example of figures whose stoicism he admires. In the first instance his treatment of memory approaches that of mystical religion, in the second it approaches that of the more mundane religion of the popular sermon; in both cases memory is bound up with notions of morality and religious duty. Wordsworth is one of the first English poets to use poetry for such ultimately religious purposes; in his early visionary work he does not so much expound formal doctrine (an exercise managed by many of his predecessors) as embody and exemplify his own insights into what he took to be religious truth.

His concentration on memory as his primary source of inspiration meant that his poetry, far more than that of most poets, is almost exclusively concerned with himself; where other characters appear they are there finally as an admonition and example for the author. The concern with memory also meant that his subject was not so much the external world as the mind that perceived and remembered that world – he is less the poet of natural than of psychological truth. His early belief that spiritual and external truth were finally one, though the identity may be apparent only at rare moments, is at the root of his dislike of eighteenth-century poetic diction. With Rousseau he believed that social convention obscured rather than ordered nature; his concern was with a validity underlying appearances, and he believed that a simplicity of diction and anecdote could best present such truths. His fidelity to his own standard of a selection of 'language really used by men' was however intermittent – his diction had its sources as much in Milton and Spenser as in the speech of Westmorland peasants.

Dick Davis

Editions: *Poetical Works*, ed. T. Hutchinson (1969); *Poetry and Prose*, ed. D.N. Smith (1973); *The Prelude*: *A Parallel Text*, ed. J.C. Maxwell (1971). See: H. Darbishire, *The Poet Wordsworth* (1950); J. Jones, *The Egotistical Sublime* (1954); M. Moorman, *William Wordsworth*: *A Biography* (2 vols, 1957 and 1965); C. Salveson, *The Landscape of Memory* (1965); J. Wordsworth, *The Music of Humanity* (1969).

491
WUNDT, Wilhelm 1832–1920

German experimental psychologist

Wundt's long career offers an interesting paradox for historians of science. He was a laborious but not a clever man who personally made no useful discoveries nor ever had any valid theoretical insights. He was an immensely hard-working systematizer who opposed and devalued the contributions of better scientists. He was touchy and reacted to imagined slights with personal attacks. Yet his life's work, more than that of gifted contemporaries, launched human experimental psychology as an academic discipline.

Until the eighteenth century it had been thought impossible (and perhaps blasphemous) to suppose that we may learn anything about the human mind by experiments or observations. Systematic theories related personality type (e.g. choleric, sanguine, phlegmatic or melancholic) to physique and even to diet. But it was thought impossible to understand perception, or memory, or to measure the speed of human thought processes because these functions involved a non-material entity whose functions were, in principle, unmeasurable and unquantifiable. Two conceptual steps were necessary: the first was to bring techniques of measurement and mathematical modelling successfully to bear on the study of human thought, as they had been brought to bear on the movements of the stars or the physics of the everyday world; the second step was to relate these measurements to the physiology of the sense organs, and eventually of the brain, in order to discover what happens in the nervous system to produce the vivid world of our conscious experience. Most of the necessary work had been completed by people who taught Wundt.

By 1860 J. Muller and E.H. Weber had shown that people can very reliably indicate the relative magnitudes of their sensations (touch, brightness, loudness, etc.) and that sensory thresholds and difference thresholds were remarkably constant across different individuals. G.T. Fechner had added the idea of a regular 'psychophysical law' for sensation. The great Herman von Helmholtz* had published the early volumes of a *Handbook of Physiological Optics*, and a work on audition which were to remain useful until 1950.

Helmholtz had put forward a useful theory of colour vision and, in about 1850, had shown that the speed of nerve-conduction (on which the 'speed of thought' must depend) was not infinite, as had been supposed, but was rather a lethargic and easily measurable process. The philosophical implications of this are greater than we can now realize. The capacities of the mind were now suddenly seen to be limited by the efficiency of human neurophysiology. Helmholtz's father saw another important point, and brilliantly captured it in two significant errors, in a letter to his son: 'Dear Son, I would as soon believe your result as that we see the light of a star that burned a million years ago'. Indeed both examples show that Helmholtz had discovered that humans never can experience the present, but merely an immediate past which was dated by nerve-conduction just as the finite velocity of light dates their knowledge of distant stars to the remote past.

Wundt's early schooling as a pastor's son was remote from these intellectual debates. He was an ungifted pupil whose social awkwardness further hindered his progress. He went to the University of Tübingen in 1851 and then to Heidelberg to study medicine. He abandoned medicine, it is said because he grew bored with his patients, and went to Berlin to study for a year in J. Muller's physiological laboratory. He returned, took his degree in 1856, and began to teach. His great stroke of fortune was to be offered an assistant's position in Helmholtz's laboratory. Partly to aid his teaching he produced textbooks on the physiology of sensory perception and of movement control, among a steady flood of other publications. These gained him the Chair of Inductive Logic in Zürich in 1874, the year when his textbook *Principles of Physiological Psychology* (*Grundzüge der physiologischen Psychologie*, 2 vols, 1893, trans. 1904) was produced. This, in turn, with the approval of Muller and Fechner, may have resulted in the further, unexpected, offer of the Chair of Philosophy at Leipzig in 1875.

Wundt settled at Leipzig for the rest of his long life and his career there offers a choice of years from which anniversaries of the foundation of experimental psychology may be dated. In 1875 he requested space for demonstrations of psychological experiments and in 1879 began, in a single room, the Institute of Psychology at Leipzig, the first psychological laboratory in the world. To publish work carried out there he founded the first journal of psychology (*Philosophische Studien*, later *Psychologische Studien*) in 1881. His phenomenal rate of publication never slackened and even in his seventies and eighties, blind in one eye and only partially sighted in the other, he published continual revisions of his monumental *Outlines of Psychology* (*Grundiss der Psychologie*, 1896, trans. 1902), brought out a series of volumes on *Volkerpsychologie* ('Social Psychology and Anthropology') and published an autobiography which was published, with impeccable timing, in the year of his death. Like his life, this autobiography was devoted to his ideas and his work. His marriage and his family were disposed of in a single paragraph.

Wundt regarded psychology as the study of human consciousness, resting on the physiological study of the central nervous system and culminating in the study of man's social and technological achievements (*Volkerpsychologie*). This attitude committed him to experiments in which laboriously trained subjects would attempt precisely to describe their emotions, feelings and sensations, or to describe the 'mental events' they experienced while they responded, as fast as possible, to a light or a sound. We may now agree with his discovery that people cannot reliably do this. But we also know that the efforts he made are not worth while since most mental events do not involve language, and cannot be described in language, and the categorizations imposed by language or subjective experience may be irrelevant and misleading. But it is likely that these interests in subjective experience were the reason for the extraordinary success of his public lectures. These were encyclopedic in coverage, and his contemporaries have described them as dull and badly delivered. But they must have left an impression of *total* coverage of a discipline, from the physiology of sense-organs through the taxonomy of human emotions, through introspective studies of consciousness, mental illness, social psychology, sociology and anthropology. He was fascinated by the precise description of *experience* rather than of *behaviour*. By attempts to make precise distinctions between qualities of emotions (on a 'three-dimensional' plot of 'pleasant-unpleasant, tense-relaxed and excited-calm'). By the nature of experience at the moment of death. By the phenomena of attention and of intellectual creativity. He tackled all these problems without wit or imagination, but with honest labour. He attracted students who were no longer interested in hearing more brilliant scientists produce convincing reasons why these problems should be avoided.

Possibly his main contribution to his subject lies in the careers of his students. Kraepelin dominated German psychiatry. Lehrman, Lange and Munsterberg were influential psychologists, and when William James* wished to establish psychology at Harvard he persuaded Munsterberg to teach there. Wundt had some students like Kulpe, who set up a rival school at Wurzburg, who strongly differed from him. But collectively the people he trained achieved a curious pheno-

menon – the transformation of an area of personal intellectual interest into an established academic discipline. Wundt was even more influential in American universities. J. McKeen Cattell at Columbia, E.B. Titchener at Cornell and G.M. Stratton at California all went on to carry out far more important research than he ever achieved. He also taught G. Stanley Hall of Clarke and C.H. Judd of Chicago who, like himself, were formidably influential personalities rather than distinguished scientists. Some of his talent for systematization was passed on to H.C. Warren who produced the first dictionary of psychology.

Wundt's career shows the distinction to be made between science as an intellectual game and as a public, social phenomenon involving the acquisition of funds, the construction of buildings, the acknowledgment of academic colleagues on committees and the trappings of professional establishments. The steps from 'psychological phenomena' as a minority interest among physiologists to the status of the 'science of experimental psychology' was a very long one indeed. It could hardly have been made by a less learned, less totally respectable man, whose enormous personal output of publications covered and defined the entire field of investigations possible in his time. Among Wundt's younger contemporaries the brilliantly neurotic Freud found a different kind of influence. Men of genuinely original ideas like Exner or Kulpe could not have pulled it off. Later workers like Koffka, Kohler and Wertheimer benefited from the security of the established academic position which Wundt had defined and continued to maintain.

Wundt is in some ways the paradigmatic comic scientist, the learned dullard, a Dr Strabismus (whom God Preserve) of Leipzig. A caricature of pedantic obsessionality. In other respects he is a most admirable figure. Isolated by awkwardness, overcoming lack of capacity by sheer industry, and maintaining that industry through extreme old age and blindness long after all reasonable personal ambitions had been gratified. A man whose extreme, even heroic, absorption in a line of work he had chosen led him to no personal intellectual achievement but left behind the foundations on which his successors have built a science.

P.M.A. Rabbitt

See: *Volkerpsychologie* (10 vols, 1900–20). About Wundt: J.C. Flugel and D.J. West, *A Hundred Years of Psychology*, 1833 -1933 (1933); E.G. Boring, *History of Experimental Psychology* (1950);

Y

492
YOUNG, Thomas 1773–1829

British physicist

At the beginning of the nineteenth century the Newtonian corpuscular theory of light (according to which light consists of streams of particles) was still widely accepted. Thomas Young is chiefly remembered for having revived and, according to some commentators, even experimentally established the rival wave theory of light (according to which luminous bodies emit not particles but energy in the form of oscillations transmitted through an all-pervading medium – the 'luminiferous aether'). Young's main papers on physical optics were published in 1802–4.

Young was born of wealthy Quaker stock in Milverton, Somerset, in 1773. He was something of an infant prodigy, showing precocious talent in many areas including languages. He continued throughout his career to have a wide range of interests. Professionally he was a physician, having received his medical training at Edinburgh, Cambridge (where he picked up the nickname 'Phaenomenon Young') and Göttingen. He was interested in physiology, especially the physiology of the eye and produced in particular some speculations about colour vision which were subsequently developed much more systematically by Helmholtz* into what is nowadays still called the 'Young-Helmholtz Theory'. Young also contributed something to the understanding of surface tension of liquids and of the properties of elastic substances ('Young's modulus'). He became interested in the famous Rosetta Stone which had been discovered in Egypt by the French in 1799 and ceded to Britain in 1801. The stone is inscribed in three different languages: Greek, an Egyptian running script (subsequently called 'demotic') and hieroglyphics. It was assumed that these were three renditions of the same message; and hence the stone provided a unique opportunity to unravel the meaning of the hieroglyphs. Young is often regarded as the first correctly to understand some of the symbols (indeed his memorial tablet in Westminster Abbey reads, in part, 'he first penetrated the obscurity which had veiled for ages the hieroglyphics of Egypt'). A substantial body of opinion holds, however, that the real credit here belongs to Young's French contemporary, J.F. Champollion. There is no doubt that Young's work preceded Champollion's, nor that Champollion went much further than had Young; the real question seems to be whether what Young achieved constituted a substantial enough step forward to merit separate recognition.

Young became involved in something of a priority dispute with Champollion. Nor was this his only such dispute. He seems generally to have felt that his achievements were not sufficiently recognized. He was rather unpopular and unsuccessful as a doctor; and he felt, above all, that his achievements in physical optics were obscured by a general bias against his views within the scientific community of the time. He became involved in a famous public quarrel on optics with Henry Brougham, founding co-editor of the *Edinburgh Review*, scientist and later Lord Chancellor. Young's claims of bias do not seem to fit very well with his worldly success. Despite being only an amateur physicist, he was appointed foreign secretary of the Royal Society in 1802, professor at the Royal Institution in 1807 and was invited three times to give the prestigious Bakerian lecture to the Royal Society. It is difficult to avoid feeling that Young tended to spread his talents too widely and, although full of good ideas, often did not work them out fully enough to make as substantial contributions to knowledge as he might have done. Certainly in the sphere of physical optics, his own picture of the development of the wave theory (that he had 'sowed the seeds' whilst his young French contemporary Fresnel* had 'gathered the fruit') is rather far from the truth.

None the less, Young's contributions to physical optics were important and it is for these that he is chiefly remembered. He pointed out that if light is indeed a periodic wave motion then, if two light beams oscillating in unison affect the same area, at certain points the two series of light waves will reinforce one another, whilst at other points (to arrive at which the two disturbances would have travelled distances differing by an odd number of half wavelengths) they will destroy one another. Young reported a series of experiments which he saw as directly confirming this 'principle of interference'. The one best remembered nowadays (although Young himself gave it no prominence at all) is the 'two slit experiment'. This consists of allowing light diverging from a single slit to fall on a screen with two narrow and closely adjoining slits, the effects being observed on an 'observation screen' some distance away. The result of this experiment is that a series of light and dark bands appear on the observation screen, just as the wave theory predicts (the bright and dark bands corresponding to areas of, respectively, constructive and destructive interference of the light waves).

Young was also the first to suggest in print that the waves constituting light might be transverse rather than longitudinal as had hitherto been universally believed by wave theorists. Young was (understandably) lukewarm, however, about this revolutionary hypothesis and it was left to Fresnel (who arrived at the hypothesis independently) really to develop it vigorously and grapple with the problems it brings in its train. Young's other wave theoretical ideas were also developed independently by Fresnel and the wave theory became dominant in optics for the rest of the century.

John Worrall

Young's collected works were edited in three volumes by George Peacock, *Miscellaneous Works of the late Thomas Young*, 1855. The standard biography is also by Peacock: *Life of Thomas Young* (1855).

Z

493
ZOLA, Émile 1840–1902

French novelist

Zola was a naturalized French citizen, his family origins being Italian on the side of his father who left his native Venice in 1821 eventually to set up practice as a civil engineer in Marseilles. The future novelist was born in Paris and spent his working career there, but his attachment to the sunlit landscapes of his childhood in Provence contributes to the sense in his writing of the power and beauty of nature behind the artifices and constraints of urban and industrialized society. Equally, the combination of being a first-generation immigrant, of reported persecution at school and of poverty brought on the family by the death, in 1847, of the energetic Francesco Zola, seems to have left the only child with feelings of insecurity and an intense desire to succeed which are translated into his whole approach to novel writing and into the values contained in his major novel series, *Les Rougon-Macquart* (1871–93).

Zola's early novels, of which the best known are *Claude's Confession* (*La Confession de Claude* 1865, trans. 1888), *Thérèse Raquin* (1867, trans. 1962) and *Madeleine Férat* (1868, trans. 1957), reveal a characteristic preoccupation with sexual guilt and a taste for melodrama, though here can also be discerned the radical conception of the individual as a complex of physiological forces which will find complete expression in the *Rougon-Macquart* volumes of the next two decades. In the 1868 preface to the second edition of *Thérèse Raquin*, Zola shows that he is aware of the dangers of oversimplification inherent in the confined scale of his first attempts at fiction and, in the broad canvases and massed characters of novels such as *Germinal* (1885, trans. 1954) and *Earth* (*La Terre*, 1887, trans. 1954), he will develop a literary form more appropriate to his dramatic social vision. Concerned to give a philosophical framework to his art, the novelist is drawn, during the 1860s, to contemporary work in physiology and biology, absorbing the general spirit of Darwinian* evolutionary thought and the emphasis accorded by the positivist movement to the methods and achievements of science. After consulting, among other writings, Michelet's* essays on women (*La Femme*, *L'Amour*), the study of Prosper Lucas on heredity (*Trai-*té *de l'hérédité naturelle*), and Taine's* work on the influence of cultural and environmental factors on societies (*Introduction à l'histoire de la littérature anglaise*), Zola prepares, during the period 1868–9, a plan for his *Rougon-Macquart* series which is conceived as a natural and social history of a family under the Second Empire, subjected to the determinants of descent and the impact of the contemporary social and physical milieu.

Appreciation of Zola's novels was, for many years, clouded by legend and misunderstanding. What was seen as his gratuitous delight in the sordid and brutal side of life became a source of constant controversy, from brushes with the public prosecutor over his early books to the famous *Manifeste des cinq* ('The Manifesto of Five'), a public statement of protest made in 1887 by a group of young writers against the admittedly earthy *La Terre*. The novels of the series which deal with the problems of the working class, particularly *L'Assommoir* (1877, trans. 1970) and *Germinal*, were seized upon as political commentaries by those who chose to find in Zola's portrait of the proletariat a condemnation of the prevailing social order or who, alternatively, detected a patronizing and unfeeling demonstration to a middle-class reading public of the bestiality of the lower orders. A whole group of religiously inspired or disenchanted writers, among them Brunetière, Huysmans*, Vogüé, would help to typecast Zola as the representative of a pessimistic and crudely materialist view of man as part of their call for a morally or spiritually uplifting literature as the century came to a close. A more enduring critical viewpoint, however, is that which challenges Zola's consistency in the theory and practice of literary Naturalism, particularly when the lyrical passages to be found in many of his novels and their barely concealed mythopoeic substructure are set against the claims made in such theoretical essays as *The Experimental Novel* (*Le Roman expérimental*, 1880) that his fiction is modelled on the procedures of experimental science. The case that Zola is at heart a romantic poet posing as a writer of sobriety and detachment appears easily substantiated when readers are confronted with descriptions such as those of 'Le Paradou', the exotic garden in *The Abbé Mouret's Sin* (*La Faute de l'abbé Mouret*, 1875, trans. 1957), or in *The Beast in Man* (*La Bête humaine*, 1890, trans. 1958) of the railway engine, 'Lison', with a personality of its own. The strong impression of unity offered by the series, as well as by individual novels, nevertheless belies the presumption of an incoherent aesthetic or a novelist of incongruous objectives.

It is notably misleading to think of Zola's social vision as primarily political or economic; nor, despite the context given to the *Rougon-Macquart* series, should it be thought of as authentically historical. A superficial chronological framework locates the events of the series between the Coup d'État of 1851 and the fall of the Second Empire in 1870, but an element of anachronism is apparent lending to the early books in the series such as *The Kill* (*La Curée*, 1872, trans. 1895) the immediate atmosphere of a society in decay and to the later ones, including the war novel, *The Debacle* (*La Débâcle*, 1892, trans. 1972), a mood of optimism and regenerative hope. It is sometimes held that this change of tone may be related to Zola's liaison, after eighteen years of childless marriage, with Jeanne Rozerot, a mistress some twenty-seven years his junior, and the birth (1889) of the first of two children by her. Beyond this, however, Zola's whole conception of time, in contrast with the linear historical perspective on the present to be found in Balzac's* *Comédie humaine*, is both evolutionary and cyclical in that it is governed by the rhythms of all-powerful nature – for Zola the ultimate reality and force in the universe. While developing towards perfection, men and societies are conceived as subject to the seasonal flux of plant and animal life, so that the period of the Second Empire assumes the character of a phase of sickness or sterility, eventually emerging from the blood-letting of the 1870 war into new or potential fruitfulness. The constant ambivalence of a novel series which opens in an ancient graveyard (*La Fortune des Rougon, The Fortune of the Rougons*, 1871, trans. 1898) and ends in a celebration of the birth of a child (*Doctor Pascal, Le Docteur Pascal*, 1893, trans. 1957) is found in the idea that life and death are eternally interdependent. The intervening books of the series reinforce the correspondence between the ebb and flow of the natural cycle and that of human moral and social behaviour, a link which Zola, following Michelet, sees most clearly manifest in the biological cycle of woman, alternating between the destructively barren and the redemptively fertile. In Naturalism instead of the environment of woman being man, the environment of man is woman, elevated through her association with the maternal deity, nature, to a representative of the space of man's world and a metaphor of human existence. For the individual, as for the microscopic seed, life is experienced as an arena of bewildering uncertainty, a vast uterine system, as suggested by the reiterated image of the labyrinth, whether formed by the vaults and avenues of the Paris market in *Savage Paris* (*Le Ventre de Paris*, 1873, trans. 1955), the 'terrible machine' of the department store in *Ladies' Delight* (*Au Bonheur des dames*, 1883, trans. 1957) or, more obviously, the mine of *Germinal* with its endless passages and tunnels. Subject to nature's own experimental plan, humanity is faced with the uncompromising test of its capacity to fulfil a purpose which is unknown, apart from the characteristics revealed by nature herself. Energy, dynamism and fertility thus become the necessary qualities for evolutionary success by contrast with those which bring deceptive reward in an abortive society: sloth, self-indulgence, infertile lust. This stoical but fundamentally positive code of values is clearly very close to that adopted by the novelist in his personal cult of effort and self-discipline and one which, subordinating the struggles of politics and class to the spontaneous selection of the life force, is reflected in Étienne Lantier, still driving forward at the end of *Germinal*, as much as it is absent in his mother, the generous but passive and backward-looking Gervaise of *L'Assommoir*. Determinism vies with determination in Zola's thought. The thread of hereditary patterning connecting the members of his fictional family also represents for him the icy grip of the past always threatening progress and natural fulfilment.

The philosophical vision behind Zola's Naturalism embracing the individual, society and organic nature in a single whole, governs rather than being dictated by the mimetic considerations of his art. While Naturalism clearly derives many of its formal techniques from existing realism, Zola's literary theories and working notes tend to focus less on the problems of mimesis as an end in itself and to emphasize the importance of balance, logic and coherence as the instruments of a necessary verisimilitude. As his cycle of twenty books, each dealing with a separate social organ, may suggest, the novelist sets out to portray an integrated world, the validity of the picture being found in the whole rather than the individual constituents, in the combination of features which may appear in themselves distorted or exaggerated. Beginning with his boyhood friendship with Cézanne*, who provided the inspiration for his novel *The Masterpiece* (*L'Oeuvre*, 1886, trans. 1950), Zola showed a keen interest in contemporary painting and particularly the work of the Impressionists. What Naturalism and Impressionism have most in common is that both represent a departure from academic realism in positing a phenomenological relationship between artist and subject, allowing eye or imagination to compose the perceived elements into a synthesis which is the sum of imprecise detail. 'We are all of us liars, more or less,' wrote Zola in an important letter of 1885 to his friend Céard, 'but what is the mechanism and the spirit of that falsehood? . . . I consider my lies to be directed towards the truth.' It is here that the much questioned analogy with experimental procedures begins to have its meaning: even if, in *The Experimental Novel*, Zola can justly be accused of neglecting the specifically literary qualities of fiction in relation to science and its methods, the experimental is a definition of man's and the novelist's relationship to an enigmatic universe; forever seeking to advance, through trial and error, towards clarification and understanding.

It was perhaps as a natural conclusion to the inquiring stance of *Les Rougon-Macquart* that Zola should devote the last years of his life to writing novels concerned with advancing social solutions. Many of the values of these late works can be traced retrospectively to the twenty-volume series, but with a corresponding loss of literary and dramatic power as explicit statement and blatant moralizing replace the conflicts and suggestive imagery of the classic texts. The trilogy, *Les Trois villes* ('The Three Cities': *Lourdes*, 1894; *Rome*, 1896; *Paris*, 1898), represents Zola's affirmation of faith in scientific rationalism in the face of the mounting tide of contemporary religious reaction; the unfinished tetralogy, *Les Quatre évangiles* ('The Four Gospels': *Fécondité*, 1899; *Travail*, 1901; *Vérité*, 1903), the elaboration of his utopian vision of reform through prolific family life, the brotherhood of labour and enlightened education. If such works have interest for the modern reader, it lies, as Professor Hemmings suggests, in what they record of the prevailing social and intellectual climate at the turn of the century. It was this same climate which gave the novelist his final claim to public attention when in January 1898 under the title 'J'accuse', the editor of the newspaper *L'Aurore* published Zola's famous open letter to the president of the republic on the subject of the Dreyfus Affair. In an outburst of anger which was as uncharacteristic as the personal courage entailed was familiar, Zola denounced the conduct of the court-martial which, by acquitting Esterhazy of espionage in the face of all the evidence, served to confirm the trumped-up charge levelled four years before against the Jewish Captain Dreyfus. Zola himself was faced with a libel suit and forced to spend an uncomfortable year's exile in England to escape a prison sentence. He died in Paris in September 1902, poisoned by the fumes from a coal fire. The circumstances were judged accidental but, in view of his support for Dreyfus in a period of nationalist and anti-Semitic fervour, these have never been entirely free of suspicion.

David Lee

Works: *Oeuvres complètes*, ed. H. Mitterand (1966–9); *Les Rougon-Macquart*, ed. H. Mitterand (1960–7). Standard modern translations are referred to above; see also *Nana*, (trans. 1972), and *Zest for Life* (*La Joie de vivre*, trans. 1955). See: E.M. Grant, *Emile Zola* (1966); F.W.J. Hemmings, *Emile Zola* (1966), and *The Life and Times of Emile Zola* (1977); G. King, *Garden of Zola* (1978); J.C. Lapp, *Zola before the 'Rougon-Macquart'* (1964); Joanna Richardson, *Zola* (1978); P. Walker, *Emile Zola* (1968); Angus Wilson, *Emile Zola: An introductory study of his Novels* (1952).

Index

INDEX OF NAMES AND KEY TERMS

Note: Numbers refer to individual entries, *not* pages. Numbers in bold type refer to main entries for particular individuals. * denotes that the person is the subject of his or her own entry in this volume, while ** denotes that he or she is the subject of an entry in another volume of the *Makers of Culture* series, according to period.